Strategic Management

Competitiveness and Globalization

CONCEPTS

Third Edition

Michael A. Hitt
Texas A&M University

R. Duane Ireland
Baylor University

Robert E. Hoskisson
The University of Oklahoma

South-Western College Publishing
an International Thomson Publishing company I(T)P®

Cincinnati • Albany • Boston • Detroit • Johannesburg • London • Madrid • Melbourne • Mexico City
New York • Pacific Grove • San Francisco • Scottsdale • Singapore • Tokyo • Toronto

Publishing Team Director: Dave Shaut
Acquisitions Editor: John Szilagyi
Developmental Editor: Katherine Pruitt-Schenck
Production Editor: Shelley Brewer
Media Technology Editor: Kevin Von Gillern
Media Production Editor: Robin Browning
Production House: WordCrafters Editorial Services, Inc.
Internal Design: Ellen Pettengell Design
Cover Design: Tin Box Studio
Cover Image: © 1998 Tamsin Jarzebowska/Photonica
Photography Manager: Cary Benbow
Marketing Manager: Rob Bloom
Manufacturing Coodinator: Sue Kirven

Library of Congress Cataloging-in-Publication Data

Hitt, Michael A.
Strategic management : competitiveness and globalization : concepts and cases / Michael A. Hitt, R. Duane Ireland, Robert E. Hoskisson.—3rd ed.
p. cm.
Includes bibliographical references and index.
ISBN 0-538-88182-8 (Student Edition)
ISBN 0-324-00011-1 (Annotated Instructor's Edition)
ISBN 0-538-88188-7 (Concepts Edition)
ISBN 0-538-88189-5 (Cases Edition)
1. Strategic planning. 2. Industrial management. I. Ireland, R. Duane. II. Hoskisson, Robert E. III. Title.
HD30.28.H586 1999
658.4'012—dc21 98-20413
CIP

1 2 3 4 5 6 7 8 9 WE 7 6 5 4 3 2 1 0 9 8

Printed in the United States of America

International Thomson Publishing
South-Western College Publishing is an ITP Company. The ITP trademark is used under license.

To Frankie, Shawn, Angie, and Tamara. Thanks for everything: I love you.

To my wife, Mary Ann, and our children, Rebecca and Scott. The three of you are the centerpiece of my life. I love all of you and treasure the blessing of being your husband and father.

To Kathy, Robyn, Luke, Dale, Allison, Becky, Angela, Joseph, and Matthew. Our family is the most important concern of my life.

Contents

PART I

Strategic Management Inputs

CHAPTER 1

Strategic Management and Strategic Competitiveness 2

Opening Case: A New World Order in the Telecommunications Industry 3

The Challenge of Strategic Management 7

STRATEGIC FOCUS: The Impermanence of Success 8

The New Competitive Landscape 10

The Global Economy 10

The March of Globalization 12

STRATEGIC FOCUS: The March of Globalization: Wal-Mart, China, and Beyond 12

Technology and Technological Changes 15

The I/O Model of Above-Average Returns 19

The Resource-Based Model of Above-Average Returns 21

Strategic Intent and Strategic Mission 24

Strategic Intent 24

Strategic Mission 25

Stakeholders 26

STRATEGIC FOCUS: Stakeholders Are on Both Sides 26

Classification of Stakeholders 27

Organizational Strategists 31

The Work of Effective Strategists 33

The Strategic Management Process 33

Summary 35

Review Questions 36

Application Discussion Questions 37

Ethics Questions 37

Internet Exercise 37

Notes 38

CHAPTER 2

The External Environment: Opportunities, Threats, Industry Competition, and Competitor Analysis 42

Opening Case: Transformation of the Electric Utility Industry 43

The General, Industry, and Competitor Environments 47

External Environmental Analysis 48

Scanning 49

Monitoring 49

Forecasting 49

Assessing 50

Segments of the General Environment 50

The Demographic Segment 50

The Economic Segment 53

The Political/Legal Segment 54

The Sociocultural Segment 55

The Technological Segment 56

The Global Segment 58

STRATEGIC FOCUS: The Strategic Effect of the Chinese Takeover of Hong Kong 60

Industry Environment Analysis 61

Threat of New Entrants 63

Bargaining Power of Suppliers 66

STRATEGIC FOCUS: Why Other Computer Firms Want To Imitate Dell Computer 66

Bargaining Power of Buyers 67

Threat of Substitute Products 68

Intensity of Rivalry among Competitors 68

Interpreting Industry Analyses 71

Strategic Groups 71

The Value of Strategic Group Analysis 72

Competitor Analysis 73

STRATEGIC FOCUS: A New Law Safeguards Corporate Secrets 74

Summary 77

Review Questions 77

Application Discussion Questions 78

Ethics Questions 78

Internet Exercise 78

Notes 79

CHAPTER 3

The Internal Environment: Resources, Capabilities, and Core Competencies 82

Opening Case: People as a Source of Competitive Advantage 83

The Importance of Internal Analysis 87

The Challenge of Internal Analysis 88

Resources, Capabilities, and Core Competencies 91
Resources 91
Capabilities 94
Core Competencies 96
Building Core Competencies 98
Criteria of Sustainable Competitive Advantage 98
STRATEGIC FOCUS: Toyota's New Product Development and Production Systems Are Difficult to Copy 102
Value Chain Analysis 104
STRATEGIC FOCUS: Costco Companies Inc.: The Retail Warehouse Store Revolution 108
Outsourcing 110
Core Competencies—Cautions and Reminders 112
STRATEGIC FOCUS: Silicone Graphics: Disappearing Core Competence 112
Strategic Inputs and Strategic Actions 114
Summary 116
Review Questions 117
Application Discussion Questions 117
Ethics Questions 118
Internet Exercise 118
Notes 119

PART II
Strategic Actions: Strategy Formulation

CHAPTER 4
Business-Level Strategy 124

Opening Case: Focus Strategies: Achieving Strategic Competitiveness by Serving Narrow Market Segments 125
Customers: Who, What, and How 130
Who: Determining the Customers to Serve 130
What: Determining the Customer Needs to Satisfy 134
How: Determining Core Competencies Necessary to Satisfy Customers' Needs 134
Types of Business-Level Strategy 135
Cost Leadership Strategy 136
STRATEGIC FOCUS: Manufacturing a Truck Chassis: Dana Corp.'s Efforts to Continuously Reduce Its Production Costs 137
Competitive Risks of the Cost Leadership Strategy 141
Differentiation Strategy 142
STRATEGIC FOCUS: Intel Corp.: Achieving Strategic Competitiveness Through the Differentiation Strategy 143
Competitive Risks of the Differentiation Strategy 146
Focus Strategies 147
Competitive Risks of Focus Strategies 149
Integrated Low-Cost/Differentiation Strategy 149
Competitive Risks of the Integrated Low-Cost/Differentiation Strategy 152

STRATEGIC FOCUS: Efforts to Avoid Becoming Stuck in the Middle in the Specialty Coffee Business 153
Summary 155
Review Questions 156
Application Discussion Questions 156
Ethics Questions 156
Internet Exercise 156
Notes 157

CHAPTER 5
Competitive Dynamics 160
Opening Case: Global Competitive Dynamics among Steel Manufacturers 161
Increased Rivalry in the New Competitive Landscape 164
Model of Competitive Dynamics and Rivalry 166
Market Commonality 168
Resource Similarity 169
Likelihood of Attack 170
First, Second, and Late Movers 170
Likelihood of Response 172
Type of Competitive Action 174
Actor's Reputation 175
Dependence on the Market 176
STRATEGIC FOCUS: Burger King and McDonald's: The Battle of Burgers and Fries 176
Competitor Resource Availability 177
Firms' Abilities to Take Action and Respond 178
Relative Firm Size 178
Speed of Competitive Actions and Competitive Responses 180
Innovation 181
Quality 183
Outcomes of Interfirm Rivalry 185
Competitive Market Outcomes 186
STRATEGIC FOCUS: Of Toothpaste and Home Appliances: Competitive Dynamics in Standard-Cycle Markets 188
Competing in Fast-Cycle Markets 190
STRATEGIC FOCUS: Fast-Cycle Competition between Caterpillar and Komatsu 191
Competitive Dynamics and Industry Evolution Outcomes 192
Summary 195
Review Questions 196
Application Discussion Questions 197
Ethics Questions 197
Internet Exercise 197
Notes 198

CHAPTER 6

Corporate-Level Strategy 202

Opening Case: The Diversification of United Parcel Service 203

History of Diversification 207

Levels of Diversification 209

Low Levels of Diversification 209

Moderate and High Levels of Diversification 210

STRATEGIC FOCUS: Changes in Diversification Strategies at Hanson PLC, Terex, and Westinghouse 211

Reasons for Diversification 212

Related Diversification 213

Sharing Activities 214

STRATEGIC FOCUS: The Sharing of Activities to Create Value 214

Transferring of Core Competencies 216

Market Power 217

Unrelated Diversification 218

Efficient Internal Capital Market Allocation 218

Restructuring 220

Diversification: Incentives and Resources 220

Incentives to Diversify 221

Resources and Diversification 225

Extent of Diversification 226

Managerial Motives to Diversify 226

STRATEGIC FOCUS: Issues to Evaluate When Considering Diversification 230

Summary 231

Review Questions 232

Application Discussion Questions 232

Ethics Questions 232

Internet Exercise 233

Notes 233

CHAPTER 7

Acquisition and Restructuring Strategies 236

Opening Case: Today MCI, Tomorrow the World for WorldCom? 237

Mergers and Acquisitions 239

Reasons for Acquisitions 240

STRATEGIC FOCUS: The Flood of Cross-Border Acquisitions 242

Problems in Achieving Acquisition Success 246

STRATEGIC FOCUS: Chaos on the Railroads After Acquisition 251

Effective Acquisitions 254

Restructuring 255

Downsizing 256

Downscoping 257

STRATEGIC FOCUS: Cast Out, Orphaned, or Spun Off? 258
Leveraged Buyoust 260
Restructuring Outcomes 262
Summary 263
Review Questions 264
Application Discussion Questions 264
Ethics Questions 265
Internet Exercise 265
Notes 266

CHAPTER 8
International Strategy 270
Opening Case: Globalization: The Driving Force of International Strategy 271
Identifying International Opportunities: The Incentive to Pursue an International Strategy 274
Increased Market Size 277
Return on Investment 278
Economies of Scale and Learning 279
Location Advantages 279
International Strategies 280
International Business-Level Strategy 280
STRATEGIC FOCUS: Air Service and Discount Retailing: Achieving Strategic Competitiveness by Using the International Low-Cost Strategy 282
STRATEGIC FOCUS: Focusing Internationally on Specific Market Segments 285
International Corporate-Level Strategy 287
STRATEGIC FOCUS: Using the Transnational Strategy as a Pathway to Strategic Competitiveness 289
Environmental Trends 290
Regionalization 290
Choice of International Entry Mode 292
Exporting 293
Licensing 293
Strategic Alliances 294
Acquisitions 295
New, Wholly Owned Subsidiary 296
Dynamics of Mode of Entry 296
Strategic Competitiveness Outcomes 297
International Diversification and Returns 297
International Diversification and Innovation 298
Complexity of Managing Multinational Firms 299
Risks in an International Environment 299
Political Risks 299
Economic Risks 300

Limits to International Expansion: Management Problems 301
Other Management Problems 302
Summary 303
Review Questions 304
Application Discussion Questions 304
Ethics Questions 305
Internet Exercise 305
Notes 305

CHAPTER 9

Cooperative Strategy 310

Opening Case: Increasing Numbers of Small and Large Firms Are Collaborating to Compete 311
Types of Cooperative Strategies 314
Reasons for Alliances 315
Business-Level Cooperative Strategies 318
Complementary Alliances 319
STRATEGIC FOCUS: The Star Alliance System: An Example of a Horizontal Airline Alliance 321
Competition Reduction Strategies 323
Competition Response Strategies 325
Uncertainty Reduction Strategies 325
STRATEGIC FOCUS: Alliances in Both the U.S. and Europe Help Firms Overcome Uncertainty in the Telecommunications Industry 326
Assessment of Competitive Advantage 328
Corporate-Level Cooperative Strategies 328
Motives for Corporate-Level Cooperative Strategies 332
International Cooperative Strategies 332
Strategic Intent of Partner 334
Network Strategies 335
STRATEGIC FOCUS: Cooperative Strategy Often Develops in Economic Districts 335
R&D Consortia and Other Network Strategies 338
Competitive Risks with Cooperative Strategies 339
Trustworthiness as a Strategic Asset 340
Strategic Approaches to Managing Alliances 341
Summary 342
Review Questions 343
Application Discussion Questions 343
Ethics Questions 344
Internet Exercise 344
Notes 344

PART III

Strategic Actions: Strategy Implementation

CHAPTER 10

Corporate Governance 350

Opening Case: AT&T's Board Overcomes Difficulties in Choosing a New CEO 351

Separation of Ownership and Managerial Control 356

Agency Relationships 357

Product Diversification as an Example of an Agency Problem 358

Agency Costs and Governance Mechanisms 360

Ownership Concentration 361

The Growing Influence of Institutional Owners as Large-Block Shareholders 361

STRATEGIC FOCUS: CalPERS Initiates New Shareholder Activist Approaches 363

Shareholder Activism: How Much Is Possible? 364

Boards of Directors 366

Enhancing the Effectiveness of the Board of Directors as a Governance Mechanism 367

STRATEGIC FOCUS: Examples of Board of Directors Reforms 368

Executive Compensation 371

A Complicated Governance Mechanism 372

The Effectiveness of Executive Compensation 372

The Multidivisional Structure 375

Market for Corporate Control 376

Managerial Defense Tactics 376

International Corporate Governance 377

Corporate Governance in Germany 377

Corporate Governance in Japan 379

Other Global Governance Reforms 380

STRATEGIC FOCUS: Reforms in International Corporate Governance 380

Governance Mechanisms and Ethical Behavior 382

Summary 383

Review Questions 385

Application Discussion Questions 385

Ethics Questions 386

Internet Exercise 386

Notes 386

CHAPTER 11

Organizational Structure and Controls 390

Opening Case: Changes in Organizational Structure at Raytheon Company 391

Evolutionary Patterns of Strategy and Organizational Structure 395

Simple Structure 396

Functional Structure 398

Multidivisional Structure 399

Implementing Business-Level Strategies: Organizational Structure and Controls 401
Using the Functional Structure to Implement the Cost Leadership Strategy 401
Using the Functional Structure to Implement the Differentiation Strategy 403
Using the Functional Structure to Implement the Integrated
Low-Cost/Differentiation Strategy 404
Using the Simple Structure to Implement Focused Strategies 405
Movement to the Multidivisional Structure 406
Implementing Corporate-Level Strategies: Organizational Structure and Controls 406
Using the Cooperative Form to Implement the Related-Constrained Strategy 406
STRATEGIC FOCUS: Using the Cooperative Form of the Multidivisional Structure to Achieve Strategic Competitiveness in the Transportation, Information and Entertainment, and Financial Services Industries 409
Using the SBU Form to Implement the Related-Linked Strategy 410
Using the Competitive Form to Implement the Unrelated Diversification Strategy 412
The Effect of Structure on Strategy 414
STRATEGIC FOCUS: Deverticalization: Sara Lee's Path to Lower Levels of Diversification 415
Implementing International Strategies: Organizational Structure and Controls 417
Using the Worldwide Geographic Area Structure to Implement the Multidomestic Strategy 417
Using the Worldwide Product Divisional Structure to Implement the Global Strategy 419
STRATEGIC FOCUS: Using the Worldwide Product Divisional Structure as a Means of Increased Internationalization 420
Using the Combination Structure to Implement the Transnational Strategy 421
Implementing Cooperative Strategies: Organizational Structure and Controls 422
Implementing Business-Level Cooperative Strategies 424
Implementing Corporate-Level Cooperative Strategies 425
Implementing International Cooperative Strategies 426
Contemporary Organizational Structures: A Cautionary Note 427
Summary 428
Review Questions 428
Application Discussion Questions 429
Ethics Questions 429
Internet Exercise 429
Notes 430

CHAPTER 12

Strategic Leadership 434

Opening Case: Strategic Leadership in the Twenty-First Century 435
Strategic Leadership 439
Managers as an Organizational Resource 440
Top Management Teams 442

Managerial Labor Market 445
Determining Strategic Direction 448
Exploiting and Maintaining Core Competencies 450
Developing Human Capital 450
STRATEGIC FOCUS: Human Resource Shortages: Temporary Workers Versus Creative Recruiting and Building Commitment 451
Sustaining an Effective Organizational Culture 454
Entrepreneurial Orientation 455
STRATEGIC FOCUS: Fastenal's Culture for Selling Nuts and Bolts 456
Changing Organizational Culture and Business Reengineering 458
Emphasizing Ethical Practices 460
Establishing Balanced Organizational Controls 462
STRATEGIC FOCUS: Balancing Controls in Large, Diversified Business Groups 463
Summary 465
Review Questions 466
Application Discussion Questions 466
Ethics Questions 467
Internet Exercise 467
Notes 467

CHAPTER 13
Corporate Entrepreneurship and Innovation 472
Opening Case: Killer Chips, Wimps, and Other Things 473
Innovation and Corporate Entrepreneurship 475
Need for Innovation and Entrepreneurship 475
Entrepreneurship and Innovation Defined 476
STRATEGIC FOCUS: The Razor's Edge: An Innovation Machine 478
International Entrepreneurship 479
Internal Corporate Venturing 480
STRATEGIC FOCUS: The Mean Innovative Machine 483
Implementing Internal Corporate Ventures 484
Implementing Product Development Teams and Facilitating Cross-Functional Integration 484
Barriers to Integration 485
Facilitating Integration 485
Appropriating (Extracting) Value from Innovation 486
Strategic Alliances: Cooperating to Produce and Manage Innovation 488
Buying Innovation: Acquisitions and Venture Capital 489
Acquisitions 490
Venture Capital 491
STRATEGIC FOCUS: Are Venture Capitalists and Entrepreneurs from the Same Mold? 492
Entrepreneurship and the Small Firm 494
Summary 497

Review Questions 498
Application Discussion Questions 498
Ethics Questions 499
Internet Exercise 499
Notes 499

NAME INDEX I-1

COMPANY INDEX I-10

SUBJECT INDEX I-16

PHOTO CREDITS PC-1

Preface

The third edition of *Strategic Management: Competitiveness and Globalization (Concepts)* continues the tradition from previous editions of integrating "cutting edge" concepts with an engaging writing style. As such, the many new features and careful revisions enhance the value of our market-leading textbook.

NEW FEATURES

- All new **chapter opening cases** and **strategic focus segments**
- Many new **company-specific examples** in each chapter
- Expanded **global coverage** throughout the book with more emphasis on the international context and issues in both the text materials and cases
- A complete view of **strategy formulation** and **implementation** at all levels
- New and current research integrated throughout the chapters' conceptual presentations

These new features provide a unique **competitive advantage** *to this book over other alternatives.* With all new opening cases and three new strategic focus segments for each chapter, there are 52 major case examples in the concepts portion of the book. In addition, over 50 percent of the shorter examples used throughout each chapter are completely new.

This new edition also emphasizes a **global advantage** with comprehensive coverage of international concepts and issues. In addition to comprehensive coverage in **Chapter 8: International Strategy,** references to and discussions of the international context and issues are included throughout the other chapters. The chapter opening cases, strategic focus segments and individual examples in each chapter cover numerous global issues and markets.

Importantly, this new edition solidifies a **research advantage** for the book. For example, each chapter has over 100 references. An average of over 50 new references has been added in each chapter for this edition. Additionally, we maintain our position as the only text on the market that offers a full four-color format that enhances the presentation of our materials and the overall text design.

Our primary goal in preparing this revised edition was to **define our advantage** by presenting the most complete learning mechanism and instructional tool. Our strategic intent continues to be to present readers with a complete, accurate, and up-to-date explanation of the strategic management process.

INTRODUCTION

The strategic management process is the focus of this book. Described in Chapter 1, organizations (both for-profit companies and not-for-profit agencies) use the strategic management process to understand competitive forces and to develop competitive advantages systematically and consistently. The magnitude of this challenge is greater today than it has been historically. A new competitive landscape is developing as a result of the technological revolution and increasing globalization. The technological revolution has placed increased importance on firm innovation and the ability to rapidly introduce new goods and services to the marketplace. The global economy, one in which goods and services flow freely among nations, continuously pressures firms to become more competitive. By offering either valued goods or services to customers, competitive firms increase the probability of earning above-average returns. Thus, the strategic management process helps organizations identify what they intend to achieve and how they will accomplish valued outcomes.

This book is intended for use primarily in strategic management and business policy courses. The materials presented in the 13 chapters have been researched thoroughly. Both the academic, scholarly literature and the business, practitioner literature were studied and then integrated to design, write, and revise this book. The academic literature provided the foundation to develop an accurate, yet meaningful description of the strategic management process. The business practitioner literature yielded a rich base of current domestic and global examples to show how the concepts, tools, and techniques of the strategic management process are applied in different types of organizations.

THE STRATEGIC MANAGEMENT PROCESS

Our treatment of the strategic management process is both *traditional* and *contemporary*. In maintaining tradition, we examine important materials that have historically been a part of understanding strategic management. For example, we thoroughly examine how to analyze a firm's external environment and internal environment as a part of the strategic management process.

Contemporary Treatment In explaining the aforementioned important activities, we strive to keep our treatments contemporary. In Chapter 3, for example, we emphasize the importance of identifying and determining the value-creating potential of a firm's resources, capabilities, and core competencies. The strategic actions taken as a result of understanding a firm's resources, capabilities, and core competencies have a direct link with the company's ability to establish a sustainable competitive advantage, achieve strategic competitiveness, and earn above-average returns.

Our contemporary treatment of the strategic management process is also exemplified in the chapters on the dynamics of strategic change in the complex global economy. In Chapter 5, for example, we discuss how the dynamics of competition between firms affect the outcomes achieved by individual companies. This chapter's discussion suggests that in most industries, the strategic actions taken by a firm are influenced by a series of competitive actions and responses initiated by competitors. Thus, competition in the global economy is fluid, dynamic, and significantly influences a firm's performance. Similarly, in Chapter 7, we explain the dynamics of strategic change at the corporate level, specifically addressing the motivation and consequences of mergers, acquisitions, and restructuring (e.g., divestitures) in the global economy.

We also emphasize that the total set of strategic actions known as *strategy formulation* and *strategy implementation* (see Figure 1.1 in Chapter 1) must be integrated carefully if a firm is to achieve strategic competitiveness and earn above-average returns. Thus, this book shows that strategic competitiveness is achieved and above-average returns are earned only when firms use implementation tools and actions that are consistent with the firm's chosen business-level (Chapter 4), corporate-level (Chapter 6), acquisition (Chapter 7), international (Chapter 8), and cooperative (Chapter 9) strategies.

Contemporary Concepts Contemporary topics and concepts are the foundation for our in-depth analysis of strategic actions firms take to implement their chosen strategies. In Chapter 10, for example, we describe how different corporate governance mechanisms (e.g., boards of directors, institutional owners, executive compensation, etc.) affect strategy implementation. Chapter 11 explains how firms can gain a competitive advantage by effectively using organizational structures to implement business-level and corporate-level strategies. The vital contributions of strategic leaders are discussed in Chapter 12. Chapter 13 addresses the important topic of corporate entrepreneurship and innovation through internal corporate venturing, strategic alliances, and external acquisition or venture capital investments. Through integration of the traditional and contemporary topics, readers of this book should be able to fully understand the strategic management process and how to use it successfully in an organizational setting.

A number of contemporary topics and issues are examined in the book as well. These include stakeholder analyses, core competencies, total quality management (TQM), strategic flexibility, transnational strategy, strategic refocusing (downsizing, downscoping), strategic change and reengineering, teamwork and horizontal organization, and the importance of business ethics.

KEY FEATURES OF THIS TEXT

To increase the value of this book for readers, several features are included, each of which is described below.

Learning Objectives Each chapter begins with clearly stated learning objectives. These objectives inform readers of key points they should master from each chapter. To both facilitate and verify learning, students can revisit each chapter's learning objectives by preparing answers to the review questions appearing at the end of each chapter.

Opening Cases Following the learning objectives is an opening case. These cases describe current strategic actions taken by modern companies including Bang & Olufsen, Nippon Steel, British Telecommunications, WorldCom, and Hoechst AG, among others. The purpose of these cases is to demonstrate how a specific firm applies the strategic management concepts that are examined in individual chapters. Thus, the opening cases provide a distinct link between the theory and application of the strategic management process in different organizations.

Key Terms Key terms critical to understanding the strategic management process are boldfaced throughout the book. Definitions of these key terms appear in chapter margins as well as in the text. Other terms and concepts throughout the text are italicized, signifying their importance.

Strategic Focus Segments Three all new Strategic Focus segments are presented in each chapter. As with the opening case, the Strategic Focus segments highlight a variety of high-profile organizations. Each segment demonstrates the application of an important part of the strategic management process in the pursuit of strategic competitiveness.

End-of-Chapter Summaries Each chapter ends with a summary that revisits the concepts outlined in the learning objectives. These summaries are presented in a bulleted format to highlight concepts, tools, and techniques examined in each chapter.

Review Questions Review questions are pointedly tied to the learning objectives, prompting students to re-examine the most important concepts in each chapter.

Application Discussion Questions These questions challenge readers to directly apply the part of the strategic management process highlighted in that chapter. They are intended to stimulate thoughtful classroom discussions and to help students develop critical thinking skills.

Ethics Questions At the end of each chapter, readers are challenged by a set of questions about ethical issues that require careful thought and analysis. Preparing answers to these questions helps students recognize and confront ongoing ethical issues facing management teams. Discussing these difficult issues in class heightens awareness of the ethical challenges encountered in global organizations and markets today.

Internet Exercises The Internet is an invaluable source for the exchange of information worldwide. No other mechanism has had the ability to disseminate business information on such a large scale so quickly and effectively as the Internet. As such, a set of Internet exercises, developed by Bruce Barringer of the University of Central Florida, is included at the end of each chapter. Each set of exercises is designed so that students develop the ability to effectively recognize valid information sources and use this to further their business knowledge and management skills.

Examples In addition to the opening cases and Strategic Focus segments, each chapter contains many other real-world examples. Grounded in descriptions of actual organizations' actions, these examples are used to illustrate key strategic management concepts and to provide realistic applications of the strategic management process.

Indices Besides the traditional end of book subject and name indices, a company index is provided. This index includes the names of all organizations discussed in the text for easier accessibility.

Full Four-Color Format Our presentation and discussion of the strategic management process is facilitated by the use of a full four-color format. This format provides the foundation for an interesting and visually appealing treatment of all parts of the strategic management process. Exhibits and photos further enhance the presentation by giving visual insight into the workings of the global business environment.

The Strategic Advantage

The title of this book highlights the importance of strategic competitiveness and globalization to our examination of the strategic management process. The strategic management process is critical to organizational success. As described in Chapter 1, strategic competitiveness is achieved when a firm develops and exploits a sustained competitive advantage. Attaining such an advantage results in the earning of above-average returns; that is, returns that exceed those an investor could expect from other investments with similar amounts of risk. For example, Gillette developed and sustained a competitive advantage over time because of its significant emphasis on innovation even though it operates largely in low-technology industry(ies). Its innovation has helped it to remain one of the top firms in each of the industries in which it competes.

The Competitive Advantage

Success in the new competitive landscape requires specific capabilities, including the abilities to (1) use scarce resources wisely to maintain the lowest possible costs, (2) constantly anticipate frequent changes in customers' preferences, (3) adapt to rapid technological changes, (4) identify, emphasize, and effectively manage what a firm does better than its competitors, (5) continuously structure a firm's operations so objectives can be achieved more efficiently, and (6) successfully manage and gain commitments from a culturally diverse workforce.

The Global Advantage

Also critical to the approach used in this text is the fact that all firms face increasing global competition. Firms no longer operate in relatively safe domestic markets as U.S. auto firms have discovered. In the past, many companies, including most in the United States, produced large quantities of standardized products. Today, firms typically compete in a global economy that is complex, highly uncertain, and unpredictable. To a greater degree than in a primarily domestic economy, the global economy rewards effective performers, whereas poor performers are forced to restructure significantly to enhance their strategic competitiveness. As noted earlier, increasing globalization and the technological revolution have produced a new competitive landscape. The new competitive landscape presents a challenging and complex environment for firms, but one that also has opportunities. The importance of developing and using these capabilities in the new competitive landscape of the twenty-first century should not be underestimated.

CASES

There are two other versions of our book. The combined edition (ISBN 0-538-88182-8) includes the 13 text chapters featured in this book along with 40 comprehensive cases. These 40 cases are also available in a cases-only edition (ISBN 0-538-88189-5). All of these cases are new to the third editions of our work and represent a variety of business and organizational situations and strategic issues. For example, there are cases representing manufacturing, service, consumer goods, and industrial goods industries. Furthermore, many of the cases include an international perspective. Also, cases with high technology, entertainment, and food or retail firms are represented. Some cases focus specifically on social or ethical issues, whereas others emphasize strategic issues of entrepreneurial or small- and medium-sized firms. Finally, a significant number of the cases also provide an effective perspective on the industry examined.

The cases were reviewed carefully and selected personally by the authors. Our goal was to choose cases that were well written and that are focused on clear and important strategic management issues. In addition, the variety of cases provides a rich learning experience for those performing case analyses. The cases are multidimensional. For the readers' convenience, a matrix listing all 40 cases and the dimensions/characteristics of each one is provided following the table of contents. Although most of these cases are concerned with well-known national and multinational companies, several depict the strategic challenges involved in smaller and entrepreneurial firms (e.g., Pasta Perfect, Amazon.com, Harold's).

Given the global economy emphasized in our work, approximately 65 percent of the cases include an international perspective (e.g., Enron Development Corporation, Motorola in China, Birra Moretti). There are also cases of special interest or topics (e.g., Bank of America, Southwest Airlines, Starbucks, Benetton, China Eastern Airlines and Columbia/HCA). Several of these cases have won special awards for their excellence (e.g., Telefónica España and Cap Gemini Sogeti). In summary, the cases represent a wide variety of important and challenging strategic issues and provide an exciting setting for case analyses and presentations. Additional support is available to instructors desiring to use a selected set of the 40 new cases. Further information about the Custom Case Program can be obtained from your ITP sales representative.

SUPPORT MATERIAL*

The third edition's support materials are authored by most of the same top instructors as the previous editions. We present to you one of the most compre-

*Adopters: Please contact your ITP sales representative to learn more about the supplements you are qualified to receive.

hensive and quality learning packages available for teaching strategic management. These materials have been authored by a top support team and were carefully guided by ourselves, to ensure quality and consistency.

For the Instructor

Annotated Instructor's Edition (ISBN: 0-324-00011-1) A comprehensive Annotated Instructor's Edition (combined text and cases version) has been prepared by Kendall W. Artz of Baylor University. The annotations, provide background information and suggestions to facilitate class discussion of important concepts from the book. The annotations also provide the instructor with additional company examples that give further insight into a particular topic. In addition, most chapter opening cases are accompanied by at least one URL so that further information related to the featured company can be researched using the World Wide Web.

Instructor's Manual with Video Guide & Transparencies (ISBN: 0-538-88183-6) A complete Instructor's Manual has been prepared by Richard A. Menger of St. Mary's University. The instructor's manual provides teaching notes, suggestions, and summaries. The teaching notes include discussion summaries or highlights of each opening case, Strategic Focus segment, table, and figure appearing in the text. Teaching suggestions provide the instructor with a choice of strategies for integrating various text features into a lecture format.

Video Guide (ISBN: 0-538-88183-6) An exclusive video guide has been developed by Bruce Barringer of the University of Central Florida to accompany the video package and provide information on length, alternative points of usage within the text, subjects to address, and discussion questions to stimulate classroom discussion. Suggested answers to these questions are also provided.

Transparency Acetates (ISBN: 0-324-00888-0) The full-color transparency acetates include important figures from the text and additional transparencies from the PowerPoint Presentation Files. To provide comprehensive coverage, 150 transparency acetates are included in the set.

Transparency Masters (ISBN: 0-538-88183-6) More than 200 transparency masters are printed from the PowerPoint Presentation Files and include figures from the text and innovative adaptations to enhance classroom presentation.

Instructor's Case Notes (ISBN: 0-538-88185-2) Samuel M. DeMarie of the University of Nevada at Las Vegas prepared the Case Notes that accompany the book. Each note provides details about the case within the framework of case analysis that is presented in the text. The authors selected the 40 new cases, based on the variety of strategy topics and industry types they represent. The structure of these case notes allows instructors to organize case discussions along common themes and concepts. For example, each case note details the firm's capabilities and resources, its industry and competitive environment (if applicable), and key factors for success in the industry. The case notes also feature aspects of the cases that make them unique.

Test Bank (ISBN: 0-538-88184-4) The Test Bank, prepared by Debora J. Gilliard of Metropolitan State College of Denver, has been thoroughly revised for this new edition. The test bank contains more than 1,200 multiple choice, true/false, and essay questions. Each question has been coded according to Bloom's taxonomy, a widely known testing and measurement device used to classify questions according to level (easy, medium, or hard) and type (application, recall, or comprehension).

World Class Test Computerized Testing Software (ISBN: 0-324-0059-6) New this year, World Class Test allows instructors to create, edit, store, and print exams easily and efficiently.

PowerPoint Presentation Files (ISBN: 0-0-538-88190-9) Jay Dial of Case Western Reserve University has developed more than 800 PowerPoint slides for this text. These unique slides feature figures from the text, lecture outlines, and innovative adaptations to enhance classroom presentation. These files are available on disk in PowerPoint 4.0. The PowerPoint Presentation File slides are integrated with *PowerNotes* (see below).

South-Western College Publishing's Strategy Internet Site and Resource Center The new strategy site includes a wealth of information for both students and instructors. Link directly to the Hitt/Ireland/Hoskisson section and see updates to the cases, strategy terms defined, a full Internet index with important strategy URL listings, and a section on how to write a case analysis. For the instructor, there are sample syllabi that demonstrate both traditional and nontraditional teaching of the course. This online service is available to everyone. We encourage you to access our site and our explore your strategic advantage at:
http://strategy.swcollege.com

Videos (ISBN: 0-538-00377-3) A new, very unique video package is available that features video segments exclusive to the South-Western College Publishing management team. Written and directed by Learnet, these video segments run 10-15 minutes each and focus on both small and large companies as they utilize the strategic management process. During the video segment, questions are posed and students are asked to analyze different evolving management situations. Each chapter has its own video segment, focusing on the topics presented therein.

For the Student

Insights: Readings in Strategic Management, Third Edition (ISBN: 0-538-88186-0) Prepared by Timothy B. Palmer of Louisiana State University, *Insights* has been revised and expanded for this edition and includes multiple selected readings from academic and popular business periodicals such as the *Academy of Management Executive*, the *Wall Street Journal*, *Forbes*, and *Fortune*. Each chapter features 3-4 business articles.

PowerNotes (ISBN: 0-538-88187-9) PowerNotes (a student note-taking guide), prepared by Jay Dial of Case Western Reserve University, provides a simple solution for the majority of students who spend their time during lectures copying material from the overheads. PowerNotes contains reduced images of the PowerPoint Presentation Files with space for lecture notes on each page.

ACKNOWLEDGMENTS

We gratefully acknowledge the help of many people in the development of this edition of our book. The professionalism, guidance, and support provided by the editorial team of John Szilagyi (Executive Editor), Katherine Pruitt-Schenck (Project Manager), Shelley Brewer (Production Editor), and Rob Bloom (Marketing Manager) are gratefully acknowledged. We appreciate the excellent work of Sam DeMarie, Jay Dial, Debora Gilliard, Richard Menger, Kendall Artz, Bruce Barringer, and Timothy Palmer in preparing the supplemental materials accompanying this book. Also, we appreciate the excellent secretarial assistance provided by Adrian Elton. In addition, we owe a debt of gratitude to our colleagues at Texas A&M University, Baylor University, and the University of Oklahoma. Finally, we gratefully acknowledge the help of many who read and provided feedback on drafts of our chapters for the three editions of our book. Their insights enhanced our work. Those who contributed through reviews and evaluations are:

Kendall W. Artz
Baylor University

Kimberly B. Boal
Texas Tech University

Garry D. Bruton
Texas Christian University

Victoria L. Buenger
Texas A&M University

Lowell Busenitz
University of Oklahoma

Gary R. Carini
Baylor University

Roy A. Cook
Fort Lewis College

James H. Davis
University of Notre Dame

Samuel M. DeMarie
University of Nevada at Las Vegas

Derrick E. Dsouza
University of North Texas

W. Jack Duncan
University of Alabama at Birmingham

Karin Fladmoe-Lindquist
University of Utah

Karen A. Froehlich
North Dakota State University

Debora J. Gilliard
Metropolitan State College of Denver

Ching-Der Horng
National Sun Yat-Sen University

Veronica Horton
Middle Tennessee State University

Sharon G. Johnson
Cedarville College

Anne T. Lawrence
San Jose State University

Franz T. Lohrke
University of Southern Mississippi

Richard A. Menger
St. Mary's University

Joseph E. Michlitsch
Southern Illinois University at Edwardsville

Paul Miesing
University at Albany, SUNY

Douglas D. Moesel
University of Missouri, Columbia

Benjamin M. Oviatt
Georgia State University

George M. Puia
Indiana State University

Woody Richardson
University of Alabama at Birmingham

Michael V. Russo
University of Oregon

Ronald J. Salazar
Idaho State University

Hugh Sherman
Ohio University

Clayton G. Smith
Oklahoma City University

David C. Snook-Luther
University of Wyoming

Kathleen M. Sutcliffe
University of Michigan

Thomas A. Turk
Chapman University

Margaret A. White
Oklahoma State University

Robert Wiseman
Michigan State University

FINAL COMMENT

Organizations face exciting and dynamic competitive challenges as the 1990s come to a close and the twenty-first century begins. These challenges, and effective responses to them, are explored in this third edition of *Strategic Management: Competitiveness and Globalization.* The strategic management process offers valuable insights for those committed to successfully leading and managing organizations in the 1990s and beyond. We hope that you will enjoy the exposure to the strategic management process provided by this book. In addition, we wish you success in your careers and future endeavors.

Strategic Management Inputs

Chapters

1 Strategic Management and Strategic Competitiveness

2 The External Environment: Opportunities, Threats, Industry Competition, and Competitor Analysis

3 The Internal Environment: Resources, Capabilities, and Core Competencies

Strategic Management and Strategic Competitiveness

CHAPTER 1

Learning Objectives

After reading this chapter, you should be able to:

1. Define strategic competitiveness, competitive advantage, and above-average returns.
2. Discuss the challenge of strategic management.
3. Describe the new competitive landscape and how it is being shaped by global and technological changes.
4. Use the industrial organization (I/O) model to explain how firms can earn above-average returns.
5. Use the resource-based model to explain how firms can earn above-average returns.
6. Describe strategic intent and strategic mission and discuss their value to the strategic management process.
7. Define stakeholders and describe the three primary stakeholder groups' ability to influence organizations.
8. Describe the work of strategists.
9. Explain the strategic management process.

A New World Order in the Telecommunications Industry

The telecommunications industry will never be the same. Perhaps the changes are best exemplified by the $37 billion acquisition of MCI by WorldCom Inc. This acquisition came on the heels of offers from British Telecommunications and GTE. British Telecommunications and MCI first agreed on a merger reportedly worth between $18 and $19 billion. British Telecommunications then had second thoughts, and GTE offered $28 billion. WorldCom, about 40 percent the size of MCI, made the offer to make it the largest merger in history at that point in time. The combined firms will have total annual revenue of $27.8 billion. The series of offers seemed to spur AT&T into action when it began talks with SBC regarding an acquisition. The talks made progress in the beginning, but they broke down with much external criticism and government scrutiny. Such a merger would have been worth approximately $50 billion.

http://www.mci.com
http://www.worldcom.com

All of this frenetic activity in the telecommunication industry is due to the major changes occurring in and predicted for this industry. In other words, firms are trying to prepare themselves to be competitive as changes occur. Some predict changes in the telecommunications industry as profound as occurred in the computer industry with the advent of the microcomputer. One major change that has occurred in many domestic industries is deregulation and thus increasing competition. Deregulation is also spreading globally. For example, the Federal Communications Commission voted in 1997 to allow foreign companies increased access to the U.S. telecommunications markets. This step is the first among the countries who were a party to a World Trade Organization agreement in which 69 countries pledged to open their telecommunications markets. To compete in a global mar-

ket, many telecommunications' executives feel that their firms must be large to have the necessary market power. Annual spending in the global telecommunications industry is expected to grow to $1 trillion by 2001. Furthermore there are new markets opening up such as in China that will require massive investments to compete. China alone represents a $1 trillion opportunity. Of course, it is not only the size of the market affecting major investments but also the need to be at the forefront of rapidly advancing technology. In 1996 the required investment in the telecommunications infrastructure globally was $160 billion.

Changes in the industry are clearly not limited to U.S. firms. For example, a consortium of European phone companies agreed to merge their international phone networks to create the largest service provider in Europe. The Unisource consortium was formed by PTT Nederland NV of the Netherlands, Telia AB of Sweden and Swiss Telecom. Unisource will compete mainly with two joint ventures, one between British Telecommunications and MCI and one formed by Sprint, Deutsche Telecom AG, and France Telecom SA. Unisource also has a joint venture with AT&T that will be aided by this new development. Tato, a large Italian firm, formed a strategic alliance with Deutsche Telecom to bid for Italy's third cellular telephone license and to make a $5 billion move into the fixed line market. STET, another Italian company, already controls the largest cellular phone network in Europe. It has bought into systems in Austria, Serbia, and Spain. A final example comes from Asia. Four competitors are cooperating to develop a common format of the code division multiple access (CDMA), a digital transmission technology. The firms, Lucent Technologies, Motorola, Northern Telecom, and Qualcomm, are also cooperating to help Nippon Telephone & Telegraph (NTT) to develop a world CDMA. Improving the CDMA will help Asian carriers such as NTT because of the tremendous growth in Asian markets.

These changes are some of the examples of the transformation occurring in the global telecommunications industry. The changes are required to remain competitive in a rapidly developing and dynamic industry.

SOURCE: C. Arnst, G. McWilliams and A. Barrett, 1997, The return of Ma Bell? *Business Week*, June 3, www.businessweek.com; P. Elstrom, C. Yang and J. Flynn, 1997, The New World Order, *Business Week*, October 13, 26–33; Europe's Unisource confirms its merger of global networks, 1997, *The Wall Street Journal Interactive Edition*, June 5, http://www.interactive5.wsj.com; Four wireless rivals link up to work for CDMA standards, 1997, *The Wall Street Journal Interactive Edition*, June 4, http://www.interactive5.wsj.com; GTE presses its bid for MCI, calling merger a home run, 1997, *The Wall Street Journal Interactive Edition*, http://www.interactive5.wsj.com; D.E. Kalish, 1997, WorldCom-MCI deal makes merger history, *Houston Chronicle*, November 11, C1; J.J. Keller and S. Lipin, 1997, Jumping off sidelines, GTE makes a cash bid for MCI, *The Wall Street Journal Interactive Edition*, October 16, http://www.interactive5.wsj.com; A. Kupfer, 1997, Transforming Telecom: the big switch, *Fortune*, October 13, 105–116; J. Rossant, 1997, Lean, mean—and state-owned Italian companies, *Business Week*, June 16, http://www.businessweek.com; U.S. to open up telecommunications to foreign firms, *Houston Chronicle*, November 26, C3.

Strategic competitiveness is achieved when a firm successfully formulates and implements a value-creating strategy.

The actions undertaken by firms such as WorldCom, PTT Nederland NV, Deutsche Telecom AG, STET, and Nippon Telephone and Telegraph among others are designed to help the firms achieve strategic competitiveness and earn above-average returns. **Strategic competitiveness** is achieved when a firm successfully formulates and implements a value-creating strategy. When a firm implements a value-creating strategy of which other companies are unable to duplicate the benefits or find it too costly to imitate,[1] this firm has a **sustained** or **sustainable competitive advantage** (hereafter called simply competitive advantage). A firm is assured of a competitive advantage only after others' efforts to duplicate its strategy have ceased or failed.[2] Even if a firm achieves a competitive advantage, it normally can sustain it only for a certain period of time.[3] The speed with which competitors are able to acquire the skills needed to duplicate the benefits of a firm's value-creating strategy determines how long a competitive advantage will last.[4] Understanding how to exploit its competitive advantage is necessary for a firm to earn above-average returns.[5]

A **sustained** or **sustainable competitive advantage** occurs when a firm implements a value-creating strategy of which other companies are unable to duplicate the benefits or find it too costly to imitate.

By achieving strategic competitiveness and successfully exploiting its competitive advantage, a firm is able to accomplish its primary objective—the earning of above-average returns. **Above-average returns** are returns in excess of what an investor expects to earn from other investments with a similar amount of risk. **Risk** is an investor's uncertainty about the economic gains or losses that will result from a particular investment.[6] Firms that are without a competitive advantage or that are not competing in an attractive industry earn, at best, only average returns. **Average returns** are returns equal to those an investor expects to earn from other investments with a similar amount of risk. In the long run, an inability to earn at least average returns results in failure. Failure occurs because investors will choose to invest in firms that earn at least average returns and will withdraw their investments from those earning less.

Above-average returns are returns in excess of what an investor expects to earn from other investments with a similar amount of risk.

Risk is an investor's uncertainty about the economic gains or losses that will result from a particular investment.

Average returns are returns equal to those an investor expects to earn from other investments with a similar amount of risk.

Dynamic in nature, the **strategic management process** (see Figure 1.1) is the full set of commitments, decisions, and actions required for a firm to achieve strategic competitiveness and earn above-average returns.[7] Relevant *strategic inputs*, from analyses of the internal and external environments, are necessary for effective strategy formulation and strategy implementation actions. In turn, effective *strategic actions* are a prerequisite to achieving the desired outcomes of strategic competitiveness and above-average returns. Thus, the strategic management process is used to match the conditions of an ever-changing market and competitive structure with a firm's continuously evolving resources, capabilities, and competencies (the sources of strategic inputs). Effective *strategic actions* that take place in the context of carefully integrated strategy formulation and strategy implementation processes result in desired *strategic outcomes*.[8]

The **strategic management process** is the full set of commitments, decisions, and actions required for a firm to achieve strategic competitiveness and earn above-average returns.

In the remaining chapters of this book, we use the strategic management process to explain what firms should do to achieve strategic competitiveness and earn above-average returns. Through these explanations, it becomes clear why some firms consistently achieve competitive success and others fail to do so.[9] As you will see, the reality of global competition is a critical part of the strategic management process.[10]

Several topics are discussed in this chapter. First, we examine the challenge of strategic management. This brief discussion highlights the fact that the strategic actions taken to achieve and then to maintain strategic competitiveness demand the best of managers, employees, and their organizations on a continuous basis. Second, we describe the new competitive landscape, created primarily by the emergence of a global economy and rapid technological changes. The new competitive landscape establishes the contextual opportunities and threats within which the strategic management process is used by firms striving to meet the competitive challenge raised by demanding global standards.

We next examine two models that suggest conditions organizations should study to gain the strategic inputs needed to select strategic actions in the pursuit of strategic competitiveness and above-average returns. However, the emphases of these

Figure 1.1 ***The Strategic Management Process***

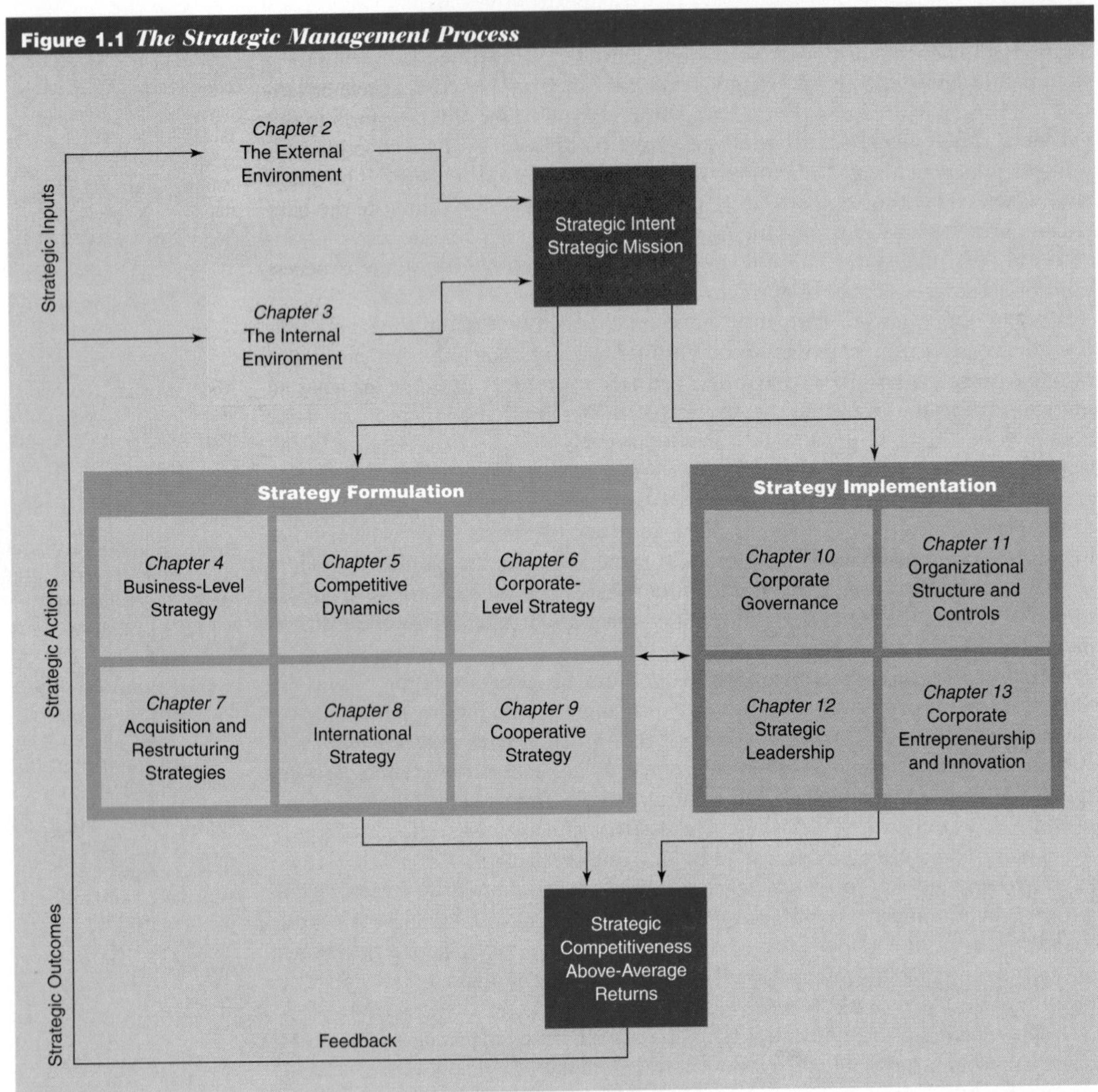

two models differ. The first model (industrial organization) suggests that the *external environment* should be the primary determinant of a firm's strategic actions. The key to this model is locating and competing successfully in an attractive (that is, profitable) industry. The second model (resource based) suggests that a firm's unique resources and capabilities are the critical link to strategic competitiveness. Comprehensive explanations of these two models in this first chapter and the next two show that through combined use of these two models, firms obtain the full set of strategic inputs needed to formulate and implement strategies successfully.

Analyses of its external and internal environments provide a firm with the information it needs to develop its strategic intent and strategic mission (intent and mission are defined later in this chapter). As shown in Figure 1.1, strategic intent and strategic mission influence strategy formulation and implementation actions.

The chapter's discussion then turns to the stakeholders served by organizations. The degree to which stakeholders' needs can be met increases directly with enhancements in a firm's strategic competitiveness and its ability to earn above-average returns. Closing the chapter are introductions to organizational strategists and the elements of the strategic management process.

THE CHALLENGE OF STRATEGIC MANAGEMENT

The goals of achieving strategic competitiveness and earning above-average returns are challenging—not only for firms as large as WorldCom, but also for those as small as your local dry cleaners. The performance of some companies, of course, more than meets strategic management's challenge. At the end of a recent year, for example, Coca-Cola and General Electric had created more wealth (as measured by market value added) than other U.S. firms (approximately $125 billion in the case of Coca-Cola; roughly $122 billion for GE). The top 10 wealth creators for 1997, including Coca-Cola and GE, are shown in Table 1.1. Microsoft moved from 14 in 1992 to 3 in 1997. More dramatically, Intel exploded from 74 in 1992 to 4 in 1997.[11] The fact that only 2 of the 25 largest U.S. industrial corporations in 1900 are still competitive today attests to the rigors of business competition and the challenge of strategic management. The remaining 23 companies have failed, been merged with other firms, or are no longer of significant size relative to competitors.[12] Moreover, in a recent year, almost 150,000 U.S. businesses either failed or filed for bankruptcy.[13] Results such as these support the view that competitive success is transient.[14] Thomas J. Watson, Jr., formerly IBM's chairman, once cautioned people to remember that "corporations are expendable and that success—at best—is an impermanent achievement which can always slip out of hand."[15]

TABLE 1.1 ***Top Ten Wealth Creators***

1997	1996	1992	Company	Market Value Added (Millions)[a]
1	1	4	Coca-Cola	$124,894
2	2	6	General Electric	121,874
3	5	14	Microsoft	89,957
4	12	74	Intel	86,481
5	3	2	Merck	78,246
6	4	3	Philip Morris	66,608
7	9	12	Exxon	55,532
8	8	10	Procter & Gamble	55,102
9	6	7	Johnson & Johnson	51,119
10	11	5	Bristol-Myers Squibb	42,910

Source: R. Teitelbaum, 1997, America's Greatest Wealth Creators, *Fortune,* November 10, 265–276.

[a]Market Value Added is defined as a company's market value minus the capital tied up in the company.

Successful performance may be transient and impermanent, at least as reflected by *Fortune*'s Most Admired Corporation list. In 1986 IBM held the number one position on *Fortune's* list for the fourth consecutive year. By 1995, IBM's position had slipped to number 281. Of course, IBM has come back as have The Limited and Honda. However, not all companies are fortunate enough for their problems to be temporary. Woolworth and Color Tile are no longer in business as explained in the Strategic Focus on the impermanence of success.

While The Limited and Honda are making changes to return to their days of success, questions remain about whether their efforts will result in the success they once enjoyed. Both have significant competition. The U.S. market drives Honda and so it is vital for the firm to reestablish its relationship with the U.S. consumer. The Limited must do the same by offering consumers smart and unique fashions in the clothing it markets. In both cases, Honda's world car and The Limited's new fashions, the success of these efforts will make the difference in the firm's ability to again achieve strategic competitiveness and to earn above-average returns.[16]

Some firms create their own problems by formulating the wrong strategy or poorly implementing a strategy. Such was the case in Union Pacific Corporation's acquisition of Southern Pacific Rail Corporation. While Union Pacific promised higher efficiency, the opposite occurred after the two firms were merged. There have been many service problems causing widespread shipping delays for many of Union Pacific's largest customers. These delays are costly to Union Pacific's customers, several of whom resorted to trucking their products to their markets. In fact, some of its customers had to halt production for a time because of the firm's inability to transport products to their customers. Union Pacific also experienced a series of fatal accidents, which complicated the problem of untangling the web of delays in freight service. The string of accidents was investigated by 80 inspectors from the Federal Railroad Administration (FRA). The head of the FRA, Jolene Molitoris, suggested that many of the problems being experienced were due to the merger. Thus, Union Pacific acquired Southern Pacific promising improved service but has only angered its best customers and courted problems with the federal regulatory agency. In the final analysis, the cost of the acquisition to Union Pacific may be much greater than the $3.9 billion paid for Southern Pacific.[17]

STRATEGIC FOCUS

The Impermanence of Success

The Limited, the largest specialty retailer in the United States, was started by Les Wexner in 1963 with $5,000 of borrowed capital. The Limited experienced incredible growth and success in its first 29 years of existence. In 1997, it had $8.6 billion in annual revenue from its 13 separate store chains and catalogs (which include Bath & Body Works and Victoria's Secret). However, The Limited has experienced problems in recent years. Competition began to eat into the company's market, with the most damage in the Women's Division. As a result the firm had significantly lower earnings in 1996. Analysts and Wexler agree that some of the problems stemmed from bad fashions; in fact, the clothes being sold by The Limited's stores became boring to the customers. To revive its operations, Wexler is changing the management team and closing unprofitable stores, 200 in 1997 alone. While it has a long way to go, analysts are cautiously optimistic about the firm's future.

Some other retailers have not been as fortunate. For example, in 1997, Woolworth closed all of its existing 400 five and dime stores. A one-time market leader, Color Tile closed its doors in 1997 as well. Woolworth's market niche became less valuable and was usurped by competitors such as Wal-Mart. Furthermore its downtown locations lost customers as shoppers fled to the suburbs. At its pinnacle, Woolworth had 2,100 stores globally. In an attempt to change with the times, Woolworth created Woolco. However, it was never able to compete effectively in the discount variety store market. At its demise, Color Tile had 103 stores. It started to lose market share when superstores such as Lowe's and Home Depot began to offer floor and wall coverings. The industry became hypercompetitive and Color Tile lacked the resources to compete with the superstores and could not make the necessary changes to successfully find a new market niche.

While not as severe as those explained above, Honda also experienced problems and is now making major changes to reassert itself in the global automobile market. A few years ago, it redesigned its popular Accord to make it more sporty. However, it had too little internal space to satisfy U.S. customers and was not adequately sporty for the Japanese consumers. As a result, Honda began to lose market share in several major markets around the world. This was quite an awakening for the Honda executives who had become perhaps too complacent with the strong demand for the firm's autos. Honda took drastic action and is now trying to build a "world car." This car has the same basic design but is adapted for consumer tastes in different markets. For example, in 1997 Honda launched two versions of the Accord, one in the U.S. and one in Japan. The U.S. version is 189 inches long and 70 inches wide to be a mid-size competitor of the Ford Taurus. The Accord in Japan is six inches shorter and four inches thinner. The Japanese version is a sporty compact with many high technology features. In 1998 a European Accord was introduced that had a short narrow body designed for maneuvering on narrow streets. There are other versions as well. Analysts are optimistic; but Honda also must fight to maintain its efficiency as cost is becoming a major factor in global auto sales.

SOURCE: K. Abdullah, 1997, Color Tile to cease operations by Aug. 30, *Dallas Morning News*, August 1, D1, D2; T. Box, 1997, Consumers put increasing emphasis on price when considering new cars, *Dallas Morning News*, September 2, D1, D8; W. Kates, 1997, Woolworth legacy fading with store chain, *Dallas Morning News*, October 20, D1, D4; K. Naughton, E. Thorton, K. Kerwin and H. Dawley, 1997, Can Honda build a world car? *Business Week*, September 8, 100–108; M. Williams, 1997, The Limited tries to rebuild after losing some of its appeal, *Dallas Morning News*, November 2, H5.

In recognition of strategic management's challenge, Andrew Grove, Intel's CEO, observed that only paranoid companies survive and succeed. Intel is the number one computer chip manufacturer in the world with market capitalization greater than the top three U.S. automakers combined. Such firms know that current success does not guarantee future strategic competitiveness and above-average returns. Accordingly, these companies strive continuously to improve so they can remain competitive. To be strategically competitive and earn above-average returns through implementation of a world car, Honda must compete differently than in the past. IBM, The Limited, Motorola, Nippon Telephone and Telegraph, and WorldCom, too, must compete differently in a world being shaped increasingly by globalization, technological changes, and the information revolution. For all these companies and others that are competing in the new competitive landscape, Andrew Grove believes that a key challenge is to try to do the impossible—namely, to anticipate the unexpected.[18]

THE NEW COMPETITIVE LANDSCAPE[19]

The fundamental nature of competition in many of the world's industries is changing.[20] The pace of this change is relentless and is increasing. Even determining the boundaries of an industry has become challenging. Consider, for example, how advances in interactive computer networks and telecommunications have blurred the definition of the "television" industry. Because of these advances, the near future will find firms such as ABC, CBS, NBC, and HBO competing not only among themselves but also with AT&T, Microsoft, and Sony. An example of this new form of competition occurred in late 1995 when News Corporation, which owns Fox Broadcasting Company, formed a strategic alliance with Tele-Communications Inc., the largest U.S. cable system. Viewed as a venture that would control a global web of sports TV networks, this alliance was considered quickly to be a major competitor for ESPN and other sources interested in delivering sports events to customers around the world.[21]

Still other characteristics of the new competitive landscape are noteworthy. Conventional sources of competitive advantage such as economies of scale and huge advertising budgets are not as effective in the new competitive landscape. Moreover, the traditional managerial mind-set cannot lead a firm to strategic competitiveness in the new competitive landscape. In its place, managers must adopt a new mind-set—one that values flexibility, speed, innovation, integration, and the challenges that evolve from constantly changing conditions.[22] The conditions of the new competitive landscape result in a perilous business world, one where the investments required to compete on a global scale are enormous and the consequences of failure are severe.[23]

Hypercompetition is a term that is used often to capture the realities of the new competitive landscape (mentioned briefly here, hypercompetitive environments are discussed further in Chapter 5). According to Richard A. D'Aveni, hypercompetition:

> results from the dynamics of strategic maneuvering among global and innovative combatants. It is a condition of rapidly escalating competition based on price-quality positioning, competition to create new know-how and establish first-mover advantage, competition to protect or invade established product or geographic markets, and competition based on deep pockets and the creation of even deeper pocketed alliances.[24]

Several factors have created hypercompetitive environments and the new competitive landscape. As shown in Figure 1.2, the emergence of a global economy and technology, coupled with rapid technological changes, are the two primary drivers.

The Global Economy

A **global economy** is one in which goods, services, people, skills, and ideas move freely across geographic borders.

A **global economy** is one in which goods, services, people, skills, and ideas move freely across geographic borders. Relatively unfettered by artificial constraints, such as tariffs, the global economy significantly expands and complicates a firm's competitive environment.[25]

Interesting opportunities and challenges are associated with the global economy's emergence. For example, Europe, instead of the United States, is now the

Figure 1.2 *The New Competitive Landscape*

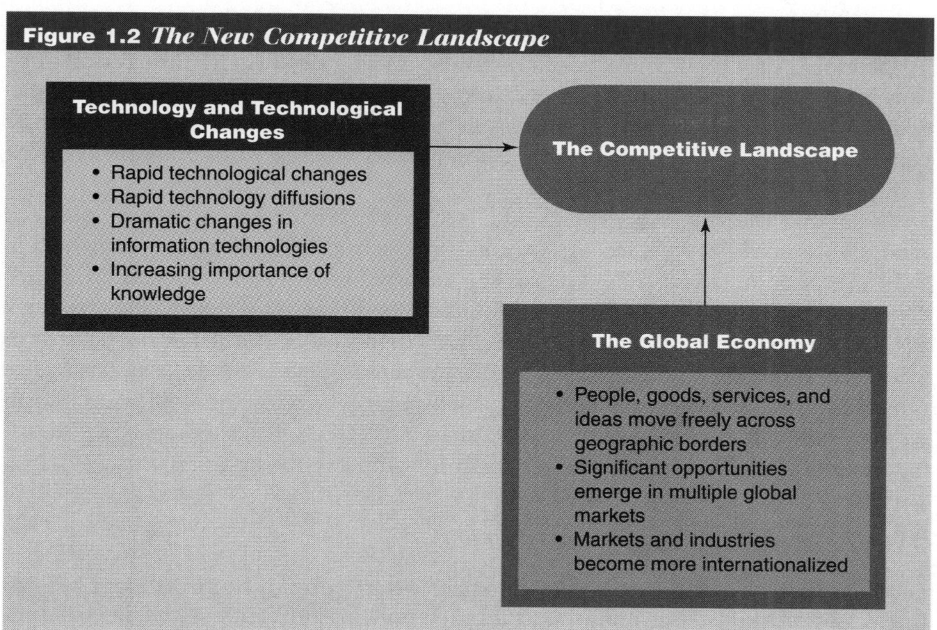

world's largest single market. If countries from the former Soviet Union and other Eastern block nations are included, the European market has a gross domestic product (GDP) of $5 trillion with 700 million potential customers.[26] In addition, by 2015 or perhaps sooner, China's total GDP will be greater than Japan's, although its per capita output will be much lower.[27] Some believe that the United States, Japan, and Europe are relatively equal contenders in the battle to be the most competitive nation, or group of nations, in the twenty-first century. Achieving this status will allow the "winner's citizens to have the highest standard of living."[28]

To achieve strategic competitiveness in the global economy, a firm must view the world as its marketplace. For example, Procter & Gamble believes that it still has tremendous potential to grow internationally where the demand for household products is not as mature (such as in China) as it is in the United States.

A commitment to viewing the world as a company's marketplace creates a sense of direction that can serve the firm well. For example, Whirlpool Corporation, the world's largest manufacturer of major home appliances, intends to maintain its global leadership position. With production facilities in 12 countries and through its marketing efforts in 120 nations, the company's sales volume outside the United States is now over 40 percent. Recently Whirlpool had investments in three appliance companies in Brazil, one in Canada, a subsidiary in Argentina, and joint ventures in Mexico, India, Taiwan, and China. Lawrence Bossidy, CEO of AlliedSignal (a manufacturer of aerospace components, automotive parts for original equipment markets, and engineered materials, such as chemicals and plastics), is convinced that globalization is a key to his firm's growth. To achieve his goal of AlliedSignal generating 45 percent of its sales volume outside the United States by 1997, Bossidy aggressively led his company into China and India, two markets he believes have great potential.[29]

Large firms such as Whirlpool and AlliedSignal often commit to competition in the global economy quicker than do midsize and small firms. In the recent past, however, the number of U.S. midsize and small firms competing in the global economy has increased. For example, the percentage of U.S. midsize companies competing in markets outside of their home nation increased to 56 percent of the total in 1995.[30]

Overall, as measured by exports, U.S. companies' strategic actions in globalized markets are increasing. In fact, in a recent time period, 42 percent of the growth in the U.S. economy was based on increasing exported goods. In 1997, exports and imports accounted for 28.4 percent of the U.S. gross domestic product. This percentage was up from 25.5 percent in 1996 and less than 21 percent in 1992. The growth in exports of U.S. firms has been particularly acute in capital goods. Experts suggest that U.S. firms have a strong competitive advantage over foreign rivals in the capital goods industries. These same experts predict that U.S. firms' competitive advantage in global technology will power them into the twenty-first century.[31]

The March of Globalization

Globalization is the spread of economic innovations around the world and the political and cultural adjustments that accompany this diffusion. Globalization encourages international integration, which has increased substantially during the last generation. In globalized markets and industries, financial capital might be obtained in one national market and used to buy raw materials in another one. Manufacturing equipment bought from a third national market can be used to produce products that are sold in yet a fourth market.[32] Thus, globalization increases the range of opportunities for firms competing in the new competitive landscape. As noted in the Strategic Focus, this is the case for Wal-Mart.

STRATEGIC FOCUS

The March of Globalization: Wal-Mart, China, and Beyond

Wal-Mart is the world's largest retailer. The world should be beware, however, because it is now moving aggressively into international markets. For example, the firm recently invested $1.2 billion to buy a controlling interest in Cifra SA a large Mexican retailer with which it had a six-year joint venture. This move is the first direct investment in one of its foreign partners. While the international division of Wal-Mart is currently small compared to the rest of Wal-Mart's organization, analysts estimate that international sales could reach $27 billion (17 percent of Wal-Mart's annual revenues) by 2000. Currently, other retailers have much more foreign sales such as Tengelmann and Aldi from Germany, Ahold from the Netherlands, and Carrefour from France.

Wal-Mart is trying to achieve boundaryless retailing with global pricing, sourcing, and logistics. Most of Wal-Mart's international investments have been in Canada and Mexico, with close proximity to the United States. However, it has moved recently into Argentina, Brazil, Indonesia, and China. Supercenter stores in Buenos Aires sell as many as 15,000 items in a day, twice as many as in comparable U.S. superstores. Wal-Mart plans to export its North American dominance to other regions of the world as well. Additional descriptions of Wal-Mart's international expansion plans are presented in Chapter 8.

One of the regions Wal-Mart intends to enter is China. China is trying to boldly reform its economy, moving toward a more open and entrepreneurial system. Currently, the Chinese government plans to sell a majority of the 13,000 large and mid-sized state-owned enterprises, along with many of the small firms as well. President Jiang Zemen has stated, "We should encourage mergers of enterprises, standardize bankruptcy procedures, divert laid-off workers, increase efficiency by downsizing staff and encourage re-employment projects." Wal-Mart plans to expand operations in China because its managers estimate that purchasing power in China will equal current levels in the U.S. within seven years. Others are venturing into China as well ranging from Motorola's $2 billion fabrication plant to the joint venture between Enron and Singapore Power. This joint venture is designed to develop small scale power projects that are expected to explode in number over the next several years in China.

Another example of the increasing globalization is the fact that the largest gasoline retailer in the U.S. is owned by a foreign firm. Petroleos de Venezuela owns Citgo which has 14,054 gasoline outlets in the U.S. The number two retailer is Texaco with 13,023 outlets. Citgo, Mobil, and Shell (headquartered in the Netherlands) account for 30 percent of the U.S. gasoline market.

SOURCE: S. Faison, 1997, Bold economic reforms proposed at opening of China Congress, *New York Times*, September 13, nytimes.com; M. M. Hamilton, 1997, At gasoline pumps, an urge to merge, *Washington Post*, July 15, washingtonpost.com; L. Lee and J. Millman, 1997, Wal-Mart to invest $1.2 billion for control of Mexican retailer, *Wall Street Journal Interactive Edition*, June 4, http://www.interactive3.wsj.com; *Wall Street Journal*, Singapore Power, Enron units form joint venture in China, June 21, http://www.wsj.com; W. Zellner, L. Shepard, I. Katz and D. Lindorff, 1997, Wal-Mart spoken here, *Business Week*, June 16, http://www.businessweek.com.

The internationalization of markets and industries makes it increasingly difficult to think of some firms as domestic companies. For example, in a recent year, Honda Motor Company (1) employed 14,000 people in the United States; (2) sold 660,000 units in the United States, 480,000 (73 percent) of which it produced there; (3) manufactured its automobiles with 75 percent local U.S. content (parts/assemblies manufactured in the United States); (4) purchased $2.9 billion worth of parts from U.S. suppliers; (5) paid $2.5 billion in federal income tax; (6) invested $3 billion in a research and development center in the United States; and (7) exported 40,000 cars from its U.S. facilities to other nations' markets. At the same time, Chrysler Corporation was producing minivans in Canada and LeBarons in Mexico. Similarly, Toyota Motor Corporation continues to reduce its total employment in Japan while expanding its global workforce. Toyota's Kentucky facility is the only place where the company builds its Avalon sedan and Camry Coupe and station wagon. In 1997, this plant became the sole producer of Toyota's new minivan and in 1998, the firm began to build its T100 pickup in the United States.[33] Likewise, a few years ago, Bridgestone Corporation, headquartered in Japan, acquired Firestone Corporation, then an American firm. Now, Bridgestone is planning to build a $400 million manufacturing facility in the U.S. The intent is to enhance its competitive position in the U.S. market with its ninth plant in the U.S. in addition to its $430 million upgrade of existing facilities.[34]

Given their operations, these firms should not be thought of as Japanese or American. Instead, they can be classified more accurately as global companies striv-

Toyota Motor Corporation has reduced its work force in Japan while expanding globally. Its Georgetown, Kentucky, facility is the sole producer of Toyota minivans, Avalon sedans, and Camry coupes and station wagons.

ing to achieve strategic competitiveness in the new competitive landscape. Some believe that because of its enormous economic benefits, globalization will not be stopped. It has been predicted, for example, that genuine free trade in manufactured goods among the United States, Europe, and Japan would add 5 to 10 percent to the triad's annual economic outputs; free trade in the triad's service sector would boost aggregate output by another 15 to 20 percent. Realizing these potential gains in economic output requires a commitment from the industrialized nations to cooperatively stimulate the higher levels of trade necessary for global growth. Eliminating national laws that impede free trade is an important stimulus to increased trading among nations.[35]

Global competition has increased performance standards in many dimensions, including those of quality, cost, productivity, product introduction time, and smooth, flowing operations. Moreover, these standards are not static; they are exacting, requiring continuous improvement from a firm and its employees. As they accept the challenges posed by these increasing standards, companies improve their capabilities and individual workers sharpen their skills. Thus, in the new competitive landscape, competitive success will accrue only to those capable of meeting, if not exceeding global standards. This challenge exists for large firms and for small and midsize companies that develop cooperative relationships (e.g., joint ventures) with larger corporations in order to capitalize on international growth opportunities.[36]

The development of newly industrialized countries is changing the global competitive landscape and significantly increasing competition in global markets. The economic development of Asian countries outside of Japan is increasing the significance of Asian markets. Firms in the newly industrialized Asian countries such as South Korea, however, are becoming major competitors in global industries. For instance, Samsung has become a market leader in the semiconductor industry taking market share away from Japanese and American firms. Samsung is also moving into the aerospace industry. With increasing globalization and the spread of information technology, other countries are likely to develop their industrial bases as well. As this occurs, global markets will expand but competition in those markets will also become more intense.

Firms such as Wal-Mart, Motorola, and Enron are making major moves into international markets. In particular, each of these firms is making important investments in Asia. Of course there are also firms such as Petroleos de Venezuela that have made major investments in North America. Thus, international investments come from many directions and are targeted for many different regions of the world. There are risks with these investments, however. We discuss a number of these risks in Chapter 8. Some have referred to these risks as the liability of foreignness.[37] Critical to success in international markets is a firm's ability to manage international operations such that it takes advantage of the opportunities presented by operating in these markets and overcomes or avoids most of the challenges that exist in these markets. Recent research suggests that firm's are challenged in their early ventures into international markets and can have difficulties if they enter too many different or challenging international markets. In other words, performance may suffer in early efforts to globalize until the skills to manage it are developed. Moverover, performance may suffer with substantial amounts of globalization. In this instance, firms may overdiversify internationally beyond their ability to manage the diversified operations that have been created.[38] The outcome can sometimes be quite painful to firms.[39] Thus, movement into international markets, even for firms with substantial experience in such markets, requires careful planning and selection of the appropriate markets to enter and the most effective strategies to operate successfully in those markets.[40]

Global markets are attractive strategic options for some companies, but they are not the only source of strategic competitiveness. In fact, for most companies, even for those capable of competing successfully in global markets, it is critical to remain committed to the domestic market. In the words of the director of economic studies at the Brookings Institution, "Imported goods are components of a larger share of goods produced and sold in the United States, and international trade is likely to grow in significance. Still, the great bulk of the goods and services Americans consume and invest in is entirely domestic."[41] In the new competitive landscape, firms are challenged to develop the optimal level of globalization, a level that results in appropriate concentrations on a company's domestic and global operations.

In many instances then, strategically competitive companies are those that have learned how to apply competitive insights gained locally (or domestically) on a global scale. These companies do not impose homogeneous solutions in a pluralistic world. Instead, they nourish local insights so they can, as appropriate, modify and apply them in different regions around the world.

Technology and Technological Changes

There are three categories of technological trends and conditions through which technology is significantly altering the nature of competition.

Increasing Rate of Technological Change and Diffusion Both the rate of technology changes and the speed at which new technologies become available and are used have increased substantially over the last 15 to 20 years. *Perpetual innovation* is a term used to describe how rapidly and consistently new, information-intensive technologies replace older ones. The shorter product life cycles resulting from these rapid diffusions of new technologies place a competitive premium on being able to quickly introduce new goods and services into the marketplace. In fact, when products become somewhat indistinguishable because of the widespread and rapid diffusion of technologies, speed to market may be the only source of competitive advantage (see Chapter 5).[42]

There are other indicators of rapid technology diffusion. Some evidence suggests that after only 12 to 18 months, companies likely will have gathered information about their competitors' research and development and product decisions. Often, merely a few weeks pass before a new American-made product introduced in U.S. markets is copied, manufactured, and shipped to the United States by one or more companies in Asia.

Once a source of competitive advantage, today's rate of technological diffusion stifles the protection firms possessed previously through their patents. Patents are now thought by many to be an effective way of protecting proprietary technology primarily in the pharmaceutical and chemical industries. Many firms competing in the electronics industry often do not apply for patents to prevent competitors from gaining access to the technological knowledge included in the patent application.

The Information Age Dramatic changes in information technology have occurred in recent years. Personal computers, cellular phones, artificial intelligence, virtual reality, and massive databases (e.g., Lexis/Nexis) are a few examples of how information is used differently as a result of technological developments. Intel's Andrew Grove believes that electronic mail (e-mail) systems are the first manifestation of a revolution in the flow and management of information in companies throughout the world. In Grove's view, "The informed use of e-mail has two simple but startling implications: It turns days into minutes, and allows each person to reach hundreds of co-workers with the same effort it takes to reach just one."[43] An important outcome of these changes is that the ability to access and effectively use information has become an important source of competitive advantage in virtually all industries.

Companies are now being wired to build electronic networks linking them to customers, employees, vendors, and suppliers. IBM has made this a major thrust in its drive to reorient and revive its business. These networks are often referred to as E-business by IBM and others. E-business is big business. For example, Internet trade is predicted to reach $105 billion by 2000 from only $7.8 billion in 1997. It is even predicted that E-business will eventually represent 75-80 percent of the U.S. gross domestic product. This means that most transactions will be accomplished electronically.[44]

Both the pace of change in information technology and its diffusion will continue to increase. It is predicted, for example, that the number of personal computers in use will grow from over 150 million today to 278 million in 2010.

America Online (AOL) is trying to position itself to take advantage of this brave new world. Steve Case started the firm in 1985 and has experienced many problems since then, the most recent of which occurred in 1996. Case was a dreamer, a visionary who wanted to connect common people, not only the techies. There were many naysayers, particularly at the beginning. Regardless of the naysayers and the significant challenges that America Online has had to overcome, the firm's announcement that it was acquiring Compuserve, the oldest and largest online service, has been hailed as a major feat for AOL. It resulted from a three-way deal

Jeff Bezos, founder of Amazon.com, the largest bookstore in the world, began the company when he realized the enormous potential of selling via the Internet. The company, which sells only via the Internet, has an electronic network that connects it to its customers, employees, and suppliers.

with WorldCom. WorldCom bought Compuserve and then sold the online company's 2.6 million subscribers to AOL's networking and Internet access division. AOL is now the number one provider of online services. It adds 6,000 subscribers per day and has increased revenues from $53 million in 1993 to $2 billion in 1997. AOL expects to have 25 million subscribers by 2000. Case suggests that AOL "wants to be the Coca-Cola of the online world."[45]

The declining costs of information technologies and the increased accessibility to them are also evident in the new competitive landscape. The global proliferation of relatively inexpensive computing power and its linkage on a global scale via computer networks combine to increase the speed and diffusion of information technologies. Thus, the competitive potential of information technologies is now available to companies throughout the world rather than only to large firms in Europe, Japan, and North America.[46]

An important electronic pathway through which relatively inexpensive data and information are being distributed is the Internet. Combined, the Internet and World Wide Web create an infrastructure that allows the delivery of information to computers in any location. Access to significant quantities of relatively inexpensive information yields strategic opportunities for a range of industries and companies. Retailers, for example, use the Internet to provide abundant shopping privileges to customers in multiple locations. The power of this means of information access and application results in an almost astonishing array of strategic implications and possibilities.[47]

Anticipating and even creating users' future needs for access to and competitive use of information is challenging. The nature of this complex situation in an emerging industry seems to argue against a firm's long-term competitive success. Bill Gates, Microsoft's CEO, observed recently that while his firm may be the most dominant force in the personal computer industry today, "the landscape is changing fast enough that the company's continued role is far from guaranteed." This opinion was offered at a time when Microsoft controlled more than 80 percent of the world market for PC operating systems.[48] Thus, even for companies holding dominant positions such as Microsoft, the information age's rapid changes yield an uncertain and ambiguous future.

Increasing Knowledge Intensity *Knowledge* (information, intelligence, and expertise) is the basis of technology and its application. In the new competitive landscape, knowledge is a critical organizational resource and is increasingly a valuable source of competitive advantage. Because of this, many companies now strive to transmute the accumulated knowledge of individual employees into a corporate asset. Some argue that the value of intangible assets, including knowledge, is growing as a proportion of total shareholder value.[49] The probability of achieving strategic competitiveness in the new competitive landscape is enhanced for the firm that realizes that its survival depends on the ability to capture intelligence, transform it into usable knowledge, and diffuse it rapidly throughout the company.[50] Companies that accept this challenge shift their focus from obtaining the information to exploiting the information to gain a competitive advantage over rival firms.[51]

Our discussion of conditions in the new competitive landscape shows that firms must be able to adapt quickly to achieve strategic competitiveness and earn above-average returns. The term strategic flexibility describes a firm's ability to do this. **Strategic flexibility** is a set of capabilities firms use to respond to various demands and opportunities that are a part of dynamic and uncertain competitive environments.[52] Firms should develop strategic flexibility in all areas of their operations. Such capabilities in terms of manufacturing, for example, allow firms to "switch gears—from, for example, rapid product development to low cost—relatively quickly and with minimum resources."[53]

Strategic flexibility is a set of capabilities firms use to respond to various demands and opportunities that are a part of dynamic and uncertain competitive environments.

To achieve strategic flexibility, many firms have to develop organizational slack. Slack resources allow the firm some flexibility to respond to environmental changes.[54] When the changes required are large, firms may have to undergo strategic reorientations. Such reorientations can change drastically a firm's competitive strategy.[55] Strategic reorientations are often the result of a firm's poor performance. For example, when a firm earns negative returns, its stakeholders (see discussion later in this chapter) are likely to place pressure on the top executives to make major changes.[56] To achieve continuous strategic flexibility, a firm has to develop the capacity to learn. As such, the learning is continuous, thereby providing the firm with new and current sets of skills. This allows it to adapt to its environment as the environment changes.[57]

Through careful strategic decisions, Coca-Cola has created strategic flexibility. It has done so by developing effective distribution of its products. For example, several years ago it developed a subsidiary bottling operation. It wanted to build an experienced and large bottling network to benefit from economies of scale and have significant capital to invest in distribution systems to enhance sales of Coca-Cola. Today this small set of anchor bottlers serves as the base for Coca-Cola's global distribution system. While the economies of scale and slack resources for investment provide flexibility of action for Coca-Cola, the real source of flexibility is in the way these anchor bottlers are managed. For example, CCE, the anchor domestic bottler in the United States, is substantially decentralized. In this way, the bottling operation in one region of the country can use different advertising campaigns from bottlers in other regions. Because of its success, CCE is becoming Coca-Cola's primary bottler in Great Britain, France, Belgium, the Netherlands and Luxembourg. Thus, CCE has the resources and expertise to move into different regions of the world, which only increases its economies of scale.[58]

Next, we describe two models used by firms to generate the strategic inputs needed to successfully formulate and implement strategies and to maintain strategic flexibility in the process of doing so.

THE I/O MODEL OF ABOVE-AVERAGE RETURNS

From the 1960s through the 1980s, the external environment was thought to be the *primary* determinant of strategies firms selected to be successful.[59] The I/O (industrial organization) model explains the dominant influence of the external environment on firms' strategic actions. This model specifies that the chosen industry in which to compete has a stronger influence on a firm's performance than do the choices managers make inside their organizations.[60] Firm performance is believed to be predicted primarily by a range of an industry's properties, including economies of scale, barriers to entry, diversification, product differentiation, and the degree of concentration[61] (these industry characteristics are examined in Chapter 2).

Grounded in the economics discipline, the I/O model has four underlying assumptions. First, the external environment is assumed to impose pressures and constraints that determine the strategies that would result in above-average returns. Second, most firms competing within a particular industry, or within a certain segment of an industry, are assumed to control similar strategically relevant resources and pursue similar strategies in light of those resources. The I/O model's third assumption is that resources used to implement strategies are highly mobile across firms. Because of resource mobility, any resource differences that might develop between firms will be short lived. Fourth, organizational decision makers are assumed to be rational and committed to acting in the firm's best interests as shown by their profit maximizing behaviors.[62]

The I/O model challenges firms to locate the most attractive industry in which to compete. Because most firms are assumed to have similar strategically relevant resources that are mobile across companies, competitiveness generally can be increased only when they find the industry with the highest profit potential and learn how to use their resources to implement the strategy required by the structural characteristics in that industry. The *five forces model of competition* is an analytical tool used to help firms with this task. This model (explained in detail in Chapter 2) encompasses many variables and tries to capture the complexity of competition.[63]

The five forces model suggests that an industry's potential profitability (i.e., its rate of return on invested capital relative to its cost of capital) is a function of interactions among five forces (suppliers, buyers, competitive rivalry among firms currently in the industry, product substitutes, and potential entrants to the industry).[64] Using this tool, a firm is challenged to understand an industry's profit potential and the strategy that should be implemented to establish a defensible competitive position, given the industry's structural characteristics. Typically, this model suggests that firms can earn above-average returns by manufacturing standardized products at costs below those of competitors (a cost leadership strategy) or differentiated products for which customers are willing to pay a price premium (a differentiation strategy). Cost leadership and differentiation strategies are described fully in Chapter 4.

As shown in Figure 1.3, the I/O model suggests that above-average returns are earned when firms implement the strategy dictated by the characteristics of the general, industry, and competitive environments. Companies that develop or acquire the internal skills needed to implement strategies required by the external environment are likely to succeed, while those that do not are likely to fail. As such, above-average returns are determined by external characteristics rather than the firm's unique internal resources and capabilities.

Let us consider the bagel industry as an example. It is a high growth industry with substantial potential to earn above-average returns. U.S. industry sales in-

Figure 1.3 *The I/O Model of Superior Returns*

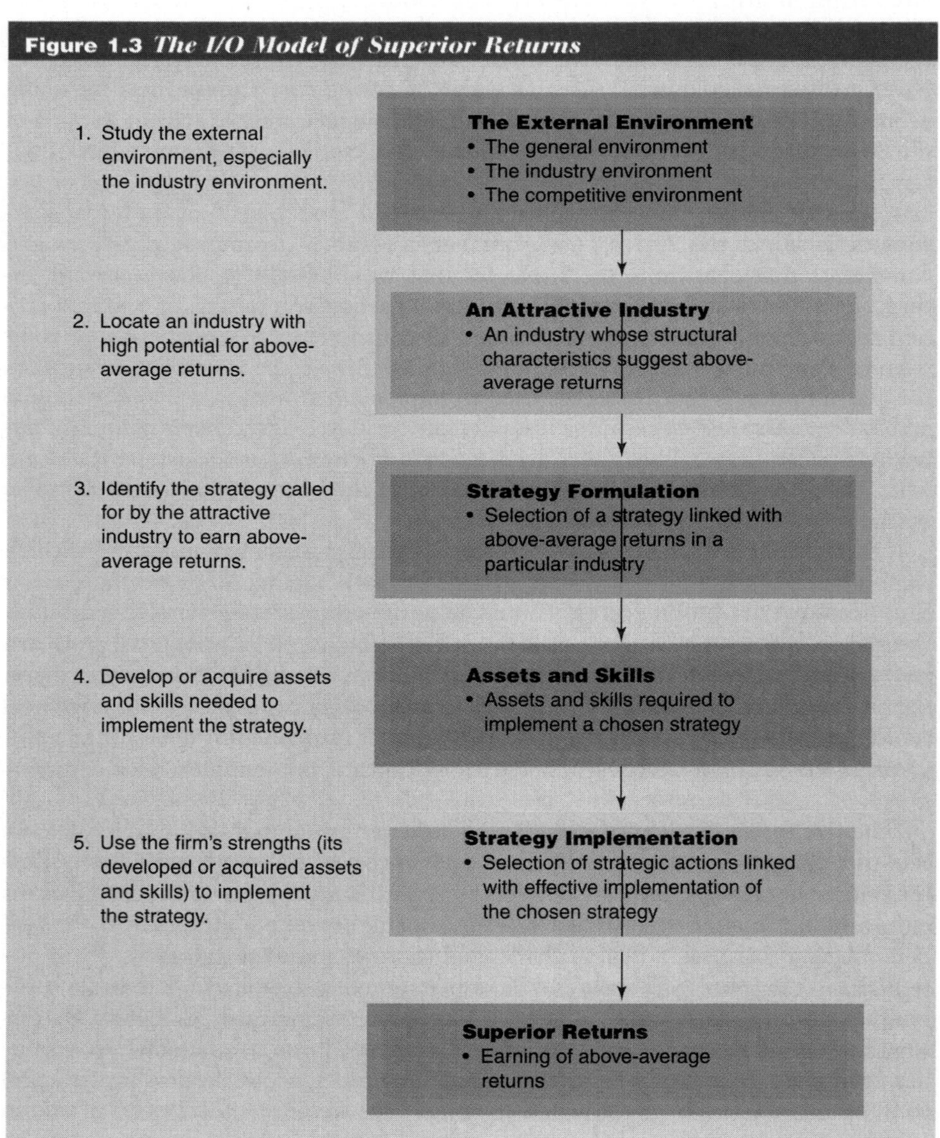

creased from $1.6 billion in 1995 to $2.3 billion in 1996, over a 40 percent rise in one year. Industry experts predict this growth trend for global sales as well. Interestingly, the bagel industry is in its infancy and thus has much potential. Evidence of this fact is shown by the growth of The Great Canadian Bagel Ltd. It was started in 1993 and by the end of 1996, it had 112 bakeries in operation. Other bagel firms are opening operations in Europe and Asia. Clearly it is an attractive industry to enter.[65]

Recent research provides support for the I/O model. It showed that approximately 20 percent of firm profitability was explained by industry. In other words, 20 percent of a firm's profitability is determined by the industry(ies) in which it chooses to operate. This research also showed, however, that 36 percent of the variance in profitability could be attributed to firm characteristics and actions.[66] The results of this research suggest that both the environment and firm characteristics play a role in determining a firm's specific level of profitability. Thus, there is likely a reciprocal relationship between the environment and firm strategy, and this interrelationship affects firm performance.[67]

As the research results suggest, successful competition in the new competitive landscape mandates that a firm build a unique set of resources and capabilities. This should be done, however, within the framework of the dynamics of the industry (or industries) in which a firm competes. In this context, a firm is viewed as a bundle of market activities and a bundle of resources. Market activities are understood through application of the I/O model. The development and effective use of a firm's resources, capabilities, and competencies is understood through application of the resource-based model. Through an effective combination of results gained by using both the I/O and resource-based models, firms dramatically increase the probability of achieving strategic competitiveness and earning above-average returns.

THE RESOURCE-BASED MODEL OF ABOVE-AVERAGE RETURNS

The resource-based model assumes that each organization is a collection of unique resources and capabilities that provides the basis for its strategy and is the *primary* source of its returns. In the new competitive landscape, this model argues that a firm is a collection of evolving capabilities that is managed dynamically in pursuit of above-average returns.[68] Thus, according to this model, differences in firms' performances across time are driven *primarily* by their unique resources and capabilities rather than by an industry's structural characteristics.[69] This model also assumes that over time, a firm acquires different resources and develops unique capabilities. As such, all firms competing within a particular industry may not possess the same strategically relevant resources and capabilities. Another assumption of this model is that resources may not be highly mobile across firms. The differences in resources form the basis of competitive advantage.[70]

Resources are inputs into a firm's production process, such as capital equipment, the skills of individual employees, patents, finance, and talented managers. In general, a firm's resources can be classified into three categories: physical, human, and organizational capital.[71] Described fully in Chapter 3, resources are both tangible and intangible in nature.

Resources are inputs into a firm's production process, such as capital equipment, the skills of individual employees, patents, finance, and talented managers.

Individual resources alone may not yield a competitive advantage. For example, a sophisticated piece of manufacturing equipment may become a strategically relevant resource only when its use is integrated effectively with other aspects of a firm's operations (such as marketing and the work of employees). In general, it is through the combination and integration of sets of resources that competitive advantages are formed. A **capability** is the capacity for a set of resources to integratively perform a task or an activity.[72] Through continued use, capabilities become stronger and more difficult for competitors to understand and imitate.[73] As a source of competitive advantage, a capability ". . . should be neither so simple that it is highly imitable, nor so complex that it defies internal steering and control."[74]

A **capability** is the capacity for a set of resources to integratively perform a task or an activity.

Amazon has taken the retail book market by storm. It was the first firm to sell books on the Internet. As such Amazon has developed important capabilities for marketing and distributing books online. This firm has shown that a large inventory and beautiful facilities are not necessary to sell books. However, Amazon's capabilities can be imitated. In fact, they are being imitated by the large and powerful Barnes & Noble. Barnes & Noble is the leading book marketer in the United States. It recently opened its own online bookshop. Developing Web pages and online order taking is copied easily. Barnes & Noble's action could be bad news for Amazon. It remains to be seen whether Amazon will enjoy many first mover advantages. (See Chapter 5 for a full discussion of first mover advantages.) Analysts are betting that Barnes & Noble will win this competitive battle if for no other reason than it has the resources to wage cutthroat competition.[75]

The resource-based model of competitive advantage is shown in Figure 1.4. In contrast to the I/O model, the resource-based view is grounded in the perspective that a firm's internal environment, in terms of its resources and capabilities, is more critical to the determination of strategic actions than is the external environment. Instead of focusing on the accumulation of resources necessary to implement the strategy dictated by conditions and constraints in the external environment (I/O model), the resource-based view suggests that a firm's unique resources and capabilities provide the basis for a strategy. The strategy chosen should allow the firm to best exploit its core competencies relative to opportunities in the external environment.

Not all of a firm's resources and capabilities have the potential to be the basis for competitive advantage. This potential is realized when resources and capabilities are valuable, rare, costly to imitate, and nonsubstitutable.[76] Resources are *valuable* when they allow a firm to exploit opportunities and/or neutralize threats in its external environment; they are *rare* when possessed by few, if any, current and potential competitors; they are *costly to imitate* when other firms either cannot obtain them or are at a cost disadvantage to obtain them compared to the firm that already possesses them; and they are nonsubstitutable when they have no structural equivalents.[77]

When these four criteria are met, resources and capabilities become core competencies. **Core competencies** are resources and capabilities that serve as a source of competitive advantage for a firm over its rivals.[78] Often related to a firm's functional skills (e.g., the marketing function is a core competence at Philip Morris), the development, nurturing, and application of core competencies throughout a firm may be highly related to strategic competitiveness. Managerial competencies are important in most firms. For example such competencies have been shown to be critically important to successful entry into foreign markets.[79] Such competen-

Core competencies are resources and capabilities that serve as a source of competitive advantage for a firm over its rivals.

Figure 1.4 *The Resource-Based Model of Superior Returns*

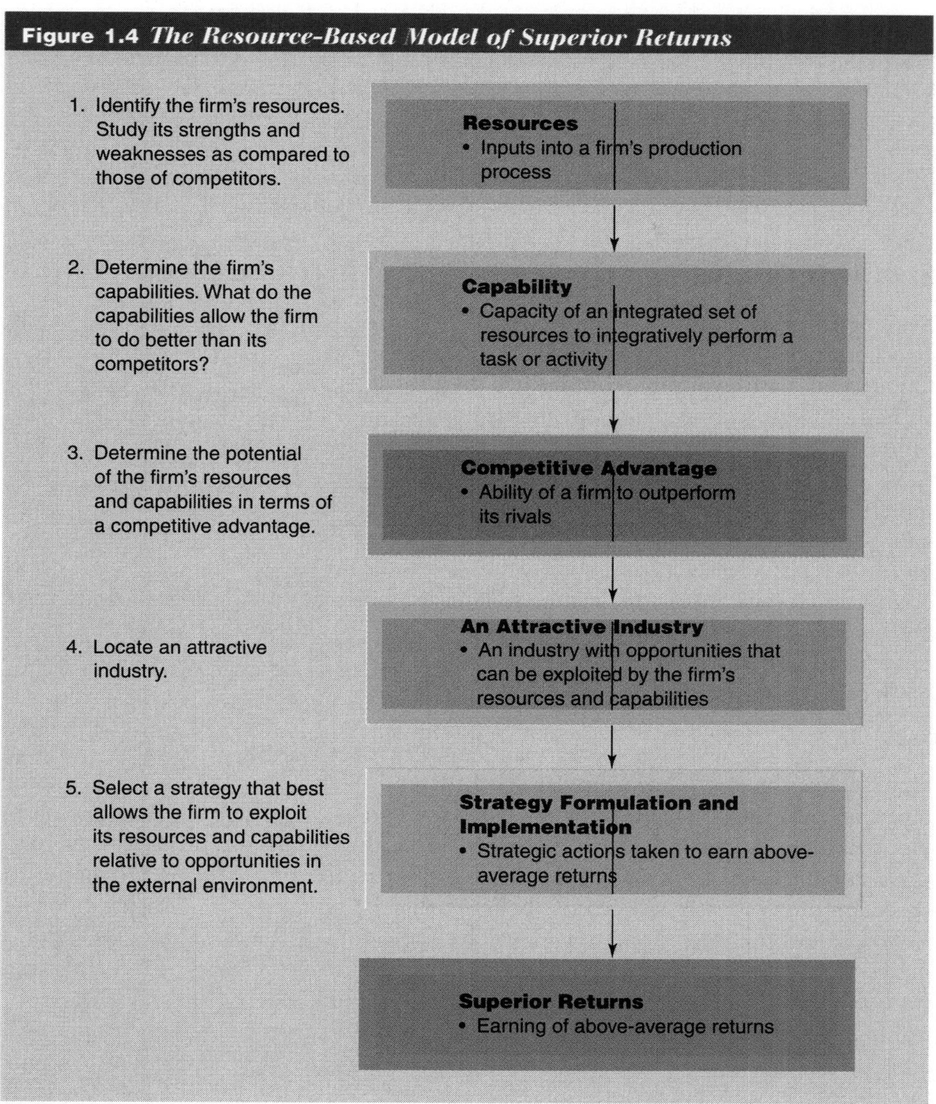

cies may include the capability to effectively organize and govern complex and diverse operations and the capability to create and communicate a strategic vision.[80] Another set of important competencies is product related. Included among these competencies are the capability to develop innovative new products and to reengineer existing products to satisfy changing consumer tastes.[81] Competencies must also be under continuous development to keep them up-to-date. This requires a systematic program for updating old skills and learning new ones.[82] Dynamic core competencies are especially important in rapidly changing environments such as those that exist in high technology industries.[83] Thus, the resource-based model argues that core competencies are the basis for a firm's competitive advantage, its strategic competitiveness, and its ability to earn above-average returns.

STRATEGIC INTENT AND STRATEGIC MISSION

Resulting from analyses of a firm's internal and external environments is the information required to form a strategic intent and develop a strategic mission (see Figure 1.1). Both intent and mission are linked with strategic competitiveness.

Strategic Intent

Strategic intent is the leveraging of a firm's internal resources, capabilities, and core competencies to accomplish the firm's goals in the competitive environment.

Strategic intent is the leveraging of a firm's internal resources, capabilities, and core competencies to accomplish the firm's goals in the competitive environment.[84] Concerned with winning competitive battles and obtaining global leadership, strategic intent implies a significant stretch of an organization's resources, capabilities, and core competencies. When established effectively, a strategic intent can cause people to perform in ways they never imagined would be possible.[85] Strategic intent exists when all employees and levels of a firm are committed to the pursuit of a specific (and significant) performance criterion. Some argue that strategic intent provides employees with the only goal worthy of personal effort and commitment—to unseat the best or remain the best, worldwide.[86] Strategic intent has been formed effectively when people believe fervently in their product and industry and when they are focused totally on their firm's ability to outdo its competitors.[87]

The following examples are expressions of strategic intent. Unocal Corporation intends "to become a high-performance multinational energy company—not the biggest, but the *best*." According to Eli Lilly and Company, "It's our strategic intent that customers worldwide view us as their most valued pharmaceutical partner." Phillips Petroleum Company seeks "to be the top performer in everything" the company does. Intel intends to become the premier building-block supplier to the computer industry. Microsoft believes that its "holy grail" is to provide the Yellow Pages for an electronic marketplace of on-line information systems. Canon desires to "beat Xerox" and Honda strives to become a second Ford (a company it identified as a pioneer in the automobile industry). The CEO of Pep Boys does not believe in friendly competition; instead, he wants to dominate the competition and, by doing so, put them out of business. At Procter & Gamble (P&G), employees participate in a program the CEO calls "combat training." The program's intent is to focus on ways P&G can beat the competition. AlliedSignal wants to rank with General Electric and Merck as one of America's premier profitmakers. One way AlliedSignal seeks to achieve this strategic intent is to record 6 percent annual productivity improvements "forever." Chrysler Corporation's strategic intent is to be the world's premier car and light truck manufacturer by 2000.[88]

Because of its emotional edge, strategic intent may even be described metaphorically. In a recent annual report, Reebok International showed a series of pictures depicting an athlete crossing a high-jump bar. In her own handwriting, the athlete described her commitment to being the best and to winning:

> It's about raising the bar. I can jump higher. I know it. I can see it. I'm stronger, faster, I've learned more. The key is to focus, to concentrate on each basic element that goes into a jump. Jumping is my gift and it's a privilege to improve the gift. When everything works right, when you're focused and relaxed, it's kind of like flying. One thing that keeps you involved in jumping is that you

are always trying to clear the next height. Even if you miss, you come away from every jump knowing you can go higher.[89]

The words of this athlete appear to reflect Reebok's intent to focus and concentrate on every part of its business in order to constantly improve its performance and, by doing so, achieve strategic competitiveness and earn above-average returns.

But it is not enough for a firm to only know its own strategic intent. To perform well demands that we also identify our competitors' strategic intent. Only when intentions of others are understood can a firm become aware of the resolve, stamina, and inventiveness (traits linked with effective strategic intents) of those competitors.[90] A company's success may be grounded in a keen and deep understanding of the strategic intent of customers, suppliers, partners, and competitors.[91]

Strategic Mission

As our discussion shows, strategic intent is *internally focused.* It is concerned with identifying the resources, capabilities, and core competencies on which a firm can base its strategic actions. Strategic intent reflects what a firm is capable of doing as a result of its core competencies and the unique ways they can be used to exploit a competitive advantage.

Strategic mission flows from strategic intent. Externally focused, the **strategic mission** is a statement of a firm's unique purpose and the scope of its operations in product and market terms.[92] A strategic mission provides general descriptions of the products a firm intends to produce and the markets it will serve using its internally based core competencies. The interdependent relationship between strategic intent and strategic mission is shown in Figure 1.5.

The **strategic mission** is a statement of a firm's unique purpose and the scope of its operations in product and market terms.

An effective strategic mission establishes a firm's individuality and is exciting, inspiring, and relevant to all stakeholders.[93] Together, strategic intent and strategic mission yield the insights required to formulate and implement the firm's strategies.

Based partially on a firm's strategic intent and mission, top executives develop a *strategic orientation,* a predisposition to adopt a certain strategy(ies) over others.[94] Strategic orientation is also affected by the national culture in an executive's home

Figure 1.5 *The Interdependent Relationship Between Strategic Intent and Strategic Mission*

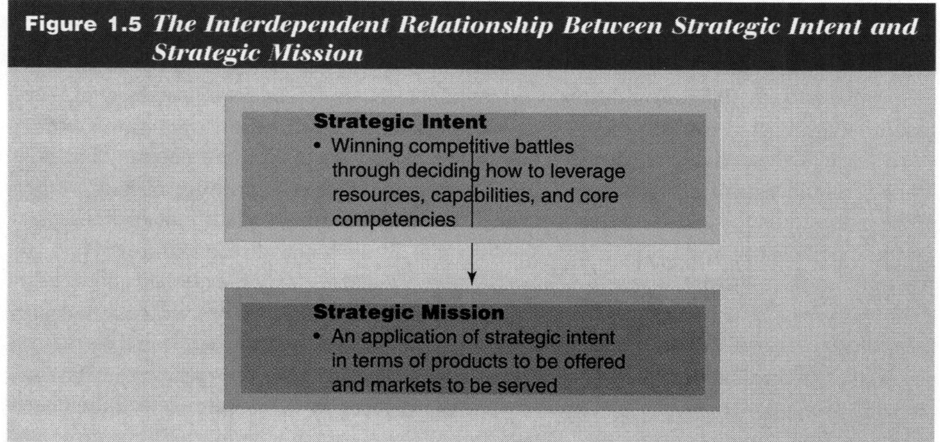

country and the institutional environment where the firm's operations are located.[95] A competitor's strategic orientations can be predicted based on knowledge of its strategic intent and mission, the institutional environment where its home office is located, and the cultural values of the top executives' home country.

When a firm is strategically competitive and earning above-average returns, it has the capacity to satisfy its stakeholders' interests. The stakeholder groups a firm serves are examined next.

STAKEHOLDERS

Stakeholders are the individuals and groups who can affect and are affected by the strategic outcomes achieved and who have enforceable claims on a firm's performance.

An organization is a system of primary stakeholder groups with whom it establishes and manages relationships.[96] **Stakeholders** are the individuals and groups who can affect and are affected by the strategic outcomes achieved and who have enforceable claims on a firm's performance.[97] Claims against an organization's performance are enforced through a stakeholder's ability to withhold participation essential to a firm's survival, competitiveness, and profitability.[98] Stakeholders continue to support an organization when its performance meets or exceeds their expectations.

Thus, organizations have dependency relationships with their stakeholders. Firms, however, are not equally dependent on all stakeholders at all times; as a consequence, every stakeholder does not have the same level of influence. The more critical and valued a stakeholder's participation is, the greater a firm's dependency on it. Greater dependence, in turn, results in more potential influence for the stakeholder over a firm's commitments, decisions, and actions. In one sense, the challenge strategists face is to either accommodate or find ways to insulate the organization from the demands of stakeholders controlling critical resources.[99]

STRATEGIC FOCUS

Stakeholders Are on Both Sides

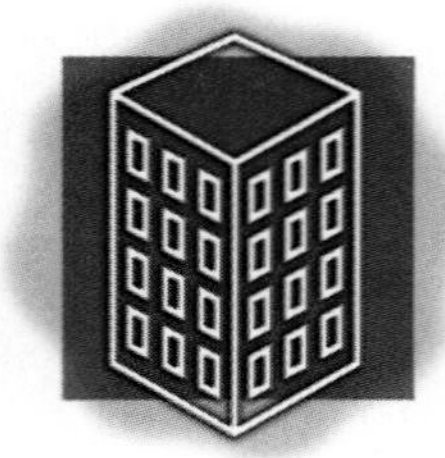

There are several types of stakeholders and firms must be sensitive to the needs of all of them if they are to earn above-average returns. General Motors, for example, must deal with the United Auto Workers (UAW) union (product market stakeholder) that represents many of its employees while at the same time satisfying its shareholders and potential shareholders (capital market stakeholders). This can be challenging. In 1997, GM had the lowest productivity in the auto industry. GM requires 47 worker-hours to produce an automobile while Nissan can do it in 28 worker-hours. Chrysler and Ford require 38 and 41 worker-hours respectively. This productivity gap costs GM $700 more per car than Nissan. Shareholders and analysts on Wall Street placed significant pressure on GM to improve its productivity. To do so, GM planned to eliminate 50,000 plant jobs over a several year span. However, the UAW fought GM on this decision and threatened to strike.

Unions have employees, too. For example, the Teamsters Union experienced a threatened strike from its office and professional employees. The employees were dissatisfied with the union's proposal that would require employees to have 33 years service to reach the top pay scale, the introduction of time clocks, and restrictions on the use of flextime. The office and professional employees union forced the dispute to be submitted to a mediator. Not all unions are as tough in their negotiations. The German Chemical Union agreed to a reduction in wages. Because of financial problems in German companies, the union agreed to a 10 percent decrease in wages. The union has been pressured by the federal government in Germany to make concessions because of 11 percent unemployment. The German union negotiator called the agreement a reaction to the changing economy.

Another important product market stakeholder is the customer. When a firm has one primary customer, that customer often has significant power as Lockheed Martin Corporation has discovered. The Defense Department, Lockheed's primary customer, expressed substantial concern and scrutinized the potential merger between Lockheed and Northrop Grumman Corporation. Defense leaders are particularly concerned about the potential for less innovation and higher costs. There are discussions about requiring Lockheed to spin off businesses for the deal to be approved. If approved, the new company of Lockheed and Northrop would own 80 percent of the electronic machinery that jams radar equipment and protect aircraft. These firms must be careful not to anger their biggest customer, the powerful federal government.

SOURCE: S. Crock, S. Browder and W. Echikson, 1997, Lockheed: A deal too far? *Business Week*, July 31, businessweek.com; F. Swoboda, 1997, Teamsters on unusual side in labor tiff, *Washington Post*, July 16, washingtonpost.com; *Wall Street Journal Interactive Edition*, 1997, German chemical union agrees to let companies cut wages, http://www.interactive5.wsj.com; B. Vlasic, 1997, GM can't afford to budge: To compete on productivity, it risks strikes, *Business Week*, June 16, http://www.businessweek.com.

The discussion in the Strategic Focus regarding GM's stakeholders suggests the potential differences in power among stakeholders. GM's shareholders and Wall Street are more powerful than the union representing GM workers. GM is willing to accept a strike if necessary in order to achieve the increase in productivity desired by the shareholders. Lockheed's case shows the firm's dependency on its stakeholder, the U.S. government. The Strategic Focus also provides examples of several different types of stakeholders, the topic of our next discussion.

Classification of Stakeholders

The parties involved with a firm's operations can be separated into three groups.[100] As shown in Figure 1.6, these groups are the *capital market stakeholders* (shareholders and the major suppliers of a firm's capital), the *product market stakeholders* (the firm's primary customers, suppliers, host communities, and unions representing the workforce), and the *organizational stakeholders* (all of a firm's employees, including both nonmanagerial and managerial personnel).

Each of these stakeholder groups expects those making strategic decisions in a firm to provide the leadership through which their valued objectives will be accomplished.[101] But these groups' objectives often differ from one another, sometimes placing managers in situations where tradeoffs have to be made.

Grounded in laws governing private property and private enterprise, the most obvious stakeholders, at least in U.S. firms, are *shareholders*—those who have invested capital in a firm in the expectation of earning at least an average return on their investments. Shareholders want the return on their investment (and, hence, their wealth) to be maximized. This could be accomplished at the expense of investing in a firm's future. Gains achieved by reducing investment in research and development, for example, could be returned to shareholders (thereby increasing the short-term return on their investments). However, a short-term enhancement

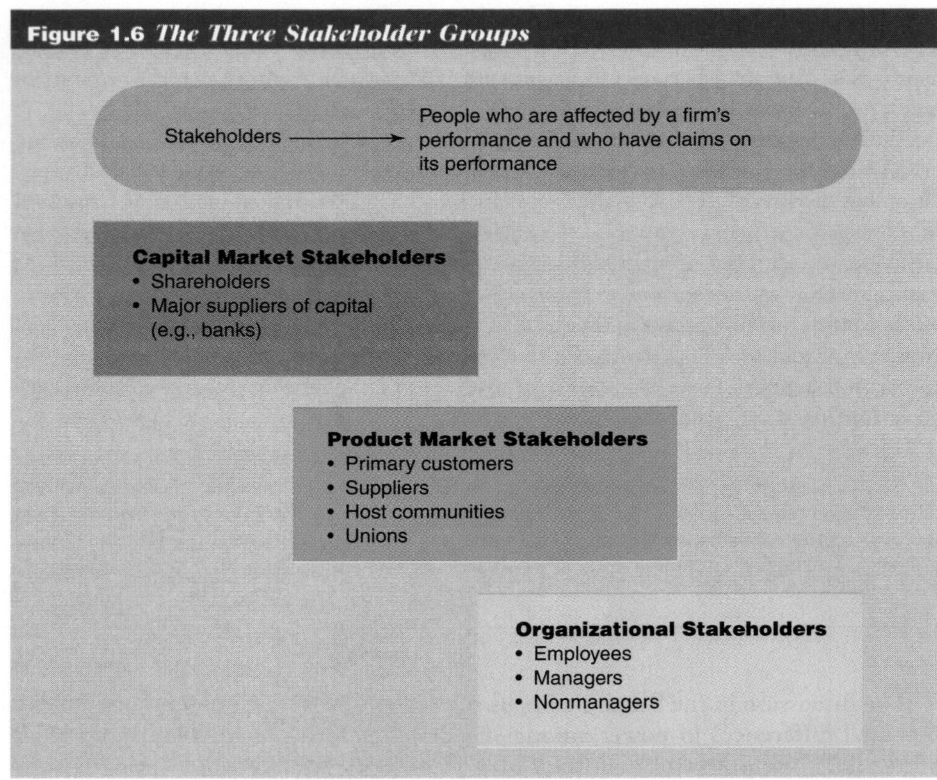

Figure 1.6 *The Three Stakeholder Groups*

of shareholders' wealth can negatively affect the firm's future competitive ability. Sophisticated shareholders, with diversified portfolios, may sell their interests if a firm fails to invest in its future. This is exemplified in the Strategic Focus as GM's shareholders are exerting pressure to increase the firm's productivity. Those making strategic decisions are responsible for a firm's survival in both the short and the long terms. Accordingly, it is in the interests of neither the organizational stakeholders nor the product market stakeholders for investments in the company to be unduly minimized.

In contrast to shareholders, customers prefer that investors receive a minimum return on their investments (also see the Strategic Focus discussion of the Defense Department's concerns about Lockheed's strategy). As such, customers could have their interests maximized when the quality and reliability of a firm's products are improved, but without a price increase. High returns to customers might come at the expense of lower returns negotiated with capital market shareholders.

Because of potential conflicts, each firm is challenged to manage its stakeholders. First, a firm must carefully identify all important stakeholders. Second, it must prioritize them in case it cannot satisfy all of them. In doing this, power is the most critical criterion. Other criteria might include the urgency of satisfying each particular stakeholder and the degree of importance to the firm.[102] When earning above-average returns, this challenge is lessened substantially. With the capability and flexibility provided by above-average returns, a firm can more easily satisfy all stakeholders simultaneously.

When earning only average returns, however, a firm may find the management of stakeholders to be more difficult. In these situations, tradeoffs must be made. With average returns, a firm is unlikely to maximize the interests of all stakeholders. The objective becomes one of at least minimally satisfying each stakeholder. Tradeoff decisions are made in light of how dependent the firm is on the support of the stakeholder groups. An example of how stakeholders can demand satisfaction of their claims on a firm's performance is provided in the next subsection. A firm earning below-average returns does not have the capacity to minimally satisfy all stakeholders. The managerial challenge in this case is to make tradeoffs that minimize the amount of support lost from stakeholders.

Societal values influence the general weightings allocated among the three stakeholder groups. Although all three groups are served by firms in at least the major industrialized nations, the priorities in their service vary somewhat because of cultural differences. These differences are shown in the following commentary:

> In America . . . shareholders have a comparatively big say in the running of the enterprises they own; workers . . . have much less influence. In many European countries, shareholders have less say and workers more . . . In Japan . . . managers have been left alone to run their companies as they see fit—namely for the benefit of employees and of allied companies, as much as for shareholders.[103]

Thus, it is important that those responsible for managing stakeholder relationships in a country outside their native land use a global mind-set. A **global mind-set** is the "capacity to appreciate the beliefs, values, behaviors, and business practices of individuals and organizations from a variety of regions and cultures."[104] Use of a global mind-set allows managers to better understand the realities and preferences that are a part of the world region and culture in which they are working.

A **global mind-set** is the capacity to appreciate the beliefs, values, behaviors, and business practices of individuals and organizations from a variety of regions and cultures.

In the next three subsections, additional information is presented about the stakeholder groups that firms manage.

Capital Market Stakeholders Both shareholders and lenders expect a firm to preserve and enhance the wealth they have entrusted to it. The returns expected are commensurate with the degree of risk accepted with those investments (i.e., lower returns are expected with low-risk investments; higher returns are expected with high-risk investments).

If lenders become dissatisfied, they can impose stricter covenants on subsequent capital borrowing. Shareholders can reflect their dissatisfaction through several means, including the sale of their stock. When aware of potential or actual dissatisfactions among capital market stakeholders, a firm may respond to their concerns. The firm's response to dissatisfied stakeholders is affected by the nature of its dependency relationship with them (which, as noted earlier, is also influenced by a society's values). The greater and more significant the dependency relationship, the more direct and significant a firm's response will be.

The power and influence of capital market stakeholders are exemplified in their effects on Rubbermaid in 1997. Rubbermaid announced that its earnings were going to be over 30 percent below the expected amount. At the first announcement of this downward revision of estimated earnings, investors signaled their dissatisfaction by driving down the share price by 11 percent. With the second announcement of bad news, shareholders increased pressure on management to make changes to improve shareholder value. This pressure has led to changes with many managers being forced to resign while others have left voluntarily. Top-level managers are making other changes as well. For example, they are seeking new ways to distribute the firm's products in addition to the traditional outlets such as Wal-Mart. The firm recently formed an alliance with Amway Corp. and is trying to tap specialty stores and the Internet. Thus, shareholders have prompted significant actions on the part of Rubbermaid's top management.[105] At least in the short run, this additional support for the capital market stakeholders may come at the expense of returns to other stakeholders.

Product Market Stakeholders Initial observation of customers, suppliers, host communities, and unions representing workers might suggest little commonality among their interests. However, close inspection indicates that all four parties can benefit as firms engage in competitive battles. For example, depending on product and industry characteristics, marketplace competition may result in lower product prices being charged to a firm's customers and higher prices paid to its suppliers (the firm might be willing to pay higher supplier prices to ensure delivery of the types of goods and services linked with competitive success).

As noted in Chapter 4, customers, as stakeholders, demand reliable products at the lowest possible prices. Suppliers seek assured customers willing to pay the highest sustainable prices for the goods and services they receive. Host communities want companies willing to be long-term employers and providers of tax revenues, without placing excessive demands on public support services. Union officials are interested in secure jobs, under ideal working conditions, for employees they represent. Thus, product market stakeholders are generally satisfied when a firm's profit margin yields the lowest acceptable return to capital market stakeholders (i.e., the lowest return lenders and shareholders will accept and still retain their interests in the firm).

All product market stakeholders are important in a competitive business environment. However, in many firms, customers are being emphasized. Jack Welch, CEO of General Electric, is known for his position that satisfied customers are the only source of job security for the firm's organizational stakeholders. At AT&T, one of the company's top-level executives cautions employees to ask why customers (and/or competitors) are not being discussed after the first 15 minutes of any meeting. If they are not being talked about after a second 15-minute period, the executive believes people should leave the meeting.[106]

In 1946, PepsiCola Co. made a pioneering move that established a new market niche for its product. It hired Edward F. Boyd to develop a sales team to market PepsiCola to African-Americans. Mr. Boyd was one of very few African-Americans in a professional position with a major U.S. corporation. Because of other actions taken by PepsiCola before this time (e.g., scholarships and job programs), the firm had a generally positive image in the African-American community. Mr. Boyd changed the image of African-Americans used in advertisements (e.g., he developed an ad in 1948 for a store display showing a smiling African-American woman serving her family PepsiCola) as opposed to the Aunt Jemima ads, for example. One of his models was Ron Brown, the future Secretary of Commerce. As a result of these efforts, PepsiCola captured a large share of this market niche and outsold Coca-Cola in Chicago for the first time in the late 1940s. Thus, PepsiCola targeted, satisified, and captured this set of customers.[107] The relationship between satisfaction of customers' needs and strategic competitiveness is examined in detail in Chapter 4.

Organizational Stakeholders Employees, nonmanagerial and managerial, expect a firm to provide a dynamic, stimulating, and rewarding working environment. These stakeholders are usually satisfied working for a company that is growing and developing their skills, especially the skills required to be effective team members and to meet or exceed global work standards. Workers who learn how to productively use rapidly developing knowledge are thought to be critical to organizational success. In a collective sense, the education and skills of a nation's workforce may be its dominant competitive weapon in a global economy.[108]

In the next section, we describe the people responsible for the design and execution of strategic management processes. Various names are given to these people—top-level managers, executives, strategists, the top management team, and general managers are examples. Throughout this book, these names are used interchangeably. But, in all cases, they describe the work of persons responsible for designing and implementing a successful strategic management process.

As is discussed in Chapter 12, top-level managers can be a source of competitive advantage. The decisions and actions these people make to *combine* resources to create capabilities can also result in a competitive advantage.

ORGANIZATIONAL STRATEGISTS

Small organizations may have a single strategist. In many cases, this person owns the firm and is deeply involved with its daily operations. At the other extreme, large, diversified firms have many top-level managers. In addition to the CEO and other top-level officials (e.g., chief operating officer and chief financial officer), they have managers who are responsible for the performance of individual business units.

Typically, stakeholders have high expectations of top-level managers, particularly the CEO. These expectations place significant pressure on top executives. Because of these pressures and the complexity and challenges of the job, many people do not want to be managers, particularly top-level managers. In the current global economy and new competitive landscape, top managers hold insecure positions. Many middle management positions have been eliminated through restructurings, placing more stress on the remaining top- and lower-level managers. These problems are exemplified in Solid State Measurements Inc.'s search for new members for its top management team. The CEO had significant problems locating adequate applicants for the positions. Charles Thomas, Solid State's CEO, said he found the talent pool to be very thin. As a result the search was long, arduous, and frustrating.[109]

Top-level managers play critical roles in firms' efforts to achieve desired strategic outcomes. In fact, some believe that every organizational failure is actually a failure of those who hold the final responsibility for the quality and effectiveness of a firm's decisions and actions.[110]

Decisions for which strategists are responsible include how resources will be developed or acquired, at what price they will be obtained, and how they will be used. Managerial decisions also influence how information flows in a company, the strategies a firm chooses to implement, and the scope of its operations. In making these decisions, managers must assess the risk involved in taking the actions being considered. This risk is then factored into the decision.[111] The firm's strategic intent (discussed earlier) will affect the decisions managers make. Also, managers' strategic orientations, which include their personal values and beliefs, will affect the decisions.[112] Additionally, how strategists complete their work and their patterns of interactions with others significantly influence the way a firm does business and affect its ability to develop a competitive advantage.

Organizational culture refers to the complex set of ideologies, symbols, and core values shared throughout the firm and that influences the way it conducts business. It is the social energy that drives—or fails to drive—the organization.

How a firm does business is captured by the concept of organizational culture. Critical to strategic leadership practices and the implementation of strategies, **organizational culture** refers to the complex set of ideologies, symbols, and core values shared throughout the firm and that influences the way it conducts business. Thus, culture is the "social energy that drives—or fails to drive—the organization."[113] Andersen Consulting's core values include the requirement that employees attend company-sponsored training classes in professional attire, an expectation of hard work (up to 80 hours per week), and a willingness to work effectively with others in order to accomplish all tasks that are parts of the company-wide demanding workload.[114] These core values at Andersen Consulting provide a particular type of social energy that drives the firm's efforts. As we discuss in Chapters 2, 12, and 13, organizational culture is a potential source of competitive advantage.[115]

After evaluating available information and alternatives, top-level managers must frequently choose from among similarly attractive alternatives. The most effective strategists have the self-confidence necessary to select the best alternatives, allocate the required level of resources to them, and effectively explain to interested parties why certain alternatives were selected.[116]

When choosing among alternatives, strategists are accountable for treating employees, suppliers, customers, and others with fairness and respect. Evidence suggests that trust can be a source of competitive advantage, thereby supporting an organizational commitment to treat stakeholders fairly and with respect.[117] Nonetheless, firms cannot succeed without people who, following careful and

Organizational culture is the social energy that drives a firm and influences the way it does business. In many high-level corporate environments, core values include attending training classes, wearing professional attire, and working hard and effectively with other employees.

sometimes difficult analyses, are willing to make tough decisions—the types of decisions that result in strategic competitiveness and above-average returns.[118]

The Work of Effective Strategists

Perhaps not surprisingly, hard work, thorough analyses, a willingness to be brutally honest, a penchant for always wanting the firm and its people to accomplish more, and common sense are prerequisites to an individual's success as a strategist.[119] John Sculley, former CEO of Apple Computer, describes the reality of work in the 1990s, suggesting that sleeping through the night is an outmoded remnant of the agrarian and industrial ages. "People don't live that way anymore," Sculley believes. "It's a 24-hour day, not an 8-to-5 day."[120]

In addition to the characteristics mentioned, effective strategists must be able to think clearly and ask many questions. Their strategic effectiveness increases as they find ways for others also to think and inquire about what a firm is doing and why. But, in particular, top-level managers are challenged to "think seriously and deeply . . . about the purposes of the organizations they head or functions they perform, about the strategies, tactics, technologies, systems and people necessary to attain these purposes and about the important questions that always need to be asked."[121] Through this type of thinking, strategists, in concert with others, increase the probability of identifying bold, innovative ideas. When these ideas lead to the development of core competencies—that is, when the ideas result in exploiting resources and capabilities that are valuable, rare, costly to imitate, and nonsubstitutable—they become the foundation for taking advantage of environmental opportunities.

Our discussion highlights the nature of a strategist's work. Instead of simplicity, the work is filled with ambiguous decision situations—situations for which the most effective solutions are not always easily determined. However, the opportunities suggested by this type of work are appealing. These jobs offer exciting chances to dream and to act. The following words, given as advice by his father to Steven J. Ross, the former chairman and co-CEO of Time-Warner, describe the opportunities in a strategist's work: "There are three categories of people—the person who goes into the office, puts his feet up on his desk, and dreams for 12 hours; the person who arrives at 5 A.M. and works for 16 hours, never once stopping to dream; and the person who puts his feet up, dreams for one hour, then does something about those dreams."[122] The organizational term used for a dream that challenges and energizes a company is strategic intent.[123]

Strategists have opportunities to dream and to act, and the most effective ones provide a vision (strategic intent) to effectively elicit the help of others in creating a firm's competitive advantage.

THE STRATEGIC MANAGEMENT PROCESS

The pursuit of competitiveness is at the heart of strategic management and the choices made when designing and using the strategic management process. Firms are in competition with one another—to gain access to the resources needed to earn above-average returns and to provide superior satisfaction of stakeholders' needs. Effective use of the interdependent parts of the strategic management process results in selecting the direction the firm will pursue and its choices to achieve the desired outcomes of strategic competitiveness and above-average returns.

As suggested by Figure 1.1, the strategic management process is intended to be a rational approach to help a firm respond effectively to the challenges of the new competitive landscape. This process calls for a firm to study its external (Chapter 2) and internal (Chapter 3) environments to identify its marketplace opportunities and threats and determine how to use its core competencies in the pursuit of desired strategic outcomes. With this knowledge, the firm forms its strategic intent so it can leverage its resources, capabilities, and core competencies and win battles in the global economy. Flowing from strategic intent, the strategic mission specifies, in writing, the products a firm intends to produce and the markets it will serve when leveraging its resources, capabilities, and competencies.

A firm's strategic inputs provide the foundation for its strategic actions to formulate and implement strategies. As strategic actions, both formulation and implementation are critical to achieving strategic competitiveness and earning above-average returns.

As suggested by the horizontal arrow linking the two types of strategic actions (see Figure 1.1), formulation and implementation must be integrated simultaneously. When formulating strategies, thought should be given to implementing them. During implementation, effective strategists seek feedback that allows improvement of the selected strategies. Thus, the separation of strategy formulation from strategy implementation in Figure 1.1 is for discussion purposes only. In reality, these two sets of actions allow the firm to achieve its desired strategic outcomes only when they are carefully integrated.

Figure 1.1 shows the topics we examine to study the interdependent parts of the strategic management process. In Part II of this book, actions related to the formulation of strategies are explained. The first set of actions studied is the formulation of strategies at the business-unit level (Chapter 4). A diversified firm, one competing in multiple product markets and businesses, has a business-level strategy for each distinct product market area. A company competing in a single product market has but one business-level strategy. In all instances, a business-level strategy describes a firm's actions designed to exploit its competitive advantage over rivals. But, as is explained in Chapter 5, business-level strategies are not formulated and implemented in isolation. Competitors respond to and try to anticipate each other's actions. Thus, the dynamics of competition are an important input to the formulation and implementation of all strategies, but especially to business-level strategies.

For the diversified firm, corporate-level strategy (Chapter 6) is concerned with determining the businesses in which the company intends to compete, how resources are to be allocated among those businesses, and how the different units are to be managed. Other topics vital to strategy formulation, particularly in the diversified firm, include the acquisition of other companies and, as appropriate, the restructuring of the firm's portfolio of businesses (Chapter 7) and the selection of an international strategy that is consistent with the firm's resources, capabilities, and core competencies and its external opportunities (Chapter 8). Chapter 9 examines cooperative strategies. Increasingly important in a global economy, firms use the strategies to gain competitive advantage by forming advantageous relationships with other companies.

To examine more direct actions taken to implement strategies successfully, we consider several topics in Part III of this book. First, the different mechanisms used to govern firms are considered (Chapter 10). With demands for improved corporate governance voiced by various stakeholders, organizations are challenged to manage in ways that will result in the satisfaction of stakeholders' interests and the attainment of desired strategic outcomes. Finally, the matters of organizational structure and actions needed to control a firm's operations (Chapter 11), the patterns of strategic leadership appropriate for today's firms and competitive environments (Chapter 12), and the link among corporate entrepreneurship, innovation, and strategic competitiveness (Chapter 13) are addressed.

As noted earlier, competition requires firms to make choices to survive and succeed. Some of these choices are strategic in nature, including those of selecting a firm's strategic intent and strategic mission, determining which strategies to implement to offer a firm's products to customers, choosing an appropriate level of corporate scope, designing governance and organization structures that will properly coordinate a firm's work, and, through strategic leadership, encouraging and nurturing organizational innovation.[124] When made successfully, choices in terms of any one of these sets of actions have the potential to result in a competitive advantage for a firm over its rivals.

Primarily because they are related to how a firm interacts with its stakeholders, almost all strategic decisions have ethical dimensions.[125] Organizational ethics are revealed by an organization's culture; that is to say, a firm's strategic decisions are a product of the core values that are shared by most or all of a company's managers and employees. Especially in the turbulent and often ambiguous new competitive landscape, those making strategic decisions are challenged to recognize that their decisions do affect capital market, product market, and organizational stakeholders differently and to evaluate the ethical implications of their decisions. Certainly, top executives at Columbia/HCA should have heeded this suggestion. In 1997, allegations of misconduct by top managers in Columbia/HCA affected shareholders and consumers alike. U.S. federal government officials issued indictments against several Columbia/HCA employees for alleged false statements regarding interest payments on debt that led to overpayments of Medicare and the Department of Defense insurance organization.[126] (Additional descriptions of actions taken in this firm are offered in other parts of the book.) Relationships between organizational ethics and particular strategic decisions are described in virtually all of the remaining chapters of this book.

As you will discover, the strategic management process examined in this text calls for disciplined approaches to the development of competitive advantages. These approaches provide the pathway through which firms will be able to achieve strategic competitiveness and earn above-average returns in the twenty-first century. Mastery of this strategic management process will effectively serve readers and the organizations for whom they choose to work.

SUMMARY

- Through their actions, firms seek strategic competitiveness and above-average returns. Strategic competitiveness is achieved when a firm has developed and learned how to implement a value-creating strategy successfully. Above-average returns—returns in excess of what investors expect to earn from other investments with similar levels of risk—allow a firm to simultaneously satisfy all of its stakeholders.

- A new competitive landscape—one in which the fundamental nature of competition is changing—has emerged. This landscape challenges those responsible for making effective strategic decisions to adopt a new mind-set, one that is global in nature. Through this mind-set, firms learn how to compete in what are highly turbulent and chaotic environments that produce disorder and a great deal of uncertainty. The globalization of industries and their markets and rapid and significant technological changes are the two primary realities that have created the new competitive landscape. Globalization—the spread of economic innovations around the world and the political and cultural adjustments that accompany this diffusion—is likely to continue. Globalization also increases the standards of performance companies must meet or exceed to be strategically competitive in the new competitive landscape. Developing the ability to satisfy these global performance standards also helps firms compete effectively in their critical domestic markets.

- There are two major models of what a firm should do to earn above-average returns. The I/O model argues that the external environment is the *primary* determinant of the firm's strategies. Above-average returns are earned when the firm locates an attractive industry and sucessfully implements the strategy dictated by the characteristics of that industry. The resource-based model assumes that each firm is a collection of unique resources and capabilities that determines a firm's strategy. In this model, above-average returns are earned when the firm uses its valuable, rare, costly to imitate, and nonsubstitutable resources and capabilities (i.e., core competencies) to establish a competitive advantage over its rivals.
- Strategic intent and strategic mission are formed in light of the information and insights gained from studying a firm's internal and external environments. Strategic intent suggests how resources, capabilities, and core competencies will be leveraged to achieve desired outcomes in the competitive environment. The strategic mission is an application of strategic intent. The mission is used to specify the product markets and customers a firm intends to serve through the leveraging of its resources, capabilities, and competencies.
- Stakeholders are those who can affect and are affected by a firm's strategic outcomes. Because a firm is dependent on the continuing support of stakeholders (shareholders, customers, suppliers, employees, host communities, etc.), they have enforceable claims on the company's performance. When earning above-average returns, a firm can adequately satisfy all stakeholders' interests. However, when earning only average returns, a firm's strategists must carefully manage all stakeholder groups in order to retain their support. A firm earning below-average returns must minimize the amount of support it loses from dissatisfied stakeholders.
- Organizational strategists are responsible for the design and execution of an effective strategic management process. Today, the most effective of these processes are grounded in ethical intentions and conduct. Strategists themselves, people with opportunities to dream and to act, can be a source of competitive advantage. The strategist's work demands decision tradeoffs, often among attractive alternatives. Successful top-level managers work hard, conduct thorough analyses of situations, are brutally and consistently honest, and ask the right questions, of the right people, at the right time.

REVIEW QUESTIONS

1. What are strategic competitiveness, competitive advantage, and above-average returns? Why are these terms important to those responsible for an organization's performance?
2. What *is* the challenge of strategic management?
3. What are the two factors that have created the new competitive landscape? What meaning does this landscape have for those interested in starting a business firm in the near future?
4. According to the I/O model, what should a firm do to earn above-average returns?
5. What does the resource-based model suggest a firm should do to achieve strategic competitiveness and earn above-average returns?
6. What are the differences between strategic intent and strategic mission? What is the value of the strategic intent and mission for a firm's strategic management process?

7. What are stakeholders? Why can they influence organizations? Do stakeholders always have the same amount of influence over an organization? Why or why not?
8. How would you describe the work of organizational strategists?
9. What are the parts of the strategic management process? How are these parts interrelated?

APPLICATION DISCUSSION QUESTIONS

1. As suggested in the opening case, the outcomes in the telecommunications industry are uncertain. Go to your library to study WorldCom's current performance. Based on your reading, do you judge WorldCom to be a success? Why or why not?
2. Choose several firms in your local community with which you are familiar. Describe the new competitive landscape to them and ask for their feedback about how they anticipate the landscape will affect their operations during the next five years.
3. Select an organization (e.g., school, club, church) that is important to you. Describe the organization's stakeholders and the degree of influence you believe each has over the organization.
4. Are you a stakeholder at your university or college? If so, of what stakeholder group, or groups, are you a part?
5. Think of an industry in which you want to work. In your opinion, which of the three primary stakeholder groups is the most powerful in that industry today? Why?
6. Reject or agree with the following statement: "I think managers have little responsibility for the failure of business firms." Justify your view.
7. Do strategic intent and strategic mission have any meaning in your personal life? If so, describe it. Are your current actions being guided by an intent and mission? If not, why not?

ETHICS QUESTIONS

1. Can a firm achieve a competitive advantage and thereby strategic competitiveness without acting ethically? Explain.
2. What are a firm's ethical responsibilities if it earns above-average returns?
3. What are some of the critical ethical challenges to firms competing in the global economy?
4. How should ethical considerations be included in analyses of a firm's internal and external environments?
5. Can ethical issues be integrated into a firm's strategic intent and mission? Explain.
6. What is the relationship between ethics and stakeholders?
7. What is the importance of ethics for organizational strategists?

INTERNET EXERCISE

The following is a list of well-recognized American companies:

Exxon: **http://www.exxon.com**
Southwest Airlines: **http://www.iflyswa.com**
General Motors: **http://www.gm.com**
Wal-Mart: **http://www.wal-mart.com**
McDonald's: **http://www.mcdonalds.com**

Select two of these companies. For each company, use the Internet to collect sufficient information to compile a list of the company's major stakeholders. In what ways are the stakeholders of each company similar and in what ways are they different? In your research, did you find any evidence that the companies you studied are actively managing their stakeholder groups?

Strategic Surfing

Strategy & Business is a publication that prints a variety of thoughtful articles, interviews, and case studies focused on strategic management and general business issues. The online version of this publication can be accessed at the following website:

http://www.strategy-business.com

NOTES

1. J. B. Barney, 1994, Commentary: A hierarchy of corporate resources, in P. Shrivastava, A. Huff, and J. Dutton (eds.), *Advances in Strategic Management* 10A, (Greenwich, Conn.: JAI Press), 119.
2. J. B. Barney, 1991, Firm resources and sustained competitive advantage, *Journal of Management* 17: 99–120.
3. D. J. Collis and C. A. Montgomery, 1995, Competing on resources: Strategy in the 1990s, *Harvard Business Review* 73, no. 4: 118–128.
4. R. M. Grant, 1995, *Contemporary Strategy Analysis*, 2nd ed. (Cambridge, Mass.: Blackwell Business), 138–140.
5. R. A. D'Aveni, 1995, Coping with hypercompetition: Utilizing the new 7S's framework, *Academy of Management Executive* IX, no. 3: 54; D. Schendel, 1994, Introduction to the Summer 1994 special issue—Strategy: Search for new paradigms, *Strategic Mangement Journal* (Special Summer Issue) 15: 3.
6. P. Shrivastava, 1995, Ecocentric management for a risk society, *Academy of Management Review* 20: 119.
7. R. P. Rumelt, D. E. Schendel, and D. J. Teece (eds.), 1994, *Fundamental Issues in Strategy* (Boston: Harvard Business School Press), 527–530; A. D. Meyer, 1991, What is strategy's distinctive competence? *Journal of Management* 17: 821–883.
8. Schendel, Introduction to the Summer 1994 special issue, 1–3.
9. Rumelt, Schendel, and Teece, *Fundamental Issues in Strategy*, 534–547.
10. M. E. Porter, 1994, Toward a dynamic theory of strategy, in R. P. Rumelt, D. E. Schendel, and D. J. Teece (eds.), *Fundamental Issues in Strategy* (Boston: Harvard Business School Press), 423–425.
11. R. Teitelbaum, 1997, America's greatest wealth creators, *Fortune*, November 10, 265–276.
12. C. J. Loomis, 1993, Dinosaurs, *Fortune*, May 3, 36–42.
13. *The State of Small Business: A Report of the President*, 1994, Washington, D.C., 41–42.
14. Rumelt, Schendel, and Teece, *Fundamental Issues in Strategy*, 530.
15. Loomis, Dinosaurs, 36.
16. K. Naughton, E. Thorton, K. Kerwin and H. Dawley, 1997, Can Honda build a world car? *Business Week*, September 8, 100–108; M. Williams, 1997, The Limited tries to rebuild after losing some of its appeal, *Dallas Morning News*, November 2, H5.
17. D. Machalaba, 1997, Union Pacific battles problems as crashes continue to pile up, *Wall Street Journal Interactive Edition*, August 29, http://www.wsj.com.
18. A. Reinhardt, 1997, Paranoia, aggression, and other strengths, *Business Week*, October 13, 14; A. S. Grove, 1995, A high-tech CEO updates his views on managing and careers, *Fortune*, September 18, 229–230; S. Sherman, 1993, The secret to Intel's success, *Fortune*, February 8, 14.
19. This section is based largely on information featured in two sources: M. A. Hitt, B. W. Keats, and S. M. DeMarie, 1998, Navigating in the new competitive landscape: Building competitive advantage and strategic flexibility; in the 21st century, *Academy of Management Executive*, in press. R. A. Bettis and M. A. Hitt, 1995, The new competitive landscape, *Strategic Management Journal* (Special Summer Issue) 16: 7–19.
20. S. Kotha, 1995, Mass customization: Implementing the emerging paradigm for competitive advantage, *Strategic Management Journal* 16: 21–42.
21. Associated Press, 1995, Fox-TCI to challenge ESPN, *Dallas Morning News*, November 1, D1, D11.
22. C. K. Prahalad, 1995, forward in R. Ashkenas, D. Ulrich, T. Jick, and S. Kerr (eds.), *The Boundaryless Organization: Breaking the Chains of Organizational Structure*, (San Francisco: Jossey-Bass Publishers), xiii-xvii.
23. R. D. Ireland and M. A. Hitt, 1998, Achieving and maintaining strategic competitiveness in the 21st century: The role of strategic leadership, *Academy of Management Executive*, in press.
24. D'Aveni, Coping with hypercompetition, 46.
25. K. Ohmae, 1995, Letter from Japan, *Harvard Business Review* 73, no. 3: 154–163; P. Gyllenhammar, 1993, The global economy: Who will lead next? *Journal of Accountancy* 175: 61–67.
26. J. C. Madonna, 1992, If it's markets you need, look abroad, *New York Times Forum*, January 5, F13.
27. T. A. Stewart, 1993, The new face of American power, *Fortune*, July 26, 70–86.
28. L. C. Thurow, 1992, Who owns the twenty-first century? *Sloan Management Review* 33, no. 3: 5–17.
29. Whirlpool Corp., 1995, *Standard & Poor Stock Reports*, August 31, 2474; Whirlpool Corp., 1995, *Value Line*, June 16, 135; S. Tully, 1995, So, Mr. Bossidy, we know you can cut. Now show us how to grow, *Fortune*, August 21, 70–80.
30. The big picture, 1995, *Business Week*, November 13, 8.
31. G. Koretz, 1997, America's edge in capital goods, *Business Week*, September 22, 26.
32. P. Krugman, 1994, Location and competition: Notes on economic geography, in R. P. Rumelt, D. E. Schendel, and D. J. Teece (eds.), *Fundamental Issues in Strategy*, (Boston: Harvard Business School Press), 463–493; W. W. Lewis and M. Harris, 1992, Why globalization must prevail, *McKinsey Quarterly* 2: 114–131.
33. Crain News Service, 1995, Toyota plans to build T100 in U.S., boost plants' autonomy, *Dallas Morning News*, Octo-

ber 28, D39; M. G. Harvey, 1993, "Buy American": Economic concept or economic slogan? *Business Horizons* 36, no. 3: 40–46.

34. R. Narisetti, 1997, Bridgestone plans to build a factory for tires in U.S., *Wall Street Journal*, July 15, B12.
35. Lewis and Harris, Why globalization must prevail, 115; J. Newmith and E. Jaspin, 1993, Japan's patents pending no more, *Waco Tribune-Herald*, January 24, A1, A10.
36. R. M. Kanter, 1995, Thriving locally in the global economy, *Harvard Business Review* 73, no. 5: 151–160; M. E. Porter and C. van der Linde, 1995, Green and competitive: Ending the stalemate, *Harvard Business Review* 73, no. 5: 120–134.
37. S. Zaheer and E. Mosakowski, 1997, The dynamics of the liability of foreignness: A global study of survival in financial services, *Strategic Management Journal* 18: 439–464.
38. M. A. Hitt, R. E. Hoskisson, and H. Kim, 1997, International diversification: Effects on innovation and firm performance in product-diversified firms, *Academy of Management Journal* 40: 767–798.
39. R. W. Moxon and C. Bourassa-Shaw, 1997, The global free-trade dilemma: Can you control the personal gale of creative destruction? *Business* 18(Spring): 6–9.
40. W. Hopkins and S. A. Hopkins, 1997, Strategic planning-financial performance relationships in banks: A casual examination, *Strategic Management Journal* 18: 635–652.
41. H. J. Aaron, 1992, Comments included in a debate called "How real is America's decline?" *Harvard Business Review* 70, no. 5: 172.
42. *Business Week*, 1997, The rich ecosystem of Silicon Valley, August 25, 202.
43. Grove, A high-tech CEO, 229.
44. B. Morris, 1997, IBM really wants your E-business, *Fortune*, November 10, 36–38.
45. J. C. Ramo, 1997, How AOL lost the battles but won the war, *Time*, September 15, http//www.pathfinder.com.
46. A. L. Sprout, 1995, The Internet inside your company, *Fortune*, November 27, 161–168.
47. Liberation, courtesy of the Internet, 1995, *Business Week*, December 4, 136; Sprout, The Internet inside your company, 161–168.
48. A. Goldstein, 1995, Microsoft may not always be king of the hill, Gates says, *Dallas Morning News*, November 24, D4.
49. T. A. Stewart, 1995, Mapping corporate brainpower, *Fortune*, October 30, 209–212; T. A. Stewart, 1995, Trying to grasp the intangible, *Fortune*, October 2, 157–161; T. A. Stewart, 1995, The information wars: What you don't know will hurt you, *Fortune*, June 12, 119–121.
50. C. A. Bartlett and S. Ghoshal, 1995, Changing the role of top management: Beyond systems to people, *Harvard Business Review* 73, no. 3: 141.
51. T. A. Stewart, 1995, Getting real about brainpower, *Fortune*, November 27, 201–203.
52. R. Sanchez, 1995, Strategic flexibility in product competition, *Strategic Management Journal* (Special Summer Issue) 16: 135–159.
53. Kotha, Mass customization, 21.
54. J. L. C. Cheng and I. F. Kesner, 1997, Organizational slack and response to environmental shifts: The impact of resource allocation patterns, *Journal of Management* 23: 1–18.
55. V. L. Barker III and I. M. Duhaime, 1997, Strategic change in the turnaround process: Theory and empirical evidence, *Strategic Management Journal* 18: 13–38.
56. W. Boeker, 1997, Strategic change: The influence of managerial characteristics and organizational growth, *Academy of Management Journal* 40: 152–170.
57. N. Rajagopalan and G. M. Spreitzer, 1997, Toward a theory of strategic change: A multi-lens perspective and integrative framework, *Academy of Management Review* 22: 48–79.
58. N. Deogun, 1997, Coca-Cola Enterprises uncaps a global bottling play, *Wall Street Journal*, October 29, B4.
59. Our discussion of the I/O model is informed by the following works: Barney, Firm resources, 99–120; A. A. Lado, N. G. Boyd, and P. Wright, 1992, A competency based model of sustainable competitive advantage: Toward a conceptual integration, *Journal of Management* 18: 77–91; R. M. Grant, 1991, The resource-based theory of competitive advantage: Implications for strategy formulation, *California Management Review* 33 (Spring): 114–135.
60. D. Schendel, 1994, Introduction to competitive organizational behavior: Toward an organizationally-based theory of competitive advantage, *Strategic Management Journal* (Special Winter Issue) 15: 2.
61. A. Seth and H. Thomas, 1994, Theories of the firm: Implications for strategy research, *Journal of Management Studies* 31: 165–191.
62. Seth and Thomas, Theories of the firm, 169–173.
63. Porter, Toward a dynamic theory of strategy, 428.
64. M. E. Porter, 1985, *Competitive Advantage* (New York: Free Press); M. E. Porter, 1980, *Competitive Strategy* (New York: Free Press).
65. C. Mulhern, 1997, Bagel boom: Rising star of food franchising takes the world by storm, *Entrepreneur Magazine Online*, June 3, entrepreneurmag.com.
66. A. M. McGahan and M. E. Porter, 1997, How much does industry matter, really? *Strategic Management Journal* 18 (Summer Special Issue): 15–30.
67. R. Henderson and W. Mitchell, 1997, The interactions of organizational and competitive influences on strategy and performance, *Strategic Management Journal* 18 (Summer Special Issue): 5–14; C. Oliver, 1997, Sustainable competitive advantage: Combining institutional and resource-based views, *Strategic Management Journal* 18: 697–713; J. L. Stimpert and I. M. Duhaime, 1997, Seeing the big picture: The influence of industry, diversification, and business strategy on performance, *Academy of Management Journal* 40: 560–583.
68. J. R. Williams, 1994, Strategy and the search for rents: The evolution of diversity among firms, in R. P. Rumelt, D. E. Schendel, and D. J. Teece (eds.), *Fundamental Issues in Strategy* (Boston: Harvard Business School Press), 229–246.
69. K. Cool and I. Dierickx, 1994, Commentary: Investments in strategic assets: Industry and firm-level perspectives, in P. Shrivastava, A. Huff, and J. Dutton (eds.), *Advances in Strategic Management* 10A (Greenwich, Conn.: JAI Press), 35–44; Rumelt, Schendel, and Teece, *Fundamental Issues in Strategy*, 553; R. Rumelt, 1991, How much does industry matter? *Strategic Management Journal* 12: 167–185.
70. Barney, Commentary, 113–125.
71. Barney, Firm resources; Grant, Resource-based theory; Meyer, What is strategy's distinctive competence?
72. Grant, Resource-based theory, 119–120.

73. Rumelt, Schendel, and Teece, *Fundamental Issues in Strategy*, 31.
74. P. J. H. Schoemaker and R. Amit, 1994, Investment in strategic assets: Industry and firm-level perspectives, in P. Shrivastava, A. Huff, and J. Dutton (eds.), *Advances in Strategic Management* 10A (Greenwich, Conn.: JAI Press), 9.
75. R. E. Stross, 1997, Why Barnes & Noble may crush Amazon, *Fortune*, September 13, pathfinder.com.
76. J. B. Barney, 1995, Looking inside for competitive advantage, *Academy of Management Executive* IX, no. 4: 56.
77. Barney, Firm resources.
78. Lado, Boyd, and Wright, A competency based model; Grant, Resource-based theory; M. A. Hitt and R. D. Ireland, 1986, Relationships among corporate level distinctive competencies, diversification strategy, corporate structure, and performance, *Journal of Management Studies* 23: 401–416.
79. A. Madhok, 1997, Cost, value and foreign market entry mode: The transaction and the firm, *Strategic Management Journal* 18: 39–61.
80. A. A. Lado, N. G. Boyd and S. C. Hanlon, 1997, Competition, cooperation, and the search for economic rents: A syncretic model, *Academy of Management Review* 22: 110–141.
81. A. Arora and A. Gambardella, 1997, Domestic markets and international competitiveness: Generic and product specific competencies in the engineering sector, *Strategic Management Journal* 18 (Summer Special Issue): 53–74.
82. D. J. Teece, G. Pisano and A. Shuen, 1997, Dynamic capabilities and strategic management, *Strategic Management Journal* 18: 509–533.
83. D Lei, M. A. Hitt and R. A. Bettis, 1996, Dynamic core competences through meta-learning and strategic context, *Journal of Management* 22: 547–567.
84. G. Hamel and C. K. Prahalad, 1989, Strategic intent, *Harvard Business Review* 67, no. 3: 63–76.
85. S. Sherman, 1995, Stretch goals: The dark side of asking for miracles, *Fortune*, November 13, 231–232; G. Hamel and C. K. Prahalad, 1994, *Competing for the Future* (Boston: Harvard Business School Press), 129–136.
86. Hamel and Prahalad, Strategic intent, 66.
87. S. Sherman, 1993, The secret to Intel's success, 14.
88. Unocal Corporation, 1994, *Annual Report*, 4; Phillips Petroleum Company, 1994, *Health, Environmental and Safety Report*, 4; Eli Lilly and Company, 1993, *Annual Report to Shareholders*, 1; M. Loeb, 1993, It's time to invest and build, *Fortune*, February 22, 4; S. Sherman, 1993, The new computer revolution, *Fortune*, June 14, 56–84; C. A. Bartlett and S. Ghoshal, 1995, Changing the role of top management: Beyond systems to people, *Harvard Business Review* 73, no. 3: 136–137; A. Taylor III, 1993, How to murder the competition, *Fortune*, February 22, 87–90; Z. Schiller, 1992, No more Mr. nice guy at P&G—not by a long shot, *Business Week*, February 3, 54–56; S. Tully, 1995, So, Mr. Bossidy, we know you can cut, 73; AlliedSignal, 1995, *Value Line*, August 11, 1357.
89. Reebok, 1992, *Annual Report*, 2–12.
90. Hamel and Prahalad, Strategic intent, 64.
91. M. A. Hitt, D. Park, C. Hardee, and B. B. Tyler, 1995, Understanding strategic intent in the global marketplace, *Academy of Management Executive* IX, no. 2: 12–19.
92. R. D. Ireland and M. A. Hitt, 1992, Mission statements: Importance, challenge, and recommendations for development, *Business Horizons* 35, no. 3: 34–42.
93. A. D. DuBrin and R. D. Ireland, 1993, *Management and Organization*, 2nd ed. (Cincinnati, Ohio: Southwestern), 140.
94. N. Rajagopalan, 1992, Strategic orientations, incentive plan adoptions, and firm performance: Evidence from electric utility firms, *Strategic Management Journal* 18: 761–785.
95. M. A. Geletkanycz, 1997, The salience of culture's consequences: The effects of cultural values on top executive commitment to the status quo, *Strategic Management Journal* 18: 615–634, M. A. Hitt, M. T. Dacin, B. B. Tyler and D. Park, 1997, Understanding the differences in Korean and U.S. Executives' strategic orientation, *Strategic Management Journal* 18: 159–167.
96. M. B. E. Clarkson, 1995, A stakeholder framework for analyzing and evaluating corporate social performance, *Academy of Management Review* 20: 92–117; T. Donaldson and L. E. Preston, 1995, The stakeholder theory of the corporation: Concepts, evidence, and implications, *Academy of Management Review* 20: 65–91; T. M. Jones, 1995, Instrumental stakeholder theory: A synthesis of ethics and economics, *Academy of Management Review* 20: 404–437.
97. Clarkson, A stakeholder framework; R. E. Freeman, 1984, *Strategic Management: A Stakeholder Approach* (Boston: Pitman), 53–54.
98. G. Donaldson and J. W. Lorsch, 1983, *Decision Making at the Top: The Shaping of Strategic Direction* (New York: Basic Books), 37–40.
99. Rumelt, Schendel, and Teece, *Fundamental Issues in Strategy*, 33.
100. Donaldson and Lorsch, *Decision Making at the Top*, 37.
101. M. J. Polonsky, 1995, Incorporating the natural environment in corporate strategy: A stakeholder approach, *Journal of Business Strategies* 12: 151–168.
102. R. K. Mitchell, B. R. Agle and D. J. Wood, 1997, Toward a theory of stakeholder identification and salience: Defining the principle of who and what really count, *Academy of Management Review* 22: 853–886.
103. Donaldson and Preston, The stakeholder theory of the corporation, citing a quote from *The Economist*, 1994, Corporate governance special section, September 11, 52–62.
104. Don't be an ugly-American manager, 1995, *Fortune*, October 16, 225.
105. T. Aeppel, 1997, Rubbermaid warns 3rd-quarter profit will come in far below expectations, *Wall Street Journal*, September 19, A4.
106. D. Kirkpatrick, 1993, Could AT&T rule the world? *Fortune*, May 17, 55–66.
107. T. Petzinger, Jr., 1997, Boyd overcame race barriers to build a market for Pepsi, *Wall Street Journal Interactive Edition*, August 29, http://www.wsj.com.
108. New paths to success, 1995, *Fortune*, June 12, 90–94; T. A. Stewart, 1995, Mapping corporate brainpower, 209–211; S. Lee, 1993, Peter Drucker's fuzzy future, *Fortune*, May 17, 136.
109. T. Schellhardt, 1997, Talent pool is shallow as corporations seek executives for top jobs, *Wall Street Journal*, June 26, A1, A10; T. Schellhardt, 1997, Want to be a manager? Many people say no, calling job miserable, *Wall Street Journal*, April 4, A1, A4.

110. J. O. Moller, 1991, The competitiveness of U.S. industry: A view from the outside, *Business Horizons* 34, no. 6: 27–34.
111. G. McNamara and P. Bromiley, 1997, Decision making in an organizational setting: Cognitive and organizational influences on risk assessment in commercial lending, *Academy of Management Journal* 40: 1063–1088.
112. L. Markoczy, 1997, Measuring beliefs: Accept no substitutes *Academy of Management Journal* 40: 1228–1242.
113. M. A. Hitt and R. E. Hoskisson, 1991, Strategic competitiveness, in L. W. Foster (ed.), *Advances in Applied Business Strategy* (Greenwich, Conn.: JAI Press), 1–36.
114. Bartlett and Ghoshal, Changing the role of top management, 139.
115. K. Weigelt and C. Camerer, 1988, Reputation and corporate strategy, *Strategic Management Journal* 9: 443–454; J. B. Barney, 1986, Organizational culture: Can it be a source of sustained competitive advantage? *Academy of Management Review* 11: 656–665.
116. R. D. Ireland, M. A. Hitt, and J. C. Williams, 1992, Self-confidence and decisiveness: Prerequisites for effective management in the 1990s, *Business Horizons* 35, no. 1: 36–43.
117. R. C. Mayer, J. H. Davis, and F. D. Schoorman, 1995, An integrative model of organizational trust, *Academy of Management Review* 20: 709–734, J. H. Davis, F. D. Schoorman, and R. C. Mayer, 1995, The trusted general manager and firm performance: Empirical evidence of a strategic advantage, paper presented at the Strategic Management Society conference; J. B. Barney and M. H. Hansen, 1994, Trustworthiness as a source of competitive advantage, *Strategic Management Journal* 15: 175–190.
118. G. Belis, 1993, Beware the touchy-feely business book, *Fortune*, June 28, 147; A. E. Pearson, 1988, Tough-minded ways to get innovative, *Harvard Business Review* 66, no. 3: 99–106.
119. J. S. Harris, 1995, Bill Dodson, *Dallas Morning News*, September 3, H1, H2; Tully, So, Mr. Bossidy, we know you can cut, 70–80; K. W. Chilton, M. E. Warren, and M. L. Weidenbaum (eds.), 1990, *American Manufacturing in a Global Market* (Boston: Kluwer Academic Publishers), 72.
120. A. Deutschman, 1993, Odd man out, *Fortune*, July 26, 42.
121. T. Leavitt, 1991, *Thinking About Management* (New York: Free Press), 9.
122. M. Loeb, 1993, Steven J. Ross, 1927–1992, *Fortune*, January 25, 4.
123. Hamel and Prahalad, *Competing for the Future*, 129.
124. Rumelt, Schendel, and Teece, *Fundamental Issues in Strategy*, 9–10.
125. Our discussion of ethics and the strategic management process, both here and in other chapters, is informed by materials appearing in J. S. Harrison and C. H. St. John, 1994, *Strategic Management of Organizations and Stakeholders: Theory and Cases* (St. Paul, Minn.: West Publishing Company).
126. M. Brockhaus, L. Haynes, J. Ogletree and D. Parcel, 1997, Columbia/HCA: One-stop shopping in the health care industry, working paper, University of Oklahoma.

CHAPTER 2

The External Environment: Opportunities, Threats, Industry Competition, and Competitor Analysis

Learning Objectives

After reading this chapter, you should be able to:

1. Explain the importance of studying and understanding the external environment.
2. Define the general and industry environments.
3. Discuss the four activities of the external environmental analysis process.
4. Name and describe the six segments of the general environment.
5. Identify the five competitive forces and explain how they determine an industry's profit potential.
6. Define strategic groups and describe how they influence a firm's competitive actions.
7. Describe what firms need to know about their competitors and different methods used to collect competitive intelligence.

Transformation of the Electric Utility Industry

The electric power industry in the United States is on the verge of a historic transformation. This $250 billion industry has in the past pursued a vertical integration strategy while operating in protected geographic but regulated markets. In the future, however, participants in the electric power marketplace will have many diverse core competencies and product offerings. Some will operate in narrow product markets while others will cross state and even national geographic boundaries to create business. There are conditions within three general environmental segments driving the changes that will radically restructure the competitive market segments in this industry.

http://www.eia.doe.gov

Changes occurring in the *political/legal segment*, for example, are having a dramatic effect on the electric power industry. It is estimated that the amount spent on electric power by its customers could drop by 20 to 30 percent over the next five to ten years due to deregulation. The move toward deregulation in the United States began in the 1970s with oil shocks to the economy. Utilities, saddled with higher costs, sought to increase their rates considerably. But a public outcry pressured many states to force utilities to hold down rates, effectively halting the companies' ability to increase capacity. To deal with this concern, independent power producers were authorized through the Capital Public Utility Regulatory Policy Act of 1978 to create new alternative power suppliers to the market. This led to a new set of independent power producers focusing on cogeneration technology. Cogeneration is produced by independent producers as a byproduct from normal production

processes. This allowed many manufacturers who use steam, hot water, hot gases, or electrical/mechanical sources of power to become independent power producers.

Furthermore, because some households geographically adjacent to these manufacturers were paying utility rates as much as 50 percent higher than their neighbors, there was an untenable political situation. As such, consumers have not allowed regulatory barriers to restrict their economic interests. In addition, many firms have threatened to move their multibillion dollar operations to other areas of the country where utility rates are lower. Thus, conditions in the *economic segment* are at work to foster the changes emerging in this industry. There have also been a number of mergers and acquisitions in the utility industry. Because producers have been limited in growth and are facing declining earning prospects, this type of competitive behavior is likely to continue. Therefore, electric utilities are preparing for brutal competition, similar to that experienced in other deregulated industries, such as airlines, trucking, and telecommunications.

Significant changes in the *technological segment* are also affecting the U.S. electric power industry. From 1949 to 1965, the cost of producing a kilowatt of power fell 37 percent as the size of the generators increased. Additionally, new generation technologies such as combined-cycle and cogeneration plants have been producing power at efficiency levels of 50 to 60 percent with advanced technology targeting an efficiency level of 70 percent or better for the use of fuels by the year 2005. This productivity compares to standard conventional power plant efficiency levels of 30 to 40 percent of fuel use. Furthermore, renewable sources of power such as wind and solar are making advancements. Also, information technology is emerging as a powerful force. It allows highly automated real-time meters and other gateways to home electrical use to market and sell electricity much more efficiently. This has allowed markets to merge and develop so that power can be traded as a commodity. Not only is this happening in the United States, but many power utility companies are expanding their reach to global markets including China, India, and Latin America.

It is also likely that the Internet will facilitate the trading of electrical power. There was a reported experiment between Northern Telecom (a Canadian firm) and United Utilities (a British utilities firm) to use power lines as an Internet provider. If the technology materializes, utilities firms with transmission capability may become the largest provider of telecommunications in the world.

These environmental changes are likely to realign the competition in the electric utilities industry into a number of different competitive arenas. First, it is likely that there will be generation companies that will become mega-generators, controlling perhaps 80 percent of the total generation capacity across all U.S. geographical markets. Second, there will also be large intelligent networks that will manage the transmission of power. Finally, there will be distribution companies or wire companies that own and maintain the wires through which the power is distributed to various markets.

Another set of competitors likely to emerge is energy service companies. First, there will be companies that will meter the energy and develop customer service relationships with consumers and businesses. Second, power markets probably will develop where power is exchanged as a commodity on stock exchanges. Finally, there are likely to be companies dealing in information technology products and services that will provide information and appliances to improve power use efficiency. Thus, it is highly probable that the entire context of competition in the industry will change. This will alter the nature of the customer and supplier relationships and allow for many new entrants as well as possible product substitutes. Because electric power can be a huge operating expense, a large savings in this category could result in above-average returns for firms. On the other hand, this may create significant competitive problems for utilities with inefficient generating plants. Thus, this change portends substantial opportunities and threats for electric power customers at large as well as threats to the management of the electric utility companies. Change will be the common theme and adaptation must follow.

SOURCE: AP-Dow Jones News Service, 1997, Electric utilities announces Internet access via power lines, http://www.interactive.wsj.com, October 8; B. O'Reilly, 1997, Transforming the power business, *Fortune*, September 29, 143–156; M. Weiner, N. Nohria, A. Hickman and H. Smith, 1997, Value networks—the future of the U.S. utility industry, *Sloan Management Review* 37, no. 4, 21–34; P. Navarro, 1996, Electric utilities: The argument for radical deregulation, *Harvard Business Review*, 75, no. 1, 112–125.

Research has shown that the external environment plays a significant role in the growth and profitability of firms,[1] as dramatically demonstrated in the case of significant changes taking place in certain segments of the general environment facing firms competing in the electric utilities industry. Which companies will succeed in the changing utilities industry will be determined largely by firms' reactions to the changes in their environment. This chapter focuses on how firms should analyze and understand their external environment, as shown in Figure 1.1 in Chapter 1.

As noted in the first chapter, the environmental conditions facing firms currently are different from those of past decades. Many companies now compete in global, rather than domestic, markets. Technological changes and the explosion in information gathering and processing capabilities demand more timely and effective competitive actions and responses.[2] The rapid sociological changes occurring in many countries affect labor practices and the nature of products demanded by increasingly diverse consumers. Governmental policies and laws affect where and how firms choose to compete. Deregulation and local government changes such as those emerging in the electric utilities industry illustrate the importance these changes are likely to have on the strategic direction and competitive environment of both foreign and domestic firms. Companies must be aware of and understand the implications of these environmental realities to compete effectively in the global economy.

In high-performing, strategically competitive organizations, managers seek patterns to help them understand their external environment, which may be different from what they expect.[3] It is vital for decision makers to have a precise and accurate understanding of their company's competitive position. For example, one of the first decisions Louis Gerstner, Jr., made when chosen as IBM's CEO from outside the firm was to visit with each member of IBM's senior management team. A key reason for these visits was to learn about each business area's competitive standing in the industry (or industries) in which it competed.[4] Strategic decision makers know that understanding their firm's external environment helps to improve a company's competitive position, increase operational efficiency, and win battles in the global economy.[5]

Through a variety of means, firms attempt to understand their external environments by gaining information about competitors, customers, and other stakeholders in the external environment. In particular, firms are attempting to gain information to build their own base of knowledge and capabilities.[6] These firms may attempt to imitate the capabilities of able competitors or even successful firms in other industries or build new knowledge and capabilities to develop a competitive advantage. Based on this new information, knowledge, and capabilities, firms may take actions to buffer environmental effects on them or to build relationships with stakeholders in that environment.[7] To build knowledge and firm capabilities and to take actions that buffer or build bridges to external stakeholders, organizations must effectively analyze their external environment.

In this chapter, we discuss the external environment. Through an integrated understanding of the external and the internal environments, firms gain the information needed to understand the present and predict the future.[8] As shown in Figure 2.1, a firm's external environment has three major components: the general, industry, and competitor environments.

FIGURE 2.1 *The External Environment*

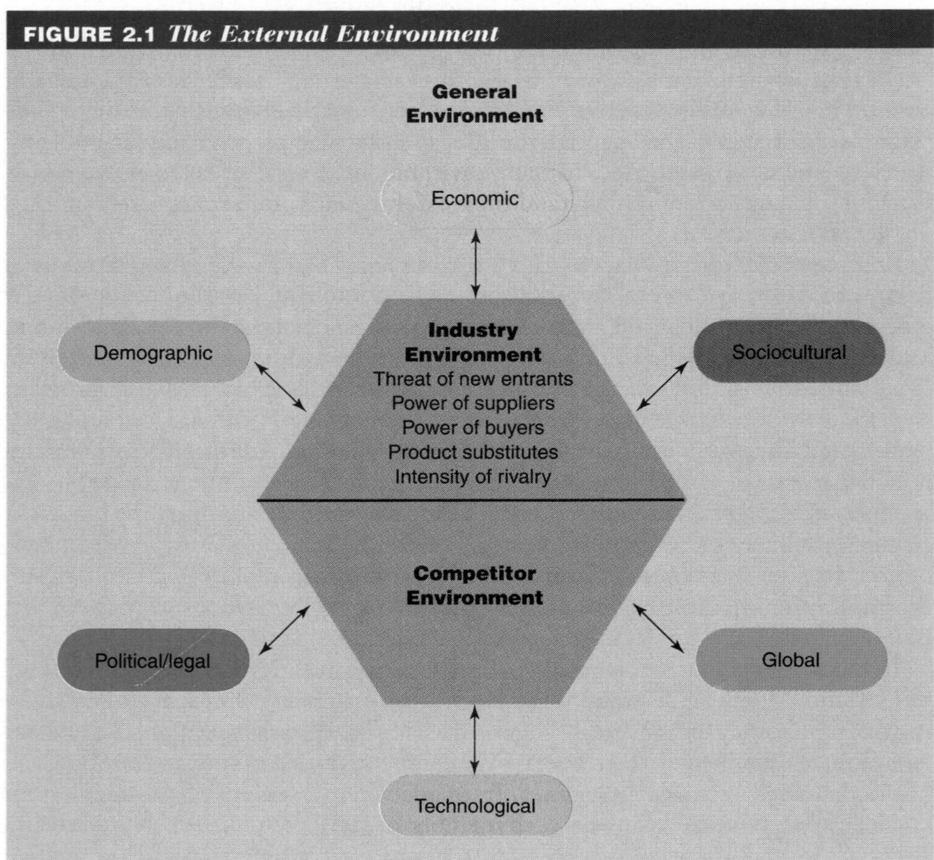

THE GENERAL, INDUSTRY, AND COMPETITOR ENVIRONMENTS

The **general environment** is composed of elements in the broader society that can influence an industry and the firms within it.[9] We group these elements into environmental *segments* called the demographic, economic, political/legal, sociocultural, technological, and global segments. Examples of *elements* analyzed in these six segments are shown in Table 2.1. Firms cannot directly control these elements. Instead, the strategic challenge is to understand each segment and its implications so appropriate strategies can be formulated and implemented.

The **general environment** is composed of elements in the broader society that can influence an industry and the firms within it.

The **industry environment** is the set of factors—the threat of new entrants, suppliers, buyers, product substitutes, and the intensity of rivalry among competitors—that directly influences a firm and its competitive actions and responses. In total, the interactions among these five factors determine an industry's profit potential. The challenge is to locate a position within an industry where a firm can favorably influence these factors or where it can successfully defend against their influence. The greater a firm's capacity to favorably influence its industry environment, the greater the likelihood that it will earn above-average returns.

The **industry environment** is the set of factors—the threat of new entrants, suppliers, buyers, product substitutes, and the intensity of rivalry among competitors—that directly influences a company and its competitive actions and responses.

We also discuss in this chapter how companies gather and interpret information about their competitors. Called *competitor analysis*, a firm's understanding of its current competitors complements the insights provided by study of the general and industry environments. In combination, the results of these three analyses influence the development of a firm's strategic intent, strategic mission, and strategic actions.

TABLE 2.1 ***The General Environment: Segments and Elements***

Demographic Segment	■ Population size ■ Age structure ■ Geographic distribution	■ Ethnic mix ■ Income distribution
Economic Segment	■ Inflation rates ■ Interest rates ■ Trade deficits or surpluses ■ Budget deficits or surpluses	■ Personal savings rate ■ Business savings rates ■ Gross domestic product
Political/Legal Segment	■ Antitrust laws ■ Taxation laws ■ Deregulation philosophies	■ Labor training laws ■ Educational philosophies and policies
Sociocultural Segment	■ Women in the workforce ■ Workforce diversity ■ Attitudes about quality of work life	■ Concerns about the environment ■ Shifts in work and career preferences ■ Shifts in preferences regarding product and service characteristics
Technological Segment	■ Product innovations ■ Process innovations ■ Applications of knowledge	■ Focus of private and government-supported R&D expenditures ■ New communication technologies
Global Segment	■ Important political events ■ Critical global markets	■ Newly industrialized countries ■ Different cultural and institutional attributes

Analysis of the general environment is focused on the future; analysis of the industry environment is focused on understanding the factors and conditions influencing a firm's profitability; and, analysis of competitors is focused on predicting the dynamics of competitors' actions, responses, and intentions. Although each analysis is discussed separately, a firm's performance improves when the insights from analyses of the general environment, the industry environment, and the competitive environment are integrated.

The process of external environmental analysis is discussed next.

EXTERNAL ENVIRONMENTAL ANALYSIS

Most firms face external environments that are growing more turbulent, complex, and global, which makes them increasingly difficult to interpret.[10] To cope with what are often ambiguous and incomplete environmental data and to increase their understanding of the general environment, firms engage in a process called external environmental analysis. This process includes four activities: scanning, monitoring, forecasting, and assessing (see Table 2.2). It should be conducted on a continuous basis.[11]

An important objective of studying the general environment is identification of opportunities and threats. **Opportunities** are conditions in the general environment that may help a company achieve strategic competitiveness. **Threats** are conditions in the general environment that may hinder a company's efforts to achieve strategic competitiveness. In essence, external environmental opportunities represent *possibilities* while threats are potential *constraints.*

Opportunities are conditions in the general environment that may help a company achieve strategic competitiveness.

Threats are conditions in the general environment that may hinder a company's efforts to achieve strategic competitiveness.

To analyze the general environment, several sources are used. Included among these are a wide variety of printed materials (e.g., trade publications, newspapers, business publications, the results of academic research and of public polls); attendance and participation in trade shows; the content of conversations with suppliers, customers, and employees of public-sector organizations; and, business-related "rumors" provided by many different people.[12] Additional sources of information and data include individuals in "boundary spanning" positions who interact with external constituents such as salespersons, purchasing managers, public relations directors, and human resource managers. Decision makers should verify the validity and reliability of the sources on which their environmental analyses are based.[13]

TABLE 2.2 *Components of the External Analysis*

Scanning	■ Identifying early signals of environmental changes and trends
Monitoring	■ Detecting meaning through ongoing observations of environmental change and trends
Forecasting	■ Developing projections of anticipated outcomes based on monitored changes and trends
Assessing	■ Determining the timing and importance of environmental changes and trends for firms' strategies and their management

Scanning

Scanning entails the study of all segments in the general environment. Through scanning, firms identify early signals of potential changes in the general environment and detect changes that are already under way.[14] When scanning, analysts typically deal with ambiguous, incomplete, and unconnected information and data. Environmental scanning has been found critically important for effective performance in firms that operate in highly volatile environments.[15] Additionally, scanning activity must be aligned with the organizational context; a scanning system designed for a volatile environment is inappropriate for a firm in a stable environment.[16]

In the 1990s, analysts in financial institutions are observing several changes in the general environment. First, some government officials and security analysts believe a combination of personal savings, private pensions, and Social Security income may be insufficient to support U.S. baby boomers' (those born between 1947 and 1964) retirement. It has even been suggested that financing baby boomers' retirement needs threatens the financial stability of most industrial nations, including the United States. The first of the baby boomer generation will retire in 2011. These retirements will push the total number of retirees from 25 million in 1991 to more than 33 million in 2011.[17] Changes in lifestyles and health care systems may result in longer average life spans for the baby boomers. By combining this information with data gleaned from scanning other environmental segments (e.g., the demographic, sociocultural, and political/legal segments), analysts can determine trends to monitor, forecast, and assess. Such analyses might result in an opportunity for financial institutions to serve effectively the baby boomers' retirement needs.

Monitoring

When *monitoring*, analysts observe environmental changes to see if, in fact, an important trend is emerging.[18] Critical to successful monitoring is an ability to detect meaning in different environmental events. For example, an emerging trend regarding education might be suggested by changes in federal and state funding for educational institutions, changes in high school graduation requirements, and changes in the content of high school courses. In this instance, analysts should determine whether these different events suggest an educational trend and, if so, whether other information and data should be studied to monitor it.

Forecasting

Scanning and monitoring are concerned with events in the general environment at a point in time. When *forecasting*, analysts develop feasible projections of what might happen, and how quickly, as a result of the changes and trends detected through scanning and monitoring.[19] For example, analysts might forecast the time that will be required for a new technology to reach the marketplace. Or they might forecast the length of time before different corporate training procedures are required to deal with anticipated changes in the composition of the workforce or how much time will elapse before changes in governmental taxation policies affect consumers' purchasing patterns. At Gillette, a recent forecast of slower sales and earnings growth led to a downturn in the firm's stock price. As this example shows, because markets respond so quickly, forecasts can lead to negative outcomes quickly.[20]

Assessing

The objective of *assessing* is to determine the timing and significance of the effects of environmental changes and trends on the strategic management of a firm.[21] Through scanning, monitoring, and forecasting, analysts are able to understand the general environment. Going a step further, the intent of assessment is to specify the implications of that understanding for the organization. Without assessment, analysts are left with data that are interesting but of unknown relevance.

Rubbermaid is an example of a firm that has learned to be careful about scanning, monitoring, forecasting, and assessing its external environment to avoid future problems with its customers and losing market share to emerging competitors. Rubbermaid has been ranked among the top 10 in *Fortune's* most admired companies list. During 1994 and 1995, it was ranked the number one company in corporate America. Recently, however, Rubbermaid experienced a number of problems. For example, it was confronted by several new competitors. In addition, Rubbermaid experienced major increases in the cost of resin (an important raw material in many of its products) and attempted to pass these costs to customers through large price increases. Wal-Mart was particularly angered by the large price increases because it is a huge customer of Rubbermaid. In response, Wal-Mart refused to stock a number of Rubbermaid products and deleted others from its promotional materials provided to customers. Instead, Wal-Mart featured Sterilite, one of Rubbermaid's prominent new competitors, in its promotional materials. Given that Wal-Mart is Rubbermaid's largest customer, accounting for more than 15 percent of Rubbermaid's total household-product sales, the discount store executives' anger seems well founded. Rubbermaid suffered from these forecasting errors and miscalculations. Expert competitive assessments in the future will contribute to Rubbermaid's efforts to avoid these types of difficulties.[22]

SEGMENTS OF THE GENERAL ENVIRONMENT

The general environment is composed of segments (and their individual elements) that are external to the firm (see Table 2.1). Although the degree of impact varies, these environmental segments affect each industry and its firms. The challenge is to scan, monitor, and assess those elements in each segment that are of the greatest importance to a firm. Results should include recognition of environmental changes, trends, opportunities, and threats. Opportunities are then matched with a firm's core competencies. When these matches are successful, the firm achieves strategic competitiveness and earns above-average returns.

The Demographic Segment

The **demographic segment** is concerned with a population's size, age, structure, geographic distribution, ethnic mix, and income distribution.

The **demographic segment** is concerned with a population's size, age, structure, geographic distribution, ethnic mix, and income distribution.[23] As noted previously, executives must analyze the demographics of the global areas potentially rel-

Demographic changes in populations are one of the key segments of the general environment. A few advanced countries have zero population growth; in others, such as the U.S., couples are having fewer than two children. In contrast, the populations of some developing nations are increasing, causing a depletion of resources and a reduction in the standard of living.

evant to their firms, rather than only those of the domestic population. In the following materials, each demographic element is discussed briefly.

Population Size Observing the demographic changes in populations highlights the importance of this environmental segment. For example, in some advanced nations, there is negative population growth (discounting the effects of immigration). In some countries, including the United States and several European nations, couples are averaging fewer than two children. Such a birth rate will produce a loss of population over time (even with the population living longer on average).[24] Population loss may require that a country increase immigration to have an adequate labor pool.

In contrast to advanced nations, the rapid growth rate in the populations of some Third World countries is depleting those nations' natural resources and reducing citizens' living standards. This rapid growth rate in the populations of some Third World countries may be a major challenge into the twenty-first century.

Age Structure In some countries, and certainly in the United States, the population's average age is increasing. In the U.S., for example, the percent of the population aged 55 and older is expected to increase from roughly 6 percent in 1995 to approximately 37.5 percent in 2019.[25] Contributing to this change are declining birth rates and increasing life expectancies. Among other outcomes, these changes create additional pressures on health care systems. Beyond this, these trends may suggest numerous opportunities for firms to develop goods and services to meet the needs of an increasingly older population.

It has been projected that some people alive today might live to the age of 200 or more. If such a life span becomes a reality, a host of interesting opportunities and problems will emerge. For example, the effect on individuals' pension plans will be significant and will create potential opportunities and threats for financial institutions.[26]

Geographic Distribution For several decades, the United States has experienced a population shift from the North and East to the West and South. Similarly, the trend of moving from metropolitan to nonmetropolitan areas continues. Among other effects, these trends have changed local and state governments' tax bases. In turn, the locations of business firms are influenced by the degree of support different taxing agencies offer.

The geographic distribution of populations throughout the world is being changed by the capabilities resulting from advances in communications technology. For example, through computer technologies, people can remain in their homes and communicate with others in remote locations to complete their work. In these instances, people can live where they prefer while being employed by a firm located in an unattractive location. Approximately 25 percent of U.S. employees may work out of their homes by the year 2000.[27]

Partially because of the advances in communication technology, approximately 29.5 percent of the more than 100 million employed workers in the United States in 1997 were contingency workers. Contingency workers include those who are part time, temporary, and on contract. As a result, these employees are more mobile. It is estimated that the number of contingency workers will continue to grow to as much as 50 percent of the U.S. workforce by the year 2000. This trend exists in other parts of the world as well, including Western Europe, Japan, Latin America, and Canada. Interestingly, the fastest growing segment of contingency workers is in the technical and professional area.[28]

Ethnic Mix The ethnic mix of countries' populations continues to change. Within the United States, the ethnicity of states, and of cities within the states, varies significantly. For business firms, the challenge is to be aware of and sensitive to these changes. Through careful study, firms can develop and market goods and services intended to satisfy the unique needs and interest of different ethnic groups.

Ethnic mix changes also affect a workforce's composition. In the United States, for example, by the mid-1990s, only 15 percent of the new workers entering the workforce were Caucasian males. The remainder of those entering the workforce during the 1990s were Caucasian, U.S.-born women (42 percent) and immigrants and U.S.-born minorities (43 percent).[29] The Hispanic population is predicted to be the fastest growing segment of the U.S. workforce in the 1990s. By 2000, Hispanics will account for 9.2 percent of the workforce, up from 7.8 percent in 1991. Because a labor force can be critical to competitive success, firms are challenged to work effectively with an increasingly diverse labor force.[30] Diversity in the workforce is also a sociocultural issue.

Effective management of a culturally diverse workforce can produce a competitive advantage. For example, heterogeneous work teams have been shown to produce more effective strategic analyses, more creativity and innovation, and higher quality decisions than homogeneous work teams.[31] Because of these potential outcomes, a number of companies promote cultural diversity in their workforce and facilitate effective management of such diversity through specialized management training. Among these companies are American Express, Northern States Power

Company, General Foods, US West, and British Petroleum. For example, all US West employees (more than 60,000) attend a diversity training program.[32]

Income Distribution Understanding how income is distributed within and across populations informs firms of different groups' purchasing power and discretionary income. Study of income distributions suggests that while living standards have improved over time, there are variances within and between nations.[33] Of interest to firms are the average incomes of households and individuals. For instance, a notable change is the increase of dual career couples. Although real income has been going down, dual career couples have increased their income. These figures yield strategically relevant information.

The Economic Segment

Clearly, the health of a nation's economy affects the performance of individual firms and industries. As a result, strategists study the economic environment to identify changes, trends, and their strategic implications.

The **economic environment** refers to the nature and direction of the economy in which a firm competes or may compete.[34] As shown in Table 2.1, indicators of an economy's health include inflation rates, interest rates, trade deficits or surpluses, budget deficits or surpluses, personal and business savings rates, and gross domestic product. However, because of the interconnectedness of the global financial community, analysts often must also scan, monitor, forecast, and assess the health of other countries' economies. For example, the economic status of nations with which the United States exchanges many products, such as Japan and Germany, can affect the overall health of the U.S. economy. In this regard, some worry that billions of dollars, yen, and deutsche marks move across national borders without much control by central banks. The delicately balanced global financial system permitting these easy transfers might contribute to an international economic crisis if the balance in the system were lost.[35]

The **economic environment** refers to the nature and direction of the economy in which a firm competes or may compete.

Of course, some of these problems might be eliminated if European countries are able to achieve their goal of a single currency for all of Europe. European countries have set target dates for a European monetary union in which countries will agree on irrevocable exchange rates by 1999 and change completely to a new single currency by 2002. Some speculate that European countries will not be able to meet these target dates nor will they be able to establish a single currency. Alternatively, the single currency may begin with the union of several financially strong nations, such as Germany, Belgium, and France, allowing the others to join later as they are able to meet the requirements. The interrelatedness among different national economies is shown in ways other than currency exchange rates and similarities of their currencies.[36] Agreements to lower or eliminate trade barriers between nations, such as the North American Free Trade Agreement (NAFTA), have potentially significant economic consequences for the nations involved.

Economic issues can also have significant influences on political and legal issues. For example, some argue that the United States cannot afford to cancel favored-nation status for China, even though it has threatened to do so because of perceived human rights concerns. To take such action might have significant negative economic consequences for U.S. firms. The recent devaluation of multiple currencies in Asia shocked many fast paced economies into slow growth economies in the short term. For firms with significant assets in the Philippines, Thailand, Malaysia, and Indonesia, the devaluations had a significant negative effect. On the other hand, those who expect to build in these areas in the future may find significantly lower property and labor costs.[37]

The Political/Legal Segment

The **political/legal segment** is the arena in which organizations and interest groups compete for attention and resources and the body of laws and regulations guiding these interactions.

The **political/legal segment** is the arena in which organizations and interest groups compete for attention and resources and the body of laws and regulations guiding these interactions.[38] Essentially, this segment represents how organizations try to influence government and how government entities influence them. Constantly changing, this segment (see Table 2.1) influences the nature of competition. Because of this, firms must analyze carefully a new administration's business-related policies and philosophies. Antitrust laws, taxation laws, industries chosen for deregulation, labor training laws, and the degree of commitment to educational institutions are areas where an administration's policies can affect the operations and profitability of industries and individual firms.

As indicated in the opening case, deregulation in the electric power industry will force many firms to restructure their competitive practices. It is estimated that the $250 billion spent on electric power could decrease by 20 or 30 percent over the next five to ten years due to deregulation.[39] The electric power industry is the largest U.S. industry to be deregulated. "It's about twice the size of long-distance telephone service and dwarfs gas, airline, trucking, and railroad industries," states Kenneth Lay, CEO of Enron Corporation.[40] Because electric power can be such a huge operating expense, a large savings in this category could enhance corporate profitability substantially. Of course, this is the "great nightmare" for utilities with high-cost inefficient generating plants. Who will pay the cost of these stranded assets? Consumers? Electric utilities? These issues will be determined by the interactions occurring in the political/legal environment.

Viewpoints regarding government philosophies and policies (federal, state, and local), the most effective means of competition, and the ideal relationship between government and business can vary substantially. In addition to political perspectives, these viewpoints are affected by the nature of the industry in which a firm competes. As the 1990s come to a close, business firms across the globe are confronted by an interesting array of political/legal questions and issues. For example, the debate continues over trade policies. Some believe a nation should erect trade barriers to protect its domestic products. Others argue that free trade across nations serves the best interests of individual countries and their citizens. With the NAFTA and GATT agreements now in place, the trend seems to be toward free trade.

For instance, Central America, which was once a proving ground for guerrilla-warfare tactics, is joining most of the rest of Latin America as a proving ground for free-market reform.[41] Guatemala, for instance, is implementing one of the most aggressive telecommunication reform laws in Latin America. It is essentially opening its market to full competition in all segments; local, long-distance, paging, and cellular services. Motorola and 14 other foreign telecommunications companies are negotiating to provide these services. Furthermore, Guatemala has already privatized railroad, radio, and electrical utilities companies and has begun the process to privatize its telecommunications company, Guatel. Other Central American countries are taking similar if not identical actions. El Salvador ended 14 years of civil war and is reforming social security and tax collection systems. Nicaragua has attracted 19 factories to its free-trade zone and has slated its state phone company for sale.

In the United States, frequent debates occur over the appropriate amount of regulation of business. Many want less regulation; others, however, believe that more regulation is required to ensure appropriate business practices. Cases from both ends of the spectrum have been observed recently. For example, the Justice Department investigated Anheuser-Busch, Inc.'s sales practices to determine if it is abusing its dominant market position in its "100% share of mind program." Many microbrewers say the program is creating a situation where they have been dropped by Anheuser's distributors because of the incentive program. Often the distributor places them with Anheuser's microbrew label, Redhook.[42] At the other end of the spectrum, the Federal Communications Commission has been liberalizing its control over television networks and program ownership. This loosening of federal government controls over the entertainment industry has allowed the Disney Company to purchase Capital Cities/ABC. Outside of the fact that it involves well-known entertainment industry firms, the acquisition is interesting because it represents a vertical integration for Disney. It provides a means to distribute Disney products and thus is a related diversification move within the same industry (types of diversification are explained in Chapter 6). Certainly, it gives the Disney Company more power within the entertainment industry.[43]

The Sociocultural Segment

The **sociocultural segment** is concerned with different societies' social attitudes and cultural values. Because attitudes and values are a society's cornerstone, they often drive demographic, economic, political/legal, and technological changes. Firms are challenged to understand the meaning of attitudinal and cultural changes across global societies.

The **sociocultural segment** is concerned with different societies' social attitudes and cultural values.

As mentioned earlier, a significant workforce trend in many countries concerns diversity. In the United States, for example, 76.3 million women are expected to participate in the labor force by 2011.[44] In addition, a large percentage of new entrants into the workforce will be ethnic minorities. As a result, the workforce will become increasingly diverse.

In the United States, approximately 46 percent of the workforce is composed of women. In Sweden, it's 50 percent, Japan, 41 percent, and Mexico, 37 percent. In the United States, 43 percent of the managerial jobs are held by women. In Sweden, 17 percent are held by women and in Japan, it is only 9.4 percent. In Japan, many women head businesses, but they are self-employed. The same is true in the United States, but approximately 17 percent of all U.S. businesses are headed by women, excluding those who are self-employed. In the United States, women are paid approximately 76 percent of the compensation paid to men. In Sweden, it's 77 percent, in Japan, 61.6 percent, and in Mexico, 68.2 percent. Thus, while women have experienced employment problems in the United States, the barriers to their participation in the workplace in many other countries seem to be greater.[45]

The influx of women and the increasing ethnic and cultural diversity in the workforce yield exciting challenges and significant opportunities.[46] Included among these are the needs to combine the best of both men's and women's leadership styles for a firm's benefit and to identify ways to facilitate all employees' contributions to their firms. An example of a firm attempting to do this is Avon. Four out of the eleven members of the board are women, and more than 40 percent of its global managers are women.[47] Some companies now provide training to nurture women's and ethnic minorities' leadership potential. Changes in organizational structure and management practices also often are required to eliminate subtle barriers that may exist. Learning to manage diversity in the domestic workforce can increase a firm's effectiveness in managing a globally diverse workforce, as it acquires more international operations. The results from these commitments to promote and manage diversity enhance a company's performance.[48]

Many women now choose to start their own businesses, as implied earlier, oftentimes because of frustration in dealing with the glass ceiling (a subtle barrier to the advancement of women and ethnic minorities in corporations). In 1982, there were 2.4 million female entrepreneurs in the United States; in 1991, that number exceeded 3 million. In 1994, women owned 7.7 million businesses, more than one-third of all U.S. firms. If this rate of start-ups continues, women will own one-half of U.S. businesses by the year 2000. The number of businesses owned by minority women continues to grow, increasing 153 percent between 1987 and 1996. The same trend has been observed in other countries such as Japan.[49]

The number of women in the corporate world who are relocating was up to 26 percent in 1996 from 16 percent in 1993. Many of these women relocate without their families and thereby lead complex lifestyles while trying to maintain their family life. Dorrit J. Bern, for example, is having a significant influence on the corporation she is leading. She is CEO of Charming Shoppes, Inc., which is headquartered in Philadelphia, but her family lives in Chicago. She didn't want to uproot her family, but the chance to turn around this business after being a successful executive with Sears was a significant opportunity. She maintains an apartment in Philadelphia Monday through Friday and a family life in Chicago on weekends. Her husband is a consultant and has more flexibility to manage the home and the lives of their three children.[50]

Moreover, the number of single fathers with custody of their children has increased dramatically to 1.86 million in 1996 from 393,000 in 1970. There are still more single mothers at 9.86 million, but single-father families have been growing by 10 percent annually. Demographers and marketers are noting this change.[51]

The Technological Segment

Pervasive and diversified in scope, technological changes affect many parts of societies. These effects occur primarily through new products, processes, and materials. The **technological segment** includes the institutions and activities involved with creating new knowledge and translating that knowledge into new outputs, products, processes, and materials.

The **technological segment** includes the institutions and activities involved with creating new knowledge and translating that knowledge into new outputs, products, processes, and materials.

Given the rapid pace of technological change, it is vital that firms carefully study different elements in the technological segment. For example, research has shown that early adopters of new technology often achieve higher market shares and earn higher returns. Thus, executives must continuously scan the environment to identify potential substitutes for their firm's technology as well as newly emerging technologies from which their firm could benefit. They need to identify the speed with

Research has shown that firms adopting new technology early often achieve greater market share and earn higher returns. The CAD system—a technological innovation—in the photo is being used to design cars.

which substitute technologies are likely to emerge and the timing of any major technological changes.[52]

A technology with important implications for business is the Internet, sometimes referred to as "the information superhighway." The Internet is a global web of more than 25,000 computer networks. It provides a quick, inexpensive means of global communication (i.e., with strategic alliance partners) and access to information. For example, GE engineers often use the Internet to communicate with their counterparts when doing development work for other companies. The Internet provides access to experts on such topics as chemical engineering and semiconductor manufacturing, to the Library of Congress, and even to satellite photographs. Other information available on the Internet includes Security and Exchange Commission (SEC) filings, Commerce Department data, Census Bureau information, new patent filings, and stock market updates.[53] Not only is the Internet an excellent source of data on a firm's external environment, there are a number of firms that provide Internet software that pushes data into customers' computers or other communication devices as soon as it happens. Tibco and Pointcast are two firms that specialize in products that keep their clients informed continuously about noteworthy news that is customized to the customers' interests.[54]

A number of firms have benefited from the popularity and use of the Internet. U.S. Robotics is one example. U.S. Robotics makes modems and other communications devices for computers and its sales are booming. Modems are important for connecting personal computers to phone lines that help gain access to the Internet. The technology in the manufacture of modems has advanced rapidly. Their speed may only be curtailed by the limits of conventional phone lines.[55] Encyclopedia Britannica Inc. is using the Internet to revive its business. For example, the firm now offers a free search engine with sites screened by its editors.[56] As Encyclopedia Britannica's actions demonstrate, the Internet can allow a firm to be both flexible and innovative with its product introductions.[57]

Microsoft is now changing its strategy not only to provide software for the Internet, but also to make sure that a new operating system does not displace its Windows business for PCs when a "Web lifestyle" emerges. As a result, Microsoft is working with phone companies and investing in cable companies Comcast and TCI. Similarly, Bill Gates has invested in WebTV Networks Inc. to obtain technology to deliver a high-speed digital stream that can be viewed—as movies, Web sites or advertising—on televisions with its equipment. Oracle Corporation, through its unit Network Computer, Inc. is developing a rival design for a cable box, which was given a significant boost by support from Intel.[58]

Another new technology that is gaining rapid popularity is satellite imaging. Several aerospace companies have invested up to $1 billion in corporate earth-imaging systems. For example, Space Imaging, Inc., a joint venture of Lockheed Martin, E-Systems, Mitsubishi Corporation, and Eastman Kodak Company, is a $500 million venture that provides images from an advanced satellite. Many expect this technology to compete in the global information trade industry and some anticipate that it will create a revolution. There are a number of uses for this technology. For example, Coldwell Banker Corporation uses it to offer real estate shoppers photographs from space of homes, neighborhoods, and traffic patterns. Television networks, such as ABC, use the technology to provide detailed images of battle zones for evening news broadcasts. Even urban planners are using the technology to update property tax rolls, while other firms may use it to plot new phone lines without using crews to study the terrain beforehand.[59]

Many firms are making significant revenues in the space-related businesses with demand for satellites the key driving factor.[60] For instance, the military now has a backpack-sized communicator called Manpack that gives the soldier on any battlefield in the world a direct satellite voice- and data-link. A soldier in a foxhole can talk directly with the Pentagon. Furthermore, the technology by ViaSat lets thousands of soldiers use one satellite simultaneously.[61] Spacehab is building research modules that could expand the amount of pressurized space on the shuttle and, thus, house more experiments. Demand for more space was created when the Challenger disaster created a backlog of 400 experiments with the suspension of space shuttle flights.

The Global Segment

The **global segment** includes relevant new global markets and existing ones that are changing, important international political events, and critical cultural and institutional characteristics of relevant global markets.

The **global segment** includes relevant new global markets and existing ones that are changing, important international political events, and critical cultural and institutional characteristics of relevant global markets. Although the previous segments should be analyzed in terms of their domestic and global implications, some additional specific global factors should be analyzed as well.

Firms must also attempt to identify critical new global markets and/or those that are changing. It is clear that many global markets are fast becoming borderless and integrated.[62] For example, firms may examine emerging markets such as those in South American countries or markets in newly industrialized countries such as in Asia (e.g., South Korea, Taiwan) for new opportunities. They should also be cognizant of the potential threats from these countries.

Newly industrialized countries, such as South Korea, have significant buying power but also have globally competitive firms. Based on significant support and economic planning from the government, the predominant goal of major South

Korean firms is growth. Thus, many South Korean firms place less emphasis on earning net profits and more on attaining major growth goals through their strategic actions.[63] An example of this is shown by Samsung's new venture into passenger-car production, partially because of executives' concerns at being ranked number two in size to Hyundai. Although Samsung is predicted to invest approximately $4.5 billion in developing its auto manufacturing venture, it also plans to invest up to $150 million in the development of a 100-seat jetliner, $3 billion to build semiconductor manufacturing plants in North America, Europe, and Southeast Asia, and $2 to $3 billion to establish a hypermedia city of offices, shops, entertainment centers, and housing in downtown Seoul by 2000. Recently, Samsung invested approximately $9.92 billion in expansion opportunities.[64]

Firms must also have a reasonable understanding of the different cultural and institutional attributes of global markets in which they operate or hope to operate. For example, a firm operating in South Korea must understand the value placed on hierarchical order, formality, self-control, and on duty rather than rights. Furthermore, Korean ideology places emphasis on communitarianism, a characteristic of many Asian countries. Korea's approach differs from that of Japan and China with its focus on *Inhwa* or harmony. *Inhwa* is based on a respect of hierarchical relationships and an obedience to authority. Alternatively, the approach in China is focused on *Guanxi* or personal relationships and in Japan on *Wa* or group harmony and social cohesion.[65] The institutional context of Korea suggests a major emphasis on centralized planning by the government. The emphasis placed on growth by many South Korean firms is the result of a government policy to promote economic growth in South Korea.[66]

The cultural and institutional contexts in which firms must operate in global markets can be critical. For example, in India there is a current nationalist campaign against multinational firms. This campaign led to the recent closing of a Kentucky Fried Chicken (KFC) restaurant in New Delhi. Although the official statement was that the KFC outlet was closed for health reasons after an inspection, executives of several U.S. food companies blamed political posturing related to an upcoming election. Also, those who oppose KFC's opening are often those who lobby against meat eating. KFC was one of the first major fast food giants to open a facility in India. Furthermore, it has been quite successful in Asia with more than 2,200 restaurants operating in that region of the world. Still, even a firm that has been as successful as KFC must carefully and thoroughly analyze the institutional and cultural environments of its global markets.[67]

As explained in the Strategic Focus on the takeover of Hong Kong, China offers potential opportunities but also threats to a number of firms with domestic headquarters outside its borders. Even more so with Hong Kong now a part of China, its growing economic prowess makes its firms potentially significant competitors, particularly in labor-intensive industries. As a result, firms operating in such industries worldwide must view the development of Chinese entrepreneurial operations as an environmental threat. Alternatively, firms that can invest in China may be able to take advantage of the low-cost labor; and, China also offers a huge and growing market for products, as evidenced by the success of Procter & Gamble's (P&G) products there.[68] P&G sells approximately 50 percent of the shampoo used in China, and its nationwide distribution system may be the best in that country. P&G owes its success to being an early mover in China, and its aggressiveness has paid dividends. It has been successful even though its prices are sometimes 300 percent greater than local brands. The development of the Chinese economy is one that must be analyzed carefully by firms operating in many industries, regardless of their home country.

STRATEGIC FOCUS

The Strategic Effect of the Chinese Takeover of Hong Kong

The Chinese takeover of Hong Kong was accomplished July 1, 1997. The effects of the environmental policy changes portend to be dramatic. There is now one country with two systems and a new economy for the capitalist hub of Asia, Hong Kong. It's not clear whether Hong Kong will become the cosmopolitan capital of Chinese capitalism or whether Chinese-style bureaucrats will change what has made it special. The economic environment that evolves will tell the ultimate outcome of the Chinese takeover of Hong Kong. Either of these scenarios may be inaccurate because China and Hong Kong are major investors in each other. Top officials in the special administrative region (SAR), which will be the official government of the Hong Kong territories, are determined to be more active than were the British. They use Singapore as an example of the type of policy to be implemented. Although Hong Kong will continue to be a standard setter in real estate and financial services, even more important is that it is likely to be the media and pop-culture hub for all of China. Although it will certainly be a financial and fashion hub, it may become too dependent on the Chinese economy. If it focuses too much on China, it may lose its standing as a regional center for all of Southeast Asia. If it is exposed to too many of the economic upheavals because of China's political and economic difficulties, Hong Kong may jeopardize its current standing.

As the change has been anticipated for some time, "red chip" companies—such as corporations controlled by mainland interests but listed in Hong Kong—are emerging as the new pillars of Hong Kong. They are restructuring the old order of local property developers and bankers who previously dominated the Hong Kong stock market. It is conceivable that many of the red chip companies will swallow major Hong Kong companies just as earlier Hong Kong entrepreneurs acquired British-owned companies in the 1980s. There is a question as to who will regulate the red chip companies. Will China be able to dictate who can list companies on the exchange or will this be determined solely by free market options?

Hong Kong has another concern. Because it does not have a strong manufacturing base, policy and administrative leaders are wondering if it will lose its central economic role as it competes with other economic coastal centers such as Shanghai. Because housing costs are so high in Hong Kong, some suggest that it will cost half as much to employ an engineer in California as in Hong Kong. Therefore, there is little incentive to invest in R&D and staff training in Hong Kong. Hong Kong companies rely on young laborers from China's interior who go home after a few years. These workers lack the technical skills required to manufacture more advanced products. Because costs are so high, manufacturers may simply shop for cheaper labor elsewhere in Asia. Thus, there is no clear evidence that Hong Kong will be able to maintain its financial and service center role without a strong manufacturing base such as that held by Shanghai.

Additionally, protecting the rule of law which has been the foundation of Hong Kong's economic success may be difficult if civil liberties erode under the Chinese system. There will be severe temptations by Chinese and/or Hong Kong firms to use their mainland connections to special advantage after the takeover. This can lead to corruption, which undermines the rule of law and the current economic success of Hong Kong. An additional factor is what the overseas Chinese, especially in Southeast Asia, will do with the Hong Kong takeover. The expatriate Chinese have kept their distance from the mainland politics. Their loyalties do not lie with the Chinese nation-state but rather with the returns that can be earned there. They have invested only in special economic zones that are protected and where they are free to move their capital. Many of them would not be willing to relinquish their foreign passport and go back to China. They will invest in China if that is where money can be earned, but if labor costs increase and productivity levels off, they are just as likely to turn to Vietnam to establish operations, or to other areas such as India, Bangladesh, Fiji, or Guatemala. If China attacks Taiwan or crushes the spirit and rule of law of Hong Kong, the overseas Chinese will not likely continue to invest in China. Loyalties to China will be overcome by economic pressures and fundamental loyalties to families.

How policy changes and ultimate government changes affect the economy will decide the nature of competition among firms and whether the Hong Kong takeover succeeds or fails. Potential demographic changes of foreign expatriate Chinese coming home or immigrants from the mainland will have an effect on these strategies. Certainly, politics and the rule of law will affect the nature of strategic exchange between firms. Thus, what happens in Hong Kong will have a strong influence on the strategic environment of the firms in Hong Kong and on the Chinese mainland, as well as all the multinational firms established there.

SOURCES: J. Barnathan, 1997, Hong Kong, *Business Week*, June 9, 45–49; M. Elliott and D. Elliott, 1997, Hong Kong: Why the world watches, *Newsweek*, May 19, 30–35; P. Engardio and J. Barnathan, 1997, Red chips rising, *Business Week*, June 9, 50–51; P. H. Kahn, 1997, Waiting for the shoe to drop in Hong Kong, *Wall Street Journal*, October 7, A18; P. Kwong, 1996, The Chinese Diaspora, *World Business* 2, no. 2: 26–31.

A key objective of analyzing the general environment is identification of anticipated significant changes and trends among external elements. With a focus on the future, the analysis of the general environment allows firms to identify opportunities and threats. Also critical to a firm's future operations is an understanding of its industry environment and its competitors, which are considered next.

INDUSTRY ENVIRONMENT ANALYSIS

An **industry** is a group of firms producing products that are close substitutes. In the course of competition, these firms influence one another. Typically, industries include a rich mix of competitive strategies that companies use in pursuing strategic competitiveness and above-average returns.[69]

An **industry** is a group of firms producing products that are close substitutes.

Compared to the general environment, the industry environment has a more direct effect on strategic competitiveness and above-average returns. The intensity of industry competition and an industry's profit potential (as measured by the long-run return on invested capital) are a function of five competitive forces: the threat of new entrants, suppliers, buyers, product substitutes, and the intensity of rivalry among competitors (see Figure 2.2).

Developed by Michael Porter, the five forces model of competition expands the arena for competitive analysis. Historically, when studying the competitive environment, firms concentrated on companies with which they competed directly. But

FIGURE 2.2 *The Five Forces Model of Competition*

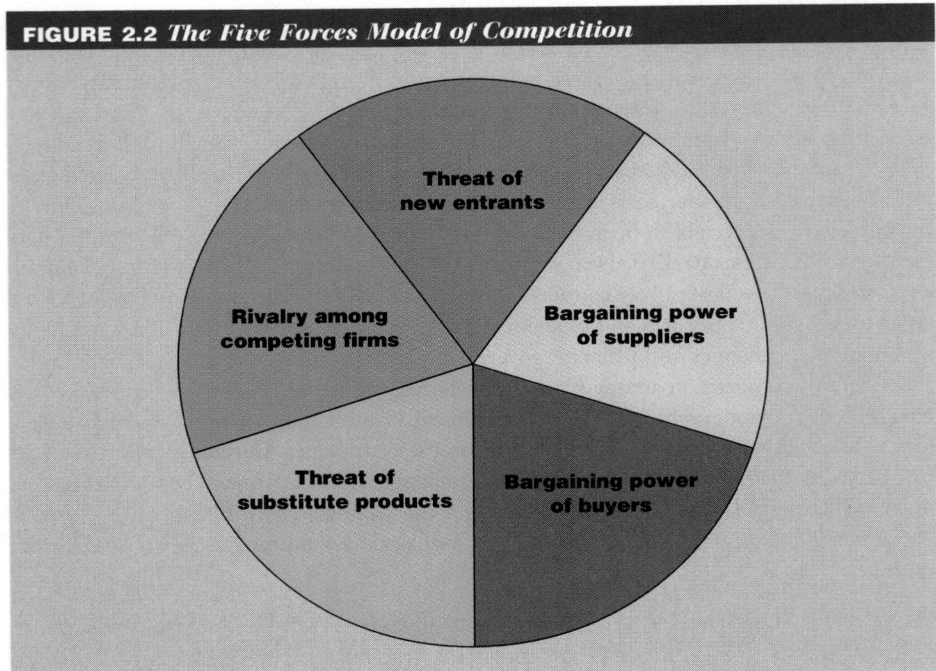

today, competition is viewed as a grouping of alternative ways for customers to obtain the value they desire, rather than being limited to direct competitors. This is particularly important because in recent years industry boundaries have become blurred. For example, in the electrical utilities industry, as the opening case indicates, cogenerators, firms that also produce power, are competing for customers along with regional utility companies. Moreover, telecommunications companies now compete with broadcasters, software manufacturers also provide personal financial services, airlines now sell mutual funds, and automakers sell insurance and provide financing.[70] In addition to focusing on customers to define markets rather than specific industry boundaries, one should examine geographic boundaries as well. Research has shown that different geographic markets for the same product can have considerable differences in the competitive conditions.[71]

The five forces model recognizes that suppliers could become a firm's competitor (by integrating forward), as could buyers (by integrating backward). This is illustrated graphically in the pharmaceuticals industry where Merck & Company acquired Medco Containment Services, a mail-order pharmacy and prescription benefits management company. In so doing, Merck integrated forward and became a competitor of other pharmacies and prescription benefits management companies. Perhaps most importantly, Merck guaranteed a major source of distribution for its products. Shortly after Merck's acquisition, SmithKline Beecham and Eli Lilly announced plans to acquire similar companies and integrate forward as well.[72] Additionally, firms choosing to enter a new market and those producing products that are adequate substitutes could become competitors for an existing company.

Threat of New Entrants

New entrants to an industry can threaten existing competitors. New entrants bring additional production capacity. Unless product demand is increasing, additional capacity holds consumers' costs down, resulting in less sales revenue and lower returns for all firms in the industry. Often, new entrants have substantial resources and a keen interest in gaining a large market share. As such, new competitors may force existing firms to be more effective and efficient and to learn how to compete on new dimensions (e.g., computer-driven distribution channels). The likelihood that firms will enter an industry is a function of two factors: barriers to entry and the retaliation expected from current industry participants. When firms find entry into a new industry difficult or when firms are at a competitive disadvantage entering a new industry, entry barriers exist.

Barriers to Entry Existing competitors try to develop barriers to market entry. Alternatively, potential entrants seek markets where the entry barriers are relatively insignificant. The absence of entry barriers increases the probability a new entrant can operate profitably in an industry. There are several potentially significant entry barriers.

Economies of Scale. As the quantity of a product produced during a given time period increases, the costs of manufacturing each unit declines. These benefits are referred to as *economies of scale.*

Scale economies can be gained through most business functions (e.g., marketing, manufacturing, research and development, and purchasing). New entrants face a dilemma when existing competitors have scale economies. Small-scale entry places them at a cost disadvantage. However, large-scale entry, where the new entrant manufactures large volumes of a product to gain scale economies, risks strong reactions from established competitors.

Although still important in some industries (automobile manufacturing, for example), the competitive realities of the 1990s and the approaching twenty-first century may reduce the significance of scale economies as an entry barrier. Many companies now customize their products for large numbers of small customer groups. Customized products are not manufactured in the volumes necessary to achieve economies of scale. Customization is made possible by new flexible manufacturing systems. In fact, the new manufacturing technology facilitated by advanced computerization has allowed the development of mass customization in some industries. Mass customized products can be individualized to the customer in a very short period of time (e.g., within a day). Mass customization may become the norm in manufacturing products by the end of the 1990s.[73] Companies manufacturing customized products learn how to respond quickly to customers' desires, rather than developing scale economies.

Product Differentiation. Over time, customers may come to believe that an existing firm's product is unique. This belief can result from service to the customer, effective advertising campaigns, or the firm being the first to market a particular product. Many firms such as Coca-Cola and PepsiCo spend significant amounts of money on advertising to convince potential customers of the distinctiveness of their products. The belief that a firm's product is unique results in loyal customers who have strong brand identification. Typically, new entrants must allocate significant resources over a long period of time to overcome existing customer loyalties. To combat the perception of uniqueness, new entrants frequently offer their products at lower prices. This can result, however, in lower profitability or even a loss for the new entrant.

Capital Requirements. Competing in a new industry requires resources to invest. In addition to physical facilities, capital is needed for inventories, marketing activities, and other critical business functions. Although competing in a new industry may appear attractive, the capital required for successful market entry may not be available.

Switching Costs. Switching costs are the one-time costs customers incur when buying from a different supplier. The costs of buying new ancillary equipment and of retraining employees and even the psychic costs of ending a relationship may be incurred in switching to a new supplier. In some cases, switching costs are low, such as switching soft drink brands, although cost may be higher for the bottler than the ultimate consumer. Sometimes larger companies help to pay the switching costs as Anheuser Busch is doing through an incentive program for beer distributors. At other times, switching costs are high even for the ultimate consumer; for instance, switching from cassette tapes to CDs as a music format. The consumer not only has to buy a CD player but CDs are more costly than cassettes. If switching costs are high, a new entrant must offer either a substantially lower price or a much better product to attract buyers. Usually, the more established the relationship, the greater the switching costs.

Access to Distribution Channels. Over time, industry participants can develop effective means of distributing products. Once developed, firms nurture their relationship with distributors. Such nurturing creates switching costs for distributors. Access to distribution channels can be a strong entry barrier for potential new entrants, particularly in consumer nondurable goods industries (e.g., in grocery stores, shelf space is limited). Thus, new entrants must persuade distributors to carry their products, either in addition to or in place of existing firms' products. Price breaks and cooperative advertising allowances may be used for this purpose, but their use reduces the new entrant's potential to earn above-average returns.

Cost Disadvantages Independent of Scale. In some instances, established competitors have cost advantages that new entrants cannot duplicate. Proprietary product technology, favorable access to raw materials, favorable locations, and government subsidies may provide such cost advantages. Successful competition requires new entrants to finds ways to reduce the strategic relevance of these factors. For example, the advantage of a favorable location can be reduced by offering direct delivery to the buyer (a number of food establishments, with unattractive locations, deliver goods directly to the consumer).

Government Policy. Through licensing and permit requirements, governments can control entry into an industry. Liquor retailing, banking, and trucking are examples of industries where government decisions and actions affect industry entry. Also, governments restrict entrance into some utility industries because of the need to provide quality service to all and the capital requirements necessary to do so.

Expected Retaliation Decision makers will also anticipate existing competitors' reactions to a new entrant. If retaliation is expected to be swift and vigorous, a decision could be reached against entry. Strong retaliation can be anticipated from firms with a major stake in an industry (e.g., having fixed assets with few, if any, alternative uses), from firms with substantial resources, and when industry growth is slow or constrained. Sometimes, a company will publicly announce its intentions.

The Cable News Network, better known as CNN and now part of Time Warner, has had a monopoly on the broadcast of 24-hour news. Capital Cities/ABC launched a 24-hour news service in 1997, using ABC News correspondents and anchors. Britain's BBC is also attempting to start a global news channel. GE's NBC has allied with Microsoft to initiate its national news network MSNBC. MSNBC also has a parallel Web site, allowing news and information to be distributed over the Internet. Time Warner intends to respond to these competitive actions by developing a parallel Web site called CityWeb. It will attempt to distribute programs to the main network affiliates (the local TV stations of ABC, NBC, Fox, and CBS) through the Internet and help them establish their own Web sites. The main networks do not have a Web site strategy. Fox indicated that the firm would eventually try to collaborate with its affiliates on co-branding and revenue sharing on Web traffic flowing in both directions. Thus, it will be interesting to see the outcome of both the 24-hour news market and how the Internet strategies evolve as competitors launch one initiative in response to other's actions.[74]

Firms can avoid entry barriers by searching out market niches that are not being served by the primary competition. Small entrepreneurial firms are generally best suited for searching out and serving these neglected market segments. A number of years ago when Honda entered the U.S. market, it concentrated on small engine motorcycles, a market that firms such as Harley-Davidson ignored. By targeting this neglected market segment, Honda avoided competition. After consolidating its position, however, Honda used its new strength to attack its rivals by

Honda sought a market niche by concentrating on small-engine motorcycles, which Harley-Davidson did not produce. Once it established itself in the small-engine niche, Honda was able to introduce larger motorcycles and compete in a broader market.

introducing larger motorcycles and competing in the broader market.[75] Competitive actions and responses are discussed in more detail in Chapter 5.

Bargaining Power of Suppliers

Increasing prices and reducing the quality of products sold are potential means through which suppliers can exert power over firms competing within an industry. If unable to recover cost increases through its pricing structure, a firm's profitability is reduced by the suppliers' actions. A supplier group is powerful when

- it is dominated by a few large companies and is more concentrated than the industry to which it sells;
- satisfactory substitute products are not available to industry firms;
- industry firms are not a significant customer for the supplier group;
- suppliers' goods are critical to buyers' marketplace success;
- the effectiveness of suppliers' products has created high switching costs for industry firms; and
- suppliers are a credible threat to integrate forward into the buyers' industry (e.g., a clothing manufacturer might choose to operate its own retail outlets). Credibility is enhanced when suppliers have substantial resources and provide the industry's firms with a highly differentiated product.

The Strategic Focus on Dell Computer Corporation illustrates how a supplier can use its power and save money for the ultimate consumer. Dell's strategy of selling directly to the corporate market is now being duplicated by Compaq and others. Dell has reduced its cost relative to other rivals and has increased its power relative to its buyers. Also, Dell is pursuing the direct consumer market.[76] Gateway 2000 sells directly to the consumer market and has now decided to pursue the corporate market by moving into larger servers.[77]

STRATEGIC FOCUS

Why Other Computer Firms Want to Imitate Dell Computer

Dell Computer Corporation's approach to selling PCs has focused on direct distribution using distributors or computer resellers. Because Dell's business model costs less to produce and distribute, the industry leaders, Compaq, IBM, Packard Bell, and Hewlett-Packard (HP) have tried to copy Dell's approach rather than use computer resellers to whom they have outsourced much of their business in this highly competitive industry.

The typical approach to distribution with the leading PC manufacturers is based on a forecast of demand. For instance, Compaq builds its machines based on this forecast. It test inspects and stores the PCs before sending them to a reseller's warehouse until customers purchase them. Often, the average time between inventory and purchase is six to eight weeks. Furthermore, the reseller's markup is generally between 7 and 9 percent. The reseller often unpacks the product, removes the computer, loads software and tests the whole thing before it is sold to the customer. The entire process is quite expensive because of packaging and repackaging as well as paying for the reseller's markup. In a fast-paced industry such as personal computers, time is money.

Compaq has unveiled recently an optimized-distribution model with much fanfare. The firm will not build a computer until it receives an order for one. Therefore, Compaq will begin to customize PCs in its own plants and ship them directly to the reseller. Similarly, HP has sought to reduce inventories and force reseller inventory down to two weeks. Compaq, IBM, and HP's advantage is that they can sell computers even through resellers; they have much broader computer lines and sell half of their product abroad. The international consumer base often does not buy computers over the phone or the Internet which is Dell's approach, but competition with Dell has required this firm's competitors to squeeze their resellers. The problem with squeezing the margins of the resellers is that there is no longer an incentive for resellers to provide the service to the larger producers.

For instance, both Compaq and HP have suggested that they will make a series of changes in reforming dealer relationships. Rather than shipping finished PCs, they would ship components, which dealers themselves would assemble into a finished unit.

One of the resellers, MicroAge, Inc., has dealt with this pressure by transforming itself into an assembler for the giants such as IBM, HP, Compaq, and Acer. MicroAge installs software and adds components requested by the customer. Furthermore, the firm collects fees for operating help desks for other companies and helps manage other companies' computer buying needs. Thus, MicroAge is searching for creative ways to increase its financial returns.

Except for Dell's approach, the buyer's power is increasing relative to seller's. Resellers are losing power and customers are gaining power and more customization. Competition is increasing dramatically among the PC producers. Dell's advantage is eroding as other computer companies and their resellers respond. Dell will struggle to maintain a competitive edge. It appears that without a direct selling advantage, the large firms will have to maintain an incentive for resellers, even though they sell a significant portion of their computers directly as well. Moreover, Dell is moving toward Gateway 2000's turf, the consumer or home market. Gateway 2000 also sells direct and has responded to Dell's actions by seeking to move to the corporate market. Dell is now trying to improve its inventory management system and has reduced its parts inventory to 12 days. This reduction in parts inventory improves Dell's efficiency and power over suppliers.

SOURCE: D. Darlin, 1997, Channel change, *Forbes*, August 25, 80; D. Kirkpatrick, 1997, Now everyone in PCs wants to be like Mike, *Fortune*, September 8, 91–92; A. Zipser, 1997, In search of greener pasters, Gateway moves on Dell's turf, *Barron's* Online, http://www.interactive.wsj.com, September 15; L. Zuckerman, 1997, Dell Computer taking aim at consumers, *New York Times* on the Web, http://www.nytimes.com, August 29; L. Zuckerman, 1997, Corporations betting that computers can buy productivity gains, *New York Times* on the Web, http://www.nytimes.com, January 2.

Bargaining Power of Buyers

Firms seek to maximize the return on their invested capital. Buyers (customers of the focal industry/firm) prefer to purchase products at the lowest possible price, at which the industry earns the lowest acceptable rate of return on its invested capital. To reduce their costs, buyers bargain for higher quality, greater levels of service, and lower prices. These outcomes can be achieved by encouraging competitive battles among firms in an industry. Customers (buyer groups) are powerful when

- they purchase a large portion of an industry's total output;
- the product being purchased from an industry accounts for a significant portion of the buyers' costs;

- they could switch to another product at little, if any, cost; and
- the industry's products are undifferentiated or standardized, and they pose a credible threat if they were to integrate backward into the sellers' industry.

Relations with customers and the service provided such customers have assumed significant meaning in recent years. For example, one study showed that a firm's value on the stock market increased with improvements in its customer service.[78] Poor relations with customers can also hurt a firm's performance. Without good relations, retail firms may give less shelf space to its products, similar to the action Wal-Mart took against Rubbermaid. In fact, this example is an excellent one where the buyer, Wal-Mart, has significant power over the seller, Rubbermaid. This is exemplified by the fact that Wal-Mart executives openly criticized Rubbermaid for the actions taken, but Rubbermaid only publicly stated positive comments about Wal-Mart. Of course, the differences in power are readily seen in the statistics showing Wal-Mart with $105 billion in 1997 sales compared to Rubbermaid's $2.35 billion.[79]

Just as Wal-Mart forced many of its suppliers into electronic data exchange (EDI), the Internet creates more power for the general consumer. For instance, *Amazon.com*, the largest book Internet seller, forced Barnes & Noble to create an Internet site. The ultimate result is a reduction in prices for the buyer. Thus, the Web may create a buyer-centric compared to a seller-centric environment shifting more power to buyers.[80] Rubbermaid is now searching for ways to deal with the power of retailers such as Wal-Mart.[81] Selling to specialty retailers and directly to consumers through direct-seller firms such as Amway and on the Internet is one way the company is trying to solve the problem. It may find, however, that the Internet creates more powerful consumers as well.

Threat of Substitute Products

Substitute products are different goods or services that can perform similar or the same functions as the focal product (functional substitute). Because it is available as an alternative or substitute, Nutrasweet places an upper limit on the prices sugar manufacturers can charge. Nutrasweet and sugar perform the same service but with different characteristics. Other product substitutes include fax machines instead of overnight delivery of correspondence, plastic containers instead of glass jars, paper versus plastic bags, and tea, with its lower caffeine content, as a healthier substitute for coffee.[82] Capable of satisfying similar customer needs, but with different characteristics, substitute products place an upper limit on the prices firms can charge. In general, the threat of substitute products is strong when customers face few, if any, switching costs and when the substitute product's price is lower and/or its quality and performance capabilities are equal to or greater than the industry's products. To reduce the attractiveness of substitute products, firms are challenged to differentiate their offerings along dimensions that are highly relevant to customers (e.g., price, product quality, service after the sale, and location).

Intensity of Rivalry among Competitors

In many industries, firms compete actively with one another to achieve strategic competitiveness and earn above-average returns. Competition among rivals is stimulated when one or more firms feel competitive pressure or when they identify an opportunity to improve their market position. Competition among rivals is often based on price, product innovation, and other actions to achieve product differentiation (such as extensive customer service, unique advertising campaigns, and extended product warranties).

Because firms in an industry are mutually dependent, one firm's actions often invite retaliation from competitors. An industry in which this pattern of action and reaction (competitive actions and responses) occurs repeatedly is the deregulated airline industry. Quick reactions to one firm's price cuts are normal in this industry. Similarly, reactions to the introduction of innovative products, such as frequent flyer programs, usually are swift. Originated by American Airlines, virtually all major airlines rapidly developed similar frequent flyer programs. Thus, in the airline industry, as in many industries, firms often *simultaneously* apply two or all three of the principal means of competition (price changes, product/service innovations, and different means of differentiation) used by rivals when trying to gain a favorable marketplace position. Robert Crandall, former CEO of American Airlines, stated that the airline "business is intensely, vigorously, bitterly, savagely competitive."[83] The *intensity* of competitive rivalry among firms is a function of several factors, as described next.

Numerous or Equally Balanced Competitors Industries populated by many participants tend to be characterized by intense rivalry. With many participants, often a few firms believe they can take actions without eliciting a response. Other firms generally notice these actions and choose to respond. Frequent patterns of actions and responses create intense rivalry. At the other extreme, industries with only a few firms of equivalent size and power also tend to have high degrees of competitive rivalry. The resource bases of these firms permit vigorous actions and responses. The marketplace battles between fast food chains and footwear companies (e.g., Nike versus Reebok) exemplify an intense rivalry between relatively equivalent competitors.

Slow Industry Growth When a market is growing, firms are challenged to use resources effectively to serve an expanding customer base. In this instance, fewer actions may be taken to attract competitors' customers. The situation changes, however, when market growth either slows or stops. Under these conditions, rivalry becomes much more intense; an increase in one firm's market share usually comes at the expense of competitors' shares.

To protect their market shares, firms engage in intense competitive battles. Such battles introduce market instability, often reducing industry profitability. Parts of the fast food industry are characterized by this situation. In contrast to years past, the market for these products is growing more slowly. To expand market share, many of these companies (e.g., McDonald's, Burger King, and Wendy's) are competing aggressively in terms of pricing strategies, product introductions, and product and service differentiation. These firms also search for new international markets to achieve their growth goals.[84]

High Fixed or Storage Costs When fixed costs account for a large part of total costs, companies are challenged to utilize most, if not all, of their productive capacity. Operating in this manner allows the costs to be spread across a larger volume of output. Such actions by many firms in an industry can result in excess supply. To reduce inventories, companies typically decrease product prices and offer product rebates as well as other special discounts. These practices often intensify rivalry among competitors. This same phenomenon is observed in industries with high storage costs. Perishable products, for example, lose their value rapidly with the passage of time. When inventories grow, perishable goods producers often use pricing strategies to sell their products quickly.

Lack of Differentiation or Low Switching Costs Differentiated products engender buyer identification, preferences, and loyalty. Industries with large numbers of companies that have successfully differentiated their products have less rivalry. When buyers view products as commodities (i.e., as products with few differentiated features or capabilities), rivalry intensifies. In these instances, buyers' purchasing decisions are based primarily on price and service.

The effect of switching costs is identical to that described for differentiated products. The lower the buyers' switching costs, the easier it is for competitors to attract them (through pricing and service offerings). High switching costs, however, at least partially insulate firms from rivals' efforts to attract their customers.

Capacity Augmented in Large Increments In some industries, the realities of scale economies dictate that production capacity should be added only on a large scale (e.g., in the manufacture of vinyl chloride and chlorine). Additions of substantial capacity can be disruptive to a balance between supply and demand in the industry. Price cutting is used often to bring demand and supply back into balance. Achieving balance in this manner has, however, a negative effect on the firm's profitability.

Diverse Competitors Not all companies seek to accomplish the same goals, nor do they operate with identical cultures. These differences make it difficult to identify an industry's competitive rules. Moreover, with greater firm diversity, it becomes increasingly difficult to pinpoint a competing firm's strategic intent. Often firms engage in various competitive actions, in part to see how their competitors will respond. This type of competitive interaction can reduce industry profitability.

High Strategic Stakes Competitive rivalry becomes more intense when attaining success in a particular industry is critical to a large number of firms. For example, diversified firms' successes in one industry may be important to their effectiveness in other industries in which they compete. This is the case when firms follow a corporate strategy of related diversification (where the separate businesses are often interdependent. This strategy is explained in detail in Chapter 6).

High strategic stakes can also exist in terms of geographic locations. For example, Japanese automobile manufacturers are committed to a significant presence in the U.S. marketplace. Because of the stakes involved, for Japanese and U.S. manufacturers, rivalry in the automobile industry is quite intense.

High Exit Barriers Sometimes companies continue to compete in an industry even though the returns on their invested capital are low or even negative. Firms making this choice face high exit barriers. *Exit barriers* are economic, strategic, and emotional factors causing companies to remain in an industry even though the profitability of doing so may be in question. Common sources of exit barriers are

- specialized assets (assets with values linked to a particular business or location);
- fixed costs of exit (e.g., labor agreements);
- strategic interrelationships (mutual dependence relationships between one business and other parts of a company's operations, such as shared facilities and access to financial markets);

- emotional barriers (aversion to economically justified business decisions because of fear for one's own career, loyalty to employees, and so forth); and
- government and social restrictions (common outside the United States, restrictions often are based on government concerns for job losses and regional economic effects).

INTERPRETING INDUSTRY ANALYSES

Industry analyses can be challenging and are a product of careful study and interpretation of information and data from multiple sources. A wealth of industry-specific data is available for analyzing an industry. Because of the globalization described in Chapter 1, analysts must include international markets and rivalry in their analyses. In fact, research has shown that international variables are more important than domestic variables in the determination of competitiveness in some industries. Furthermore, because of the development of global markets, industry structures are no longer bounded by a country's borders; industry structures are often global.[85]

In general, the stronger the competitive forces, the lower the profit potential for firms in an industry. An *unattractive industry* has low entry barriers, suppliers and buyers with strong bargaining positions, strong competitive threats from product substitutes, and intense rivalry among competing firms. These industry attributes make it very difficult for firms to achieve strategic competitiveness and earn above-average returns. Alternatively, an attractive industry has high entry barriers, suppliers and buyers with little bargaining power, few competitive threats from product substitutes, and relatively moderate rivalry.[86]

A good example of global rivalry is that between Kimberly-Clark and Procter & Gamble. In 1995, Kimberly-Clark paid $7.36 billion to acquire Scott Paper Company and became the largest manufacturer of tissue products, greatly expanding its presence in Europe. This added strength was intended to help it compete more effectively in the global marketplace with P&G. In 1993 and 1994, Kimberly-Clark had to absorb losses from its European operations, which encountered difficulties in competing against P&G's aggressive promotion of its diapers and other paper products. In the United States, Kimberly-Clark is the dominant manufacturer of diapers with 40 percent of the market, compared to P&G's 36 percent. However, in Europe, P&G has a substantial market share with 68 percent of the British diaper market and up to 55 percent of the French diaper market. The Scott acquisition will accelerate Kimberly-Clark's expansion in Europe, to include the northern countries of Britain, Germany, and the Netherlands, and into southern countries, such as Spain and Italy.[87] Most recently the battle has begun to rage in emerging markets such as Brazil.[88] Both Kimberly-Clark and P&G are investing heavily in corporate R&D to develop and market new and more competitive products.

STRATEGIC GROUPS

More than 20 years ago, Michael Hunt studied the home appliance industry. He introduced the term *strategic group* to describe competitive patterns observed in that industry. Although he found differences in characteristics and strategies, Hunt

A **strategic group** is a group of firms in an industry following the same or a similar strategy along the same strategic dimensions.

also discovered that many firms were following similar strategies. He chose to label the groups following similar strategies strategic groups.[89] Formally, a **strategic group** is "a group of firms in an industry following the same or a similar strategy along the [same] strategic dimensions."[90] Examples of strategic dimensions include the extent of technological leadership, the degree of product quality, pricing policies, the choice of distribution channels, and the degree and type of customer service. Thus, membership in a particular strategic group defines the essential characteristics of a firm's strategy.[91] While the strategies of firms within a group are similar, they are different from the strategies being implemented by firms in other strategic groups.

The notion of strategic groups is popular for analyzing an industry's competitive structure.[92] Contributing to its popularity is the assertion that strategic group analysis is a basic framework that should be used in diagnosing competition, positioning, and the profitability of firms within an industry.[93]

Use of strategic groups for analyzing industry structure requires that dimensions relevant to the firms' performances within an industry (e.g., price and image) be selected. Plotting firms in terms of these dimensions helps to identify groups of firms competing in similar ways. For example, Dodge, Chevrolet, and Toyota form a strategic group, as do Mercedes and BMW. The products in each of these groups are similar in price and image (within the group).

There are several implications of strategic groups. First, a firm's major competitors are those within its strategic group. Because firms within a group are selling similar products to the same customers, the competitive rivalry among them can be intense. The more intense the rivalry, the greater the threat to each firm's profitability. Second, the strengths of the five competitive forces differ across strategic groups. As a result, firms within the various strategic groups have different pricing policies. Third, the closer the strategic groups in terms of strategies followed and dimensions emphasized, the greater the likelihood of competitive rivalry between the groups. For example, Nissan and Pontiac are more likely competitors for Dodge than for Mercedes and Porsche. In contrast, strategic groups that differ significantly in terms of strategic dimensions and strategies do not compete directly.

The Value of Strategic Group Analysis

Opinions vary about the value of strategic group analysis for understanding industry dynamics and structure. Some argue that there is no convincing evidence that strategic groups exist or that a firm's performance depends on membership in a particular group.[94] Another criticism of strategic groups is that the variances in many firms' product lines make it difficult to capture the nature of a company's outputs through study of a few strategic dimensions. For example, automobile companies manufacture many products with varying attributes. Dodge, for instance, manufactures some relatively inexpensive cars with a family orientation. However, the firm also sells the Dodge Viper, a sports car that is expensive and not family oriented.

These criticisms notwithstanding, strategic group analysis yields benefits. It helps in the selection and partial understanding of an industry's structural characteristics, competitive dynamics, evolution, and strategies that historically have allowed companies to be successful within an industry.[95] As is always the case, a tool's strengths and limitations should be known before it is used.

COMPETITOR ANALYSIS

Having an understanding of the general environment, the industry environment, and strategic groups, the final activity in the study of the external environment is competitor analysis. Competitor analysis focuses on each company with which a firm competes directly. Although important in all industry settings, competitor analysis is especially critical for firms facing one or a few powerful competitors.[96] For example, Nike and Reebok are keenly interested in understanding each other's objectives, strategies, assumptions, and capabilities. In successful companies, the process of competitor analysis is used to determine:

- what drives the competitor as shown by its *future objectives*;
- what the competitor is doing and can do as revealed by its *current strategy*;
- what the competitor believes about itself and the industry as shown by its *assumptions*; and
- what the competitor's capabilities are as shown by its *capabilities*.[97]

Information on these four issues helps strategists prepare an anticipated response profile for each competitor (see Figure 2.3). Thus, the results of an effective com-

FIGURE 2.3 *Competitor Analysis Components*

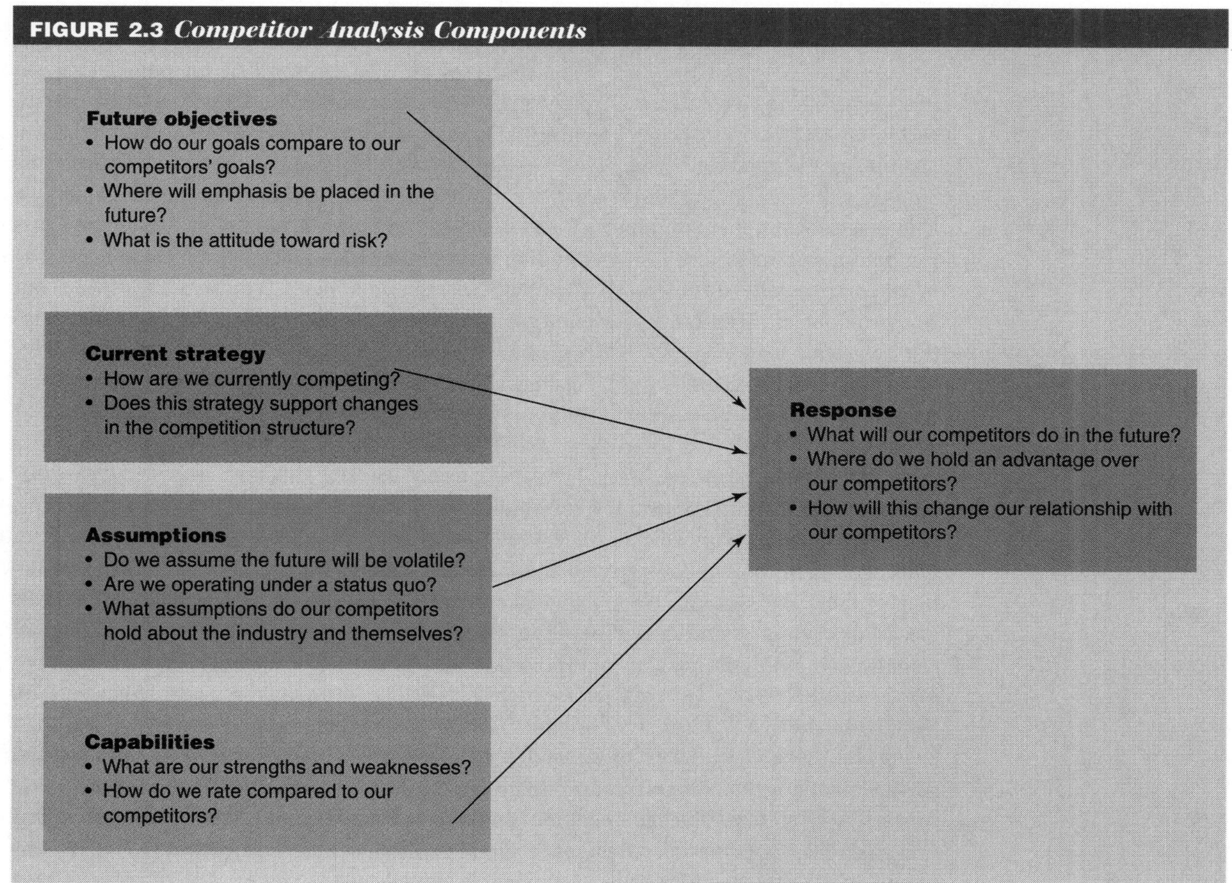

petitor analysis help a firm understand, interpret, and predict its competitors' actions and initiatives.[98]

Critical to effective competitor analysis is the gathering of needed information and data, referred to as *competitor intelligence.* Analysts are challenged to obtain information and data ethically that inform them about competitors' objectives, strategies, assumptions, and capabilities. Intelligence gathering techniques commonly considered to be both legal and ethical include (1) obtaining publicly available information (e.g., court records, competitors' help-wanted advertisements, annual reports, financial reports of publicly held corporations, and Uniform Commercial Code filings, and (2) attending trade fairs and shows to obtain competitors' brochures, view their exhibits, and listen to discussions about their products.

However, as the Strategic Focus on corporate spying indicates, many firms are not being ethical in the way they pursue competitive intelligence. In fact, much of the spying is being supported by government agencies that formerly were focused on political causes. Economics, it appears, is becoming more prominent as the main impetus for state supported intelligence gathering.

STRATEGIC FOCUS

A New Law Safeguards Corporate Secrets

The Economic Espionage Act of 1996 (EEA) for the first time makes theft of trade secrets a federal offense. Since the end of the cold war, the FBI reports that spying did not stop but merely changed its focus. Foreign spies, who might otherwise be out of work, are focusing on corporations. Louis Freeh, FBI Director, suggests that more than $24 billion in proprietary information is being stolen each year. The FBI estimates that its economic espionage caseload jumped to 800 in 1995 from 400 in 1994. Because computer technology is so powerful and makes it much easier to copy and transmit information, intangible assets can be expropriated more easily without arousing immediate suspicion. Nothing is missing when computer files are copied and the originals remain in place. The victim only finds out later when his or her strategic advantage evaporates. Congress listened and responded with the Economic Espionage Act. EEA prescribes prison sentences of up to 15 years and fines of up to $500,000 for individuals. Furthermore, prosecutors can seize property used in commission of the crime. Several examples of spying are given below.

In January of 1997, a chemical engineer at Avery-Dennison Corporation crept into a colleague's office at the labelmaker's plant, clicked off the lights and, wearing gloves, began rifling confidential plans for expansion in the Far East. In fact, the engineer, Dr. Lee, had been stealing Avery secrets since 1989. Trained in the U.S. with three advanced degrees, he began to work for Avery in 1986. He had been selling secrets to P.Y. Yang, chairman of the Taiwanese Adhesive-Tapemaker Four-Pillars Enterprise Co. Mr. Yang offered Dr. Lee periodic payments of $10,000 to $15,000 for Avery trade secrets. The thefts became so common that Dr. Lee kept pre-addressed labels to Mr. Yang in Taiwan. Prosecutors estimated that he provided more than $15 million of secrets in return for a total of $150,000 paid to a Taiwan account controlled by his mother-in-law.

At one point, the head of office supply retailer Staples had his wife seek and receive a position working for Office Depot. She investigated Office Depot's delivery system work, how many people were in the operation, and how it trained employees. Under the current law, this type of competitor intelligence would be illegal. A company could violate the law by hiring an employee who brings a Rolodex from his past employer. The contacts on that

Rolodex would be considered trade secrets. In the past, there was an informal agreement among employers that companies would not sue each other in exchanging employees. More recently, there have been several lawsuits based on the theory that information inevitably will be disclosed as one company hires another's executives.

In January 1997, Volkswagen settled a dispute with General Motors Corp. GM's German Opal A.G. unit accused Volkswagen of industrial espionage, related to the hiring of VW purchasing and production manager Jose Ignacio Lopez de Arriortua. Volkswagen paid GM and Opal $100 million and agreed to purchase $1 billion worth of parts over a 7-year period.

A number of companies have developed significant business to protect corporate secrets. Sensormatic, for example, is working on technology with Sigma Circuits to develop a program that will embed security labels into circuit boards of computers during the initial manufacturing process. Theoretically, any information transferred from one machine to another would have this embedded label in the data processed on the individual computer. Many corporations, seeking to maintain their competitive advantage, are putting in state-of-the-art security systems. The American Society for Industrial Security (ASIS) annual meeting attracts more than 15,000 security practitioners, suppliers, and consultants from around the world. Thus, competitive intelligence is an important consideration in protecting one's trade secrets and competitive advantage in an era where spying has moved from political to economic espionage.

SOURCE: D. Starkman, 1997, Secrets and lies: The dual career of a corporate spy, *Wall Street Journal*, October 23, B1, B12; A. Farnham, 1997, How safe are your secrets?, *Fortune*, September 8, 114–120; M. G. Gotschall, 1997, Corporate security goes high tech: Protecting your people and assets makes good business sense, Special Advertising Section, *Fortune*, September 8, S1–S8.

Interestingly, a report by Deloitte & Touche suggests that 42 percent of major companies do not have a competitor intelligence system. In other words, they do not have a formal process for gathering and analyzing information about competitors. Undoubtedly, many of these firms have informal and less systematic means of gathering information about competitors. For example, 87 percent of these firms obtain information about competitor activities and 82 percent obtain information about changing market structures. Seventy-six percent of the firms also felt that they needed better information on competitor activities and 67 percent felt a need for better information on changing market structures. Nearly all of the firms felt that competitors had used intelligence techniques to gather information on their activities. Thus, firms understand the need for competitor information and gather it, even though in some firms the process may not be systematic.[99]

Competitor analysis has grown more important as a new competitive landscape has evolved. The following statements by major firm executives and investors suggest the reality of the new competitive landscape:

> I don't believe in friendly competition. I want to put them out of business.
> —Mitchell Leibovitz, CEO of Pepboys

> Major sustainable competitive advantages are almost nonexistent in the field of financial services.
> —Warren Buffett, investor[100]

Therefore, firms need to develop a more systematic means of capturing knowledge about a firm's competitive context. In effect, employees have substantial knowledge about their firms and about external constituencies and stakeholders, but few companies are able to transform this particular knowledge into a company-wide asset. Firms that are able to do so refer to this as *structural intellectual capital.* Companies such as Monsanto are attempting to link key individuals (e.g., sales representatives) across the globe to share information they obtain about competitors and other important external stakeholders. Some refer to these as knowledge networks and linking employees through networks can provide a breadth of knowledge representing a sum of employees' collective experiences and information. Furthermore, the sharing of information helps pass on organizational learning and thus becomes a true organizational asset.[101]

Obtaining competitor information is important, particularly given the statements noted earlier about significant competition and the competitive battlefield. Of course, because of systematic competitor intelligence systems, some firms have trouble maintaining critical secrets about their products, technology, or other operations. Sometimes, competitors steal information by using insiders (employees of the focal company) as illustrated in the Strategic Focus. For example, one study showed that about 75 percent of the Fortune 1000 companies believed that information they desired to remain secret was stolen from them or at least there were attempted thefts within the past five years. Thus, significant pressures can lead to the use of questionable practices to obtain desired information about competitors.[102]

Also, to deal with this situation, some firms communicate misinformation. For instance, Dell Computer Corporation set out to secretly produce a monitor for its PCs that was nearly the size of a big screen television. The purpose was to allow corporations as well as individual consumers to open many work-areas on one screen without overlap, thereby increasing their productivity. After much research and analysis, it was decided that this type of monitor was inefficient and uneconomical. Researchers decided that it would be more economical for consumers to purchase multiple small monitors and load each with whatever they needed. The top-secret plan was scrapped totally.

Immediately after the plan was eliminated, Dell allowed its secret to leak out in hopes that one of its main competitors (e.g., Gateway) would undertake the project. Gateway has often been a second-mover to Dell. After it learned of Dell's secret monitor, Gateway announced publicly that the firm would build a monitor the size of a television, and they would be the first in the industry to do so. Without much research or analysis, the monitor, named Destination, was produced and sold. From the beginning, sales were extremely slow, and constant problems existed with the few monitors that were sold. The project was a complete failure. Approximately 52 percent of all units sold were returned for repair. It wasn't long after this failure that Gateway realized that it had been set up by Dell. Dell knew that Gateway longed to be a 'first mover" and would seize the opportunity quickly. Of course, Michael Dell states that he has no idea how Gateway obtained the information, but found it quite amusing. Industry analysts referred to this action by Dell as "a corporate headfake." Sometimes in an intensely competitive industry the leader can act as if it intends to make a competitive move, when in reality it is only trying to get the followers to react, wasting both time and money.[103]

Certain techniques, eavesdropping, trespassing, blackmail, and the theft of drawings, samples, or documents, are unethical and considered to be illegal.[104] While a number of intelligence gathering techniques are legal, decision makers must determine if their use is ethical. In highly competitive environments, employees may feel greater pressure to rely on these techniques. Interestingly, evidence suggests that most business people believe their competitors use questionable intelligence gathering techniques far more frequently than they do.[105] Perhaps an appropriate guideline is to use intelligence gathering techniques that respect the principles of common morality and the right of competitors not to reveal certain information about their products, operations, and strategic intentions.[106]

As with analysis of the general environment, analyses of the industry and competitor environments should result in the identification of opportunities and threats for the focal firm. A procedure for identification of opportunities and threats is explained in the "Introduction to Preparing an Effective Case Analysis" (beginning of Part IV).

SUMMARY

- Firms' external environments are often challenging and complex. Because of their effect on performance, firms must develop the skills required to identify opportunities and threats existing in their external environments.
- The external environment has three major parts: the general environment (elements in the broader society that affect industries and their firms), the industry environment (factors that influence a firm and its competitive actions and responses—the threat of entry, suppliers, buyers, product substitutes, and the intensity of rivalry among competitors), and specific analyses of each major competitor.
- Environmental analyses often must assume a nationless and borderless business environment.
- The external environmental analysis process includes four steps: scanning, monitoring, forecasting, and assessing. Analysis of the external environment leads to the identification of opportunities and threats.
- The general environment includes six segments: demographic, economic, political/legal, sociocultural, technological, and global. For each, the objective is to identify and study the strategic relevance of different changes and trends.
- As compared to the general environment, the industry environment has a more direct effect on a firm's efforts to achieve strategic competitiveness and earn above-average returns.
- The five forces model of competition includes characteristics that determine the industry's profit potential. Through study of the five forces, firms select a position in the industry in which they can match their core competencies with an opportunity to achieve strategic competitiveness and earn above-average returns.
- Different strategic groups exist within industries (a strategic group is a collection of firms that follow similar strategies). The competition within each strategic group is more intense than is the competition between strategic groups.
- Competitor analysis informs a firm about the objectives, strategies, assumptions, and capabilities of the companies with which it competes.
- Different techniques are available for gathering the intelligence (information and data) needed to understand competitors' actions and intentions. Analysts must determine the appropriate and ethical techniques for use in their firm.

REVIEW QUESTIONS

1. Why is it important for firms to study and understand the external environment?
2. What are the differences between the general environment and the industry environment? Why are these differences important?
3. What is the environmental analysis process? What do analysts try to learn as they scan, monitor, forecast, and assess?
4. What are the six segments of the general environment? Explain the differences among them.

5. Using information in the chapter, can you justify accepting the following statement: "There are five competitive forces that determine an industry's profit potential." Explain.
6. What is a strategic group? Of what value is the strategic group concept in choosing a firm's strategy?
7. Why do firms seek information about competitors and how is that information best collected?

APPLICATION DISCUSSION QUESTIONS

1. Given the importance of understanding an external environment, why do some managers, and their firms, fail to do so? Provide an example of a firm that understood poorly its external environment and discuss the implications.
2. Select a firm and describe how you characterize the nature of the external environment facing it. As someone who will soon enter the business world, how do you react to these environmental conditions? Why?
3. Describe how it would be possible for one firm to think of a condition in the general environment as an opportunity, whereas a second firm would see that condition as a threat. Provide an example of an environmental characteristic that could be perceived this way.
4. Choose a firm in your local community. Explain the course of action you would follow and the materials you would read to understand its industry environment.
5. Select an industry and describe what firms could do to create barriers to entry in this industry.
6. What conditions would cause a firm to retaliate aggressively against a new entrant in the airline industry?
7. Is it possible for an industry to exist with only a single strategic group? If so, how? Please provide an example of such an industry.

ETHICS QUESTIONS

1. How can a firm apply its "code of ethics" in the study of its external environment?
2. What ethical issues, if any, may be relevant in a firm's monitoring of its external environment?
3. For each segment of the general environment, identify an ethical issue to which companies should be sensitive.
4. What is the importance of ethical practices between a firm and its suppliers and distributors? Explain.
5. In an intense rivalry, especially one that involves competition in the global marketplace, how can a firm undertake ethical practices and yet maintain its competitiveness? Discuss.
6. While differences in strategies may exist between strategic groups, should commonly accepted ethical values/practices be the same across strategic groups within an industry? Explain.
7. What are the primary ethical issues associated with competitor intelligence practices?

INTERNET EXERCISE

Go to Boeing's home page at:

http://www.boeing.com

Familiarize yourself with Boeing's current products, services, and worldwide operations. Also, using one of the popular search engines such as Yahoo or Excite, search the Internet for other timely information about Boeing. After you have completed your search, make a list of the issues affecting Boeing in its external environment. Organize your list into the different segments of the external environment shown in Figure 2.1.

Strategic Surfing

There are many on-line periodicals available that can help firms remain abreast of their external environment. Some examples include:

Business Week: **http://www.businessweek.com**
Fortune: **http://pathfinder.com/fortune**
Forbes: **http://www.forbes.com**
Inc.: **http://www.inc.com**

NOTES

1. J. A. Wagner and R. Z. Gooding, 1997, Equivocal information and attribution: An investigation of patterns of managerial sensemaking, *Strategic Management Journal* 18: 275–286; S. Kotha and A. P. Nair, 1995, Strategy and environment as determinants of performance: Evidence from the Japanese machine tool industry, *Strategic Management Journal* 16: 497–518.
2. C. M. Grimm and K. G. Smith, 1997, *Strategy As Action: Industry Rivalry and Coordination* (Cincinnati: Southwestern); C. J. Fombrun, 1992, *Turning Point: Creating Strategic Change in Organizations,* (New York: McGraw-Hill), 13.
3. K. E. Weick, 1995, *Sensemaking in Organizations* (Thousand Oaks: Sage).
4. Lou Gerstner's first 30 days, 1993, *Fortune,* May 31, 57–62.
5. Fombrun, *Turning Points,* 16–18.
6. M. Farjoun and L. Lei, 1997, Similarity judgments in strategy formulation: Role, process, and implications, *Strategic Management Journal* 18: 255–273; U. Zander and B. Kogut, 1995, Knowledge and the speed of the transfer and imitation of organizational capabilities: An empirical test, *Organization Science* 6: 76–92.
7. M. B. Meznar and D. Nigh, 1995, Buffer or bridge? Environmental and organizational determinants of public affairs activities in American firms, *Academy of Management Journal* 38: 975–996.
8. D. J. Teece, G. Pisano, and A. Shuen, 1997, Dynamic capabilities and strategic management, *Strategic Management Journal* 18: 509–533.
9. L. Fahey and V. K. Narayanan, 1986, *Macroenvironmental Analysis for Strategic Management* (St. Paul: West Publishing Company), 49–50.
10. M. A. Hitt, B. W. Keats, and S. M. DeMarie, 1998, Navigating in the new competitive landscape: Building strategic flexibility and competitive advantage in the 21st century, *Academy of Management Executive,* in press.
11. J. F. Preble, 1992, Environmental scanning for strategic control, *Journal of Managerial Issues* 4: 254–268; K. Gronhaug and J. S. Falkenberg, 1989, Exploring strategy perceptions in changing environments, *Journal of Management Studies* 26: 349–359.
12. Fombrun, *Turning Points,* 77; Gronhaug and Falkenberg, Exploring strategy perceptions, 350.
13. H. Courtney, J. Kirkland, and P. Visuerie, 1997, Strategy under uncertainty, *Harvard Business Review* 75, no. 6: 66–79; L. S. Richman, 1993, Why the economic data misleads us, *Fortune,* March 8, 108–114.
14. D. S. Elenkov, 1997, Strategic uncertainty and environmental scanning: The case for institutional influences on scanning behavior, *Strategic Management Journal* 18: 287–302.
15. I. Goll and A. M. A. Rasheed, 1997, Rational decision-making and firm performance: The moderating role of environment, *Strategic Management Journal* 18: 583–591; R. L. Priem, A. M. A. Rasheed, and A. G. Kotulic, 1995, Rationality in strategic decision processes, environmental dynamism and firm performance, *Journal of Management* 21: 913–929.
16. M. Yasai-Ardekani and P. C. Nystrom, 1996, Designs for environmental scanning systems: Tests of contingency theory, *Management Science* 42: 187–204.
17. R. Dodge, 1997, Summit turns attention to economics of aging, *Dallas Morning News,* June 21, F1, F2; S. Shepard, 1993, Baby boom could bust retirement system, *WacoTribune-Herald,* May 23, A1; How America will change over the next 30 years, 1993, *Fortune,* May 2, 12.
18. Fahey and Narayanan, *Macroenvironmental Analysis,* 39.
19. Ibid., 41.
20. M. Maremont, 1997, Gillette tries to soothe analyst fears on profit growth, *Wall Street Journal,* September 24, B1.
21. Fahey and Narayanan, *Macroenvironmental Analysis,* 42.
22. T. Aeppel, 1997, Rubbermaid warns 3rd-quarter profits will come in far below expectations, *Wall Street Journal,* September 19, A4; A. B. Fisher, 1996, Corporate reputations, *Fortune,* March 6, 90–93; L. Smith, 1995, Rubbermaid goes thump, *Fortune,* October 2, 90–104.
23. Fahey and Narayanan, *Macroenvironmental Analysis,* 58.
24. E. Cornish, 1990, Issues of the '90s, *Fortune,* February 11, 136–141.
25. R. Stodghill II, 1997, The coming job bottleneck, *Business Week,* March 24, 184–185.
26. G. Colvin, 1997, How to beat the boomer rush, *Fortune,* August 18, 59–63.
27. D. Kunde, 1997, Well connected, *Dallas Morning News,* October 22, D1, D2; Associated Press, 1997, Telecommuters say they'd walk before going back to the office, *Dallas Morning News,* October 21, D1.
28. R. Dodge, 1997, Labor complications, *Dallas Morning News,* September 1, D1, D2; M. N. Martinez, 1995, Contingency workers shed the bad rap, *HR Magazine* 40, no. 4: 16–18.
29. M. McLaughlin, 1989, A change of mind, *New England Business,* April, 42–53.
30. J. R. W. Joplin and C. S. Daus, 1997, Challenges of leading a diverse workforce, *Academy of Management Executive* XI, no. 3: 32–47; G. Robinson and K. Dechant, 1997, Building a business case for diversity, *Academy of Management Executive* IX, no. 3: 21–31.
31. S. Finkelstein and D. C. Hambrick, 1996, *Strategic Leadership: Top Executives and Their Effect on Organizations* (Minneapolis: West); T. Cox and S. Blake, 1991, Managing cultural diversity: Implications for international competitiveness, *Academy of Management Executive V,* no. 3: 45–46.
32. J. P. Fernandez, 1993, *The Diversity Advantage* (New York: Lexington Books).
33. J. Landers, 1997, Incomes rising around world, *Dallas Morning News,* September 15, D1, D4.
34. Fahey and Narayanan, *Macroenvironmental Analysis,* 105.
35. J. Landers, 1997, High labor costs slow investment in German economy, *Dallas Morning News,* October 27, D1, D4; New York Times Service, 1997, U.S. deficit at its lowest in 23 years, *Dallas Morning News,* October 27, D1, D3.
36. R. Norton, 1995, There go these Eurocrats again, *Fortune,* September 18, 51.
37. R. Henkoff, 1997, Asia: Why business is still bullish, *Fortune,* October 27, 139–142.
38. Fahey and Narayanan, *Macroenvironmental Analysis,* 139–157.

39. B. O'Reilly, 1997, Transforming the power business, *Fortune*, September 29, 143–156.
40. Ibid., 143.
41. T. Vogel, 1997, Central America goes from war zone to enterprise zone, *Wall Street Journal*, September 25, A18.
42. J. R. Wike and B. Ortega, 1997, Anheuser's sales practices under probe, *Wall Street Journal*, October 3, A3.
43. K. Harris, 1995, Lights! Camera! Regulation! *Fortune*, September 4, 83–86.
44. How America will change over the next 30 years, 12.
45. P. Thomas, 1995, Success at a huge personal cost: Comparing women around the world, *Wall Street Journal*, July 26, B1.
46. J. B. Roesner, 1991, Ways women lead, *Harvard Business Review* 69, no. 3: 119–125.
47. B. Morris, 1997, If women ran the world it would look a lot like Avon, *Fortune*, July 21, 74–79.
48. F. N. Schwartz, 1992, Women as a business imperative, *Harvard Business Review* 70, no. 2: 105–113; C. Torres and M. Bruxelles, 1992, Capitalizing on global diversity, *HR Magazine*, December, 30–33; B. Geber, 1990, Managing diversity, *Training*, July, 23–30.
49. E. H. Buttner and D. P. Moore, 1997, Women's organizational exodus to entrepreneurship: Self-reported motivations and correlations with success, *Journal of Small Business Management* 35, no. 1: 34–46; *USA Today*, 1997, More minority owners, June 27, B10; J. Files, 1996, Texas 2nd in women-owned businesses, *Dallas Morning News*, January 30, D5.
50. J. S. Lublin, 1997, How one CEO juggles a job and a family miles apart, *Wall Street Journal*, October 8, B1, B15.
51. D. Milbank, 1997, More dads raise families without mom, *Wall Street Journal*, October 3, B1, B2.
52. B. L. Dos Santos and K. Peffers, 1995, Rewards to investor in innovative information technology applications: First movers and early followers in ATMs, *Organization Science* 6: 241–259; S. A. Zahra, S. Nash, and D. J. Bickford, 1995, Transforming technological pioneering into competitive advantage, *Academy of Management Executive* IX, no. 1: 17–31.
53. R. Tetzeli, 1994, The Internet and your business, *Fortune*, March 7, 89–96.
54. E. W. Desmond, 1997, How data may soon seek you out, *Fortune*, September 8, 149–150.
55. S. McCartney, 1995, U.S. Robotics dials up dollars in market for modems, *Wall Street Journal*, July 27, B8.
56. R. A. Melcher, 1997, Dusting off the Britannica, *Business Week*, October 20, 143–146.
57. M. Iansiti and A. MacCormack, 1997, Developing products on Internet time, *Harvard Business Review* 75, no. 5: 108–117.
58. D. Bank, 1997, Microsoft's talks with TCI are part of a broader strategy, http://www.interactive.wsj.com, October 16; D. Bank, 1997, Microsoft claims digital breakthrough, *Wall Street Journal*, September 16, B14.
59. J. Cole, 1995, New satellite imaging could soon transform the face of the earth, *Wall Street Journal*, November 30, A1, A5.
60. E. Schonfeld, 1997, The space business heats up, *Fortune*, November 24, 142–152.
61. S. Woolley, 1997, ViaSat: Slow and steady does it, *Forbes*, November 3, 178–180.
62. J. Birkinshaw, A. Morrison, and J. Hulland, 1995, Structural and competitive determinants of a global integration strategy, *Strategic Management Journal* 16: 637–655.
63. G. R. Ungson, R. M. Steers, and S.H. Park, 1997, *Korean Enterprise: The Quest for Globalization* (Boston: Harvard Business School Press).
64. S. Glain, 1995, Going for growth: Korea's Samsung plans very rapid expansion into autos, other lines, *Wall Street Journal*, March 2, A1, A6; L. Nakarmi and R. Neff, 1994, Samsung's radical shakeup, *Business Week*, February 28, 74–76.
65. J. P. Alston, 1989, Wa, guanxi, and inhwa: Managerial principals in Japan, China and Korea, *Business Horizons*, March-April, 26–31.
66. M. A. Hitt, M. T. Dacin, B. B. Tyler, and D. Park, 1997, Understanding the differences in Korean and U.S. executives' strategic orientations, *Strategic Management Journal* 18: 159–167; S. Yoo and S. M. Lee, 1987, Management style and practice of Korean chaebols, *California Management Review* 29, Summer: 95–110.
67. K. Singh, 1996, Fried chicken's fearsome foes, *Far Eastern Economic Review*, January 25, 30; M. Jordan, 1995, U.S. food firms head for cover in India, *Wall Street Journal*, November 21, A14.
68. J. Kahn, 1995, P&G viewed China as a national market and is conquering it, *Wall Street Journal*, September 12, A1, A6.
69. S. M. Oster, 1994, *Modern Competitive Analysis*, 2nd edition (New York: Oxford University Press).
70. R. A. Bettis and M. A. Hitt, 1995, The new competitive landscape, *Strategic Management Journal* 16 (Special Summer Issue): 7–19.
71. G. R. Brooks, 1995, Defining market boundaries, *Strategic Management Journal* 16: 535–549.
72. A. M. McGahan, 1994, Industry structure and competitive advantage, *Harvard Business Review* 72, no. 5: 115–124.
73. J. H. Gilmore and B. J. Pine, II, 1997, The four faces of mass customization, *Harvard Business Review*, 75, no. 1: 91–101; S. Kotha, 1995, Mass customization: Implementing the emerging paradigm for competitive advantage, *Strategic Management Journal* 16 (Special Summer Issue): 21–42; B. Pine, 1993, *Mass Customization* (Boston: Harvard Business School Press); B. Pine, B. Victore, and A. C. Boynton, 1993, Making mass customization work, *Harvard Business Review* 71, no. 5: 108–119.
74. R. E. Calem, 1997, Time Warner goes after affiliates of TV networks. New York Times on the Web, http://www.nytimes.com, January 16; E. Jensen and J. Lippman, 1995, New competition may mean bad news for CNN, *Wall Street Journal*, December 6, B1, B4.
75. Take on the giants, 1996, *Success*, January/February, 30.
76. L. Zuckerman, 1997, Dell Computer taking aim at consumers, New York Times on the Web, http://www.nytimes.com, August 29.
77. A. Zipser, 1997, In search of greener pastures, Gateway moves on Dell's turf, Barron's Online, http://www.interactive.wsj.com, September 15.
78. P. R. Nayyar, 1995, Stock market reactions to customer service changes, *Strategic Management Journal* 16: 39–53.
79. Briefing Book, 1997, http://www.interactive.wsj.com, November 15; L. Smith, 1995, Rubbermaid goes thump, *Fortune*, October 2, 90–104.

80. J. W. Gurley, 1997, Seller, beware: The buyers rule e-commerce, *Fortune*, November 10, 234–236.
81. Aeppel, Rubbermaid warns 3rd-quarter profits will come in far below expectations, A4.
82. S. Browder, 1997, Tea is bagging a bigger crowd, *Business Week*, August 25, 6.
83. R. A. D'Aveni, 1995, Coping with hypercompetition: Utilizing the new 7S's framework, *Academy of Management Executive* IX, no. 3: 45.
84. R. Gibson, 1997, Burger wars sizzle as McDonald's clones the Whopper, *Wall Street Journal*, September 17, B1.
85. H. J. Moon and K. C. Lee, 1995, Testing the diamond model: Competitiveness of U.S. software firms, *Journal of International Management* 1: 373–387.
86. Much of the preceding discussion of competitive forces is based on Porter, *Competitive Strategy*.
87. H. S. Bryne, 1996, Global war: Beefed-up Kimberly-Clark prepares to battle P&G, *Barron's*, April 22, 17; P. Thomas, 1995, Kimberly-Clark and P&G face global warfare, *Wall Street Journal*, July 18, B1, B6.
88. R. Narisetti and J. Friedland, 1997, Diaper wars of P&G and Kimberly-Clark now heat up in Brazil, *Wall Street Journal*, June 4, A1, A10.
89. M. S. Hunt, 1972, Competition in the major home appliance industry, 1960–1970 (doctoral dissertation, Harvard University).
90. Porter, *Competitive Strategy*, 129.
91. R. K. Reger and A. S. Huff, 1993, Strategic groups: A cognitive perspective, *Strategic Management Journal* 14: 103–123; J. McGee and H. Thomas, 1986, Strategic groups: A useful linkage between industry structure and strategic management, *Strategic Management Journal* 7: 141–160.
92. J. B. Barney and R. E. Hoskisson, 1990, Strategic groups: Untested assertions and research proposals, *Managerial and Decision Economics* 11: 198–208.
93. M. Peteraf and M. Shanley, 1997, Getting to know you: A theory of strategic group identity, *Strategic Management Journal* 18 (Special Issue), 165–186; R. M. Grant, 1995, *Contemporary Strategy Analysis*, 2nd ed. (Cambridge, MA: Blackwell Publishers), 98.
94. D. Nath and T. Gruca, 1997, Covergence across alternatives for forming strategic groups, *Strategic Management Journal* 18: 745–760; Barney and Hoskisson, Strategic groups, 202.
95. K. G. Smith, C. M. Crimm, and S. Wally, 1997, Strategic groups and rivalrous firm behavior: Towards a reconciliation, *Strategic Management Journal* 18: 149–157.
96. S. Ghoshal and D. E. Westney, 1991, Organizing competitor analysis systems, *Strategic Management Journal* 12: 17–31.
97. Porter, *Competitive Strategy*, 49.
98. S. A. Zahra and S. S. Shaples, 1993, Blind spots in competitive analysis, *Academy of Management Executive* VII, no. 2: 7–28.
99. U.S. companies slow to develop business intelligence, 1995, *Deloitte & Touche Review*, October 16, 1–2.
100. D'Aveni, Coping with hypercompetition, 45.
101. T. A. Stewart, 1995, Getting real about brain power, *Fortune*, November 27, 201–203; T. A. Stewart, 1995, Mapping corporate brain power, *Fortune*, October 30, 209–211.
102. M. Geyelin, 1995, Why many businesses can't keep their secrets, *Wall Street Journal*, November 20, B1, B3.
103. A. Zipser, 1997, In search of greener pastures, Gateway moves on Dell's turf, Barron's Online, http://www.interactive.wsj.com, September 15.
104. K. A. Rehbeing, S. A. Morris, R. L. Armacost, and J. C. Hosseini, 1992, The CEO's view of questionable competitor intelligence gathering practices, *Journal of Managerial Issues* 4: 590–603.
105. S. A. Zahra, 1994, Unethical practices in competitive analysis: Patterns, causes, and effects, *Journal of Business Ethics* 13: 53–62; W. Cohen and H. Czepiec, 1988, The role of ethics in gathering corporate intelligence, *Journal of Business Ethics* 7: 199–203.
106. J. H. Hallaq and K. Steinhorst, 1994, Business intelligence methods—How ethical?, *Journal of Business Ethics* 13: 787–794; L. S. Paine, 1991, Corporate police and the ethics of competitor intelligence gathering, *Journal of Business Ethics* 10: 423–436.

The Internal Environment: Resources, Capabilities, and Core Competencies

CHAPTER 3

Learning Objectives

After reading this chapter, you should be able to:

1. Explain the importance of studying and understanding the internal environment.
2. Define value and discuss its importance.
3. Describe the differences between tangible and intangible resources.
4. Define capabilities and discuss how they are developed.
5. Describe four criteria used to determine if a firm's resources and capabilities are core competencies.
6. Explain how value chain analysis is used to identify and evaluate a firm's resources and capabilities.
7. Define outsourcing and discuss the reasons for its use.
8. Discuss the importance of preventing a firm's core competencies from becoming core rigidities.
9. Explain the relationship between a firm's strategic inputs and its strategic actions.

People as a Source of Competitive Advantage

In a *Fortune* survey featuring the most admired corporations worldwide, a critical theme emerged. Although no one strength was judged sufficient to place a company on top of the global list of most admired firms, a capability for finding, nurturing, and keeping intelligent and talented employees was most strongly related to a company's overall score. For instance, Disney received the highest score for being the most innovative company. Michael Eisner indicated that "we create a new product—a book, a movie, something—every five minutes and each one has to be superb. Our goal is to do it better every time out. But our real product is managing talent. That's what we really do here, and we never lose sight of that—because without that, what have you got?" Similarly, Jack Welch, GE's CEO, says, "All we can do is bet on the people who we pick. So my whole job is picking the right people." In fact, Welch personally interviews candidates for the top five hundred jobs at GE. Most companies in the survey found that the ability to attract and hold talented employees was the single most reliable predictor of excellence.

http://

http://www.disney.com
http://www.ge.com
http://www.saic.com
http://www.levi.com
http://www.microsoft.com

The Hay Group that conducted the survey for *Fortune* found that seven basic themes contribute to corporate excellence in hiring and career development practices:

1. Top managers at the most admired companies take their firm's mission statements seriously and expect everyone else to do likewise.
2. Success attracts the best people and the best people sustain success.
3. Top companies know precisely what they're looking for, often through intense psychological testing.
4. They see career development as an investment, not a chore.
5. Whenever possible, they promote from within.
6. They reward performance.
7. They measure workforce satisfaction.

In essence, the most admired firms in the survey are experts at managing human resources.

A number of private companies also take managing human resources seriously. Robert Beyster, the chief executive officer and founder of Science Applications International Corp. (SAIC), built a scientific consulting firm starting with twelve employees in 1969 to a 25,000-employee high-tech research and engineering firm. SAIC recently bought Bellcore, the former research arm of the Bell operating companies and improved its ranking to the forty-first largest private firm in *Forbes*'s ranking of the five hundred largest private companies. At SAIC, employees own 90 percent of the company and the other 10 percent is held by consultants or employees who left the company before SAIC required that departing employee owners were required to sell their shares back to the firm. Although Beyster has 1.5 percent of the $2 billion net worth of the firm instead of owning 100 percent, his philosophy has turned employees into committed and motivated stakeholders. The firm has four different employee-ownership programs that are among the most sophisticated in the country. As Narri Cooper indicates, "When I'm making a decision, I don't just make it as an information technology manager, I make it as an owner." Furthermore, nine employees sit on the twenty-two-person board alongside such luminaries as U.S. Navy Admiral B. R. Inman.

Because private firms compete with public companies for star talent, private companies have had to take actions such as those initiated by SAIC to attract the most qualified personnel. In a 1997 study, consultants found that 30 percent of the largest U.S. companies have stock option plans for more than half their employees. Although SAIC is exemplary, most private companies have yet to deal with the problem of the incentives that public companies are offering. To compete more effectively, Levi Strauss & Co., a privately owned firm that completed a leveraged buyout, has sought to revamp its profit sharing plan. It replaced its ESOP because it benefited mostly middle managers and because workers located outside the U.S. could not participate. The new plan rewards all 37,000 employees with a cash payment equal to their 1996 salaries if the company meets a cash flow target of $7.6 billion by the year 2001. In essence, the plan makes Levi Strauss employees implicit owners of the company.

Microsoft views human resources as an organizational capability. Microsoft has sought to make large new product teams work as efficiently as small teams. Although small teams of talented people may be the most desired way to develop new products, this is impossible when the product is complex and short deadlines are required to be competitive. As a result, firms such as Microsoft find it necessary to manage large teams (perhaps hundreds) of talented engineers to develop new complex software products. Because of this reality, Microsoft has developed innovative ways of managing teams of talented people. These managerial approaches help Microsoft produce innovative products.

In summary, human resources are critical. Developing the ability to hire, manage, motivate, and orchestrate people is an important capability that adds to a firm's core competence. If it can effectively manage this critical capability, the company may become one of the top firms on *Fortune*'s most admired corporations list or be highlighted in *Forbes*'s examples of outstanding private companies.

SOURCE: M.A. Cusumano, 1997, How Microsoft makes large teams work like small teams, *Sloan Management Review* 39, no. 1: 9–20; A. Fisher, The world's most admired companies, *Fortune*, October 27, 220–240; C.T. Geer, 1997, Turning employees into stakeholders, *Forbes*, December 1, 155–157; C.T. Geer, 1997, Sharing the wealth, capitalist-style, *Forbes*, December 1, 158–160; M.A. Huselid, S.E. Jackson and R.S. Schuler, 1997, Technical and strategic human resource management effectiveness as determinants of firm performance, *Academy of Management Journal* 40: 171–188; P. Cappelli and A. Crocker-Hefter, 1996, Distinctive human resources are firms' core competencies, *Organizational Dynamics* 24, no. 3: 7–22.

Disney, GE, Science Applications International Corp. and Microsoft have developed capabilities to manage their human resources. Each of these firms is interested in developing a *sustainable competitive advantage.* A sustainable competitive advantage is achieved when firms implement a value-creating strategy that is grounded in their own unique resources, capabilities, and core competencies (terms defined in Chapter 1). Firms achieve strategic competitiveness and earn above-average returns when their unique core competencies are leveraged effectively to take advantage of opportunities in the external environment. As the opening case indicates, one way to develop competitive advantage is through people, the firm's employees.[1]

Over time, the benefits of every firm's value-creating strategy can be duplicated. In other words, all competitive advantages have a limited life.[2] The question of duplication is not *if* it will happen, but *when.* During the 1980s, for example, the competitive advantage of brand names began to dissipate. Among the factors causing a temporary erosion of the competitive advantage yielded by brand names for some firms was a technological development—the checkout scanner. Studying data available to them from scanners allowed retailers (such as grocery stores) to determine quickly how price promotions on various products affected their sales volume. In the words of one analyst, this new technology "gave retailers tremendous new muscle over the brandmakers, and with all the increased emphasis on discounts and promotions, consumers learned how to bargain."[3]

Effective duplication by competitors may have contributed to Home Depot's performance difficulties. "Home Depot isn't such a nimble category killer anymore," says a business writer. Competitors such as Lowe's and Eagle Hardware have built hangar-size warehouses that offer an array of goods similar to that available from Home Depot. Moreover, these competitors' actions have reduced the service gap between them and Home Depot.[4] Although in Chapter 4 we describe actions Home Depot is taking to counteract this duplication, competitors' actions have contributed to Home Depot's reduced performance.

In general, the sustainability of a competitive advantage is a function of three factors: (1) the rate of core competence obsolescence due to environmental changes, (2) the availability of substitutes for the core competence, and (3) the imitability of the core competence.[5] The challenge for strategists in all firms—a challenge that can be met through proper use of the strategic management process—is to manage current core competencies effectively while simultaneously developing new ones to use when the competitive advantage derived from application of current ones has been eroded.[6] Only when firms develop a continuous stream of competitive advantages (as explained further in Chapter 5) do they achieve strategic competitiveness, earn above-average returns, and remain ahead of competitors. Intel and Microsoft continuously make investments that are intended to enhance their current sources of competitive advantage and simultaneously spur the creation of new ones.[7] These investments appear to contribute significantly to these firms' ability to achieve and maintain strategic competitiveness.

In Chapter 2, we examined the general environment, the industry environment, and rivalry among competing firms. Armed with knowledge about their firm's environments, managers have a better understanding of the marketplace opportunities and the products necessary to pursue them.

In this chapter, we focus on the firm. Through an analysis of the internal environment, a firm determines *what it can do*—that is, the actions permitted by its unique resources, capabilities, and core competencies. As discussed in Chapter 1, core competencies are a firm's source of competitive advantage. The magnitude of that competitive advantage is a function primarily of its uniqueness compared to competitors' competencies.[8] The proper matching of what a firm *can do* with what it *might do* allows the development of strategic intent, a strategic mission, and the formulation of strategies. When implemented effectively, a value-creating strategy is the pathway to strategic competitiveness and above-average returns. Outcomes resulting from internal and external environmental analyses are shown in Figure 3.1.

Several topics are examined in this chapter. First, the importance and the challenge of studying a firm's internal environment are addressed. We then discuss the roles that resources, capabilities, and core competencies play in the development of sustainable competitive advantage. Included in these discussions are descriptions

FIGURE 3.1 ***Outcomes from External and Internal Environmental Analyses***

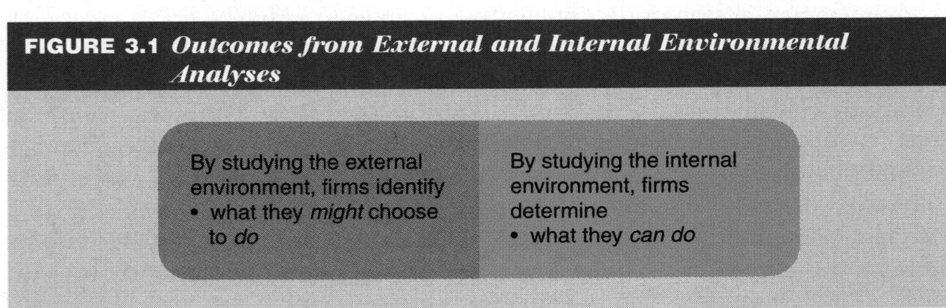

of the techniques used to identify and evaluate resources and capabilities and the criteria used to select the firm's core competencies from among its resources and capabilities. While studying these materials, it is important to recall that resources, capabilities, and core competencies are not valuable alone; they have value only because they allow the firm to perform certain activities that result in a competitive advantage. To have sustained competitive advantage these activities must be unique.[9]

As shown in Figure 1.1 in Chapter 1, strategic intent and strategic mission, coupled with insights gained through analyses of the internal and external environments, determine the strategies a firm will select and the actions it will take to implement them successfully. In the final part of the chapter, we describe briefly the relationship between intent and mission and a firm's strategy formulation and implementation actions.

THE IMPORTANCE OF INTERNAL ANALYSIS

In the new competitive landscape, traditional conditions and factors, such as labor costs, access to financial resources and raw materials, and protected or regulated markets, can still provide competitive advantage but to a lesser degree now than in the past.[10] A key reason for this decline is that the advantages created by these sources can be overcome through an international strategy (international strategies are discussed in Chapter 8). As a result, overcapacity is the norm in a host of industries, increasing the difficulty of forming competitive advantages. In this challenging competitive environment, few firms are able to make consistently the right strategic decisions. Additionally, less job security for individual employees is an inevitable consequence of operating in this more challenging competitive environment. It is interesting, for example, that a number of firms, including Kodak, Citicorp, Levi Strauss, Whirlpool, Apple, and Kimberly-Clark among others, announced layoffs in 1997 and early 1998, at a time when the economy was very strong.[11]

The demands of the new competitive landscape make it necessary for top-level managers to rethink the concept of the corporation. Although corporations are difficult to change, earning strategic competitiveness in the 1990s and into the twenty-first century requires development and use of a different managerial mind-set.[12] Most top-level managers recognize the need to change their mind-sets but many hesitate to do so. In the words of a European CEO of a major U.S. company, "It is more reassuring for all of us to stay as we are, even though we know the result will be certain failure . . . than to jump into a new way of working when we cannot be sure it will succeed."[13]

Critical to the managerial mind-set required is the view that a firm is a *bundle* of heterogeneous resources, capabilities, and core competencies that can be used to create an exclusive market position.[14] This view suggests that individual firms possess at least some resources and capabilities that other companies do not have, at least not in the same combination. Resources are the source of capabilities, some of which lead to the development of a firm's core competencies. By using their core competencies, firms are able to perform activities *better* than competitors or that competitors are unable to duplicate. Essentially, the mind-set required in the new competitive landscape defines its strategy in terms of unique competitive position rather than in terms of operational effectiveness. For instance, Michael Porter argues that quest for productivity, quality, and speed from a number of management techniques (total quality management, benchmarking, time-based competition, reengineering) have resulted in operational efficiency but not strong sustainable strategy.[15]

Increasingly, managers are being evaluated in terms of their ability to identify, nurture, and exploit their firm's unique core competencies.[16] By emphasizing competence acquisition and development, organizations learn how to learn—a skill that is linked with the development of competitive advantage. As a process, learning how to learn requires commitment, time, and the active support of top-level executives. At Deere & Co., managers have created an "in-house Yellow Pages" to help them find an expert inside or outside the firm.[17] The system is quite inexpensive, about the cost of one engineer to operate it, but it has paid for itself annually, at least six times over, especially when there is a crisis, say in production, and an expert is needed to solve it. In the final analysis, a corporate-wide obsession with the development and use of knowledge and core competencies more broadly may characterize companies able to compete effectively on a global basis in the twenty-first century.[18]

Value consists of the performance characteristics and attributes provided by companies in the form of goods or services for which customers are willing to pay.

By exploiting their core competencies and meeting the demanding standards of global competition, firms create value for their customers. **Value** consists of the performance characteristics and attributes provided by companies in the form of goods or services for which customers are willing to pay. Ultimately, customer value is the source of a firm's potential to earn average or above-average returns. In Chapter 4, we note that value is provided to customers by a product's low cost, by its highly differentiated features, or by a combination of low cost and high differentiation, as compared to competitors' offerings. Core competencies, then, are actually a value-creating system through which a company seeks strategic competitiveness and above-average returns (these relationships are shown in Figure 3.2). In the new competitive landscape, managers need to determine if their firm's core competencies continue to create value for customers.[19]

During the last several decades, the strategic management process was concerned largely with understanding the characteristics of the industry in which a firm was competing and, in light of those characteristics, determining how the firm should position itself relative to competitors. The emphasis on industry characteristics and competitive strategy may have understated the role of organizational resources and capabilities in developing competitive advantage. A firm's core competencies, in addition to the results of an analysis of its general, industry, and competitive environments, should drive the selection of strategies. In this regard, core competencies, in combination with product-market positions or tactics, are the most important sources of competitive advantage in the new competitive landscape. Emphasizing core competencies when formulating strategies causes companies to learn how to compete primarily on the basis of firm-specific differences rather than seeking competitive advantage solely on the structural characteristics of their industries.[20]

The Challenge of Internal Analysis

The decisions managers make in terms of resources, capabilities, and core competencies have a significant influence on a firm's ability to develop competitive advantages and earn above-average returns.[21] Making these decisions—that is, identifying, developing, protecting, and deploying resources, capabilities, and core

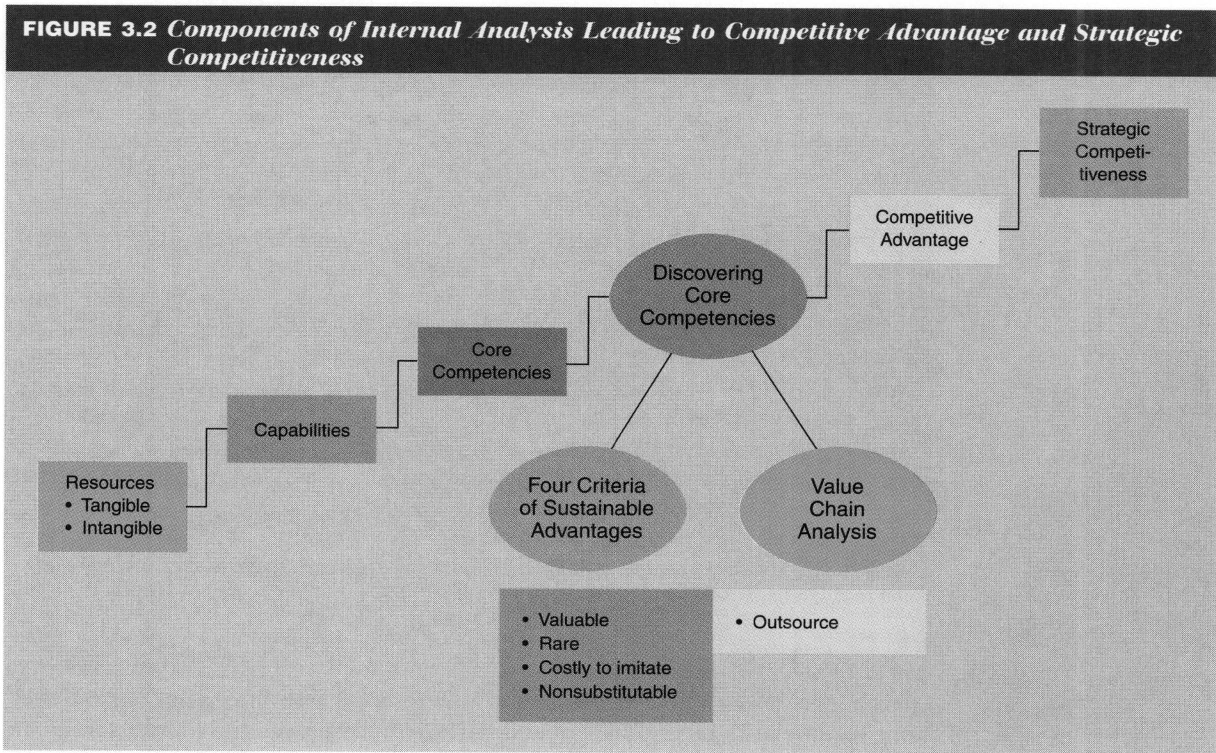

FIGURE 3.2 *Components of Internal Analysis Leading to Competitive Advantage and Strategic Competitiveness*

competencies—may appear to be relatively easy tasks. In fact, this work is as challenging and difficult as any other with which managers are involved; and, it is becoming increasingly internationalized and linked with the firm's success.[22]

Sometimes mistakes are made when conducting an internal analysis. Managers might, for example, select resources and capabilities as a firm's core competencies that do not, in fact, yield a competitive advantage. When this occurs, strategists must have the confidence to admit the mistake and take corrective actions. Firm growth can occur through well-intended errors. Indeed, learning generated by making and correcting mistakes can be important to the creation of new competitive advantages.[23]

To manage the development and use of core competencies, managers must have courage, self-confidence, integrity, the capacity to deal with uncertainty and complexity, and a willingness to hold people accountable for their work.[24] Successful strategists also seek to create an organizational environment in which operating units feel empowered to use the identified core competencies to pursue marketplace opportunities.

Difficult managerial decisions concerning resources, capabilities, and core competencies are characterized by three conditions: uncertainty, complexity, and intraorganizational conflicts (see Figure 3.3).

Managers face *uncertainty* in terms of the emergence of new proprietary technologies, rapidly changing economic and political trends, changes in societal values, and shifts in customer demands. Such environmental uncertainty increases the *complexity* and the range of issues managers examine when studying the internal

FIGURE 3.3 ***Conditions Affecting Managerial Decisions About Resources, Capabilities, and Core Competencies***

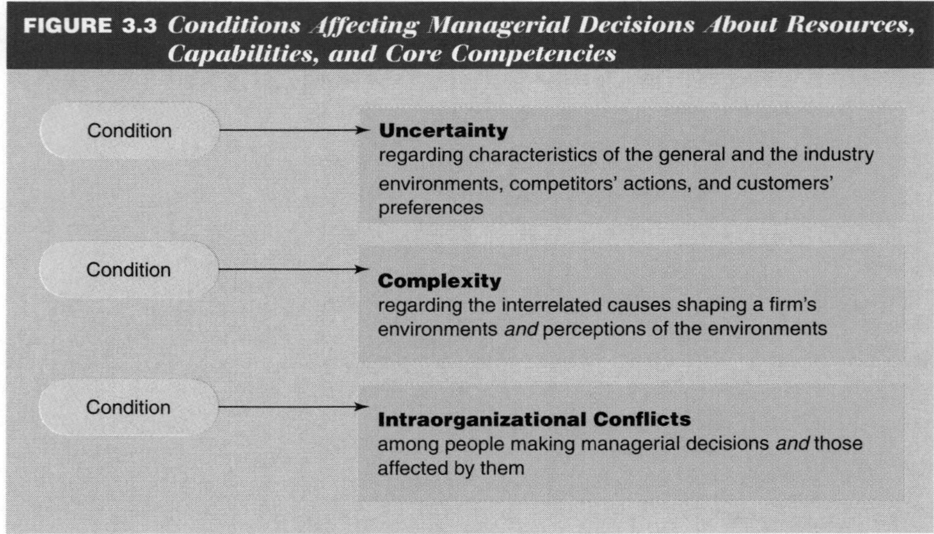

Source: Adapted from R. Amit and P. J. H. Schoemaker, 1993, Strategic assets and organizational rent, *Strategic Management Journal* 14: 33.

environment. Managerial biases about how to cope with uncertainty affect decisions about the resources and capabilities that will become the foundation of the firm's competitive advantage. Finally, *intraorganizational conflict* surfaces when decisions are made about core competencies that are to be nurtured and about how the nurturing is to take place.

When making decisions affected by these three conditions, managers should use their judgment. *Judgment* is a capacity for making successful decisions when no obviously correct model or rule is available or when relevant data are unreliable or incomplete.[25] In this situation one must be aware of possible cognitive biases. For instance, one must compare internal firm resources and make a judgment whether a resource is a strength or a weakness. When exercising judgment, the strategist demonstrates a willingness to take intelligent risks in a timely manner. In the new competitive landscape, executive judgment can be a particularly important source of competitive advantage. One reason judgment can result in a competitive advantage is that over time, effective judgment allows a firm to retain the loyalty of stakeholders whose support is linked to above-average returns.[26]

Significant changes in the value-creating potential of a firm's resources and capabilities can occur in a rapidly changing global economy. Because these changes affect a company's power and social structure, inertia or resistance to change may surface. Firms should not deny the changes needed to assure strategic competitiveness; nonetheless, managers sometimes deny the need for organizational and/or personal change. *Denial* is an unconscious coping mechanism used to block out and not initiate painful changes.[27] Occasionally, an entire industry is accused of being in denial. Some analysts recently cited the automobile manufacturing industry as an example of this. In light of saturation in some major markets (such as the United States), automakers have had to increase incentives. The alternative is to reduce production, a difficult decision.[28] GE's CEO, Jack Welch, believes that top-level executives must demonstrate unflinching candor when making strategic decisions. Part of this candor demands that decision makers cause their firms and their people to face reality as it is—not as it once was or as they want it to be.[29] Successful strategists have learned that involving many people in decisions about changes reduces denial and intraorganizational conflict.

RESOURCES, CAPABILITIES, AND CORE COMPETENCIES

Our attention now turns to a description of resources, capabilities, and core competencies—characteristics that are the foundation of competitive advantage. As shown in Figure 3.2, some combination of resources and capabilities can be managed to create core competencies. This subsection defines and provides examples of these internal aspects.

Resources

Defined in Chapter 1, *resources* are inputs into a firm's production process such as capital equipment, the skills of individual employees, patents, finance, and talented managers. Broad in scope, resources cover a spectrum of individual, social, and organizational phenomena.[30] Resources alone do not typically yield a competitive advantage. A professional football team may benefit from employing the league's most talented running back, but it is only when the running back integrates his running style with the blocking schemes of the offensive linemen and the team's offensive strategy that a competitive advantage may develop. Similarly, a firm's production technology, if not protected by patents or other constraints, can be purchased or imitated by competitors, but when that production technology is in-

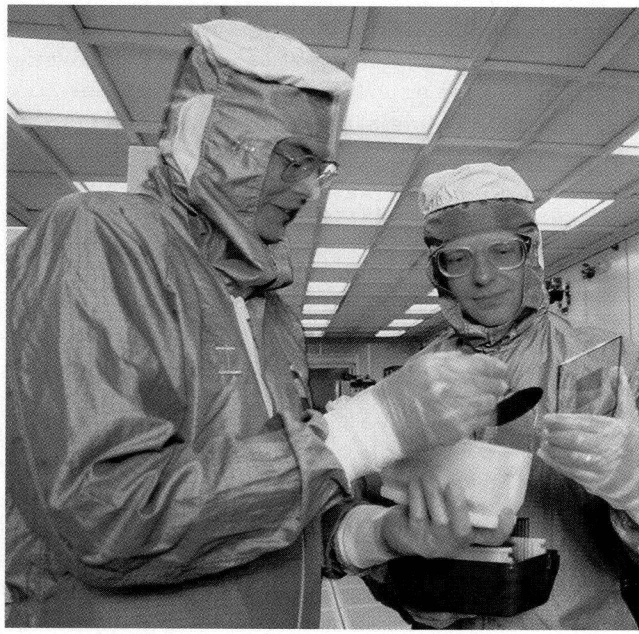

If a firm does not protect its technology with patents or other constraints, it can be purchased or imitated by competitors.

Tangible resources are assets that can be seen and quantified.

Intangible resources range from the intellectual property rights of patents, trademarks, and copyrights to the people-dependent or subjective resources of know-how, networks, organizational culture, and a firm's reputation for its goods or services and the ways it interacts with people (e.g., employees, suppliers, and customers).

tegrated with other resources to form a capability, a core competence may develop that results in competitive advantage. Thus, a competitive advantage can be created through the *unique bundling of several resources.*[31] Physical assets alone usually cannot provide a firm with a sustainable competitive advantage.[32]

Some of a firm's resources are tangible; others are intangible. **Tangible resources** are assets that can be seen and quantified. **Intangible resources** range from the intellectual property rights of patents, trademarks, and copyrights to the people-dependent or subjective resources of know-how, networks, organizational culture, and a firm's reputation for its goods or services and the ways it interacts with people (e.g., employees, suppliers, and customers).[33]

Reputation is viewed as an intangible resource that can endow companies with a competitive advantage. Some equate reputation to "what accountants call goodwill and marketers call brand equity."[34] Among other competitive benefits, a positive reputation allows the firm to charge premium prices for its goods or services and to reduce its marketing costs.[35] Harley-Davidson is a brand that may drive sales on any two-wheeled vehicle. Using the Harley-Davidson brand, GT Bicycles has been licensed to offer the Velo Glide for $1700. GT sold 1,000 Limited Edition Bicycles for $2,500 each in 1996 that were snapped up quickly by collectors. These bikes have real Harley paint jobs, a fake gas tank, and chrome fenders similar to a Harley soft-tail motorcycle.[36]

The four types of tangible resources are financial, physical, human, and organizational (see Table 3.1). The three types of intangible resources (*technological* and those resulting from the firm's *innovation* and *reputation*) are shown in Table 3.2.

Tangible Resources As tangible resources, a firm's borrowing capacity and the status of its plant and equipment are visible to all. The value of many tangible resources can be established through financial statements, but these statements do not account for the value of all of a firm's assets in that they disregard some intangible resources.[37] As such, sources of a firm's competitive advantage often are not reflected on its financial statements.

Managers are challenged to understand fully the strategic value of their firm's tangible and intangible resources. The *strategic value of resources* is indicated by the degree to which they can contribute to the development of capabilities and core competencies and, ultimately, a competitive advantage. For example, as a tangible

TABLE 3.1 *Tangible Resources*

Financial Resources	■ The firm's borrowing capacity ■ The firm's ability to generate internal funds
Physical Resources	■ Sophistication and location of a firm's plant and equipment ■ Access to raw materials
Human Resources	■ The training, experience, judgment, intelligence, insights, adaptability, commitment, and loyalty of a firm's individual managers and workers
Organizational Resources	■ The firm's formal reporting structure and its formal planning, controlling, and coordinating systems

Source: Adapted from J.B. Barney, 1991, Firm resources and sustained competitive advantage, *Journal of Management* 17: 101; R.M. Grant, 1991, *Contemporary Strategy Analysis* (Cambridge, England: Blackwell Business), 100–102.

TABLE 3.2 *Intangible Resources*

Technological Resources	■ Stock of technology such as patents, trademarks, copyrights, and trade secrets ■ Knowledge required to apply it successfully
Resources for Innovation	■ Technical employees ■ Research facilities

Reputation	■ Reputation with customers
	  ■ Brand name
	  ■ Perceptions of product quality, durability, and reliability
	■ Reputation with suppliers
	  ■ For efficient, effective, supportive, and mutually beneficial interactions and relationships

Source: Adapted from R. Hall, 1992, The strategic analysis of intangible resources, *Strategic Management Journal* 13: 136–139; R.M. Grant, 1991, *Contemporary Strategy Analysis* (Cambridge, England: Blackwell Business), 101–104.

resource, a distribution facility will be assigned a monetary value on the firm's balance sheet. The real value of the facility as a resource, however, is grounded in other factors such as its proximity to raw materials and customers and the manner in which workers integrate their actions internally and with other stakeholders such as suppliers and customers.[38]

As shown in Figure 3.2, resources are the source of a firm's capabilities. Capabilities are the source of a firm's core competencies, which are the basis of competitive advantages. Intangible resources, as compared to tangible resources, are a superior and more potent source of core competencies.[39] In fact, in today's competitive environment, ". . . the success of a corporation lies more in its intellectual and systems capabilities than in its physical assets. [Moreover], the capacity to manage human intellect—and to convert it into useful products and services—is fast becoming the critical executive skill of the age."[40] Some evidence also suggests that the value of intangible assets is growing as a proportion of a firm's total shareholder value. In a recent 10-year period, for example, one study's results indicate that the relationship between tangible assets (defined as property, plant, and equipment in this study) and total market value for U.S. mining and manufacturing companies declined from 62 to 38 percent.[41]

Intangible Resources Because they are less visible and more difficult for competitors to understand, purchase, imitate, or substitute, managers prefer to use intangible resources as the foundation for a firm's capabilities and core competencies. In fact, it may be that the more unobservable (that is, intangible) a resource is, the more sustainable will be the competitive advantage based on it.[42]

Brand names are an intangible resource that helps to create a firm's reputation and are recognized widely as an important source of competitive advantage for many companies, especially for those manufacturing and selling consumer goods and services.[43] When effective, brand names inform customers of a product's performance characteristics and attributes. When products with strong brand names provide value across time, customers become very loyal by refusing to buy competitors' offerings, including private-label generic products.

When a brand name yields a competitive advantage, companies sometimes strive to find additional ways to exploit it in the marketplace as the earlier example of Harley-Davidson using its brand name to sell bicycles demonstrates. Century 21 Real Estate seeks to use its brand name to offer and sign up customers for a wide range of discounted home services.[44] Disney has used its brand name to offer clothes representing Disney figures. Currently, Disney is entering the restaurant business through a chain of sport theme restaurants based on its ESPN cable sports network brand. Disney has also launched ESPN merchandise stores.[45]

One way brand-name products are supported is through advertising. Advertising is considered one of the best ways to build brand equity, as suggested by the fact that spending on advertising continues to increase and exceeded $182 billion in the United States in 1997.[46] Consumer products giant Procter & Gamble was the largest advertiser in the United States in 1995, spending a total of $1.51 billion to advertise Crest toothpaste, Tide detergent, and its other well-known consumer goods. Close behind P&G in advertising spending in 1995 were General Motors, $1.5 billion, and Philip Morris, $1.4 billion. Nevertheless, the ad dollar is becoming diffused over many more alternative providers. For instance, advertising revenue on the Web reached $217 million through the first six months of 1997, which is more than triple the $61 million spent in the first six months of 1996.[47]

As a source of capabilities, tangible and intangible resources are a critical part of the pathway to the development of competitive advantage (see Figure 3.2). As discussed previously, resources' strategic value is increased when they are integrated or combined. Defined formally in Chapter 1, *capability* is the capacity for a set of resources to integratively perform a task or activity. Capabilities are unique combinations of the firm's information-based tangible resources (see Table 3.1) and/or intangible resources (see Table 3.2) and are what the firm is able to do as a result of teams of resources working together.

Capabilities

As just explained, capabilities represent the firm's capacity to deploy resources that have been purposely *integrated* to achieve a desired end state. As the glue that binds an organization together, capabilities emerge over time through complex interactions between and among tangible and intangible resources. As explained in the opening case, they are often based on developing, carrying, and exchanging information and knowledge through the firm's human capital. Thus, the firm's knowledge base is embedded in and reflected by its capabilities and is a key source of advantage in the new competitive landscape.[48] Because a knowledge base is grounded in organizational actions that may not be understood explicitly by all employees, the firm's capabilities become stronger and more valuable strategically through repetition and practice.

As illustrated in Figure 3.4, the primary base for the firm's capabilities is the skills and knowledge of its employees and often their functional expertise. As such, the value of human capital in the development and use of capabilities and, ultimately, core competencies cannot be overstated. Microsoft, for example, believes that its best asset is the "intellectual horsepower" of its employees. To assure continued development of this capability and the core competence that follows, the firm strives continuously to hire people who are more talented than the current set of employees.[49]

FIGURE 3.4 *Capabilities*

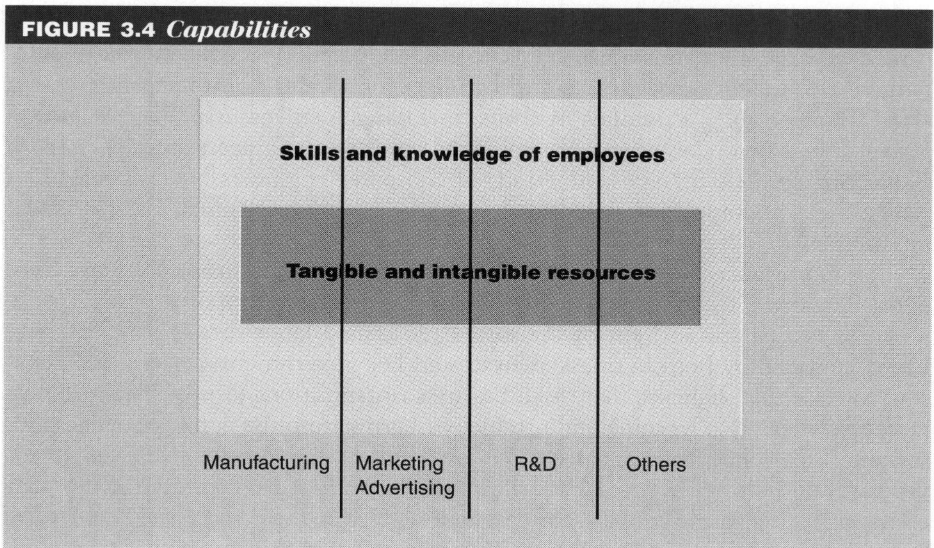

Some believe that the knowledge possessed by the firm's human capital is among the most significant of an organization's capabilities and may ultimately be at the root of all competitive advantages. In the words of one business analyst, "Companies have come to understand that one of the strongest competitive advantages is absolute knowledge."[50] Some even view knowledge as "the sum of everything everybody in [a] company knows that gives [the firm] a competitive edge in the marketplace."[51] Moreover, the *rate* at which firms acquire new knowledge and develop the skills necessary to apply it in the marketplace is a key source of competitive advantage.[52] To facilitate knowledge acquisition, development, and application, some firms (such as Coca-Cola, GE, and General Motors) have created a new top management team (this term is discussed in Chapter 12) position—the chief knowledge officer or the chief learning officer (CLO). Regardless of the title, the task for these strategists is primarily to help the firm become a learning organization that is open to making the changes required to establish and exploit competitive advantages.

Some evidence suggests that workforces throughout the global economy may lack the skills and knowledge firms require to exploit them as a source of competitive advantage. For instance, a National Association of Manufacturers study indicated that, "nearly nine out of 10 U.S. manufacturers are reporting shortages of qualified workers, and a growing gap has emerged between job requirements in the high technology economy and the skills available."[53] One manager has noted that "high tech is exploding. . . . And the only thing stopping growth from being even stronger is the lack of qualified high-tech professionals."[54] In particular, this concern, which exists across all types of industries, is directed toward the future. "These concerns are not about the existing workforce so much as about the people coming into the workforce."[55] The shortage is not only being felt by large firms. The report, *The Survey of Small and Mid-Sized Businesses*, prepared by the 63,000-member National Small Business United and Arthur Andersen Enterprise Group showed a similar concern. The survey reported that the single most important challenge was labor quality. When confronted with a possible shortage of skilled workers, companies desiring to develop their knowledge as a source of competitive advantage sometimes scan the global economy to find the required labor skills. For example, a number of firms, including Siemens, Motorola, Hewlett-Packard, and Digital Equipment, employed computer engineers from the city of Bangalore, India. The city's thousands of computer engineers have signaled that Bangalore is an important global source of information technology and workforce capabilities.[56]

The importance of human capital and knowledge to the firm's strategic competitiveness and the need to provide continuous learning opportunities for employees, particularly in light of the forecasted skilled labor force shortages, have been suggested by both business analysts and key government officials. One analyst, for example, believes that in all business organizations (especially those providing services) ". . . learning and productivity grow from the cumulative decision-making experiences of employees in long-term relationships with customers, vendors and fellow employees."[57] It has also been argued that the United States' competitiveness in the global economy and its ability to increase the standard of living of individual citizens is influenced strongly by the degree to which the nation's human capital is nourished and increased.[58]

As illustrated in Figure 3.4 and Table 3.3, capabilities are often developed in specific functional areas (e.g., manufacturing, R&D, marketing, etc.) or in a part (e.g., advertising) of a functional area. Research results suggest a relationship between distinctive competencies (or capabilities) developed in particular functional areas and the firm's financial performance at both the corporate and business-unit levels.[59] Thus, firms should seek to develop functional area distinctive competencies or capabilities in individual business units and at the corporate level (in the case of diversified firms). Table 3.3 shows a grouping of organizational functions and the capabilities certain companies are thought to possess in terms of all or parts of those functions.

As mentioned in the opening case, Science Applications International Corp, Levi Strauss, and Microsoft are respected for their different functional abilities to develop their human resources. In particular, Microsoft has a creative ability to make large new product teams work as efficiently as small teams.[60]

Armed with knowledge about resources and capabilities, managers are prepared to identify their firm's core competencies. As defined in Chapter 1, *core competencies* are resources and capabilities that serve as a source of competitive advantage for a firm over its rival.

Core Competencies

As the source of competitive advantage for a firm, core competencies distinguish a company competitively and reflect its personality. Core competencies emerge over time through an organizational process of accumulating and learning how to deploy different resources and capabilities. As a capacity to take action, core competencies ". . . are the essence of what makes an organization unique in its ability to provide value to customers over a long period of time."[61]

Not all of a firm's resources and capabilities are strategic assets—that is, assets that have competitive value and the potential to serve as a source of competitive advantage.[62] Some resources and capabilities may result in incompetence because they represent competitive areas in which the firm is weak compared to competitors. Thus, some resources or capabilities may stifle or prevent the development

TABLE 3.3 *Examples of Firms' Capabilities*

Functional Areas	Capabilities	Firm Examples
Distribution	Effective use of logistics management techniques	Wal-Mart
Human resources	Motivating, empowering, and retaining employees	AEROJET
Management information systems	Effective and efficient control of inventories through point-of-purchase data collection methods	Wal-Mart
Marketing	Effective promotion of brand-name products	Gillette Ralph Lauren Clothing McKinsey & Co.
	Effective customer service	Nordstrom Norwest Solectron Corporation Norrell Corporation
	Innovative merchandising	Crate & Barrel
Management	Effective execution of managerial tasks	Hewlett-Packard
	Ability to envision the future of clothing	The Gap
	Effective organizational structure	PepsiCo
Manufacturing	Design and production skills yielding reliable products	Komatsu
	Product and design quality	The Gap
	Production of technologically sophisticated automobile engines	Mazda
	Miniaturization of components and products	Sony
Research & development	Exceptional technological capability	Corning
	Development of sophisticated engineered elevator control solutions	Motion Control Engineering Inc.
	Rapid transformation of technology into new products and processes	Chaparral Steel
	Deep knowledge of silver-halide materials	Kodak
	Digital technology	Thomson Consumer Electronics

of a core competence. Firms with insufficient financial capital, for example, may be unable to purchase facilities or hire the skilled workers required to manufacture products that yield customer value. In this situation, financial capital (a tangible resource) would be a weakness. Armed with in-depth understandings of their firm's resources and capabilities, strategic managers are challenged to find external environmental opportunities that can be exploited through the firm's capabilities while avoiding competition in areas of weakness.

Additionally, an important question is: How many core competencies are required for the firm to have a competitive advantage? Responses to this question vary. McKinsey & Co. recommends that clients identify three or four competencies around which their strategic actions can be framed.[63] Note the consistency of Rolls-Royce's decisions with this advice to focus on only four competencies. The company has outsourced a number of peripheral activities such as making car bodies and fasteners so it can concentrate "on its core competencies—engines, paint, leather, (and) wood."[64] Trying to support and nurture more than four core competencies may prevent the firm from developing the focus it needs to exploit fully its competencies in the marketplace.

From an impoverished city in southern Italy called Santeramo Del Colle, Pasquale Natuzzi has taken his firm Industrie Natuzzi SpA from selling 100 leather sofas to Macy's in 1982 to having an estimated 25 percent of the U.S. leather furniture market.[65] Because his clients in Italy were pressuring him to send two or three sofas but only bill them for one or two to avoid taxes, he decided to begin selling his furniture overseas. He has focused his firm's competencies on design flair and quality leathers, highly skilled craftsmen, each with a computer to maintain efficient operations, and low labor costs with strong worker incentives. Because of Natuzzi's focus on a few critical core competencies, his furniture has maintained attractive designs that meet the needs of this fashion conscious industry at a price that is 20 percent less than what Macy's paid in 1982.

Not all resources and capabilities are core competencies. The following section discusses two approaches for identifying core competencies.

BUILDING CORE COMPETENCIES

Two conceptual tools can help to identify and build competencies and the achievement of competitive advantage. First, we discuss four specific criteria to determine which of a firm's resources and capabilities are core competencies. Because they have satisfied the four criteria of sustainable competitive advantage, the capabilities shown in Table 3.3 are core competencies for the firms processing them. Following this discussion, we describe value chain analysis for deciding what value-creating competencies should be maintained, upgraded, or developed and which activities should be outsourced.

Criteria of Sustainable Competitive Advantage

As shown in Table 3.4, capabilities that are valuable, rare, costly to imitate, and nonsubstitutable are strategic capabilities and a source of competitive advantage.[66] Capabilities failing to satisfy these criteria are not core competencies. Thus, as shown in Figure 3.5, every core competence is a capability, but every capability is not a core competence.

A sustained competitive advantage is achieved only when competitors have tried, without success, to duplicate the benefits of a firm's strategy or when competitors lack the confidence to attempt imitation. For some period of time, a firm may earn a competitive advantage through the use of capabilities that are, for example, valu-

TABLE 3.4 ***Four Criteria for Determining Strategic Capabilities***

Valuable Capabilities	■ Help a firm neutralize threats or exploit opportunities
Rare Capabilities	■ Are not possessed by many others
Costly to Imitate Capabilities	■ Historical: A unique and a valuable organizational culture or brand name
	■ Ambiguous cause: The causes and uses of a competence are unclear
	■ Social complexity: Interpersonal relationships, trust and friendship among managers, suppliers, and customers
Nonsubstitutable Capabilities	■ No strategic equivalent

FIGURE 3.5 ***Core Competence as a Strategic Capability***

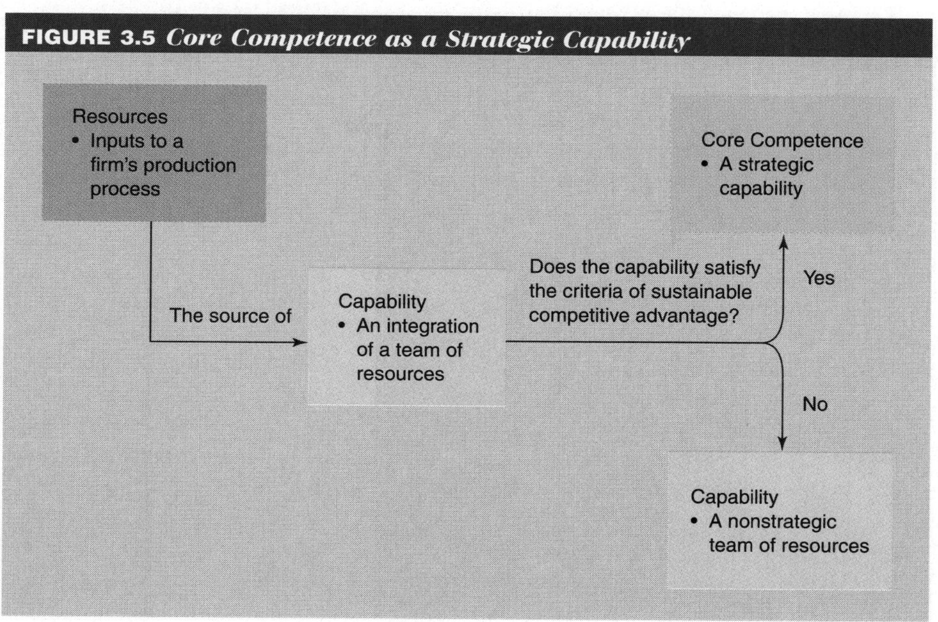

able and rare,[67] but are imitable. In such an instance, the length of time a firm can expect to retain its competitive advantage is a function of how quickly competitors can successfully imitate a good, service, or process. It is only through the combination of conditions represented by all four criteria that a firm's capabilities have the potential to create a sustained competitive advantage.

Valuable **Valuable capabilities** are those that create value for a firm by exploiting opportunities and/or neutralize threats in its external environment. Valuable capabilities enable a firm to formulate and implement strategies that create value for specific customers. Sony Corp. has used its valuable capabilities dealing with the designing, manufacturing, and selling of miniaturized electronic technology to exploit a range of marketplace opportunities, including those for portable disc players and easy-to-hold 8mm video cameras.[68]

Valuable capabilities are those that create value for a firm by exploiting opportunities and/or neutralize threats in its external environment.

Rare **Rare capabilities** are those possessed by few, if any, current or potential competitors. A key question managers seek to answer when evaluating this criterion is "How many rival firms possess these valuable capabilities?" Capabilities possessed by many rival firms are unlikely to be a source of competitive advantage for any one of them. Instead, valuable but common (i.e., not rare) resources and capabilities are sources of competitive parity.[69] Competitive advantage results only when firms develop and exploit capabilities that differ from those they share with competitors.

Rare capabilities are those possessed by a few, if any, current or potential competitors.

Costly to Imitate **Costly to imitate capabilities** are those that other firms cannot develop easily. Capabilities that are costly to imitate can occur because of one or a combination of three reasons (see Table 3.4).

Costly to imitate capabilities are those that other firms cannot develop easily.

First, a firm sometimes is able to develop capabilities because of *unique historical conditions.* "As firms evolve, they pick up skills, abilities, and resources that are unique to them, reflecting their particular path through history."[70] A firm with a

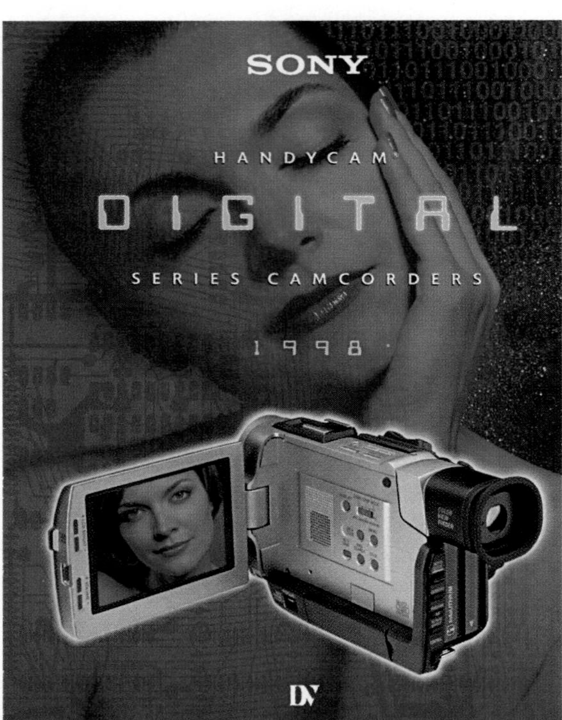

Sony Corp. used its valuable capabilities to design, manufacture, and sell its hand-held digital camcorders.

unique and valuable organizational culture that emerged in the early stages of the company's history ". . . may have an imperfectly imitable advantage over firms founded in another historical period"[71]—a period of time in which less valuable values and beliefs strongly influence the development of a firm's culture. This may be the case for the consulting firm McKinsey & Co.

McKinsey's culture is thought by competitors, clients, and analysts alike to be a primary source of competitive advantage. As testimony to the intangibility of culture, even to some of those familiar with it, consider the following description of culture as McKinsey's source of advantage: "It is that culture, unique to McKinsey and eccentric, which sets the firm apart from virtually any other business organization and which often mystifies even those who engage (its) services." The historical foundation for McKinsey's culture was established by Marvin Bower, the company's founding father. In fact, "much of what McKinsey is today harks back to the early 1930s" when Bower entered the consulting business. Bower's concept of how his consulting firm would operate was that it should provide advice about effective managerial practices to top-level executives. As guidance for McKinsey's consultants, Bower developed a set of principles. Cited frequently and with intensity, these principles actually define what McKinsey was and is today. As such, they are the backbone of the company's unique, and what some think is an enigmatic, culture. According to Bower's principles, a McKinsey consultant should (1) put the interests of the client ahead of increasing the company's revenues, (2) remain silent about the client's business operations, (3) be truthful and not fear challenging a client's opinion, and (4) perform only work that s/he believes is in the client's best interests and is something McKinsey can do well.[72]

A second condition of being costly to imitate occurs when the link between the firm's competencies and its competitive advantage is *causally ambiguous*.[73] In these instances, competitors are unable to understand clearly how a firm uses its competencies as the foundation for competitive advantage. As a result, competitors are uncertain about the competencies they should develop to duplicate the benefits of a competitor's value-creating strategy. Gordon Forward, CEO of Chaparral Steel, allows competitors to tour his firm's facilities. In Forward's words, competitors can be shown almost ". . . everything and we will be giving away nothing because they can't take it home with them."[74]

Social complexity is the third reason that capabilities can be costly to imitate. Social complexity means that at least some, and frequently many, of the firm's capabilities are the product of complex social phenomena. Examples of socially complex capabilities include interpersonal relationships, trust and friendships among managers, and a firm's reputation with suppliers and customers. Hewlett-Packard's culture is recognized widely as socially complex and as a source of competitive advantage. Socially complex capabilities resulting from this culture include the nurturing of innovation across divisional boundaries and the effective use of cross-functional work teams. Recently this culture provided the capability HP needed to develop work processes through which the firm was able to improve operations dramatically in its North American distribution organization. Designed by a cross-functional work team of 35 people from HP and two other companies, the distribution center's new work processes reduced the number of days required to deliver products to customers from 26 to 8.[75]

Nonsubstitutable **Nonsubstitutable capabilities** are those that do not have strategic equivalents. This final requirement for a capability to be a source of competitive advantage ". . . is that there must be no strategically equivalent valuable resources that are themselves either not rare or imitable. Two valuable firm resources (or two bundles of firm resources) are strategically equivalent when they each can be exploited separately to implement the same strategies."[76] In general the strategic value of capabilities increases the more difficult they are to substitute.[77] The more invisible capabilities are, the more difficult it is for firms to find substitutes and the greater the challenge is to competitors trying to imitate a firm's value-creating strategy. Firm-specific knowledge and trust-based working relationships between managers and nonmanagerial personnel are examples of capabilities that are difficult to identify and for which finding substitutes is challenging.

Nonsubstitutable capabilities are those that do not have strategic equivalents.

To summarize this discussion, we reiterate that sustainable competitive advantage results only through the use of capabilities that are valuable, rare, costly to imitate, and nonsubstitutable. Table 3.5 shows the competitive consequences and performance implications resulting from combinations of the four criteria of sustainability. The analysis suggested by the contents of the table helps managers determine the strategic value of the firm's capabilities. Resources and capabilities falling into the first row in the table (that is, resources and capabilities that aren't valuable or rare and that are imitable and for which strategic substitutes exist) are ones the firm should not emphasize to formulate and implement strategies. Capabilities yielding competitive parity and either temporary or sustainable competitive advantage, however, will be supported. Large competitors such as Coca-Cola and PepsiCo may have capabilities that can yield only competitive parity. In such cases, the firms will nurture these capabilities while simultaneously emphasizing those that can yield either a temporary or sustainable competitive advantage.

TABLE 3.5 ***Outcomes from Combinations of the Criteria for Sustainable Competitive Advantage***

Is the Resource or Capability Valuable?	Is the Resource or Capability Rare?	Is the Resource or Capability Costly to Imitate?	Is the Resource or Capability Nonsubstitutable?	Competitive Consequences	Performance Implications
No	No	No	No	Competitive disadvantage	Below-average returns
Yes	No	No	Yes/no	Competitive parity	Average returns
Yes	Yes	No	Yes/no	Temporary competitive advantage	Above-average returns to average returns
Yes	Yes	Yes	Yes	Sustainable competitive advantage	Above-average returns

What about Toyota's advantage in new product development and production systems in the Strategic Focus? First, its strategy appears to create value because is has been successful with selling its designs at a low cost. Its production systems and new product development capabilities are obviously rare. Others have had difficulty reproducing this system even though many competitor executives have visited Toyota plants. Although the techniques may not be causally ambiguous, Toyota's system is socially complex. Furthermore, the firm continues to learn and maintain its early advantage in efficient production systems and new product development. Establishing early advantage and maintaining that advantage will be discussed more fully in Chapter 5. Also, because of the complexity and idiosyncrasy of Toyota's production system, the system is nonsubstitutable. In fact, Toyota has had trouble transferring its production system to other locations such as the Georgetown facility in Kentucky. Therefore, Toyota appears to have a sustainable competitive advantage.

STRATEGIC FOCUS

Toyota's New Product Development and Production Systems Are Difficult to Copy

Toyota's secret of competitive success has been its new product development and production systems. Toyota has a large manufacturing complex in Georgetown, Kentucky. Two days a month, more than 50 auto executives and engineers travel to this complex and participate in five hour tours. The tours include an intensive question and answer session for visiting executives of competing car companies. Even though Toyota shows competitors how it makes cars, no other company has succeeded in beating Toyota as the most efficient auto company in the world. Mercedes-Benz has sophisticated engineering; Honda has excellent engine technology; and Chrysler is excellent in styling. But Toyota sets the standard in efficiency, quality, and productivity.

Furthermore, although it has been considered conservative and slow-moving, the firm's new CEO, Hiroshi Okuda, seeks to make Toyota even more efficient. Speed is becoming more important as the twenty-first century approaches. Additionally, Okuda intends to not only increase Toyota's global market share but also to improve its operating margins. In Japan, Toyota has set a 40 percent market share as its goal while its closest rival, Nissan, currently has 22 percent. Furthermore, Toyota has 21 percent of the market in Southeast Asia. Additionally, Toyota ranks fourth in unit sales behind the Big Three in the U.S. with an 8 percent share. Okuda has set a 10 percent goal of market share in the United States.

Competitors understand the techniques and practices Toyota uses but cannot reproduce the firm's production system. Although the principles of Toyota's productivity are not complicated, its implementation and coordination require "an incredible amount of detail, planning, discipline, hard work and painstaking attention to detail." Therefore, although it is not causally ambiguous, it is highly socially complex. What makes imitation of the production system even more difficult is that Toyota continues to improve its own system.

Some believe that Toyota's exceptional strength lies in its ability to learn. Its employees are always problem-conscious and strongly customer-oriented. It has a simple ability to learn from its mistakes and improve continually. Although the 1997 Previa was an engineering marvel, it was powered by a small engine and buyers found it sluggish and too expensive at $30,000. In 1998, the Sienna XLE may not be an engineering marvel, but it has a larger engine, inventive technology, and a $22,000 price tag.

Toyota's new product development is unrivaled in the industry. The firm produces a new car in eighteen months. Some U.S. competitors are down to 30 months. Besides its speed at producing a new model, Toyota now develops similar models simultaneously. The industry approach is to develop a sedan and then follow sequentially with a coupe or some other variety. Toyota's approach is to develop these products simultaneously. Through this method, Toyota has doubled its engineering output over the past four years while increasing its budget by only 20 percent.

Toyota is also excelling as the first automobile maker to sell a mass production vehicle with a hybrid engine. A hybrid engine combines gasoline engine technology with an electric motor that receives electricity both from a battery pack and from the car's movement. Using this technology, the Prius, the first hybrid technology model car, gets 66 miles per gallon and generates half the normal amount of carbon dioxide. Toyota hopes to produce a thousand cars a month even though the Prius won't be profitable because it costs twice as much to make as its $17,900 price tag.

Toyota has also provided a breakthrough in engine design. It has designed a 120-horsepower engine for its 1998 Corolla, which uses 25 percent fewer parts, making it 10 percent lighter and 10 percent more fuel-efficient. This has allowed Toyota to slash the price of its '98 Corolla by $1,500 compared to its 1997 model. Toyota realizes that it is also dependent on its suppliers. As such, "it has consciously institutionalized a set of practices for transferring knowledge between itself and the suppliers, so that the whole group learns faster." On average, Toyota's independent suppliers are 59 miles away from its assembly plants. By comparison, GM's supplier average is 425 miles from the plants they serve. This results in a larger inventory for both the supplier and General Motors' plants.

Although Toyota is unexcelled in productivity as the above factors denote, the firm has had difficulty establishing its systems for production and product development outside of Japan. Therefore, Toyota remains Japan-centric. In the long run, this is likely to be a strong hindrance to future growth. In its Georgetown complex, decisions are often referred back to Tokyo. This has created a problem of relatively high turnover at the Georgetown complex. Toyota realizes that with the Japanese market quite saturated, growth will have to come in international markets; therefore, the company is pursing foreign direct investment. As such, production in Japan has dipped from the peak of four million in 1991 to 3.4 million in 1996. Notwithstanding the difficulties, no one has been able to determine how to duplicate Toyota's product development and production systems.

SOURCE: A. Taylor III, 1997, How Toyota defies gravity, *Fortune*, December 8, 100–108; A. Pollack, 1997, At Toyota, ten percent share is viewed as a start, http://www.nytimes.com, October 24; M. Krebs, 1997, Toyota ahead of pack on hybrid production, http://www.nytimes.com, July 25; B. Bremner, L. Armstrong, K. Kerwin, and K. Naughton, 1997, Toyota's crusade, *Business Week*, http://www.businessweek.com, April 7.

The Gap, a specialty retailer, operates more than 1,600 company outlets under the store names The Gap, GapKids, Banana Republic, and Old Navy. Through the presentation of dressed-down clothes at affordable prices, the firm is thought to have revolutionized the casual-apparel market for women, men, and children. The firm relied on various capabilities to develop competitive advantages in terms of its attention to quality and design and the use of clever advertising slogans and campaigns. To exploit what it saw as an opportunity to serve customers interested in dressed-down clothes but unable to afford The Gap's goods, the firm decided to use its capabilities and competencies to establish Old Navy stores.[78]

What type of advantage, if any, results from the use of some of The Gap's capabilities such as product design and quality, creative advertising, and store design and layout to develop the Old Navy format? It seems that the capabilities being used in this new retailing format are valuable and rare, but at least with respect to The Gap's major competitors, these capabilities can be imitated. For example, The Gap's CEO suggested that ". . . there are no secrets in retailing. The minute something new—a store or a look—is created in this industry, it is instantly visible, there for all the world to examine and replicate."[79] Strategic equivalents for these capabilities may or may not exist. Thus, an analysis of these capabilities suggests that The Gap has established a temporary competitive advantage with its Old Navy stores (see Table 3.5). In terms of the performance implications, the firm should earn above-average returns until competitors learn how to duplicate the value Old Navy stores creates through exploitation of The Gap's.

In the next section, we discuss another framework firms use to examine their resources and capabilities to discover core competencies. Value chain analysis allows the firm to understand the parts of its operations (see Figure 3.2) that create value and those that do not. Understanding these issues is important because the firm earns above-average returns only when the value it creates is greater than the costs incurred to create that value.[80]

Primary activities are involved with a product's physical creation, its sale and distribution to buyers, and its service after the sale.

Support activities provide the support necessary for the primary activities to take place.

Value Chain Analysis

The value chain is a template that firms use to understand their cost position and to identify the multiple means that might be used to facilitate the implementation of their business-level strategy.[81] As shown in Figure 3.6, a firm's value chain can be segmented into primary and support activities. **Primary activities** are involved with a product's physical creation, its sale and distribution to buyers, and its service after the sale. **Support activities** provide the support necessary for the pri-

FIGURE 3.6 ***The Basic Value Chain***

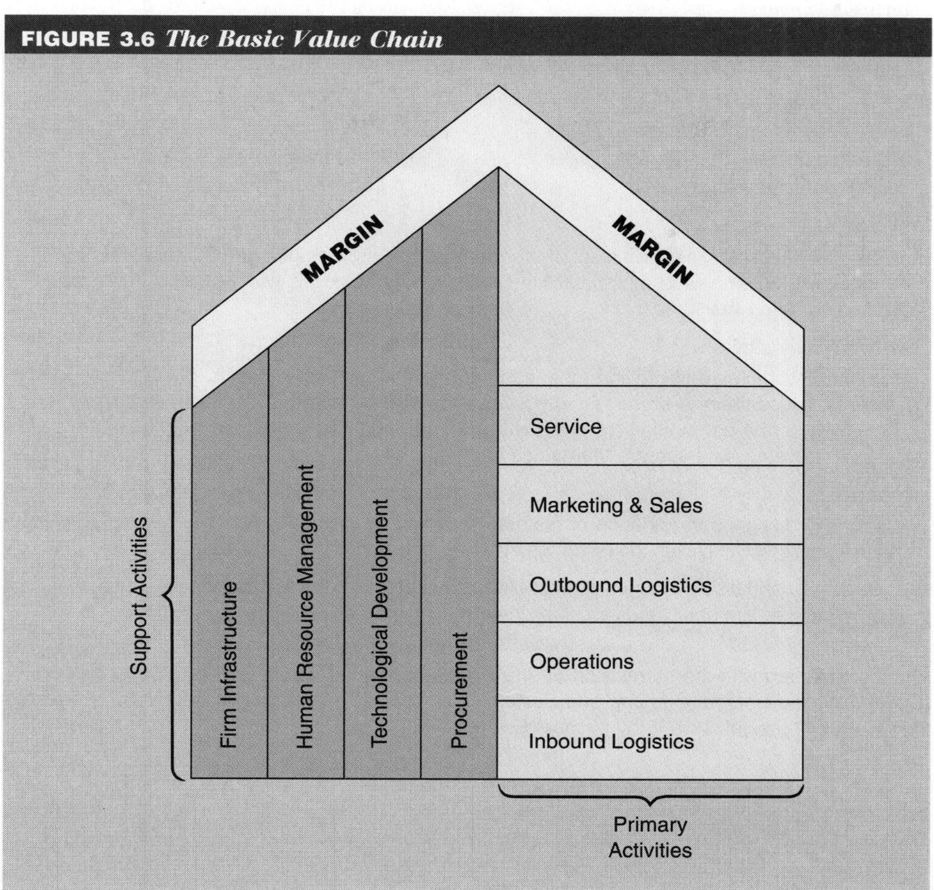

mary activities to take place. The value chain shows how a product moves from the raw material stage to the final customer. For individual firms, the essential idea of the value chain "... is to add as much value as possible as cheaply as possible, and, most important, to capture that value." In a globally competitive economy, "... the most valuable links on the chain tend to belong to people who own knowledge—particularly about customers."[82]

Table 3.6 lists the items to be studied to assess the value-creating potential of primary activities. In Table 3.7, the items to consider when studying support activities are shown. As with the analysis of primary activities, the intent in examining these items is to determine areas where the firm has potential to create and capture value. All items included in both tables are to be evaluated with competitors' capabilities in mind. To be a source of competitive advantage, a resource or capability must allow a firm to (1) perform an activity in a manner that is superior to competitors' performances or (2) perform a value-creating activity that competitors cannot complete. Only under these conditions does a firm create value for customers and have opportunities to capture that value. Sometimes, this requires firms to reconfigure or recombine parts of the value chain in unique ways. As shown in Figure 3.7, Federal Express (FedEx) changed the nature of the delivery

TABLE 3.6 ***Examining the Value–Creating Potential of Primary Activities***

Inbound Logistics

Activities, such as materials handling, warehousing, and inventory control, used to receive, store, and disseminate inputs to a product.

Operations

Activities necessary to convert the inputs provided by inbound logistics into final product form. Machining, packaging, assembly, and equipment maintenance are examples of operations activities.

Outbound Logistics

Activities involved with collecting, storing, and physically distributing the final product to customers. Examples of these activities include finished goods warehousing, materials handling, and order processing.

Marketing and Sales

Activities completed to provide means through which customers can purchase products and to induce them to do so. To effectively market and sell products, firms develop advertising and promotional campaigns, select appropriate distribution channels, and select, develop, and support their sales force.

Service

Activities designed to enhance or maintain a product's value. Firms engage in a range of service-related activities, including installation, repair, training, and adjustment.

Each activity should be examined relative to competitors' abilities. Accordingly, firms rate each activity as *superior, equivalent,* or *inferior.*

Source: Adapted with the permission of The Free Press, a division of Simon & Schuster from *Competitive Advantage: Creating and Sustaining Superior Performance* by Michael E. Porter, pp. 39–40, Copyright © 1985 by Michael E. Porter.

TABLE 3.7 ***Examining the Value–Creating Potential of Support Activities***

Procurement

Activities completed to *purchase* the inputs needed to produce a firm's products. Purchased inputs include items fully consumed during the manufacture of products (e.g., raw materials and supplies as well as fixed assets—machinery, laboratory equipment, office equipment, and buildings).

Technological Development

Activities completed to improve a firm's product and the processes used to manufacture it. Technology development takes many forms, such as process equipment, design, both basic research and product design, and servicing procedures.

Human Resource Management

Activities involved with recruiting, hiring, training, developing, and compensating all personnel.

Firm Infrastructure

Firm infrastructure includes activities such as general management, planning, finance, accounting, legal support, and governmental relations that are required to support the work of the entire value chain. Through its infrastructure, the firm strives to effectively and consistently identify external opportunities and threats, identify resources and capabilities, and support core competencies.

Each activity should be examined relative to competitors' abilities. Accordingly, firms rate each activity as *superior, equivalent,* or *inferior.*

Source: Adapted with the permission of The Free Press, a division of Simon & Schuster from *Competitive Advantage: Creating and Sustaining Superior Performance* by Michael E. Porter, pp. 40–43, Copyright © 1985 by Michael E. Porter.

FIGURE 3.7 ***Increased Value in Human Resource Management and Outbound Logistics Created a Core Competency for Federal Express***

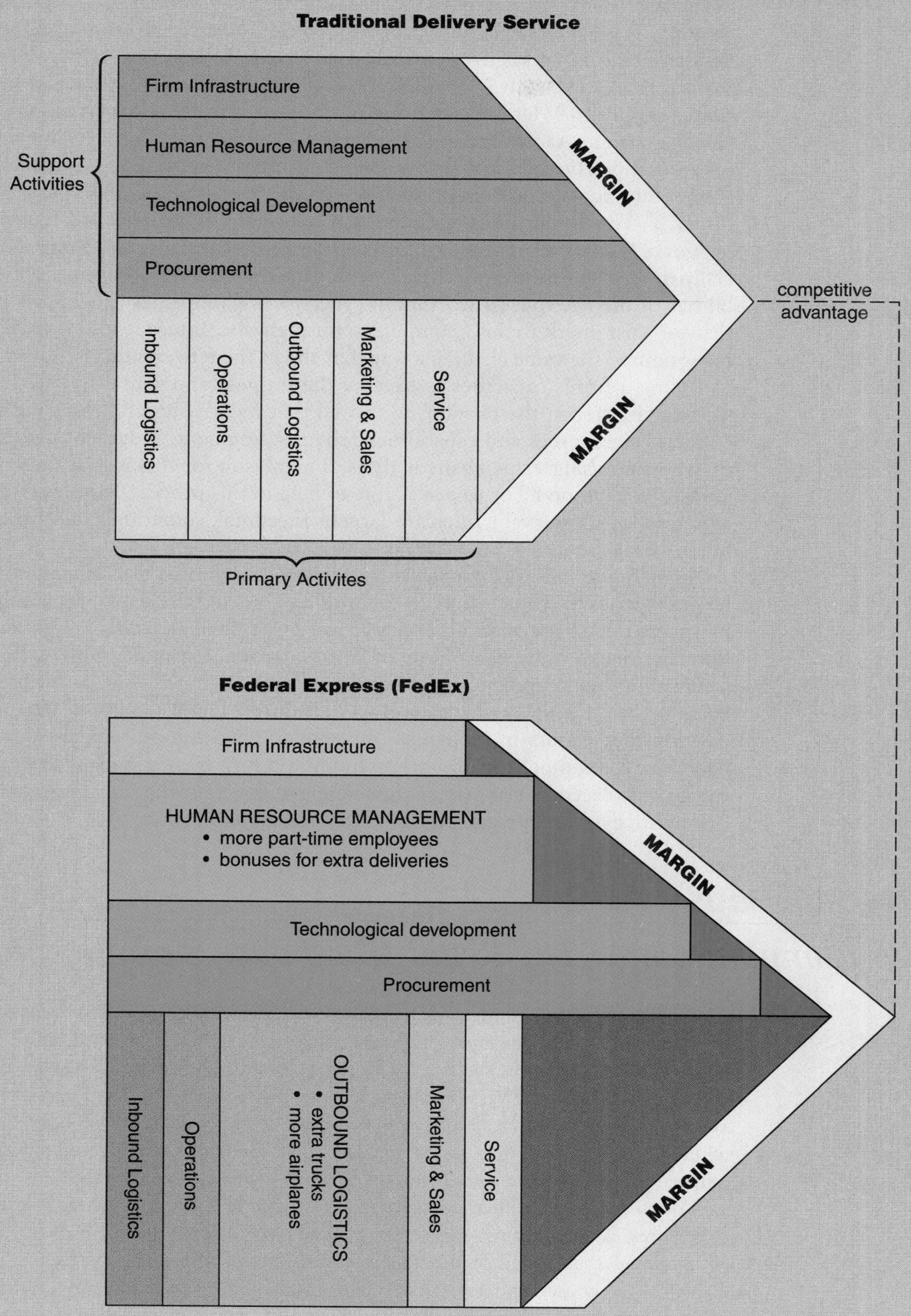

Traditional Delivery Service

Support Activities

Firm Infrastructure

Human Resource Management

Technological Development

Procurement

Inbound Logistics

Operations

Outbound Logistics

Marketing & Sales

Service

Primary Activites

MARGIN

MARGIN

competitive advantage

Federal Express (FedEx)

Firm Infrastructure

HUMAN RESOURCE MANAGEMENT
- more part-time employees
- bonuses for extra deliveries

Technological development

Procurement

Inbound Logistics

Operations

OUTBOUND LOGISTICS
- extra trucks
- more airplanes

Marketing & Sales

Service

MARGIN

MARGIN

business by reconfiguring both its outbound logistics (primary activity) and human resource management (support activity) to originate the overnight delivery business, creating value for itself in the process of doing so.

In combination with Federal Express, Calyx and Corolla launched a mail-order flower service in 1989. Through the inventiveness of Ruth M. Owades, Calyx and Corolla changed radically the way flowers are distributed. Through this firm, flowers are shipped directly from growers to customers. Prices are reduced because middlemen are cut out and the flowers are fresher, creating better value for the customer.[83] The opportunity to purchase automobiles through on-line computer networks is another example of firms' efforts to reconfigure the value chain, especially in terms of primary activities. Companies such as Auto-By-Tel use the capabilities of the Internet to sell cars in cyberspace. Companies providing opportunities for customers to buy computers through the Internet also appear to have reconfigured the value chain in a way that allows them to create and capture value.[84]

Rating a firm's capacities to execute the primary and support activities is challenging. Earlier in the chapter, we noted that identifying and assessing the value of a firm's resources and capabilities requires judgment. Judgment is equally necessary when using value chain analysis. The reason for this is that there is no obviously correct model or rule available to help in this process. Moreover, most data available for these evaluations are largely anecdotal, sometimes unreliable, or difficult to interpret.

An effective value chain analysis results in the identification of new ways to perform activities to create value. In the Strategic Focus on Costco, we see that a firm has been able to focus on appropriate aspects of the value chain. This concentration has created significant value for customers and shareholders alike. Because the innovations employed at Costco are firm specific—that is, they are grounded in a company's unique way of combining its resources and capabilities—they are difficult for competitors to recognize, understand, and imitate. The greater the time necessary for competitors to understand how a firm is creating and capturing value through its execution of primary and support activities, the more sustainable is the competitive advantage gained by the innovating company.

STRATEGIC FOCUS

Costco Companies Inc.: The Retail Warehouse Store Revolution

Although Sam's Club (affiliated with Wal-Mart) has approximately 42 percent more members than Costco and 70 percent more stores, Costco's 1997 sales were $1 billion more than Sam's Club. Accordingly, the average Costco store outsells Sam's Clubs by an almost two-to-one margin. Because Wal-Mart has such a strong reputation in retailing, it seems almost counterintuitive to find a set of stores that can out-merchandise Wal-Mart. Even in such an unattractive, low margin business as warehouse retailing, there is room for strong competence and competitive advantage, as evidenced by the Costco approach.

Costco operates an international chain of Costco and Price Club warehouse membership stores. The company seeks to carry quality brand name merchandise at substantially lower prices than found at other conventional warehouse and retail outlets. Although Costco's warehouse approach offers one of the largest product category selections found under a single roof, it only has about 4,000 stock-keeping units (SKUs). Comparatively, a typical supermarket such as Safeway will carry 30,000 units while stores such as Kmart and

Wal-Mart will carry 40,000 to 60,000 and Fred Myers has as many as 200,000. Therefore, Costco's approach focuses on stocking a few branded items in each category such that, in essence, it has done the comparison shopping for its customer. Costco demands the best prices from the vendors and passes these savings on to customers through very low margins. Costco's gross margins were about 12.5 percent in 1997. Its closest competitor is Wal-Mart at 21.5 percent. Fred Myers' gross margins range as high as 32.5 percent, and comparatively, Home Depot, a category killer or competitor focused on home improvement and hardware, is at 29 percent.

Costco's approach also entails picking high priced items that are priced competitively and trying to create repeat business. Furthermore, its vendors largely finance Costco's inventory. For instance, Costco's accounts payable is only 80 percent of its inventory, while at Wal-Mart the ratio is 48 percent. Thus, relative to Wal-Mart, Costco requires little working capital.

In addition to well-regarded brand-name items, Costco stocks over 200 private-label items that account for 11 percent of sales. It also sells top-quality products using its Kirkland signature brand. Kirkland, Washington, is the former hometown of the now Issaquah, Washington, headquartered firm.

Costco also seeks to build customer trust through its Signature label. For instance, it sells a superior Procter & Gamble paper towel because the private-label brand was an inferior product. It does not offer extended service warranties or service contracts on appliances because "In our view, those programs are a rip-off." In addition, as James D. Sinegal, the current CEO, indicates, they also try to give before they get. "One way or another, the vendor is going to cheat you if you take too much out of his hide." Therefore, Costco managers try to cooperate with vendors to help them reduce the margins and offer valuable suggestions for increasing product value and reducing manufacturing cost.

Costco also promotes from within. Sinegal is an example, having started in the warehouse working under Sol Price, who founded the Price Club chain in 1976. There are very few formal meetings and virtually no bureaucracy. For instance, there is no press or investor relations staff. Virtually all the firm's energy is dedicated to the value chain activities of buying and merchandising products. Costco also has a line of periphery stores that provides pharmaceutical, optical, gasoline pumps, and even a business center that competes with Kinko's in some areas.

As a result of Costco's strategic approach, even with very low margins, it earned an 11.5 percent return on capital, which is near the same level as Wal-Mart's 13 percent. Costco's membership renewal rate is 97 percent among active small businesses. That type of loyalty is more than the average patient's loyalty to physicians. Costco also seeks to screen members (a support activity) to reduce bad checks and shrinkage (loss to pilferage), which is only 2 percent of sales. This level is one-tenth of that of many supermarkets and is a significant way to hold down overhead costs. Costco can drive down margins so low relative to its competitors that it creates significant and cascading amounts of value for its customers.

SOURCE: T.W. Ferguson, 1997, A revolution that has a long way to go, *Forbes*, August 11, 106–112; Costco Companies Inc. home page, 1997, http://www.pricecostco.com, December 5; Costco companies on the Forbes 500, 1997, http://www.forbes.com, December 11.

What should a firm do with respect to primary and support activities in which its resources and capabilities are not a source of competence and competitive advantage? For instance, if Costco moves too far from its competencies with its periphery stores, it may consider using subcontractors. In these instances, as discussed next, firms should study the possibility of outsourcing the work associated with primary and support activities in which they cannot create and capture value.

OUTSOURCING

Outsourcing is the purchase of a value-creating activity from an external supplier.

Outsourcing is the purchase of a value-creating activity from an external supplier. In the view of one consultant, "outsourcing is a strategic concept—a way to add value to the business that converts an in-house cost center into a customer-focused service operation."[85] Sometimes, virtually all firms within an industry seek the strategic value that can be captured through effective outsourcing. The automobile manufacturing industry is an example of this. Based on an observation of the outsourcing trend in this industry an analyst concluded that the "whole strategy worldwide now in the auto industry is to get down to your core vehicle-producing operations. . . . That means shedding everything but stamping, powertrains and final assembly . . . and getting rid of everything that doesn't contribute to those areas."[86]

Several statistics demonstrate the increasing scope of outsourcing. For example, Dun and Bradstreet estimated that global outsourcing would increase to $180 billion in 1998; a 23 percent increase from $146 billion in 1997. Approximately two-thirds of this amount was to come from North American companies.[87] U.S. corporations spent more than $38 billion on information technology outsourcing alone in 1995. This amount represented a full 8 percent of total expenditures by U.S. firms on information technology during that year. In fact, approximately 20 percent of the largest U.S. companies use some form of information technology outsourcing.[88] Similar growth rates in outsourcing activities are expected in other fields, including health care, customer service, and human resources. This has been one of the trends that has increased the importance of cooperative strategy (e.g., the more frequent use of strategic alliances, as described in Chapter 9).

Perhaps the major reason outsourcing is being used prominently is that few, if any, firms possess the resources and capabilities required to achieve competitive superiority in all primary and support activities. With respect to technologies, for example, research suggests that few companies can afford to develop internally all the technologies that might lead to competitive advantage in the future. By nurturing a few core competencies, the firm increases its probability of developing a competitive advantage. Additionally, by outsourcing activities in which it lacks capabilities, the firm can concentrate fully on those areas in which it can create value.[89]

Universities are outsourcing food service and bookstore management. For instance, Marriott and Aramark have license agreements with Burger King, Blimpies, and other franchises to establish restaurants on university campuses. More than half of the 3,500 U.S. campuses now have at least one national brand restaurant. Similarly, Follett College Stores and Barnes & Noble bookstores operate 550 and 360 university bookstores, respectively.[90] Also, universities are turning to private firms to run dorms. Because on-campus housing is costly to build and universities are unsure about continued enrollments, there is reluctance to build new dorms. In Texas more than a dozen institutions have made arrangements with private developers to build space for about 6,500 students. The largest managers are American Campus Lifestyles, Camden Property Trust, and Century Development.[91] University administrators are trying to focus on their core mission—education.

Boeing Co. has decided to expand its outsourcing program. To increase efficiency and eventually save an estimated $600 million annually, the firm has elected to buy more aircraft components and parts from outside suppliers instead of making them. Airplane doors, landing gear components, interiors, and control surfaces are examples of products Boeing decided to outsource. Core products such as engine struts and wings will still be manufactured in house. With these outsourcing decisions, the firm now manufactures approximately 52 percent of the components that comprise its airplanes, outside of engines. Of the remaining 48 percent, 34 percent is purchased from American suppliers with 14 percent coming from suppliers in other nations. Although some workers reacted negatively to Boeing's decision to outsource more of its work, the company felt that these actions were necessary to help it remain the largest aerospace manufacturer in the world. A review of the firm's choices suggests that no work was being outsourced in which the company's capabilities yielded a core competence that was a source of competitive advantage.[92]

When outsourcing, a firm seeks the greatest value. In other words, a company wants to outsource only to firms possessing a core competence in terms of performing the primary or support activity that is being outsourced. For companies to whom others outsource, being able to create value is the pathway through which they achieve strategic competitiveness and earn above-average returns.

When evaluating resources and capabilities, firms must be careful not to decide to outsource activities in which they can create and capture value. Additionally, companies should not outsource primary and support activities that are used to neutralize environmental threats or complete necessary ongoing organizational tasks. Called a "nonstrategic team of resources" in Figure 3.5, firms must verify that they do not outsource capabilities that are critical to their success, even though the capabilities are not actual sources of competitive advantage.

Another risk that is part of outsourcing concerns the firm's knowledge base. As discussed earlier in the chapter, knowledge continues to increase in importance as a source of competence and competitive advantage for firms in the new competitive landscape. In part, organizations learn through a continuous and integrated sharing of experiences employees have as they perform primary and support activities. One reason for the success of a learning organization is that with continuous and integrated sharing of experiences, it is able to evaluate thoroughly the ongoing validity of the key assumptions it holds about the nature and future of its business operations. Outsourcing activities in which the firm cannot create value can have an unintended consequence of damaging the firm's potential to continuously evaluate its key assumptions, learn, and create new capabilities and core competencies. Therefore, managers should verify that the firm does not outsource activities that stimulate the development of new capabilities and competencies.[93]

Occasionally, a firm discovers that areas in which it could perhaps develop a competence can and should be outsourced. For example, many believe that banks should develop a core competence in the area of information technology (IT). Following careful analysis of its resources and capabilities, however, managers at Continental Bank concluded that the bank lacked the skills required to develop a core competence in the IT area. As a result, the managers decided to outsource the firm's IT activities so the bank could "focus on its true core competencies—intimate knowledge of customers' needs and relationships with customers."[94]

In the next section, important cautions about core competencies are discussed.

CORE COMPETENCIES–CAUTIONS AND REMINDERS

An attractive attribute of a firm's core competencies is that, unlike physical assets, they tend to become more valuable through additional use. A key reason for this is that they are largely knowledge based.[95] Sharing knowledge across people, jobs, and organizational functions often results in an expansion of that knowledge in competitively relevant ways.[96] At Chaparral Steel, for example, the CEO believes that one of his firm's ". . . core competencies is the rapid realization of new technology into steel products."[97] As a learning organization, Chaparral extends significant efforts to verify that learning is shared across the entire firm. Thus, in a manner that is consistent with the most effective learning organizations, it seems that Chaparral Steel has a healthy disrespect for the status quo. Resulting from this "disrespect" is a commitment to constant self-examination and experimentation.[98]

Evidence and company experiences show that the value of core competencies as sources of competitive advantage should never be taken for granted. Moreover, the ability of any particular core competence to provide competitive advantage on a permanent basis should not be assumed. The reason for these cautions is due to the central dilemma that is associated with the use of core competencies as sources of competitive advantage. This dilemma is that all core capabilities simultaneously have the potential to be *core rigidities.* All capabilities, then, are both a strength and a weakness. They are strengths because they are the source of competitive advantage and, hence, strategic competitiveness; they are a weakness because if emphasized when they are no longer competitively relevant, they can be the seeds of organizational inertia.[99] Additionally, as explained in the Strategic Focus concerned with Toyota, some capabilities may be difficult to transfer even within the firm.[100] Toyota has had difficulties in transferring its productions systems to a U.S. environment.

Events occurring in the firm's external environment create conditions through which core competencies can become core rigidities and create inertia. "Often the flip side, the dark side, of core capabilities is revealed due to external events when new competitors figure out a better way to serve the firm's customers, when new technologies emerge, or when political or social events shift the ground underneath."[101] It really isn't changes in the external environment that cause core capabilities to become core rigidities; rather, it is strategic myopia and inflexibility on the part of a firm's managers that results in core competencies being emphasized to the point that strategic inertia strangles the firm's ability to grow and to adapt to environmental changes.[102] The experiences at Silicone Graphics, as described in the Strategic Focus, demonstrate these relationships.

STRATEGIC FOCUS

Silicone Graphics: Disappearing Core Competence

In 1997, Silicone Graphics (SGI) announced a layoff of up to 1,000 of its 10,500 employees. Furthermore, Edward R. McCracken, chairman and chief executive officer, stepped down after thirteen years at the helm. Additionally, SGI took a $50 million restructuring charge in 1997. Besides these internal difficulties, disgruntled shareholders filed a lawsuit against the firm. The plaintiffs alleged that SGI officers made "false and misleading comments" to "artificially inflate" the stock price while the company proceeded with a convertible debt transaction. Following the debt transaction and insider selling, the stock price fell from a high of $30 to $14 per share.

Silicone Graphics, Inc., has focused on making unique computers that manipulate three-dimensional graphics better than any other workstation. The dinosaurs on *Jurassic Park* were created on SGI machines. These machines are also used to design jets for Boeing and model cars for companies such as Ford. SGI's core strategy was to control the design of the microprocessor chips used in its computers. Although its products are scalable, which allows buyers to choose their entry point and then grow to larger systems, this focus may have turned out to be myopic. Until recently, this strategy has worked quite well for SGI. It allowed the firm to have close association between the microprocessor hardware and software development that could track the hardware chip design quite closely. It also facilitated its leadership in three-dimensional graphics and powerful Web servers. Having its core competence focus intertwined between both hardware and software became problematic as the Wintel standard (the combination of Intel chips and Microsoft software) began to increase in power and graphics capabilities. Furthermore, Microsoft's Windows NT seems to be approaching the de facto standard for corporate workstations. This is giving companies such as Dell Computer an advantage on servers using the Wintel standard. Because there is opportunity for software producers to make more money from a standard platform, these software makers inevitably write code for the Windows NT standard first, instead of closed platform producers such as SGI. For instance, Hewlett-Packard announced a machine to be used as a server that linked up to eight Pentium Pro Intel microprocessors running at two hundred megahertz each. The next version of Windows NT will enable up to eight microprocessors to work together. This type of "symmetric multi-processing" has been a standard practice in the Unix-based servers produced by Sun Microsystems and Silicone Graphics. Thus, the Hewlett-Packard and soon-to-follow products by Compaq and others are climbing the performance ladder and providing significant competition for the previous leaders in the workstation market.

Recognizing these difficulties, SGI sought to maintain its strategy by moving further up the performance ladder as well. In February 1996, the firm announced a planned acquisition of Cray Computer, the supercomputer maker. This would make SGI the number one high-performance computer company in the world. However, not only was the strategic value of the acquisition fuzzy, it added significant risk because Cray's research culture was much different than the fast paced one at Silicone Graphics. Thus, the acquisition of Cray Computer seemed to add to Silicone Graphic's woes rather than relieve them.

It may have been better for SGI to pursue software for the Wintel standard and manage its hardware business as a mature or even declining business. Focusing on software would allow SGI to take advantage of the Wintel standard and sell its graphics packages to those companies using this more high-volume approach. Of course, it is very difficult to change the strategic direction of a company when its core competence is built on high margin machines with proprietary operating system software and chips (hardware). Switching to a focus on market share from a focus on profit margin is also difficult when the core competence is built to create profit margins rather than market share.

SOURCE: Dow Jones Newswire, 1997, Shareholders file lawsuit against Silicone Graphics: *Wall Street Journal Interactive Edition*, http/wwww.wsj.com, December 3; L. Gomes, 1997, Hewlett-Packard to unveil computer with eight Pentium chips, *Wall Street Journal Interactive Edition*, http://www.wsj.com, December 1; R.D. Hof, I. Sager, and L. Himelstein, 1997, The sad saga of Silicone Graphics, *Business Week*, August 4, 67–68; R. Liu, 1997, SGI cuts jobs, CEO to leave, *CNN Financial News*, http://www.cnnfn.com, October 29; D. Darlin, 1996, The core problem, *Forbes*, February 26, 48.

FIGURE 3.8 ***Declining Competitive Advantage***

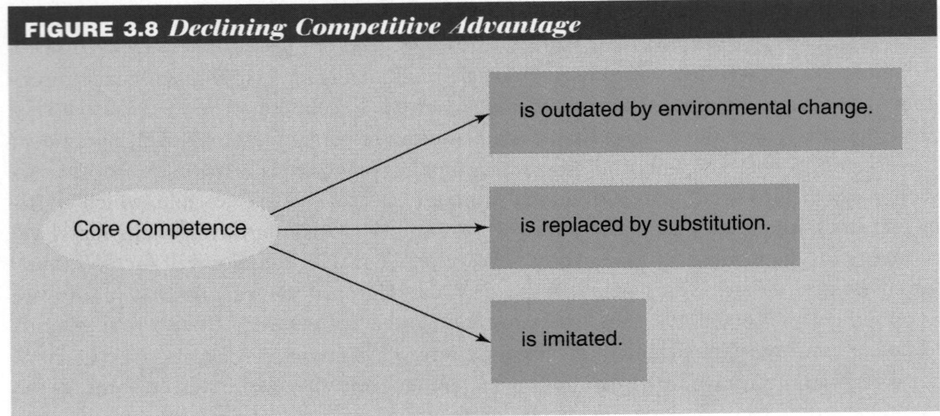

As evidenced by the Strategic Focus, managers operating in the new competitive landscape must remember that core competencies that are allowed to become core rigidities prevent the firm from changing when necessary. Firms that have achieved strategic competitiveness and earned above-average returns for extended periods of time are sometimes hesitant to change what they are doing. Capabilities are competencies only when they are strategically relevant; that is, when their use permits exploitation of opportunities in the external environment. Rapid and significant changes in the global economy prevent firms from permanently exploiting the same competencies. Firms failing to recognize this reality may quickly find themselves at a competitive disadvantage. Thus, executives must seek to strike a balance between nurturing and supporting existing core competencies while simultaneously encouraging the type of forthright appraisals that will cause the development of *new* competencies.

Figure 3.8 summarizes how competitive advantage declines. A firm may not adapt well to changes in the external environment, its core competence may be substituted by other firms and/or it may be imitated by competitors. All three of these things happened to Silicone Graphics. If it had been able to adapt and create a new competence, however, it may have retained its position.

STRATEGIC INPUTS AND STRATEGIC ACTIONS

Shown in Figure 1.1 in Chapter 1, the results gained through analyses of the external and internal environments provide the strategic inputs a firm needs to develop its strategic intent and strategic mission. The value of intent and mission is that they describe what a firm seeks to achieve in light of its internal competencies and external opportunities.

To close our discussion of strategic inputs, we offer a few final comments about intent and mission. Defined in Chapter 1, *strategic intent* is the leveraging of a firm's resources, capabilities, and core competencies (hereafter called capabilities for the purpose of this discussion) to accomplish the firm's goals in the competitive environment.[103] Recent evidence suggests that, indeed, successful companies competing in the global economy have learned how to leverage their capabilities to reach challenging goals.[104] For instance, Chaparral Steel's strategic intent may be captured by the following statement: ". . . the goal for every hour, the criterion for every person's activity, is crystal clear: make ever more steel, increasingly better than anyone else."[105] Other firms such as Silicone Graphics and Apple Computer may have overextended the firms' resources and capabilities. Apple, traditionally a niche player in education and publishing, sought to extend its capabilities into the business market, but because the company continued to focus on profit margins of its proprietary system rather than market share through an open systems approach, it was displaced by industry PC leaders such as Compaq and Dell.[106]

Strategic managers are challenged to stimulate the formation of stretch goals for each employee, even when some may not understand the importance of doing so. Individual stretch goals must be consistent with the objective embedded within the firm's strategic intent. When employees are motivated by a well-articulated strategic intent, properly established stretch goals leverage all of a firm's competencies and may create future success for both individual employees and their firm.[107] Moreover, when handled correctly, pursuing accomplishment of a firm's strategic intent ". . . causes employees to perform in ways they never imagined possible."[108]

The thoughts of an assistant brand manager at Procter & Gamble's location in Rotterdam, Netherlands, describe positive outcomes from the application of strategic intent. When first exposed to the firm's strategic intent, this employee thought to himself, "You've got to be kidding!" However, after working toward his personal stretch goals that were consistent with the firm's strategic intent, he concluded that the concept works! Describing his view about intent, the employee

Apple Computer, which had a niche in the education and publishing markets, may have overextended its resources and capabilities by trying to enter the business market.

stated that "Even though I might not reach a specific goal, I do get near it, and that is a greater achievement than I would ever have expected."[109]

Andersen Consulting is a firm stretching its capabilities to reach its strategic intent. Viewing itself as the "world's premier business and technology consultancy," the firm intends to become the world's first and foremost full-service consulting emporium, capable of serving clients by rewiring computer systems, recrafting strategies, reeducating employees, and reengineering work processes. Already earning more than 51 percent of its revenues from outside the United States, Andersen's work in 46 countries reflects its commitment to remain what some believe is the leading global consulting firm.[110] The capabilities Andersen is using to achieve its strategic intent include its knowledge, skills, and experiences in terms of logistics and operations strategies, total supply chain management processes, and information and technology strategies.[111] Challenging as it should be, this strategic intent may be reached through effective use of Andersen Consulting's capabilities and core competencies.

Strategic intent defines the framework for a firm's strategic mission. The strategic mission is a statement of a firm's unique purpose and the scope of its operations in product and market terms.[112] Because it specifies the products a firm will offer in particular markets, and presents a framework within which the firm will work, the strategic mission is an application of strategic intent.[113] In a small private school, for example, the strategic intent is the vigorous pursuit of excellence. The strategic mission flowing from this intent is to serve intellectually gifted or highly motivated students from a six-county region seeking a college preparatory educational experience.

In the case of all firms and organizations, once formulated, the strategic intent and strategic mission are the basis for the development of business-level, corporate-level, acquisition, restructuring, international, and cooperative strategies (see Chapter 4 and Chapters 6 through 9). The first of these strategy types—business-level strategy—is discussed in the next chapter.

SUMMARY

- In the new competitive landscape, traditional conditions and factors, including labor costs and effective access to financial resources and raw materials, can still provide a competitive advantage but to a lesser degree. In this new landscape, a firm's internal environment (that is, its resources, capabilities, and core competencies) may have a stronger influence on the development of competitive advantage and the formulation and implementation of strategies than do the characteristics and conditions of the external environment. But, no competitive advantage lasts forever. Over time, the benefits provided by all competitive advantages can be duplicated. Because of this, firms are challenged to exploit their current competitive advantage while simultaneously using their resources, capabilities, and core competencies to develop advantages that will be relevant in the future.
- Effective management of core competencies requires careful analysis of a firm's resources (inputs to the production process) and capabilities (capacities for teams of resources to perform a task or activity integratively). To complete these analyses successfully, strategic managers must be self-confident, courageous, and willing to hold people accountable for their work.
- Individually, resources are typically not sources of competitive advantage. Capabilities, which result from groupings of both tangible and intangible resources, are more likely to yield an advantage. A key reason for this is that how the firm forms, nurtures, and exploits core competencies that are

grounded in capabilities is less visible to competitors and, hence, more difficult to understand and costly to imitate.

- The skills and knowledge of the firm's human capital may be the primary basis for all of its capabilities. Capabilities of this type emerge by developing human capital and sharing information regarding how tangible and intangible resources can be combined in strategically relevant ways.
- Not all of the firm's capabilities are core competencies. Only capabilities that are valuable, rare, costly to imitate, and nonsubstitutable are sources of competitive advantage and, as such, can be selected as core competencies. Over time, core competencies must be supported and nurtured, but they cannot be allowed to become core rigidities. Competencies result in competitive advantage over the firm's rivals only when they allow the firm to create value by exploiting external environmental opportunities. When this is no longer the case, the firm's attention must be shifted to other capabilities that do satisfy the four criteria of sustainable competitive advantage.
- Value chain analysis is used to identify and evaluate a firm's resources and capabilities. By studying their primary and support activities, firms better understand their cost structure and the activities in which they can create and capture value.
- In the cases of primary and support activities that must be performed, but for which the firm lacks the resources and capabilities required to create value, outsourcing is considered. Used frequently in the new competitive landscape, outsourcing is the purchase of a value-creating activity from an external supplier. The firm should outsource only to companies that possess a competitive advantage in terms of the primary or support activity being outsourced. Strategic managers must verify that their firm does not outsource activities in which it can create and capture value. Additionally, firms must avoid outsourcing nonstrategic capabilities that are not a source of competitive advantage, yet are important to the firm's ongoing efforts to develop continuously value-adding knowledge.
- Strategic intent and strategic mission are grounded in the results obtained through analyses of the firm's external and internal environments. Taken together, the results of environmental analyses and the formation of the firm's strategic intent and mission provide the information needed to formulate and implement an array of strategies, including business-level, corporate-level, acquisition, restructuring, international, and cooperative.

REVIEW QUESTIONS

1. Why is it important for firms to study and gain an understanding of their internal environment?
2. What is value? How do firms earn value and why is it important that they be able to do so?
3. What are the differences between tangible and intangible resources? Which of these two categories of resources typically contributes more to the development of competitive advantage, and why?
4. What are capabilities? How are capabilities developed?
5. What are the four criteria used to determine which of a firm's resources and capabilities are its core competencies? Why is it important for strategic managers to use these criteria?
6. How is value chain analysis used in organizations? What knowledge can strategic managers gain by using value chain analysis?
7. What is outsourcing? Why is it so valuable to companies competing in the new competitive landscape?
8. Why is it important for firms to prevent their core competencies from becoming core rigidities?
9. What is the relationship between strategic inputs and strategic actions?

APPLICATION DISCUSSION QUESTIONS

1. Several companies are discussed in the opening case. Which of these companies are likely to have a sustainable competitive advantage based on their human resource management capability?

2. Select a store in your local community from which you purchase items. Ask one of the store's strategic managers to describe the value the firm provides to its customers. Do you agree with the strategic manager's assessment? Did the manager describe the value for which you pay when purchasing goods or services from this store? If not, what might account for the difference in opinions?
3. For an organization or club in which you are a member, prepare a list of what you think are its tangible and intangible resources. Using the categories shown in Tables 3.1 and 3.2, group the resources you identified. Show your list to other members of your organization and ask for their assessment. Did they agree with your groupings? If not, why not?
4. Refer to the third question. Was it easier for you to list the tangible or intangible resources? Why?
5. What competitive advantage does your college or university possess? On what core competencies is this advantage based? What evidence can you provide to support your opinions?
6. Discuss how Silicone Graphics, as described in a Strategic Focus, could have overcome the change in its competitive environment and its potential loss of core competence. Please obtain information from business sources to support your assessment.

ETHICS QUESTIONS

1. Can an emphasis on developing a competitive advantage result in unethical practices such as the use of questionable techniques to gather information about competitors? If so, do you believe these unethical practices occur frequently? Please provide evidence to support your opinion.
2. Can ethical practices facilitate development of a brand name and a corporate reputation? If so, explain how.
3. What is the difference between exploiting human capital and nurturing human capital to arrive at a competitive advantage? Can exploitation of human capital lead to a competitive advantage? If so, how?
4. Ethically, are strategic managers challenged to use their firm's resources to help train members of their society to reduce the shortage of skilled workers in their country? Why or why not?
5. What, if any, ethical dilemmas are associated with the use of outsourcing? How should strategic managers deal with them?
6. What ethical issues do strategic managers face when they conclude that their firm cannot earn above-average returns if thousands of employees are not laid off?

INTERNET EXERCISE

Go to Coca-Cola's home page at:

http://www.coca-cola.com

Search the Internet for information on the Coca-Cola Corporation. After you have completed your search, make a list of the company's tangible and intangible resources (see Tables 3.1 and 3.2). How do both sets of resources contribute to Coca-Cola's sustained competitive advantage?

Strategic Surfing

An increasing number of companies are establishing "internal" or "corporate" universities to facilitate their training needs and help build core competencies. Corporations are using this innovative concept to strengthen their internal environments. Following are several examples of corporate universities:

Motorola University:

http://www.mot.com/MU

Sears University:

http://www.sears.com/company/hr/suniv.html

Iams University:

http://www.iams.com/employ/universi.html

Dell University:

http://www.dell.com/dell/careers/benefits/dellu.htm

Intel University:

http://wiche.edu/telecom/membership/Sharing/forms/techintel.html

NOTES

1. M. A. Huselid, S. E. Jackson, and R. S. Schuler, Technical and strategic human resource management effectiveness as determinants of firm performance, *Academy of Management Journal* 40: 171–188.
2. D. J. Teece, G. Pisano, and A. Shuen, 1997, Dynamic capabilities and strategic management, *Strategic Management Journal* 18: 509–534; R. G. McGrath, I. C. MacMillan, and S. Venkataraman, 1995, Defining and developing competence: A strategic process paradigm, *Strategic Management Journal* 16: 251–275.
3. B. Morris, 1996, The brand's the thing, *Fortune*, March 4, 72–80.
4. P. Sellers, 1996, Can Home Depot fix its sagging stock? *Fortune*, March 4, 139–146.
5. P. C. Godfrey and C. W. L. Hill, 1995, The problem of unobservables in strategic management research, *Strategic Management Journal* 16: 519–533.
6. D. Leonard-Barton, 1995, *Wellsprings of Knowledge: Building and Sustaining the Sources of Innovation* (Boston: Harvard Business School Press); McGrath, MacMillan, and Venkataraman, 1995, Defining and developing competence, 253.
7. A. Reinhardt, I. Sager, and P. Burrows, 1997, Can Andy Grow keep profits up in an era of cheap PCs?, *Business Week*, December 22, 70–77; R. E. Stross, 1997, Mr. Gates builds his brain trust, *Fortune*, December 8, 84–98.
8. Godfrey and Hill, 1995, The problem of unobservables, 522.
9. J. B. Barney, 1996, The resource-based theory of the firm, *Organization Science* 7: 469–480; M. E. Porter, 1996, What is strategy? *Harvard Business Review* 74, no. 6: 61–78.
10. A. Mehra, 1996, Resource and market based determinants of performance in the U.S. banking industry, *Strategic Management Journal* 17: 307–322; J. Pfeffer, 1994, *Competitive Advantage Through People: Unleashing the Power of the Work Force* (Boston: Harvard Business School Press), 6–14.
11. F. R. Bleakley, 1997, New round of layoffs may be beginning, *Wall Street Journal*, November 13, A2.
12. R. Henderson and W. Mitchell, 1997, The interaction of organizational and competitive influences on strategy and performance, *Strategic Management Journal* 18 (Summer Special Issue), 5–14; A. A. Lado, N. G. Boyd, and S. C. Hanlon, 1997, Competition, cooperation and the search for economic rents: A syncretic model, *Academy of Management Review* 22: 110–141; Porter, 1996, What is strategy?; J. B. Barney, 1995, Looking inside for competitive advantage, *Academy of Management Journal Executive* IX, no. 4: 59–60.
13. S. Ghoshal and C. A. Bartlett, 1995, Changing the role of top management: Beyond structure to processes, *Harvard Business Review* 73, no. 1: 96.
14. Barney, 1996, Resource-based theory; Porter, 1996, What is strategy?; M. A. Peteraf, 1993, The cornerstones of competitive strategy: A resource-based view, *Strategic Management Journal* 14: 179–191.
15. Porter, 1996, What is strategy?, 61.
16. K. E. Marino, 1996, Developing consensus on firm competencies and capabilities, *Academy of Management Executive* X, no. 3: 40–51.
17. T. A. Stewart, 1997, Does anyone around here know. . . ?, *Fortune*, September 29, 279.
18. C. E. Helfat, 1997, Know-how and asset complementarity and dynamic capability accumulation: The case of R&D, *Strategic Management Journal* 18: 339–360; C. M. Christensen, 1997, Making strategy: Learning by doing, *Harvard Business Review* 75, no. 6: 141–156; R. M. Grant, 1996, Prospering in dynamically-competitive environments: Organizational capability as knowledge integration, *Organization Science* 7: 375–387; D. Lei, M. A. Hitt, and R. Bettis, 1996, Dynamic core competencies through metalearning and strategic context, *Journal of Management* 22: 247–267; H. Rheem, 1995, The learning organization, *Harvard Business Review* 73, no. 2: 10; G. Hamel and C. K. Prahalad, 1994, *Competing for the Future* (Boston: Harvard Business School Press).
19. A. Campbell and M. Alexander, 1997, What's wrong with strategy? *Harvard Business Review* 75, no. 6: 42–51.
20. C. Oliver, 1997, Sustainable competitive advantage: Combining institutional and resource-based views, *Strategic Management Journal* 18: 697–713; D. J. Collis and C. A. Montgomery, 1995, Competing on resources: Strategy in the 1990s, *Harvard Business Review* 73, no. 4: 118–128; B. Wernerfelt, 1995, The resource-based view of the firm: Ten years after, *Strategic Management Journal* 16: 171–174; J. B. Barney, 1994, Commentary; A hierarchy of corporate resources, *Advances in Strategic Management* 10A, 113–125.
21. J. H. Dyer, 1996, Specialized supplier networks as a source of competitive advantage: Evidence from the auto industry, *Strategic Management Journal* 17: 271–291; R. L. Priem and D. A. Harrison, 1994, Exploring strategic judgment: Methods for testing the assumptions of prescriptive contingency theories, *Strategic Management Journal* 15: 311–324; R. Amit and P. J. H. Schoemaker, 1993, Strategic assets and organizational rent, *Strategic Management Journal* 14: 33–46.
22. W. Boeker, 1997, Executive migration and strategic change: The effect of top manager movement on product-market entry, *Administrative Science Quarterly* 42: 213–236; C. R. Schwenk, 1995, Strategic decision making, *Journal of Management* 21: 471–493.
23. H. W. Jenkins, 1996, 40,000 job cuts! Where does he get off? *Wall Street Journal*, March 5, A15; McGrath, MacMillan, and Venkataraman, 1995, Defining and developing competence, 253.
24. D. Kunde, 1996, Self-control guru, *Dallas Morning News*, February 5, D1, D4; T. A. Stewart, 1996, Looking out for number 1, *Fortune*, January 15, 33–48.
25. M. Farjoun and L. Lai, 1997, Similarity judgments in strategy formulation: Role, process and implications, *Strategic Management Journal* 18: 255–273.
26. H. W. Vroman, 1996, The loyalty effect: The hidden force behind growth, profits, and lasting value (book review), *Academy of Management Executive* X, no. 1: 88–90.
27. W. Kiechel, 1993, Facing up to denial, *Fortune*, October 18, 163–165.
28. H. Ha, 1997, GM seen needing to cut production or raise

incentives, *Wall Street Journal Interactive Edition*, http://www.interactive.wsj.com, December 8.

29. P. Sellers, 1996, What exactly is charisma? *Fortune*, January 15, 68–75.
30. Teece, Pisano, and Shuen, 1997, Dynamic capabilities, 513–514; Barney, 1995, Looking inside for competitive advantage, 50.
31. McGrath, MacMillan, and Venkataraman, 1995, Defining and developing competence, 252.
32. T. Chi, 1994, Trading in strategic resources: Necessary conditions, transaction cost problems, and choice of exchange structure, *Strategic Management Journal* 15: 271–290; R. Reed and R. DeFillippi, 1990, Causal ambiguity, barriers to imitation, and sustainable competitive advantage, *Academy of Management Review* 15: 88–102.
33. R. Hall, 1991, The contribution of intangible resources to business success, *Journal of General Management* 16, no. 4: 41–52.
34. N. E. Grund, 1996, Reputation: Realizing value from the corporate image, *Academy of Management Executive* (book review section) X, no. 1: 100.
35. C. J. Fombrun, 1996, *Reputation: Realizing Value from the Corporate Image* (Boston: Harvard Business School Press).
36. R. Furchgott, 1997, Rebel without an engine, *Business Week*, September 15, 8.
37. T. A. Stewart, 1996, Coins in a knowledge bank, *Fortune*, February 19, 230–233.
38. S. Sherman, 1996, Secrets of HP's "muddled team," *Fortune*, March 18, 116–120.
39. McGrath, MacMillan, and Venkataraman, 1995, Defining and developing competence, 252; Porter, 1996, What is strategy?
40. J. B. Quinn, P. Anderson, and S. Finkelstein, 1996, Making the most of the best, *Harvard Business Review* 74, no. 2: 71–80.
41. T. A. Stewart, 1995, Trying to grasp the intangible, *Fortune*, October 2, 157–161.
42. Godfrey and Hill, 1995, The problem of inobservables, 522–523.
43. D. A. Aaker, 1996, *Building Strong Brands* (New York: Free Press).
44. S. Woolley, 1996, I want my Century 21! *Business Week*, January 15, 72–73.
45. B. Orwell, 1997, Disney is to enter restaurant business, and chain will sport an ESPN theme, *Wall Street Journal*, October 15, B6.
46. Fortune, 1996, Top stories for Monday, December 9, http://www.fortune.com.
47. A. R. Sorkin, 1997, Ad revenue on Web rises in first six months of 1997, *The New York Times* on the Web, http://www.nytimes.com, August 4.
48. Grant, 1996, Prospering in dynamically-competitive environments; Lei, Hitt, and Bettis, 1996, Dynamic core competencies; J. B. Quinn, 1994, *The Intelligent Enterprise* (New York: Free Press).
49. Stross, 1997, Mr. Gates builds his brain trust; E. M. Davies, 1996, Wired for hiring: Microsoft's slick recruiting machine, *Fortune*, February 5, 123–124.
50. D. Kunde, 1996, Corporations thinking ahead with chief knowledge officers, *Dallas Morning News*, January 14, D1.
51. T. A. Stewart, 1991, Brainpower, *Fortune*, June 3, 44.
52. Helfat, 1997, Know-how and asset complementarity; Lei, Hitt, and Bettis, 1996, Dynamic core competencies.
53. N. Dunne, 1997, US manufacturers see huge skill shortage, *Financial Times*, November 11, 4.
54. S. Kaufman, 1996, Firm offers essential high-tech component: People, *Dallas Morning News*, January 22, D2.
55. R. C. Monson, 1995, Firms worry about finding skilled workers, survey shows, *Dallas Morning News*, December 15, D10.
56. J. Landers, 1995, New jewel in the crown! *Dallas Morning News*, December 17, H1, H2.
57. F. F. Reichheld, 1996, Solving the productivity puzzle, *Wall Street Journal*, March 2, A1, A4.
58. R. Lowenstein, 1996, Why primary voters are so angry, *Wall Street Journal*, February 22, C1.
59. M. A. Hitt and R. D. Ireland, 1986, Relationships among corporate level distinctive competencies, diversification strategy, corporate structure, and performance, *Journal of Management Studies* 23: 401–416; M. A. Hitt and R. D. Ireland, 1985, Corporate distinctive competence, strategy, industry, and performance, *Strategic Management Journal* 6: 273–293; M. A. Hitt, R. D. Ireland, and K. A. Palia, 1982, Industrial firms' grand strategy and functional importance, *Academy of Management Journal* 25: 265–298; M. A. Hitt, R. D. Ireland, and G. Stadter, 1982, Functional importance and company performance: Moderating effects of grand strategy and industry type, *Strategic Management Journal* 3: 315–330; C. C. Snow and E. G. Hrebiniak, 1980, Strategy, distinctive competence, and organizational performance, *Administrative Science Quarterly* 25: 317–336.
60. M. A. Cusumano, 1997, How Microsoft makes large teams work like small teams, *Sloan Management Review* 39, no. 1: 9–20.
61. D. Leonard-Barton, H. K. Bowen, K. B. Clark, C. A. Holloway, and S. C. Wheelwright, 1994, How to integrate work and deepen expertise, *Harvard Business Review* 72, no. 5: 123.
62. Chi, 1994, Trading in strategic resources, 272; Porter, 1996, What is strategy?
63. C. Ames, 1995, Sales soft? Profits flat? It's time to rethink your business, *Fortune*, June 26, 142–146; S. Fatsis, 1993, Bigger is not necessarily better, *Waco Tribune-Herald*, January 17, B1, B6.
64. A. Taylor, III, 1993, Shaking up Jaguar, *Fortune*, September 6, 66.
65. R. C. Morais, 1997, A methodical man, *Forbes*, August 11, 70–72.
66. This section is drawn primarily from two sources: Barney, 1995, Looking inside for competitive advantage, J. B. Barney, 1991, Firm resources and sustained competitive advantage, *Journal of Mangement* 17: 99–120.
67. Barney, 1995, Looking inside for competitive advantage, 53.
68. Ibid., 50.
69. Ibid., 52.
70. Ibid., 53.
71. Barney, 1991, Firm resources, 108.
72. J. Huey, 1993, How McKinsey does it, *Fortune*, November 1, 56–81.
73. R. Reed and R. J. DeFillippi, 1990, Causal ambiguity, barriers to imitation, and sustainable competitive advantage, 88–102.
74. Leonard-Barton, 1995, *Wellsprings of Knowledge*, 7.
75. Sherman, 1996, Secrets of HP's "muddled team."

76. Barney, 1991, Firm resources, 111.
77. Amit and Schoemaker, 1993, Strategic assets, 39.
78. S. Caminiti, 1996, Will Old Navy fill the Gap? *Fortune*, March 18, 59–62.
79. Ibid., 60.
80. M. E. Porter, 1985, *Competitive Advantage* (New York: Free Press), 33–61.
81. G. G. Dess, A. Gupta, J-F. Hennart, and C. W. L. Hill, 1995, Conducting and integrating strategy research at the international, corporate, and business levels: Issues and directions, *Journal of Management* 21: 376; Porter, 1996, What is strategy?
82. T. A. Stewart, 1995, The information wars: What you don't know will you hurt you, *Fortune*, June 12, 119–121.
83. Calyx & Corolla home page, 1997, http://www.calyxandcorolla.com; Computerworld, 1994, Being the leader of the pack in the mail-order catalog industries doesn't require cutting-edge technology—just smart use of existing technology, *Computerworld*, March 7, 79.
84. D. Darlin, 1997, Channel change, *Forbes*, August 25, 80; D. Kirkpatrick, 1997, Now everyone in PC's wants to be like Mike, *Fortune*, September 8, 91–92.
85. Outsourcing: How industry leaders are reshaping the American corporation, 1996, *Fortune*, Special Advertising Section.
86. T. Box, 1996, Outsourcing to cut jobs in Arlington, *Dallas Morning News*, March 23, F1, F11.
87. M. R. Ozanne, 1997, Outsourcing: Managing strategic partnerships for the virtual enterprise, *Fortune*, Special Advertising Section, September 29, S1–S48.
88. J. W. Verity, 1996, Let's order out for technology, *Business Week*, May 13, 47.
89. H. W. Chesbrough and D. J. Teece, 1996, When is virtual virtuous? Organizing for innovation, *Harvard Business Review* 74, no. 1: 70.
90. M. Halkias, 1997, Fast-food firms, book sellers become big trend on campus, *Dallas Morning News*, September 8, D1, D8.
91. M. Totty, 1997, Flooded by students, colleges turn to private firms to manage dorms, *Wall Street Journal*, August 20, T1, T4.
92. J. Haley, 1995, Boeing strategy angers workers, *Daily Herald*, July 14, H2.
93. N. A. Wishart, J. J. Elam, and D. Robey, 1996, Redrawing the portrait of a learning organization: Inside Knight-Ridder, Inc., *Academy of Management Executive* X, no. 1: 7–20; D. Lei and M. A. Hitt, 1995, Strategic restructuring and outsourcing: The effect of mergers and acquisitions and LBOs on building firm skills and capabilities, *Journal of Management* 21: 835–859.
94. R. L. Huber, 1993, How Continental Bank outsourced its "crown jewels," *Harvard Business Review* 71, no. 2: 128.
95. J. C. Spender and R. M. Grant, 1996, Knowledge and the firm: Overview, *Strategic Management Journal* 17 (Winter Special Issue): 5–10.
96. Lei, Hitt, and Bettis, 1996, Dynamic core competences; Leonard-Barton, 1995, *Wellsprings of Knowledge*, 59–89.
97. Leonard-Barton, 1995, *Wellsprings of Knowledge*, 7.
98. Wishart, Elam, and Robey, 1996, Redrawing the portrait, 8.
99. M. Hannan and J. Freeman, 1977, The population ecology of organizations, *American Journal of Sociology* 82: 929–964.
100. G. Szulanski, 1996, Exploring internal stickiness: Impediments to the transfer of best practices within the firm, *Strategic Managment Journal* 17 (Winter Special Issue): 27–44.
101. Leonard-Barton, 1995, *Wellsprings of Knowledge*, 30–31.
102. R. Sanchez and J. T. Mahoney, 1996, Modularity, flexibility, and knowledge management in procut and organization design, *Strategic Management Journal* 17 (Winter Special Issue): 63–76; C. A. Bartlett and S. Ghoshal, 1994. Changing the role of top management. Beyond strategy to purpose. *Harvard Business Review* 72, no. 6: 79–88
103. G. Hamel and C. K. Prahalad, 1989, Strategic intent, *Harvard Business Review* 67, no. 3: 63–76.
104. P. Almeida, 1996, Knowledge sourcing by foreign multinationals: Patent citation analysis in the U.S. semiconductor industry, *Strategic Management Journal* 17 (Winter Special Issue): 155–165.
105. Leonard-Barton, 1995, *Wellsprings of Knowledge*, 8.
106. J. Heilemann, 1997, The perceptionist: How Steve Jobs took back Apple, *The New Yorker*, September 8, 34–41.
107. M. S. S. El-Namaki, 1992, Creating a corporate vision, *Long Range Planning* 25, no. 2: 119–121.
108. S. Sherman, 1995, Stretch goals: The dark side of asking for miracles, *Fortune*, November 13, 231–232.
109. H. W. Mentink, 1996, An employee's goals, *Fortune*, February 5, 26.
110. J A. Byrne, 1995, Hired guns packing high powered knowhow, *Business Week*, September 18, 92–96.
111. 1996, Andersen Consulting advertisement appearing in *Wall Street Journal*, February 6; R. Henkoff, 1993, Inside Andersen's army of advice, *Fortune*, October 4, 78–86.
112. R. D. Ireland and M. A. Hitt, 1992, Mission statements: Importance, challenge and recommendations for development, *Business Horizons* 35, no. 3: 34–42.
113. C. Marshall, 1996, A sense of mission, *The Strategist* 7, no. 4: 14–16.

Strategic Actions: Strategy Formulation

Chapters

4 Business-Level Strategy
5 Competitive Dynamics
6 Corporate-Level Strategy
7 Acquisition and Restructuring Strategies
8 International Strategy
9 Cooperative Strategy

Business-Level Strategy

CHAPTER 4

Learning Objectives

After reading this chapter, you should be able to:

1. Define strategy and explain business-level strategies.
2. Describe the relationship between customers and business-level strategies.
3. Discuss the issues firms consider when evaluating customers in terms of *who*, *what*, and *how*.
4. Define the integrated low-cost/differentiation strategy and discuss its increasing importance in the new competitive landscape.
5. Describe the capabilities necessary to develop competitive advantage through the cost leadership, differentiation, focused low-cost, focused differentiation, and the integrated low-cost/differentiation business-level strategies.
6. Explain the risks associated with each of the five business-level strategies.

Focus Strategies: Achieving Strategic Competitiveness by Serving Narrow Market Segments

A Danish company Bang & Olufsen manufactures upscale electronics products. Using its core competencies in product design and manufacturing, the firm produces an array of what have been labeled as "fantastic-looking" luxury items. Among its offerings are $1,800 to $5,000 stereo speakers, and $15,000 television sets. Striving deliberately for high style and quality, the firm's top-of-the-line products are targeted to audiophiles and video buffs that are willing to pay premium prices. In describing the company's product design, Ole Bek, director of Bang & Olufsen's international distribution center, noted that he learns much more by window shopping at Louis Vuitton in Paris than by looking at consumer electronics outlets.

http://
http://www.snapon.com
http://www.iamsco.com

To highlight more clearly and consistently the uniqueness of its products and to better serve the specialized interests and needs of its target customers, the firm decided recently to launch a string of impeccably designed stores that sell only its own products. Simultaneously, Bang & Olufsen discontinued the practice of distributing its products through what it considered to be "downscale" shops. The practice of concentrating on its own dedicated shops as the primary means of product distribution is consistent with actions taken by other companies that serve upscale customer needs. Louis Vuitton, for example, sells its bags only in its own boutiques. Cartier International Inc. and Guicci Group have pulled their products from the shelves of hundreds of stores in the United States. The key reason for these withdrawals was to eliminate markdowns in the prices of their products. Moreover, selling products through its own retailing outlets allows Bang & Olufsen to move even further upscale. Doing this, the firm's executives believe, will allow the company to avoid having to compete against other electronics manufacturers on the basis of price. Bang & Olufsen recognized the disasters that have befallen other European companies (including Grundig, Ferguson, Brion Vega, and Telefunken) that tried and failed to compete successfully against primarily Asian manufacturers on the price dimension. This recognition solidified Bang & Olufsen's strategic decision to focus on the upscale, highly differentiated part of the electronics market.

Snap-on Tools also serves the needs of a particular customer segment. This firm's high-quality and high-priced tools are targeted to mechanics and other professionals who are deeply passionate about their tools, but have little time to shop for them. To deal with the time constraint faced by this customer group, the founders of Snap-on Tools developed a system through which the firm's products are delivered to customers on the same day of every week. In commenting about this strategy, one analyst noted, "Snap-on found a way to reach a group of customers who weren't being served and created a way to make its high-quality products affordable." Very successful, the firm's sales volume has grown from approximately $670 million in 1986 to an expected $1.8 billion in 1998. Snap-on Tools has exported its strategy of serving the unique needs of a particular market segment to other countries, such as Germany.

The Iams Company is another firm with a strategy that is built around serving the unique needs of certain customer groups. When this company was established in Dayton, Ohio, in 1946, pet food was relatively inexpensive, not very nutritious, and sold exclusively in supermarkets and some feed stores. Convinced that premium foods that could serve pets' nutritional needs would appeal to certain groups, Paul Iams, the firm's founder and an animal nutritionist, decided to bypass what had been the traditional distribution channels for pet foods. Instead of selling to supermarkets and feed stores, Iams went directly to veterinarians, breeders, and pet stores. Annual sales at this firm have grown from $16 million in 1982 to over $500 million. Study of the firm's success caused one analyst to observe, "In hindsight, I find it amazing that Ralston Purina and others didn't spot this market, but none of them did. A couple of guys in Dayton outsmarted a whole bunch of sophisticated marketers." Today, this firm continues to be guided by its mission: "To enhance the well-being of dogs and cats by providing world-class quality foods."

SOURCE: T. Brophy, 1997, Snap-on Tools Inc., *Value Line*, August 8, 1334; E. Davies, 1997, Selling sex and cat food, *Fortune*, June 9, 36; W. Echikson, Bang & Olufsen's class act gets classier, *Business Week*, October 20, 142F; The Iams Company, 1997, *The Iams Company Home Page*, October 20, http://www.iams.com.

The three firms mentioned in the opening case implement strategies that are intended to serve customers' unique needs. For this service and the high quality of the products being purchased, these companies' customers are willing to pay premium prices. Callaway Golf Company also strives to serve the unique needs of a particular group of customers. Offering products with exceptional performance capabilities, the essence of the firm's strategic intent and strategy is suggested by the following statements:

> Callaway Golf Company designs, manufactures, and markets high quality, innovative golf clubs. The Company's basic objective is to design and manufacture its clubs in such a way that they are demonstrably superior to, and pleasingly different from, competitors' golf clubs. The Company's golf clubs are sold at premium prices to both average and skilled golfers on the basis of performance, ease of use and appearance.[1]

To achieve strategic competitiveness and earn above-average returns, as Callaway Golf Company has done, a company analyzes its external environment, identifies opportunities in that environment, determines which of its internal resources and capabilities are core competencies, and selects an appropriate strategy to implement.[2] A **strategy** is an integrated and coordinated set of commitments and actions designed to exploit core competencies and gain a competitive advantage. In this sense, strategies are purposeful and precede the taking of actions to which they apply.[3] An effectively formulated strategy marshals, integrates, and allocates a firm's resources, capabilities, and competencies so it can cope successfully with its external environment.[4] Such a strategy also rationalizes a firm's strategic intent and strategic mission and what will be done to achieve them.[5] Information about a host of variables, including markets, customers, technology, worldwide finance, and the changing world economy[6] must be collected and analyzed to formulate and implement strategies properly. In the final analysis, the test of a strategy's effectiveness is its ability to allow the firm to offer a good or service to customers that provides greater value relative to the value provided by competitors' products.[7]

A **strategy** is an integrated and coordinated set of commitments and actions designed to exploit core competencies and gain a competitive advantage.

Recall from Chapters 1 and 3 that *core competencies* are resources and capabilities that serve as a source of competitive advantage for a firm over its rivals. Strategic competitiveness and the earning of above-average returns hinge on a firm's ability to develop and exploit new core competencies faster than competitors can mimic the competitive advantages yielded by the current ones.[8] When focused on the continuous need to develop new core competencies, firms are able to drive competition in the future as well as the present.[9] Thus, especially in the new competitive landscape, with its continuing globalization and rapid technological changes, only firms with the capacity to improve, innovate, and upgrade their competitive advantages over time can expect to achieve long-term success.[10]

As explained in this chapter, successful firms use their core competencies to satisfy customers' needs. The relationship between appropriate strategic actions and the achievement of strategic competitiveness is increasingly important in today's turbulent and competitive environment.[11] These relationships are shown in Figure 1.1 in Chapter 1. As displayed in that figure, a firm's *strategic inputs* (gained through study of the external and internal environments) are used to select the *strategic actions* (the formulation and implementation of value-creating strategies) that will yield desired *strategic outcomes.*

Actions taken at The Iams Company exemplify these relationships. Through an examination of the general, industry, and competitor external environments, Paul Iams envisioned an opportunity to serve a particular segment of the pet food market—people interested in providing their pets with high-quality and nutritionally sound food products. Today, The Iams Company is recognized as a world leader in dog and cat nutrition. Through work completed at the Paul F. Iams Technical Center and Animal Care Facility, the firm is able to continuously discover new ways to improve its products, and in doing so, the health of its customers' pets.[12] As is the case with Bang & Olufsen and Snap-on Tools, focused differentiation is the business-level strategy (defined and discussed later in the chapter) The Iams Company chose to implement to achieve strategic competitiveness and above-average returns.

The initial environmental opportunity pursued by The Iams Company was identified through careful study. Opportunities to continue implementing a chosen business-level strategy can also surface somewhat unexpectedly for established firms. For example, Anheuser-Busch's initial announcement of its intention to sell the Eagle Snacks unit so it could refocus on its world-leading beer business provided an opportunity for Frito-Lay (a division of PepsiCo) to expand its already dominant share of the salty snack market.[13] Similarly, in light of major competitors' financial woes (identified through study of the firm's industry environment), Luby's Cafeterias decided to aggressively build additional units in one of its key Southwest locations. Because of its superior financial position (a source of competitive advantage), Luby's CEO concluded that "The stagnation of our competitors from the standpoint of expansion has allowed us a unique opportunity to continue to expand. . . ."[14] The August 1997 shutdown of United Parcel Service Inc. (UPS) resulted in a decrease of 5 percent in the firm's shipping volume. Estimates are that the Teamsters' strike cost UPS at least $700 million in lost revenue. Feeling emboldened by the UPS customers they serviced during the strike, UPS competitors, including FedEx and the U.S. Postal Service, are aggressively seeking to take additional customers from UPS. Through its acquisition of Caliber System Inc., FedEx is attacking UPS on its home turf—nonexpress ground delivery. To gain business from UPS, the U.S. Postal Service is offering cheaper rates and invested $270 million in advertising in 1998 to inform people about its overnight and parcel services.[15] Additional information about UPS is presented in Chapter 6's opening case.

At a broader level, companies committed to the importance of competing successfully in the global economy constantly study developments in the world's markets to identify emerging opportunities to exploit their competitive advantages. The breakup of the former Soviet Union in 1991, for example, has resulted in numerous commercial opportunities, especially for consumer goods companies. To succeed in the Russian consumer revolution, companies are advised to ". . . quickly seize opportunities to position themselves, and then prepare for keener competition."[16] Firms must exercise caution, however, when entering emerging markets such as Russia. Although they are, indeed, the new frontier for many of the world's companies, emerging markets come with a mix of opportunity and risk. Companies should be aware of this reality. In general, firms that establish deep local roots and align their strategies with the long-term goals of the host country have the greatest likelihood of being successful.[17]

Rapid development of Poland is yielding opportunities that are somewhat unexpected for many types of companies. Some observers of the Polish business environment feel that Poland "is emerging as Europe's star performer" following a difficult beginning. Reasons for this emergence include a commitment among Polish firms to benchmark their operations against the world's best performers and the restructuring of state-owned corporations. Foreign investment in Poland is on the rise "because foreign companies see the potential of Poland's domestic market and its attractiveness as a supply base for both West and East." In light of the country's extensive infrastructure needs and the projects already on its books, Asea Brown Boveri (ABB) expects annual sales of $1 billion in Poland by 2000. (ABB's sales in Poland were only $260 million in 1994.) Korea's Daewoo Motor Co. selected Poland as its center for automobile production in Europe. In addition, "a number of French and German retail chains have also been quietly positioning themselves to supply Poland's rising middle class."[18]

Business-level strategy, the focus of this chapter, is an integrated and coordinated set of commitments and actions designed to provide value to customers and gain a competitive advantage by exploiting core competencies in specific, individual product markets.[19] Thus, a business-level strategy reflects a firm's belief about where and how it has an advantage over its rivals.[20]

A **business-level strategy** is an integrated and coordinated set of commitments and actions designed to provide value to customers and gain a competitive advantage by exploiting core competencies in specific, individual product markets.

Customers are the foundation of successful business-level strategies. In the words of one CEO, "When you get people focused on customers, it has a very remarkable effect" on the firm's performance outcomes.[21] Because of their strategic importance, we begin this chapter with a discussion of customers. Three issues are considered in this analysis. Each firm determines (1) *who* it will serve, (2) *what* needs target customers have that it will satisfy, and (3) *how* those needs will be satisfied through implementation of a chosen strategy. For Bang & Olufsen, *who* the firm serves is audiophiles and video buffs; the *what* (or customer need) the company satisfies is for premium top-of-the-line electronics components; and, *how* these customer needs are satisfied is through use of Bang & Olufsen's competitive advantages in product design and manufacturing.

Following the discussion on customers, we describe four generic business-level strategies. These strategies are called *generic* because they can be implemented in both manufacturing and service industries.[22] Our analysis of the generic strategies includes descriptions of how each one allows a firm to address the five competitive forces discussed in Chapter 2. In addition, we use the value chain (see Chapter 3) to show examples of primary and support activities necessary to implement each generic strategy successfully. Risks associated with each generic strategy are also presented in this chapter. Organizational structures and controls required for the successful implementation of business-level strategies are explained in Chapter 11.

A fifth business-level strategy that both manufacturing and service firms are implementing more frequently is considered in the chapter's final section. Some believe that this integrated strategy (a combination of attributes of the cost leadership and differentiation strategies) is essential to establishing and exploiting competitive advantages in the global economy.[23]

CUSTOMERS: WHO, WHAT, AND HOW

Organizations must satisfy some group of customers' needs to be successful. *Needs* refer to the benefits and features of a good or service that customers want to purchase.[24] A basic need of all customers is to buy products that provide value.

A key reason that firms must be able to satisfy customers' needs is that in the final analysis, returns earned from relationships with customers are the lifeblood of all organizations.[25] Relationships with customers are strengthened when the firm is committed to providing *superior* value to those it serves. Superior value is often created when a firm's product helps a customer enhance the business's own competitive advantage.[26]

The challenge of identifying and determining how to satisfy the needs of what some business analysts believe are increasingly sophisticated, knowledgeable, and fickle customers is difficult.[27] Moreover, it is only through *total* satisfaction of their needs that customers develop the type of firm-specific loyalty companies seek. The belief of the president and chief operating officer (COO) of the Ritz-Carlton® Hotel Company describes the relationship between total need satisfaction and customer loyalty: "Unless you have 100 percent customer satisfaction—and I don't mean that they are just satisfied, I mean that they are excited about what you are doing—you have to improve."[28] Although difficult to earn, the estimate that "raising customer retention rates by five percentage points increases the value of an average customer by 25 percent to 100 percent"[29] is another indicator of the value of loyal customers. Increasingly, databases are linked with customer retention rates. Among other useful outcomes, information gleaned from these databases allows a firm to tailor its offerings more precisely to satisfy individualized customer needs.[30]

Strategically competitive organizations in the latter part of the 1990s and into the twenty-first century will (1) think continuously about who their customers are, (2) maintain close and frequent contacts with their customers, (3) determine how to use their core competencies in ways that competitors cannot imitate, and (4) design their strategies to allow them to satisfy customers' current, anticipated, and even unanticipated needs.[31] The chairman of AlliedSignal, a manufacturer of aerospace equipment, automobile parts, and a range of engineered materials, observes that there is a near unanimous opinion in his firm that its businesses should be run primarily by customer-oriented processes[32] such as the four mentioned here. Companies study their corporate memory (research stored documents) to enhance their understanding of product attributes that may appeal to current customers. Through these efforts, it might be discovered, for example, that a product being evaluated for possible introduction to the marketplace is quite similar to one the firm produced and sold previously. By analyzing customer reactions to the earlier product, the firm may be able to enhance the value that the new, yet similar product can offer to customers.[33]

Who: Determining the Customers to Serve

Customers can be divided into groups based on differences in their needs. Doing this is more effective than deciding that the firm will serve the needs of the "average customer." Averages sometimes do not provide in-depth insights about an issue that is relevant to decision makers. Shown in Table 4.1 are characteristics of the average American, the average woman, and the average man. Although inter-

TABLE 4.1 *Characteristics of the Average American*

The Average American

- Watches television seven hours daily, makes 1,029 telephone calls annually and eats 198 meals out a year.
- Wastes 150 hours a year sifting through clutter searching for things.
- Receives 49,060 pieces of mail in a lifetime. A third of it is junk.
- Charges $2,750 a year on credit cards.
- Owns 16 denim items, including seven pairs of jeans.
- Laughs 15 times daily. The average adult cusses once every eight words at leisure and every 29 words at work.
- Eats 11,113 M&M's in a lifetime.
- Has 40 hours of leisure a week. In an average week, the average American parent spends six hours shopping and 40 minutes playing with the kids.

Average Woman

- Lives 78.6 years.
- Has a body with 28 percent fat.
- Owns 30 pairs of shoes.
- Tries on 16 pairs of jeans to find a perfect fit.
- Spends 15.7 minutes on her hair each morning.

Average Man

- Lives 71.6 years
- Has a body with 15 percent fat.
- Owns 15 dress shirts, six pairs of slacks, six sport shirts, five knit shirts and three sweaters.
- Spends four hours a year tying his tie.
- Devotes 3,350 hours to shaving during his lifetime.

Sources: Columbus Dispatch; *In an Average Lifetime* and *On an Average Day* (Fawcett Columbine) by Tom Heymann; *Your Vital Statistics* (Citadel) by Gyles Brandreth; *American Averages* (Doubleday) *by Mike Feinsilber and William B. Mead; The Statistical Abstract of the United States.*

esting, these descriptors are of less value to a company seeking to target customers than attributes and needs associated with *specific* and *identifiable* customer segments.

Almost any identifiable human or organizational characteristic can be used to subdivide a large potential market into segments that differ from one another in terms of that characteristic.[34] Common characteristics on which customers' needs vary include (1) demographic variables (e.g., age, gender, income, occupation, education, race, nationality, and social class), (2) geographic segmentation (e.g., regions, countries, states, counties, cities, and towns), (3) lifestyle choices (lifestyle refers to a set of values or tastes exhibited by a group of customers, especially as they are reflected in consumption patterns[35]), (4) individual personality traits, (5) consumption patterns (e.g., usage rate and brand loyalty), (6) industry structural characteristics, and (7) organizational size.[36]

Recent experiences at Kmart demonstrate the importance of continuously focusing on the needs of a firm's target customer group. Kmart's core U.S. customer is over 55 years of age with an average income of under $20,000 and no children at home. Wal-Mart's average customer is under 44 and has an annual income of slightly under $40,000. These data suggest that compared to competitor Wal-Mart, Kmart's core customer seeks to purchase discounted products. Recent surveys also show that only 19 percent of Kmart shoppers are loyal to the chain. In comparison, 46 percent of Wal-Mart's customers are considered to be loyal (recall our earlier discussion about the positive effects of customer loyalty).

Even though women in the 25–44 age group are an important customer group for Kmart, the firm continues to experience weak results in women's apparel. Analysts believe that the primary reason for this weakness is that Kmart's women's apparel has become geared for a crowd that is younger than the 25- to 44-year-old group. The failure to serve effectively the needs of its target customers may be contributing to the lack of productivity at Kmart's stores as compared to Wal-Mart and Target. Kmart averages $195 in sales per square foot, as compared to $350 at Wal-Mart and $240 at Target. In late 1997, Kmart, one of the world's largest mass merchandise retailers, announced that it was offering early retirement to 28,500 hourly employees, or 11 percent of its workforce. This decision was made to reduce its high operating costs, but analysts have concluded that Kmart will not be able to return its core stores to healthy profitability until the core merchandising problems are solved.[37]

Increasing Segmentation of Markets In the new competitive landscape, many firms have become adept at identifying precise differences among customers' needs. Armed with these understandings, companies segment customers into *competitively relevant groups*—groups of customers with unique needs. As shown by the following statement, General Motors believes that four of its automobile product groups serve the unique needs of four competitively relevant groups: "The Chevy is squarely aimed at people shopping for a low price. The Pontiac targets performance enthusiasts. The Olds is for upscale buyers who might normally shop for import sport sedans, and the Buick will appeal to older buyers who want premium cars with conservative styling and room for six riders."[38] Named after a piece of legislation that was passed in the United States in 1972, Title 9 Sports sells athletic products to women of all ages. The firm's offerings are intended to support women's efforts to reach their personal fitness goals.[39]

In the United States, estimates are that at least 62 distinct classes of citizens exist, each with its own beliefs, aspirations, tastes, and needs. Some believe that, if anything, the trend toward fragmentation into smaller classes and subgroups is accelerating in the United States and throughout the world's markets.[40]

Nevertheless, companies' efforts to create a huge set of goods and services that is intended to satisfy unique needs may be confusing for some customers. This confusion can result from the sheer number of products available to consumers, particularly those in the United States. In fact, Americans today face by far the widest array of options they have ever confronted. The average number of items in a grocery store grew from 24,531 to over 30,000 between 1987 and 1997. During this time period, new products emerged on grocers' shelves at incredible rates, resulting in a peak of over 22,000 introductions in 1995. Of these introductions, nearly 70 percent fail. Given these realities, companies are challenged to provide sufficient detail to their target customers regarding the superiority of their product relative to competitors' offerings.[41]

U.S. teenagers represent a large but competitively relevant group whose purchasing power continues to expand (some of the spending patterns of this group are shown in Table 4.2). Teenagers are the target customer at Gadzooks, a successful specialty retailer of clothing and accessories. Just because individuals are 15 years old, says a Gadzooks store manager, doesn't mean they don't deserve good service.[42] JCPenney Co. uses its competitive advantage of private brands to design, manufacture, and sell its Arizona jeans. Launched in 1989, this brand is targeted to and driven by teens. In only five years, sales from the brand's tops, jeans, and

American consumers are confronted with over 30,000 products in the grocery store. In 1995, over 22,000 products were introduced, with approximately 70 percent doomed to failure.

jackets exceeded $500 million. In discussing reasons for the Arizona brand's success, a Penney's spokeswoman observed that teenagers identify with the brand, ". . . and even have given the brand their own pet name. They're calling it Zonez—with a 'z' at the end."[43]

Evidence suggests, though, that teenagers can be fickle customers. For example, during a recent spring season, Gadzooks carried a full stock of "retro" wear such as lizard-skin bell bottoms. Unfortunately for the firm, young shoppers failed to materialize as buyers for these items. After trying on a pair of the lizard-skin bell bottoms, a 15-year-old noted that while the clothing item was "cool," she had no interest in wearing it. In evaluating this situation, Gadzook's CEO observed

TABLE 4.2 ***Spending Patterns of United States' Teenagers***

- They eat a lot, spending an average of $2,648.36 a year on food. As a group that is $64.48 billion a year, not including what parents purchase on weekly shopping trips to the supermarket.
- They read little. They spend an average of $13.82 a year on books for a total of $120.7 million.
- They like music, spending an average of $17.40 on compact disks and $12.96 on cassette tapes a year. Annual tab: $195.4 million on CDs and $129.6 million on tapes.
- Teens fork over an average of $62.10 a year of their own money for jeans or about $1 billion as a group.
- Teens spend an average of $95.35 of their own money each year for sneakers and athletic shoes. That represents about $1.4 billion a year.

Source: Simmons Market Research Bureau Inc. as reported in M. Halkias, 1995, To buy for—at least today, *Dallas Morning News,* October 14, F1, F2.

that his firm is in the business of trends and that, this time, it simply missed on its prediction about the popularity of retro wear.[44] Similarly, Guess clothing items appear to be losing some of their appeal to teenagers. By late 1997, the brand that teenagers judged third in "coolness" only two years earlier had fallen to number 23. Some analysts feel that the firm's products are no longer as innovative as they were in the 1980s. During a recent shopping trip, one teenager, for example, was observed to pass by Guess's low-waist, deep-blue-rinse jeans (priced at $48 per pair) in favor of a $39 pair of Levi's. When asked what drove her decision, the teen said simply, "Levi's are much cooler than Guess."[45]

What: Determining the Customer Needs to Satisfy

As a firm decides who it will serve, it must simultaneously identify the needs of the chosen customer group that its goods or services can satisfy. Top-level managers play a critical role in efforts to recognize and understand customers' needs. Their capacity to gain valuable insights from listening to and studying customers influences product, technology, and distribution decisions.

At Staples, which is the second-largest office supply superstore chain in the United States, top-level managers spend significant amounts of time analyzing reports about their customers' buying habits and solving customer problems. Spending executive time in this manner sends a strong signal to all employees that "Staples cares deeply, very deeply, about [understanding and] pleasing customers."[46] These efforts by top-level managers may contribute meaningfully to the firm's superior performance. Annual sales in 1998 were expected to increase by approximately 30 percent as compared to 1997. This rapid sales growth is four times faster than the overall North American office-supply-distribution industry. To further fuel its growth, Staples intends to continue with an aggressive store-opening program and to spend additional time seeking success in European markets.[47] Thus, in firms that achieve strategic competitiveness, such as Staples, customer contact is a key responsibility for top-level managers as well as marketing and sales personnel.[48]

An additional competitive advantage accrues to firms capable of anticipating and then satisfying needs that were unknown to target customers. Firms able to do this provide customers with unexpected value—that is, a product performance capability or characteristic they did not request, yet do value.[49] Moreover, anticipating customers' needs yields opportunities for firms to shape their industry's future and gain an early competitive advantage (an early competitive advantage is called a *first mover advantage* and is discussed in Chapter 5). For example, Sprint, a diversified telecommunications company, believes that it "set the standard in long distance with its fiber optic network." In terms of the future, the firm also believes that "by joining with our cable partners in a revolutionary venture, we will be setting the standard once again. We're creating the blueprint that other communications companies will have to follow: a new kind of company that delivers the entire interconnected world of globe-spanning voice, video and data—all from a single source."[50]

How: Determining Core Competencies Necessary to Satisfy Customers' Needs

Firms use their core competencies to implement value-creating strategies and satisfy customers' needs. One of the strategic imperatives at IBM is to more quickly convert the firm's technological competence into commercial products that customers value. IBM's intensive knowledge of its customers' businesses helps the firm accomplish this objective.[51] Honda's motorcycle, car, lawn mower, and generator businesses are all based on the company's core competence in engines and power trains. Honda continues to bolster its commitment to research and development to strengthen this core competence.[52] At Canon, core competencies in optics, imaging, and microprocessor controls provide the foundation to satisfy customer needs in a range of product markets including copiers, laser printers, cameras, and image scanners. One of the most solid and trusted suppliers in the electronics and computer industries, Hewlett-Packard uses its engineering core competence to manufacture products that are renowned for their quality.[53]

Next, we discuss the business-level strategies firms implement in the pursuit of strategic competitiveness and above-average returns.

TYPES OF BUSINESS-LEVEL STRATEGY

Business-level strategies are concerned with a firm's industry position relative to competitors.[54] Companies that have established favorable industry positions are better able to cope with the five forces of competition (see Chapter 2). To position itself, a firm must decide if its intended actions will allow it to perform activities differently or to perform different activities than its rivals.[55] Thus, favorably positioned firms may have a competitive advantage over their industry rivals. This is important in that the universal objective of all companies is to develop and sustain competitive advantages.[56]

Originally, it was determined that firms choose from among four generic business-level strategies to establish and exploit a competitive advantage within a particular competitive scope: *cost leadership*, *differentiation*, *focused low cost*, and *focused differentiation* (see Figure 4.1). A fifth generic business-level strategy, the integrated low-cost/differentiation strategy, has evolved through firms' efforts to find the most effective ways to exploit their competitive advantages.

When selecting a business-level strategy, firms evaluate two types of competitive advantage: "lower cost than rivals, or the ability to differentiate and command a premium price that exceeds the extra cost of doing so."[57] Having lower cost than rivals denotes the firm's ability to perform activities differently than rivals; being able to differentiate indicates a capacity to perform different activities.[58] Competitive advantage is achieved within some scope. Scope has several dimensions, including the group of product and customer segments served and the array of geographic markets in which a firm competes. Competitive advantage is sought by competing in many customer segments when implementing either the cost leadership or the differentiation strategy. In contrast, through implementation of focus strategies, firms seek either a cost advantage or a differentiation advantage in a *narrow competitive scope* or *segment*. With focus strategies, the firm "selects a segment or group of segments in the industry and tailors its strategy to serving them to the exclusion of others."[59]

None of the five business-level strategies is inherently or universally superior to the others.[60] The effectiveness of each strategy is contingent on the opportunities and threats in a firm's external environment *and* the possibilities permitted by the firm's unique resources, capabilities, and core competencies. It is critical, therefore, for the firm to select a strategy that is appropriate in light of its com-

FIGURE 4.1 *Four Generic Strategies*

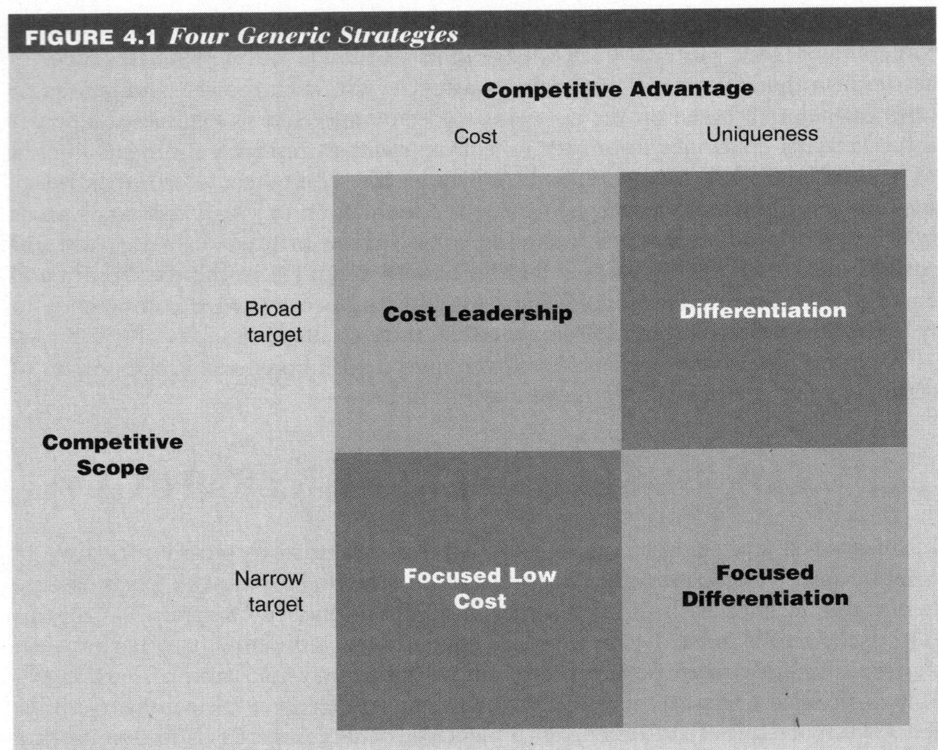

Source: Adapted with the permission of The Free Press, a division of Simon & Schuster from COMPETITIVE ADVANTAGE: Creating and Sustaining Superior Performance by Michael E. Porter, Fig. 1-3, 12. Copyright © 1985 by Michael E. Porter.

petencies and environmental opportunities; once selected, the strategy should be implemented carefully and consistently. Recently some criticized the Volkswagen group for what they saw as the firm's failure in terms of these strategic requirements. Indecision regarding the exact segments of the automobile industry in which the firm wanted to compete and how it intended to compete within chosen segments caused at least a temporary setback in the value of the firm's stock.[61]

Cost Leadership Strategy

A **cost leadership strategy** is an integrated set of actions designed to produce products at the lowest cost, relative to competitors, with features that are acceptable to customers.

A **differentiation strategy** is an integrated set of actions designed to produce products that customers perceive as being different in ways that are important to them.

A **cost leadership strategy** is an integrated set of actions designed to produce products at the lowest cost, relative to competitors, with features that are acceptable to customers. A **differentiation strategy** is an integrated set of actions designed to produce products that customers perceive as being different in ways that are important to them.[62] The differentiation strategy calls for firms to sell nonstandardized products to customers with unique needs. The cost leadership strategy should achieve low cost relative to competitors while not ignoring means of differentiation that customers value. Alternatively, the differentiation strategy should consistently upgrade a product's differentiated features that customers value without ignoring costs to customers. Thus, although their nature differs, firms can create value (recall that value is defined in Chapter 3 as the product's set of characteristics and attributes for which customers are willing to pay) through either cost leadership or the differentiation strategy.[63]

Firms seeking competitive advantage by implementing the cost leadership strategy often sell no-frills, standardized products to the most typical customers in the industry. In the new competitive landscape, it is increasingly difficult for firms implementing this type of strategy to differentiate between product features that are standard and those providing benefits that exceed the price the company's target customers are willing to pay.[64]

Successful implementation of the cost leadership strategy requires a consistent focus on driving costs lower, relative to competitors' costs. Firms often drive their costs lower through investments in efficient-scale facilities, tight cost and overhead control, and cost minimizations in such areas as service, sales force, and R&D. For example, Unifi Inc., one of the world's largest texturizers of filament polyester and nylon fiber, makes significant investments in its manufacturing technologies to drive its costs lower in an environment of upward pressure on prices of raw materials and packaging supplies. Already one of the most efficient producers in its industry, the company recently completed a modernization program for texturing polyester. Unifi also intends to modernize and expand its nylon, covered yarn, and dyed yarn operations. Combined, these actions are expected to increase the firm's technological lead over its rivals and further reduce its production costs.[65] Similarly, Nova Corp.'s chemical business is the low-cost leader in the manufacture of ethylene and polyethylene. To foster profitable growth as the twenty-first century begins, the firm intends to use its superior cost position to add pipeline miles in Canada and other locations in North America.[66]

Emerson Electric Co., a U.S. manufacturer that has earned above-average returns during both favorable and unfavorable economic climates, bases its operations on several principles—continuous cost reduction, use of state-of-the-art equipment, and open communications. The firm's adherence to these principles has resulted in impressive outcomes; "Adjusted for inflation, Emerson Electric's revenues have barely increased in the past half-dozen years. Yet in that period its earnings, cash flow and dividends per share have all increased by about 50 percent."[67]

As described in the Strategic Focus, the cost leadership strategy is being used in one of Dana Corp.'s business groups. While reading this Strategic Focus, notice the actions taken in one of the business group's plants to drive costs lower.

STRATEGIC FOCUS

Manufacturing a Truck Chassis: Dana Corp.'s Efforts to Continuously Reduce Its Production Costs

Dana Corp. is a global leader in the engineering, manufacture, and distribution of products and systems for the vehicular, off-highway, and industrial markets. A diversified firm (diversification strategies are explained in Chapter 6), Dana is organized into seven core business groups. With facilities in approximately 20 countries and over one-half of sales revenues earned outside the United States, Drivetrain components is the most global of Dana's business groups. Technological skills are the core competence on which this group's actions and growth objectives are based. Use of this competence recently helped the group develop the ability to build a complete rolling chassis for trucks and off-highway vehicles.

Less expensive on a per-unit basis, being able to purchase this type of chassis is important to automobile manufacturers as they seek ways to reduce parts and labor costs in their assembly plants.

Since 1995, Dana's plant in Stockton, California (a plant that is part of the Drivetrain components group) has been manufacturing truck chassis for a single customer: Toyota Motor Corp. Critical to Toyota's selection of this particular supplier was Dana's agreement to strive for a 2 percent price cut in the cost of its product. This reduction, which was to be reached by 1997, created a need for the Dana facility to find ways to drive its costs still lower. Reaching this objective has proved to be difficult, however. In 1995, the Stockton plant was already producing its products at world-class efficiency levels. Moreover, the fact that this plant essentially serves as a link in a transcontinental assembly line constrains its flexibility in terms of seeking ways to drive its costs lower. Approximately every 90 minutes, the plant receives steel parts from a Toyota facility located in Japan. With roughly 180 parts and 115 feet of welding involved, Dana builds a truck chassis that weighs roughly 300 pounds. At regular intervals, completed chassis are sent to a Toyota assembly plant that is located 63 miles from Stockton.

To find ways to drive costs lower in what was already a world-class manufacturing facility, the plant manager decided that the only hope was to create a culture of inventiveness—a culture in which every worker was challenged to find more efficient ways to produce the truck chassis. Believing that no change was too small, the manager insisted that every worker learn each job in the plant (to understand how each part fits into the whole) and that no person be given a permanent assignment (to maintain a fresh supply of perspectives). Challenged to question absolutely every activity completed in the facility, even down to the sequencing of individual welds, workers were required to submit two ideas in writing each month. Always oriented to actions that would increase efficiency and reduce costs, 81 percent of these ideas proved to be worth implementing during the facility's first two years of operation. One employee alone developed 180 ideas in a single year. Included among these were the installation of backup welding guns and the use of an electronic eye to assist in placing a cross-member.

Continuous feedback about plant productivity is provided to employees through use of electronic signs, similar to gymnasium scoreboards. The reaching of every efficiency goal, no matter how small, is celebrated openly. Multiple reinforcements, including free sodas for a day, the hosting of a family barbecue, and financial rewards, are used to acknowledge workers' achievements.

In late 1996, the plant reached an aggressive and long-sought threshold goal of producing 33 units hourly. As soon as it was reached, a new goal of manufacturing 36 chassis per hour was set. Developing the efficiencies required to reach this goal would reduce costs further and contribute to achievement of the 2 percent price-cut objective. Although not yet reached (Dana cut Toyota's price by .84 percent in early 1997), the facility continues to seek ways to increase its efficiencies and reduce its costs.

SOURCE: Dana Corp., 1997, Dana Corp. Home Page, December 7, http://www.dana.com; J.W. Milner, 1997, Dana Corp., *Value Line*, October 10, 814; T. Petzinger, Jr., 1997, A plant manager keeps reinventing his production line, *Wall Street Journal*, September 19, B1.

As described in Chapter 3, a firm's value chain determines which parts of its operations create value and which do not. Primary and support activities that allow a firm to create value through a cost leadership strategy are shown in Figure 4.2. Companies that cannot link the activities included in this figure lack the re-

FIGURE 4.2 ***Examples of Value-Creating Activities Associated with the Cost Leadership Strategy***

Support Activities			
Firm Infrastructure	Cost-effective management information systems.	Relatively few managerial layers in order to reduce overhead costs.	Simplified planning practices to reduce planning costs.
Human Resource Management	Consistent policies to reduce turnover costs.	Intense and effective training programs to improve worker efficiency and effectiveness.	
Technology Development	Easy-to-use manufacturing technologies.	Investments in technologies in order to reduce costs associated with a firm's manufacturing processes.	
Procurement	Systems and procedures to find the lowest cost (with acceptable quality) products to purchase as raw materials.	Frequent evaluation processes to monitor suppliers' performances.	

Inbound Logistics	**Operations**	**Outbound Logistics**	**Marketing and Sales**	**Service**
Highly efficient systems to link suppliers' products with the firm's production processes.	Use of economies of scale to reduce production costs. Construction of efficient-scale production facilities.	A delivery schedule that reduces costs. Selection of low-cost transportation carriers.	A small, highly trained sales force. Products priced so as to generate significant sales volume.	Efficient and proper product installations in order to reduce the frequency and severity of recalls.

MARGIN

MARGIN

Source: Adapted with the permission of The Free Press, a division of Simon & Schuster from *Competitive Advantage: Creating and Sustaining Superior Performance* by Michael E. Porter. Copyright © 1985 by Michael E. Porter.

sources and capabilities (and hence the core competencies) required to implement the cost leadership strategy successfully.

When implementing the cost leadership strategy, firms must be careful not to ignore completely sources of differentiation (e.g., innovative designs, service after the sale, product quality, etc.) that customers value. Emerson Electric Co. implements what it calls a best-cost producer strategy—"achieving the lowest cost consistent with quality."[68] Thus, the firm's products provide customers with a level of quality that at least meets, and often exceeds, their expectations relative to the purchase price.

Recently some worldwide travelers expressed dissatisfaction with the value they received from budget-priced hotels. In the words of one customer in response to her stay in a budget-priced Paris hotel, "Budget to me means clean, comfortable service for a good rate. But what I ended up getting was mediocre for a high price."[69] This feedback shows that customers evaluate a cost leader's product in terms of its cost, relative to the benefits its features provide.

As explained next, effective implementation of a cost leadership strategy allows a firm to earn above-average returns in spite of the presence of strong competitive forces.

Rivalry with Existing Competitors Having the low-cost position serves as a valuable defense against rivals. Because of the cost leader's advantageous position, rivals hesitate to compete on the basis of price. Instead, rivals try to compete against cost leaders through some means of differentiation. In South America, for example, top-level executives at Disco SA concluded that they could not compete against giant retailers Wal-Mart and Carrefour of France on the basis of price alone. Offering products at prices nearly as low as its largest competitors, Disco believes that it provides more convenience and service to customers. Carrying a wide range of brands and perishables, Disco stores offer home delivery, telephone ordering, and child care. Strategically, the firm's executives believe customers will accept a slight increase in product cost in return for the store's conveniences and services.[70] However, if rivals do challenge the firm to compete on the basis of price, the low-cost firm can still earn at least average returns after its competitors have lost theirs through competitive rivalry.[71]

Bargaining Power of Buyers (Customers) Powerful customers can force the low-cost leader to reduce its prices, but price will not be driven below the level at which the next-most-efficient industry competitor can earn average returns. Although powerful customers could force the low-cost leader to reduce prices even below this level, they probably would not choose to do so. Still lower prices would prevent the next-most-efficient competitor from earning average returns, resulting in its exit from the market and leaving the low-cost leader in a stronger position. Customers lose their power, and pay higher prices, when forced to buy from a firm operating in an industry without rivals.

Occasionally, a firm's bargaining power allows it to transfer increased costs to customers. Recently, for example, Unifi incurred substantially higher costs for raw materials and packaging products, but because it is a dominant supplier in many of its markets (up to a 70 percent share in some), Unifi was able to pass through higher costs to customers.[72]

Bargaining Power of Suppliers A firm in the low-cost position operates with margins greater than those of its competitors. Recently, for example, Emerson Electric Co. earned a net profit margin of 9 cents per sales dollar, a figure "... that's far higher than the industry average."[73] Moreover, analysts' expectations are that the firm's margins should continue to expand, especially in light of its efforts aimed at productivity gains and lower payroll costs (gained partly by directing production to low-wage regions).[74]

Among other benefits, higher margins relative to competitors make it possible for the low-cost firm to absorb price increases from suppliers. When an industry is faced with substantial increases in the cost of its supplies, the low-cost leader may be the only one able to pay the higher prices and continue to earn either average or above-average returns. Alternatively, powerful low-cost leaders may be able to force suppliers to hold down their prices, reducing their margins in the process.

Potential Entrants Through continuous efforts to reduce costs to levels below those of competitors, low-cost leaders become very efficient. Because they enhance profit margins, ever-improving levels of efficiency serve as a significant entry barrier to an industry for potential entrants. New entrants must be willing to accept no better than average returns until they gain the experience required to approach the efficiency of the low-cost leader. To earn even average returns, new entrants must have the competencies required to match the cost levels of other competitors.

The low-cost leader's low profit margins (relative to the margins earned by firms implementing the differentiation strategy) make it necessary for the firm to sell large volumes of its product to earn above-average returns. At Acer, the firm's CEO notes that the margins on his company's products, including its personal computers, are "shell-thin." "But sell enough of them," he believes, "and a formula emerges: Low margins and high turnover can be a recipe for success."[75] The cost leadership strategy, and the resulting emphasis on high volume and low margins, are the foundation for the firm's 20-plus-year effort to become Taiwan's first global brand-name powerhouse, similar to IBM or Sony Corp.[76] However, firms striving to be the low-cost leader must avoid pricing their products at a level that precludes them from earning above-average returns and encourages new industry entrants. Another computer manufacturer, Packard Bell, is sometimes thought to price its products too low in efforts to gain volume. "A favorite with first-time PC buyers seeking the latest multimedia features at rock-bottom prices," Packard Bell is challenged to sell its products at prices that permit the earning of at least average returns.[77]

Product Substitutes As compared to its industry rivals, the low-cost leader holds an attractive position in terms of product substitutes. When faced with the possibility of a substitute, the low-cost leader has more flexibility than its competitors. To retain customers, the low-cost leader can reduce its product's price. With still lower prices and features of acceptable quality, the low-cost leader increases the probability that customers will prefer its product, rather than a substitute.

Competitive Risks of the Cost Leadership Strategy

The cost leadership strategy is not without risks. One risk is that the low-cost leader's manufacturing equipment could become obsolete because of competitors' technological innovations. These innovations may allow rivals to produce at costs lower than those of the original cost leader.

A second risk is too much focus. Because of their focus on continuously driving costs lower, firms implementing a cost leadership strategy sometimes fail to detect significant changes in customers' needs or in competitors' efforts to differentiate what has traditionally been an undifferentiated, commodity-like product.

Before Orville Redenbacher and Charles Bowman launched Orville Redenbacher's Gourmet Popping Corn, for example, popcorn was thought to be a humble, commodity-like product. Convinced that people would pay more for high-quality popcorn, Orville Redenbacher developed a popcorn hybrid that produced fuller popping corn. He also perfected harvesting and packaging techniques that minimized kernel damage. In a tribute to Mr. Redenbacher, who died recently at the age of 88, the executive director of The Popcorn Institute observed that "He pioneered the gourmet popcorn niche. He promoted it very effectively and helped bring popcorn to a new level of acceptance."[78]

A final risk of the cost leadership strategy concerns imitation. Competitors sometimes learn how to imitate the low-cost leader's strategy successfully. When this occurs, the low-cost leader is challenged to find ways to increase the value provided by its good or service. Usually, value is increased by selling the current product at an even lower price or by adding features customers value while maintaining price. Even low-cost leaders must be careful when reducing prices to a still lower level. If the firm prices its good or service at an unrealistically low level (a level at which it will be difficult to retain satisfactory margins), customers' expectations about what they envision to be a reasonable price become difficult to reverse.[79]

Differentiation Strategy

With the differentiation strategy, the *unique* attributes and characteristics of a firm's product (other than cost) provide value to customers. Because a differentiated product satisfies customers' unique needs, firms implementing the differentiation strategy charge premium prices. To do this successfully, a "firm must truly be unique at something or be perceived as unique."[80] It is the ability to sell its differentiated product at a price that exceeds what was spent to create it that allows the firm to outperform its rivals and earn above-average returns.

Rather than costs, the focus of the differentiation strategy is on continuously investing in and developing features that differentiate products in ways that customers value. Overall, a firm using the differentiation strategy seeks to be different from its competitors along as many dimensions as possible. The less similarity between a firm's goods or services and those of competitors, the more buffered the firm is from rivals' actions. Commonly recognized differentiated products include Toyota's Lexus ("the relentless pursuit of perfection"), Ralph Lauren's and Tommy Hilfiger's clothing lines (image), Caterpillar (a heavy equipment and manufacturing firm committed to providing rapid delivery of spare parts to any location in the world), Maytag appliances (product reliability), McKinsey & Co. (the highest priced and most prestigious consulting firm in the world), and Rolex watches (prestige and image).

A product can be differentiated in an almost endless number of ways. Unusual features, responsive customer service, rapid product innovations and technological leadership, perceived prestige and status, different tastes, and engineering design and performance are examples of approaches to differentiation. In fact, virtually anything a firm can do to create real or perceived value for customers is a basis for differentiation. The challenge is to determine which features create value for the customer.

Starbucks Coffee Co., for example, believes that listening—a vital component of customer service—is one way the firm creates value. A company spokesperson notes, "We expect our employees to listen to customers." Catering to customers who value being able to "travel the world without leaving home," the ResidentSea cruise ship has only 250 apartments. These units range from 1,105 to 2,700 square feet, including penthouses and duplexes. Prices began at $1.2 million for the smallest units and peak at $5.4 million for the largest ones. Each apartment is equipped with a private terrace and whirlpool, home entertainment center, and three separate phone lines for phone, fax, and Internet access. Shapiro Marketing provides value through its Tie Protector. This product uses a little screen that retracts from a tie clip, shielding the customer's tie from damage that can result from spills.[81]

A leading manufacturer of integrated circuits, Intel Corp. creates value through implementation of the differentiation strategy. Intended to meet the needs of current and future sophisticated software applications, speed, innovation, and manufacturing expertise are core competencies Intel uses to differentiate its products from competitors' offerings. Additional information about Intel and its differentiation strategy are presented in the Strategic Focus.

STRATEGIC FOCUS

Intel Corp.: Achieving Strategic Competitiveness Through the Differentiation Strategy

Market share is one indicator of the success Intel has achieved through implementation of its differentiation strategy. With nearly 90 percent of new PCs using its chips, Intel's annual sales exceeded $25 billion in 1997. Some analysts believe that the firm's sales volume may reach $50 billion by 2000.

To maintain and enhance the differentiated features of its chips, Intel allocates significant financial resources to research and development (approximately 8.7 percent of sales) and capital improvements. Through these allocations and investments, Intel has developed an ability to convert more rapidly to new process technologies it is using to manufacture higher speed microprocessors. At least in part because of these investments, Intel's 1996 gross margin was 56 percent.

Impressive innovations that result in greater differentiation between Intel's products and those of its competitors continue to flow. In late 1997, for example, Intel announced that it had discovered how to double the amount of information that can be placed onto a transistor. This innovation overcomes a fundamental barrier in the design of integrated circuits. Initially, Intel intended to use this breakthrough to create more powerful memory chips for an array of products, including cellular phones, networking equipment, video arcade games, and other consumer electronics items. With this technology, a digital answering machine could have twice as much room to store messages. At the time of its announced discovery, this technology was good only for flash memory—chips that retain information even after the products in which they reside are turned off. As such, it could not be used for regular computer memory or for microprocessors such as Intel's Pentiums.

A more stunning innovation was also made known to the public in late 1997. Considered to be Intel's next-generation microprocessor, the firm developed the capability of producing a chip that can process 64 bits of information at a time. This compares to the simultaneous processing of 32 bits of information that Intel's most recent chip can handle. Industry experts estimated that the new chip, with Merced as its code name, will operate at 900 megahertz rather than the 300-megahertz capability of Intel's then-faster chip, the Pentium II. Moreover, the Merced will have approximately four times the 7.5 million transistors included on the Pentium II chip. The Merced's novel design features a change in the fundamental instructions that tell microprocessors what to do. Intel intends to use the new chip in high-end computers in 1999. Current plans call for the Merced to appear in desktop machines sometime after 2003.

Because of the chip's complexity, Intel's competitors such as Advanced Micro Devices (AMD) and Cyrix Corp. will find it difficult to duplicate the Merced and its capabilities. Thus, the chip, and the technology on which it is based, may serve to differentiate Intel's products for a reasonable period of time into the future.

Competing aggressively against AMD and Cyrix is consistent with Intel's objective of retaining its dominant market position. Because of the proliferation of computers costing less than $1,000, and some PC manufacturers' decisions to buy chips for these machines from AMD and Cyrix, Intel has had to cut the prices of its Pentium chips at a faster and steeper rate than usual. In commenting about this, an analyst stated that "back in the 486 era, Intel very satisfactorily thwarted the bid by AMD for a share of the CPU market. It then was able to maintain a clear technology lead as well as margins, despite price reductions that made the rival's offerings obsolescent. Now, however, AMD claims parity in performance, and so does a new entrant, Cyrix." Even in spite of these competitive challenges, the general consensus was that Intel's strengths would allow it to continue differentiating its products and to earn above-average returns as a result of doing so, even after sharing some of its markets with others.

SOURCE: *Bloomberg News*, 1997, Intel to give chip details, *Dallas Morning News*, October 13, D3; Intel Corp., 1997, *Intel Corp. Home Page*, http://www.intel.com; *San Francisco Chronicle*, Intel says it can double data storage on transistors, *Dallas Morning News*, September 17, D2; E. B. Swort, 1997, Advanced Micro, *Value Line*, October 24, 1053; E. B. Swort, 1997, Intel, *Value Line*, October 24, 1061; D. Takahashi, 1997, Intel's chip innovations could scramble PC industry, *Wall Street Journal*, October 21, B4.

A firm's value chain can also be used to determine if it can link the activities required to create value through implementation of the differentiation strategy. Examples of primary and support activities that are used commonly to differentiate a good or service are shown in Figure 4.3. Companies without the core competencies needed to link these activities cannot expect to implement the differentiation strategy successfully.

As explained next, successful implementation of the differentiation strategy allows a firm to earn above-average returns in spite of the presence of strong competitive forces.

Rivalry with Existing Competitors Customers tend to be loyal purchasers of products that are differentiated in ways meaningful to them. As their loyalty to a brand increases, their sensitivity to price increases lessens. This relationship between brand loyalty and price sensitivity insulates a firm from competitive rivalry. Thus, McKinsey & Co. is insulated from its competitors, even on the basis of price, as long as it continues to satisfy the differentiated needs of what appears to be a loyal customer group. The same outcome is true for Tommy Hilfiger, as long as its "classic preppy . . . with a twist" clothes[82] continue to satisfy the needs of "America's multicultural society" for garments with unique features.[83]

FIGURE 4.3 *Examples of Value-Creating Activities Associated with the Differentiation Strategy*

Support Activities			
Firm Infrastructure	Highly developed information systems to better understand customers' purchasing preferences.	A company-wide emphasis on the importance of producing high-quality products.	
Human Resource Management	Compensation programs intended to encourage worker creativity and productivity.	Somewhat extensive use of subjective rather than objective performance measures.	Superior personnel training.
Technology Development	Strong capability in basic research.	Investments in technologies that will allow the firm to produce highly differentiated products.	
Procurement	Systems and procedures used to find the highest quality raw materials.	Purchase of highest quality replacement parts.	

Inbound Logistics	**Operations**	**Outbound Logistics**	**Marketing and Sales**	**Service**
Superior handling of incoming raw materials so as to minimize damage and improve the quality of the final product.	Consistent manufacturing of attractive products. Rapid responses to customers' unique manufacturing specifications.	Accurate and responsive order-processing procedures. Rapid and timely product deliveries to customers.	Extensive granting of credit buying arrangements for customers. Extensive personal relationships with buyers and suppliers.	Extensive buyer training to assure high-quality product installations. Complete field stocking of replacement parts.

MARGIN

MARGIN

Source: Adapted with the permission of The Free Press, a division of Simon & Schuster from *Competitive Advantage: Creating and Sustaining Superior Performance* by Michael E. Porter, Fig 4-1, 122. Copyright © 1985 by Michael E. Porter.

Bargaining Power of Buyers (Customers) The *uniqueness* of differentiated goods or services insulates the firm from competitive rivalry and reduces customers' sensitivity to price increases. Based on a combination of unique materials and brand image, Ralph Lauren's clothes satisfy certain customers' unique needs better than do competitors' offerings. A key reason that some buyers are willing to pay a premium price for this firm's clothing items is that for them, other products do not offer a comparable combination of features and cost. The lack of perceived acceptable alternatives increases the firm's power relative to its customers.

Bargaining Power of Suppliers Because a firm implementing the differentiation strategy charges a premium price for its products, suppliers must provide it with high-quality parts. However, the high margins the firm earns when selling effectively differentiated products partially insulate it from the influence of suppliers. Higher supplier costs can be paid through these margins. Alternatively, because of buyers' relative insensitivity to price increases, the differentiated firm might choose to pass the additional cost of supplies on to the customer by raising the price of its unique product.

Potential Entrants Customer loyalty and the need to overcome the uniqueness of a differentiated product are substantial entry barriers faced by potential entrants. Entering an industry under these conditions typically demands significant investments of resources and a willingness to be patient while seeking the loyalty of customers.

Product Substitutes Firms selling brand-name goods and services to loyal customers are positioned effectively against product substitutes. In contrast, companies without brand loyalty are more subject to their customers switching either to products that offer differentiated features that serve the same function as the current product, particularly if the substitute has a lower price, or to products that offer more features that perform more attractive functions.

As our discussion shows, firms can gain competitive advantage through successful implementation of the differentiation strategy. Nonetheless, several risks are associated with this strategy.

Competitive Risks of the Differentiation Strategy

One risk of the differentiation strategy is that customers might decide that the price differential between the differentiator's and the low-cost leader's product is too significant. In this instance, a firm may be providing differentiated features that exceed customers' needs. When this happens, the firm is vulnerable to competitors that are able to offer customers a combination of features and price that is more consistent with their needs.

Another risk of the differentiation strategy is that a firm's means of differentiation no longer provide value for which customers are willing to pay. Upscale retailer Bloomingdale's discovered that its focus on "glitz" as a means of differentiation no longer provided value to at least some of its customers, especially those shopping in the store's new locations. A review of the firm's situation resulted in one analyst concluding that "The mystique of the store hasn't been transferable" from New York City. Moreover, the analyst felt that the stores were "either too avant-garde or too humdrum. And in many cases, their prices were too high." In response to its situation, Bloomingdale's decided to emphasize comfort—a means of differentiation the firm thought would provide customer value—rather than glitz. Among other actions taken to focus on comfort was renovation of the chain's stores to provide customers with user-friendly designs.[84]

A third risk of the differentiation strategy is that learning can narrow customers' perceptions of the value of a firm's differentiated features. The value of the IBM name on personal computers was a differentiated feature for which some customers were willing to pay a premium price as the product emerged. However, as customers familiarized themselves with the standard features and as a host of PC clones entered the market, IBM brand loyalty began to fail. Clones offered customers features similar to those of the IBM product at a substantially lower price, reducing the attractiveness of IBM's product. Even currently, IBM's relatively new Aptiva line is failing to meet company expectations. In assessing the situation, one dealer observed that while the Aptiva is a "cool" machine, it simply costs too much for the features that it provides relative to the combination of features and price of products from competitors such as Compaq and Hewlett-Packard.[85]

Focus Strategies

In contrast to the cost leadership and differentiation strategies, a company implementing a focus strategy seeks to use its core competencies to serve the needs of a certain industry segment (e.g., a particular buyer group, segment of the product line, or geographic market).[86] A **focus strategy** is an integrated set of actions designed to produce products that serve the needs of a particular competitive segment. Although the breadth of a target is clearly a matter of degree, the essence of the focus strategy "is the exploitation of a narrow target's differences from the balance of the industry."[87] For example, the Dallas, Garland & Northeastern (DGNO) railroad firm runs from central Dallas, to Garland, and on to Greenville, Texas. Only a 92-mile line, the firm serves a segment (large firms including Kraft Foods and Sherwin-Williams) that is in need of rail transportation in a constrained geographic area.[88] Through successful implementation of a focus strategy, a company can gain a competitive advantage in its chosen target segments even though it does not possess an industry-wide competitive advantage.[89]

A **focus strategy** is an integrated set of actions designed to produce products that serve the needs of a particular competitive segment.

The foundation of focus strategies is that a firm can serve a particular segment of an industry more effectively or efficiently than can industry-wide competitors. Success with a focus strategy rests on a firm's ability either to find segments where unique needs are so specialized that broad-based competitors choose not to serve them or locate a segment being served poorly by the broad-based competitors.[90] When AT&T was in the process of selecting C. Michael Armstrong to replace then current CEO Robert Allen, smaller competitors began to move quickly to steal customers from the telecommunications giant. Behind these attempts was the belief that AT&T, as a broad-based competitor, was, at least at a point in time, poorly serving the needs of some segments.[91]

Value can be provided to customers through two types of focus strategies: focused low cost and focused differentiation.

Focused Low-Cost Strategy Using a double-drive-through format, Rally's Hamburgers Inc. implements the focused low-cost strategy. At the end of a recent year, Rally's had approximately 500 restaurants operating in 20 U.S. states.[92] These restaurants have limited menus and no indoor seating. According to the firm's CEO,

Rally's serves "the little-spare-time-or-cash crowd that McDonald's and Burger King have all but abandoned." Concentrating on the value-adding dimensions of price and speed, the firm recently sold and delivered to customers in 45 seconds a "fully-dressed burger, a 16-ounce soft drink and a good-sized fries for $1.97."[93]

No longer an independent entity, AST Research Inc., a maker of personal computers, is a wholly owned subsidiary of South Korea's Samsung Electronics Co., Ltd. This firm continues to struggle as it loses market share to larger rivals. To respond to its competitive challenges, AST decided, in December of 1997, to slash its worldwide workforce by over 1,100 jobs (about 37 percent of all employees). Additionally, executives concluded that AST could no longer compete effectively on an industry-wide basis. Now committed to implementing the focused low-cost strategy, AST is positioning itself as a company that can serve better the specialized needs of small- and medium-size businesses than can industry-wide competitors. Analysts, however, were not particularly optimistic, noting that "other leading PC makers are already pursuing that niche and that AST would be hard-pressed to separate itself from the rest of the pack."[94]

Focused Differentiation Strategy Other firms (such as Bang & Olufsen, Snap-on Tools, and The Iams Company, the firms described in the opening case) implement the focused differentiation strategy. The number of ways products can be differentiated to serve the unique needs of particular competitive segments is virtually endless. Consider the following examples.

Located in strip shopping centers that are accessible to the public, Sally Beauty Supply stores stock more than 4,000 hair, skin, and nail care products and salon equipment. Some of the chain's sales are to the general public, but the majority of its business is selling to professional hair and nail stylists. Because of its target customer, Sally Beauty Supply competes mainly with wholesalers rather than retailers. The key to the firm's success appears to be its ability to locate and offer new and "hot" products to a group of professionals that is interested in purchasing and using cutting-edge products. One analyst has suggested that the firm has "found a niche that others haven't tried to exploit."[95]

Other firms also implement the focused differentiation strategy, including Security Passions, located in Ciudad Juarez, Mexico. For less than $2,000, the firm will line a customer's favorite mink coat or leather jacket with material that is designed to deflect bullets from large-calibre handguns. Security Passions developed this product because its town is home to one of Mexico's most notorious drug cartels. Especially in the state of Texas in the United States, log homes are becoming popular. Aimed at middle-age professionals seeking upscale simulations of rugged living, technological advances are being used to build what are thought to be comfortable, yet unique dwellings. A fourth-generation bread baker is delighting customers throughout Europe with a variety of unique (and pricey) breads. Among the items he bakes are 10 different Bavarian and French loaves, two types of plaited Israeli cholla, loaves baked in a tin especially important from Australia to give a slice worthy of a sandwich, and a loaf with very expensive Italian sun-dried onions. Using its competitive advantages of unimpeachable quality and brand recognition, Patek Philippe, a family business, manufactures only 18,000 watches annually. Prices range from $7,000 for a plain wind-it-yourself Patek to $250,000 for a top-of-the-line model. In part, these watches are marketed as investments, which they seem to be. A 1989 limited edition that sold for $9,150 recently fetched $26,000 at an auction.[96]

Firms must be able to complete various primary and support activities in a competitively superior manner to achieve strategic competitiveness and earn above-average returns when implementing a focus strategy. The activities that must be completed to implement the focused low-cost and the focused differentiation strategies are virtually identical to those shown in Figures 4.2 and 4.3, respectively. Similarly, the manners in which the two focus strategies allow a firm to deal successfully with the five competitive forces parallel those described with respect to the cost leadership and the differentiation strategies. The only difference is that the competitive scope changes from industry wide to a narrow competitive segment of the industry. Thus, a review of Figures 4.2 and 4.3 and the text regarding the five competitive forces yields a description of the relationship between each of the two focus strategies and competitive advantage.

Competitive Risks of Focus Strategies

When implementing either type of focus strategy, a firm faces the same general risks as does the company pursuing the cost leadership or the differentiation strategy on an industry-wide basis. However, focus strategies have three additional risks beyond these general ones. First, a competitor may be able to focus on a more narrowly defined competitive segment and "outfocus" the focuser. For example, a firm might decide that it can better serve the specialized needs of one or the other of Sally Beauty Supply's two key customer groups—professional hair stylists and nail stylists. Second, a firm competing on an industry-wide basis may decide that the market segment being served by the focus-strategy firm is attractive and worthy of competitive pursuit. No longer content with its traditional customer group only, Home Depot now has plans to concentrate on more narrow segments that it has not tried to serve previously, such as people who make large-ticket home renovations. In addition, the firm has entered the institutional maintenance and cleaning business with its purchase of Maintenance Warehouse America Corp.[97] Because of its size and capabilities, firms now competing in focused market segments may be threatened by Home Depot's entrance into their market domains. The third risk of a focus strategy is that the needs of customers within a narrow competitive segment may become more similar to those of customers as a whole. When this occurs, the advantages of a focus strategy are either reduced or eliminated.

Next, we describe a business-level strategy that is being used more prominently in the new competitive landscape. A key reason for this is the requirements of global competition.

Integrated Low-Cost/Differentiation Strategy

Particularly in global markets, a firm's ability to blend the low-cost and the differentiation approaches may be critical to sustaining competitive advantages. Compared to firms relying on one dominant generic strategy for their success, a company capable of successfully implementing an integrated low-cost/differentiation strategy should be in a better position to adapt quickly to environmental changes, learn new skills and technologies more quickly, and effectively leverage its core competencies across business units and product lines.

A growing body of evidence supports the relationship between implementation of an integrated strategy and the earning of above-average returns.[98] Some time ago, for example, a researcher found that the most successful firms competing in low-profit potential industries were able to effectively combine the low-cost and differentiation strategies.[99] In a more recent comprehensive study, it was discovered that "businesses which combined multiple forms of competitive advantage outperformed businesses that only were identified with a single form."[100] Other research found that the highest performing companies in the Korean electronics industry were those combining both the differentiation and cost leadership strategies, suggesting the viability of the integrated strategy in different nations.[101]

A key reason firms capable of successfully implementing the integrated strategy can earn above-average returns is that the benefits of this strategy are additive: "differentiation leads to premium prices at the same time that cost leadership implies lower costs."[102] Thus, the integrated strategy allows firms to gain competitive advantage by offering two types of value to customers—some differentiated features (but often fewer than those provided by the product-differentiated firm) and relatively low cost (but not as low as the products of the low-cost leader).

Mabuchi Motor, a Japanese company, implements the integrated low-cost/differentiation strategy. This firm manufacturers the small electric motors that power compact disk players, toy airplanes, and car windows. Mabuchi's focus is singular and consistent. The firm's objective is to produce "high-quality products at low prices, but in limited variety." Approximately 99 percent of revenues are earned from the sales of motors. Costs are kept low by the firm's decision to design and manufacture a limited variety of its products. The company produces 4.9 million motors daily, but fills 55 percent of its orders with just 10 different models. These products are differentiated through the firm's "obsession" with its miniature devices. At a modern technical center, Mabuchi scientists constantly research ways to differentiate their firm's products from competitors' offerings, seeking ways to make their motors "lighter, quieter, hardier and cheaper." Indicators of Mabuchi's strategic competitiveness include control of more than one-half of the world's market for small motors and routine double-digit operating margins.[103]

Firms must be strategically flexible to implement successfully the integrated low-cost/differentiation strategy. Discussed next are three approaches to organizational work that can increase the strategic flexibility that is associated with implementation of this strategy.

Flexible Manufacturing Systems Made possible largely as a result of the increasing capabilities of modern information technologies, flexible manufacturing systems increase the "flexibilities of human, physical and information resources"[104] that are integrated to create differentiated products at low costs. A *flexible manufacturing system* (FMS) is a computer-controlled process used to produce a variety of products in moderate, flexible quantities with a minimum of manual intervention.[105]

The goal of FMS is to eliminate the low-cost versus product-variety trade-off inherent in traditional manufacturing technologies. The flexibility provided by an FMS allows a plant to "change nimbly from making one product to making another."[106] When used properly, an FMS can help a firm become more flexible in response to changes in its customers' needs, while retaining low-cost advantages and consistent product quality. Because an FMS reduces the lot size needed to manufacture a product efficiently, a firm's capacity to serve the unique needs of a narrow competitive scope is increased. Thus, FMS technology is a significant technological advance that allows firms to produce a large variety of products at a low cost. Levi Strauss, for example, uses an FMS to make jeans for women that meet their exact measurements. Andersen Windows lets customers design their own windows through use of proprietary software the firm has developed. Motorola successfully uses an FMS to customize pagers in different colors, sizes, and shapes.[107]

Effective use of an FMS is linked with a firm's ability to understand constraints these systems may create (in terms of materials handling and the flow of supporting resources in scheduling, for example) and to design an effective mix of machines, computer systems, and people.[108] As a result, this type of manufacturing technology facilitates the implementation of complex competitive strategies such as the integrated low-cost/differentiation strategy that lead to strategic competitiveness in global markets.[109]

Incorporated into firms' processes somewhat slowly at first, the number of companies anticipating their use of FMSs in the near future is substantial. For example, among U.S. firms with more than 10,000 employees, "68 percent of electrical equipment manufacturers, 78 percent of machinery producers, 93 percent of automobile makers, and 100 percent of aerospace companies expect to have some form of FMS by the year 2000.[110] Although these expressed intentions are impressive, it is interesting to note that according to a researcher's results, "the bulk of the major firms in Japan, Western Europe and the United States will have begun using FMS by (2000), but the percentage will still be higher in Japan than in the United States or Western Europe."[111] Contributing to the slower rate of adoption of FMSs in the United States is the reality that U.S. firms, as compared to European and especially Japanese companies, tend to require higher rates of return to justify investments in these systems.[112] Moreover, evidence to date suggests that Japanese manufacturing firms have derived greater benefits from investments in FMSs as compared to their U.S. counterparts. The cause of this outcome may be that FMSs are managed less effectively in U.S. firms.[113]

Information Networks Across Firms New information networks linking manufacturers with their suppliers, distributors, and customers are another technological development that increases a firm's strategic flexibility and responsiveness.[114] Recent changes in a range of information technologies facilitated the development of competitively valuable information networks. Examples of these technologies include CADD (computer-assisted design and development) systems, CIM (computer-integrated manufacturing) systems, and EDI (electronic data integration). Ford Motor Co., Allen Bradley, Hitachi, Motorola, and Boeing are but a few of the many companies using information networks to coordinate the development, production, distribution, and marketing of their products. Among many benefits, these computer-based information links substantially reduce the time needed to design and test new products and allow a firm to compete on the basis of fast delivery (a differentiated feature) and low cost.[115]

Total Quality Management Systems Although difficult to implement,[116] many firms have established total quality management (TQM) systems (also see Chapter 5). Important objectives sought through use of TQM systems include increases in the quality of a firm's product and the productivity levels of the entire organization.[117] Enhanced quality focuses customers' attention on improvements in product performance, feature utility, and reliability. This allows a firm to achieve differentiation and ultimately higher prices and market share. An emphasis on quality in production techniques lowers manufacturing and service costs through savings in rework, scrap, and warranty expenses. These savings can result in a competitive

CADD systems are an example of a competitively valuable information network. These computer-based links substantially reduce the time needed to design and test new products, such as the Airbus plane shown in the photograph. Firms with CADD systems are better able to compete on the basis of fast delivery and lower costs.

advantage for a firm over its rivals. Thus, TQM programs integrate aspects of the differentiation and cost leadership strategies.

Four key assumptions are the foundation of TQM systems. The first assumption is that "the costs of poor quality (such as inspection, rework, lost customers and so on) are far greater than the costs of developing processes that produce high-quality products and services."[118] The second assumption is that employees naturally care about their work and will take initiatives to improve it. These initiatives are taken only when the firm provides employees with the tools and training they need to improve quality and when managers pay attention to their ideas. The third assumption is that "organizations are systems of highly interdependent parts."[119] Problems encountered in such systems often cross traditional functional (e.g., marketing, manufacturing, finance, etc.) lines. Solving interdependent problems requires integrated decision processes with participation from all affected functional areas. The fourth assumption is that the responsibility for an effective TQM system rests squarely on the shoulders of upper-level managers. These people must openly and totally support use of a TQM system and accept the responsibility for an organizational design that allows employees to work effectively.

As with the other business-level strategies, there are risks associated with use of the integrated low-cost/differentiation strategy.

Competitive Risks of the Integrated Low-Cost/Differentiation Strategy

The potential of the integrated strategy, in terms of above-average returns, is significant, but this potential comes with substantial risk. Selecting a business-level strategy calls for firms to make choices about how they intend to compete. Achieving the low-cost position in an industry, or a segment of an industry (e.g., a focus strategy), demands that the firm be able to reduce its costs consistently relative to competitors. Use of the differentiation strategy, with either an industry-wide or a focused competitive scope (see Figure 4.1), results in above-average returns only when the firm provides customers with differentiated products they value and for which they are willing to pay a premium price.

The firm failing to establish a leadership position in its chosen competitive scope, as the low-cost producer or as a differentiator, risks becoming "*stuck-in-the-middle*."[120] Being stuck in the middle prevents firms from dealing successfully with the five competitive forces and from earning above-average returns. Indeed, some research results show that the lowest performing businesses are those lacking a distinguishable competitive advantage. Not having a clear and identifiable competitive advantage results from a firm being stuck in the middle.[121] Such firms can earn average returns only when an industry's structure is highly favorable or when the firm is competing against others that are in the same position.[122]

Midsize accounting firms (those with as many as 50 partners and 300 employees) appear to be stuck in the middle. These companies lack the size and resources to offer the wide array of services available from the Big Six giants; at the same time, their overhead rates prevent them from matching the low prices charged by small accounting firms and solo practitioners. Thus, these firms' services seem to be too expensive to compete with the low-cost small firms and too undifferentiated to provide the value offered by the large, differentiated accounting firms. In an accounting firm consultant's opinion, these conditions suggest that by the year 2000, middle size accounting firms may be "as extinct as the dodo."[123]

As explained in the Strategic Focus, some firms competing in the specialty coffee business also face the possibility of becoming stuck-in-the-middle. If it materializes, this outcome would be a product primarily of the dynamics of competition within this industry.

STRATEGIC FOCUS

Efforts to Avoid Becoming Stuck in the Middle in the Specialty Coffee Business

Evidence suggests that some firms competing in the coffee-bar business may be stuck in the middle. The leader in this industry is Starbucks Corp. As shown by the following comments, the founder and CEO, Howard Schultz, has always wanted this firm to be more than a profitable enterprise: "We had a mission, to educate consumers everywhere about fine coffee. We had a vision, to create an atmosphere in our stores that drew people in and gave them a sense of wonder and romance in the midst of their harried lives."

Vertically integrated (the firm controls operations for its coffee sourcing, roasting, packaging, and distribution), Starbucks continues to expand rapidly. With approximately 1,250 units at the beginning of 1998, the company planned to add more than 400 stores in 1998 alone; 2,000 total units are expected by 2000. To better serve its customers, including the growing number of teenagers who see coffee houses as an alternative to the movies or the mall, Starbucks has introduced larger units in select markets. With 50 or more seats rather than the standard seating capacity of 20 to 25, these larger locations permit expanded menus and live entertainment.

Based in part on the prediction that sales in the specialty coffee industry will reach $3 billion in 1999 (up from only $44 million in 1969), an explosive growth is anticipated in the total number of coffee bars in the United States. This growth, through which the number of total units will likely double between 1996 and 2000, will lead to an industry shakeout. One analyst noted that the intensity of competition in this industry makes it highly improbable that all players in the business will survive. Even more directly, Michael Bergman, CEO of a coffee-bar business called Second Cup, believes that as a result of events occurring in the industry, "You will have the strong, big players and the small, well-run chains that really understand their particular customer. The victims are going to be marginal players in the middle."

Aware of these industry realities, some firms are taking actions in an effort to avoid become stuck in the middle. Timothy's World Coffee operates the bulk of its 28 U.S. stores in what is known to be a brutally competitive market in New York City. To differentiate itself and to serve the needs of a narrow customer group, the firm established Timothy's World-News Café. At these locations, customers can buy coffee as well as purchase and read their favorite magazines while in the store.

Chock Full O'Nuts roasts, packs, and markets regular, instant, decaffeinated, and specialty coffees and teas. The firm's products are sold to retail, foodservice, and private-label customers. Because of competitive difficulties, the company discontinued its Chock Full O'Nuts cafés in October 1996. In an effort to avoid being stuck in the middle in the coffee specialty business, Chock Full O'Nuts then decided to expand its Quikava coffee chain as the foundation of a focused differentiation strategy. Each Quikava unit is a tiny, double-drive-through that sells coffee, road-ready sandwiches, and baked goods. Because these units continue to operate in the red, analysts believe that the company will likely have to do more than double its number of stores to reach break even (an outcome that is not expected until at least fiscal 1999). Thus, at least in terms of the short run, Chock Full O'Nuts may not have developed a successful specialty coffee business concept—one that will allow it to remain a viable participant in an industry that may experience a shakeout in the near future.

SOURCE: *Bloomberg News*, 1997, Upscale coffee chains show signs of overheating, *Dallas Morning News*, August 3, H3; R. Coleman, 1997, Java Juniors, *Dallas Morning News*, June 9, D1, D4; R. M. Greene, 1997, Chock Full O'Nuts, *Value Line*, August 15, 1467; Starbucks: Making values pay, 1997, *Fortune*, September 29, 261–272; D. Vlassis, 1997, Starbucks Corp., *Value Line*, August 22, 1747; S. Caminiti, 1995, Coffee chains are getting the jitters, *Fortune*, November 27, 42, 44.

Once a firm has selected its business-level strategy, it must both anticipate and be prepared to respond to competitors' actions and responses. Recently, for example, Coffee Station, Inc., initiated competitive actions that have the potential to affect Starbucks. In a bid to become the number-two operator of specialty coffee outlets, the firm purchased the 61-store Pasqua Inc. chain. Some analysts suggested that Coffee Station might be seeking to gain the size required to compete against Starbucks. Because of the high visibility of Coffee Station and Pasqua outlets in New York City, San Francisco, and Los Angeles, respectively, it is possible that Coffee Station's attempt to consolidate part of the specialty coffee market will enhance the firm's strategic competitiveness. Increasing success by competitors will elicit competitive responses from Starbucks and other industry participants.[124] Competitive dynamics such as these that occur as firms implement their strategies are examined in the next chapter. These dynamics take place with respect to all types of strategies (see Chapters 6 through 9), but the majority of competitive actions and competitive responses are initiated in efforts to implement a firm's business-level strategy.

SUMMARY

- A business-level strategy is an integrated and coordinated set of commitments and actions designed to provide value to customers and gain a competitive advantage by exploiting core competencies in specific, individual product markets. Five business-level strategies are examined in this chapter. Strategic competitiveness is enhanced when a firm is able to develop and exploit new core competencies faster than competitors can mimic the competitive advantages yielded by its current competencies.
- Customers are the foundation of successful business-level strategies. When considering customers, firms simultaneously examine three issues: *who*, *what*, and *how*. Respectively, these issues cause the firm to determine the customer groups it will serve, the needs those customers have that it seeks to satisfy, and the core competencies it possesses that can be used to satisfy customers' needs. The increasing segmentation of markets occurring throughout the world creates multiple opportunities for firms to identify unique customer needs.
- Firms seeking competitive advantage through the cost leadership strategy often produce no-frills, standardized products for an industry's typical customer. Above-average returns are earned when firms continuously drive their costs lower than those of their competitors while providing customers with products that have low prices and acceptable levels of differentiated features.
- Competitive risks associated with the cost leadership strategy include (1) a loss of competitive advantage to newer technologies, (2) a failure to detect changes in customers' needs, and (3) the ability of competitors to imitate the low-cost leader's competitive advantage through their own unique strategic actions.
- Through implementation of the differentiation strategy, firms provide customers with products that have different (and valued) features. Because of their uniqueness, differentiated products are sold at a premium price. Products can be differentiated along any dimension that is valued by some group of customers. Firms using this strategy seek to differentiate their products from competitors' goods or services along as many dimensions as possible. The less similarity with competitors' products, the more buffered a firm is from competition with its rivals.
- Risks associated with the differentiation strategy include (1) a customer group's decision that the differences between the differentiated product and the low-cost leader's product are no longer worth a premium price, (2) the inability of a differentiated product to create the type of value for which customers are willing to pay a premium price, and (3) the ability of competitors to provide customers with products that have features similar to those associated with the differentiated product, but at a lower cost.
- Through the low-cost and the differentiated focus strategies, firms serve the needs of a narrow competitive segment (e.g., buyer group, product segment, or geographic area). This strategy is successful when firms have the core competencies required to provide value to a narrow competitive segment that exceeds the value available from firms serving customers on an industry-wide basis.
- The competitive risks of focus strategies include (1) a competitor's ability to use its core competencies to "outfocus" the focuser by serving an even more narrowly defined competitive segment, (2) decisions by industry-wide competitors to serve a customer group's specialized needs that the focuser has been serving, and (3) a reduction in differences of the needs between customers in a narrow competitive segment and the industry-wide market.
- Firms using the integrated low-cost/differentiation strategy strive to provide customers with relatively low-cost products that have some valued differentiated features. The primary risk of this strategy is that a firm might produce products that do not offer sufficient value—in terms of either low cost or differentiation. When this occurs, the company is "stuck in the middle." Firms stuck in the middle compete at a disadvantage.

REVIEW QUESTIONS

1. What is a strategy and what are business-level strategies?
2. What is the relationship between a firm's customers and its business-level strategy? Why is this relationship important?
3. When studying customers in terms of *who*, *what*, and *how*, what questions are firms trying to answer?
4. What is the integrated low-cost/differentiation strategy? Why is this strategy becoming more important to firms?
5. How is competitive advantage achieved through successful implementation of the cost leadership strategy? The differentiation strategy? The focused low-cost strategy? The focused differentiation strategy? The integrated low-cost/differentiation strategy?
6. What are the risks associated with selecting and implementing each of the five strategies mentioned in question 5?

APPLICATION DISCUSSION QUESTIONS

1. You are a customer of your university or college. What actions does your school take to understand *what* your needs are? Be prepared to discuss your views.
2. Choose a firm in your local community that is of interest to you. Based on interactions with this company, which business-level strategy do you believe the firm is implementing? What evidence can you provide to support your belief?
3. Assume that you have decided to establish and operate a restaurant in your local community. *Who* are the customers you would serve? *What* needs do these customers have that you could satisfy with your restaurant? *How* would you satisfy those needs? Be prepared to discuss your responses.
4. What business-level strategy is your school implementing? What core competencies are being used to implement this strategy?
5. Assume you overheard the following comment: "It is impossible for a firm to produce a low-cost, highly differentiated product." Accept or reject this statement and be prepared to defend your position.

ETHICS QUESTIONS

1. Can a commitment to ethical conduct on issues such as the environment, product quality, and fulfilling contractual agreements affect competitive advantage? If so, how?
2. Is there more incentive for differentiators or low-cost leaders to pursue stronger ethical conduct? Think of an example to support your answer.
3. Can an overemphasis on low-cost leadership or differentiation lead to ethical problems (such as poor product design and manufacturing) that create costly problems (e.g., product liability lawsuits)?
4. Reexamine the assumptions about effective TQM systems presented in this chapter. Do these assumptions urge top-level managers to maintain higher ethical standards? If so, how?
5. A brand image is one way a firm can differentiate its good or service. However, many questions are now being raised about the effect brand images have on consumer behavior. For example, considerable concern has arisen about brand images that are managed by tobacco firms and their effect on teenage smoking habits. Should firms be concerned about how they form and use brand images? Why or why not?

INTERNET EXERCISE

Go to Dayton Hudson's home page at:

http://www.shop-at.com

The Dayton Hudson Corporation owns a family of retail stores including Dayton's, Hudson's, Marshall Field's, Target, and Mervyn's. Dayton Hudson is unusual in that some of its stores pursue a low-cost strategy and some pursue a differentiation strategy. Visit Dayton Hudson's Web site and the Web sites of each of the individual chains of stores. Which of the stores pursue a low-cost strategy and which stores pursue a differentiation strategy? Provide examples of how each of the stores supports its respective strategy.

Strategic Surfing

Hoover's Online provides free access to information and current news stories about American companies. This resource is valuable to managers and students who are interested in learning more about the background, performance, and strategies of U.S. companies.

http://www.hoovers.com/

NOTES

1. Callaway Golf Company, 1997, *Annual Report*, 1.
2. A. Campbell and M. Alexander, 1997, What's wrong with strategy? *Harvard Business Review* 75, no. 6: 42–51; D. J. Collis and C. A. Montgomery, 1995, Competing on resources: Strategy in the 1990s, *Harvard Business Review* 73, no. 4: 118–128.
3. This particular view of strategy is mentioned in D. P. Slevin and J. G. Covin, 1997, Strategy formation patterns, performance, and the significance of context, *Journal of Management* 23: 189–209.
4. C. E. Helfat, 1997, Know-how and asset complementarity and dynamic capability accumulation: The case of R&D, *Strategic Management Journal* 18: 339–360; A. Seth and H. Thomas, 1994, Theories of the firm: Implications for strategy research, *Journal of Management Studies* 31: 167.
5. N. Rajagopalan and G. M. Spreitzer, 1997, Toward a theory of strategic change: A multi-lens perspective and integrative framework, *Academy of Management Journal* 22: 48–79; R. R. Nelson, 1994, Why do firms differ, and how does it matter? in R. P. Rumelt, D. E. Schendel, and D. J. Teece (eds.), *Fundamental Issues in Strategy* (Boston: Harvard Business School Press), 247–269.
6. H. Courtney, J. Kirkland, and P. Viguerie, 1997, Strategy under uncertainty, *Harvard Business Review* 75, no. 6: 67–79; P. F. Drucker, 1997, The future that has already happened, *Harvard Business Review* 75, no. 5: 20–24.
7. G. S. Day and D. J. Reibstein, 1997, *Wharton on Dynamic Competitive Strategy* (New York: John Wiley & Sons), 3.
8. G. S. Day, 1997, Maintaining the competitive edge: Creating and sustaining advantages in dynamic competitive environments, in G. S. Day and D. J. Reibstein (eds.), 1997, *Wharton on Dynamic Competitive Strategy* (New York: John Wiley & Sons), 48–75; D. Leonard-Barton, 1995, *Wellsprings of Knowledge* (Boston: Harvard Business School Press).
9. C. Oliver, 1997, Sustainable competitive advantage: Combining institutional and resource-based views, *Strategic Management Journal* 18: 697–713.
10. T. T. Baldwin, C. Danielson, and W. Wiggenhorn, 1997, The evolution of learning strategies in organizations: From employee development to business redefinition, *Academy of Management Executive* XI, no. 4: 47–58; D. Lei, M. A. Hitt, and R. Bettis, 1996, Dynamic core competences through meta-learning and strategic context, *Journal of Management* 22: 549–569.
11. C. M. Christensen, 1997, Making strategy: Learning by doing, *Harvard Business Review* 75, no. 6: 141–156.
12. The Iams Company, 1997, *The Iams Company Home Page*, October 20, http://www.iams.com.
13. M. Zimmerman, 1995, Frito-Lay stands to gain from rival's exit, *Dallas Morning News*, October 26, D1, D10.
14. M. Zimmerman, 1995, Luby's adds units as rivals face troubles, *Dallas Morning News*, November 6, D1, D4.
15. N. Harris, 1997, UPS puts its back into it, *Business Week*, October 27, 50.
16. J. Jenk, C. H. Michel, and V. Margotin-Roze, 1995, The Russian consumer revolution, *The McKinsey Quarterly*, no. 2: 35–46.
17. J. E. Garten, 1997, Troubles ahead in emerging markets, *Harvard Business Review* 75, no. 3: 38–50.
18. K. L. Miller, F. J. Comes, and P. Simpson, 1995, Poland: Rising star of Europe, *Business Week*, December 4, 64–70.
19. G. G. Dess, A. Gupta, J.-F. Hennart, and C. W. L. Hill, 1995, Conducting and integrating strategy research at the international, corporate, and business levels: Issues and directions, *Journal of Management* 21: 357–393.
20. Day and Reibstein (eds.), *Wharton on Dynamic Competitive Strategy*, 20.
21. B. Saporito, 1993, How to revive a fading firm, *Fortune*, March 22, 80.
22. M. E. Porter, 1980, *Competitive Strategy* (New York: The Free Press).
23. Lei, Hitt, and Bettis, Dynamic core competencies.
24. A. J. Slywotzky, 1996, *Value Migration* (Boston: Harvard Business School Press), 13.
25. A. W. H. Grant and L. A. Schlesinger, 1995, Realize your customers' full profit potential, *Harvard Business Review* 73, no. 5: 59–72.
26. Freightliner: Growing through innovation and agility, 1997, *Fortune*, December 8, S10.
27. T. A. Stewart, 1997, A satisfied customer isn't enough, *Fortune*, July 21, 112–113.
28. T. O. Jones and W. E. Sasser, Jr., 1995, Why satisfied customers defect, *Harvard Business Review* 73, no. 6: 88–99.
29. T. A. Stewart, 1995, After all you've done for your customers, why are they still not happy? *Fortune*, December 11, 182.
30. J. Hagel, III and J. F. Rayport, 1997, The coming battle for customer information, *Harvard Business Review* 75, no. 1: 53–65.
31. Slywotzky, *Value Migration*, 13; R. McKenna, 1995, Real-time marketing, *Harvard Business Review* 73, no. 4: 87–95; S. F. Wiggins, 1995, New ways to create lifetime bonds with your customers, *Fortune*, October 30, 115.

32. A master class in radical change, 1993, *Fortune*, December 13, 82–90.
33. V. Griffith, 1997, Treasures in the corporate memory, *The Financial Times*, November 10, 14.
34. T. C. Kinnear, K. L. Bernhardt, and K. A. Krentler, 1995, *Principles of Marketing*, 4th ed. (New York: HarperCollins), 149–150.
35. Ibid., 153.
36. Ibid., 149–161; D. F. Abell, 1980, *Defining the Business: The Starting Point of Strategic Planning* (Englewood Cliffs, NJ: Prentice-Hall).
37. R. Berner, 1997, Kmart makes early-retirement offer to 28,500, *Wall Street Journal*, November 14, B4; M. H. Gerstein, 1997, Kmart Corp., *Value Line*, August 22, 1654; K. Naughton, 1995, Bright lights, big city won't cut it for Kmart, *Business Week*, May 26, 57.
38. Associated Press, 1996, Automakers rolling out new models, *Dallas Morning News*, January 4, D2.
39. Title 9 Sports, 1997, *General Merchandise Catalog*, December, 12.
40. K. Labich, 1994, Class in America, *Fortune*, February 7, 114–126.
41. E. Osnos, 1997, Cornucopia of choices proves confusing for today's consumer, *Dallas Morning News*, September 29, D1, D5.
42. Strong holiday sales enable Gadzooks to expand, 1996, *Dallas Morning News*, January 4, D11; M. Halkias, 1995, To buy for—at least today, *Dallas Morning News*, October 14, F1, F2.
43. Halkias, To buy for, F2.
44. R. Coleman, 1997, Slow teen sales force Gadzooks to trim forecast, *Dallas Morning News*, July 22, D1, D5.
45. F. Rose and J. R. Emshwiller, 1997, Guess, "coolness" fading, plans sultry ads, *Wall Street Journal*, November 19, B4.
46. R. Jacob, 1995, How one red-hot retailer wins customer loyalty, *Fortune*, July 10, 72–79.
47. D. R. Cohen, 1997, Staples, *Value Line*, October 24, 1135.
48. R. McKenna, Real-time marketing; F. J. Gouillart and F. D. Sturdivant, 1994, Spend a day in the life of your customers, *Harvard Business Review* 72, no. 1: 116–125.
49. The future for strategy: An interview with Gary Hamel, 1993, *European Management Journal* 14: 179–191.
50. Sprint, 1994, *1994 Annual Report to Shareholders*, 1.
51. G. A. Niemond, 1997, International Business Machines, *Value Line*, October 24, 1099.
52. Honda Motor Company, 1997, *Honda Motor Company Home Page*, December 6, http://www.honda.com.
53. Trendy yet traditional, 1997, *The Financial Times*, November 14, 19.
54. M. E. Porter, 1985, *Competitive Advantage* (New York: The Free Press), 26.
55. M. E. Porter, 1996, What is strategy? *Harvard Business Review* 74, no. 6: 61–78.
56. Campbell and Alexander, What's wrong with strategy? 43; G. Colvin, 1997, The changing art of becoming unbeatable, *Fortune*, November 24, 299–300.
57. M. E. Porter, 1994, Toward a dynamic theory of strategy, in R. P. Rumelt, D. E. Schendel, and D. J. Teece (eds.), *Fundamental Issues in Strategy* (Boston: Harvard Business School Press), 423–461.
58. Porter, What is strategy? 62.
59. Porter, *Competitive Advantage*, 15.
60. P. M. Wright, D. L. Smart, and G. C. McMahan, 1995, Matches between human resources and strategy among NCAA basketball teams, *Academy of Management Journal* 38: 1502–1074; Porter, Toward a dynamic theory, 434.
61. G. Bowley and H. Simonian, 1997, Volkswagen makes series of U-turns, *The Financial Times*, November 21, 19.
62. Porter, *Competitive Strategy*, 35–40.
63. Campbell and Alexander, What's wrong with strategy? 42.
64. J. C. Anderson and J. A. Narus, 1995, Capturing the value of supplementary services, *Harvard Business Review* 73, no. 1: 75–83.
65. C. Sirois, 1997, Unifi, Inc., *Value Line*, August 22, 1640.
66. J. Arbitman, 1997, Nova Corp., *Value Line*, September 26, 439.
67. S. Lubove, 1994, It ain't broke, but fix it anyway, *Forbes*, August 1, 56–60.
68. Ibid., 56.
69. J. Simmons, 1995, Budget hotels aren't bargains abroad, *Wall Street Journal*, November 17, B1, B4.
70. J. Friedland, 1997, Latin American retailer fights giants, *Wall Street Journal*, September 19, A10.
71. Porter, *Competitive Strategy*, 36.
72. Sirois, Unifi, Inc., 1640.
73. Lubove, It ain't broke, 57.
74. P. M. Seligman, 1997, Emerson Electric, *Value Line*, October 24, 1007.
75. L. Kraar, 1995, Acer's edge: PCs to go, *Fortune*, October 30, 192.
76. J. Moore and P. Burrows, 1997, A new attack plan for Acer America, *Business Week*, December 8, 82–83.
77. Intel filing suggests trouble at PC maker Packard Bell, 1995, *Dallas Morning News*, November 28, D6.
78. T. Zorn, 1995, Orville Redenbacher leaves premium legacy, *Dallas Morning News*, September 24, H5.
79. Day and Reibstein (eds.), *Wharton on Dynamic Competitive Strategy*, 10.
80. Porter, *Competitive Advantage*, 14.
81. C. Crossen, 1997, The crucial question for these noisy times may just be: "Huh?" *Wall Street Journal*, July 10, A1, A6; A. Faircloth, 1997, Ultra-Lux condos of the high seas, *Fortune*, November 10, 40; M. J. McCarthy, 1997, New maneuvers in the necktie-spot war, *Wall Street Journal*, July 13, B1.
82. It's Tommy's world, 1996, *Vanity Fair*, February, 110.
83. F. Rice, 1995, Hilfiger's bipartisan fashions are hot, *Fortune*, October 30, 32.
84. S. Chandler and A. T. Palmer, 1995, Bloomie's tries losing the attitude, *Business Week*, November 13, 52.
85. I. Sager and P. Burrows, 1997, I'm not gonna pay a lot for this Aptiva, *Business Week*, October 13, 59.
86. Porter, *Competitive Strategy*, 38.
87. Porter, *Competitive Advantage*, 15.
88. T. Maxon, 1997, General manager works her way up the line at RailTex, *Dallas Morning News*, July 20, H2.
89. Porter, *Competitive Advantage*, 15.
90. Ibid., 15–16.
91. New York Times News Service, 1997, AT&T may name chief today, *Dallas Morning News*, October 20, D1, D4.

92. Rally's Hamburgers Inc., 1995, *Wall Street Journal*, December 6, B8.
93. N. J. Perry, 1992, Hit'em where they used to be, *Fortune*, October 19, 112–113.
94. A. Goldstein, 1997, PC maker cutting staff 37%, *Dallas Morning News*, December 4, D1, D12.
95. M. Halkias, 1995, Blush is on at Sally Beauty, *Dallas Morning News*, October 23, D1, D4.
96. L. Crawford, 1997, The bullet-proof fashions to die for on wild frontier of Mexico's drug war, *The Financial Times*, November 15, 132; A. Dworkin, 1997, Hewing a housing trend, *Dallas Morning News*, July 21, D1, D4; *The Financial Times*, 1997, A cosmopolitan crust, November 23, II; D. Weisgall, 1997, Buying time, *Fortune*, September 8, 192.
97. N. Harris, 1997, Home Depot: Beyond do-it-yourselfers, *Business Week*, June 30, 86–88; B. Sharav, 1997, Home Depot, *Value Line*, October 17, 888.
98. Insights presented in this section are drawn primarily from Dess, Gupta, Hennart and Hill, Conducting and integrating strategy research, 376–379.
99. W. K. Hall, 1980, Survival strategies in a hostile environment, *Harvard Business Review* 58, no. 5: 75–87.
100. Dess, Gupta, Hennart, and Hill, Conducting and integrating strategy research, 377.
101. L. Kim and Y. Lim, 1988, Environment, generic strategies, and performance in a rapidly developing country: A taxonomic approach, *Academy of Management Journal* 31: 802–827.
102. Porter, *Competitive Advantage*, 18.
103. R. Henkoff, 1995, New management secrets from Japan—really, *Fortune*, November 27, 135–146.
104. R. Sanchez, 1995, Strategic flexibility in product competition, *Strategic Management Journal* 16 (Special Summer Issue): 140.
105. Ibid., 105.
106. D. M. Upton, 1995, What really makes factories flexible? *Harvard Business Review* 73, no. 4: 74–84.
107. J. Martin, 1997, Give 'em exactly what they want, *Fortune*, November 10, 283–85.
108. R. S. Russell and B. W. Taylor, III, 1998, *Operations Management*, Second Edition (Upper Saddle River, NJ: Prentice-Hall), 255–257; S. W. Flanders and W. J. Davis, 1995, Scheduling a flexible manufacturing system with tooling constraints: An actual case study, *Interfaces* 25, no. 2: 42–54.
109. D. Lei, M. A. Hitt, and J. D. Goldhar, 1996, Advanced manufacturing technology, organization design and strategic flexibility, *Organization Studies* 17: 501–523.
110. E. Mansfield, 1993, The diffusion of flexible manufacturing systems in Japan, Europe and the United States, *Management Science* 39: 149–159 as quoted in Sanchez, Strategic flexibility in product competition, 141.
111. Mansfield, The diffusion of flexible manufacturing systems, 153–154.
112. Ibid., 158.
113. R. Garud and S. Kotha, 1994, Using the brain as a metaphor to model flexible production systems, *Academy of Management Review* 19: 671–698.
114. S. A. Melnyk and D. R. Denzler, 1996, *Operations Management: A Value-Driven Approach* (Chicago: Irwin).
115. A. Baxter, 1997, Designs for survival, *The Financial Times*, November 20, 14.
116. T. Y. Choi and O. C. Behling, 1992, Top managers and TQM success: One more look after all these years, *Academy of Management Executive* XI, no. 1: 37–47; R. K. Reger, L. T. Gustafson, S. M. DeMarie, and J. V. Mullane, 1994, Reframing the organization: Why implementing total quality is easier said than done, *Academy of Management Review* 19: 565–584.
117. J. D. Westphal, R. Gulati, and S. M. Shortell, 1997, Customization or conformity? An institutional and network perspective on the content and consequences of TQM adoption, *Administrative Science Quarterly* 42: 366–394.
118. J. R. Hackman and R. Wagemen, 1995, Total quality management: Empirical, conceptual, and practical issues, *Administrative Science Quarterly* 40: 310.
119. Ibid., 311.
120. Porter, *Competitive Advantage*, 16.
121. A. Miller and G. G. Dess, 1993, Assessing Porter's (1980) model in terms of its generalizability, accuracy and simplicity, *Journal of Management Studies* 30: 553–585.
122. Porter, *Competitive Advantage*, 17.
123. L. Berton, 1995, Midsize accountants lose clients to firms both large and small, *Wall Street Journal*, November 15, A1, A4.
124. D. Clark, 1997, Coffee Station, Inc. to acquire Pasqua, a specialty chain, *Wall Street Journal*, June 13, A6.

Competitive Dynamics

CHAPTER 5

Learning Objectives

After reading this chapter, you should be able to:

1. Define the conditions for undertaking competitive actions.
2. Identify and explain factors affecting the probability that a competitor will initiate a response to competitive actions.
3. Describe first, second, and late movers and the advantages and disadvantages of each.
4. Understand the factors that contribute to the likelihood of a response to a competitive action.
5. Explain the effects of firm size, speed of strategic decision making and implementation, innovation, and quality on a firm's ability to take competitive action.
6. Understand three basic market situations as outcomes of competitive dynamics.
7. Discuss the types of competitive actions most relevant for each of the three stages of an industry evolution.

Global Competitive Dynamics among Steel Manufacturers

Global market conditions are changing rapidly for steel manufacturing companies. Facilities that were previously government owned in some countries are being privatized. Once privatized, these companies often develop an active export strategy. Minimills, once dismissed as minor players, are increasing their share of various domestic markets, especially in the United States. Relying on highly efficient technologies, minimills typically remelt scrap metal to make rough products. New technology is allowing them to make finer steel products, which traditionally were manufactured solely by vertically integrated steel companies. Additionally, the trend of following customers to other countries continues. In the 1980s, this competitive action was quite visible in the United States. As Japanese automobile manufacturers built U.S. facilities, many of their suppliers, including steel companies, followed. The practice of following one's customer to provide superior service has expanded to other industry settings. Producers of appliances, heavy equipment, and machine tools are globalizing their operations and challenging suppliers to accompany them or risk losing business. Whirlpool Corporation, for example, has manufacturing facilities in 13 countries and recently built a second plant in India to produce frost-free refrigerators.

http://www.nsc.co.jp

Steel companies with plants close to Whirlpool's operations increase the probability that they will earn the firm's business. The result of changes in global market conditions such as the ones cited here has increased rivalry among competitors.

In combination, this array of competitive actions and competitive responses is forcing steel manufacturers to globalize rapidly. Toward the end of the 1980s, for example, French steelmaker Usinor (the world's fourth largest manufacturer of crude steel and the largest supplier of steel to the European automobile manufacturing industry) decided to increase its global presence. Largely European-oriented at the time of this decision, Usinor chose to focus mainly on partnerships with local companies in the pursuit of globalization. Recently Usinor formed a relationship with Dofasco of Canada to build a galvanizing facility in Hamilton, Ontario. This effort will allow Usinor to supply galvanized sheet metal (one of the firm's most competitive products) for the first time to General Motors, Ford, and Chrysler on their home turf. The firm's chairman described this cooperative relationship as a "significant demonstration of the company's strategy of trying to globalize (its) strong points."

Large, vertically integrated steelmakers such as Bethlehem Steel are also taking strategic actions in response to the changing nature of the world's steel industry (the vertical integration strategy is discussed in Chapter 6). The second largest U.S. steelmaker, Bethlehem recently acquired Lukens. Analysts saw this acquisition as a reflection of the pressure on traditional integrated steelmakers to cut costs and close inefficient plants in the face of mounting competition from competitors located all over the world as well as from U.S. minimills. Bethlehem officials believed that ownership of Lukens, which was a leading North American specialty steel manufacturer producing stainless, alloy, and carbon products, would yield "significant strategic benefits." Synergies across product lines and an opportunity to reduce costs were the major anticipated benefits. For example, immediate plans called for closing one of Bethlehem's two steel plate mills and one of Lukens' in order to reduce costs and integrate product offerings.

Nippon Steel, Japan's largest steelmaker, also is making competitive decisions that are intended to enhance its global presence. Nippon has entered into a joint venture with Brazilian steel manufacturer Usiminas to produce steel for vehicle bodies. This venture (with 60 percent ownership by Usiminas and 40 percent by Nippon), is aimed at supplying a growing number of vehicle makers in South America, particularly Brazil, with high-grade steel products. Affected adversely by declining demand in its home markets and in other Asian markets as the 1990s came to a close, Nippon Steel remains interested in establishing other global operations to enhance its competitiveness.

Other firms competing in the world's increasingly globalized steel industry are also initiating competitive actions in light of environmental changes and the resulting competitive challenges that are facing them. For instance, British Steel PLC agreed to merge its production of large-diameter pipes into Europipe GmbH, which is the pipe-producing joint venture between German steel conglomerate Mannesmann AG and Usinor. Company officials indicated that this merger would help the firms cover a wider market spectrum, allowing Europipe to supply large-diameter pipes across the entire range of qualities and sizes.

Viewed collectively, the array of competitive actions being taken by steelmakers is likely to increase dramatically the rivalrous actions among these companies throughout the world.

SOURCE: M. Marshall, 1998, British Steel to merge unit into Europipe, *Wall Street Journal,* January 20, A14; N. Tait, 1998, Bethlehem increases bid for Lukens, *Financial Times,* January 6, 14; *Lukens Home Page,* 1998, January 21, http://www.lukens.com; *Usinor Home Page,* 1998, January 21, http://www.usinor.com; C. Adams, 1997, Steelmakers scramble in a race to become global powerhouse, *Wall Street Journal,* August 26, A1, A10; M. Nakamoto, 1997, Nippon Steel move in Brazil, *Financial Times,* December 15, 20; D. Owen and S. Wagstyl, 1997, French steel company targets US car industry, *Financial Times,* December 18, 13; R. Waters, 1997, Bethlehem pays $400m for Lukens, *Financial Times,* December 16, 20.

Characteristics and conditions associated with the global steel industry demonstrate the type of competitive landscape facing most firms as the twenty-first century nears. More volatile and unpredictable, companies competing in this landscape must learn how to cope successfully with the challenges presented by discontinuous environmental changes, the increasing globalization of their industries, and the array of competitive actions and competitive responses that are being taken by aggressive competitors.[1] In addition, top-level managers must be willing to make the type of difficult decisions that are called for by the nature of competitors' actions and responses. In fact, some believe that one of the most important skills that will be linked to strategic competitiveness in the twenty-first century will be managers' willingness and perhaps even eagerness to make significant, and sometimes painful decisions. Many of these decisions will be necessitated by the competitive dynamics affecting the firm's operations.[2]

As explained in the opening case, Bethlehem Steel's recent competitive actions are being influenced by the efforts of competitors to exploit their individual and unique competitive advantages in the pursuit of strategic competitiveness. The importance of Bethlehem's intention to reduce its overall costs, at least partially through the acquisition of Lukens, is supported by the competitive actions being considered by two minimill competitors.

In 1998's first calendar quarter, U.S.-based Nucor Corp. and Regina, Saskatchewan's, Ipsco Inc. were strongly considering building new mills to roll steel plate. Interestingly, both steelmakers acknowledged that the steel plate market was not expected to grow much and that the boost in manufacturing capability created by the new mills would result in production overcapacity on an industry-wide basis. To describe the reason for this competitive action, an Ipsco executive stated the following: "We assume steel is mature. We'd build because we think we'd be low-cost and high-quality and somebody would be knocked out of the market. We think we can take over a share of the market somebody else has." The "somebody else" could be Bethlehem Steel. Both new plants would be built in the eastern or southern United States, locations that would put the plants in approximately the same geographic market as Bethlehem's plate mill in Sparrows Point, Maryland. Already recognized as an inefficient facility, some analysts believed that Bethlehem would close the Sparrows Point plant if Nucor and Ipsco were to build their new facilities.[3]

INCREASED RIVALRY IN THE NEW COMPETITIVE LANDSCAPE

Conditions in the new competitive landscape are increasing competitive rivalry and require many companies (including steelmakers, as described previously) to compete differently to achieve strategic competitiveness and earn above-average returns. For instance, the current nature of competition for bus manufacturers (such as Daimler-Benz, Volvo, Scania, Fiat, Iveco, and Renault) is quite different from the past. One of the last big manufacturing industries to experience the worldwide changes of modernization and industry rationalization, some bus manufacturers are buying market share through acquisitions. Volvo, for example, purchased Carrus, which had been the largest independent manufacturer of bus bodies in the Nordic region. Renault now sells buses to price-sensitive European buyers from Karossa, the Czech bus and coachmaker, in which it purchased a controlling interest. Another competitive action being taken in the global bus industry is to scour international markets for customers to compensate for tougher conditions in the firm's domestic market. Mercedes-Benz, for instance, views Turkey as an important market as well as an export base for eastern Europe and the former Soviet Union.[4]

In the entertainment industry, megaplex theaters are changing the nature of competition. Transforming the way customers pick and watch movies, companies are scrambling to build theaters with as many as 30 screens. With each megaplex costing up to $30 million to build, movie entertainment at the local theater is becoming a capital-intensive business. The chairman of Regal Cinemas Inc., the fifth largest chain in the United States, believes that "middle-tier companies with limited resources have to wonder how they are going to play" in what the entertainment industry is becoming. Competitive actions being taken in this industry are as tactical as increasing individual ticket prices and as strategic as consolidation. (Regal, for example, recently purchased Cobb Theaters to gain control of the firm's 643 screens.) Other actions being considered by companies trying to differentiate themselves from competitors include building units with amenities such as babysitting services and cappuccino bars in addition to a still larger number of screens.[5]

Several reasons account for the changes in competition taking place in many industries.[6] First, in most industries, an emphasis on a single domestic market is decreasing; in its place is an increasing emphasis on international and global markets. This is certainly the outcome being witnessed among the world's automobile manufacturers. Thought to be a brutally competitive industry, the share of the U.S. market held by that nation's Big Three auto companies (General Motors, Ford, and Chrysler) continues to decline. In fact, these companies' combined share of car sales in the United States fell from 74 percent in 1985 to 61 percent at the end of 1997. Some analysts predicted that without successful competitive responses and innovative competitive actions, the Big Three's market share could decline another five percentage points by the end of 2002.[7]

Contributing partially to the decline in domestic market share held by the U.S. Big Three auto companies were ineffective decisions regarding the nature of competitive practices and the interests of consumers with respect to several product lines, including small cars.[8] However, a global managerial mind-set (see Chapter 1) that calls for an emphasis on international markets also accounts for some of this decline in market share. Toyota executives appear to operate from such a mind-set.

Currently the third largest auto manufacturer in the world, Toyota is initiating a series of competitive actions that is intended to result in the firm replacing Ford Motor Company as the world's second largest car company. Viewing the world as its marketplace, the firm wants to supply 65 percent of its sales in large markets such as the United States and Europe from local sources rather than from Japan. To reach this goal, Toyota is engaged in what has been labeled "breakneck" expansion plans in both the United States and Europe. As a result, Toyota will be able to produce more than one million units in its North American plants by 1999.[9] Furthermore, Toyota believes that its current competitive actions will allow it to increase its European market share to 5 percent (from its current 3 percent share) in the near future. (Toyota holds 10 percent of the U.S. market and between 20 percent and 30 percent of Asian markets.)[10]

As these examples demonstrate, once the firm begins to look outside its domestic market to enhance its strategic competitiveness, the effective managerial mind-set expands quickly to include consideration of the need to compete in multiple global markets. This seems to be the case for Mahindra & Mahindra, India's largest manufacturer of utility vehicles and tractors. With 70 percent and 27 percent domestic market shares, respectfully, this firm intends to establish a global presence within five to six years. Following initial introductions of some of its products to the southern parts of the United States, Mahindra & Mahindra plans to move into African, South American, and eventually, European markets.[11]

Significant advances in communications technologies that allow more effective coordination across operations in multiple markets and faster decision making and competitive responses are the second reason for the changes taking place in many industries' competitive landscapes.[12] Third, new technology and innovations, particularly in the information technology and computer industries, have changed competitive landscapes in ways that facilitate small and medium-sized businesses' efforts to compete more effectively. Finally, the increasing number of agreements to allow free trade across country borders (such as the 1993 North American Free Trade Agreement, NAFTA) is facilitating a growing cross-border focus.[13]

The changing competitive landscape even has former competitors cooperating in such areas as new technology development and forming strategic alliances to compete against other competitors (as discussed in Chapter 9).[14] For example, a set of companies has formed two major alliances to battle for a Latin American pay television audience that is estimated to be as many as 45 million homes. Composed of Rupert Murdoch's News Corporation, Mexico's Grupo Televisa, and Brazil's Organizacoes Globo, Sky Latin America is the larger of the two alliances. Competing against this cooperative arrangement is Galaxy Latin America, a combination of the Cisneros group of Venezuela, Grupo Abril of Brazil, and Multivison, a family-run Mexican media company, and Hughes Electronics.[15] Global alliances have also been formed among many of the world's telephone companies to pursue business in Europe.[16] (Additional information about some of these telecommunications alliances is presented in a Strategic Focus in Chapter 9.) Increasingly, cooperative R&D arrangements are also being developed in the new competitive landscape. These arrangements are vehicles through which firms overcome their resource constraints by acquiring skills and capabilities from alliance partners.[17]

This chapter focuses on competitive dynamics. The essence of this important topic is that a firm's strategies and their implementation (see Figure 1.1) are dynamic in nature. Actions taken by one firm often elicit responses from competitors. These responses, in turn, typically result in responses from the firm that acted originally as illustrated by the opening case concerned with the competitive actions begin taken by some of the world's steel manufacturers. The series of competitive actions and competitive responses among firms competing within a particular industry creates **competitive dynamics**. Such dynamic competitive interaction often shapes the competitive position of firms undertaking the business-level strategies described in the previous chapter and to some extent, corporate strategies (product diversification, international diversification, and cooperative strategies) described in later chapters. Thus, because of the reality of competitive dynamics, the effectiveness of any type of strategy is determined not only by the initial move, but also by how well the firm "anticipates and addresses the moves and countermoves of competitors and shifts in customer demands over time."[18]

Competitive dynamics results from a series of competitive actions and competitive responses among firms competing within a particular industry.

To discuss the part of the strategic management process called competitive dynamics, we introduce a model (see later discussion of Figure 5.1) of competitive dynamics; the remainder of the chapter describes it. Firms able to understand and deal successfully with competitive dynamics increase the probability of avoiding US Airways' recent situation. Caught in a competitive squeeze between lower-cost regional carriers, which were picking off the firm's best routes, and larger carriers with national and global route structures, US Airways lacked the resources to match, the company's executives were committed to finding a more attractive competitive position for their firm.[19]

After the overall model is introduced, we examine the factors that lead to competitive attack and potential response. This is followed by a discussion of the incentives of market leadership (first-mover advantages) and its disadvantages. We also discuss the advantages and disadvantages of followership (second or late movers). Once a competitive action is taken, a number of factors help determine the potential response. These factors are discussed next. We then examine firms' capabilities for attack and response, including firm size, speed of decision making, innovation, and product and process quality. Following these descriptions is a discussion of three different types of market competition (defined later as slow cycle, standard cycle, and fast cycle) that result from competitive interaction. In particular, we explore the nature of rivalry and propose strategies for competition in fast-cycle markets where competitive rivalry has escalated to an intense level and where the new competitive landscape is probably the most evident. This discussion examines the strategy of competitive disruption, in which firms capitalize on temporary compared to sustained competitive advantage by cannibalizing their past new product entry to introduce the next product or process innovation. Finally, we describe competitive rivalry outcomes as industries move through the emerging, growth, and maturity stages.

MODEL OF COMPETITIVE DYNAMICS AND RIVALRY

Competitive rivalry exists when two or more firms jockey with one another in the pursuit of an advantageous market position.

Over time, firms competing in an industry are involved with a number of competitive actions and competitive responses.[20] **Competitive rivalry** exists when two or more firms jockey with one another in the pursuit of an advantageous market position. Competitive rivalry takes place between and among firms because one or more competitors feel pressure or see opportunities to improve their market position. Rivalry is possible because of competitive asymmetry. The principle of individual differences, competitive asymmetry exists when firms differ from one another in terms of their resources, capabilities, and core competencies (see Chapter 3) and in terms of the opportunities and threats in their industry and competitive environments (see Chapter 2). Strategies, and, especially business-level strategies, are formed to exploit the asymmetric relationships existing among competitors.[21]

In most industries, a firm's competitive actions have observable effects on its competitors and typically cause responses designed to counter the action.[22] In early 1998, for instance, Renault, France's largest car and truck manufacturer, announced plans to increase its output by 500,000 units a year through 2002. In addition, the carmaker indicated that it was committed to improving the efficiency of its manufacturing operations to reduce its overall costs. Renault's competitive decisions were made partly in response to Toyota's previously announced intention to build a new small-car manufacturing plant in France. Even in light of chronic overcapacity in the world's automobile manufacturing industry, Renault officials believed that the firm's response was required for it to become more competitive in its home market and to prevent Renault from falling behind more efficient rivals such as Toyota.[23]

As the example of competitive actions and competitive responses among the world's steel manufacturers demonstrates, firms are mutually interdependent with their competitors.[24]

Mutual interdependence among firms means that strategic competitiveness and above-average returns result only when companies recognize that their strategies are not implemented in isolation from their competitors' actions and responses. Eastman Kodak Co. and Fuji Photo Film Co., for example, continue to engage in a series of competitive actions and responses in efforts to establish competitive advantages. Competition in the United States with Fuji has affected Kodak's performance. To reduce the decline in its domestic market share, Kodak priced its film products aggressively during the 1997 Christmas season. Company officials indicated that this pricing decision boosted the firm's U.S. film sales 2 percent during the year's last quarter. Ted McGrath, president of Fuji's U.S. photo imaging operations, said, "Fuji is evaluating its 1998 strategy. We're not going to sit back and be submissive, but we're not going to do anything alarming."[25] Thus, because it affects strategic competitiveness and returns, firms are concerned about the pattern of competitive dynamics and the rivalry it creates.[26]

Mutual interdependence among firms means that strategic competitiveness and above-average returns result only when companies recognize that their strategies are not implemented in isolation from their competitors' actions and responses.

Figure 5.1 illustrates a summary model of interfirm rivalry and the likelihood of attack and response. As can be seen from the model, competitor analysis begins with analyzing competitor awareness and motivation to attack and respond to competitive action. *Awareness* refers to whether or not the attacking or responding firm is aware of the competitive market characteristics such as the market commonality and the resource similarity of a potential attacker or respondent (these terms are defined in a subsequent section).[27] Managers may have "blind spots" in their industry and competitor analyses due to underestimation or an inability to analyze these factors.[28] This may be the case in the U.S. blue-jeans market. Levi Strauss & Co.'s failure to pay close attention to changes in teenagers' interests appears to have contributed to the decline in the firm's share of its core market. In 1990, Levi had 30.9 percent of the U.S. blue jeans market; at the end of 1997, this percentage had declined to 18.7. During this time period, competition in this part of the clothing fashion industry intensified considerably, affecting Levi Strauss in the

FIGURE 5.1 *A Summary Model of Interfirm Rivalry: The Likelihood of Attack and Response*

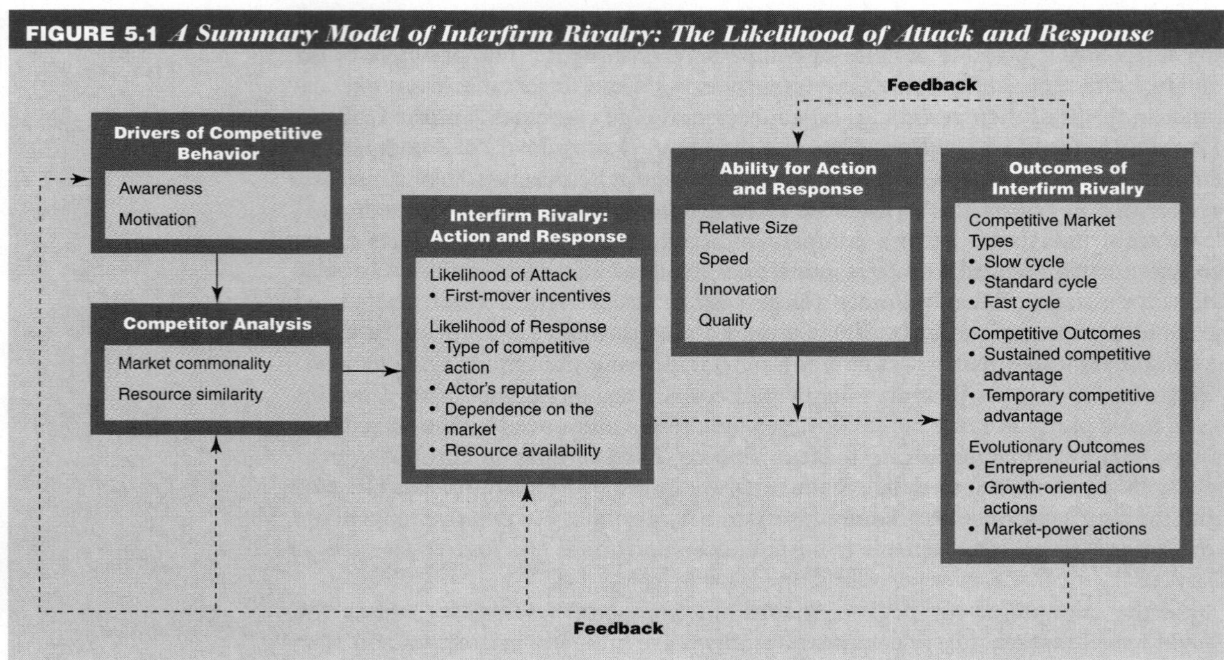

Source: Adapted from M. J. Chen, 1996, Competitor analysis and interfirm rivalry: Toward a theoretical integration, *Academy of Management Review* 21: 100–134.

process: "Top-end designers such as Tommy Hilfiger and Ralph Lauren have squeezed Levi on one end, while private labels sold by low-priced retailers such as J.C. Penney Co. and Sears Roebuck and Co. have come on strong from the other direction.[29] This lack of awareness may lead to such things as industry overcapacity and excessive competition.[30] *Motivation* relates to the incentives a firm has to attack and respond if attacked. A firm may perceive advantages to moving first, given the potential for interaction.

As Figure 5.1 suggests, both market commonality and resource similarity mediate the awareness and motivation to undertake actions and responses. The likelihood of action and response will result in the competitive outcomes. These outcomes, however, will be moderated by a firm's ability to undertake strategic actions and responses. Furthermore, Figure 5.1 illustrates that feedback from the nature of rivalry will also influence the nature of a competitor's view of the previous exchange and may change the nature of awareness and motivation.

Market Commonality

Many firms, for example, those in the airlines, chemical, pharmaceutical, breakfast cereals, and electronics industries, compete in the same multiple markets. In the brewery industry, many beer producers compete in the same regional markets.[31] Regional competition is also evident in international markets through "triad" competition or the necessity for multinational corporations to have businesses in Asia (traditionally Japan), Europe, and North America.[32] When multimarket overlap exists between firms, this presents opportunities for **multipoint competition**, a situation in which firms compete against each other simultaneously in several product or geographic markets.[33] In the airline industry for instance, there are opportunities for multipoint competition. The three largest U.S. airlines, United, American, and Delta, have substantial market overlap and therefore substantial awareness and motivation to respond to competitive actions. Research has shown that such commonality reduces the likelihood of competitive interaction in the industry.[34] Because these three airlines operate in many common markets, competitive peace will reign until one firm makes a competitive move, then the competitive response will be swift.[35]

multipoint competition occurs when firms compete against each other simultaneously in several product or geographic markets.

There are many other examples of firms whose competitive actions involve them in situations of multipoint competition. For example, Bayerische Motoren Werke (BMW) and Honda Motor Company engage in multipoint competition as they both manufacture and sell cars and motorcycles. Hoechst AG and DuPont compete against each other in the specialty chemicals and plastic markets. Compaq, IBM, and Dell encounter multipoint competition as they compete in the home and business personal computer markets and the expanding server market.[36]

Resource Similarity

The intensity of competitive rivalry often is based on a potential response and is of great concern for an attacker. An attacker may not be motivated to target a rival that seems likely to retaliate. This is especially true for firms with strategic resources similar to those of a potential attacker.[37] (Resource similarity refers to the extent of resource overlap between two firms.)[38] In addition, resource dissimilarity likely plays a vital role in a competitor's motivation to attack or respond. In fact, "the greater is the resource imbalance between the acting firm and competitors or potential responders, the greater will be the delay in response."[39] Although the degree of market commonality is quite visible to the strategists of both firms, strategic resources, because of their possible indeterminable nature (due to, for example, causal ambiguity and social complexity as described in Chapter 3), tend to be much less identifiable. The difficulty in identifying and understanding relationships among the competing firms' resources (including its capabilities and core competencies) also contributes to response delays, especially in instances of resource dissimilarity.

Coca-Cola and Pepsi's decisions to compete in the bottled water market demonstrate an imbalance in resources between the acting firms (Coke and Pepsi) and the potential responding companies (Perrier Group, Suntory International, McKesson, Great Brands of Europe, and Crystal Geyser). Attracted by the then-current size ($3.6 billion in 1997) and rapid growth (8 percent annually) of the bottled water market, Coke and Pepsi decided to engage the industry's incumbents in competitive battle. Seeking to become the nation's number-one bottled water company, Pepsi introduced Aquafina in 1997. In addition to the several bottled waters it sells outside the United States, Coca-Cola intended to introduce such products in the U.S. market no later than 1998. In response to these intended competitive actions, an industry analyst observed, "Anytime Coke and Pepsi get into the market, they're going to shake things up." Indications are that executives at the Perrier Group are preparing their firm's competitive responses to the two giant firms' market entries. Kim Jeffery, president of the Perrier Group, suggested that "no one's going to dethrone us. The competition will only make us better."

However, the resource dissimilarity between the Perrier Group and Coca-Cola and Pepsi may delay initiation of the competitive responses the company will take to protect its key bottled water brands—Arrowhead, Poland Spring, and Great Bear.[40]

LIKELIHOOD OF ATTACK

A **competitive action** is a significant competitive move taken by a firm that is designed to gain a competitive advantage in a market.

Although awareness and motivation to respond are derived largely from competitor analysis of market commonality and resource similarity, there are strong incentives to be the first mover in a competitor battle if the attacking firm believes it has potential to win. A **competitive action** is a significant competitive move taken by a firm that is designed to gain a competitive advantage in a market.[41] Some competitive actions are large and significant; others are small and designed to help fine-tune or implement a strategy. The first mover in a competitive interaction may be able to gain above-average returns while competitors consider potential countermoves. Furthermore, the first mover may be able to deter counterattack if given enough time. Therefore, there are significant incentives to be a first mover and the order of each competitive action and response influences an industry's competitive dynamics. Of greatest importance are first movers, second movers, and late movers.

First, Second, and Late Movers

A **first mover** is a firm that takes an initial competitive action.

A **first mover** is a firm that takes an initial competitive action. The concept of first movers has been influenced by economist Joseph Schumpeter. In particular, he believed that firms achieve competitive advantage through entrepreneurial discovery and innovative competitive action.[42] In general, first movers "allocate funds for product innovation and development, aggressive advertising, and advanced research and development."[43] Through competitive actions such as these, first movers hope to gain a competitive advantage. For example, Mitsubishi Consumer Electronics America Inc. decided to discontinue selling tube-based television sets in the United States in the latter part of 1998. Seeking to "stake out a leading role in digital TV," Mitsubishi intended to concentrate all of its technological skills on the development of advanced sets.[44] The merger between Renaissance Capital Group, a Western-operated investment bank, and Russia's International Co. for Finance & Investment (ICFI) resulted in Russia's largest investment bank. Combining Renaissance's access to global capital with ICFI's extensive domestic operations made the bank the first in Russia to compete on an international scale. The merged unit was hopeful that its operational capacities would result in first mover advantages.[45]

Several competitive advantages can accrue to the firm that is first to initiate a competitive action. Successful actions allow a firm to earn above-average returns until other competitors are able to respond effectively. In addition, first movers have the opportunity to gain customer loyalty, thereby making it difficult for responding firms to capture customers. For instance, Harley-Davidson has been able to maintain a competitive lead in large motorcycles due to intense customer loyalty. Across time, though, the competitive advantage of a first mover begins to erode (recall from discussions in Chapter 1 that every competitive advantage can be imitated eventually). Consider Harley-Davidson's situation as an example. Since its turnaround in the early 1980s, Harley-Davidson has set the standard for loud,

Harley-Davidson has been able to maintain a competitive lead in large motorcycles because of intense customer loyalty.

low-riding, heavyweight V-twin cruisers. For most of the past 20 years, the firm has derived competitive benefits from being the first mover in its market segment and as a result of emphasizing its reputation and brand name as competitive advantages. Recently, however, competitors are achieving some success in competing against Harley. Big Dog Motorcycles is one of several new U.S. motorcycle manufacturers trying to produce products that emulate the characteristics and performance attributes of Harley's cruisers. For the most part, these competitors seek to offer customers a product that is of quality similar to Harley's, but at a lower price.[46]

The advantages and their duration vary by type of competitive action and industry. First-mover advantages also vary based on the ease with which competitors can imitate the action. The more difficult and costly an action is to imitate, the longer a firm may receive the benefits of being a first mover. When core competencies are the foundation of a competitive action, first-mover advantages tend to last for a longer period of time. Core competence-based competitive actions have a high probability of resulting in a sustained competitive advantage.

However, potential disadvantages may result from being the first firm to initiate a competitive action. Chief among these is the degree of risk taken by first movers. Risk is high because it is not easy to predict the amount of success a particular competitive action will produce prior to its initiation.[47] Oftentimes, first movers have high development costs. Second movers can avoid these costs through reverse engineering (taking apart a new product and then reassembling it to learn how it works). Another potential disadvantage of being a first mover may exist if the market in which the firm is competing is dynamic and uncertain. In other words, the extent and range of marketplace competition heighten the potential risk. In fact, in a highly uncertain market, it may be more appropriate to be a second or late mover.

A **second mover** is a firm that responds to a first mover's competitive action, often through imitation or a move designed to counter the effects of the action.

A **second mover** is a firm that responds to a first mover's competitive action, often through imitation or a move designed to counter the effects of the action.

When the second mover responds quickly to a first mover's competitive action, it may earn some of the first-mover advantages without experiencing the potential disadvantages. For example, a fast second mover may gain some of the returns and obtain a portion of the initial customers and thereby customer loyalty, while avoiding some of the risks encountered by the first mover. The firm taking a second action as a competitive response to the first mover can do so after evaluating customers' reactions to the first mover's action.[48] To be a successful first or fast second mover, a company must be able to analyze its markets and identify critical strategic issues.[49]

In some instances, it may not be possible to move quickly in response to a first mover's action. For example, if the first mover introduces a sophisticated new product and competitors have not undertaken similar research and development, considerable time may be required to respond effectively. Therefore, there are some risks involved in being a follower, as opposed to a leader, in the market. There are no blueprints for first-mover success. Followers may be able to respond without significant market development costs by learning from a first mover's successes and mistakes. Thus, the actions and outcomes of the first firm to initiate a competitive action may provide a more effective blueprint for second and later movers.[50] Table 5.1 provides a list of classic cases where imitators were able to overcome the pioneers' early entries.

New Balance Inc. is a second mover in the athletic shoe industry. Currently, it spends only $4 million annually to advertise its products. Mark Coogan, a marathoner who placed forty-first in the 1996 Olympics in his event, is the firm's best-known endorser. In contrast, Nike spent $1 billion on sponsored endorsements and advertising during 1997; in the same year for the same purposes, Reebok spent over $400 million.[51] Unlike Nike and Reebok, New Balance's market share is increasing rapidly. In fact, while the industry's sales increased 3 percent in 1997, New Balance recorded a sales gain of 16 percent.

Accounting for New Balance's success as a second mover is its ability to satisfy baby boomers' needs. The firm's target market is demonstrated by customers' average ages—Nike (25), Reebok (33), and New Balance (42). As a second mover, the firm's shoes are not particularly innovative as compared to industry leader Nike. In contrast to many competitors that introduce new models roughly every six weeks, New Balance introduces a new one approximately every 17 weeks. New Balance's competitive success as a second mover appears to be based on its ability to offer high-quality products at moderate prices but in multiple-sized widths. Unlike most companies, which produce shoes in two widths—medium and wide—New Balance offers customers five choices, ranging from a narrow AA to an expansive EEEE. The varying widths is a valued competitive feature, in that about 20 to 30 percent of the U.S. population has narrower, or wider, than average feet.[52]

A **late mover** is a firm that responds to a competitive action, but only after considerable time has elapsed after the first mover's action and the second mover's response. Although some type of competitive response may be more effective than no response, late movers tend to be poorer performers and often are weak competitors.

LIKELIHOOD OF RESPONSE

Once firms take competitive action, the success of the particular action will often be determined by the likelihood and nature of response. A **competitive response**

TABLE 5.1 *Cases Where Second/Late Movers Surpassed First Movers*

Product	First Movers	Second/Late Movers	Comments
35mm cameras	Leica (1925) Contrax (1932) Exacta (1936)	Canon (1934) Nikon (1946) Nikon SLR (1959)	The German pioneers were the technology and market leader for decades until the Japanese copied their technology, improved on it, and lowered prices. The pioneers then failed to react and ended up as incidental players.
Ballpoint pens	Reynolds (1945) Eversharp (1946)	Parker "Jotter" (1954) Bic (1960)	The pioneers disappeared when the fad first ended in the late 1940s. Parker entered eight years later. Bic entered last and sold pens as cheap disposables.
Caffeine-free soft drinks	Canada Dry's "Sport" (1967) Royal Crown's RC1000 (1980)	Pepsi Free (1982) Caffeine-free Coke, Tab (1983)	The pioneers had a three-year head start on Coke and Pepsi but could not hope to match the distribution and promotional advantages of the giants.
CAT scanners (computed axial tomography)	EMI (1972)	Pfizer (1974) Technicare (1975) GE (1976) Johnson & Johnson (1978)	The pioneers had no experience in the medical equipment industry. Imitators ignored its patents and drove the pioneer out of business with marketing, distribution, and financial advantages, as well as extensive industry experience.
Commercial jet aircraft	deHavilland Comet 1 (1952)	Boeing 707 (1954) Douglas DC-8 (1955)	The British pioneer rushed to market with a jet that crashed frequently. Boeing followed with safer, larger, and more powerful jets unsullied by tragic crashes.
Diet soft drinks	Kirsch's No-Cal (1952) Royal Crown's Diet Rite Cola (1962)	Pepsi's Patio Cola (1963) Coke's Tab (1963) Diet Pepsi (1964) Diet Coke (1982)	The pioneers could not match the distribution advantages of Coke and Pepsi. Nor did they have the money needed for massive promotional campaigns.
Dry beer	Asahi (1987)	Kirin, Sapporo, and Suntory in Japan (1988) Michelob Dry (1988) Bud Dry (1989)	The Japanese pioneer could not match Anheuser-Busch's financial, marketing, and distribution advantages in the U.S. market.
Light beer	Rheingold's Gablinger's (1966) Meister Brau Lite (1967)	Miller Lite (1975) Natural Light (1977) Coors Light (1978) Bud Light (1982)	The pioneers entered nine years before Miller and sixteen years before Bud Light, but financial problems drove both out of business. Marketing and distribution determined the outcome. Costly legal battles were commonplace.
MRI (magnetic resonance imaging)	Fonar (1978)	Johnson & Johnson's Technicare (1981) General Electric (1982)	The tiny pioneer faced the huge medical equipment suppliers, who easily expanded into the MRI arena. The pioneer could not hope to match their tremendous market power.
Operating systems personal computers	CP/M (1974)	MS-DOS (1981) Microsoft Windows (1985)	The pioneer created the early standard but did not upgrade for the IBM-PC. Microsoft bought an imitative upgrade and became the new standard. Windows entered later and borrowed heavily from predecessors, then emerged as the leading interface.
Personal computers	MITS Altair 8800 (1975) Apple II (1977) Radio Shack (1977)	IBM-PC (1981) Compaq (1982) Dell (1984) Gateway (1985)	The pioneers created computers for hobbyists, but when the market turned to business uses, IBM entered and quickly dominated, using its reputation and its marketing and distribution skills. The second movers then copied IBM's standard and sold at lower prices.
Pocket calculators	Bowmar (1971)	Texas Instruments (1972)	The pioneer assembled calculators using TI's integrated circuits. TI controlled Bowmar's costs, which rose as calculator prices fell. Vertical integration was the key.

Source: S. P. Schnaars, 1994, *Managing Imitation Strategies: How Later Entrants Seize Markets from Pioneers* (New York: The Free Press).

A **late mover** is a firm that responds to a competitive action, but only after considerable time has elapsed after the first mover's action and the second mover's response.

A **competitive response** is a move taken to counter the effects of an action by a competitor.

is a move taken to counter the effects of an action by a competitor. Firms considering offensive action need to be cognizant of the potential response from competition. An offensive action may escalate rivalry to a point where action becomes self-defeating and an alternative strategy may be necessary. A *deescalation strategy* is an attempt to reduce overly heated competition that has become self-defeating. As Figure 5.1 shows, the probability of a competitor response to a competitive action is based on the type of action, the reputation of the competitor taking the action, the competitor's dependence on the market, and competitor resource availability.

Type of Competitive Action

A **strategic action** represents a significant commitment of specific and distinctive organization resources; it is difficult to implement and to reverse.

The two types of competitive actions are strategic and tactical.[53] A **strategic action** represents a significant commitment of specific and distinctive organizational resources; it is difficult to implement and to reverse. The introduction of an innovative product to a market, Compaq Computer's purchase of Digital Equipment Corporation, and the recent decision by some high-tech companies to allocate significant financial resources to build brand names for their products are all examples of strategic actions.

Manufacturers of the hardware and software that drive computer networks are becoming powerful global competitors, but few of these companies are known outside of the business markets in which their products are sold. Recently three of the largest firms in the network-computing business (Cisco Systems, Oracle, and Sun Microsystems) concluded that their future success requires recognition and admiration by a wider public. Expensive in nature (analysts estimate that the three firms collectively will spend billions of dollars), each company's newly developed long-term marketing campaign is intended to promote its image with the general public.

The effort to build a brand name for its products was inspired by the success of the "Intel Inside" campaign. Market research results suggest that for many PC buyers, the Intel Inside logo that is positioned on computer manufacturers' products has become a "trustmark"—a trademark on which a significant part of the purchase decision is based. Cisco, Oracle, and Sun hope to duplicate Intel's brand-image accomplishment among buyers of computer networks. Oracle, for example, which is the world's second largest software firm, chose the slogan "Oracle—Enabling the Information Age" for its advertising campaign. Initially, Sun used the logo "100% Pure Java" to support its brand-building efforts; Cisco coined the Cisco Powered Network (CPN) logo for the same purpose.[54] Because of the expense and the commitment being made to the marketplace, each firm's decision to enter into brand-building marketing campaigns is an example of a strategic competitive action.

A **tactical action** is taken to fine-tune a strategy; it involves fewer and more general organizational resources and is relatively easy to implement and reverse.

In contrast to strategic actions, a **tactical action** is taken to fine-tune a strategy; it involves fewer and more general organizational resources and is relatively easy to implement and reverse. A price increase in a particular market (e.g., in airfares) is an example of a tactical action. This action involves few organizational resources (e.g., communicating new prices/changing prices on products), its implementation is relatively easy, and it can be reversed (through a price reduction, for example) in a relatively short period of time.

Responses to a strategic action, as compared to a tactical action, are more difficult because they require more organizational resources and are more time consuming. As compared to strategic actions, tactical actions usually have more immediate effects. The announcement of a price increase in a price-sensitive market such as airlines could have immediate effects on competitors. As such, it is not uncommon to find airlines responding quickly to a competitor's price change, particularly if the announced change represents a price decrease because without a response other airlines may lose market share.[55]

Airline companies also respond quickly to tactical actions taken regarding frequent flier programs. For example, American Airline's recent creation of an Executive Platinum level of service for the "ultra frequent flyer" was imitated quickly by Trans World Airlines.[56] Rapid competitive responses are often initiated in low-cost goods and services markets. Cash flow is critical to firms (such as airline companies) competing in these markets, and consumers are price-sensitive because there is relatively little differentiation in the services provided. Moreover, attempted differentiated efforts tend to be imitated rapidly. In addition to imitations of frequent flyer program changes, those competing in the airline industry in the latter part of the 1990s imitated actions being taken to (1) refurbish airplanes, (2) set aside the best seats for the firm's best customers, (3) add food to more flights and increase the amount of food on flights currently receiving such service, and (4) assure on-time arrivals and effective and safe handling of luggage.[57]

Not all competitive actions will elicit or require a response from competitors. On the whole, there are more competitive responses to tactical than to strategic actions.[58] It is usually easier to respond to tactical than to strategic actions and sometimes more necessary, at least in the short term. For example, responding to changes in a competitor's frequent flier program is much easier and requires far fewer resources as compared to responding to a major competitor's decision to upgrade its fleet of jets and to form strategic alliances to enter new markets.

Actor's Reputation

An action (either strategic or tactical) taken by a market leader is likely to serve as a catalyst to a larger number of and faster responses from competitors and to a higher probability of imitation of the action. In other words, firms are more likely to imitate the actions of a competitor that is a market leader. For instance, Anheuser-Busch's decision to deepen its ties with Mexican brewer Grupo Modelo is a competitive action that may elicit rapid and imitative actions. By increasing its ownership position in Modelo to 37 percent, U.S. market leader Anheuser-Busch signaled to competitors its renewed commitment to broaden its profit base and to establish Budweiser as a global brand.[59] Similarly, FedEx's merger with Caliber System is the type of competitive action that will be evaluated carefully by the firm's competitors. With Caliber System's RPS subsidiary now in its fold, analysts thought that FedEx would be able to grow more rapidly than it could have alone. Using RPS's fleet of 13,500 trucks, FedEx enhanced its ability to compete against United Parcel Service, "because both companies move nonexpress parcels primarily by ground when they don't absolutely, positively have to arrive by the next day"[60] (additional information about UPS appears in Chapter 6).

Firms also often react quickly to imitate successful competitor actions. An example is the personal computer market, where IBM quickly dominated the market as a second mover but was also imitated by Compaq, Dell, and Gateway (see Table 5.1). Alternatively, firms that have a history as strategic players that take risky, complex, and unpredictable actions are less likely to solicit responses to and imitation of their actions.[61] Finally, firms that are known to be price predators (frequently cutting prices to hurt competitors and obtain market share, only to raise prices later) also do not elicit a large number of responses or imitation. In fact, there is less imitation and a much slower response to price predators than to either of the other two types of firms (market leader and strategic player).[62]

Dependence on the Market

Firms with a high dependency on a market in which a competitive action is taken are more likely to respond to that action. For example, firms with a large amount of total sales from one industry are more likely to respond to a particular competitive action taken in their primary industry than is a firm with businesses in multiple industries (e.g., conglomerate). Thus, if the type of action taken has a major effect on them, firms are likely to respond, regardless of whether it is a strategic or a tactical action. A pattern of competitive actions and competitive responses occurring between two firms that are highly dependent on their core market is described in the Strategic Focus about Burger King and McDonald's.

STRATEGIC FOCUS

Burger King and McDonald's: The Battle of Burgers and Fries

Burger King and McDonald's are both completely dependent on sales in the fast food industry. As such, it is not surprising that the firms monitor each other's strategic and tactical actions quite carefully. Moreover, competitive actions taken by one of these companies, whether strategic or tactical, almost certainly will result in a competitive response. Following are examples of such competitive actions and responses.

McDonald's is much larger than its counterpart. In the United States, McDonald's had almost 12,500 units at the beginning of 1998, compared to Burger King's total of about 7,500 in the same market at the same time. Burger King has 2,000-plus units outside the United States, which is substantially fewer than the over 10,000 units that bear the McDonald's name. But, recent experiences may suggest that being the biggest does not assure recording the best performance. In fact, difficulties at McDonald's in the latter part of the 1990s contributed to Burger King's willingness to engage in a series of competitive actions and competitive responses with McDonald's. Examples of McDonald's end-of-the-1990s woes include the following: (1) a low-fat hamburger that was launched in 1991 and abandoned in 1996, (2) the Arch Deluxe that was introduced in 1996 and whose future was in doubt in 1998 (the company even conceded that in consumer taste tests, the Arch Deluxe was not seen, at least by some survey participants, as delivering value versus Burger King's Whopper), and (3) the ineffectiveness of 1997's 55-cent promotion program. (Consumers were annoyed that 55-cent burgers, including the Big Mac, at one point, were available only when other full-priced food items were purchased simultaneously.)

Sensing that the firm might be more vulnerable to competitive attack as a result of these difficulties, Burger King took several actions. On August 28, 1997, the company launched the Big King. A direct competitor of McDonald's Big Mac, this was Burger King's first new sandwich offering since introducing the BK Broiler in 1990. A Big Mac lookalike, the Big King had 75 percent more beef and considerably less bread than the Big Mac. Describing the initial success of the product's introduction, Burger King officials suggested that the "personality" of the Big King would allow it to compete well in direct competition with the Big Mac. "Get ready for the taste that beats the Big Mac" was the advertising slogan accompanying the Big King's introduction.

McDonald's did not take Burger King's decision to attack its 30-year-old core product lightly, especially because customer's initial reaction to the Big King was positive. In fact, less than one month after the Big King was introduced, McDonald's launched its lookalike challenge to the Whooper, which is Burger King's flagship sandwich. Called "The Big 'n Tasty," analysts observed the remarkable similarity between this product and the Whopper, "right down to the 4.5-inch diameter of its sesame-seed bun."

Also, the competitive battle between these two firms escalated beyond burgers to fries. Because fries had long been acknowledged as one of McDonald's competitive advantages, Burger King's decision to fight McDonald's in terms of this particular product was significant. Burger King used another slogan that attacked McDonald's product directly—"The taste that beat McDonald's fries"—to introduce its new fries to the marketplace. As suggested by the following statement, a different production process is what Burger King believes creates its superior product: "The new fries are made with a process in which fresh-cut potatoes are sprayed with a potato-based coating before they are frozen, shipped and then cooked, as before, in vegetable oil. The result is fries that are tastier, crispier, and stay hot longer." To promote the new product, Burger King declared Friday, December 26, 1997, Free FryDay in the United States. On this day, anyone could visit a Burger King unit and receive a free bag of french fries. Company officials indicated that about 15 million bags were handed out through this promotion.

Burger King executives interpreted the results of blind french fry taste tests positively. In these tests, 57 percent of consumers preferred Burger King's new fries against 35 percent preferring McDonald's, with the 8 remaining percent expressing no opinion. The history of competitive dynamics between these two firms suggests that each firm should expect a rapid competitive response to the competitive actions it has taken in regard to both burgers and french fries.

SOURCE: R. Tomkins, 1998, Burger King fires harder, *The Financial Times*, January 5, 19; Associated Press, 1997, Frying in the face of McDonald's, *Dallas Morning News*, December 11, D1; E. S. Browning and R. Gibson, 1997, McDonald's arches lose golden luster, *Wall Street Journal*, September 3, C1, C2; G. DeGeorge, 1997, Can it make hash out of Big Mac? *Business Week*, September 8, 42; M. H. Gerstein, 1997, McDonald's Corp., *Value Line*, September 19, 321; R. Gibson, 1997, Burger wars sizzle as McDonald's clones the Whopper, *Wall Street Journal*, September 17, B1.

Competitor Resource Availability

A competitive response to a strategic or tactical action also requires organizational resources. Firms with fewer resources are more likely to respond to tactical actions than to strategic ones because responses to tactical actions require fewer resources and are easier to implement. In addition, firm resources may dictate the type of response. For example, local video stores have relatively limited resources to respond to competitive actions taken by Blockbuster, one of the large retail chains competing in the video business and the industry's dominant firm. Typically, a local store cannot imitate a Blockbuster strategic action to establish multiple units within a particular geographic area in the pursuit of blanket market coverage. In contrast, the smaller local firm is far more likely to respond to a Blockbuster tactical action of reduced prices. However, because of its lower volume and lack of purchasing power, relative to the large chains, initiating a competitive response in the form of a tactical price reduction can also be difficult for the local store. To compete against Blockbuster, the local video store often relies on personalized customer service and a concentration on being willing to stock or search for hard-to-find videos as the sources of its competitive advantage. A focus on mass availability of the most popular titles and a desire to hold operating costs as low as possible suggest that a large video chain such as Blockbuster will not necessarily respond to the local store's service-oriented competitive actions, even though it has the resources to do so.[63]

As this example suggests, small firms can respond effectively to their larger counterparts' competitive actions. In the toy industry, some small, localized competitors are initiating an array of competitive responses to the big toy store chains' (e.g., Toys "R" Us and Kay-Bee Toys) promotions, discount prices, and enormous merchandise variety. Children's General Store, for example, seeks to carry specialized products that the chains don't stock. Sullivan's Toy Store in Washington, D.C., expects its clerks to spend as much as a half-hour helping customers find the "perfect" gift. The store's owners believe that such personalized service is of significant value to customers. Located in Essex Junction, Vermont, Timeless Toys Inc. specializes in what it considers to be "beautiful dolls." Janet's Thingamajigs focuses on classic, second-hand toys. This store seems to benefit competitively from the enjoyment some parents derive from watching their children play with toys they used during their youth. Thus, even without the level and types of resources required to imitate larger firms' competitive actions, small companies can achieve success when their competitive responses allow them to use their unique resources to create value for a specialized customer segment.[64]

FIRMS' ABILITIES TO TAKE ACTION AND RESPOND

As indicated earlier, resource availability and ability to respond affect the probability of a company's response to a competing firm's competitive actions. Firms' abilities therefore moderate the relationship between interfirm rivalry and the competitive outcomes (see Figure 5.1). There are four general firm abilities to take action that influence competitive interaction within a market or industry: (1) relative firm size within a market or industry, (2) the speed at which competitive actions and responses are made, (3) the extent of innovation by firms in the market or industry, and (4) product quality.

Relative Firm Size

The *size* of a firm can have two important, but opposite, effects on an industry's competitive dynamics. First, the larger a firm, the greater its market power. Of course, the extent of any firm's market power is relative to the power of its competitors. Boeing Company (with roughly a 65 percent share of the world's commercial aircraft market) and Airbus Industrie (with approximately a 33 percent market share) both have substantial market power. Relatively, however, Boeing's market power exceeds that of Airbus.[65] In the U.S. automobile manufacturing industry, all three major competitors are large; as such, no individual firm has relative and critical market power over the others. Nonetheless, it is difficult for small firms to enter the market because the sheer size of the Big Three creates substantial entry barriers to the industry. On a global level, Toyota continues to increase its market power as a result of its growth. This power will increase again if it is able to reach the objective discussed earlier in the chapter—namely, replacing Ford Motor Company as the world's second largest car and truck manufacturer.

Another example of market power is shown by Sega's recent problems. A Japanese maker of video games and the equipment on which the games are played, Sega encounters stiff competition throughout the world. In particular, Sony's PlayStation recently was able to outpace sales of Sega's Saturn machine. Following analysis of the competitive situation, Sega decided not to pursue sales of the Saturn because of the belief that to do so would result in further damage to the firm's profitability. Also contributing to this decision was Sony's market signal to Sega that the PlayStation would be priced even more competitively. Relative to Sega, Sony has a much stronger resource base to support this tactical competitive action. Because of declining volume and Sony's market power, Sega executives concluded that it could not continue to compete primarily on the basis of price with its more powerful competitor. Instead of selling the Saturn machine, Sega decided to focus on software sales where the firm's profit margins were more attractive.[66]

Problems created by firm size are demonstrated by events—both historical and current—in the computer industry. Although the giant in the industry, IBM, was highly successful, it did not invent or first introduce the microcomputer, which is the primary basis of the industry today. It took entrepreneurial ventures, such as Apple Computer, Dell Computer, and Compaq, to introduce the innovations in goods and services that revolutionized the industry. Small firms often do this by fostering what Joseph Schumpeter referred to as creative destruction.[67] As Steven Jobs and his partner Steve Wozniak revolutionized the computer industry, Michael Dell, who was in high school when Apple introduced its computers, revolutionized the way computers were produced and distributed.

Some believe that the success of the revolution credited to Dell Computer Corp. is demonstrated by the view that the firm had become the driving force in the PC business as the 1990s came to a close. In suggesting this perspective, one business writer noted, "In just a few years the company has gone from a compelling sideshow in the industry to a fast-charging threat to big boys like Compaq and IBM. Thanks to a low-cost, direct-sales model . . . Dell's global-market-share rank has climbed to a virtual tie for No. 3, from No. 8"[68] at the beginning of 1997.

Dell's superior marketplace performance quickly attracted a host of competitors. PC makers Hewlett-Packard, Compaq, and IBM, as well as retailers CompUSA, OfficeMax, and Computer City, all announced in 1997 that they were entering Dell's stronghold—the build-to-order (BTO) business. Some of these firms, CompUSA, for example, reported initial success with their direct sales approach.[69] As another indicator of the potential challenge to Dell's success, Compaq's CEO Eckhard Pfeiffer noted that his firm had been able to quickly erase Dell's cost advantages through the methods it was using in its newly created BTO business.[70] After surveying the late 1990s competitive landscape, Compaq's Pfeiffer suggested, "The future belongs to whichever company provides the right bundle of products, technology, solutions, and services with the lowest cost of ownership to customers."[71] History suggests that entrepreneurial ventures may be the ones to first discover ways to satisfy what CEO Pfeiffer sees as his industry's competitive challenges. On the other hand, Compaq's acquisition of Digital Equipment Corp. in 1998 and its selection as the sole provider of PCs to be sold in Tandy Corp.'s Radio Shack stores in the same year suggested that the firm was making progress toward its goal of becoming a full-service company with a solutions-oriented approach for customers.[72]

A quote attributed to Herbert Kelleher, co-founder and CEO of Southwest Airlines, best describes the approach needed by large firms. In Kelleher's words, "Think and act big and we'll get smaller. Think and act small and we'll get bigger."[73] This suggests that large firms should use their size to build market power, but that they must think and act like a small firm (e.g., move quickly and be innovative) in order to achieve strategic competitiveness and earn above-average returns over the long run. A commitment to the value of each employee and to the use of organizational structures that encourage individuals to demonstrate initiative appear to facilitate large firms' efforts to act entrepreneurially.[74] Thermo Electron, 3M, GTE, and Xerox are examples of large companies that are following these prescriptions to overcome the liabilities of size through the creation and support of entrepreneurship.[75]

Speed of Competitive Actions and Competitive Responses

Our world is one in which time and speed are important. We go to fast food restaurants and use microwave ovens. We regularly use e-mail, overnight express mail (public and private), and fax machines. The same is true with competition. The

"Think and act big and we'll get smaller. Think and act small and we'll get bigger," says Herb Kelleher, co-founder and CEO of Southwest Airlines.

speed with which a firm can initiate competitive actions and competitive responses may determine its success. In the global economy, speed in developing a new product and moving it to the marketplace is becoming critical to a firm's efforts to establish a sustainable competitive advantage and earn above-average returns.[76]

Executives at British Telecommunications (BT) have consciously increased the speed at which competitive decisions are made within the firm. Top-level managers considered the ability to make decisions more rapidly as vital if BT were to be able to take advantage of opportunities produced by various market liberalization policies. Making swift decisions, BT moved into new product territories, including advanced media services, as the twenty-first century approached. To compete successfully in this particular product area, BT formed an alliance, called British Interactive Broadcasting, with BskyB, Matsushita, and HSBC Midland. BT also created a 50–50 joint venture with the industrial group Viag to compete in Germany, which is Europe's largest telecommunications market. In France, BT has become a partner with Compagnie Generale des Eaux in Cegetel. Analysts expected this union to become the chief competitor to France Telecom. Through a series of alliances and partnerships such as these, BT has rapidly extended its influence outside of its home market. Some analysts believe that BT's decision-making speed and the competitive actions resulting from it indicate that the firm "can claim European leadership in moves to exploit market liberalisation."[77]

Speed to the marketplace is one of the problems U.S. automobile manufacturers have experienced in competing with Japanese firms. Some time ago, Japanese auto companies were able to design a new product and introduce it to the market within three years. In comparison, U.S. firms required between five and eight years to complete these activities. This time differential made it possible for Japanese firms to design and move to the market two or three new automobiles in the same time it took a U.S. automaker to do one.

In a global economy, although time is a critical source of competitive advantage, managing for speed requires more than attempting to have employees work faster. Essentially, it requires working smarter, using different types of organizational structures, and having the time required for completion as a primary work-related goal.[78] Research has shown that the pace of strategic decision making may be affected by an executive's cognitive ability, use of intuition, tolerance for risk, and propensity to act.[79] Executives who use intuition and have a greater tolerance for risk are predisposed to make faster strategic decisions than do those without such characteristics. It is also known that decisions are likely to occur faster in centralized organizations because they will not have to go through as many levels or get approval from as many people. More formalized and bureaucratic organizations, however, may find it difficult to make fast strategic decisions[80] because they require more layers of approval.

Jack Welch, chairman and CEO of General Electric, states that speed is the ability sought by all of today's organizations.[81] He suggests that companies are striving to develop products faster, speed up production cycles in moving them to the market, and improve response time to customers. In Welch's opinion, having faster communications and moving with agility are critical to competitive success.

Innovation

A third general factor, innovation, has long been known in some industries, such as pharmaceuticals and computers, to have a strong influence on firm performance.[82] The strategic importance of innovation is explored further in Chapter 13. In today's global economy, research suggests that innovation (both product innovation and process innovation) is becoming linked with above-average returns in a growing number of industries.[83] One study, for example, found that companies with the highest performance also invested the most in research and development. In 1960, U.S. firms held more than two-thirds of the world market in 10 of the top 15 major industries. By 1970, the United States continued to dominate 9 of those 15 industries. However, by 1980, U.S. domination was limited to only 3 of the 15 industries. The study found that this was due largely to changes in innovation. Firms from other countries were move innovative than U.S. firms in many of the industries.[84] In fact, a contributing factor to the productivity and technology problems experienced by U.S. firms has been managers' unwillingness to bear the costs and risks of long-term development of product and process innovations.[85]

In general, the dynamics of competition among firms competing in high-tech industries encourage significant allocations to each company's research and development function.[86] This is the case of Taiwan's Thunder Tiger, one of the world's leading manufacturers of radio-controlled model aircraft. Between 1987 and 1996, Thunder Tiger spent between 5 and 7 percent of its sales revenue on R&D. These allocations contributed to the firm's development of high-quality precision engineering skills as well as rigorous quality control techniques. These core competencies were the ones on which Thunder Tiger relied to develop and manufacture innovative, high-quality products over the years.

In 1997, the firm allocated 15 percent of revenues to R&D; similar if not identical allocations are expected in future years. Thunder Tiger's executives believe that the additional resources for R&D will support the company's new contract with the Taiwanese government that calls for it to develop an innovative prototype thrust engine for military and industrial purposes. The military will use Thunder Tiger's engine for remote-controlled decoy aircraft; in the industrial field, the engine will be used in turbine generators. In commenting about the nature of this contract, the firm's founder, Aling Lai, observed the following: "From toys to aerospace—sounds crazy, doesn't it? But, we see a lot of opportunities in the aerospace field and our R&D team is capable of developing advanced technology products."[87] Thus, innovation skills can be a great equalizer for small firms competing against large companies (see Chapter 13).

Firms competing in industries in which the pattern of competitive dynamics calls for innovation-related abilities should recognize that implementing innovations effectively can be difficult. Some researchers believe that implementation failure, not innovation failure, increasingly is the cause of a firm's inability to derive adequate competitive benefits from its product and process innovations.[88] Among other capabilities, a firm requires executives who are able to integrate its innovation strategy with other strategies (such as the business-level strategies discussed in Chapter 4) and an ability to recruit and select high-tech workers to successfully implement innovations.[89]

Our discussion of factors influencing an industry's competitive dynamics suggests that large firms with significant market power that act like small firms—making strategic decisions and implementing them with speed—and that are innovative are strong competitors and are likely to earn above-average returns. However, no matter how large, fast, and innovative an organization is, product quality also affects an industry's competitive dynamics and influences a firm's ability to achieve strategic competitiveness in domestic and global markets.

Quality

Product quality has become a universal theme in the global economy and continues to shape the competitive dynamics in many industries.[90] Today product quality is important in all industry settings and is a necessary, but not sufficient, condition to successful strategy implementation. Without quality goods or services, strategic competitiveness cannot be achieved. Quality alone, however, does not guarantee that a firm will achieve strategic competitiveness or earn above-average returns. In the words of the president of the National Center for Manufacturing Sciences, a nonprofit research consortium, "Quality used to be a competitive issue out there, but now it's just the basic denominator to being in the market."[91]

This is the case in the café-bakery business, for example. Accepting product quality as a given, executives heading competitors La Madeleine and Corner Bakery believe that their products are more than simply food. They suggest that their establishments and products contribute to a way of life for those interested in purchasing items from neighborhood bakeries with a family atmosphere.[92]

Quality involves meeting or exceeding customer expectations in the goods and/or services offered.[93] The quality dimensions of goods and services are shown in Table 5.2. As a competitive dimension, quality is as important in the service sector as it is in the manufacturing sector.[94]

Quality involves meeting or exceeding customer expectations in the goods and/or services offered.

Quality begins at the top of the organization. Top management must create values for quality that permeate the entire organization.[95] These values should be built into strategies that reflect long-term commitments to customers, stockholders, and other important stakeholders.[96]

TABLE 5.2 ***Quality Dimensions of Goods and Services***

Product Quality Dimensions	*Service Quality Dimensions*
1. *Performance*—Operating characteristics	1. *Timeliness*—Performed in promised time period
2. *Features*—Important special characteristics	2. *Courtesy*—Performed cheerfully
3. *Flexibility*—Meeting operating specifications over some time period	3. *Consistency*—All customers have similar experiences each time
4. *Durability*—Amount of use before performance deteriorates	4. *Convenience*—Accessible to customers
5. *Conformance*—Match with preestablished standards	5. *Completeness*—Fully serviced, as required
6. *Serviceability*—Ease and speed of repair or normal service	6. *Accuracy*—Performed correctly each time
7. *Aesthetics*—How a product looks and feels	
8. *Perceived quality*—Subjective assessment of characteristics (product image)	

Source: Adapted from J.W. Dean, Jr., and J.R. Evans, 1994, *Total Quality: Management, Organization and Society* (St. Paul, Minn.: West Publishing Company); H.V. Roberts and B.F. Sergesketter, 1993, *Quality Is Personal* (New York: The Free Press); D. Garvin, 1988, *Managed Quality: The Strategic and Competitive Edge* (New York: The Free Press).

Recent actions taken by Michael Dell demonstrate top managerial support for product quality. Although Dell Computer products have long had some of the highest quality ratings in the PC industry, Dell himself remains obsessed with the need for continuous quality improvements. To reduce the already relatively low failure rate of Dell's PCs, Dell became convinced that it was necessary to find a way to reduce the number of times a computer's hard drive—the most sensitive part of the PC—was handled during the assembly process. Based on this conviction, he insisted "that the number of touches be dramatically reduced from an existing level of more than 30 per drive." By revamping production lines, Dell employees were able to cut the number of touches by 50 percent. The results from this particular quality-based activity are impressive. After eliminating one-half of the hard drive touches, "the rate of rejected hard drives fell by 40 percent, and the overall failure rate for the company's PC dropped by 20 percent."[97] When top-level managers emphasize product quality in the manner demonstrated by Michael Dell, a process of total quality management pervades the firm in all activities and processes.

Quality and total quality management are closely associated with the philosophies and teachings of W. Edwards Deming (and, to a lesser extent, Armand Feigenbaum and Joseph Juran).[98] These individuals' contributions to the practice of management are based on a simple, yet powerful, insight; the understanding that it costs less to make quality products than defect-ridden ones.

Total quality management (TQM) is a "managerial innovation that emphasizes an organization's total commitment to the customer and to continuous improvement of every process through the use of data-driven, problem-solving approaches based on empowerment of employee groups and teams."[99] Actually a philosophy about how to manage, TQM "combines the teachings of Deming and Juran on statistical process control and group problem-solving processes with Japanese values concerned with quality and continuous improvement."[100] Statistical process control (SPC) is a technique used to upgrade continually the quality of the goods or services a firm produces. SPC benefits the firm through the detection and elimination of variations in processes used to manufacture a good or service.[101]

Total quality management is managerial innovation that emphasizes an organization's total commitment to the customer and to continuous improvement of every process through the use of data-driven, problem-solving approaches based on empowerment of employee groups and teams.

Although there are skeptics, when applied properly, the principles of total quality management can help firms achieve strategic competitiveness and earn above-average returns.[102] Three principal goals sought when practicing total quality management are boosting customer satisfaction, reducing product introduction time, and cutting costs. As discussed in this chapter, achievement of these goals can be expected to have a positive effect on a firm's performance. To reach these goals, firms must provide their employees and leaders with effective TQM training.[103]

Ironically, Deming's and Juran's ideas on quality and continuous improvement were adapted and implemented by Japanese firms long before many U.S. firms acknowledged their importance. For this reason, a host of Japanese firms developed a competitive advantage in product quality that has been difficult for U.S. firms to overcome.[104] Deming's 14 points for managing and achieving quality (see Table 5.3) have become a watchword in many businesses globally.

Embedded within Deming's 14 points for management is the importance of striving continuously to improve how a firm operates and the quality of its goods or services. In fact, Deming did not support use of the TQM term, arguing that he did not know what total quality was and that it is impossible for firms to reach a goal of "total quality." The pursuit of quality improvements, Deming believed, should be a never-ending process.

TABLE 5.3 ***Deming's 14 Points for Management***

1. Create and publish to all employees a statement of the aims and purposes of the company or other organization. The management must demonstrate constantly their commitment to this statement.
2. Learn the new philosophy, top management and everybody.
3. Understand the purpose of inspection, for improvement of processes and reduction of costs.
4. End the practice of awarding business on the basis of price tag alone.
5. Improve constantly and forever the system of production and service.
6. Institute training.
7. Teach and institute leadership.
8. Drive out fear. Create trust. Create a climate for innovation.
9. Optimize toward the aims and purposes of the company—the efforts of teams, groups, staff areas.
10. Eliminate exhortations for the workforce.
11. (a) Eliminate numerical quotas for production. Instead, learn and institute methods for improvement. (b) Eliminate management by objective. Instead, learn the capabilities of processes and how to improve them.
12. Remove barriers that rob people of pride of workmanship.
13. Encourage education and self-improvement for everyone.
14. Take action to accomplish the transformation.

Source: Reprinted from *Out of the Crisis* by W. Edwards Deming by permission of MIT and The W. Edwards Deming Institute. Published by MIT, Center for Advanced Engineering Study, Cambridge, MA 02139. Copyright © 1986 by W. Edwards Deming.

Newer methods of TQM use benchmarking and emphasize organizational learning.[105] Benchmarking facilitates TQM by developing information on the best practices of other organizations and industries. This information is often used to establish goals for the firm's own TQM efforts. Benchmarking provides a process from which a firm can learn from the outcomes of other firms.[106] Because of the importance of product (both goods and service) quality in achieving competitive parity or a competitive advantage, many firms in the United States and around the world are emphasizing total quality management and integrating it with their strategies.

As our discussions have indicated, relationships between each of the four general abilities (size, speed, innovation, and quality) influence a firm's competitive actions and outcomes. Those responsible for selecting a firm's strategy should understand these relationships and anticipate that competitors will take competitive actions and competitive responses designed to exploit the positive relationships depicted in Figure 5.2. In the next section, we describe the different outcomes of competitive dynamics.

OUTCOMES OF INTERFIRM RIVALRY

Figure 5.1 illustrates potential outcomes of interfirm rivalry. In some competitive environments, sustainable competitive advantage may be more likely. As discussed in Chapter 3, one of the key determinants of sustainability is whether a firm's prod-

FIGURE 5.2 ***Effects of Firm Size, Speed of Decision Making/Actions, Innovation, and Quality on Sustainability of Competitive Actions and Outcomes***

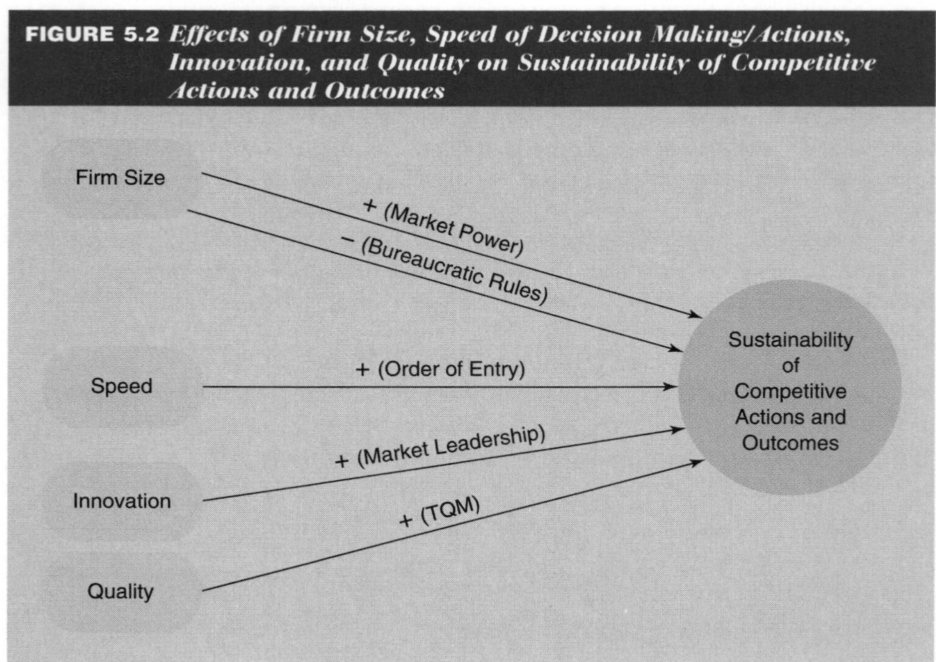

*Plus and minus signs indicate effects on performance.

ucts are costly to imitate. A sustainability framework, therefore, might focus on different market types where product imitability is largely or partially shielded.[107] All major markets have seen their foreign rivals make inroads into what had been their domestic markets. However, even with strong rivalry and increasing potential for imitability, some markets have been shielded from such competition. These markets are described as slow-cycle or sheltered markets. In other markets, product imitability is moderate. As such, they are labeled standard-cycle markets, often described as oligopolistic. In still other markets, firms are in rapid, dynamic, and often entrepreneurial environments where changes are identified as fast cycle.[108]

Competitive Market Outcomes

Products in **slow-cycle markets** reflect strongly shielded resource positions where competitive pressures do not readily penetrate a firm's sources of strategic competitiveness.

Products in **slow-cycle markets** reflect strongly shielded resource positions where competitive pressures do not readily penetrate the firm's sources of strategic competitiveness. This is often characterized in economics as a monopoly position. A firm that has a unique set of product attributes or an effective product design may dominate its markets for decades as did IBM with large mainframe computers. This type of competitive position can be established even in markets where there is significant technological change, such as Microsoft's position with difficult to imitate, complex software systems. Drug manufacturers often have established such a position legally under patent laws. Shielded advantages may be geographic; as such, the opening of huge emerging markets in Eastern Europe, Russia, China, and India offers strong motivation for firms to pursue such opportunities.

Although the idea of a monopoly, which has a single seller, restricted output, and high prices, is not likely to be attained in the United States because of government policy restrictions, subtle and more complex variations are possible with a local monopoly approach. This is what Wal-Mart did in its early years. It established a local monopoly in rural areas in the southwest United States, especially when coupled with efficient distribution systems. Many airlines also seek to establish a shielded advantage by the innovation of hub control at airports. Examples included American Airlines' dominance in Dallas and Delta's hubs in Atlanta and Salt Lake City.

Effective product designs may be able to dominate their markets for many years. For example, the McIlhenny family of Louisiana has dominated the hot sauce industry for 125 years with a singe product unchanged since its inception: Tabasco sauce.[109] These firms may be closely associated with the main idea of the resource-based view of the firm because their resources and capabilities are difficult to imitate. The sustainability of competitive action associated with a slow-cycle market is depicted in Figure 5.3.

Products in **standard-cycle markets** reflect moderately shielded resource positions where competitive interaction penetrates a firm's sources of strategic competitiveness; but with improvement of its capabilities, the firm may be able to sustain a competitive advantage.

Standard-cycle markets may be more closely associated with the industrial organization economics approach following Porter's five force model on competitive strategy. In these organizations, strategy and organization are designed to serve high-volume or mass markets. The focus is on coordination and market control as in automobile and appliance industries.[110] These organizations, even though they may be able to sustain world-class products for decades (e.g., Kellogg, Coca-Cola), may experience severe competitive pressures. Extended dominance and, in fact, world leadership is possible through continuing capital investment and superior learning as is the case with Coca-Cola. This contrasts with protected markets because there is not such a high rate of ongoing investment into the production of Tabasco sauce. Although it may be difficult to enter standard-cycle markets because of the competitive intensity, if successful and if duplicated by competitors, more intense competitive pressures can be brought to bear. More intense competition may be similar to that found in fast-cycle markets.[111]

FIGURE 5.3 *Gradual Erosion of a Sustained Competitive Advantage*

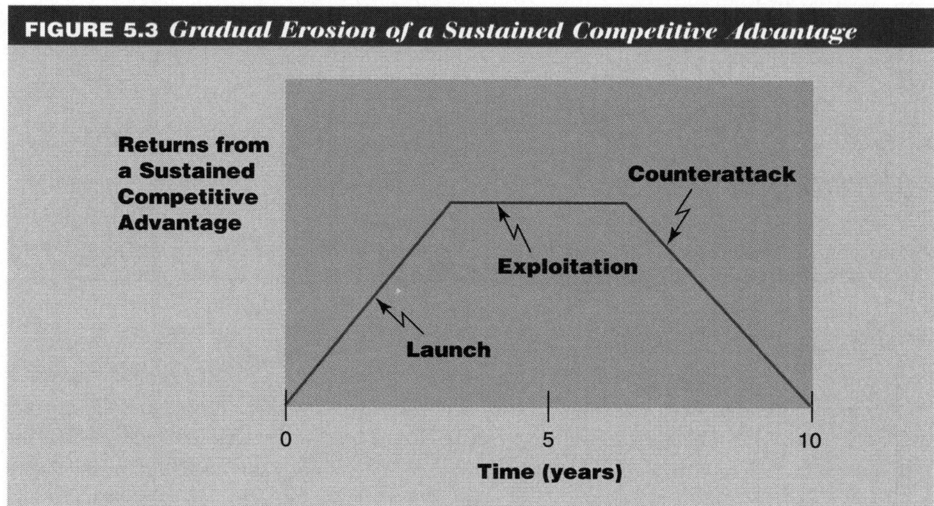

Source: Adapted from I.C. MacMillan, 1988, Controlling competitive dynamics by taking strategic initiative, *Academy of Management Executive* II, no. 2: 111–118.

Although Coca-Cola has been able to sustain world-class products for decades, it is still under pressure from competitors. Through continued capital investment and superior learning, the firm is able to maintain world dominance.

Competitive pressures facing Procter & Gamble (P&G) and Whirlpool Corp. are described in the Strategic Focus. Both of these firms have long held dominant positions while serving mass markets on a global basis, but as discussed in the Strategic Focus, competitors continue to challenge their positions through aggressive competitive actions. Thus, these two firms are experiencing significant competitive pressures while competing in standard-cycle markets.

STRATEGIC FOCUS

Of Toothpaste and Home Appliances: Competitive Dynamics in Standard-Cycle Markets

Competing in mature, slow-growth markets that tend to be overrun with products, Colgate-Palmolive (C-P) is being credited with revitalizing its North American operations in toothpaste, detergent, and personal care products.

Although New York-based, C-P generates almost 70 percent of its sales revenue from outside the United States and Canada. Nonetheless, the lack of a growth focus in the North American market was of deep concern to top-level executives for several years. To correct its deficiencies in this market, the firm recently closed inefficient facilities, revamped production processes, and invested heavily in new products. The results of these efforts were impressive for the 1997 fiscal year: North American sales increased 23 percent, gross margins expanded 5 percentage points (from 50 percent to 55 percent), and operating profits grew by 73 percent.

Toothpaste is one of the products that is of keen interest to C-P, primarily because oral care accounts for roughly one-third of the firm's revenues. For the first time, C-P's toothpaste market share in the United States now exceeds Procter & Gamble's. This accomplishment is impressive in that P&G held the top spot in this market for 35 consecutive years before being unseated by C-P in 1997.

To stimulate toothpaste sales even further, C-P recently introduced Total toothpaste into the United States (the product is also sold in 103 other countries). Analysts see Total as a potential blockbuster for C-P in terms of revenue and profit growth. It is the first oral pharmaceutical ever approved by the Food and Drug Administration. Total contains Triclosan, which is a broad-spectrum antibiotic that helps heal gingivitis. Gingivitis is a bleeding-gum disease that is afflicting an increasing number of aging baby boomers. To promote Total, C-P intended to spend $100 million in 1998 on an advertising campaign. None of C-P's rivals were even close to launching a similarly effective gum-disease-fighting toothpaste at the time Total was introduced. Having studied C-P's recent performance and intended future competitive actions, one analyst suggested that while Colgate-Palmolive was an underdog to P&G in the past, it is now "sucker-punching" the company through product and process innovations.

Whirlpool is the world's largest manufacturer of home appliances. To be competitive, the firm has taken a number of actions over the years, including investing in three appliance companies in Brazil and one in Canada and forming joint ventures with companies in Mexico, India, Taiwan, and China. Whirlpool now faces an attack from long-time rival General Electric (GE).

Under Jack Welch's leadership, GE seeks the number-one market position in businesses in which it competes. But, for all of its efforts, GE has never been able to unseat Whirlpool from its position as the largest appliance maker in the United States. As an indicator of the intensity of the rivalry between these two firms, consider the fact that based on its 35 percent share of the U.S. market as compared to GE's 32 percent, Whirlpool referred to GE in one of its recent annual reports as the "number-two company."

GE is redoubling its commitment to gain the top market share position from Whirlpool. The company spent approximately $100 million to develop what it sees as an innovative plastic basket for its new clothes washer. It is this basket on which GE is grounding its competitive attacks. GE claims that the clothes basket in Whirlpool's machines is made of steel covered with porcelain and that the porcelain chips. When told of this view, Whirlpool's CEO David Whitwam said, "You'd have to throw a brick in there to make it chip."

Of course, Whirlpool and GE face additional competitors. Haier Group, for example, is the number-one consumer electronics company in China. This firm accounts for almost 40 percent of China's refrigerator sales and a third of the country's washing machine and air-conditioner sales. Committed to aggressive growth, Haier's president wants his company to become an export powerhouse and achieve status as a global brand name. More aggressive pressure from other global competitors such as Haier Group suggests that Whirlpool and GE must continue to examine the full range of competitors when making decisions about how to compete in what historically has been a standard-cycle market.

SOURCE: L. Grant, 1998, Outmarketing P&G, *Fortune*, January 12, 150–162; W. M. Carley, 1997, GE, no. 2 in appliances, is agitating to grab share from Whirlpool, *Wall Street Journal*, July 2, A1, A6; K. Chen, 1997, Would America buy a refrigerator labeled "made in Qingdao"? *Wall Street Journal*, September 17, A1, A14; M. Moffett, 1997, Brasmotor's success draws competitors, *Wall Street Journal*, July 11, A10; C. Quintanilla and J. Carlton, 1997, Whirlpool unveils global restructuring effort, *Wall Street Journal*, September 19, A3, A6; P. H. Roth, 1997, Whirlpool Corp., *Value Line*, September 12, 134.

In **fast-cycle markets**, a competitive advantage cannot be sustained; firms attempt to gain temporary competitive advantages by strategically disrupting the market.

In **fast-cycle markets**, such as cellular telephones and DRAM computer chips, it does not appear that a first-mover advantage yields sustained competitive advantage. One way to examine the intensity of dynamics in these industries is to study the long-run pricing patterns of some products. For instance, in 1988, the cost per megabyte of DRAM computer chips was $378. Three years later, the market price for a one-megabyte chip had dropped to $35.[112] When cellular phones were introduced, they were priced at around $3,500, but five years later the price dropped below $100 and now cellular phone equipment is often given away if you subscribe to a cellular system service. Perpetual innovation and shorter product cycles dominate this market class. Standard-cycle markets are scale oriented, whereas fast-cycle markets are idea driven.

Competing in Fast-Cycle Markets

To this point in the chapter, the focus has been on trying to obtain a sustained competitive advantage. Sustained competitive advantage is possible in slow- and standard-cycle markets. Figure 5.3 focuses on this type of competitive advantage. Usually there is an entrepreneurial launch stage of the strategy, a period of exploitation, and, ultimately, a period of counterattack where the competitive advantage erodes. In fast-cycle markets, a sustained competitive advantage may be a goal that creates inertia and exposes one to aggressive global competitors. Even though GM and IBM have economies of scale, huge advertising budgets, the best distribution systems in their industry, cutting edge R&D, and deep pockets, many of their advantages have been eroded by global competitors in Europe, Japan, and now Korea.

A new competitive advantage paradigm is emerging where a firm seizes the initiative through a small series of steps as illustrated in Figure 5.4. As you can see from this figure, the idea is to create a counterattack before the advantage is eroded.

FIGURE 5.4 *Obtaining Temporary Advantages to Create Sustained Advantage*

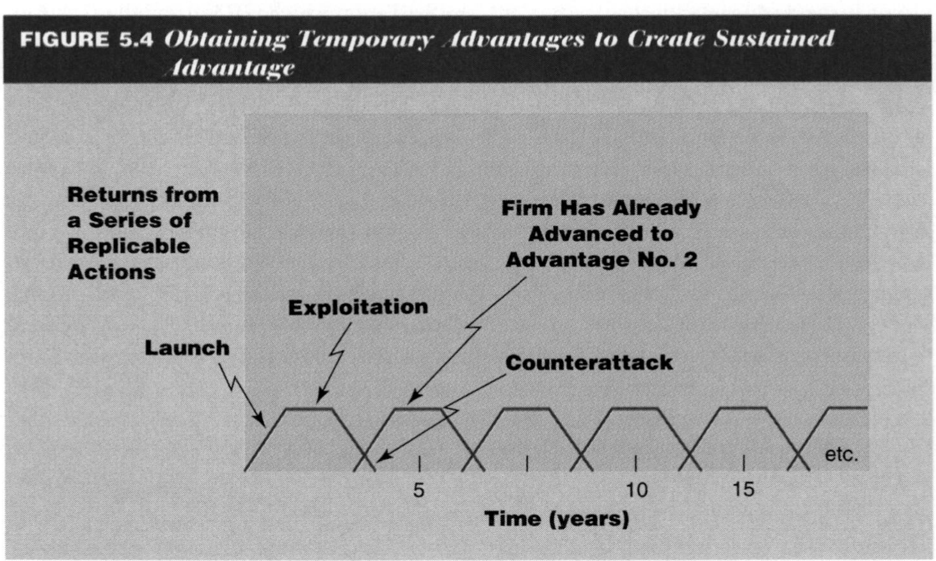

Source: Adapted from I. C. MacMillan, 1988, Controlling competitive dynamics by taking strategic initiative, *Academy of Management Executive* II, no. 2: 111–118.

This actually leads to cannibalizing your own products through the next stage of product evolution and entry.[113] Thus, the focus of this new paradigm is competitive disruption.[114] In this competitive approach, one can escalate competition in an arena such as price and quality only so far, then the dominant competitor should seek to jump to another level of competition such as speed and know-how or innovation. As explained in the Strategic Focus, this is the approach that Komatsu took in competing with Caterpillar and that Caterpillar is now taking to compete against Komatsu.

STRATEGIC FOCUS

Fast-Cycle Competition between Caterpillar and Komatsu

In the early to middle part of the 1980s, Komatsu initiated a series of successful competitive actions against Caterpillar. First, Komatsu developed a line of effective products that it priced competitively. When Caterpillar responded in a similar fashion, Komatsu, in turn, used process innovations to enhance the value of its products and then introduced them into niche markets. Additionally, Komatsu entered emerging markets where Caterpillar was not strong.

However, competition between these two firms today may be even more rivalrous as compared to a decade ago; and, as a result of a series of seemingly effective competitive actions and responses, Caterpillar is now a stronger competitor. Some of its current strength is a product of the firm's decade-long program of cost cutting, targeted investments, and market-based reorganizations.

Caterpillar has long been the world's largest manufacturer of construction and mining equipment, natural gas engines and industrial gas turbines, and remains a leading global supplier of diesel engines. The firm's major markets include road building, mining, logging, agriculture, petroleum, and general construction. Coupled with the firm's size is a vast array of knowledge and capabilities that are being used as the foundation for its competitive rivalry with Komatsu.

It is generally acknowledged that Caterpillar has beaten off the challenge to its dominant position in the large-scale equipment market. Critical to Caterpillar's ability to counterattack Komatsu's invasion to its dominance in the large-scale equipment market were the firm's innovation skills and well-developed dealer network. Called the firm's single largest strategic weapon by its chairman Donald Fites, Caterpillar has 192 dealers serving customers in nearly 200 countries. For the last ten-plus years, extensive efforts have been completed to cement the links between Caterpillar and its dealer network. A technologically sophisticated worldwide computer network that provides instant information about parts availability and new machines to all dealers is one example of what the firm does to derive competitive advantages from the links with its dealers.

Caterpillar is also initiating competitive actions that will allow it to attack Komatsu in markets that traditionally have been strongholds for that firm. For example, through the results of a $100 million investment, Caterpillar launched a family of "compact" building equipment in 1998. (This attack parallels in nature the one Komatsu launched against Caterpillar in the large-scale equipment market.) The compact building equipment line features products that are targeted to the mini-excavators' field. At the time of the launch, this market was dominated by Komatsu, although two other Japanese manufacturers, Yanmar and Kubota, also held significant shares of this market. Producing its new machines in the United

Kingdom, United States, and Japan, Caterpillar's goal was to gain quickly one-fifth of the $3.5 billion a year market for compact equipment.

Caterpillar's current competitive actions include geographic as well as product launches. When Komatsu initiated its competitive attacks, Caterpillar was not strong in the world's emerging markets (as noted previously). Today, however, Caterpillar is pushing intensely into China and other developing countries where rapid growth for construction equipment is expected. In fact, Caterpillar is committed deeply to extending its global presence in the pursuit of strategic competitiveness: "Mr. Fites envisages domestic sales will fall from roughly half total revenues this year (1997) to 25 percent within the next two decades. The company is expecting particularly large returns from China, where it is half way through a $90 million investment programme and where annual sales are projected to climb from about $200 million to up to $1 billion by early next century."

SOURCE: Caterpillar Home Page, 1998, January 27, http://www.caterpillar.com; D. Weimer, 1998, A new Cat on the hot seat, *Business Week*, March 9, 56–61; J. Beisler, 1997, Caterpillar, *Value Line*, November 7, 1310; P. Marsh and S. Wagstyl, 1997, The hungry Caterpillar, *Financial Times*, December 2, 22.

The array of competitive actions and competitive responses occurring between Caterpillar and Komatsu described in the Strategic Focus demonstrate the four strategic steps shown in Table 5.4. At different times and in terms of different products and markets, each of these firms has been able to (1) identify a competitive opportunity that disrupted the status quo, (2) create a temporary advantage that was eroded through aggressive responses by its competitor, (3) seize the initiative from its competitor through effective competitive actions, and (4) sustain its momentum by continually offering new products and entering new markets. As this example about Caterpillar and Komatsu shows, firms must exhibit strategic flexibility if they are to be successful while competing in fast-cycle markets. Thus, when facing these market conditions, firms must learn how to respond quickly to technological change and market opportunities by offering more new products, broader product lines, and product upgrades more rapidly.[115]

Competitive Dynamics and Industry Evolution Outcomes

Because industries and markets evolve over time, so do the competitive dynamics between firms in the industry. We have examined how firms interact in a short span of time using an action–reaction framework, but we have not yet considered how competitive interaction evolves over longer periods of time. Three general stages of industry evolution are relevant to our study of competitive dynamics: emerging entrepreneurial, larger growth-oriented, and mature firms. These are shown in Figure 5.5.

Firms entering emerging industries attempt to establish a niche or an initial form of beginning dominance within an industry. Competitive rivalry for the loyalty of customers is serious. In these industries, depending on the types of products, firms often attempt to establish product quality, technology, and/or advantageous relationships with suppliers in order to develop a competitive advantage in the pursuit of strategic competitiveness. These firms are striving to build their reputation. As a result, a variety of different competitive strategies may be employed in such an industry. This diversity can be beneficial to many of the firms

TABLE 5.4 ***Strategic Steps for Seizing the Initiative in Fast-Cycle Markets***

1. *Disrupting the status quo.*	Competitors disrupt the status quo by identifying new opportunities to serve the customer and by shifting the rules of competition. These moves end the old pattern of competitive interaction between rivals. This requires speed and variety in approach.
2. *Create temporary advantage.*	Disruption creates temporary advantages. These advantages are based on better knowledge of customers, technology, and the future. They are derived from customer orientation and employee empowerment throughout the entire organization. These advantages are short lived and eroded by fierce competition.
3. *Seizing the initiative.*	By moving aggressively into new areas of competition, acting to create a new advantage or undermine a competitor's old advantage, the company seizes the initiative. This throws the opponent off balance and puts it at a disadvantage for a while. The opponent is forced to play catch up, reacting rather than shaping the future with its own actions to seize the initiative. The initiator is proactive, whereas competitors are forced to be reactive.
4. *Sustaining the momentum.*	Several actions in a row are taken to seize the intiative and create momentum. The company continues to develop new advantages and does not wait for competitors to undermine them before launching the next initiative. This succession of actions sustains the momentum. Continually offering new initiatives is the only source of sustainable competitive advantage in fast-cycle environments.

Source: Adapted from R.A. D'Aveni, 1995, Coping with hypercompetition: Utilizing the new 7's framework, *Academy of Management Executive* IX, no. 3: 45–60.

FIGURE 5.5 ***An Action-Based Model of the Industry Life Cycle***

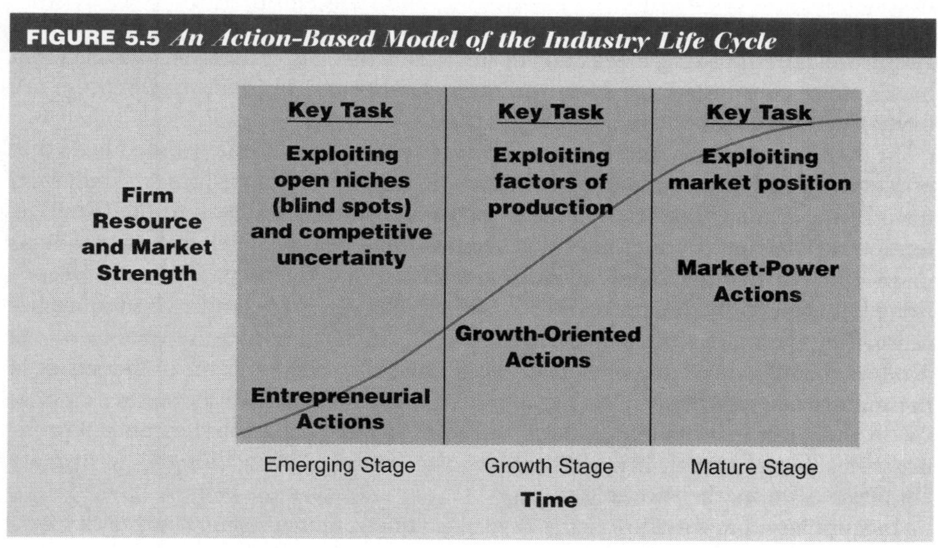

Source: Adapted from C.M. Grimm and K.G. Smith, 1997, *Strategy as Action: Industry Rivalry and Coordination* (St. Paul, MN: West Publishing Co.).

in the industry. The diversity of competitive strategies may avoid direct competition and help firms gain dominance in market niches.[116] Although speed is important in new emerging industries, access to capital is often the critical issue. Therefore, it is not uncommon to have strategic alliances develop between a new firm entering the market and a more established firm that wishes to gain a foothold in the new industry.[117]

These firms often rely on top management to develop market opportunities. Stephen Jobs and Bill Gates were able to foresee the future possibilities of the microcomputer and the standardized microcomputer operating system. Their vision of an uncertain environment gave rise to both Apple Computer and Microsoft. Thus, firms in the emerging stage take *entrepreneurial actions* which focus on entrepreneurial discovery in uncertain environments.

Growth-oriented firms are the survivors from the emerging industry stage. In the growth stage, *growth-oriented actions* are emphasized, which tend to create product standardization as consumer demand creates a mass market with growth potential. Thus, many of these firms are more established, but no less competitive. In fact, as the industry begins to mature, the variety of strategies being implemented tends to decrease.[118] As such, entrepreneurial actions are still taking place but there is more emphasis on growth-oriented actions. Oftentimes, groups of firms will follow a similar strategy and thus become directly competitive. However, the rivalry between groups may be more indirect.[119] In industries where there is considerable within-strategic-group rivalry and competitive rivalry between firms in separate strategic groups, firms frequently earn below-average returns.[120]

Some of these industries may also be fragmented. Fragmented markets, such as fast food restaurants, tend to offer standardized facilities and products, but decentralized decision making to the local units. The standardization allows for low-cost competition. The primary value added comes from services provided. These markets offer a prime opportunity for franchising because of the ability to standardize facilities, operations, and products.[121]

In nonfragmented industries, the speed of new product development and introduction to the marketplace becomes an important competitive weapon. Consumers tend to be more sophisticated and expect not only quality products, but also product designs that meet their needs. Firms that can move new products that better meet consumers' needs to the market more quickly than competitors are likely to gain a competitive advantage.

In mature industries, there are usually fewer surviving competitors. Those that do survive tend to be larger with dominant market share positions. Therefore, firms in the mature stage emphasize *market-power actions* which focus the firm's attention on offering product lines that are profitable and producing those products in an efficient manner. New product innovation or entrepreneurial actions continue but are greatly deemphasized. Process innovations are emphasized more because they maintain dominance through cost efficiencies and the quality of the product manufactured and provided to customers.[122] Finally, firms in industries in the mature stage frequently seek international expansion or an increasing emphasis on their international operations and sales, a move that often extends a product's life. Thus, growth-oriented actions also continue even though the primary emphasis is on market-power actions.

In summary, once mature firms have a dominant market share, they seek to exploit their market power and extensive resources and capabilities in an attempt to maintain dominance. In a study examining the 1950–1972 period, market leaders

Kellogg, General Mills, General Foods, and Quaker Oats introduced more than 80 new brands without significant product innovation in an attempt to fill all niches and deter entry.[123] This strategy was very successful until the private-label producers grew powerful enough to counter this strategy.

This chapter concludes our emphasis on business-level strategy, although some business-level issues are discussed in future Chapters (e.g., Chapters 8, 9 and 11). The next chapter begins our discussion of corporate-level strategy.

SUMMARY

- Competitive rivalry entails actions and responses to competitive actions taken by other firms. Competitive attack and response are more likely when awareness, motivation, and abilities to attack or respond are present.
- Market commonality, as determined by multimarket contact in such industries as airlines, is likely to lead to dampening of a potential attack. However, if an offensive action is taken, a response is more likely in the presence of market commonality.
- Awareness of competitors' ability to attack or respond is facilitated by resource similarity among competitors. Those with similar resources are more likely to attack and respond than are those with fewer resources.
- First movers can gain a competitive advantage and customer loyalty by being the first in the market. First movers also take more risks. However, first movers often are higher performers. Second movers, particularly those that are larger and faster, can also gain a competitive advantage and/or earn at least average returns because they imitate, but do not take some of the risk that first movers do. The longer the time required to respond, the higher the probability that the first mover will enjoy strong performance gains. Late movers (those that respond a long time after the original action was taken) tend to be lower performers and much less effective.
- The probability of a response by a competitor to a competitive action is based partially on the extent to which the competitor is dependent on the particular market in which the action was taken. In addition, the probability of response is based on the type of action, the reputation of the firm taking the strategic action (the expectation of success), and the resources available to the competitor contemplating response.
- The two types of competitive actions are strategic and tactical. Strategic actions are more long term in nature, require many specific resources, and are difficult to reverse. Alternatively, tactical actions tend to be more short term in orientation, require fewer and more general resources, and can be more easily reversed. More tactical, rather than strategic, actions are taken and more responses are made to tactical than to strategic actions. It is easier to respond to a tactical action, partly because it requires fewer resources. In addition, a tactical action is likely to have a shorter term effect than a strategic action. Responses to strategic actions are more difficult, require more resources, and require a longer-term investment.
- When competitors are highly dependent on a market in which competitive actions are taken, there is a high probability that they will respond to such actions. However, firms that are more diversified across markets are less likely to respond to a particular action that affects only one of the markets in which they compete.
- The highest probability of a response comes when an action is taken by a market leader. Furthermore, when an action is taken by a market leader, it is more likely that a competitor will imitate the action taken. Alternatively, if the firm has a reputation as a strategic player (a firm that takes more complex and risky actions), there is a lower probability of response. A price predator is also less likely to elicit a response from competitors.
- Those with more resources are more likely to respond to strategic actions than are those with fewer resources. Furthermore, the probability of response is determined not only by the amount of

resources, but by the ability to use those resources in taking competitive action.

- Abilities needed to engage in competitive actions and responses include the relative size of the acting and responding firms, the function of speed in the market or industry, the importance of innovation in competitive moves, and product quality.
- Large firms often have strong market power. Alternatively, as firms grow larger, they often institute bureaucratic rules, procedures, and structures. These have the effect of reducing the probability that a firm will take actions and respond to others' actions. In addition, they reduce the speed with which a firm may be able to implement an action or respond to competitors' actions.
- Speed is becoming increasingly important in many industries in order to gain and hold a competitive advantage. In fact, many large firms must act like small firms (flexible and agile) to be competitive. This may require that they decentralize many responsibilities and decisions and that they create cross-functional teams in order to speed multiple processes (e.g., the innovation process).
- Both product and process innovation are becoming more important in the competitive posture of many industries. Some research has shown that firms that invest more in R&D and that are more innovative tend to have higher performance in multiple industries. Product innovation tends to be more important in emerging and growth industries, while mature industries may emphasize process innovation.
- Product quality has become critical in order to maintain competitive parity in most industries. Total quality management must be infused throughout the organization by top management and integrated with firm strategies. Benchmarking is used to help make comparative judgments about quality relative to other firms' best practices.
- There are three basic market outcomes from interfirm rivalry. Slow-cycle markets allow a firm to establish competitive advantage in a near monopoly situation. Until recently, many utility firms were in this position. Standard-cycle markets allow market situations where sustainability is possible. Firms that have multimarket contact may dampen competition somewhat. Fast-cycle markets create a situation where only temporary competitive advantage is possible such as in the electronics and pharmaceutical industries.
- In fast-cycle markets, a new paradigm of competitive action may be necessary, competitive disruption. This usually involves cannibalization of a previous product entry through decreasing prices, while establishing the new innovative product at the high end of the market, with increased product performance at a premium price.
- Industry evolution is important in determining the type of competition and the type of competitive actions that are emphasized. For example, firms in an emerging stage attempt to establish a reputation and develop a market niche in technology or quality of products provided. The main task is to establish an entrepreneurial action, usually in an uncertain environment. In growth firms, special emphasis may be placed on innovation to increase economies of scale. Speed of competitive actions taken is also important. The key task is to pursue growth-oriented actions by exploiting factors of production to increase dominance. In mature industries with fewer competitors, special emphasis is placed on market-power actions designed to defend the most profitable product lines and processes in order to produce and distribute those products with the greatest efficiency (lowest cost). However, entrepreneurial, growth-oriented, and market-power actions are taken at all stages, although the emphasis is different at each stage.

REVIEW QUESTIONS

1. What two factors contribute to awareness, motivation, and ability in competitor analysis?
2. What are the advantages and disadvantages of being a first, second, or late mover?
3. On what four factors is the likelihood of a response to a competitive action based?
4. What is the likelihood of response to a tactical action, a strategic action, and actions taken by market leaders? Explain why.
5. What are the advantages and the disadvantages of size regarding strategic actions and responses thereto?
6. Why is speed important in many industries? What can

firms do to increase the speed at which they make and implement strategic decisions?

7. In what types of industries is innovation important for competitive advantage? Explain the importance of different types of innovation (product and process) for success in different industries.
8. Describe three types of markets and the nature of rivalry in each.
9. How does industry evolution affect interfirm rivalry? Identify three stages of industry evolution, and briefly explain the types of competitive actions emphasized in those stages.

APPLICATION DISCUSSION QUESTIONS

1. Read the popular business press (e.g., *Business Week*, *Fortune*) and identify a strategic action and a tactical action taken by firms approximately two years ago. Next, read the popular business press to see if, and how, competitors responded to those actions. Explain the actions and the responses, linking your findings to the discussion in this chapter.
2. Why would a firm regularly choose to be a second-mover? Likewise, why would a firm purposefully be a late mover?
3. Explain how Sun Microsystems' strategic actions affected its primary competitors (e.g., IBM, DEC, HP, Silicone Graphics).
4. Choose a large firm and examine the popular business press to identify how its size, speed of actions, level of innovation, and quality of goods or services have affected its competitive position in its industry. Explain your findings.
5. Identify a firm in a fast-cycle market and trace why its strategy was successful or unsuccessful over several strategic actions.

ETHICS QUESTIONS

1. In your opinion, are some industries known for ethical practices, while others are not? If so, name industries thought to be ethical and those that are evaluated less favorably in terms of ethics. How might the competitive actions and competitive responses differ between an "ethical" and an "unethical" industry?
2. When engaging in competitive rivalry, firms jockey for a market position that is advantageous, relative to competitors. In this jockeying, what kind of competitor intelligence gathering approaches are ethical?
3. A second mover is a firm that responds to a first mover's competitive actions, often through imitation. Is there anything unethical about how a second mover engages in competition? Why or why not?
4. Standards for competitive rivalry differ in countries throughout the world. What should firms do to cope with these differences?
5. Is it possible that total quality management practices could result in firms operating more ethically than before such practices were implemented? If this is possible, what might account for an increase in the ethical behavior of a firm when using TQM principles?
6. What ethical issues are involved in fast-cycle markets?

INTERNET EXERCISE

The following companies are past winners of the Malcolm Baldrige National Quality Award:

ADAC Laboratories: **http://www.adaclabs.com**
Ames Rubber Corporation: **http://www.amesrubber.com**
Eastman Chemical: **http://www.eastman.com**
Federal Express: **http://www.fedex.com**
Motorola: **http://www.mot.com**
Trident Precision: **http://www.tridentprecision.com**

The Malcolm Baldrige National Quality Award, which is administered by the National Institute of Standards and

Technology and the U.S. Commerce Department, recognizes U.S. firms for excellence in quality management. Select one of the past winners of this award. Use the Internet to find information that enables you to write a short critique of how this company uses an emphasis on quality management to enhance its competitiveness.

Strategic Surfing

DePaul University maintains a Web site that provides links to a variety of Web sites that focus on quality management issues.

http://condor.depaul.edu/~mgt/om_sub11.html

NOTES

1. J. Kurtzman, 1998, An interview with C. K. Prahalad, in J. Kurtzman (ed.), *Thought Leaders* (San Francisco: Jossey-Bass), 40–51; C. M. Grimm and K. G. Smith, 1997, *Strategy as Action: Industry Rivalry and Coordination* (Cincinnati: South-Western College Publishing); A. Y. Illinitch and R. A. D'Aveni, 1996, New organizational forms and strategies for managing in hypercompetitive environments, *Organization Science* 7: 211–220.
2. G. Colvin, 1997, The most valuable quality in a manager, *Fortune*, December 29, 279–280.
3. C. Adams, 1998, Two steelmakers may build new mills, *Wall Street Journal*, January 7, A2.
4. H. Simonian, 1997, No stopping them, *Financial Times*, November 7, 15.
5. R. Grover, 1997, Now playing on screen 29 . . . , *Business Week*, July 7, 46.
6. K. Nobeoka and M. A. Cusumano, 1997, Multiproject strategy and sales growth: The benefits of rapid design transfer in new product development, *Strategic Management Journal* 18: 169–186; R. A. Bettis and M. A. Hitt, 1995, The new competitive landscape, *Strategic Management Journal* 16 (Special Summer Issue), 7–19.
7. K. Kerwin and K. Naughton, 1997, Can Detroit make cars that baby boomers like? *Business Week*, December 1, 134–148.
8. B. Vlasic and K. Naughton, 1997, The small-car wars are back, *Business Week*, September 22, 40–42.
9. T. Box, 1997, Toyota steers a solid course of growth, *Dallas Morning News*, November 30, H1, H2; H. Simonian, 1997, A steady drive around the world, *Financial Times*, December 5, 14.
10. M. Nakamoto, 1998, Japan carmakers renew their European offensive, *The Financial Times*, January 15, 7; M. Nakamoto, 1997, Toyota targets European sales, *Financial Times*, November 20, 21.
11. J. Kurtzman, 1998, An interview with Keshub Mahindra, in J. Kurtzman (ed.), *Thought Leaders* (San Francisco: Jossey-Bass), 29–39.
12. E. K. Clemons, 1997, Technology-driven environmental shifts and the sustainable competitive disadvantage of previously dominant companies, in G. S. Day and D. J. Reibstein (eds.), *Wharton on Dynamic Competitive Strategy* (New York: John Wiley & Sons), 99–126.
13. B. S. Silverman, J. A. Nickerson, and J. Freeman, 1997, Profitability, transactional alignment, and organizational mortality in the U.S. trucking industry, *Strategic Management Journal* 18 (Special Summer Issue), 31–52.
14. A. C. Inkpen and P. W. Beamish, 1997, Knowledge, bargaining power, and the instability of international joint ventures, *Academy of Management Review* 22: 177–202; J. Stiles, 1995, Collaboration for competitive advantage: The changing world of alliances and partnerships, *Long Range Planning* 28: 109–112.
15. S. Fidler, 1997, Big guns target a sky wars victory, *Financial Times*, December 19, 5.
16. E. Tucker, 1997, Euro-regulator spectre hovers backstage, *Financial Times*, December 19, 3.
17. M. Sakakibara, 1997, Heterogeneity of firm capabilities and cooperative research and development: An empirical examination of motives, *Strategic Management Journal* 18 (Special Summer Issue), 143–164.
18. G. S. Day and D. J. Reibstein, 1997, The dynamic challenges for theory and practice, in G. S. Day and D. J. Reibstein (eds.), *Wharton on Competitive Strategy* (New York: John Wiley & Sons) 2.
19. D. Foust and W. Zellner, 1997, US Airways: Not much room to maneuver, *Business Week*, October 13, 40.
20. S. J. Marsh, 1998, Creating barriers for foreign competitors: A study of the impact of anti-dumping actions on the performance of U.S. firms, *Strategic Management Journal* 19: 25–37; K. G. Smith, C. M. Grimm, and S. Wally, 1997, Strategic groups and rivalrous firm behavior: Towards a reconciliation, *Strategic Management Journal* 18: 149–157.
21. R. A. Klavans, C. A. Di Benedetto, and J. J. Prudom, 1997, Understanding competitive interactions: The U.S. commercial aircraft market, *Journal of Managerial Issues* IX, no. 1: 13–36.
22. Day and Reibstein, *Wharton on Competitive Strategy;* M. E. Porter, 1980, *Competitive Strategy* (New York: The Free Press), 17.
23. H. Simonian, 1998, Renault expands horizons, *Financial Times*, January 2, 10.
24. Porter, *Competitive Strategy*.
25. L. Johannes, 1998, Kodak reports loss of $744 million including big restructuring charge, *Wall Street Journal*, January 16, A4.
26. C. R. Henderson and W. Mitchell, 1997, The interactions of organizational and competitive influences on strategy and performance, *Strategic Management Journal* 18 (Special Summer Issue), 5–14.
27. W. Ocasio, 1997, Towards an attention-based view of the firm, *Strategic Management Journal* 18 (Special Summer Issue), 187–206.
28. Grimm and Smith, *Strategy as Action*, 75–102.
29. L. Himelstein, 1997, Levi's is hiking up its pants, *Business Week*, December 1, 70–75.

30. G. P. Hodgkinson and G. Johnson, 1994, Exploring the mental models of competitive strategists: The case for a processual approach, *Journal of Management Studies* 31: 525–551; J. F. Porac and H. Thomas, 1994, Cognitive categorization and subjective rivalry among retailers in a small city, *Journal of Applied Psychology* 79: 54–66.
31. N. Houthoofd and A. Heene, 1997, Strategic groups as subsets of strategic scope groups in the Belgian brewing industry, *Strategic Management Journal* 18: 653–666; G. P. Carroll and A. Swaminathan, 1992, The organizational ecology of strategic groups in the American brewing industry from 1975–1988, *Industrial and Corporate Change* 1: 65–97.
32. K. Ohmae, 1985, *Triad Power* (New York: The Free Press).
33. Grimm and Smith, *Strategy as Action*, 84; f. i. smith and R. L. Wilson, 1995, The predictive validity of the Karnani and Wernerfelt model of multipoint competition, *Strategic Management Journal* 16: 143–160.
34. J. Gimeno and C. Y. Woo, 1996, Hypercompetition in multimarket environment: The role of strategic similarity and multimarket contact in competitive deescalation, *Organization Science* 7: 322–344; W. N. Evans and I. N. Kessides, 1994, Living by the "golden rule": Multimarket contact in the U.S. airline industry, *Quarterly Journal of Economics* 109: 341–366.
35. M. J. Chen, 1996, Competitor analysis and interfirm rivalry: Toward a theoretical integration, *Academy of Management Review* 21: 100–134.
36. L. Kehoe and P. Taylor, 1998, Compaq achieves goal of joining top three ahead of time, *Financial Times*, January 25, 5; Hoechst, 1996, *Annual Report.*
37. M. A. Peteraf, 1993, Intraindustry structure and response toward rivals, *Journal of Managerial Decision Economics* 14: 519–528.
38. Grimm and Smith, *Strategy as Action*, 84; Chen, Competitor analysis.
39. Grimm and Smith, *Strategy as Action*, 125.
40. B. Horovitz, 1997, Coca-Cola, Pepsi tap bottled water market, *USA Today*, August 27, B10.
41. Smith and Grimm, *Strategy as Action*, 53–74.
42. A. A. Lado, N. G. Boyd, and S. C. Hanlon, 1997, Competition, cooperation, and the search for economic rents: A syncretic model, *Academy of Management Review* 22: 110–141.
43. J. L. C. Cheng and I. F. Kesner, 1997, Organizational slack and response to environmental shifts: The impact of resource allocation patterns, *Journal of Management* 23: 1–18.
44. E. Ramstad, 1998, Mitsubishi unit bets big on digital TV, to end sales of standard sets in U.S., *Wall Street Journal*, January 19, B10.
45. B. McKay, 1997, Merger to create Russia's largest investment bank, *Wall Street Journal*, July 10, A12.
46. K. Stevens and K. Kurschner, 1997, That vroom! you hear may not be a Harley, *Business Week*, October 20, 159–160.
47. M. B. Lieberman and D. B. Montgomery, 1988, First-mover advantages, *Strategic Management Journal* 9: 41–58.
48. K. G. Smith, C. M. Grimm, and M. J. Gannon, 1992, *Dynamics of Competitive Strategy* (Newberry Park, CA: Sage).
49. A. Ginsberg and N. Venkatraman, 1992, Investing in new information technology: The role of competitive posture and issue diagnosis, *Strategic Management Journal* 13 (Special Summer Issue): 37–53.
50. Smith, Grimm, and Gannon, *Dynamics of Competitive Strategy.*
51. V. Griffith, 1998, Reebok to cut sponsorships, *Financial Times*, January 15, 15.
52. I. Pereira, 1998, Sneaker company tags out-of-breath baby boomers, *Wall Street Journal*, January 16, B1, B2.
53. G. S. Day, 1997, Assessing competitive arenas: Who are your competitors? In G. S. Day and D. J. Reibstein, *Wharton on Competitive Strategy* (New York: John Wiley & Sons) 25–26.
54. *The Economist*, 1997, Soap power, with added logic, December 7, 68–73.
55. K. Labich, 1994, Air wars over Asia, *Fortune*, April 4, 93–98.
56. T. Maxon, 1998, American to bolster flier plan, *Dallas Morning News*, January 22, D3.
57. T. Maxon, 1997, Return trip, *Dallas Morning News*, June 10, D1, D14.
58. Grimm and Smith, *Strategy as Action*, 134.
59. E. Malkin and R. A. Melcher, 1997, On the prowl for more suds, *Business Week*, October 6, 154D–154F.
60. L. Grant, 1997, Why FedEx is flying high, *Fortune*, November 10, 156–160.
61. Smith, Grimm, and Gannon, *Dynamics of Competitive Strategy.*
62. Ibid.
63. B. Pinsker, 1997, Rental block, *Dallas Morning News*, June 14, C5, C8.
64. H. Stout, 1997, Tiny toy stores scramble for ways to lure customers, *Wall Street Journal*, December 9, B2.
65. M. Skapinker, 1998, Airbus boasts year of record orders, *Financial Times*, January 8, 6.
66. M. Nakamoto, 1997, Sega sales suffer as competition bites, *Financial Times*, November 21, 17.
67. J. A. Schumpeter, 1961, *Theory of Economic Development* (New York: Oxford University Press).
68. A. E. Serwer, 1997, Michael Dell turns the PC world inside out, *Fortune*, September 8, 76–86.
69. M. Halkias, 1998, CompUSA Inc., *Dallas Morning News*, January 29, D10; S. A. Forest and P. Burrows, 1997, And give me an extra-fast modem with that, please, *Business Week*, September 29, 38; K. Lyons, 1997, CompUSA to offer built-to-order PCs, *Dallas Morning News*, July 16, D1, D12.
70. A. Goldstein, 1997, Dell surpasses analyst expectations as profits soar 71% in third quarter, *Dallas Morning News*, November 25, D7.
71. A. Goldstein, 1997, Compaq CEO sees industry consolidation, *Dallas Morning News*, November 18, D6.
72. Bloomberg News, 1998, Radio Shack to sell only Compaq PCs, *Dallas Morning News*, January 29, D2; A. Goldstein, 1998, Compaq to buy Digital, *Dallas Morning News*, January 27, D1, D6.
73. R. A. Melcher, 1993, How Goliaths can act like Davids, *Business Week* (Special Issue), 193.
74. J. Kurtzman, 1998, An interview with Charles Handy, in J. Kurtzman (ed.), *Thoughts Leaders* (San Francisco: Jossey-Bass), 4–15; J. Birkinshaw, 1997, Entrepreneurship in multinational corporations: The characteristics of subsidiary initiatives, *Strategic Management Journal* 18: 207–229.
75. Harvard Business Review Perspectives, 1995, How can big companies keep the entrepreneurial spirit alive? *Harvard Business Review* 73, no. 6: 183–192.

76. E. H. Kessler and A. K. Chakrabarti, 1996, Innovation speed: A conceptual model of context, antecedents, and outcomes, *Academy of Management Review* 21: 1143–1191; S. L. Brown and K. M. Eisenhardt, 1995, Product development: Past research, present findings, and future directions, *Academy of Management Review* 20: 343–378; K. M. Eisenhardt and B. N. Tabrizi, 1995, Accelerating adaptive processes: Product innovation in the global computer industry, *Administrative Science Quarterly* 40: 84–110.
77. A. Cane, 1997, Long-distance visionary, *Financial Times*, December 19, 3.
78. R. R. Nayyar and K. A. Bantel, 1994, Competitive agility: A source of competitive advantage based on speed and variety, *Advances in Strategic Management* 10A, 193–222.
79. S. Wally and J. R. Baum, 1994, Personal and structural determinants of the pace of strategic decision-making, *Academy of Management Journal* 37: 932–956.
80. Ibid.
81. T. Smart and J. H. Dobrzynski, 1993, Jack Welch on the art of thinking small, *Business Week*, (Special Enterprise Issue), 212–216.
82. J. Kurtzman, 1998, An interview with Gary Hamel, in J. Kurtzman (ed.), *Thought Leaders* (San Francisco: Jossey-Bass), 134–149; J. Wind, 1997, Preemptive strategies, in G. S. Day and D. J. Reibstein, *Wharton on Dynamic Competitive Strategy* (New York: John Wiley & Sons), 256–276; S. C. Wheelwright and K. B. Clark, 1995, *Leading Product Development* (New York: The Free Press).
83. B. N. Dickie, 1998, Foreword, in J. Kurtzman (ed.), *Thought Leaders* (San Francisco: Jossey-Bass), xi–xvii; J. Kurtzman, 1998, An interview with Paul M. Romer, in J. Kurtzman (ed.), *Thought Leaders* (San Francisco: Jossey-Bass), 66–83.
84. L. G. Franko, 1989, Global corporate competition: Who's winning, who's losing, and the R&D factor as one reason why, *Strategic Management Journal* 10: 449–474.
85. R. E. Hoskisson and M. A. Hitt, 1994, *Downscoping: How to Tame the Diversified Firm* (New York: Oxford University Press).
86. K. J. Klein and J. S. Sorra, 1996, The challenge of innovation implementation, *Academy of Management Review* 21: 1055–1080.
87. L. Tyson, 1997, Model Taiwan company becomes a high flyer, *Financial Times*, December 18, 16.
88. Klein and Sorra, The challenge of innovation implementation.
89. N. Dunne, 1998, American goldmine for high-tech workers, *Financial Times*, January 15, 4; V. Griffith, 1998, Learning to wear two hats, *Financial Times*, January 5, 20; N. Timmins, 1998, Manufacturers face skills shortfall, *Financial Times*, January 9, 4.
90. J. W. Dean, Jr., and D. E. Bowen, 1994, Management theory and total quality: Improving research and practice through theory development, *Academy of Management Review* 19: 392–419.
91. J. Aley, 1994, Manufacturers grade themselves, *Fortune*, March 21, 26.
92. M. Halkias, 1997, Rising competition, *Dallas Morning News*, November 13, D1, D12.
93. J. Heizer and B. Render, 1996, *Production and Operations Management*, 4th ed. (Upper Saddle River, NJ: Prentice-Hall), 75–106.
94. M. van Biema and B. Greenwald, 1997, Managing our way to higher service-sector productivity, *Harvard Business Review* 75, no. 4: 87–95.
95. S. Chatterjee and M. Yilmaz, 1993, Quality confusion: Too many gurus, not enough disciples, *Business Horizons* 36, no. 3: 15–18.
96. B. Render and J. Heizer, 1997, *Principles of Operations Management*, 2nd ed. (Upper Saddle River, NJ: Prentice Hall), 89–113.
97. Serwer, Michael Dell.
98. W. S. Sherman and M. A. Hitt, 1996, Creating corporate value: Integrating quality and innovation programs, in D. Fedor and S. Ghoshal (eds.), *Advances in the Management of Organizational Quality* (Greenwich, CT: JAI Press), 221–244.
99. J. D. Westphal, R. Gulati, and S. M. Shortell, 1997, Customization or conformity: An institutional and network perspective on the content and consequences of TQM adoption, *Administrative Science Quarterly* 42: 366–394.
100. E. E. Lawler, III, 1994, Total quality management and employee involvement: Are they compatible? *Academy of Management Executive* VIII, no. 1: 68.
101. R. S. Russell and B. W. Taylor, III, 1998, *Operations Management*, 2nd ed. (Upper Saddle River, NJ: Prentice Hall), 130–165.
102. A. M. Schneiderman, 1998, Are there limits to total quality management?, *Strategy Business* 11, second quarter, 35–45; R. Krishnan, A. B. Shani, and G. R. Baer, 1993, In search of quality improvement: Problems of design and implementation, *Academy of Management Executive* VII, no. 3: 7–20.
103. R. Blackburn and B. Rosen, 1993, Total quality and human resources management: Lessons learned from Baldridge award-winning companies, *Academy of Management Executive* VII, no. 3: 49–66.
104. H. V. Roberts and B. F. Sergesketter, 1993, *Quality Is Personal* (New York: The Free Press).
105. S. B. Sitkin, K. M. Sutcliffe, and R. G. Schroeder, 1994, Distinguishing control from learning in total quality management: A contingency perspective, *Academy of Management Review* 19: 537–564.
106. J. R. Hackman and R. Wageman, 1995, Total quality management: Empirical, conceptualization and practical issues, *Administrative Science Quarterly* 40: 309–342.
107. J. R. Williams, 1992, How sustainable is your competitive advantage? *California Management Review* 34 (Spring): 29–51.
108. G. S. Day, 1997, Maintaining the competitive edge: Creating and sustaining advantages in dynamic competitive environments, in G. S. Day and D. J. Reibstein, *Wharton on Dynamic Competitive Strategy* (New York: John Wiley & Sons) 48–75.
109. J. H. Perser, 1993, McIlhenny used shrewd marketing to keep Tabasco a hot export product, *Traffic World*, April 5, 15–16.
110. A. D. Chandler, 1990, The enduring logic of industrial success, *Harvard Business Review* 68, no. 2: 130–140.
111. J. L. Bower and T. M. Hout, 1988, Fast-cycle capability for competitive power, *Harvard Business Review* 66, no. 6: 110–118.

112. Williams, How sustainable is your competitive advantage?
113. K. R. Conner, 1995, Obtaining strategic advantage from being imitated: When can encouraging "clones" pay? *Management Science* 41: 209–225; K. R. Connor, 1988, Strategies for product cannibalism, *Strategic Management Journal* 9 (Special Summer Issue), 135–159.
114. R. A. D'Aveni, 1995, Coping with hypercompetition: Utilizing the new 7's framework, *Academy of Management Executive* IX, no. 3: 45–60.
115. R. Sanchez, 1995, Strategic flexibility in product competition, *Strategic Management Journal* 16 (Special Summer Issue), 9–26.
116. M. A. Hitt, B. B. Tyler, C. Hardee, and D. Park, 1994, Understanding strategic intent in the global marketplace, *Academy of Management Executive* IX, no. 2: 12–19.
117. G. Miles, C. Snow, and M. P. Sharfman, 1993, Industry variety and performance, *Strategic Management Journal* 14: 163–177.
118. D. Lei, 1989, Strategies for global competition, *Long-Range Planning* 22: 102–109.
119. Miles, Snow, and Sharfman, Industry variety.
120. K. Cool and I. Dierickx, 1993, Rivalry, strategic groups and firm profitability, *Strategic Management Journal* 14: 47–59.
121. S. A. Shane, 1996, Hybrid organizational arrangements and their implications for firm growth and survival: A study of new franchisors, *Academy of Management Journal* 39: 216–234.
122. D. M. Schroeder, 1990, A dynamic perspective on the impact of process innovation upon competitive strategies, *Strategic Management Journal* 11: 25–41.
123. R. Schmalensee, 1978, Entry deterrence in the ready-to-eat breakfast cereal industry, *Bell Journal of Economics* 9: 305–328.

Corporate-Level Strategy

CHAPTER 6

Learning Objectives

After reading this chapter, you should be able to:

1. Define corporate-level strategy and discuss its importance to the diversified firm.
2. Describe the advantages and disadvantages of single-business and dominant-business strategies.
3. Explain three primary reasons why firms move from single-business and dominant-business strategies to more diversified strategies.
4. Describe how related-diversified firms use activity sharing and the transfer of core competencies to create value.
5. Discuss the two ways an unrelated diversification strategy can create value.
6. Discuss the incentives and resources that encourage diversification.
7. Describe motives that can encourage managers to further diversify a firm.

The Diversification of United Parcel Service

Founded in 1970 in Seattle, Washington, United Parcel Service (UPS) is the world's largest package distribution company, transporting over 3.1 billion parcels and documents annually. UPS offers its services in over 200 countries through the efforts of approximately 340,000 employees. To improve both effectiveness and efficiency, the firm's package operations are grouped into five geographic sections to handle deliveries outside the United States—Asia Pacific, Canada, Europe, Latin America/Caribbean, and Middle East/Africa. UPS utilizes more than 500 aircraft, 147,000 vehicles, and 2,400 facilities to deliver packages. In fact, UPS believes that it operates the world's largest airline. As the twenty-first century approaches, company leaders suggest that the firm's commitment to learning how to continuously increase its competitiveness in global markets represents the cornerstone of the future for UPS.

http://www.ups.com

During August 1997, the operational capacities of UPS were damaged severely by a two-week strike that was called by the firm's unionized personnel. The strike resulted in a loss of over $600 million in sales revenue and highlighted the company's dependence on the core part of its business operations. This dependence is illustrated by the fact that at the

end of 1997, roughly 97.8 percent of UPS's sales revenue was generated through the delivery of parcels and documents. The remaining 2.2 percent of revenue was earned by a wholly owned, independently managed subsidiary called UPS Worldwide Logistics.

Established in 1991, UPS Worldwide Logistics is a third-party provider of global supply-chain management solutions, including transportation management, warehouse operations, inventory management, documentation for import and export, and network optimization practices, among other services. In essence, as a group to whom others outsource their need for a service, UPS Worldwide Logistics has the ability required "to partner with its customers to move goods from the source of raw materials through to the end consumer, meeting every need in the distribution chain along the way."

The 1997 strike's effect on sales revenues created a renewed interest among UPS executives to derive additional sales revenue from the diversification represented by the firm's Worldwide Logistics unit. Focused on logistics management, which is the science of moving and storing products, UPS top-level managers believe that the Logistics unit can grow sevenfold in only six years. If this objective is reached, the revenues generated by the Logistics unit through the early part of the twenty-first century would approximate 13 percent of UPS's total sales revenue.

Predicted growth in the market for the outsourcing of logistics to companies such as UPS Worldwide Logistics and Electronic Data Systems Corp. (one of UPS's major competitors in the logistics business) encourages the belief among UPS executives that its diversification effort will benefit the entire company. In 1997, U.S. firms spent approximately $10 billion on outsourced logistics services; this figure is expected to increase to over $50 billion by 2000. By transferring its distribution system core competence from the major part of UPS to the Worldwide Logistics unit, the firm believes it possesses a competitive advantage that will allow it to succeed in the burgeoning logistics business.

Currently, the Logistics unit offers a variety of transportation-related services. For example, to provide a batch of independent components to Dell Computer Corp.'s customers simultaneously, various portions of computer shipments from different distributors are collected and then combined into a single shipment for the Round Rock, Texas-based firm. To expand its operations, the unit intends to offer more services. Data handling and "electronic commerce," such as taking care of billing for customers, are examples of services being planned for the future. Committed to the global marketplace in providing its services, UPS Worldwide Logistics has warehouse and distribution centers in Singapore; Cologne, Germany; and Best, Netherlands, as well as a facility in Louisville, Kentucky.

SOURCE: C. Batchelor, 1998, UPS sets up rail service in Germany, *Financial Times*, March 17, 27; Associated Press, 1998, UPS, pilots reach tentative labor deal, *Dallas Morning News*, January 20, D2; A. Dworkin, 1997, Delivering the goods, *Dallas Morning News*, September 14, H1, H6; UPS Home Page, 1998, January 12, http://www.ups.com.

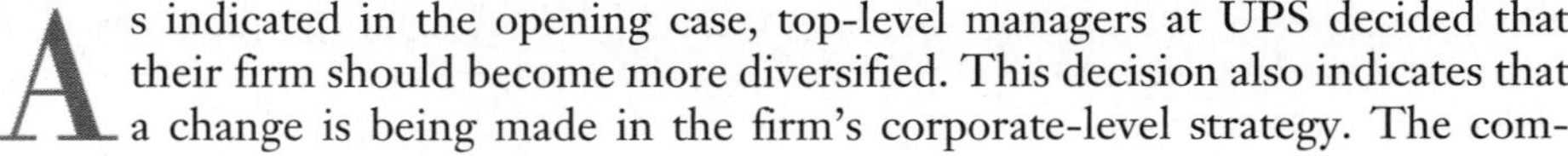

As indicated in the opening case, top-level managers at UPS decided that their firm should become more diversified. This decision also indicates that a change is being made in the firm's corporate-level strategy. The company had been implementing what is called a *single-business* corporate-level strategy (see Figure 6.1). With a low level of diversification (recall that in 1997, approximately 2.2 percent of revenue was earned outside its core business), UPS sought strategic competitiveness and above-average returns by concentrating on the distribution of packages and documents. For many years, this strategy was successful. Based on the competitive advantage yielded by the firm's core competency in distribution, UPS became the world's largest package distribution company. The sales revenue and financial returns that UPS has earned historically suggest that this firm has achieved a position of strategic competitiveness.

However, 1997 proved to be the year in which UPS's almost total reliance on the package distribution business for its revenue and profitability became an issue. As explained previously, a strike by the firm's unionized personnel resulted in a loss of approximately $600 million in sales revenue in a two-month period. This situation caused some UPS customers to consider the wisdom of relying on a single source for distribution of their products. Similarly, UPS executives concluded that some diversification away from its core business would benefit their company.

The focal point of the interest in additional diversification quickly became the firm's own Worldwide Logistics unit. Convinced that it can be a "big player" in the logistics management field, UPS executives established an ambitious set of sales revenue goals for this subsidiary. Revenues of roughly $700 million in 1997 (up from $500 million in 1996) were expected to reach $1 billion in 1998 and increase by $700 or $800 million annually through 2003. If achieved, this pace of growth will exceed the expected 8 percent annual growth rate in the firm's core parcel-shipping business.

FIGURE 6.1 *Levels and Types of Diversification*

Low Levels of Diversification

Single business:	More than 95% of revenue comes from a single business.	A
Dominant business:	Between 70% and 95% of revenue comes from a single business.	A / B

Moderate to High Levels of Diversification

Related constrained:	Less than 70% of revenue comes from the dominant business, and all businesses share product, technological, and distribution linkages.	A / B — C
Related linked: (mixed related and unrelated)	Less than 70% of revenue comes from the dominant business, and there are only limited links between businesses.	A / B — C

Very High Levels of Diversification

Unrelated:	Less than 70% of revenue comes from the dominant business, and there are no common links between businesses.	A B C

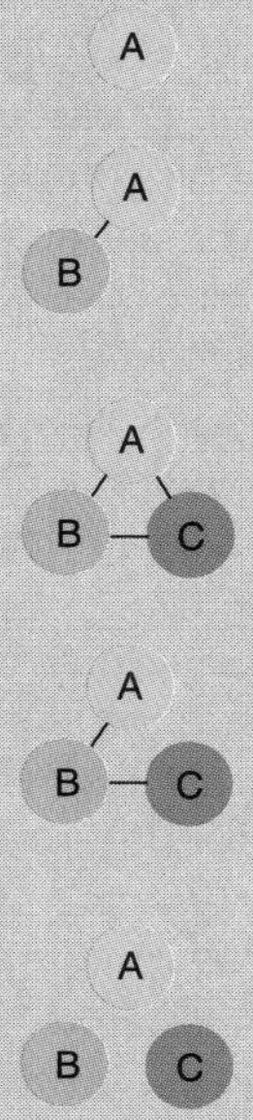

Source: Adapted from R. P. Rumelt, 1974, *Strategy, Structure and Economic Performance* (Boston: Harvard Business School).

Although aggressive in nature, some analysts believe these revenue goals are attainable. The CEO of Armstrong & Associates Inc., a logistics analysis company, noted that he had "been expecting great things from UPS Logistics for a long time." Moreover, in this analyst's view, "UPS has got so many resources, they ought to be able to build a worldwide logistics operation that could force others out of business."[1] If this type of success is achieved, and the firm is able to earn 13 percent or more of sales revenue from the operations of its Worldwide Logistics unit, UPS's corporate-level strategy will have changed from *single business* to *dominant business* (see Figure 6.1). The success of UPS's additional diversification is not assured, however. Diversification strategies are difficult to manage.[2] Nonetheless, the risk UPS executives believed their firm would face by failing to become more diversified exceeded the risk associated with learning how to effectively manage a more diversified corporation. Beyond the matter of risk, UPS executives were convinced that the firm's financial returns would increase through proper management of a greater amount of diversification.

In Chapters 4 and 5, our discussions focused on the selection and use of business-level strategies.[3] Our discussions of different business-level strategies (Chapter 4) and the competitive dynamics associated with their use (Chapter 5) were focused primarily on firms competing in a single industry or product market.

When a firm chooses to diversify its operations beyond a single industry and to operate businesses in several industries, it is pursuing a corporate-level strategy of diversification. As is the case with business-level strategies, a corporate-level strategy of diversification allows a firm to adapt to conditions in its external environment.[4] An influential strategic choice in firms, diversification strategies play a major role in the behavior of large firms.[5] Strategic choices regarding diversification are, however, fraught with uncertainty.[6]

A diversified company has two levels of strategy: a business-level (or competitive) strategy and a corporate-level (or company-wide) strategy.[7] In diversified firms, each business unit chooses a business-level strategy to implement to achieve strategic competitiveness and earn above-average returns. But diversified firms must also choose a strategy that is concerned with the selection and management of its businesses. Defined formally, a **corporate-level strategy** is action taken to gain a competitive advantage through the selection and management of a mix of businesses competing in several industries or product markets. In essence, a corporate-level strategy is what makes "the corporate whole add up to more than the sum of its business unit parts."[8] Corporate-level strategy is concerned with two key questions: what businesses the firm should be in and how the corporate office should manage its group of businesses.[9] Roberto Goizueta, former CEO of Coca-Cola, captured the essence of these two questions by suggesting that top-level executives were responsible for verifying that the firm could develop effective strategies across time and knew how to allocate capital effectively and efficiently.[10] In the current complex global environment, top-level managers should view their firm's businesses as a portfolio of core competencies when seeking answers to these critical questions.[11]

A **corporate-level strategy** is action taken to gain a competitive advantage through the selection and management of a mix of businesses competing in several industries or product markets.

Relating back to Figure 1.1 in Chapter 1, our focus herein is on the formulation of corporate-level strategy. The corporate-level strategy should evolve from the firm's strategic intent and mission. Also, as with business-level strategies, corporate-level strategies are expected to help the firm earn above-average returns (create value).[12] Some have suggested that few corporate-level strategies actually create value.[13] In the final analysis, the value of a corporate-level strategy "must be that the businesses in the portfolio are worth more under the management of the company in question than they would be under any other ownership."[14] Thus, the corporate-level strategy should be expected to contribute a given amount to the returns of all business units that exceeds what those returns would be without the implementation of such a strategy.[15] When managed effectively, corporate-level strategies enhance a firm's strategic competitiveness and contribute to its ability to earn above-average returns.[16] In the latter part of the 1990s and into the twenty-first century, corporate-level strategies will be managed in a global business environment characterized by high degrees of risk, complexity, uncertainty, and ambiguity.[17]

A primary approach to corporate-level strategy is diversification, which requires corporate-level executives to craft a multibusiness strategy. One reason for the use of a diversification strategy is that managers of diversified firms possess unique, general management skills that can be used to develop multibusiness strategies and enhance a firm's strategic competitiveness.[18] To derive the greatest benefit from their skills, managers must focus their energies on the tasks associated with managing a diversification strategy.[19] The prevailing theory of diversification suggests that firms should diversify when they have excess resources, capabilities, and core competencies that have multiple uses.[20] Multibusiness strategies often encompass many different industry environments, and, as discussed in Chapter 11, these strategies require unique organizational structures.

This chapter begins by addressing the history of diversification. Included in this discussion are descriptions of the advantages and disadvantages of single-business and dominant-business strategies. We next describe different levels of diversification (from low to high) and reasons firms pursue a corporate-level strategy of diversification. Two types of diversification strategies that denote moderate to very high levels of diversification—related and unrelated—are then examined.

Large diversified firms often compete against each other in several markets. This is called *multipoint competition*. For instance, RJR Nabisco competes against Philip Morris in both cigarettes and consumer foods. Svenska Aeroplan Aktiebolaget (Saab) and Daimler-Benz AG compete against one another in both automobiles and aircraft engines. Vertical integration strategies designed to exploit market share and gain power over competitors are also explored. Closing the chapter is a brief discussion of questions firms should consider when examining the possiblility of becoming a diversified company. For the already-diversified firm, these questions can be used to determine if additional levels of diversification should be pursued.

Of course, there are alternatives to diversification. These options entail long-term contracts, such as strategic alliances and franchising, discussed in Chapter 9, and expanding into new geographic markets such as international diversification, discussed in Chapter 8.

HISTORY OF DIVERSIFICATION

In 1950, only 38.1 percent of the *Fortune* 500 U.S. industrial companies generated more than 25 percent of their revenues from diversified activities. By 1974, this figure had risen to 63 percent. In 1950, then, more than 60 percent of the largest *Fortune* 500 industrial companies were either single-business or dominant-business firms; by 1974, this had dropped to 37 percent.[21]

Beginning in the late 1970s, and especially through the middle part of the 1980s, a significant trend toward refocusing and divestiture of business units unrelated to core business activities took place in many firms. In fact, approximately 50 percent of the *Fortune* 500 companies refocused on their core businesses from 1981–1987.[22] As a result, by 1988, the percentage of single- or dominant-business firms on the *Fortune* 500 list of industrial companies had increased to 53 percent.[23] Although many diversified firms have become more focused, this is somewhat masked because extensive market and international diversification (compared to product diversification) has occurred that is not included in these statistics. As Chapter 8's discussion reveals, international strategy has been increasing in importance and has led to greater financial performance relative to product diversification.[24]

The trend toward product diversification of business organizations has been most significant among U.S. firms. Nonetheless, large business organizations in Europe, Asia, and other parts of the industrialized world have also implemented diversification strategies. In the United Kingdom, the number of single- or dominant-business firms fell from 60 percent in 1960 to 37 percent in 1980. A similar, yet less dramatic trend toward more diversification occurred in Japan. Among the largest Japanese firms, 60 percent were dominant- or single-business firms in 1958, although this percentage fell only to 53 percent in 1973.

These trends toward more diversification, which have been partially reversed due to restructuring (see Chapter 7), indicate that learning has taken place regarding corporate diversification strategies. The main lesson learned is that firms performing well in their dominant business may not want to diversify. Moreover, firms that diversify should do so cautiously, choosing to focus on a relatively few, rather than many, businesses.[25]

Deciding to become more diversified in terms of both product offerings and geographic locations appears to have contributed to Cott Corporation's recent difficulties. Originally, Cott produced and sold (at discount prices) an array of private-label beverages including soft drinks, New Age beverages, iced teas, juice drinks, sport drinks, and bottled water. Cott's customers were large retail chains such as Wal-Mart and Safeway. Through effective implementation of its strategy, this Toronto, Canada, company grew, in less than 10 years, from a small family business to a multinational corporation with annual sales of over $1 billion. This growth resulted in the firm becoming the leading worldwide supplier of premium retailer branded beverages and the world's fourth largest soft drink company. The company believes that product innovation, employee creativity, high-quality products, and world-class packaging are its core competencies.

As one analyst observed recently, the firm followed its initial success with expansions "into things it had no business expanding into, such as the Canadian beer market and faraway countries." In addition to these product and geographic forays, Cott also planned, but did not execute, a strategy that called for it to pattern a major line of private-label foods after the approach it used to sell its private-label soft drinks. Given the problems created by ill-advised diversification efforts, Cott Corporation sold its beer business and reorganized its international operations to cut costs.[26]

Thus, for Cott Corporation, diversification outside its core business area did not result in additional financial returns. Sometimes, however, the failure to pursue appropriate types of diversification may have a negative effect on the firm's strategic competitiveness. Some analysts believe that this may have been the case recently for AT&T. During the time AT&T was searching for a new CEO, its competitors, such as WorldCom, GTE, and MCI Communications, completed transactions to achieve dominant market positions in different segments of the telecommunications industry. Inactive during the search for its new CEO, AT&T may have lost some opportunities to buy assets required to do battle (see the opening case in Chapter 10). As a result, AT&T may find itself competing against a raft of fortified new rivals. The breadth of its rivals' strengths suggests that AT&T is facing the "fight of its life" in everything from local phone services to the Internet as the twenty-first century approaches. Calling for the firm to pursue a strategy of related diversification, some proposed that AT&T should have been adding to its communications assets at the same time competitors were adding to theirs. AT&T pursued related diversification earlier (in the mid-1990s) when it filled a hole in its wireless services capabilities through the purchase of McCaw Cellular Communications for more than $12 billion.[27]

As these examples about Cott and AT&T suggest, strategic competitiveness can be increased when the firm pursues a level of diversification that is appropriate for its resources (especially financial resources) and core competencies and the opportunities and threats that exist in its external environment. For some companies, however, the match between competencies and external environmental conditions indicates that they can flourish by focusing on single or highly related businesses. Two prominent examples include Wal-Mart and Coca-Cola. In fact, when he became Coca-Cola's CEO, Roberto Goizueta went against then-current wisdom when he decided to change the firm from a highly diversified company to one that was focused tightly on its core products. Goizueta explained, "There's a perception in this country that you're better off if you're in two lousy businesses than if you're in a good one—that you're spreading the risk. It's crazy."[28]

Another example of a firm that achieves success through highly focused operations is Mabuchi Motor, a midsize but highly successful Japanese firm. Ninety-nine percent of its annual revenue comes from the sale of motors. The focus on motors allows company scientists to continuously examine ways to improve the motors, such as making them lighter, quieter, more enduring, and cheaper.[29]

LEVELS OF DIVERSIFICATION

Diversified firms vary according to the level of diversification and connection between and among their businesses. Figure 6.1 lists and defines five categories of businesses according to increasing levels of diversification. Besides single- and dominant-business categories, more fully diversified firms are classified into related and unrelated categories. A firm is related through its diversification when there are several links between business units; for example, units share products or services, technologies, and/or distribution channels. The more links among businesses, the more "constrained" the relatedness of diversification. Unrelatedness refers to a lack of direct links between businesses.

Low Levels of Diversification

A firm pursing a low level of diversification focuses its efforts on a single or a dominant business. The Wm. Wrigley Jr. Company is an example of a firm with little diversification. Its primary focus is on the chewing gum market.[30] A firm is classified as a single business when revenue generated by the dominant business is greater than 95 percent of the total sales.[31] Dominant businesses are firms that generate between 70 percent and 95 percent of their total sales within a single category. Because of the sales it generates from breakfast cereals, Kellogg is an example of a dominant business firm.

Hershey Foods Corp. (the largest U.S. producer of chocolate and nonchocolate confectionery items) is another dominant business firm. Although Hershey manufactures some food products (principally San Giorgio, American Beauty, Delmonico, Skinner, and Ronzoni pastas), the bulk of the firm's revenue is earned through the selling of its confectionery items. To generate interest in its candies across time, the company introduces new products carefully and deliberately. Commenting about this approach, an analyst suggested the following: "Announcing that a new candy is on the way, then keeping it under wraps until it is ready increases sales and sparks a general feeling of enthusiasm for Hershey stock."[32]

As a result of recent decisions to become less diversified, Volvo AB now follows the dominant business corporate-level strategy. Although still diversified, with varied business interests including its agricultural equipment, the car and heavy-truck units are the firm's core businesses. Together, these units account for 70 percent of sales revenue and 50 percent of profits. To enhance its competitiveness in these units, Volvo embarked on a three-year strategic drive in late 1997 that was intended to "cut purchasing costs, slim management and lift productivity by 5 percent a year."[33] Often dominant business firms have some level of vertical integration. Many firms (such as Texaco) started as single businesses and evolved to use a dominant-business strategy involving vertical integration.

Moderate and High Levels of Diversification

When a firm earns more than 30 percent of its sales volume outside a dominant business, and when its businesses are related to each other in some manner, the company is classified as a related-diversified firm. With more direct links between the businesses, the firm is defined as related constrained. Examples of related-constrained firms include Campbell Soup, Procter & Gamble, Xerox, and Merck & Company. If there are only a few links between businesses, the firm is defined as a mix related and unrelated business, or a related-linked firm, (see Figure 6.1). Johnson & Johnson, Westinghouse, General Electric, and Schlumberger are examples of related-linked firms. Related-constrained firms share a number of resources and activities between businesses. Related-linked firms have less sharing of actual resources and assets and relatively more transfers of knowledge and competencies between businesses. Highly diversified firms, which have no relationships between businesses, are called unrelated-diversified firms. Examples of firms pursuing an unrelated diversification strategy include Dart Group, Tenneco, Textron, and Thailand's Charoen Pokphand (with department stores and business units operating in the petrochemicals and telecommunications industries, this firm's annual sales revenue approximates $8 billion).[34]

In general, there are more unrelated-diversified firms in the United States than in other (e.g., European) countries. In Latin America and other emerging economies such as Korea and India, conglomerates (firms following the unrelated diversification strategy) continue to dominate the private sector.[35] For example, typically family controlled, these corporations account for more than two-thirds of the 33 largest private business groups in Brazil. Similarly, the largest business groups in Mexico, Argentina, and Colombia are family-owned, diversified enterprises.[36]

Consistent with a global trend of refocusing, some companies decide to become less diversified. As indicated in the Strategic Focus, less diversification allows the firm to concentrate on fewer business lines. A decision to refocus could be a product of an inability to effectively manage greater levels of diversification or recognition of the fact that a lower level of diversification would permit a superior match between the firm's core competencies and its environmental opportunities and threats.

STRATEGIC FOCUS

Changes in Diversification Strategies at Hanson PLC, Terex, and Westinghouse

Cited historically as perhaps the world's most successful follower of the unrelated diversification strategy, Hanson PLC nonetheless decided in the mid-1990s to become less diversified and to streamline its operations. Thus, Hanson either sold or spun off a number of its operating businesses; those remaining were structured into four independent business units. Spinning off 34 operating companies created one of these new business units, U.S. Industries. After completing all of its streamlining actions, top-level executives were convinced that the firm's newly created ability to concentrate on its core holdings would lead to increased financial returns. Also contributing to an anticipated enhancement of the firm's strategic competitiveness was the elimination of $1.4 billion of debt through the spin-offs and divestitures.

Terex was also once more diversified than it is today. After divestitures, the firm is now focused more tightly on its related constrained diversification strategy (roughly 33 percent of revenue comes from the Terex Trucks unit; the remaining 67 percent is generated by Terex Cranes). Terex implements the cost leadership strategy in both its truck and crane business units. Emphasizing efficiency, the company uses streamlined assembly lines to produce simple, standardized equipment that is priced 10 to 15 percent lower than competitors' offerings.

Terex's former chairman and CEO relied on high-yield debt to finance an acquisition strategy during the late 1980s and early 1990s. Among the acquisitions were truck trailer manufacturer Fruehauf Trailer Corp. and forklift maker Clark Material Handling Company. Related to the firm's other units, Terex was, nonetheless, unable to successfully implement the cost leadership strategy to manufacture truck trailers and forklifts. Although substantial progress was made by the firm's new CEO to reduce costs and increase efficiencies at Clark Material (a $20 million profit in 1996 was a significant improvement over a $30 million loss in 1993), Terex sold Clark in 1996. This transaction followed the finalization of the divestment of the Fruehauf unit in January 1995. Selling these units has allowed Terex to refocus on the core truck and crane businesses rather than allocating its energies and resources across four units that shared some commonalties.

As a 100-year-plus-old industrial manufacturer, Westinghouse Electric Corp. implemented the related-linked diversification strategy for many years. The significant reduction in the amount of this firm's diversification began with the August 1995 acquisition of CBS for $5.4 billion in cash. Convinced that the firm's future was in broadcasting, CEO Michael H. Jordan initiated a process that culminated in the official changing of the firm's name to CBS Corporation. To create its broadcasting focus, two business units were sold in 1997 (Thermo King and Westinghouse Power Generation). Jordan intended to complete the sales of the remaining major business units—energy systems, process control, and government operations—by mid-1998.

During these divestitures, CBS Corp. acquired American Radio Systems' radio broadcasting operations. Calling this transaction "strategically attractive," a top-level CBS executive stated, "This investment will significantly strengthen CBS's position in the fast growing radio industry. It will enable CBS Radio to expand into new top 50 markets and increase its position in its existing markets." Thus, to expand its single product line of broadcasting, a line that includes CBS Network, CBS radio, the TV station group, cable, and "other" broadcasting, CBS Corp. was committed to making selective acquisitions.

SOURCE: *CBS Corporation Home Page*, 1998, January 13, http://www.cbs.com; *Terex Corporation Home Page*, 1998, January 13, http://www.terex.com; *The Economist*, 1997, Westinghouse RIP, November 29, 63–65; T. Aeppel, 1997, How Westinghouse's famous name simply faded away, *Wall Street Journal*, November 20, B4; G. Fairclough, 1997, Terex's fortunes improve after tough cost-cutting, *Wall Street Journal*, September 30, B4; L. L. Brownlee and J. R. Dorfman, 1995, Birth of U.S. industries isn't without complications, *Wall Street Journal*, May 18, B4.

REASONS FOR DIVERSIFICATION

Firms implement a diversification strategy as their corporate-level strategy for many reasons. A partial list of these is shown in Table 6.1. These reasons are discussed throughout the remainder of this chapter in relationship to specific diversification strategies.

Most firms implement a diversification strategy to enhance the strategic competitiveness of the entire company. This is the case at UPS, as explained in the

TABLE 6.1 ***Motives, Incentives, and Resources for Diversification***

Motives to Enhance Strategic Competitiveness

- Economies of scope (related diversification)
  - Sharing activities
  - Transferring core competencies
- Market power (related diversification)
  - Blocking competitors through multipoint competition
  - Vertical integration
- Financial economies (unrelated diversification)
  - Efficient internal capital allocation
  - Business restructuring

Incentives and Resources with Neutral Effects on Strategic Competitiveness

- Antitrust regulation
- Tax laws
- Low performance
- Uncertain future cash flows
- Firm risk reduction
- Tangible resources
- Intangible resources

Managerial Motives (Value Reduction)

- Diversifying managerial employment risk
- Increasing managerial compensation

opening case, and for Saab and Daimler-Benz as well. With headquarters in Brussels, this is also true for the Solvay Group. In pursuit of above-average returns, Solvay concentrates on diversified activities in five sectors—alkalis, peroxygens, plastics, processing, and health.[37] When a diversification strategy does enhance strategic competitiveness, the firm's total value is increased. Value is created through either related diversification or unrelated diversification when those strategies allow a company's business units to increase revenues and/or reduce costs while implementing their business-level strategies.

Another reason for diversification is to gain market power relative to competitors. To increase its market power by building a national home-care network, Integrated Health Services, Inc. purchased RoTech Medical Corp. for $615 million in stock. Integrated Health officials suggested that the additional diversification this transaction created would enable the firm to provide a broad spectrum of home health services, from nursing to respiratory care to intravenous medication and nutrition. Similarly, the purchase of a Cleveland-based retail real estate brokerage firm by Trammel Crow Co., a prominent Dallas-based industrial real estate company, was intended to increase quickly the firm's retail penetration on a national scale. In commenting about the purchase, a Trammel Crow executive observed, "We think that this acquisition advances our progress by a number of years."[38] In the instance of both Integrated Health and Trammel Crow, additional diversification was expected to help each firm gain a competitive advantage over its rivals.

Other reasons for implementing diversification may not enhance strategic competitiveness; in fact, diversification could have neutral effects or actually increase costs or reduce a firm's revenues. These reasons include diversification (1) to neutralize a competitor's market power (e.g., to neutralize the advantage of another firm by acquiring a distribution outlet similar to those of the competitors) or (2) to expand a firm's portfolio to reduce managerial employment risk (e.g., if a single business fails, a top-level manager remains employed in a diversified firm). Because diversification can increase firm size and thus managerial compensation, managers may have motives to diversify a firm. This type of diversification may reduce the firm's value.

RELATED DIVERSIFICATION

As suggested earlier in the chapter, related diversification is a strategy through which the firm intends to build upon or extend its existing resources, capabilities, and core competencies in the pursuit of strategic competitiveness.[39] Thus, firms that have selected related diversification as their corporate-level strategy seek to exploit economies of scope between business units. Available to firms operating in multiple industries or product markets,[40] **economies of scope** are cost savings attributed to transferring the capabilities and competencies developed in one business to a new business without significant additional costs.

Economies of scope are cost savings attributed to transferring the capabilities and competencies developed in one business to a new business without significant additional costs.

Firms seek to create value from economies of scope through two basic kinds of operational economies: sharing activities and transferring core competencies. The difference between sharing activities and transferring competencies is based on how separate resources are used jointly to create economies of scope. Tangible resources, such as plant and equipment or other business-unit physical assets, often must be shared to create economies of scope. Less tangible resources, such as sales forces, also can be shared. However, when know-how is transferred between separate activities and there is no physical or tangible resource involved, a core competence has been transferred as opposed to sharing activities.

Sharing Activities

Activity sharing is quite common, especially among related-constrained firms. At Procter & Gamble, a paper towels business and a baby diapers business both use paper products as a primary input to the manufacturing process. Having a joint paper production plant that produces inputs for both divisions is an example of a shared activity. In addition, these businesses are likely to share distribution sales networks because they both produce consumer products.

In Chapter 3, primary and support value chain activities were discussed. In general, primary activities, such as inbound logistics, operations, and outbound logistics, might have multiple shared activities. Through efficient sharing of these activities, firms may be able to create core competencies. In terms of inbound logistics, the business units may share common inventory delivery systems, warehousing facilities, and quality assurance practices. Operations might share common assembly facilities, quality control systems, or maintenance operations. With respect to outbound logistics, two business units might share a common sales force and sales service desk. Support activities could include the sharing of procurement and technology development efforts. The sharing of activities occurring at Honeywell and TRW is described in the Strategic Focus.

STRATEGIC FOCUS

The Sharing of Activities to Create Value

Implementing the related-constrained diversification strategy, Honeywell has a single product focus—controls. A worldwide manufacturer and marketer of control systems and components, the firm has three major business units—home and building controls, industrial controls, and space and aviation controls. These units account for approximately 45 percent, 31 percent, and 22 percent of total sales revenue, respectively. (The remaining 2 percent is earned by what the firm classifies as "other" businesses.) Controls for homes and buildings are intended to create comfortable, safe, efficient environments. The firm's industrial control systems and components are designed to improve productivity, optimize the use of raw materials, help companies comply with environmental regulations, ensure plant safety, and enhance overall competitiveness. The space and aviation controls unit is the world's leading supplier of avionics systems for commercial, military, and space markets.

Seeking total sales revenue of $10 billion by 2000 (revenues were expected to reach $8.8 billion in 1998), Honeywell established a new division to reach this goal and to increase its financial returns. Called Consumer Goods, this division's creation was stimulated by results generated through market research. To Honeywell's surprise, recent market research indicated that the firm's name is recognized widely by the public. In fact, researchers "discovered that although consumers knew little about most Honeywell products, they had seen its name on about 140 million central heating and air conditioning controls installed in the U.S. and Europe."

Honeywell is now using the technology and manufacturing core competencies that were developed in its three major business units to produce consumer goods such as fans, humidifiers, dehumidifiers, and air cleaners. Offered initially in the United States, Honeywell executives believe that Europe and East Asia are promising markets for its consumer goods. By sharing some of the activities required to manufacture high-quality controls among its major units, and through an emphasis on the value provided by Honeywell's reputation as a manufacturer of high-quality products, the firm hopes to achieve sales of $1 billion in its Consumer Goods division by 2002.

In September 1996, TRW sold its information services business. With two business units remaining (automotive components, generating 66 percent of sales revenue, and space and defense, accounting for the remaining 34 percent), TRW is following the related-linked diversification strategy. Several divisions exist within each of the two units to serve different customer groups' unique needs. Nonetheless, the firm is now less diversified than it was before the information services unit was sold.

In early 1998, TRW formed a new division in its space and defense unit. Called Telecommunications, this division uses technologies TRW developed originally to manufacture components for use in top-secret military satellites. The firm's objective was for this division to achieve sales revenues of up to $4 billion annually by 2008. The technologies committed to this new division via internal transfers are used to manufacture a range of hardware aimed at operators of commercial telecommunication satellites and suppliers of ground-based communication equipment.

Analysts had a favorable view of TRW's attempt to share some of its activities and skills. One reason for this reaction could be TRW's success in early efforts to use military technologies in the commercial sector. For example, the firm learned how to produce ultra-fast semiconductor chips for use in mobile telephone handsets such as those manufactured by Motorola and Ericsson. These commercial chips are based on "gallium arsenide that [TRW had] developed for digital processing jobs on defense satellites, such as the Pentagon's Milstar telecoms spacecraft."

Over time, top-level executives want activities to be shared between TRW's two major units as well as within the divisions of each unit. Learning how to share activities between the major units could result in dramatic successes in the marketplace. Although important to the firm's future success, this objective will not be achieved easily. In fact, TRW's president and chief operating officer observed recently that one of his company's biggest challenges is to find ways of transferring military-related technologies from the company's space division to the automotive sector.

SOURCE: Honeywell Inc. Home Page, 1998, January 14, http://www.honeywell.com; TRW Inc. Home Page, 1998, January 14, http://www.trw.com; T. Brophy, 1997, TRW Inc., *Value Line*, November 7, 1381; P. Marsh, 1997, TRW to form new telecoms division, *Financial Times*, December 15, 19; P. M. Seligman, 1997, Honeywell, *Value Line*, October 24, 1013; S. Wagstyl, 1997, Honeywell bows to consuming passions, *Financial Times*, November 28, 23.

As explained in the Strategic Focus, firms expect the sharing of activities across units to result in increased strategic competitiveness and financial returns. Other matters affect the degree to which these outcomes will be achieved through activity sharing. For example, firms should recognize that sharing activities requires sharing business-unit strategic control. Moreover, one business-unit manager may feel that another business-unit manager is receiving more benefit from the activity sharing. Such a perception could create conflicts between division managers. Activity sharing is also risky because business-unit ties create links between outcomes. If demand for the product of one business is reduced, there may not be sufficient revenues to cover the fixed costs of running the joint plant. Shared activities create interrelationships that affect the ability of both businesses to achieve strategic competitiveness. Activity sharing may be ineffective if these costs are not taken into consideration.

The costs of activity sharing notwithstanding, research shows that the sharing of activities and resources across businesses within a firm can increase the firm's value. For example, recent research examining acquisitions of firms in the same industry (referred to as horizontal acquisitions) such as in the banking industry, has found that sharing resources and activities (thereby creating economies of scope) contributed to postacquisition performance increases and higher returns to shareholders.[41] Additionally, research suggests that firms selling off related units where resource sharing is a possible source of economies of scope produced lower returns than selling off businesses unrelated to the firm's core business.[42] Still other research found that firms with more related units had lower risk.[43] These results suggest that gaining economies of scope by sharing activities and resources across businesses within a firm may be important to reduce risk and gain positive returns from diversification efforts.

Transferring of Core Competencies

Over time, a strategically competitive firm's intangible resources, such as know-how, become the foundation for competitively valuable capabilities and core competencies. Thus, in diversified firms, core competencies are complex sets of resources and capabilities that link different businesses primarily through managerial and technological knowledge, experience, and expertise.[44]

Marketing expertise is an example of a core competence that could be used this way. Because the expense of developing such a competence has already been incurred, and because competencies based on intangible resources are less visible and more difficult for competitors to understand and imitate, transferring these types of competencies from an original business unit to another one may reduce costs and enhance an entire firm's strategic competitiveness.[45] A key reason Philip Morris decided to acquire Miller Brewing Company was that it believed that a competitive advantage could be achieved by transferring its marketing core competence to Miller.

As a cigarette company, Philip Morris developed a particular expertise in marketing. When Philip Morris purchased Miller Brewing, the beer industry had efficient operations, but no firm in the industry had established marketing competence as a source of competitive advantage. The marketing competence transferred from Philip Morris to Miller resulted in the introduction of improved marketing practices to the brewing industry. These practices, especially in terms of advertising, proved to be the source of competitive advantage that allowed Miller Brewing to earn above-average returns for a period of time. In fact, several years passed before Anheuser-Busch, the largest firm in the brewing industry, developed the capabilities required to duplicate the benefits of Miller's strategy. A strong competitive response from Anheuser-Busch was predictable, however, in that beer is the firm's core business.

Some firms discover that they either are unable to transfer competencies or they transfer competencies that do not help a business unit establish a competitive advantage. One way managers facilitate the transfer of competencies is to move key people into new management positions. Although Philip Morris accomplished competence transfer to Miller Brewing in this way, a business-unit manager of an older division may be reluctant to transfer key people who have accumulated the knowledge and experience necessary to transfer the competencies. Thus, managers with the ability to facilitate the transfer of a core competence may come at a premium or may not want to transfer, and the top-level managers from the transferring division may not want them to be transferred to a new division to fulfill a diversification objective.

Market power exists when a firm is able to sell its products above the existing competitive level or reduce the costs of its primary and support activities below the competitive level, or both.

Market Power

Related diversification can also be used to gain market power. **Market power** exists when a firm is able to sell its products above the existing competitive level or reduce the costs of its primary and support activities below the competitive level, or both.[46]

One approach to gaining market power through diversification is multipoint competition. *Multipoint competition* exists when two or more diversified firms compete in the same product areas or geographic markets.[47] For example, when Philip Morris moved into foods by buying General Foods and Kraft, RJR's competitive response was the acquisition of another foods company, Nabisco. The competitive rivalry between these two companies is an example of multipoint competition.

If these firms compete head to head in each market, multipoint competition will not create potential gains; instead, it will generate excessive competitive activity. Over time, if these firms refrain from competition and in effect realize mutual forbearance, this may be classified as a form of related diversification that creates value for each firm through less competitive activity (see discussion in Chapter 5). *Mutual forbearance* is a relationship between two or more firms in which excessive competition leads to a situation where all firms in the competitive set see that such competition is self-destructive and, without formal agreement, cease the self-destructive competitive actions and responses.

Walt Disney and Time Warner operate in similar businesses—theme parks, movie and television production, and broadcasting activities. Disney has spent considerable amounts of money advertising its theme parks in Time Warner magazines. Time Warner, however, began an aggressive advertising campaign aimed at taking Disney's theme park customers. Disney retaliated by canceling its advertising in Time Warner's publications. Time Warner responded by canceling corporate meetings in Florida at a Disney resort. Disney responded by canceling Time Warner advertisements of its theme parks on a Los Angeles television station owned by Disney.[48] This illustrates the potential negative side of multipoint competition. Disney's actions represents a counterattack mode, argued to be a prominent strategic action when multipoint competition exists.[49] Counterattacks are not common where multipoint competition exists because the threat of a counterattack may prevent strategic actions from being taken or, more likely, firms may retract their strategic actions with the threat of counterattack.[50]

Another approach to creating value by gaining market power is the strategy of vertical integration. **Vertical integration** exists when a company is producing its own inputs (backward integration) or owns its own source of distribution of outputs (forward integration). It is also possible to have partial vertical integration where some inputs and outputs are sold by company units, while other inputs and outputs are produced or sold by outside firms.

A company pursuing vertical integration is usually motivated to strengthen its position in its core business by gaining market power over competitors. This is done through savings on operations costs, avoidance of market costs, better control to establish quality, and, possibly, protection of technology.

Vertical integration exists when a company is producing its own inputs (backward integration) or owns its own source of distribution of outputs (forward integration).

In response to prominent threats in their external environment (such as changes in environmental regulations and third-party reimbursement practices) in the early to mid-1990s, some firms competing in the pharmaceutical industry pursued a strategy of vertical integration. In November 1993, for example, Merck & Company, at the time the world's largest prescription drug manufacturer, paid $6.6 billion to acquire Medco Containment Services Inc. (one of the largest mail-order pharmacy and managed care companies at the time of its purchase). With Medco, Merck controls a dominant supplier of its products. Further contributing to an increase in Merck's market power as a result of pursuing vertical integration was its opportunity to have detailed and immediate access to information regarding customers' marketing-related needs. In identical fashion, SmithKline Beecham PLC attempted to increase its market power through the forward vertical integration purchase of United HealthCare's pharmacy-benefit services unit, Diversified Pharmaceutical Services Inc.; Eli Lilly & Company's purchase of McKesson's PCS Health Systems unit was completed for the same strategic reason.[51] Important benefits accruing to Merck & Company, SmithKline Beechman, and Eli Lilly as a result of the decision to vertically integrate in a forward direction include reductions in market transaction costs and some additional protection of proprietary technologies.

Of course, there are limits to vertical integration. For example, an outside supplier may produce the product at a lower cost. As a result, internal transactions from vertical integration may be expensive and reduce profitability. Also, bureaucratic costs are incurred when implementing this strategy. Because it can require that substantial sums of capital be invested in specific technologies, vertical integration may be problematic when technology changes quickly. Changes in demand also create capacity balance and coordination problems. If one division is building a part for another internal division, but achieving economies of scale requires the division to build it at a scale beyond the capacity of the internal buyer to absorb demand, sales outside the company would be necessary. However, if demand slackens, an overcapacity would result because the internal users cannot absorb total demand. Thus, although vertical integration can create value and contribute to strategic competitiveness, especially in gaining market power over competitors, it is not without risks and costs.

UNRELATED DIVERSIFICATION

Financial economies are cost savings realized through improved allocations of financial resources based on investments inside or outside the firm.

An unrelated diversification strategy can create value through two types of financial economies. **Financial economies** are cost savings realized through improved allocations of financial resources based on investments inside or outside the firm.[52]

The first type of financial economy involves efficient internal capital allocations. This type also seeks to reduce risks among the firm's business units. This can be achieved, for example, through development of a portfolio of businesses with different risk profiles, thereby reducing business risk for the total corporation. A second approach of financial economies is concerned with purchasing other corporations and restructuring their assets. This approach allows a firm to buy and sell businesses in the external market with the intent of increasing its total value.

Efficient Internal Capital Market Allocation

Capital allocation is usually distributed efficiently in a market economy by capital markets. Efficient distribution of capital is induced because investors seek to purchase shares of firm equity (ownership) that have high future cash-flow values.

Capital is allocated not only through equity, but also through debt, where shareholders and debtholders seek to improve the value of their investment by investing in businesses with high growth prospects. In large diversified firms, however, the corporate office distributes capital to divisions to create value for the overall company. Such an approach may provide potential gains from internal capital market allocation, relative to the external capital market.[53] The corporate office, through managing a particular set of businesses, may have access to more detailed and accurate information as well as actual business and performance prospects.

Compared to corporate office personnel, investors would have relatively limited access to internal information and can only estimate actual divisional performance and future business prospects. Although businesses seeking capital must provide information to capital providers (e.g., banks, insurance firms), firms with internal capital markets may have at least two informational advantages. First, information provided to capital markets through annual reports and other sources may not include negative information, but rather only positive prospects and outcomes. External sources of capital have limited ability to know *specifically* what is taking place inside large organizations. Although owners have access to information, they have no guarantee of full and complete disclosure.[54]

Second, although a firm must disseminate information, this information becomes available to potential competitors simultaneously. With insights gained by studying this information, competitors might attempt to duplicate a firm's competitive advantage. Without having to reveal internal information, a firm may protect its competitive advantage through an internal capital market.

If intervention from outside the firm is required to make corrections, only significant changes are possible, such as forcing the firm into bankruptcy or changing the dominant leadership coalition (e.g., the top-management team described in Chapter 12). Alternatively, in an internal capital market, the corporate office may choose to adjust managerial incentives or suggest strategic changes in the division to make fine-tuned corrections. Thus, capital allocation can be adjusted according to more specific criteria than is possible with external market allocation. The external capital market may fail to allocate resources adequately to high-potential investments, compared to corporate office investments, because it has less accurate information. The head office of a diversified company can more effectively perform such tasks as disciplining underperforming management teams and allocating resources.[55]

Intensely devoted to the unrelated diversification strategy, Harold Geneen is recognized by some for his ability to organize what was, for a certain period of time, a highly effective corporate office—an office that disciplined operating units through the imposition of strict financial controls. As CEO of then highly diversified ITT, Geneen based his leadership practices on the belief "that sound financial management could be applied successfully to any business, from rental cars to bakeries to insurance."[56] Known also for his unshakable commitment to "facts" that were generated through detailed quantitative analyses, Geneen expected long hours and unquestionable loyalty from those working with and for him. At the height of his success, perhaps no other corporate leader exceeded Geneen's ability to guide a firm following the unrelated diversification strategy.[57]

Although ITT no longer follows the unrelated diversification strategy, other firms do. One of Europe's oldest and most powerful industrial dynasties, Ifil is rapidly becoming more diversified. Historically, this Italian firm's major holding has been its 30 percent ownership of Fiat. Since 1986, however, Ifil has diversified aggressively and extensively through entries into food, cement, tourism, and retailing. Current plans include a possible acquisition-based movement into the telecommunications industry. As a result of becoming more diversified, Ifil's holdings in Fiat now represent less than 45 percent of its $4.1 billion in net assets.[58] In this firm, the primary function of the corporate office is the efficient allocation and management of resources. As such, financial economies are critical to attempts to earn above-average returns at Ifil. However, such risk reduction strategies may not be valuable to all firms' stakeholders. Shareholders and debtholders have lower cost ways of reducing their risk through diversification of their own investment portfolios. Successful implementation of an unrelated diversification strategy requires that a firm incur fewer costs to reduce an individual investor's risks as compared to the costs that investor would experience to diversify his or her own portfolio.[59]

Restructuring

Another alternative, similar to the internal capital market approach, focuses exclusively on buying and selling other firm assets in the external market. It is similar to the real estate business, where profits are earned by buying assets low, restructuring them, and selling them as high as possible. The restructuring approach usually entails buying the firm, selling off assets such as corporate headquarters, and terminating corporate staff members.

Selling underperforming divisions and placing the remaining divisions under the discipline of rigorous financial controls are other often used restructuring actions. Rigorous controls require divisions to follow strict budgets and account regularly for cash inflows and outflows to corporate headquarters. A firm pursuing this approach may have to use hostile takeovers or tender offers. Hostile takeovers have the potential to increase the resistance of the target firm's top-level managers. In these cases, corporate-level managers often are dismissed, while division managers are retained.

Creating financial economies through the purchase of other companies and the restructuring of their assets requires an understanding of significant trade-offs. First, success usually calls for a focus on mature, low-technology businesses. Otherwise, resource allocation decisions become too complex because the uncertainty of demand for high-technology products requires information-processing capacities beyond the smaller corporate staffs of unrelated-restructuring firms. Service businesses are also difficult to buy and sell in this way because of their client or sales orientation. Sales staffs of service businesses are more mobile than those of manufacturing-oriented businesses and may seek jobs with a competitor, taking their clients with them. This is true in professional service businesses such as accounting, law, advertising, and investment banking. As such, these businesses probably would not create value if acquired by an unrelated-restructuring firm.

DIVERSIFICATION: INCENTIVES AND RESOURCES

The economic reasons given in the last section summarize the conditions under which diversification strategies increase a firm's value. Diversification, however, is often undertaken with the expectation that doing so will prevent a firm from reducing its value. Thus, there are reasons to diversify that are value neutral. As we explain next, several incentives may lead a firm to pursue further diversification.[60]

Incentives to Diversify

Incentives provide reasons to diversify; they come from both the external environment and a firm's internal environment. The term *incentive* implies that managers have some choice whether to pursue the incentive or not. Incentives external to the firm include antitrust regulation and tax laws. Internal firm incentives include low performance, uncertain future cash flows, and overall firm risk reduction.

Antitrust Regulation and Tax Laws Government antitrust policies and tax laws provided incentives for U.S. firms to diversify in the 1960s and 1970s. Applications of antitrust laws regarding mergers that create increased market power (vertical and horizontal integration) were stringent in the 1960s and 1970s.[61] As a result, many of the mergers during this time were unrelated—that is, they involved companies pursuing different lines of business. Thus, the merger wave of the 1960s was "conglomerate" in character. Merger activity leading to conglomerate diversification was encouraged primarily by the Celler-Kefauver Act (which discouraged horizontal and vertical mergers). For example, in the 1973–1977 period, 79.1 percent of all mergers were conglomerate.[62]

The mergers of the 1980s, however, were different. Antitrust enforcement ebbed, permitting more and larger horizontal mergers (acquisition of the same line of business, such as a merger between two oil firms).[63] In addition, investment bankers became more freewheeling in the kinds of mergers they would try to facilitate; as a consequence, hostile takeovers increased to unprecedented numbers.[64] The conglomerates or highly diversified firms of the 1960s and 1970s became more "focused" in the 1980s and 1990s as merger constraints were relaxed and restructuring implemented.[65]

Tax effects on diversification stem not only from individual tax rates but also from corporate tax changes. Some companies (especially mature companies) may have activities that generate more cash than they can reinvest profitably. Michael Jensen, a prominent financial economist, believes that such *free cash flows* (liquid financial assets for which investments in current businesses are no longer economically viable) should be redistributed to shareholders in the form of dividends.[66] However, in the 1960s and 1970s, dividends were taxed more heavily than ordinary personal income. As a result, in the pre-1980s, shareholders preferred that companies retain these funds for use in buying and building companies in high-performance industries. If the stock value appreciated over the long term, shareholders might receive a better return for these funds than through dividends because they would be taxed more lightly under capital gains rules.

In 1986, however, the top ordinary individual income tax rate was reduced from 50 percent to 28 percent, and the special capital gains tax was changed, causing capital gains to be treated as ordinary income. These changes suggested that shareholders would no longer encourage firms to retain funds for purposes of diversification. Moreover, the elimination of personal interest deductions, as well as the lower attractiveness of retained earnings to shareholders, has prompted the use of more leverage by firms (interest expense is tax deductible for firms). These tax law changes also influenced an increase in divestitures of unrelated business units after 1984. Thus, individual tax rates for capital gains and dividends may have created a shareholder incentive for increased diversification before 1986, but an incentive for reduced diversification after 1986, unless funded by tax-deductible debt.

Regarding corporate taxation, acquisitions typically increase a firm's depreciable asset allowances. Increased depreciation (non–cash-flow expense) produces lower taxable income, thereby providing additional incentive for acquisitions. Before 1986, acquisitions may have been the most attractive means for securing tax benefits.[67] The tax incentives are particularly important because acquisitions represent the primary means of firm diversification, but the 1986 Tax Reform Act reduced some of the corporate tax advantages of diversification.[68]

As this discussion notes, across different time periods, U.S. government policy has provided incentives for both increased and reduced levels of diversification. Recently, a loosening of federal regulations, coupled with a desire to expand their product offerings to hold onto and build upon their existing franchises, have provided incentives for large U.S. banks to become more diversified through the pursuit of related diversification. By acquiring securities firms, investment banks, and other financial services companies, some large banks have diversified their revenue streams considerably. Banc One, for example, paid $7.3 billion to purchase credit-card issuer First USA. Similarly, NationsBank acquired the investment firm Montgomery Securities for $1.2 billion.[69] Commenting favorably about this acquisition, NationsBank's chief financial officer suggested that the acquisition enabled his firm "to provide [its] clients true 'one-stop-shopping' capabilities." Moreover, the CFO observed, "The combination of our businesses will give all our clients access to the financial products and services they need to reach their goals, from bank loans and bridge financings to debt and equity underwriting and risk management. Simply put, this new organization gives all of us more freedom to put creative solutions on the table for our clients."[70]

In addition to the external incentive to diversify that antitrust regulation and tax laws provide, there are incentives internal to the firm that increase the likelihood that diversification will be pursued.

Low Performance It has been proposed that "high performance eliminates the need for greater diversification,"[71] as in the example of the Wm. Wrigley Jr. Co. Conversely, low performance may provide an incentive for diversification. Firms

A loosening of federal regulations and a desire to expand their product offerings have given large U.S. banks the incentive to become more diversified through acquisitions. Banc One Corp. paid $7.3 billion for First USA Inc., a credit-card issuer.

plagued by poor performance often seek to take higher risks.[72] Interestingly, though, some researchers have found that low returns are related to greater levels of diversification.[73] Poor performance may lead to increased diversification, especially if resources exist to pursue additional diversification. Continued poor returns following additional diversification, however, may slow the pace of diversification and even lead to divestitures. Thus, an overall curvilinear relationship, as illustrated in Figure 6.2, may exist between diversification and performance.

Germany's Daimler-Benz provides an example of poor performance fueled by diversification. Under its former CEO, Edzard Reuter, Daimler-Benz diversified to become a manufacturer of jets, helicopters, trains, and electronics in addition to its core automotive and truck businesses. The purpose of this diversification was to transform the firm into an "integrated technology company."[74]

Unfortunately, the acquisitions were less than sterling; furthermore, attempts to integrate the various businesses that had been acquired faltered. In 1993 and in 1995, Daimler-Benz had substantial net losses, largely attributed to the new businesses added in previous years. Its core business, Mercedes-Benz Automotive and Truck Division, continued to be profitable during this time period. The CEO following Reuter, Juergen Schrempp, was under increasing pressure to reverse the diversification strategy begun by Reuter.[75]

Recent evidence suggests that Juergen Schrempp is dealing successfully with the challenges that were created partly by the firm's failed diversifications. Since assuming leadership control for the firm in May 1995, Schrempp has taken decisive actions.[76] Money-losing operations, including the firm's electronics business and its 24 percent stake in Cap Gemini, the French software-services company, were sold. Fokker, the Dutch airplane manufacturer, was liquidated (interestingly, when serving as head of Daimler-Benz's aerospace division, Schrempp himself orches-

FIGURE 6.2 ***The Curvilinear Relationship Between Diversification and Performance***

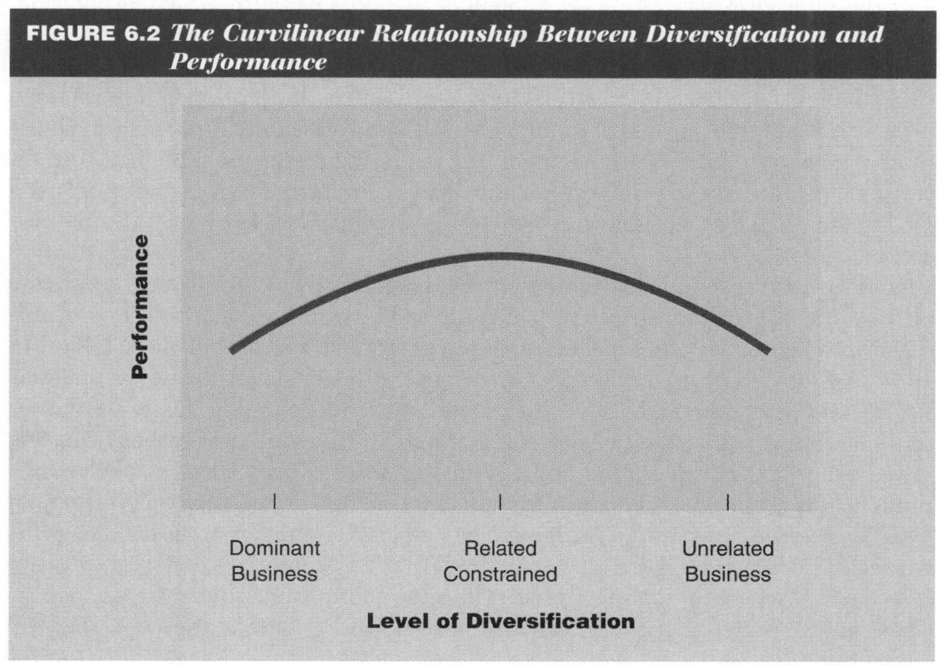

trated the acquisition of Fokker).[77] In addition, Schrempp eliminated a layer of upper-level executives and is trying to instill a culture of responsibility and entrepreneurship. Thought of as a cultural revolution, one in which each of Daimler's 23 remaining business units is expected to earn at least 12 percent on its invested capital, innovation is the driving force being used to create the new culture. Cross-disciplinary project teams, called function groups, represent one technique created to stimulate process and product innovations.[78] The fact that 1997 sales revenue and earnings exceeded those of 1996 (revenues, for example, increased almost 20 percent) suggests the possibility that the poor performance that was stimulated by Daimler-Benz's diversification efforts is being reversed.

Uncertain Future Cash Flows As a firm's product line matures and/or is threatened, diversification may be perceived as an important defensive strategy. Firms in mature or maturing industries sometimes find it necessary to diversify to survive over the long term.[79] Certainly, this has been one of the dominant reasons for diversification among railroad firms during the 1960s and 1970s. Railroads diversified primarily because the trucking industry was perceived to have significant negative effects on the demand for rail transportation. Uncertainty, however, can be derived from both supply and demand sources.

Diversification because of uncertainty also pertains to firms in industries where foreign competitors with lower average costs have penetrated domestic markets. The diversification in the steel industry in the 1970s exemplifies this type of supply-side uncertainty as an incentive. To reduce its dependence on steel, U.S. Steel bought Marathon Oil and Texas Oil and Gas. This competitive action was taken because international integrated steel makers (such as Nippon Steel) were able to produce steel at a lower cost due to lower labor costs and newer, more efficient production facilities.

In 1986, in recognition of the fact that its diversification decisions had created a vastly different organization, U.S. Steel changed its name to USX Corporation. Today, with three independent business units (Marathon, U.S. Steel, and Delhi Groups), this firm "is a major worldwide producer of oil and natural gas, the nation's largest producer of steel products and one of the largest U.S. gatherers, processors, and transporters of natural gas. USX today is really three separate businesses, each with its own management, yet operating under the USX board of directors."[80] Once the world's dominant steel manufacturer, sales revenue from USX's U.S. Steel group now accounts for approximately 27 percent of total corporate sales.

The U.S. defense industry has downsized significantly in recent years and many of the firms in this industry have had to diversify to survive. An indicator of this downsized industry is the decline in the Pentagon's budget from $370 billion in 1987 to $259 billion in 1997.[81] Major defense industry diversification is demonstrated by General Dynamics' decision to sell all of its defense industry businesses so it could diversify into other product markets. At the same time, other firms followed a horizontal integration strategy in the pursuit of the market power they thought was required to remain competitive in the downsized defense industry. In 1997 alone, Boeing acquired McDonnell Douglas, Raytheon purchased Texas Instruments' defense business, and Lockheed Martin sought to acquire Northrop Grumman. Occurring among firms in the same lines of business, these acquisitions caused some to conclude that the entire defense industry would become less competitive.[82]

Thus, demand uncertainties about expected future cash flows have affected diversification strategy decisions in some defense firms and horizontal, market power-oriented integration strategies in others.[83] Because of evidence regarding the results of such actions, the effects of the decision to diversify into other businesses by a firm such as General Dynamics will be interesting to observe. In general, existing evidence indicates that although diversification may increase shareholder wealth and reduce the uncertainty of future cash flows in selected instances, these outcomes are achieved often at the expense of profitability.

Firm Risk Reduction Because diversified firms pursuing economies of scope often have investments that are too inflexible to realize synergy between business units, several potential problems exist. **Synergy** exists when the value created by business units working together exceeds the value those same units create when working independently. For example, as a firm increases its relatedness between business units, it increases its risk of corporate failure because synergy produces joint interdependence between business units and the firm's flexibility of response is constrained. This threat may force two basic decisions.

Synergy exists when the value created by business units working together exceeds the value those same units create when working independently.

First, the firm may reduce the level of technological change by operating in more certain environments. This may make the firm risk averse and, thus, uninterested in pursuing new product lines that have potential but are not proven. Alternatively, the firm may constrain the level of activity sharing and forego the benefits of synergy. Either or both decisions may lead to further diversification. The former would lead to related diversification into industries where more certainty exists. The latter result may produce further, but unrelated, diversification.[84]

Resources and Diversification

Although incentives to diversify may exist, a firm must possess the resources required to make diversification economically feasible. As mentioned earlier, tangible, intangible, and financial resources may facilitate diversification. Resources vary in their utility for value creation, however, because of differences in rarity and mobility; that is, some resources are easier for competitors to duplicate because they are not rare, valuable, costly to imitate, and nonsubstitutable. For instance, free cash flows may be used to diversify the firm. Because financial resources such as free cash flows are more flexible and common, they are less likely to create value as compared to other types of resources.[85] The diversification mentioned earlier for steel firms was facilitated significantly by the presence of free cash flows.

This is also likely true of the diversification efforts by Anheuser-Busch. Anheuser-Busch was a very profitable company and significant cash flows were created from the success of the brewery business. These resources were then used to purchase the St. Louis Cardinals, to invest almost $400 million in the development and operation of the Eagle snack food business, and to acquire the Campbell Taggart bakery business. The use of these resources, however, did not produce significant positive returns for Anheuser-Busch. As a result, the firm decided to spin off Campbell Taggart, sell the St. Louis Cardinals, and close the Eagle snacks business.[86] Still the world's largest brewing organization, Anheuser-Busch continues to use free cash flows to support its business interests in theme park operations, manufacturing and recycling aluminum beverage containers, rice milling, real estate development, turf farming, railcar repair and transportation, and paper label printing, among others.[87] It is the diversification created by this particular mix of businesses that the corporation's executives are able to manage in a way that creates value.

Tangible firm resources usually include the plant and equipment necessary to produce a product. Such assets may be less flexible. Any excess capacity of these resources (plant and equipment) often can be used only for very closely related products, especially those requiring highly similar manufacturing technologies. Excess capacity of other tangible resources, such as a sales force, can be used to diversify more easily. Again, excess capacity in a sales force would be more effective with related diversification because it may be utilized to sell similar products. The sales force would be more knowledgeable about related product characteristics, customers, and distribution channels. Tangible resources may create resource interrelationships in production, marketing, procurement, and technology, defined earlier as activity sharing.

Intangible resources would, of course, be more flexible than actual tangible physical assets in facilitating diversification. Although the sharing of tangible resources may induce diversification, intangible resources could encourage even more diversification. Clearly, there were some potential intangible resource synergies that could be achieved by Anheuser-Busch. For example, Anheuser-Busch's knowledge of yeast products may have been useful in the use of yeast within Campbell Taggart. This did not, however, produce significant positive synergies between the brewery and bakery businesses as hoped by Anheuser-Busch executives.[88] Apparently, there was little sharing of tangible or intangible resources; thus, little value was created.

Extent of Diversification

If a firm has incentives and resources to diversify, the extent of diversification will be greater than if it just has incentives or resources alone.[89] The more flexible, the more likely the resources will be used for unrelated diversifications; the less flexible, the more likely the resources will be used for related diversification. Thus, flexible resources (e.g., free cash flow) are likely to lead to relatively greater levels of diversification. Also, because related diversification requires more information processing to manage links between businesses, more unrelated units can be managed by a small corporate office.[90]

MANAGERIAL MOTIVES TO DIVERSIFY

Managerial motives for diversification may exist independent of incentives and resources. These motives include managerial risk reduction and a desire for increased compensation.[91] For instance, diversification may reduce top-level managers' *employment risk* (risk of job loss or income reduction). That is, corporate executives may diversify a firm in order to diversify their employment risk, as long as profitability does not suffer excessively.[92] Diversification also provides an additional benefit to managers that shareholders do not enjoy. Diversification and firm size are highly correlated and, as size increases, so does executive compensation.[93] Large firms are more complex and harder to manage and, thus, managers of larger firms are compensated more highly.[94] As a result, diversification provides an avenue for increased compensation and therefore may serve as a motive for managers to engage in greater diversification. Governance mechanisms, such as the board of directors, ownership monitoring, executive compensation, and the market for corporate control may limit managerial tendencies to overdiversify. These governance mechanisms are discussed in more detail in Chapter 10.

Governance mechanisms may not be strong and, in some instances, managers may diversify the firm to the point that it fails to earn even average returns.[95] Resources employed to pursue each diversification are most likely to include financial assets (e.g., free cash flows), but may also involve intangible assets. Thus, this type of diversification is not likely to lead to improved performance. The loss of adequate internal governance may result in poor relative performance, thereby triggering a threat of takeover. Although external controls, such as the threat of takeover, may create improved efficiency by replacing ineffective managerial teams, managers may avoid takeovers through defensive tactics (golden parachutes, poison pills, etc.) Therefore, an external governance threat, although having a restraining influence on managers, does not provide flawless control of managerial motives for diversification.[96]

Most of the large, publicly held firms are profitable because managers are positive agents and many of their strategic actions (e.g., diversification moves) contribute to this success. As mentioned, governance devices are designed to deal with exceptions to the norms of achieving strategic competitiveness and increasing shareholder wealth in the process. It is overly pessimistic to assume that managers will usually act in their own self-interest as opposed to their firm's interest.[97]

Managers may also be held in check by concerns for their reputation in the labor market. If reputation facilitates power, a poor reputation may also reduce power. Likewise, a market for managerial talent may constrain managerial abuse of power to pursue inappropriate diversification.[98] In addition, some diversified firms also provide policing of other diversified firms. These large, highly diversified firms seek out poorly managed diversified firms for acquisition to restructure the target firm's asset base. Knowing that their firms could be acquired if not managed successfully, managers are encouraged to find ways to achieve strategic competitiveness.

In summary, although managers may be motivated to increase diversification, governance mechanisms are in place to discourage such action merely for managerial gain. However, this governance is imperfect and may not always produce the intended consequences. Even when governance mechanisms cause managers to correct a problem of overdiversification, these moves are not without trade-offs. For instance, spinoff firms may not realize productivity gains, although it is in the best interest of the divesting firm.[99] As such, the assumption that managers need disciplining may not be entirely correct, and sometimes governance may create consequences that are worse than those resulting from overdiversification.[100]

Therefore, as this discussion suggests, the level of diversification the firm chooses should be based on the optimal levels that are indicated by market and strategic characteristics (resources) owned or available to each company. Optimality may be judged by the factors examined in this chapter: resources, managerial motives, and incentives.

As shown in Figure 6.3, the level of diversification that can be expected to have the greatest positive effect on performance (in terms of strategic competitiveness and the earning of above-average returns) is based partly on how the interaction of resources, managerial motives, and incentives affects the adoption of particular diversification strategies. As indicated earlier, the greater the incentives and the more flexible the resources, the higher the level of expected diversification. Financial resources (the most flexible) should have a stronger relationship to the extent of diversification than either tangible or intangible resources. Tangible resources (the most inflexible) would be useful primarily for related diversification.

The model suggests that implementation issues are important to whether diversification creates value or not (see Chapter 11). It also suggests that governance mechanisms are important to the level and type of diversification implemented (see Chapter 10).

As we have discussed, diversification strategies can enhance a firm's strategic competitiveness and allow it to increase its financial returns. This appears to be the case for Estee Lauder. One of the world's largest cosmetics companies with brands such as Clinque, Aramis, Origins, and Prescriptives, as well as its flagship Lauder products, this firm follows a long-term strategy of diversifying into niche

FIGURE 6.3 ***Summary Model of the Relationship Between Firm Performance and Diversification***

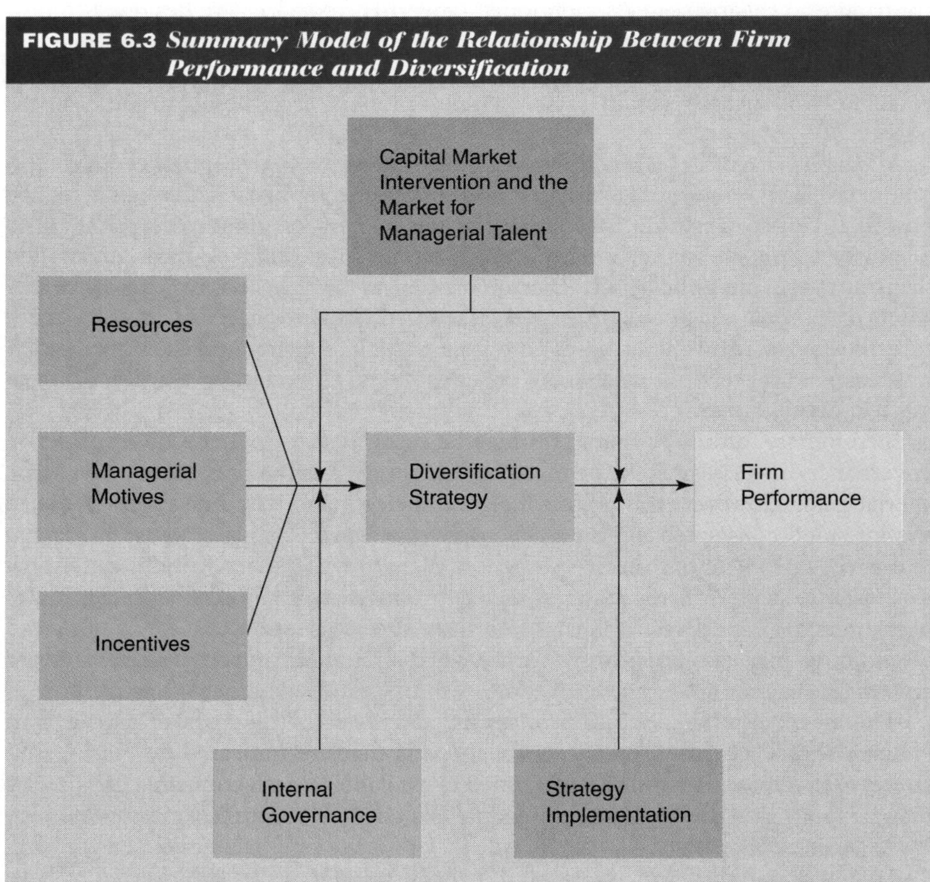

Source: R. E. Hoskisson and M. A. Hitt, 1990, Antecedents and performance outcomes of diversification: A review and critique of theoretical perspectives, *Journal of Management* 16: 498.

areas of the beauty business. To diversify, Lauder purchases firms with high-profile brands and then uses its managerial and organizational skills to create value. Recently Lauder pursued still more related diversification through its acquisition of Aveda Corporation. Aveda's natural beauty products are made from flower and plant essences, using aromatherapy principles. Attracted to Aveda because of its unique market position and entrepreneurial management team, Lauder executives believed that Aveda's products would augment its existing portfolio by extending its presence in hair care and by introducing Lauder into a new distribution channel of specialist hair salons. (At the time of its acquisition, Aveda's products were sold in 30,000 salons worldwide.)[101]

Positive outcomes from diversification such as those experienced by Estee Lauder are achieved only when the company has pursued a proper amount of diversification. Presented in this chapter's final Strategic Focus is a set of questions that should be considered when deciding if the firm should diversify or, for the already diversified company, if additional levels of diversification should be pursued. Preparing forthright answers to these questions improves the probability that top-level managers will make an informed and effective decision regarding diversification. If the answers to these questions are in the direction opposite to that which suggests an ability to create value through diversification, then a decision not to become more diversified is required.

While reading this Strategic Focus, recall that any corporate-level diversification strategy will enhance a firm's strategic competitiveness and increase its financial returns only when it creates value. At the corporate level, value is created through the selection and management of a particular group of businesses that is worth more under the ownership of the company than it would be under any other ownership.[102]

Estee Lauder acquired Aveda Corporation, whose natural beauty products are based on aromatherapy principles. Aveda's products enhanced Lauder's portfolio by extending the firm's presence in hair care and giving it a presence in specialist hair care salons.

STRATEGIC FOCUS

Issues to Evaluate When Considering Diversification

As suggested in this chapter, decisions regarding diversification are among the most challenging a firm and its top-level managers face. More effective decisions can be reached through analysis of the following six questions.

- What resources, capabilities, and core competencies do we possess that would allow us to outperform competitors?

To create value across businesses from the corporate level, top-level managers must determine precisely what it has the capacity to do that would increase the competitiveness of an acquired company or that would allow it to move successfully into a new geographic market. (Geographic diversification, which is movement into different market areas, is discussed in detail in Chapter 8.) The work of creative employees, excellent distribution capabilities, and superior knowledge about the transfer of information are examples of competencies on which the firm could rely to create value when diversifying. Borders, one of North America's largest book and music retailers, opened its first European store in 1998 on London's Oxford Street. This store was the largest bookshop built in Britain in 50 years. The company intended to open at least three or four additional stores in 1998 (one in Leeds) and 1999. The value to be created through Borders' geographic diversification was the building of what some in the United Kingdom view as "cultural superstores"—stores with vast collections of CDs and computer games as well as the offering of coffees and cakes to those browsing through the firm's huge book collection. To create value in its new geographic locations, Borders intended to rely on its ability to determine the particular set of diverse and unique cultural products that would be of interest to customers. Once identified, additional value is created for customers by Borders' capacity to offer this array of products in a single site.

- What core competencies must we possess to succeed in a new product or geographic market?

To compete successfully, companies typically must own or have access to all competencies that are linked to the earning of above-average returns in a given market. Coca-Cola, for example, concluded that its superior distribution capabilities and marketing and branding expertise were sufficient to allow the firm to be successful through its diversification into the wine business, but because the company lacked intimate knowledge about the wine business, its diversification effort failed. Similarly, Tomkins, a United Kingdom conglomerate, divested its distribution operations. Although the firm has the competencies (including possession of the detailed knowledge about how to allocate capital effectively and efficiently across and within business units) that are necessary to add value to its food, automotive parts manufacturing, and building and industrial companies, it was not able to add value in the distribution business.

- Is it possible for us to leapfrog competitors?

If the firm lacks the competencies required to create value in an area into which it seeks to diversify, it can try to purchase the skill that it lacks or develop that skill inhouse. Additionally, the firm could use the competencies it does possess to redefine the rules of competition. To diversify from its core camera business into photocopiers, Canon rewrote the competitive rules in an industry dominated by Xerox. Relying on its photographic technology and dealer management skills, Canon targeted small businesses and the consumer market rather than large companies, sold its machines through a network of dealers rather than through a direct sales force, and focused on quality and price in the manufacturing of its products rather than speed.

- Will diversification break up capabilities and competencies that should be kept together?

Sometimes, the firm's strategic competitiveness is a product of the synergy that results from a unique combination of resources and capabilities. If those are broken apart so one or two skills can be transferred to a new setting, the diversification effort may fail. In Markides' words, "Too many companies mistakenly assume that they can break up clusters of competencies or skills that, in fact, work only because they are together, reinforcing one another in a particular competitive context. Such a misjudgment can doom a diversification move."

- Will we only be a player in the new product or geographic market or will we emerge as a winner?

Corporate-level capabilities and competencies create value through diversification efforts only when they are valuable, rare, costly to imitate, and nonsubstitutable (see Chapter 3). Thus, to earn above-average returns through diversification, firms must be able to create something that is unique.

- What can the firm learn through its diversification and is it organized properly to acquire such knowledge?

To create value on a long-term basis, the firm should view each diversification effort as an opportunity to learn. Acquired knowledge should then become the foundation upon which future diversification possibilities are evaluated.

SOURCE: A. Davis, 1998, Distribution sell-off likely at Tomkins, *Financial Times*, January 5, 27; A. Rawsthorn, 1998, US book chain to open first European store, *Financial Times*, January 7, 10; C. C. Markides, 1997, To diversify or not to diversify, *Harvard Business Review* 75, no. 6: 93–99; A. Roseno and C. Nokkentved, 1997, *Management Processes and Corporate-Level Strategy* (Copenhagen, Denmark: Management Process Institute).

SUMMARY

- Pursuing a single- or dominant-business corporate-level strategy may be preferable to a more diversified-business strategy, unless a corporation can develop economies of scope or financial economies between businesses, or obtain market power through additional levels of diversification. These economies and market power are the main sources of value creation for firm diversification.
- The primary reasons a firm pursues increased diversification are value creation through economies of scope, financial economies, or market power; actions because of government policy, performance problems, or uncertainties about future cash flow; and managerial motivations (e.g., to increase their compensation).
- Managerial motives to diversify can lead to overdiversification. On the other hand, managers can also be good stewards of the firm's assets.
- The level of firm diversification is a function of the incentives, firm resources, and the managerial motives to diversify.
- Related diversification can create value by sharing activities or transferring core competencies.
- Activity sharing usually involves sharing tangible resources between businesses. Core competence

transfer involves transferring the core competencies developed in one business to another business. It also may involve transferring competencies between the corporate office and a business unit.

- Activity sharing is usually associated with related-constrained diversification. Activity sharing is costly to implement and coordinate, may create unequal benefits for the divisions involved in sharing, and may lead to fewer risk-taking behaviors.
- Successful unrelated diversification is accomplished by efficiently allocating resources or restructuring a target firm's assets and placing them under rigorous financial controls.

REVIEW QUESTIONS

1. What is corporate-level strategy? Why is it important to a diversified firm?
2. Identify the advantages and disadvantages of single- and dominant-business strategies as compared to firms with higher levels of diversification.
3. What are three reasons why firms choose to move from either a single- or a dominant-business position to a more diversified position?
4. How do firms share activities and transfer core competencies to obtain economics of scope, while pursuing a related diversification strategy?
5. What are the two ways to obtain financial economies when pursuing an unrelated diversification strategy?
6. What incentives and resources encourage diversification in firms?
7. What motives might encourage managers to engage a firm in more diversification?

APPLICATION DISCUSSION QUESTIONS

1. This chapter suggests that there is a curvilinear relationship between diversification and performance. How can this relationship be modified so that the negative relationship between performance and diversification is reduced and the downward curve has less slope or begins at a higher level of diversification?
2. The *Fortune* 500 industrial firms are very large, and many of them have significant product diversification. Are these large firms overdiversified currently and experiencing lower performance than they should? Explain.
3. What is the primary reason for overdiversification, industrial policies, such as taxes and antitrust regulation, or because managers pursue self-interest, increased compensation, and reduced risk of job loss? Why?
4. One rationale for pursuing related diversification is to obtain market power. In the United States, too much market power, however, may result in a challenge by the Justice Department (because it may be perceived as anticompetitive). Under what situations might related diversification be considered unfair competition?
5. Assume you have received two job offers—one from a dominant-business firm and one from an unrelated-diversified firm (the beginning salaries are virtually identical). Which offer would you accept and why?
6. By the year 2010, do you believe large firms will be more or less diversified than they are today? Why? Will the trends regarding diversification be identical in Europe, the United States, and Japan? Explain.

ETHICS QUESTIONS

1. Assume you overheard the following statement: "Those managing an unrelated-diversified firm face far more difficult ethical challenges than do those managing a dominant-business firm." Based on your reading of this chapter, do you accept or reject this statement? Why?
2. Is it ethical for managers to diversify a firm rather than return excess earnings to shareholders? Provide reasoning in support of your answer.
3. What unethical practices might occur when a firm restructures its operations? Explain.
4. Do you believe ethical managers are unaffected by the managerial motives to diversify discussed in this chapter? If so, why? In addition, do you believe ethical managers should help their peers learn how to avoid making diversification decisions on the basis of the managerial motives to diversify? Why or why not?

INTERNET EXERCISE

Go to the *Fortune* 500 List at:

http://www.pathfinder.com/fortune/fortune500/500list.html

Select three firms from the *Fortune* 500 and visit their Web sites. From their Web sites and other Internet resources, determine each firm's level of diversification (see Figure 6.1). For each firm, comment on the appropriateness of its level of corporate diversification given the overall nature of the firm.

Strategic Surfing

NewsPage-Company Lookup is a very helpful Web site for accessing current news stories about U.S. corporations. These stories, which are selected from major American periodicals, provide current insight into the corporate and business-level company strategies.

http://www.companylink.com

NOTES

1. A. Dworkin, 1997, Delivering the goods, *Dallas Morning News*, September 14, H1, H6.
2. D. D. Bergh, 1997, Predicting divestiture of unrelated acquisitions: An integrative model of *ex ante* conditions, *Strategic Management Journal* 18: 715–731; J. L. Stimpert and I. M. Duhaime, 1997, Seeing the big picture: The influence of industry, diversification, and business strategy on performance, *Academy of Management Journal* 40: 560–583.
3. M. E. Porter, 1980, *Competitive Strategy* (New York: The Free Press), xvi.
4. K. Ramaswamy, 1997, The performance impact of strategic similarity in horizontal mergers: Evidence from the U.S. banking industry, *Academy of Management Journal* 40: 697–715.
5. M. A. Hitt, R. E. Hoskisson, and H. Kim, 1997, International diversification: Effects on innovation and firm performance in product-diversified firms, *Academy of Management Journal* 40: 767–798; W. G. Rowe and P. M. Wright, 1997, Related and unrelated diversification and their effect on human resource management controls, *Strategic Management Journal* 18: 329–338.
6. W. Boeker, 1997, Executive migration and strategic change: The effect of top manager movement on product-market entry, *Administrative Science Quarterly* 42: 213–236; H. A. Haverman, 1993, Organizational size and change: Diversification in the savings and loan industry after deregulation, *Administrative Science Quarterly* 38: 20–50.
7. M. E. Porter, 1987, From competitive advantage to corporate strategy, *Harvard Business Review* 65, no. 3: 43–59.
8. Ibid., 43.
9. Boeker, Executive migration and strategic change; C. A. Montgomery, 1994, Corporate diversification, *Journal of Economic Perspectives* 8: 163–178.
10. J. Huey, 1997, In search of Roberto's secret formula, *Fortune*, December 29, 230–234.
11. J. Kurtzman, 1998, An interview with C. K. Prahalad, in J. Kurtzman (ed.), *Thought Leaders* (San Francisco: Jossey-Bass), 40–51; D. Lei, M. A. Hitt, and R. Bettis, 1996, Dynamic core competencies through meta-learning and strategic context, *Journal of Management* 22: 547–567.
12. C. C. Markides, 1997, To diversify or not to diversify, *Harvard Business Review* 75, no. 6: 93–99.
13. C. C. Markides and P. J. Williamson, 1996, Corporate diversification and organizational structure: A resource-based view, *Academy of Management Journal* 39: 340–367; M. Goold and K. Luchs, 1993, Why diversify? Four decades of management thinking, *Academy of Management Executive* VII, no. 3: 7–25.
14. A. Roseno and C. Nokkentved, 1997, *Management Processes and Corporate-Level Strategy* (Copenhagen, Denmark: Management Process Institute); A. Campbell, M. Goold, and M. Alexander, 1995, Corporate strategy: The question for parenting advantage, *Harvard Business Review* 73, no. 2: 120–132.
15. T. H. Brusch and P. Bromiley, 1997, What does a small corporate effect mean? A variance components simulation of corporate and business effects, *Strategic Management Journal* 18: 825–835.
16. J. B. Barney, 1997, *Gaining and Sustaining Competitive Advantage* (Reading, MA: Addison-Wesley).
17. M. A. Hitt, B. W. Keats, and S. DeMarie, 1998, Navigating in the new competitive landscape: Building strategic flexibility and competitive advantage in the 21st century, *Academy of Management Executive* (in press); T. Mroczkowski and M. Hanaoka, 1997, Effective rightsizing strategies in Japan and America: Is there a convergence of employment practices? *Academy of Management Executive* XI, no. 2: 57–67.
18. Campbell, Goold, and Alexander, Corporate strategy; Goold and Luchs, Why diversify?, 8.
19. R. Simons and A. Davila, 1998, How high is your return on management? *Harvard Business Review* 76, no. 1: 71–80.
20. D. Collis and C. A. Montgomery, 1995, Competing on resources: Strategy in the 1990s, *Harvard Business Review* 73, no. 4: 118–128; M. A. Peteraf, 1993, The cornerstones of competitive advantage: A resource-based view, *Strategic Management Journal* 14: 179–191.
21. R. P. Rumelt, 1974, *Strategy, Structure and Economic Performance* (Cambridge, MA: Harvard University Press).
22. C. C. Markides, 1995, Diversification, restructuring and economic performance, *Strategic Management Journal* 16: 101–118.
23. R. E. Hoskisson, M. A. Hitt, R. A. Johnson, and D. S. Moesel, 1993, Construct validity of an objective (entropy) categorical measure of diversification strategy, *Strategic Management Journal* 14: 215–235.

24. Hitt, Hoskisson, and Kim, International diversification; M. A. Hitt, R. E. Hoskisson, and R. D. Ireland, 1994, A mid-range theory of the interactive effects of international and product diversification on innovation and performance, *Journal of Management* 20: 297–326.
25. W. M. Bulkeley, 1994, Conglomerates make a surprising comeback—with a '90s twist, *Wall Street Journal*, March 1, A1, A6.
26. M. Heinzl and N. Deogun, 1998, Cott loses sparkle due to price war, chairman's health, *Wall Street Journal*, January 6, B8; G. G. Marcial, Why Cott may bubble up, *Business Week*, March 2, 108; *Cott Corporation Home Page*, 1998, January 13, http://www.cott.com.
27. J. J. Keller, 1997, As AT&T seeks CEO, megadeals pass by, *Wall Street Journal*, October 17, A8.
28. J. Talton, 1997, Late Coke CEO built empire with quiet grace, *Dallas Morning News*, October 26, H3.
29. R. Henkoff, 1995, New management secrets from Japan—really, *Fortune*, November 27, 135–146.
30. *Value Line*, 1994, Edition 10 (February 18): 1494.
31. Rumelt, *Strategy, Structure, and Economic Performance;* L. Wrigley, 1970, Divisional autonomy and diversification (Ph.D. dissertation, Harvard Business School).
32. P. M. Seligman, 1997, Hershey Foods, *Value Line*, November 14, 1478; Associated Press, 1997, Psst! Hershey's up to something, *Dallas Morning News*, October 14, D1.
33. G. McIvor, 1997, Volvo unveils profit drive, *Financial Times*, December 9, 15; B. Mitchener, 1997, Volvo proves small players can perform, *Wall Street Journal*, October 22, A19.
34. B. Einhorn and S. Prasso, 1997, Thailand's anxious giant, *Business Week*, October 27, 70E4–70E16; P. J. Williamson, 1997, Asia's new competitive game, *Harvard Business Review* 75, no. 5: 55–67; *Business Week*, 1997, Corporate scoreboard, August 25, 163.
35. T. Khanna and K. Palepu, 1997, Why focused strategies may be wrong for emerging markets, *Harvard Business Review* 75, no. 4: 41–50.
36. *The Economist*, 1997, Inside story, December 6, 7–9.
37. M. Smith, 1998, Solvay thaws 15% advance, *Financial Times*, February 6, 16; Solvay Group, 1996, *Annual Report*, 2.
38. S. Brown, 1997, Crow signals expansion into retail, *Dallas Morning News*, August 27, D3; R. Winslow, 1997, Integrated Health to buy RoTech for $615 million, *Wall Street Journal*, July 8, A3, A8.
39. D. J. Teece, G. Pisano, and A. Shuen, 1997, Dynamic capabilities and strategic management, *Strategic Management Journal* 18: 509–533.
40. M. E. Porter, 1985, *Competitive Advantage* (New York: The Free Press), 328.
41. T. H. Brusch, 1996, Predicted change in operational synergy and post-acquisition performance of acquired businesses, *Strategic Management Journal* 17: 1–24; H. Zhang, 1995, Wealth effects of U.S. bank takeovers, *Applied Financial Economics* 5: 329–336.
42. D. D. Bergh, 1995, Size and relatedness of units sold: An agency theory and resource-based perspective, *Strategic Management Journal* 16: 221–239.
43. M. Lubatkin and S. Chatterjee, 1994, Extending modern portfolio theory into the domain of corporate diversification: Does it apply? *Academy of Management Journal* 37: 109–136.
44. Barney, *Gaining and Sustaining Competitive Advantage*, 367; A. Mehra, 1996, Resource and market based determinants of performance in the U.S. banking industry, *Strategic Management Journal* 17: 307–322; S. Chatterjee and B. Wernerfelt, 1991, The link between resources and type of diversification: Theory and evidence, *Strategic Management Journal* 12: 33–48.
45. N. Argyres, 1996, Capabilities, technological diversification and divisionalization, *Strategic Management Journal* 17: 395–410.
46. W. G. Shepherd, 1986, On the core concepts of industrial economics, in H. W. deJong and W. G. Shepherd (eds.), *Mainstreams in Industrial Organization* (Boston: Kluwer Publications).
47. K. Hughes and C. Oughton, 1993, Diversification, multi-market contact and profitability, *Economica* 60: 203–224.
48. L. Landro, P. M. Reilly, and R. Turney, 1993, Disney relationship with Time Warner is a strained one, *Wall Street Journal*, April 14, A1, A9.
49. A. Karnani and B. Wernerfelt, 1985, Multipoint competition, *Strategic Management Journal* 6: 87–96.
50. f. i. smith and R. L. Wilson, 1995, The predictive validity of the Karnani and Wernerfelt model of multipoint competition, *Strategic Management Journal* 16: 143–160.
51. E. Karrer-Rueedi, 1997, Adaptation to change: Vertical and horizontal integration in the drug industry, *European Management Journal* 15: 461–469.
52. Bergh, Predicting divestiture of unrelated acquisitions; C. W. L. Hill, 1994, Diversification and economic performance: Bringing structure and corporate management back into the picture, in R. P. Rumelt, D. E. Schendel, and D. J. Teece (eds.), *Fundamental Issues in Strategy* (Boston: Harvard Business School Press), 297–321.
53. O. E. Williamson, 1975, *Markets and Hierarchies: Analysis and Antitrust Implications* (New York: Macmillan Free Press).
54. R. Kochhar and M. A. Hitt, 1998, Linking corporate strategy to capital structure: Diversification strategy, type, and source of financing, *Strategic Management Journal* (in press).
55. Ibid.; P. Taylor and J. Lowe, 1995, A note on corporate strategy and capital structure, *Strategic Management Journal* 16: 411–414.
56. *The Economist*, 1997, Harold Geneen, December 6, 99.
57. Ibid., 99.
58. J. Rossant, 1997, When the Agnellis go shopping, they really go shopping, *Business Week*, October 27, 70E28–70E30.
59. R. Amit and J. Livnat, 1998, A concept of conglomerate diversification, *Journal of Management* 14: 593–604.
60. M. Lubatkin, H. Merchant, and M. Srinivasan, 1997, Merger strategies and shareholder value during times of relaxed antitrust enforcement: The case of large mergers during the 1980s, *Journal of Management* 23: 61–81.
61. D. L. Smart and M. A. Hitt, 1998, A test of the agency theory perspective of corporate restructuring, working paper, Texas A&M University.
62. R. M. Scherer and D. Ross, 1990, *Industrial Market Structure and Economic Performance* (Boston: Houghton Mifflin).
63. A. Shleifer and R. W. Vishny, 1994, Takeovers in the 1960s and 1980s: Evidence and implications, in R. P. Rumelt, D. E. Schendel, and D. J. Teece (eds.), *Fundamental Issues in Strategy* (Boston: Harvard Business School Press), 403–422.
64. Lubatkin, Merchant, and Srinivasan, Merger strategies and shareholder value; D. J. Ravenscraft and R. M. Scherer,

1987, *Mergers, Sell-Offs and Economic Efficiency* (Washington, DC: Brookings Institution), 22.

65. P. L. Zweig, J. P. Kline, S. A. Forest, and K. Gudridge, 1995, The case against mergers, *Business Week*, October 30, 122–130; J. R. Williams, B. L. Paez, and L. Sanders, 1988, Conglomerates revisited, *Strategic Management Journal* 9: 403–414.
66. M. C. Jensen, 1986, Agency costs of free cash flow, corporate finance, and takeovers, *American Economic Review* 76: 323–329.
67. R. Gilson, M. Scholes, and M. Wolfson, 1988, Taxation and the dynamics of corporate control: The uncertain case for tax motivated acquisitions, in J. C. Coffee, L. Lowenstein, and S. Rose-Ackerman (eds.), *Knights, Raiders, and Targets: The Impact of the Hostile Takeover* (New York: Oxford University Press), 271–299.
68. C. Steindel, 1986, Tax reform and the merger and acquisition market: The repeal of the general utilities, *Federal Reserve Bank of New York Quarterly Review* 11, no. 3: 31–35.
69. M. Murray, 1997, Banks look afield to satisfy appetite for expansion, *Wall Street Journal*, July 9, B4.
70. PR Newswire Association, Inc., 1997, NationsBank completes acquisition of Montgomery Securities, October 1.
71. Rumelt, *Strategy, Structure and Economic Performance*, 125.
72. E. H. Bowman, 1982, Risk seeking by troubled firms, *Sloan Management Review* 23: 33–42.
73. Y. Chang and H. Thomas, 1989, The impact of diversification strategy on risk-return performance, *Strategic Management Journal* 10: 271–284; R. M. Grant, A. P. Jammine, and H. Thomas, 1988, Diversity, diversification, and profitability among British manufacturing companies, 1972–1984, *Academy of Management Journal* 31: 771–801.
74. A. Taylor, III, 1997, Revolution at Daimler-Benz, *Fortune*, November 10, 144–152.
75. J. Templeman, 1995, The shocks for Daimler's new driver, *Business Week*, August 21, 38–39.
76. Daimler-Benz Home Page, 1998, January 15, http://www.Daimler-Benz.com.
77. Taylor, Revolution at Daimler-Benz, 147.
78. B. Mitchener, 1997, Daimler's Alabama M-class experiment gives a transatlantic jolt to Stuttgart, *Wall Street Journal*, October 17, A18.
79. C. G. Smith and A. C. Cooper, 1988, Established companies diversifying into young industries: A comparison of firms with different levels of performance, *Strategic Management Journal* 9: 111–121.
80. USX Corporation Home Page, 1998, January 15, http://www.usx.com.
81. L. Smith, 1997, Air power, *Fortune*, July, 134–136.
82. A. Dworkin, 1997, Defense mergers raise fears, *Dallas Morning News*, July 5, F1, F9.
83. S. Crock, 1997, Can this farm boy keep Lockheed in orbit? *Business Week*, October 27, 103–115; J. Dial and K. J. Murphy, 1995, Incentives, downsizing, and value creation at General Dynamics, *Journal of Financial Economics* 37: 261–314.
84. N. M. Kay and A. Diamantopoulos, 1987, Uncertainty and synergy: Towards a formal model of corporate strategy, *Managerial and Decision Economics* 8: 121–130.
85. Jensen, Agency costs.
86. R. A. Melchor and G. Burns, 1996, How Eagle became extinct, *Business Week*, March 4, 68–69.
87. Anheuser-Busch Companies, Inc. Home Page, 1998, January 15, http://www.anheuser-busch.com.
88. R. Gibson, 1995, Anheuser-Busch will sell snacks unit, Cardinals, and the club's home stadium, *Wall Street Journal*, October 26, A3, A5; M. Quint, 1995, Cardinals and snack unit are put on block by Busch, *New York Times*, October 26, D2.
89. R. E. Hoskisson and M. A. Hitt, 1990, Antecedents and performance outcomes of diversification: Review and critique of theoretical perspectives, *Journal of Management* 16: 461–509.
90. C. W. L. Hill and R. E. Hoskisson, 1987, Strategy and structure in the multiproduct firm, *Academy of Management Review* 12: 331–341.
91. A. A. Cannella, Jr., and M. J. Monroe, 1997, Contrasting perspectives on strategic leaders: Toward a more realistic view of top managers, *Journal of Management* 23: 213–237; S. Finkelstein and D. C. Hambrick, 1996, *Strategic Leadership: Top Executives and Their Effects on Organizations* (St. Paul, MN: West Publishing Company).
92. D. L. May, 1995, Do managerial motives influence firm risk reduction strategies? *Journal of Finance* 50: 1291–1308; Y. Amihud and B. Lev, 1981, Risk reduction as a managerial motive for conglomerate mergers, *Bell Journal of Economics* 12: 605–617.
93. S. R. Gray and A. A. Cannella, Jr., 1997, The role of risk in executive compensation, *Journal of Management* 23: 517–540; H. Tosi and L. Gomez-Mejia, 1989, The decoupling of CEO pay and performance: An agency theory perspective, *Administrative Science Quarterly* 34: 169–189.
94. S. Finkelstein and R. A. D'Aveni, 1994, CEO duality as a double-edged sword: How boards of directors balance entrechment avoidance and unity of command, *Academy of Management Journal* 37: 1070–1108.
95. R. E. Hoskisson and T. Turk, 1990, Corporate restructuring: Governance and control limits of the internal market, *Academy of Management Review* 15: 459–477.
96. J. K. Seward and J. P. Walsh, 1996, The governance and control of voluntary corporate spin offs, *Strategic Management Journal* 17: 25–39; J. P. Walsh and J. K. Seward, 1990, On the efficiency of internal and external corporate control mechanisms, *Academy of Management Review* 15: 421–458.
97. Finkelstein and D'Aveni, CEO duality as a double-edged sword.
98. E. F. Fama, 1980, Agency problems and the theory of the firm, *Journal of Political Economy* 88: 288–307.
99. R. A. Johnson, 1996, Antecedents and outcomes of corporate refocusing, *Journal of Management* 22: 439–483; C. Y. Woo, G. E. Willard, and U. S. Dallenbach, 1992, Spin-off performance: A case of overstated expectations, *Strategic Management Journal* 13: 433–448.
100. H. Kim and R. E. Hoskisson, 1996, Japanese governance systems: A critical review, in S. B. Prasad (ed.), *Advances in International Comparative Management* (Greenwich, CT: JAI Press), 165–189.
101. A. Rawsthorn, 1997, Estee Lauder agrees to buy Aveda for $300m, *Financial Times*, November 20, 25.
102. D. J. Collis and C. A. Montgomery, 1998, Creating corporate advantage, *Harvard Business Review* 76, no. 3: 71–83.

Acquisition and Restructuring Strategies

CHAPTER 7

Learning Objectives

After reading this chapter, you should be able to:

1. Describe why acquisitions have been a popular strategy.
2. List and explain the reasons why firms make acquisitions.
3. Describe seven problems that work against developing a competitive advantage when making acquisitions.
4. Name and describe the attributes of acquisitions that help make them successful.
5. Define restructuring and distinguish among its common forms.
6. Describe how a firm can achieve successful outcomes from a restructuring strategy.

Today MCI, Tomorrow the World for WorldCom?

The 1998 WorldCom acquisition of MCI has been one of the largest to date. The two firms initially agreed to a price of $37 billion, $9 billion more than the second largest bid made by GTE. Originally, British Telecom (BT) and MCI had agreed to an acquisition, but BT later decided to reduce its offer, making it worth approximately $18 billion. Analysts have said that BT may have made a large error in reducing the amount of its offer and driving MCI into the arms of a different suitor. Due to stock price changes the acquisition is worth approximately $42 billion.

http://www.mci.com
http://www.worldcom.com

WorldCom is the product of a brash entrepreneur, Bernard J. Ebbers. The fact that WorldCom is smaller than MCI does not bother Ebbers. Over the last ten years, WorldCom has been built through over 50 acquisitions. Included among these acquisitions have been several billion dollar deals. The MCI deal is worth approximately four times the budget of the state of Mississippi, where WorldCom's headquarters is located.

WorldCom's acquisition of MCI makes it the third largest telecommunications firm behind AT&T. The combined firm controls over 60 percent of the traffic on the global com-

puter network in the United States. The newly combined firm controls four of the six largest Internet service providers. Furthermore, WorldCom is now the only telecommunications company to provide nationwide local phone service and long distance service for both business and residential customers. WorldCom is saving considerable money partly because it owns local networks and thus no longer has to pay a 45 percent tariff on long distance revenues to the Baby Bells as MCI did. It also is saving about $700 million annually because the newly combined firm has the needed infrastructure.

The new company's name, MCI WorldCom, created some debate, but when the dust settled, analysts and investors alike gave the acquisition a positive review. Its ultimate success, however, may depend on what other telecommunications firms do in response. For example, some analysts are speculating that this huge acquisition may pave the way for AT&T to make an acquisition (and SBC) that will not be rejected by the Justice Department. Because the telecommunications market is global, there could be other actions in Europe in response to this acquisition.

SOURCE: D. A. Blackmon, 1997, WorldCom's massive bid shakes up little town, *Wall Street Journal*, October 13, B1, B9; P. Elstrom, C. Yang, and S. Jackson, 1997, WorldCom + MCI: How it all adds up, *Business Week*, November 4, 44; J. Files, 1997, GTE offers $28 billion for MCI in all-cash deal, *Dallas Morning News*, October 16, A1, A20; H. Goldblatt and N. D. Schwartz, 1997, Telecom in play, *Fortune*, November 10, 83–88; S. Pulliam, 1997, WorldCom bid for MCI raises question: Who's next? *Wall Street Journal*, October 2, C1, C2; WorldCom and MCI engaged, 1997, *The Economist*, November 15, 69–70; WorldCom bid to alter telecom industry, 1997, *Wall Street Journal*, October 2, A1, A10; T. E. Weber and R. Quick, 1997, Would WorldCom-MCI deal lift tolls on net? *Wall Street Journal*, October 2, B1, B2; S. Young, 1997, MCI merger could smooth the way for AT&T deal. *WSJ Interactive Edition*, http://www.interactive.wsj.com/edition.

Chapter 6 examined corporate-level strategy and, in particular, discussed types and levels of product diversification that can build core competencies. The dominant means for fashioning a diversification strategy is through acquisitions. Although acquisitions have been a popular strategy among U.S. firms for many years, the decade of the 1980s was labeled by some as "merger mania." In fact, depending on whether only whole-firm acquisitions or partial (ownership) acquisitions are included, the number of acquisitions completed in the United States during the 1980s varies from slightly over 31,000 to as many as 55,000. The total value of these acquisitions exceeded $1.3 trillion.[1]

While these numbers are impressive, they are small compared to the current "merger mania." The total value of mergers and acquisitions during 1997 was $1.6 trillion, more than the total amount for the whole decade of the 1980s. Furthermore, there were more than 22,000 transactions in 1997, 40 percent of the total number of transactions in the decade of the 1980s. The 40 percent increase in total value of the transactions over 1996 is due mostly to the large deals, exemplified by the WorldCom acquisition of MCI. The large acquisitions are primarily because of the need to consolidate for market power to be competitive in global markets. Also, deregulation, low interest rates, and growing stock values in 1997 fueled the large increase in activity. Another trend is also evident, the growing number of cross-border acquisitions.[2]

With the large number of acquisitions in the 1980s and 1990s and the substantial capital investment required to support this activity, one would expect that it was driven by strong positive returns to shareholders of the acquiring firms. However, the outcomes do not fully support this expectation. For example, research has shown that *shareholders of acquired firms* often earn above-average returns from the acquisition, but that *shareholders of acquiring firms* are less likely to gain such returns. The average returns earned by shareholders of acquiring firms was close to zero.[3] The significant negative returns earned from some acquisition activity and the overdiversification of some firms (see Chapter 6) have produced a need for restructuring strategies. Restructuring involves acquiring and divesting businesses or assets to position a firm's operations strategically and develop effective core competencies.[4] Furthermore, many firms including AT&T, ITT, Hanson PLC, 3M, Melville, W. R. Grace, Sprint, Tenneco, Sears, Roebuck and Company, and General Motors have been spinning off or breaking up their diversified portfolios to create greater returns for shareholders. Often these firms reduce employment levels in corporate headquarters where highly integrated corporate structures exist.[5]

The purpose of this chapter is to explore the reasons for acquisitions and the potential problems firms encounter in attempting to achieve strategic competitiveness through an acquisition strategy (see Figure 1.1). As the opening case illustrates, the WorldCom acquisition of MCI positions the newly combined firm as a major presence in the telecommunications market. It is third in size only to AT&T and the complementary resources provide special synergies. An example is the access to long distance customers provided by MCI and the local phone networks provided by WorldCom. These features alone will save the new firm millions of dollars in tariff fees that MCI had to pay to the Baby Bells in the past. However, merging and integrating two large firms will be no easy task. Effective integration will be required to realize the expected synergies. We also describe acquisitions that have been disastrous because efforts to merge the two firms effectively were not successful. The primary reasons for the lack of strategic competitiveness among acquiring firms, along with the attributes of acquisitions that create competitive advantage, are discussed next. Thereafter, we explore the phenomenon of restructuring, the reasons for its use, and the restructuring alternatives that create strategic competitiveness. Finally, we explain how a few unique firms are able to create a competitive advantage through unrelated diversification. These firms may obtain a core competence of continually acquiring other firms, restructuring them, and retaining certain firm assets, while divesting others.

MERGERS AND ACQUISITIONS

A **merger** is a transaction in which two firms agree to integrate their operations on a relatively coequal basis because they have resources and capabilities that together may create a stronger competitive advantage. The transaction between Reading & Bates and Falcon Drilling is an example of a merger with a new ten-member board of directors composed of five members from each company. This merger created a firm with major market power in deep-water oil and gas drilling.[6] Alternatively, an **acquisition** is a transaction in which one firm buys controlling or 100 percent interest in another firm with the intent of more effectively using a core competence by making the acquired firm a subsidiary business within its portfolio. Usually, the management of the acquired firm reports to the management

A **merger** is a transaction in which two firms agree to integrate their operations on a relatively coequal basis because they have resources and capabilities that together may create a stronger competitive advantage.

An **acquisition** is a transaction in which one firm buys controlling or 100 percent interest in another firm with the intent of more effectively using a core competence by making the acquired firm a subsidiary business within its portfolio.

A **takeover** is an acquisition in which the target firm did not solicit the bid of the acquiring firm.

of the acquiring firm. Most mergers represent friendly agreements between the two firms, whereas acquisitions include unfriendly takeovers. A **takeover** is an acquisition in which the target firm did not solicit the bid of the acquiring firm. Only a small minority of these transactions are mergers; most are acquisitions. Therefore, the primary focus in this chapter is on acquisitions.

Reasons for Acquisitions

Firms follow an acquisition strategy and/or make selected acquisitions for several potential reasons.[7] Among them are achieving a competitive advantage through greater market power, overcoming barriers to entry, increasing the speed of market entry, the significant costs involved in developing new products, avoiding the risks of new product development, achieving diversification (either related or unrelated), and, finally, avoiding competition.[8] These reasons are described more fully in the following sections.

Increased Market Power A primary reason for acquisitions is to achieve greater market power. Many firms may have core competencies but lack the size to exercise their resources and capabilities. Market power usually is derived from the size of the firm and the firm's resources and capabilities to compete in the marketplace. Therefore, most acquisitions designed to achieve greater market power entail buying a competitor, supplier or distributor, or a business in a highly related industry to allow exercise of a core competence and gain competitive advantage in the acquiring firm's primary market. Acquisition of a competing firm is referred to as a *horizontal acquisition.* A *vertical acquisition* refers to a firm acquiring a supplier or distributor of its good or service. Acquisition of a firm in a highly related industry is referred to as a *related acquisition.* Recent research suggests that horizontal acquisitions of firms with similar characteristics result in higher performance than when firms with dissimilar characteristics are acquired. Similar characteristics of importance include strategy, managerial styles, and resource allocation patterns. Similarities in these characteristics makes the integration of the two firms proceed more smoothly.[9] An example of a horizontal acquisition between firms with similar characteristics was Ernst & Young's acquisition of KPMG Peat Marwick. The Chairman and Chief Executive Officer of Ernst & Young, Philip Laskawy, stated, "we concluded that our global practices, our personality and our chemistry matched perfectly." This acquisition was driven by the need for market power because of the requirement to provide global full-service operations.[10]

The opportunity to make horizontal and vertical acquisitions was enhanced by changes in the interpretation and enforcement of U.S. antitrust laws in the early 1980s (see Chapter 10).[11] Prior to that time, very few acquisitions of direct competitors were allowed by the U.S. government. Of course, this action by the federal government represented a major impetus to an acquisition strategy. Firms that gain greater share and/or have more resources for gaining competitive advantage have more power to use against competitors in their markets.[12]

Market power dominance was probably the driving force behind many mergers in the drug industry such as Merck's vertical acquisition of Medco Containment Services, Inc., a drug distribution company. Other pharmaceutical companies such as Eli Lilly and SmithKline Beecham PLC have made similar vertical acquisitions to ensure distribution of their drug product lines by managing prescription plans.[13] Sandoz AG's acquisition of Gerber Products, however, was a related acquisition. Many of these pharmaceutical mergers—vertical, horizontal, and related—are directed at increased market power because managed-care and potential regulatory changes in the health care industry challenged the traditional power of pharmaceutical firms. The trade-off for pharmaceutical firms, however, is that they will likely reduce spending on R&D and new product development as they invest money in acquisitions and the transaction costs associated with them.[14]

Overcome Entry Barriers Barriers to entry (introduced in Chapter 2) represent factors associated with the market and/or firms currently operating in the market that make it more expensive and difficult for a new firm to enter that market. For example, it may be difficult to develop a new venture in a market because large and established competitors may already occupy the niche of interest. Such an entry may require substantial investments in a large manufacturing facility and substantial advertising and promotion to produce adequate sales for the manufacturer to achieve economies of scale and offer products at a competitive price. Market entry also requires a firm to have an efficient distribution system and outlets to reach the consumer. If consumers have loyalty to existing brands already in the market, even these actions may not be adequate to produce a successful new venture. In this case, a firm may find it easier to enter the market by acquiring an established company. Although the acquisition can be costly, the acquiring firm can achieve immediate access to the market and can do so with an established product that may have consumer loyalty. In fact, the higher the barriers to entry are, the more likely it is that acquisitions will be used to enter a particular market.

In 1997, Caterpillar acquired the Perkins Engine unit from Lucas Varity to gain a presence in the small engine market. This acquisition provided entry for Caterpillar into a fast growing market and simultaneously allowed the firm to gain control over a major supplier. This acquisition will also help Caterpillar build the capability to manufacture and market smaller-scale construction equipment that is growing in popularity. There were no overlaps in the two businesses (thus, an entry into a new market), but there are substantial opportunities for synergy.[15] Caterpillar's acquisition of Perkins Engine represents related diversification (see Chapter 6). Computer Services' acquisition of Continuum also represents related diversification. Computer Services provides computer services such as information systems integration and outsourcing with its main competitors being IBM and Electronic Data Systems. Continuum, on the other hand, provides supplies and support software to the insurance and banking industry. This acquisition allowed Computer Services to enter the market for computer and other support services for these two important and related industries. In particular, the strategic action moves Computer Services into a new and lucrative market of software services for the financial sector.[16]

Acquisitions are used commonly to enter new international markets as explained in Chapter 8. For example, cross-border acquisitions currently acount for approximately 30 percent of all acquisitions in Europe. Acquisitions are a popular means of entering new international markets because they are perhaps the fastest way to enter new markets, and they enable the acquirer to achieve a critical mass (presence) in a market and more control over foreign operations (compared to strategic alliances with a foreign partner, for example).[17] Because of this control, an acquiring firm can also make changes in the acquired firm if desired or use its resources and capabilities to make changes in the acquired firm's operations. The emphasis on cross-border acquisitions is particularly evident in the telecommunications industry as described in the opening case in Chapter 1.[18] This recent surge in international acquisitions is also exemplified in the Strategic Focus on cross-border acquisitions.

STRATEGIC FOCUS

The Flood of Cross-Border Acquisitions

Merger mania has now reached Europe and is spreading globally. Of particular importance is the increasing number of cross-border acquisitions that help firms either enter a new regional market or increase their market power in that region of the world. For example, in 1997 there were a number of large cross-border acquisitions in Europe. Among those were the largest hostile takeover attempt in French history with Assicurazioni General (Italy) acquiring Assurances Generales de France (AGF) and the British based Reed Elsevier PLC's acquisition of Wolters Kluwer to form one of the world's largest publishing firms. Interestingly, Germany's Allianz outbid Italy's Generali and acquired AGF. Part of the incentives for these acquisitions is the need to reduce costs and to develop market power. To compete with other international firms, European companies must have a global or at least a European presence. Some of the acquisitions are needed to attain critical mass to compete with U.S. and Asian firms in certain markets.

The merger mania extends well beyond Europe to other parts of the world. For example, Mexico's Cemex has embarked on a worldwide expansion strategy, primarily using acquisitions to expand into new markets. Cemex made its first move into Asia paying $70 million for a 30 percent stake in Rizal, a Philippine cement firm. Since 1989, Cemex has grown through acquisitions to become the third largest cement maker globally. Its primary operations outside of Mexico are in the United States, Spain, Central America, South America, and the Caribbean. Acquisitions are also increasing in other Latin American countries such as Brazil, an attractive market for acquisitions for foreign firms. Brazilian companies in the financial and retail sectors particularly have suffered recently and are thus good buys. Examples include England's BBA Group PLC's acquisition of Brazil's polyester manufacturer, Bidim Ltda and Swiss Bank Group's acquisition of Banco Omega Group S.A., a bank headquartered in Rio de Janeiro.

Surging growth in Shiseido, a Japanese cosmetics firm, has been fueled by acquisitions. In 1997 Shiseido bought the Japanese division of Helene Curtis from Unilever, a large European firm. The union between B.A.T. Industries PLC, headquartered in London and Zurich Insurance of Switzerland also represent this major trend toward cross-border acquisitions. The integration of the two firms financial services businesses exemplifies a global trend toward consolidation in this field. Consolidation provides market power and the cross-border acquisition provides an increased global presence.

This merger trend, however, is being observed closely for antitrust actions by European governments. Several of the transactions noted above were scrutinized closely by the respective governments of the countries involved. For example, the B.A.T. and Zurich insurance union was reviewed carefully by antitrust officials in the European Union. The compelling need for market power and more global presence in order to be competitive in international markets makes it less likely that these acquisitions will be disapproved. The trend toward global merger mania probably will continue for years to come.

SOURCE: C. Adams, 1997, Cemex firm paves expansionary path, *Houston Chronicle*, December 26, C1, C4; E. Beck, 1997, B.A.T., Zurich Insurance discuss merger, *Wall Street Journal*, October 13, A3, A10; B. Coleman, 1997, EU antitrust officials brace themselves for merger wave, *Wall Street Journal Inter-*

active, October 15, http://www.wsj.com; B. Coleman, 1997, Giant European mergers facing review, *Wall Street Journal*, October 15, A17; P. Druckerman, 1997, Mergers still hot in Brazil despite jitters, *Wall Street Journal*, November 17, A20, A22; T. Kamm and R. Frank, 1997, Eurodeal day: Four bids, pacts hop borders, *Wall Street Journal*, October 14, A16, A19; B. Hutton, 1997, Acquisitions behind surge at Shiseido, *Financial Times*, November 12, 17; J. Rossant, 1997, Why merger mania is rocking the continent, *Business Week*, October 27, 64.

Cost of New Product Development Oftentimes, the development of new products internally and the start-up of new ventures can be quite costly and require significant time to develop the products and achieve a profitable return. For example, new ventures require an average of 8 years to achieve profitability and 12 years to generate adequate cash flows.[19] In addition, it has been estimated that almost 88 percent of innovations fail to achieve adequate returns on investment.[20] Furthermore, about 60 percent of innovations are effectively imitated within 4 years after patents are obtained. Therefore, internal development is often perceived by managers as entailing high risk.[21] The basic problem is that the costs of developing and bringing a new product to market can be substantial.[22] As a result, managers may prefer other means of market entry that are much quicker and less risky. This is an important strategy in the pharmaceutical industry, for example. Acquiring an established firm, although sometimes costly, is less risky than a new venture because there is a track record on which that firm can be evaluated. Furthermore, an acquisition offers immediate access to the market with an established sales volume and customer base.[23] Alternatively, new ventures often have to build their sales volume over time, working hard to develop a relationship with customers. One of the reasons Johnson & Johnson acquired Cordis was to more fully establish its name among doctors and hospitals who were worrying about the cost of its stent device to open clogged arteries. Cordis also provides devices that facilitate the opening of clogged arteries. This built credibility for Johnson & Johnson's stent device and resulted in reduced R&D and distribution costs.[24] Therefore, acquisition of an established firm provides a significant presence in the market and can provide profitability in the short term. Thus, reduced cost compared to new product development can be one reason why acquisitions have been a popular strategy.

Increased Speed to Market Firms can increase their speed to market by pursuing an acquisition rather than new product development.[25] Compaq Computer bought Tandem Computers for $3 billion to expand its product line into larger computers for the business market, for example. Tandem is a manufacturer of large, powerful computers that are targeted for the banking, financial, retail, and telecommunications industries. It would have taken Compaq a substantial amount of time to develop the computers of the size and power that Tandem manufactures and then to establish a presence in the business market. One analyst remarked that, "with one signature on the checkbook, all of Compaq's research and development gets compressed into a one-day event." This action also gives Compaq a more complete product line allowing it to provide one-stop shopping for business customers.[26]

Lucent Technologies, the technologically advanced telecommunications manufacturer spun off from AT&T, purchased Octel Communications to fill a void in its product line. While Lucent has the technological capabilities to develop products such as voice mail systems manufactured by Octel, it is much faster and possibly cheaper when all costs are considered over time to acquire a firm already established in the market. Lucent executives believe that by offering a more complete product line, the firm will experience greater sales even of its established product lines.[27]

Firms use acquisitions to enter foreign markets more quickly as well. Acquiring a company with established operations and relations in a new foreign market is a much faster way to enter these markets than to try to establish a new facility and new relationships with stakeholders in the new country. For example, Merrill Lynch purchased Mercury Asset Management, a London based money manager, in the largest international acquisition by a U.S. securities firm. The purchase gave Merrill a greater global presence that would have taken years for the company to develop on its own. In fact, the acquisition made Merrill the fourth largest asset manager in the world.[28]

There has been a record number of bank mergers and acquisitions recently and an increasing number in the insurance industry as well. These are representative of attempts to reduce costs available through technological change and increase market power in the banking and insurance industry rapidly as regulations have been relaxed to allow entry into new markets.

Lower Risk Compared to Developing New Products Internally developed new ventures can be quite risky. New ventures have high failure rates and take longer to achieve adequate cash flows and profitability. Alternatively, acquisitions provide outcomes that are more certain and can be estimated more accurately. This is because the target firms (e.g., Octel) have a track record that can be carefully analyzed, and forecasts of future revenues and costs can be based on historical records.[29] No such records exist for newly developed products such as Johnson & Johnson's coronary stent innovation.

It has been suggested that acquisitions have become a common means of avoiding risky internal ventures (and therefore risky R&D investments). In fact, acquisition may become a substitute for innovation.[30] Firms also may use acquisitions to avoid internal ventures because constraints on their resources and capabilities require decisions on whether to invest their scarce resources in developing new products or in making acquisitions. Of course, acquisitions are not riskless ventures. The risks of making an acquisition are discussed later in the chapter.

Increased Diversification A firm may find it easier to develop new products and new ventures within its current market because its managers better understand the products and the market. However, it is often more difficult for a firm to develop new products that are quite different from its existing set of products and to enter new markets because its managers may have less understanding of such markets. Thus, it is uncommon for a firm to develop new products and ventures internally as a means of diversifying its product line.[31] Instead, a firm usually opts to diversify through acquisition.

Research shows that acquisitions are a common means of diversification. Acquisitions provide the fastest and perhaps the easiest way to change a firm's portfolio of businesses.[32] Acquisitions are used often by firms to reduce dependence on a provider of resources or major supplier of parts or other items necessary to conduct business. Caterpillar's acquisition of Perkins Engine involved the purchase of a major supplier. Such acquisitions provide more control and reduce a firm's dependence on an external organization.[33] Nevertheless, acquisitions that diversify a firm's product lines must be undertaken after careful study and evaluation. Research shows that horizontal acquisitions usually are more successful than diversifying acquisitions. The difference in performance can be even greater when an acquired firm operates in highly diverse markets from those of the acquiring firm.[34]

In addition, as mentioned earlier, until the early 1980s, the U.S. government did not favor horizontal acquisitions and often precluded them through the enforcement of antitrust laws. As noted in Chapter 6, changes in the interpretation and enforcement of such laws led to a substantial number of horizontal acquisitions within the same market and acquisitions of firms in related businesses. Therefore, acquisitions have become a popular means of expanding market share and/or moving into related markets (and thus, achieving related diversification) as well as making unrelated diversification moves.

Avoiding Excessive Competition Firms sometimes use acquisitions to move into related and unrelated markets to decrease dependence on markets with substantial competitive pressure, frequently from foreign firms. In the 1980s, U.S. firms in many industries experienced problems maintaining their competitiveness in markets where Japanese, German, and other foreign firms had a strong presence. This is probably best exemplified by the U.S. automobile market. At the start of the 1980s, General Motors had approximately a 50 percent share of the U.S. automobile market. By the early 1990s, GM's share of the U.S. market fell to near 30 percent. Much of the lost market share was captured by Japanese and German and later South Korean firms. During the mid-1980s, General Motors acquired Electronic Data Systems (EDS) and Hughes Aerospace, possibly to avoid competition with the Japanese. Now, U.S. firms are becoming more competitive and GM sold its stakes in these two businesses to refocus on the automobile market.

U.S. Steel's acquisitions of Marathon Oil and Texas Oil and Gas were, in part, an attempt to avoid competition with imported steel from Japan. The Japanese do not have a strong industrial sector in petroleum and natural gas. Therefore, many U.S. firms attempted to spread their risks and diversify into other industries because of significant foreign competition. This has not been an effective strategy because it did not help U.S. firms gain strategic competitiveness or earn above-average returns, although, in some cases, it prevented below-average returns.

The Japanese have been much less active in acquisitions than have U.S. firms, and many of the earlier acquisitions in Japan, such as the merger to create Nippon Steel, were designed primarily to increase the market power of firms within Japanese markets.[35] Sony's acquisition of CBS Records and Bridgestone's acquisition of Firestone Tire and Rubber, on the other hand, illustrate that the Japanese were becoming important players in the international market for acquisitions in the 1980s. The increase in Japanese acquisitions at this time was partly motivated by the lower value of the dollar relative to the yen; as the yen appreciates in value relative to the dollar, U.S. assets can be bought with yen that are worth more dollars.

There were multiple reasons for these acquisitions. In both the Sony and the Bridgestone cases, the acquisitions provided the acquiring firms with significant footholds in the market. Sony's acquisition of CBS Records and Columbia Pictures provided vertical integration and outlets for some of Sony's new technology and products. For instance, despite poor performance of this business, Sony's president, Noboyuki Idei, refused to sell the firm's entertainment division (previously CBS Records and Columbia Pictures) in order to help standardize the digital video disk (DVD) format on which Sony and other consumer electronic producers have temporarily agreed.[36] After the final standard emerges, Sony's entertainment unit will provide the firm with an important distribution presence to market its products. (Matsushita, on the other hand, sold its film producer, MCA, to Seagram's and took a significant charge on its earnings because of competitive pressure.) Also, these acquisitions helped both Sony and Bridgestone overcome significant barriers to entry in U.S. markets, were completed rapidly, and seemed to entail less risk because of the known markets and past performance of each firm.

The Bridgestone acquisition of Firestone Tire and Rubber was a horizontal acquisition. Therefore, while it did not represent product diversification, it did represent international diversification, an important topic covered in Chapter 8. Alternatively, Sony's acquisitions of CBS Records and Columbia Pictures represented related diversification moves. As such, neither seemed to entail significant risk because of potential increased capabilities for market power and synergies from these acquisitions. These and other primary reasons for making acquisitions are summarized in Figure 7.1.

Although advantages can be gained from acquisitions, potentially significant problems can also accrue. Sometimes, these problems may equal or exceed the benefits gained. As a result, the average returns on acquisitions have varied closely around zero, as noted earlier in this chapter. Next, we examine some of these potential problems.

Problems in Achieving Acquisition Success

Among the potential problems of an acquisition strategy are difficulties integrating the acquired firm into the acquiring firm, inadequate analysis of target firm and managerial hubris, the large or extraordinary debt assumed to complete the acquisition, an inability to achieve synergy (no complementarities), too much diversification, managers who are overly focused on acquisitions, and acquiring firms that become too large.[37] These problems are also shown in Figure 7.1.

Integration Difficulties Integrating two companies after an acquisition can be quite difficult.[38] Among the problems that can arise are melding two disparate corporate cultures,[39] linking different financial and control systems, building effective working relationships (particularly when management styles differ), and resolving problems regarding the status of acquired firm executives.[40]

PhyCor acquired its major rival, MedPartners, in 1997. The newly combined company operates in 50 states and has 35,000 physicians affiliated with it. Although some analysts predicted the union would produce the "tiger" in the industry, others questioned whether their previous rivalry and two significantly different cultures and operating styles would allow an effective integration. PhyCor has a slow and deliberate style of operating while MedPartners is much more aggressive. Because of the different styles, PhyCor grew at a steady pace by acquisitions but MedPartners' growth was more rapid and erratic. The differences in style are similar to the childrens' story about the race between the tortoise and the hare. There is concern that MedPartners was built too fast and not well developed. As such, it may cause PhyCor indigestion when integration is attempted. That is the reason that PhyCor's stock suffered when the acquisition was announced. Prior to the acquisition, PhyCor's stock price declined because of investors' concerns. PhyCor has 53 well-established group practice clinics, while MedPartners had a more di-

FIGURE 7.1 ***Reasons for Acquisitions and Problems in Achieving Success***

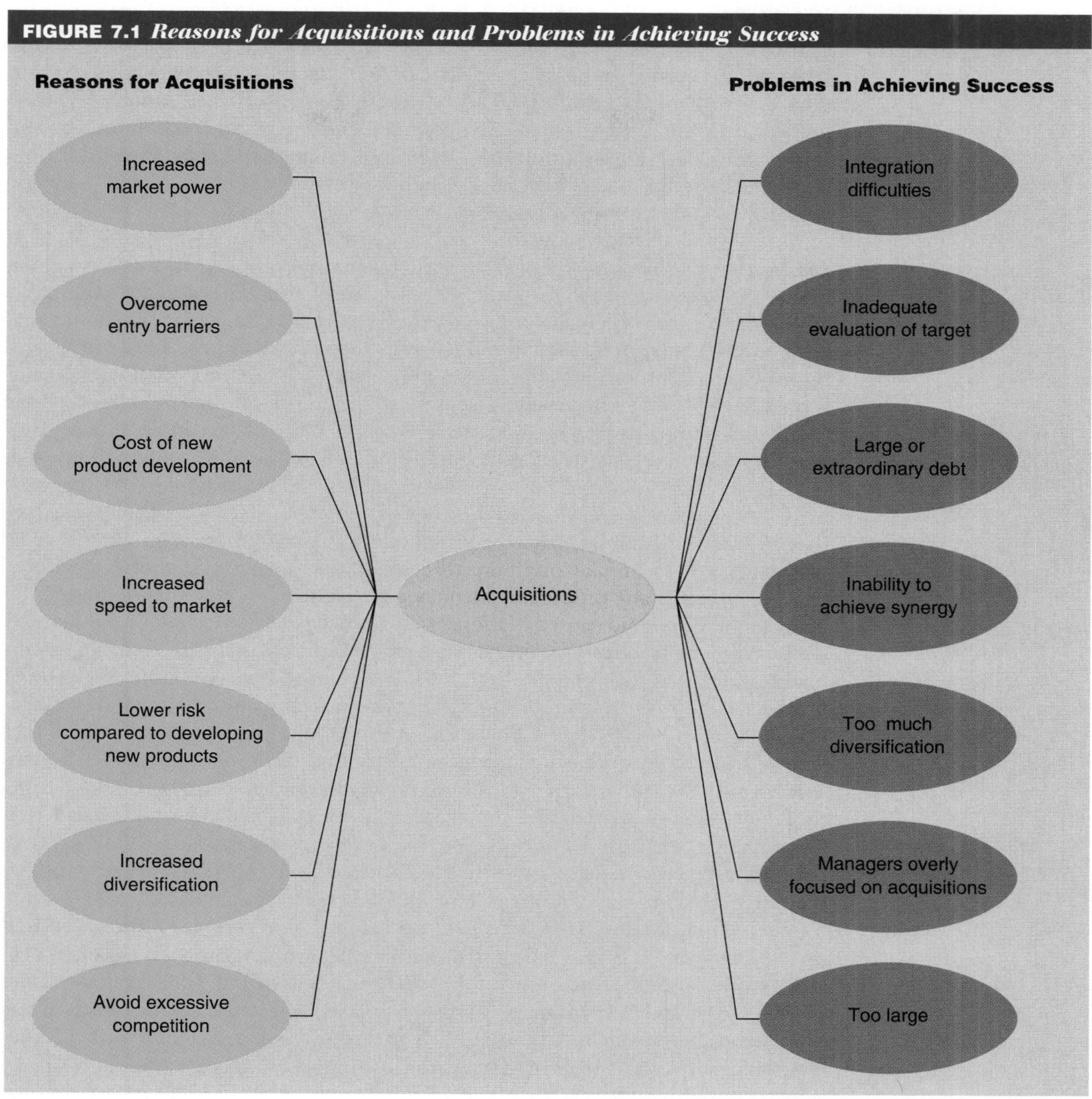

verse and fragmented physician base. The CEO of MedPartners was offered a position on the Board of the combined company but was not offered a management position. Time will tell whether the two companies can be integrated effectively. PhyCor management has its share of challenges to regain the confidence of investors.[41] One of the biggest challenges for the acquiring company after the acquisition is how to effectively integrate the two firms so that they operate as one.[42]

Robert Frankenberg, the CEO of Novell, Inc., which at one point was the second largest personal computer software company next to Microsoft, took over for Raymond Noorda. Novell became smaller when Frankenberg divested WordPerfect software and other application programming assets. Frankenberg found it necessary to sell WordPerfect for $124 million, compared to a purchase price of $855 million, in part, due to fierce competition from Microsoft. There was an extraordinary clash between the staffs of Novell and WordPerfect that crippled the integration after the acquisition and compounded management errors. Thus, the culture clash added significantly to the decreased value in the company and further necessitated selling WordPerfect. As the next section discusses, Novell may also have paid too much for WordPerfect.[43]

Inadequate Evaluation of Target Another potential problem is that a firm may pay too much for an acquisition. If a firm does not thoroughly analyze the target and fails to develop adequate knowledge of its market value, too much money may be offered to acquire it. In addition, current shareholders in the target firm must be enticed to sell their stock. To do so, they often require a premium over the current stock price. The bank acquisitions are requiring significant premiums. These premiums frequently are between 40 and 60 percent. For example, late in 1997 National City agreed to acquire First of America Bank for $6.78 billion. This price is approximately 3.8 times the book value of First of America and 22.9 times the bank's estimated 1998 earnings. The CEO of National City, David Daberko, stated that he knew his bank was paying a premium for First of America, but that it would have had to pay a similar premium three or four years ago. Of course, having to pay a premium at any time is not adequate justification and investors suggested this because the price paid caused National City's stock price to decline by 5.9 percent. Analysts were also critical of the acquisition, particularly the price paid, suggesting that National City's aggressive cost cutting plans may not be realistic.[44] A similar problem may be encountered by First Union, which acquired CoreStates Financial at a cost of $16.3 billion. The CEO of First Union, Edward Crutchfield, previously had vowed to reject acquisition targets that could not contribute to earnings within 18 months of the acquisition. However, the acquisition price is 5.3 times the book value of CoreStates, much larger than that paid for First of America. Thus, there is concern about the price paid in this instance as well. While Crutchfield has been largely successful with the 75 acquisitions in the last decade, analysts are skeptical about this one because of the high premium paid.[45]

The seemingly large premiums paid for banks pale in comparison to what Federated Department Stores paid for Broadway Department Stores. Federated paid a huge premium of $8 per share for a stock that was selling for less than $2 per share in a $1.6 billion transaction. In fact, between 1994 and 1996, Federated made two huge acquisitions of R.H. Macy's (centered in New York City) with 123 department stores and Broadway (based in Los Angeles) with 82 stores.[46]

Managerial hubris has been blamed for overpayment and inadequate rational evaluation of many targets.[47] Raymond Noorda may have also been influenced by hubris when he was CEO of Novell before Robert Frankenberg. Noorda completed the failed acquisition of WordPerfect. Ex-employees indicate that Noorda may have been overly obsessed with William Gates, Microsoft's chairman, causing Noorda to jump at the chance to acquire WordPerfect and Borland International's Quattro Pro spreadsheet software.[48]

Large or Extraordinary Debt Many of the acquisitions completed in the 1980s and 1990s were financed with significant debt. In fact, the 1980s produced an innovation called *junk bonds*.[49] Junk bonds represented a new financing option in which risky acquisitions were financed with money (debt) that provided a high return to the lenders (often referred to as the bondholders). Some of the interest rates on junk bonds were as high as 18 and 20 percent because they are unsecured (not tied to specific assets as collateral) and thus, are risky. Furthermore, firms were encouraged to take on significant debt because it was believed to positively discipline managerial actions. Some well-known finance scholars argued that debt disciplines managers not to misuse funds and, therefore, executives were often encouraged to utilize significant leverage to complete large acquisitions.[50] However, there are dramatic and unfortunate examples of the significant costs entailed in financing acquisitions. Federated Department Stores took on substantial debt to buy Macy's and Broadway. The debt and other transaction expenses resulted in a $62 million loss on Federated's 1995 $43 billion annual sales. A study by Stern Stewart, a consulting firm that tracks market value created in the last decade, indicated that Federated had destroyed $2.6 billion in capital. This performance ranked close to the bottom of the 1,000 firms tracked in the study.[51] A great deal of the number and dollar value of bankruptcies has been attributed to the use of excess leverage, the cost of such debt, and the reduced managerial flexibility resulting from high leverage.[52]

Some of the use of leverage was fueled by the sale of junk bonds, described earlier, and by the notion that the use of high levels of debt constrains managers from taking opportunistic actions in their own interest and forces them to act more in shareholders' interests.[53] Although this is an accurate characterization of the effects of debt, it fails to recognize the potential trade-offs that firms may have to make when large amounts of debt are used, particularly when the costs of debt are high. Obviously, resources are finite, and when payments for interest and principal on the debt are high, those dollars cannot be invested in other opportunities. A substantial amount of evidence suggests that when a firm has significant debt, managers forego investments that are likely to have long-term payoffs. These investments may include research and development and capital equipment. In both cases, these types of investments appear to be important for long-term firm competitiveness.[54]

Therefore, we conclude that the use of debt has both positive and negative effects. On the one hand, leverage can be a positive force in the development of a firm, allowing it to take advantage of attractive expansion opportunities. However, the use of too much leverage (e.g., extraordinary debt) can lead to negative outcomes, such as postponing or eliminating investments necessary to maintain strategic competitiveness. As such, many acquisitions in the 1990s are using more equity offerings instead of debt.[55] For instance, the acquisition of First of America by National City, mentioned earlier, used a tax-free stock swap to accomplish the transaction.

Inability to Achieve Synergy Another significant problem in achieving success with acquisitions is assessing the potential synergy involved and/or the benefits of such synergy. To achieve a competitive advantage through an acquisition, a firm must realize private synergy and core competence that cannot be imitated easily by competitors. Private synergy refers to the benefit from merging the acquiring and target firms that is due to a unique resource or a capability (set of resources) that is complementary between the two firms and not available among other potential bidders for that target firm.[56] Unfortunately, private synergy that is not easily imitated by competitors is uncommon. Perhaps this is one of the primary reasons that acquisitions rarely provide significant positive returns to acquiring firms' shareholders.

Early in 1996, Anheuser-Busch, the largest brewer in the United States, admitted defeat in two of its acquired businesses, snack foods and bread. It bought Eagle Snacks in 1979 because it saw that it could not only distribute beer but also salty snacks on regular beer routes to taverns and supermarkets. Anheuser also bought Campbell Taggart, a bakery unit. In doing so, Anheuser felt that because one of beer's main ingredients is yeast, it could also use this expertise in bread making. Furthermore, it could use its distribution process and network associated with its other products. Eagle boosted quality and began expanding from peanuts and pretzels to potato and tortilla chips. This created a significant strategic response from Frito-Lay. Frito launched an array of new products and upgraded its distribution while cutting costs. Frito's market share jumped to around 50 percent from 40, while Anheuser's never topped 6 percent and poor returns were realized year after year. As competition increased in Anheuser's main market, beer, these added businesses were distractions and diverted top managers' attention. This led to delays in new brand rollouts and the need to rebuild beer momentum. Instead of focusing on product diversification as it did earlier, Anheuser-Busch is now focusing on international markets where synergies are more likely to be realized in their dominant beer market.[57]

Synergy is not necessarily easy to achieve as described in the Strategic Focus regarding the purchase of Southern Pacific Rail by Union Pacific for $3.9 billion. After Union Pacific acquired Southern Pacific, numerous problems ensued including substantial railroad congestion. In short, Union Pacific had significant problems in merging the two companies and the firm's performance deteriorated. One could speculate that Union Pacific has actually achieved negative synergy. Because of the poor performance caused by the acquisition, customers that use the railroad are suffering and are expected to lose as much as $1.3 billion.

Synergy between two firms is not always easy to achieve. Union Pacific may have achieved negative synergy by acquiring Southern Pacific. Union Pacific's performance deteriorated after the acquisition.

Acquisitions entail many indirect costs, often referred to as transaction costs.[58] There are many costs involved in selecting acquisition targets and negotiating the acquisition. There are direct costs such as legal fees and fees of investment bankers in addition to those charged by consultants. There are also indirect costs such as the time of managers and staff evaluating proposals and in negotiating the deal. After the acquisition is consummated, there is considerable time spent evaluating the assets and employees of the acquiring firm and deciding how to integrate them into the acquiring firm's operations. Another indirect cost is the loss of key managers and employees after the acquisition.[59] Sometimes the acquiring firm lays off employees from the acquiring firm who work in redundant activities; this reduces costs. In other cases, the managers and employees experience a loss of autonomy after the merger and look for new jobs in other companies that give them more autonomy.[60] Interestingly, research shows that acquisitions of foreign firms results in higher turnover of acquired firm employees.[61] The differences in national culture and general means of operation may exacerbate other differences that normally exist in acquisitions. These costs, particularly the indirect ones, are often underestimated when considering the potential synergies.

STRATEGIC FOCUS

Chaos on the Railroads After Acquisition

Union Pacific acquired Southern Pacific Rail for $3.9 billion in September 1996. In early 1997, it began experiencing significant problems as it tried to integrate Southern Pacific's operations into its own. The problems continued throughout 1997 and into 1998. Union Pacific expected to obtain large returns from the acquisition through reduced costs and promised to improve delivery times by 20 percent after the acquisition. Unfortunately, neither of these benefits materialized.

Union Pacific faced substantial challenges because Southern Pacific Rail was a weak and ineffectively managed company. It had suffered from inadequate investment and performed poorly. Union Pacific underestimated the crews and locomotives needed to staff the trains and to transport the freight. The consequences of Union Pacific's miscalculations were significant traffic snarls and delays, along with mishaps such as derailments and equipment breakdowns. Furthermore, because Union Pacific encouraged many key Southern Pacific personnel to leave, there was a substantial loss of institutional knowledge. These same key personnel kept the Southern railroad operating under bad conditions. With these people gone, there was no one to help solve the problems when they occurred. At times, more than 10,000 railroad cars were stuck in limbo on the Union Pacific rails.

The logjam created many hardships for Union Pacific customers that depended on the railroad to move their goods to market. One Union Pacific customer suggested that the problems were similar to a cancer that spread to affect at least 20 percent of the railroad's system. Many customers could not get their goods to their customers. For example, the chemical companies using the railroad lost millions of dollars in sales and had to absorb extra costs, such as inventory costs and higher shipping fees from alternative shippers. As some firms discovered, using trucks for shipping can cost as much as 20 percent more with bulky orders, and trucks were not always available causing substantial delays in some cases. The costs were estimated to be as much as $1.3 billion. This does not include the lost business and goodwill suffered by Union Pacific. Clearly, Union Pacific was not able to achieve synergy through its acquisition of Southern Pacific Rail.

SOURCE: C. Boisseau, 1998, Union Pacific reports progress on slowdown, *Houston Chronicle*, January 14, C2; Big railroad merger quickly goes awry, 1997, *Wall Street Journal*, October 2, A1, A8; C. Boisseau, 1997, Rail customers want end to delays, *Houston Chronicle*, August 30, C1, C3; D. Machalaba and A. W. Mathews, 1997, Union Pacific tie-ups reach across economy, *Wall Street Journal*, October 8, B1, B10; Logjam costs $762 million, professor says, 1997, *Bryan-College Station Eagle*, November 27, A22.

Too Much Diversification An outcome of the trend toward acquisitions over the 1960s, 1970s, and 1980s was that firms often became overdiversified. Research suggests that the long-term performance of many acquisitions is not positive. It is not uncommon for prior acquisitions to be divested several years thereafter, primarily because of poor performance.[62] As noted earlier, acquisition has been used as a primary means of diversifying a firm's product line. When a firm becomes overdiversified, it is difficult to manage effectively. The level at which a firm becomes overdiversified differs for each firm. This is because each firm's type of diversification and managerial expertise determine when a firm reaches a point of diversification that is too complex and unmanageable. Because related diversification requires more information processing than unrelated diversification, overdiversification is reached with fewer business units than with unrelated diversification.[63] When overdiversification occurs, firm performance usually suffers.[64]

In addition, high diversification often is accompanied by other attributes that can produce lower long-term performance. For example, when a firm becomes more diversified, top-level executives often emphasize financial controls over strategic controls in the evaluation of divisional performance.[65] Defined and explained more extensively in Chapters 11 and 12, strategic control in the diversified firm refers to top executive understanding of business unit strategy and operations, whereas financial control refers to objective evaluation (e.g., ROI) criteria of business unit performance. The change in emphasis comes about because the top executives do not have adequate knowledge of the various businesses to evaluate effectively the strategies and strategic actions taken by division general managers. As a result, the division general managers become short-term oriented because strategic controls do not balance the risk that is shifted to them. Oftentimes, their compensation is tied to the achievement of certain financial outcomes. As a result, they may reduce long-term investments (e.g., R&D, capital investment) that entail some risk in order to boost short-term profits.[66] When they do so, long-term performance may suffer.

Too much diversification through acquisition creates significant problems for the management of the firm. Top-level managers may not effectively manage each of the businesses and maintain strategic competitiveness. Over time, this may result in lower innovation in those businesses.[67]

Firms following an acquisition strategy may begin to use acquisitions as a substitute for innovation. They become locked into a self-reinforcing cycle. They make several acquisitions that produce less innovation over time. As they encounter significantly stronger competition and lose their competitive advantage in certain markets, they may seek to acquire firms in other markets. This reinforces the cycle. As a result, if firms use acquisitions as a substitute for innovation, eventually they are likely to encounter performance problems.[68]

Managers Overly Focused on Acquisitions An active acquisition strategy often requires much managerial time and energy. For example, the process of making acquisitions requires extensive preparation and sometimes lengthy negotiations. Searches for viable acquisition candidates must be conducted that involve extensive data gathering and analyses. Although executives are rarely involved in the data gathering and analyses, they must review the results and select the best candidate from the alternatives. After selecting the acquisition candidate, an effective acquisition strategy must be formulated and implemented. Negotiations with target firm representatives can consume considerable time, particularly if the acquisition is an unfriendly takeover. Therefore, because the process involves much time and energy, executives may become overly focused on the process. Such focused energy can divert managerial attention from other important matters within the firm, particularly those that are long term in nature and require significant time and attention.[69] Furthermore, these negotiations often do not consider potential postmerger integration problems.[70]

Target firm executives also may spend substantial amounts of time and energy on the acquisition. Operations in target firms being pursued for acquisition have been described as being in a state of virtual suspended animation.[71] While day-to-day operations continue, albeit sometimes at a slower pace, most target firm executives are unwilling to make long-term commitments. Long-term decisions are frequently postponed until the negotiation process has been completed. Therefore, the acquisition process can create a short-term perspective and greater risk aversion among top-level executives in the target firm.[72]

Besides creating a short-term perspective and greater risk aversion among top-level managers, acquisitions and change of ownership can foster neglect of the firm's core business. For instance, in the 1980s and early 1990s, car rental companies neglected their core business because of many changes of ownership through acquisitions. Since its start-up in the 1940s, Avis has been owned by 12 different parents, including ITT, Beatrice Companies, and Wesray Capital. In 1990, GM owned a small stake in Avis and in National Car Rental System, which is also now independent. Ford controlled Budget and part of Hertz. Chrysler owned Snappy, Dollar, and Thrifty rental car companies. In the early 1990s, the car rental companies were receiving so many incentives to take new cars from the Detroit Big Three that they made more money buying and selling cars than they did in the rental business. However, between 1992 and 1996, the cash incentives to rental car companies were eliminated. During this period, many of the rental car companies lost the focus of their business, did not update technology and reservation systems, ended up with too many cars, and did not have consistent brand identities. For instance, Alamo pioneered the off-airport rental plaza but now is in more airport locations. To improve performance, these firms must refocus on their core business, car rentals. It is hoped that the employee ownership programs at Avis and National will help facilitate an improved focus on their core business.[73]

Additionally, it is not unusual for significant layoffs to occur after acquisitions, particularly in the acquired business. For example, when Ciba-Geigy and Sandoz merged to form Novartis AG, they laid off about 12,000 employees.[74] Given the large amount of turnover in the executive ranks of acquired firms, it is not surprising that many executives are reluctant to make major decisions for fear that they may be evaluated negatively by acquiring firm executives and laid off after the acquisition is completed.[75] This loss of managerial personnel can be problematic. In addition to losing significant managerial experience and expertise, those championing new products may leave and, therefore, the development and transfer of those new products to the market may be postponed or eliminated.[76]

Too Large Most acquisitions create a larger firm. In theory, increased size should help the firm gain economies of scale and therefore develop more efficient operations. This would be true, for example, in research and development operations and, thus, larger firms should over time produce greater amounts of innovation. However, it has been found that increases in size create efficiencies only when the acquiring firm is not too large. After reaching some level of size, the problems created by large size outweigh the benefits gained from increased size. For example, larger firms can become unwieldy to manage. If too many levels of managers exist, approval for the development and implementation of innovations can become lengthy and burdensome. Furthermore, to manage the larger size, firms often use more bureaucratic controls. **Bureaucratic controls** are formalized supervisory and behavioral rules and policies that are designed to ensure consistency of decisions and actions across different units. Although these more formalized rules and policies can be beneficial to the organization, they sometimes produce more rigid and standardized behavior among managers.

It is not uncommon for the acquiring firm to adopt and implement centralized controls within the acquired firm in order to facilitate integration. This reduces flexibility and, in the long run, may produce less innovation and less creative decision making, thus harming long-term firm performance.[77]

The preceding discussion provides reasons to pursue acquisitions and delineates the problems in realizing success. Next, we summarize the characteristics of effective acquisitions.

Bureaucratic controls are formalized supervisory and behavioral rules and policies that are designed to ensure consistency of decisions and actions across different units.

EFFECTIVE ACQUISITIONS

As noted, evidence suggests acquisition strategies rarely produce positive returns for the acquiring firm's shareholders. However, an acquisition strategy can have positive outcomes. Some of the specific attributes of acquisitions are more likely than others to produce positive outcomes and therefore may require the careful attention of top executives considering an acquisitions strategy.

Recent research identified some potentially important attributes of successful and unsuccessful acquisitions.[78] The research indicated that successful acquisitions entailed target firms that had complementary assets or resources for the acquiring firm. As a result, when the acquired firm was integrated into the acquiring firm, positive synergy and capability were created. In fact, the integration of the two firms frequently produced unique resources, a requirement to build strategic competitiveness, as described earlier.[79] Thus, the acquisitions were generally highly related to the acquiring firm's businesses. In fact, the acquiring firm maintained its focus on core businesses and leveraged those core businesses with the complementary assets and resources from the acquired firm. Oftentimes targets were selected and "groomed" by establishing a working relationship sometime prior to the acquisition (e.g., through strategic alliances).[80]

In addition, friendly acquisitions normally facilitate integration of the two firms. The two parties work together to find ways to integrate their firms and achieve positive synergy. In hostile takeovers, animosity often results between the two top management teams, which can permeate the new joint organization. As a result, more key personnel in the acquired firm may be lost, and those who remain may resist the changes necessary to integrate the two firms and create synergy.[81] With effort, cultural clashes can be overcome, and fewer key managers and employees will become discouraged and leave.[82] Thus, successful acquisitions tend to be friendly, although there are exceptions.

Research suggests that successful acquirers often conduct a deliberate and careful selection of target firms and also consider the ensuing negotiations. In addition, the acquiring and frequently the target firms have considerable financial slack in the form of cash and/or debt capacity. A significant attribute is that the merged firm continues to maintain a low or moderate debt position, even if a substantial amount of leverage is used to finance the acquisition. Where substantial debt is used to finance the acquisition, it is reduced quickly by selling off assets from the acquired firm. Often the assets sold are not complementary to the acquiring firm's businesses or are performing poorly. Also, the acquiring firm may sell its own lower performing businesses after making an acquisition. In this way, high debt and debt costs are avoided. Therefore, the debt cost does not prevent long-term investments such as R&D, and managerial discretion in the use of cash flow is relatively flexible.

Another characteristic of firms that launch successful acquisitions is that they emphasize innovation and continue to invest in R&D as part of their overall strategy. As a result, they maintain a high managerial commitment to innovation. This is clearly evidenced in the case of Johnson & Johnson that has made a number of acquisitions over the years. Nonetheless, it continues to focus on creating internal innovation as well. Although the firm recently developed a new R&D lab, it has continued to make excellent acquisitions that are complementary to its various product lines, such as the Cordis acquisition, which aligns with Johnson & Johnson's coronary stent.[83] Johnson & Johnson also maintains its manufacturing skills and improves the operations of its acquired firms.

The final two characteristics of successful acquisitions are flexibility and adaptation skills. When both the acquiring and the target firms have experience in managing change, they will be more skilled at adapting their capabilities to new environments. As a result, they are more adept at integrating the two organizations, which is particularly important when disparate cultures are encountered. Adaptation skills allow the two firms to integrate more quickly, efficiently, and effectively both firms' assets. As a result, the merged firm begins to produce the positive synergy and capabilities envisioned more quickly.

The attributes of a successful acquisition and their results are summarized in Table 7.1. Although some acquisitions have been successful, the majority of acquisitions completed during the last three decades have not been highly successful. Because of their lack of success and the growth of some firms to unmanageable sizes with too much diversity, a number of firms, in the United States and internationally, have restructured.

RESTRUCTURING

A significant wave of restructuring began in the late 1980s and increased in the 1990s that changed the composition of many U.S. and international firms.[84] Although restructuring was a common strategy among many U.S. firms during this period, it has spread internationally to countries such as Japan, Germany, and South Korea. **Restructuring** refers to changes in the composition of a firm's set of businesses and/or financial structure.[85] Much restructuring has entailed downsizing and the divestiture of businesses.[86] During this restructuring, a significant reduction in the number of acquisitions occurred, as firms attempted to "get their houses in or-

Restructuring refers to changes in the composition of a firm's set of businesses and/or financial structure.

TABLE 7.1 ***Attributes of Successful Acquisitions***

Attributes	Results
1. Acquired firm has assets and/or resources that are complementary to the acquiring firm's core business	High probability of positive synergy and competitive advantage by maintaining strengths
2. Friendly acquisition	Faster and more effective integration; possibly lower premiums
3. Careful and deliberate selection of target firms and conduct of negotiations	Acquire firms with strongest complementarities and avoid overpayment
4. Financial slack (cash and/or favorable debt position)	Financing (debt or equity) easier to obtain and less costly
5. Merged firm maintains low-to-moderate debt position	Lower financing cost, lower risk (e.g., of bankruptcy and avoids trade-offs associated with high debt)
6. Has experience with change and is flexible and adaptable	Faster and more effective integration; facilitates achievement of synergy
7. Sustained and consistent emphasis on R&D and innovation	Maintain long-term competitive advantage in markets

der." The primary impetus for restructuring was poor performance, along with correction of overdiversification.[87] For example, International Paper announced plans to sell $1 billion of its noncore assets to refocus the firm and improve financial performance. In particular, it will sell businesses that have failed to achieve market share and profitability goals. The announcement came after posting a loss equal to $1.39 a share. Businesses expected to be sold include the imaging business and those marketing printing supplies. In addition to the divestitures, other restructuring actions were announced. Among those was a planned layoff of more than 40 percent of International Paper's work force or about 9,000 employees. The intent is to refocus on its core businesses and to substantially improve performance.[88]

Although restructuring has been a worldwide phenomenon, some of the most significant restructuring has taken place in U.S. firms. Next, we examine some common means of restructuring—downsizing, downscoping, and leveraged buyouts.

Downsizing

Downsizing is a reduction in the number of employees, and sometimes in the number of operating units, but it may or may not change the composition of businesses in the corporation's portfolio.

One of the most common means of making changes within U.S. firms is that of downsizing. **Downsizing** is a reduction in the number of employees, and sometimes in the number of operating units, but it may or may not change the composition of businesses in the corporation's portfolio. The late 1980s and 1990s evidenced the loss of thousands of jobs in private and public organizations throughout the United States. There have been significant workforce reductions at General Motors, IBM, Kodak, Procter & Gamble, TRW, Unisys, and Xerox, among many others. In fact, one study estimates that 85 percent of the *Fortune* 1000 firms have implemented some downsizing.[89] The intent of these downsizings was to become "lean and mean."[90] However, results of a survey published in the *Wall Street Journal* suggest that many of the firms that downsized did not meet their goals. Eighty-nine percent of the firms surveyed suggested that the downsizing had a goal of reducing expenses, but only 46 percent achieved this goal. Another 71 percent suggested that their goal was to improve productivity, but only 22 percent of the respondents said that they met their goal for increasing productivity. Finally, 67 percent stated a goal of increasing competitive advantage, but only 19 percent noted that this goal was achieved.[91] These results have been confirmed in a study sponsored by the American Management Association and by other studies as well.[92]

Recent research shows that firms from both the United States and Japan received lower returns after downsizing. In effect, the stock markets in the respective countries evaluated the downsizings negatively (i.e., they evaluated that the downsizings would have negative outcomes for the firms over the long term). The researcher concluded that downsizing is not a panacea for problems that firms have and that they must take positive actions to deal with the problems directly and strategically. Normally, downsizing occurs because of other problems the firm is experiencing.[93]

When overcapacity exists, as in the defense industry, downsizing can produce above-average returns as it did for General Dynamics as the first mover to reduce the overcapacity.[94] Thus, although downsizing can be successful, it has not generally been as successful as intended. Furthermore, it has other unintended and potentially negative consequences. For instance, it is often problematic because corporations do not have total control over which employees stay and which seek new positions elsewhere. Often the best employees take advantage of separation payments during layoffs because they have other employment options. Research has shown that downsizing improves shareholder wealth when it is done for strategic purposes as in the General Dynamics case.[95] This has also been confirmed in other studies where the term *rightsizing* is used to mean that when downsizing is necessary firms should make certain that cuts are not done too deeply so that the changes to the firm's human capital do not affect strategic competitiveness.[96]

Despite the problems, downsizing continues in many large firms in the United States and worldwide. Many of the downsizings occur because of poor performance such as the case with International Paper, as discussed earlier. The downsizings announced in 1997 by Kodak and Ericsson were also due to poor performance. Kodak was suffering market share losses and thus stock price reductions because Fuji, a Japanese firm, was substantially undercutting its price for film. Kodak had to cut costs to reduce the price of its film to combat Fuji.[97] Similar to Kodak, Ericsson announced a 10,000 employee reduction in its Infocom business because of declining profits due to margin and price reductions.[98] Kimberly Clark announced a layoff of 5,000 employees because of a profit shortfall in 1997 and to reduce its overcapacity.[99] Even in these cases, care must be taken not to cut too many employees and to try to keep the most talented ones, both of which can be a significant challenge.

Downscoping

Other firms have downscoped and met more success.[100] **Downscoping** refers to divestiture, spin-offs, or some other means of eliminating businesses that are unrelated to a firm's core businesses. This is often referred to as strategically refocusing on the firm's core businesses. A firm that downscopes often also downsizes as noted in the example of International Paper described earlier.[101] However, it does not eliminate key employees from its primary businesses, which could lead to loss of core competence. The firm reduces its size by reducing the diversity of businesses in its portfolio. When accomplished, the top management team can more effectively manage the firm. This is because the firm becomes less diversified, and the top management team can better understand and manage the remaining businesses, primarily the core and other related businesses.[102] (Strategic leadership exercised by the top management team is the focus of Chapter 12.)

Downscoping refers to divestiture, spin-offs, or some other means of eliminating businesses that are unrelated to a firm's core businesses.

Rather than downscoping, some firms are spinning off businesses. PepsiCo chose to spin off KFC, Pizza Hut, and Taco Bell; the three fast-food businesses are known as Tricon. PepsiCo spun off the three businesses in part because of their poor performance.

A number of very large spin-offs have been undertaken in recent times. EDS was successfully spun off from General Motors. The EDS spin-off created the largest independent computer services company. EDS has grown with the outsourcing of computer systems, but it is now designing software and selecting hardware and training clients to use the software and hardware. EDS also operates one of the world's top six management consulting practices.[103]

Several other recent spin-offs are described in the Strategic Focus. These include spin-offs by PepsiCo of its fast-food businesses, by U.S. West, and by Cordiant. The spin-off by PepsiCo is dissimilar from the spin-off of EDS by GM in that the fast-food businesses have been underperforming PepsiCo's core business. The opposite was true at GM. In both cases, however, the spin-offs allowed the firms to focus on their core businesses. Thus, this strategic move can be considered a form of downscoping for both firms. Thus, while many of the firms, both the parent and the spin-off, increase shareholder value and accounting performance, some do not (see the Strategic Focus).[104]

STRATEGIC FOCUS

Cast Out, Orphaned, or Spun Off?

Through divestitures of various businesses, many firms have downscoped or refocused on their core businesses. However, in recent years, the trend has been to spin off businesses rather than to sell them to new owners. In many cases, this approach has been more lucrative for shareholders and allows the firm to refocus on its core business. The popularity of this approach is seen in recent announcements of spin-offs by PepsiCo and U.S. West in the United States and by Cordiant, a London-based advertising holding company.

PepsiCo decided to spin off its three fast-food businesses, KFC, Pizza Hut, and Taco Bell, while U.S. West and Cordiant chose to split theirs into two separate businesses. The new PepsiCo spin-off is known as Tricon for the three icons. In 1997, both KFC and Taco

Bell increased their sales over the previous year. This represents a trend for KFC but is the first increase in recent years for Taco Bell. Alternatively, Pizza Hut's sales declined during both 1996 and 1997. Thus, part of the reason that PepsiCo decided to spin off these businesses was their performance. They did not meet PepsiCo's criterion. Some analysts suggest that the new firm, Tricon, will have a challenge in handling its $4.7 billion debt, 10 times the businesses' cash flow, and a negative $740 million shareholder equity. On the other hand, Tricon managers expect these businesses to be more innovative without "big brother" PepsiCo looking over their shoulders. Already several fast food innovations are planned for both Pizza Hut and Taco Bell. There are also positive feelings about the top two executives for Tricon, David Novak, who turned around the performance of KFC, and Andrall Pearson, former president of PepsiCo. That said, the hypercompetition in the fast-food industry makes it difficult for any firm to succeed. Even the perennial market leader, McDonald's, has encountered problems in recent years (as explained in a Strategic Focus in Chapter 5).

One common reason for spin-offs is poor performance as in the case with PepsiCo. In others, it may be a lack of synergy, as in the case of U.S. West and Cordiant. U.S. West was the only Baby Bell to move into the cable business to take advantage of the expected synergy between the cable and communications businesses. Unfortunately, this synergy never materialized. Communications companies no longer expect to use cable systems as a means to carry communications into homes. Such plans changed with new Internet technology and with growing knowledge of the expense of using a universal cable communications system. Because of these changes, there has been little interaction between the two separate businesses at U.S. West. Therefore, the top executive felt that spinning them off into two separate companies would allow each to focus on its business without distractions. At Cordiant, the two separate advertising businesses did not mix well, possibly because of differing cultures when they were merged. Thus, the two new firms, Saatchi & Saatchi and Cordiant Communications Group, are reestablishing separate identities. Saatchi & Saatchi was considered the much stronger of the two originally and thus, is expected to flourish alone.

It should be noted that spin-offs are not a cure-all for performance problems. For example, AT&T's spin-off of Lucent Technologies and NCR did not improve NCR's performance. Similarly, AT&T has not performed as well as hoped after the spin-off. Actually, because of the highly disappointing performance of NCR within AT&T, many referred to the change as a cast-off. Lucent Technologies is the only one of the three businesses that seems to have benefited from the separation. Analysts also question whether the spin-offs and divestitures planned by the poorly performing Tele-Communications Inc. (TCI) will improve its performance. Thus, the popular new trend seems to have some benefits but cannot cure all the ills of companies with multiple businesses.

SOURCE: P. Galuska, 1997, Still waiting for the new NCR, *Business Week*, December 15, 142–146; R. Gibson, 1997, Fast-food spin-off enters Pepsi-free era, *Wall Street Journal*, B1, B10; R. Grover, 1997, The dismantling of an empire, *Business Week*, June 30, 94–95; S. Lipin, 1997, U.S. West to split into two companies, *Wall Street Journal*, October 27, A3; Y. Ono, 1997, Cordiant breakup fails to impress market, *Wall Street Journal*, December 16, B10; S. Pulliam, 1997, Pepsi's fast-food spin-off may cause some indigestion, *Wall Street Journal*, September 17, C1, C2; P. Sellers, 1997, Pepsi's eateries go it alone, *Fortune*, August 4, 27–30.

Probably one of the best known cases of downscoping outside of AT&T is Hanson PLC. Hanson was a British conglomerate well known for its strategy of acquiring unrelated businesses often operating in declining markets that were poor performers and undervalued. Hanson would immediately implement actions designed to increase efficiency, reduce costs, and improve profits. Oftentimes after these actions were accomplished and successful, Hanson would sell the firm for a profit. For years, this strategy seemed to work well for Hanson. However, as the global environment for business changed and the markets became increasingly competitive, Hanson management was unable to adapt. As a result, the firm's performance declined.[105] Hanson managers decided that the way to deal with these problems was to downscope by splitting the firm into four separate businesses. It began the process in 1995 by spinning off a set of unrelated businesses located in the United States. It finished the process in 1996 by spinning off three more businesses, Energy, Imperial Tobacco, and Millenium Chemicals. Thus, while Hanson referred to this as a separation into four businesses, it actually split into five separate businesses with the original Hanson firm remaining after spinning off four groups of businesses. The U.S. businesses spin-off, USI, was successful as its stock price increased 55 percent within one year after the action. The performance of Hanson after the spin-offs in 1996 was mixed.[106] There are a number of other firms that have downscoped or are currently in the process of downscoping in hopes of improving performance. Among these is Campbell Soup. This company announced that it was spinning off seven of its noncore businesses, which generate annual revenues of $1.4 billion, in order to refocus.[107] Thus, downscoping appears to be a major restructuring strategy in the 1990s.

Leveraged Buyouts

A **leveraged buyout (LBO)** is a restructuring action whereby the managers of the firm and/or an external party buys all of the assets of the business, largely financed with debt, and takes the firm private.

Although downscoping is a prominent and generally successful restructuring strategy, another restructuring strategy, leveraged buyouts, has received significant attention in the popular press. A **leveraged buyout (LBO)** is a restructuring action whereby the managers of the firm and/or an external party buys all of the assets of the business, largely financed with debt, and takes the firm private. The firm is bought by a few owners often in partnership associations, such as Kolberg, Kravis and Roberts (KKR), primarily by obtaining significant amounts of debt. Through this action, the stock of the firm is no longer traded publicly. This form of restructuring was predicted by a prominent finance scholar to be the corporate form of the future.[108] Oftentimes the new owners of the LBO firm also sell a significant number of assets after the purchase and, in so doing, downscope the firm.[109] Some of these assets are sold to help reduce the significant debt costs. In addition, it is frequently the intent of the new owners to increase the efficiency of the firm and sell it within a period of five to eight years. It is interesting to note, however, that recent research suggests that increased efficiency does not come from pressures of debt. Researchers have found that managerial ownership creates more effective incentives in the buyout than debt.[110] This is supported by anecdotal evidence at Clayton, Dubilier & Rice, Inc., a firm that facilitates leveraged buyouts.[111] This firm reports that managers who received ownership incentives help implement performance improvements. It is the equity incentive rather than the fear of not making debt payments that creates improvement.

The three types of leveraged buyouts are (1) management buyouts (MBO), (2) employee buyouts (EBO), and (3) an LBO in which another firm or partnership such as KKR buys the whole firm, as opposed to a part of the firm, and takes it private. MBOs have been found to lead to downscoping, increased strategic focus, and improved performance.[112] As part of CBS, Fender Musical Instruments was a poor performer. In 1981, William Schultz was brought in to fix it, but ended up putting together an MBO in 1985. Fender's independence proved Schultz's strategy to be correct. It began with $11 in debt for every $1 in equity, but the brand name was strong. In 1995, Fender's sales were $300 million with nearly 50 percent of the guitar market share. Recent evaluation has seen the equity of Schultz's group grow to more than $100 million compared to an initial investment of $500,000.[113]

Improvements at UAL (parent of United Airlines) and Avis Rent-A-Car are attributed to EBOs at these firms. The UAL arrangement appears to be working better than the situation at Avis. At UAL there has been more of a cooperative spirit with gains in market share and above-average returns.[114] At Avis and other EBOs, difficulties have arisen between management and employees. Furthermore, few employee owners have been requested to sit on boards.[115] These problems are very similar to the problems of the employee buyouts experienced in Russia. Needed restructuring is hard to accomplish because of employee job security fears.[116] When change is needed, more problems usually occur between managers and employees.

Whole-firm LBOs, on the other hand, see improvements through downsizing and retrenchment. This approach was illustrated through a buyout at Dr Pepper by Forsmann Little, a leveraged buyout specialist like KKR. Dr Pepper was successful enough to receive a new infusion of capital through an initial public offering. It subsequently was bought out by Cadbury Schweppes PLC.[117]

While LBOs have been hailed as a significant innovation in the financial restructuring of firms, there are potentially negative trade-offs. First, the large debt increases the financial risk of the firm, as evidenced by the number of LBO firms that have had to file for bankruptcy in the 1990s. The intent of owners to increase the efficiency of the LBO firm and sell it within five to eight years sometimes creates a short-term and risk-averse managerial focus. As a result, many of these firms fail to invest in R&D or take other major actions designed to maintain or improve the core competence of the firm.[118]

Most scholars believe LBOs occur because of poor corporate governance (discussed in Chapter 10). The poor governance allows managers to take actions that

Employee buyouts (EBOs) do not always have a positive effect on a firm. At Avis, for example, there have been problems between management and employees.

are not in the best interests of the firm but from which the managers may profit. Thus, many scholars argue the LBO occurs to correct the inefficiencies created by this environment. Because the managerial actions often entail acquiring businesses that do not create value for the firm, LBOs lead frequently to divestitures of these businesses. Some research supports this explanation of LBOs.[119] Others argue that the problems are not due to weaknesses in corporate governance but rather to managerial mistakes.[120] There is research to support this view as well.[121] We conclude that in reality there may be several reasons that LBOs are undertaken.

Restructuring Outcomes

The restructuring alternatives, along with typical short- and long-term outcomes, are presented in Figure 7.2. As shown in the figure, the most successful restructuring actions are those that help top management regain strategic control of the firm's operations. Thus, downscoping has been the most successful because it refocuses the firm on its core business(es). Executives can control the strategic actions of the businesses because they are fewer, less diverse, and deal with operations with which top management is more knowledgeable.

Jack Welch, CEO of General Electric, has created significant wealth for GE shareholders. He has done so largely by restructuring the firm to create greater efficiencies and by developing an excellent management team. In 1997, Welch again decided that GE needed to restructure one more time before he retired. His intent was to increase the efficiencies in GE's industrial businesses. He believed this was necessary if these businesses were to compete effectively in global mar-

FIGURE 7.2 ***Restructuring and Outcomes***

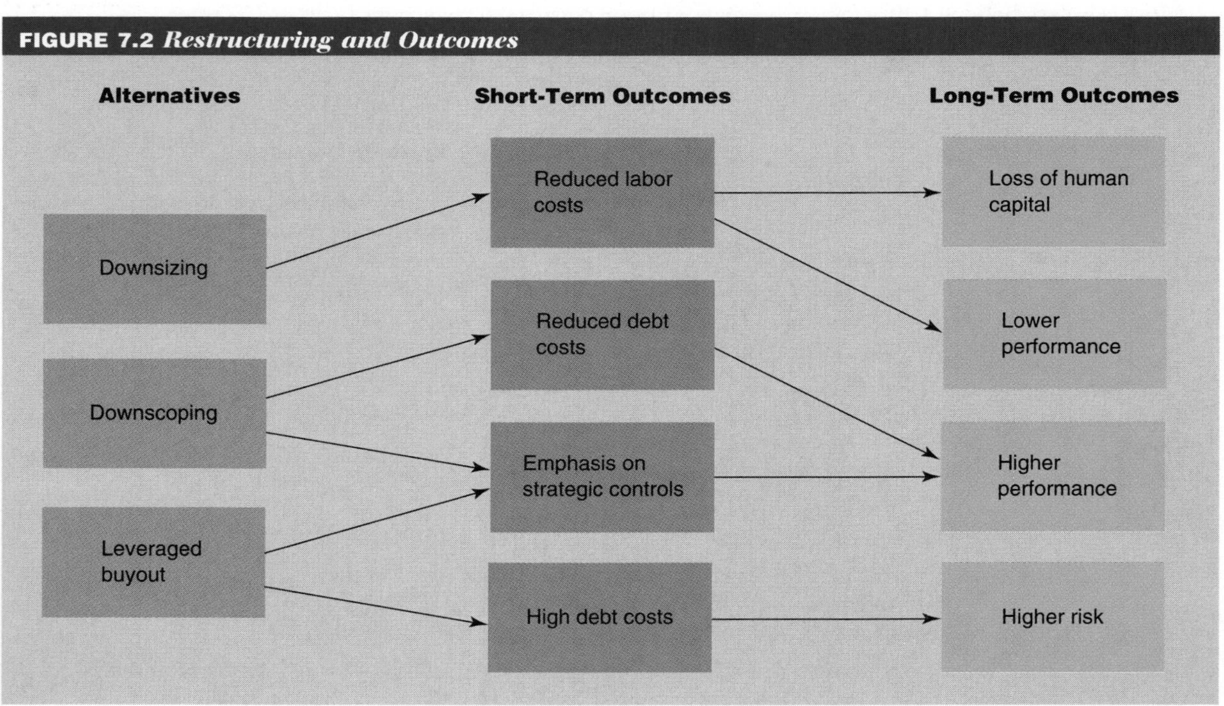

kets. By increasing efficiencies, he intended to improve these businesses' profitability. The restructuring was aimed at reducing costs and increasing productivity. Most expect him to be successful because of his past performance.[122]

Lastly, takeover bids and managerial resistance have been found to affect performance of an acquisition. For example, research has shown that hostile takeover bids often do not produce the outcomes expected. The raiders in hostile bids argue the takeover is the result of an entrenched management that has not acted in the best interests of the shareholders. This kind of acquisition, however, produces problems in integrating the two firms. The target firm managers often leave or are forced out and the remaining employees may be resentful. Sometimes, losing key people means a loss of knowledge and experience that could be helpful in making the acquired business productive for the acquiring firm. One study found no instances where acquisitions involving hostile bids were effective. Only friendly acquisitions produced high performance after the merger of the two firms.[123] Also, hostile bids induce managerial resistance. Research has shown that managerial resistance increases the acquisition offer which enhances the market value for the target firm shareholders.[124] Therefore, acquirers should carefully consider the situation before making a hostile bid for a target firm.

SUMMARY

- Acquisition has been a popular strategy for many years, but the number and the size of acquisitions increased greatly during the 1980s and 1990s. The popularity of acquisitions was facilitated by a change in the interpretation of U.S. antitrust laws and innovations in the financing of large acquisitions (i.e., junk bonds).
- Firms might make acquisitions for several reasons. Among these are increasing their market power, overcoming barriers to entry, avoiding the costs involved in developing new products internally and bringing them to market, increasing the speed at which the firm can enter a new business, reducing the risk of entering a new business, diversifying the firm more easily, and avoiding severe competition, often from foreign firms.
- Acquisitions produce their share of problems for the acquiring firm as well. It is often difficult to achieve effective integration between the acquiring and the acquired firms. Firms sometimes inadequately evaluate the target firm because of the bidding process. In addition, firms can overestimate the potential capabilities and synergy that can be created between the acquiring and the acquired firms. The costs of acquisition can be significant. These include the costs of obtaining financing and arranging for the acquisition of another firm. When a firm takes on large or extraordinary levels of debt to complete an acquisition, problems can arise. Other firms have been unsuccessful because the acquiring firm became too diversified. Managers have also become overly focused on making acquisitions, which may lead to inappropriate managerial oversight over other firm operations. Finally, a firm may become too large in size through acquisition, which makes the firm more difficult to manage.
- However, acquisitions can be successful. Successful acquisitions often require deliberate and careful selection of the target and firm negotiations. In addition, both the acquiring and the target firms in successful mergers frequently have considerable slack in the form of cash and/or debt capacity. Successful acquiring firms often maintain a low or moderate debt position. Even if significant leverage is used to finance the acquisition, the firm quickly reduces the debt and debt costs by selling off portions of the acquired firm or some of its own lower performing businesses. Successful acquisitions involve firms with complementary assets/resources, and those complementary resources are used to leverage the core competence of the joint firm. Related to this point, friendly acquisitions often lead to more success. Acquisi-

tions also tend to be more successful when both the acquiring and the target firms have experience in adapting to change and therefore are better able to achieve effective integration. Finally, many of the successful acquiring firms maintain an emphasis on innovation and R&D as a part of their overall strategy.

- In the late 1980s and 1990s, restructuring became a common and important strategic action. Oftentimes this restructuring is undertaken to downsize the firm. The approach requires employee layoffs and also seeks to reduce the number of hierarchical levels in an organization. Although it does reduce formal behavioral controls, it is problematic because corporations do not have total control of which employees stay and which seek new positions elsewhere. Therefore, a firm may lose many high-performing employees.
- Another approach to restructuring is downscoping. The goal of downscoping is to reduce the level of a firm's diversification. This form of restructuring is often accomplished by divesting unrelated businesses, whereby the firm's top executives can strategically refocus on the firm's core business. It is often accompanied by downsizing as well. This approach has been more successful than downsizing alone.
- Another popular form of restructuring is known as the leveraged buyout (LBO). In a leveraged buyout, the management or an external party buys 100 percent of the firm's stock, largely financed with debt, and takes the firm private. The three types of LBOs are management buyouts (MBOs), employee buyouts (EBOs), and whole-firm LBOs. MBOs have functioned best because they provide clear incentives for managers. EBOs provide the potential for improved cooperation, but power struggles can occur between managers and workers if significant change is required. In general, LBOs have met with mixed success. Oftentimes, the intent is to improve the firm's efficiency and performance and to sell the firm (or take it public) within five to eight years after the leveraged buyout. Some LBO firms have been successful because of improved incentives for managers, but in recent years some have experienced performance problems, primarily because of the high debt and debt costs.
- The main goal of corporate restructuring, in most cases, is to gain or regain strategic control of the firm. Downscoping and strategic refocusing on core businesses reduce the pressure for processing information to manage a wider diversity of businesses and allow the top executives to control the businesses by evaluating strategic actions, as opposed to placing an emphasis on financial outcomes. This generally produces higher performance and achieves strategic competitiveness over the long term.

REVIEW QUESTIONS

1. Why have acquisitions been a popular strategy?
2. For what reasons might firms follow an acquisition strategy?
3. What problems might be encountered by firms following an acquisition strategy?
4. What are some of the approaches that firms employ to complete an acquisition strategy successfully?
5. What are the common forms of restructuring and their goals?
6. How can a firm successfully implement a restructuring strategy?

APPLICATION DISCUSSION QUESTIONS

1. Given the evidence that the shareholders of many acquiring firms gain little or nothing in value from acquisitions, why do so many firms follow such a strategy?
2. Of the reasons for following an acquisition strategy described in the chapter, which are positive, and which are more negative and likely to create performance problems over the long term?

3. After reading popular press accounts of large acquisitions, choose a recent one and detail the important characteristics of the acquiring and the acquired firms. Based on these characteristics and other information, do you think this acquisition will succeed in achieving high performance? Explain why or why not.
4. Search popular press accounts to find an acquisition that has the attributes necessary for success. Why do you feel this acquisition has a high probability of success over the long term?
5. What is meant by the term *synergy?* Explain how the merger of two separate businesses can create synergy. How can firms create private synergy that cannot be imitated easily by other companies?
6. How can top executives in a firm determine the most appropriate level of diversification and thereby avoid becoming overdiversified? How can they determine the appropriate level of debt/leverage to utilize?
7. Why have LBOs not become the organization of the future, as proposed by a prominent finance scholar? Why have MBOs been more successful than EBOs?
8. In comparing acquiring a business with developing a new product/business internally, what are the advantages and disadvantages of each?

ETHICS QUESTIONS

1. If there is a relationship between the size of the firm and a top executive's compensation, is there an inducement for top executives to engage in mergers and acquisitions in order to increase their compensation? What is the board of directors' role in maintaining the integrity of the compensation system?
2. When a manager seeks to restructure (acquire or divest firm assets), are there incentives to do it in a way that builds the manager's power relative to shareholders or other stakeholders such as employees, rather than the firm's power relative to the market in order to achieve strategic competitiveness? Could this motive be related to the lack of success among acquiring firms?
3. If shareholders increase their wealth through a downsizing, does this come at the expense of employees who have invested a considerable portion of their life in the firm or at the expense of whole communities dependent on employment from the downsizing firm?
4. Do "corporate raiders" always target firms that are performing poorly and thus have a rational reason for pursuing the restructuring due to mismanagement, or is there also an incentive to pursue firms that have resources to "buy off" hostile suitors ("green mail")?
5. When a leveraged buyout is attempted, shareholders often increase their wealth (e.g., stock price increases), but debtholders may find their investment at risk because bond ratings are often downgraded. Are there any ethical issues associated with the transfer of wealth from debtholders to shareholders?
6. Before an LBO, should a manager reveal information about planned new products that might bring personal gain (e.g., when the manager becomes an owner through the LBO) rather than gain to public shareholders, once the firm is private?

INTERNET EXERCISE

Go to M&A Marketplace at:

http://www.mergernetwork.com/default.html

At the Web site, go to "News Headlines" and select the link that provides access to recent announcements of corporate mergers. Select one of the mergers and visit the Web sites of the companies involved. From what you learn about the companies, speculate on the reason for the merger. Does the merger make sense to you? Why or why not?

Strategic Surfing

Of the many sites on the Internet that provide merger-related information, two are particularly useful. The first site, Pointers to the World of Mergers and Acquisitions, provides links to other merger-related Web sites and newsgroups. The second site, Securities Data Company, provides a broad array of merger-related information, news, and data.

http://www.gwdg.de/~ifbg/mergers.html

http://www.secdata.com

NOTES

1. M. A. Hitt, R. E. Hoskisson, R. D. Ireland, and J. S. Harrison, 1991, Effects of acquisitions on R&D inputs and outputs, *Academy of Management Journal* 34: 693–706; M. Sikora, 1990, The M&A bonanza of the '80s and its legacy, *Mergers and Acquisitions*, March/April, 90–95; J. F. Weston and K. S. Chung, 1990, Takeovers and corporate restructuring: An overview, *Business Economics* 25, no. 2: 6–11.
2. S. R. Curry, 1997, First: The year of the very big deals, *Fortune*, November 24, 36–38; Mergers, acquisitions up record 40%, 1997, *Dallas Morning News*, January 3, F11; The business of travel, 1997, *Financial Times*, November 20, 1.
3. M. C. Jensen, 1988, Takeovers: Their causes and consequences, *Journal of Economic Perspectives* 1, no. 2: 21–48.
4. D. Lei and M. A. Hitt, 1995, Strategic restructuring and outsourcing: The effect of mergers and acquisitions and LBOs on building firm skills and capabilities, *Journal of Management* 21: 835–860.
5. J. S. Lublin, 1995, Spinoffs may establish new companies but they often spell the end of jobs, *Wall Street Journal*, November 21, B1, B8.
6. S. Lipin and P. Fritsch, 1997, Falcon Drilling to merge with Reading & Bates, *Wall Street Journal Interactive Edition*, July 15, http://www.wsj.com.
7. P. C. Haspeslagh and D. B. Jemison, 1991, *Managing Acquisitions: Creating Value Through Corporate Renewal* (New York: The Free Press).
8. D. K. Datta, G. E. Pinches, and V. K. Naravyanan, 1992, Factors influencing wealth creation from mergers and acquisitions: A metaanalysis, *Strategic Management Journal* 13: 67–84; G. F. Davis and S. K. Stout, 1992, Organization theory and the market for corporate control: A dynamic analysis of the characteristics of large takeover targets, 1980–1990, *Administrative Science Quarterly* 37: 605–633; W. B. Carper, 1990, Corporate acquisitions and shareholder wealth: A review and exploratory analysis, *Journal of Management* 16: 807–823.
9. K. Ramaswamy, 1997, The performance impact of strategic similarity in horizontal mergers: Evidence from the U.S. banking industry, *Academy of Management Journal* 40: 697–715.
10. E. MacDonald, 1997, Ernst & Young to merge with KPMG, *Wall Street Journal*, October 20, A3, A13.
11. A. Shleifer and R. W. Vishny, 1991, Takeovers in the '60s and the '80s: Evidence and implications, *Strategic Management Journal* 12 (Special Winter Issue): 51–59.
12. M. Lubatkin, N. Srinivasan, and H. Merchant, 1997, Merger strategies and shareholder value during times of relaxed antitrust enforcement: The case of large mergers during the 1980s, *Journal of Management* 23: 59–81.
13. J. Wyatt, 1995, Drug stocks—where M&A pays off, *Fortune*, October 30, 222.
14. E. Tanouye and G. Anders, 1995, Drug industry takeovers mean more cost-cutting, less research spending, *Wall Street Journal*, February 1, B1, B4.
15. C. Quintanilla, 1997, Caterpillar to buy small-engine maker, Lucas Varity's Perkins, for $1.33 billion, *Wall Street Journal*, December 12, A3, A4.
16. L. Bannon, 1997, Computer Services to buy Continuum, *Wall Street Journal*, April 30, A3, A5.
17. D. Angwin and B. Savill, 1997, Strategic perspectives on European cross-border acquisitions: A view from the top European executives, *European Management Review* 15: 423–435.
18. L. Capron and W. Mitchell, 1997, Outcomes of international telecommunications acquisitions: Analysis of four cases with implications for acquisitions theory, *European Management Review*, 15: 237–251.
19. R. Biggadike, 1979, The risky business of diversification, *Harvard Business Review* 57, no. 3: 103–111.
20. E. Mansfield, 1969, *Industrial Research and Technological Innovation* (New York: Norton).
21. L. H. Clark, Jr., and A. L. Malabre, Jr., 1988, Slow rise in outlays for research imperils U.S. competitive edge, *Wall Street Journal*, November 16, A1, A5; E. Mansfield, M. Schwartz, and S. Wagner, 1981, Imitation costs and patents: An empirical study, *Economic Journal* 91: 907–918.
22. J. K. Shank and V. Govindarajan, 1992, Strategic cost analysis of technological investments, *Sloan Management Review* 34 (Fall): 39–51.
23. M. A. Hitt, R. E. Hoskisson, R. A. Johnson, and D. D. Moesel, 1996, The market for corporate control and firm innovation, *Academy of Management Journal* 39: 1084–1119.
24. E. Tanouye and S. Lipin, 1995, Cordis agrees to be acquired by J&J in a stockswap valued at $1.8 billion, *Wall Street Journal*, November 7, B6; R. Winslow, 1995, Going for flow: Simple device to prop clogged arteries open changes coronary care: Johnson & Johnson's 'stent' is a hit, but the cost is worrying hospitals, *Wall Street Journal*, October A1, A8.
25. K. F. McCardle and S. Viswanathan, 1994, The direct entry versus takeover decision and stock price performance around takeovers, *Journal of Business* 67: 1–43.
26. D. Silverman, 1997, Compaq to acquire Tandem, *Houston Chronicle*, June 24, C1, C8.
27. T. Weber, 1997, Lucent to acquire Octel for $1.8 billion, *Wall Street Journal*, July 18, A3, A4.
28. A. Raghavan and S. Callan, 1997, Merrill's $5.3 billion global bet, *Wall Street Journal*, November 20, C1, C22.
29. M. A. Hitt, R. E. Hoskisson, and R. D. Ireland, 1990, Mergers and acquisitions and managerial commitment to innovation in M-form firms, *Strategic Management Journal* 11 (Special Summer Issue): 29–47.
30. Hitt et al., The market for corporate control and innovation; J. Constable, 1986, Diversification as a factor in U.K. industrial strategy, *Long Range Planning* 19: 52–60.
31. Hitt et al., Effects of acquisitions; Hitt, Hoskisson, and Ireland, Mergers and acquisitions.
32. D. D. Bergh, 1997, Predicting divestiture of unrelated acquisitions: An integrative model of *ex ante* conditions, *Strategic Management Journal* 18: 715–731.
33. S. Finkelstein, 1997, Interindustry merger patterns and resource dependence: A replication and extension of Pfeffer (1972), *Strategic Management Journal* 18: 787–810.
34. J. Anand and H. Singh, 1997, Asset redeployment, acquisitions and corporate strategy in declining industries, *Strategic Management Journal*, 18 (Special Summer Issue): 99–118.

35. W. C. Kester, 1991, *Japanese Takeovers: The Global Contest for Corporate Control* (Boston: Harvard Business School Press), 94–95.
36. P. Newcomb, 1996, Video games, *Forbes,* May 6, 45.
37. M. A. Hitt, J. S. Harrison, R. D. Ireland, and A. Best, 1998, Attributes of successful and unsuccessful acquisitions of U.S. firms, *British Journal of Management,* in press.
38. D. K. Datta, 1991, Organizational fit and acquisition performance: Effects of post-acquisition integration, *Strategic Management Journal* 12: 281–297; J. Kitching, 1967, Why do mergers miscarry? *Harvard Business Review* 45, no. 6: 84–101.
39. H. Aaron, 1994, A poisoning of the atmosphere, *Wall Street Journal,* August 29, A10; P. M. Elsass and J. F. Veiga, 1994, Acculturation in acquired organizations: A force field perspective, *Human Relations* 47: 453–471.
40. A. F. Buono and J. L. Bowditch, 1989, *The Human Side of Mergers and Acquisitions* (San Francisco: Jossey-Bass).
41. A. Bianco, 1997, Will these blood types mix? *Business Week,* November 24, 82–83; PhyCor to purchase rival MedPartners, 1997, *Houston Chronicle,* C3.
42. D. B. Jemison and S. B. Sitkin, 1986, Corporate acquisitions: A process perspective, *Academy of Management Review* 11: 145–163.
43. R. Tamburri and D. Clark, 1996, Technology: Corel to acquire Novell's WordPerfect for $124 million in cash and stock, *Wall Street Journal,* February 1, B5; D. Clark, 1996, Software firm fights to remake business after ill-fated merger, *Wall Street Journal,* January 12, A1, A6.
44. M. Murray, 1997, National City to acquire First of America in a stock swap valued at $6.78 billion, *Wall Street Journal,* December 2, A3, A8.
45. D. Greising and N. Harris, 1997, You paid how much for that bank? *Business Week,* December 1, 152; S. Lipin and S. E. Frank, 1997, First Union to acquire CoreStates for stock valued at $16.3 billion, *Wall Street Journal,* November 19, A3, A4.
46. L. Grant, 1996, Miracle or mirage on 34th Street? *Fortune,* February 5, 84–90.
47. R. Roll, 1986, The hubris hypothesis of corporate takeovers, *Journal of Business* 59: 197–216.
48. Clark, Software firm fights.
49. G. Yago, 1991, *Junk Bonds: How High Yield Securities Restructured Corporate America* (New York: Oxford University Press), 146–148.
50. M. C. Jensen, 1987, A helping hand for entrenched managers, *Wall Street Journal,* November 4, A6; M. C. Jensen, 1986, Agency costs of free cash flow, corporate finance, and takeovers, *American Economic Review* 76: 323–329.
51. Grant, Miracle or mirage on 34th Street?, 85.
52. M. A. Hitt and D. L. Smart, 1994, Debt: A disciplining force for managers or a debilitating force for organizations? *Journal of Management Inquiry* 3: 144–152.
53. M. C. Jensen, 1989, Is leverage an invitation to bankruptcy? On the contrary—it keeps shaky firms out of court, *Wall Street Journal,* February 1, A14; Jensen, A helping hand.
54. B. H. Hall, 1990, The impact of corporate restructuring on industrial research and development, in M. N. Baily and C. Winston (eds.), *Brookings Papers on Economic Activity* 3: 85–135; B. Baysinger and R. E. Hoskisson, 1989, Diversification strategy and R&D intensity in multi-product firms, *Academy of Management Journal* 32: 310–332.
55. L. Grant, 1993, Corporate connections: Mergers are on the rise, but unlike deals of the 80s they aren't debt laden, *U.S. News & World Report,* August 2, 46–49.
56. Hitt et al., Effects of acquisitions; J. B. Barney, 1988, Returns to bidding firms in mergers and acquisitions: Reconsidering the relatedness hypothesis, *Strategic Management Journal* 9 (Special Summer Issue): 71–78.
57. R. Gibson, 1996, Anheuser-Busch plans to spin off baking unit, ending costly foray, *Wall Street Journal,* February 29, B3; R. A. Melcher and G. Burns, 1996, How Eagle became extinct: Anheuser saw synergies in beer and snacks, *Business Week,* March 4, 68–69.
58. J-F. Hennart and S. Reddy, 1997, The choice between mergers/acquisitions and joint ventures: The case of Japanese investors in the United States, *Strategic Management Journal* 18: 1–12.
59. Hitt, Hoskisson, Johnson, and Moesel, The Market for Corporate Control.
60. P. Very, M. Lubatkin, R. Calori, and J. Veiga, 1997, Relative standing and the performance of recently acquired European firms, *Strategic Management Journal* 18: 593–614.
61. J. A. Krug and H. Hegarty, 1997, Post-acquisition turnover among U.S. top management teams: An analysis of the effects of foreign vs domestic acquisitions of U.S. targets, *Strategic Management Journal* 18: 667–675.
62. M. E. Porter, 1987, From competitive advantage to corporate strategy, *Harvard Business Review* 65, no. 3: 43–59; D. J. Ravenscraft and R. M. Scherer, 1987, *Mergers, Sell Offs and Economic Efficiency* (Washington, D.C.: Brookings Institute).
63. C. W. L. Hill and R. E. Hoskisson, 1987, Strategy and structure in the multiproduct firm, *Academy of Management Review* 12: 331–341.
64. R. A. Johnson, R. E. Hoskisson, and M. A. Hitt, 1993, Board of director involvement in restructuring: The effects of board versus managerial controls and characteristics, *Strategic Management Journal* 14 (Special Issue): 33–50; C. C. Markides, 1992, Consequences of corporate refocusing: *Ex ante* evidence, *Academy of Management Journal* 35: 398–412.
65. R. E. Hoskisson and M. A. Hitt, 1988, Strategic control systems and relative R&D investment in large multiproduct firms, *Strategic Management Journal* 9: 605–621.
66. Hitt, Hoskisson, and Ireland, Mergers and acquisitions.
67. Hitt et al., The market for corporate control and innovation.
68. Hitt, Hoskisson, and Ireland, Mergers and acquisitions.
69. Ibid.
70. Jemison and Sitkin, Corporate acquisitions.
71. Hitt et al., Effects of acquisitions.
72. R. E. Hoskisson, M. A. Hitt, and R. D. Ireland, 1994, The effects of acquisitions and restructuring (strategic refocusing) strategies on innovation, in G. von Krogh, A. Sinatra, and H. Singh (eds.), *Managing Corporate Acquisitions* (London: Macmillan Press), 144–169.
73. L. Miller and G. Stern, 1996, Car rental companies neglect core business, often skid into losses, *Wall Street Journal,* February 15, A1, A8.
74. M. R. Sesit and G. Steinmetz, 1997, UBS, Swiss Bank are expected to merge, *Wall Street Journal,* December 2, A3, A4.

75. J. P. Walsh, 1988, Top management team turnover following mergers and acquisitions, *Strategic Management Journal* 9: 173–183.
76. M. A. Hitt, R. E. Hoskisson, R. D. Ireland, and J. Harrison, 1991, Are acquisitions a poison pill for innovation?, *Academy of Management Executive* V, no. 4: 22–34.
77. Hitt, Hoskisson, and Ireland, Mergers and acquisitions.
78. Hitt et al., Attributes of successful and unsuccessful.
79. J. S. Harrison, M. A. Hitt, R. E. Hoskisson, and R. D. Ireland, 1991, Synergies and post acquisition performance: Differences versus similarities in resource allocations, *Journal of Management* 17: 173–190; Barney, Returns to bidding firms.
80. M. A. Lubatkin and P. J. Lane, 1996, Psst . . . The merger mavens still have it wrong! *Academy of Management Executive* X, no. 1: 21–39.
81. J. P. Walsh, 1989, Doing a deal: Merger and acquisition negotiations and their impact upon target company top management turnover, *Strategic Management Journal* 10: 307–322.
82. L. S. Lublin, 1995, Strategies for preventing post-takeover defections, *Wall Street Journal*, April 28, B1, B8.
83. Tanouye and Lipin, Cordis agrees to be acquired by J&J; G. P. Pisano and S. C. Wheelwright, 1995, The new logic of R&D, *Harvard Business Review* 73, no. 5: 93–105.
84. R. A. Johnson, 1996, Antecedents and outcomes of corporate refocusing, *Journal of Management* 22: 437–481.
85. J. E. Bethel and J. Liebeskind, 1993, The effects of ownership structure on corporate restructuring, *Strategic Management Journal* 14 (Special Summer Issue): 15–31.
86. E. Bowman and H. Singh, 1990, Overview of corporate restructuring: Trends and consequences, in L. Rock and R. H. Rock (eds.), *Corporate Restructuring* (New York: McGraw-Hill).
87. R. E. Hoskisson, R. A. Johnson, and D. D. Moesel, 1994, Divestment intensity of restructuring firms: Effects of governance, strategy and performance, *Academy of Management Journal* 37: 1207–1251.
88. J. Welch, 1997, International Paper to cut work force and sell $1 billion of noncore assets, *Wall Street Journal*, July 4, A4.
89. W. McKinley, C. M. Sanchez, and A. G. Schick, 1995, Organizational downsizing: Constraining, cloning, learning, *Academy of Management Executive* IX, no. 3: 32–44.
90. R. E. Hoskisson and M. A. Hitt, 1994, *Downscoping: How to Tame the Diversified Firm* (New York: Oxford University Press).
91. A. Bennet, 1991, Downsizing doesn't necessarily bring an upswing in corporate profitability, *Wall Street Journal*, June 4, B1, B4.
92. K. S. Cameron, S. J. Freeman, and A. K. Mishra, 1991, Best practices in white-collar downsizing: Managing contradictions, *Academy of Management Executive* V, no. 3: 57–73.
93. P. M. Lee, 1997, A comparative analysis of layoff announcements and stock price reactions in the United States and Japan, *Strategic Management Journal* 18: 879–894.
94. J. Dial and K. J. Murphy, 1995, Incentives, downsizing and value creation at General Dynamics, *Journal of Financial Economics* 37: 261–314.
95. D. L. Worrell, W. M. Davidson, and V. M. Sharma, 1991, Layoff announcements and stockholder wealth, *Academy of Management Journal* 34: 662–678.
96. M. A. Hitt, B. W. Keats, H. F. Harback, and R. D. Nixon, 1994, Rightsizing: Building and maintaining strategic leadership and long-term competitiveness, *Organizational Dynamics* 23 (Autumn), 18–32; J. S. Lublin, 1994, Don't stop cutting staff, study suggests, *Wall Street Journal*, September 27, B1.
97. R. Waters, 1997, Eastman Kodak to cut 10,000 jobs, *Financial Times*, November 12, 13.
98. T. Burt, 1997, Ericsson plans to cut 10,000 jobs, *Financial Times*, December 3, 17.
99. J. Kirkpatrick, 1997, Kimberly-Clark to slash up to 5,000 jobs, *Dallas Morning News*, November 22, F1, F11; R. Langreth, 1997, Kimberly-Clark's sweeping cutbacks should ease overcapacity, analysts say, *Wall Street Journal*, November 24, A3.
100. Hoskisson and Hitt, *Downscoping*.
101. J. Kose, H. P. Lang, and J. Nitter, 1992, The voluntary restructuring of large firms in response to performance decline, *Journal of Finance* 47: 891–917; J. S. Lublin, 1995, Spin offs may establish new companies, but they often spell the end of jobs, *Wall Street Journal*, November 21, B1, B8.
102. Johnson, Hoskisson, and Hitt, Board of directors involvement; R. E. Hoskisson and M. A. Hitt, 1990, Antecedents and performance outcomes of diversification: A review and critique of theoretical perspectives, *Journal of Management* 16: 461–509.
103. N. Templin, 1996, Under Alberthal, EDS is out of limelight but triples revenue, *Wall Street Journal*, February 21, A1, A6.
104. Johnson, Antecedents and outcomes.
105. P. Stonham, 1997, Demergers and the Hanson experience. Part one: The prelude, *European Management Journal* 15: 266–274.
106. P. Stonham, 1997, Demergers and the Hanson experience. Part two: Demerger tactics, *European Management Journal* 15: 413–422.
107. Campbell's higher-margin diet, 1997, *Business Week*, September 22, 43; E. Jensen, 1997, Campbell Soup may shed some noncore soup lines, *Wall Street Journal*, July 14, A4.
108. M. C. Jensen, 1989, Eclipse of the public corporation, *Harvard Business Review* 67, no. 5: 61–74.
109. M. F. Wiersema and J. P. Liebeskind, 1995, The effects of leveraged buyouts on corporate growth and diversification in large firms, *Strategic Management Journal* 16: 447–460.
110. P. H. Phan and C. W. L. Hill, 1995, Organizational restructuring and economic performance in leveraged buyouts: An ex-post study, *Academy of Management Journal* 38: 704–739.
111. W. C. Kester and T. A. Luehrman, 1995, Rehabilitating the leveraged buyout, *Harvard Business Review* 73, no. 3: 119–130.
112. A. Seth and J. Easterwood, 1995, Strategic redirection in large management buyouts: The evidence from post-buyout restructuring activity, *Strategic Management Journal* 14: 251–274.
113. M. Matzer, 1996, Playing solo, *Forbes*, March 25, 80–81.
114. S. Chandler, 1996, United we own, *Business Week*, March 18, 96–100.
115. A. Bernstein, 1996, Why ESOP deals have slowed to a crawl, *Business Week*, March 18, 101–102.
116. I. Filatochev, R. E. Hoskisson, T. Buck, and M. Wright, 1996, Corporate restructuring in Russian privatizations:

Implications for US investors, *California Management Review* 38, no. 2: 87–105.

117. B. Ortega, 1995, Cadbury seeking a new king of pop to oversee no. 3 soft-drink business, *Wall Street Journal,* January 30, B2.
118. W. F. Long and D. J. Ravenscraft, 1993, LBOs, debt, and R&D intensity, *Strategic Management Journal* 14 (Special Issue, Summer): 119–135.
119. D. D. Bergh and G. F. Holbein, 1997, Assessment and redirection of longitudinal analysis: Demonstration with a study of the diversification and divestiture relationship, *Strategic Management Journal* 18: 557–571.
120. C. Markides and H. Singh, 1997, Corporate restructuring: A symptom of poor governance or a solution to past managerial mistakes? *European Management Journal* 15: 213–219.
121. D. L. Smart and M. A. Hitt, 1997, A test of the agency theory perspective of corporate restructuring, working paper, University of Nebraska.
122. A. Bernstein, S. Jackson, and J. Byrne, 1997, Jack cracks the whip again, *Business Week,* December 15, 34–35.
123. Hitt, Harrison, Ireland, and Best, Attributes of successful and unsuccessful acquisitions.
124. P. Holl and D. Kyriazis, 1997, Wealth creation and bid resistance in U.K. takeover bids, *Strategic Management Journal* 18: 483–498.

International Strategy

CHAPTER 8

Learning Objectives

After reading this chapter, you should be able to:

1. Explain traditional and emerging motives for firms to pursue international diversification.
2. Explore the four factors that lead to a basis for international business-level strategies.
3. Name and define generic international business-level strategies.
4. Define the three international corporate-level strategies: multidomestic, global, and transnational.
5. Discuss the environmental trends affecting international strategy.
6. Name and describe the five alternative modes for entering international markets.
7. Explain the effects of international diversification on firm returns and innovation.
8. Name and describe two major risks of international diversification.
9. Explain why the positive outcomes from international expansion are limited.

Globalization: The Driving Force of International Strategy

Introduced in Chapter 1, globalization is a reality around which our study of the strategic management process is framed. An increasingly globalized world is dramatically changing today's economic landscape from that of only 20 years ago. Moreover, the pace of global economic expansion will increase, perhaps significantly so, in the next 20 years.

Defined earlier as the spread of economic innovations around the world and the political and cultural adjustments that accompany this diffusion, globalization can be viewed through different lenses that represent specific levels of analysis. At a *worldwide level*, globalization concerns the increasing economic interdependence among countries. This growth in interdependence is demonstrated by increases in the cross-border flow of goods, services, capital, and knowledge. Public policy analysts focus on *country-level* globalization, which is the extent of interlinkages between their country's economy and those of the rest of the world. The *industry level* of globalization refers to the degree to

http://www.nike.com
http://www.reebok.com
http://www.adidas.com
http://www.toyota.co.jp
http://www.sony.com
http://www.hoechst.com

which a firm's competitive position within a particular industry is interdependent with its position in another country. The pharmaceutical industry is an example of one that is highly globalized. In globalized industries, markets across the world tend to be dominated by the same companies. Nike, Reebok, and Adidas, for example, are dominant in the athletic footwear industry. For the *individual firm,* globalization refers to the extent to which the company has expanded its revenue and asset base across countries and the degree to which it engages in cross-border flows of capital, goods, services, and knowledge across subsidiaries.

Toyota is an example of a highly globalized company (Toyota's effective use of its core competencies is described in a Strategic Focus in Chapter 3; its innovation ability is explained in a Strategic Focus in Chapter 13). Approximately 35 percent of the firm's global output is generated from wholly or partially owned affiliates in over 25 countries in Europe, Asia, and the Americas. Furthermore, "Toyota exported 38 percent of its domestic production from Japan to foreign markets and engaged in significant intra-firm flows among its affiliates. For example, within its Southeast Asian regional network, Toyota exported diesel engines from Thailand, transmissions from the Philippines, steering gears from Malaysia and engines from Indonesia." With over $20 billion in cash, Toyota has allocated $13.5 billion to global expansion through the year 2000. The intent of these investments is to create the automobile manufacturing industry's first truly globally organized company.

Toyota follows the multidomestic international strategy (discussed in this chapter) at the corporate level and the integrated/low-cost differentiation strategy at the business unit level (see Chapter 4). Through the multidomestic strategy, Toyota seeks to use its vast manufacturing clout to customize vehicles for regional markets. Manufacturing hubs in Asia, North America, and Europe rely on locally based suppliers and design teams to tailor vehicles to local tastes. Through its integrated supplier networks, world-standard setting manufacturing efficiencies, and superior product development skills, Toyota is able to reduce costs continuously relative to competitors while simultaneously offering differentiated features (e.g., product quality and reliability) to customers that create value for them.

Sony Corporation is another example of a highly globalized and successful company. Sony's better-than-expected year-end 1997 profits were in sharp contrast to many of its rivals, especially its Japanese counterparts. In light of results such as these, some analysts believe that "Sony has built a competitive advantage that is sustainable; its strategy is very well defined and [is] absolutely right."

In recognition of the increasingly globalized nature of the world's markets and the industries in which it competes, Hoechst AG is becoming a globalized firm rather than a German company. The company's CEO indicates that the change processes required for Hoechst to become a globalized company were initiated some 15 or 20 years ago. Although Hoechst is not yet truly an international company, neither is it still a typical German company. Following a significant reorganization, Hoechst is a widely diversified corporation with operations in pharmaceuticals, animal health, polyester products, industrial gases, paints and coatings, agribusiness, and basic chemicals and cellulose acetate. In light of this reorganization, one in which decision making responsibility has been decentralized to those managing the strategic business units, the firm's top-level managers are making decisions regarding Hoechst's strategic positioning for the next 10 to 20 years. This is a time period in which Hoechst executives believe the world's economies will become more interdependent. The decision areas the executives are examining include choices about the company's portfolio of businesses and how capital will be allocated among those divisions (recall that these are corporate-level strategy issues). Within individual strategic business units, decisions must be made regarding products to be offered and in which global markets, the pace at which the business will globalize, and the methods for entering different global markets, among others. Thus, to achieve strategic competitiveness in the global economy, Hoechst AG must choose and implement international strategies at both the corporate and business unit levels. The international strategy choices available to firms, such as Hoechst AG, that have decided to internationalize their operations are the focus of this chapter.

SOURCE: V. Govindarajan and A. Gupta, 1998, Setting a course for the new global landscape, in Part One of As business goes global, *Financial Times*, February 10–11, 3–5; M. Nakamoto, 1998, Sony posts 45% rise as games beat rivals, *Financial Times*, January 30, 13; T. Box, 1997, Toyota steers a solid course of growth, *Dallas Morning News*, November 30, H1, H6; B. Bremner, L. Armstrong, K. Kerwin, and K. Naughton, 1997, Toyota's crusade, *Business Week*, April 7, 104–114; C. Cookson, Interview with Jurgen Dormann, 1997, *Fortune* (Special edition), November 10, 106E6–106E26; M. Nakamoto, 1997, Toyota targets European sales, *Financial Times*, November 20, 21; H. Simonian, 1997, A steady drive around the world, *Financial Times*, December 5, 14.

In the 1980s, the dramatic success of Japanese firms and products, such as Toyota and Sony, in the United States and other international markets provided a powerful jolt to U.S. managers and awakened them to the importance of international competition and global markets. In the 1990s, Russia and China represent potential major international market opportunities for firms from many countries, including the United States, Japan, Korea, and European nations. They also represent formidable competitors, particularly China in low-technology manufacturing industries. There is some debate, however, regarding the relative attractiveness of the Russian and Chinese markets for companies competing in the global marketplace. Some believe that for at least a period of time, foreign investors will continue to favor China. The reason for this preference is that China is more orderly while Russia remains full of risks. Moreover, it may be that Russia's movement to more of a free-market economy could depend on homegrown developments instead of foreign direct investments (FDI) and other modes firms use to internationalize their operations.[1]

Thus, the international arena features both opportunities and threats for firms seeking strategic competitiveness in global markets. This chapter examines opportunities facing firms as they seek to develop and exploit core competencies by diversifying into global markets. In addition, we discuss different problems and complexities that can be associated with implementation of the firm's chosen international strategies.[2] The importance of learning how to respond successfully to these opportunities and threats should not be underestimated. Some executives, for example, believe that goods and services may be imitated somewhat easily by effective global competitors, but it is much more difficult to duplicate the competitive benefits resulting from a firm's ability to become a truly global corporation. Selecting and implementing appropriate international strategies allows the firm to become a global corporation.[3]

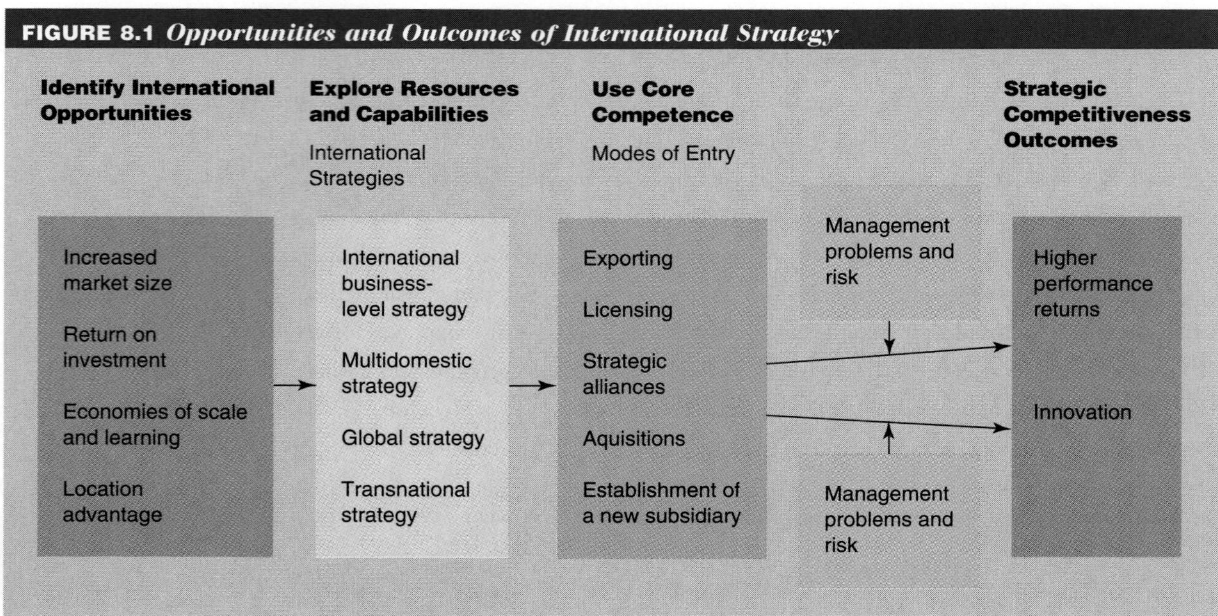

In this chapter, as illustrated in Figure 1.1 in Chapter 1, we discuss the importance of international strategy as a source of strategic competitiveness and above-average returns. The chapter focuses first on the incentives to internationalize. Once the firm decides to compete internationally, it must select its strategy and choose a mode of entry. It may enter international markets by exporting from domestic-based operations, licensing, forming joint ventures with international partners, acquiring a foreign-based firm, or establishing a new subsidiary. Such international diversification can extend product life cycles, provide incentives for more innovation, and produce above-average returns. These benefits are tempered by political and economic risks and the problems of managing a complex international firm with operations in multiple countries. Figure 8.1 provides an overview of these choices and outcomes. The relationships among international opportunities, exploration of resources and capabilities that result in strategies and modes of entry that are based on core competencies are explored in this chapter.

IDENTIFYING INTERNATIONAL OPPORTUNITIES: THE INCENTIVE TO PURSUE AN INTERNATIONAL STRATEGY

An **international strategy** refers to the selling of products in markets outside the firm's domestic market.

An **international strategy** refers to the selling of products in markets outside the firm's domestic market.[4] One of the primary reasons for implementing an international strategy (as opposed to a strategy focused on the domestic market) is that international markets yield potential new opportunities. Raymond Vernon captured the classic rationale for international diversification.[5] He suggested that typically a firm discovers an innovation in its home country market, especially in an advanced economy such as that found in the United States. Some demand for the product may develop in other countries and, thus, exports are provided by domestic operations. Increased demand in foreign countries justifies direct foreign investment in production capacity abroad, especially as foreign competitors also organize to meet increasing demand. As the product becomes standardized, the firm may rationalize its operations by moving production to a region where manufacturing costs are low. Vernon, therefore, suggests that firms pursue international diversification to extend a product's life cycle.

Another traditional motive for firms to become multinational is to secure key resources. Key supplies of raw material, especially minerals and energy, are important in some industries. For instance, aluminum producers need a supply of bauxite, tire firms need rubber, and oil companies scour the world to find new petroleum reserves.

Others seek to secure access to low-cost factors of production. Clothing, electronics, watchmaking, and many other industries have moved portions of their operations to foreign locations in pursuit of lower costs. To enhance its cost competitiveness in the deflationary environment at the end of the 1990s, GE continued to shift some of its appliance manufacturing operations to various locations throughout the world. All of the firm's gas ranges are now made in San Luis Potosi, Mexico, through the firm's joint venture with Mabe, a Mexican company. In total, GE employs over 24,000 people in Mexico, primarily to manufacture appliances.[6]

Ireland's low labor costs and its use of the English language have helped make it the fastest growing telesales location in the European Union. To date, over 50 international companies have established telephone-based operations in Ireland. In American Airlines' Dublin office, now responsible for all of the firm's European reservations, approximately 300 Irish telephone operators complete the work that was handled previously by eight separate reservation centers scattered across Europe.[7]

Turkey's wage rates are among the lowest in Europe. In fact, the nation's hourly rates average one-half of those in Portugal, the poorest country in the European Union. Moreover, wages are lower than in some eastern European countries and

GE moved some of its appliance manufacturing operations to other locations around the world to enhance its cost competitiveness in the deflationary environment of the late 1990s. All of GE's gas ranges are now made in Mexico through a joint venture with Mabe, a Mexican company.

many developing nations. Because of these wage rates, coupled with the fact that workers' productivity is increasing by 3.6 percent annually, compared to the OECD average of 2.8 percent, many multinational companies are establishing operations in Turkey. In fact, these investments have caused Turkey's economy to grow at a rate that has actually created labor shortages.[8]

Low cost production factors are sometimes influenced by government actions. For example, Alabama outbid North and South Carolina for the first U.S. Mercedes-Benz car plant.[9] The state provided land and training wages for new workers and made commitments that government agencies and utilities would buy large quantities of the four-wheel-drive recreational vehicles the plant will produce.

Although these traditional motives continue to exist, as the Mercedes example illustrates, other emerging motivations have been driving international expansion (see Chapter 1). For instance, pressure has increased for global integration of operations, mostly driven by more universal product demand. As nations industrialize, demand for commodity products appears to become more similar.[10] This nationless or borderless demand for products may be due to lifestyle similarities in developed nations. Also, increases in global communication media facilitate the ability of people in different countries to visualize and model lifestyles in disparate cultures.[11]

In some industries, technology is driving globalization because economies of scale necessary to reduce costs to the lowest level often require efficient scale investment greater than that needed to meet domestic market demand.[12] There is also pressure for cost reductions in purchasing from the lowest cost global suppliers. For instance, R&D expertise for a new emerging business start-up may not be found in the domestic market.[13]

New large-scale markets, such as Russia, China, and India, also provide a strong incentive because of potential demand. And, because of currency fluctuations, firms may desire to have their operations distributed across many countries to reduce the risk of currency devaluation in one country.[14] This desire notwithstanding, the unique nature of countries such as China and Russia should not be overlooked. China, for example, differs from Western countries on many contextual variables, including culture, politics, and the precepts of its economic system.[15] The serious challenges these differences pose for Western competitive paradigms emphasize the need for global competitors to possess the skills to manage financial, economic, and political risks. Moreover, the vast percentage of U.S.-based companies' overseas business is in European markets. In addition, 60 percent of U.S. firms' assets that are located outside the domestic market are in Europe; and, two-thirds of all foreign R&D spending by U.S. affiliates takes place in Europe.[16] Therefore, companies seeking to internationalize their operations should also be aware of increased pressure for local country or regional responsiveness, especially where goods or services require customization because of cultural differences.[17] For example, with operations in 104 nations, McDonald's tailors its food products from country to country. In India, the McMaharajah, a mutton-based sandwich, replaces the Big Mac. Bolivian units sell McSaltenas as well as the standard U.S.-style offerings. The McSaltenas is a typical Andean dish of beef, potatoes, peas, and hot peppers, all encased in pastry.[18]

The frequent need for local repair and service is another factor influencing an increased desire for local country responsiveness. This localization may even affect industries that are seen as needing more global economies of scale such as white goods (e.g., refrigerators and other appliances.)[19] For large products, such as heavy earthmoving equipment, transportation costs become significant. Employment contracts and labor forces differ significantly. It is more difficult to negotiate employee layoffs in Europe than in the United States because of employment contract differences. Often host governments demand joint ownership, which allows the entering firm to avoid tariffs. Also, host governments frequently require a high percentage of local procurements, manufacturing, and R&D. These issues increase the need for local investment and responsiveness compared to seeking global economies of scale.

Given the traditional and emerging motivations for expanding into international markets, firms may achieve four basic opportunities through international diversification: increased market size; greater returns on major capital investments and/or investments in new product and process developments; greater economies of scale, scope, and/or learning; and/or a competitive advantage through location (e.g., access to low-cost labor, critical resources, or customers). These potential opportunities to enhance the firm's strategic competitiveness are examined relative to the costs incurred to pursue them and the managerial challenges that accompany both product and geographic international diversification decisions. Higher coordination expenses, a lack of familiarity with local cultures, and a lack of full access to knowledge about political influences in the host country are examples of costs firms incur when pursuing international diversification.[20]

Increased Market Size

Firms can expand the size of their potential market, sometimes dramatically, by moving into international markets. As part of its expansion efforts, Tupperware chose to market its storage containers in Russia. Sold initially in St. Petersburg, this strategic decision was based on market research indicating that the company's products appealed to Russian consumers. A company spokesperson noted, "With the large number of households and significant underemployment in Russia, we see this country as a great market opportunity and are investing time and training to build a strong sales force."[21]

To expand the size of its markets, Friday's Hospitality Worldwide Inc. is establishing its Friday's American Bar concept in major urban settings and airports throughout Europe and Asia. Geographic diversification is expected to be a major part of the company's growth. The company's CEO noted that his firm's different concepts, including the flagship TGI Friday's units, are very successful in countries outside the United States.[22] Frito-Lay plans to continue pursuing international growth opportunities through strategic acquisitions. Recently the firm purchased several snack food operations from United Biscuits Holdings PLC (this company is headquartered in the United Kingdom). Frito-Lay officials indicated that this acquisition improved the firm's European market position by giving it much needed production capacity.[23]

Following an international strategy is a particularly attractive option to firms competing in domestic markets that have limited growth opportunities. For example, the U.S. soft drink industry is relatively saturated. Most changes in market share for any single firm must come at the expense of competitors' share. Given this competitive reality, the two major soft drink manufacturers, Coca-Cola and PepsiCo, decided to enter international markets to take advantage of growth opportunities. Pepsi moved into the former Soviet Union years ago; later, Coke entered China. Originally, each firm obtained an exclusive franchise in those countries; today however, markets in Russia and China are more open. Coke has gained competitive parity and has now surpassed Pepsi in Russia. Beyond this, Coke's volume exceeds Pepsi's in Europe, Latin America, and Asia. In terms of overall volume, Coke outsells Pepsi almost three to one outside the United States. To combat this challenge and to increase its international market size, Pepsi is pushing hard in developing markets such as India and Indonesia where Coke is not entrenched completely. In an effort to use its resources wisely, Pepsi is lowering its market share expectations in Brazil and Japan, two countries in which Coke holds strong market positions. In discussing this decision, an analyst noted, "Pepsi is saying we'll be a profitable no. 2 in these two large markets."[24]

Across time, the competitive battle between these two giants seeking to increase the size of their served markets will continue to expand into product areas other than traditional soft drinks. Coke, for example, recently purchased the Orangina brand from Pernod Ricard of France. This acquisition gives Coke a new sparkling orange drink. A leading brand in France, Orangina had limited exposure in other European countries and small sales in the United States at the time of Coke's purchase. Coke executives believed that their company's global distribution system would result in significant sales increases for Orangina in Europe and other markets as well.[25] This acquisition demonstrates the belief of Coke's top-level managers that product and geographic diversification can enhance their firm's strategic competitiveness.

Return on Investment

Large markets may be crucial for earning a return on significant investments, such as plant and capital equipment and/or R&D. Therefore, most R&D-intensive industries are international. For example, the aerospace industry requires heavy investments to develop new aircraft. To recoup investments, aerospace firms may need to sell new aircraft in both domestic and international markets. This is the case for Boeing and Airbus Industrie. International sales are critical to the ability of each firm to earn satisfactory returns on its invested capital. In light of this reality, Boeing and Airbus are deciding how to allocate their production capacities to satisfy the major portion of demand projected for commercial jets between 1997 and 2006. During this time period, it is estimated that 2,460 jets can be sold in North America, 2,070 in Europe, 1,750 in the Asia/Pacific area, and another 1,100 in other countries throughout the world.[26] As these projected deliveries of commercial jets suggest, international sales are linked strongly to the strategic competitiveness of both Boeing and Airbus.

In addition to the need for a large market to recoup heavy investment in R&D, the development pace for new technology is increasing. As a result, new product obsolescence occurs more rapidly. Therefore, investments need to be recouped more quickly. Beyond this, firms' abilities to develop new technologies are expanding, and because of different patent laws across country borders, competitor imitation is more likely. Through reverse engineering, competitors are able to take apart a competitive product, learn the new technology, and develop a similar product that imitates the new technology (see Chapters 5 and 13). Because of competitors' abilities to do this relatively quickly, the need to recoup new product development costs rapidly is increasing. Therefore, the larger markets provided by international expansion are particularly attractive in many industries (e.g., computer hardware) because they expand the opportunity to recoup large capital investment and large-scale R&D expenditures.[27]

Economies of Scale and Learning

When firms expand their markets, they may be able to enjoy economies of scale, particularly in their manufacturing operations. Thus, to the extent that firms are able to standardize products across country borders and use the same or similar production facilities, coordinating critical resource functions, they are likely to achieve more optimal economic scale.[28] This is the goal of many firms in Europe as the common market continues to evolve. Sweden's Volvo, for example, has reduced its car manufacturing platforms from three to two. This action eliminated a costly indulgence for a relatively small manufacturer, and lowered the firm's break-even point through economies of scale.[29]

This is the case, too, for Korean automobile companies. By 2002, current plans call for Korea's five care manufacturers to increase their worldwide vehicle-making capacity by 60 percent. Other global automobile manufacturers criticized this expansionary decision. The essence of this criticism was that additional output by Korean car companies would contribute to an emerging glut in worldwide manufacturing capacity. In response, Korean automobile manufacturing executives indicated that they intended to develop additional capacity to gain the economies of scale required to compete effectively in the global marketplace.[30]

Firms may also be able to exploit core competencies across international markets. This allows resource and knowledge sharing between units across country borders.[31] It generates synergy and helps the firm produce higher quality goods or services at lower cost.

Location Advantages

Firms may locate facilities in other countries to lower the basic costs of the goods and/or services provided.[32] For example, they may have easier access to lower cost labor, energy, and other natural resources. Other location advantages include access to critical supplies/resources and to customers. Once positioned favorably through an attractive location, firms must manage their facilities effectively to gain the full benefit of a location advantage.[33]

Toyota, for example, may use one of its European facilities (in either Britain or France) to produce a new sporty car that is replacing the Tercel. Saying that the firm's goal is to ". . . get a car that gives young people goosebumps," Toyota executives indicated that the company would not abandon the entry-level youth market in spite of the seriousness of the competitive challenge from rival Honda's Civic line. A key location advantage associated with either one of these European sites is that Toyota could hold down the flow of imports to Europe from its Japanese facilities.[34] Ford Motor Company believes the initial success of its joint venture with Jiangling Motors in China gives it a location advantage relative to General Motors. Through this venture, Ford was the first of the two giant firms to actually produce a minibus in China. Ford executives are hopeful that first-mover advantages will result from this achievement.[35]

We have explored why international strategies may be important and some of their advantages. Next, we describe the types and content of international strategies that might be formulated and then implemented.

INTERNATIONAL STRATEGIES

An international strategy may be one of two basic types, business or corporate level. At the business level, firms follow generic strategy types: low cost, differentiation, focused low cost, focused differentiation, or integrated low cost/differentiation. At the corporate level, firms can formulate three types: multidomestic, global, or transnational (a combination of multidomestic and global). However, to create competitive advantage, each of these strategies must realize a core competence based on difficult to duplicate resources and capabilities.[36] As discussed in Chapters 4 and 6, the firm expects to create value through the implementation of a business-level and a corporate-level strategy.[37]

International Business-Level Strategy

Each business must develop a competitive strategy focused on its own domestic market. We discussed business-level generic strategies in Chapter 4 and competitive dynamics in Chapter 5. However, international business-level strategies have some unique features. In pursuing an international business-level strategy, the home country of operation is often the most important source of competitive advantage.[38] The resources and capabilities established in the home country often allow the firm to pursue the strategy beyond the national boundary. Michael Porter developed a model that describes the factors contributing to the advantage of firms in a dominant global industry and associated with a specific country or regional environment.[39] His model is illustrated in Figure 8.2.

FIGURE 8.2 ***Determinants of National Advantage***

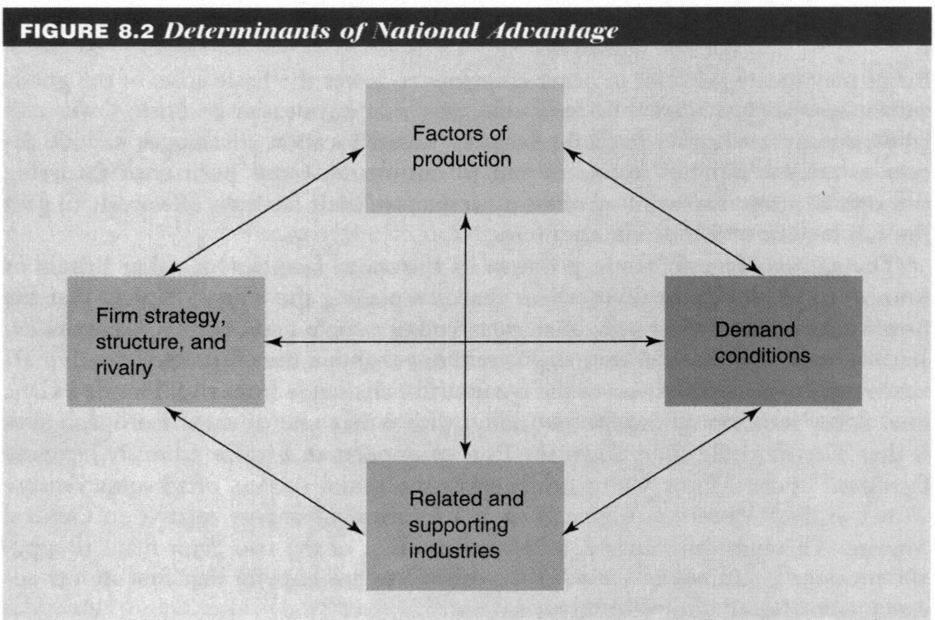

Source: Adapted and reprinted with the permission of The Free Press, an imprint of Simon & Schuster from *The Competitive Advantages of Nations* by Michael E. Porter, p. 72. Copyright © by Michael E. Porter.

The first dimension in the model, *factors of production*, refers to the inputs necessary to compete in any industry, such as labor, land, natural resources, capital, and infrastructure (e.g., highway, postal, and communication systems). Of course, there are basic (e.g, natural and labor resources) and advanced (e.g., digital communication systems and highly educated workforces) factors. There are also generalized (highway systems, supply of debt capital) and specialized factors (skilled personnel in a specific industry, such as a port that specializes in handling bulk chemicals). If a country has both advanced and specialized production factors, it is likely that this will serve an industry well in spawning strong home-country competitors that can become successful global competitors. Ironically, countries often develop advanced and specialized factor capabilities because they lack critical basic resources. Some Asian countries, such as Korea, lack abundant natural resources, but the strong work ethic, the large number of engineers, and the systems of large firms have created an expertise in manufacturing. Germany developed a strong chemical industry, partially because Hoechst and BASF spent years developing a synthetic indigo dye to reduce their dependence on imports. This was not the case in Britain because large supplies of natural indigo were available in the colonies.[40]

The second dimension, *demand conditions*, is characterized by the nature and size of the buyers' needs in the home market for the industry's goods or services. The sheer size of a sales segment could produce the demand necessary to create scale-efficient facilities. This efficiency could also lead to domination of the industry in other countries. However, specialized demand may also create opportunities beyond national boundaries. For example, Swiss firms have long led the world in tunneling equipment because of the need to tunnel through mountains for rail and highway passage. Japanese firms have created a niche market for compact, quiet air conditioner units. Small, but quiet units are required in Japan because homes are often small and packed together tightly. Under these conditions, large, noisy units would be unacceptable.[41]

Related and supporting industries is the third dimension in the model. Italy has become the leader in the shoe industry because of related and supporting industries. The leather supplies necessary to build shoes are furnished by a well-established industry in leather processing. Also, many people travel to Italy to purchase leather goods. Thus, there is support in distribution. In addition, supporting industries in leather-working machinery and design services contribute to the success of the shoe industry. In fact, the design services industry supports many related industries, such as ski boots, fashion apparel, and furniture. In Japan, cameras and copiers have been related industries. In Denmark, the dairy products industry is related to an industry focused on food enzymes.

Firm strategy, structure, and rivalry, the final country dimension, also fosters the growth of certain industries. The pattern of firm strategy, structure, and rivalry among firms varies greatly from nation to nation. Earlier, much attention was placed on examining U.S. enterprise managers; more recently, the Japanese have been scrutinized and emulated. In Germany, because of the excellent technical training system, there is a strong inclination toward methodological product and process improvement. In Japan, unusual cooperative and competitive systems have facilitated cross-functional management of complex assembly operations. In Italy, the national pride of its designers has spawned strong industries in sports cars, fashion apparel, and furniture. In the United States, competition among computer manufacturers and software producers has favored the development of these industries.

The four basic dimensions of the "diamond" model shown in Figure 8.2 emphasize the environmental or structural attributes of a national economy that may contribute to national advantage. One could therefore conclude that chance or luck has led to the competitive advantage of individual firms in these industries. To a degree this is true, but government policy also had contributed to the success and failure of firms and industries. This is certainly the case in Japan, where the Ministry of International Trade and Investment (MITI) has contributed significantly to the corporate strategies followed. Nevertheless, each firm must create its own success. Not all firms have survived to become global competitors, given the same country factors that spawned the successful firms. Therefore, the actual strategic choices managers make may be the most compelling reason for success or failure. The factors illustrated in Figure 8.2, therefore, are likely to lead to competitive advantages for a firm only when an appropriate strategy is applied, taking advantage of distinct country factors. We therefore reiterate examples of the low-cost, differentiation, focused low-cost, focused differentiation, and integrated low-cost/differentiation generic strategies that are discussed in Chapter 4.

International Low-Cost Strategy The international low-cost strategy is likely to develop in a country with a large demand. Usually the operations of such an industry are centralized in a home country, and obtaining economies of scale is the primary goal. Outsourcing of low value-added operations may take place, but high value-added operations are retained in the home country. As such, products are often exported from the home country.

As explained in the Strategic Focus, certain global air carriers are seeking strategic competitiveness through use of the international low-cost strategy. Through a variety of entry modes (entry modes are discussed in detail later in the chapter), Wal-Mart, too, follows this strategy as it continues to globalize its operations.

STRATEGIC FOCUS

Air Service and Discount Retailing: Achieving Strategic Competitiveness by Using the International Low-Cost Strategy

EasyJet is a London-based low-cost airline that was founded after the liberalization of the European Union (EU) aviation market. The market's liberalization permits European airlines to begin services anywhere in the EU without obtaining government permission. This company has modeled its operations after U.S. low-fare carriers such as Southwest Airlines. Along with others using the international low-cost strategy, including Ryanair and Debonair, EasyJet's business practices have resulted in lower airfares in the United Kingdom and Ireland. One reason for the companies' initial success is the inducement their low fares create for previous nonflyers to use their services. Brussels-based Virgin Express, a part of Richard Branson's group, is achieving the same outcomes in continental Europe.

The low-cost airlines claim that a large percentage of their customers are business travelers. The fares offered to these people are enticing. Recently, for example, Ryanair sold tickets for a one-way trip from London to Glasgow for nine pounds (before tax). Customers are promised safe passage, but little else is provided. Most do not serve meals. Passengers wanting something to drink must pay for the product. These practices, as well as others, are followed to drive costs lower.

To reduce its costs of servicing a plane once it is on the ground and to turn units around quicker for departures, Ryanair discontinued carrying cargo. With less loading and unloading to complete, aircraft are now turned around in 20 minutes. Ryanair offers no frills and a single class of seating. The essence of the firm's low-cost strategy is captured by the following statement by Michael O'Leary, the firm's CEO: "We said that we're not going to feed you or put you up in hotels or give you frequent flyer points or any of that rubbish." To reduce its maintenance and staff costs, Ryanair flies only one type of aircraft—the Boeing 737-200. Moreover, the firm operates from secondary airports. In London, for example, it uses Stansted and Luton rather than Gatwick or Heathrow. To reduce yet another cost, Ryanair's CEO informed travel agents that his firm would pay a seven and one-half percent commission instead of the industry standard of 9 percent. Ryanair is expanding its market coverage. It now offers flights between the British Isles and continental Europe, Dublin and Paris and Dublin and Brussels, and from London to Stockholm and to Oslo. The firm is also negotiating with airports in eight additional European countries to establish more routes.

The essence of Wal-Mart's international low-cost strategy is demonstrated by founder Sam Walton's words: "We'll lower the cost of living for everyone, not just in America." One of the keys to implementing its low-cost strategy, both domestically and internationally, is the firm's advanced retail technology. This technology enables Wal-Mart to have the correct quantities of goods in the appropriate place at the right time while minimizing inventory costs. The latest variation of this sophisticated system has employees carrying hand-held computers that allow them to reorder merchandise. Simultaneously, backroom computers link each store with a sophisticated satellite system.

Wal-Mart started to internationalize its operations in 1991. Since then, the firm has already become the largest retailer in Canada (144 stores) and Mexico (396 stores). Wal-Mart also operates eight stores in Argentina, two in Brazil, three in China, and two in Indonesia through joint ventures. To continue diversifying internationally, Wal-Mart decided to enter the European market. This process was started with the purchase of the Wertkauf hypermarket company from Germany's Mann family. Suggesting that no German retailer was capable of matching Wal-Mart's logistics core competency, analysts viewed Wal-Mart's movement into Germany positively. The challenge to Wal-Mart in Germany is to gain quickly the volume it requires for its international low-cost strategy to be effective. Combining its volume with the firm's logistics skills and merchandising savvy may yield the combination required for Wal-Mart to achieve strategic competitiveness in Germany and perhaps the European market in general.

SOURCE: L. Lee, 1998, Wal-Mart net rose 17% in quarter, fueling optimism, *Wall Street Journal*, February 19, B2; M. Skapinker, 1997, Cut to the bone . . . fares, service and turnaround, *Financial Times*, November 20, VII; M. Skapinker, 1997, No-frills airlines travelling on a wing and a fear, *Financial Times*, November 20, VI; Sam's Travels, 1997, *Financial Times*, December 19, 13; R. Tomkins, 1997, Wal-Mart comes shopping in Europe, *Financial Times*, December 21, 23; R. Tomkins, 1997, Wal-Mart enters Europe, *Financial Times*, December 19, 15.

As the Strategic Focus discussion suggests, using the international low-cost strategy to diversify their operations may be reasonable strategic choices for several of Europe's no-frills airlines and for Wal-Mart. In fact, some analysts do believe Wal-Mart should aggressively pursue international growth opportunities using its low-cost strategy to further enhance its strategic competitiveness.[42]

For all of these firms, there are risks associated with implementing the international low-cost strategy. The airline companies, for example, may face competition from their larger and better-resourced competitors. Recently EasyJet found itself engaged in a pricing battle with KLM, the Dutch airline. This competition evolved when EasyJet starting flying from its base at Luton airport, near London, to Shiphol airport in Amsterdam. British Airways and Germany's Lufthansa are both considering starting their own low-cost companies to compete against Debonair and Ryanair.[43]

A major risk for Wal-Mart is that it may not learn quickly how to compete successfully in what is seen to be Europe's unique retailing environment. Does Wal-Mart have the confidence it needs to make small adjustments to satisfy local tastes while maintaining the discipline required to drive costs lower on a continuous basis? Will first German and then other European retailers retain their customers by learning how to create value either through differentiation strategies or by driving their costs lower relative to Wal-Mart's? These issues pose strategic challenges to Wal-Mart's executives; but, the fact that the company hopes to generate one-third of its profit growth annually through international sales suggests its intentions in Europe and other world markets.[44]

International Differentiation Strategy A country with advanced and specialized factor endowments is likely to develop an international differentiation strategy. Germany has a number of world-class chemical firms. The differentiation strategy followed by many of these firms to develop specialized chemicals was possible because of the factor conditions surrounding the development of this industry. The Kaiser Wilhelm (late Max Planck) Institutes and university chemistry programs were superior in research and produced the best chemistry education in the world. Also, Germany's emphasis on vocational education fostered strong apprenticeship programs for workers.[45] Today, German companies competing in retailing consumer goods are learning how to improve their service to battle against competitors (e.g., Lands' End and Marks & Spencer) who are implementing their international differentiation strategies in Germany.[46]

The Japanese capabilities in consumer electronics have given them an advantage in memory chips and integrated circuits, the basic components in this industry. However, differentiation by Sharp Corporation, a Japanese electronics firm, has given it the lead in liquid crystal displays (LCDs), which are used with laptop computer and camcorders.[47] Alternatively, the United States is the leader in logic chips, the main components of computers, telecommunications equipment, and defense electronics. Intel is the world's leading producer of computer logic chips, and its products are differentiated worldwide by the slogan "Intel inside."

International Focus Strategies Many firms remain focused on small market niches as they pursue international focus strategies.[48] The ceramic tile industry in Italy contains a number of medium and small fragmented firms that produce approximately 50 percent of the world's tile.[49] These tile firms, clustered in the Sassuolo area of Italy, have formed a number of different focus strategies. Firms such as Marazzi, Iris, Cisa-Cerdisa, and Flor Gres invest heavily in technology to improve product quality, aesthetics, and productivity. These firms have close relationships with equipment manufacturers. They tend to emphasize the focused low-cost strategy, while maintaining a quality image. Another group, including Piemme and Atlas Concorde, attempts to compete more on image and design. Firms in this group invest heavily in advertising and showroom expositions. Because they try to appeal to selected customer tastes, they emphasize the focused differentiation strategy.[50]

Other uses of the international focus strategy are described in the Strategic Focus. While reading these materials, notice each firm's intent to serve exceptionally well a particular need of a particular market segment.

STRATEGIC FOCUS

Focusing Internationally on Specific Market Segments

Volvo earns 70 percent of its sales revenue from manufacturing and selling cars and trucks (other businesses include construction equipment and marine engines). To reverse the firm's recent declines, the CEO initiated a new product development drive to put cars on a more stable footing and to expand trucks globally. The two competitive advantages on which Volvo's automobiles have been sold are product security (safety) and reliability.

New cars are being manufactured for what the firms calls "niche customers." Two new models were introduced in 1998. Sharing a common platform, one product introduction was a replacement for the aging 900 series; the second was a smaller successor to the S70 and V70 cars. In describing the firm's new design philosophy, the CEO explained, "We are defining lifestyle segments and trying to shoot off sharply designed products based on a few basic platforms." Aware of the global challenge facing his small firm, the CEO notes that Volvo is interested in following a niche strategy that allows it to capture 10 percent to 15 percent of its chosen markets.

The efficiency of the highly capitalized domestic institutions, coupled with their large branch networks and use of high quality, sophisticated technologies, creates a retail banking environment in Spain in which it is difficult for foreign firms to compete successfully. Because of the domestic banks' competitive advantages, foreign rivals now concentrate on niche activities. Chase Manhattan, for example, focuses on a range of niches including corporate finance, capital markets and derivatives businesses, and peseta clearing activities. Chase's recent performance based on its international focus strategy in Spain is impressive—a return on earnings of 23 percent and a return on assets of 5.9 percent.

Because of what they envision as significant growth potential in terms of mutual and pension funds, U.K.-based Barclays and U.S.-based Citibank are focusing on the private banking sector. Citibank has converted the 83 branches it operates in Spain into product advisory centers. In each location, customers have access to computer systems that help them determine their desired risk levels; once known, a set of investment alternatives is recommended. As is the case for Citibank, Barclays has ". . . scaled back its retail operations in Spain, concentrated on the big cities and focused on asset management of medium to big private accounts according to a carefully elaborated segmentation of potential clients." Barclays operates 180 branches as it competes against Citibank and others to serve the unique needs of the private banking market segment.

Denizli, Turkey, has a long history as a town with multiple textiles manufacturing facilities. The town and its new factories are an example of the success being achieved as a result of recent Turkish industrial modernization efforts.

Denizli's factories specialize in the manufacture of towels, sheets, and garments. In the past, however, these facilities concentrated on selling their output to domestic markets. Now, many of the town's textile companies are looking abroad to sell goods to the lucrative but demanding consumer outlets of Western Europe and the United States. This expansion into global markets with niche textile products is being helped by bank support and state encouragement.

Nesa Textiles is one of Denizli's factories that is striving to compete globally. Through a substantial investment program, Nesa has acquired high technology machinery that it uses to weave, dye, and prepare bath towels and gowns—the firm's primary products. Nesa's focus is on the manufacture of products that are targeted to the high quality, high value market segment. The firm's modern technology permits the focus. Nesa's marketing manager believes that the success of Denizli's textile factories make it impossible for them to compete on a low-cost basis with countries, such as Pakistan and Indonesia, where manufacturing expenses, including labor costs, are much lower. (As mentioned earlier in this chapter, Turkey's overall wage rates are quite low, but in Denizli's textile factories the wage rates exceed the country's average by quite a margin.) With an MBA from Izmir University and fluency in three foreign languages, Nesa's marketing manager is confident of his firm's success as well as the success of other Turkish firms. This confidence is suggested by the following comment: "You in Western Europe will have to watch out, the Anatolian tiger is coming."

In 1990, Western companies such as Smirnoff's owner Diageo PLC of Britain and Absolut's V&S Vin & Spirit AB of Sweden expressed high hopes for the success of their vodka products in Russia. With famous brand names and well-honed marketing skills, these firms anticipated being able to sell their products to a consumer segment that was willing to pay for a product that was differentiated from local vodkas. Thus, these companies intended to follow the international focused differentiation strategy to compete in the Russian market.

To date, these firms' performances are disappointing. With a combined market share of less than 1 percent, they are discovering that the segment of the market willing to trade up to Western brands and to pay a higher price for the opportunity to do so is apparently quite small. Moreover, Russia's private and state vodka producers are challenging Western producers' differentiation strategy as they introduce new niche brands into the market and hawk them with clever, eye-catching packaging and advertising campaigns.

SOURCE: E. Beck, 1998, Why foreign distillers find it so hard to sell vodka to the Russians, *Wall Street Journal*, January 15, A1, A9; T. Burns, 1997, Niche goals bring away results, *Financial Times*, November 17, II; H. Simonian, 1997, Volvo's lights burn brighter, *Financial Times*, December 9, 17; R. Taylor, 1997, Global markets beckon for old weaving centre, *Financial Times*, December 12, VI.

International Integrated Low-Cost/Differentiation Strategy The integrated strategy has become more popular because of flexible manufacturing systems, improved information networks within and across firms, and total quality management systems (see Chapter 4). Because of the wide diversity of markets and competitors, following an integrated strategy may be the most effective in global markets.[51] Therefore, competing in global markets requires sophisticated and effective management.[52] Komatsu illustrates a classic case where this strategy was well executed. Komatsu was able to gain on a strong competitor, Caterpillar, by pursuing the integrated low-cost/differentiation strategy. Caterpillar had a very strong brand image in world markets, but Komatsu was able to overcome this differentiation advantage by improving its image and reducing its costs. It was initially able to do this because of lower labor costs and steel prices. Furthermore, in the 1970s, the dollar was strong, and this allowed a successful export strategy. Although Komatsu has remained very competitive, it faces critical challenges today due to the competitive actions being taken by Caterpillar.[53] Some of the competitive actions and competitive responses occurring between Caterpillar and Komatsu were considered in a Strategic Focus in Chapter 5.

International Corporate-Level Strategy

The business-level strategies discussed previously depend, to a degree, on the type of international corporate-level strategy the firm is following. Some corporate strategies give individual country units the authority to develop their own strategies; other corporate strategies require that country business-level strategies be compromised because of dictates from the home office to accomplish standardization of products and sharing of resources across countries. International corporate-level strategy is distinguished from international business-level strategy by the scope of the operations in both product and geographic diversification. International corporate-level strategy is required when the level of product complexity increases to multiple industries and multiple countries or regions.[54] Corporate strategy is guided by headquarters, rather than by business or country managers. The three international corporate-level strategies are shown in Figure 8.3.

A **multidomestic strategy** is one in which strategic and operating decisions are decentralized to the strategic business unit in each country in order to tailor products to the local market.

Multidomestic Strategy A **multidomestic strategy** is one in which strategic and operating decisions are decentralized to the strategic business unit in each country in order to tailor products to the local market.[55] A multidomestic strategy focuses on competition within each country. It assumes that the markets differ and

FIGURE 8.3 *International Corporate-Level Strategies*

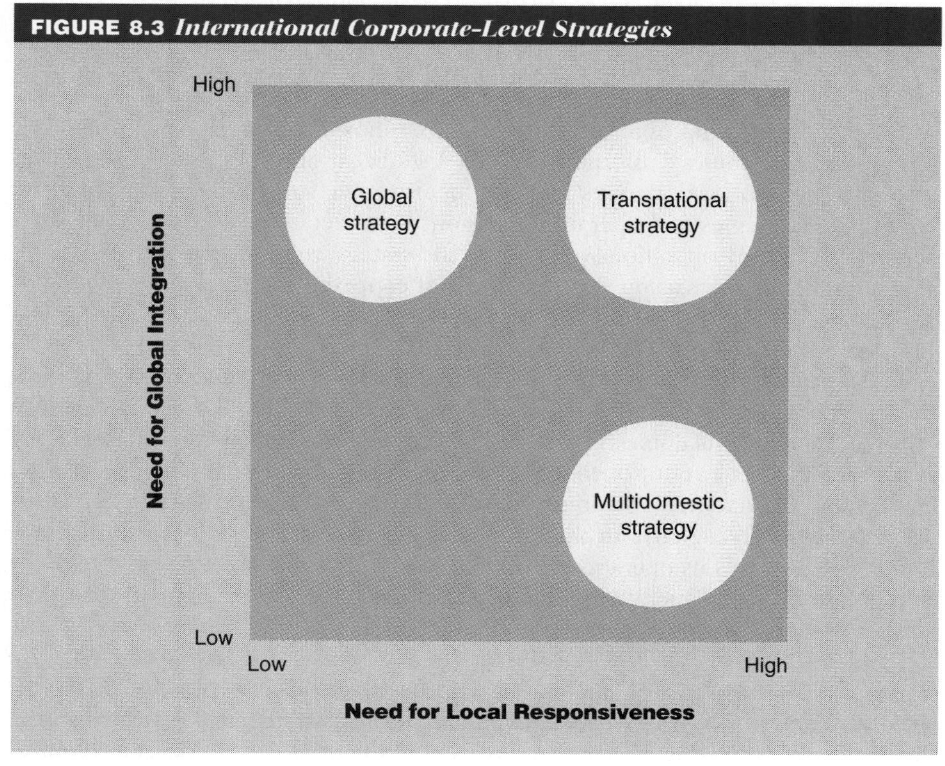

A **global strategy** is one in which standardized products are offered across country markets and competitive strategy is dictated by the home office.

therefore are segmented by country boundaries. In other words, consumer needs and desires, industry conditions (e.g., number and type of competitors), political and legal structures, and social norms vary by country. Multidomestic strategies allow for the customization of products to meet the specific needs and preferences of local customers. Therefore, they should be able to maximize competitive response to the idiosyncratic requirements of each market. However, multidomestic strategies do not allow for the achievement of economies of scale and thus can be more costly. As a result, firms employing a multidomestic strategy decentralize strategic and operating decisions to the business units operating in each country. The multidomestic strategy has been more prominent among European multinational firms because of the varieties of cultures and markets found in Europe.

Owning some of the world's best known food brands (e.g., Knorr soups and sauces, Hellmann's salad dressings, Skippy peanut butter, and Entenmann's baked goods), Bestfoods follows the multidomestic strategy. The company is organized around three worldwide businesses. To implement the multidomestic strategy, Bestfoods' managers are given a great deal of autonomy to adapt products to local tastes. This is necessary, says the firm's CEO, because food brands have geographical limitations. An example of these limitations is suggested by the following comment from the CEO: "The day I teach Americans to eat Marmite will be the day I teach the French to eat peanut butter."[56] (Marmite is a thick, dark, spread that is a staple of the national diet in Britain).

Global Strategy Alternatively, a global strategy assumes more standardization of products across country markets.[57] As a result, competitive strategy is centralized and controlled by the home office. The strategic business units operating in each country are assumed to be interdependent, and the home office attempts to achieve integration across these businesses. Therefore, a **global strategy** is one in which standardized products are offered across country markets and competitive strategy is dictated by the home office. Thus, a global strategy emphasizes economies of scale and offers greater opportunities to utilize innovations developed at the home office or in one country in other markets. A global strategy, however, often lacks responsiveness to local markets and is difficult to manage because of the need to coordinate strategies and operating decisions across country borders. Therefore, achieving efficient operations with a global strategy requires the sharing of resources and an emphasis on coordination and cooperation across country boundaries. This requires more centralization and central headquarters control. The Japanese have often pursued this strategy with success.[58]

CMS Energy is the fourth largest integrated utility in the United States. Over the last several years, CMS has spent approximately $3 billion to become involved in projects outside its domestic market (current projects include ones in Argentina and Morocco). As a result of these investments, 25 percent of the firm's earnings come from international operations. The CEO wants this percentage to be at least 50 percent by 2002. Active in the entire energy chain, from wellhead to the end-user, CMS controls its operations from its Detroit, Michigan, home office. Across time, CMS hopes to operate in a total of between six and nine countries as it provides standardized products through implementation of the global strategy.[59]

Transnational Strategy A **transnational strategy** is a corporate-level strategy that seeks to achieve both global efficiency and local responsiveness. Realizing the diverse goals of the transnational strategy is difficult because one goal requires close global coordination, while the other requires local flexibility. Thus, "flexible coordination" is required to implement the transnational strategy.[60] It requires building a shared vision and individual commitment through an integrated network. In reality, it is difficult to achieve a pure transnational strategy because of the conflicting goals.

A **transnational strategy** is a corporate-level strategy that seeks to achieve both global efficiency and local responsiveness.

Examples of firms following the transnational strategy are presented in the Strategic Focus. Notice that each of these firms is attempting the difficult task of simultaneously achieving the benefits of global efficiency and local responsiveness.

STRATEGIC FOCUS

Using the Transnational Strategy as a Pathway to Strategic Competitiveness

Headquartered in Switzerland, Nestlé is the world's largest food company. Well over two-thirds of the firm's sales revenue is earned outside its domestic market. Nestlé operates almost 500 factories and employs approximately 225,000 people worldwide. The company produces more than 8,500 products that are sold in more than 100 countries. Decentralization is important to how Nestlé's conducts business. In fact, the firm notes that its policy is ". . . to adapt as much as possible to local customs and circumstances while allowing decisions about products, marketing and personnel to be made at the local level." Simultaneously, however, efforts are undertaken at the corporate office to introduce as many efficiencies as possible across Nestlé's widely dispersed product operations.

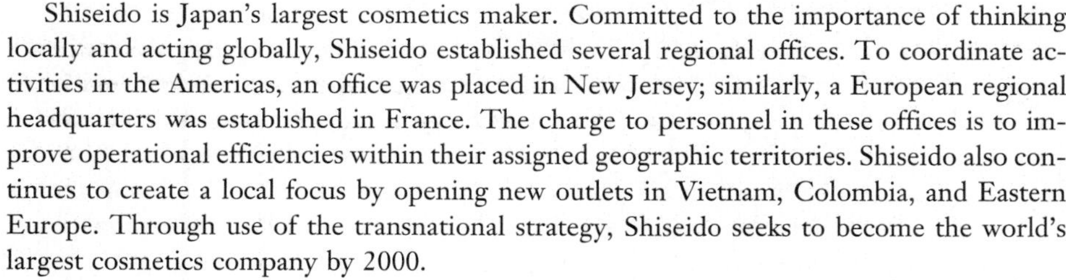

Shiseido is Japan's largest cosmetics maker. Committed to the importance of thinking locally and acting globally, Shiseido established several regional offices. To coordinate activities in the Americas, an office was placed in New Jersey; similarly, a European regional headquarters was established in France. The charge to personnel in these offices is to improve operational efficiencies within their assigned geographic territories. Shiseido also continues to create a local focus by opening new outlets in Vietnam, Colombia, and Eastern Europe. Through use of the transnational strategy, Shiseido seeks to become the world's largest cosmetics company by 2000.

GE is using what it calls a "smart bomb" strategy to design, manufacture, and sell appliances. In essence, this strategy, one that GE top-level managers believe allows them to manage markets rather than factories, proceeds as follows: "GE executives examine each country's idiosyncrasies microscopically, then tailor a mix of products, brands, manufacturing facilities, marketing, and retail approaches to wring the best performance from each. They measure factors such as the quality and strength of local competitors, the market's growth potential, and the availability of skilled labor. Their unyielding goal: to generate the handsomest returns possible on the smallest investment possible." Complementing the efforts to satisfy unique local needs is a commitment to derive the greatest number of economies of scale as possible from the firm's various manufacturing facilities. Additionally, once discovered, innovations are applied across GE's various Asian factories.

Results obtained in Asia from these actions continue to be impressive. For example, appliance sales are growing at a 12 percent annual rate. Although used initially in GE's appliance businesses in Asia, smart bombing is now sweeping across all of GE's other business units. Thus, GE appears to be moving toward use of the transnational strategy in many if not all of its strategic business units as it seeks to become even more competitive internationally.

The Thomson Corporation is widely diversified in terms of both products and geographic areas. The company is involved in over 350 businesses or product lines; its products are sold in over 200 countries. Thomson's principal business focus, however, is specialized information and publishing. These activities are directed at participants in its core markets of regulatory, financial services, higher education, scientific, technical and medical/healthcare, and reference.

In the pursuit of strategic competitiveness and above-average returns, Thomson remains committed to a decentralized organizational structure. This structure, executives believe, allows business unit decision makers to offer customers products that satisfy their unique tastes. Accompanying this structure, however, are rigorous financial controls and operating criteria. Thomson's headquarters personnel use these controls to increase the efficiency of each operating unit. The performance criteria influence the selection of businesses to add to the firm's corporate portfolio (Thomson pursues growth and diversification through an acquisition strategy) and determine when an individual unit's performance warrants divestiture. Thus, Thomson also uses the transnational strategy to achieve both global efficiency and local responsiveness.

SOURCE: S. P. Khu, 1998, Thomson plans $2.5bn listing for travel arm, *Financial Times*, March 19, 15; Nestlé Home Page, 1998, February 8, http://www.nestle.com; The Thomson Corporation Home Page, 1998, February 8, http://www.thomcorp.com; L. Grant, 1997, GE's 'smart bomb' strategy, *Fortune*, July 21, 109–110; Shiseido to launch new brand, *Financial Times*, February 20, 29; Shiseido, 1997, *Fortune* (Special Advertising Section), August 4, S–39.

ENVIRONMENTAL TRENDS

Although the transnational strategy is difficult to implement, emphasis on the need for global efficiency is increasing as more industries begin to experience global competition as well as an increased emphasis on local requirements. Moreover, as discussion in the Strategic Focus suggested, global goods and services often require some customization to meet government regulations within particular countries or to fit customer tastes and preferences. In addition, most multinational firms desire to achieve some coordination and sharing of resources across country markets to hold down costs. Furthermore, some products and industries may be better suited for standardization across country borders than others. As a result, most large multinational firms with diverse products may employ a partial multidomestic strategy with certain product lines and global strategies with others. This may be the case with GE's smart bomb strategy. Because the strategy is intended to satisfy the unique appliance needs of different groups of Asian customers, it possesses some of the characteristics of a multidomestic strategy. In addition, though, central headquarters personnel are establishing operational guidelines to pursue economies of scale and a limited degree of standardization across products.

Regionalization

Regionalization in world markets is becoming more common. Location can affect a firm's strategic competitiveness.[61] Firms must decide whether to compete in all (or many) world markets or to focus on a particular region(s).[62] The advantage of attempting to compete in all markets relates to the economies that can be achieved because of the combined market size. However, if the firm is competing in industries where the international markets differ greatly (e.g., it must employ a multidomestic strategy), it may wish to narrow its focus to a particular region of the world. In so doing, it can better understand the cultures, legal and social norms, and other factors important for effective competition in those markets. Therefore, a firm may focus on Far East markets only, rather than attempting to compete in the Middle East, Europe, and the Far East. It may choose a region of the world where the markets are more similar and thus some coordination and sharing of resources would be possible. In this way, the firm may be able not only to understand the markets better, but also to achieve some economies, even though it may have to employ a multidomestic strategy.

Sometimes, however, regional opportunities surface unexpectedly for companies carefully analyzing their external environments (see Chapter 2). Based in Houston, Texas, Service Corporation International (SCI) is the world's largest undertaker (annual revenues exceed $2.3 billion). Recently the firm identified an opportunity in Germany's funeral industry. Specifically, SCI observed that approximately 95 percent of Germany's 4,500 undertakers are small, family-run businesses (discussed further in Chapter 9, Germany's business economy has long been dominated by small family firms). Because of size constraints, these companies typically do not offer services such as helping relatives arrange for flowers and the purchase of a headstone and a cemetery plot. In contrast, SCI provides customers with a one-stop shopping option, flexible hours, and amenities (e.g., an optional photographer). Even with these additional services, SCI's prices are competitive with the average $5,000 cost of a German funeral. SCI entered the German market in 1995 to pursue this opportunity. To date, the firm has purchased all or parts of 15 funeral homes located in major German cities. With sales exceeding $8 million annually, SCI is committed to further extending its operations in Germany.[63] Seeking to be competitive on a global basis, SCI also has operations in Britain, Canada, and France.

Regional strategies may be promoted by countries that develop trade agreements to increase the economic power of a region. The European Community (EC) and the Organization of American States (OAS, South America) are collections of countries that developed trade agreements to promote the flow of trade across country boundaries within the region.[64] For example, many European firms have been acquiring and integrating their businesses in Europe to better rationalize pan-European brands as the EC creates more unity in European markets. The North American Free Trade Agreement (NAFTA), signed by the United States, Canada, and Mexico, is designed to facilitate free trade across country borders in North America and may be expanded to include other countries in South America, such as Argentina, Brazil, and Chile.[65] These agreements loosen restrictions on international strategies within a region and provide greater opportunity to realize the advantages of international strategies. NAFTA does not exist for the sole purpose of U.S. businesses going north and south. Bernardo Dominguez, a Mexican businessman, arranged to purchase Westin Hotels Group in North America, South America, and Europe for $708 million for Aoki Corp. of Japan.[66] Also, Cementos de Mexico (CEMEX), the largest cement company in Mexico, has been buying cement makers in Spain and Venezuela as well as in the southwestern United States to extend its market share after the NAFTA agreement was confirmed. Anticipating entry by foreign competitors into Mexico, CEMEX is readying itself to compete globally, especially in emerging markets. For instance, it is stepping up exports to Asia. It received orders for 2 million tons of cement in 1995 from Taiwan, Thailand, and Indonesia.[67]

NAFTA, signed by the United States, Canada, and Mexico, was designed to facilitate free trade across North American borders. It gives firms the opportunity to realize the advantages of international strategies, as evidenced by Pennzoil's automotive business in Guadalajara, Mexico.

After firms decide on their international strategies and whether to employ them in regional or world markets, they must decide how to accomplish such international expansion.[68] Therefore, the next section discusses how to enter new international markets.

CHOICE OF INTERNATIONAL ENTRY MODE

International expansion is accomplished through exporting, licensing, strategic alliances, acquisitions, and establishing new wholly owned subsidiaries. These means of entering international markets and their characteristics are shown in Table 8.1. Each has its advantages and disadvantages as described in the following subsections.

TABLE 8.1 ***Global Market Entry: Choice of Entry Mode***

Type of Entry	**Characteristics**
Exporting	high cost, low control
Licensing	low cost, low risk, little control, low returns
Strategic alliances	Shared costs, shared resources, shared risks, problems of integration (e.g., two corporate cultures)
Acquisition	Quick access to new market, high cost, complex negotiations, problems of merging with domestic operations
New wholly owned subsidiary	Complex, often costly, time consuming, high risk, maximum control, potential above-average returns

Exporting

Many industrial firms initially begin international expansion by exporting their goods or services to other countries.[69] Exporting does not require the expense of establishing operations in the host countries, but exporters must establish some means of marketing and distributing their products. In so doing, exporting firms must develop contractual arrangements with host country firms. Its disadvantages include the often high costs of transportation and possible tariffs placed on incoming goods. Furthermore, the exporter has less control over the marketing and distribution of its products in the host country and must pay the distributor and/or allow the distributor to add to the price to recoup its costs and make a profit. As a result, it may be difficult to market a competitive product through exporting or to provide a product that is customized to each international market through exporting.

Historically, Japanese firms have succesfully used exporting as an international entry mode. This is the case for Canon, a world leader in imaging and information technology. The firm began in 1937 as a producer of high-quality cameras. At that time, Canon's products were relatively expensive for consumers in its domestic market. This situation, according to current president Fujio Mitarai, forced the firm to learn how to compete internationally. Thus, almost from its founding, Canon has used exporting as a mode of entry to multiple global markets.[70]

As the 1990s come to a close, the number of Japanese firms interested in exporting their products to different countries, but especially to the United States, is increasing. Declining domestic demand is significantly influencing this interest, as is the devaluation of Japan's currency. For instance, Rheon Automatic Machinery, a manufacturer of pastry-making machines, seeks to triple exports to the United States by 2000. Suffering from a softening in demand for its products in Japan, the firm's general manager also observes that the "U.S. market is huge and we can't afford not to be there." The managers at plastics producer Iris Ohyama felt that they faced a simple choice in 1994—export or die. Increased domestic competition, coupled with the nation's then-weakened economy, caused company executives to conclude that additional sales of its flower pots, storage containers, and garbage bins in Japan, its only market, were problematic. A decision was reached to export extensively, particularly to North America. Building on the success of its exporting entry mode, the firm soon established two American factories. These facilities now generate all of the company's U.S. sales, which today, account for 10 percent of total revenue.[71]

Licensing

A licensing arrangement allows a foreign firm to purchase the right to manufacture and sell the firm's products within a host country or set of countries.[72] The licenser is normally paid a royalty on each unit produced and sold. The licensee takes the risks and makes the monetary investments in facilities for manufacturing, marketing, and distributing the goods or services. As a result, licensing is possibly the least costly form of international expansion.

Licensing is also a way to expand returns based on previous innovations. For instance, Sony and Philips codesigned the audio CD. In 1994, makers of CDs and CD-ROM players and disks generated $50 billion in revenues. Sony and Philips collected 5 cents for every CD sold.[73] As the Sony–Philips example demonstrates, many firms can stand on the shoulders of their past innovations. Continual focus on research and patent licensing allows a firm to gain strong returns from its innovations for many years in the future.[74]

Today, however, the returns to Sony and Philips from CD sales are threatened somewhat. Knockoff disks, which are cheap counterfeits of original products, are a growth business. Sales of counterfeit disks in China alone are estimated to exceed $1 billion annually. Interestingly, technological advances are contributing to the severity of the problem. In fact, innovation makes it easier for counterfeiters to improvise. Pressing machinery used to manufacture disks is so advanced and compact in size that it can be operated in the smallest of quarters. Located commonly in housing tenements, it is difficult for officials to find counterfeiters' production lines. Corporations are seeking legal remedies to their situation but with limited success to date.[75]

Of course, licensing has its disadvantages. For example, this approach to international expansion provides the firm very little control over the manufacture and marketing of its products in other countries. In addition, licensing provides the least potential returns because returns must be shared between the licenser and the licensee. The international firm may learn the technology and, after the license expires, produce and sell a similar competitive product. Komatsu, for example, first licensed much of its technology from U.S. companies International Harvester, Bucyrus-Erie, and Cummins Engine to enter the earthmoving equipment business to compete against Caterpillar. It subsequently dropped these licenses and developed its own products using the technology it gained from the U.S. companies.[76]

Strategic Alliances

Strategic alliances have enjoyed popularity in recent years as a primary means of international expansion.[77] Strategic alliances allow firms to share the risks and the resources required to enter international markets.[78] Moreover, alliances can facilitate the development of new core competencies that can contribute to the firm's future strategic competitiveness.[79] In addition, most strategic alliances are with a host country firm that has knowledge of the competitive conditions, legal and social norms, and cultural idiosyncrasies that should help the firm manufacture and market a competitive product. Alternatively, the host firm may find access to technology and new products attractive. Therefore, each partner in an alliance brings knowledge and/or resources to the partnership.[80]

Ford Motor Company has joined an alliance that existed previously between Germany's Daimler-Benz AG and Canada's Ballard Power Systems. This new and larger alliance, between two manufacturers and an alternative energy company, was organized so the three companies could work together to develop automotive engines and drive trains that produce power more efficiently and cleanly compared to products used currently. By participating in this alliance, Ford and Daimler-Benz are showing their support for the concept of electric cars that do not need batteries but can create their own electricity with a device called a fuel cell. Ballard's knowledge as a leader in fuel-cell technology is critical to the work to be completed through the formation of the alliance. In addition to their knowledge regarding electric vehicles, Ford and Daimler-Benz are committing significant amounts of financial resources ($420 million from Ford alone) to this alliance. Thus, the three partners to this alliance are contributing in ways that are intended to result in the alliance's success.[81] Strategic alliances are discussed in more depth in Chapter 9.

Acquisitions

Cross-border acquisitions have been increasing significantly with free trade in global markets.[82] They have also been increasing among Japanese and German firms because the value of the dollar has fallen relative to their home countries' currencies.[83] As explained in Chapter 7, acquisitions can provide quick access to a new market. In fact, acquisitions may provide the fastest and often the largest initial international expansion of any of the alternatives. This was the case with BMW's acquisition of Rover Cars in order to enter the sport utility vehicle market. Although acquisitions have become a popular mode of entering international markets, they are not without their costs. International acquisitions carry some of the same disadvantages that exist for domestic acquisitions, as discussed in Chapter 7. In addition, they can be expensive and often require debt financing (which also carries an extra cost). International negotiations for acquisitions can be exceedingly complex—generally more complicated than in domestic acquisitions. Dealing with the legal and regulatory requirements in the foreign host country of the target firm and obtaining appropriate information for effective negotiation of the agreement frequently present significant problems. Finally, the problems of merging the new firm into the acquiring firm often are more complex than for domestic acquisitions. The acquiring firm must deal not only with different corporate cultures, but also with potentially different social cultures and practices. Therefore, while international acquisitions have been popular because of the rapid access to new markets they provide, they also carry with them important costs and multiple risks.

Some analysts believe that South Korea may be a country targeted by companies seeking to expand internationally through acquisitions. Chase Manhattan, General Motors, and GE were considering such acquisitions early in 1998. In part, these interests were being fueled by the requirement for the South Korean government to open its nation's economy as part of a $60 billion international bailout. In concert with Robert Bosch GmbH and Sachs AG, General Motors is examining the possibility of acquiring Mando Machinery, a large but ailing auto parts company. GE's approach to South Korea's economic crises was expressed by a company spokesperson who explained that "sometimes when there are situations with uncertainty, it can create acquisition opportunities for us."[84]

Forestry company UPM-Kymmene also uses acquisitions as an entry mode into global markets. This Finnish firm was created in 1996 through a merger of two rivals. A string of strategic acquisitions has allowed UPM-Kymmene to establish itself "as one of the few genuinely transcontinental producers in a traditionally fragmented industry." Now the world's largest pulp and paper producer after U.S.-based International Paper, some analysts see UPM-Kymmene's actions as setting a cross-border consolidation trend in its industry. Collectively, the company's acquisitions have created a worldwide producer and a worldwide seller. Although the firm is currently concentrating on integrating its acquisitions into its existing operations, the CEO does not rule out the possibility of further acquisitions if attractive opportunities were to surface.[85]

The world's largest retailer, Wal-Mart, is using several entry modes to globalize its operations. For example, in China, the firm used a joint venture mode of entry. To begin the firm's foray into Germany, an acquisition was completed. In all likelihood, the same entry mode will be used to establish Wal-Mart's presence in Japan. The head of Wal-Mart's international operations describes the reason-

Wal-Mart is planning to use a combination of entry modes into the Japanese market. Some areas of Japanese industry are open to greenfied start-ups and others are more conducive to acquisitions.

ing for this decision: In Japan, "there may be isolated pockets where you could do greenfield start-ups, but Japan has a very sophisticated, well-developed retail industry. When you have that situation, critical mass is more difficult to obtain, so acquisitions are a more appropriate first step."[86]

New, Wholly Owned Subsidiary

A **greenfield venture** is one in which a new, wholly owned subsidiary is established.

The establishment of a new, wholly owned subsidiary is referred to as a **greenfield venture**. This is often a complex and potentially costly process. This alternative has the advantage of providing maximum control for the firm and, therefore, if successful, has the most potential to provide above-average returns. The risks are also great because of the costs involved in establishing a new business operation in a new country. The firm may have to acquire the knowledge and expertise of the existing market by hiring host country nationals, possibly from competitive firms, and/or consultants (which can be costly). It maintains control over the technology, marketing, and distribution of its products through this process. Alternatively, it must build new manufacturing facilities, establish distribution networks, and learn and implement appropriate marketing strategies to compete in the new market.

Dynamics of Mode of Entry

Choice of mode of entry is determined by a number of factors.[87] Initial market entry will often be through export because this requires no foreign manufacturing expertise and investment only in distribution. Licensing can also facilitate the product improvement necessary to enter foreign markets, as in the Komatsu example. Strategic alliances have been popular because they allow partnering with an experienced player already in the targeted market. Strategic alliances also reduce risk through the sharing of costs. These modes therefore are best for early market development tactics.

To secure a stronger presence, acquisitions or greenfield ventures may be required. Many Japanese automobile manufacturers, such as Honda, Nissan, and Toyota, have gained presence in the United States through a greenfield venture in addition to joint ventures. Both acquisitions and greenfield ventures are likely to come at later stages in the development of an international diversification strategy.

Thus, there are multiple means of entering new global markets. As is the case with Wal-Mart, firms select the entry mode that is suited best to the situation at hand. In some instances, these options will be followed sequentially, beginning with exporting and ending with greenfield ventures. In other cases, the firm may use several but not all of the different entry modes. The decision regarding the entry mode to use is primarily a result of the industry's competitive conditions, the country's situation and government policies, and the firm's unique set of resources, capabilities, and core competencies.

STRATEGIC COMPETITIVENESS OUTCOMES

Once the strategy and mode of entry have been selected, firms need to be concerned about overall success. International expansion can be risky and may not result in a competitive advantage. The following strategic competitiveness issues are discussed, as suggested in Figure 8.1.

International Diversification and Returns

International diversification is the primary international corporate-level strategy. In Chapter 6, we discussed the corporate-level strategy of product diversification. Through this strategy, the firm engages in the manufacture and sale of multiple diverse products. **International diversification** is a strategy through which a firm expands the sale of its goods or services across the borders of global regions and countries into different geographic locations or markets. The number of different markets in which it operates and their importance shows the degree to which a firm is diversified internationally. The percentage of total sales is often used to measure a region's or country's importance to the firm.[88]

International diversification is a strategy through which a firm expands the sales of its goods or services across the borders of global regions and countries into different geographic locations or markets.

As noted earlier, multiple reasons exist for firms to diversify internationally. Because of its potential advantages, international diversification should be related positively to firm returns. Research has shown that as international diversification increases, firm returns increase, whereas domestic product diversification is often related negatively to firm returns.[89] There are many reasons for the positive effects of international diversification, such as the potential economies of scale and experience, location advantages, increased market size, and potential to stabilize returns. The stabilization of returns helps reduce a firm's overall risk.[90]

Firms in the Japanese automobile industry have found that international diversification may allow a company to better exploit its core competencies. Therefore, the sharing of knowledge resources can produce synergy among the operations in different countries/international markets as it has among Japanese automakers.[91]

On the other hand, firm returns may affect international diversification. For example, poor returns in a domestic market may encourage a firm to expand internationally to enhance its profit potential. In addition, internationally diversified firms may, in turn, have access to more flexible labor markets, as the Japanese do in the United States, and benefit from global scanning for competition and market opportunities.[92] As a result, multinational firms with efficient and competitive operations are more likely to produce above-average returns for their investors and better products for their customers than are solely domestic firms.[93] However, as explained later, international diversification can be carried too far.

International Diversification and Innovation

In Chapter 1, we noted that the development of new technology is at the heart of strategic competitiveness. Michael Porter stated that a nation's competitiveness depends on the capacity of its industry to innovate and suggested that firms achieve competitive advantage in international markets through innovation. Competitors eventually and inevitably outperform firms that fail to innovate and improve their operations and products. Therefore, the only way to sustain a competitive advantage is to upgrade it continually.[94]

International diversification provides the potential for firms to achieve greater returns on their innovations (through larger and/or more numerous markets) and thus lowers the often substantial risks of R&D investments. Therefore, international diversification provides incentives for firms to innovate. In addition, international diversification may be necessary to generate the resources required to sustain a large-scale R&D operation. An environment of rapid technological obsolescence makes it difficult to invest in new technology and the capital-intensive operations required to take advantage of it. Firms operating solely in domestic markets may find such investments difficult because of the length of time required to recoup the original investment. Furthermore, if the time is extended, it may not be possible to recover the investment before the technology becomes obsolete.[95] As a result, international diversification improves the firm's ability to appropriate additional and necessary returns from innovation before competitors can overcome the initial competitive advantage created by the innovation.

The relationship among international diversification, innovation, and returns is complex. Some level of performance is necessary to provide the resources to generate international diversification. International diversification provides incentives and resources to invest in research and development. Research and development, if done appropriately, should enhance the returns of the firm, which, in turn, provides more resources for continued international diversification and investment in R&D.

Because of the potential positive effects of international diversification on performance and innovation, some have argued that such diversification may even enhance returns in product diversified firms. International diversification would increase market potential in each of the product lines, but the complexity of managing a product diversified and internationally diversified firm is significant. Therefore, it is likely that international diversification can enhance the returns of a firm that is highly product diversified, but only when it is managed well.

Asea Brown Boveri (ABB) may demonstrate these relationships. This firm's operations involve high levels of both product and international diversification; yet, ABB's performance is quite strong. Some believe that the firm's ability to effectively implement the transnational strategy contributes to its strategic competitiveness. To manage itself, ABB assembles culturally diverse corporate and divisional management teams. These teams are used to facilitate simultaneous achievement of global integration and local responsiveness. Evidence suggests that more culturally diverse top management teams often have a greater knowledge of international markets and idiosyncrasies.[96] (Top management teams are discussed further in Chapter 12.) Moreover, an in-depth understanding of diverse markets among top-level managers facilitates intra-firm coordination and the use of long-term, strategically relevant criteria to evaluate the performance of managers and their units. In turn, this approach facilitates improved innovation and performance.[97]

Complexity of Managing Multinational Firms

Although many potential benefits can be realized by implementing an international strategy, problems and complexities can also arise. For example, multiple risks are involved when operating in several different countries. Firms can become only so large and diverse before becoming unmanageable or the costs of managing them exceed their benefits. Other complexities include the highly competitive nature of global markets, multiple cultural environments, potentially rapid shifts in the value of different currencies, and the possible instability of some national governments.

Political risks are related to instability in national governments and to war, civil or international.

RISKS IN AN INTERNATIONAL ENVIRONMENT

International diversification carries with it multiple risks. International expansion is difficult to implement and manage after implementation because of these risks. Primary among these are the political and economic risks. Because of these risks, highly diversified firms are accustomed to market conditions yielding competitive situations that differ from what was predicted. Sometimes, these situations contribute positively to the firm's efforts to enhance its strategic competitiveness; on other occasions, they have a negative effect on the firm's efforts.[98] Specific examples of political and economic risks are shown in Figure 8.4.

Political Risks

Political risks are related to instability in national governments and to war, civil or international. Instability in a national government creates multiple problems. Among these are economic risks and the uncertainty created in terms of government regulation, many legal authorities, and potential nationalization of private assets. For example, foreign firms that are investing in Russia may have concerns about the stability of the national government and what might happen to their investments/assets in Russia should there be a major change in government.

Different concerns exist for foreign firms investing in China. They are less worried about the potential for major changes in China's national government than about the uncertainty of China's regulation of foreign business investments. Tensions among Hong Kong, Taiwan, and China create concern about investment in the region. Taiwan is the second largest investor in China behind Hong Kong. Much of the tension is political: Taiwan and Hong Kong have been a laboratory in which capitalism was tested against socialism in China.[99]

FIGURE 8.4 ***Risks in the International Environment***

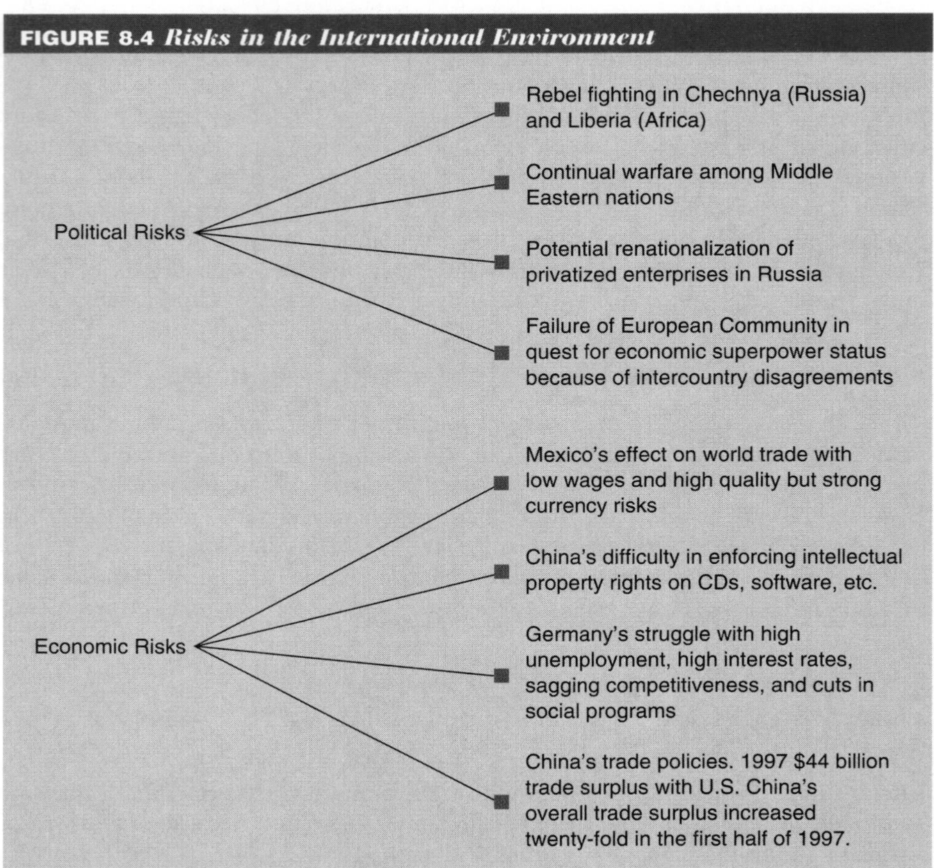

Source: N. Banerjee, 1996, Russia's many regions work to attract funds from foreign investors, *Wall Street Journal,* April 30, A1, A8; P. Engardio and D. Roberts, 1996, Rethinking China, *Business Week,* March 4, 57–64; R.S. Greenberger, 1996, U.S. sharply attacks China over intellectual property, *Wall Street Journal,* May 1, A3, A4; A.D. Marcus, 1996, Israel seems to target Lebanon economy, *Wall Street Journal,* April 17, A16; C. Rosett, 1996, Russian Communists target privatizers, *Wall Street Journal,* February 13, A11; P. Stein, 1996, Hong Kong feels heavy hand of China, *Wall Street Journal,* April 17, A16; J. Templeman, 1996, The economy that fell to earth, *Business Week,* January 15, 46.

Economic Risks

Economic risks are interdependent with political risks, as noted earlier. However, there are other economic risks associated with international diversification. Chief among these are the differences and fluctuations in the value of different currencies. For example, with U.S. firms, the value of the dollar relative to other currencies determines the value of their international assets and earnings. An increase in the value of the dollar can reduce the value of U.S. multinational firms' international assets and earnings in other countries. Furthermore, the value of different currencies can, at times, dramatically affect a firm's competitiveness in global markets because of its effect on the prices of goods manufactured in different countries. For example, an increase in the value of the dollar can harm U.S. firms' exports to international markets because of the price differential of the products.

Miller Brewing Company's recent experience with a joint venture demonstrates how political and economic risks are interwoven. Formed with Brazil's Cia, Cervejaria Brahma SA, Miller held a 50 percent ownership in this alliance. Brazil's Administrative Council of Economic Defense (Cade) ruled that the alliance between Miller and Brahma, both among the largest brewers in the world, deprived consumers of the benefits of head-to-head competition between the two giants. The agency allowed Miller 24 months to sell its stake in the alliance. Analysts suggested that this decision cast a cloud over efforts by multinational corporations to penetrate fast-growing Brazilian markets. Thus, this decision raised the possibility that other companies seeking to expand their operations through entry into Brazil's markets via cooperative arrangements such as a joint venture would either delay or cancel such expansion plans. The following comment from a lawyer representing the two brewers suggests this as well as the possibility that a different market entry mode may be appropriate for use in Brazil: "This decision is a yellow light, which says that if foreign companies wish to come into Brazil, they should not joint venture with Brazilian companies but should come in and make investments themselves."[100]

Limits to International Expansion: Management Problems

Research has shown that there are positive returns to early international diversification, but they tend to level off and become negative as the diversification increases past some point.[101] There are multiple reasons for the limits to the positive effects of international diversification. For example, greater geographic dispersion across country borders increases the costs of coordination between units and the distribution of products. Additionally, trade barriers, logistical costs, cultural diversity, and other differences by country (e.g., access to raw materials, different employee skill levels) greatly complicate the implementation of international diversification.[102]

Institutional and cultural factors often represent strong barriers to the transfer of a firm's competitive advantages from one country to another. Marketing programs often have to be redesigned and new distribution networks established when firms expand into new countries. In addition, they may encounter different labor costs and capital charges. Therefore, it is difficult to effectively implement, manage, and control international operations.[103]

Amway Corporation's recent experiences in South Korea demonstrate the managerial challenges in international diversification. Long committed to the relationship between international diversification and financial returns, Amway competes extensively in what it calls the Asian-Pacific region. Countries into which Amway has expanded in this region include Japan, South Korea, Taiwan, Thailand, Australia, China, Hong Kong, and New Zealand. The importance of South Korea to Amway is indicated by the fact that this country is the firm's third largest market on a worldwide basis. As a result of attacks by local consumer groups and environmental activities and competitive actions taken by South Korea's domestic competitors, Amway's sales in this important market plunged recently by 64 percent. Contributing to this precipitous decline was the decision by approximately 70,000 of the firm's 140,000 distributors to discontinue working for the company. Following a study of the situation, an analyst suggested that "Amway's continuing woes in Korea . . . underscore how cultural land mines and informal trade barriers still make it tough for many foreign companies to make it in this market."

At the center of Amway's problem was a detergent called Dish Drops. To express their concerns, 82 consumer and environmental groups formed an Anti-Amway Committee. These groups alleged that Amway was misleading consumers by advertising that Dish Drops was an environmentally friendly product. Moreover, the groups asserted that Amway was overcharging consumers by a factor of two or three relative to the costs of local manufacturers' detergents. In light of these claims, some of the consumer groups suggested that "Amway is not a moral company; and, they have the wrong attitude in marketing their products." To publicize these allegations, the Korea Soap and Detergent Association, a trade group for local manufacturers, sponsored advertisements.

Brian Chalmers, the president of Amway's Korean operation, responded to these allegations. For example, Amway asserted that the tests used to determine that Dish Drops was not an environmentally friendly product were flawed. Instead of complying with the international standard of eight days or more of testing to determine a detergent's biodegradability, Amway officials noted that the Dish Drops product was studied in only one and two days of testing. Furthermore, Chalmers denied that Amway was overcharging customers. He explained that Dish Drops is economical if the customer dilutes the concentrated soap as directed on the package. Chalmers suggested that because consumer groups refuse to accept Amway's guidelines for using the concentrate, they mistakenly concluded that the product is too expensive.

In spite of these difficulties, Chalmers remains positive about Amway's market potential in South Korea. To explain his decision to expand the firm's product line in South Korea, Chalmers said, "The opportunity this market provides is still absolutely unbounded."[104]

The amount of international diversification that can be managed will vary by firm and the abilities of the managers. The problems of central coordination and integration are reduced if the firm diversifies into more friendly countries that have similar cultures. In so doing, there are fewer trade barriers, a better understanding of the laws and customs, and the product is easier to adapt for local markets. For example, U.S. firms may find it less difficult to expand their operations into Canada and Western European countries (e.g., Great Britain, France) than into Asian countries (e.g., Japan, Korea).[105] The difficulties Amway is having in South Korea appear to support the contention that U.S. firms may find entry into Asian markets more challenging as compared to entries into more culturally similar markets.

Other Management Problems

One critical concern is that the global marketplace is highly competitive. Firms accustomed to a highly competitive domestic market experience more complexities in international markets. That is caused not only by the number of competitors encountered, but also by the differences of those competitors. A U.S. firm expanding operations into a European country may encounter competitors not only from Great Britain, Germany, France, and Spain, but also from countries outside of Europe, such as Hong Kong, Japan, Korea, Taiwan, Canada, and possibly even South America. Firms from each of these countries may enjoy different competitive advantages. Some may have low labor costs, others may have easy access to financing and low capital costs, and still others may have access to new high technology. Finally, attempting to understand the strategic intent of a competitor is more complex because of the different cultures and mind-sets.[106]

Another problem focuses on the relationships between the host government and the multinational corporation. For example, while Japanese firms face few trade barriers in competing in U.S. markets, U.S. firms often encounter many barriers to selling their products and operating in Japanese markets.[107] These regulations have traditionally kept the yen high relative to the dollar by keeping out imports and reducing the value of Japanese exports. This increases the price of Japanese products abroad. As noted earlier, the problem has been reversing itself somewhat, but much more remains to be done to reduce entry barriers. Many firms, such as Toyota and General Motors, are turning to strategic alliances to overcome entry barriers.

The nature of managerial complexity not only in international markets, but in domestic ones as well, has led managers to seek help in meeting this challenge. The next chapter focuses on how firms are cooperating with each other to meet some of their management challenges.

SUMMARY

- International diversification is increasing not only because of traditional motivations, but also for emerging reasons. Traditional motives include extending the product life cycle, securing key resources, and having access to low-cost labor. Emerging motivations focus on increased pressure for global integration as the demand for commodity products becomes borderless, and yet pressure for local country responsiveness is increasing.
- An international strategy usually attempts to capitalize on four important opportunities: potential increased market size; opportunity to earn a return on large investments, such as plant and capital equipment and/or research and development; economies of scale and learning; and potential location advantages.
- International business-level strategies are similar to the generic business-level strategy types: international low cost, international differentiation, international focus, and international integrated low cost/differentiation. However, each of these strategies is usually grounded in some home country advantage, as Porter's diamond model suggests. The diamond model emphasizes four determinants: factors of production; demand conditions; related and supporting industries; and patterns of firm strategy, structure, and rivalry.
- International corporate-level strategies are classified into three types. A multidomestic strategy focuses on competition within each country in which the firm operates. Firms employing a multidomestic strategy decentralize strategic and operating decisions to the strategic business units operating in each country so each can tailor its goods and services to the local market. A global strategy assumes more standardization of products across country boundaries. Therefore, competitive strategy is centralized and controlled by the home office. A transnational strategy seeks to combine aspects of both multidomestic and global strategies in order to emphasize both local responsiveness and global integration and coordination. The strategy is difficult to implement, requiring an integrated network and a culture of individual commitment.
- Although the transnational strategy is difficult to implement, environmental trends are causing many multinational firms to consider the needs for both global efficiencies and local responsiveness. Most large multinational firms, particularly those with many diverse products, may use a multidomestic strategy with some product lines and a global strategy with others.
- Some firms decide to compete only in certain regions of the world, as opposed to viewing all markets in the world as potential opportunities. Competing in regional markets allows firms and managers to focus their learning on specific markets, cultures, location resources, etc.
- Firms may enter international markets in one of several different ways, including exporting, licensing, forming strategic alliances, making acquisitions, and establishing new, wholly owned

subsidiaries, often referred to as greenfield ventures. Most firms begin with exporting and/or licensing because of their lower costs and risks, but later may expand to strategic alliances and acquisitions. The most expensive and risky means of entering a new international market is through the establishment of a new, wholly owned subsidiary. Alternatively, it provides the advantages of maximum control for the firm and, if successful, potentially the greatest returns as well.

- International diversification facilitates innovation in the firm. It provides a larger market to gain more and faster returns from investments in innovation. In addition, international diversification may generate the resources necessary to sustain a large-scale R&D program.
- In general, international diversification is related to above-average returns, but this assumes effective implementation of international diversification and management of international operations. International diversification provides greater economies of scope and learning. These, along with the greater innovation, help produce above-average returns.
- Several risks are involved with managing multinational operations. Among these are political risks (e.g., instability of national governments) and economic risks (e.g., currency value fluctuations).
- There are also limits to the ability to manage international expansion effectively. International diversification increases coordination and distribution costs, and management problems are exacerbated by trade barriers, logistical costs, and cultural diversity, among other factors.
- Additionally, international markets are highly competitive and firms must maintain an effective working relationship with the host government.

REVIEW QUESTIONS

1. What are the traditional and emerging motives that are causing firms to expand internationally?
2. What four factors are a basis for international business-level strategies?
3. What are the generic international business-level strategies? How do they differ from each other?
4. What are the differences among the following corporate-level international strategies: multidomestic, global, and transnational?
5. What environmental trends are affecting international strategy?
6. What five modes of international expansion are available, and what is the normal sequence of their use?
7. What is the relationship between international diversification and innovation? How does international diversification affect innovation? What is the effect of international diversification on firm returns?
8. What are the risks involved in expanding internationally and managing multinational firms?
9. What are the factors that create limits to the positive outcomes of international expansion?

APPLICATION DISCUSSION QUESTIONS

1. Given the advantages of international diversification, why do some firms choose not to expand internationally?
2. How do firms choose among the alternative modes for expanding internationally and moving into new markets (e.g., forming a strategic alliance versus establishing a wholly owned subsidiary)?
3. Does international diversification affect innovation similarly in all industries? Why or why not?
4. What is an example of political risk in expanding operations into China or Russia?
5. Why do some firms gain competitive advantages in international markets? Explain.
6. Why is it important to understand the strategic intent of strategic alliance partners and competitors in international markets?
7. What are the challenges associated with pursuing the transnational strategy? Explain.

ETHICS QUESTIONS

1. As firms attempt to internationalize, there may be a temptation to locate where product liability laws are lax to test new products. Are there examples where this motivation is the driving force behind international expansion?
2. Regulation and laws regarding the sale and distribution of tobacco products are stringent in the U.S. market. Undertake a study of selected U.S. tobacco firms to see if sales are increasing in foreign markets compared to domestic markets. In what countries are sales increasing and why? What is your assessment of this practice?
3. Some firms may outsource production to foreign countries. Although the presumed rationale for such outsourcing is to reduce labor costs, examine the liberality of labor laws (for instance, the strictness of child labor laws) and laws on environmental protection in another country to evaluate the ethics of this action.
4. Are there markets that the U.S. government protects through subsidy and tariff? If so, which ones and why?
5. Should the United States seek to impose trade sanctions on other countries such as China because of human rights violations?
6. Latin America has been experiencing a significant change in both political orientation and economic development. Describe these changes. What strategies should foreign international businesses implement, if any, to influence government policy in these countries? Is there a chance these political changes will reverse? How would business strategy change if Latin American politics reverses its current course?

INTERNET EXERCISE

Go to International Business Resources at:

http://www.ciber.bus.msu.edu/busres.html

This Web site is an award-winning site maintained by the Center for International Business and Research at Michigan State University. The site contains numerous links to other international business sites. Put yourself in the place of the manager of a firm that is thinking about exporting for the first time. Which links on the above site would be valuable to you as a first-time exporter? Explain the merits of each of the links that you feel would be helpful.

STRATEGIC SURFING

To help U.S. businesses understand foreign markets, the U.S. Central Intelligence Agency and the U.S. State Department produce "country profiles" that are available to the public free of charge. These profiles are available at the following Web sites:

CIA World Factbook:

http://www.odci.gov/cia/publications/nsolo/wfb-all.html

U.S. State Department Country Reports on Economic Policy and Trade Practices:

http://www.state.gov/www/issues/economic/trade_reports/index.html

NOTES

1. G. Mellon, 1997, Which has the brightest future, China or Russia? *Wall Street Journal*, August 29, A19.
2. B. L. Kirkman and D. L. Shapiro, 1997, The impact of cultural values on employee resistance to teams: Toward a model of globalized self-managing work team effectiveness, *Academy of Management Review* 22: 730–757.
3. P. Martin, 1997, A future depending on choice, *Financial Times*, November 7, 12.
4. C. W. L. Hill, 1998, *Global Business Today* (Boston: Irwin/McGraw Hill), 336; B. J. Punnett and D. A. Ricks, 1997, *International Business*, second edition, (Cambridge, MA: Blackwell Publishers), 8.
5. R. Vernon, 1996, International investment and international trade in the product cycle, *Quarterly Journal of Economics* 80: 190–207.
6. A. Bernstein, S. Jackson, and J. Byrne, 1997, Jack cracks the whip again, *Business Week*, December 15, 34–35.
7. J. M. Brown, 1997, World eyes Ireland for telesales growth, *Financial Times*, November 7, 2.
8. *Financial Times*, 1997, Flexible and cheap, December 12, II.
9. D. Woodruff and K. L. Miller, 1995, Mercedes' maverick in Alabama, *Business Week*, September 11, 64–65.
10. J. N. Kapferer, 1998, Making brands work around the world,

in Part One of As business goes global, *Financial Times*, February 12–13.

11. Punnett and Ricks, *International Business*, 334–337.
12. S. Batholomew, 1997, National systems of biotechnology innovation: Complex interdependencies in the global system, *Journal of International Business Studies* 28: 241–266; A. Madhok, 1997, Cost, value and foreign market entry mode: The transaction and the firm, *Strategic Management Journal* 18: 39–61.
13. W. Kuemmerle, 1997, Building effective R&D capabilities abroad, *Harvard Business Review* 75, no. 2: 61–70; B. J. Oviatt and P. P. McDougall, 1995, Global start-ups: Entrepreneurs on a worldwide stage, *Academy of Management Executive* IX, no. 2: 30–44.
14. J. J. Choi and M. Rajan, 1997, A joint test of market segmentation and exchange risk factor in international capital markets, *Journal of International Business Studies* 28: 29–49.
15. J. L. Xie, 1996, Karasek's model in the People's Republic of China: Effects of job demands, control, and individual differences, *Academy of Management Journal* 39: 1594–1618.
16. J. P. Quinlan, 1998, Europe, not Asia, is corporate America's key market, *Wall Street Journal*, January 12, A20.
17. M. A. Hitt, M. T. Dacin, B. B. Tyler, and D. Park, 1997, Understanding the differences in Korean and U.S. executives' strategic orientations, *Strategic Management Journal* 18: 159–167.
18. McDonald's adapts Mac attack to foreign tastes with expansion, 1997, *Dallas Morning News*, December 7, H3.
19. Berstein, Jackson, and Byrne, Jack cracks the whip again.
20. S. Zaheer and E. Mosakowski, 1997, The dynamics of the liability of foreignness: A global study of survival in financial services, *Strategic Management Journal* 18: 439–464.
21. Tupperware snaps at chance to sell in Russia, 1997, *Dallas Morning News*, November 25, D4.
22. M. Halkias, 1997, Friday's outlines growth, *Dallas Morning News*, December 3, D1, D10.
23. M. Halkias, 1997, Frito-Lay to buy snack brands abroad, *Dallas Morning News*, November 18, D1, D7.
24. N. Harris, 1997, If you can't beat 'em, copy 'em, *Business Week*, November 17, 50.
25. R. Tomkins and A. Jack, 1997, Coca-Cola to buy Orangina for $840 million, *Financial Times*, December 23, 15.
26. M. Skapinker, 1998, Airbus boasts year of record orders, *Financial Times*, January 7, 6; F. M. Biddle, 1997, Boeing's effort to cushion itself from cycle backfires, *Wall Street Journal*, October 24, B4; C. Goldsmith, 1997, Airbus plans to spend $2.9 billion on jets to compete with Boeing, *Wall Street Journal*, December 9, B4.
27. W. Shan and J. Song, 1997, Foreign direct investment and the sourcing of technological advantage: Evidence from the biotechnology industry, *Journal of International Business Studies* 28: 267–284.
28. A. J. Venables, 1995, Economic integration and the location of firms, *The American Economic Review* 85: 296–300.
29. H. Simonian, 1997, Volvo's lights burn brighter, *Financial Times*, December 9, 17.
30. M. Schuman and V. Reitman, 1997, A world-wide glut doesn't sway Samsung from auto business, *Wall Street Journal*, August 25, A1, A11.
31. J. Birkinshaw, 1997, Entrepreneurship in multinational corporations: The characteristics of subsidiary initiatives, *Strategic Management Journal* 18: 207–229.
32. S. Makino and A. Delios, 1996, Local knowledge transfer and performance: Implications for alliance formation in Asia, *Journal of International Business Studies* 27 (Special Issue), 905–927.
33. K. Ferdows, 1997, Making the most of foreign factories, *Harvard Business Review* 75, no. 2: 73–88.
34. V. Reitman, 1998, Toyota plans new lost-cost car to replace its struggling Tercel, *Wall Street Journal*, January 9, B4.
35. Ford beats GM to be first to make cars in China, 1997, *Wall Street Journal*, December 2, A17.
36. D. J. Teece, G. Pisano, and A. Shuen, 1997, Dynamic capabilities and strategic management, *Strategic Management Journal* 18: 509–533.
37. A. Campbell and M. Alexander, 1997, What's wrong with strategy? *Harvard Business Review* 75, no. 6: 42–51.
38. A. Rugman, 1998, Multinationals as regional flagships, in Part One of As business goes global, *Financial Times*, February 10–11, 6–9.
39. M. E. Porter, 1990, *The Competitive Advantage of Nations* (New York: The Free Press).
40. Ibid., 84.
41. Ibid., 89.
42. N. D. Schwartz, 1998, Why Wall Street's buying Wal-Mart again, *Fortune*, February 16, 92–94.
43. R. B. Lieber, 1997, Flying high, going global, *Fortune*, July 7, 195–197; M. Skapinker, 1997, No-frills airlines travelling on a wing and a fear, *Financial Times*, November 20, VI.
44. Schwartz, Why Wall Street's buying Wal-Mart again, 94; Sam's travels, 1997, *Financial Times*, December 19, 13.
45. Porter, *Competitive Advantage*, 133.
46. D. Woodruff, 1997, Service with a what? *Business Week*, September 8, 130F–130H.
47. J. Friedland, 1994, Sharp's edge: Prowess in LCD screens puts it ahead of Sony, *Far Eastern Economic Review*, July 28, 74–76.
48. T. Burns, 1997, Niche goals bring away results, *Financial Times*, November 17, II; Oviatt and McDougall, Global start-ups.
49. Porter, *Competitive Advantage*, 210–225.
50. M. J. Enright and P. Tenti, 1990, How the diamond works: The Italian ceramic tile industry, *Harvard Business Review* 68, no. 2: 90–91.
51. D. Lei, M. A. Hitt, and J. D. Goldhar, 1996, Advanced manufacturing technology: The impact on organization design and strategic flexibility, *Organization Studies* 17: 501–523.
52. R. D. Ireland and M. A. Hitt, 1998, Achieving and maintaining strategic competitiveness in the 21st century: The role of strategic leadership, *Academy of Management Executive* (in press).
53. D. Weimer, 1998, A new Cat on the hot seat, *Business Week*, March 9, 56–61; A. E. Johnson, 1997, Caterpillar pays $1.3 billion for Varity Perkins, *Financial Times*, December 12, 1; P. Marsh and S. Wagstyl, 1997, The hungry Caterpillar, *Financial Times*, December 2, 22.
54. M. A. Hitt, R. E. Hoskisson, and R. D. Ireland, 1994, A midrange theory of the interactive effects of international and product diversification on innovation and performance, *Journal of Management* 20: 297–326.

55. S. Ghoshal, 1987, Global strategy: An organizing framework, *Strategic Management Journal* 8: 425–440.
56. R. Tomkins, 1998, US market benefits from Knorr know-how, *Financial Times*, January 20, 19.
57. Ghoshal, Global strategy.
58. J. K. Johaansson and G. S. Yip, 1994, Exploiting globalization potential: U.S. and Japanese strategies, *Strategic Management Journal* 15: 579–601.
59. N. Tait, 1998, CMS pumps up its power across the world, *Financial Times*, January 8, 17.
60. C. A. Bartlett and S. Ghoshal, 1989, *Managing Across Borders: The Transnational Solution* (Boston: Harvard Business School Press).
61. Govindarajan and Gupta, Setting a course; A. Saxenian, 1994, *Regional Advantage: Culture and Competition in Silicon Valley and Route 128* (Cambridge, MA: Harvard University Press).
62. Rugman, Multinationals as regional flagships, 6.
63. Woodruff, Service with a what?
64. L. Allen and C. Pantzalis, 1996, Valuation of the operating flexibility of multinational corporations, *Journal of International Business Studies* 27: 633–653.
65. J. I. Martinez, J. A. Quelch, and J. Ganitsky, 1992, Don't forget Latin America, *Sloan Management Review* 33 (Winter): 78–92.
66. P. B. Carroll, 1994, Buyer of Westin deal may represent new breed of Mexican businessman, *Wall Street Journal*, March 1, A15.
67. G. Smith and J. Person, 1996, CEMEX: Solid as Mexico sinks, *Business Week* February 27, 58–59.
68. V. Govindarajan and A. Gupta, 1998, How to build a global presence, in Part One of As business goes global, *Financial Times*, February 10–11; Madhok, Cost, value and foreign market entry mode, 41.
69. Punnett and Ricks, *International Business*, 249–250; G. M. Naidu and V. K. Prasad, 1994, Predictors of export strategy and performance of small- and medium-sized firms, *Journal of Business Research* 31: 107–115.
70. Canon: Sixty Years of Progress, 1998, *Fortune* (Special Advertising Section), August 4, S-5.
71. S. Glain, 1997, A whole new wave of Japanese exports is headed westward, *Wall Street Journal*, November 14, A1, A6.
72. Hill, *Global Business Today*, 361–363.
73. B. Schlender, 1995, Sony on the brink, *Fortune*, June 12, 66.
74. J. R. Green and S. Schotchmer, 1995, On the division of profit in sequential innovation, *The Rand Journal of Economics* 26: 20–33.
75. B. Einhorn, 1997, China's CD pirates find a new hangout, *Business Week*, December 15, 138F.
76. C. A. Bartlett and S. Rangan, 1992, Komatsu limited, in C. A. Bartlett and S. Ghoshal (eds.), *Transnational Management: Text, Cases and Readings in Cross-Border Management* (Homewood, IL: Irwin), 311–326.
77. A. C. Inkpen and P. W. Beamish, 1997, Knowledge, bargaining power, and the instability of international joint ventures, *Academy of Management Review* 22: 177–202; S. H. Park and G. R. Ungson, 1997, The effect of national culture, organizational complementarity, and economic motivation on joint venture dissolution, *Academy of Management Journal* 40: 279–307.
78. Y. Pan and D. K. Tse, 1996, Cooperative strategies between foreign firms in an overseas country, *Journal of International Business Studies* 27 (Special Issue): 929–946.
79. M. A. Hitt, B. W. Keats, and S. M. DeMarie, 1998, Navigating in the new competitive landscape: Building strategic flexibility and competitive advantage in the 21st century, *Academy of Management Executive* (in press).
80. M. A. Lyles and J. E. Salk, 1996, Knowledge acquisition from foreign parents in international joint ventures: An empirical examination in the Hungarian context, *Journal of International Business Studies* 27 (Special Issue): 877–903.
81. Ford joins global alliance on electric cars, *Dallas Morning News*, December 16, D6.
82. M. A. Hitt, R. E. Hoskisson, and H. Kim, 1997, International diversification: Effects on innovation and firm performance in product-diversified firms, *Academy of Management Journal* 40: 767–798.
83. J. F. Hennart and S. Reddy, 1997, The choice between mergers/acquisitions and joint ventures: The case of Japanese investors in the United States, *Strategic Management Journal* 18: 1–12.
84. U.S. firms consider growth into S. Korea, 1997, *Dallas Morning News*, December 27, F1, F3.
85. G. McIvor, 1998, Paper-maker unwraps global aims, *Financial Times*, January 6, 16.
86. R. Tomkins, 1997, Wal-Mart on the prowl for retail acquisitions in Europe and Japan, *Financial Times*, December 23, 15.
87. W. C. Kim and P. Hwang, 1992, Global strategy and multinationals' entry mode choice, *Journal of International Business Studies* 23: 29–53.
88. Hitt, Hoskisson, and Kim, International diversification, 767.
89. R. Buhner, 1987, Assessing international diversification of West German corporations, *Strategic Management Journal* 8: 25–37.
90. J. M. Geringer, P. W. Beamish, and R. C. daCosta, 1989, Diversification strategy and internationalization: Implications for MNE performance, *Strategic Management Journal* 10: 109–119; R. E. Caves, 1982, *Multinational Enterprise and Economic Analysis* (Cambridge, MA: Cambridge University Press).
91. B. Bremner, L. Armstrong, K. Kerwin, and K. Naughton, 1997, Toyota's crusade, *Business Week*, April 7, 104–114.
92. S. J. Kobrin, 1991, An empirical analysis of the determinants of global integration, *Strategic Management Journal* 12 (Special Issue): 17–37.
93. M. Kotabe, 1989, Hollowing-out of U.S. multinationals and their global competitiveness, *Journal of Business Research* 19: 1–15.
94. Porter, *Competitive Advantage*.
95. M. Kotabe, 1990, The relationship between off-shore sourcing and innovativeness of U.S. multinational firms: An empirical investigation, *Journal of International Business Studies* 21: 623–638.
96. S. Finkelstein and D. C. Hambrick, 1996, *Strategic Leadership: Top Executives and Their Effects on Organizations* (St. Paul, MN: West Publishing Company).
97. Hitt, Hoskisson, and Kim, International diversification, 790.
98. A lorry-load of trouble in Asia, 1997, *The Economist*, December 6, 65–66.

99. A. Tanzer, 1996, How Taiwan is invading China, *Forbes*, April 8, 86–91.
100. M. Moffett, 1997, Miller Brewing is ordered to sell its stake in Brazilian joint venture, *Wall Street Journal*, June 13, A14.
101. Hitt, Hoskisson, and Kim, International diversification; S. Tallman and J. Li, 1996, Effects of international diversity and product diversity on the performance of multinational firms, *Academy of Management Journal* 39: 179–196; Hitt, Hoskisson, and Ireland, A mid-range theory of interactive effects; Geringer, Beamish, and daCosta, Diversification strategy.
102. Porter, *Competitive Advantage*.
103. Hitt, Hoskisson, and Kim, International diversification.
104. M. Schuman, 1997, Amway finds itself washed over in a South Korean soap drama, *Wall Street Journal*, October 22, A16.
105. Hitt, Dacin, Tyler, and Park, Understanding the differences.
106. M. A. Hitt, B. B. Tyler, and C. Hardee, 1996, Understanding strategic intent in the global marketplace, *Academy of Management Executive* IX, no. 2: 12–19.
107. D. P. Hamilton, M. Williams, and N. Shirouzu, 1995, Japan's big problem: Freeing its economy from over regulation, *Wall Street Journal*, April 25, A1, A6.

Cooperative Strategy

CHAPTER 9

Learning Objectives

After reading this chapter, you should be able to:

1. Identify and define different types of cooperative strategy.
2. Explain the rationale for a cooperative strategy in three types of competitive situations: slow-cycle, standard-cycle, and fast-cycle markets.
3. Understand competitive advantages and disadvantages and competitive dynamics of cooperative strategies at the business level.
4. Describe uses of cooperative strategies at the corporate level.
5. Identify appropriate applications of cooperative strategies when pursuing international strategies.
6. Distinguish the competitive risks of cooperative strategies.
7. Understand the nature of trust as a strategic asset in forming cooperative strategies.
8. Describe the two basic management approaches for managing strategic alliances.

Increasing Numbers of Small and Large Firms Are Collaborating to Compete

Trends in both large firms such as multinational enterprises and small entrepreneurial firms have begun to emphasize a cooperative strategy or partnering with other companies. As explained in Chapter 8, large multinational enterprises have formed to exploit firm-specific advantages on a worldwide basis. However, many of these large firms have found their potential profits dissipating because internal governance and organizational structure costs outweigh their benefits. To improve this situation, many large multinationals are spinning off businesses they own and forming partnerships with other companies. These firms have moved away from a wholly-owned approach toward managing a business network of partners. Some of the better known of these networks or firms have been created by the Japanese. Often known as *vertical keiretsus* (a flagship firm with associated suppliers and distributors as partners), these networks have succeeded in forming strong global competitive positions in such diverse fields as consumer electronics (Sony, Matsushita), automobiles (Toyota, Nissan), and computers (NEC, Toshiba).

http://www.microsoft.com

Microsoft is an example of a firm that has a large system of partnerships with smaller software producers. Nowhere is this more evident than at the Comdex trade show where Microsoft's partner pavilion exhibits the nearly three hundred firms that eagerly show their relationship to the giant company. As the industry consolidates around Microsoft's Windows operating system, many firms are finding considerable momentum selling into this mass market. Because of their investment decisions, even IBM's global services division found its customers asking for software supporting the Windows NT operating system.

With the convergence of technologies, however, Microsoft is worried that if the Internet web moves to the television screen, the market may change to a direction that is not compatible with the software standard it has pursued. As a result, the company has been interested in developing a partnership or ownership stake in the cable TV industry. For instance, it has talked with Tele-Communications, Inc. (TCI), one of the largest cable television operators. TCI pays a large amount for digital cable boxes that have the capability of providing high-speed Internet access, besides hundreds of digital cable channels. Microsoft has been trying to influence the design of these new set-top boxes that will help bring the Internet into living rooms through cable wires by pressuring computer desktop manufacturers to adopt CE Windows (Microsoft's operating system for apparatus other than computers). It would be impossible for even Microsoft to purchase subsidiaries in all the areas of technology where the Internet will be established; therefore, it must forge these relationships through partnering or at the very most, partial ownership.

For small firms, forming cooperative relationships with other small companies as well as large ones is becoming a necessity. Although advances in technology, communications, and transportation have created many opportunities for growing small companies, it is almost impossible for single, entrepreneurial firms to exploit them on their own. Market pressures force small companies to work together in cooperative relationships. Today, large companies (e.g., those in the automobile industry) are winnowing their base and focusing on "tier one" suppliers (those who handle multiple parts and often supervise other subcontracting suppliers). These actions force smaller firms farther down the supply chain in two opposite directions—specialization and comprehensiveness. Quality is forcing more specialization, while suppliers are expected to provide all-encompassing or "do-it-all" solutions. This forces the smaller companies into cooperation with other firms, even former competitors. Such small-firm networks are being used in Italy and Denmark as well as other places throughout the world.

In the United States, for example, Harry Brown bought a Rust Belt company, Erie Bolt, now EBC Industries and transformed it by building alliances with many of his former competitors. Brown works with a machine shop to produce metal studs because both companies can produce a higher quality product for their customers. Brown and his former competitors, numbering about fifty, jointly market their capabilities to create business that they couldn't generate as individual firms. Furthermore, they share information about quality systems, consult with each other before investing in machinery, use each other's sales reps, and refer customers to each other. They can now offer a far more comprehensive product and a single point of contact for a variety of products. These alliances are not without their drawbacks. Harry Brown has had to take on the nearly full-time job of coordinating the group's efforts.

Other businesses form hybrid trade associations or work through an umbrella organization such as the Center for Advanced Fiber Optics Applications. This center is comprised of 12 companies that formed a separate non-profit entity to help them market separate new business opportunities. Usually with each network, you will find a leader behind it (and a strategic-center firm as explained later in the chapter) that champions the network firms. Although a particular CEO of a company, such as Brown, can be the champion, a third party can also offer an outside perspective needed to plant the seed necessary to develop the network. Often network brokers, whose very existence is a testimony to the trend, have a flair for getting overburdened CEOs to see the picture of the usefulness of such business network strategies.

SOURCE: S. Hamm, A. Cortese, and S.B. Garland, 1998, Microsoft's future, *Business Week*, January 19, 58–69; D. Fenn, 1997, Sleeping with the enemy, INC Online, http://www.inc.com, November; A. Rugman and J. D'Cruz, 1997, The theory of the flagship firm, *European Management Journal* 15: 403–412; D. Bank, 1997, Microsoft emphasizes its role as a partner at Comdex, *Wall Street Journal*, November 19, B4; E. Shapiro, 1997, TCI may get investment by Microsoft, *Wall Street Journal*, October 15, A3, A4; S.E. Human and K.G. Provan, 1997, An emergent theory of structure and outcomes in small-firm strategic manufacturing networks, *Academy of Management Journal* 40: 368–404.

Cooperative strategies have become increasingly popular since the mid-1980s. For example, the number of petitions to the U.S. Department of Justice for clearance of joint ventures increased by 423 percent during the 1986–1995 time period. Some have referred to this new trend as "coopetition" in that major competitors are now forming cooperative alliances to fend off other competition, oftentimes from foreign firms.[1] For instance, two U.S.-based competitors, Nucor Corporation and USX Corporation, formed an alliance to take advantage of each firm's unique competencies. USX researchers developed the idea for a revolutionary new steel-making process that eliminates the use of blast furnaces and coke batteries. They estimated this new process would reduce the cost of steel production by 20 to 25 percent.[2] As in the USX-Nucor partnership, alliances help firms obtain new technology rapidly and reduce the investment necessary to develop and introduce new products, to enter new markets, or to survive in their current ones. Also, as the opening case shows, cooperative strategies help firms overcome managerial and size limits to growth.[3] An increasing number of small and medium-sized companies, such as EBC Industries in the opening case, are engaging in cooperative strategies.[4] A Coopers and Lybrand survey of small companies found that such firms participating in alliances increased their revenues faster by generating 23 percent more goods and services than those not involved in them.[5] Alliances have become even more popular in international markets (between firms with headquarters in different countries) in recent years as the Japanese keiretsus mentioned in the opening case demonstrate.[6] Chrysler and other auto firms have been seeking to develop keiretsu type networks among their suppliers.[7]

Although strategic alliances, a prominent cooperative strategy, can serve a number of purposes and many are successful, managing them can be difficult.[8] The failure rate for alliances is notably high.[9] A study on the airline industry, for example, found that less than 30 percent of the alliances between international carriers have been successful.[10] As discussed in this chapter, firms must be careful when selecting alliance partners. They need to understand their potential partner's strategic intent and should attempt to develop trust among the partners to facilitate a more effective operation.[11] Because of the high failure rate, top executives who are considering entering into an alliance must develop a good understanding of the appropriate cooperative strategy to use and how to best implement it.

To this point in the book, competition among firms has been our focus. The previous chapters facilitate understanding of competitive advantage and strategic competitiveness through strong positions against external challenges, maximizing of core competencies, and minimizing of weaknesses. This chapter focuses on gaining competitive advantage through cooperation with other firms.[12]

TYPES OF COOPERATIVE STRATEGIES

Strategic alliances are a primary cooperative strategy. **Strategic alliances** are partnerships between firms whereby their resources, capabilities, and core competencies are combined to pursue mutual interests in developing, manufacturing, or distributing goods or services. Strategic alliances are explicit forms of relationships between firms. They come in three basic types.

One type of strategic alliance is a **joint ventures** in which two or more firms create an independent company. For instance, Dow Corning and Owens Corning were joint ventures created by Corning (formerly Corning Glass) with Dow Chemical Corporation and Owens Corporation, respectively. In joint ventures, each partner typically owns 50 percent of the equity.

A second type of strategic alliance is an **equity strategic alliance**, in which the partners own different percentages of equity in the new venture such as 60 and 40 percent. Many foreign direct investments are completed through equity strategic alliances such as those by Japanese and U.S. companies in China.[13] Unisource is an equity strategic alliance among three European telecommunication companies: Netherland's Koninklijke PTT, Sweden's Telia, and Swiss Telecom PTT. Chrysler Corporation and Mitsubishi Motors and Ford Motor Company and Mazda Motor Corporation have also formed significant equity strategic alliances. Equity strategic alliances are considered better at transferring know-how between firms because they are closer to hierarchical control than nonequity alliances.[14]

Finally, **nonequity strategic alliances** are formed through contract agreements given to a company to supply, produce, or distribute a firm's goods or services without equity sharing. Chrysler's network of supplier partners was mentioned earlier. This firm's approach to suppliers used to be based on a supplier's ability to build components at the lowest possible cost. There were no consultations concerning product design or the supplier's profit margins. Today, Chrysler's suppliers are involved deeply such that each partner works closely with Chrysler engineers. As a result, these mostly nonequity alliances have created $1.7 billion in annual savings for Chrysler; the supplier-partner's profits have increased as well.[15] Other types of cooperative contractual arrangements concern marketing and in-

Strategic alliances are partnerships between firms whereby their resources, capabilities, and core competencies are combined to pursue mutual interests in developing, manufacturing, or distributing goods or services.

A **joint venture** is when two or more firms create an independent company, with each of the partners typically owning equal shares in the new enterprise.

An **equity strategic alliance** consists of partners who own different percentages of equity in the new venture.

Nonequity strategic alliances are formed through contact agreements given to a company to supply, produce, or distribute a firm's goods or services without equity sharing.

formation sharing. Airlines, for example, use flight code sharing arrangements. Many of these additional relationships demonstrate nonequity strategic alliances.

Although this chapter focuses primarily on the explicit forms of strategic alliances as noted above, there are also implicit cooperative arrangements. One is called tacit collusion. **Tacit collusion** exists when several firms in an industry cooperate tacitly in reducing industry output below the potential competitive level, thereby increasing prices above the competitive level.[16] Most strategic alliances, however, exist not to reduce industry output but to increase learning, facilitate growth, or increase returns and strategic competitiveness.[17]

Tacit collusion exists when several firms in an industry cooperate tacitly in reducing industry output below the potential competitive level, thereby increasing prices above the competitive level.

Cooperative agreements may also be explicitly collusive, which is illegal in the United States unless regulated by the government as was the case in the telecommunications industries until recent deregulation. *Mutual forbearance* (another term for tacit collusion) is tacit recognition of interdependence, but it has the same effect as explicit collusion in that it reduces output and increases prices. (Mutual forbearance is defined and explained in Chapter 6.)

The following sections explain strategic alliances in depth. We first discuss reasons for engaging in strategic alliances. This is followed by examining strategic alliances at the business-unit level, then at the corporate and international levels. Additionally, we describe network strategies where the cooperative relations among firms produce multiple alliances, including large consortia and different types of business networks. As such, we discuss how strategies among multiple alliance partnerships differ from those with two partner alliances. The major risks of pursuing the various types of alliances are considered. Finally, we discuss the importance of trust as a strategic asset to foster cooperative strategies that create competitive advantage and endure over time.

Reasons for Alliances

A number of different rationales support participation in strategic alliances.[18] The reasons for cooperation differ based on three types of basic market situations: slow-cycle, standard-cycle, and fast-cycle.[19] These three market situations were introduced in Chapter 5. As noted earlier, *slow-cycle* markets refer to markets that are sheltered or near monopolies such as railroads and, historically, telecommunications companies and utilities. Often, these companies cooperate to develop standards (e.g., to regulate air or train traffic), but because they can also collude to reduce competition, the government usually provides significant regulation to avoid consumer price discrimination. *Standard-cycle* market cooperation can result from firms trying to avoid overcapacity rather than attempting to increase their opportunities. As such, these cooperative arrangements are often focused on obtaining market power. *Fast-cycle* markets frequently involve entrepreneurial firms offering new goods or services with short life cycles that are imitated quickly. In these markets, a cooperative strategy is used to increase the speed of product development or market entry as well as to gain strategic competitiveness. The reasons for strategic alliances in each of these markets are listed in Table 9.1.

Firms in slow-cycle markets tend to seek entry into markets that are restricted or try to establish franchises in new markets. For instance, many firms in slow-cycle markets consider cooperative strategic alliances in emerging markets that usually have restricted entry. In emerging markets in Eastern Europe, Russia, Latin America, India, China, and elsewhere, utility firms from developed countries are strongly motivated to form strategic alliances with local partners. For example, as

TABLE 9.1 ***Reasons for Strategic Alliances by Market Type***

Market	Reason
Slow Cycle	■ Gain access to a restricted market
	■ Establish a franchise in a new market
	■ Maintain market stability (e.g., establishing standards)
Standard Cycle	■ Gain market power (reduce industry overcapacity)
	■ Gain access to complementary resources
	■ Overcome trade barriers
	■ Meet competitive challenge from other competitors
	■ Pool resources for very large capital projects
	■ Learn new business techniques
Fast Cycle	■ Speed up new goods or service entry
	■ Speed up new market entry
	■ Maintain market leadership
	■ Form an industry technology standard
	■ Share risky R&D expenses
	■ Overcome uncertainty

deregulation occurs in the United States, U.S. telecommunications firms have the opportunity to share in establishing a near-monopoly franchise in these emerging markets. Firms operating in emerging markets desire these alliances because they need the expertise and technological know-how that can be provided by firms from developed countries. France's Alcatel has established a strong market position through joint ventures with local partners in Mexico and China.[20] It is also a leading telecommunications equipment supplier in South Africa and other emerging markets.[21] Unisource, itself a joint venture among three national telecommunication monopolies (from the Netherlands, Sweden, and Switzerland), is launching a venture in Hungary. The partners, previously state monopolies, are Hungarian oil and gas company MOL rt. (21 percent), Hungarian railways MAV rt. (25 percent), and a technological research institute KFKI (5 percent). Called MKM-Tel, this venture "hopes to blanket the country with a fiber optic network by the end of 1999," initially providing telecom services to businesses.[22] This approach has also been used by utility firms participating in energy, electricity, and gas pipeline projects such as one in India arranged by Enron Corporation.

Cooperation, however, may be difficult to establish in slow-cycle markets. Near monopolies usually seek to be self-sustaining rather than be maintained jointly by partners. For example, as competition for telecommunication services emerges in Europe, a number of telecommunication firms that were previously state monopolies have sought to cooperate and form strategic alliances. The Global One Alliance, formed by France Telecom and Deutsche Telekom, which is also allied with Sprint, has had difficulties. In this joint venture, the two original partners often compete with one another and thereby pull in opposite directions. These partners have significantly different corporate cultures and technical infrastructures and are scrutinized frequently by government agencies. Both the Unisource alliance mention above and the now defunct British Telecom (BT) and MCI alliance have had similar difficulties.[23] On the other hand, deregulation and privatization (e.g., in Russia) create opportunities for establishing monopoly franchises in emerging market countries; slow-cycle market firms often seek to take advantage of these opportunities.

In standard-cycle markets, which are often large and oriented toward economies of scale (e.g., automobile and commercial aerospace), alliances are more likely to be between partners with complementary resources, capabilities, and core competencies (see Table 9.1). In these markets where economies of scale are important for competitive advantage or parity, large international alliances are useful because national markets may be too small to support the scale-efficient nature of the businesses. Therefore, the increasing globalization of markets presents opportunities to combine resources, capabilities, and competencies. This is a primary reason for alliances between automobile firms such as Ford and Mazda.

A new venture, Teledesic, based in Seattle, Washington, is a partnership between Craig McCaw and Bill Gates. McCaw and Gates want to circle the globe with 288 satellites supplying high-speed Internet access around the world. Other competing companies also see the potential of this service. Although the network speed is not as great as that proposed by Teledesic, Motorola has launched 5 of its intended 66 satellites for its Iridium system. Alcatel's network called SkyBridge is another threat to Teledesic because the company's subsidiary has experience in launching satellites. To counter this competition, Teledesic is partnering with Boeing, granting it the rights to launch Teledesic's satellites. Boeing is also conveniently headquartered in Seattle as is Gate's Microsoft. Teledesic's plan to resell the service through local country telephone companies to overcome regulatory barriers may also give it a competitive edge.[24]

Firms also may cooperate in standard-cycle markets to reduce industry overcapacity and pool resources to meet capital needs. Although mergers can help to overcome overcapacity, such as in the defense industry (e.g., between Martin Marietta and Lockheed to form Lockheed Martin), they are not forms of cooperative strategy (this is because merged firms do not remain independent). The European alliances in aerospace, for instance Airbus Industrie, have been designed to help the partners become more competitive with U.S. aerospace firms. Airbus aircraft are manufactured under a consortium composed of France's Aerospatiale and Germany's Daimler-Benz Aerospace, each with 37.9 percent of the business; British Aerospace, with 20 percent, and Spain's Construcciones Aeronauticas, with 4.2 percent.[25] Because most aerospace projects require huge capital outlays, pooling resources is often a rational step. Also, when a firm has a project that requires significant R&D investment, as in a new casting approach for a steel mill, it may be necessary to seek a partner to share in these outlays.[26] Finally, firms in standard-cycle markets also may form alliances to overcome trade barriers (see Chapter 8) and to learn new business techniques.

Fast-cycle markets, which have short product cycles, such as those among electronics firms, create incentives for cooperation because development, manufacture, and distribution of a new product can happen more quickly. Furthermore, cooperation can lead to the development of standard products in a high-technology market.[27] For instance, Sematech, a cooperative strategic alliance among multiple electronic and semiconductor firms, was quite important in establishing the adoption of the UNIX standard operating system for workstation computer producers.[28] Intel and Hewlett-Packard (HP) are collaborating to offer a new chip that would process data in 64-bit chunks instead of Intel's Pentium standard 32 bits. The chip would be able to run today's Window's software as well as programs written for HP's version of UNIX, without modification. This innovation portends to take the microprocessor revolution to a level that will allow competition with mainframes; Intel will be able to compete across the full sprectrum of computing. This vision is reminiscent of the great expectations for the Power PC, a joint venture among IBM, Motorola, and Apple that was to propel the companies into a leadership position by combining the best of the PC with the best of Apple. The Power PC, however, failed to meet the expectations the partnering firms had of it.[29]

Uncertainty is also a rationale for increased cooperation among fast-cycle market firms. Cable television firms are collaborating on moving interactive television and Internet service through cable systems. As discussed in the opening case, Microsoft is trying to influence this movement's direction. The ultimate cable set-top box is likely to be the outcome of this activity. This device may bring together digital TV channels, interactive TV, and Internet access. Because the technology is still uncertain as to how to combine these technologies and because the expertise for each technology is held by a different company, strategic alliances are the preferred approach until a standard emerges. An amalgam of microprocessor and chip companies (Intel, Motorola, SGS Thompson, LSI Logic, and others), operating system and Internet software firms (Microsoft, Oracle, and Netscape), set-top manufacturers (NextLevel Systems, Scientific-Atlantic, Sony, and others), and cable and Internet service providers (AtHome Corp., America Online, TCI, NBC, and AT&T) are joining forces to establish this market.[30] This example suggests the uncertain and competitive nature of fast-cycle markets. As such, alliances between firms in fast-cycle markets also may be formed to share risky R&D investments, maintain market leadership, and develop an industry technology standard.[31]

These rationales are used to pursue strategy at different levels. The next section describes business-level cooperative strategies.

BUSINESS-LEVEL COOPERATIVE STRATEGIES

In this section, we explain four types of business-level cooperative strategies: complementary strategies, competition reduction strategies, competition response strategies, and uncertainty reduction strategies (see Figure 9.1). Following our dis-

FIGURE 9.1 ***Types of Business- and Corporate-Level Strategic Alliances***

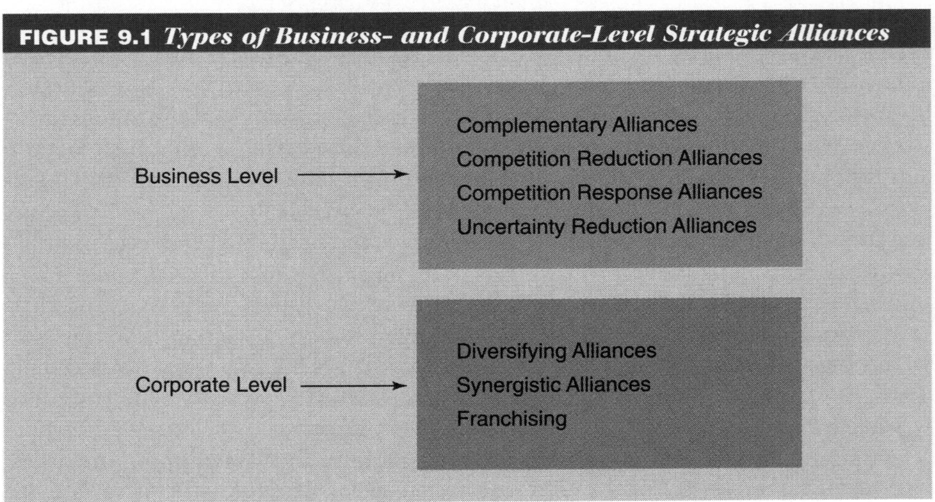

cussion of these four general types of business-level cooperative strategies is an assessment of the potential competitive advantages associated with each one.

Complementary Alliances

Complementary strategic alliances are designed to take advantage of market opportunities by combining partner firm assets in complementary ways to create new value.[32] As the race toward a standard in cable TV set-top boxes suggests, firms often form alliances because they lack certain resources or competencies held by other companies. As Figure 9.2 illustrates, there are two types of complementary strategic alliances, vertical and horizontal. The vertical complementary strategic alliance involves distribution, supplier, and outsourcing functions that are at different stages in the value chain. Benetton and Marks and Spencer are successful clothing firms that use alliances for suppliers and distributors of their products.

Complementary strategic alliances are designed to take advantage of market opportunities by combining partner firms assets in complementary ways to create new value.

Many large U.S. firms have adopted a supply partnership approach that does not entail ownership positions. Traditionally large U.S. firms have preferred vertical integration (ownership of the supply source). This has been especially true in the U.S. automobile industry. In comparison, Japanese auto manufacturers use supply partnerships in a system of cooperation and competition between partner suppliers.[33] Performance of supply partnerships suggests that they provide an effective substitute for vertical integration.[34] Chrysler, as mentioned earlier, has been developing a keiretsu-type network of partners among its suppliers.[35] Just-in-time inventory systems for the suppliers and distributors require significant amounts of cooperation between partnering firms. Such systems can reduce costs for both parties and increase the solidarity of the relationship between manufacturers and their suppliers and distributors.

Outsourcing (discussed in Chapter 3) has been an important means of reducing costs and the basis for an increasing number of strategic alliances. For instance, many large firms such as Xerox, Delta Air Lines, and Kodak outsource their information technology (IT) function.[36] Sears, Ameritech, Lucent Technologies (an AT&T spin-off), and J.P. Morgan have outsourced their data and computer support as well.[37] For instance, J.P. Morgan has not only outsourced to reduce costs, but also to maintain currency. It outsourced its IT function to Pinnacle Alliance, a consortium of Andersen Consulting, AT&T Solutions, Computer Sciences Corporation, and Bell Atlantic Network Integration. J.P. Morgan's chairman, Douglas A. Warner III, explained, "Technology is critical to J.P. Morgan's success—so critical, and on so many specialized fronts, that no one firm can be a leader in all of them. . . . Teaming up with these firms will [increase] our ability to exploit new technologies, manage costs, and create competitive advantage."[38]

A growing number of traditional consulting firms have added managing outsourced functions such as IT because of their ability in these functional areas. For example, in addition to EDS, Andersen Consulting performs outsourced IT operations along with IT consulting. Magna International has increased its revenues by performing outsourced manufacturing and design work for the Big Three U.S. automakers.[39] Although Magna faces increased competition, it possesses the capabilities not only to manufacture goods effectively, but also to design high value-added goods. In fact, Magna can perform initial design, engineering, and development of whole vehicles and thus, has become a strong supplier. Significant outsourcing such as this might be of concern to traditional automakers because it could give their suppliers more power, resulting in in-

FIGURE 9.2 ***Vertical and Horizontal Complementary Strategic Alliances***

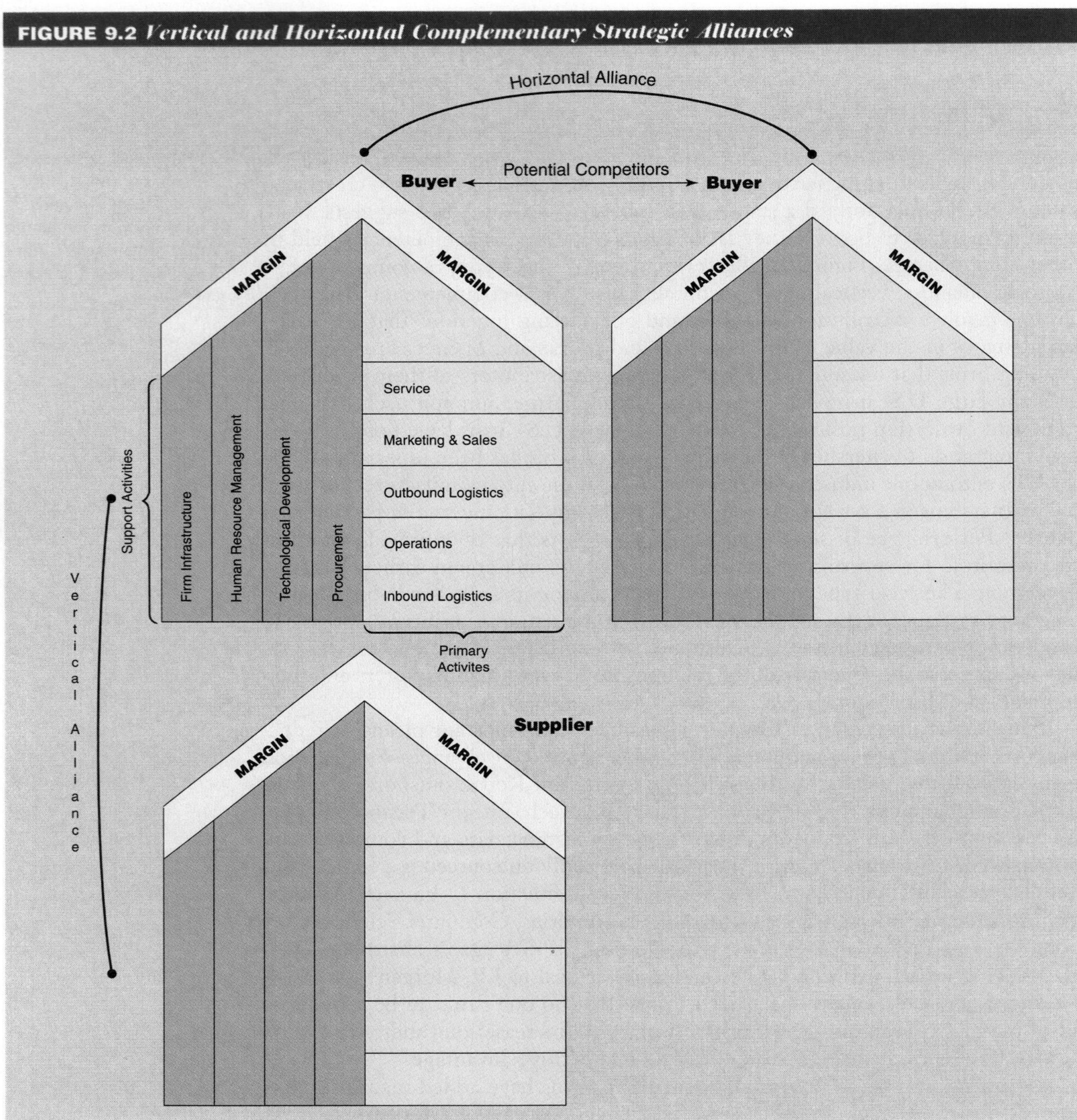

creased costs. As Chapter 3 indicates, outsourcing critical resources and capabilities can also harm the development and maintenance of a firm's core competence. A firm needs to ensure that critical functions are not outsourced in order to maintain its core competencies.[40] Also, partnerships with firms completing work that is outsourced may not be necessary when the purchase is nonstrategic. Because partnerships can be expensive, it may be better to manage the relationship using a free market approach.[41] Therefore, a balanced approach is required. A firm does not want to outsource a strategic competence nor enter into a costly partnership, so selectively choosing partners where they are critical to complement capabilities in suppliers is important.

Some firms that have market power use it in detrimental ways. Manufacturing suppliers and retailers, for example, have traditionally seen each other as adversaries. Wal-Mart's power over Rubbermaid may not be the most effective approach to foster a relationship with a supplier. If the balance of power changes, use of power can come back to haunt a company. Victims will seek ways to resist as Rubbermaid did in its relationship with Wal-Mart (see Chapter 2). Working together often encourages partners to provide greater value to customers than when they try to exploit their power. Understanding this dynamic has been the key to Marks and Spencer's success.[42] Research also shows that such "soft" relationship aspects are important to the long-term success of foreign exporters.[43]

Horizontal complementary strategic alliances (partners at the same stage in the value chain) are often used to increase the strategic competitiveness of the partners involved. Although horizontal chain alliances usually focus on long-term product and service technology development,[44] many competitors also form joint marketing agreements. Some of these agreements not only reduce costs but increase revenues and market power. As described in the Strategic Focus, European airlines have formed many joint marketing agreements inside and outside of Europe. For example, Lufthansa and Scandinavian Airlines have outlined a strategic alliance in Europe and extended their reach internationally.[45] Their Star Alliance system contains Lufthansa, UAL's United Airlines, Scandinavian Airlines, Air Canada and Thai Airways International. Similarly, Delta has extended its agreements with SwissAir, Sabena World, and Austrian Airlines in Europe.[46] Since these partnerships can increase market power substantially and reduce competition, there have been calls to regulate the international airline links and route allocations.[47]

STRATEGIC FOCUS

The Star Alliance System: An Example of a Horizontal Airline Alliance

In May 1997 Lufthansa Airlines announced its Star Alliance with UAL's United Airlines, Scandinavian Airlines, Air Canada, and Thai Airways International. More recently, the Star Alliance announced an attempt to broaden its bilateral agreements through negotiations with Asian Airlines Systems, Singapore Airlines, and Cathay Pacific Airways. This alliance has the potential to offer "seamless global service," and would be a competitive threat to the alliance sought by British Airways (BA) and AMR Corp.'s American Airlines. The BA/AMR alliance was unveiled a year before Star's system but to date, has failed to win regulatory approval.

The Star Alliance also threatens the established Global Alliance system composed of Delta, Swissair, Sabena, Austrian Airlines, and Singapore Airlines. Because Singapore Airlines is a part of the Swissair-Delta team, Global's network would be disrupted. Swissair has taken a 30 percent ownership position in Italian airline AirOne, Alitalia's leading Italian competitor. But this still leaves Delta without access to a major hub in Europe (major hubs include Rome, London, Amsterdam, and Frankfurt). If Global can establish an alliance with Air France, which is pending, then it may get entry to Paris.

Northwest and KLM Royal Dutch Airlines also have a competing network airline system. Although Alitalia had been pressured by some government factions to choose Air France because both airlines remain state run, it chose to link with KLM as a strategic partner and plans to have European hubs in Milan's Malpensa, Rome's Fiumicino, and Amsterdam's Schiphol airports. It will also allow Alitalia to have better global links and may lead to a three-way link with KLM and Northwest, which could save the airline partners several hundred million dollars within two years. The cooperative agreement could facilitate privatization of Alitalia, which the government scheduled for 1998. However, the agreement likely will cause Alitalia to renegotiate its alliance with Continental Airlines of the U.S. because of KLM's agreement with Northwest. Continental and Northwest have been in joint discussions for a potential partnership as well.

The instability among these alliances may cause partners to rethink their alliance plans. For instance, prior to the attempted agreement between American Airlines and British Airways, British Airways had a relationship with USAir. To form the British Air-American alliance, the former alliance with USAir had to be broken. If Singapore Air joins the Star Alliance, it likely will have to break its alliance with Swissair and Delta. As with the USAir alliance with BA, the changeover to the Star Alliance may create mistrust of forming future alliances with competitors. Similarly, Alitalia may have to renegotiate its alliance agreement with Continental. Another concern is the possibility of these alliances creating monopolistic power. This potential has been the reason the British Air-American Airlines alliance has been unable, to date, to win regulators' approval. Regulators have demanded that the two carriers give away, rather than sell, 350 valuable slots a week, mostly at the all-important London Heathrow hub. Although American may have to retreat to a simple co-sharing agreement rather than a more comprehensive alliance system, the firm probably will execute an alliance that is allowable under the current regulations.

SOURCE: T.Y. Jones, 1998, Musical chairs, *Forbes*, January 12, 60–63; AP-Dow Jones News Service, 1997, Swissair to take 30% stake in Italy's AirOne, *Wall Street Journal* Interactive edition, http://www.wsj.com, December 30; D. Ball, 1997, Alitalia may be ready for takeoff, profit, KLM link signal rebound, *Wall Street Journal* Interactive edition, http://www.wsj.com, December 22; AP-Dow Jones News Service, 1997, Alitalia/Continental–2: Few $100M Saving in two years, *Wall Street Journal* Interactive edition, http://www.wsj.com, December 19; C. Goldsmith, 1997, Lufthansa looks to broaden its alliances, *Wall Street Journal*, September 15, A18; H. Banks, 1997, Trans-Atlantic headache, *Forbes*, September 8, 165.

A few observations may be useful about horizontal versus vertical alliance situations. The perception of partner trustworthiness may be different in horizontal alliances where the potential partners are competitors and vertical alliances where the partners are buyers and suppliers. For example, the relationship that Chrysler is developing with its supplier network may be built on trustworthiness that has evolved through previous business transactions.

Horizontal alliances, formed among competitors, may have less of a basis for trust. For example, as mentioned earlier, although Nucor Steel and USX Corporation formed an alliance to produce a new steel-making process, the perceptions of trustworthiness may be relatively low in the relationship because the two companies are former competitors. Similarly, the level of trust among airlines may be quite low because they continue to compete, even with current partners, on many routes. It is not likely that horizontal alliances, therefore, will prove long lasting. This seems to be clear in the airline alliance systems discussed in the Strategic Focus. The airline partnerships appear to be quite tenuous and opportunistic. Such alliances, although they do provide scale advantages, do not appear to be fertile ground for trust and long-standing partnerships.

Competition Reduction Strategies

In the heat of rivalry, many firms may seek to avoid destructive or excessive competition. One means of avoiding such competition is tacit collusion or mutual forbearance (see Chapter 6). This may be accomplished in some markets through cartels such as OPEC that seek to manage the price and output of companies (e.g., oil companies in member countries) in a specific industry.

In the mid-1990s, Russia had a huge surplus of aluminum. When these aluminum manufacturing firms were privatized, they began to export the metal in large quantities, which caused the world price to drop precipitously. These Russian producers undercut the western price by as much as 50 percent. The Aluminum Association, a trade association of aluminum manufacturers, met and called for the United States to file anti-dumping trade charges, claiming that Russia was "dumping" aluminum below market rates. The Russians argued that they needed foreign hard currency to deal with a difficult transitional economy; to cut them off from foreign markets would create a difficult political problem. As a result, there was a meeting by government and industry officials in Brussels in 1994 that resulted in a government pact calling for "voluntary" cuts in production. Although the politicians claimed this was not a cartel, it had the same result: production cuts to sustain a world price.[48] Aluminum prices in the late 1990s increased. Prices rose from near 50 cents per pound to 65 in 1996 and 72 in 1997.[49]

Japan's economy entails a number of entrenched cartels and significant collusion. Even though economic and political forces have been working against cartels and collusion, approximately 50 percent of the manufacturing industries in Japan engage in some form of price fixing. Because some cartels date back to the 1600s, such anticompetitive activity in Japan is accepted and tolerated, which makes it difficult to change cartels and collusive practices. Although the situation is complex, Eastman Kodak argues that cartels and collusion have given Japanese competitors excessive returns against which it is difficult for international firms to compete.[50] More recently, some have argued that problems suffered by Asian economies such as South Korea have resulted because large Korean chaebols, industrial groups mentioned in Chapters 5 and 7, have followed collusive practices similar to the Japanese keiretsus. The basic problem is that cartels have restricted output, while governments restrict imports, and as a result, the countries' currencies have been devalued. The cartels have proven to be problematic for country competitiveness in a global economy.[51]

There is an opposing view. Some claim Japan's firms are less profitable because domestically they are hypercompetitive against each other.[52] For instance, Japan has 10 car firms compared to three competing in the United States. These firms engage in intense competitive battles. If, however, this is harmful, why do the 10 auto firms continue to survive? In the United States, they would have been forced into bankruptcy. Part of the answer lies in Japan's industrial policies, such as lifetime employment.

Even more telling is the comparison between South Korea and Taiwan, two "Asian tigers." Industrial policy in South Korea has placed economic development in the hands of the large family-dominated conglomerates or chaebols. In Taiwan, investment decisions are more decentralized because small and medium-sized firms dominate economic development. Although the large chaebols have developed economies of scale and scope in manufacturing, and even moved into more complex and technologically sophisticated industries such as auto, steel, and semi-conductors, their image is not that of leading edge technology firms.[53] Taiwan, on the other hand, has many small firms that often collaborate with one another such as in electronic components, computer peripherals, and machine tools. In the recent downturn among Asian tigers, Taiwan's approach to economic development appears to have faired much better than South Korea's. The close chaebol-government ties may have led Korean companies to make less effective investments because of government guarantees. More capital was in the hands of a larger number of investors in Taiwan, resulting in less collusion and superior investment decisions. For instance, as with Japan, Korea has too many automobile firms; it has five offerings through the chaebols when its economy can really only support two, even with an export-oriented strategy.[54] The bottom line also provides impetus for this interpretation; the average return on equity was 14 percent in Taiwan versus 4 percent in South Korea in 1996.[55]

Reduction of competition also can be accomplished through industry trade organizations or government policy that is designed to reduce excessive competition, as the aluminum example illustrates above.[56] Some firms follow pricing rules that have developed without direct coordination among competitors. For instance, banks have set rules for lowering or raising mortgage or prime interest rates. This keeps the pricing system for interest rates coordinated among competitors.

Sometimes firms use direct collusion. Consider the ADM example where managers were accused of trying to fix prices on farm commodities with other competitors.[57] Similarly, Toys 'R' Us, the dominant toy retailer, was found to be in violation of federal trade laws by colluding with toy manufacturers to not sell popular toy lines to its chief competitors, warehouse clubs such as Price/Costco or Sam's Club. By getting toy manufacturers to refuse to sell their products to these large powerful retailers, the price could be higher for toy manufacturers and Toys

Toys 'R' Us was found to be in violation of federal trade laws because it was alleged to be in collusion with toy manufacturers to prevent them from selling popular toys to its competitors—primarily warehouse clubs. By keeping manufacturers from selling to other retailers, Toys 'R' Us could charge higher prices.

'R' Us, even though Toys 'R' Us argued that they have to sell toys year round and not just during hot selling cycles.[58]

Competition Response Strategies

As Chapter 5 suggests, some firms enter into strategic alliances to respond to competitors' major strategic actions. For example, as competition for telecommunications services in emerging markets has mushroomed, alliance formation in these areas has increased. Mexico is a country in which these developments are being witnessed. When MCI formed an alliance in Mexico with Grupo Financiero Banamex in January 1994, it was followed by other strategic alliances among competitors to battle for this emerging market. Specifically, AT&T and Grupo Alpha and Sprint and Texmex formed partnerships in November and December 1994, respectively.[59] The airline alliances mentioned in the Strategic Focus are generally complementary, but may also be considered competition response alliances. Susan Snider, director of international alliances for Delta Air Lines, said: "Alliances are not an option anymore. The only way you can fill in the voids is through global partnerships."[60] As businesses go global, travelers are demanding more seamless travel. If one airline can provide it through an alliance system, others are forced to form similar alliances.

DirecTV, a unit of General Motor's Hughes Electronics subsidiary, is the dominant provider of direct satellite broadcasting with 3 million subscribers. Primestar Partners, a joint venture among a consortium of cable television operators, has approximately 2 million subscribers. EchoStar Communications is in the third position with 1 million subscribers, but it is the fastest growing. This competition has forced the price of satellite receiver systems down from $699 to $199, with some discounting even as low as $100, through offers of free installation ($100 value), free pay-per-view movie coupons or do-it-yourself installation kits. Since DirecTV's breakup with AT&T, it has tried to deal with its competitors by following two strategies. First, the firm is trying to offer exclusive programming to its subscribers by forming partnership agreements with media producers. For instance, it has an agreement with Time Warner to produce a weekly music series, resembling MTV programming, exclusively for DirecTV subscribers. Second, the firm is exploring alliances with Bell firms to continue to expand its subscriber base. For instance, SBC, a San Antonio based Bell system, now owns Pacific Telesis Group and thereby has access to the Southern California market. An alliance between DirecTV and SBC would give SBC an entry into the video market, which it has been hesitant to enter. Alternatively, an alliance with Bell Atlantic would support Chairman Raymond Smith's ardent strategy for the video market. Also, Bell Atlantic recently increased its market power through the acquisition of Nynex Corp.[61]

Uncertainty Reduction Strategies

Strategic alliances also can be used to hedge against risk and uncertainty.[62] For instance, the recent changes in regulation of the telecommunications industry have led to a significant number of alliances. Although President Clinton signed the 1996 Telecommunications Act into law in February, the Federal Communications Commission did not set up its rules implementing the law until August. A New Year's Eve ruling in 1997 struck down the telecommunication industries' rules of competition in a ruling by a U.S. judge in Texas. The result came from a suit filed by GTE and the local Bell system contesting pricing and especially the restriction on offering long-distance service in their home territories.[63] This legislation and subsequent court battles have created significant uncertainty for the firms involved.

Similarly, in Europe, a law implementing deregulation went into effect on January 1, 1998. The law dismantled inefficient state monopolies and opened a $130 billion market for competition. To deal with the uncertainty involved, a number of firms formed alliances in the United States, Europe, and throughout the world. Examples of these alliances are explored in the Strategic Focus.

STRATEGIC FOCUS

Alliances in Both the U.S. and Europe Help Firms Overcome Uncertainty in the Telecommunications Industry

AT&T recently announced its intended acquisition of Teleport for approximately $11.3 billion. This strategic action is a way of dealing with the uncertainty associated with telecommunication deregulation and subsequent regulatory court battles. Robert Annunziata helped to create Teleport Communications when he left AT&T in 1983. He went to work for Merrill Lynch as an internal satellite communications manager, but he eventually told his new employer to abandon its satellite strategy and instead build a fiber-optic network to bypass the Bell monopolies and save a significant amount on their phone bills. This advice was followed, and the effort ultimately evolved into Teleport, a provider of telecommunications services to business customers. Teleport recruited the United Nations and several large banking firms as its first major business customers. In the early 1990s, cable companies realized that they could partnership with Teleport using their cable systems to install fiber-optic cable.

In 1992, Comcast, Continental Cablevision, Cox Communications, and Tele-communications joined in a partnership to acquire Teleport. Later, Continental Cablevision, which had been acquired by U.S. West, sold its Teleport shares to get federal approval for the accord. Teleport has now become the nation's largest independent, competitive local carrier. Because laying fiber-optic and developing a local business is very capital-intensive, AT&T chose to make this acquisition as an entry into the local market.

Teleport's cable partners originally entered this market as a strategic option because it was unclear what would happen with their businesses with deregulation pending. Various cable companies have found it difficult and costly to enter the telephone business. For instance, Teleport's cable partners also have a separate wireless-phone partnership with Sprint. Maintaining the relationship with AT&T and Sprint will allow Teleport's partners to watch what happens in the industry from the sidelines. It also gives them the option of returning to the telecommunications industry more aggressively when cable upgrades allow transmission of an array of voice, data, and video services to consumers nationwide.

Teleport's partners are not only dealing with the uncertainty of the regulatory environment, but also with technological uncertainty. At some point, cable lines will have greater capability for two-way communications, which is less flawed and expensive. Furthermore, the Bell firms and long distance companies such as AT&T and MCI have more to lose in the telecommunications business. They can let the telecommunications giant AT&T determine how to handle the local phone service and then enter at a later date when there is less uncertainty.

In Europe, the large telecommunication monopolies have been confronting the uncertainty of the regulatory change with alliances as well. As of January 1, 1998, a competitor from any country in the Common Market could offer traditional phone services to all customers in any other country. It could do this by either renting part of the country monopoly provider's network or by building its own new network. In anticipation of this, several giant telecommunication monopoly providers formed alliances as mentioned earlier in the chapter. Unisource is an alliance between the Netherlands' Koninklijke PTT, Sweden's Telia, and Swiss Telecom PTT. British Telecom and MCI had allied prior to the MCI acquisition by WorldCom. WorldCom's international arm has planned to sink $3 billion into building a pan-European network. Although Spain won the opportunity to postpone deregulation until 1999, it recently changed its mind and is offering some alternatives to Telefonica de Espana's monopoly. Retevision SA is the second firm offering international and interprovincial telephone service in Spain. A third operator's license has been approved by the Spanish government. The Global One alliance of Deutsche Telekom, France Telecom, and Sprint has expressed an interest as has Cable Europa, a cable company controlled by General Electric, Capital Bank of America, and Callahan Associates. Furthermore, the Retevision enterprise is supported by a consortium led by the Spanish Utility Empresa Nationalde Electricidad and Telecom Italia, which outbid Global One. The Spanish utility and Italian telecom consortium acquired 70 percent of the Retevision franchise.

SOURCE: L. Cauley, 1998, AT&T deal offers three cable giants some wiggle room, *Wall Street Journal*, January 9, B1, B16; S. N. Mehta, 1998, Why Ma Bell called Teleport CEO, *Wall Street Journal*, January 9, B1, B7; K. Pope and E. Ramstead, 1998, HDTV sets: Too pricey too late? *Wall Street Journal*, January 7, B1, B11; In the shark pond, 1998, *The Economist*, January 3, 59–60; J. R. Wilke and S. N. Mehta, 1998, U.S. plans immediate appeal of Telecom ruling, *Wall Street Journal*, January 2, 3; C. Vitzthum, 1997, Retevision will offer services charging Telefonica's might, *Wall Street Journal* Interactive Edition, http://www.wsj.com, December 31; G. Naik, 1997, Firms vie to ring in new year in Europe, *Wall Street Journal*, December 18, A18; J. Brinkley, 1997, U.S. and Europe in battle over digital TV, *The New York Times* on the Web, http://www.nytimes.com, August 25.

Although much of the uncertainty leading to the formation of these alliances has been caused by deregulation in the United States and Europe, technology and anxiety regarding potential demand also leads to multiple alliances. The technical standards for high definition TV (HDTV), which will use digital technology, have not been set. A number of alliance systems have been created to establish and market technological standards. Furthermore, broadcasters and TV set manufacturers are unsure of the demand for digital transmission programming.

A number of alliances have been formed to share the risk and uncertainty associated with the market potential of HDTV. The Grand Alliance system was formed in the United States. by AT&T, General Instruments, the Massachusetts Institute of Technology, Thompson Consumer Electronics, and the Sarnoff Research Center and others to help create a standard to deal with the technological uncertainty. Realizing that, ultimately, digital television is expected to be worth billions of dollars in sales to broadcasters and consumers around the world, European firms have also formed an alliance called Digital Video Broadcast (DVB). Although the U.S. alliance system was created before the European one, the Europeans have completed their work and marketing started about the same time that the deployment of the Grand Alliance system was set to begin marketing. Even though neither system is set completely, both alliances are competing in the world marketplace for countries seeking to establish digital television broadcast systems and equipment.[64]

Another uncertainty concerns the broadcasters who haven't decided when to offer high-definition programs, which require special digital transmitters and eventually upgraded cameras. It is a chicken and egg problem. Broadcasters simply don't know how many viewers will have the necessary receiving equipment, and TV makers haven't decided when to launch the sets, uncertain as to when programming will begin. Hitachi and Thompson Consumer Electronics have jointly produced a real projection HDTV that can transmit digital video. Samsung, Sony, and Zenith all are demonstrating different types of receiving and broadcasting equipment, most through partnership arrangements.

In summary, uncertainty can come from a number of sources: regulatory, technological, and demand. Regardless of the source of uncertainty, it leads to firms working together to manage the uncertainty in a collaborative way through strategic alliances. These systems of alliances, however, are often short lived once the uncertainty disappears.

Assessment of Competitive Advantage

Although all alliances are undertaken for strategic purposes, it does not mean that they will realize complementary assets, achieve strategic competitiveness, and earn above-average returns. For instance, alliances to reduce competition are more likely to achieve competitive parity than competitive advantage. In fact, they are usually undertaken to blunt or slow other competitive strategic or tactical moves, which more than likely results in only average returns. An alliance that is formed by a firm lagging behind its competitors for the purpose of improving its capabilities is also likely to achieve no more than competitive parity.

Complementary alliances, however, are more likely to create competitive advantage, achieve strategic competitiveness, and earn above-average returns. When potential complementary capabilities between two firms are realized, there is usually a cost saving advantage or creation of new capabilities or both, which enhances performance. Furthermore, when a firm is able to enter a market quicker through alliance activities than it could otherwise, it may gain at least a short-term competitive advantage. Many supplier and distributor agreements are of this nature.

Uncertainty reduction strategies, however, are likely to realize only average returns because they attempt to buffer uncertainty and rely, to some degree, on luck. This type of alliance increases the number of options a firm has and thus increases its flexibility and ultimate survival.[65] As such, these alliances are important because without them, a firm may experience below-average returns. For example, earlier entrants into the market have established relationships with key firms and, thus, may create stronger barriers to the entry of new competitors.

CORPORATE-LEVEL COOPERATIVE STRATEGIES

Strategic alliances designed to facilitate product and/or market diversification are called **corporate-level cooperative strategies.**

Diversifying strategic alliances allow a firm to expand into new product or market areas without an acquisition.

Strategic alliances designed to facilitate product and/or market diversification (see Chapter 6) are called **corporate-level cooperative strategies**. The three types of corporate-level cooperative strategies are diversifying, synergistic, and franchising (see Figure 9.1).

Diversifying strategic alliances allow a firm to expand into new product or market areas without an acquisition. Large diversified firms generally seek growth through mergers and acquisitions, as explained in Chapters 6 and 7. However, two firms that do not want to merge can still achieve diversified growth by forming a strategic alliance.[66]

South Korea's Samsung Group is a large conglomerate or chaebol that uses strategic alliances to expand into new markets first. Currently, Samsung is investing $4.5 billion to develop cars with Nissan. Samsung Aerospace is also heading a strategic alliance with the Chinese government and aerospace contractors to develop a 100-seat jetliner by the end of the decade. Additionally, Samsung negotiated with Boeing and Airbus Industrie of Europe to buy three 100- to 200-seat commercial jetliners. Some speculate that it is trying to create a domestic airline that would compete with Korean Air and Asiana Airlines. Samsung is also a part owner of movie producer DreamWorks SKG and has had discussions with Disney about a possible multimedia alliance.[67] The late 1990s' financial crisis throughout much of Asia, however, has Samsung pondering the wisdom of such far flung investments.[68] Further analyses may cause Samsung to change some of its investment plans.

Joint ventures have some similar strategic characteristics to mergers and acquisitions. In the United States, legal restrictions can constrain the ability of firms to make major acquisitions. Historically, the U.S. government has tried to prevent horizontal acquisitions that created excessive market power. Such acquisitions may be prohibited because they are viewed as fostering explicit collusion. Acquisitions lack the flexibility that is accommodated by strategic alliances. As mentioned earlier, strategic alliances are similar to financial options that create flexibility and reduce risk when moving into uncertain markets.[69] Large diversified firms may adopt diversifying strategic alliances to increase flexibility and reduce risk. Firms also may use a strategic alliance as an experimental step prior to acquisition.[70] If the alliance proves successful, the firm can then acquire its alliance partner.

If potential business partners have unique resources or capabilities that cannot be imitated easily by competitors, strategic alliances may be more efficient than acquisitions. These characteristics may be lost in the acquisition process. To buy them on the open market may be very expensive because of their unique qualities and value.[71]

Additionally, some firms are using alliances as a preliminary step to ease the difficulty of other forms of restructuring.[72] For instance, Daimler-Benz Aerospace (DASA) has had significant performance problems, given the downturn of the defense industry. DASA and Thomson CSF, a French missile component and armament sales firm, formed a joint venture known as TDA. This alliance, along with others, will allow DASA and Thomson to circumvent local politics in both countries. It will provide more flexibility to consolidate operations and alleviate excess capacity in the defense and aerospace industries.[73]

Synergistic strategic alliances create joint economies of scope between two or more firms. They are similar to horizontal strategic alliances at the business level, but they create synergy across multiple functions or multiple businesses between partner firms. Two firms might, for example, create joint research and manufacturing facilities that they both use to their advantage and thus attain economies of scope without a merger. Sony Corporation shares its know-how through strategic alliances with multiple small firms. A key reason Sony forms these strategic alliances is to acquire commercially useful economies of scope without incurring the costs of acquisitions.[74]

Synergistic strategic alliances create joint economies of scope between two or more firms.

As mentioned in the opening case, the main corporate strategy of Microsoft historically has been its strategic use of partnerships. Microsoft got its start through a strategic alliance with IBM, which had been reluctant through the 1970s to use collaboration. In launching its entry into personal computers, IBM again began to rely on outside partners: Intel for logic chips, Microsoft for operating system software, Epson for peripherals, and a number of Asian vendors for other components.[75] Its success with the IBM partnership allowed Microsoft to improve its competition with Apple. With Windows and Windows 95, it achieved a strong market reliance on PC manufacturer partnerships. Although a collaboration to develop OS/2, an alternative operating system, with IBM failed, Microsoft's collaborations with PC producers succeeded; Windows 95 and soon Windows 98 is the operating system sold with virtually every new PC. It also has used collaboration to establish its Internet browser, Explorer, and to pursue a multimedia strategy with a joint venture with NBC called MSNBC, along with other strategic alliances (e.g., DreamWorks SKG). The centerpiece of Bill Gates' strategy is to take large chunks of the corporate market by dominating the server and mainframe world through Windows NT and BackOffice software.

Windows NT is directed at running the corporate network to which the desktop is connected. BackOffice is the suite of applications that runs on NT. Most client server networks have been run on UNIX, an operating system invented at AT&T's Bell Labs. Microsoft approached Bell Labs about developing and jointly standardizing the operating system, but Bell Labs chose to go it alone. As a result, sales of UNIX-based machines have been replaced by NT-based machines. Also, the dominant network software firm, Novell, faces stiff competition as well because NT incorporates the networking software as part of the operating system. This has been possible because Intel has produced chips (e.g., Pentium Pro chips) that are competitive with chips that run servers produced by competitor firms. This has allowed traditional PC partners such as Compaq and Hewlett-Packard to produce NT-based machines. The acceptance of NT has contributed to precipitous declines for some firms such as Silicone Graphics (see the Strategic Focus in Chapter 3).

In part, NT has been more profitable than Windows 95 because it is being sold by larger computer firms, which have higher margins, in partnership with Microsoft. Digital Equipment has also developed a strategic partnership with Microsoft. Even though Digital has had difficulties, Microsoft signed the deal because it needs large firms to serve corporate clientele. Often when a large server network system is sold, the selling corporation leaves a representative on site to serve the client. Microsoft, coming from the PC market, has no extensive sales service capability. It needs Digital even with its problems. It has HP. It could use the help of IBM. Although IBM is working with Microsoft because of the potential business it might lose otherwise, it is reluctant to form a strategic partnership because IBM sells competing software, Notes (former Lotus Notes, e-mail and networking software) and DB2 (database software). Sun, at this point, continues to focus on high-end UNIX-based servers, although it has an entry level machine that competes strongly with Intel-based machines running Windows NT.[76]

Besides microcomputers and servers, Microsoft has created Windows CE, an operating system for smaller systems such as hand-held computers or palmtops. It can also be used in a number of mobile communicators and other gadgets. For instance, Microsoft is hoping to have Windows CE become the standard system for TV set-top boxes to bring the Internet to the television. To achieve this, Microsoft has purchased part ownership in Comcast, the fourth-largest cable company, for $1 billion. In addition, as mentioned earlier, Microsoft has also attempted to form an alliance with TCI. Alternatively, Microsoft has acquired WebTV for $425 million, which delivers interactive content to ordinary television sets. Thus, a small $299 box will allow a television to be used to view and interact with Internet Web sites.[77]

Small firms also partner with Microsoft because such partnerships bring market credibility. Commerce One announced a "strategic relationship" with Microsoft in electronic commerce, that is, business-to-business electronic commerce software. Once SAP, a popular network software producer, understood that the relationship with Microsoft was clear, Commerce One got an equity investment from SAP.[78]

Microsoft's successes at partnerships have brought inordinate market power to the firm and Bill Gates in particular. There is concern that Microsoft will dominate the industry as well as exert political influence. Although Gates hired nine lobbying and law firms with offices in Washington, D.C., Microsoft recently lost its battle to have Internet Explorer bundled with Windows 95.[79] Daniel Goodhope, a special assistant in the Texas Attorney General's office, likened Microsoft's form of collaboration as similar to the fictional Star Trek race called the Borg. Part flesh and part machine, the Borg beings prowl the universe conquering other races. Goodhope uses the Borg as a metaphor for Microsoft: "Resistance is futile. You will be assimilated."[80] Gates' claim is that being a software company, he simply wants to move into every business where software matters.

Microsoft has a corporate strategy of strategic alliances with partnerships across many businesses and functions. However, its dominant partnerships in operating systems are synergistic across all its businesses and functions. While this strategy has given Microsoft extraordinary market power that it shares with its partners, it has also brought on the scrutiny of the U.S. government, spurred by other industry participants.

Franchising is another alternative to diversification that may be considered a cooperative strategy based on contracting.[81] Franchising provides an alternative to vertical integration and has been a popular strategy.[82] It allows relatively strong centralized control and facilitates knowledge transfer without significant capital investment.[83] Approximately one-third of all retail sales in the United States and Canada are made through franchised outlets.[84] Firms often diversify because focus on a single business is risky (i.e., potential for loss of demand for goods and services without counterbalancing demand from other markets). Service firms may diversify some of their business and financial risk by creating franchises. Many hotels and fast food restaurants (e.g., Hilton Hotels and McDonald's) use this cooperative alternative to diversify into new markets. Real estate firms, such as Century 21, also create nationwide chains through franchising. Examples of other firms that pursue franchising include Charles Schwab in financial services, HCA/Columbia in hospitals, and Service Corporation International in mortuaries. Franchising reduces financial risk because franchisers invest their own capital to expand the service. This capital investment motivates franchisers to perform well by perpetuating the quality, standards, and reputation of the original business. As such, franchising may provide growth at less risk than diversification. Of course, the franchising firm loses some control, but the franchise contract usually provides for performance and quality audits.

Franchising is another alternative to diversification that may be considered a cooperative strategy based on contracting.

In real estate many of the large referral networks, which have served as referral services for local brokers, are losing market share to firms that are wholly owned or that have strong national or international alliance systems. As corporations have downsized and outsourced, there is a stronger demand for property management services and also a stronger relationship with client companies. As firms expand globally, there is also a need to offer services in more international areas such as Hong Kong. Thus, national chains with strong affiliations both domestically and internationally are providing a broader range of service than has been offered traditionally by national or international networks. Strong relationships are being created as the local independent company broker systems appear to be breaking down. The networks of affiliate independent brokers can work, but they need to assume the appearance of a corporation. Colliers International Property Consultants has developed such as system. It can offer broker partners a 12-person research department that a purely local firm could not support.[85]

Motives for Corporate-Level Cooperative Strategies

Because corporate-level cooperative strategies involve not only motives for obtaining competitive advantage but also for reducing risk, assessment of the effects of these motives is essential (for a related discussion, see motives for diversification in Chapter 6). Managers have incentives to increase sales when performance is low as well as to increase their salaries by expanding the size of the business. Alliances can help managers achieve both of these objectives similar to diversification. For example, they can expand the size of the business and thus increase their compensation. Unless a corporation has strong corporate governance to guard against managers using strategic alliances inappropriately (see Chapter 10 regarding governance mechanisms), they may be used for purposes that do not enhance a firm's strategic competitiveness. Managers, for example, may use the intricacy of alliance networks to enrich their own position in the firm. Alliances built on a CEO's contacts and relationships may be lost if that person leaves the company. He or she may be the only one who effectively understands the complex web of relationships existing in the corporate network of alliance partners.[86] These understandings can entrench the manager, making dismissal difficult.

Alternatively, the capability to manage a large number of strategic alliances may exist in very few firms and may be difficult for competitors to imitate. In this light, managing a cooperative network may result in another competitive advantage for the firm. Research shows that firms capable of learning from their collaborations develop know-how that can be distinguished from mere experience with strategic alliances.[87] Although networks of alliances can be used to diversify the firm, to create competitive advantage, and possibly to enrich managers' positions, the cost and difficulty of managing them should not be underestimated. Monitoring these relationships and maintaining cordial and trusting relations require time and effort. Such costs should be considered before entering into numerous strategic alliances.[88]

INTERNATIONAL COOPERATIVE STRATEGIES

In general, multinational corporations have achieved higher performance than firms operating domestically.[89] Also, as domestic economics have grown more global, the importance of international cooperative strategies has increased.[90] Often, firms that develop distinct resources and capabilities in their home markets may be able to leverage them by making direct investments in international markets as opposed to licensing or exporting their products. Cooperative strategies (e.g., international strategic alliances) are a common mode for making such investments in international markets.

Firms can create more corporate flexibility and extend or leverage their core competencies in new geographic regions by developing international strategic alliances.[91] However, such alliances are more complex and risky than domestic ones. For example, there is a higher failure rate for international joint ventures than for international greenfield ventures (establishing a wholly owned subsidiary).[92] Although strategic alliances allow partner firms to share risks, and thus are less risky for each individual partner than a greenfield venture, they are difficult to manage. The need to coordinate and cooperate to share skills and knowledge requires significant processing of information on the part of all partner managers.[93] Where significant demands are placed on partners' managers to achieve quick returns, there is less alliance success. Thus, while international cooperative strategies can have significant positive outcomes, care must be taken when choosing the particular partners, managers, and ventures to ensure success.[94]

As indicated in Chapter 8, some countries regard local ownership as an important national policy objective. In general, western governments, though nervous about foreign ownership in some industries, are less concerned than many other governments. India, on the other hand, strongly prefers to license local companies as opposed to foreign ownership and joint ventures with a local firm or wholly foreign-owned subsidiaries. Another example is South Korea, whose government increased the ceiling on foreign investment in South Korean firms from 15 to 18 percent in 1996.[95] Accordingly, in some countries, managers may not have the full range of entry mode choices discussed in Chapter 8. Investment by foreign firms may only be allowed through cooperative agreements such as a joint venture. This is often true in newly industrialized and developing countries with emerging markets. Joint ventures can be helpful to foreign partners because the local partner can provide information about local markets, capital sources, and management skills.

As trade agreements have proliferated globally, the rules of competition have changed and, therefore, cooperative strategies have likewise changed. More than 100 countries are signatories to the World Trade Organization (WTO) and the International Monetary Fund (IMF). With other treaties, such as the North American Free Trade Agreement (NAFTA), only two or three countries are involved. Accordingly, the strategies have changed to adjust to these agreements. In the European Union, for instance, firms have increased their direct control over subsidiaries and use Pan-European strategies rather than individual country strategies. In other words, these firms establish a strategy for all of their operations in Europe as opposed to a different strategy for each European country. However, in general, the trade agreements spawned more cooperative ventures between partners from those countries that were a party to the agreement. These trade agreements promote freer trade and therefore increase the opportunity for more foreign direct investment, at least from firms headquartered in countries covered by the agreement. As illustrated by the Strategic Focus on telecommunication firms, this trend is occurring in the European Union and in North America and also in Asia through the Asia-Pacific Economic Cooperation Forum (APEC).

As mentioned earlier, joint ventures are more prominent in emerging markets. For instance, international joint ventures represent 52 percent of the value of new manufacturing ventures in China.[96] Additionally, since 1985, alliances between U.S. and international firms have been growing at a 27 percent annual rate across all industries.[97] This growth occurs even though many alliances are eventually replaced by mergers or acquisitions.[98]

Strategic Intent of Partner

With the increased number of international cooperative strategies comes a greater variance in the partner's strategic intent. For example, a partner may intend to learn a technology and use it later to become a competitor. Thus, it is important to assess potential partners' strategic intent in forming cooperative relationships.[99]

Emerging economies, such as Russia's, have a distinct need for foreign investment and technology transfer. Although approximately 75 percent of the Russian economy has been privatized, there has been no large influx of capital. The Russian process was intended more to establish private property rights. As the nature of the Russian economy changes, there is a dire need for new investment, but the Russians are wary of foreign investment in their country.[100] They are quite sensitive about the strategic intent of foreign partners who want to establish cooperative agreements and operations in their country, although this is beginning to change with more market-oriented and entrepreneurial managers.[101]

A recent partnership, for example, between Khanty-Mansiyskneftegazgeologia (KMNNG), a privatized Russian oil exploration company, and UPC, a private Delaware-based oil exploration and production company, could be an example for other international alliances between Russian and western partners. The interests of each partner have been better aligned than most typical 50/50 Russian joint ventures. In previous oil industry joint ventures, the Russian partner desires quick cash and the foreign partner wants ownership of reserves to bolster its balance sheet. Russian partners do not want to cede control and the foreign partner does not want to bankroll them. In contrast, UPC and KMNGG fused themselves into a complicated cash and stock transaction. Technically, KMNGG is an 86 percent owned subsidiary of UPC named KMOC. With this structure, it was possible to win a $55 million private placement investment. Gerard de Geer, a Swedish businessman who founded a Moscow-based Brunswick investment bank, which is a large shareholder, has become the chairman of KMOC. He has the deciding vote on all business deals. This arrangement was a key in winning foreign investment. Perhaps the deal would not have taken place if it were in the hands of tradition-bound oil industry executives from both sides.[102]

Some countries, and the firms within them, have distinct needs for the transfer of technology to facilitate their economic development. Oftentimes, companies in these countries, especially in Asia, have an organizational culture that promotes and facilitates learning. These firms then have the strategic intent in cooperative arrangements of learning from their partner(s). Firms that have different strategic intents may realize a loss of the competitive advantage of their core competence if their alliance partner learns it; therefore, technology and knowledge transfer must be controlled carefully.[103]

On the other hand, Texas Instruments (TI) and Hitachi began conducting joint research in 1988 and incrementally expanded their relationship. During the early part of the relationship, managers from the two firms had to bridge cultural differences. For example, there were significant differences in decision-making processes. TI used a common American approach in which managers held a meeting to discuss an issue, then spent time brainstorming, followed by a decision. Hitachi executives, on the other hand, more commonly held informal discussions and came to a decision prior to the meeting. The actual meeting was used to ratify the final decision. Over time, the two companies learned to work together effectively and eventually developed a joint venture to produce memory chips. Although it took almost six months of negotiations, it was decided that the new venture would sell its chips to both companies at the same time and Hitachi and TI would then be free to sell the chips in competition with each other. TI's executives suggest that it intends to provide better services for its customers to differentiate itself from Hitachi.[104]

NETWORK STRATEGIES

To this point, the focus has been on the cooperative relations between two (or a very few) firms, such as joint ventures or contractual arrangements.[105] However, networks are an important complement to other forms of cooperative strategy. Often networks of smaller firms work together because they are located in geographic industrial districts such as Silicon Valley. Networks such as these are described in the Strategic Focus.

STRATEGIC FOCUS

Cooperative Strategy Often Develops in Economic Districts

Cooperative strategy has been fostered widely in the Silicon Valley of California where many electronic, computer, and biotech firms create innovation and cooperative relationships between large and startup firms. The "Cambridge phenomenon" was a phrase coined more than a decade ago as Britain tried to create its own Silicon Valley. The Cambridge area of Britain has a network of technologically able and entrepreneurial people. Some 1,200 "knowledge-based" companies are located here, employing 30,000 people and generating more than three billion pounds of sales. About 85 percent of the startup companies in the area survive beyond five years, which is well above the British norm of 50 percent. Cambridge University has been a magnet for technological developments. It boasts 50 Nobel prize winners and has many research institutes such as the Laboratory for Molecular Biology where Watson and Crick first discovered the structure of DNA.

The seemingly tranquil lifestyle of this small community will be difficult to maintain as fast growing companies locate in the area. For example, in the summer of 1997, Microsoft announced plans to build a £50 million research laboratory, the first such facility for Microsoft outside of the United States. Additionally, Bill Gates donated $20 million toward a new computer studies building at Cambridge. He is also helping to develop a £30 million venture capital pool, managed by Amadeus Fund Management Group.

Throughout Italy, a number of cooperative districts can be found focusing on specific industry groups. In northeast Lombardy, the small town of Lumezzane is the world leader in silverware, faucet, and valve production with more than two thousand small companies manufacturing these items. In this town of 24,000, most companies have 20 or fewer employees with each worker specializing in particular crafts, such as shaping forks, sculpting their edges, and polishing the specific piece of silverware.

There is a tight network among family, friends and colleagues in Lumezzane. For example, when a business is threatened with bankruptcy, a set of phone calls usually yields a group of six to eight unofficial "trustees" who help bring the company safely back into the black. Townspeople are fiercely loyal to Lumezzane. They usually don't sell their businesses to outsiders, and they stick to the geographic area even though better housing prices are available in nearby Brescia.

There are a number of districts such as these throughout the world where cooperative strategy is often developed among smaller and larger companies. For instance, Dalton, Georgia, is the center for carpet manufacturers. Similar clothes design districts are found in New York City and vicinity. These areas frequently foster significant interrelationships between networks of firms that are often competitors but also collaborators.

SOURCE: T. Mueller, 1997, A town where cooperation is king, *Business Week*, December 15, 155; T. Buerkle, 1997, Cambridge: Britain's I-technology hotbed, *International Herald-Tribune*, October 8, 13; R. Pouder and C.H. St. John, 1996, Hot spots and blind spots: Geographical clusters of firms and innovation, *Academy of Management Review* 21: 1192–1225.

A **network strategy** involves a group of interrelated firms that works for the common good of all.

Although clustered groups of firms often form cooperative networks, it does not mean that the firms in the district are more competitive.[106] A **network strategy** involves a group of interrelated firms that works for the common good of all. The intent of the network strategy is to increase performance of a network of firms.[107] The relationships may be formal or informal. Examples of such networks include Japanese keiretsus and U.S. R&D consortia.

In the 1950s, the emphasis was on larger and stronger firms as product diversification grew popular and larger firms expanded into new product and geographic markets. Similarly, in the multinational and matrix organizations of the 1970s, a combination of functional and divisional structures was used to create large firms of enormous strength and complexity. More recently, however, a newer type of strategy known as a network has emerged. The structural characteristics of a network organization are discussed in Chapter 11. Herein, we outline the strategic approach of these networks. There are three types of networks: stable, dynamic, and internal.[108]

Stable networks often appear in mature industries with largely predictable market cycles and demand. In Japan, these relationships usually include some shared ownership among the network firms as part of a keiretsu.[109] Among U.S. firms, ties have grown stronger and, thus, stable relationships are more common. For example, in the athletic footwear and apparel business, Nike has long established relationships with a network of suppliers and distributors throughout the world.

Dynamic networks often emerge in industries where rapid technological innovations are introduced, frequently because of the short life cycles of products. Apple Computer employed a dynamic network with its innovative Newton, a personal digital assistant. Although the product was developed by Apple, Newtons are manufactured almost entirely by Sharp Corporation. Apple is also involved in an alliance with Motorola and IBM to develop a new microprocessor. Along with this relationship, Apple provided its partners, suppliers, dealers, and consultants with access to its internal electronic mail system, which greatly reduced the boundaries across these organizations.[110] Unfortunately, Apple's network of alliances has not proven very successful.

Internal networks can also be implemented to facilitate firm operations. For example, the global electric products firm, Asea Brown Boveri (ABB), buys and sells a multitude of products across many country boundaries using an internal network for coordination. Benetton, serving as a chief broker among many independent specialist suppliers and distributors, has an external network similar to ABB's internal network.[111]

Each of these network types has a focal **strategic center** or firm that manages the network. The main bank is the strategic center in *horizontal Japanese keiretsus* that entail loosely coupled, diverse businesses. The primary relationship among these diverse businesses is common ownership and arrangements with the same bank or set of banks. In *vertical keiretsus,* such as Toyota and Nissan automobile manufacturers, a dominant firm manages a supplier network.[112] Firms such as Nike, Nintendo, Benetton, Apple, Sun Microsystems, and IKEA (a Swedish furniture maker) are strategic centers associated with network structures. These companies are not "virtual firms" where all central competence is outsourced;[113] instead, they have capabilities and core competencies that allow them to shift important activities to other companies which creates value when these companies are better able to perform such activities.[114]

Strategic center refers to the firm that manages a network.

Monorail is a small company that produces personal computers under $1,000 that fit into a FedEx optimal-size shipping box. These computers now account for approximately one-third of the computers sold. Douglas Johns, a former Compaq employee, started the company. He decided that the computer was becoming a commodity where superior logistics would become the main competitive advantage. He hired designers and managers and contracted for everything else, including manufacturing and shipping through FedEx. Although the company has had significant success and has garnered retail support through CompUSA, the largest computer superstore chain in the United States, its strategy is easily copied. Compaq and IBM have added low-priced computers and Power Computing, recently purchased by Apple, is designing a PC company with product designers but no factory. Also, Dell and Gateway 2000, who ship directly to the customer, are still more efficient than Monorail. When it introduces a new product, Monorail will stick with proven technology and try to keep inventory and other logistic costs low.[115]

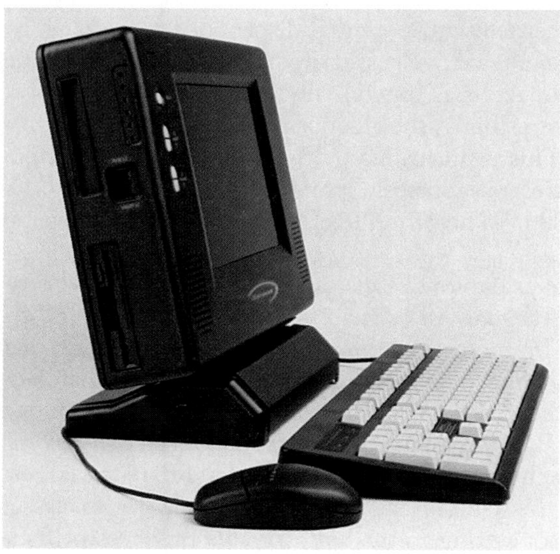

Douglas Johns, a former Compaq employee, started Monorail because he felt that superior logistics would become a major competitive advantage in the PC industry. Monorail computers sell for under $1,000 and fit into FedEx shipping boxes.

As with Monorail, virtual companies go beyond alliances and depend totally on their network to sustain performance. For instance, when a Monorail contractor's die used for stamping out steel computer cases broke, it took five days for a subcontractor to build a new one. By the time the system was back on line, store shelves were empty of Monorail products. Thus, while a virtual company is the ultimate form of network and can be powerful, it also is vulnerable to its network partners. If the partners do not perform well, the virtual company may fail.[116]

R&D Consortia and Other Network Strategies

R&D consortia represent a form of a network strategy where there is a strong need for cooperation among firms (often direct competitors) in an industry.[117] The U.S. National Cooperative Research Act of 1984 allowed the formation of joint venture and research consortia among domestic competitors fostering the development and realization of R&D objectives for industrial progress. These network organizations have been in existence for some time in Japan, Korea, and more recently in the European Union.[118] For example, the Japanese government's industrial policy and the Japanese Machine Tool Building Association (a trade group) have fostered the successful development of the machine tool industry in Japan.[119] The Japanese machine tool industry accounted for less than 1 percent of world production in 1955; in 1991 it accounted for 28 percent of world output. In contrast, the American share of world machine tool production declined from about 40 percent in 1955 to 6.6 percent in 1991.

In high-technology industries, where there is significant uncertainty, coalitions among firms are likely to form to develop an industry technological standard, thereby reducing consumer uncertainty. The videotape VHS Alliance, coordinated by Matsushita to sponsor video recorder standards and the Technical Workstation Alliance created in 1988 to develop and sponsor the UNIX operating system standards, are two examples of this phenomenon.[120] Such alliances may be developed by a sponsoring firm that offers a technology license at a low cost to induce other firms to adopt its technology. In these cases, there is an incentive to make the consortium as large as possible so that there is broad acceptance of the standard across firms using the technology. However, these firms still often compete with one another. Participating firms are concerned with potential disproportionate gains by rival firms. This is most likely when alternative standards are being proposed. The firms proposing a standard try to make it as functionally equivalent to their pre-alliance technology as possible. Interestingly, the alliance partners frequently compete in similar market segments. This is illustrated by the nine computer companies that participated in two different alliances sponsoring competing UNIX operating systems standards in 1988.[121] Therefore, R&D consortia tend to develop naturally as competition evolves.

Sematech is one of the successful examples of a major research consortium headquartered in the United States.[122] Its goal was to help the U.S. semiconductor industry regain its competitiveness by increasing the number of usable chips that could be manufactured from each wafer of silicon and make each chip capable of being more productive. Because the U.S. semiconductor industry has rebounded and is currently very strong, several critics have argued that Sematech has accomplished its goals. Currently, Sematech's corporate members include 10 of the largest semiconductor manufacturers in the United States. These companies invest in Sematech to hedge their risks for operating in this industry. Its predecessor, Microelectronics Computer Cooperation (MCC), was not as successful in transferring R&D technology products to the marketplace as Sematech. MCC's top management concluded that its main value was in the collaboration and shared technology generated by the industry cooperation. The cooperation among industry competitors has probably generated many intangible benefits as well. Although there are multiple potential benefits from the use of cooperative strategies, there continues to be some significant competitive risks.

COMPETITIVE RISKS WITH COOPERATIVE STRATEGIES

Even as companies attempt to cooperate, they also compete, both with firms in and outside their alliances. As such, there are significant risks with a cooperative strategy, including such actions or outcomes as poor contract development, misrepresentation of partner firms' competencies, failure of partners to make complementary resources available, being held hostage through specific investments associated with the alliance or the partner, and misunderstanding of a partner's strategic intent.

While there are incentives to cooperate in strategic alliances, there are also incentives to act opportunistically. If a poor contract is developed, the partnership is likely to dissolve in time. The strategic intent of the parties forming an alliance should be identified and incorporated into the contract to guard against potential opportunistic behaviors.

Some partnerships may dissolve because firms misrepresent their potential competencies to partners. Such misrepresentation is more likely when a partner offers intangible resources such as "knowledge of local conditions." Some partnerships may fail because partners refuse to allow their complementary resources to be available to the venturing firm. Contractual arrangements can sometimes discourage this form of adverse behavior, but once a firm makes an investment, in a joint venture for example, the local partner may hold those assets hostage if foreign countries do not have laws protecting them.

An alliance between Foote, Cone & Belding (FCB) of Chicago and Publicis of Paris, two premiere advertising agencies, suited the needs of each partner. FCB needed help to support its international clients, while Publicis could use FCB's experience in North and South America. However, the trust between the two chief executives who formed the alliance began to dissolve soon after the deal was struck. The divorce came in 1997 after many aspersions were cast on both sides; but, that did not end the fight. Publicis made a hostile takeover for the parent of FCB, True North Communications. Both companies, but especially FCB, are worse off than before the alliance was established.[123]

In addition to the moral hazards (potential cheating by partner firms), there are other risks. One of those risks is having the ability to form and manage a joint venture effectively. Prior experience may not be adequate for collaborative strategies to endure. Another risk is having the ability to collaborate. Alternatively, it may be difficult to identify trustworthy partners with which to collaborate.

Substitutes for alliances include mergers and acquisitions or internal development of new products. To the extent that there are reasonable substitutes (e.g., acquisitions) and significant risks, such cooperative strategies may lose their attractiveness. The increasing number of strategic alliances suggests that they may be

FIGURE 9.3 ***Managing Competitive Risks in Cooperative Strategies***

imitated easily by competitors. Many firms form alliances with other companies because their competitors have done so. The different risks and means of managing them in strategic alliances are shown in Figure 9.3.

TRUSTWORTHINESS AS A STRATEGIC ASSET

A component critical to the success of alliances is trust between partners.[124] The fact that there are incentives to pursue cooperative strategies does not mean that partnering firms have the capability to manage such cooperative relationships and maintain them. Corning, over time, has developed a strong reputation for collaborative venturing. Because of Corning's reputation, potential partners know that a strategic alliance is likely to be successful because it has a reputation for being trustworthy. If a firm takes advantage of other firms in cooperative relationships, it will develop a reputation that will prevent future cooperative opportunities; the firm will be considered untrustworthy by potential partners.[125] Trustworthiness is a strategic asset in cooperative relations because it can be rare. Because all aspects of a cooperative relationship cannot be specified in a contract, trustworthiness is an important attribute. As previously mentioned, horizontal strategic alliances have been found to be successful in developing and bringing new products to the market. However, because this form of cooperation often occurs between competitors, trust is critical to its success. Over time, collaborators gain knowledge about the reliability of partner firms as well as knowledge about partner capabilities.[126]

Frito-Lay and Sara Lee formed a new strategic alliance to produce a product line of sweet snack items for sale in convenience stores, vending machines, and supermarkets. Frito-Lay, a unit of PepsiCo, has approximately $5 billion in annual sales and controls more than 50 percent of the U.S. market for salty snacks such as pretzels and potato chips. Sara Lee is an $18 billion consumer products firm that has other food businesses such as Jimmy Dean and Hillshire Farm as well as consumer businesses such as Playtex, Hanes, and L'Eggs. While not competitors, both Sara Lee and Frito-Lay have strong reputations in the food business. The products from the new alliance will be made in Sara Lee bakeries and marketed under the brand name BreakAways carrying the Sara Lee logo. The products will be distributed by Frito-Lay, which has one of the best distribution systems in the food industry. This new product line will provide both firms their first entry into the $914 million a year snack cake market. Some analysts have estimated that the joint venture could eventually generate as much as $500 million in annual sales. While each firm brings distinct and important capabilities to the alliance, the need to work together closely will require a significant degree of trust. For example, the new snacks will be produced in Sara Lee bakeries but with help from Frito-Lay technical teams. The manufacture and distribution of these goods will require careful coordination between the two parent firms. The alliance will have to fend off a powerful competitor who also just entered the market, Nabisco. Thus, time will tell whether this alliance between two highly successful snack food producers and marketers will lead to the success predicted.[127]

STRATEGIC APPROACHES TO MANAGING ALLIANCES

Two basic approaches to managing assets and liabilities are associated with cooperative strategies (see Figure 9.3).[128] One approach, based on minimizing alliance costs, requires that firms develop capabilities to create effective partner contracts and to monitor such contracts. The other approach, focused on maximizing value-creation opportunities, requires trustworthy partners with complementary assets and emphasizes trusting relationships. The first approach may produce successful joint ventures, but it is costly to write protective contracts and to develop effective monitoring systems. Furthermore, protective contracts and monitoring systems shield parts of the organization from both participating partners. Although monitoring systems can largely prevent opportunism and cheating among partner firms, they also preclude spontaneous opportunities that might develop between cooperating partners. Thus, they may preclude both firms from realizing the venture's full potential.

If trust can be used as a strategic asset in choosing partners, monitoring costs will be lower and opportunities between collaborating firms can be maximized. This second approach to governance is referred to as *opportunity maximizing* because partners in such alliances are able to pursue potential rent-generating opportunities that would simply be unavailable to partners in more contractually restricted alliances.[129] It is important, then, for firms to consider both the assets and liabilities of monitoring systems that will be used to manage the alliance.[130] For example, AT&T entered an alliance with a much smaller credit card technology firm to develop a new credit card service. To ensure secrecy so that the alliance could maintain a critical lead in the industry, no contract was used for the first several months of this relationship. During this time the firms worked collaboratively, sharing information and resources, while relying on the character and goodwill of each other to guide the relationship. In examining this relationship, AT&T was more concerned with maximizing the opportunities of the alliance than with the minimization of potential opportunism within the alliance.[131]

In summary, trust is not required for cooperation between two parties, but without it, monitoring costs will be higher. Furthermore, trust will increase risk-taking behavior between partners to take advantage of opportunities.[132] Trust has distinct advantages, but it also has increased liabilities associated with the risks of cooperative strategies.

Our focus in the next major section of the book is the strategic actions taken to implement formulated strategies. The first topic examined is corporate governance: how firms align managers' interests with those of the shareholders and control their operations to affect their strategic competitiveness.

SUMMARY

- Strategic alliances are partnerships between firms whereby resources, capabilities, and core competencies are combined to pursue mutual interests. Usually, firms' complementary assets are combined in strategic alliances. Strategic alliances have three basic varieties: joint ventures, equity strategic alliances, and nonequity strategic alliances.

- Other types of cooperative strategies are usually implicit rather than explicit. These include mutual forbearance or tacit collusion, in which firms in an industry tacitly cooperate to reduce industry output below the potential competitive output level and thereby raise prices above the competitive level. Firms might also explicitly collude, which is an illegal practice unless it is sanctioned through government regulations such as in the case of electric and telecommunications utilities.
- Cooperative strategies are often used at the business-unit level. We identified four types of business-level strategic alliances. Complementary strategic alliances are firm partnerships created to take advantage of market opportunities that combine assets between partner firms in ways that create value. Often, vertical complementary strategic alliances are organized in a way to facilitate supply or distribution. Outsourcing strategies are also of this type when complementarities are possible. Highly visible examples of outsourcing are shown in large firms such as Xerox, Delta Air Lines, and Kodak, which have outsourced their information technology functions.
- Horizontal complementary strategic alliances facilitate business-level strategies. These alliances include marketing agreements and joint product development between competitors and other complementary firms (e.g., domestic and international airlines).
- Competition reduction and response alliances are formed to respond to competitive interactions between firms. Competition reduction alliances are proposed to avoid excessive competition and are used to respond to competitors' actions.
- Uncertainty also fosters the use of strategic alliances. Strategic alliances can be used to hedge against risks if there is significant uncertainty about performance or new technologies.
- All business-level strategic alliances may not result in strategic competitiveness and above-average returns. Complementary alliances are most likely to create strategic competitiveness, whereas competition reduction and competitive response alliances are more likely to achieve competitive parity. Uncertainty reduction alliances may prevent a firm from experiencing below-average returns.
- Strategic alliances also can be used at the corporate level. Corporate-level diversifying strategic alliances reduce risk but, at the same time, can be highly complex. Strategic alliances may also help to avoid government prohibitions against horizontal mergers. Furthermore, strategic alliances may be used as an experimental step before acquisition.
- Corporate-level synergistic alliances create economies of scope between two firms. Such alliances facilitate achievement of synergy across multiple businesses and functions at the corporate level.
- Franchising is an additional corporate-level cooperative strategy that provides an alternative to diversification. Firms following a franchising strategy can diversify their risk associated with a single business (even those in many markets) without adding new products. McDonald's has used this strategy extensively.
- A number of international cooperative strategies exist. Many firms pursue cooperative international strategies because some countries regard local ownership as an important national policy objec-

tive. Furthermore, the new trade agreements (e.g., World Trade Organization, NAFTA, etc.) have facilitated an increased number of cooperative ventures as firms are allowed to participate in more foreign investments. This is especially true in emerging markets where foreign partners are often essential. International strategic alliances can be risky. One of the most serious errors managers make in forming foreign ventures is not understanding the strategic intent of the partner.

- Adding to the number of cooperative strategies is the network organization. Network organizations are associations of firms with formal or informal relationships that work for the common good of all. These networks can be one of three types: stable, dynamic, or internal.
- Stable networks appear in mature industries with predictable cycles and market demands. The Japanese horizontal keiretsu is an example of this type of network.
- Dynamic networks produce rapid techonological innovations, where product life cycles are short and shifts in consumer tastes alter frequently. Often, these networks are formed to create more stability and facilitate adoption of a new industry technology standard such as the VHS format in video recorders.
- Internal networks occur in firms that have established entities across countries that facilitate coordination between headquarters and subsidiary organizations. ABB and Benetton are examples of firms with significant internal networks.
- A number of competitive risks are associated with cooperative strategies. If a contract is not developed appropriately or if a potential partner firm misrepresents its competencies or fails to make available promised complementary resources, failure is likely. Furthermore, a firm may be held hostage through asset-specific investments made in conjunction with a partner, which may be exploited.
- Trust is an important asset in many strategic alliances. Firms recognize other firms that have a reputation for trustworthiness in cooperative strategic relations. This suggests that firms pursuing cooperative relations may have two competing objective functions, one fostering strong governance and contract development capabilities and another focusing on selecting trustworthy partners where complementary assets exist.

REVIEW QUESTIONS

1. What are the three types of cooperative strategies?
2. What are the different rationales for cooperative strategies in slow-cycle, standard-cycle, and fast-cycle markets?
3. What are the advantages and disadvantages of the four different types of cooperative strategies at the business level?
4. How are cooperative strategies used at the corporate level of strategic analysis? When would these strategy types be used and what are the potential problems associated with each one?
5. How are cooperative strategies applied in international operations?
6. What are the four competitive risks of engaging in cooperative strategies?
7. Why is trust important in cooperative strategies?
8. How is the cost minimization approach different from the opportunity maximization approach to managing strategic alliances?

APPLICATION DISCUSSION QUESTIONS

1. Select an issue of the *Wall Street Journal* and identify all of the articles that focus on cooperative strategies. Classify the particular type of cooperative strategy and identify the strategic objective of the cooperative venture for each.
2. Find two articles describing a cooperative strategy, one where trust is being used as a strategic asset and another where contracts and monitoring are being emphasized. Examine the differences between the management approaches and describe advantages and disadvantages of each approach.
3. Choose a *Fortune* 500 firm that has a significant need to outsource some aspect of its business such as its information technology function. Describe the potential

outsourcing opportunities available and explain the approach you would use to achieve the outsourcing objective.

4. Find an example of a research consortia and examine its organization and strategic approaches. Provide an alternative strategy using the network organization that you think would be equivalent in performance.
5. How can corporate-level cooperative strategies help achieve a boundaryless organization? Describe the advantages and disadvantages to such an organization.

ETHICS QUESTIONS

1. Think about the idea of asset-specific investment and hostage taking in cooperative relations. Is hostage taking, as described in the chapter, a central problem in strategic alliances or is it more of a problem in vertical relationships between firms (e.g., suppliers, distributors)? Please explain.
2. "A contract is necessary because most firms cannot be trusted to act ethically in a cooperative venture such as a strategic alliance." Please explain whether you think this statement is true or false.
3. Ventures in foreign countries without strong contract law are more risky because managers are subject to bribery and lack of commitment once assets have been invested in the country. How can managers deal with these problems?
4. Monopoly firms are regulated in the United States. However, a monopoly enterprise is often considered unethical if it seeks to enter an emerging country. Please explain why.
5. Firms with a reputation for ethical behavior in strategic alliances are likely to have more legitimate venture opportunities than firms without this reputation for good character. How do firms develop such positive reputations?

INTERNET EXERCISE

The following companies have information about their business alliances on their Web sites:
British Airways: **http://www.british-airways.com**
First Virtual: **http://www.firstvirtual.com**
Unisys: **http://www.unisys.com**
General Magic: **http://www.genmagic.com**
Select two of these companies. For each company, go to its Web site and locate the section that discusses the company's business alliances. Then write a critique of how an involvement in business alliances helps each of these companies achieve its business objectives.

STRATEGIC SURFING

The *Alliance Analyst* is the only management publication dedicated solely to the topic of strategic alliances. Although it is not available on-line, the *Alliance Analyst* does maintain a Web site that features past articles and other alliance-related information.

http://www.allianceanalyst.com/

NOTES

1. A. N. Brandenburger and B. J. Nalebuff, 1996, *Co-opetition* (New York: Doubleday).
2. N. Templin, 1995, Strange bedfellows: More and more firms enter joint ventures with big competitors, *Wall Street Journal*, November 1, Al, A12.
3. D. Fenn, 1997, Sleeping with the enemy, INC Online, http://www.inc.com, November; S.A. Shane, 1996, Hybrid organizational arrangements and their implications for firm growth and survival: A study of new franchisers, *Academy of Management Journal* 39: 216–234.
4. S. E. Human and K. G. Provan, 1997, An emergent theory of structure and outcomes in small-firm strategic manufacturing networks, *Academy of Management Journal* 40: 368–404.
5. S. Gruner, 1996, Benchmark: Partnering for products, INC online, http://www.inc.com, February.
6. S. H. Park and G. R. Ungson, 1997, The effect of national culture, organizational complementarity, and economic motivation on joint venture dissolution, *Academy of Management Journal* 40: 279–307; A. Rugman and J. D'Cruz, 1997, The theory of the flagship firm, *European Management Journal* 15: 403–412
7. J. H. Dyer, 1996, How Chrysler created an American keiretsu, *Harvard Business Review* 74, no. 4: 42–56.

8. D. Fenn and S. Greco, 1997, Details, details, details, INC homepage, http://www.inc.com, July.
9. S. H. Park and M. Russo, 1996, When cooperation eclipses competition: An event history analysis of joint venture failures, *Management Science* 42: 875–890.
10. Airline alliances: Flying in formation, 1995, *The Economist,* July 22, 59.
11. T. Saxton, 1997, The effects of partner and relationship characteristics, *Academy of Management Journal* 40: 443–462; Park and Ungson, The effect of national culture, organizational complementarity and economic motivation on joint venture dissolution.
12. B. Gomes Casseres, 1996, *The Alliance Revolution: The New Shape of Business Rivalry* (Cambridge, MA: Harvard University Press).
13. Y. Pan, 1997, The formation of Japanese and U.S. equity joint ventures in China, *Strategic Management Journal* 18: 247–254.
14. D. C. Mowery, J. E. Oxley, and B. S. Silverman, 1996, Strategic alliances and interfirm knowledge transfer, *Strategic Management Journal* 17 (Special Winter Issue): 77–92.
15. Dyer, How Chrysler created an American keiretsu.
16. J. B. Barney, 1997, *Gaining and Sustaining Competitive Advantage* (Reading, MA: Addison Wesley), 255.
17. B. Kogut, 1988, Joint ventures: Theoretical and empirical perspectives, *Strategic Management Journal* 9: 319–332.
18. A. A. Lado, N. G. Boyd, and S. C. Hanlon, 1997, Competition, cooperation, and the search for rents: A syncretic model, *Academy of Management Review* 22: 110–141; F. J. Contractor and P. Lorange, 1988, Why should firms cooperate? The strategic and economic bases for cooperative strategy, in F. J. Contractor and P. Lorange (eds.), *Cooperative Strategies in International Business* (Lexington, MA: Lexington Books).
19. E. E. Bailey and W. Shan, 1995, Sustainable competitive advantage through alliances, in E. Bowman and B. Kogut (eds.), *Redesigning the Firm* (New York: Oxford University Press); J. R. Williams, 1992, How sustainable is your competitive advantage? *California Management Review* 34, no. 2: 29–51.
20. J. Kahn, 1996, Alcatel's local call paying off in China, *Wall Street Journal,* January 15, A5.
21. J. C. Huertas and J. P. Chapon, 1997, Alcatel awarded major contract in South Africa, Alcatel home page, http://www.alcatel.com, press release, July 23.
22. M. Feher, 1997, Unisource to invest $250 Mln in Hungary Telecoms Co., *Wall Street Journal* Interactive Edition, http://www.wsj.com, December 22.
23. J. L. Schenker and J. Pressley, 1997, Feared French-German telecom venture poses little threat so far, *Wall Street Journal* Interactive Edition, http://www.wsj.com, December 23.
24. P. Wayner, 1997, Sky-high dreams for the Internet, *The New York Times* on the Web, http://www.nyt.com, May 22.
25. J. Tagliabue, 1997, Airbus partners agree to form independent corporation. *The New York Times* on the Web, http://www.nyt.com, January 14.
26. Templin, Strange bedfellows: More and more firms enter joint ventures.
27. C. W. L. Hill, 1997, Establishing a standard: Competitive strategy and technological standards in winner-take-all industries, *Academy of Management Executive* XI, no. 2: 7–25.
28. R. Axelrod, W. Mitchell, R.E. Thomas, D.S. Bennett, and E. Bruderer, 1995, Coalition formation in standard-setting alliances, *Management Science* 41: 1493–1508; L. D. Browning, J. M. Beyer, and J. C. Shetler, 1995, Building cooperation in a competitive industry: Sematech and the semiconductor industry, *Academy of Management Journal* 38: 113–151.
29. B. Schlender and A. H. Moore, 1997, Killer chip, *Fortune,* http://www.pathfinder.com/fortune, November 10.
30. D. Bank, 1997, TCI uses hi-tech "layer cake" to ward off Microsoft, *Wall Street Journal,* December 16, B4.
31. Hill, Establishing a standard.
32. Park and Ungson, The effect of national culture, organizational compementarity, and economic motivation on joint venture dissolution; R. Johnston and P. Lawrence, 1988, Beyond vertical integration—The rise of the value adding partnership, *Harvard Business Review* 66, no. 4: 94–101.
33. X. Martin, W. Mitchell, and A. Swaminathan, 1995, Recreating and extending Japanese automobile buyer-supplier links in North America, *Strategic Management Journal* 16: 589–619; J. Dyer and W. S. Ouchi, 1993, Japanese style partnerships: Giving companies a competitive edge, *Sloan Management Review* 35, no. 1: 51–63; B. Asanuma, 1989, Manufacturer-supplier relationships in Japan and the concept of relation-specific skill, *Journal of the Japanese and International Economies* 3: 1–30.
34. J. H. Dyer, 1996, Specialized supplier networks as a source of competitive advantage: Evidence from the auto industry, *Strategic Management Journal* 17: 271–291; J. T. Mahoney, 1992, The choice of organizational form: Vertical financial ownership versus other methods of vertical integration, *Strategic Management Journal* 13: 559–584.
35. J. H. Dyer, How Chrysler created an American keiretsu.
36. L. Willcocks and C. J. Choi, 1995, Cooperative partnership and "total" IT outsourcing: From contractual obligation to strategic alliance? *European Management Journal* 13, no. 1: 67–78.
37. J. W Verity, 1996, Let's order out for technology, *Business Week,* May 13, 47.
38. As quoted in P. Hapaaniemi, 1997, Side by side, *Chief Executive,* June, S4–S10.
39. M. Heinzl, 1995, Magna International profits on big three outsourcing, *Wall Street Journal,* August 24, B5.
40. R. A. Bettis, S. R Bradley, and G. Hamel, 1992, Outsourcing and industrial decline, *Academy of Management Executive* VI, no. 1: 7–22.
41. V. Kapoor and A. Gupta, 1997, Aggressive sourcing: A free-market approach, *Sloan Management Review* 39, no. 1: 21–31.
42. K. Nirmalya, 1996, The power of trust in manufacturing-retailer relationships, *Harvard Business Review* 74, no. 6: 92–106.
43. N. F. Piercy, C. S. Katsikeas, and D. W. Cravens, 1997, Examining the role of buyer-seller relationships in export performance, *Journal of World Business* 32, no. 1: 73–86.
44. M. Kotabe and K. S. Swan, 1995, The role of strategic alliances in high technology new product development, *Strategic Management Journal* 16: 621–636.
45. B. Coleman, 1995, Lufthansa and Scandinavian Airlines unveil plans for a strategic alliance, *Wall Street Journal,* May 12, A9.
46. E. McDowell, 1995, Delta seeks to expand its tie with three airlines in Europe, *New York Times,* September 9, 34.

47. M. Brannigan, 1995, Airlines' "code sharing" helps them, hinders travelers, *Wall Street Journal*, October 13, B1; T.H. Oum and A.J. Taylor, 1995, Emerging patterns in intercontinental air linkages and implications for international route allocation policy, *Transportation Journal* 34 (Summer): 5–27.
48. E. Norton and M. DuBois, 1994, Foiled competition: Don't call it a cartel, but world aluminum has forged a new order, *Wall Street Journal*, June 9, A1, A6.
49. C. Adams, 1998, Aluminum companies earnings increased in the fourth quarter, *Wall Street Journal* Interactive Edition, http://www.wsj.com, January 8.
50. D. P. Hamilton and N. Shirouzu, 1995, Japan's business cartels are starting to erode, but change is slow, *Wall Street Journal*, December 4, Al, A6.
51. G. Melloan, 1997, This year's economic lesson: Japan's model failed, *Wall Street Journal*, December 30, A11.
52. H. Tezuka, 1997, Success as the source of failure? Competition and cooperation in the Japanese economy, *Sloan Management Review* 39, no. 2: 83–93.
53. G. R. Ungson, R. M. Steers and S. H. Park, 1997, *Korean Enterprise: The Quest for Globalization* (Cambridge, MA: Harvard Business School Press), 163.
54. M. Ihlwan and B. Bremner, 1998, Korea Inc. balks, *Business Week*, January 19, 44–46.
55. A. Tanzer, 1998, Tight little island, *Forbes*, January 12, 52–53.
56. R. Brahm, 1995, National targeting policies, high technology industries, and excessive competition, *Strategic Management Journal* 16 (Special Issue, Summer): 71–92.
57. H. S. Bryne, 1995, Damage control at ADM, *Barrons*, October 23, 14.
58. J. M. Broder, 1997, Toys 'R' Us led price collusion, judge rules in upholding F.T.C., *The New York Times* on the Web, http://www.nytimes.com, October 1.
59. C. Torres, 1996, Mexican phone competition heats up, *Wall Street Journal*, April 23, Al5.
60. As quoted in T.Y. Jones, 1998, Musical chairs, *Forbes*, January 12, 60–63.
61. F. M Biddle and L. Cauley, 1997, DirecTV seeks new partners, fresh programs, *Wall Street Journal*, December 17, B1, B3.
62. R. G. McGrath, 1997, A real options logic for initiating technological positioning investments, *Academy of Management Review* 22: 974–996; B. Kogut, 1991, Joint ventures and the option to expand and acquire, *Management Science* 37: 19–33.
63. J. R. Wilke and S. N. Mehta, 1998, U.S. plans immediate appeal of telecom ruling, *Wall Street Journal*, January 2, A3.
64. J. Brinkley, 1997, U.S. and Europe in battle over digital TV, *The New York Times* on the Web, http://www.nytimes.com, August 25; D. Caruso, In debate on advanced TV, FCC can be assertive, *The New York Times* on the Web, http://www.nytimes.com, June 17.
65. K. Singh, 1997, The impact of technolgical complexity and interfirm cooperation on business survival, *Academy of Management Journal* 40: 339–367.
66. J.-F. Hennart and S. Ready, 1997, The choice between mergers/acquisitions and joint ventures in the United States, *Strategic Management Journal* 18: 1–12.
67. S. Glain, 1995, Korea's Samsung plans very rapid expansion into autos, other lines, *Wall Street Journal*, March 2, A1, A11.
68. Ihlwan and Bremner, Korea Inc. balks.
69. H. Ingham and S. Thompson, 1994, Wholly owned versus collaborative ventures in diversifying financial services, *Strategic Management Journal* 15: 325–334.
70. J. Bleeke and D. Ernst, 1995, Is your alliance really a sale? *Harvard Business Review* 73, no. 1: 97–105.
71. J. B. Barney, 1988, Returns to bidding firms in mergers and acquisitions: Reconsidering the relatedness hypothesis, *Strategic Management Journal* 9 (Special Summer Issue): 71–78.
72. A. Nanda and P.J, Williamson, 1995, Use joint ventures to ease the pain of restructuring, *Harvard Business Review* 73, no. 6: 119–128.
73. C. Covault, 1995, German, French firms merge armaments units, *Aviation Week & Space Technology*, January 30, 25.
74. U. Gupta, 1991, Sony adopts strategy to broaden ties with small firms, *Wall Street Journal*, February 28, B2.
75. M. J. Yoshino and U. S. Rangan, 1995, *Strategic Alliances: An Entrepreneurial Approach to Globalization* (Cambridge, MA: Harvard Business School Press).
76. D. Kirkpatrick, 1997, Gates wants all your business—and he's starting to get it, *Fortune*, May 26, 58–68.
77. Windows on the whole world, 1997, *The Economist*, November 29, 68; Set-top boxing, 1997, *The Economist*, November 29, 67–68.
78. D. Kirkpatrick, 1998, These days, everybody needs a Microsoft strategy, *Fortune*, January 12, 134–135.
79. J. H. Birnbaum, 1998, D.C.'s anti-Gates lobby, *Fortune*, January 12, 135.
80. S. Hamm, A. Cortese, and S.B. Garland, 1998, Microsoft's future, *Business Week*, January 19, 58.
81. Shane, Hybrid organizational arrangements and their implications for firm growth and survival.
82. R. Martin and R. Justis, 1993, Franchising, liquidity constraints and entry, *Applied Economics* 25: 1269–1277; S. W. Norton, 1988, Franchising, brand name capital, and the entrepreneurial capacity problem, *Strategic Management Journal* 9 (Special Summer Issue): 105–114.
83. P. Ingram and J.A.C. Baum, 1997, Opportunity and constraint: Organizations' learning from the operating and competitive experience of industries, *Strategic Management Journal*, 18 (Special Summer Issue): 75–98.
84. G. F. Mathewson and R. H. Winter, 1985, The economies of franchise contracts, *Journal of Law and Economics* 28: 503–526.
85. J. Holusha, 1997, As industry changes, networks feel a ripple, *The New York Times* on the Web, http://www.nyt.com, January 26.
86. R. E. Hoskisson, W. P. Wan and M. H. Hansen, 1998, Strategic alliance formation and market evaluation: Effects of parent firm's governance structure, in M. A. Hitt, J. Ricart and R.D. Nixon (eds.), Managing Strategically in an Interconnected World (London: John Wiley & Sons), in press.
87. B. L. Simonin, 1997, The importance of collaborative knowhow: An empirical test of the learning organization, *Academy of Management Journal* 40: 1150–1174.
88. P. J. Buckley and M. Casson, 1996, An economic model of international joint venture strategy, *Journal of International Business Studies* 27: 849–876; J. E. McGee, M. J. Dowling, and W. L. Megginson, 1995, Cooperative strategy and new ven-

ture performance: The role of business strategy and management experience, *Strategic Management Journal* 16: 565–580.

89. M. A. Hitt, R. E. Hoskisson, and H. Kim, 1997, International diversification: Effects on innovation and firm performance in product diversified firms, *Academy of Management Journal* 40: 767–798; R. Morck and B. Yeung, 1991, Why investors value multinationality, *Journal of Business* 64, no. 2: 165–187.
90. L. K. Mytelka, 1991, *Strategic Partnerships and the World Economy* (London: Pinter Publishers).
91. J. Hagedoorn, 1995, A note on international market leaders and networks of strategic technology partnering, *Strategic Management Journal* 16: 241–250.
92. J. Li, 1995, Foreign entry and survival: Effects of strategic choices on performance in international markets, *Strategic Management Journal* 16: 333–351.
93. R. Madhavan and J. E. Prescott, 1995, Market value impact of joint ventures: The effect of industry information-processing load, *Academy of Management Journal* 38: 900–915.
94. J. L. Johnson, J. B. Cullen, and T. Sakano, 1996, Setting the stage for trust and strategic integration in Japanese-U.S. cooperative alliances, *Journal of International Business Studies* 27: 981–1004; J.M. Geringer, 1991, Measuring performance of international joint ventures, *Journal of International Business Studies* 22, no. 2: 249–263.
95. M. Schuman, 1996, South Korea raises limit to 18% on foreign investment in firms, *Wall Street Journal*, February 27, A12.
96. *The Bulletin of the Ministry of Foreign Trade and Economic Cooperation of the People's Republic of China*, 1995, issues no. 1 and no. 2.
97. J. Blecke and W. Ernst, 1992, The way to win in cross-border alliances, *Harvard Business Review* 70, no. 6: 475–481.
98. J. J. Reuer and K. D. Miller, 1997, Agency costs and the performance implications of international joint venture internalization, *Strategic Management Journal* 18: 425–438.
99. M. T. Dacin, M. A. Hitt, and E. Levitas, 1997, Selecting partners for successful international alliances: Examinations of U.S. and Korean firms, *Journal of World Business* 32, no. 1: 3–16; M. A. Hitt, M. T. Dacin, B. B. Tyler, and D. Park, 1997, Understanding the differences in Korean and U.S. executives strategic orientations, *Strategic Management Journal* 18: 159–168.
100. M. Wright, R. E. Hoskisson, I. Filatochev, and T. Buck, 1998, Revitalizing privatized Russian enterprises, *Academy of Management Executive*, in press; I. Filatochev, R.E. Hoskisson, T. Buck, and M. Wright, 1996, Corporate restructuring in Russian privatizations: Implications for U.S. investors, *California Management Review* 38, no. 2: 87–105.
101. S. M. Puffer, D. J. McCarthy, and A. I. Naumov, 1997, Russian managers' beliefs about work: Beyond the stereotypes, *Journal of World Business* 32, no. 2: 258–275.
102. J. Thornhill, 1997, Prospects for partnership, *Financial Times*, December 1, 10.
103. G. Hamel, 1991, Competition for competence and inter-partner learning with international strategic alliances, *Strategic Management Journal* 12: 83–103.
104. Dacin, Hitt, and Levitas, Selecting partners for successful international alliances; Templin, 1995, Strange bedfellows: More and more firms enter joint ventures.
105. C. Jones, W. S. Hesterly, and S. P. Borgatti, 1997, A general theory of network governance: Exchange conditions and social mechanisms, *Academy of Management Review* 22: 911–945; T. J. Rowley, 1997, Moving beyond dyadic ties: A network theory of stakeholder influences, *Academy of Management Review* 22: 887–910.
106. R. Pouder and C. H. St. John, 1996, Hot spots and blind spots: Geographical clusters of firms and innovation, *Academy of Management Review* 21: 1192–1225.
107. Rugman and D'Cruz, 1997, The theory of the flagship firm; D.B. Holm, K. Eriksson and J. Johanson, 1996, Business networks and cooperation in international business relationships, *Journal of International Business Studies* 27: 1033–1053.
108. R. Miles and C. C. Snow, 1994, *Fit, Failure and the Hall of Fame: How Companies Succeed or Fail* (New York: The Free Press).
109. M. L. Gerlach, 1992, *Alliance Capitalism: The Social Organization of Japanese Business* (Berkeley, CA: University of California Press).
110. H. Bahrami, 1992, The emerging flexible organization: Perspectives from Silicon Valley, *California Management Review* 34, no. 3: 33–52.
111. J. Levine, 1996, Even when you fail, you learn a lot, *Forbes*, March 11, 58–62.
112. T. Nishiguchi and J. Brookfield, 1997, The evolution of Japanese subcontracting, *Sloan Management Review* 39, no. 1: 89–101; T. Nishiguchi, 1994, *Strategic Industrial Sourcing* (New York: Oxford University Press).
113. W. Davidow and M. Malone, 1992, *A Virtual Corporation: Structuring and Revitalizing the Corporation of the 21st Century* (New York: Harper Business).
114. G. Lorenzoni and C. Baden-Fuller, 1995, Creating a strategic center to manage a web of partners, *California Management Review* 37, no. 3: 146–163.
115. E. Ramstad, 1997, A PC maker's low-tech formula: Start with the box, *Wall Street Journal*, December 29, B1, B6.
116. H. W Chesbrough and D. J. Teece, 1996, When is virtual virtuous? Organizing for innovation, *Harvard Business Review* 74, no. 1: 65–73.
117. P. Olk and C. Young, 1997, Why members stay in or leave an R&D consortium: Performance and conditions of membership as determinants of continuity, *Strategic Management Journal* 18: 855–877; M. Sakakibara, 1997, Hetergeneity of firm capabilities and cooperative research and development: An empirical examination of motives, *Strategic Management Journal* 18 (Special Summer Issue): 143–164.
118. Brahm, National targeting policies.
119. S. Kotha and A. Nair, 1995, Strategy and environment as determinants of performance: Evidence from the Japanese machine tool industry, *Strategic Management Journal* 16: 497–518.
120. G. Saloner, 1990, Economic issues in computer interface standardization, *Economic Innovation and New Technology* 1: 135–156.
121. Axelrod, Mitchell, Thomas, Bennett, and Bruderer, Coalition formation in standard-setting alliances.
122. L. D. Browning, J. M. Beyer, and J. C. Shetler, 1995, Building cooperation in a competitive industry: Sematech and the semiconductor industry, *Academy of Management Journal* 38: 113–151.

123. R. A. Melcher and G. Edmundson, 1997, A marriage made in hell, *Business Week*, December 22, 40–42.
124. J. B. Barney and M. H. Hansen, 1994, Trustworthiness: Can it be a source of competitive advantage? *Strategic Management Journal* 15 (Special Winter Issue): 175–203.
125. M. J. Dollinger, P. A. Golden, and T. Saxton, 1997, The effect of reputation on the decision to joint venture, *Strategic Management Journal* 18: 127–140; C. W. L. Hill, 1990, Cooperation, opportunism, and the invisible hand: Implications for transaction cost theory, *Academy of Management Review* 15: 500–513.
126. R. Gulati, 1996, Social structure and alliance formation patterns: A longitudinal analysis, *Administrative Science Quarterly* 40: 619–652.
127. M. Zimmerman, 1996, A BreakAway success? *Dallas Morning News,* January 8, Dl, D4.
128. J. H. Dyer, 1997, Effective interfirm collaboration: How firms minimize transaction costs and maximize transaction value, *Strategic Management Journal* 18: 535–556; M. Hansen, R. E. Hoskisson, and J. B. Barney, 1997, Trustworthiness in strategic alliances: Opportunism minimization versus opportunity maximization, Working paper, Brigham Young University.
129. P. Moran and S. Ghoshal, 1996, Theories of economic organization: The case for realism and balance, *Academy of Management Review* 21: 58–72.
130. A. Parke, 1993, Strategic alliance structuring: A game theoretic and transaction cost examination of interfirm cooperation, *Academy of Management Journal* 36: 794–829.
131. C. S. Sankar, W. R. Boulton, N. W. Davidson, C. A. Snyder, and R. W. Ussery, 1995, Building a world-class alliance: The universal card—TSYS case, *Academy of Management Executive* IX, no. 2: 20–29.
132. R. C. Mayer, J. H. Davis, and F. D. Schoorman, 1995, An integrative model of organizational trust, *Academy of Management Review* 20: 709–734.

Strategic Actions: Strategy Implementation

PART III

Chapters

10 Corporate Governance
11 Organizational Structure and Controls
12 Strategic Leadership
13 Corporate Entrepreneurship and Innovation

Corporate Governance

CHAPTER 10

Learning Objectives

After reading this chapter, you should be able to:

1. Define corporate governance and explain why it is used to monitor and control managers' strategic decisions.
2. Explain how ownership came to be separated from managerial control in the modern corporation.
3. Define an agency relationship and managerial opportunism and describe their strategic and organizational implications.
4. Explain how four internal corporate governance mechanisms—ownership concentration, board of directors, executive compensation, and the multidivisional (M-form) structure—are used to monitor and control managerial decisions.
5. Discuss trends among the three types of compensation executives receive and their effects on strategic decisions.
6. Describe how the external corporate governance mechanism—the market for corporate control—acts as a restraint on top-level managers' strategic decisions.
7. Discuss the use of corporate governance in Germany and Japan.
8. Describe how corporate governance mechanisms can foster ethical strategic decisions and behaviors on the part of top-level executives.

AT&T's Board Overcomes Difficulties in Choosing a New CEO

A *Business Week* special report classified AT&T's board of directors as one of the worst in the country. AT&T suffered through a year-long CEO succession fiasco because, some feel, the board failed to exercise effective control over its previous CEO, Robert E. Allen. AT&T recently hired C. Michael Armstrong, former CEO of Hughes Electronics. The board had considered hiring Armstrong but was then sidetracked by Allen who recommended John Walter to ultimately succeed him. Walter, the former CEO of printing leader R.R. Donnelley & Sons, left eight months after coming to AT&T. In fact, Walter quit, seemingly a victim of behind-the-scenes lobbying by Allen to deny him the CEO job. Apparently, it was difficult for Allen to actually terminate his position as AT&T's CEO.

http://www.att.com

Four out of ten money managers and governance experts who responded to the *Business Week* survey said that AT&T's board was among the worst in corporate America. They accused it of harmful acquisitions (e.g., the acquisition of NCR), a number of costly write-offs including the NCR acquisition, and layoffs and spin-offs where AT&T lost a significant amount of its human capital, including personnel working at Bell Labs.

John D. Zeglis, who sought to succeed the outgoing Allen before Armstrong was nominated, has become the number two man and likely heir apparent to Armstrong when he retires. When Armstrong took over as CEO, he required Allen, who had been in trouble even before the Walter debacle, to step down from all his positions within the company. Zeglis matches well with Armstrong, and as a lawyer, he understands the institutional network of key legislators and regulators including knowledge of the Federal Communications Commission. As their first move, Armstrong and Zeglis announced the acquisition of Teleport Communications, a local carrier based in New York City. AT&T's competitiveness declined during its leadership crises. WorldCom took over MCI and many other acquisitions occurred, which put AT&T behind in possible strategic moves that it could have taken (see the discussion in Chapter 6).

Many expect significant changes in AT&T's board of directors. Over the last two years, outside directors who are CEOs from Eastman Kodak, Johnson & Johnson, Chevron, and Caterpillar have joined the board. Some outside directors have come on with significant commitment as shareholders. For instance, George M.C. Fisher, Kodak's CEO, bought nearly five thousand shares a month before coming on the board. Other directors who collectively own ten thousand shares may not have as great a commitment. These are former CBS CEO Thomas H. Wyman, Columbia University ex-president Michael I. Sovern, and consultants Donald F. McHenry and Kathryn Eickhoff. Because AT&T's reputation has been tarnished with major institutional investors, it sought to employ its directors in an effort to rebuild the company's image.

Campbell Soup Company, on the other hand, won the honors in the *Business Week* survey for the best board of directors for the second year in a row. Chairman David W. Johnson has sought to build the reputation of its board as a progressive governance pioneer. Outside directors took control of the search for the new CEO and therefore created a new role for boards in management succession. Furthermore, Campbell has initiated performance evaluations for board members, making individual members more concerned with self-improvement and more attuned to creating effective processes. Typically, boards are packed with trusted friends and colleagues who rarely challenge the CEO's policies and directives. This has given a country club atmosphere to the perception of many boards. Campbell's board members have been trained to focus on one purpose: acting in the shareholders' best interest.

The emphasis of institutional investors, such as the California Public Employees' Retirement System (CalPERS), has fueled pressures for stronger corporate governance practices. Pfizer, for instance, has a new innovative position, vice president for corporate governance. A critical characteristic of board members, from the investor viewpoint, is that they should be independent of the CEO. That does not mean that board members should micromanage or circumvent the CEO; rather, they should provide strong oversight without rubber-stamping the CEO's plans. This suggests that all strategic plans should be scrutinized rigorously and managers should be evaluated against high performance standards.

Furthermore, as the Campbell example illustrates, board members are taking more control of the leadership succession process. Outside directors are becoming more free of all ties to either the CEO or the company. Many suggest a minimum of inside managers and no consultants who work with the firm should be on the board. Also of concern is the idea of interlocking directorships, where CEOs serve on each other's boards.

More firms are now insisting directors own significant stock in the company for which they provide oversight. Although some CEOs argue that board governance doesn't matter as much as shareholder value, a critical goal of many boards today is the prevention of future problems. If problems do occur with the CEO's leadership, a proactive board of independent directors who own shares has more of an incentive to spot problems in advance and act swiftly than a board packed with management loyalists.

However, some see boards as having overcorrected for the years when rubber-stamping was the norm. Their basic fear is that if a board receives unfair criticism, this will make directors hesitant to take strategic risks. Often, a firm's wrong-headedness is an honest strategic mistake and not a substantive governance problem.

The size of the board can also change its group dynamics. Smaller boards may be more effective than larger boards. Smaller boards are likely to have informal but in-depth communication. In contrast, larger boards are likely to have more ceremonial presentations and be more formalized and thereby go into less depth when making strategic decisions.

Boards of directors, owners, and the decisions they make in governing the corporation have a strong influence on a firm's strategic direction. Corporate governance is an important issue in examining the implementation of a firm's strategies.

SOURCES: A. Bryant, 1998, How the mighty have fallen and managed to profit handsomely, *The New York Times* on the Web, http://www.nytimes.com, January 5; S. Lipin, 1998, AT&T to buy Teleport for $11.3 billion, *Wall Street Journal*, January 9, A3, A6; T. Elstrom, 1997, Honeymoon in Jersey, *Business Week*, December 15, 40; J. A. Byrne, R. Grover, and R. A. Melcher, 1997, The best and worst boards: Our special report on corporate governance, *Business Week*, December 8, 91–98; J. J. Keller, 1997, AT&T's board faces many twists and turns in search for new CEO, *Wall Street Journal*, October 13, A1, A6; J. A. Byrne, 1997, AT&T: How to turn a dud into a dynamo, *Business Week*, December 8, 95; K. Day, 1997, Big investors say Walter's exit is latest sign that directors are unequal to their task, *Washington Post*, July 18, G1.

As the opening case illustrates, corporate governance is increasingly important as a part of the strategic management process.[1] If the board makes the wrong decision in selecting the firm's strategic leader, the CEO, the whole firm suffers as well as its shareholders. This may have been the case at AT&T. On the other hand, solid governance procedures can create credibility for the firm and its strategy as in the instance of Campbell Soup.[2]

Corporate governance is a relationship among stakeholders that is used to determine and control the strategic direction and performance of organizations.[3] At its core, corporate governance is concerned with identifying ways to ensure that strategic decisions are made effectively.[4] Additionally, governance can be thought of as a means used in corporations to establish order between parties (the firm's

Corporate governance is a relationship among stakeholders that is used to determine and control the strategic direction and performance of organizations.

owners and its top-level managers) whose interests may be in conflict.[5] In modern corporations, especially those in the United States and the United Kingdom, a primary objective of corporate governance is to ensure that the interests of top-level managers are aligned with shareholders' interests. Corporate governance involves oversight in areas where owners, managers, and members of boards of directors may have conflicts of interest. These areas include the election of directors, general supervision of CEO pay and more focused supervision of director pay, and the corporation's overall structure and strategic direction.[6]

Effective governance of the modern organization is of interest to shareholder activists, businesspeople, business writers, and academic scholars. One reason for this interest is the belief held by some that corporate governance mechanisms have failed to adequately monitor and control top-level managers' strategic decisions.[7] Although perhaps more frequently associated with firms in the United States and the United Kingdom, this perspective is causing changes in governance mechanisms in corporations throughout the world, especially with respect to efforts intended to improve the performance of boards of directors.[8] This attention and interest, however, are understandable for a second and more positive reason; namely, evidence suggests that a well-functioning corporate governance and control system can result in a competitive advantage for an individual firm.[9] For example, with respect to one governance mechanism—the board of directors—it has been suggested that the board's role is rapidly evolving into a major strategic force in U.S. business firms.[10] Thus, in this first chapter describing strategic actions used to implement strategies, we describe monitoring and controlling mechanisms that, when used properly, ensure that top-level managerial decisions and actions contribute to the firm's strategic competitiveness and its ability to earn above-average returns.

Effective corporate governance is also of interest to nations. As stated by a researcher, "Every country wants the firms that operate within its borders to flourish and grow in such ways as to provide employment, wealth, and satisfaction, not only to improve standards of living materially but also to enhance social cohesion. These aspirations cannot be met unless those firms are competitive internationally in a sustained way, and it is this medium- and long-term perspective that makes good corporate governance so vital."[11] Thus, in many individual corporations, shareholders are striving to hold top-level managers more accountable for their decisions and the results they generate. As with individual firms and their boards, nations that govern their corporations effectively may gain a competitive advantage over rival countries.

In a range of countries, but especially in the United States and the United Kingdom, the fundamental goal of business organizations is to maximize shareholder value.[12] Traditionally, shareholders are treated as the firm's key stakeholder because they are the company's legal owners. The firm's owners expect top-level managers and others influencing the corporation's actions (e.g., the board of directors) to make decisions that will result in the maximization of the company's value and, hence, of their own wealth.

In this chapter's first section, we describe the relationship that is the foundation on which the modern corporation is built. For the most part, this relationship provides an understanding of how U.S. firms operate. The majority of this chapter is then devoted to an explanation of various mechanisms owners use to govern managers and ensure that they comply with their responsibility to maximize shareholder value.

In many corporations, shareholders expect top-level managers to make decisions that result in the maximization of the company's value—and of their own wealth.

Four internal governance mechanisms and a single external one are used in the modern corporation (see Table 10.1). The four internal governance mechanisms examined here are (1) ownership concentration, as represented by types of shareholders and their different incentives to monitor managers, (2) the board of directors, (3) executive compensation, and (4) the multidivisional (M-form) organizational structure. (As explained in Chapter 11, in addition to governing managers'

TABLE 10.1 ***Corporate Governance Mechanisms***

Internal Governance Mechanisms

Ownership Concentration

- Relative amounts of stock owned by individual shareholders and institutional investors

Board of Directors

- Individuals responsible for representing the firm's owners by monitoring top-level managers' strategic decisions

Executive Compensation

- Use of salary, bonuses, and long-term incentives to align managers' interests with shareholders' interests

Multidivisional Structure

- Creation of individual business divisions to closely monitor top-level managers' strategic decisions

External Governance Mechanism

Market for Corporate Control

- The purchase of a firm that is underperforming relative to industry rivals in order to improve its strategic competitiveness decisions, the M-form structure is the one required to implement successfully different types of related and unrelated corporate-level diversification strategies.)

We next consider the market for corporate control, an external corporate governance mechanism. Essentially, the market for corporate control is a set of potential owners seeking to "raid" undervalued firms and earn above-average returns on their investments by replacing ineffective top-level management teams.[13] The chapter's focus then shifts to the issue of international corporate governance. We briefly describe governance approaches used in German and Japanese firms whose traditional governance structures are being affected by the realities of competing in the global economy. In part, this discussion suggests the possibility that the structures used to govern global companies in many different countries, including Germany, Japan, the United Kingdom, and the United States, are becoming more, rather than less, similar. Closing our analysis of corporate governance is a consideration of the need for these control mechanisms to encourage and support ethical behavior in organizations.

Before we begin, we need to highlight two matters related to corporate governance. First, research results suggest that the mechanisms explained in this chapter have the potential to influence positively the governance of the modern corporation. This evidence is important, because the development of the modern corporation has placed significant responsibility and authority in the hands of top-level managers. The most effective of these managers hold themselves accountable for their firm's performance and respond positively to the demands of the corporate governance mechanisms explained in this chapter.[14] Second, it is the appropriate use of a variety of mechanisms that results in the effective governance of a corporation. The firm's owners should not expect any single mechanism to govern the company effectively across time. It is through the proper use of several mechanisms that owners are able to govern the corporation in ways that maximize strategic competitiveness and increase the financial value of their firm.[15]

SEPARATION OF OWNERSHIP AND MANAGERIAL CONTROL

Historically, U.S. firms were managed by their founder-owners and their descendants. In these cases, corporate ownership and control resided in the same person(s). As firms grew larger, ". . . the managerial revolution led to a separation of ownership and control in most large corporations, where control of the firm shifted from entrepreneurs to professional managers while ownership became dispersed among thousands of unorganized stockholders who were removed from the day-to-day management of the firm."[16] These changes created the modern public corporation, which is based on the efficient separation of ownership and managerial control. A basic legal premise supporting this efficient separation is that the primary objective of a firm's activities should be to increase the corporation's profit and the financial gains of the owners, that is, the shareholders.[17]

The separation of ownership and managerial control allows shareholders to purchase stock, which entitles them to income (residual returns) from firm operations after expenses have been paid. This right, however, requires they also take a risk that the firm's expenses may exceed its revenues. To manage this investment risk, shareholders seek to maintain a diversified portfolio by investing in several companies to reduce their overall risk.

In small firms, managers often are the owners, so there is no separation between ownership and managerial control, but as firms grow and become more complex, owners/managers may contract with managerial specialists. These managers oversee decision making in the owner's firm and are compensated on the basis of their decision-making skills. Managers, then, operate a corporation through use of their decision-making skills and are viewed as agents of the firm's owners.[18] In terms of the strategic management process (see Figure 1.1 in Chapter 1), managers are expected to form a firm's strategic intent and strategic mission and then formulate and implement the strategies that realize them. Thus, in the modern public corporation, top-level managers, especially the CEO, have primary responsibility for initiating and implementing an array of strategic decisions.

As shareholders diversify their investments over a number of corporations, their risk declines (the poor performance or failure of any one firm in which they invest has less overall effect). Shareholders thus specialize in managing their investment risk; managers specialize in decision making. Without management specialization in decision making and owner specialization in risk bearing, a firm probably would be limited by the abilities of its owners to manage and make effective strategic decisions. Therefore, the separation and specialization of ownership (risk bearing) and managerial control (decision making) is theoretically economically efficient.

Agency Relationships

The separation between owners and managers creates an agency relationship. An **agency relationship** exists when one or more persons (the principal or principals) hire another person or persons (the agent or agents) as decision-making specialists to perform a service.[19] Thus, an agency relationship exists when one party delegates decision-making responsibility to a second party for compensation (see Figure 10.1).[20] In addition to shareholders and top-level managers, other examples of agency relationships include consultants and clients and insured and insurer. Moreover, within organizations, an agency relationship exists between managers and their employees as well as between top-level executives and the firm's owners.[21] In the modern corporation, managers must understand the links between these relationships and the firm's effectiveness.[22] Although the agency relationship between managers and their employees is important, this chapter focuses on the agency relationship between the firm's owners (the principals) and top-level managers (the principals' agents) because this relationship is related directly to the strategies implemented by managers.

An **agency relationship** exists when one or more persons (the principal or principals) hire another person or persons (the agent or agents) as decision-making specialists to perform a service.

The separation between ownership and managerial control can be problematic. Research evidence documents a variety of agency problems in the modern corporation.[23] Problems can surface because divergent interests exist between the principal and the agent, or because shareholders often lack direct control of large publicly traded corporations. Problems arise when an agent makes decisions that result in the pursuit of goals that conflict with those of the principals. Thus, when ownership and control are separated, a relationship is formed that *potentially* allows divergent interests (between principals and agents) to surface, which can lead to managerial opportunism.[24] **Managerial opportunism** is the seeking of self-interest with guile (cunning, deceit).[25] Opportunism is both an attitude (e.g., an inclination or proclivity) and a set of behaviors (i.e., specific acts of self-interest that are sought with guile).[26] Although few agents act opportunistically, the inclination and proclivity to engage in opportunistic behaviors varies among individuals and across cultures.[27] The prob-

Managerial opportunism is the seeking of self-interest with guile.

FIGURE 10.1 *An Agency Relationship*

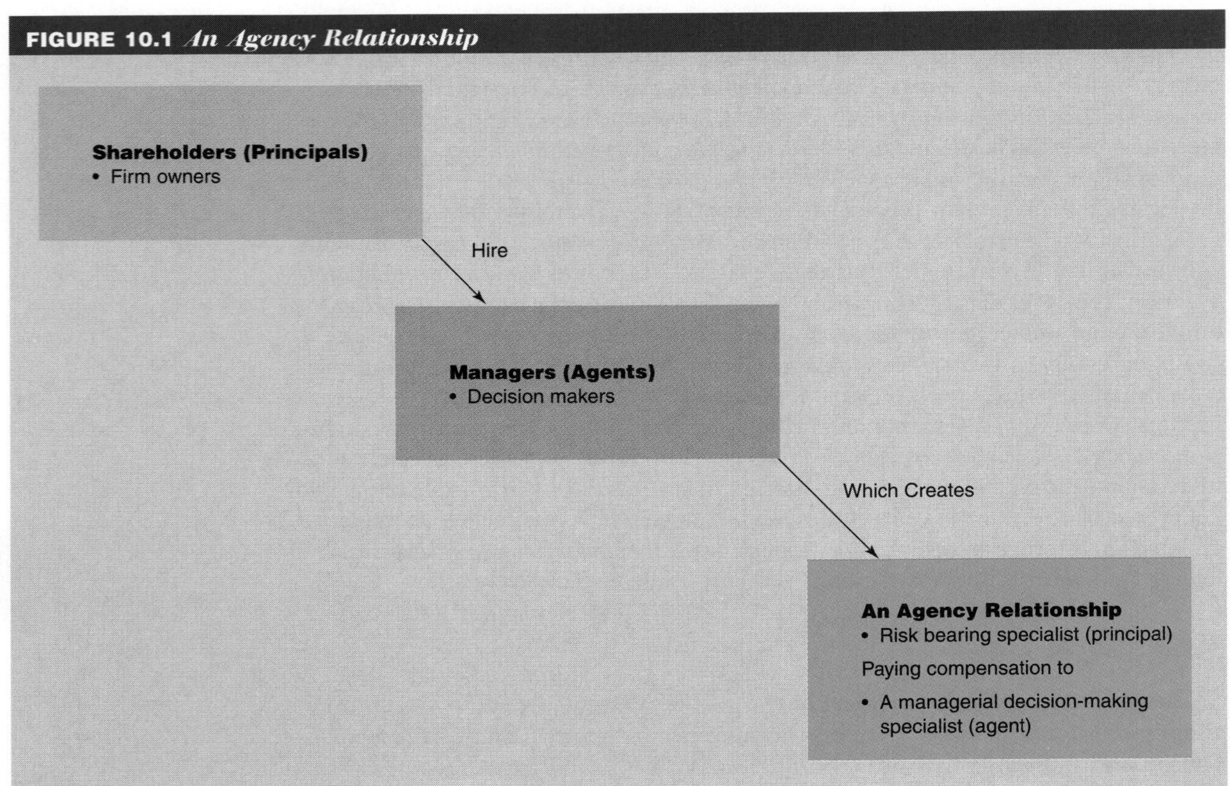

lem for principals, however, is that it is impossible to know beforehand which agents will or will not engage in opportunistic behavior. Because a top-level manager's reputation is an imperfect guide to future behavior, and because opportunistic behavior cannot be observed until it has taken place, principals establish governance and control mechanisms on the assumption that some agents might act opportunistically.[28] Thus, the principals' delegation of decision-making responsibilities to agents creates the opportunity for conflicts of interest to surface. Top-level managers, for example, may make strategic decisions that maximize their personal welfare and minimize their personal risk.[29] Decisions such as these prevent the maximization of shareholder wealth. Decisions regarding product diversification demonstrate these possibilities.

Product Diversification as an Example of an Agency Problem

As explained in Chapter 6, corporate-level strategies involving product diversification can enhance a firm's strategic competitiveness and increase its returns, both of which serve the interests of shareholders and top-level managers. However, because product diversification can provide two benefits to managers that shareholders do not enjoy, top-level executives sometimes prefer more product diversification than do shareholders.[30]

The first managerial benefit occurs because of the positive relationships between diversification and firm size and between firm size and executive compensation. Thus, increased product diversification provides an opportunity for higher compensation for top-level managers through growth in firm size.[31]

The second managerial benefit is that product diversification and the resulting diversification of the firm's portfolio of businesses can reduce top-level managers' employment risk.[32] *Managerial employment risk* is the risk of job loss, loss of compensation, and loss of managerial reputation. These risks are reduced with increased diversification because a firm and its upper-level managers are less vulnerable to the reduction in demand associated with a single or a limited number of product lines or businesses. Furthermore, the firm may have free cash flows over which top-level managers have discretion. *Free cash flows* are resources generated after investment in all projects that have positive net present values within the firm's current product lines.[33] In anticipation of positive returns, managers may decide to use these funds to invest in products that are not associated with the current lines of business, even if the investments increase the firm's level of diversification. The managerial decision to consume free cash flows to increase the firm's diversification inefficiently is an example of self-serving and opportunistic managerial behavior. In contrast to managers, shareholders may prefer that free cash flows be returned as dividends so they will have control over reinvestment decisions.[34]

Curve *S* in Figure 10.2 depicts shareholders' optimal level of diversification. Owners seek the level of diversification that reduces the risk of the firm's total failure while simultaneously increasing the company's value through the development of economies of scale and scope (see Chapter 6). Of the four corporate-level diversification strategies shown in Figure 10.2, shareholders might prefer the diver-

FIGURE 10.2 *Manager and Shareholder Risk and Diversification*

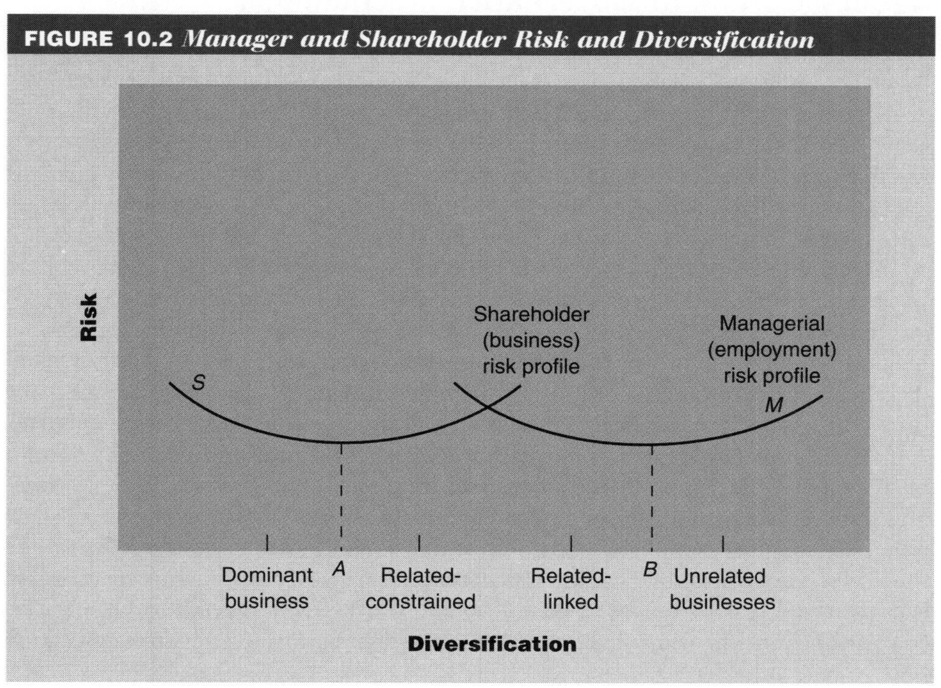

sified position noted by point *A* on curve *S*—a position that is located between the dominant business and related-constrained diversification strategies. Of course, the optimum level of diversification sought by owners varies from firm to firm. Factors that affect shareholders' preferences include the firm's primary industry, the intensity of rivalry among competitors in that industry, and the top management team's experience with implementing diversification strategies.

As with principals, upper-level executives—as agents—seek what they perceive to be an optimal level of diversification. Declining performance resulting from too much product diversification increases the probability that a firm will be acquired through the market for corporate control. Once acquired, the employment risk for the firm's top-level managers increases substantially. Furthermore, a manager's employment opportunities in the external managerial labor market (discussed in Chapter 12) are affected negatively by a firm's poor performance. Therefore, top-level managers prefer diversification, but not to a point that it increases their employment risk and reduces their employment opportunities.

Curve *M* (in Figure 10.2) shows that executives prefer higher levels of product diversification than shareholders. Top-level managers might prefer the level of diversification shown by point *B* on curve *M*. In general, shareholders prefer riskier strategies with more focused diversification and reduce their risk through holding a diversified portfolio of equity investments. Alternatively, managers cannot work for a diverse portfolio of firms to balance their employment risk. As such, top-level managers may prefer more diversification in order to maximize firm size and executive compensation and reduce employment risk. Product diversification, therefore, is a potential agency problem that could result in principals incurring costs to control their agents' behaviors.

Agency Costs and Governance Mechanisms

The potential conflict illustrated in Figure 10.2, coupled with the fact that principals do not know which managers might act opportunistically, demonstrates why principals establish governance mechanisms. But establishing and using the governance mechanisms discussed in this chapter is not without costs. **Agency costs** are the sum of incentive, monitoring, enforcement costs, and individual financial losses incurred by principals because it is impossible to use governance mechanisms to guarantee total compliance by the agent.[35]

Agency costs are the sum of incentive, monitoring, enforcement costs, and individual financial losses incurred by principals because it is impossible to use governance mechanisms to guarantee total compliance by the agent.

In general, managerial interests may prevail when governance mechanisms are weak. For example, the firm's level of diversification will move closer to curve *M* in Figure 10.2 when governance mechanisms allow managers a significant amount of autonomy in making strategic decisions. If, however, the board of directors controls managerial autonomy, or if other strong governance mechanisms are used, the firm's diversification level will approach that desired by shareholders (see curve *S*).

In the following sections, we explain the effects of various means of governance on managerial decisions to formulate and implement the firm's different strategies, especially corporate-level diversification strategies. We focus on this strategy type because the relationship between principals and agents, developed through the use of governance mechanisms, is observed easily. Moreover, this relationship is critical in diversified firms. The failure to govern strategic decisions properly in companies implementing diversification results in significant negative effects on the firm's performance as measured by strategic competitiveness and financial returns.[36]

OWNERSHIP CONCENTRATION

Ownership concentration is defined by both the number of large-block shareholders and the total percentage of shares they own. **Large-block shareholders** typically own at least five percent of a corporation's issued shares. Ownership concentration as a governance mechanism has been researched extensively.[37] One reason for this level of interest and analysis is that large-block shareholders are increasingly active in their demands that corporations adopt effective governance mechanisms to control the decisions of their managerial agents.[38]

Ownership concentration is defined by both the number of large-block shareholders and the total percentage of shares they own.

Large-block shareholders typically own at least five percent of a corporation's issued shares.

In general, *diffuse ownership* (a large number of shareholders with small holdings and few if any large-block shareholders) produces weak monitoring of managerial decisions. Among other problems, diffuse ownership makes it difficult for owners to coordinate their actions effectively. An outcome of weak monitoring might be diversification of the firm's product lines beyond the shareholders' optimum level. Higher levels of monitoring could encourage managers to avoid levels of diversification that exceed shareholders' preferences. Such monitoring could also disallow excessive compensation paid to managers by holding down diversification and thereby the size of the firm. In fact, research evidence shows that ownership concentration is associated with lower levels of firm diversification.[39] Thus, with high degrees of ownership concentration, the probability is greater that managers' strategic decisions will be intended to maximize shareholder value.

Typically, shareholders monitor managerial decisions and firm actions through the board of directors. Shareholders elect members to their firm's board. Elected members are expected to oversee managerial agents and to ensure that the corporation is operated in ways that will maximize shareholders' wealth.

The Growing Influence of Institutional Owners as Large-Block Shareholders

A classic work published in the 1930s argued that the "modern" corporation had become characterized by a separation of ownership and control.[40] This change occurred as firm growth prevented founders-owners from maintaining their dual positions as owners and managers of their corporations. More recently, another shift has occurred. Ownership of many modern corporations is now concentrated in the hands of institutional investors rather than individual shareholders.[41]

Institutional owners are financial institutions such as stock mutual funds and pension funds that control large-block shareholder positions. Because of their prominent ownership positions, institutional owners, as large-block shareholders, are a powerful governance mechanism.[42] Institutions of these types now own more than 50 percent of the stock in large U.S. corporations. Of the top 1,000 corporations, they own on average 59 percent of the stock.[43] Pension funds alone are expected to control at least one-half of corporate equity by 2000.[44] Thus, as these ownership percentages suggest, institutional owners have both the size and incentive to discipline ineffective top-level managers and are able to influence significantly a firm's choice of strategies and overall strategic decisions.[45]

Institutional owners are financial institutions such as stock mutual funds and pension funds that control large-block shareholder positions.

Research evidence indicates that institutional and other large-block shareholders are becoming more active in efforts to influence a corporation's strategic decisions. Initially, the focus seemed to be on the accountability of CEOs. After focusing on the performance of many CEOs, which has contributed to the ouster of a number of them, shareholder activists and institutional investors are targeting what they perceive as ineffective boards of directors (see AT&T opening case example).

Anthony J.F. O'Reilly, former CEO of H.J. Heinz, Inc., was the target of activist shareholders, even though his corporation had earned above-average returns. Both Teachers Insurance and Annuity Association—College Retirement Equities Fund (TIAA-CREF) and California Public Employees' Retirement System (CalPERS) believed that Heinz's board of directors was an example of what a board should not be: "a cozy club of loyalists headed by a powerful and charismatic chieftain."[46] O'Reilly held lavish parties for company officials and analysts. Activists believe that a stronger board would have reined in such costly events. O'Reilly fought such board reforms because Heinz had performed well. However, as the opening case illustrates, Campbell Soup, a rival of Heinz, has found that higher accountability for the board of directors is paying dividends. Recall that Campbell placed first in the *Business Week* survey of corporate governance two years in a row.[47]

CalPERS provides retirement and health coverage to more than one million current and retired public employees.[48] It is the largest public employee pension fund in the United States, with a portfolio approximating $135 billion invested in more than 1,200 companies. As an active institutional owner, the organization's actions have earned it a reputation for bullying some U.S. companies into adopting its recommendations. CalPERS is generally thought to act aggressively to promote decisions and actions that it believes will enhance shareholder value in companies in which it invests. To pressure boards of directors to make what it believes are needed changes, CalPERS annually issues a target list of companies in which it owns stock that it believes are underachieving. This list is based on corporations' relative rates of shareholder return, their degree of responsiveness to CalPERS' inquiries, labor practices, and the percentage of shares owned by CalPERS. Once published, CalPERS usually demands meetings with top-level managers from companies included on the list and is known to flex its muscle to oust directors when its requests are denied.[49] According to CalPERS officials, the intent of these sessions is to persuade corporate boards to force management to initiate appropriate strategic changes inside the targeted company. Based on inputs from this institutional investor, some believe that top-level executives at various companies, including GM, IBM, and Kodak, have lost their jobs.

Public pension funds such as CalPERS also must achieve strategic success through their operations, but research results suggest that the activism of large public pension funds such as CalPERS has not been universally successful. These findings indicate that activists' proposals to top-level managers that are not focused on firm performance issues can have a negative effect on the company's efforts to earn above-average returns. Thus, questions exist regarding the practice of shareholder activists and the long-term performance effects of their actions on targeted firms.[50]

The Strategic Focus discusses CalPERS recent change in its strategic approach to pursue increased investments in international companies. As CalPERS and other pension funds begin to invest overseas, they are actively trying to change corporate governance procedures. Also, as pointed out in the Strategic Focus, institutional investors may consider taking board seats on firms in which they are invested heavily.

STRATEGIC FOCUS

CalPERS Initiates New Shareholder Activist Approaches

Many of the rules of corporate governance have changed because of activist shareholders such as public pension funds like the California Public Employees' Retirement System (CalPERS). Historically, CalPERS has been proud of its intolerance of poor corporate performance. The policies of institutional activists such as CalPERS have changed the way most boards are structured and managed: boards are not overly large now so that they can have more effective group processes. Most board members are composed of outside directors who are non-employees and independent. Outside directors chair key committees such as the audit and compensation committees. Furthermore, new proxy rules have been required by the Security and Exchange Commission because activist investors such as CalPERS have pushed for more accurate information on those who perform the corporate governance role (e.g., board members and large stockholders).

U.S.-style shareholder activism is now being adopted in other areas of the world. For instance, in Europe, the International Corporate Governance Network drew 35 people to an inaugural meeting in London in 1996. Its second meeting in Paris in the summer of 1997 drew 125 people. The French Business Council was addressed by Richard Koppes, the former general council of CalPERS. The top managers of French firms were concerned about governance issues because U.S. institutions already own 25 to 40 percent of the shares of many French companies. Many of these top managers expect to be majority owned by U.S. institutional investors within the next few years. Although many union and civil service employee funds limit investments in non-U.S. companies, others have been increasing the size of their international portfolios. CalPERS, for instance, invests more than $25 billion overseas. This suggests that the organization's fiduciary duty should also challenge it to be more active in overseas governance matters.

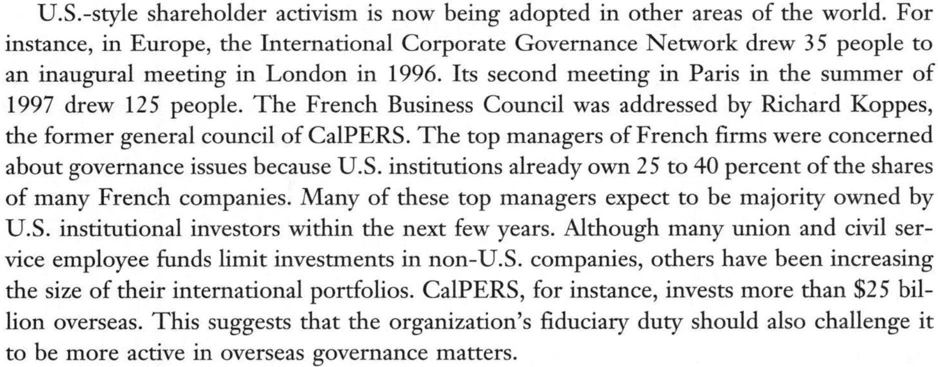

Recent actions indicate that CalPERS is, in fact, beginning to flex its muscles overseas. In 1997, it established corporate governance principles for investments in Britain and France. It is now developing similar principles for Germany and Japan. It does not rule out giving foreign companies the same treatment that it has given to U.S. companies in its annual list of underperforming management teams. CalPERS funds invested in foreign shares have risen from $8 billion at the end of 1993 to over $25 billion. CalPERS decided to address corporate governance issues in Britain, France, Germany and Japan because these are the countries where it has the largest holdings.

Britain has a set of guidelines aimed at developing more effective board structures and has improved on the disclosure of compensation. France has also been improving. However, Germany and Japan have large bank ownership stakes and in Japan, cross ownership between companies is common. Therefore, CalPERS is concerned about companies' ability to appoint independent directors, one of its key principles, in these countries. After a significant bear market in Japan, CalPERS expects the Japanese to be more responsive to advice on corporate governance related issues.

Domestically, CalPERS is also considering a new initiative. Until recently, it did not seek direct board seats as a way to further evangelize its principles of corporate governance. Recently, however, trustees of the organization have approved a draft policy that could end the longstanding practice of avoiding directorships. If CalPERS pursues board memberships because of increasing ownership positions, other influential activist funds may follow its lead. The Council of Institutional Investors, a 110-member pension fund group, which holds more than $1 trillion in assets, suggests that the potential implications for such a move would be substantial.

There are concerns about such a move. Terence J. Gallagher, corporate-governance vice president at Pfizer, observed, "You'd be getting sort of a contingency director, which is generally not considered to be good corporate governance. It could lead to friction on the board." It also could lead to micromanagement of the corporation, something that CalPERS has said it opposes. Micromanagement could lead to managers being risk-averse when significant strategic decisions are at issue. As CalPERS and other institutional investors become more proactive, not only in their own domestic economies but also toward international companies, they must avoid taking actions that could reduce a firm's competitiveness.

SOURCE: CalPERS Home Page, 1998, http://www.calpers.ca.gov.may; J. S. Lublin, 1997, CalPERS considers seeking board seats, *Wall Street Journal*, A3, A4; T. A. Stewart, 1997, A visitor from the dark side, The Pathfinder Network, http://www.fortune.com, November 10; S. Webb, 1997, CalPERS sets its sight overseas, *Wall Street Journal*, October 20, C1, C18; S. S. Hemmerick, 1997, CalPERS lends muscle to governance effort, *Pensions & Investments*, March 31, 20.

Shareholder Activism: How Much Is Possible?

The U.S. Securities and Exchange Commission (SEC) has issued several rulings that support shareholder involvement and control of managerial decisions. One such action is the easing of the rule regarding communications among shareholders. Historically, shareholders could communicate among themselves only through what had proved to be a cumbersome and expensive filing process. With a simple notification to the SEC of the intended meeting, shareholders can now meet to discuss a corporation's strategic direction. If a consensus on an issue exists, shareholders can vote as a block. For example, the 20 largest shareholders of Philip Morris own approximately 25 percent of the firm's stock. Coalescing around a position and voting as a block would send a powerful message to Philip Morris' top-level managers and its board of directors. This voting capability has been referred to as *shareholder empowerment*.

Others argue that even greater latitude should be extended to those managing the funds of large institutional investor groups. Allowing these individuals to hold positions on the boards of directors of corporations in which their organization has significant investments might allow fund managers to better represent the interests of those they serve.[51] As the Strategic Focus indicates, CalPERS is considering this because it would enable institutional investors to influence corporations' strategic decisions more effectively. Additionally, this capability would foster more direct disciplining of poor performing or dissident top-level managers when needed.

The type of shareholder and board of director activism we have described sometimes provokes reactions from top-level managers. Unintended and not always anticipated, these reactions require still further attention by those monitoring the decisions being made by the firm's agents. A reaction articulated by one corporate CEO demonstrates this issue. When asked to evaluate results achieved through shareholder activism, the CEO believed that at least some of the actions requested by shareholder activists exceed the roles specified by the separation of ownership and managerial control. When this occurs, the CEO argued, owners and directors begin to micromanage the corporation, which is not their job. Faced with this situation, executives may reduce their managerial employment risk. Implementing strategies with greater diversification, as explained earlier, is one path top-level managers can pursue to achieve this objective. O'Reilly, for instance, did not increase Heinz's diversification, but he held ownership positions and board responsibilities in a number of other enterprises.[52] Of course, such a course reduces the time he was able to spend on Heinz strategic issues.

For this reason, a number of CEOs are deciding to decline to be outside directors on other firms' boards. CEOs that are on too many boards have been criticized. The National Association of Corporate Directors (NACD) has urged that CEOs hold no more than three directorships in publicly held firms. Gordon Bethune of Continental Airlines asks, "How much time do I want to spend doing somebody else's work?" Instead of serving on other firms' boards, top-level managers, such as those at Continental Airlines, increasingly desire to spend time improving their own firm's performance. Improved performance reduces the likelihood that a firm will become a takeover candidate.[53]

Executives may protect themselves against employment risks when institutional investors have major investments in their firm. Besides the offensive protection of doing a better job, they may seek defensive protection from a possible acquisition. Evidence suggests that the number of executives receiving such protection is increasing. In mid-1996, 57 percent of U.S. public companies offered severance packages to top-level executives in case a firm changed hands. The percentage of firms engaging in these practices in 1987 was only 35 percent.[54] A *golden parachute*, a type of managerial protection that pays a guaranteed salary for a specified period of time in the event of a takeover and the loss of one's job, is sought by many top-level managers, particularly the CEO. There are a number of other anti-takeover provisions that allow a firm to defend itself if a takeover is attempted.[55] A more recently developed protection is called "the golden goodbye." A golden goodbye provides automatic payments to top-level executives if their contracts are not renewed, regardless of the reason for nonrenewal. Michael Ovitz, former president

Many top-level executives seek a golden parachute, which will guarantee a salary for a specified period of time in the event of a takeover or loss of a job.

of Walt Disney, had a five-year contract that included a $10 million golden goodbye. However, when he stepped down after only one year on the job, he was able to collect $93 million in cash and stock options.[56] Similarly, John R. Walter received a severance package valued at $26 million after working at AT&T for only eight months. In theory, the golden goodbye arrangement protects top-level managers working at corporations whose long-term prospects are uncertain.

In general, though, the degree to which institutional investors can actively monitor the decisions being made in all of the companies in which they are invested is questionable. CalPERS, for instance, targets 12 companies at a time. The New York Teachers Retirement Fund, another activist institutional investor, focuses on 25 of the 1,300 plus companies in its portfolio. Given limited resources, even large-block shareholders tend to concentrate on corporations in which they have significant investments. Thus, although shareholder activism has increased, institutional investors face barriers to the amount of active governance they can realistically employ.[57]

Next, we examine boards of directors—another governance mechanism used to control managerial decisions and align owners' and managers' interests.

BOARDS OF DIRECTORS

As we have described, the practices of large institutional investors have resulted in an increase in ownership concentration in U.S. firms. Nonetheless, diffuse ownership still describes the status of most U.S. firms,[58] which means that monitoring and control of managers by individual shareholders is limited in large corporations. Furthermore, large financial institutions, such as banks, are prevented from directly owning firms and from having representatives on boards of directors. These conditions highlight the importance of the board of directors for corporate governance. Our analysis of the board of directors shows that, although they are imperfect, there is a respected body of thought and research supporting the view that boards of directors can positively influence both managers and the companies they serve.

The **board of directors** is a group of elected individuals whose primary responsibility is to act in the owners' interests by formally monitoring and controlling the corporation's top-level executives.

The **board of directors** is a group of elected individuals whose primary responsibility is to act in the owners' interests by formally monitoring and controlling the corporation's top-level executives.[59] This responsibility is a product of the American legal system, which "... confers broad powers on corporate boards to direct the affairs of the organization, punish and reward managers, and protect the rights and interests of shareholders."[60] Thus, an appropriately structured and effective board of directors protects owners from managerial opportunism.

Generally, board members (often called directors) are classified in one of three groups (see Table 10.2). *Insiders* are active top-level managers in the corporation who are elected to the board because they are a source of information about the firm's day-to-day operations.[61] *Related outsiders* have some relationship with the firm—contractual or otherwise—that may create questions about their independence, but these individuals are not involved with the corporation's day-to-day activities. *Outsiders* are individuals elected to the board to provide independent counsel to the firm and may hold top-level managerial positions in another company or have been elected to the board prior to the beginning of the current CEO's tenure.[62]

Some argue that many boards are not effectively fulfilling their primary fiduciary duty to protect shareholders. Among other possibilities, it may be that boards are a managerial tool—a tool that largely rubber stamps managers' self-serving ini-

TABLE 10.2 ***Classifications of Boards of Directors' Members***

Insiders

- The firm's CEO and other top-level managers

Related outsiders

- Individuals not involved with the firm's day-to-day operations, but who have a relationship with the company

Outsiders

- Individuals who are independent of the firm—in terms of day-to-day operations and other relationships

tiatives.[63] In general, those critical of boards as a governance device believe that inside managers dominate boards and exploit their personal ties with them. A widely accepted view is that a board with a significant percentage of its membership from the firm's top-level executives tends to result in relatively weak monitoring and control of managerial decisions.[64] Board critics advocate reforms to ensure that independent outside directors represent a significant majority of the total board's membership.[65] Practitioners and academics, however, disagree over the most appropriate role of outside directors in a firm's strategic decision-making process.[66]

Because of external pressures, board reforms have been initiated. To date, these reforms have generally called for an increase in the number of outside directors, relative to insiders, serving on a corporation's board. For example, in 1984, the New York Stock Exchange started requiring that listed firms have board audit committees composed solely of outside directors.[67] As a result of external pressures, more boards of large corporations are now dominated by outsiders. But with fewer insiders and related outsiders on a firm's board, legitimate managerial concerns may not be adequately represented. Thus, there are potential strategic implications associated with the movement toward having corporate boards dominated by outsiders.

Outsiders do not have contact with the firm's day-to-day operations. This lack of contact precludes easy access to the rich information about managers and their skills that is required to evaluate managerial decisions and initiatives effectively. Valuable information may be obtained through frequent interactions with insiders during board meetings. Insiders possess such information by virtue of their organizational positions. Thus, boards with a critical mass of insiders can be informed more effectively about intended strategic initiatives—both in terms of the reasons for them and the outcomes expected through their accomplishments.[68] Without this type of information, outsider-dominated boards may emphasize financial, as opposed to strategic, evaluations. Such evaluations shift risk to top-level managers, who, in turn, may make decisions to maximize their interests and reduce their employment risk. Reductions in R&D investments, additional diversification of the firm, and pursuit of greater levels of compensation are examples of decisions managers could make to achieve these objectives.

Enhancing the Effectiveness of the Board of Directors as a Governance Mechanism

Our discussion has suggested that the board of directors is an important source of control and governance in the modern corporation. Because of this importance, and as a result of increased scrutiny from shareholders, particularly large institutional investors, the performances of individual board members and of entire boards are being evaluated more formally and with greater intensity.[69] Some believe that directors increase the probability of fulfilling their responsibilities effectively when they are honest and act with prudence and integrity for the good of the entire firm and are committed to reaching independent judgments on an informed basis rather than rubber stamping management proposals.[70]

Given the demand for greater accountability and improved performance, many boards of directors have initiated voluntary changes. Among these changes are (1) increases in the diversity of board members' backgrounds (e.g., a greater number of directors are being selected from public service, academic, and scientific settings; the percentage of boards with ethnic minorities has increased; and more U.S. boards now have members from different countries), (2) the strengthening of internal management and accounting control systems, and (3) the establishment and consistent use of formal processes to evaluate the board's performance. The result of changes such as these should be enhancements in the effectiveness of the board of directors as a means of control.

The following Strategic Focus also indicates that other innovative board approaches are being pursued. Managers are becoming more interested and aggressive in putting outside directors on their company's boards. One reason for this is that CEOs are finding that including a top-notch outside director can increase a firm's stock price. McKinsey & Co., in a hypothetical survey, found that when companies in which outsiders constitute a majority of the board, owned significant amounts of stock, were subjected to formal evaluation, and were not personally tied to top management, institutional shareholders were willing to pay up to 11 percent more for their shares.[71] Also, top boards, its seems, are becoming smaller, especially in high-technology firms, such as many found in Silicon Valley. Increasingly, outside directors are being required to hold significant equity stakes as a prerequisite to holding a board position. A recent study also suggests that inside director performance increases if they hold an equity position. The announcement of an inside director with less than 5 percent ownership decreases shareholder wealth, but an insider with ownership between 5 percent and 25 percent increases shareholder wealth. Therefore, an inside director's knowledge of the firm can be used appropriately. Finally, an inside director's relationship to the CEO does not necessarily lead to CEO entrenchment if the inside director has a strong ownership position.[72]

STRATEGIC FOCUS

Examples of Board of Directors Reforms

Shareholder activism has pressured many boards to undertake significant reforms. Many CEOs are also seeking to use the board as a way to improve strategy and corporate performance. The Business Roundtable, which includes 200 CEOs of the largest U.S. companies, has openly endorsed ideas on corporate governance once considered radical. The Roundtable is endorsing that the utmost duty of both management and corporate boards is to ensure that shareholder wealth is created.

During the time that Louis E. Platt has been CEO at Hewlett-Packard (HP), he indicates that he has benefited significantly from his board and the right level of independence. He suggests that there needs to be an effective balance between collaboration and independence to function appropriately. HP's board emphasizes three fundamental elements that create effective governance. First, there is an emphasis on performance. If the firm is not performing well, the board is not likely to perform well either. This is the foundational governance principle. The second element is to make sure that each board member is an effective representative of the company's shareholders. Board service then is not just supplemental income for board members. They must realize that if something goes wrong, shareholders expect accountability from not only the company managers but also board members for not performing well as their representatives. Finally, they seek to have a culture of openness between the CEO and board members. If the company stumbles and the board struggles to deal effectively with its poor performance, the board may have been kept in the dark about the real issues facing the company.

HP's board, in coordination with the CEO, has developed a set of guidelines and duties for directors that has been approved by CalPERS. In addition, the board has established the following mission statement: "The mission of the board of directors of Hewlett-Packard Company is to monitor and support management in creating long term value for its shareholders, customers and employees in an ethically and socially responsible manner while maintaining the standard of excellence that has become associated with Hewlett-Packard."

Although the board's approach has improved governance substantially and HP's performance is exemplary, Albert Dunlap, the former CEO of Sunbeam, pursued a more radical approach to board reform. When he came to Sunbeam, the first thing he did was pay the board 100 percent in stock. Additionally, he had them buy stock in the firm as a condition of being on the board. He also did this at Scott Paper, and it was considered to be revolutionary. He has even undertaken to put governance activists on his boards. For instance, Charles Elson, a professor at Stetson University of Law, and a noted writer and theorist on the role of the board and the value of shareholder activism, was put on Sunbeam's board. As a legal academic, buying five thousand shares at $23 per share was a significant commitment. He indicated that the investment was significantly more than he had equity in his home. He obviously had to put his money where his mouth was since he had been writing about governance activism for some time. Dunlap has also suggested board term limits of five years.

Interestingly, Dunlap believes that the CEO should also be the chairperson. This view is contrary to many of the governance views held by institutional investors such as CalPERS. In support of this belief, he says the following: "The professional chairman comes to that meeting, and although these are capable, well-meaning people, they don't have enough background in the company to raise the important issues. They are not conversant enough with what's going on. The board meeting becomes highly inefficient and many times misses the most important points." However, he also suggests that he needs a strong board: "If you don't have a strong board, you will fail. I need people who will stand up and say, 'That's nonsense.' "

He also suggests that a board should never have more than ten people. In fact, the ideal board would probably have eight people, according to Dunlap. One other insider would be useful on the board, the chief financial officer, because he or she has to be so intimately involved in board communications. He would also seek to have a board with a variety of backgrounds to help a company deal with international, marketing, and financial market issues. Dunlap has criticized the typical board as "a group of CEOs who have failed miserably running companies, and yet they are on a multiplicity of other boards."

Although Al Dunlap has run large companies, his approach is similar to that of smaller more entrepreneurial firms such as those found in Silicon Valley. Because today's firms are intensely competitive, the role of the board of directors has become a lot less ceremonial and more proactive in the oversight and actual running of the corporation. The high-technology sector, which accounts for approximately one quarter of U.S. wage growth, has an approach that may be useful in creating more successful boards. For most Silicon Valley boards, their role is to be active in the strategic direction of the company. Rather than sheer oversight, each director brings to the board some specialized skill in specific areas (sales and marketing, legal, technical, financial, etc.). The board helps the CEO by asking hard questions to ensure that the strategic direction is sound and viable. The boards that are able to do this have several characteristics in common.

These boards have far fewer members than most boards of comparable companies outside the technology industry. For instance, Sun Microsystems, Seagate, Oracle, and Cisco each have fewer than 10 directors on their boards. Smaller and faster growing successful companies often have as few as five directors where traditional companies will have a dozen or more such board members. Large boards create communication difficulties, which tend to make boards less efficient. Some view small boards as too cohesive, thus stifling dissent. Experience shows, however, that smaller group dynamics allows for freer exchange of views because dissent in a smaller group is less imposing than being an outcast in a larger group. Also, small boards put a premium on the effectiveness of individual directors. "Glamour" directors who do not have specific knowledge or expertise relevant to the company are not justifiable. In contrast, effective boards feature people who are familiar with the company, including its venture capitalists, lawyers, and consultants. Although these people are considered outsiders, they have a closer relationship with the company and understand internal operations better than those who would be recommended under traditional governance theory. The best Silicon Valley directors are quite independent, but they also have a large equity stake in the firms they run. Meetings are more frequent and informal exchange of information takes place on a regular basis. Usually firms' boards meet every eight weeks and more frequently in a crisis situation.

The high ownership position is particularly true of venture capitalists and early advisers and investors in high-technology companies. High-technology companies usually also make sure that management teams have large equity stakes and therefore a common interest with shareholders. The large equity ownership of officers, directors and employees ensures common interest among all stakeholders. Although boards of high-technology companies have instituted practices that don't necessarily fit with current governance procedures, they may be worth considering as a model because of the success of many of these firms.

SOURCES: J. A. Byrne, 1997, Governance: CEOs catch up with shareholder activists, *Business Week*, September 22, 36; J. A. Byrne, 1997, The CEO and the board, *Business Week*, September 15, 106–116; Reforming the Board, 1997, *The Economist*, August 9, 16–17; A. Dunlap, 1997, On "Dunlapping" the Board, *Corporate Board*, January-February, 102–108; D. J. Berger, 1997, The Silicon Valley board, *Corporate Board*, July-August, 105–110; L. E. Platt, 1997, Governance the H-P Way, *Directors & Boards*, 21; no. 4: 20–25; Charles Elson: The board outsider goes inside, 1997, *Corporate Board*, March-April, 32.

Besides the board reforms mentioned in the Strategic Focus, a number of analysts have suggested that more women need to be represented on boards. Approximately 10.6 percent of board seats are held by women.[73] Korn/Ferry International, an executive search firm, reports that 71 percent of boards surveyed had at least one woman on the board, up from 46 percent a decade ago. Catalyst, a nonprofit group that studies women in business, notes that among the *Fortune* 500, 84 percent have at least one woman on their board. However, the increase in 1997 was only 3 percent, following jumps of 9 percent and 7 percent the previous two years; thus, among *Fortune* 500 firms the rate of inclusion is slowing.[74] However, Korn/Ferry's survey found that 36 percent of companies reported that at least one other woman has joined after the first woman or women were put on a board. The survey, however, reported that although their influence was increasing, female board members believed their opinions were weighed less heavily in executive succession and compensation decisions. Thus, it appears that more board reform is necessary in regard to diversity and board functioning.[75]

Next, we discuss a highly visible corporate governance mechanism—executive compensation.

EXECUTIVE COMPENSATION

A reading of the business press shows that the compensation of top-level managers, and especially of CEOs, generates a great deal of interest and strongly held opinions. What factors account for this level of visibility and interest? In response to the issues suggested by this question, two researchers observed that while "widespread interest in CEO pay can be traced to a natural curiosity about extremes and excesses . . . it also stems from a more substantive reason. Namely, to observe CEO pay is to observe in an indirect but very tangible way the fundamental governance processes in large corporations. Who has power? What are the bases of power? How and when do owners and managers exert their relative preferences? How vigilant are boards? Who is taking advantage of whom?"[76]

The purpose of executive compensation is to improve the alignment of management and shareholder interests and reward managers for effort rendered.[77] The board of directors is responsible for determining the extent to which the firm's executive compensation structure provides incentives to top-level managers to act in the owners' best interests.[78]

Executive compensation is a governance mechanism that seeks to align managers' and owners' interests through salary, bonuses, and long-term incentive compensation such as stock options. Stock options are a mechanism used to link executives' performance to the performance of their company's stock.[79] Increasingly, long-term incentive plans are becoming a critical part of compensation packages in U.S. firms.[80] At Baxter International, for example, more than 70 senior-level managers were extended an opportunity to take out personal loans from a bank to buy up to several times their annual compensation in the company's common stock.[81] This decision is supported by the conviction of many board directors that linking more of top-level management's overall compensation to the corporation's financial performance is a superior way to align managers' and owners' interests.

Executive compensation is a governance mechanism that seeks to align managers' and owners' interests through salary, bonuses, and long-term incentive compensation such as stock options.

Using executive compensation effectively as a governance mechanism is particularly challenging in firms implementing international strategies. For example, preliminary evidence suggests that the interests of owners of multinational corporations are served best when there is less uniformity among the firm's foreign subsidiaries' compensation plans rather than more.[82] Developing an array of unique compensation plans requires additional monitoring and increases the firm's agency costs. For instance, this study also found that the cultural distance between the headquarters country and the foreign subsidiary country (e.g., U.S. headquarters is more culturally distant from a subsidiary in Japan than one in the U.K.) increases the agency problem. Pay must, therefore, align correctly with the situation.

A Complicated Governance Mechanism

For several reasons, executive compensation, especially long-term incentive compensation, is complicated. First, the strategic decisions made by top-level managers are typically complex and nonroutine; as such, direct supervision of executives is inappropriate for judging the quality of their decisions. Because of this, there is a tendency to link the compensation of top-level managers to measurable outcomes such as financial performance. Second, an executive's decision often affects a firm's financial outcome over an extended period of time, making it difficult to assess the effect of current decisions on the corporation's performance. In fact, strategic decisions are more likely to have long-term, rather than short-term, effects on a company's strategic outcomes. Third, a number of variables intervene between top-level managerial decisions and behavior and firm performance. Unpredictable economic, social, or legal changes (see Chapter 2) make it difficult before implementation to discern the effects of strategic decisions. Thus, although performance-based compensation may provide incentives to managers to make decisions that best serve shareholders' interests, such compensation plans alone are imperfect in their ability to monitor and control managers.

Although incentive compensation plans may increase firm value in line with shareholder expectations, they are subject to managerial manipulation. For instance, annual bonuses may provide incentives to pursue short-run objectives at the expense of the firm's long-term interests. Supporting this conclusion, some research has found that bonuses based on annual performance were negatively related to investments in R&D, which may affect the firm's long-term strategic competitiveness.[83] Although long-term performance-based incentives may reduce the temptation to underinvest in the short run, they increase executive exposure to risks associated with uncontrollable events, such as market fluctuations and industry decline.[84] The longer the focus of incentive compensation, the greater the long-term risks borne by top-level managers.

The Effectiveness of Executive Compensation

In recent times, many stakeholders, including shareholders, have been angered by the compensation received by some top-level managers, especially CEOs. CEOs have a different perspective. George Fisher, chairman and CEO of Eastman Kodak, stated that "We all should be compensated based on competitive issues. If you want a world-class shortstop, you pay. The good news is that many CEOs are getting well-compensated for really good performances."[85] Indeed, it is the rare CEO who does not sincerely believe that she or he has earned a reward.[86] Thus, some executives argue that they are being rewarded for effectively making critical decisions that affect their firm's performance in the highly competitive global economy.[87]

The level and intensity of the dissatisfaction with executive compensation appears to be influenced by layoffs announced by a host of corporations in the United States and across the world.[88] Some of those critical of executive compensation as a means of corporate governance cited the experiences of AT&T's workers and the firm's CEO.[89] During 1996, the year in which AT&T decided to lay off as many as 40,000 employees, then current CEO Robert E. Allen received $16.2 million in salary and stock payouts. As an indication of the complexity of achieving strategic competitiveness in the global economy, AT&T expected to hire as many as 15,000 new employees during 1996 while laying off thousands of others in order to restructure the businesses in its diversified portfolio.[90] At the beginning of 1998, the new CEO of AT&T, C. Michael Armstrong, suggested that AT&T might lay off as many as 18,000 plus 7,000 announced earlier. Although in the short run the stock fell 5.8 percent, Armstrong's compensation package will be based on future performance.[91]

In general, it may be that organizational employees, a key stakeholder, are feeling disenfranchised, discouraged, and angry in a time period of significant downsizings, stagnant wages, and ever more burdensome work loads for layoff survivors.[92] Contributing to these feelings is the fact that during 1996, the average salary and bonus for CEOs increased by 39 percent. When stock options are included total compensation rose 54 percent. This increase compares to an average gain of 3.2 percent for white-collar professionals and of 3 percent for factory employees during the same year.[93] Moreover, the spread between the pay of the typical worker and CEOs concerns employees. In the 1960s the ratio between a worker's pay and that of the CEO was 30-to-1; by the end of 1995 it was 100-to-1.[94]

Among several challenges facing board directors striving to use executive compensation to align managers' interests with shareholders' interests is the determination of what represents "fair" compensation for top-level managers. As guidance for making this decision, board directors should remember that the most important criterion to consider is shareholder wealth creation. This is necessary because the economic principles on which executive compensation is based are concerned not with fairness but with productivity.[95] At least at a point in time, the situation at Green Tree Financial demonstrated the effectiveness of linking an executive's compensation with her or his performance.

At Green Tree, the CEO, Lawrence M. Coss, received a $65.1 million bonus during 1995 and a $102.4 million bonus in 1996.[96] Based in St. Paul, Minnesota, this company finances manufactured housing and home improvement loans. Green Tree had been one of the best performing stocks on the New York Stock Exchange. Between 1991 and 1996, its stock had compounded annual returns of 53 percent. As a result of the creation of wealth for shareholders at a point in time, ". . . Green Tree isn't getting gripes from stockholders about Mr. Coss's compensation," said John Dolphin, Green Tree's vice president for investor relations. Dolphin further noted that Coss's contract was entirely performance based and that shareholders were thrilled with his work and the corporation's financial performance.[97] His compensation was 2.5 percent of pretax earnings paid in shares pegged to the 1991 value of $3 per share. When the stock soared above $45 dollars per share, so did his compensation.

Somewhat similarly, GE's CEO Jack Welch saw his salary and bonus increase 22.3 percent between 1994 and 1995 and 18 percent between 1995 and 1996. Welch was also awarded stock-appreciation rights valued at a potential $12.9 and $21.3 million at the close of the firm's 1995 and 1996 fiscal years, respectively. In 1996, GE's compensation committee observed that Welch's compensation was appropriate in light of the corporation's financial performance and the CEO's decisive management of both operational and strategic issues.[98] The amount of shareholder wealth created at GE during Welch's tenure as CEO appears to support the compensation committee's position.

However, in *Business Week*'s special report on executive pay for 1996, both these executives were criticized because the size of the compensation was so great relative to the actual shareholder value created.[99] In regard to Green Tree, although most shareholders have not complained, Mr. Coss and Green Tree's board have been sued by several small pension funds for excessive compensation. When Green Tree reported a charge to fourth quarter 1997 earnings due to the high rate of refinancing among its clientele, its stock price began to fall. When Green Tree restated its earnings, Coss was asked to repay part of his compensation. Also, because the company had been overly aggressive in its accounting for earnings, it changed its procedure. Furthermore, Coss's compensation was changed to a more standard plan where he received stock options instead of stock as a percentage of earnings. In 1998, Green Tree was acquired by Conseco, partly because its stock price was low.[100]

As the example of Green Tree seems to suggest, executive compensation is an imperfect means of corporate governance. (Individually, each governance mechanism discussed in this chapter is imperfect.) The dissatisfaction with executive compensation being expressed by shareholders and other stakeholders as well may have surfaced because of the mechanism's imperfection and/or ineffective use. Specifically, there is criticism of excessive stock option packages such as that of Michael Eisner at Disney.[101] It is possible that members of corporate boards of directors have not been effective in their use of this governance mechanism. If executive compensation plans are not aligning top-level managers' interests with the interests of other stakeholders, especially those of shareholders, appropriate changes must be made. For instance, one proposal is that, to be awarded the intended stock option, the executive must outperform peer companies. Alternatively, boards may be rewarding mediocre performance when the stock market is going up in general and executives are able to take advantage of the increased value without appropriate accountability.

Thus, the proactive positions concerning executive compensation taken by institutional investors and individual shareholders have been effective. Input from these stakeholders should result in modifications to executive compensation that will improve its value as a means of corporate governance.

Many stakeholders are dissatisfied with executive compensation as a means of corporate governance. The excessive stock option package commanded by Michael Eisner at Disney, for example, has been severely criticized.

A company's organizational structure also influences the alignment of principals' and agents' interests. As indicated in the next section, structure can be an especially valuable governance mechanism in diversified firms.

THE MULTIDIVISIONAL STRUCTURE

Oliver Williamson, an economist, argues that organizational structure, particularly the multidivisional (M-form) structure, serves as an internal governance mechanism in that it controls managerial opportunism.[102] The corporate office that is a part of the M-form structure, along with the firm's board of directors, closely monitors the strategic decisions of managers responsible for the performance of the different business units or divisions that are a part of the diversified corporation's operations. Active monitoring of an individual unit's performance suggests a keen managerial interest in making decisions that will maximize shareholders' wealth. Williamson believes that the M-form structure brings forth a greater managerial interest in wealth maximization than do other organizational structures such as the variations of the functional structure (another type of structure that is discussed in Chapter 11).

To improve his firm's financial performance, Domenico Cempella, CEO of the Italian flag carrier Alitalia SpA, announced a restructuring plan that calls for use of the M-form structure. To provide managerial incentives and controls so Alitalia could better compete in what was to become a deregulated European market after 1998, the CEO intended to split the company into two separate, highly competitive carriers—one for long routes and one for medium and short routes—as well as other operating divisions.[103] Recently GE, another corporation using a multidivisional organizational structure, allocated $200 million to a program (called Six Sigma, which refers in statistical terms to a very high level of quality) that was designed to sharply improve the quality of the firm's vast array of products. At the time of the announced allocation, GE generated approximately 35,000 defects per million products. The objective of the program was to reduce defects to less than 4 per million. To align the interests of division managers with those of the CEO and the program being implemented to enhance shareholder wealth, CEO Jack Welch decided that GE would weight 40 percent of bonus compensation on the intensity of managers' efforts and progress being made toward achieving Six Sigma quality.[104]

While the M-form may limit division managers' opportunistic behaviors, it may not limit corporate-level managers' self-serving actions. For example, research evidence suggests that diversified firms organized through the M-form structure are likely to implement corporate-level strategies that cause them to become even more diversified.[105] In fact, one of the potential problems with the divisionalization that is a part of the M-form structure is that it will be used too aggressively.[106] As discussed in Chapters 6 and 10, beyond some point, diversification serves managers' interests more than it serves shareholders' interests.

In addition, a depth-for-breadth trade-off often occurs in an extensively diversified firm with an M-form structure. Because of the diversification of product lines (breadth of businesses), top-level executives do not have adequate information to evaluate the strategic decisions and actions of divisional managers (depth). To complete their evaluations, they must wait to observe the financial results achieved by individual business units. In the interim period, division managers may be able to act opportunistically.

Where internal controls are limited because of extensive diversification, the external market for corporate control and the external managerial labor market may be the primary controls on managers' decisions and actions, such as pursuing acquisitions to increase the size of their firm and their compensation.[107] Because external markets lack access to relevant information inside the firm, they tend to be less efficient than internal governance mechanisms for monitoring top-level managers' decisions and performance. Therefore, in diversified firms, corporate executive decisions can be controlled effectively only when other strong internal governance mechanisms (e.g., the board of directors) are used in combination with the M-form structure. When used as a single governance mechanism, the M-form structure may actually facilitate overdiversification and inappropriately high compensation for corporate executives.[108]

MARKET FOR CORPORATE CONTROL

The **market for corporate control** is composed of individuals and firms that buy ownership positions in (or take over) potentially undervalued corporations so they can form new divisions in established diversified companies or merge two previously separate firms.

The market for corporate control is an external governance mechanism that becomes active when a firm's internal controls fail.[109] The **market for corporate control** is composed of individuals and firms that buy ownership positions in (or take over) potentially undervalued corporations so they can form new divisions in established diversified companies or merge two previously separate firms. Because they are assumed to be the party responsible for formulating and implementing the strategy that led to poor performance, the top management team of the purchased corporation is usually replaced. Thus, when operating effectively, the market for corporate control ensures that managerial incompetence is disciplined.[110] This governance mechanism should be activated by a firm's poor performance relative to industry competitors. A firm's poor performance, often demonstrated by the earning of below-average returns, is an indicator that internal governance mechanisms have failed—that is, their use did not result in managerial decisions that maximized shareholder value.

Michael Price is a participant in the market for corporate control. He is head of Franklin Mutual which oversees $28 billion in assets. Known by various terms, including value investor and corporate raider, individuals such as Price purchase shares of an underperforming company's stock. Through their ownership position, such individuals pressure firms to maximize shareholder value by breaking up assets or selling out. He has recently tried to put Dow Jones, a publishing company, into play. His plan was to merge assets of Dow Jones with the Washington Post. Dow Jones has good potential capabilities, but has been underperforming lately. Price has also been involved in forcing out management teams, directly or indirectly at Sunbeam, Dial, and Chase Manhattan. For instance, partly as a result of his pressure, Chemical Bank bought Chase Manhattan.[111]

Managerial Defense Tactics

Historically, the increased use of the market for corporate control has enhanced the sophistication and variety of managerial defense tactics that are used to reduce the influence of this governance mechanism. The market for corporate control tends to increase risk for managers. As a result, managerial pay is often increased indirectly through *golden parachutes* (where a CEO can receive up to three years' salary if his or her firm is taken over). Among other outcomes, takeover defenses increase the costs of mounting a takeover and can entrench incumbent management while reducing the chances of introducing a new management team.[112] Some defense tactics require the type of asset restructuring that results from divesting one or more divisions in the diversified firm's portfolio. Others necessitate only financial structure changes such as repurchasing shares of the firm's outstanding stock.[113] Some tactics (e.g., a change in the state of incorporation) require shareholder approval, but the greenmail tactic (wherein money is used to repurchase stock from a corporate raider to avoid the takeover of the firm) does not.

A potential problem with the market for corporate control is that it may not be totally efficient. A study of several of the most active corporate raiders in the 1980s showed that approximately 50 percent of their takeover attempts targeted firms with above-average performance in their industry—corporations that were neither undervalued nor poorly managed.[114] The targeting of high-performance businesses may lead to acquisitions at premium prices and to decisions by target firm managers to establish what may prove to be costly takeover defense tactics to protect their corporate positions.

Although the market for corporate control lacks the precision possible with internal governance mechanisms, the fear of acquisition and influence by corporate raiders is an effective constraint on the managerial growth motive.[115] The market for corporate control has been responsible for significant changes in many firms' strategies and has, when used appropriately, served the best interests of corporate owners—the shareholders. For instance, the announcement of Compaq's purchase of Digital Equipment shares lifted the Digital share price by 25 percent.[116] Although unthinkable a few years ago, Digital has been performing poorly recently, and the link with Compaq appears to be a positive result for Digital shareholders.

Next, we address the topic of international corporate governance primarily through a description of governance structures used in Germany and Japan.

INTERNATIONAL CORPORATE GOVERNANCE

Comparisons of corporate governance structures used in other economic systems with the one used in the United Kingdom and the United States are interesting.[117] In this section, we describe the governance structures used in Germany and Japan among others. Our brief discussion of the governance of German and Japanese corporations shows that the nature of corporate governance in these two nations is being affected by the realities of the global economy and the competitive challenges that are a part of it.[118] Thus, while the stability associated with German and Japanese governance structures has been viewed historically as an asset, some believe that it may now be a burden.[119]

We chose to examine Germany and Japan here because of their prominent positions in the global economy. Furthermore, their governance structures contrast with those of the United States and the United Kingdom. The strategic management process should be used to study governance processes throughout the world to increase understanding.

Corporate Governance in Germany

In many private German firms, the owner and manager are still the same individual. In these instances, there is no agency problem. Even in publicly traded corporations, there is often a dominant shareholder.

Historically, banks have been at the center of the German corporate governance structure, which is the case in many continental European countries such as Italy and France. As lenders, banks become major shareholders when companies they had financed earlier seek funding on the stock market or default on loans. Although stakes are usually under 10 percent, there is no legal limit on how much of a firm's stock banks can hold (except that a single ownership position cannot exceed 15 percent of the bank's capital). Today, various types of specialized institutions—savings banks, mortgage banks, savings and loan associations, leasing firms, and insurance companies—are also important sources of corporate funds.

Through their own shareholdings and by casting proxy votes for individual shareholders who retain their shares with the banks, three banks in particular—Deutsche, Dresdner, and Commerzbank—exercise significant power. Although individual shareholders can tell the banks how to vote their ownership position, they generally elect not to do so. A combination of their own holdings with their proxies results in majority positions for these three banks in many German companies. These banks, as well as others, monitor and control managers both as lenders and as shareholders by electing representatives to supervisory boards.

German firms with more than 2,000 employees are required to have a two-tier board structure. Through this structure, the supervision of management is separated from other duties normally assigned to a board of directors, especially the nomination of new board members. Thus, Germany's two-tiered system places the responsibility to monitor and control managerial (or supervisory) decisions and actions in the hands of a separate group.[120] One of the reasons underlying this division is that the stronger management is the less safe it is to assume that its interests coincide with those of the owners of the business. The application of this principle is to place all the functions of direction and management in the hands of the management board—the Vorstand—except appointment to the Vorstand itself, which is the responsibility of the supervisory tier—the Aufsichtsrat. Employees, union members, and shareholders appoint members to the Aufsichtsrat.

As implied by our discussion of the importance of banks in Germany's corporate governance structure, private shareholders do not have major ownership positions in their country's firms. Historically, continental Europeans have held the belief that the control of large corporations is too important an asset to be left only to the discretion of public shareholders.[121] Large institutional investors such as pension funds and insurance companies are also relatively insignificant owners of corporate stock. Thus, at least historically, top-level managers in German corporations generally have not been dedicated to the proposition that their decisions and actions should result in maximization of shareholder value. This lack of emphasis on shareholder value is changing in some German firms.

At Veba AG, a diversified industrial giant that builds shopping malls, runs a cable-television system, and is Germany's largest operator of gasoline stations, CEO Ulrich Hartmann has taken actions that are quite different from those observed normally in German firms. To become less vulnerable to a takeover and to create shareholder value, Hartmann evaluated and changed Veba's portfolio. Veba exited the coal-trading business, reduced the workforce by 12,000 in its chemical operations, closed its tire-rubber business, and sold its synthetic-rubber operation. In addition, it initiated an investor relations program where it explained its actions to key investors. As a result, its stock price doubled between 1991 and 1995, and it has consistently outperformed the German stock market in recent years. Many German companies such as Veba are listing on stock exchanges outside of Germany, which often require more transparency and accounting disclosure.[122] As this practice continues, German firms will likely move toward a greater emphasis on creating shareholder value.

Corporate Governance in Japan

Attitudes toward corporate governance in Japan are affected by the concepts of obligation, family, and consensus. In Japan, obligation does not result from broad general principles; rather, it is a product of specific causes or events. In this context, an obligation "... may be to return a service for one rendered or it may derive from a more general relationship, for example, to one's family or old alumni, or one's company (or Ministry), or the country. This sense of particular obligation is common elsewhere but it feels stronger in Japan."[123] As part of a company family, individuals are members of a unit that envelops their lives to an unusual degree. Families command the attention and allegiance of parties from the top to the bottom in corporations. Moreover, a keiretsu (defined in Chapter 9) is more than an economic concept—it, too, is a family. Consensus, the most important influence on the Japanese corporate governance structure, calls for the expenditure of significant amounts of energy to win the hearts and minds of people when possible as opposed to proceeding by edict of top-level managers. Consensus is highly valued, even when a firm's commitment to it results in a slow and cumbersome decision-making process.

As in Germany, banks play a more important role in financing and monitoring large public firms in Japan. The bank owning the largest share of stocks and largest amount of debt, the main bank, has the closest relationship with the company's top-level managers. The main bank not only provides financial advice to the firm, but also is responsible for closely monitoring managerial agents. Thus, Japan has a bank-based financial and corporate governance structure while the United States has a market-based financial and governance structure.

Aside from lending money (debt), a Japanese bank can hold up to 5 percent of a firm's total stock; a group of related financial institutions can hold up to 40 percent. In many cases, main-bank relationships are part of a horizontal keiretsu (see Chapter 9). A horizontal keiretsu is a group of firms tied together by cross-shareholdings. Thus, firms in such a keiretsu develop interrelationships and are interdependent. A keiretsu firm usually owns less than 2 percent of any other member firm; however, each company typically has a stake of that size in every firm in the keiretsu. As a result, somewhere between 30 percent and 90 percent of a firm is owned by other members of the keiretsu. Thus, a keiretsu is a system of relationship investments.

Other characteristics of Japan's corporate governance structure include (1) powerful government intervention (the Japanese Ministry of Finance maintains strong regulatory control of all of Japan's businesses), (2) close relationships between corporations and government sectors, (3) passive and stable shareholders (individuals and groups who exercise little monitoring and control of managerial agents), and (4) the virtual absence of an external market for corporate control, although mergers are common.

As is the case in Germany and the United States, Japan's corporate governance structure is changing. For example, because of their continuing development as economic organizations, the role of banks in the monitoring and control of managerial behavior and firm outcomes is less significant than it has been.[124] As with

German firms, the availability of global capital increases the sources of funds for Japanese corporations. Additionally, the business arrangements resulting from keiretsus and relationships between companies and government agencies are being studied. Some observers of Japan's corporate governance structure suggest that significant competition from global rivals and the strong yen are among factors stimulating efforts to study governance practices that may not be as effective as they have been historically.[125] Also, some noticeable changes are taking place in annual shareholder meetings. Executives are lengthening meetings and listening carefully to shareholder complaints.[126]

Other Global Governance Reforms

As our explanation of governance structures suggests, it is possible that the new competitive landscape (see Chapters 1 and 5) and the global economy that is a critical part of it will foster the creation of a relatively uniform governance structure that will be used by firms throughout the world.[127] As markets become more global and customer demands become more similar, shareholders are becoming the focus of managerial agents' efforts in an increasing number of companies. This is true of German and Japanese systems that are becoming more shareholder oriented. In turn, however, U.S. firms are becoming increasingly tied to financial institutions with higher debt levels and increased institutional investor activism. Thus, regardless of their national origin, the structures used to govern corporations will tend to become more similar than is the case today.

This is illustrated in the Strategic Focus about corporate governance reforms taking place in companies around the world. The Japanese model of corporate governance that has been followed by Korean chaebols, large conglomerate firms, is being questioned and reforms in governance are expected. European countries such as France and Italy, which have bank-centered governance approaches, are moving to more shared ownership. In Italy and other western European countries, much of this increased focus on equity markets is coming through privatization of large previously state-owned enterprises. The privatization process has also fostered much of the increases in equity in Russia and Eastern Europe as well. It is interesting to note that research has found that privatization has not led to decreases in employment as was previously feared by countries that had initiated the privatization process.[128] China is also undertaking reforms that have affected corporate governance. Although China has not truly privatized, except through the joint venture process, it has decentralized its system to provide much more local control.

STRATEGIC FOCUS

Reforms in International Corporate Governance

In both developed and developing economies, corporate governance is being reformed. For several decades, intellectuals and policymakers worried that the U.S. financial system was forcing businesses to pursue short-term profits at the expense of long-term investment. In fact, there was a national commission headed by Professor Michael Porter of Harvard Business School that recommended significant changes to the U.S. approach to capitalism. Many looked to the Japanese and German systems and found that the capital was more "patient" in those economies. Therefore, it was suggested that the U.S. system of corporate governance become more relationship oriented as was the case with the financial systems in Japan and Germany.

However, the financial systems across Asia, many of which are based on the Japanese-style approach, such as the Korean model, had serious difficulties in 1997 and into 1998. Many of the Asian and continental European economies are bank and debt based. A World Bank study found that total bank loans in the U.S. equal 50 percent of the nation's gross domestic product. This compares with 100 percent in Malaysia, 150 percent in Japan, and 170 percent in Germany. The bond market, on the other hand, totals 100 percent of annual U.S. gross domestic product, compared with 90 percent in Germany, 75 percent in Japan, 50 percent in Korea, and less than 10 percent in Thailand and Indonesia. Therefore, in most of Asia and a significant part of Europe, banks are at the center of providing capital. Additionally, in many of these economies, banks can hold equity, unlike the U.S. economy where the Glass Stegall Act prevents banks from having equity holdings. For this reason, the Germanic and Japanese approaches have been credited with providing patient and long-term oriented capital to corporations.

Lately, a number of countries have been questioning whether this is true. The chaebols of Korea, for instance, have been accused of being unresponsive and pursuing "wrong-headed" long-term investments. For instance, Chapter 9 discusses Samsung's investment into the car industry that continued even when there was significant overcapacity in the global auto industry.

France, as well as Italy, has significant bank-oriented financial systems. France, for instance, has been undergoing gradual but significant changes as demands for increasing shareholder value have become more important. As with Italy, France's system has been based on cross-shareholdings and reciprocal board memberships. However, with the large numbers of mergers, privatizations and restructurings taking place, shareholders are becoming more influential in the governance of large corporations. One active investor in France, G. Guy Wyser-Pratte, suggests, "France is a banana republic when it comes to corporate governance." It is difficult for shareholder power to prosper in a country such as France. The Paris Bourse lists only 681 stocks of French companies, compared with more than 2,100 on the London Stock Exchange and more than 7,700 on the New York and NASDAQ exchanges combined. Italy's stock market is even smaller compared to Germany, France, and Spain. Italy's system of corporate governance also includes significant amounts of cross-shareholdings and reciprocal board arrangements between and among companies.

Of course, some systems of corporate governance are built to focus not solely on shareholder concerns. For instance, in the Netherlands and Germany, a two-tiered system of corporate governance is at work. German corporations have a supervisory board with half the members representing shareholders and the other half representing employees. Shareholders have the ultimate control over the supervisory board and thus have the ability to influence decisions. The chairman is one of the shareholder representatives and in cases where voting results in a deadlock, he or she can cast an additional vote to break the logjam. However, there have been some recent challenges to the two-tiered board system. The argument by corporate officials is that the constant search for social consensus among workers and managers has led to a compromise of Germany's competitive edge in world markets. This lack of competitiveness creates large levels of unemployment, not only in Germany but also in other countries such as France where corporate governance has not been incisive.

Board reforms have also been taking place in emerging economies such as Russia and China. In Russia, privatization of numerous banks combined with broad licensing rules has allowed the Russian bank industry to become 75 percent private. Furthermore, privatized firms have wrestled control from "red directors" (former Communist managers who were previously managers of state-owned enterprises) as investment companies. Such concentrated ownership after the privatization process has allowed many Russian firms to be more rapidly revitalized than would have been the case under less diffused ownership.

Although there are significant differences between the Russian approach and the Chinese approach, China is adopting a corporate governance restructuring scheme as well. The China approach has decentralized operations by giving local control to previously centralized state enterprises. This is a separation of ownership approach—one that requires accountability in terms of spending and debt payment by these local managers over financial resources. Improvements could be made by providing performance-based incentives for managers, better private financial institutions, and a stronger application of bankruptcy law for poor performance. These issues, as well as stronger private enterprises, would ensure more effective corporate governance.

SOURCES: "More consensus" in Germany, 1997, *Financial Times*, December 18, 11; Italian governance, 1997, *Financial Times*, December 15, 18; A. Murray, 1997, New economic models fail while America Inc. keeps rolling, *Wall Street Journal*, September 8, A1, A13; Comic opera: Italy's stock exchange, 1997, *The Economist*, August 30, 54–55; S. Douma, 1997, The two-tier system of corporate governance, *Long Range Planning* 30, no. 4: 612–615; S. Li and T. Zhu, 1997, Put onus on managers in China, *Asian Wall Street Journal Weekly*, July 21, 12; A. Osterland, 1997, France is a banana republic: Corporate governance is changing in France . . . slowly, *Financial World*, July-August, 40–43; Co-termination, 1997, *Industry Week*, July 21, 54; A. Jack, 1997, New tricks for old dog, *Financial Times*, June 26, 29; J. S. Abarbanell and A. Meyendorff, 1997, Bank privatization in post-Communist Russia: The case of Zhilsotsbank, *Journal of Comparative Economics* 25: 62–97; S. Liesman, 1997, Outsiders at Russia's Rao Gazpron vie for crucial first seat on firm's board, *Wall Street Journal*, June 25, A18.

GOVERNANCE MECHANISMS AND ETHICAL BEHAVIOR

In this chapter's final section, we discuss the need for governance mechanisms to support ethical behaviors. The governance mechanisms described in this chapter are designed to ensure that the agents of the firm's owners—that is, the corporation's top-level managers—make strategic decisions that best serve the interests of the entire group of stakeholders as described in Chapter 1. In the United States at least, shareholders are recognized as a company's most significant stakeholder. As such, the focus of governance mechanisms is on the control of managerial decisions to increase the probability that shareholders' interests will be served, but product market stakeholders (e.g., customers, suppliers, and host communities) and organizational stakeholders (e.g., managerial and nonmanagerial employees) are important as well.[129] In this regard, at least the minimal interests or needs of all stakeholders must be satisfied by outcomes achieved through the firm's actions. Without satisfaction of at least minimal interests, stakeholders will decide to withdraw their support or contribution to one firm and provide it to another (e.g., customers will purchase products from a supplier offering an acceptable substitute).

John Smale, an outside member of General Motors' board of directors, believes that all large capitalist enterprises must be concerned with goals in addition to serving shareholders. In Smale's opinion, "A corporation is a human, living enterprise. It's not just a bunch of assets. The obligation of management is to perpetuate the corporation, and that precedes their obligation to shareholders."[130] The argument, then, is that the firm's strategic competitiveness is enhanced when its governance mechanisms are designed and implemented in ways that take into consideration the interests of all stakeholders. Although subject to debate, some believe that ethically responsible companies design and use governance mechanisms that serve all stakeholders' interests. There is, however, a more critical relationship between ethical behavior and corporate governance mechanisms.

Evidence demonstrates that all companies are vulnerable to a display of unethical behaviors by their employees, including, of course, top-level managers. For example, in March 1997, federal agents raided Columbia/HCA facilities in El Paso, Texas. In July, they took documents from 35 different hospitals. The probe involved 700 governance agents and sent Columbia/HCA stock price plummeting. Several executives were indicted on charges of Medicaid fraud. Thomas Frist, Jr., started HCA, which was later sold to a smaller partner, Columbia. Richard L. Scott took over and started an aggressive plan to increase returns, which had slowed. Scott pushed to transform the traditional arm's-length distance between doctors and hospitals. He wanted doctors to hold equity in Columbia/HCA hospitals. However, federal law prohibits doctors from referring patients to laboratories and certain other health-care facilities in which they have ownership. The exception is in rural areas, where hospitals might not exist if doctors couldn't invest in them. Columbia/HCA made the most of this exception to increase performance. Scott also pushed cost-cutting efforts, which created an incentive to squeeze as much revenue as possible from patients. This created an incentive for hospital administrators to push beyond ethical limits. It is clear that for the federal probe, the main administrators stepped over the line. Scott spent little time forging a strong board and, therefore, little oversight was provided. Although the board pushed Scott out and brought back Frist, the board, including Frist, must take some responsibility for the failure and try to restore the company's image and improve its performance.[131] (Additional information about this firm appears in Chapter 12.)

The decisions and actions of a corporation's board of directors can be an effective deterrent to unethical behaviors. In fact, some believe that the most effective boards participate actively in setting boundaries for business ethics and values.[132] Once formulated, the board's expectations related to ethical decisions and actions by all of the firm's stakeholders must be communicated clearly to top-level managers. Moreover, these managers should be made to understand that the board will hold them fully accountable for the development and support of an organizational culture that results in only ethical decisions and behaviors. As explained in Chapter 12, CEOs can be positive role models for ethical behavior.

It is only when the proper controls of governance mechanisms are in place that strategies are formulated and implemented in ways that result in strategic competitiveness and above-average returns. As this chapter's discussion suggests, corporate governance mechanisms are a vital, yet imperfect part of firms' efforts to implement strategies successfully.

SUMMARY

- Corporate governance is a relationship among stakeholders that is used to determine the firm's direction and control its performance. How firms monitor and control top-level managers' decisions and actions, as called for by governance mechanisms, affects the implementation of strategies. Effective governance that aligns managers' interests with shareholders' interests can result in a competitive advantage for the firm.
- In the modern corporation, there are four internal governance mechanisms—ownership concen-

tration, board of directors, executive compensation, and the multidivisional structure—and one external—the market for corporate control.

- Ownership is separated from control in the modern corporation. Owners (principals) hire managers (agents) to make decisions that will maximize the value of their firm. As risk specialists, owners diversify their risk by investing in an array of corporations. As decision-making specialists, top-level managers are expected by owners to make decisions that will result in the earning of above-average returns. Thus, modern corporations are characterized by an agency relationship that is created when one party (the firm's owners) hires and pays another party (top-level managers) because of their decision-making skills.
- Separation of ownership and control creates an agency problem when an agent pursues goals that are in conflict with the principals' goals. Principals establish and use governance mechanisms to control this problem.
- Ownership concentration, an internal governance mechanism, is defined by the number of large-block shareholders and the percentage of shares they own. With significant ownership percentages such as those held by large mutual funds and pension funds, institutional investors often are able to influence top-level managers' strategic decisions and actions. Thus, unlike diffuse ownership, which tends to bring about relatively weak monitoring and control of managerial decisions, concentrated ownership results in more active and effective monitoring of top-level managers. An increasingly powerful force in corporate America, institutional owners are actively using their positions of concentrated ownership in individual companies to force managers and boards of directors to make decisions that maximize a firm's value. These owners (e.g., CalPERS) have caused executives in prominent companies to lose their jobs because of their failure to serve shareholders' interests effectively.
- In the United States and the United Kingdom, the board of directors, composed of insiders, related outsiders, and outsiders, is a governance mechanism shareholders expect to represent their collective interests, especially because ownership is diffuse. The percentage of outside directors on most boards now exceeds the percentage of insider directors. This relative percentage of outsiders seems appropriate. These individuals are expected to be more independent of a firm's top-level managers than are those selected from inside the firm.
- A highly visible and often criticized governance mechanism is executive compensation. Through the use of salary, bonuses, and long-term incentives, the mechanism is intended to strengthen the alignment of managers' and shareholders' interests. A strong emphasis on executive incentives has widened the gap between the pay of the typical worker and CEOs. A firm's board of directors has the responsibility of determining the degree to which executive compensation is succeeding as a governance mechanism and to initiate all appropriate corrective actions when required.
- As an internal governance mechanism, the multidivisional (M-form) structure is intended to reduce managerial opportunism and to align principals' and agents' interests as a result. The M-form makes it possible for the corporate office to monitor and control managerial decisions in the individual divisions in diversified firms. However, at the corporate level, the M-form may actually stimulate managerial opportunism, resulting in top-level executives overdiversifying.
- In general, evidence suggests that shareholders and board directors have become more vigilant in their control of managerial decisions. Nonetheless, these mechanisms are insufficient to govern the diversification of many large companies. As such, the market for corporate control is an important governance mechanism. Although it, too, is imperfect, the market for corporate control has been effective in causing corporations to downscope and reduce their degree of inefficient diversification.
- Corporate governance structures used in Germany and Japan differ from each other and from the one used in the United States. Historically, the U.S. governance structure has focused on maximizing shareholder value. In Germany, employees, as a stakeholder group, have a more prominent role in governance than is the case in the United States. Until recently, Japanese shareholders played virtually no role in the monitoring and control of top-level managers. However, these

systems are becoming more similar as are many governance systems in both developed countries such as France and Italy and developing countries such as Russia and China.

- Effective governance mechanisms ensure that the interests of all stakeholders are served. Thus, long-term strategic success results when firms are governed in ways that permit at least minimal satisfaction of capital market stakeholders (e.g., shareholders), product market stakeholders (e.g., customers and suppliers), and organizational stakeholders (managerial and nonmanagerial employees). Moreover, effective governance causes the establishment and consistent use of ethical behavior as the firm formulates and implements its strategies.

REVIEW QUESTIONS

1. What is corporate governance? What factors account for the considerable amount of attention corporate governance receives from several parties, including shareholder activists, business press writers, and academic scholars? Why are governance mechanisms used to control managerial decisions?
2. What does it mean to say that ownership is separated from control in the modern corporation? What brought about this separation?
3. What is an agency relationship? What is managerial opportunism? What assumptions do owners of modern corporations make about managerial agents? What are the strategic implications of these assumptions?
4. How are the four internal governance mechanisms—ownership concentration, boards of directors, executive compensation, and the multidivisional (M-form) structure—used to align the interests of managerial agents with those of the firm's owners?
5. What trends exist in terms of executive compensation? What is the effect of increased use of long-term incentives on executives' strategic decisions?
6. What is the market for corporate control? What conditions generally cause this external governance mechanism to become active? How does this mechanism constrain top-level managers' decisions?
7. What is the nature of corporate governance mechanisms used in Germany and Japan?
8. How can corporate governance mechanisms foster ethical strategic decisions and behaviors on the part of managerial agents?

APPLICATION DISCUSSION QUESTIONS

1. The roles and responsibilities of top-level managers and members of a corporation's board of directors are different. Traditionally, executives have been responsible for determining the firm's strategic direction and implementing strategies to achieve it, whereas the board has been responsible for monitoring and controlling managerial decisions and actions. Some argue that boards should become more involved with the formulation of a firm's strategies. In your opinion, how would the board's increased involvement in the selection of strategies affect a firm's strategic competitiveness? What evidence can you offer to support your position?
2. Do you believe that large U.S. firms have been overgoverned by some corporate governance mechanisms and undergoverned by others? Provide an example of a business firm to support your belief.
3. How can corporate governance mechanisms create conditions that allow top-level managers to develop a competitive advantage and focus on long-term performance? Search the business press to find an example of a firm in which this occurred and prepare a description of it.
4. Some believe that the market for corporate control is not an effective governance mechanism. If this is an accurate view, what factors might account for the ineffectiveness of this method of monitoring and controlling managerial decisions?
5. Assume that you overheard the following comments: "As a top-level manager, the only agency relationship I am concerned about is the one between myself and the firm's owners. I think that it would be a waste of my time and energy to worry about any other agency relationship." How would you respond to this person? Do you accept or reject this view? Be prepared to support your position.

ETHICS QUESTIONS

1. As explained in this chapter, the use of corporate governance mechanisms should establish order between parties whose interests may be in conflict. Do firm owners have any ethical responsibilities to managers when using governance mechanisms to establish order? If so, what are they?
2. Is it ethical for a firm owner to assume that agents (managers hired to make decisions that are in the owner's best interests) are averse to work and risk? Why or why not?
3. What are the responsibilities of the board of directors to stakeholders other than shareholders?
4. What ethical issues are involved with executive compensation? How can we determine if top-level executives are paid too much?
5. Is it ethical for firms involved in the market for corporate control to target companies performing at levels exceeding the industry average? Why or why not?
6. What ethical issues, if any, do top-level managers face when asking their firm to provide them with either a golden parachute or a golden goodbye?
7. How can governance mechanisms be designed to ensure against managerial opportunism, ineffectiveness, and unethical behaviors?

INTERNET EXERCISE

Go to CalPERS at:

http://www.calpers.ca.gov

To ensure an acceptable return on their investment, the major stockholders of public corporations are becoming increasingly involved in corporate governance issues. The California Public Employees Retirement Fund, which is referred to as CalPERS, exemplifies this trend. CalPERS is the largest public pension system in America, with more than $128 billion in assets. In recent years, CalPERS has become very aggressive in terms of applying pressure on low-performing companies to improve their governance practices. With this in mind, visit the CalPERS Web site. From this site and other Internet resources, make a list of the activities that CalPERS has engaged in to try to influence the governance practices of the companies in which it invests.

Strategic Surfing

Corporate Governance is a Web site that is dedicated solely to corporate governance issues. The site is very extensive and contains information pertaining to a broad spectrum of corporate governance issues. Executive Paywatch is another site of interest to observers of corporate governance issues. This site is sponsored by the AFL-CIO and monitors the compensation packages of the CEOs of major American corporations.

http://www.corpgov.net
http://www.aflcio.paywatch.org/ceopay

NOTES

1. R. D. Ward, 1997, *21st Century Corporate Board* (New York: John Wiley & Sons).
2. J. A. Byrne, R. Grover, and R. A. Melcher, 1997, The best and worst boards: Our special report on corporate governance, *Business Week*, December 8, 91–98.
3. R. K. Mitchell, B. R. Agle, and D. J. Wood, 1997, Toward a theory of stakeholder identification and salience: Defining the principle of who and what really counts, *Academy of Management Review* 22: 853–886.
4. J. H. Davis, F. D. Schoorman, and L. Donaldson, 1997, Toward a stewardship theory of management, *Academy of Management Review* 22: 20–47.
5. O. E. Williamson, 1996, Economic organization: The case for candor, *Academy of Management Review* 21: 48–57.
6. E. F. Fama and M. C. Jensen, 1983, Separation of ownership and control, *Journal of Law and Economics* 26: 301–325.
7. Ward, *21st Century Corporate Board*, 3–144.
8. C. Arnolod and K. Breen, 1997, Investor activism goes worldwide, *Corporate Board* 18, no. 2: 7–12.
9. M. Kroll, P. Wright, L. Toombs, and H. Leavell, 1997, Form of control: A critical determinant of acquisition performance and CEO rewards, *Strategic Management Journal* 18: 85–96; J. K. Seward and J. P. Walsh, 1996, The governance and control of voluntary corporate spinoffs, *Strategic Management Journal* 17: 25–39.
10. J. D. Westphal and E. J. Zajac, 1997, Defections from the inner circle: Social exchange, reciprocity and diffusion of board independence in U.S. corporations, *Administrative*

Science Quarterly 42: 161–212; Ward, *21st Century Corporate Board.*

11. J. Charkham, 1994, *Keeping Good Company: A Study of Corporate Governance in Five Countries* (New York: Oxford University Press), 1.
12. Cadbury Committee, 1992, *Report of the Cadbury Committee on the Financial Aspects of Corporate Governance* (London: Gee).
13. M. A. Hitt, R. E. Hoskisson, R. A. Johnson, and D. D. Moesel, 1996, The market for corporate control and firm innovation, *Academy of Management Journal* 39: 1084–1119; J. P. Walsh and R. Kosnik, 1993, Corporate raiders and their disciplinary role in the market for corporate control, *Academy of Management Journal* 36: 671–700.
14. Davis, Schoorman, and Donaldson, Toward a stewardship theory of management.
15. C. Sundaramurthy, J. M. Mahoney, and J. T. Mahoney, 1997, Board structure, antitakeover provisions, and stockholder wealth, *Strategic Management Journal* 18: 231–246; K. J. Rediker and A. Seth, 1995, Boards of directors and substitution effects of alternative governance mechanisms, *Strategic Management Journal* 16: 85–99.
16. G. E. Davis and T. A. Thompson, 1994, A social movement perspective on corporate control, *Administrative Science Quarterly* 39: 141–173.
17. M. A. Eisenberg, 1989, The structure of corporation law, *Columbia Law Review* 89, no. 7: 1461 as cited in R. A. G. Monks and N. Minow, 1995, *Corporate Governance* (Cambridge, MA: Blackwell Business), 7.
18. E. E. Fama, 1980, Agency problems and the theory of the firm, *Journal of Political Economy* 88: 288–307.
19. M. Jensen and W. Meckling, 1976, Theory of the firm: Managerial behavior, agency costs, and ownership structure, *Journal of Financial Economics* 11: 305–360.
20. H. C. Tosi, J. Katz, and L. R. Gomez-Mejia, 1997, Disaggregating the agency contract: The effects of monitoring, incentive alignment, and term in office on agent decision making, *Academy of Management Journal* 40: 584–602; P. C. Godfrey and C. W. L. Hill, 1995, The problem of unobservables in strategic management research, *Strategic Management Journal* 16: 519–533.
21. P. Wright and S. P. Ferris, 1997, Agency conflict and corporate strategy: The effect of divestment on corporate strategy, *Strategic Management Journal* 18: 77–83.
22. T. M. Welbourne and L. R. Gomez Meiia, 1995, Gainsharing: A critical review and a future research agenda, *Journal of Management* 21: 577.
23. P. Wright, S. P. Ferris, A. Sarin, and V. Awasthi, 1996, Impact of corporate insider, blockholder, and institutional equity ownership on firm risk taking, *Academy of Management Journal* 39: 441–463.
24. P. B. Firstenberg and B. G. Malkiel, 1994, The twenty-first century boardroom: Who will be in charge? *Sloan Management Review*, Fall, 27–35, as cited in C. M. Daily, 1996, Governance patterns in bankruptcy reorganizations, *Strategic Management Journal* 17: 355–375.
25. O. E. Williamson, 1996, *The Mechanisms of Governance* (New York: Oxford University Press), 6; O. E. Williamson, 1993, Opportunism and its critics, *Managerial and Decision Economics* 14: 97–107.
26. S. Ghoshal and P. Moran, 1996, Bad for practice: A critique of the transaction cost theory, *Academy of Management Review* 21: 13–47.
27. Williamson, Economic organization, 50.
28. Godfrey and Hill, The problem of unobservables in strategic management research.
29. Y. Amihud and B. Lev, 1981, Risk reduction as a managerial motive for conglomerate mergers, *Bell Journal of Economics* 12: 605–617.
30. R. E. Hoskisson and T. A. Turk, 1990, Corporate restructuring: Governance and control limits of the internal market, *Academy of Management Review* 15: 459–477.
31. S. Finkelstein and D. C. Hambrick, 1989, Chief executive compensation: A study of the intersection of markets and political processes, *Strategic Management Journal* 16: 221 239; H. C. Tosi and L. R. Gomez-Mejia, 1989, The decoupling of CEO pay and performance: An agency theory perspective, *Administrative Science Quarterly* 34: 169–189.
32. Hoskisson and Turk, 1990, Corporate restructuring.
33. M. S. Jensen, 1986, Agency costs of free cash flow, corporate finance, and takeovers, *American Economic Review* 76: 323–329.
34. C. W. L. Hill and S. A. Snell, 1988, External control, corporate strategy, and firm performance in research intensive industries, *Strategic Management Journal* 9: 577–590.
35. A. Sharma, 1997, Professional as agent: Knowledge asymmetry in agency exchange, *Academy of Management Review* 22: 758–798.
36. R. Comment and G. Jarrell, 1995, Corporate focus and stock returns, *Journal of Financial Economics* 37: 67–87.
37. A. Shleifer and R. W. Vishny, 1986, Large shareholders and corporate control, *Journal of Political Economy* 94: 461–488.
38. J. A. Byrne, 1997, The CEO and the board, *Business Week*, September 15, 107–116.
39. R. E. Hoskisson, R. A. Johnson, and D. D. Moesel, 1994, Corporate divestiture intensity in restructuring firms: Effects of governance, strategy, and performance, *Academy of Management Journal* 37: 1207–1251.
40. A. Berle and G. Means, 1932, *The Modern Corporation and Private Property* (New York: Macmillan).
41. M. P. Smith, 1996, Shareholder activism by institutional investors: Evidence from CalPERS, *Journal of Finance* 51: 227–252.
42. J. D. Bogert, 1996, Explaining variance in the performance of long-term corporate blockholders, *Strategic Management Journal* 17: 243–249.
43. M. Useem, 1998, Corporate leadership in a globalizing equity market, *Academy of Management Executive* XII, in press.
44. C. M. Dailey, 1996, Governance patterns in bankruptcy reorganizations, *Strategic Management Journal* 17: 355–375.
45. Useem, Corporate leadership in a globalizing equity market; R. E. Hoskisson and M. A. Hitt, 1994, *Downscoping: How to Tame the Diversified Firm* (New York: Oxford University Press).
46. Byrne, The CEO and the board, 109.
47. Byrne, Grover, and Melcher, The best and worst boards.
48. E. Schine, 1997, CalPERS' grand inquisitor, *Business Week*, February 24, 120.
49. CalPERS highlights retailers in its list of underperformers, 1996, *Wall Street Journal*, February 7, Cl8.

50. B. Rehfeld, 1997, Low-cal CalPERS, *Institutional Investor*, March 31, 4–12; Smith, Shareholder activism.
51. M. J. Roe, 1993, Mutual funds in the boardroom, *Journal of Applied Corporate Finance* 5, no. 4: 56–61.
52. Byrne, The CEO and the board, 114.
53. J. S. Lublin, 1997, More CEOs decide: No time for seats, *Wall Street Journal*, October 28, A2.
54. *Bloomberg Business News*, 1996, More companies add severance package for execs, survey says, *Dallas Morning News*, July 6, F3.
55. Sundaramurthy, Mahoney, and Mahoney, Board structure, antitakeover provisions, and stockholder wealth; C. Sundaramurthy, 1996, Corporate governance within the context of antitakeover provisions, *Strategic Management Journal* 17: 377–394.
56. R. Grover and E. Schine, 1997, At Disney, Grumpy isn't just a dwarf, *Business Week*, February 24, 38.
57. B. S. Black, 1992, Agents watching agents: The promise of institutional investors voice, *UCLA Law Review* 39: 871–893.
58. Rediker and Seth, Boards of directors, 85.
59. J. K. Seward and J. P Walsh, 1996, The governance and control of voluntary corporate spinoffs, *Strategic Management Journal* 17: 25–39.
60. P. Mallete and R. L. Hogler, 1995, Board composition, stock ownership, and the exemption of directors from liability, *Journal of Management* 21: 861–878.
61. B. D. Baysinger and R. E. Hoskisson, 1990, The composition of boards of directors and strategic control: Effects on corporate strategy, *Academy of Management Review* 15: 72–87.
62. E. J. Zajac and J. D. Westphal, 1996, Director reputation, CEO-board power, and the dynamics of board interlocks, *Administrative Science Quarterly* 41: 507–529.
63. J. D. Westphal and E. J. Zajac, 1995, Who shall govern? CEO/board power, demographic similarity, and new director selection, *Administrative Science Quarterly* 40: 60–83.
64. R. P. Beatty and E. J. Zajac, 1994, Managerial incentives, monitoring, and risk bearing: A study of executive compensation, ownership, and board structure in initial public offerings, *Administrative Science Quarterly* 39: 313–335.
65. A. Bryant, 1997, CalPERS draws a blueprint for its concept of an ideal board, *New York Times*, June 17, C1.
66. I. M. Millstein, 1997, Red herring over independent boards, *New York Times*, April 6, F10; W. Q. Judge, Jr., and G. H. Dobbins, 1995, Antecedents and effects of outside directors' awareness of CEO decision style, *Journal of Management* 21: 43–64.
67. I. E. Kesner, 1988, Director characteristics in committee membership: An investigation of type, occupation, tenure and gender, *Academy of Management Journal* 31: 66–84.
68. S. Zahra, 1998, Governance, ownership and corporate entrepreneurship among the *Fortune* 500: The moderating impact of industry technological opportunity, *Academy of Management Journal* 41: in press.
69. J. A. Conger, D. Finegold, and E. E. Lawler III, 1998, Appraising boardroom performance, *Harvard Business Review* 76, no. 1: 136–148; J. A. Byrne and L. Brown, 1997, Directors in the hot seat, *Business Week*, December 8, 100–104.
70. H. Kaback, 1996, A director's guide to board behavior, *Wall Street Journal*, April 1, A14.
71. J. A. Byrne, 1997, Putting more stock in good governance, *Business Week*, September 15, 116; A. Bianco and J. A. Byrne, 1997, The rush to quality on corporate boards, *Business Week*, March 3, 34–35.
72. S. Rosenstein and J. G. Wyatt, 1997, Inside directors, board effectiveness, and shareholder wealth, *Journal of Financial Economics* 44: 229–250.
73. E. Cetera, 1997, *Business Week*, October 13, 44.
74. It's lonely at the top: Women's progress in gaining company directorships slows to crawl, 1997, *Dallas Morning News*, October 2, D11.
75. A boardroom gender gap, *Business Week*, November 24, 1997, 32.
76. D. C. Hambrick and S. Finkelstein, 1995, The effects of ownership structure on conditions at the top: The case of CEO pay raises, *Strategic Management Journal* 16: 175.
77. L. R. Gomez-Mejia and R. Wiseman, 1997, Reframing executive compensation: An assessment and review, *Journal of Management* 23: 291–374.
78. D. Bilimoria, 1997, Perspectives on corporate control: Implications for CEO compensation, *Human Relations* 50: 829–858; S. Werner and H. L. Tosi, 1995, Other people's money: The effects of ownership on compensation strategy and managerial pay, *Academy of Management Journal* 38: 1672–1691.
79. S. Finkelstein and B. K. Boyd, 1998, How much does the CEO matter?: The role of managerial discretion in the setting of CEO compensation, *Academy of Management Journal* 41: 179–199; I. Kristol, 1996, What is a CEO worth? *Wall Street Journal*, June 5, A14.
80. L. Wines, 1996, Compensation plans that support strategy, *Journal of Business Strategy* 17, no. 4: 17–20.
81. V. R. Loucks, Jr., 1995, An equity cure for managers, *Wall Street Journal*, September 26, Al9.
82. K. Roth and S. O'Donnell, 1996, Foreign subsidiary compensation: An agency theory perspective, *Academy of Management Journal* 39: 678–703.
83. R. E. Hoskisson, M. A. Hitt, and C. W. L. Hill, 1993, Managerial incentives and investment in R&D in large multiproduct firms, *Organization Science* 4: 325–341.
84. K. A. Merchant, 1989, *Rewarding Results: Motivating Profit Center Managers* (Cambridge, MA: Harvard Business School Press); J. Eaton and H. Rosen, 1983, Agency, delayed compensation, and the structure of executive remuneration, *Journal of Finance* 38: 1489–1505.
85. C. Duff, 1996, Top executives ponder high pay, decide they're worth every cent, *Wall Street Journal*, May 15, Bl.
86. Kristol, What is a CEO worth?
87. L. Uchitelle, 1996, Performance pay made 1995 bonus year for executives, *Houston Chronicle*, March 30, C3.
88. R. E. Yates, 1995, Restless in the ranks, *Dallas Morning News*, October 12, D1, D10.
89. S. Puri, 1997, The problem with stock options: Pay for underperformance, *Fortune*, December 8, 52–56.
90. Associated Press, 1996, Downsized firms start adding staff, *Dallas Morning News*, May 29, D2.
91. J. J. Keller, 1998, AT&T revamping to trim 18,000 jobs, *Wall Street Journal*, January 27, A3.
92. Special Report, 1996, How high can CEO pay go? *Business Week*, April 22, 100–121.
93. J. Reingold, 1997, Executive pay: Special report, *Business Week*, April 21, 58–64.

94. Uchitelle, Performance pay.
95. D. Machan, 1996, The last article you will ever have to read on executive pay? No way! *Forbes*, May 20, 176–234.
96. Reingold, Executive pay: Special report, 60.
97. Associated Press, 1996, Low-profile exec gets high-profile bonus, *Dallas Morning News*, April 11, D2.
98. GE chief's salary, bonus rose 22.3% to $5.32 million in '95, 1996, *Wall Street Journal*, March 13, B5.
99. Reingold, Executive pay: Special report, 60.
100. J. Bailey, 1998, Conseco agrees to acquire Green Tree, *Wall Street Journal*, April 8, A2, A6; J. Bailey, 1998, Green Tree's Coss must repay part of '96 bonus, *Wall Street Journal*, January 28, A3, A11; A. Osterland, 1997, How Green Tree got pruned, *Business Week*, December 1, 37.
101. J. Reingold, 1997, The folly of jumbo stock options, *Business Week*, December 22, 36–37.
102. O. E. Williamson, 1985, *The Economic Institutions of Capitalism: Firms, Markets and Relational Contracting* (New York: Macmillan Free Press).
103. New CEO presents plan for restructuring airline, 1996, *Wall Street Journal*, May 17, B8.
104. W. M. Carley, 1996, GE implements $200 million program to slash number of defects per product, *Wall Street Journal*, April 25, A4.
105. B. W. Keats and M. A. Hitt, 1988, A causal model of linkages among environmental dimensions, macro organizational characteristics, and performance, *Academy of Management Journal* 31: 570–598.
106. O. E. Williamson, 1994, Strategizing, economizing, and economic organization, in R. P. Rumelt, D. E. Schendel, and D. J. Teece (eds.), *Fundamental Issues in Strategy* (Cambridge, MA: Harvard Business School Press), 380.
107. Hoskisson and Turk, Corporate restructuring: Governance and control limits of the internal market.
108. M. A. Hitt, R. E. Hoskisson, and R. D. Ireland, 1990, Mergers and acquisitions and managerial commitment to innovation in M-form firms, *Strategic Management Journal* 11 (Special Summer Issue): 29–47.
109. Hitt, Hoskisson, Johnson, and Moesel, The market for corporate control and firm innovation; Walsh and Kosnik, Corporate raiders.
110. Mallette and Hogier, Board composition, 864.
111. A. E. Serwer, 1997, Michael Price has a plan for Dow Jones, *Fortune*, November 10, 137–140.
112. Sundaramurthy, Mahoney and Mahoney, Board structure, antitakeover provisions, and stockholder wealth.
113. R. A. Johnson, R. E. Hoskisson, and M. A. Hitt, 1998, The effects of environmental uncertainty on the mode of corporate restructuring, working paper University of Missouri.
114. Walsh and Kosnik, Corporate raiders.
115. S. Johnston, 1995, Managerial dominance of Japan's major corporations, *Journal of Management* 21: 191–209.
116. E. Ramstad and J. G. Auerback, 1998, Compaq buys Digital, an unthinkable event just a few years ago, *Wall Street Journal*, January 28, A1, A14.
117. Useem, Corporate leadership in a globalizing equity market.
118. Our discussion of corporate governance structures in Germany and Japan is drawn from Monks and Minow, *Corporate Governance*, 271–299; Charkham, *Keeping Good Company*, 6–118.
119. H. Kim and R. E. Hoskisson, 1996, Japanese governance systems: A critical review, in B. Prasad (ed.), *Advances in International Comparative Management* (Greenwich, CT: JAI Press), 165–189.
120. S. Douma, 1997, The two-tier system of corporate governance, *Long Range Planning* 30, no. 4: 612–615.
121. A. Osterland, 1997, France is a banana republic; corporate governance is changing in France . . . slowly, *Financial World*, July-August, 40–43; B. Riley, 1996, French leave for shareholders, *Financial Times*, June 23, XX.
122. Shake it up, 1997, *Wall Street Journal*, July 15, A18; G. Steinmetz, 1996, Satisfying shareholders is a hot new concept at some German firms, *Wall Street Journal*, March 6, A1, A6.
123. Charkham, *Keeping Good Company*, 70.
124. Williamson, *The Mechanisms*, 320.
125. D. P. Hamilton and N. Shirouau, 1996, Japan's business cartels are starting to erode, but change is slow, *Wall Street Journal*, December 4, A1, A6.
126. Japanese firms change meeting format, invite shareholder questions, 1997, *Dallas Morning News*, June 28, F2.
127. M. E. Porter, 1992, Capital disadvantages: America's failing capital investment system, *Harvard Business Review* 70, no. 5: 65–82.
128. W. L. Megginson, R. C. Nash, and M. van Randenborgh, 1994, The financial and operating performance of newly privatized firms: An international empirical analysis, *Journal of Finance* 49: 403–452.
129. E. Freeman and J. Liedtka, 1997, Stakeholder capitalism and the value chain, *European Management Journal* 15, no. 3: 286–295.
130. A. Taylor, III, 1996, GM: Why they might break up America's biggest company, *Fortune*, April 29, 84.
131. L. Lagnado, A. Sharpe, and G. Jaffe, 1997, Doctors' orders: How Columbia/HCA changed health care, for better or worse, *Wall Street Journal*, August 1, A1, A4.
132. R. F. Felton, A. Hudnut, and V. Witt, 1995, Building a stronger board, *McKinsey Quarterly 1995*, no. 2: 169.

Organizational Structure and Controls

CHAPTER 11

Learning Objectives

After reading this chapter, you should be able to:

1. Explain the importance of integrating strategy implementation and strategy formulation.
2. Describe the dominant path of evolution from strategy to structure to strategy again.
3. Identify and describe the organizational structures used to implement different business-level strategies.
4. Discuss organizational structures used to implement different corporate-level strategies.
5. Identify and distinguish among the organizational structures used to implement three international strategies.
6. Describe organizational structures used to implement cooperative strategies.

Changes in Organizational Structure at Raytheon Company

A diversified company, Raytheon follows the related-linked corporate-level strategy (see Figure 6.1 in Chapter 6). The firm's newly created size (close to $21 billion in sales revenue), expansive product focus, and geographic diversity (the company has customers in more than 80 countries) call for the use of a particular type of the multidivisional organizational structure (this structural type is explained fully later in the chapter) to implement its chosen corporate-level strategy of related-linked diversification. The organizational structure now in place at this firm and actions being taken to use it effectively are the focus of this opening case.

http://www.raytheon.com

Strategic decisions made recently at the corporate level have influenced Raytheon's organizational structure. In 1997, the firm completed two acquisitions to increase its competitiveness in the defense businesses. In July, Texas Instruments' defense lines were bought at a price of $2.9 billion; in December, $9.5 billion was spent to acquire Hughes Electronics' defense business from General Motors Corporation. Combining these acquisitions with the firm's existing operations created the third largest defense company in the United States and spurred changes in Raytheon's organizational structure.

To exploit fully the competitive advantage corporate executives believed these acquisitions provided their firm, Raytheon Systems was created as a division or strategic business

unit, with five operating segments. As shown below, the company's other three strategic business units are Raytheon Electronics, Raytheon Aircraft Co., and Raytheon Engineers & Constructors. Believing that the combination of this business unit's products creates a "defense powerhouse," the company stated, "With products that cover air, land and sea, Raytheon brings together a unique set of skills, experience, and state-of-the-art technologies to provide total defense systems solutions to the U.S. and its allies around the world."

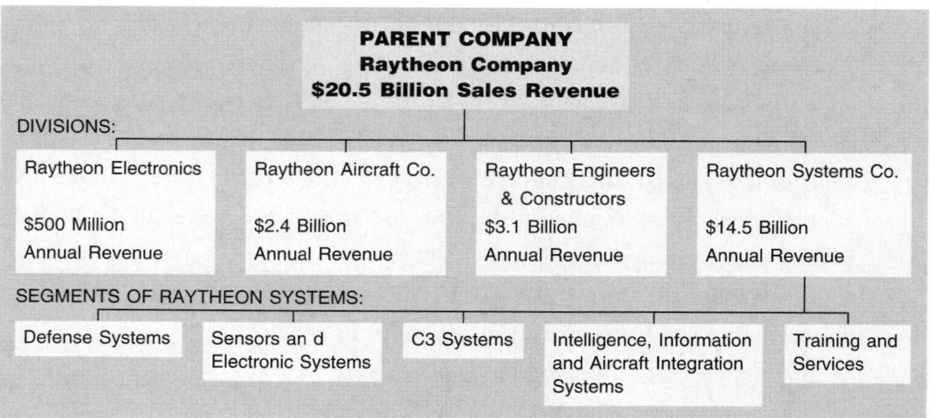

The structure shown above is an example of the strategic business unit (SBU) form of the multidivisional structure. Discussed fully in this chapter, this structure is appropriate for use by firms following a corporate-level strategy of related-linked diversification. This structure allows each of the business units to operate independently which means interactions between and among these units are infrequent. The reason for this is that relatively few product and geographic market relationships exist across the strategic business units. Within each unit, however, segments are related by products manufactured and/or geographic markets served. For example, while Raytheon Electronics and Raytheon Engineers & Constructors are not related, the five segments that have been grouped to form Raytheon Systems produce similar products and/or serve similar markets.

The SBU structural form calls for mechanisms to be used to integrate activities among a business unit's segments when doing so can enhance the unit's overall performance. Product similarities, for example, sometimes allow the sharing of a segment's resources and capabilities to produce components that are common to products being manufactured in more than one segment.

At Raytheon Systems, Centers of Excellence are used as an integrating mechanism. These "centers of excellence are cross-functional organizations that design and manufacture key components and subassemblies. The Centers of Excellence allow a focus on best-of-class engineering and manufacturing practices; maximize design efficiency and standardization; eliminate duplication of work and underutilization of facilities; and provide productivity through a reduced number of processes." One Center of Excellence is called Printed Wiring Board Fabrication. Located in Austin, Texas, this cross-functional unit combines work that had been completed previously at six different facilities. Two or more of Raytheon Systems' five segments share some of the products produced by this Center.

Corporate executives were optimistic about the potential of the Raytheon Systems' unit. As a result of strategic and structural changes made at the corporate level, the firm's top-level managers suggested that the System's strategic business unit could grow 10 percent annually. Some analysts concurred with this assessment, noting that ". . . Raytheon Systems was poised to dominate the defense electronics business, which is the main growth area of defense spending." Challenges to the business unit's potential include well-positioned competitors such as Lockheed Martin and the significant amount of debt the firm incurred to acquire Hughes Electronics and Texas Instruments' defense lines. To enhance the efficiency of its newly created Raytheon Systems business unit and to reduce its corporate debt, the company announced a reduction of 8,500 employees in early 1998. To have an even more positive effect on the corporation's operational efficiency, another 1,000 jobs in Raytheon Engineers & Constructors' unit were eliminated at the same time.

SOURCE: J. G. Auerbach, 1998, Raytheon expects to post charge of $500 million for revamping, *Wall Street Journal*, January 26, B4; A. Dworkin, 1998, Raytheon cuts may herald industry changes, *Dallas Morning News*, January 24, F1, F2; V. Griffith, 1998, Raytheon set to axe 9,700 jobs, *Financial Times*, January 26, 17; L. Johannes, 1998, Raytheon has loss following charges, but sales rise 18 percent, *Wall Street Journal*, January 27, B4; Raytheon Company Home Page, 1998, February 3, http://www.raytheon.com; A. Dworkin, 1997, Raytheon Systems unveiled, *Dallas Morning News*, December 19, D1, D11; T. A. Schwartzman, 1997, Raytheon, *Value Line*, October 3, 567.

In the previous chapter, we described mechanisms companies use to govern their operations and to align various parties' interests, especially the interests of top-level executives, with those of the firm's owners. Governance mechanisms can influence a company's ability to implement formulated strategies successfully and thereby facilitate competitive advantage.[1]

In this chapter, our focus is on the organizational structures and controls used to implement the strategies discussed previously (e.g., business-level, Chapter 4; corporate-level, Chapter 6; international, Chapter 8; and cooperative, Chapter 9). Moreover, as the discussion about actions taken at Raytheon Company suggests, the proper use of an organizational structure and its accompanying integrating mechanisms and controls can contribute to the firm's strategic competitiveness.[2] In fact, the most productive global competitors are those with effective product innovation skills and an organizational structure in place that facilitates successful and timely applications of internal capabilities and core competencies.[3] Thus, organizational structure influences managerial work and the decisions made by top-level managers.[4]

Organizational structure alone, however, does not create a competitive advantage;[5] rather, a competitive advantage is created when there is a proper match between strategy and structure. For example, it may be that what makes 3M's competitive advantage somewhat sustainable ". . . is its unique blend of practices, values, autonomous structures, funding processes, rewards, and selection and development of product champions."[6] Similarly, the Acer Group, manufacturer of Acer personal computers, is known as an innovative competitor. Some analysts believe that a unique organizational structure (which the CEO labels "global brand, local touch") contributes significantly to the firm's strategic competitiveness.[7] On the other hand, ineffective strategy/structure matches may result in firm rigidity and failure given the complexity and need for rapid changes in the new competitive landscape.[8] Thus, effective strategic leaders (see Chapter 12) seek to develop an organizational structure and accompanying controls that are superior to those of their competitors.[9] Using competitively superior structures and controls explains in part why some firms survive and succeed while others do not.[10] Executives at Bayerische Motoren Werke AG (BMW), for example, believe that the recently created process-oriented organizational structure will contribute to the firm's future success. The objective of this structure is to enable BMW to strengthen its focus on customers and markets and to improve further the efficiency of its manufacturing operations.[11] As with the other parts of the strategic management process, top-level managers bear the final responsibility to make choices about organizational structures that will enhance firm performance.[12] Following its acquisition of Digital Equipment Corporation (DEC), Compaq Computer Corporation executives, for example, must make structural decisions that will facilitate a successful integration of DEC's businesses into their own. Although generally optimistic, analysts see developing an organizational structure that could integrate what had been two different businesses operating within the guidelines of two different cost structures to be challenging.[13]

Selecting the organizational structure and controls that result in effective implementation of chosen strategies is a fundamental challenge for managers, especially top-level managers. A key reason is that in the global economy, firms must be flexible, innovative, and creative to exploit their core competencies in the pursuit of marketplace opportunities.[14] They also require a certain degree of stability in their structures so that day-to-day tasks can be completed efficiently. Accessible and reliable information is required for executives to reach decisions regarding the selection of a structure that can provide the desired levels of flexibility and stability. By helping executives improve their decision making, useful information contributes to the formation and use of effective structures and controls.[15]

Executives at Barclays, the United Kingdom banking group, recently made decisions regarding the firm's strategy and organizational structure. Information flows from investor groups and a desire to improve its stock market rating were instrumental in stimulating the executives' strategic and structural decisions. To bring its retail financial services to the forefront, Barclays' CEO decided to regroup the company's operations into four business units: retail financial services, asset management, investment banking, and business banking. The purpose of this structural reorganization was to split personal and business banking, which the firm believes have different managerial requirements, risk profiles, and cost structures. The largest of the four units is the newly created retail financial services. This unit includes personal banking in the United Kingdom and Europe, private banking, the African and Caribbean banks, mutual funds, and Barclay Trust. By concentrating on the retail financial services division, as permitted by changes to the firm's organizational structure, Barclays' top-level managers hope to reduce the volatility of the company's earnings flow that a focus on corporate banking had engendered.[16]

To examine organizational structure and controls, this chapter first describes a pattern of growth and accompanying changes in organizational structure experienced by strategically competitive firms. This pattern is one in which structural change follows strategic growth and success. In turn, structural adjustments can affect future formulations of strategies.

The chapter's second major section discusses organizational structures and controls that are used to implement different business-level strategies. The dominant structures and control characteristics that contribute to the effective implementation of each of the business-level strategies described in Chapter 4 are explained in this part of the chapter.

Corporate-level strategy implementation is then described. The transition from the functional to the multidivisional structure is highlighted in this section. This major structural innovation took place in several firms during the 1920s, including DuPont. In fact, noted business historian Alfred Chandler cites DuPont as the innovator in both the strategy of diversification and the multidivisional structure.[17] Specific variations of the multidivisional structure are discussed in terms of their relationship with effective implementation of related and unrelated diversification strategies.

Next, we describe structures that are used to implement different international strategies. Because of the increasing globalization of many industries, the number of firms implementing international strategies continues to grow. As noted in previous chapters, the trend toward globalization is significant and pervasive.[18] In the words of Joe Gorman, CEO of TRW, a large diversified firm with operations in defense, auto parts, and data, "There's no question in my mind that a great transformational change is occurring. It's a change from regional economies and industries to truly global ones."[19] Almost identically, a business historian believes that the "global restructuring of industries and work [that is occurring today] is the most significant economic change in 100 years."[20] Having observed conditions such as these, GE's CEO and chairman, Jack Welch, suggested that the speed at which the future is approaching the firm creates a discontinuous set of environmental conditions.[21] To cope successfully with the strategic challenges associated with discontinuous changes, the firm must develop and use organizational structures that facilitate meaningful conversations among all stakeholders regarding opportunities and threats facing the company at different points in time.[22] To examine the use of structure to implement international strategies effectively, we first describe the structure and control characteristics of the multidomestic strategy. This section is followed by a similar discussion of the global strategy. The transnational strategy is examined next, along with the variations in structure that are required to implement it. In the chapter's final two sections, we discuss the use of organizational structures to implement cooperative strategies and a few issues concerning organizational forms that should be of interest to those responsible for effective use of a firm's strategic management process.

EVOLUTIONARY PATTERNS OF STRATEGY AND ORGANIZATIONAL STRUCTURE

All firms require some form of organizational structure to implement their strategies. In this section, we describe how organizational structures have evolved in response to managerial and organizational needs.

Principally, structures are changed when they no longer provide the coordination, control, and direction managers and organizations require to implement strategies successfully.[23] The ineffectiveness of a structure typically results from increases in a firm's revenues and levels of diversification. In particular, the formulation of strategies involving greater levels of diversification (see Chapter 6) demands structural change to match the strategy. Some structures become elaborate while others become focused on financial rather than strategic control.

Organizational structure is a firm's formal role configuration, procedures, governance and control mechanisms, and authority and decision-making processes.

Organizational structure is a firm's formal role configuration, procedures, governance and control mechanisms, and authority and decision-making processes.[24] Influenced by situational factors including company size and age, organizational structure reflects managers' determination of *what* the firm does and *how* it completes that work given its chosen strategies.[25] Strategic competitiveness can be attained only when the firm's selected structure is congruent with its formulated strategy.[26] As such, a strategy's potential to create value is reached only when the firm configures itself in ways that allow the strategy to be implemented effectively. Thus, as firms evolve and change their strategies, new structural arrangements are required. Additionally, existing structures influence the future selection of strategies. Accordingly, the two key strategic actions of strategy formulation and strategy implementation continuously interact to influence managerial choices about strategy and structure.

Figure 11.1 shows the growth pattern many firms experience. This pattern results in changes in the relationships between the firm's formulated strategies and the organizational structures used to support and facilitate their implementation.

Simple Structure

A **simple structure** is an organizational form in which the owner-manager makes all major decisions directly and monitors all activities, while the staff serves as an extension of the manager's supervisory authority.

A **simple structure** is an organizational form in which the owner-manager makes all major decisions directly and monitors all activities, while the staff serves as an extension of the manager's supervisory authority. This structure involves little specialization of tasks, few rules, and limited formalization. Although important, information systems are relatively unsophisticated, and owner-managers participate directly in the firm's day-to-day operations. Typically, this structure is used by firms offering a single product line in a single geographic market. Because of the small organization size, the simple structure is used frequently in firms implementing either the focused low-cost or focused differentiation strategy. Restaurants, repair businesses, and other specialized enterprises are examples of firms whose limited complexity calls for the use of the simple structure. In this structure, communication is frequent and direct, and new products tend to be introduced to the market quickly, which can result in a competitive advantage. Because of these characteristics, few of the coordination problems that are common in larger organizations exist.

The simple structure, the operations it supports, and the strategies being implemented in these companies play important roles in the success of various economies. Job creation data are one indicator of this importance. In the United States, for example, companies with between 100 and 500 employees have become the largest job creators.[27] These small firms created approximately 85 percent of the new jobs in the United States between 1991 and 1996. The value of small firms to the United Kingdom's economy has also been recognized. In the U.K., some analysts believe that the simple organizational structure may result in competitive advantages for some small firms relative to their larger counterparts. A broad-based openness to innovation, greater structural flexibility, and an ability to respond more rapidly to environmental changes are examples of these potential competitive ad-

FIGURE 11.1 ***Strategy and Structure Growth Pattern***

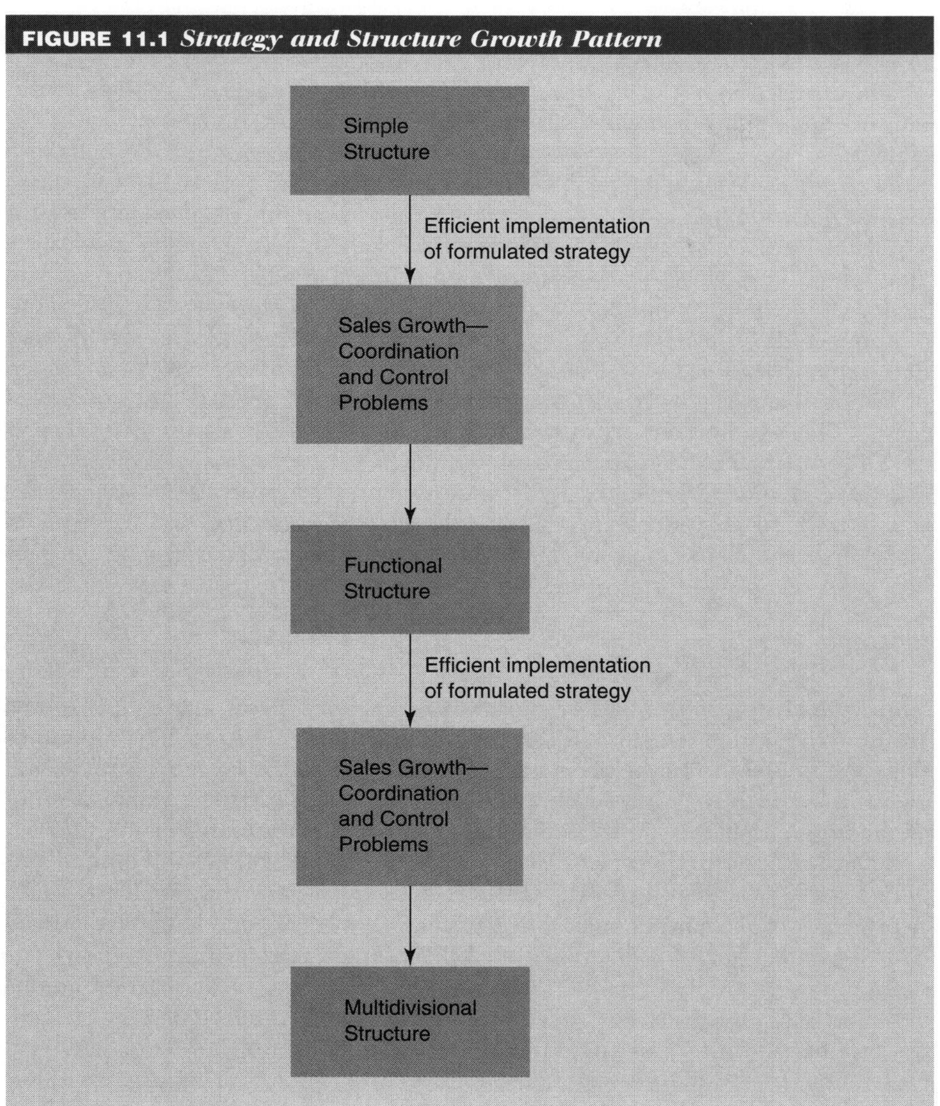

vantages.[28] Thus, although large corporations are indeed vital to the health of the world's economies, the importance of small firms should not be overlooked. The simple organizational structure properly supports the implementation of the focused strategies that are chosen most often by small firms (see Chapter 4).

However, as the small firm grows larger and more complex, managerial and structural challenges emerge. For example, the amount of competitively relevant information requiring analysis increases substantially. These more complicated information processing needs place significant pressures on the simple structure and the owner-manager. Commonly, owner-managers lack the organizational skills and experiences required to manage effectively the specialized and complex tasks involved with multiple organizational functions. Owner-managers or the top-level managers employed by the small firm's owner bear the responsibility to recognize the inadequacy of the firm's current organizational structure and the need to change to one that is consistent with the firm's strategy.[29]

The experiences of Yo! provide a useful illustration. Established as a sushi restaurant in London, this company achieved immediate success. In its first year of operation, Yo! grew by adding products related directly to its restaurant business such as a London-wide sushi delivery service and an event catering service. After its first year of operation, the company's founder announced ambitious plans to move the Yo! name into new areas including supermarkets and hotels. The objective was to establish Yo! as a mass-market youth brand. Initial product line expansions included clothing for young adults and children and toys. A more contemporary style of hotel—to be called Yotel—was also planned. Beyond this, the founder also believed that there was ". . . an opportunity for Yo! at the convenience-store level, providing a new retail environment involving home delivery and Internet shopping."[30] These ambitious growth objectives, however, create significant pressures on Yo!'s managers and its simple organizational structure. As the firm's product lines become more diverse (recall that increased product diversity signals a change in strategy), an appropriate response to the pressures the firm and its top-level managers face includes movement to a functional organizational structure or perhaps even one of the forms of the multidivisional structure.

The **functional structure** consists of a chief executive officer and limited corporate staff, with functional line managers in dominant organizational areas such as production, accounting, marketing, R&D, engineering, and human resources.

Functional Structure

To coordinate more complex organizational functions, firms such as Yo! should abandon the simple structure in favor of the functional structure. The functional structure is used by larger firms implementing one of the business-level strategies and by firms with low levels of diversification (for instance, companies implementing either the single- or dominant-business corporate-level strategy).

The **functional structure** consists of a chief executive officer and limited corporate staff, with functional line managers in dominant organizational areas such as production, accounting, marketing, R&D, engineering, and human resources. This structure allows for functional specialization, thereby facilitating knowledge sharing and idea development.[31] Because the differences in orientation among organizational functions can impede communication and coordination, the central task of the CEO is to integrate the decisions and actions of individual business functions for the benefit of the entire corporation.[32] This organizational form also facilitates career paths and professional development in specialized functional areas.

An unintended negative consequence of the functional structure is the tendency for functional-area managers to focus on local versus overall company strategic issues. Such emphases cause specialized managers to lose sight of the firm's overall strategic intent and strategic mission. When this situation emerges, the multidivisional structure often is implemented to overcome this difficulty.

Another condition that encourages a change from the functional to the multidivisional structure is greater diversification. Strategic success often leads to growth and diversification. Deciding to offer the same products in different markets (market diversification) and/or choosing to offer additional products (product diversification) creates control problems. The multidivisional structure provides the controls required to deal effectively with additional levels of diversification. In fact, the firm's returns may suffer when increased diversification is not accompanied by a change to the multidivisional structure.

Multidivisional Structure

The chief executive's limited ability to process increasing quantities of strategic information, the focus of functional managers on local issues, and increased diversification are primary causes of the decision to change from the functional to the multidivisional (M-form) structure. According to Alfred Chandler, "The M-form came into being when senior managers operating through existing centralized, functionally departmentalized . . . structures realized they had neither the time nor the necessary information to coordinate and monitor day-to-day operations, or to devise and implement long-term plans for the various product lines. The administrative overload had become simply too great."[33]

The **multidivisional (M-form) structure** is composed of operating divisions where each division represents a separate business or profit center and the top corporate officer delegates responsibilities for day-to-day operations and business-unit strategy to division managers. Because the diversified corporation is the dominant form of business in the industrialized world, the M-form is being used in most of the corporations competing in the global economy.[34] However, only effectively designed M-forms enhance a firm's performance. Thus, for all companies, and perhaps especially for diversified firms, performance is a function of the goodness of fit between strategy and structure.[35]

The **multidivisional (M-form) structure** is composed of operating divisions where each division represents a separate business or profit center and the top corporate officer delegates responsibility for day-to-day operations and business-unit strategy to division managers.

Chandler's examination of the strategies and structures of large American firms documented the M-form's development.[36] Chandler viewed the M-form as an innovative response to coordination and control problems that surfaced during the 1920s in the functional structures being used by large firms such as DuPont and General Motors.[37] Among other benefits, the M-form allowed firms to greatly expand their operations.[38]

Use of the Multidivisional Structure at DuPont and General Motors Chandler's studies showed that firms such as DuPont began to record significant revenue growth through the manufacture and distribution of diversified products while using the functional structure. Functional departments such as sales and production, however, found it difficult to coordinate the conflicting priorities of the firm's new and different products and markets. Moreover, the functional structures being used allocated costs to organizational functions rather than to individual businesses and products. This allocation method made it virtually impossible for top-level managers to determine the contributions of separate product lines to the firm's return on its investments. Even more damaging for large firms trying to implement newly formulated diversification strategies through use of a functional structure that was appropriate for small companies and for those needing proprietary expertise and scale[39] was the increasing allocation of top-level managers' time and energies to short-term administrative problems. Focusing their efforts on these issues caused executives to neglect the long-term strategic issues that were their primary responsibility.

To cope with similar problems, General Motors CEO Alfred Sloan, Jr., proposed a reorganization.[40] Sloan conceptualized separate divisions, each representing a distinct business, that would be self-contained and have its own functional hierarchy. Implemented in 1925, Sloan's structure delegated day-to-day operating responsibilities to division managers. The small staff at the corporate level was responsible for determining the firm's long-term strategic direction and for exercising overall financial control of semiautonomous divisions. Each division was to make its own business-level strategic decisions, but because the corporate office's focus was on the outcomes achieved by the entire corporation rather than the performance of separate units, decisions made by division heads could be superseded by corporate office personnel. Sloan's structural innovation had three important outcomes: "(1) it enabled corporate officers to more accurately monitor the performance of each business, which simplified the problem of control; (2) it facilitated comparisons between divisions, which improved the resource allocation process; and (3) it stimulated managers of poor performing divisions to look for ways of improving performance."[41]

The Use of Internal Controls in the Multidivisional Structure The M-form structure holds top-level managers responsible for formulating and implementing overall corporate strategies; that is, they are responsible for the corporate-level acquisition and restructuring, international, and cooperative strategies that we examined in Chapters 6 through 9.

Strategic and financial controls are the two major types of internal controls used to support implementation of strategies in larger firms.[42] Properly designed organizational controls provide clear insights to employees regarding behaviors that enhance the firm's competitiveness and overall performance.[43] Effective implementation of diversification strategies results when firms appropriately use both types of controls. For example, when Ford Motor Company increased its ownership in Mazda Motor Corp. to a controlling interest of approximately 33 percent, top-level managers acknowledged the need to use strategic controls when evaluating the performance of all Ford units. Simultaneously, however, the appointment of Ford executive Henry D. G. Wallace as Mazda's new president (Wallace was the first foreigner to head a Japanese automaker) was a partial signal of the need for financial controls to manage Mazda's extensive product line and base of supplier costs.[44] Similarly, top-level managers at CKS Group, a leader in Internet-related advertising, concluded recently through the use of strategic controls that the firm should reduce its roster of businesses from 10 operating units to four. Additionally, the need for financial controls was emphasized as demonstrated by realignments in reporting relationships between units and managers and the stated need for costs to be reduced on a company-wide basis.[45]

Strategic control entails the use of long-term and strategically relevant criteria by corporate-level managers to evaluate the performance of division managers and their units.

Strategic control entails the use of long-term and strategically relevant criteria by corporate-level managers to evaluate the performance of division managers and their units. Strategic control emphasizes largely subjective judgments and may involve intuitive evaluation criteria. Behavioral in nature, strategic controls typically require high levels of cognitive diversity among top-level managers. Cognitive diversity captures the differences in beliefs about cause-effect relationships and desired outcomes among top-level managers' preferences.[46] Corporate-level managers rely on strategic control to gain an operational understanding of the strategies being implemented in the firm's separate divisions or business units. Because strategic control allows a corporate-level evaluation of the full array of strategic actions—those concerned with both the formulation and implementation of a business-unit strategy—corporate-level managers must have a deep understanding of a division's or business unit's operations and markets.[47] The use of strategic controls also demands rich information exchanges between corporate and divisional managers. These exchanges take place through both formal and informal (i.e., unplanned) face-to-face meetings.[48] As diversification increases, strategic control can be strained.[49] Sometimes, this strain results in a commitment to reduce the firm's level of diversification. For example, Black & Decker's top-level managers decided recently to divest some divisions to reduce the firm's overall level of diversification. Units sold were the household products division in North America, Latin America, and Australia; Emhart Glass (a maker of equipment for the manufacture of glass containers); and True Temper Sports (a manufacturer of golf club shafts). Difficulties encountered when attempting to use strategic controls to evaluate the performance of these units and those managing them may have contributed to the divestment decisions. These divestments, coupled with a workforce reduction of 3,000 jobs (10 percent of the firm's workforce), were expected to generate annual savings of more than $100 million.[50]

Financial control entails objective criteria (e.g., return on investment) that corporate-level managers use to evaluate the returns being earned by individual business units and the managers responsible for their performance. Because they are oriented to financial outcomes, an emphasis on financial controls requires divisional performance to be largely independent of other divisions.[51] As such, when the firm chooses to implement a strategy calling for interdependence among the firm's different businesses, such as the related-constrained corporate-level strategy, the ability of financial control to add value to strategy implementation efforts is reduced.[52]

Financial control entails objective criteria (e.g., return on investment) that corporate-level managers use to evaluate the returns being earned by individual business units and the managers responsible for their performance.

Next, we discuss the organizational structures and controls that are used to implement different business-level strategies.

IMPLEMENTING BUSINESS-LEVEL STRATEGIES: ORGANIZATIONAL STRUCTURE AND CONTROLS

As discussed in Chapter 4, business-level strategies establish a particular type of competitive advantage (typically either low cost or differentiation) in a particular competitive scope (either an entire industry or a narrow segment of it). Effective implementation of the cost leadership, differentiation, and integrated low-cost/differentiation strategies occurs when certain modifications are made to the characteristics of the functional structure based on the unique attributes of the individual business-level strategies.

Using the Functional Structure to Implement the Cost Leadership Strategy

The structural characteristics of specialization, centralization, and formalization play important roles in the successful implementation of the cost leadership strategy. *Specialization* refers to the type and numbers of job specialties that are required to perform the firm's work.[53] For the cost leadership strategy, managers divide the firm's work into homogeneous subgroups. The basis for these subgroups is usually functional areas, products being produced, or clients served. By dividing and grouping work tasks into specialties, firms reduce their costs through the efficiencies achieved by employees specializing in a particular and often narrow set of activities.

Centralization is the degree to which decison-making authority is retained at higher managerial levels. Today, the trend in organizations is toward decentralization—the movement of decision-making authority down to people in the firm who have the most direct and frequent contact with customers. However, to coordinate activities carefully across organizational functions, the structure used to implement the cost leadership strategy calls for centralization. Thus, when designing this particular type of functional structure, managers strive to push some decision-making authority lower in the organization while remaining focused on the more general need for activities to be coordinated and integrated through the efforts of a centralized staff.

Because the cost leadership strategy is often chosen by firms producing relatively standardized products in large quantities, formalization is necessary. *Formalization* is the degree to which formal rules and procedures govern organizational activities.[54] To foster more efficient operations, R&D efforts emphasize improvements in the manufacturing process.

As summarized in Figure 11.2, successful implementation of the cost leadership strategy requires an organizational structure featuring strong task specialization, centralization of decision-making authority, and formalization of work rules and procedures. This type of functional structure encourages the emergence of a low-cost culture—a culture in which all employees seek to find ways to drive their firm's or unit's costs lower than rivals' costs. Using highly specialized work tasks, low-cost leader Southwest Airlines strives continuously to increase the efficiency of its

FIGURE 11.2 ***Functional Structure for Implementation of a Cost Leadership Strategy***

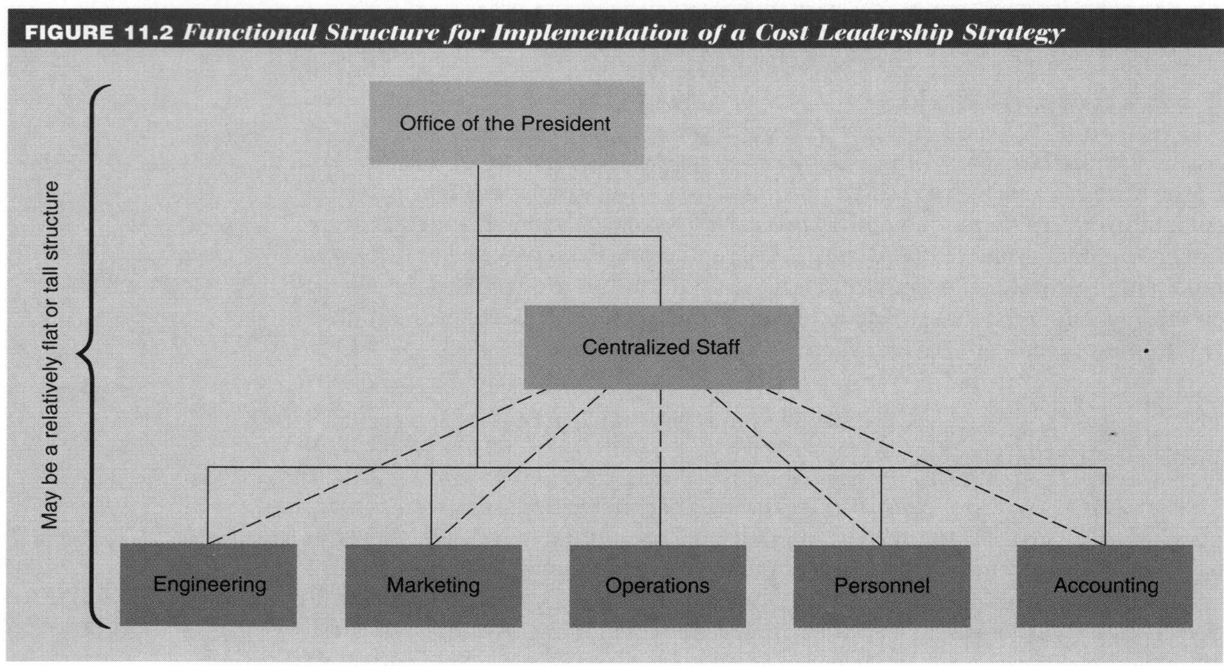

Notes:
- Operations is the main function
- Process engineering is emphasized rather than new product R&D
- Relatively large centralized staff coordinates functions
- Formalized procedures allow for emergence of a low-cost culture
- Overall structure is mechanical; job roles are very structured

production and distribution systems. For example, Southwest was one of the first carriers to sell tickets on the Internet. A travel industry consultant concluded that Southwest's simple fares and schedule make it easy to sell travel directly to consumers on the Internet.[55] Similarly, some European carriers that are preparing for privatization, including Air France, TAP Air Portugal, Alitalia, and LOT off Poland, are seeking to develop a low-cost culture that may prove to be critical to their success as deregulated firms competing in the global marketplace.[56]

Using the Functional Structure to Implement the Differentiation Strategy

Successful implementation of the differentiation strategy occurs when a functional structure is used in which decision-making authority is decentralized. Unlike the cost leadership strategy, where coordination and integration of organizational function activities occurs through centralization of decision-making authority, the functional structure used to implement the differentiation strategy demands that people throughout the firm learn how to coordinate and integrate their activities effectively. This is the expectation at Nordstrom, the successful retailer. This firm's structure calls for individual stores to employ buyers who specialize in purchasing products that will satisfy the unique tastes of customers in different geographic locales.[57]

The marketing and R&D functions are often emphasized in the differentiation strategy's functional structure. For example, because of its commitment to continuous product innovation across all of its operations, R&D is emphasized in several of FAG Kugelfischer's business units to facilitate implementation of the differentiation strategy in those individual units. This emphasis is suggested by the following comment: "All our efforts in the R&D field have only one objective—improving the performance parameters of our products for the benefit of our customers in such a way that new machinery equipped with them constitutes a clear advance in terms of purchasing costs, service, and maintenance."[58] As in the case at FAG, an emphasis on R&D in firms implementing the differentiation strategy typically is focused on those activities required to develop new products. Centralized staffs make certain that the efforts of those working in these two critical functions are integrated successfully. To properly control new product development, a centralized research facility may be established, and to maintain efficiency, the manufacturing facility also may be partially centralized. This allows integration of new products quickly while maintaining the highest possible efficiency.[59] Alternatively, many firms use decentralized cross-functional teams composed of representatives from marketing, R&D, and manufacturing to integrate these functions for new product design, manufacturing, and introduction to the marketplace.

Finally, to capitalize on emerging trends in key markets, the firm implementing the differentiation strategy often makes rapid changes based on ambiguous and incomplete information. Such rapid changes demand that the firm use a relatively flat organizational structure to group its work activities (in a relatively flat structure, workers are likely to have a number of tasks included in their job descriptions). The implementation of the differentiation strategy is affected negatively when the firm has extensive centralization and formalization, especially in a rapidly changing environment. Thus, the overall organizational structure needs to be flexible and job roles less structured. Additional characteristics of the form of the functional structure used to implement the differentiation strategy are shown in Figure 11.3.

FIGURE 11.3 ***Functional Structure for Implementation of a Differentiation Strategy***

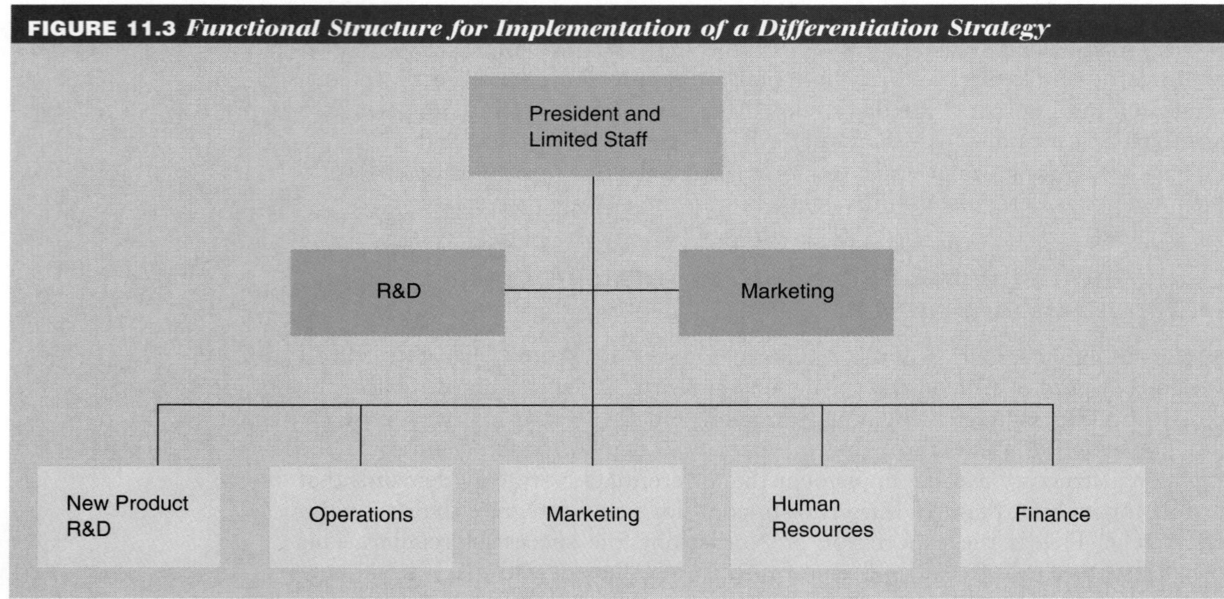

Notes:
- Marketing is the main function for keeping track of new product ideas
- New product R&D is emphasized
- Most functions are decentralized, but R&D and marketing may have centralized staffs that work closely with each other
- Formalization is limited so that new product ideas can emerge easily and change is more readily accomplished
- Overall structure is organic, job roles are less structured

Using the Functional Structure to Implement the Integrated Low-Cost/Differentiation Strategy

To implement the integrated low-cost/differentiation strategy, companies seek to provide value that differs from that offered by the low cost and the differentiated firm—low cost, relative to the cost of the differentiated firm's product, and valuable differentiated features, relative to the features offered by the low-cost firm's product.

The integrated low-cost/differentiation strategy is being formulated more frequently, especially by global firms, but it is difficult to implement. The primary reason for this is that the strategic and tactical actions required to implement the low-cost and the differentiation strategies are not the same. For example, to achieve the low-cost position, relative to rivals, emphasis is placed on production and manufacturing process engineering, with infrequent product changes. In contrast, to achieve a differentiated position, marketing and new product R&D are emphasized. But, as explained earlier, the structural characteristics used to emphasize new product development differ from those needed to emphasize process engineering. To implement this strategy successfully, managers are challenged to form an organizational structure that allows the development of differentiated product features while costs, relative to rivals' costs, are reduced. Often the functional structure has to be supplemented by horizontal coordination, such as cross-functional teams and a strong organizational culture to implement this strategy effectively.

Recent decisions made by top-level managers at Peugeot-Citroen, the French car manufacturer, and Japan's Nissan Motor Company suggest an interest on the part of both firms to use the functional structure to implement the integrated low-cost/differentiation strategy. Although committed to continuous product innovation and to launching new models more rapidly, these two companies want simultaneously to reduce their costs. At the heart of the cost control efforts are reconfigurations of the firms' assembly plants. Nissan plans to shift to five platforms from the current total of 24. Executives believe that this cost-reducing decision will also allow the firm to quickly offer nine new models to the marketplace and shorten overall product development times to a mere 12 months. Similarly, officials at Peugeot-Citroen seek to prune the number of its car platforms from seven to three. Both companies also announced organizational structural changes that were intended to facilitate implementation of their car manufacturing strategies.[60]

Using the Simple Structure to Implement Focused Strategies

As noted earlier, many focused strategies—strategies through which a firm concentrates on serving the unique needs of a narrow part or scope of the industry—are implemented most effectively through the simple structure. At some point, however, the increased sales revenues resulting from success necessitate changing from a simple to a functional structure. The challenge for managers is to recognize when a structural change is required to coordinate and control effectively the firm's increasingly complex operations.

The intent of companies manufacturing regional soft drinks is to serve the needs of a narrow group of customers better than do giants Coca-Cola and PepsiCo. People targeted by the regional manufacturers are those with individualized tastes for soft drinks. To describe these firms and their products, an analyst noted that "... obscure soft drinks like Cheerwine are thriving in local markets across the country. These regional or 'cult' brands—with down-home names like Moxie, Big Red, Sun-drop, and Kickapoo Joy Juice—grew up in mostly rural areas. Many es-

To attain its goals of continuous product innovation and cost reduction, Nissan Motor Company is planning to reconfigure its assembly plants with 5 platforms instead of 24.

chew marketing, relying on the appeal of long histories, local pride and wild formulas, including one derived from a Russian cake-icing recipe and another that sprang from a failed pharmaceutical experiment."[61] Revolving around flexible production functions, these manufacturers have low levels of specialization and formalization. Additionally, as demonstrated by the nature of their marketing efforts, the regional soft drink companies centralize few of the decisions about the activities of different organizational functions.

Regional or "cult" brand colas, such as Moxie, Big Red, and Sun-drop, serve a narrow group of customers with individualized tastes for soft drinks.

Service Performance Corporation (SPC) also uses the simple organizational structure. Serving approximately 100 customers, SPC provides janitorial and facilities services in office buildings, malls, airports, laboratories, and manufacturing facilities. The firm's founder and CEO believes that service is his company's only product. To describe the character of SPC's organizational structure, the CEO noted that his nine-year-old company had retained its "aversion to bureaucracy." The simple structure is used to help all employees focus on what is believed to be the firm's competitive advantage—superior customer service.[62]

Movement to the Multidivisional Structure

The above-average returns gained through successful implementation of a business-level strategy often result in diversification of the firm's operations. This diversification can take the form of offering different products (product diversification) and/or offering the same or additional products in other markets (market diversification). As explained in Chapter 6, increased product and/or market diversification demands that firms formulate a corporate-level strategy as well as business-level strategies for individual units or divisions (see Figure 6.1 to review the different corporate-level strategies and their respective levels of diversification). With greater diversification, the simple and functional structures must be discarded in favor of the more complex, yet increasingly necessary multidivisional structure.

IMPLEMENTING CORPORATE-LEVEL STRATEGIES: ORGANIZATIONAL STRUCTURE AND CONTROLS

Effective use of the multidivisional structure helps firms implement their corporate-level strategy (diversification). In this section, we describe three M-form variations (see Figure 11.4) that are required to implement the related-constrained, related-linked, and unrelated diversification strategies.

Using the Cooperative Form to Implement the Related-Constrained Strategy

The **cooperative form** (of the multidivisional structure) is an organizational structure that uses many integration devices and horizontal human resource practices to foster cooperation and integration among the firm's divisions.

To implement the related-constrained strategy, firms use the cooperative form of the multidivisional structure. The **cooperative form** is an organizational structure that uses many integration devices and horizontal human resource practices to foster cooperation and integration among the firm's divisions. The cooperative form (see Figure 11.5) emphasizes horizontal links and relationships more than the two

FIGURE 11.4 ***Three Variations of the Multidivisional Structure***

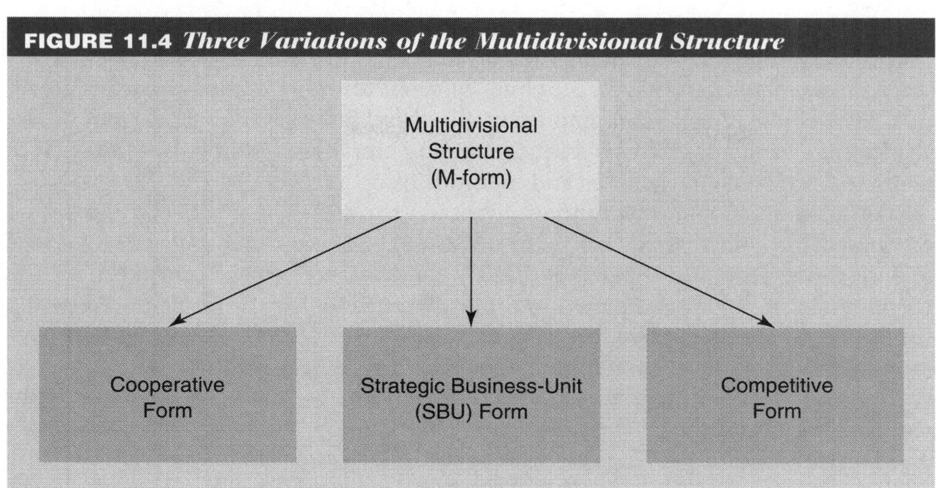

FIGURE 11.5 ***Cooperative Form of the Multidivisional Structure for Implementation of a Related-Constrained Strategy***

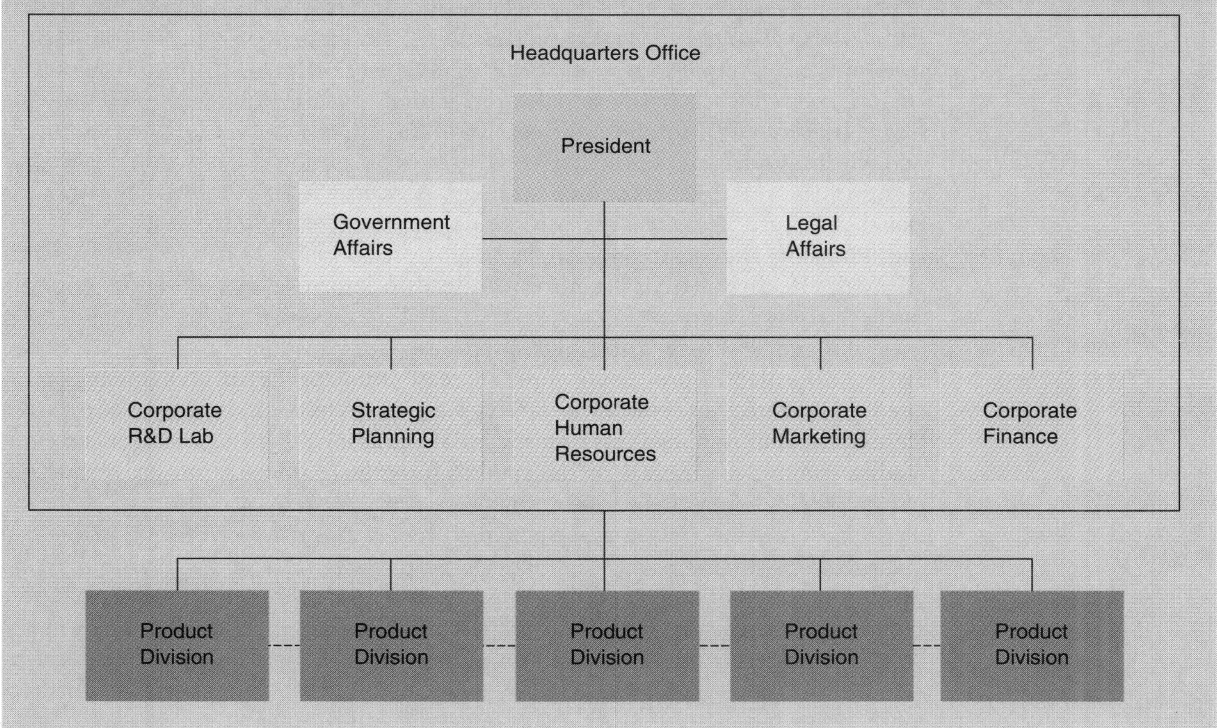

Notes:

- Structural integration devices create tight links among all divisions
- Corporate office emphasizes centralized strategic planning, human resources, and marketing to foster cooperation between divisions
- R&D is likely to be centralized
- Rewards are subjective and tend to emphasize overall corporate performance in addition to divisional performance
- Culture emphasizes cooperative sharing

other variations of the multidivisional structure described later in the chapter. Cooperation among divisions that are formed around either products or markets served is necessary to realize economies of scope and to facilitate the transferring of skills.[63] Increasingly, it is important for these links to allow and support the sharing of a range of strategic assets, including employees' "know-how" as well as tangible assets such as facilities and methods of operations.[64]

To facilitate cooperation among divisions that are either vertically integrated or related through the sharing of strategic assets, some organizational functions (e.g., human resource management, R&D, and marketing) are centralized at the corporate level. Work completed in these centralized functions is managed by the firm's central administrative, or headquarters, office. When the central office's efforts allow exploitation of commonalties among the firm's divisions in ways that yield a cost or differentiation advantage (or both) in the divisions as compared to undiversified rivals, the cooperative form of the multidivisional structure is a source of competitive advantage for the diversified firm.[65]

Besides centralization, a number of structural integration links are used to foster cooperation among divisions in firms implementing the related-constrained diversification strategy. Frequent direct contact between division managers encourages and supports cooperation and the sharing of strategic assets. Sometimes, liaison roles are established in each division to reduce the amount of time division managers spend facilitating the integration and coordination of their units' work. Temporary teams or task forces may also be formed around projects and may require the efforts of many people from separate divisions to achieve desired levels of divisional coordination. Formal integration departments might be formed in firms requiring the work of temporary teams or task forces on a continuous basis. Ultimately, a matrix organization evolves in firms implementing the related-constrained strategy. A *matrix organization* is an organizational structure in which there is a dual structure combining both functional specialization and business product or project specialization.[66] Although complicated, effective matrix structures can lead to improved coordination among a firm's various divisions.[67]

As implied by the horizontal procedures used for coordination that we described earlier, information processing must increase dramatically to implement the related-constrained diversification strategy successfully. But, because cooperation among divisions implies a loss of managerial autonomy, division managers may not readily commit themselves to the type of integrative information processing activities demanded by this organizational structure. Moreover, coordination among divisions sometimes results in an unequal flow of positive outcomes to divisional managers. In other words, when managerial rewards are based at least in part on the performance of individual divisions, the manager of the division able to derive the greatest marketplace benefit from the sharing of the firm's strategic assets might be viewed as receiving relative gains at others' expense. In these instances, performance evaluations are emphasized to facilitate sharing of strategic assets. Furthermore, using reward systems that emphasize overall company performance besides outcomes achieved by individual divisions helps overcome problems associated with the cooperative form.

The use of the cooperative form of the multidivisional structure in three companies is described in the Strategic Focus. Notice that each firm is implementing the related-constrained diversification strategy, which, it seems, results in a match between strategy and structure within these companies.

STRATEGIC FOCUS

Using the Cooperative Form of the Multidivisional Structure to Achieve Strategic Competitiveness in the Transportation, Information and Entertainment, and Financial Services Industries

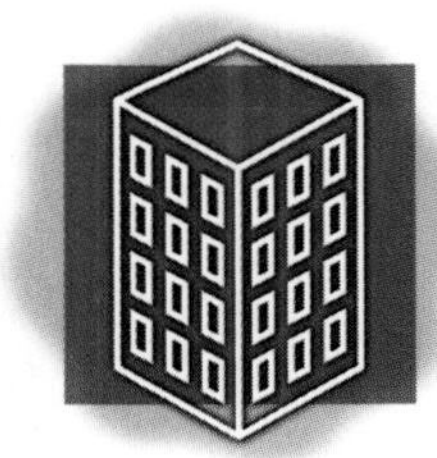

Montreal-based Bombardier is a worldwide manufacturer of transportation-related equipment. It has production facilities in eight countries in addition to Canada. The firm's corporate organizational structure features four product divisions—transportation, recreational products, aerospace, and services. Shared across the four product divisions is the firm's set of technological capabilities and competencies. As a source of competitive advantage, these capabilities and competencies allow Bombardier to introduce innovative products continuously and rapidly. To describe the factors contributing to his firm's strategic competitiveness, Bombardier's CEO observed, "We're selling technology, and we're selling new products. That's what makes us a success."

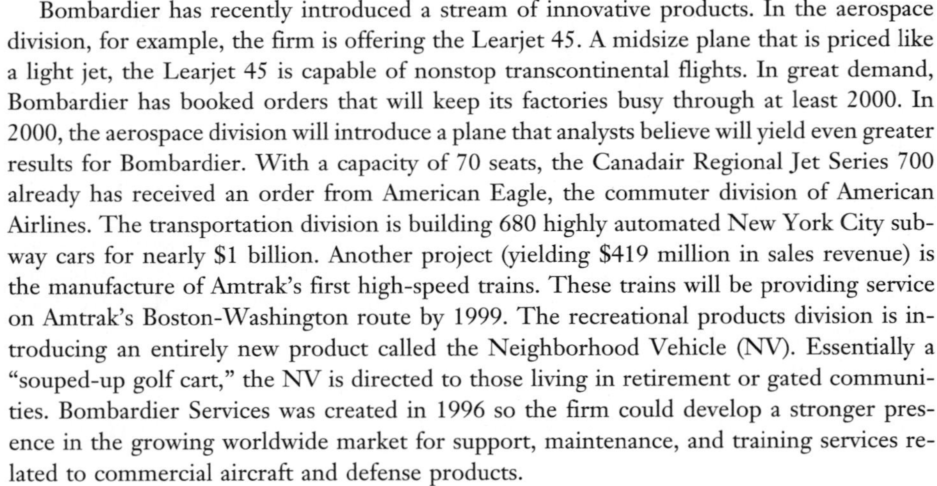

Bombardier has recently introduced a stream of innovative products. In the aerospace division, for example, the firm is offering the Learjet 45. A midsize plane that is priced like a light jet, the Learjet 45 is capable of nonstop transcontinental flights. In great demand, Bombardier has booked orders that will keep its factories busy through at least 2000. In 2000, the aerospace division will introduce a plane that analysts believe will yield even greater results for Bombardier. With a capacity of 70 seats, the Canadair Regional Jet Series 700 already has received an order from American Eagle, the commuter division of American Airlines. The transportation division is building 680 highly automated New York City subway cars for nearly $1 billion. Another project (yielding $419 million in sales revenue) is the manufacture of Amtrak's first high-speed trains. These trains will be providing service on Amtrak's Boston-Washington route by 1999. The recreational products division is introducing an entirely new product called the Neighborhood Vehicle (NV). Essentially a "souped-up golf cart," the NV is directed to those living in retirement or gated communities. Bombardier Services was created in 1996 so the firm could develop a stronger presence in the growing worldwide market for support, maintenance, and training services related to commercial aircraft and defense products.

To increase its strategic competitiveness, E. W. Scripps engaged in a year-long strategic realignment of its assets. Operations that were divested include book publishing and a cable-TV distribution system. The firm's corporate-level strategy now calls for it ". . . to be a provider of information and entertainment to particular consumer categories." To implement this strategy, three product divisions have been formed—publishing, broadcast, and entertainment. Personnel in the three divisions cooperate with one another to integrate and coordinate their operations when doing so increases the firm's competitive ability. Facilitating these integration and coordination attempts is Scripps' targeting of particular geographic locations in all three product divisions. Essentially, the firm seeks to cluster its media operations in midsize, high-growth Sun Belt markets such as Florida and Texas.

As a reflection of changes in financial markets and its own rapid growth, Morgan Stanley & Co. recently reorganized itself into two main product divisions—securities and asset management. Corporate executives viewed this structural change as a logical extension of the company's drive to build value in a rapidly changing environment. A key objective of this structural change was for the firm's investment bankers and securities salespeople and traders to work together more closely. Moreover, Morgan Stanley wanted to simplify the way it conducts business with its major corporate clients. Through use of the cooperative form of the multidivisional structure, Morgan Stanley was able to combine its various securities and investment-banking skills that previously were divided among three departments. These departments had offered separate debt, equity, and investment-banking strategies to corporate clients. According to company documents, "Morgan Stanley has improved efficiencies and established a position to provide a more effective, integrated approach to client services" as a result of changing its organizational structure.

Morgan Stanley's top-level managers suggested that their company was the first big Wall Street firm to integrate its securities businesses so closely. Analysts, however, argued that structural changes completed by Merrill Lynch in 1995 resulted in a similar outcome. To enhance its competitiveness, Merrill brought all of its investment-banking and capital-markets businesses into one group under one manager. Thus, both of these firms initiated changes that were designed to align more closely their organizational structures with their corporate level strategies. In commenting about the results of his firm's efforts, one Morgan Stanley employee noted that the structural changes would compel individuals to work together more closely.

SOURCES: Bombardier Home Page, 1998, February 4, http://www.bombardier.com; E. W. Scripps Home Page, 1998, February 4, http://www.scripps.com; Morgan Stanley Home Page, 1998, February 4, http://www.ms.com; J. Weber, W. Zellner, and G. Smith, 1998, Loud noises at Bombardier, *Business Week*, January 26, 94–95; J. P. Miller, 1997, E. W. Scripps turns page, and spots new opportunities, *Wall Street Journal*, September 23, B4; Morgan Stanley forms 2 big divisions, following industry trends, 1997, *The New York Times* on the Web, http://www.nytimes.com, December 16.

When there are fewer and/or less constrained links among the firm's divisions, the related-linked diversification strategy should be implemented. As explained next, this strategy can be implemented successfully through use of the SBU form of the multidivisional structure.

Using the SBU Form to Implement the Related-Linked Strategy

The **strategic business unit (SBU) form** of the multidivisional structure consists of at least three levels, with the top level being corporate headquarters; the next level, SBU groups; and the final level, divisions grouped by relatedness (either product or geographic market) within each SBU.

The **strategic business unit (SBU) form** of the multidivisional structure consists of at least three levels, with the top level being corporate headquarters; the next level, SBU groups; and the final level, divisions grouped by relatedness (either product or geographic market) within each SBU (see Figure 11.6). The firm's business portfolio is organized into those related to one another within a SBU group and those unrelated in other SBU groups. Thus, divisions within groups are related, but groups are largely unrelated to each other. Within the SBU structure, divisions with similar products or technologies are organized to achieve synergy. Each SBU is a profit center that is controlled by the firm's headquarters office. An important benefit of this structural form is that individual decision makers, within their strategic business unit, look to SBU executives rather than headquarters personnel for strategic guidance. Recall from the opening case that Raytheon Company also uses the SBU multidivisional structural form. Divisions within the firm's four strategic business units are related, but the business units are largely unrelated to one another.

Scotts is another company that uses the SBU form of the multidivisional structure. A producer and marketer of products for do-it-yourself lawn care, profes-

FIGURE 11.6 ***SBU Form of the Multidivisional Structure for Implementation of a Related-Linked Strategy***

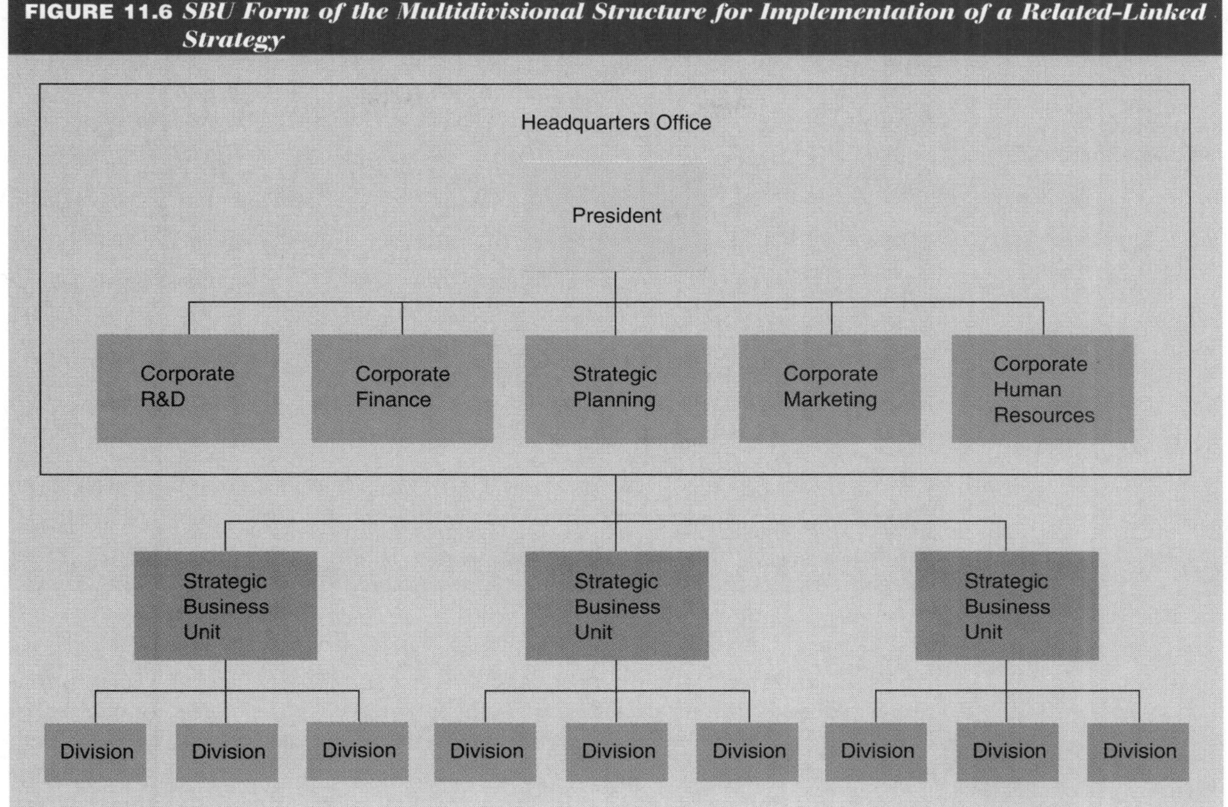

Notes:

- Structural integration among divisions within SBUs but independence across SBUs
- Strategic planning may be the most prominent function in headquarters to manage the strategic planning approval process of SBUs for the president
- Each SBU may have its own budget for staff to foster integration
- Corporate headquarters staff serve as consultants to SBUs and divisions, rather than having direct input to product strategy as in the cooperative form

sional turf care, and horticulture, the firm seeks $1 billion in sales revenues by 2000 (revenues were $606 million in 1994).[68] Recently Scotts revamped its organizational structure to help the company reach its sales revenues goal. The company is now organized into four main business units: consumer lawn (its mainstay fertilizers and other home products); consumer garden (primarily consisting of Stern's Miracle-Gro Products); professional (includes commercial applications such as golf courses); and international.[69]

The organizational structure for large diversified firms such as Scotts and Raytheon can be complex. This complexity is a reflection of the size and diversity of a diversified firm's operations. Consider the case of General Electric (GE). Implementing the related-linked corporate-level strategy, this firm's structure calls for integration among divisions within SBUs but independence between the SBUs. GE managers expect to be able to "walk, think, and talk" like a small firm and to make decisions and introduce innovative products at a pace that is equivalent to its smaller competitors.[70]

Recently GE's SBU structure featured 13 major strategic business units. GE Power Systems is one of these. Other units include GE Aircraft Engines (the world's

GE Information Services is one of the firm's 13 SBUs. The unit provides business-to-business electronic commerce solutions and manages the world's largest electronic trading company.

largest manufacturer of military and commercial aircraft jet engines), GE Information Services (a leading provider of business-to-business electronic commerce solutions, managing the world's largest electronic trading community of more than 40,000 trading partners), and GE Medical Systems (a world leader in medical diagnostic imaging technology). GE Power Systems serves those who are supplying the world's need for reliable, highly efficient electricity. Gas Turbines is one of at least 15 divisions within the Power Systems portfolio. Other divisions with which Gas Turbines is integrated to varying degrees include Steam Turbines, Hydro Turbines and Generators, Boiling Water Reactor Services, and Advanced Nuclear Reactor Systems. Featuring the broadest line of gas turbines in the industry today, GE is the acknowledged world leader with more than 5,000 units installed and more than 4,600 combustion turbines operating successfully around the globe.[71]

As noted above, GE's organizational structure is expected to enable the firm to act quickly and effectively. Thus, even for firms as large as GE, structural flexibility is as important as strategic flexibility (recall the discussion in Chapter 5 indicating that today's challenging competitive dynamics have created a need for the firm to have strategic flexibility). Through a combination of strategic and structural flexibility, GE is able to respond rapidly to opportunities as they emerge throughout the world. An example of this is GE's commitment to pursue investment and growth opportunities that senior-level executives envisioned during Asia's late 1990's economic crisis.[72]

Using the Competitive Form to Implement the Unrelated Diversification Strategy

Firms implementing the unrelated diversification strategy seek to create value through efficient internal capital allocations or by restructuring, buying, and selling businesses.[73] The competitive form of the multidivisional structure is used to implement the unrelated diversification strategy. The **competitive form** is an organizational structure in which the controls used emphasize competition between separate (usually unrelated) divisions for corporate capital. To realize benefits from efficient resource allocations, divisions must have separate, identifiable profit performance and must be held accountable for such performance. The internal capital market requires organizational arrangements that emphasize *competition* rather than *cooperation* between divisions.[74]

The **competitive form** is an organizational structure in which the controls used emphasize competition between separate (usually unrelated) divisions for corporate capital.

To emphasize competitiveness among divisions, the headquarters office maintains an arms-length relationship and does not intervene in divisional affairs except to audit operations and discipline managers whose divisions perform poorly. In this situation, the headquarters office sets rate-of-return targets and monitors the outcomes of divisional performance.[75] It allocates cash flow on a competitive basis, rather than automatically returning cash to the division that produced it. The competitive form of the multidivisional structure is illustrated in Figure 11.7.

A diversified supplier of hardware items to U.S. discount retailers, Newell Company uses the competitive form of the multidivisional structure to implement its unrelated diversification strategy. Committed to growth by acquisition, product lines added across time to the firm's independent divisions share no common characteristics. Supplying primarily large firms such as Wal-Mart, Newell sells an array of products, including pots and pans, paint brushes, and curtain rods. Newell's competitive advantage is created at the corporate level. Using a small corporate

FIGURE 11.7 ***Competitive Form of the Multidivisional Structure for Implementation of an Unrelated Strategy***

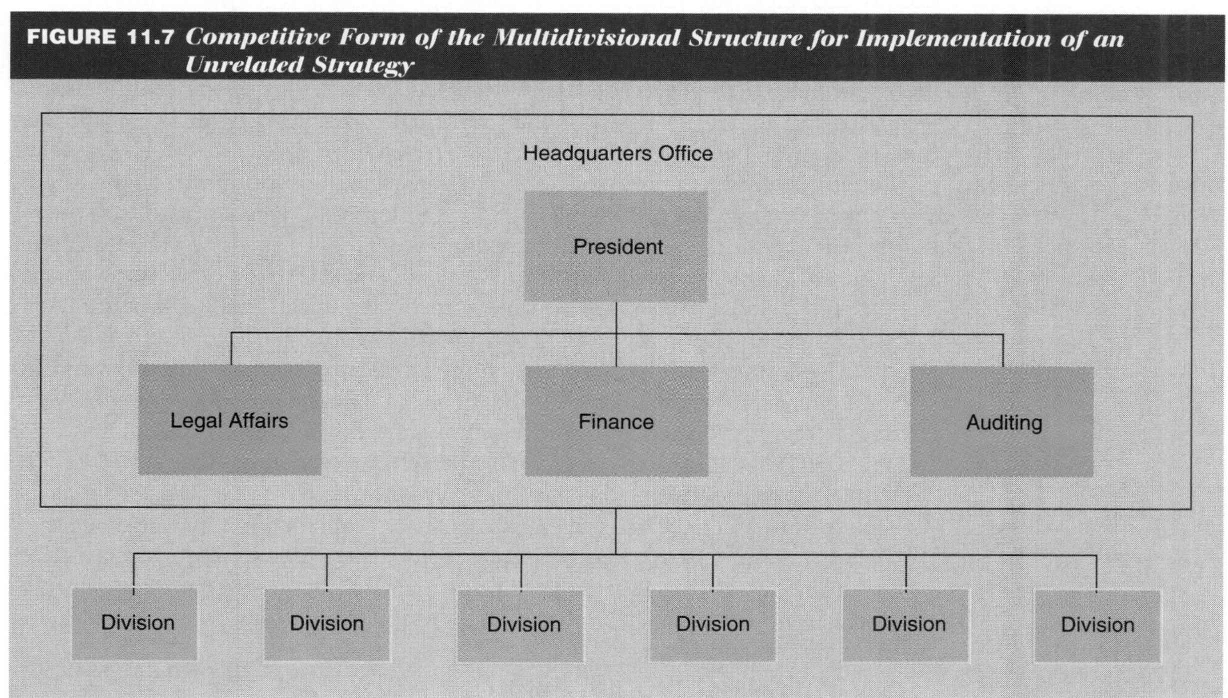

Notes:

- Corporate headquarters has a small staff
- Finance and auditing are the most prominent functions in the headquarters to manage cash flow and ensure accuracy of performance data coming from divisions
- The legal affairs function becomes important when acquiring and divesting assets
- Divisions are independent and separate for financial evaluation purposes
- Divisions retain strategic control, but cash is managed by the corporate office
- Divisions compete for corporate resources

TABLE 11.1 ***Characteristics of the Structures Necessary to Implement the Related-Constrained, Related-Linked, and Unrelated Diversification Strategies***

	Overall Structural Form		
Structural Characteristics	**Cooperative M-form (Related-Constrained Strategy[a])**	**SBU M-form (Related-Linked Strategy[a])**	**Competitive M-form (Unrelated Diversification Strategy[a])**
Centralization of operation	Centralized at corporate office	Partially centralized (in SBUs)	Decentralized to division
Use of integrating mechanisms	Extensive	Moderate	Nonexistent
Divisional performance appraisal	Emphasizes subjective criteria	Uses a mixture of subjective and objective criteria	Emphasizes objective (financial or ROI) criteria
Divisional incentive compensation	Linked to overall corporate performance	Mixed linkage to corporate, SBU, and divisional performance	Linked to divisional performance

[a]Strategy implemented with structural form.

headquarters staff, the firm has developed a sophisticated electronic, logistical system. Allocated to each of its divisions, this system is used as the basis for each division's logistics with its customers. Although not related to each other, each of Newell's divisions creates value "from the lower cost and improved customer relations provided by the Newell system."[76]

In summary, our discussion describes three major forms of the multidivisional structure and the relationship of the individual forms with particular corporate-level strategies. Table 11.1 shows the characteristics of these structures. As shown in the table, differences are seen in the degree of centralization, the focus of performance appraisal, the horizontal structures (integrating mechanisms), and the incentive compensation schemes necessary to implement the three corporate-level strategies of related-constrained, related-linked, and unrelated diversification successfully. The most centralized and most costly organizational form is the cooperative structure. The least centralized, with the lowest bureaucratic costs, is the competitive structure. The SBU structure requires partial centralization and involves some of the mechanisms necessary to implement the relatedness between divisions. Also, the divisional incentive compensation awards are allocated according to both SBU and corporate performance. In the competitive structure, the most important criterion is divisional performance.

Earlier in the chapter, we indicated that, once formed, an organizational structure can influence a firm's efforts to implement its current strategy and the selection of future strategies. Using the multidivisional structure as the foundation for the discussion, the explanation in the next section exemplifies the relationship between structure and strategy.

THE EFFECT OF STRUCTURE ON STRATEGY

As explained earlier, the M-form is a structural innovation intended to help managers deal with the coordination and control problems created by increasing product and market variety. Once established, however, the M-form structure has the potential to positively influence the firm's diversification strategy.[77] Strong and appropriate incentives, ones that encourage managers to pursue additional marketplace opportunities, coupled with improved accountability and superior internal resource allocations from the corporate office, may stimulate additional diversification. Furthermore, these additional levels of diversification can result in greater returns on the firm's investments.[78] Eventually, however, there is a tendency for the M-form to encourage inefficient levels of diversification. Following a comprehensive review of research evidence, some researchers noted that there is a growing body of evidence which suggests that adoption of the M-form structure facilitates the pursuit of inefficient diversification.[79] Again, this cause/effect relationship—that is, the influence of the M-form on a firm's pursuit of additional diversification—is not inherently negative. The complicating factor is that at some point, the additional amounts of diversification stimulated by the M-form become inefficient, thereby reducing the firm's strategic competitiveness and its returns.

Other theory and research suggests that once the M-form influences the pursuit of more diversification that yields inefficient strategic outcomes, the relationship between structure and strategy may reverse in direction.[80] In other words, firms that become inefficiently diversified implement strategies that result in less efficient levels of diversification. One researcher found, for example, that half of the diversified acquisitions made by unrelated diversified firms were later divested.[81] Another discovered that a decrease in the diversified scope of M-form firms was associated with an improvement in shareholder wealth. This finding, too, suggests that these firms' diversification had become inefficient.[82] An example of a firm that recently changed its diversification strategy to increase its efficiency and strategic competitiveness is described in the Strategic Focus. Sara Lee Corporation intends to reduce substantially its level of diversification by the year 2000. To achieve all of the potential gains from this corporate-level decision, the firm will also need to change its organizational structure to facilitate implementation of a less diversified strategy.

Sara Lee's commitment to lower levels of diversification parallels what appears to be a 1990's trend in some countries. In the United States and the United Kingdom, for example, the 1990s is a time period in which "pure plays" are in and diversified companies are out. This preference results in decisions in firms ranging from AT&T to ITT to split up into separately traded companies that focus on their core businesses.[83] The trend toward focus is not as apparent among German firms yet, but recent evidence suggests it may increase in Germany if pressure to reduce costs and improve efficiency gains strength in the near future.[84]

STRATEGIC FOCUS

Deverticalization: Sara Lee's Path to Lower Levels of Diversification

Founded by a Canadian entrepreneur, Sara Lee Corporation became a global manufacturer and marketer of high-quality, brand name products for consumers throughout the world. In 1997, the firm had operations in more than 40 countries and sold its products in over 140 nations. Using the SBU form of the multidivisional structure to implement the related-linked diversification strategy, Sara Lee was organized into four separate businesses: packaged meats and bakery (39 percent of sales revenue), coffee and grocery (14 percent), household and body care (9 percent), and personal products (38 percent). Famous brand names included in Sara Lee's portfolio of businesses were Hanes, Hanes Her Way, L'eggs, Bali, Champion, Hillshire Farm, Jimmy Dean, Sanex, and Kiwi, among others. For many years, the company's growth was fueled by what its leaders viewed to be strategic acquisitions.

Although generating record profits in 1997, the corporation's stock was languishing on Wall Street. Sara Lee's CEO and chairman, John Bryan, described the firm's status with the financial community as follows: "We were pretty boring to Wall Street, and there was a clamor to do something." The "something" Bryan and other Sara Lee top-level managers decided upon was to "deverticalize" their corporation. Through deverticalization, Sara Lee's level of diversification will be reduced substantially. In fact, this restructuring program was intended to fundamentally reshape Sara Lee in a manner that executives believed better prepared their firm to compete in the twenty-first century.

On September 15, 1997, Bryan announced formally Sara Lee's plan to deverticalize. The conglomerate intended to sell $3 billion of its assets, including entire divisions and multiple manufacturing operations. According to Bryan, the firm's ". . . deverticalization program was designed to enable us to focus our energies and talents on the greatest value-creating activities in our business, which are building and managing leadership brands. Minimizing the degree to which our business is vertically integrated reduces the capital demands on our company while enhancing our competitiveness." As a less diversified corporation, the intention was for Sara Lee to become a company similar to Nike, Coca-Cola, and Polo/Ralph Lauren. Each of these firms allocates significant amounts of its resources to marketing and to outsourcing manufacturing. Thus, the intent was for Sara Lee to move away from manufacturing the brand name goods it was selling. Executives believed that the deverticalization program would generate as much as $3 billion within a three-year period (culminating by the year 2000).

To reach its objective of building branded leadership positions through deverticalization, Sara Lee intended to divest substantial portions of its U.S. yarn and textile operations. This is a significant decision given that Sara Lee Knit Products held the number one U.S. market share position in men's and boys' and women's and girls' underwear garments. The first of the divestments in this product line was announced on January 5, 1998. On this date, National Textiles agreed to purchase nine of Sara Lee's yarn and textile operations. The yield to Sara Lee from this transaction was expected to approximate $600 million over a three-year period. Other divestments were planned for some of the company's food and nonfood businesses by 2000.

The results of these divestments and of the less diversified strategy that Sara Lee will follow at the corporate level demand a different organizational structure. Possible structural choices include the cooperative form of the multidivisional structure and even the functional structure (if Sara Lee's final set of divestments results in a highly focused firm—one with low levels of diversification).

Wall Street's initial reaction to Sara Lee's deverticalization program was positive. On September 15, 1997, the day of the program's announcement, the company's stock rose 14 percent.

SOURCES: Sara Lee Corporation Home Page, 1998, http://www.saralee.com; *The Economist*, 1997, Separate and fit, September 20, 69; R. Lowenstein, 1997, Remember when companies made things? *Wall Street Journal*, September 18, C1; R. Melcher, 1997, A finger in fewer pies, *Business Week*, September 29, 44; J. P. Miller, 1997, Sara Lee to retreat from manufacturing, *Wall Street Journal*, September 16, A3, A10.

Our discussion now turns to an explanation of organizational structures used to implement the three international strategies explained in Chapter 8.

IMPLEMENTING INTERNATIONAL STRATEGIES: ORGANIZATIONAL STRUCTURE AND CONTROLS

Increasingly, a firm's ability to achieve strategic competitiveness is a function of its competitive success in the global marketplace.[85] Although important for many firms, competing successfully in global markets is perhaps especially critical for large companies. General Motors CEO Jack Smith, for example, intends for his company to expand sales outside the United States, Canada, and Mexico to 4.5 million vehicles by 2006. Critical to accomplishing this objective is the successful implementation of GM's international strategy. Included as parts of this strategy are the manufacture of (1) an inexpensive family car in Poland, (2) Chevrolet Blazers in Russia, (3) Chevrolet Corsicas in Argentina, and (4) Buick sedans in China.[86] Supporting implementation of GM's international and domestic strategies are newly formed organizational structures designed to integrate effectively the work of engineers and manufacturing and marketing personnel.[87] As explained in this section of the chapter, international strategies such as those chosen by GM's top-level executives cannot be implemented successfully without use of the proper organizational structure.[88] As the decade closes, results from implementation of GM's international strategy through its new organizational structure are encouraging. Fueled by continuing cost-cutting efforts and stronger-than-expected factory sales, GM posted record earnings in the fourth quarter of 1997.[89]

Using the Worldwide Geographic Area Structure to Implement the Multidomestic Strategy

The *multidomestic strategy* is a strategy in which strategic and operating decisions are decentralized to business units in each country to facilitate tailoring of products to local markets. Through this strategy, Campbell Soup customizes its products to local tastes. For example, the firm's cream of pumpkin soup is Australia's largest selling canned soup. In Hong Kong, Campbell sells watercress-and-duck-gizzard soup.[90] However, it is sometimes difficult for firms to know how local their products should or can become. Lands' End, for example, is one of the U.S. mail-order firms being lured by the promise of the European market for its products and services. Interested in adapting to local preferences, the firm's director of international operations observed that the most difficult part of achieving this objective is to know in which areas to be local.[91]

Firms implementing the multidomestic strategy often attempt to isolate themselves from global competitive forces by establishing protected market positions or by competing in industry segments that are most affected by differences among local countries. The worldwide geographic area structure (see Figure 11.8) is used to implement the multidomestic strategy. The **worldwide geographic area structure** emphasizes national interests and facilitates managers' efforts to satisfy local or cultural differences.

The **worldwide geographic area structure** emphasizes national interests and facilitates managers' efforts to satisfy local or cultural differences.

Recently, Coca-Cola shed the management structure it had been using to implement the firm's strategy with its core soft drink business. Previously, soft drinks had been divided into two units—North America and International. "But given that some of [the firm's] individual operating groups outside of North America now generate income equal to that of our entire company in the mid-1980s,

FIGURE 11.8 ***Worldwide Geographic Area Structure for Implementation of a Multidomestic Strategy***

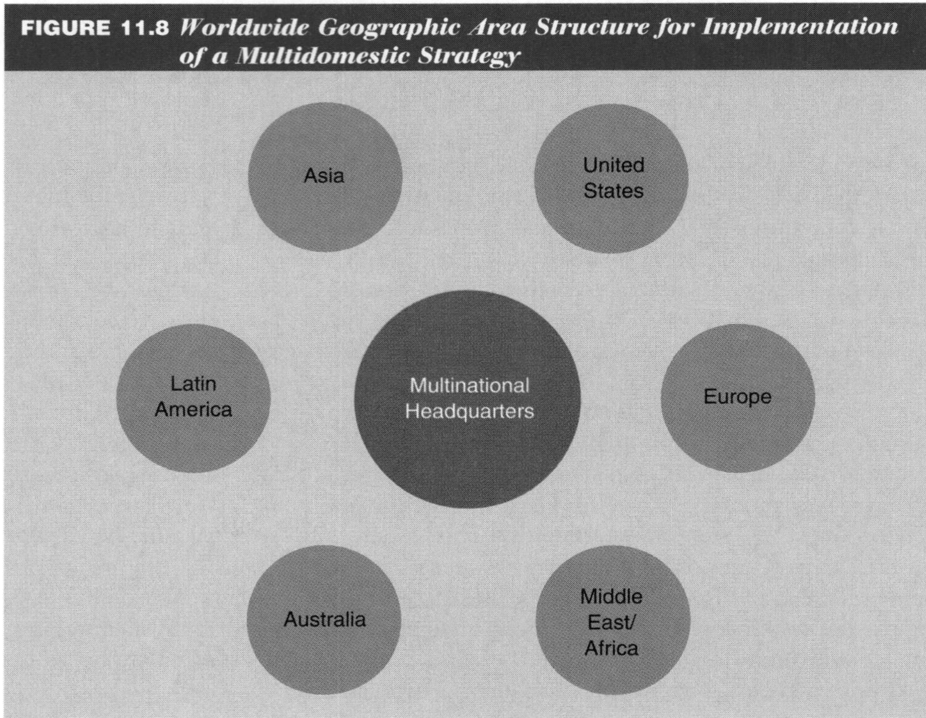

Notes:
- Blue shaded perimeter circles indicate decentralization of operations
- Emphasis is on differentiation by local demand to fit an area or country culture
- Corporate headquarters coordinates financial resources among independent subsidiaries
- The organization is like a decentralized federation

bundling those units under the title of 'International' had become artificial and impractical." Today, Coca-Cola's worldwide soft drink operations are divided into five groups, with North America but one of the five newly formed units. Forming this worldwide geographic area structure will likely enhance the firm's ability to manage its soft drink business globally.[92]

Because implementing the multidomestic strategy requires little coordination between different country markets, there is no need for integrating mechanisms among divisions in the worldwide geographic area structure. As such, formalization is low and coordination among units in a firm's worldwide geographic area structure is often informal. Because each European country has a distinct culture, the multidomestic strategy and the associated worldwide geographic structure were a natural outgrowth of the multicultural marketplace. This type of structure often was developed originally by friends and family members of the main business who were sent as expatriates into foreign countries to develop the independent country subsidiary. The relationship to corporate headquarters by divisions took place through informal communication among "family members."[93]

The primary disadvantage of the multidomestic strategy and worldwide geographic area structure combination is the inability to create global efficiency. As the emphasis on lower cost products has increased in international markets, the need to pursue worldwide economies of scale and scope has increased. These changes have fostered use of the global strategy.

Using the Worldwide Product Divisional Structure to Implement the Global Strategy

The *global strategy* is a strategy in which standardized products are offered across country markets and where competitive strategy is dictated by the firm's home office. International scale and scope economies are sought and emphasized when implementing this international strategy. Because of the important relationship between scale and scope economies and successful implementation of the global strategy, some activities of the firm's organizational functions are sourced to the most effective worldwide providers.

The worldwide product divisional structure (see Figure 11.9) is used to implement the global strategy. The **worldwide product divisional structure** is an organizational form in which decision-making authority is centralized in the worldwide division headquarters to coordinate and integrate decisions and actions among disparate divisional business units. This form is the organizational structure of choice for rapidly growing firms seeking to manage their diversified product lines effectively.[94] Integrating mechanisms also create effective coordination through mutual adjustments in personal interactions. Such integrating mechanisms include direct contact between managers, liaison roles between departments, temporary task forces or permanent teams, and integrating roles. As managers participate in

The **worldwide product divisional structure** is an organizational form in which decision-making authority is centralized in the worldwide division headquarters to coordinate and integrate decisions and actions among disparate divisional business units.

FIGURE 11.9 *Worldwide Product Divisional Structure for Implementation of a Global Strategy*

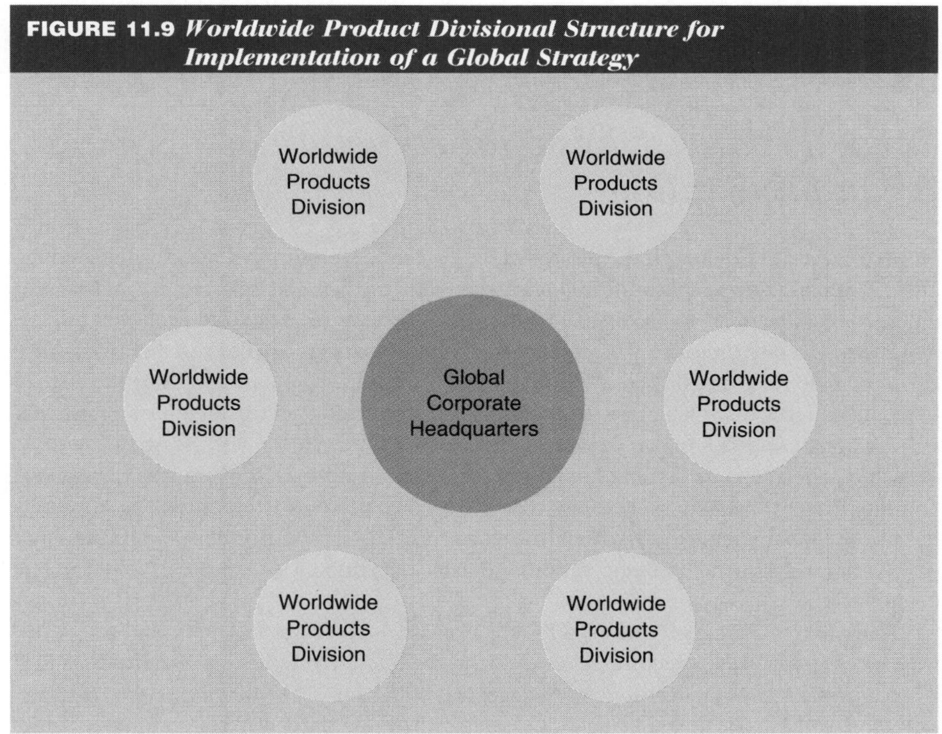

Notes:

- Orange shaded headquarters circle indicates centralization to coordinate information flow among worldwide products
- Corporate headquarters uses many intercoordination devices to facilitate global economies of scale and scope
- Corporate headquarters also allocates financial resources in a cooperative way
- The organization is like a centralized federation

cross-country transfers, they are socialized in the philosophy of managing an integrated strategy through a worldwide product divisional structure. A shared vision of the firm's strategy and structure is developed through standardized policies and procedures (formalization) that facilitate implementation of this organizational form.

Two primary disadvantages of the global strategy and its accompanying worldwide product divisional structure are the difficulty involved with coordinating decisions and actions across country borders and the inability to respond quickly and effectively to local needs and preferences. For example, Federal Express was reported to have encountered difficulties with its expansion into Asia, an area of international growth the company believed had significant potential. One problem the firm experienced concerned attempts to establish hub systems. The hub system is vital to FedEx's ability to achieve required levels of coordination across country borders. As an analyst noted, "The hub system is critical; it positions Federal Express to simultaneously pursue two massive markets—trans-Pacific and intra-Asian—at lower costs. The same planes that carry freight to the hub destined for the U.S. and Japan can also provide regular overnight delivery between cities on the continent."[95]

As explained in the Strategic Focus, H. J. Heinz uses the worldwide product divisional structure to implement the global strategy. Notice that this structure is expected to contribute to the firm's efforts to improve its international operations.

STRATEGIC FOCUS

Using the Worldwide Product Divisional Structure as a Means of Increased Internationalization

Headquartered in Pittsburgh, Pennsylvania, H. J. Heinz Company is a worldwide food producer. Perhaps known best for its ubiquitous ketchup, the firm also sells infant foods, condiments, pet foods, tuna, and is involved with weight-control products and programs as well. Heinz has a strong international presence, deriving 45 percent of sales revenue from operations outside the United States. However, the firm's newly appointed CEO, William R. Johnson, believes that Heinz has yet to derive full strategic benefit from efforts to internationalize its business (Johnson's tenure as Heinz's CEO began formally in April 1998). As such, he is convinced that Heinz can improve its overall corporate performance through renewed efforts to compete successfully outside the firm's domestic U.S. markets. Committed to the global strategy rather than the multidomestic strategy, organizational structure plays a key role in the strategic actions Johnson is taking to enhance Heinz's strategic competitiveness.

Under the leadership of Anthony O'Reilly, Johnson's predecessor, Heinz used the worldwide geographic area structure to implement the multidomestic international strategy. Through this structure, decisions were decentralized to business units in various countries or regions to facilitate the tailoring of the company's products to local tastes. Johnson, however, is organizing Heinz in terms of product categories rather than geographic areas. In this manner, ". . . tuna managers in Europe will work with tuna managers in Asia, Latin America, and other regions, allowing the best brand manager to advise all the countries." Through the operations supported by this structure, Heinz seeks to create additional value by emphasizing its brand names.

One indicator of the new organizational structure was the establishment of a new worldwide products division. Created in February of 1998, the Specialty Pet Food division was given the responsibility of marketing Heinz's specialty pet foods on a global basis. In particular, marketing efforts were to be focused on introducing Heinz's specialty pet food brands (e.g., Nature's Recipe, Vet's Choice, and Martin Pet Foods) to Europe and other developing pet food markets such as South America, Asia, Australia, and South Africa. In commenting about this new division, then-current CEO O'Reilly suggested that Specialty Pet Foods was an example of Heinz's commitment to reorganize its corporate structure to support the firm's growth initiatives and its desire to continue building international operations.

Johnson has other strategic actions that he wants Heinz to initiate. Implementation of these actions, too, will be supported by use of the worldwide product divisional structure. For example, he wants his firm to continue test-marketing products that have been successful in one country in other locations. Frozen tuna filets and flavored tuna, which have sold well in Europe, were tested recently in the United States. In fact, attempts to cross-sell products among different nations are an important component to Heinz's desire to exploit the value of its brand names internationally.

Another decision that has been made concerns performance assessments. To evaluate more effectively the performance of individual worldwide products divisions, personnel at Heinz's headquarters have assumed a more prominent role. One result of these evaluations is the decision to consider selling Weight Watchers, the weight-control business that makes frozen foods and offers classes. Although successful in the United Kingdom, the program has been a disappointment in the United States. Thus, decision making within this firm is becoming more centralized in order to identify and then group appropriately the products that can contribute to Heinz's attempts to improve its international operations.

SOURCES: Infoseek, 1998, Heinz makes appointments at three international affiliates; Announces formation of Specialty Pet Food unit, February 4, http://www.infoseek.com; R. Balu, 1997, Heinz's Johnson to divest operations, scrap management of firm by regions, *Wall Street Journal*, December 8, B22; *The Economist*, 1997, Separate and fit, September 20, 69.

Using the Combination Structure to Implement the Transnational Strategy

The *transnational strategy* is an international strategy through which a firm seeks to provide the local responsiveness that is the focus of the multidomestic strategy *and* to achieve the global efficiency that is the focus of the global strategy. The **combination structure** has characteristics and structural mechanisms that result in an emphasis on both geographic and product structures. Unilever Group uses the combination structure. The firm's operations are divided into 14 business groups. Some of the groups are framed around emerging markets; others are framed around the company's European food and drink businesses.[96] Thus, this structure has the multidomestic strategy's geographic area focus and the global strategy's product focus. The following company statements show the approach this structure supports:

The **combination structure** has characteristics and structural mechanisms that result in an emphasis on both geographic and product structures.

> Unilever describes itself as international, not global, because it does not attempt to enter all markets with the same product. Half of Unilever's business is in food, where it is often essential to take a local view. Only a few products—like ice cream, tea, and olive oil—successfully cross national or regional borders.

> Similarly, in detergents, the formulation Unilever sells in South Africa will differ from the one in France because washing habits, machines, clothes, and water quality are all different. Personal wash products, on the other hand, need to vary less, so there are strong international brands like *Lux* and *Dove*. The Unilever portfolio includes a balanced mix of local, regional and international brands which take account of the differences as well as the similarities in consumer needs.[97]

The fits between the multidomestic strategy and the worldwide geographic area structure and the global strategy and the worldwide product divisional structure are apparent. However, when a firm seeks to implement both the multidomestic and global strategies simultaneously through a combination structure, the appropriate integrating mechanisms for the two structures are less obvious. The structure used to implement the transnational strategy must be simultaneously centralized and decentralized, integrated and nonintegrated, and formalized and nonformalized. These seemingly opposing structural characteristics must be managed by a structure that is capable of encouraging all employees to understand the effects of cultural diversity on a firm's operations. Moreover, the combination structure should allow the firm to learn how to gain competitive benefits in local economies by adapting capabilities and core competencies that often have been developed and nurtured in less culturally diverse competitive environments.

In the next section, we focus on implementation of the dominant forms of the cooperative strategies that were discussed in Chapter 9.

IMPLEMENTING COOPERATIVE STRATEGIES: ORGANIZATIONAL STRUCTURE AND CONTROLS

Increasingly, companies develop multiple rather than single joint ventures or strategic alliances to implement cooperative strategies. Furthermore, the global marketplace accommodates many interconnected relationships among firms. Resulting from these relationships are networks of firms competing through an array of cooperative arrangements or alliances.[98] When managed effectively, cooperative arrangements can contribute positively to each partner's ability to achieve strategic competitiveness and earn above-average returns.

To facilitate the effectiveness of a *strategic network*—a grouping of organizations that has been formed to create value through participation in an array of cooperative arrangements such as a strategic alliance—a strategic center firm may be necessary. A *strategic center firm* facilitates management of a strategic network. Through its management, the central firm creates incentives that reduce the probability of any company taking actions that could harm its network partners, and it identifies actions that increase the opportunity for each firm to achieve competitive success through its participation in the network.[99] Illustrated in Figure 11.10, the strategic center firm is vital to the ability of companies to create value and increase their strategic competitiveness. The four critical aspects of the strategic center firm's function are

Strategic outsourcing: The strategic center firm outsources and partners with more firms than do the other network members. Nonetheless, the strategic center

FIGURE 11.10 *A Strategic Network*

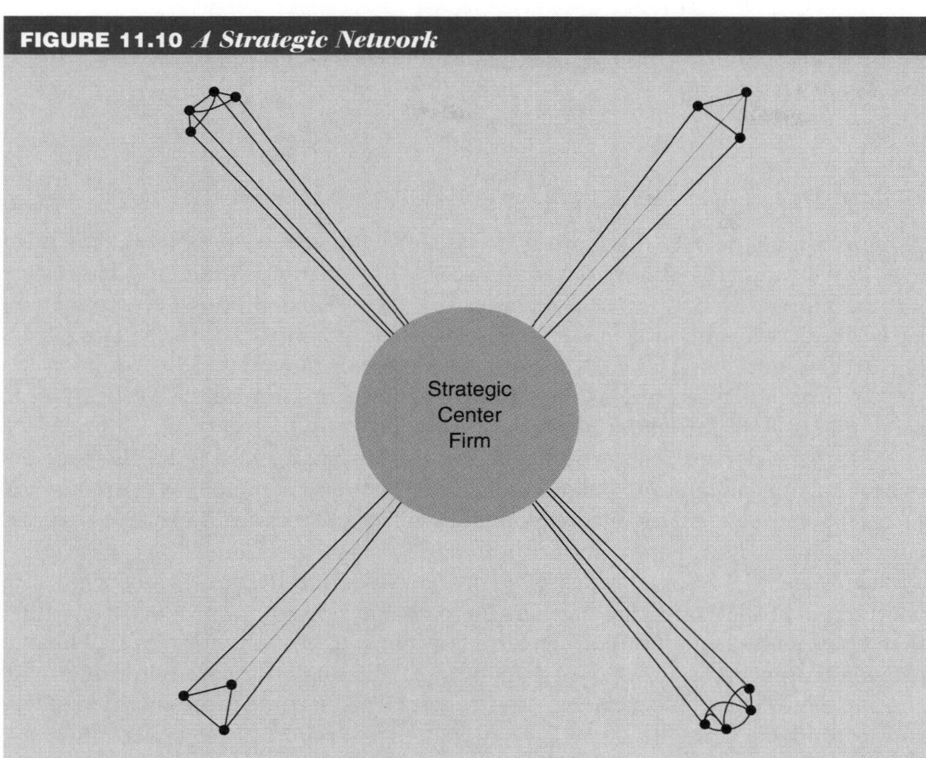

firm requires partners to be more than contractors. Partners are expected to solve problems and to initiate competitive courses of action that can be pursued by the network.

Capability: The strategic center firm has core competencies that are not shared with all network partners. To increase the network's effectiveness, the central firm attempts to develop each partner's core competencies and provides incentives for network firms to share their capabilities and competencies with partners.

Technology: The strategic center firm manages the development and sharing of technology-based ideas among network partners.

Race to learn: The strategic center firm emphasizes to partners that the principal dimension of competition in competitive environments is between value chains and networks of value chains. As a result, a strategic network is as strong as its weakest value chain link. As a value chain link, a strategic network seeks to develop a competitive advantage in a primary or support activity (see Chapter 3). The need for each firm to be strong for the benefit of the entire network encourages positive rivalry among partners to learn rapidly and effectively.[100] The most effective strategic center firms learn how to manage learning processes occurring among network members.

The dominant problem in single venture cooperative arrangements is the lack of ability to control innovation and learning. However, a well-managed strategic network can overcome this problem. Therefore, as explained in the following discussions, the managerial role of the strategic center firm is critical to the successful implementation of business-level, corporate-level, and international cooperative strategies.

Implementing Business-Level Cooperative Strategies

As noted in Chapter 9, there are two types of complementary assets at the business level—vertical and horizontal. Vertical complementary strategic alliances are formed more frequently than horizontal alliances. Focused on buyer-supplier relationships, vertical strategic networks usually have a clear strategic center firm. Japanese vertical keiretsus such as those developed by Toyota Motor Company are structured this way. Acting as the strategic center firm, Toyota fashioned its lean production system around a network of supplier firms.

A strategic network of vertical relationships in Japan such as the network between Toyota and its suppliers often includes the following implementation issues. First, the strategic center firm encourages subcontractors to modernize their facilities and provides them with technical and financial assistance if necessary. Second, it reduces its transaction costs by promoting longer term contracts with subcontractors so that supplying partners increase their long-term productivity, rather than continually negotiating short-term contracts based on unit pricing. Third, it provides engineers in upstream companies (suppliers) better communication with contractees. Thus, the contractees and center firms become more interdependent and less independent.[101]

The lean production system pioneered by Toyota has been diffused throughout the Japanese and U.S. automobile industries. However, no automobile producer is able to duplicate the effectiveness and efficiency Toyota derives from use of this manufacturing system.[102] A key factor accounting for Toyota's ability to derive a competitive advantage from this system is the cost to imitate the structural form used to support its application. In other words, Toyota's largely proprietary actions as the strategic center firm in the network it created are ones that competitors are unable to duplicate.

In vertical complementary strategic alliances, such as the one between Toyota and its suppliers, the company that should function as the strategic center firm is obvious. However, this is not always the case with horizontal complementary strategic alliances, as the following example demonstrates.

A jet engine joint venture formed between rivals GE and United Technologies' Pratt and Whitney unit promised significant returns for both firms.[103] However, other cooperative arrangements between jet engine manufacturers have not yielded anticipated results. Previously, for example, GE and Rolls-Royce's jet engine division formed a joint venture to manufacture engines for Boeing's 777 commercial jet. Bitter disputes between the partners led to the breakup of this venture. Similarly, an earlier venture among Pratt, Rolls-Royce, and other small contractors to build smaller jet engines failed. A problem common to all of these ventures was the difficulty of selecting the strategic center firm. The distrust that had formed among the joint venture companies through years of aggressive competition prevented agreements regarding the firm that should function as the strategic center of a network. Thus, because the dominant strategic center firm is evident, vertical complementary strategic alliances tend to be far more stable than horizontal complementary strategic alliances.

Joint ventures between jet engine manufacturers have not always been successful. Because the companies involved often were aggressive competitors, it is difficult for them to agree on which firm should serve as the strategic center.

Implementing Corporate-Level Cooperative Strategies

Although corporate-level cooperative strategy partnerships should select a strategic center firm to operate the network of alliances effectively, it is more difficult to choose a strategic center firm in some types of corporate-level cooperative strategies. It is easier, for example, for a strategic center firm to emerge in a centralized franchise network than in a decentralized set of diversified strategic alliances. This situation is demonstrated by McDonald's.

McDonald's has formed a centralized strategic network in which its corporate office serves as the strategic center for its franchisees. Recently, McDonald's decided that the firm should use its core competencies to better serve the adult market. Long a favorite of children, many parents of adolescents do not share their offsprings' excitement about eating at McDonald's. Developed through the strategic center's centralized R&D function, a new product, aimed at adults, was introduced in mid-1996. Called the Arch Deluxe, this food item was pitched as "the burger with a grownup taste." However, this was not a successful product introduction (see the Strategic Focus in Chapter 5). This result, coupled with other issues, caused one analyst to suggest that McDonald's was a brand in need of "radical surgery."

To cope with its problems, McDonald's, as a strategic center firm, initiated a series of actions. Framed around the need to improve the quality of its products and speed up their delivery, the company developed its "just-in-time kitchen" concept for use by franchisees. This new production system is designed to move made-to-order sandwiches to customers without increasing the preparation time. As part of this system, a computer-monitored machine dumps frozen fries into a basket that in turn is dunked into hot oil for cooking. The machine then shakes the fries and dumps them into bins for serving. Simultaneously, robot machines prepare drinks quickly as ordered by the customer. Preventing full use of this system's capabilities, however, was the delay in supplying all franchisees with the equipment.

Thus, as the strategic center firm in its centralized franchise network, McDonald's still faces significant challenges.[104]

Unlike McDonald's, Corning's corporate-level cooperative strategy has resulted in the implementation of a system of diversified strategic alliances. This has required Corning to implement a decentralized network of joint ventures and strategic alliances in which it is more difficult to form a strategic center firm among network partners. Over time, Corning has focused on intangible resources, such as a reliable reputation for being a trustworthy and committed partner, to develop competitively successful strategic networks. In these situations, the strategic network has loose connections between joint ventures or multiple centers, although Corning is typically the principal center. However, the joint ventures are less dependent on the strategic center firm and, as such, require less managerial attention from it.[105]

Implementing International Cooperative Strategies

Competing in multiple countries increases dramatically the complexity associated with attempts to manage successful strategic networks formed through international cooperative strategies.[106] A key reason for this increased complexity is the differences among countries' regulatory environments. These differences are especially apparent in regulated industries such as telecommunications and air travel.

As shown in Figure 11.11, many large, multinational firms form distributed strategic networks with multiple regional strategic centers to manage their array

FIGURE 11.11 *A Distributed Strategic Network*

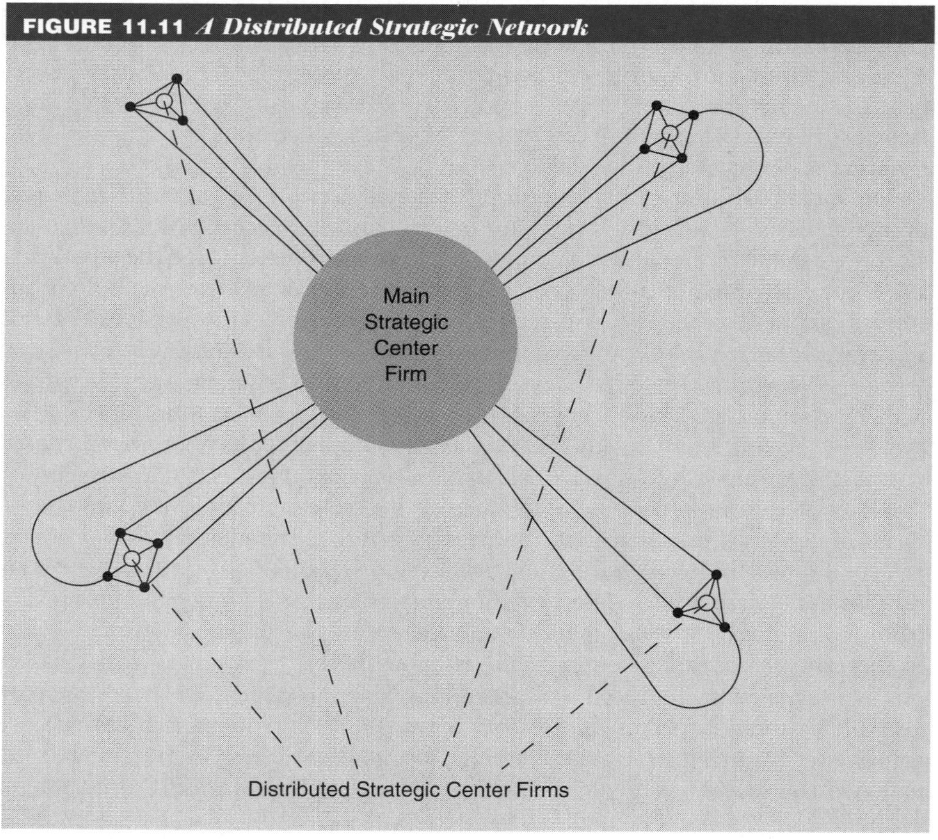

of cooperative arrangements with partner firms.[107] These networks are illustrated by several large multinational firms. Swedish firms such as Ericsson (telecommunications exchange equipment) and Electrolux (white goods, washing machines) have strategic centers located in countries throughout the world instead of only in Sweden where they are headquartered. Ericsson, for example, is active in more than 100 countries and employs over 85,000. Divided into five business areas (public telecommunications, radio communications, business networks, components, and microwave systems), the firm has cooperative agreements with companies throughout the world.

A world leader in electrical engineering, Asea Brown Boveri Group (ABB) is involved with a significant number of distributed strategic networks. Organized into four key business segments (power generation, power transmission and distribution, industrial and building systems, and financial services), ABB features 1,000 companies and 36 separate business areas. With a new, global 11-member board of directors representing seven nationalities, ABB considers itself a truly global company—one without a single country home. The firm has formed strategic networks in its key world areas of the Americas, Europe (including the former Soviet Union), the Middle East and North Africa, sub-Sahara Africa, and Asia Pacific.[108]

CONTEMPORARY ORGANIZATIONAL STRUCTURES: A CAUTIONARY NOTE

Contemporary organizational structures such as those used to implement international cooperative strategies emerge typically in response to social and technological advances.[109] However, the redesign of organizations throughout the society—indeed globally—necessarily entails losses as well as gains.[110] For example, DuPont, the world's largest chemicals concern, decided recently to scrap most of its central support groups. Primarily, these groups provided information technology, communications, and other services to the company's main operating divisions. The gains expected from this decision included elimination of some corporate bureaucracy and reductions in the amount of time required for production innovations to reach the marketplace. The primary loss associated with these gains concerned personnel. While some workers were to be transferred to other positions, many lost their jobs.[111]

With new organizational forms, many workers become deskilled—that is, their abilities are not sufficient to perform sucessfully in a new structure that often demands constant innovation and adaptation. This may describe the situation for some of the workers that are to be assigned to new positions within DuPont. The learning organization that is a part of new organizational forms requires that each worker become a self-motivated, continuous learner.[112] At least in the short run, a number of employees lack the level of confidence necessary to participate actively in organizationally sponsored learning experiences. Moreover, the flatter organizational structures that accompany contemporary structures can seem intrusive as a result of their demand for more intense and personal interactions with internal and external stakeholders. Combined, these conditions may create stress for many.

These realities do not call for managers to abandon efforts to adopt organizational structures that have the greatest probability of facilitating sucessful implementation of a firm's strategies. The challenge for those responsible for effective use of the strategic management process depicted in Figure 1.1 of Chapter 1 is to respond to various issues associated with the development and use of new organizational structures in ways that will enhance the productivity of individuals and the firm.[113] As explained in the next chapter, this responsibility belongs to strategic leaders.

SUMMARY

- Organizational structure is a formal configuration that largely determines *what* a firm will do and *how* the firm will complete its work. Different structures are required to implement different strategies. A firm's performance increases when strategy and structure are matched properly.
- Business-level strategies are usually implemented through the functional structure. The cost leadership strategy requires a centralized functional structure—one in which manufacturing efficiency and process engineering are emphasized. The differentiation strategy's functional structure decentralizes implementation-related decisions, especially those concerned with marketing, to those involved with individual organizational functions. Focus strategies, used in small firms, require a simple structure until such time that a firm begins to compete in multiple markets and/or sells multiple products.
- The evolution from the functional structure to the three types of the multidivisional structure (M-form) occurred from the 1920s to the early 1970s. The cooperative M-form, used to implement the related-constrained corporate-level strategy, has a centralized corporate office and extensive integrating mechanisms. Divisional incentives are linked to overall corporate performance. The related-linked SBU M-form structure establishes separate profit centers within the diversified firm. Each profit center may have divisions offering similar products, but the centers are unrelated to each other. The competitive M-form structure, used to implement the unrelated diversification strategy, is highly decentralized, integrating mechanisms are nonexistent, and objective financial criteria are used to evaluate each unit's performance.
- Initially, an organizational structure is chosen in light of support required to implement a firm's strategy. Once established, however, structure influences strategy. This is observed most prominently in the M-form structure stimulating additional diversification in the diversified firm.
- The multidomestic strategy, implemented through the worldwide geographic area structure, emphasizes decentralization and locates all functional activities in the country or geographic area. The worldwide product divisional structure is used to implement the global strategy. This structure is centralized to coordinate and integrate different functions' activities to gain global economies of scope and scale. Decision-making authority is centralized in the firm's worldwide division headquarters. The transnational strategy—a strategy through which the firm seeks the local responsiveness of the multidomestic strategy *and* the global efficiency of the global strategy—is implemented through the combination structure. Because it must be simultaneously centralized and decentralized, integrated and nonintegrated, and formalized and nonformalized, the combination structure is difficult to organize and manage successfully.
- Increasingly important to competitive success, cooperative strategies are implemented through organizational structures framed around strategic networks.

REVIEW QUESTIONS

1. Why is it important that the strategic actions of strategy implementation and strategy formulation be integrated carefully?
2. What is the meaning of the following statement? "In organizations, there is a consistent path of structure following strategy and then strategy following structure."

3. What organizational structures are used to implement the cost leadership, differentiation, integrated low-cost/differentiation, and focused business-level strategies?
4. What organizational structures are used to implement the related-constrained, related-linked, and unrelated corporate-level diversification strategies?
5. What organizational structures should be used to implement the multidomestic, global, and transnational international strategies?
6. What is a strategic network? What is a strategic center firm? What roles do they play in organizational structures used to implement cooperative strategies?

APPLICATION DISCUSSION QUESTIONS

1. Why do firms experience evolutionary cycles where there is a fit between strategy and structure punctuated with periods in which strategy and structure are reshaped? Provide examples of prominent U.S. firms that have experienced this pattern.
2. Select an organization (for example, an employer, a social club, or a nonprofit agency) in which you currently hold membership. What is this organization's structure? Do you believe this organization is using the structure that is appropriate, given its strategy? If not, what structure should be used?
3. Examine the popular business press to find a firm using the multidivisional structure. Which form of the multidivisional structure is the firm using? What is there about the firm that makes it appropriate for the M-form to be in use?
4. Through reading of the business press, locate one firm implementing the global strategy and one implementing the multidomestic strategy. What organizational structure is being used in each firm? Are these structures allowing each firm's strategy to be implemented successfully? Why or why not?
5. Identify a businessperson in your local community. Provide definitions to the person of strategic and financial controls. Ask that the businessperson describe to you the use of each type of control in his or her business. In which type of control does the businessperson have the greatest confidence, and why?

ETHICS QUESTIONS

1. When a firm changes from the functional structure to the multidivisional structure, what responsibilities do you believe it has to current employees?
2. Are there ethical issues associated with the use of strategic controls? With the use of financial controls? If so, what are they?
3. Are there ethical issues involved in implementing the cooperative and competitive M-form structures? If so, what are they? As a top-level manager, how would you deal with them?
4. Global and multidomestic strategies call for different competitive approaches. What ethical concerns might surface when firms attempt to market standardized products globally or when they develop different products/approaches for each local market?
5. What ethical issues are associated with the view that the "redesign of organizations throughout the society—indeed globally—necessarily entails losses as well as gains"?

INTERNET EXERCISE

Go to Eastman Kodak's Home Page at:

http://www.kodak.com

Use the Internet to conduct research on Eastman Kodak Corporation. How would you describe Kodak's organizational structure? Does Kodak's structure appropriately complement its competitive strategies?

Strategic Surfing

The Economist is a high-quality British magazine that is available on-line. The magazine publishes thoughtful articles on economics, politics, international business, management, and other issues.

http://www.economist.com

NOTES

1. M. Kroll, P. Wright, L. Toombs, and H. Leavell, 1997, Form of control: A critical determinant of acquisition performance, *Strategic Management Journal* 18: 85–96.
2. D. J. Teece, G. Pisano, and A. Shuen, 1997, Dynamic capabilities and strategic management, *Strategic Management Journal* 18: 509–533.
3. C. Hales and Z. Tamangani, 1996, An investigation of the relationship between organizational structure, managerial role expectations and managers' work activities, *Journal of Management Studies* 33: 731–756.
4. S. E. Human and K. Provan, 1997, An emergent theory of structure and outcomes in small-firm strategic manufacturing networks, *Academy of Management Journal* 40: 368–403.
5. M. H. Overholt, 1997, Flexible organizations: Using organizational design as a competitive advantage, *Human Resource Planning* 20, no. 1: 22–32.
6. J. R. Galbraith, 1995, *Designing Organizations* (San Francisco: Jossey-Bass), 6.
7. J. Kurtzman, 1998, An interview with Stan Shih, in J. Kurtzman (ed.), *Thought Leaders* (San Francisco: Jossey-Bass), 85–93.
8. A. Y. Ilinitch, R. A. D'Aveni, and A. Y. Lewin, 1996, New organizational forms and strategies for managing in hypercompetitive environments, *Organization Science* 7: 211–220.
9. D. A. Nadler and M. L. Tushman, 1997, *Competing by Design: The Power of Organizational Architecture* (New York: Oxford University Press).
10. E. F. Suarez and J. M. Utterback, 1995, Dominant designs and the survival of firms, *Strategic Management Journal* 16: 415–430.
11. *PR Newswire*, 1998, BMW prepares for the future with a process-oriented organizational structure, January 16, 116.
12. R. A. Heifetz and D. L. Laurie, 1997, The work of leadership, *Harvard Business Review* 75, no. 1: 124–134; R. H. Hall, 1996, *Organizations: Structures, Processes, and Outcomes* (6th ed.) (Englewood Cliffs, NJ: Prentice-Hall), 106–107.
13. L. Kehoe, 1998, Compaq will pay $9.6 billion in cash and stock for Digital, *Financial Times*, January 27, 22.
14. H. W. Volberda, 1996, Toward the flexible form: How to remain vital in hypercompetitive environments, *Organization Science* 7: 359–374.
15. T. R. Kayworth and R. D. Ireland, 1998, The use of information technology (IT) standards as a means of implementing the cost leadership strategy, working paper, Baylor University; Nadler and Tushman, *Competing by Design*, 9.
16. G. Graham and J. Kibazo, 1998, Barclays plans internal reorganisation, *Financial Times*, January 20, 21.
17. Suarez and Utterback, Dominant designs and the survival of firms.
17. A. D. Chandler, Jr., 1990, *Scale and Scope: The Dynamics of Industrial Capitalism* (Cambridge: The Belknap Press of Harvard University Press), 182–183.
18. F. R. Bleakly, 1996, The future of the global marketplace, *Wall Street Journal*, May 15, A13; J. Janssen-Bauer and C. C. Snow, 1996, Responding to hypercompetition: The structure and processes of a regional learning network organization, *Organization Science* 7: 413–427.
19. G. P. Zachary, 1995, Behind stocks' surge is an economy in which big U.S. firms thrive, *Wall Street Journal*, November 22, A1, A3.
20. Ibid., A1.
21. R. M. Hodgetts, 1996, A conversation with Steve Kerr, *Organizational Dynamics*, Spring, 74.
22. G. Hamel, 1997, Killer strategies, *Fortune*, June 23, 82.
23. S. Singhal, 1994, *Senior Management—The Dynamics of Effectiveness* (New Delhi: Sage Publications), 48.
24. Ibid., 48; Galbraith, *Designing Organizations*, 13; R. R. Nelson, 1994, Why do firms differ, and how does it matter? in R. P. Rumelt, D. E. Schendel, and D. J. Teece (eds.), *Fundamental Issues in Strategy* (Cambridge, MA: Harvard Business School Press), 259.
25. L. Donaldson, 1997, A positivist alternative to the structure-action approach, *Organization Studies* 18: 77–92; Hales and Tamangani, An investigation of the relationship, 738; Nelson, Why do firms? 259.
26. B. C. Esty, 1997, A case study of organizational form and risk shifting in the savings and loan industry, *Journal of Financial Economics* 44: 57–76; C. W. L. Hill, 1994, Diversification and economics performance: Bringing structure and corporate management back into the picture, in R. P. Rumelt, D. E. Schendel, and D. J. Teece (eds.), *Fundamental Issues in Strategy* (Cambridge, MA: Harvard Business School Press), 297–321.
27. R. Waters, 1997, Return of the downsizers, *Financial Times*, December 19, 13.
28. V. Griffith, 1997, Lumbering giants, *Financial Times*, December 15, 10.
29. H. M. O'Neill, R. W. Pouder, and A. K. Buchholtz, 1998, Patterns in the diffusion of strategies across organizations: Insights from the innovation diffusion literature, *Academy of Management Review* 23: 98–114.
30. M. Carter, 1998, The world according to Yo!, *Financial Times*, January 26, 11.
31. Galbraith, *Designing Organizations*, 25.
32. P. Lawrence and J. W. Lorsch, 1967, *Organization and Environment* (Cambridge, MA: Harvard Business School Press).
33. A. D. Chandler, 1994, The functions of the HQ unit in the multibusiness firm, in R. P. Rumelt, D. E. Schendel, and D. J. Teece (eds.), *Fundamental Issues in Strategy* (Cambridge, MA: Harvard Business School Press), 327.
34. W. G. Rowe and P. M. Wright, 1997, Related and unrelated diversification and their effect on human resource management controls, *Strategic Management Journal* 18: 329–338; D. C. Galunic and K. M. Eisenhardt, 1996, The evolution of intracorporate domains: Divisional charter losses in high-technology, multidivisional corporations, *Organization Science* 7: 255–282.
35. G. G. Dess, A. Gupta, J.-F. Hennart, and C. W. L. Hill, 1995, Conducting and integrating strategy research at the international, corporate, and business levels: Issues and directions, *Journal of Management* 21: 357–393.
36. A. D. Chandler, 1962, *Strategy and Structure: Chapters in the History of the American Industrial Enterprise* (Cambridge, MA: The MIT Press).

37. O. E. Williamson, 1994, Strategizing, economizing, and economic organization, in R. P. Rumelt, D. E. Schendel, and D. J. Teece (eds.), *Fundamental Issues in Strategy* (Cambridge, MA: Harvard Business School Press), 361–401.
38. Rowe and Wright, Related and unrelated diversification; S. Ghoshal and C. A. Bartlett, 1995, Changing the role of top management: Beyond structure to processes, *Harvard Business Review* 73, no. 1: 87–88.
39. Galbraith, *Designing Organizations*, 27.
40. Nadler and Tushman, *Competing by Design*, 206.
41. R. E. Hoskisson, C. W. L. Hill, and H. Kim, 1993, The multidivisional structure: Organizational fossil or source of value? *Journal of Management* 19: 269–298.
42. Rowe and Wright, Related and unrelated diversification.
43. C. M. Farkas and S. Wetlaufer, 1996, The ways chief executive officers lead, *Harvard Business Review* 74, no. 3: 110–122.
44. Associated Press, 1996, Trouble-shooter aims to galvanize Mazda, Ford, *Dallas Morning News*, April 13, F2; V. Reitman, 1996, Japan is aghast as foreigner takes the wheel at Mazda, *Wall Street Journal*, April 15, A11.
45. S. G. Beatty, 1998, CKS Group will reduce its businesses to 4 from 10 and revamp management, *Wall Street Journal*, January 20, B8.
46. C. C. Miller, L. M. Burke, and W. H. Glick, 1998, Cognitive diversity among upper-echelon executives: Implications for strategic decision processes, *Strategic Management Journal* 19: 39–58; D. J. Collis, 1996, Corporate strategy in multibusiness firms, *Long Range Planning* 29: 416–418.
47. M. A. Hitt, R. E. Hoskisson, R. A. Johnson, and D. D. Moesel, 1996, The market for corporate control and firm innovation, *Academy of Management Journal* 39: 1084–1119.
48. R. E. Hoskisson, M. A. Hitt, and R. D. Ireland, 1994, The effects of acquisitions and restructuring (strategic refocusing) strategies on innovation, in G. von Krogh, A. Sinatra, and H. Singh (eds.), *Managing Corporate Acquisitions* (London: Macmillan Press), 144–169.
49. R. E. Hoskisson and M. A. Hitt, 1988, Strategic control and relative R&D investment in large multiproduct firms, *Strategic Management Journal* 9: 605–621.
50. R. Tomkins, 1998, Black & Decker plans to cut 3,000 jobs, *Financial Times*, January 28, 15.
51. Collis, Corporate strategy, 417.
52. M. A. Hitt, R. E. Hoskisson, and R. D. Ireland, 1990, Mergers and acquisitions and managerial commitment to innovation in M-form firms, *Strategic Management Journal* 11 (Special Summer Issue): 29–47.
53. S. Baiman, D. F. Larcker, and M. V. Rajan, 1995, Organizational design for business units, *Journal of Accounting Research* 33: 205–229; Hall, *Organizations*, 13.
54. Ibid., Hall, 64–75.
55. T. Maxon, 1996, Southwest to let surfers use 'Net to arrange flights, *Dallas Morning News*, April 30, D1.
56. V. Boland, 1998, Airlines prepare to hit runway to privatisation, *Financial Times*, January 26, 17.
57. M. Halkias, 1996, Changing the retail landscape, *Dallas Morning News*, March 17, H1, H2.
58. FAG Kugelfischer, 1996, *Annual Report*, 22.
59. V. Govindarajan, 1988, A contingency approach to strategy implementation at the business-unit level: Integrating administrative mechanisms with strategy, *Academy of Management Journal* 31: 828–853.
60. D. Owen, 1998, Peugeot-Citroen unveils revamp, *Financial Times*, January 22, 19; Motor moves, 1998, *Financial Times*, January 28, 13; Nissan, 1998, *Financial Times*, January 28, 14.
61. R. Frank, 1996, Moxie, Big Red, other cult drinks thrive on being hometown heroes, *Wall Street Journal*, May 6, B1, B5.
62. Service Performance Corporation, 1998, *Fortune*, Special Advertising Section, February 2, S2.
63. C. C. Markides and P. J. Williamson, 1996, Corporate diversification and organizational structure: A resource-based view, *Academy of Management Journal* 39: 340–367; C. W. L. Hill, M. A. Hitt, and R. E. Hoskisson, 1992, Cooperative versus competitive structures in related and unrelated diversified firms, *Organization Science* 3: 501–521.
64. J. Robins and M. E. Wiersema, 1995, A resource-based approach to the multibusiness firm: Empirical analysis of portfolio interrelationships and corporate financial performance, *Strategic Management Journal* 16: 277–299.
65. C. C. Markides, 1997, To diversify or not to diversify, *Harvard Business Review* 75, no. 6: 93–99.
66. Nadler and Tushman, *Competing by Design*, 99.
67. Hall, Organizations, 186; J. G. March, 1994, *A Primer on Decision Making: How Decisions Happen* (New York: The Free Press), 117–118.
68. Master Entrepreneur Award, 1996, Netscape, May 12, http://www.sddt.com.
69. M. Murray, 1996, Massive restructuring at Scotts to include cuts in spending, staff, *Wall Street Journal*, April 3, B4.
70. P. J. Frost, 1997, Bridging academia and business: A conversation with Steve Kerr, *Organization Science* 8: 335.
71. GE Home Page, 1998, February 4, http://www.ge.com.
72. R. Waters, General Electric sees Asian opportunity, 1998, *Financial Times*, January 23, 19.
73. R. E. Hoskisson and M. A. Hitt, 1990, Antecedents and performance outcomes of diversification: A review and critique of theoretical perspectives, *Journal of Management* 16: 461–509.
74. C. W. L. Hill, M. A. Hitt, and R. E. Hoskisson, 1992, Cooperative versus competitive structures in related and unrelated diversified firms, *Organization Science* 3: 501–521.
75. J. B. Barney, 1997, *Gaining and Sustaining Competitive Advantage* (Reading, MA: Addison-Wesley), 420–433.
76. Collis, *Corporate strategy*, 418.
77. Williamson, Strategizing, economizing, 373.
78. B. W. Keats and M. A. Hitt, 1988, A causal model of linkages among environmental dimensions, macro organizational characteristics, and performance, *Academy of Management Journal* 31: 570–598.
79. Hoskisson, Hill, and Kim, The multidivisional structure, 276.
80. R. E. Hoskisson, R. A. Johnson, and D. D. Moesel, 1994, Corporate divestiture intensity: Effects of governance strategy and performance, *Academy of Management Journal* 37:1207–1251; R. E. Hoskisson and T. Turk, 1990, Corporate restructuring, governance and control limits of the internal capital market, *Academy of Management Review* 15: 459–471.
81. M. E. Porter, 1987, From competitive advantage to corporate strategy, *Harvard Business Review* 65, no. 3: 43–59.

82. C. C. Markides, 1992, Consequences of corporate refocusing: Ex ante evidence, *Academy of Management Journal* 35: 398–412.
83. S. Lipin, 1998. Cognizant, a D&B spin-off, to split in two, *Wall Street Journal*, January 15, A3.
84. V. Houlder, 1997, Fashion, focus and frontiers, *Financial Times*, December 19, 9.
85. R. D. Ireland, M. A. Hitt, and K. Artz, 1998, The effects of competitive strategies, cooperative strategies, and core competencies on superior financial performance in small manufacturing firms, working paper, Baylor University; M. A. Hitt, R. E. Hoskisson, and R. D. Ireland, 1994, A mid-range theory of the interactive effects of international and product diversification on innovation and performance, *Journal of Management* 20: 297–326.
86. Wire Reports, 1996, GM to focus on global sales market, *Dallas Morning News*, May 25, F1, F3.
87. K. Naughton and K. Kerwin, 1995, At GM, two heads may be worse than one, *Business Week*, August 14, 46.
88. M. A. Hitt, M. T. Dacin, B. B. Tyler, and D. Park, 1997, Understanding the differences in Korean and U.S. executives' strategic orientations, *Strategic Management Journal* 18: 159–167.
89. R. Blumenstein, 1998, GM doubles net on strong factory sales, *Wall Street Journal*, January 27, A3, A8.
90. L. Grant, 1996, Stirring it up at Campbell, *Fortune*, May 13, 80–86.
91. C. Rahweddeer, 1998, U.S. mail-order firms shake up Europe, *Wall Street Journal*, January 6, A15.
92. Coca-Cola Home Page, 1998, February 4, http://www.cocacola.com; G. Collins, 1996, Coke changes its recipe for administration, *Austin-American Statesman*, January 13, C1, C2; C. A. Bartlett and S. Ghoshal, 1989, *Managing Across Borders: The Transnational Solution* (Cambridge, MA: Harvard Business School Press).
93. Bartlett and Ghoshal, *Managing Across Borders.*
94. Ibid.
95. D. A. Blackmon, 1996, Fedex swings from confidence abroad to a tightrope, *Wall Street Journal*, March 15, B4.
96. C. Rohwedder, 1996, Unilever reorganizes its management as a first step in broad restructuring, *Wall Street Journal*, March 14, A11.
97. Unilever Home Page, 1998, February 5, http://www.unilever.com.
98. B. Gomes-Casseres, 1994, Group versus group: How alliance networks compete, *Harvard Business Review* 72, no. 4: 62–74.
99. G. R. Jones, 1998, *Organizational Theory* (Reading, MA: Addison-Wesley), 163–165.
100. G. Lorenzoni and C. Baden-Fuller, 1995, Creating a strategic center to manage a web of partners, *California Management Review* 37, no. 3: 146–163.
101. T. Nishiguchi, 1994, *Strategic Industrial Sourcing: The Japanese Advantage* (New York: Oxford University Press).
102. W. M. Fruin, 1992, *The Japanese Enterprise System* (New York: Oxford University Press).
103. W. M. Carley, 1996, GE–Pratt venture, like others before it, faces hurdles, *Wall Street Journal*, May 10, B3.
104. S. Branch, 1997, What's eating McDonald's? *Fortune*, October 13, 122–125; C. Edwards, 1997, Putting the fast in food, *Dallas Morning News*, July 21, D4; R. Gibson and M. Moffett, 1997, Why you won't find any egg McMuffins for breakfast in Brazil, *Wall Street Journal*, October 23, A1, A12.
105. Corning Home Page, 1998, February 5, http://www.corning.com; J. R. Houghton, 1990, Corning cultivates joint ventures that endure, *Planning Review* 18, no. 5: 15–17.
106. C. Jones, W. S. Hesterly, and S. P. Borgatti, 1997, A general theory of network governance: Exchange conditions and social mechanisms, *Academy of Management Review* 22: 911–945.
107. R. E. Miles, C. C. Snow, J. A. Mathews, G. Miles, and J. J. Coleman, Jr., 1997, Organizing in the knowledge age: Anticipating the cellular form, *Academy of Management Executive* XI, no. 4: 7–20.
108. ABB Home Page, 1998, February 5, http://www.abb.com; Nadler and Tushman, *Competing by Design*, 89.
109. Chandler, *Scale and Scope.*
110. B. Victor and C. Stephens, 1994, The dark side of the new organizational forms: An editorial essay, *Organization Science* 5: 479–482.
111. R. Waters, 1998, New DuPont shake-up to slash bureaucracy, *Financial Times*, January 8, 3; A. Barrett, 1997, At DuPont, time to both sow and reap, *Business Week*, September 29, 107–108.
112. M. A. Hitt, B. W. Keats, and S. M. DeMarie, 1998, Navigating in the new competitive landscape: Building competitive advantage and strategic flexibility in the 21st century, *Academy of Management Executive* (in press).
113. R. D. Ireland and M. A. Hitt, 1998, Achieving and maintaining strategic competitiveness in the 21st century: The role of strategic leadership, *Academy of Management Executive* (in press).

Strategic Leadership

CHAPTER 12

Learning Objectives

After reading this chapter, you should be able to:

1. Define strategic leadership and describe the importance of top-level managers as an organizational resource.
2. Define top management teams and explain their effects on the firm's performance and its ability to innovate and make appropriate strategic changes.
3. Describe the internal and external managerial labor markets and their effects on the development and implementation of firm strategy.
4. Discuss the value of strategic leadership for determining the firm's strategic direction.
5. Explain the role of strategic leaders in exploiting and maintaining core competencies.
6. Describe the importance of strategic leaders in developing a firm's human capital.
7. Define organizational culture and explain the importance of what must be done to sustain an effective culture.
8. Describe what strategic leaders can do to establish and emphasize ethical practices in their firms.
9. Discuss the importance and use of organizational controls.

Strategic Leadership in the Twenty-First Century

Given changes toward a new competitive landscape mentioned in this book (see in particular Chapters 1, 2, and 5), the role of strategic leaders is changing accordingly. Because of changes in competition and technology and an increased emphasis on customer satisfaction as well as globalization of industries, organizations face significant adaptive challenges. As a result, leaders must manage this change process in a way that facilitates competitive success. This takes more than just providing a well-designed solution. It requires an effective implementation process and commitment from people throughout the organization. It takes the collective intelligence of employees at all levels who need to use each other as resources. Working across internal and external organizational boundaries, employees must learn to work together to find solutions. Employees may look to the strategic leader for relief from stress in times of change, but rather than protecting them from outside threats, it is the role of a leader to stimulate his or her employees to adapt. Instead of maintaining norms, leaders encourage employees to change the way business is done from seemingly immutable practices bound by cultural heritage and history.

http://www.pathfinder.com

In light of the adaptive challenge to make transformation toward the twenty-first century, a number of firms are choosing CEOs who come from not only outside the firm but often outside the industry. Therefore, many CEOs are following a track outside of an individual firm rather than pursuing internal promotion and lifetime careers in one organization. Many of these CEOs are considered portable, not because they know a specific busi-

ness, but because they have the emotional stature to facilitate change in an organization. One study, for instance, found that more than a third of the CEOs hired by 369 major corporations in the 1990s came from outside the company. These include some of the largest and best-known companies in the United States, such as Eastman Kodak Co., IBM Corporation, and AT&T Corporation. The experiences of these companies have influenced other boards to go outside their company to look for their executives, particularly when the company is in trouble. Despite this trend, some companies continue to groom and pick insiders, such as the succession of M. Douglas Ivester at Coca-Cola after the death of Roberto Goizueta.

As Chapter 10 suggests, boards have grown more powerful and are taking charge of managerial succession. They are concerned about signals to investors and workers. Sometimes a new outside CEO is like a professional athlete, "a free agent," who is dynamic and charismatic and may be able to send a signal that will improve company performance, both in terms of morale and the stock price. However, there are significant risks with this approach. Consider, for example, AT&T's mistake discussed in Chapter 10. John R. Walter, who was appointed president and was the heir apparent for the CEO position, lost credibility after Robert Allen decided that he was not capable of filling the job. AT&T lost eight months between the time Walter came to the company and when he left. It was time overly focused on leadership succession and not on strategic success.

Some executives have become temporary CEOs who focus on rescuing firms in crises. Steve Miller, the temporary CEO of Waste Management Corporation, has also had a similar job at Olympia & York Developments Ltd., Morrison Knudsen Corporation, and Federal-Mogul Corporation. This role started before he left Chrysler and, ever since, has been one of coming into companies in crisis, reassuring workers and investors, and then seeking to change things to stabilize the firm. Subsequently, he leaves or takes a position on the board as they seek and hire a more permanent CEO. Gerard Roche, chairman of Heidrick & Struggles, Inc., says "I wish I had ten Steve Millers—who'd take the job."

Miller began this phase of his career at Chrysler in 1980 during negotiations for a loan bailout to rescue the firm from liquidation. When he was unable to get the CEO position at Chrysler (Lee Iacocca was the CEO at the time), he moved to help rescue the real estate giant Olympia & York. This firm had a significant $12 million debt load. Although he could not save Olympia & York because banks were able to seize individual properties and wouldn't forbear, he did oversee the organization's orderly collapse. Subsequently, he became an outside director to Sun River. That position lasted only one year because he was called on to rescue Morrison Knudsen after William Agee was dismissed. Agee had pushed the engineering construction company into a disastrous expansion program and nearly into bankruptcy. Miller held the banks off until the company could dispose of some assets. The firm was finally acquired by Washington Construction Group in 1996. Miller also served as the interim CEO at Federal-Mogul, another company that had expanded beyond its basic businesses and engaged in aggressive accounting. It failed to live up to Wall Street earnings estimates and was in a crisis. He administered a rapid and dramatic turnaround and facilitated the acquisition of Federal-Mogul by British auto parts maker T & N PLC. In the spring of 1997, Miller joined Waste Management's board. Because of some succession difficulties, Waste Management began to look for a new CEO. Miller persuaded Ronald T. LeMay, the number two executive at Spring Corporation, to take the position. After a short period on the job, LeMay quit suddenly and stock analysts expected the worst. As a result, the board asked Miller to step in and fill the role until someone more permanent could be found.

Although competitive trends are forcing firms to adapt, and outside leaders are often brought in to facilitate change to meet competitive challenges, significant changes require special leadership skills. Leaders are needed who take an interest in employees and develop a firm's human capital. Some feel that the "slash and burn" CEO who pursues significant downsizing such as Al Dunlap at Sunbeam and Robert Allen at AT&T is giving way to a new, less autocratic type of boss. For instance, Ronald W. Allen, recently hired by Delta Airlines, was chosen to help rebuild employee morale and reduce customer complaints. The board decided on a CEO who was a great listener and could capture the imagination of Delta employees. People skills and the ability to build human capital were very important to their search. John F. Welch, Jr., the renowned CEO of General Electric, is celebrated as one of the nation's most effective CEOs because of his stress on quality and customer service. He's also seeking to create the "borderless" company with better relationships among inside units and between inside and outside constituents. Henry Schacht, the CEO of Lucent Technologies, is excellent at sharing power and helping employees to feel involved.

Another leader, Alex Trotman, CEO at Ford Motor Company, keeps employees informed about both desirable and less desirable events. Some CEOs can focus on both getting the job done and facilitating employee development and relationships. Robert Crandall, American Airlines former CEO, Jack Welch at General Electric, and Andrew S. Grove, Intel's former CEO, have been considered to be strong simultaneously on task and on relationships. Because change is an essential and ongoing process, successful strategic managers will be able to make tough decisions such as downsizing and be sensitive to employee relationships.

In summary, strategic leaders are now required to be transformational managers who not only can help firms operate efficiently, but can provide visionary leadership, which empowers not only managers with good product ideas but motivates people to make the necessary changes as well.

SOURCES: J. Helyar and J. S. Lublin, 1998, Do you need an expert on widgets to head a widget company?, *Wall Street Journal,* January 21, A1, A10; J. Bailey, 1997, Steve Miller thrives in his second career: Corporate salvage, *Wall Street Journal,* December 16, A1, A9; A. A. Cannella, Jr. and M. J. Monroe, 1997, Contrasting perspectives on strategic leaders: Toward a more realistic view of top managers, *Journal of Management* 23: 213–237; S. Walsh, 1997, Captains Courteous: Era of the brutal boss may be giving way to a new sensitivity at the top, Inside Washington Post, http://www.washingtonpost.com, August 31; R. A. Heifetz and D. L. Laurie, 1997, The work of leadership, *Harvard Business Review* 75, no. 1: 124–134.

The examples of significant strategic changes with which CEOs are confronted in the opening case emphasize the importance and outcomes of effective strategic leadership. As this chapter makes clear, it is through effective strategic leadership that firms are able to use the strategic management process successfully (see Figure 1.1). Thus, as strategic leaders, top-level managers must guide the firm in ways that result in the formation of strategic intent and strategic mission. This may lead to goals that stretch everyone in the organization to improve their performance.[1] Moreover, strategic leaders are then challenged to facilitate the development of appropriate strategic actions and determine how to implement them, culminating in strategic competitiveness and above-average returns[2] (see Figure 12.1).

FIGURE 12.1 ***Strategic Leadership and the Strategic Management Process***

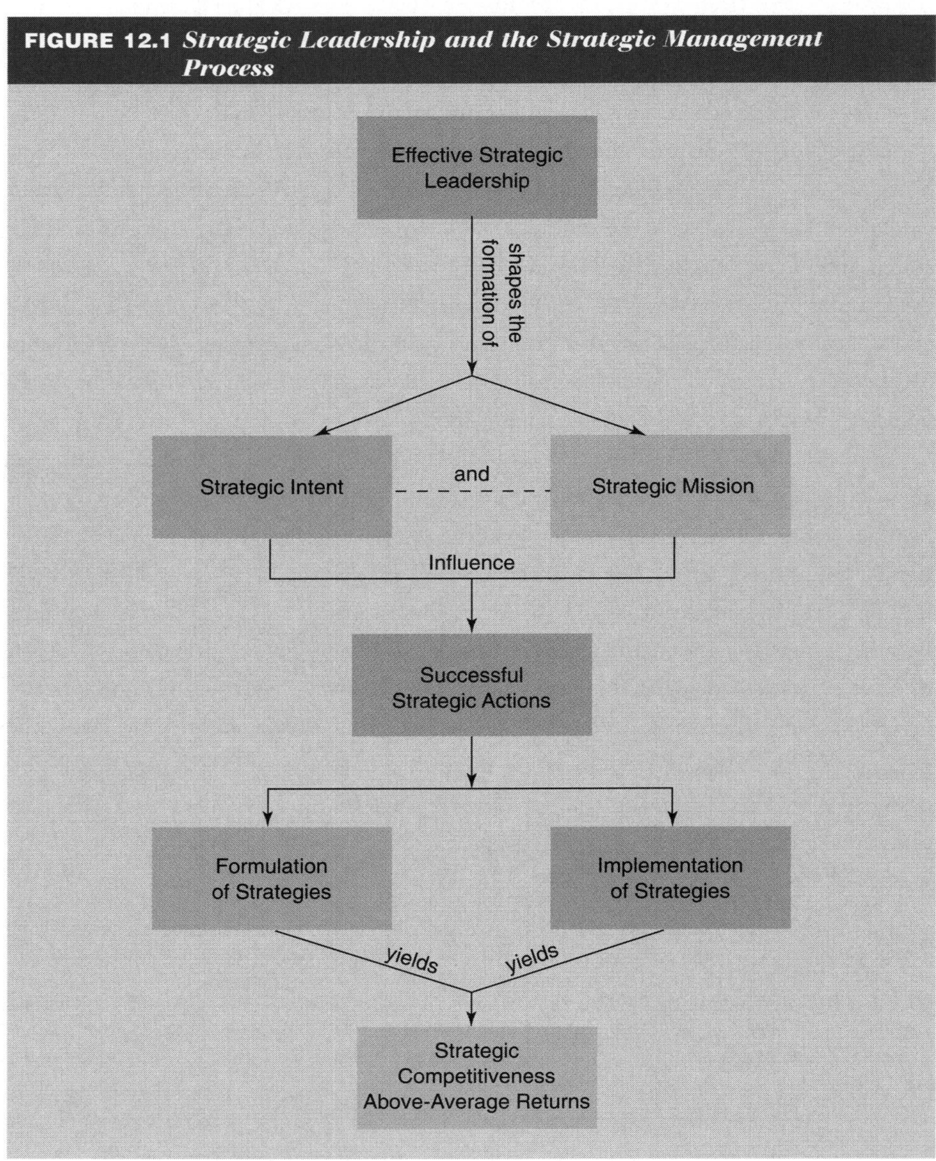

This chapter begins with a definition of strategic leadership and its importance as a potential source of competitive advantage. Next, we examine top management teams and their effects on firm innovation, strategic change, and performance. Following this discussion is an analysis of the internal and external managerial labor markets from which strategic leaders are selected. Closing the chapter are descriptions of the six key components of effective strategic leadership: determining strategic direction, exploiting and maintaining core competencies, developing human capital, sustaining an effective organizational culture, emphasizing ethical practices, and establishing balanced organizational control systems.

There is an evident consistency between many of the strategic leadership characteristics just mentioned and the actions taken by Eckhard Pfeiffer as Compaq Computer's CEO. By providing the vision for strategic intent, Pfeiffer has determined the firm's strategic direction. In 1997, not only did Compaq maintain its leading share of the PC business market and servers, it recaptured the second place position in notebook computers and was one of the top two sellers of home PCs. In addition, Compaq pushed further in the large computer business through the acquisition of Tandem Computers.[3] In early 1998, Compaq rocked the larger computer world by making a tender offer for Digital Equipment Corporation. Existing core competencies and those acquired through merger partners (e.g., brand name and distribution channels) are being used to implement the firm's new strategies in larger machines.[4] Efforts are also taken to develop and support the firm's human capital and to maintain what seems to be an effective organizational culture. This evidence suggests that Compaq Computer's CEO is an effective strategic leader.[5]

STRATEGIC LEADERSHIP

Strategic leadership is the ability to anticipate, envision, maintain flexibility, and empower others to create strategic change as necessary. Multifunctional in nature, strategic leadership involves managing through others, managing an entire enterprise rather than a functional subunit, and coping with change that seems to be increasing exponentially in today's new competitive landscape. Because of the complexity and global nature of this new landscape, strategic leaders must learn how to influence human behavior effectively in an uncertain environment. By word and/or personal example and through their ability to dream pragmatically, effective strategic leaders meaningfully influence the behaviors, thoughts, and feelings of those with whom they work.[6] The ability to manage human capital may be the most critical of the strategic leader's skills.[7] In the opinion of a well-known leadership observer, the key to competitive advantage in the 1990s and beyond "... will be the capacity of top leadership to create the social architecture capable of generating intellectual capital. . . . By intellectual capital, I mean know-how, expertise, brainpower, innovation (and) ideas."[8] Competent strategic leaders also establish the context through which stakeholders (e.g., employees, customers, and suppliers) are able to perform at peak efficiency.[9]

Strategic leadership is the ability to anticipate, envision, maintain flexibility, and empower others to create strategic change as necessary.

In the twenty-first century, many managers, who work in nations throughout the world, will be challenged to change their frames of reference to cope with the rapid and complex changes occurring in the global economy. A **managerial frame of reference** is the set of assumptions, premises, and accepted wisdom that bounds—or *frames*—a manager's understanding of the firm, the industry(ies) in which it competes, and the core competencies it uses in the pursuit of strategic

A **managerial frame of reference** is the set of assumptions, premises, and accepted wisdom that bounds—or *frames*—a manager's understanding of the firm, the industry(ies) in which it competes, and the core competencies it uses in the pursuit of strategic competitiveness.

competitiveness. A frame of reference is the foundation on which a manager's mind-set is built (see Chapter 3).

A firm's ability to achieve strategic competitiveness and earn above-average returns is compromised when strategic leaders fail to respond appropriately and quickly to mind-set-related changes that an increasingly complex and global competitive environment demands. Research suggests that a firm's "long-term competitiveness depends on managers' willingness to challenge continually their managerial frames" and that global competition is more than product versus product or company versus company—it is also a case of "mind-set versus mind-set, managerial frame versus managerial frame."[10] Competing on the basis of mind-set demands that strategic leaders learn how to deal with diverse and cognitively complex competitive situations. One of the most challenging mind-set changes is overcoming one's own successful mind-set when change is required. For instance, it was a particular mind-set that led to Wal-Mart's low-pricing strategy win over Sears. Being able to successfully complete challenging assignments that are linked to achieving strategic competitiveness early and frequently in one's career appears to improve a manager's ability to make appropriate changes to his or her mind-set.[11]

Effective strategic leaders are willing to make candid, courageous, yet pragmatic, decisions—decisions that may be difficult yet necessary in light of internal and external conditions facing the firm.[12] Effective strategic leaders solicit corrective feedback from their peers, superiors, and employees about the value of their difficult decisions. Often, this feedback is sought through face-to-face communications. The unwillingness to accept feedback may be a key reason talented executives fail, highlighting the need for strategic leaders to solicit feedback consistently from those affected by their decisions.[13]

The primary responsibility for effective strategic leadership rests at the top—in particular, with the CEO, but other commonly recognized strategic leaders include members of the board of directors, the top management team, and division general managers. Regardless of title and organizational function, strategic leaders have substantial decision-making responsibilities that cannot be delegated.[14]

Strategic leadership is an extremely complex but critical form of leadership. Strategies cannot be formulated and implemented to achieve above-average returns without effective strategic leaders. Because it is a requirement of strategic success, and because organizations may be poorly led and overmanaged, firms competing in the new competitive landscape are challenged to develop effective strategic leaders.[15] Wayne Calloway, PepsiCo's former CEO, has suggested that ". . . most of the companies that are in life-or-death battles got into that kind of trouble because they didn't pay enough attention to developing their leaders."[16]

MANAGERS AS AN ORGANIZATIONAL RESOURCE

As the introductory discussion suggests, top-level managers are an important resource for firms seeking to effectively formulate and implement strategies.[17] A key reason for this is that the strategic decisions made by top managers influence how the firm is designed and whether performance outcomes will be achieved. Thus, a critical element of organizational success is having a top management team that has superior managerial skills.[18]

Managers often use their discretion (or latitude of action) when making strategic decisions, including those concerned with the effective implementation of strategies.[19] Managerial discretion differs significantly across industries. The primary factors that determine the amount of a manager's (especially a top-level manager's) decision discretion include (1) external environmental sources (e.g., industry structure, rate of market growth in the firm's primary industry, and the degree to which products can be differentiated), (2) characteristics of the organization (e.g., size, age, resource availability, and culture), and (3) characteristics of the manager (e.g., commitment to the firm and its strategic outcomes, tolerance for ambiguity, skills to work with different people, and aspiration level) (see Figure 12.2). Because strategic leaders' decisions are intended to help the firm gain a

FIGURE 12.2 ***Factors Affecting Managerial Discretion***

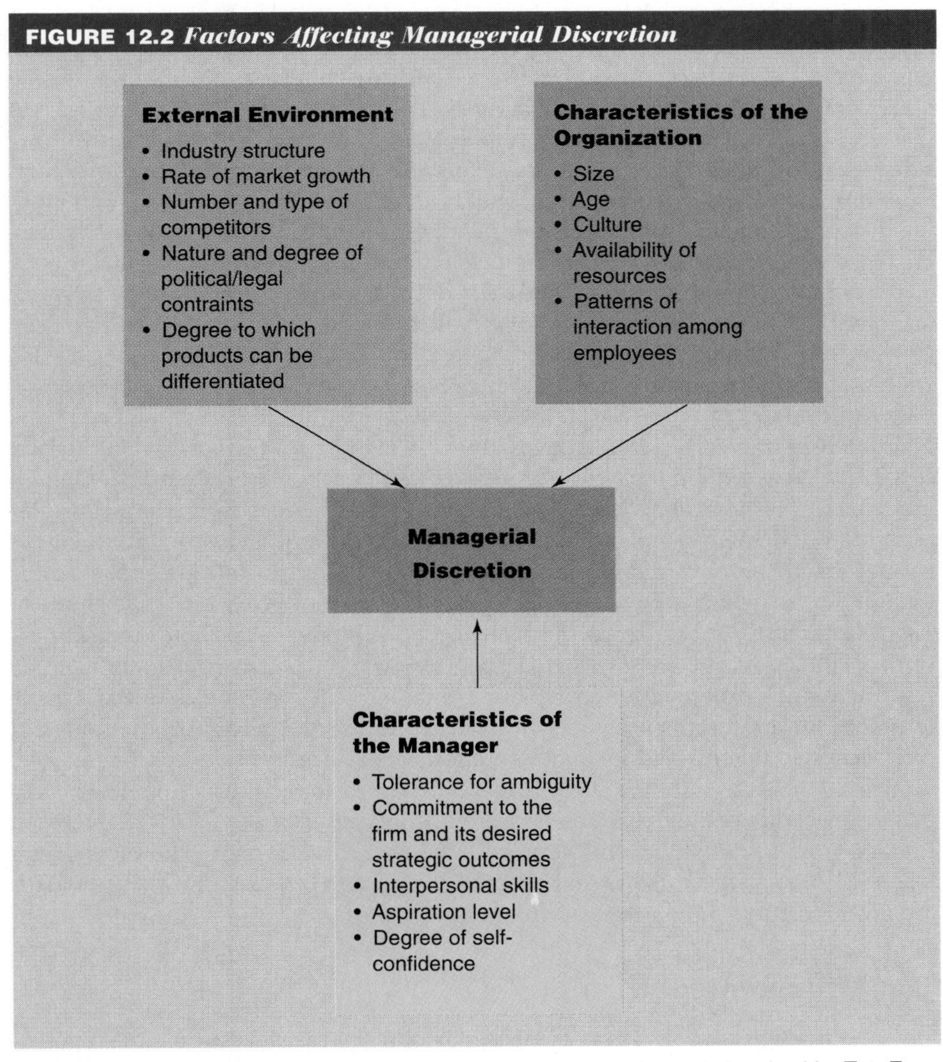

Source: Adapted from S. Finkelstein and D. C. Hambrick, 1996, *Strategic Leadership: Top Executives and Their Effects on Organizations* (St. Paul, Minn: West Publishing Co.).

competitive advantage, the way in which managers exercise discretion when determining appropriate strategic actions is critical to the firm's success.[20]

In addition to determining new strategic initiatives, top-level managers also develop the appropriate organizational structure and reward systems of a firm. (In Chapter 11, we described how organizational structure and reward systems affect strategic actions taken to implement different types of strategies.) Furthermore, top-level managers have a major effect on a firm's culture. Evidence suggests that managers' values are critical in shaping a firm's cultural values.[21] As this discussion shows, top-level managers have an important effect on organizational activities and performance.[22] The significance of this effect should not be underestimated.

The degree to which top-level managers influence a firm's performance is observed by financial markets. For example, when Eric Schmidt, chief technology officer at Sun Microsystems, was hired to be Novell's chairman of the board and CEO after a seven-month search, Novell's stock price gained 9 percent. In reaction, Sun's stock price declined 2½ percent. The market's reaction may have been due in part to Schmidt's broad experience with the Internet. Novell may also be able, with Schmidt's help, to establish important alliances with companies such as Oracle, Netscape Communications, and Sun to foster sales for Novell networking software. Novell should have been a stronger player in Internet services and has been losing business to Microsoft.[23] Thus, a strategic leader's experience and judgment, and the quality of the decisions based on them, is oftentimes of keen interest to various stakeholders, including current and potential shareholders.[24]

As the following discussion shows, the decisions and actions of some strategic leaders result in their becoming a source of competitive advantage for their firm. Consistent with the criteria of sustainability discussed in Chapter 3, strategic leaders can be a source of competitive advantage only when their work is valuable, rare, costly to imitate, and nonsubstitutable.

Effective strategic leaders focus their work on the key issues that ultimately shape the firm's ability to earn above-average returns. For example, Helmut Maucher at Nestlé and Michael Dell at Dell Computer focus their energies on determining how their companies can be market leaders and then structure their organizations to support this focus.[25] CEOs such as Maucher and Dell take actions to gain desired results. They delegate day-to-day operations to others so they can ask "big picture" questions of their managers, suppliers, shareholders, and customers. The most effective strategic leaders also travel to other companies to study successful work processes, and they build time into their schedules to think. One of the most important issues effective strategic leaders think about is the source of their firm's competitive advantage. Finding ways to release employees' brainpower influences the degree to which the firm's expertise is applied throughout the company in a competitively relevant fashion.[26] Robert Buckman, CEO of Buckman Laboratories, a specialty chemical maker, says that the most powerful incentives a CEO has are salary increases and promotions. He makes sure that these rewards are given based on how people share and borrow ideas.[27]

The **top management team** is composed of the key managers who are responsible for formulating and implementing the organization's strategies.

Top Management Teams

The **top management team** is composed of the key managers who are responsible for formulating and implementing the organization's strategies. Typically, the top management team includes the officers of the corporation as defined by the title of vice president and above and/or by service as a member of the board of directors.[28] The quality of the strategic decisions made by a top management team affects the firm's ability to innovate and engage in effective strategic change.[29]

Top Management Team, Firm Performance, and Strategic Change The job of top-level executives is complex and requires a broad knowledge of firm operations, as well as the three key parts of the firm's external environment. Therefore, firms try to form a top management team that has the appropriate knowledge and expertise to operate the internal organization, yet also deal with external stakeholders. This normally requires a heterogeneous top management team. A **heterogeneous top management team** is composed of individuals with different functional backgrounds, experiences, and education. The more heterogeneous a top management team is, with varied expertise and knowledge, the more capacity it has to provide effective strategic leadership in terms of strategy *formulation.* Members of a heterogeneous top management team benefit from discussing the different perspectives advanced by separate team members. In many cases, these discussions increase the quality of the top management team's decisions, especially when a synthesis emerges from the contesting of diverse perspectives that is generally superior to the individual perspectives.[30] For example, heterogeneous top management teams in the airline industry have the propensity to take stronger competitive actions and reactions.[31] The net benefit of these actions was positive in terms of market share and above-average returns.

A **heterogeneous top management team** is composed of individuals with different functional backgrounds, experiences, and education.

It is also important that the top management team members function cohesively. For example, some believe that an apparent inability to work together as a board affected the selection process for the new CEO at AT&T.[32] In general, the more heterogeneous and larger the top management team is, the harder it is for the team to *implement* strategies effectively.[33] The research finding that comprehensive and long-term strategic plans can be inhibited by communication difficulties when top managers of a firm come from different backgrounds and have different cognitive skills may account for these implementation-related difficulties.[34] Having members who have substantive expertise in the firm's core functions and businesses is also important to the effectiveness of a top management team. In a high-technology industry, it may be critical for a firm to have R&D knowledge and expertise included on the top management team, particularly when growth strategies are being implemented.[35]

The characteristics of top management teams are related to innovation and strategic change.[36] For example, more heterogeneous top management teams are associated positively with innovation and strategic change. Thus, firms that need to change their strategies are more likely to do so if they have top management teams with diverse backgrounds and expertise. A top management team with various areas of expertise is more likely to identify environmental changes (opportunities and threats) or changes within the firm that require a different strategic direction.[37] This fact may explain CEO Louis Gerstner's decision to change IBM's top management team. Relying more extensively on hiring from outside the company, Gerstner chose top-level managers that he believed had the skills required to help IBM better exploit the firm's core competencies.[38] The outsider approach, however, may only be temporary. Despite a significant turnaround since 1993, Gerstner suggests that the next leader may be an insider.[39]

Louis Gerstner, IBM's CEO, hired top-level managers from outside the firm whose skills would help IBM take advantage of its core competencies. Although the outsider approach led to a significant turnaround since 1993, IBM's next leader may come from within the firm.

CEO and Top Management Team Power As suggested in Chapter 10, the board of directors is an important mechanism for monitoring a firm's strategic direction and for representing the interests of stakeholders, especially those of shareholders. In fact, higher performance normally is achieved when the board of directors is involved more directly in shaping a firm's strategic direction.[40]

Boards of directors, however, may find it difficult to direct the strategic actions of powerful CEOs and top management teams. It is not uncommon for a powerful CEO to appoint a number of sympathetic outside board members, or have inside board members who are on the top management team and report to the CEO. Therefore, the CEO may have significant control over the board's actions. "A central question is whether boards are an effective management control mechanism . . . or whether they are a 'management tool,'. . . a rubber stamp for management initiatives . . . and often surrender to management their major domain of decision-making authority, which includes the right to hire, fire, and compensate top management."[41]

CEOs and top management team members can also achieve power in other ways. Holding the titles of chairperson of the board *and* chief executive officer usually gives a CEO more power than the one who is not simultaneously serving as chair of the firm's board.[42] Although the practice of CEO duality (i.e., when the CEO and the chairperson of the board are the same) has become more common in U.S. businesses, it ". . . has recently come under heavy criticism—duality has been blamed for poor performance and slow response to change in firms such as General Motors, Digital Equipment Corporation, and Goodyear Tire and Rubber."[43] Although it varies among industries, duality occurs most commonly in the largest firms. Increased shareholder activism, however, has brought CEO duality under increased scrutiny and attack in European firms as well. Historically, an independent board leadership structure in which the positions of CEO and chair were not held by one person was believed to enhance a board's ability to monitor top-level managers' decisions and actions, particularly in terms of the firm's financial performance.[44] Stewardship theory, on the other hand, suggests that CEO duality facilitates effective decisions and actions. In these instances, the increased effectiveness gained through CEO duality accrues from the individual who wants to perform effectively and desires to be the best possible steward of the firm's assets. Because of this person's positive orientations and actions, extra governance and the coordination costs resulting from an independent board leadership structure would be unnecessary.[45]

To date, the question of the effect of duality on the firm's strategic outcomes is unresolved. In a study of the relationship between duality and firm performance, researchers found that (1) the stock market is indifferent to changes in a company's duality status, (2) changes in a company's duality status has a negligible effect on its financial performance, and (3) "there is only weak evidence that duality status affects long-term performance, after controlling for other factors that might impact that performance."[46] Thus, it may be that, in general, the potential for managerial abuse created through CEO duality is unrealized in many firms.

Top management team members and CEOs who have long tenures—on the team and in the organization—have an increased ability to influence board decisions.[47] Moreover, long tenure is known to restrict the breadth of an executive's knowledge base. With the limited perspective associated with a restricted knowledge base, long-tenured top-level managers typically develop fewer alternatives to evaluate when making strategic decisions.[48] Long tenure and a restricted knowledge base increase an executive's ability to forestall or avoid board involvement in strategic decisions. However, managers of long tenure also may be able to exercise more effective strategic control, thereby obviating the need for board of director involvement because effective strategic control generally produces higher performance.[49]

In the final analysis, boards of directors should develop an effective relationship with the firm's top management team. The relative degrees of power to be held by the board and top management team members should be examined in light of an individual firm's situation. For example, the abundance of resources in a firm's external environment and the volatility of that environment may affect the ideal balance of power between boards and top management teams.[50] Through the development of effective working relationships, boards, CEOs and other top management team members are able to serve the best interests of the firm's stakeholders.

MANAGERIAL LABOR MARKET

The choice of top-level managers, especially CEOs, is a critical organizational decision with important implications for firm performance.[51] Moreover, selection of new members for a top management team represents an opportunity for the firm to adapt to changes occurring in its external environment, that is, in its general, industry, and competitive environments (see Chapter 2).

Successful companies develop screening systems to identify those with managerial and strategic leadership potential. The most effective of these systems evaluates people within the firm and gains valuable information about the capabilities of other firms' managers, particularly their strategic leaders. Screening systems are vital, in that just because a person shares the firm's values ". . . doesn't mean he or she is leadership material."[52] For current managers, training and development programs are provided to preselect and attempt to shape the skills of people who may become tomorrow's leaders.

There are two types of managerial labor markets—internal and external—from which organizations select managers and strategic leaders. An **internal mana-**

An **internal managerial labor market** consists of the opportunities for managerial positions within a firm.

An **external managerial labor market** is the collection of career opportunities for managers in organizations outside of the one for which they work currently.

gerial labor market consists of the opportunities for managerial positions within a firm. As the Opening Case illustrates, an **external managerial labor market** is the collection of career opportunities for managers in organizations outside of the one for which they work currently. Given this chapter's topic of strategic leadership, our discussion focuses on how managerial labor markets are used to select CEOs.

Several benefits are thought to accrue to a firm when the internal labor market is used to select a new CEO. Because of their experience with the firm and the industry environment in which it competes, insiders are familiar with company products, markets, technologies, and standard operating procedures. Additionally, internal hiring results in less turnover among existing personnel, many of whom possess valuable firm-specific knowledge.

It is not unusual for employees to have a strong preference for using the internal managerial labor market to select top management team members and the CEO. For example, the initial reaction among employees to the choice of outsider Ronald Zarrella as the head of all of General Motors' marketing efforts was negative. With previous executive experience at Playtex and Bausch Lomb, employees felt that Zarrella lacked the skills and background to understand the intricacies of selling cars. However, after a relatively brief time in his new position, his style and decisions earned him the respect and acceptance of many, including Jack Smith, GM's internally appointed CEO.[53]

The selection of insiders to fill top-level management positions reflects a desire for continuity and a continuing commitment to the firm's current strategic intent, strategic mission, and chosen strategies. Because of the potential importance and perceived desirability of organizational continuity, internal candidates tend to be valued over external candidates[54] when selecting a firm's CEO and other top-level managers. In fact, outside succession to the CEO position "is an extraordinary event for business firms [and] is usually seen as a stark indicator that the board of directors wants change,"[55] but as the opening case illustrates, outsiders are increasingly being used to succeed insiders.

Valid reasons exist for a firm to select an outsider as its new CEO. For example, research evidence suggests that executives who have spent their entire career with a particular firm may become "stale in the saddle."[56] Long tenure with a firm seems to reduce the number of innovative ideas top-level managers are able to develop to cope with conditions facing their firm. Given the importance of innovation for firm success in the new competitive landscape (see Chapter 13), an inability to innovate and/or to create conditions that stimulate innovation throughout the firm is a liability for a strategic leader. In contrast to insiders, CEOs selected from outside the firm may have broader, less limiting perspectives. As such, they usually encourage innovation and strategic change. Nevertheless, CEOs selected from outside the firm and even the firm's industry are sometimes disadvantaged by a lack of firm-specific knowledge and industry experience. For example, although credited with strategic leadership success at ConAgra Inc., Charles Harper's tenure as CEO of RJR Nabisco Holdings Corporation disappointed many stakeholders, including board members, employees, and financial investors. Among reasons cited for Harper 's inability to boost RJR's struggling stock price was his lack of experience running a cigarette company.[57]

Subsequently, RJR was spun off from Nabisco and an initial public offering was completed in 1995. Commencing his work as Nabisco's new CEO in 1998, James M. Kilts, a former Phillip Morris executive at Kraft Foods, has been bringing in other outsiders as well. He brought in Richard H. Lenny, who was also an executive with Philip Morris and a former president of the U.S. Business of Pillsbury Corporation, a business unit of DAIGO PLC. Lenny was brought in to run the beleagured biscuit business unit at Nabisco. Apparently, in trying to meet ambitious earnings targets promised through the initial public offering, Nabisco let its overall spending on merchandising and advertising lag behind its rivals. Nabisco spends only 2.5 percent of its sales on advertising compared with 6 percent for the average company in the food industry. Thus, significant changes need to take place to turn the flat sales and earnings around in Nabisco's basic product lines such as Oreo cookies.[58]

Figure 12.3 shows how the composition of the top management team and CEO succession (managerial labor market) may interact to affect strategy. For example, when the top management team is homogeneous (e.g., members have similar functional experiences and educational backgrounds) and a new CEO is selected from inside the firm, the firm's current strategy is unlikely to change. On the other hand, when a new CEO is selected from outside the firm and the top management team is heterogeneous, there is a high probability of a change in strategy. When the new CEO is from inside the firm, the strategy may not change, but with a heterogeneous top management team, innovation is likely to continue. An external CEO succession with a homogeneous team creates a more ambiguous situation.

As noted earlier, the type of strategic leadership that results in successful implementation of strategies is exemplified by several key actions. The most critical of these are shown in Figure 12.4. The remainder of this chapter is devoted to explaining each action. Note that many of these actions interact with each other. For example, developing human capital through executive training contributes to establishing a strategic direction, fostering an effective culture, exploiting core competencies, using effective organizational control systems, and establishing ethical practices.

FIGURE 12.3 ***Effects of CEO Succession and Top Management Team Composition on Strategy***

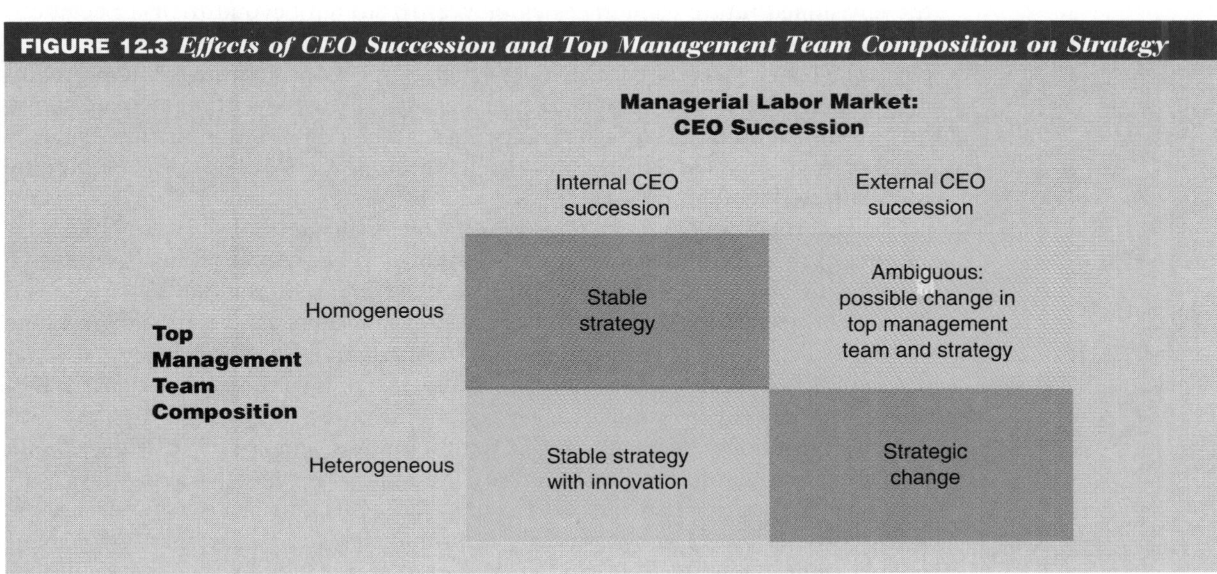

FIGURE 12.4 *Exercise of Effective Strategic Leadership*

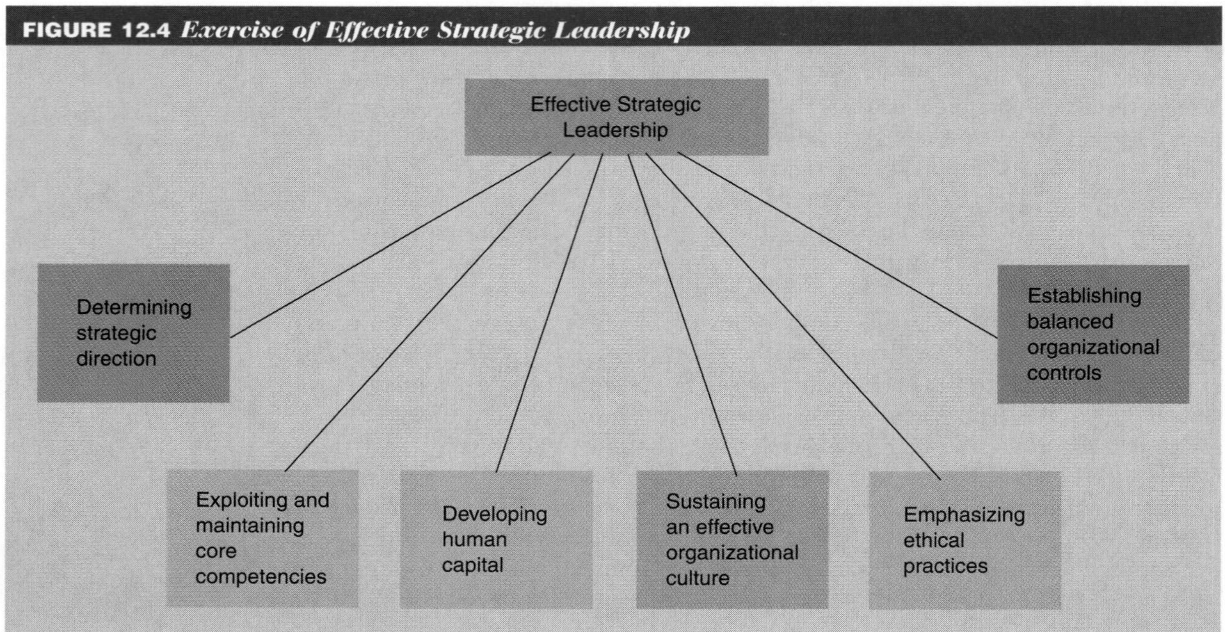

Determining the strategic direction of a firm refers to the development of a long-term vision of a firm's strategic intent.

DETERMINING STRATEGIC DIRECTION

Determining the strategic direction of a firm refers to the development of a long-term vision of a firm's strategic intent. A long-term vision normally looks at least 5 to 10 years into the future. A philosophy with goals, a long-term vision is the ideal image and character the firm seeks.[59] The ideal long-term vision has two parts, core ideology and envisioned future. While the core ideology motivates employees through the company's heritage (e.g., the "HP way" at Hewlett-Packard), the envisioned future encourages employees to stretch beyond their expectations of accomplishment and requires significant change and progress to attain.[60] The envisioned future serves as a guide to many aspects of a firm's strategy implementation process, including motivation, leadership, employee empowerment, and organizational design. For firms competing in many different industries, evidence suggests that the most effective long-term vision is one that has been accepted by those affected by it.[61]

To determine the firm's long-term vision, managers must take a sufficient amount of time to think about how it should be framed. Areas requiring executive thought include an analysis of the firm's external and internal environments and its current performance levels. Most top-level managers ask people with a range of skills to help them analyze various aspects of the firm's operations. Macroeconomists, for example, through their study of trends in the global economy, often provide insights to strategic leaders.[62]

Once the vision is determined, CEOs must motivate employees to achieve them. Some, but not all, top-level managers are thought to be charismatic strategic leaders. Theory suggests that charisma comes through interactions between leaders and followers. These interactions have been studied by examining impression management where framing, scripting, staging, and performing by the strategic leader relate to attribution of charisma by followers.[63] Although charisma is perceived as helpful, it is not a requirement for strategic leadership success. Noncharismatic people often have other skills and traits—intelligence, vision, ambition, and toughness, for example—that provide benefits similar to those gained when one is thought to be charismatic.[64] In certain situations, charismatic CEOs might facilitate better performance; in others, it might reduce leadership credibility. Jack Welch, General Electric's CEO, combines outrageous self-confidence, high-strung passion for ideas he unabashedly borrows, and unforgiving candor and appears to have charisma.[65] Tony O'Reilly, H. J. Heinz's former CEO, is a charming, pretentious Renaissance man. Although extra-curricular activities (he owns newspapers in his native Ireland) diverted his attention, until recently his star power enchanted Heinz investors. However, during his final days as Heinz's CEO, his regal ways soured institutional investors, and he came to represent the type of CEO the corporate governance advocates love to hate (see discussion in Chapter 10).[66]

Other CEOs who are typically not described as charismatic include Wal-Mart's David Glass. Though a fierce competitor, this earnest boss stands no chance in a personality contest with the larger-than-life Sam Walton. To inspire associates, Glass wisely milks the late founder's legacy. General Motors' Jack Smith is thought by some to be as charismatic as his name. He eschews TV cameras and the press. A pragmatic consensus builder, he accumulates power by giving it away. He has made GM shine even though he doesn't. Despite his lack of charisma, Smith is considered to be an effective strategic leader. Actions dedicated to enhancing one's skills (as discussed earlier) contribute positively to a strategic leader's efforts to help her or his firm reach its desired strategic outcomes.

A charismatic CEO may help gain employees' commitment to a new vision and strategic direction. Nonetheless, for all firms, it is important not to lose sight of the strengths of the organization when making changes required by a new strategic direction. Achieving this objective demands the balancing of a firm's short-term needs to adjust to a new vision while maintaining its long-term survival by emphasizing its current and valuable core competencies.

Although charisma may help a CEO motivate employees to achieve a corporate vision, it is not a requirement for strategic leadership success. Wal-Mart's former CEO Sam Walton was renowned for his larger-than-life personality, whereas his successor, David Glass, is a fierce competitor who lacks charisma.

EXPLOITING AND MAINTAINING CORE COMPETENCIES

Examined in Chapters 1 and 3, *core competencies* are resources and capabilities that serve as a source of competitive advantage for a firm over its rivals. Typically, core competencies relate to an organization's functional skills, such as manufacturing, finance, marketing, and research and development. As shown by the following descriptions, firms develop and exploit core competencies in many different functional areas in order to implement their strategies. Strategic leaders must verify that the firm's competencies are emphasized in strategy implementation efforts. Hewlett-Packard and Intel, for example, have core competencies in terms of competitive agility (an ability to act in a variety of competitively relevant ways) and competitive speed (an ability to act quickly when facing environmental and competitive pressures).[67]

In many large firms, and certainly in related diversified ones, core competencies are exploited effectively when they are developed and applied across different organizational units (see Chapter 6). Philip Morris demonstrates this by applying its marketing and promotion competencies across multiple businesses. The company's rejuvenation of Miller Beer is a classic example. Whirlpool also has well-known competencies that are emphasized to create value across country borders.[68] Some argue that the development, nurturing, and application of core competencies within multinational firms facilitates management of the complex relationships across businesses operating in different international markets.[69] Because GE Capital, a large business unit of General Electric, has made a number of acquisitions, its managers have become skilled at integrating the new businesses into GE Capital's operating culture. In the process, they have developed a new management position, that of integration manager.[70] Core competencies, however, cannot be developed or exploited effectively without appropriate human capital.

DEVELOPING HUMAN CAPITAL

Human capital refers to the knowledge and skills of the firm's entire workforce.

Human capital refers to the knowledge and skills of the firm's entire workforce. Employees, from this perspective, are viewed as a capital resource that requires investment. Much of the development of U.S. industry can be attributed to the effectiveness of its human capital. One-third of the growth in the U.S. gross national product from 1948 to 1982 was attributed to increases in the education level of the workforce. Fifty percent of this growth resulted from technical innovations and knowledge that also are based strongly on education. Only 15 percent of the growth of the gross national product during this time was attributed to investment in capital equipment.[71] Outcomes such as these support the position, as discussed in Chapter 3, that "... as the dynamics of competition accelerate, people are perhaps the only truly sustainable source of competitive advantage."[72] This suggests that the role of human resource management should be increasing in importance.[73] In turn, the effective development and management of the firm's human capital—that is, of all of the firm's managerial and nonmanagerial personnel—may be the primary determinant of a firm's ability to formulate and implement strategies successfully.[74]

As the Strategic Focus suggests, a significant problem is the lack of adequate human capital to run an organization effectively. Because of this, many firms are turning to temporary employees, while others are employing better recruiting techniques. Solving the problem, however, requires more than just hiring temporary employees; indeed, building effective commitment to organizational goals is also required. Hiring star players is also insufficient. A strategic leader needs to build an effective organizational team committed to achieving the company's vision and goals.

STRATEGIC FOCUS

Human Resource Shortages: Temporary Workers Versus Creative Recruiting and Building Commitment

The Information Technology Association of America says that about 10 percent of U.S. technical jobs remain vacant because there are no qualified workers. There has been a shortage of talent because U.S. colleges have been graduating fewer computer science and electrical and computer engineering graduates throughout the 1990s. The falling graduation rate is due partly to the decline in baby boomers of college age. The lack of sufficient numbers of workers is not only a high-tech phenomenon. The American Trucking Association reported that 400,000 truck drivers were needed in 1997. The association also suggests that 50,000 drivers leave the industry each year, while another 300,000 switch trucking jobs, hoping to find better pay and conditions. Werner Enterprises Inc., a major firm in Omaha, Nebraska, replaced 65 percent of its drivers in one year, primarily due to turnover. Demand for drivers is correlated with the expected growth for handling freight, which is projected to increase 100 millions tons a year through 2004. The United States also faces a shortage of tool-and-die workers. According to the National Tooling and Machining Association, orders of machine tools rose significantly in 1997 while at the same time there was an estimated 24,000 vacancies for tool-and-die makers.

Companies throughout the world are creatively seeking ways to overcome the shortages. For instance, the number of part-time workers is growing significantly. The *Washington Post* reported that part-time arrangements affect 57 percent of workers. Part-time workers are also being seen in areas where unemployment is high. In Japan, for instance, nearly 20 percent of the country's 10 million workers are temporary part-time employees. Almost half of Japanese companies employ part-time workers. Similarly, in Germany, part-time workers are used increasingly because of the high unemployment rate. The use of temporary workers has increased in Europe because it helps to overcome inflexible labor market regulations. Milwaukee-based Manpower Inc., which supplies temporary workers, has been opening offices across Europe. Many multinationals, especially those headquarters in the U.S., have been sensitive to Europe's high labor costs and are leading the drive to outsource some business activities to temporary workers. However, European-based multinationals are not far behind. Phillips Electronics, for instance, employs 17,000 temporary workers, nearly 7 percent of its workforce.

With significant shortages in some markets and unemployment in others, how can a company develop its human resource? Cisco Systems, a networking company in Silicon Valley, has sought to develop ways to hire top talent and maintain its high performing employees. Its recruiting team identifies exactly the kind of people the company should hire, then plans a job-hunting strategy and provides innovative hiring processes to attract new employees. Cisco has a goal of hiring the top 10–15 percent of people in its industry. CEO John Chambers says: "Our philosophy is very simple. If you get the best people in the industry to fit into your culture and you motivate them properly, then you're going to be an industry leader." Cisco has an unusual and creative technique of infiltrating art fairs and microbrewery festivals as well as home and garden shows. At these events, Cisco recruiters work the crowd, collect business cards from prospects and speak informally with them about their careers and aspirations. They also have a "friends" referral program to help them pick out those who would like to work at Cisco. Employees receive a generous referral fee, starting at $500 for those prospects who are ultimately hired. Cisco also has a Web site that allows potential employees to fill out a profile by answering a handful of questions on an applicant's background.

Besides trying to hire talented people, Cisco makes acquisitions based on the quality of the engineering and R&D talent at potential target companies. Although many companies may be able to copy Cisco's hiring efforts, the firm continues to develop additional innovative ways to recruit the industry's best employees. It was rated the top firm in a *Forbes ASAP* ranking of the one hundred top dynamic companies.

In a survey completed by *Fortune* magazine about companies that employees love to work for, three characteristics became apparent. First, the best companies to work for had inspiring leadership. As one worker from Southwest Airlines, which was at the top of *Fortune*'s list of 100 best companies to work for, said: "Working here is truly an unbelievable experience. They treat you with respect, pay you well, and empower you. They use your ideas to solve problems. They encourage you to be yourself. I love going to work!!" Effective leaders not only inspire employees to work hard and succeed, but they also expect everyone to become a mini-version of top leadership and inspire employees that work for them. Second, employees value impressive corporate facilities. For instance, at USAA, a San Antonio-based insurance and financial services company, the corporate amenities include an exceptionally well-developed child care center. If you can't drive to work, the company sponsors a van pool. USAA also provides athletic facilities where employees enjoy breaks from their tasks during the work week. Finally, employees desire to have a strong sense of purpose. For example, at Merck, a pharmaceutical and health-care company, number nine on the list of well-respected companies, workers derive satisfaction from their jobs because they feel they are producing products that help restore people's lives. Therefore, besides seeking to build shareholder value, many firms seek to create value in the human capital by motivating employees through a broader sense of purpose.

Firms are seeking not only to have excellent human capital but to build the commitment of employees to work as a team and focus their intellectual skills and energies on company goals. As suggested above, managers can buy, build, or borrow talent. Furthermore, they may get rid of those individuals who are not contributing and seek to retain employees or bind those who they want to keep by treating them properly. However, recruiting competent individual talent should not be the only focus. It can be like buying the best talent and putting those people on an All-Star team. While the individual players may be talented, they may not perform as a team. Building commitment involves gauging employees' emotional energy and attention. If employees feel overwhelmed because demands on their time and emotional energy are too high, then they are likely to become discouraged. Furthermore, if demands are high but resources to do the work are inadequate, this is likely to lead to a lack of commitment as well. Therefore, there needs to be a good balance between available resources and appropriate levels of demand on workers' time.

Tools for developing commitment include enabling employees to control decisions on how they do their work and providing employees with vision and direction. These tools create an incentive for working hard. Challenging work, which allows stimulation and development of new skills, also is motivational. At Southwest Airlines, having a fun work culture where work is done in teams and gains are shared has also instilled superior commitment.

Candid communication and concern for the people involved provides better commitment as well. Adequate training and providing employees with appropriate technology to make their work easier is motivational, too. Thus, facing the challenges of finding competent people is not enough. Developing a team spirit and treating employees appropriately is also essential to garnering employee commitment in the pursuit of organizational objectives.

SOURCES: M. Aguilera-Hellweg, 1998, The ASAP dynamic 100: Cisco's CEO John Chambers, *Forbes ASAP*, February 23, 51–52; D. Ulrich, 1998, Intellectual Capital = Competence × Commitment, *Sloan Management Review* 39, no. 2: 15–26; R. B. Lieber, 1998, Why employees love these companies, *Fortune*, January 12, 72–74; L. Grant, 1998, Happy workers, high returns, *Fortune*, January 12, 81; R. Levering and M. Moskowitz, 1998, The 100 best companies to work for in America, *Fortune*, January 12, 85–95; D. Kunde, 1997, Companies go to great lengths to fill plethora of jobs, *Dallas Morning News*, December 9, D1, D15; Number of part-timers grows, 1997, *Dallas Morning News*, December 2, D4; G. Edmondson, A tidal wave of temps in Europe, *Business Week*, December 1, 164; E. Thornton, 1997, Moral cracks in the social contract, *Business Week*, October 27, 70; P. Nakache, 1997, Cisco's recruiting edge, *Fortune*, September 29, 275–276; A. W. Mathews, Wanted: 400,000 Long-distance truck drivers, *Wall Street Journal*, September 11, B1, B6; Associated Press, 1997, U.S. faces shortage of tool-and-die workers, *Dallas Morning News*, August 11, D4.

For individuals, active participation in company-sponsored programs to develop their abilities is highly desirable, in that being able to upgrade one's skills continuously leads to more job and economic security.[75] Increasingly, part of the development required to be selected as a strategic leader is international experience. As a business analyst noted, "With nearly every industry targeting fast-growing foreign markets, more companies are requiring foreign experience for top management positions."[76] Thus, companies committed to the importance of competing successfully in the global economy provide opportunities for their future strategic leaders to work in locations other than their home nation. Also, because foreign sources of management capabilities are becoming important, managing inpatriation (the process of transferring host-country or third-country national managers into the home/domestic market of multinational firms) is becoming more important to build global core competencies.[77]

Through participation in effective training and development programs, the probability increases that a manager will be a successful strategic leader. Among other outcomes, these programs build skills, inculcate a common set of core values, and give a systematic view of the organization, thus promoting the firm's strategic vision and organizational cohesion. Furthermore, they help strategic leaders improve skills that are critical to completing other tasks associated with effective strategic leadership (e.g., determining the firm's strategic direction, exploiting and maintaining core competencies, and developing an organizational culture that supports ethical practices).

The efforts at PepsiCo demonstrate an emphasis on shaping strategic leaders so that they in turn can develop human capital in their areas of responsibility.[78] This is an important challenge, given that most strategic leaders need to enhance their human resource management abilities. When human capital investments are successful, the result is a workforce capable of learning continuously. Being able to learn continuously and to leverage the firm's expanding knowledge base is linked with strategic success in the new competitive landscape. When asked to name what accounts for Johnson & Johnson's competitive success, the firm's CEO answered that his company is ". . . not in the product business. [It] is in the knowledge business."[79]

Programs that gain outstanding results in the training of future strategic leaders become a competitive advantage for a firm. General Electric's system of training and development of future strategic leaders is comprehensive and thought to be among the best.[80] As such, this training system may be a source of competitive advantage for the firm. Similarly, Avon as been particularly effective at hiring, training, and promoting women managers. Four of its eight top officers are women and 95 percent of its sales come from Avon Ladies. Performance at the cosmetics, toiletries, and fragrance company shows that this has been not only good for diversity, but has also helped improve returns substantially.[81]

As discussed in Chapter 7, millions of managers, strategic leaders, and non-managerial personnel have lost jobs in recent years through the restructuring and downsizing in many companies. In the mid-1980s, IBM employed 405,000 workers; today, the firm employs around 225,000. During the 1990s, Sears shed 50,000 people; in 1996, AT&T announced its intended layoffs of up to 40,000 employees. The view of AT&T's former CEO, Robert Allen, about his firm's job reductions captures the sentiment of many strategic leaders facing this reality: "My company had to make the necessary, even painful changes today or forfeit the future."[82] Almost identically, Robert Eaton, Chrysler's CEO, believes, "Downsizing and layoffs are part of the price of becoming more competitive. The price for not doing it, however, is much higher in both economic and human terms."[83] A number of firms, including Kodak, Citicorp, Levi Strauss, Whirlpool, Apple, and Kimberly-Clark, among others, announced layoffs in 1997 and 1998, at a time when the economy was very strong.[84]

Regardless of the cause, layoffs can result in a significant loss of knowledge that is possessed by a firm's human capital. Although it is also not uncommon for restructuring firms to reduce their expenditures/investments in training and development programs, restructuring may be an important time to *increase* investment in such development. These firms have less slack and cannot absorb as many errors; moreover, many employees may be placed into positions without all of the skills or knowledge necessary to perform required tasks effectively.[85] In the final analysis, a view of employees as a resource to be maximized rather than a cost to be minimized facilitates successful implementation of a firm's strategies. The effectiveness of implementation processes also increases when strategic leaders approach layoffs in a manner that employees believe is fair and equitable.[86]

As described next, human capital is an important part of the firm's ability to develop and sustain an effective organizational culture.

SUSTAINING AN EFFECTIVE ORGANIZATIONAL CULTURE

An **organizational culture** consists of a complex set of ideologies, symbols, and core values that is shared throughout the firm and influences the way it conducts business. Evidence suggests that a firm can develop core competencies both in terms of the capabilities it possesses and the way the capabilities are used to produce strategic actions. In other words, because it influences how the firm conducts its business and helps regulate and control employee behavior, organizational culture can be a source of competitive advantage.[87] Thus, shaping the context within which the firm formulates and implements its strategies—that is, shaping the organizational culture—is a central task of strategic leaders.[88]

An **organizational culture** consists of a complex set of ideologies, symbols, and core values that is shared throughout the firm and influences the way it conducts business.

Hewlett-Packard provides an example of the potential power of culture. The core values of this firm's culture are in the basic belief that "men and women want to do a good job, a creative job, and that if they are provided the proper environment, they will do so."[89] An effective organizational culture encourages and supports an entrepreneurial orientation.

Entrepreneurial Orientation

Organizational culture often encourages (or discourages) the pursuit of entrepreneurial opportunities, especially in large firms.[90] At Thermo Electron, George N. Hatsopoulous, chair and CEO, has fostered an entrepreneurial spirit by offering to spin off businesses that become successful. This is opposite of conventional wisdom; when a company divests, it usually does so with its less successful businesses. Thermo Electron has completed twelve spin-offs over the years. For employees and managers involved in these spin-offs, it has provided a vehicle for ownership and significant incentive to increase value. John Hatsopoulous, the company's president, adds, "We found that the only way we could sustain the process of creating new businesses was to be able to maintain the benefits of a small company while preserving the advantages of a big company."[91]

Successful outcomes derived through employees' pursuit of entrepreneurial opportunities are a major source of growth and innovation for firms competing in today's complex, globalized environment.[92] Innovation, and a CEO that has nurtured a culture that fosters it, may account for Bombardier's recent successful innovations. As noted in Chapter 11, Laurent Beaudoin, the 59-year-old chief executive of Montreal-based Bombardier Inc., has moved ahead with a number of product innovations over the last several years. Although Bombardier has had performance difficulties, the CEO is counting on a number of new products to increase returns. He has sought to foster innovation in three of the firm's diversified businesses—aerospace, transportation, and recreational products. In 1998, Bombardier offered the Learjet 45, a mid-sized plane priced like a light jet but capable of nonstop transcontinental flights. A number of regional jet airlines such as Canada Air and American Eagle have placed orders for the plane. Its Global Express, a top of the line executive jet, has also presold a number of planes. It has also redesigned its subway cars and has a $1 billion contract for New York City featuring automatic announcements and electronic information signs. Its American Flyer high-speed rail trains will be carrying Amtrak passengers from Boston to Washington at 150 miles per hour starting in 1999. It has moved into jetskis as an offshoot from its snowmobile business. Similarly, it has developed a new two-passenger golf cart featuring an electronic motor capable of 25 miles per hour. It expects to establish a strong market share in this $33 million dollar market. The product can also be used as a neighborhood vehicle in gated or retirement communities. Bombardier also expects to introduce a new sporty all-terrain recreational vehicle to compete with models sold by Honda and Yamaha. Even though quite diversified, Bombardier is resolute in selling new technology and products in all of its product lines.[93]

Five dimensions characterize a firm's entrepreneurial orientation (EO).[94] In combination, these dimensions influence the activities a firm uses in efforts to be innovative and to launch new ventures. Discussed in Chapter 13, one of the key ways new ventures are launched in large firms is through internal corporate entrepreneurship. Particularly for firms seeking first-mover advantages (see Chapter 5), an entrepreneurial orientation among employees is critical.

Autonomy is the first of an EO's five dimensions. Autonomy is an active part of a firm's culture when employees are able to take actions that are free of stifling organizational constraints. Generally, autonomy allows individuals and groups to be self-directed. The second dimension, *innovativeness*, "reflects a firm's tendency to engage in and support new ideas, novelty, experimentation, and creative processes that may result in new products, services, or technological processes."[95] Cultures with a tendency toward innovativeness encourage employees to think beyond existing knowledge, technologies, and parameters in efforts to find creative ways to add value. *Risk taking* reflects a willingness by employees and their firm to accept risks in the pursuit of marketplace opportunities. These risks can include assuming significant levels of debt and allocating large amounts of other resources (e.g., people) to uncertain projects. Often, these risks are accepted to seize marketplace opportunities that can substantially increase the firm's strategic competitiveness and its returns. The fourth EO dimension, *proactiveness*, describes a firm's ability to be a market leader rather than a follower. Proactive organizational cultures constantly use processes to anticipate future market needs and to satisfy them before competitors learn how to do so. Finally, *competitive aggressiveness* is a firm's propensity to take actions that allow it to outperform its rivals consistently and substantially. Thus, the key dimensions that characterize an EO include autonomy, a willingness to innovate and take risks, and a tendency to be aggressive toward competitors and proactive relative to marketplace opportunities.[96]

These attributes are illustrated in the Strategic Focus about Fastenal, a service-oriented business focusing on selling fasteners to industrial companies (such as specialized nuts and bolts). Bob Kierlin, the CEO, has developed an entrepreneurial culture in the firm that provides a commonplace set of products in a way that creates value for its customers. Additional information about this firm's ability to innovate is provided in a Strategic Focus in Chapter 13 (see page 493).

STRATEGIC FOCUS

Fastenal's Culture for Selling Nuts and Bolts

Bob Kierlin founded Fastenal Company in 1967 in Winona, Minnesota. It has become the largest fastener distributor in the nation through a service-oriented business network. In addition to an in-house manufacturing division and a quality assurance department, Fastenal has a strategic system of distribution centers and a fleet of over 60 owned semi trucks and trailers with 660 branches in 48 states, Canada, and Puerto Rico. Fastenal has been on the *Forbes*' 200 Best Small Companies list for the last 10 years. When it first made the list in 1988, the company had annual sales of $22.5 million. In 1997, its sales were $339 million; almost enough to remove it from the small company list. Notwithstanding this phenomenal growth, its average return on equity has been 26.6 percent over the last five years, and 28.5 percent in 1997.

When Kierlin, current CEO of Fastenal, is asked to describe the reasons for this success, he says, "Just believe in people, give them a chance to make decisions, take risks, and work hard." Furthermore, he suggests, "We could have made this work selling cabbages." In essence, Kierlin and his top officers have facilitated an entrepreneurial culture that stimulates the kind of growth and returns experienced by Fastenal. This success apparently has nothing to do with his salary. Kierlin is paid $120,000 annually, an amount which has remained constant for the past ten years. He receives no options, bonuses, or long-term incentives. He admits, however, that his net worth is tied to the stock price, which has provided better shareholder returns than Coca-Cola or General Electric. Total returns to shareholders over the past five years have been 39.3 percent annually. This performance has come through selling nuts and bolts—49,000 different kinds of fasteners, from grade eight hex nuts to weld studs to pin bold drive anchors—in 620 stores across the United States and Canada. Furthermore, Fastenal's gross margins are 53 percent, approximately 15 percentage points higher than rivals.

Kierlin fosters a culture of decentralized decision making. Fastenal's branches can bypass the company's central purchasing department. In fact, this happens in 42 percent of purchases. Often, management-level decision making is pushed down to entry level positions. One branch decided that it required improved deliveries to increase sales. To insure that it was stocked properly, deliveries were received daily. The main focus is to furnish customers with exemplary service and charge them premiums for the value that is created by having the product available on time. The premium price works primarily because Fastenal's sales are focused on replacement parts for industrial and other kinds of machines. The company has successfully implemented a focused differentiation strategy (see Chapter 4). When something breaks, Fastenal employees provide the necessary parts in a timely manner. Rich Schmidt of Machinery Services, says, "As far as Fastenal goes, we never get told no." Of course, this kind of service builds loyalty and allows Fastenal to charge its premium price. Usually, a large factory is not likely to quibble over a three dollar bolt when its machine is down.

Many construction and equipment manufacturers outsource their inventory function to Fastenal, which means it can move to its secret weapon of cutting and machining or molding virtually any fastener or other product that it has in inventory or available from suppliers. Although such custom purchases account for only 4 percent of revenues, it is an effective sales tool and builds customer loyalty.

To foster the significant growth of Fastenal, Kierlin has kept the organizational structure very flat. There are only three management levels between branch managers and Fastenal's president, Will Oberton, who is thirty-nine years old. Often new employees work as few as six months before being given their own store to manage. Compensation for sales people after three years is likely to be split between bonus and base salary. There is no stock option, 401(K), or other pension plan available. Kierlin believes that employees should be responsible for their own retirement.

Some on Wall Street have been concerned about Fastenal's exceedingly strong growth rate and expect the fastener market to be saturated soon. Kierlin responds that he thought the smallest population that would justify a Fastenal store's presence was 25,000, but with new product lines that have similar margins to nuts and bolts, Kierlin feels that his firm can enter communities as small as 8,000 people. Accordingly, Fastenal has begun to sell power tools, saws, drills, and sanders under the FastTool brand. Although people like to comparison shop for tools that cost $150 and up, they are less likely to haggle over accessories such as drill bits, saw blades, sandpaper, and safety accessories. The margins for these replacement products rival those of fastener lines. Kierlin also suggests that its oldest stores are its most profitable ones; and, as such, sales continue to grow in already established stores. Therefore, with new lines it appears Fastenal may be able to maintain its high growth level.

Although the new locations and product lines give potential for the new growth, Kierlin is quick to remind analysts that it's not the new stores and products lines that allow for success; it's the way people are treated. Fastenal gives people a chance to make decisions and take risks and provides incentives to work hard. In essence, it's the entrepreneurial culture that Kierlin has created at Fastenal that is its true cause of underlying success.

SOURCES: B. Pappas and R. Boone, Jr., 1997, The best of the best, Forbes magazine online, http://www.forbes.com, November 3; Fastenal Company homepage, http://www.fastenal.com; R. Teitelbaum, 1997, Who is Bob Kierlin—and why is he so successful?, *Fortune*, December 8, 254–258.

Changing Organizational Culture and Business Reengineering

Changing organizational culture is more difficult than maintaining it, but effective strategic leaders recognize when change is needed. Incremental changes to the firm's culture typically are used to implement strategies. However, more significant and sometimes even radical changes to organizational culture are designed to support the selection of strategies that differ from the ones the firm has implemented historically. Regardless of the reasons for change, shaping and reinforcing a new culture requires effective communication and problem solving, along with the selection of the right people (those who have the values managers wish to infuse throughout the organization), effective performance appraisals (establishing goals and measuring individual performance toward those goals that fit with the new core values), and appropriate reward systems (rewarding the desired behaviors that reflect the new core values).[97]

Evidence suggests that cultural changes succeed only when they are supported actively by the firm's CEO, other key top management team members, and middle-level managers.[98] In fact, for large-scale changes, approximately one-third of middle-level managers need to be effective change agents. These change agents ". . . have a nice balance of capabilities: They are technically skilled people who are also very capable in personal relationships. They're an odd combination. On the one hand, they're tough decision-makers who are highly disciplined about performance results. But they also know how to get lots of people energized and aligned in the same direction."[99]

One catalyst for change in organizational culture, particularly for critical changes, is the selection of new top management team members from outside the corporation. Company founder and CEO Michael Dell of Dell Computer, who pioneered the direct marketing of computers to customers, recruited executives from companies such as Motorola, Hewlett-Packard, and Apple Computer to deal with problems the firm encountered in late 1993 and early 1994.[100] Interestingly,

Michael Dell, founder and CEO of Dell Computer, recruited top managers from Motorola, Hewlett-Packard, and Apple in the early 1990s. Market analysts wondered if Dell had the skills to compete in the PC industry, but record sales in 1996 and 1997 proved that he was more than up to the task.

Dell is 10 years younger than the next youngest member of the newly formed top management team.[101]

A key member of Dell's new team is Mort Topfer, a former Motorola executive. As vice chair, Topfer has changed Dell Computer's organizational culture. Prior to his arrival, relatively few control systems were in place. For example, the company lacked a clear understanding of the "relationships between costs and revenues and profits and losses within the different lines of business."[102] Relying on discipline and planning, Topfer designed a number of strategic and financial control systems that affect both the selection and implementation of Dell Computer's strategies. Michael Dell believes that Topfer's contributions have helped his firm change from being relatively undisciplined to one that is more focused on sustained performance and market momentum.[103] Working together effectively, Dell Computer's top management team has collectively accepted the responsibility for running the firm successfully and for initiating required changes to its organizational culture.[104] The market wondered whether Dell really had the skills to guide the company in a highly competitive industry, but huge sales increases in 1996, 1997, and early 1998 show that the direct market approach was larger than analysts anticipated and that Michael Dell was more than up to the task of getting the job done.[105]

Business reengineering is the fundamental rethinking and radical redesign of business processes to achieve dramatic improvements in performance in such areas as cost, quality, service, and speed.[106] It is a technique used by companies to survive and succeed in the new competitive landscape. Business reengineering is of significant benefit to strategic leaders seeking ways to implement chosen strategies more effectively and perhaps change the organization's culture in the process. By focusing on the activities necessary to transform materials into goods or services that are valuable to customers, business reengineering challenges firms to find ways to increase dramatically the effectiveness and efficiency of their organizational culture. For a differentiation business-level strategy (see Chapter 4), reengineering efforts are directed at finding ways to more sharply and meaningfully differentiate the firm's products from competitors' offerings. Similarly, firms implementing a cost leadership business-level strategy (see Chapter 4) use business reengineering to drive their costs lower than competitors'.

The benefits of reengineering are attained through the efforts of dedicated employees. Business reengineering success is maximized when employees believe that (1) every job in the company is essential and important, (2) all employees must create value through their work, (3) constant learning is a vital part of every person's job, (4) teamwork is essential to implementation success, and (5) problems are solved only when teams accept the responsibility for their solution.[107] These beliefs and commitments appear to exist at British Petroleum PLC (BP). In 1992, BP was forced to undergo an intense cost-cutting and restructuring plan. The company discovered that downsizing alone wasn't enough to compete in the oil-related business. For decades, BP had a corporate culture that was very traditional, formal, and predictable. The 1992 crisis was so severe that the reorganization led to making middle managers accountable for their own results and giving them a financial stake in their performance. The underlying management structure was reordered into networks or groups of employees who do similar work but are located in different countries or even different continents. The reorganization facilitated a much more decentralized structure where, although it seemed uncomfortable at first, created a much more loyal workforce. Formal titles have given way to looser roles where initiative, not conformity, is valued.[108]

EMPHASIZING ETHICAL PRACTICES

The effectiveness of strategy implementation processes increases when they are based on ethical practices. Ethical companies encourage and enable people at all organizational levels to exercise ethical judgment. Alternately, if unethical practices evolve in an organization, they become like a contagious disease.[109] To properly influence employee judgment and behavior, ethical practices must shape the firm's decision-making process and be an integral part of an organization's culture. Once accepted, ethical practices serve as a moral filter through which potential courses of action are evaluated.[110]

As discussed in Chapter 10, *managerial opportunism* occurs when managers take actions that are in their own best interests but not in the firm's best interests. In other words, managers take advantage of their positions and therefore make decisions that benefit them to the detriment of the owners (shareholders).[111] An implicit assumption of the agency model described in the discussion of corporate governance in Chapter 10 is that top-level managers may act as opportunistic agents who will capitalize on every chance to maximize personal welfare at the expense of shareholders. Individual opportunism is well documented by Wall Street insider trading scandals and other actions taken by those who financed large leveraged buyouts and acquisitions.[112] Other potential problems that have been documented include questionable hiring practices and a willingness to commit fraud by understating write-offs that reduce corporate returns.[113] It is possible, too, that very high CEO compensation is a sign of opportunism being pursued by those in the upper echelons of management.[114]

Another set of studies sheds light on these issues. Research examining managers' ethical values and beliefs in the mid-1980s and again in the early 1990s showed little change. At both times, managers emphasized utilitarian goals, that is, the achievement of economic gains for the organization's stakeholders. In fact, the earlier survey found that one of the primary reasons managers emphasized ethical practices was to achieve greater profits. Some argue that the managerial and organizational gains are mutually beneficial. In other words, firms that establish and maintain ethical practices are more likely to achieve strategic competitiveness and earn above-average returns. A key reason for this is that a reputation for ethical practices attracts loyal customers.[115]

On the other hand, recent evidence suggests that at least some individuals from different groups—including top-level executives and business students—may be willing to commit either illegal actions (e.g., fraud) or actions that many think are unethical. In one study, researchers found that 47 percent of upper-level executives, 41 percent of controllers, and 76 percent of graduate-level business students expressed a willingness to commit fraud (as measured by a subject's willingness to misrepresent his/her company's financial statements). Moreover, these researchers discovered that 87 percent of the managers made at least one fraudulent decision out of a total of seven situations requiring a decision. Another finding is that the more an individual valued a comfortable life and/or pleasure, and the less he or she valued self-respect, the greater was the probability that a fraudulent decision would be made.[116]

Another study's results appear to have important implications for organizations and those who manage them.[117] The study found that although cheating was observed, there was reluctance to report it. An unwillingness to report wrongdoing calls for the development of comprehensive organizational control systems to assure that individuals' behaviors are consistent with the firm's needs and expectations.

Thus, the findings from these studies seem to support the need for firms to employ ethical strategic leaders—ones who include ethical practices as part of their long-term vision for the firm, who desire to do the right thing, and for whom honesty, trust, and integrity are important.[118] Strategic leaders who consistently display these qualities inspire employees as they work with others to develop and support an organizational culture in which ethical practices are the expected behavioral norms.

As our discussion suggests, strategic leaders are challenged to take actions that increase the probability that an ethical culture will exist in their organization. When these efforts are successful, the practices associated with an ethical culture become institutionalized in the firm; that is, they become the set of behavioral commitments and actions accepted by most of the firm's employees and other stakeholders with whom employees interact. Actions that strategic leaders can take to develop an ethical organizational culture include (1) establishing and communicating specific goals to describe the firm's ethical standards (e.g., developing and disseminating a code of conduct), (2) continuously revising and updating the code of conduct, based on inputs from people throughout the firm and from other stakeholders (e.g., customers and suppliers), (3) disseminating the code of conduct to all stakeholders to inform them of the firm's ethical standards and practices, (4) developing and implementing methods and procedures to use in achieving the firm's ethical standards (e.g., use of internal auditing practices that are consistent with the standards), (5) creating and using explicit reward systems that recognize acts of courage (e.g., rewarding those who use proper channels and procedures to report observed wrongdoings), and (6) creating a work environment in which all people are treated with dignity.[119] The effectiveness of these actions increases when they are undertaken simultaneously since the six major actions are mutually supportive. A failure to develop and engage in all six actions reduces the likelihood that the firm can establish an ethical culture. Moreover, when strategic leaders engage successfully in these actions they serve as moral role models for the firm's employees and other stakeholders.

When ethical practices are not firmly established, trouble can emerge. For example, Columbia/HCA Health Care Corporation has been accused of wrongdoing and is under federal investigation. Although the top officers have not been charged with any crime, a number of hospital managers within the corporation have been. The main problem has been a culture that encourages managers to be overly aggressive in regard to performance, stimulates too much growth, and a weak board of directors that did not provide appropriate oversight. The system created incentives for hospital administrators to charge too much on Medicare and engage in other improper billing for services.[120] To overcome these difficulties, Columbia/HCA has appointed special ethics and compliance officers at each of its 338 hospitals. This move was spearheaded by its new ethics vice president, Alan Yuspeh, in an effort to extricate Columbia from the massive federal Medicare-fraud investigation. In most cases, Columbia is hiring external people to fill these slots. In addition, Columbia's board is forming a new committee of compliance and ethical issues headed by Judith A. Karam. This case highlights the importance of establishing ethical practices and control systems that foster strong ethics among managers and employees.[121]

As the Columbia/HCA example illustrates, organizational control systems can help to foster ethical practices and other areas important for the exercise of strategic leadership.

ESTABLISHING BALANCED ORGANIZATIONAL CONTROLS

Organizational controls have long been viewed as an important part of strategy implementation processes. Controls are necessary to help ensure that firms achieve their desired outcomes of strategic competitiveness and above-average returns.[122] Defined as the "... formal, information-based ... procedures used by managers to maintain or alter patterns in organizational activities," controls help strategic leaders build credibility, demonstrate the value of strategies to the firm's stakeholders, and promote and support strategic change.[123] Most critically, controls provide the parameters within which strategies are to be implemented as well as corrective actions to be taken when implementation-related adjustments are required. In this chapter, we focus on two organizational controls—strategic and financial—that were introduced in Chapter 11. Our discussion of organizational controls in this chapter emphasizes strategic and financial controls because strategic leaders are responsible for their development and effective use.

Although critical to the firm's success, evidence suggests that organizational controls are imperfect. Consider the example of Columbia/HCA as discussed above where the wrong incentive structure has brought the largest hospital operator to its knees over a broad federal fraud investigation. Control failures such as this have a negative effect on the firm's reputation and divert managerial attention from actions necessary to use the strategic management process effectively.

As explained in Chapter 11, financial controls are often emphasized in large corporations. Financial controls focus on short-term financial outcomes. In contrast, strategic control focuses on the *content* of strategic actions, rather than their *outcomes.* Some strategic actions can be correct but poor financial outcomes may still result because of external conditions such as recessionary economic problems, unexpected domestic or foreign government actions, or natural disasters.[124] Therefore, an emphasis on financial control often produces more short-term and risk-averse managerial decisions because financial outcomes may be due to events beyond managers' direct control. Alternatively, strategic controls encourage lower level managers to make decisions that incorporate moderate and acceptable levels of risk because outcomes are shared between the business-level executives making strategic proposals and the corporate-level executives evaluating them.

Successful strategic leaders balance strategic control and financial control (they do not eliminate financial control) with the intent of achieving more positive long-term returns.[125] In fact, most corporate restructuring is designed to refocus the firm on its core businesses, thereby allowing top-level executives to reestablish strategic control of their separate business units.[126]

Effective use of strategic control by top-level managers is integrated frequently with appropriate autonomy for the various subunits so they can gain a competitive advantage in their respective markets. Strategic control can be used to promote the sharing of both tangible and intangible resources among interdependent businesses within a firm's portfolio. In addition, the autonomy provided allows the flexibility necessary to take advantage of specific marketplace opportunities. As a result, strategic leadership promotes the simultaneous use of strategic control and autonomy.[127]

The Strategic Focus on diversified business groups suggests how important it is that diversified firms maintain a balanced control orientation. Because large diversified business groups have not maintained this balance, many throughout the world are having to restructure their operations. For instance, those in South Korea have had significant problems as the currency crisis in Southeast Asia has revealed problems in their diversification strategies.

STRATEGIC FOCUS

Balancing Controls in Large, Diversified Business Groups

Large, diversified business groups are diversified across a wide range of businesses. They often have practical financial interlocks among their holdings, and, in many cases, family ownership and control. These diversified business groups dominate private-sector industrial and service activities in many of the world economies. Even in the United States, family ownership is quite prevalent. It is estimated that over a third of the *Fortune* 500 companies are family-owned or dominated. As for the world economy as a whole, the number is certainly over 50 percent. Many diversified business groups (unrelated diversified firms or conglomerates) in the United States have been refocusing because of the market for corporate control and the ability of large investors to buy diffuse equity holdings and keep firms from overdiversifying into too many product markets.

In some developing markets, diversified business groups have provided advantages that allow them to exist more prominently throughout the world. Usually in these emerging markets, equity markets are illiquid and most financing is provided by banks, some of which are nationalized. Also, large business groups provide a significant training ground for managers in economies with few business schools where talent is usually developed. Cross-holding among business groups also facilitates contract enforcement where contract laws are often unpredictable. Thus, many economies have diversified business groups such as the chaebols in South Korea and the large diversified business groups in India and throughout Southeast Asia. Furthermore, many developed economies throughout Europe such as Italy, France, and Sweden have large diversified business groups.

Strategic leaders are seeing that the control systems they have implemented to manage large diversified business groups are becoming critical as economies become more liberal (regarding trade policies) and experience currency shocks such as those in Southeast Asia. In South Korea, many strategic leaders of the chaebols have been reorganizing to refocus on core businesses and also maintain a better balance between strategic and financial controls. For example, the Hyundai Group has indicated during the financial crises that it would scrap plans to build a $5 billion steel mill and would relinquish management of its money-losing newspaper operation. It also indicated that it would sell or merge unprofitable affiliates that can operate independently. Hyundai has 58 affiliates and sales of over $50 billion. It did not specify which of its 58 affiliates would be affected by the restructuring. Likewise, LG Group said it would cut 90 business lines worth $1.48 billion. Samsung also suggested that it will restructure as well. As with Hyundai and LG, Samsung promised that by 1999, it would adopt consolidated financial statements and eliminate cross-guarantees between affiliates for loans. This measure would provide greater transparency for the group's accounting procedures. Samsung plans to focus on three or four core industries but again, like the others, declined to name them. Because the chaebols are largely family-owned, it has been difficult to understand their operation, governance, and control procedures.

Ssangyong's restructuring has been defying the usual convention of diversified business groups in South Korea. Although it has one of the largest chaebols, Kim Suk Joon has taken his company through a long but painful restructuring that included selling its prized automobile company to a rival. Many chaebols have been too proud to scale back and often delay unveiling restructuring plans until days before declaring default. Six of the largest chaebols sought court protection from creditors in 1997. Ssangyong, in 1997, sold off its profitable paper company to Procter & Gamble for $46.7 million and sold a California cement company, Riverside Cement, to Texas Industries. Although Ssangyong's restructuring gives it an advantage because it readily undertook the restructuring process relative to other chaebols, the lesson is still the same; they have all overexpanded and overdiversified because their strategic leaders did not have adequate strategic controls in place.

Ahlstrom Corporation, a large Finnish conglomerate, restructured its governance and control systems as it confronted more competitive markets. As with many Asian firms, the Finnish conglomerate was controlled mostly by over 200 family owners. To manage the operation professionally and yet include family involvement, the Ahlstrom owners formed a family assembly that allowed them to have formal communications between family members and the board and the CEO. Furthermore, family assemblies often served as an informal sounding board for the CEO and board of directors. For instance, the family council drafted a document—the Ahlstrom Family Values and Policies—that was extensively discussed and serves as a constitution for the corporation. Ahlstrom ultimately reorganized its diversified holdings into more focused business groups after downscoping by selling off some holdings. Once the holdings were sold off and organized into four groups, the family restructured the operation so that each business group has its own board. There is an industrial holding company above the four business groups, and above that is a main board. This structure has provided much better corporate governance that is closer to the operations and allows each business group with its own subsidiaries and divisions to run more efficiently with better balance between financial controls and strategic controls, as well as better governance of management. Therefore, from a strategic leadership point of view, this structure allows for more family members to be involved and to ensure that the company is running according to the family constitution.

Many of the business groups in Southeast Asia are run by family-owned companies of expatriate Chinese. Traditionally, these firms have been in consumer industries that are nontechnical, such as shipping, commodity trading, hotel, real estate and financial services, and other light industries. As these firms seek to move into high-tech industries, such as chemicals and electronics, they have had to move away from the family-managed business concept to more professional managerial techniques. This adjustment is partly due to the change in capital markets where more transparency is required and where contracting law is becoming more prominent. Business operations, before these economic shocks, were run by their strategic leaders, mostly based on relationships between family members and friends. They are now being forced to implement better and more professional control systems as have other diversified business groups throughout the world.

Diversified business operations have also been found in India. Many Indian groups have also been restructuring, as have those in Southeast Asia such as the chaebols in Korea and in Western Europe such as the Ahlstrom Group. Their strategic leaders are seeking to develop a better balance between financial controls and strategic controls as their economies have become more liberalized and open to foreign competition.

SOURCES: P. Ghemawat and T. Khanna, 1998, The nature of diversified business groups: A research design and two case studies, *Journal of Industrial Economics*, in press; J. Magretta, 1998, Governing the family-owned enterprise: An interview with Finland's Krister Ahlstrom, *Harvard Business Review* 76, no. 1: 112–123; M. Cho, 1998, Samsung to sell units, focus on core industries, *Wall Street Journal*, January 22, A15; M. Schuman, 1998, Samsung weighs retreat on auto output, *Wall Street Journal*, January 21, A7; M. Cho, 1998, Hyundai, LG Groups to trim operations, *Wall Street Journal*, January 20, A14; M. Schuman, 1997, Seoul survivor: A giant resists the crisis, *Wall Street Journal*, December 24, A8; T. Khanna and K. Palepu, 1997, Why focused strategies may be wrong for emerging markets, *Harvard Business Review* 75, no. 4: 41–50; M. Weidenbaum, 1996, The Chinese family business enterprise, *California Management Review* 38, no. 4: 141–156.

As our discussion suggests, organizational controls establish an integrated set of analyses and actions that reinforce one another. Through effective use of strategic controls, strategic leaders increase the probability that their firms will gain the benefits of carefully formulated strategies but not at the expense of the financial control that is a critical part of the strategy implementation process. Effective organizational controls provide an underlying logic for strategic leadership, focus attention on critical strategic issues, support a competitive culture, and provide a forum that builds commitment to strategic intent.

SUMMARY

- Effective strategic leadership is required to use the strategic management process successfully, including the strategic actions associated with the implementation of strategies. Strategic leadership entails the ability to anticipate, envision, maintain flexibility, and empower others to create strategic change.
- Top-level managers are an important resource requirement for firms to develop and exploit competitive advantages. In addition, strategic leaders can be a source of competitive advantage. Top executives exercise discretion in making critical strategic decisions.
- The top management team is composed of key managers who formulate and implement strategies. Generally, they are officers of the corporation and/or members of the board of directors.
- There is a relationship among top management team characteristics, firm strategy, and performance. For example, a top management team that has significant marketing and R&D knowledge often enhances the firm's effectiveness as the team steers the firm toward implementation of growth strategies. Overall, most top management teams are more effective when they have diverse and heterogeneous skills.
- When boards of directors are involved in shaping strategic direction, firms generally improve their strategic competitiveness. Alternatively, boards may be less involved in strategic decisions about strategy formulation and strategy implementation when CEOs have more power. CEOs obtain power when they appoint people to the board and when they simultaneously serve the firm as its CEO and board chair.
- Strategic leaders are selected from either the internal or the external managerial labor market. Because of their effect on firm performance, the selection of strategic leaders from these markets has implications for a firm's effectiveness. Valid reasons exist to use both labor markets when selecting strategic leaders and managers with the potential to become strategic leaders. The internal market is used in the majority of cases to select the firm's CEO. Outsiders are selected to initiate needed change.
- Effective strategic leadership has six components: determining the firm's strategic direction, exploiting and maintaining core competencies, developing human capital, sustaining an effective organizational culture, emphasizing ethical practices, and establishing balanced organizational controls.
- Often requiring a significant amount of thinking and time to form, determining strategic direction refers to the development of a long-term vision of the firm's strategic intent. A charismatic leader can help achieve strategic intent.
- Strategic leaders must verify that their firm exploits its core competencies, which are used to create and deliver products that create value for customers, to implement strategies. In related diversified and large firms, in particular, core competencies are exploited effectively when they are shared across units and products.
- A critical element of strategic leadership and effective strategy implementation processes is the ability to develop the firm's human capital. Effective strategic leaders and firms view human capital as a resource to be maximized rather than as a cost to be minimized. Resulting from this perspective is the use of programs intended to train current and future strategic leaders so they will have the skills needed to nurture and develop the rest of the firm's human capital.
- Shaping the firm's culture is a central task of effective strategic leadership. In the new compet-

itive landscape, an appropriate organizational culture encourages the development of an entrepreneurial orientation among employees and an ability to change the culture as necessary. Reengineering can facilitate this process.

- In ethical organizations, employees are encouraged to exercise ethical judgment and to display only ethical practices. Ethical practices can be promoted through several actions, including those of setting specific goals to describe the firm's ethical standards, using a code of conduct, rewarding ethical behaviors, and creating a work environment in which all people are treated with dignity.
- The final component of effective strategic leadership is the development and use of effective organizational controls. It is through organizational controls that strategic leaders provide the direction the firm requires to flexibly, yet appropriately, use its core competencies in the pursuit of marketplace opportunities. Best results are obtained when there is a balance between strategic and financial controls.

REVIEW QUESTIONS

1. What is strategic leadership? In what ways are top-level managers considered important resources for an organization?
2. What is a top management team and how does it affect a firm's performance and its abilities to innovate and make appropriate strategic changes?
3. What are the differences between the internal and external managerial labor markets? What are the effects of each labor market type on the formulation and implementation of firm strategy?
4. How does strategic leadership affect determination of the firm's strategic direction?
5. Why is it important for strategic leaders to make certain that their firm exploits its core competencies in the pursuit of strategic competitiveness and above-average returns?
6. What is the importance of human capital and its development for strategic competitiveness?
7. What is organizational culture? What must strategic leaders do to sustain an effective organizational culture?
8. As a strategic leader, what actions could you take to establish and emphasize ethical practices in your firm?
9. What are organizational controls? Why are strategic controls and financial controls, two types of organizational controls, an important part of the strategic management process?

APPLICATION DISCUSSION QUESTIONS

1. Choose a CEO of a prominent firm you believe exemplifies the positive aspects of strategic leadership. What actions does this CEO take that demonstrate effective strategic leadership? What are the effects of these actions on the firm's performance?
2. Select a CEO of a prominent firm you believe does not exemplify the positive aspects of strategic leadership. What actions does this CEO take that are inconsistent with effective strategic leadership? How have these ineffective actions affected the firm's performance?
3. What are managerial resources? What is the relationship between managerial resources and a firm's strategic competitiveness?
4. By examining popular press articles, select an organization that has recently gone through a significant strategic change. While reading these articles, collect as much information as you can about the organization's top management team. Does your analysis suggest that there is a relationship between the top management team's characteristics and the type of change the organization experienced? If so, what is the nature and outcome of that relationship?
5. Through a reading of popular press articles, identify two new CEOs, one chosen from the internal managerial labor market and one from the external labor market. Based on your reading, why do you think these individuals were chosen? What do they bring to the job and what strategy do you think they will implement in the future?
6. In light of your reading of this chapter and popular press accounts, select a CEO you feel has exhibited vision. Has the CEO's vision been realized? If so, what have the effects been of its realization? If it has not been realized, why not?
7. Identify a firm in which you believe strategic leaders have emphasized and developed human capital. What

do you believe are the effects of this emphasis and development on the firm's performance?

8. Select an organization you think has a unique organizational culture. What characteristics of that culture make it unique? Has the culture had a significant effect on the organization's performance? If so, what is that effect?
9. Why is the strategic control exercised by a firm's strategic leaders important for long-term competitiveness? How do strategic controls differ from financial controls?

ETHICS QUESTIONS

1. As discussed in this chapter, effective strategic leadership occasionally requires managers to make difficult decisions. In your opinion, is it ethical for managers to make these types of decisions without being willing to receive feedback from employees about the effects of those decisions? Be prepared to justify your response.
2. As an employee with less than one year of experience in a firm, what actions would you pursue if you encountered unethical practices by a strategic leader?
3. In your opinion, are firms obligated ethically to promote from within, rather than relying on the external labor market to select strategic leaders? What reasoning supports your position?
4. What are the ethical issues involved, if any, with the firm's ability to develop and exploit a core competence in the manufacture of goods that may be harmful to consumers (e.g., cigarettes)? Be prepared to discuss the reasons for your response.
5. As a strategic leader, would you feel ethically responsible to develop your firm's human capital? Why or why not? Do you believe your position is consistent with the majority or minority of today's strategic leaders?
6. Select an organization, social group, or volunteer agency in which you hold membership that you believe has an ethical culture. What factors caused this culture to be ethical? Are there events that could occur that would cause this culture to become less ethical? If so, what are they?

INTERNET EXERCISE

Go to *Fortune* magazine's Ten Most Admired Companies in America at:

http://www.pathfinder.com/fortune/mostadmired/topone.html

Each year *Fortune* magazine administers a survey to top executives, outside directors, and securities analysts to determine the most admired companies in America. The results of this survey are closely watched and have been the subject of countless news articles and board-room conversations. The above Web site lists the top 10 companies from the 1997 survey. Select three of these companies and research the attributes of their CEOs using the *Fortune* Web site as a starting point. It what ways do these CEOs exemplify strategic leadership? Do the CEOs of these "most admired companies" have attributes in common? Explain your answer.

Strategic Surfing

CEO Express is a Web site designed specifically for busy executives. The site contains a menu of links to sites that appeal to CEOs and other business leaders. A similar site is referred to as The CEO Homepage. This site contains links to on-line versions of business publications valuable to CEOs and other top managers.

http://www.ceoexpress.com
http://ceohomepage.com/bizpubs.html

NOTES

1. K. R. Thompson, W. A. Hochwarter, and N. J. Mathys, 1997, Stretch targets: What makes them effective? *Academy of Management Executive* XI, no. 3: 48–59.
2. R. D. Ireland and M. A. Hitt, 1998, Achieving and maintaining strategic competitiveness in the 21st century: The role of strategic leadership, *Academy of Management Executive* XII, in press; D. Lei, M. A. Hitt, and R. Bettis, 1996, Dynamic core competencies through meta-learning and strategic context, *Journal of Management* 22: 547–567.
3. E. Ramstad, 1998, Compaq CEO takes tricky curves fast, *Wall Street Journal*, January 5, B4.
4. G. McWilliams, I. Sager, P. C. Judge, and P. Burrows, 1998,

Power play: How the Compaq-Digital deal will reshape the entire world of computers, *Business Week*, February 9, 90–97.
5. Special Report: The 25 top managers of the year, 1998, *Business Week*, January 12, 54–68.
6. H. Gardner, 1995, *Leading Minds: An Anatomy of Leadership* (New York: Basic Books); S. Sherman, 1995, How tomorrow's best leaders are learning their stuff, *Fortune*, November 27, 90–102.
7. J. B. Quinn, P. Anderson, and S. Finkelstein, 1996, Managing professional intellect: Making the most of the best, *Harvard Business Review* 74, no. 2: 71–80.
8. M. Loeb, 1994, Where leaders come from, *Fortune*, September 19, 241–242.
9. M. F. R. Kets de Vries, 1995, *Life and Death in the Executive Fast Lane* (San Francisco: Jossey-Bass).
10. G. Hamel and C. K. Prahalad, 1993, Strategy as stretch and leverage, *Harvard Business Review* 71, no. 2: 75–84.
11. Sherman, How tomorrow's best, 99; R. Calori, G. Johnson, and P. Sarnin, 1994, CEOs' cognitive maps and the scope of the organization, *Strategic Management Journal* 15: 437–457.
12. Loeb, Where leaders come from, 241; N. Nohria and J. D. Berkley, 1994, Whatever happened to the take-charge manager?, *Harvard Business Review* 72, no. 1: 128–137.
13. M. Hammer and S. A. Stanton, 1997, The power of reflection, *Fortune*, November 24, 291–296.
14. S. Finkelstein and D. C. Hambrick, 1996, *Strategic Leadership: Top Executives and Their Effects on Organizations* (St. Paul, Minn.: West Publishing Company), 2.
15. J. A. Byrne and J. Reingold, 1997, Wanted: A few good CEOs, *Business Week*, August 11, 64–70.
16. Sherman, How tomorrow's best, 102.
17. H. P. Gunz and R. M. Jalland, 1996, Managerial careers and business strategy, *Academy of Management Review* 21: 718–756.
18. C. M. Christensen, 1997, Making strategy: Learning by doing, *Harvard Business Review* 75, no. 6: 141–156; M. A. Hitt, B. W. Keats, H. E. Harback, and R. D. Nixon, 1994, Rightsizing: Building and maintaining strategic leadership and long-term competitiveness, *Organizational Dynamics* 23: 18–32; R. L. Priem and D. A. Harrison, 1994, Exploring strategic judgment: Methods for testing the assumptions of prescriptive contingency theories, *Strategic Management Journal* 15: 311–324.
19. M. J. Waller, G. P. Huber, and W. H. Glick, 1995, Functional background as a determinant of executives' selective perception, *Academy of Management Journal* 38: 943–974; N. Rajagopalan, A. M. Rasheed, and D. K. Datta, 1993, Strategic decision processes: Critical review and future directions, *Journal of Management* 19: 349–384.
20. Finkelstein and Hambrick, *Strategic Leadership*, 26–34; D. C. Hambrick and E. Abrahamson, 1995, Assessing managerial discretion across industries: A multimethod approach, *Academy of Management Journal* 38: 1427–1441; D. C. Hambrick and S. Finkelstein, 1987, Managerial discretion: A bridge between polar views of organizational outcomes, in B. Staw and L. L. Cummings (eds.), *Research in Organizational Behavior* (Greenwich, CT: JAI Press), 369–406.
21. R. C. Mayer, J. H. Davis, and F. D. Schoorman, 1995, An integrative model of organizational trust, *Academy of Management Review* 20: 709–734.
22. N. Rajagopalan and D. K. Datta, 1996, CEO characteristics: Does industry matter?, *Academy of Management Journal* 39: 197–215.
23. L. M. Fisher, 1997, Novell selects Internet guru to lead company, *The New York Times* on the Web, http://www.nytimes.com, March 19.
24. A. C. Amason, 1996, Distinguishing the effects of functional and dysfunctional conflict on strategic decision making: Resolving a paradox for top management teams, *Academy of Management Journal* 39: 123–148; Priem and Harrison, Exploring strategic judgment, 311.
25. C. M. Farkas and P. De Backer, 1996, There are only five ways to lead, *Fortune*, January 15, 109–112.
26. R. E. Stross, 1997, Mr. Gates builds his brain trust, *Fortune*, December 8, 84–98.
27. T. A. Stewart, 1997, Why dumb things happen to smart companies, *Fortune*, June 23, 159–160.
28. H. A. Krishnan, 1997, Diversification and top management team complementarity: Is performance improved by merging similar or dissimilar teams?, *Strategic Management Journal* 18: 361–374; J. G. Michel and D. C. Hambrick, 1992, Diversification posture and top management team characteristics, *Academy of Management Journal* 35: 9–37.
29. A. L. Iaquito and J. W. Fredrickson, 1997, Top management team agreement about the strategic decision process: A test of some of its determinants and consequences, *Strategic Management Journal* 18: 63–75; K. G. Smith, D. A. Smith, J. D. Olian, H. P. Sims, Jr., D. P. O'Bannon, and J. A. Scully, 1994, Top management team demography and process: The role of social integration and communication, *Administrative Science Quarterly* 39: 412–438.
30. Amason, Distinguishing the effects, 127.
31. D. C. Hambrick, T. S. Cho, and M. J. Chen, 1996, The influence of top management team heterogeneity on firms' competitive moves, *Administrative Science Quarterly* 41: 659–684.
32. J. J. Keller, 1997, AT&T's board faces many twists and turns in search for new CEO, *Wall Street Journal*, October 13, A1, A6.
33. Finkelstein and Hambrick, *Strategic Leadership*, 148.
34. C. C. Miller, L. M. Burke, and W. H. Glick, 1998, Cognitive diversity among upper-echelon executives: Implications for strategic decision processes, *Strategic Management Journal* 19: 39–58.
35. D. K. Datta and J. P. Guthrie, 1994, Executive succession: Organizational antecedents of CEO characteristics, *Strategic Management Journal* 15: 569–577; M. A. Hitt and R. D. Ireland, 1986, Relationships among corporate-level distinctive competencies, diversification strategy, corporate structure, and performance, *Journal of Management Studies* 23: 401–416; M. A. Hitt and R. D. Ireland, 1985, Corporate distinctive competence, strategy, industry, and performance, *Strategic Management Journal* 6: 273–293.
36. W. Boeker, 1997, Strategic change: The influence of managerial characteristics and organizational growth, *Academy of Management Journal* 40: 152–170; W. Boeker, 1997, Executive migration and strategic change: The effect of top manager movement on product-market entry, *Administrative Science Quarterly* 42: 213–236.
37. M. E. Wiersema and K. Bantel, 1992, Top management team demography and corporate strategic change, *Academy of Management Journal* 35: 91–121; K. Bantel and S. Jackson,

1989, Top management and innovations in banking: Does the composition of the top team make a difference? *Strategic Management Journal* 10: 107–124.

38. I. Sager and A. Cortese, 1995, At IBM, the great shrink-down may be over, *Business Week*, September 25, 58.
39. R. Narisetti, 1997, IBM's Gerstner to stay five more years, *Wall Street Journal*, November 27, A3, A14.
40. W. Q. Judge, Jr. and C. P. Zeithaml, 1992, Institutional and strategic choice perspectives on board involvement in the strategic decision process, *Academy of Management Journal* 35: 766–794; J. A. Pearce II and S. A. Zahra, 1991, The relative power of CEOs and boards of directors: Associations with corporate performance, *Strategic Management Journal* 12: 135–154.
41. J. D. Westphal and E. J. Zajac, 1995, Who shall govern? CEO/board power, demographic similarity, and new director selection, *Administrative Science Quarterly* 40: 60.
42. Ibid., 66; E. J. Zajac and J. D. Westphal, 1995, Accounting for the explanations of CEO compensation: Substance and symbolism, *Administrative Science Quarterly* 40: 283–308.
43. B. K. Boyd, 1995, CEO duality and firm performance: A contingency model, *Strategic Management Journal* 16: 301.
44. C. M. Daily and D. R. Dalton, 1995, CEO and director turnover in failing firms: An illusion of change? *Strategic Management Journal* 16: 393–400.
45. R. Albanese, M. T. Dacin, and I. C. Harris, 1997, Agents as stewards, *Academy of Management Review* 22: 609–611; J. H. Davis, F. D. Schoorman, and L. Donaldson, 1997, Toward a stewardship theory of management, *Academy of Management Review* 22: 20–47.
46. B. R. Baliga and R. C. Moyer, 1996, CEO duality and firm performance: What's the fuss? *Strategic Management Journal* 17: 41–53.
47. J. D. Westphal and E. J. Zajac, 1997, Defections from the inner circle: Social exchange, reciprocity and diffusion of board independence in U.S. corporations, *Administrative Science Quarterly* 161–183; A. K. Buchholtz and B. A. Ribbens, 1994, Role of chief executive officers in takeover resistance: Effects of CEO incentives and individual characteristics, *Academy of Management Journal* 37: 554–579.
48. Rajagopalan and Datta, CEO characteristics, 201.
49. R. A. Johnson, R. E. Hoskisson, and M. A. Hitt, 1993, Board involvement in restructuring: The effect of board versus managerial controls and characteristics, *Strategic Management Journal* 14 (Special Summer Issue): 33–50.
50. B. K. Boyd, 1995, CEO duality and firm performance: A contingency model, *Strategic Management Journal* 16: 301–312.
51. T. A. Stewart, 1998, Why leadership matters, *Fortune*, March 2, 71–82.
52. Sherman, How tomorrow's best, 92.
53. D. Woodruff and M. Maremont, 1995, GM learns to love an outsider, *Business Week*, July 3, 32.
54. Datta and Guthrie, Executive succession, 570.
55. Finkelstein and Hambrick, *Strategic Leadership*, 180–181.
56. D. Miller, 1991, Stale in the saddle: CEO tenure and the match between organization and environment, *Management Science* 37: 34–52.
57. S. L. Hwang, 1995, RJR's CEO Harper quits his position, *Wall Street Journal*, December 6, A3, A4.
58. S. L. Hwang, 1998, At Nabisco, the new chief walks into a hot kitchen, *Wall Street Journal*, February 5, B1, B2.
59. J. E. Ettlie, 1996, Review of *The Perpetual Enterprise Machine: Seven Keys to Corporate Renewal through Successful Product and Process Development*, E. Bowman (ed.), (New York: Oxford University Press), appearing in *Academy of Management Review* 21: 294–298; Hitt et al., Rightsizing, 20.
60. J. C. Collins and J. I. Porras, 1996, Building your company's vision, *Harvard Business Review* 74, no. 5: 65–77.
61. C. M. Falbe, M. P. Kriger, and P. Miesing, 1995, Structure and meaning of organizational vision, *Academy of Management Journal* 39: 740–769.
62. B. Wysocki, Jr., 1995, As firms downsize, business economists find jobs dwindling, *Wall Street Journal*, October 9, Al, A8.
63. W. L. Gardner and B. J. Avolio, 1998, The charismatic relationship: A dramaturgical perspective, *Academy of Management Review* 23: 32–58.
64. Finkelstein and Hambrick, 1996, *Strategic Leadership*, 69–72; P. Sellers, 1996, What exactly is charisma? *Fortune*, January 15, 68–75.
65. T. Smart, 1996, Jack Welch's encore, *Business Week*, October 28, 154–160.
66. J. A. Byrne, 1997, The CEO and the board, *Business Week*, September 15, 107–116.
67. P. R. Nayyar and K. A. Bantel, 1994, Competitive agility: A source of competitive advantage based on speed and variety, in P. Shrivastava, A. Huff, and J. Dutton (eds.), *Advances in Strategic Management* 10A, (Greenwich, CT: JAI Press), 193–222.
68. R. F. Maruca, 1994, The right way to go global: An interview with Whirlpool CEO David Whitwam, *Harvard Business Review* 72, no. 2: 136.
69. Lei, Hitt, and Bettis, Dynamic core competencies.
70. R. N. Askenas, L. J. DeMonaco, and S. C. Francis, 1998, Making the deal real: How GE Capital integrates acquisitions, *Harvard Business Review* 76, no. 1: 165–178.
71. B. Nussbaum, 1988, Needed: Human capital, *Business Week*, September 19, 100–102.
72. S. A. Snell and M. A. Youndt, 1995, Human resource management and firm performance: Testing a contingency model of executive controls, *Journal of Management* 21: 711–737.
73. D. Ulrich, 1998, A new mandate for human resources, *Harvard Business Review* 76, no. 1: 124–134.
74. Snell and Youndt, Human resource, 711; K. Chilton, 1994, *The Global Challenge of American Manufacturers* (St. Louis, MO: Washington University, Center for the Study of American Business); J. Pfeffer, 1994, *Competitive Advantage Through People* (Cambridge, MA: Harvard Business School Press), 4.
75. H. W. Jenkins, Jr., 1996, What price job security?, *Wall Street Journal*, March 26, Al9.
76. J. S. Lublin, 1996, An overseas stint can be a ticket to the top, *Wall Street Journal*, January 29, Bl, B2.
77. M. G. Harvey and M. R. Buckley, 1997, Managing inpatriates: Building a global core competency, *Journal of World Business* 32, no. 1: 35–52.
78. R. Frank, 1996, Enrico to lead new generation at top of Pepsi, *Wall Street Journal*, February 23, B2, B5.

79. H. Rudnitsky, 1996, One hundred sixty companies for the price of one, *Forbes*, February 26, 56–62.
80. L. Grant, 1995, GE: The envelope, please, *Fortune*, June 26, 89–90.
81. B. Morris, 1997, If women ran the world it would look a lot like Avon, *Fortune*, July 21, 74–79.
82. J. Nocera, 1996, Living with layoffs, *Fortune*, April 1, 69–71.
83. Chrysler CEO calls downsizing the price of competitiveness, 1996, *Dallas Morning News*, March 19, D8.
84. F. R. Bleakley, 1997, New round of layoffs may be beginning, *Wall Street Journal*, November 13, A2.
85. M. A. Hitt, R. E. Hoskisson, J. S. Harrison, and B. Summers, 1994, Human capital and strategic competitiveness in the 1990s, *Journal of Management Development* 13, no. 1: 35–46; C. R. Greer and T. C. Ireland, 1992, Organizational and financial correlates of a contrarian human resource investment strategy, *Academy of Management Journal* 35: 956–984.
86. C. L. Martin, C. K. Parsons, and N. Bennett, 1995, The influence of employee involvement program membership during downsizing: Attitudes toward the employer and the union, *Journal of Management* 21: 879–890.
87. C. M. Fiol, 1991, Managing culture as a competitive resource: An identity-based view of sustainable competitive advantage, *Journal of Management* 17: 191–211; J. B. Barney, 1986, Organizational culture: Can it be a source of sustained competitive advantage?, *Academy of Management Review* 11: 656–665.
88. S. Ghoshal and C. A. Bartlett, 1994, Linking organizational context and managerial action: The dimensions of quality of management, *Strategic Management Journal* 15: 91–112.
89. Sherman, How tomorrow's best, 102.
90. How can big companies keep the entrepreneurial spirit alive?, 1995, *Harvard Business Review* 73, no. 6: 183–192; S. G. Scott and R. A. Bruce, 1994, Determinants of innovative behavior: A path model of individual innovation in the workplace, *Academy of Management Journal* 37: 580–607.
91. Thermo Electron home page, 1998, http://www.thermo.com, company history.
92. C. A. Bartlett and S. Goshal, 1997, The myth of the generic manager: New personal competencies for new managerial roles, *California Management Review* 40, no. 1: 92–116.
93. J. Webber, W. Zellner, and G. Smith, 1998, Loud noises at Bombardier, *Business Week*, January 26, 94–95.
94. G. T. Lumpkin and G. G. Dess, 1996, Clarifying the entrepreneurial orientation construct and linking it to performance, *Academy of Management Review* 21: 135–172.
95. Ibid., 142.
96. Ibid., 137.
97. Ireland and Hitt, Achieving and maintaining strategic competitiveness in the 21st century.
98. J. E. Dutton, S. J. Ashford, R. M. O'Neill, E. Hayes, and E. E. Wierba, 1997, Reading the wind: How middle managers assess the context for selling issues to top managers, *Strategic Management Journal* 18: 407–425.
99. S. Sherman, 1995, Wanted: Company change agents, *Fortune*, December 11, 197–198.
100. A. E. Serwer, 1997, Michael Dell turns the PC world inside out, *Fortune*, September 8, 76–86.
101. R. Jacob, 1995, The resurrection of Michael Dell, *Fortune*, September 18, 117.
102. Ibid., 118.
103. A. Goldstein, 1995, Dell powers up, *Dallas Morning News*, September 19, D1, D4.
104. T. M. Hour and J. C. Carter, 1995, Getting it done: New roles for senior executives, *Harvard Business Review* 73, no. 6: 133–145.
105. Serwer, Michael Dell turns the PC world inside out, 84.
106. M. Hammer and J. Champy, 1995, *Reengineering the Corporation* (New York: HarperCollins).
107. Ibid.
108. S. Murray, 1997, BP alters atmosphere amid turnaround, *Wall Street Journal*, September 17, A19.
109. D. J. Brass, K. D. Butterfield, and B. C. Skaggs, 1998, Relationships and unethical behavior: A social network perspective, *Academy of Management Review* 23: 14–31.
110. J. M. Lozano, 1996, Ethics and management: A controversial issue, *Journal of Business Ethics* 15: 227–236; J. Mitchell, 1996, Professor leads attack on big business, *Dallas Morning News*, March 17, H6; J. Milton-Smith, 1995, Ethics as excellence: A strategic management perspective, *Journal of Business Ethics* 14: 683–693.
111. C. W. L. Hill, 1990, Cooperation, opportunism, and the invisible hand: Implications for transaction cost theory, *Academy of Management Review* 15: 500–513.
112. M. Zey, 1993, *Banking on Fraud* (New York: Aldine De Gruyter).
113. D. Blalock, 1996, Study shows many execs are quick to write off ethics, *Wall Street Journal*, March 26, Cl, C3; A. P. Brief, J. M. Dukerich, P. R. Brown, and J. F. Brett, 1996, What's wrong with the Treadway Commission Report? Experimental analysis of the effects of personal values and codes of conduct on fraudulent financial reporting, *Journal of Business Ethics* 15: 183–198; G. Miles, 1993, In search of ethical profits: Insights from strategic management, *Journal of Business Ethics* 12: 219–225.
114. Zajac and Westphal, Accounting for the explanations of CEO compensation.
115. S. R. Premeaux and R. W. Mondy, 1993, Linking management behavior to ethical philosophy, *Journal of Business Ethics* 12: 219–225.
116. Brief et al., What's wrong?
117. B. K. Burton and J. P. Near, 1995, Estimating the incidence of wrongdoing and whistle-blowing: Results of a study using randomized response technique, *Journal of Business Ethics* 14: 17–30.
118. Milton-Smith, Ethics as excellence, 685.
119. Brief et al., What's wrong?, 194; P. E. Murphy, 1995, Corporate ethics statements: Current status and future prospects, *Journal of Business Ethics* 14: 727–740.
120. L. Lagnado, E. M. Rodriguez, and G. Jaffe, 1997, How 'out of a loop' was Dr. Frist during Columbia's expansion?, *Wall Street Journal*, September 4, A1, A6.
121. L. Lagnado, 1997, Columbia wants hospitals to name ethics officers, *Wall Street Journal*, December 12, B7.
122. L. J. Kirsch, 1996, The management of complex tasks in organizations: Controlling the systems development process, *Organization Science* 7: 1–21.
123. R. Simons, 1994, How new top managers use control systems as levers of strategic renewal, *Strategic Management Journal* 15: 170–171.

124. K. J. Laverty, 1996, Economic "short-termism": The debate, the unresolved issues, and the implications for management practice and research, *Academy of Management Review* 21: 825–860.
125. M. A. Hitt, R. E. Hoskisson, and R. D. Ireland, 1990, Mergers and acquisitions and managerial commitment to innovation in M-form firms, *Strategic Management Journal* 11 (Special Summer Issue): 29–47.
126. R. A. Johnson, Antecedents and outcomes of corporate refocusing, *Journal of Management* 22: 437–481; R. E. Hoskisson and M. A. Hitt, 1994, *Downscoping: How to Tame the Diversified Firm* (New York: Oxford University Press).
127. Ireland and Hitt, Achieving and maintaining strategic competitiveness in the 21st century.

Corporate Entrepreneurship and Innovation

CHAPTER 13

Learning Objectives

After reading this chapter, you should be able to:

1. Describe three strategic approaches used to produce and manage innovation.
2. Discuss the two sources of internal corporate venturing: autonomous strategic behavior and induced strategic behavior.
3. Define three types of innovation.
4. Discuss how the capability to manage cross-functional teams can facilitate implementation of internal corporate ventures and innovation efforts.
5. Explain how strategic alliances can be used to produce innovation.
6. Discuss how a firm can create value by acquiring another company to gain access to its innovations or innovative capabilities.
7. Explain how large firms use venture capital to increase the effectiveness of their innovation efforts.
8. Describe the resources, capabilities, and core competencies of small versus large firms in producing innovation.

Killer Chips, Wimps, and Other Things

Intel and Hewlett-Packard are collaborating to develop a new super chip called the Merced. The project began in 1994 with the purpose of developing a more powerful chip to replace the Pentium, today's ultimate chip. The Merced, due for entry into the market in 1999, entails a new chip design. Predictions are that the Merced will be three times faster than the top Pentium. The Merced's speed and parallel processing capabilities should allow the top personal computers to handle tasks now reserved for the larger mainframe computers. If the chip works as planned, it should solidify Intel's hold on the market, eliminating any serious competition. Intel currently has about 80 percent of the microprocessor market for personal computers. Some analysts have predicted that the Merced will ensure that Intel dominates the microprocessor market for at least another 50 years. Hewlett-Packard expects to be considered one of the technology pioneers, which should boost its presence in the personal computer market.

http://
http://www.intel.com
http://www.hp.com

Intel competitors are preparing for the Merced with their own strategic moves. For example, in a move that seems to suggest that microprocessors are for wimps, Motorola is abandoning the market for the primary microprocessor chips for personal computers. Motorola will now emphasize customized highly integrated circuits. It will focus on the system chip or microcontroller. This action suggests that Motorola no longer will try to compete with Intel. However, other chip makers, including Intel, are also entering new markets. For

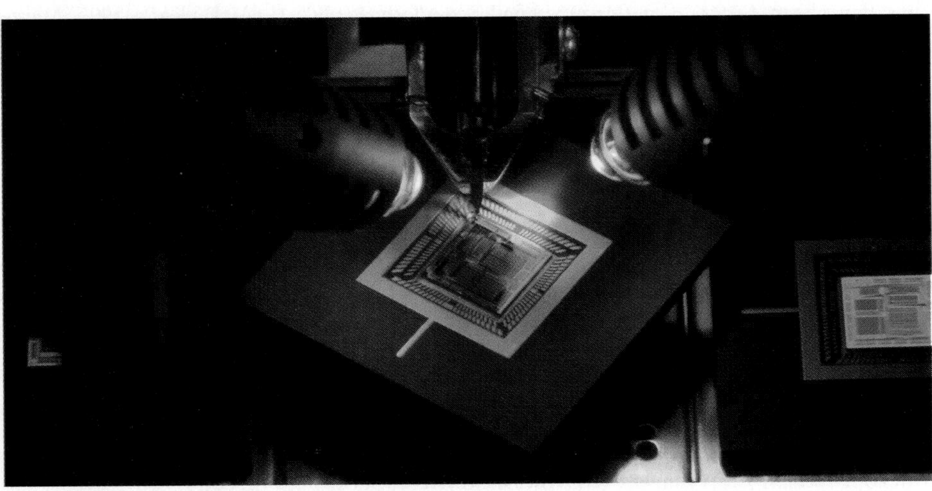

example, Texas Instruments, SJS-Thomson Electronics, and National Semiconductor are all entering specialty markets although different ones from Motorola. These firms are planning to build chips that fit into small devices such as tiny cell phones with Web access, e-mail access in automobiles, and PCs that will fit into a wallet. Some of these firms, such as SJS-Thomson Electronics, have already been successful in the system chip business. Thus, Motorola will be competing in a crowd.

Because of the expected doubling of demand, 35 new chip fabrication plants are planned by the year 2002. These plants represent a major effort. They normally require about 600,000 square feet of space, with access to an amount of water equivalent to the needs of a city with 80,000 residents. Such an undertaking may require as many as 2,000 construction workers. Within the last decade IBM took three years to complete a fabrication plant. However, in 1997, a fabrication plant was completed in half the time by a joint venture between IBM and Toshiba. Samsung built a new plant in Austin, Texas, in about the same amount of time. Thus, speed is of the essence not only in the development of new products as argued in Chapter 1 but also in the development of the plants to manufacture the new products.

Intel is not stopping with the Merced. It is also entering the market to provide support for broadcasters on digital television. In 1997, Intel announced it was investing $100 million in alliances with several other firms to develop content to be broadcast over digital TV. While still closely aligned with Microsoft and Compaq to set standards for personal computers, this action represents a break from Microsoft and Compaq's position that they would only support digital TV formats. Intel is leading the charge to ensure that interactive programs will be able to run on any delivery platform (e.g., satellite TV, cable TV) as well as digital broadcasts. Thus, Intel is not only a large and powerful company, it is also entrepreneurial. In fact, one of the main reasons that it has maintained its dominant position in the market is because of its entrepreneurial efforts.

SOURCES: D. Kirkpatrick, 1998, Three promising (non-Intel) chipmakers, *Fortune*, http://www.pathfinder.com/fortune/digitalwatch; J. Markoff, 1998, Inside Intel, the future is riding on a new chip, *The New York Times*, April 5, section 3, 1 and 6; P. Siekman, 1998, The race to build and staff America's chip plants, *Fortune*, http://www.pathfinder.com/fortune/1997; G. McWilliams, 1997, Microprocessors are for wimps, *Business Week*, December 15, 134–135; B. Schlender, 1997, Killer chip, *Fortune*, http://www.pathfinder.com/fortune/1997; D. Takahashi, 1997, Intel to support broadcasters on digital TV, *Wall Street Journal*, December 5, B3.

The opening case illustrates the importance of entrepreneurial activities for large firms, long thought the purview only of small firms. Intel is developing a new product that is likely to help it continue to dominate the microprocessor chip market. In fact, Intel's entrepreneurial capabilities have helped it develop and maintain its current dominance with the Pentium chip. The effect of Intel's entrepreneurship is substantial. One analyst predicts that its new chip, the Merced, will help it maintain its dominance in the market for another 50 years. Evidence of this possibility is shown by such large competitors as Motorola moving out of the microprocessor chip market to avoiding trying to compete directly with Intel.

Entrepreneurship is important for both large and small firms. Regardless of their size, firms in most industries have to be innovative to survive in global markets. Thus, the development of new products and new processes along with innovation in other areas of the business may be required for survival in competitive global markets. Being entrepreneurial entails risk and with risk there will be failure. Interestingly, the new competitive landscape described in Chapter 1 requires that firms take risks. Firms must take chances to align with a changing landscape. The Chinese word for crisis has two characters. The first represents danger and the other represents opportunity.[1] This is similar to entrepreneurship; it represents both risk and opportunity. Because of the clear need, many firms are increasing their entrepreneurial efforts. New businesses are being formed, by large and small firms and individuals regularly. In fact, it is estimated that approximately 3.5 million businesses are formed annually in the U.S.[2]

Relating back to Figure 1.1 in Chapter 1, our focus herein is on a critical element for implementing strategy—producing and managing innovation. (Innovation may also provide feedback for the formulation of new strategies; see the feedback loop in Figure 1.1.) In addition to the general need for innovation for a firm to be competitive, innovation is a direct requirement of specific strategies such as differentiation (product innovation) and cost leadership (process innovation). Additionally, innovation is an important capability associated with competitive dynamics (see Chapter 5). This chapter examines the resources and skills required to produce and manage innovation. Although this chapter emphasizes innovation in large companies, evidence shows that they are not the sole generators of product and process innovations. Many small and medium-sized firms are also effective innovators. Moreover, large companies often develop relationships and alliances with smaller firms to help them produce innovations. Because of the importance of their innovative abilities, the chapter's final section addresses the different capabilities of small firms that produce and manage innovation.

INNOVATION AND CORPORATE ENTREPRENEURSHIP

Some evidence suggests that effective innovation results in a sustainable competitive advantage. More specifically, innovations that are (1) difficult for competitors to imitate, (2) able to provide significant value to customers, (3) timely, and (4) capable of being exploited commercially through existing core competencies help firms develop competitive advantages.[3] Because of the link between the development of competitive advantages and the earning of above-average returns, many companies, especially those active in the global marketplace, are interested in producing innovations and in effectively managing the innovation process.

Need for Innovation and Entrepreneurship

The technological revolution and greater competition in international markets have increased the competitive importance of innovation.[4] Research has shown that firms competing in global industries that invest more in innovation also achieve the highest returns.[5] In fact, investors often react positively to new product introductions, thereby increasing the price of a firm's stock. Thus, entrepreneurship is an essential feature of high-performance firms.[6] William R. Howell, chairman of the JCPenney Company, noted that you can never "rest on your laurels. Rather, you have to try to stay ahead of the curve since competitors tend to pick up on your successes."[7]

Entrepreneurship and Innovation Defined

Entrepreneurs seek to create the future. To do so, they must take risks and be aggressive, proactive, and innovative.[8] Furthermore, they must identify anomalies in markets or opportunities where no current market exists.[9] Another important feature of entrepreneurship is growth. In fact, some authors suggest that growth is a primary differentiator of entrepreneurial firms from small businesses. Thus, effective entrepreneurial firms are fast-growth businesses. These fast-growth firms create new businesses.[10]

Corporate entrepreneurship is the set of capabilities possessed by a firm to produce or acquire new goods or services and manage the innovation process.

Corporate entrepreneurship includes the commitments, mind-sets, and actions firms take to develop and manage innovations. Formally, **corporate entrepreneurship** is the set of capabilities possessed by a firm to produce or acquire new goods or services and manage the innovation process.[11] Corporate entrepreneurship is based on effective product design and successful commercialization. Because it is a set of capabilities that results in the effective *and* efficient design and manufacture of products, corporate entrepreneurship can be a basis for strategic competitiveness.

In U.S. companies, the role of corporate entrepreneurship in both effectiveness and efficiency has been recognized only somewhat recently. After World War II, for example, U.S. manufacturers sought to satisfy worldwide demand for their goods and services by focusing on mass-production techniques that allowed them to produce products in large quantities. This focus resulted in an opportunity for other producers (e.g., those in Japan and what was then West Germany) to use a different set of strategic actions.[12] The focus of U.S. firms on quantity allowed inefficiencies, which the Japanese and the Germans exploited commercially with high levels of product quality. By the 1970s, Japanese manufacturers were more competitive than their U.S. rivals as a result of the development and use of a host of product, process, and managerial innovations. Workers in Japanese factories, for example, exercised a degree of responsibility not allowed in U.S. factories. In Japanese factories, the activities of everyone—from top-level managers to line workers to suppliers—were combined into a tightly integrated whole. Firms committed to these methods set their sights on perfection: "continually declining costs, zero defects, zero inventories, and endless product variety."[13] More has been learned about operating a manufacturing enterprise in the 1980s and 1990s than in all of the rest of the century. Regional dominance no longer exists. Global markets and competition dominate the new competitive landscape. Thus, innovations in both manufacturing and service companies are necessary for survival in a highly competitive world.[14]

Invention is the act of creating or developing a new product or process idea.

Innovation is the process of creating a commercial product from invention.

Imitation is adoption of the innovation by similar firms.

Joseph Schumpeter's classic work on management of the innovation process suggests that firms engage in three types of innovative activity.[15] **Invention** is the act of creating or developing a new product or process idea. **Innovation** is the process of creating a commercial product from invention. Finally, **imitation** is adoption of the innovation by similar firms. Imitation usually leads to product or process standardization. In the United States in particular, the most critical of these activities has been innovation. Many firms are able to create ideas that lead to in-

3M has been very successful at commercializing inventions. Thus, the firm is known to be highly innovative.

vention, but commercializing those inventions through innovation has, at times, proved to be difficult.

Strategic leaders, managers, and entrepreneurs all have roles that are critical to effective corporate entrepreneurship.[16] Especially with regard to corporate entrepreneurship, the strategic leader's role is to inspire an organization's members to work cooperatively in the pursuit of meaningful outcomes. Leaders and their words assume symbolic value to inspire organizational members to accomplish a firm's strategic intent and strategic mission. Strategic leaders have emphasized innovation at 3M for years. This company has introduced over 50,000 new products. George Allen, retired vice president of research and development at 3M, states, "3M innovates for the same reason that cows eat grass. It is a part of our DNA to do so."[17] Firms such as 3M use innovation to build a competitive advantage. Corporate entrepreneurship that produces innovation can provide a platform on which industry leadership can be built.[18]

Middle- and lower-level managers are promoters and caretakers of organizational efficiency. Their work is especially important once a product idea has been commercialized and the organization necessary to support and promote it has been formed.[19] Middle- and lower-level managers are critical to creating and implementing (commercializing) innovations at 3M.

Entrepreneurs are people who are the first to see an economic opportunity and seek to take advantage of it.[20] Often, entrepreneurs' commercial insights are not initially shared by others, forcing them to live with the social burden of not being accepted until the economic value of their insights is confirmed.

The most effective entrepreneurs are often those who work against existing product standards by behaving as if they do not exist. This mind-set seems to facilitate creativity and innovation. Within large organizations, however, effective corporate entrepreneurship can be difficult to establish and support. In large organizations, people engaged in entrepreneurial practices must fully understand the corporate culture and mind-set (see Chapter 1) that drive the firm's innovation process and the attributes of the structure, controls, and reward systems within which organizational work is completed.

STRATEGIC FOCUS

The Razor's Edge: An Innovation Machine

Gillette worked for six years to create the successor to its highly popular razor, the Sensor. The Sensor is the world's most successful razor, helping Gillette to maintain double digit growth over a period of years. In 1996 alone, Gillette achieved an increase in sales of almost 43 percent. The firm has been able to grow at phenomenal rates, particularly for a company operating in consumer goods industries, largely because of its innovation. In fact, it has been labeled an innovation machine.

Currently, about 41 percent of sales come from products introduced in the last five years. The CEO's goal is to increase that to 50 percent. Essentially, Gillette invests heavily to be the market technology leader and produce innovative products that can be sold at premium prices. This approach has paid off for Gillette. A recent study of the top 50 consumer goods companies showed that only 17 earned above the industry average growth in sales and profits for 1985–1990. Only seven of the seventeen earned above the industry average for the 1990–1995 period. Gillette was one of these seven companies. To continue significant growth in sales and profits, Gillette invests over $200 million in R&D. This annual allocation to R&D is approximately twice the average for consumer goods firms.

Its R&D is rigorous in testing newly developed products. To select the best Sensor razor design, the firm produced seven different versions and tested each one. The one design that was selected incorporated many of the best features of the other six before it was taken to the market. There were over 15,000 tests of this razor before it was placed on the market. Gillette also invests money in process innovation. It is expert at designing ways to produce its products cheaper. Thus, Gillette integrates both process and product innovation, something that few other firms are able to do.

While Gillette is best known for razors and blades, it is also a market leader in batteries (Duracell), dental care products (Oral-B), toiletries (Right Guard, White Rain), small appliances (Braun), and writing products (Parker Pen, Liquid Paper). In addition, Gillette receives over 60 percent of its revenue from outside the United States. It has significant sales of its products in Europe (particularly the United Kingdom) and Asia (particularly Japan). Its sales are also growing in South America. Gillette sells its products in more than 200 countries and has manufacturing facilities in 27 different countries. Gillette is clearly a firm that is well prepared to enter the twenty-first century.

SOURCES: W. C. Symonds and C. Matlack, 1998, Gillette's Edge: The secret of a great innovation machine? Never relax, *Business Week*, January 10, http://www.businessweek.com.premium; The Gillette Company, February 1, 1998, http://www.bigmouth.pathfinder.com/mon...vers/profiles/byid; The Gillette Company, February 1, 1998, http://www.oakland.co.uk/gilbert; The Gillette Company, February 1, 1998, *Hoovers Online*, http://www.hoovers.com.cgi-bin/brand_wp_mlist.cgi.

As described in the Strategic Focus, the Gillette Company is an excellent example of corporate entrepreneurship. It is a highly innovative company and is able to bring new products successfully to the market. It is a technology leader in all of the industries in which it competes and earns a significant amount of its annual revenue from new products introduced to the market in the last five years. The results of the firm's emphasis on innovation is also clear. Gillette has been one of the highest performing consumer goods firms for more than a decade. Its growth in sales and profits have averaged more than 17 percent annually for the last 10 years. Thus, we can conclude that corporate entrepreneurship is alive and well and, at least in some firms, such as Gillette, leads to strategic competitiveness.

While innovativeness in Japanese firms has received some attention during the last two decades, U.S. firms continue to be perceived as the most innovative. However, corporate entrepreneurship and innovation are not limited to the United States and Japan.

International Entrepreneurship

In the late 1970s, Chinese economic reforms began to allow more autonomy to market forces and legalized private entrepreneurship. Many Chinese people have more disposable income, are better informed, and have more personal freedom than at any time since 1949 when the Communists took control of the country. The outcomes are primarily the result of the reforms unleashing the entrepreneurial spirit of the Chinese people. In fact, considerable entrepreneurship is currently being exhibited in the People's Republic of China.[21] Some significant tension has arisen between the need for individualism to promote entrepreneurship and the more traditional Chinese cultural characteristics of collectivism. Individualism, a dominant characteristic in U.S. society, is important to the creativity needed for entrepreneurial behavior. Furthermore, research has shown that entrepreneurship declines as collectivism is emphasized. The same research, however, shows that exceptionally high levels of individualism can be dysfunctional for entrepreneurship as well. Thus, a balance is needed between individual initiative and the spirit of cooperation and group ownership of innovation. For firms to achieve corporate entrepreneurship, they must provide appropriate autonomy and incentives for individual initiative to surface, but also promote cooperation and group ownership of an innovation if it is to be implemented successfully. Thus, corporate entrepreneurship often requires teams of people with unique skills and resources.[22]

The importance of balancing individualism and collectivism for entrepreneurship is perhaps best exemplified by the success of Asian entrepreneurs in North America. Some have argued that the success of those of Chinese and Korean origin in North America was due to their industriousness, perseverance, frugality, and emphasis on family. Research shows, however, that there are other traits that promote their success. In North America, these individuals are allowed the autonomy necessary for creativity and entrepreneurial behavior. However, their cultural background emphasizes collectivism, which helps them promote cooperation and group ownership of innovation.[23]

Interestingly, Chinese entrepreneurs operating in China have several character traits that are similar to those of U.S. entrepreneurs, for example, achievement, independence, and self-determination. But the two sets of entrepreneurs also have different characteristics, particularly those most influenced by Confucian social philosophy.[24] Entrepreneurs of Chinese and Korean descent who operate in the

U.S. exhibit differences from all other entrepreneurs in the U.S. For example, U.S. Chinese and Korean entrepreneurs invest more equity, obtain more capital from family and friends, and receive fewer loans from financial institutions. Furthermore, they achieve higher profits than their non-Asian counterparts.[25] In contrast, a study of Israeli women showed that industry experience, business skills, and achievement were related to their performance much like other entrepreneurs in the U.S. and Europe. But, unlike others, affiliation with a network for support and advice was positively related to the success of Israeli women entrepreneurs. When they were affiliated with multiple networks, their performance suffered, possibly because of too much and potentially conflicting advice.[26]

There are other dimensions of international entrepreneurship in addition to cross cultural and ethnic comparisons. International entrepreneurship is new with activities that cross national boundaries and have the goal of creating value for the firm.[27] This definition applies to large and small firms alike. Both large and small firms are expanding their operations into new international markets and different countries. For example, in the early 1990s about 20 percent of small firms in the United States were involved in international markets. Today over 50 percent of small firms in the United States are involved in international markets.[28] Research suggests that expanding into international markets can produce higher innovation and firm performance.[29] Research also suggests that high performance firms should be first or second movers (see Chapter 5) in those markets. Order of entry (timing) is even more important than the size of the entry.[30]

INTERNAL CORPORATE VENTURING

Internal corporate venturing is the set of activities used to create inventions and innovations within a single organization.

Composed of two processes, **internal corporate venturing** is the set of activities used to create inventions and innovations within a single organization.[31] The two processes in internal corporate venturing are shown in Figure 13.1. The first in-

FIGURE 13.1 *Model of Internal Corporate Venturing*

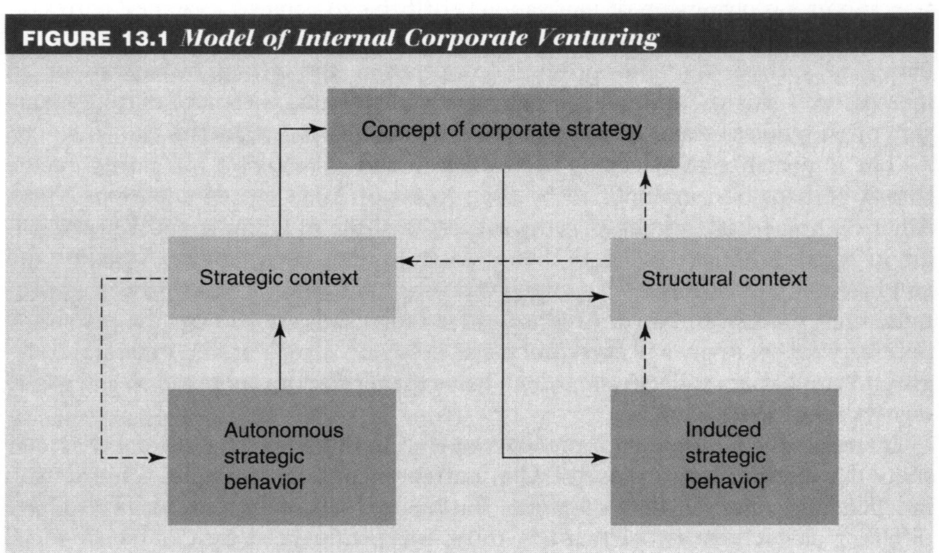

Source: Adapted from R. A. Burgelman, 1983, A model of the interactions of strategic behavior, corporate context, and the concept of strategy, *Academy of Management Review* 8: 65.

volves a bottom-up approach to the creation of product and process innovations. **Autonomous strategic behavior** is a bottom-up process in which product champions pursue new product ideas, often through a political process, whereby they develop and coordinate the commercialization of a new good or service until it achieves marketplace success. A **product champion** is a member of an organization who has an entrepreneurial vision of a new good or service and seeks to create support for its commercialization. Autonomous strategic behavior is based on a firm's wellsprings of knowledge and resources that provide the sources of a firm's innovation. Thus, a firm's capabilities and competencies are the basis for new products and processes.[32]

Autonomous strategic behavior is a bottom-up process in which product champions pursue new product ideas, often through a political process, whereby they develop and coordinate the commercialization of a new good or service until it achieves marketplace success.

A **product champion** is a member of an organization who has an entrepreneurial vision of a new good or service and seeks to create support for its commercialization.

Changing the concept of corporate-level strategy through autonomous strategic behavior results when product championing takes place within strategic and structural contexts (see Figure 13.1). The strategic context refers to the process used to arrive at strategic decisions (often requiring political processes to gain acceptance). The best firms may keep changing the strategic context and strategies because of the continuous changes in the new competitive landscape described in Chapter 1. In fact, well-known author and consultant, Gary Hamel, says that the best companies change the rules of the game. According to Hamel, they often reinvent their existing industry or develop a completely new one. For example, Nike dramatically changed the footwear industry by developing and marketing a premium-priced athletic shoe. In addition, Nike partially changed the game in the industry through a marketing blitz. In other words, firms in the industry could not

Nike dramatically changed the footwear industry by developing and marketing a premium-priced athletic shoe. The change of rules was successful because it was accompanied by a marketing blitz.

Induced strategic behavior is a top-down process whereby the current strategy and structure foster product innovations that are associated closely with the current strategy and structure.

survive without doing the same thing. This strategy clearly worked for Nike. Since 1986, its stock price has increased by an average of 47 percent annually. Interestingly, there are only a few firms that try to change the rules. Most follow similar strategies because it seems less risky.[33]

Induced strategic behavior is a top-down process whereby the current strategy and structure foster product innovations that are associated closely with the current strategy and structure. In this situation, the strategy in place is filtered through a matching structural hierarchy.

An example of induced strategic behavior is shown by Sony's decision to develop and enter the market for smart portable sensors such as Sony's portable digital assistant, the Navicam. The Navicam is the first of a new product category, portables that can sense their environment. By the year 2000, these portable sensors will serve as personal guides to major museums and shopping malls. Essentially, Sony is developing context-sensitive friendly computers. For automobiles, Sony is developing small robots with mounted TV cameras that can recognize their environment and navigate on their own.[34]

Sony also is attempting to integrate digital technologies into multiple new products in addition to personal computers, including high-resolution television and multimedia eyeglasses. CEO Nobuyuki Idei's strategic intent for Sony is to become a "digital dream kid." Thus, the vision of the firm's new CEO is to integrate digital technologies into multiple new products.[35]

Although Sony has the vision and technical experience to accomplish its goals, large firms often encounter difficulties when striving to pursue internal corporate ventures effectively. The induced processes can dominate and create strategic and structural contexts that become barriers to change. Effective internal corporate venturing processes are established only when both internal political processes and strategic and structural contexts allow a new strategic mission to emerge.

Developing and implementing an entrepreneurial strategy is a highly complex task, partly because of the significant uncertainty in the environment.[36] Such a strategy requires firms to decide and deploy corporate resources to develop new technology and then decide which innovative ideas to pursue and bring to the market, often rapidly. Some researchers have aruged that there are strategic windows of opportunity of which firms must take advantage. The windows may be open only for a short period of time; thus, it may not be possible to delay decisions to act.[37] Given the rapid changes and diffusion of technology, traditional valuation and budgeting techniques may not be useful to guide the decisions to invest and develop new technologies.[38] Thus, entrepreneurial strategies and technology investment decisions require a new managerial mind-set as discussed in Chapter 1.

While an important goal of R&D may be to create knowledge, the most successful R&D outputs (e.g., new product ideas) may lead to the development of an internal corporate venture.[39] Internal corporate ventures are often formed for radically new products, products that may not be marketed and distributed effectively by an existing business within the current corporate umbrella.[40] Also, corporate ventures emphasize different resources than independent new ventures. For example, corporate ventures emphasize internal capital, development of proprietary knowledge, and building marketing expertise. Alternatively, independent ventures primarily emphasize external capital, building technical expertise, and development of brand identification. Most corporate ventures can use the corporate reputation and so brand name will be less important. Furthermore, the technical expertise exists, flowing from the larger corporate entity.[41]

Inventing and commercializing new products is becoming more critical in many industries as stated earlier. In addition to having an effective R&D unit to develop new product ideas, firms must have a process and structure that facilitates moving these new product ideas rapidly to the market. Companies such as 3M, Pfizer, and Intel have effective processes to implement new product ideas. For example, 3M introduced 500 new products to the market in 1996, and over 50,000 new products over the life of the firm. Developing and marketing innovative new products has been referred to as a style of corporate behavior. This style, often aggressive about new ideas, change, and risk, must permeate the organization. This style includes a passion for innovation in all that the firm does.[42] It is clear that this passion exists at Toyota as explained in the Strategic Focus. Toyota continues to be a market leader for introducing new products and doing it rapidly. It has introduced a new concept auto in 15 months from inception of its idea whereas U.S. firms require on average about 36 months to do the same.

STRATEGIC FOCUS

The Mean Innovative Machine

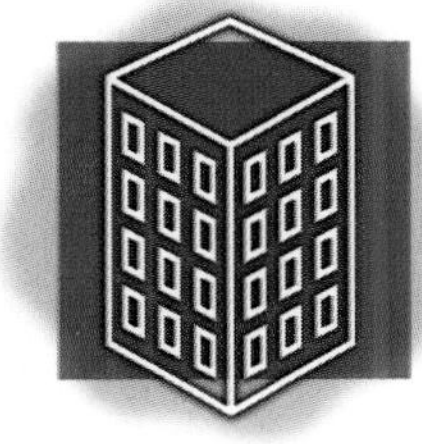

In the automobile industry, there is one firm that stands above the others when it comes to innovation, Toyota. Toyota is the industry leader in bringing new products to the market rapidly. It holds the industry mark for time, 15 months to develop a new concept car and introduce it to the market. Most other Japanese firms require about 24 months. The fastest U.S. firm can do this, on average, in about 36 months. The current president of Toyota, Hiroshi Okuda, has emphasized speed. In fact, one senior manager says that his message is speed, speed, speed.

Toyota is known for more than its speed of product development. In December 1997, the firm introduced a new automobile that is the first mass produced car with both electric and gasoline powered engines. This auto, called the Prius, produces significant economies over a traditional gasoline powered car. For example, it has an average fuel consumption of between 66 and 85 miles to the gallon. This auto also has lower emission levels than its traditional counterpart. The electric engine is used for starting and for running at low speeds. As the speed of the vehicle increases, the gasoline powered engine begins to operate. In this way, the auto has better fuel efficiency and lower emissions than traditional automobiles. The car contains a power split device to ensure that power is transmitted to the wheels continuously. While other rival automakers, Honda and Nissan, are also developing hybrid cars, Toyota was the first to the market and thus will enjoy the advantages of a first mover with respect to this particular product. Toyota has also developed a new engine that requires 25 percent fewer parts. Such an engine weighs less and is cheaper to build. This new 1.8 liter, four-cylinder engine has 560 parts compared to its predecessor with 741 parts. The engine weighs 64 pounds, about 10 percent less than its predecessor, and yet, it produces 15 percent more horsepower.

Analysts and knowledgeable industry sources believe that Toyota sets many of the standards in the industry. For example, many argue that it possesses superior skills in manufacturing, engineering, and marketing. It also manages its finances effectively. Toyota maintains $21 billion in cash and marketable securities. With this much cash available, it has the capability to move rapidly if an opportunity is identified that requires fast action to take advantage of it.

Certainly, other automakers are innovative. For example, Audi has become an aggressive innovator. Audi builds technologically innovative cars about which its customers are passionate. Also, these autos are cheaper than most of the direct competitors such as BMW, Lexus, Mercedes, Saab, and Volvo. Another example of an innovative automaker is Land Rover. This company produces vehicles not known for their fuel efficiency. Nonetheless, the firm won an energy efficiency award for energy-efficient power generation. The award was given by the Combined Heat & Power Association for Land Rover's cogeneration (combined heat and power generation) facilities at its assembly plant in Solihull, Birmingham, in the United Kingdom. Thus, Land Rover is a leading innovator in other areas of its business.

Although other auto innovations could be named, Toyota is the undisputed leader and will likely remain so for the foreseeable future. Toyota continues to invest heavily in the development of fuel cells and in producing a highly efficient, high powered electric vehicle. Many will take bets that Toyota will succeed and be the first to do so.

SOURCES: L. Boulton, 1997, Land Rover's energy drive takes a prize, *Financial Times*, November 2, 2; J. Griffiths, 1997, Global race for fuel efficiency, *Financial Times*, November 2, 8; V. Reitman, 1997, Toyota introduces new engine in the U.S. that is much lighter, cheaper to make, *Wall Street Journal*, October 8, B13; H. Simonian, 1997, Staying in the fast lane of innovation, *Financial Times*, November 7, 20; A. Taylor, III, 1997, How Toyota defies gravity, *Fortune*, December 8, 100–108; E. Thornton, K. Naughton, and D. Woodruff, 1997, Toyota's green machine, *Business Week*, December 15, 108–110; S. Zesiger, 1997, The most improved wheels, *Fortune*, November 24, 194–204.

Implementing Internal Corporate Ventures

The creation and commercialization of a new good or service is a complex process. The design and transfer of technology from engineering to manufacturing and ultimately to distribution and to the marketplace are critical. The design stage entails a high degree of integration among the various functions involved in the innovation process—from engineering to manufacturing and ultimately to market distribution. Initial design efforts that do not consider down-line aspects in the production process (manufacturing, testing, marketing, service, etc.) may result in high product costs and low product quality. Such cross-functional integration facilitates reciprocal information flows among the functions responsible for development, design, and implementation. Developing a capability to innovate rapidly using team processes, as Toyota has done, helps large firms overcome the difficulties they encounter when trying to be entrepreneurial. These matters are discussed in greater detail in the next subsection.

Implementing Product Development Teams and Facilitating Cross-Functional Integration

The importance of cross-functional integration has been recognized for some time, but it has not been practiced widely in industry until recently. However, because of an emerging emphasis on horizontal organization, firms are becoming more skilled at cross-functional integration. **Horizontal organization** refers to changes in organizational processes where managing across functional units becomes more critical than managing up and down functional hierarchies.[43] Therefore, instead of being built around vertical hierarchical functions or departments, the organization is built around core horizontal processes.

Horizontal organization refers to changes in organizational processes where managing across functional units becomes more critical than managing up and down functional hierarchies.

Evidence suggests that a key benefit that can be gained through successful application of horizontal organizational processes is effective utilization of sophisticated manufacturing technologies [e.g., the computer-aided design and manufacturing (CAD/CAM) system].[44] Thus, cross-functional integration can facilitate a firm's efforts to establish a competitive advantage.

Barriers to Integration

Barriers may exist that can stifle attempts to integrate functions effectively within an organization. For example, an emphasis on functional specialization may affect cross-functional integration. Such specialization creates distancing of divergent functions and characteristically different roles for engineering, manufacturing, and marketing. Functional departments have been found to be differentiated along four dimensions: time orientation, interpersonal orientation, goal orientation, and formality of structure.[45] Individuals from different functional departments that have different orientations understand separate aspects of product development in different ways. As such, they place emphasis on separate design characteristics and issues. For example, a design engineer may place strong importance on characteristics that make a product functional and workable. Alternatively, a person from the marketing function may place extreme importance on product characteristics that satisfy customer needs. These types of characteristics may overlap or they may differ. These different orientations can create barriers to effective communication across functions.[46] Although functional specialization may be damaging to the horizontal relationships necessary for implementing innovation, such specialization has an important purpose in creating an efficient organization. Therefore, eliminating such task specialization to overcome barriers to cross-functional integration may do more harm than good to the organization.

Another barrier to integration can be organizational politics. In some organizations, considerable political activity may center on resource allocations to the different functions. If different functions have to compete aggressively with each other to obtain adequate or needed resources, it can lead to conflict between the functions. Of course, dysfunctional conflict between functions creates a barrier to their integration.[47] Methods must be found through which cross-functional integration can be promoted without excessive concurrent political conflict and without concurrently changing the basic structural characteristics necessary for task specialization and efficiency.

Facilitating Integration

Firms can use four methods to achieve effective cross-functional integration. The first of these methods utilizes *shared values*.[48] Shared values, when linked clearly with a firm's strategic intent and mission, reduce political conflict and become the glue that promotes coupling among functional units. Hewlett-Packard has remained an accomplished technological leader because it has established the "HP way." In essence, the HP way refers to the firm's esteemed organizational culture that promotes unity and internal innovation.

Leadership is a second method of achieving cross-functional integration. Effective strategic leaders remind organizational members continuously of the value that product innovations create for the company (see Chapter 12). In the most desirable situations, this value-creating potential becomes the basis for the integration and management of functional department activities. At General Electric, Jack Welch frequently highlights the importance of integrated work, among both business units and different functions. To frame this message consistently, Welch has been instrumental in establishing and operating a managerial training center that focuses on these relationships among all levels of the company's management structure.

A third method of achieving cross-functional integration is concerned with *goals and budgets.* This method calls for firms to formulate goals and allocate the budgetary resources necessary to accomplish them. These goals are specific targets for the integrated design and production of new goods and services. Chrysler's reorganization to focus on platform teams, for example, effectively reinforced in employees' minds the importance of team processes.

A fourth means of facilitating cross-functional integration is an *effective communication system.* This may be achieved by developing a horizontal organization and emphasizing the use of cross-functional teams. More is often required, however, to overcome the barriers to integration noted earlier.[49] Shared values, effective leadership, appropriate resources to accomplish team tasks, and an information system that facilitates communications between team members and different functions contribute to an effective communication system within teams.[50] A network information system can facilitate communication among geographically dispersed team members, even those located in different countries. Because of the growing popularity of horizontal organizational structures, in particular cross-functional teams that may be geographically dispersed across international borders, firms such as IBM are emphasizing network-centered computing. According to Louis Gerstner, CEO of IBM, network-centered computing "will change the way we do business, the way we teach our children, how we communicate, how we interact as individuals."[51]

Appropriating (Extracting) Value from Innovation

Cross-functional integration, when implemented properly, may also facilitate reduced time to market, improve product quality, and create value for customers. For firms competing globally, increasing attention is being paid to the amount of time required to transfer products from the lab to the consumer.[52] A firm can gain a competitive advantage if it is able to develop a product idea and transfer it to the market sooner than competitors, especially in high-tech environments such as biotechnology.[53] If the product has wide consumer appeal, the first mover has an advantage.[54] Although there is inherent risk in being a pioneer, a first mover may be able to establish a dominant position from which to build future market share and earn above-average returns (see discussion in Chapter 5). Research evidence suggests that firms with long development cycles typically are outperformed by companies with short ones.[55] Although shorter time-to-market cycles can help firms appropriate value from their innovations, poor design can lead to expensive recalls, higher production costs, low product performance, and product liability exposure.

As noted earlier, speed has become a major factor on which firms such as Toyota compete.[56] In fact, Kim Sheridan, chairman of Avalon Software, Inc., stated that "it's not the big companies that eat the small; it's the fast that eat the slow."[57] A recent study showed that the competitive clock continues to tick while a firm delays adopting a new generation of technology. The sooner a firm innovates, the better it performs.[58] There is no single means of increasing a firm's speed. Clearly, integrating new technology into a firm's operations can increase the speed with which it accomplishes tasks. Many firms are attempting to accelerate product development and integration through cross-functional teams.[59]

Because product design teams often are composed of many different players, each of whom possesses critical knowledge and skills, cross-functional integration may reduce uncertainty and facilitate the successful introduction of innovative goods or services. In fact, the simultaneous evaluation of multiple alternatives, as is often the case with cross-functional teams, increases decision speed.[60] Hewlett-Packard, for example, is divided into global, cross-functional teams that are capable of making decisions quickly to deal with rapidly changing market conditions. However, it is essential that design teams be managed effectively. If implementation is not effective in a complex situation, uncertainty may be increased.[61]

In summary, the model presented in Figure 13.2 shows how value may be appropriated from internal innovation processes. As our discussion has indicated, the internal innovation process must be managed to facilitate cross-functional integration to appropriate the greatest amount of value from product design and commercialization efforts. Effective management of internal innovation processes can reduce both the time required to introduce innovations into the marketplace and the degree of decision uncertainty associated with the design of an innovative product and the demand for it.[62]

FIGURE 13.2 *Appropriating Value from Internal Firm Innovation*

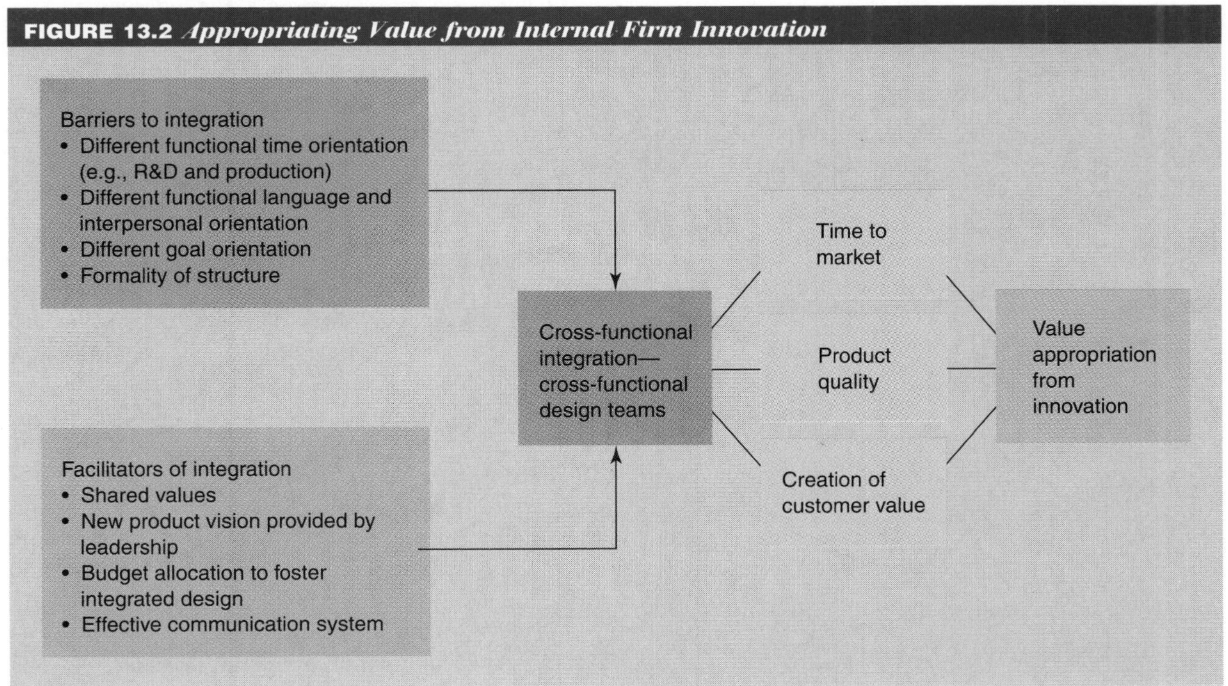

Source: Adapted from M. A. Hitt, R. E. Hoskisson, and R. D. Nixon, 1993, A mid-range theory of interfunctional integration, its antecedents and outcomes, *Journal of Engineering and Technology Management* 10: 161–185.

STRATEGIC ALLIANCES: COOPERATING TO PRODUCE AND MANAGE INNOVATION

It is difficult for most firms to possess all the knowledge required to compete successfully in their product areas over the long term. Thus, internal innovation may contribute to the development of a sustainable competitive advantage when a firm possesses the core competencies required to innovate effectively and efficiently. But because the stock of human knowledge is large and increasing at an accelerating pace, many firms, regardless of their size, cannot keep up to date on this vast pool of knowledge. Complicating this matter is the fact that the knowledge base confronting today's organizations is not only vast, but also increasingly more specialized. As such, the knowledge needed to commercialize goods and services is frequently embedded within different corporations and countries that have the ability to create specialized products.

In Chapter 9, we discussed why and how firms use strategic alliances (*strategic alliances* are partnerships between firms whereby resources, capabilities, and core competencies are combined to pursue common interests and goals)[63] to gain either competitive parity or competitive advantage relative to rivals. Moreover, one of the specific reasons to enter into a strategic alliance is to introduce innovative goods or services. Strategic alliances are often used to innovate by sharing two or more firms' knowledge and skill bases.[64]

The dreams of many biotechnology firms of becoming the next Merck are being scaled back. Most of these firms are small and many have experienced failures of new drugs, a significant problem because of their lack of resources. Thus, survival is of key concern. To avoid failure and to obtain the needed resources to continue biotechnology research, many of these companies are seeking strategic alliances with larger resource-rich firms. Over a recent 12-month period, biotechnology companies entered into 246 alliances with larger pharmaceutical firms. It is expensive and quite risky for new startup firms to operate independently in this industry. The average cost of developing a new drug is approximately $300 million and only 10 percent of the experimental drugs used in human trials are further developed and brought to the market.[65]

Similarly, large pharmaceutical firms are eagerly shopping for opportunities to team with biotechnology firms. Some of them are using the small biotechnology companies to perform the early-stage research. As such, they can reduce their in-house research costs and some of the risks as well. Forming an alliance with these firms enables the pharmaceutical firms to convert some of their fixed research costs to variable costs and to diversify their risk. Thus, the pharmaceutical firms are attempting to reduce their risk and some of their fixed costs without reducing the probability of discovering and marketing new blockbuster drugs.[66]

In a more general sense, some argue that strategic alliances can be dangerous. Supporting this argument is the contention that they allow partner firms to gain knowledge and resources that make them stronger competitors, which, if true, could ultimately lower profitability for an industry's leading firms.[67] Perhaps the most important decision with regard to alliances occurs in the selection of a partner. Not only should a firm choose a partner with complementary skills, but also one that has compatible goals and strategic orientations.[68] Thus, organizations are challenged to evaluate carefully all the risks associated with strategic alliances that might be formed in the pursuit of strategic competitiveness and above-average returns.

Across time, strategic alliances can slowly reduce the skills of a partner that does not understand the inherent risks. Collaboration within alliances can lead to competition, both in learning new skills and in refining new capabilities and core competencies that can be used to design and produce other innovative products and processes.

Japanese corporations, for example, appear to be expert in learning new technologies through strategic alliances. This skill has been instrumental in helping these firms learn how to compete in markets where they were locked out previously. For instance, all electronics products sold under the Eastman Kodak, General Electric, RCA, Zenith, and Westinghouse brand names are made by their foreign alliance partners and imported into the United States.[69]

As our discussion has suggested, alliances can lead to a company's dependence on partners through outsourcing to obtain low-cost components and inexpensive assembly. Often manufacturing skills and knowledge related to upgrading precision manufacturing and testing are lost, whereas such skills are gained by the competitors to which the firm is outsourcing.[70] Ultimately, then, a firm may lose its core competence by participating in alliances if it is not careful.

In summary, building successful strategic alliances requires focusing on knowledge, identifying core competencies, and developing strong human resources to manage these core competencies. Expecting to gain financial benefits in the short run may lead to unintended consequences in the long run. Firms may view their collaboration with other firms as an indirect form of competition for knowledge.[71]

BUYING INNOVATION: ACQUISITIONS AND VENTURE CAPITAL

In this section, we focus on the third approach firms use to produce and manage innovation. The intent of this approach is to acquire innovation, and innovative capabilities, from outside the organization. For example, in addition to strategic alliances, some pharmaceutical firms are acquiring small biotechnology companies with promising new drugs. Ciba-Geigy Ltd. bought a 50 percent interest in Chiron Corp. for $2.1 billion. The pharmaceutical firms are buying biotechnology firms not only for their promising new drugs but also their research techniques using gene-based analysis and computerization. Some time-honored techniques for creating drugs are becoming obsolete. Thus, they are attempting to buy innovation and the skills to create more innovation.[72]

As approaches to producing and managing innovation, both strategic alliances and acquisitions appear to be increasing in popularity. One reason is that the innovation prowess of companies in other countries is growing at a rapid pace. A number of indicators suggest that Japanese firms, for instance, have progressed during the post-war period from borrowing, magnifying, and successfully commercializing foreign technologies to operating at the technological frontier, especially in process innovation. The National Science Foundation reported that Japanese firms accounted for the largest single share of foreign-origin patents.[73] Japanese companies are becoming skilled at transferring technologies from Japan into their global R&D networks. One way for companies from other nations to gain competitive parity or perhaps competitive advantage is to gain access to Japanese technology by acquiring companies that have such technology.

Acquisitions

Acquiring other firms as a method of producing and managing innovation is becoming more common and may be used as a substitute for internally developed innovation.[74] A key risk of this method is that a firm may substitute the ability to buy innovations for the ability to produce innovations internally. Research suggests this tradeoff has a negative effect on the processes a firm uses to produce innovations internally.[75]

Figure 13.3 shows that firms gaining access to innovations through the acquisition of other companies risk reductions in both R&D inputs (as measured by investments in R&D) and R&D outputs (as measured by the number of patents). Evidence in Figure 13.3 shows the R&D-to-sales ratio drops after acquisitions have been completed and that the patent-to-sales ratio drops significantly after companies have been involved with large acquisitions. Additional research shows that firms engaging in acquisitions introduce fewer new products to the market.[76] These relationships indicate that firms substitute acquisitions for their internal innovation process. This may result because firms lose strategic control and emphasize financial control of original, and especially of acquired, business units.[77] Although reduced innovation may not always result, managers in acquiring firms should be aware of this potential outcome.

Innovation can be obtained in a way other than acquiring a whole firm. For example, sometimes foreign firms can acquire a license from the home country patent

FIGURE 13.3 ***Evidence of R&D Inputs (Expenditures) and Outputs (Number of Patents) per Dollar of Sales Before and After Large Acquisitions***

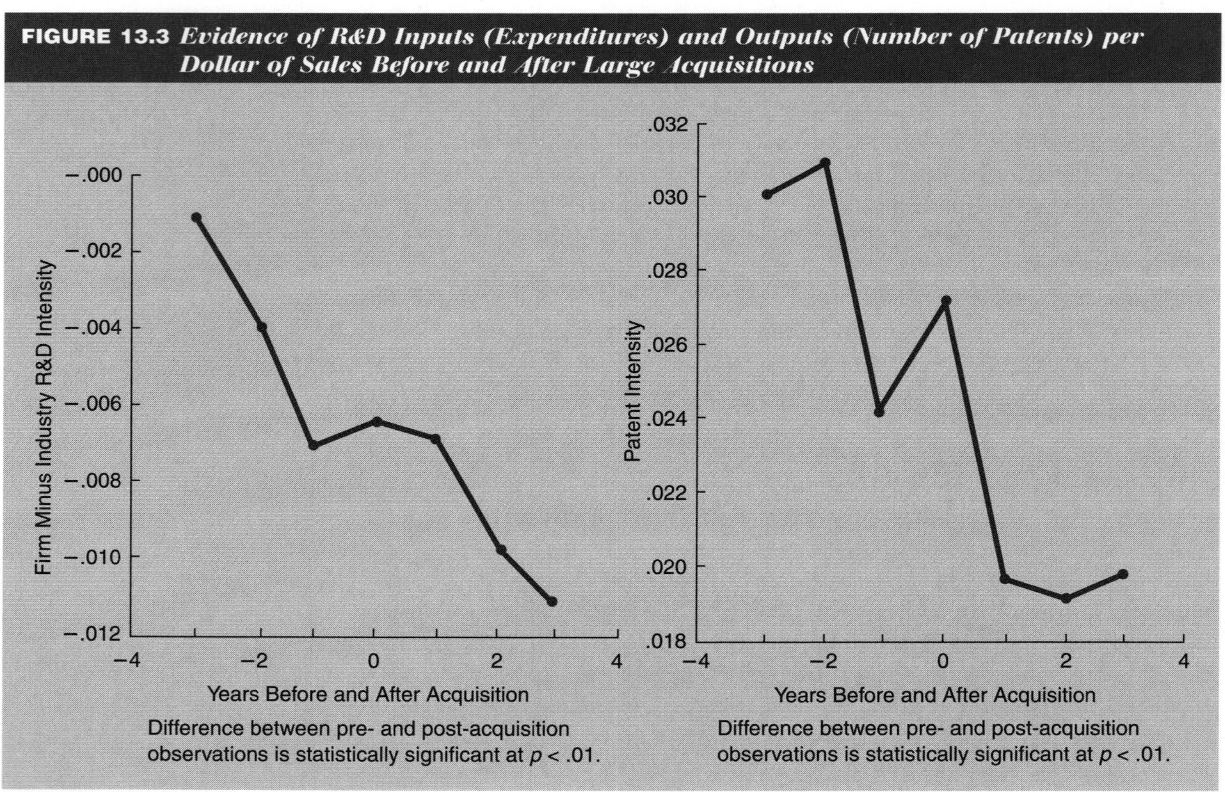

Source: M. A. Hitt, R. E. Hoskisson, R. D. Ireland, and J. S. Harrison, 1991, Are acquisitions a poison pill for innovation?, *Academy of Management Executive V,* no. 4: 24–25.

holder to use a technology. It may also buy the rights to the technology. This process is common among Indian firms. In India, most companies do not invest heavily in R&D and thus, they acquire technology and new products from firms in other countries. Interestingly, however, research shows that even modest amounts of R&D can be helpful to these firms in identifying sources of new technology.[78] Given the global marketplace and growing competition from foreign companies, firms are likely to become less willing to license or sell the rights to their technology to foreign firms. Indian firms may be forced, therefore, to invest more to develop their own technology to remain competitive.

Venture Capital

Another approach used to acquire innovations involves venture capital. Some firms choose to establish their own venture capital divisions. These divisions carefully evaluate other companies to identify those with innovations or innovative capabilities that could help the firm develop a sustainable competitive advantage. In other instances, firms decide to serve as an internal source of capital for innovative product ideas that can be spun off as independent or affiliate firms. New enterprises that are backed by venture capital provide an important source of innovation and new technology. Furthermore, they are a major source of new wealth creation in the United States. For example, these firms account annually for about one-third of all initial public offerings of stock. On average these venture capital backed new enterprises create approximately 230,000 new jobs and spend about $5 billion on R&D each year.[79]

Historically, the venture capital business has been associated primarily with independent venture capital firms, but both domestic and foreign corporations have discovered that investing in venture capital adds a new dimension to their corporate development strategies and can produce an attractive return on their investments.[80] The strategic benefits to a corporation include the ability to invest early and observe what happens to the new venture. This may lead to subsequent acquisitions, technology licensing, product marketing rights, and possibly the development of international opportunities. Large firms often view venture capital as a window on future technological development. Participation by corporations can take many forms, but usually begins with investment in several venture capital funds as a limited partner and evolves into direct investments in new business ventures. Many firms begin this strategy by forming a venture development division.

Disdain of large corporations by outside entrepreneurs can be a potential pitfall. Entrepreneurs may be wary of large corporations that seek to dominate fledgling companies. The syndication of venture funds to reduce risk may also be a factor limiting potential gains from venture capital investments. Other large firms may become part of the syndication and reduce the potential returns for the large corporate partner (through sharing of knowledge).[81] With corporate restructuring and downsizing continuing, executives seem willing to try more entrepreneurial ventures. Venture capital is apparently one way to participate and may be less risky than internal development.[82]

Larger and more experienced venture capitalists sometimes search to invest for entrepreneurs who have experience starting other ventures. These entrepreneurs have commercial experience, have knowledge about a particular industry or market sector, and ambition to succeed.[83] Alternatively some successful entrepreneurs become venture capitalists. Gary Reichling became a millionaire by selling his business to a larger corporation. In turn, he became a venture capitalist and provided capital to a small firm with little equity but a great product. Manufactured by Doumar Products, Inc., this product, un-du, is able to remove adhesives without ruining the surface product (e.g., labels, stickers, price tags, bumper stickers, etc.). Un-du can also make paper-based products temporarily transparent without harming them (e.g., making an envelope transparent to see if you signed the check sealed in it). Reichling was attracted to the product but was seriously concerned about the problems with the business plan. Eventually, Reichling took over the firm as its CEO, an unusual action for most venture capitalists, but perhaps not so unusual for former entrepreneurs.[84]

Up to this point, the focus of our discussion largely has been on corporate entrepreneurship in large firms, but small firms may even be better at producing revolutionary innovations. Although large firms often possess the significant financial resources and organizational capabilities necessary to more fully exploit innovative product opportunities, small firms may have more flexibility to produce innovations.

STRATEGIC FOCUS

Are Venture Capitalists and Entrepreneurs from the Same Mold?

Stewart Alsop is a venture capitalist and likes it because there is no ambiguity about what business he is in; he is in the business of earning money. In fact, Alsop says that he is in the business of earning lots of money. A venture capitalist who makes a small amount of money is not very good. Each year, Alsop estimates he listens to about 100 presentations and reads another 200 business plans. David Cowan is also a venture capitalist. He became interested in entrepreneurship while in college. As a freshman, he started a company that sold application software to private libraries. Later while he was a graduate student, he provided free consulting for Bessemer Ventures hoping to obtain a job with the company. He was successful. Cowan is now a partner in Bessemer Ventures and has the distinction of never losing money on one of his investments. Of course, given the risk involved, the likelihood that none of his investments will produce a negative return is very low. Recently, when Cisco Systems was sold to NetSys Technologies for $60 million, Bessemer received a 600 percent return on its investment in one year. Cowan is an aggressive investor to the point of relentlessly pursuing a person he has identified as a good CEO for a startup. If he cannot find investment opportunities fitting the appropriate criteria, he will start a company on his own, a practice that is becoming more common for venture capitalists. Thus, Cowan seems to have entrepreneurial acumen, and it would be difficult to separate him from other entrepreneurs (except that he now has equity capital).

Bob Kierlin is the highly successful CEO of Fastenal, a business selling literally nuts and bolts. His company has been providing better shareholder returns, though, than Coca-Cola or GE. Kierlin saves money in many ways. He never even thinks of flying first class and sometimes not coach either. In a recent trip from Minnesota to California, he used a company van and drove the 5,000 miles roundtrip. His salary is only $120,000 annually but his net worth is tied up in the stock. Over a recent five-year period, Fastenal produced an average 39.3 percent total return annually to shareholders. He uses what some refer to as commonsense entrepreneurship. Company policy allows branch managers to bypass company central purchasing of products if they can obtain a better deal. Branch managers bypass central purchasing 42 percent of the time. They provide exemplary service and charge premium prices. Kierlin says that the primary reason for his company's success is the philosophy that "just believe in people, give them the chance to make decisions, take risks, and work hard. We could have made this work selling cabbages."

Armando Conti is the founder of Expresso Armando, the premier manufacturer of domestic expresso machines. In 1993, Armando decided to build the world's best expresso coffee machine. This was his second entrepreneurial venture. He started his first business in 1987 and began to search for his next business in 1989. The idea for the expresso machine venture came when he purchased a $300 machine that did not produce quality expresso. He decided that there was a need for a better quality machine. With his technical skills, he designed a new expresso machine that he felt would brew superior expresso. His prototype brewed excellent coffee. It required one-and-one-half years to complete the commercial machine. The first machine was shipped to a Boston customer in December 1993. One of Armando's largest customers is Starbuck's, known throughout North America and now opening stores in Asia. In 1998, Armando's expects to sell 200 machines.

There are an increasing number of defectors from large corporations who are turning to entrepreneurship. These people often leave behind large salaries and nice offices to start or operate small new ventures. This was the case for two relatively young entrepreneurs, D. J. Edgerton and Paul Geczik. D. J. became bored with his job working in a big corporation, and Paul's employer closed his business. Paul received a piece of graphics software as severance pay and the two friends decided to use it to start a new design firm. They worked out of a run-down, rent-controlled apartment. They decided to reinvest their revenue back into their hardware and software rather than their surroundings. To establish themselves, they took almost any job, sometimes accepting last-minute jobs requiring that they work all night or all weekend to meet the deadline. One time Disney Adventure magazine needed an advertising supplement developed and completed over a weekend. No large firm could mobilize that fast so the marketing director took a chance on D. J. and Paul. They did a great job thereby winning a new customer. One of their suppliers moved back to his home in Ireland and started a new brewery. The owner wanted to establish a brand identity but had no money for a design firm to help. He proposed to give D. J. and Paul's business called Draw the Line a 5 percent stake for such work. They accepted the offer and provided about $50,000 in services. The brewery was a success, supplying dozens of pubs in Dublin. Draw the Line now has about $1 million in annual revenues with a highly successful Web-design business as a part of its portfolio and no debt.

Thus, when one examines the characteristics, it may be difficult to distinguish the entrepreneur from the venture capitalist. Many venture capitalists have prior experience as entrepreneurs and now even become involved in entrepreneurial ventures as active parties.

SOURCES: R. Teitelbaum, 1998, Who is Bob Kierlin—and why is he so successful? *Fortune*, January 10, http://www.pathfinder.com/fortune; J. Useem, 1998, The new entrepreneurial elite, *Inc. Online*, January 19, http://www.inc.com; Stewart Alsop, 1997, My secret life: The big ideas of a venture capitalist, *Fortune*, July 21, http://www.pathfinder.com/fortune; Expresso Armando, 1998, *The EM Launch Pad*, January 19, http://www.benlore.com; S. M. Mehta, 1997, The investor, *Wall Street Journal*, December 8, R28; T. Petzinger, Jr., 1997, These two young artists take tough jobs and big chances, *Wall Street Journal Interactive*, June 6, http://www.interactive6.wsj.com.

Venture capitalists and entrepreneurs play important roles in the United States and increasingly in the world economy. As noted in the Strategic Focus, they share many characteristics. In fact, it may be difficult to separate some of them as several play both roles. Clearly, entrepreneurs are important as catalysts for small businesses. Next we discuss entrepreneurship and small firms.

ENTREPRENEURSHIP AND THE SMALL FIRM

Research suggests that small firms, based in the United States and other nations throughout the world, are awarded a large number of U.S. patents.[85] Although 80 percent of the world's R&D activities in developing nations is concentrated in firms with 10,000 or more employees, these same large firms account for under half of the world's technological activity, as measured by U.S. patenting. These facts show that while large firms are important for technological advances, small firms and private individuals account for a significant share of the innovative activity and technological progress. There has been a substantial shift toward self-employment and entrepreneurial ventures in the United States.[86] Small entrepreneurial firms have become an important part of the mainstream economy and business activity in the United States.[87]

The lure of entrepreneurship is becoming far reaching. For example, women and minorities compose the largest portion of the increase in new firms. Women now own over one-third of all businesses in the United States. A majority of these firms were started in the last 10 years and may be classified as small businesses. The number of businesses owned by African Americans and Hispanic Americans has also increased dramatically in recent years.[88] One such business has thrived by providing nursing services to the inner city. Geric Home Health Care, started by an African American husband and wife team, not only serves inner city customers but also hires its employees from the inner city. Many of Geric's employees are single mothers receiving welfare. The owners found that employees assigned to the neighborhoods where they live are not afraid to work in the inner city, unlike many outsiders. To make this work, the Johnsons, who own Geric Home Health Care, had to establish a state-certified school for nursing aides. The turnover is low for this type of business, 25 percent annually. One employee explained the culture at Geric, "we're like Tom Sawyer lying in the grass dreaming about what we can do."[89]

Other entrepreneurs like Ludmila Rusakova and Jannifer Kramer, immigrants from Russia, are successful operators of a service firm. Their firm, called Master-Word Services, offers translations of documents into as many as 40 different languages. Rusakova, who is 26 and president of the firm, has nine full-time employees and 30 contractors, and the firm has revenue of approximately $2 million. The firm's customers include major oil and gas corporations, engineering companies, and law firms, and it provides services on call 24 hours a day. Currently, Rusakova is building contacts with thousands of interpreters around the world that can be hired to help on projects as needed.[90]

Even in some of the areas where large firms are effective innovators, individual entrepreneurs and small firms still make significant contributions. This relationship is demonstrated by the interactions between small and large firms operating in the electronics industry (especially among firms located in the Silicon Valley in the United States). For instance, the semiconductor industry benefited significantly by the development of new technology-based firms. Most of these firms were spin-offs created by former employees of large firms.[91] The complementarity of small and large firms in innovation is exemplified by the integration of biotechnology and pharmaceutical firms to produce innovative drugs as discussed earlier.

The balance of power between large and small companies appears to be shifting. In the United States, small and midsize companies have been responsible for nearly all of the new jobs created since 1987.[92] The Davids have what the Goliaths so desperately want: agility, resourcefulness, and flexibility. Computers and communications technologies have been great equalizers, giving individual entrepreneurs and small firms an enhanced ability to mobilize resources, hire qualified individuals, and market their goods and services (e.g., on the Internet).[93] Small firms have created most of the new jobs in the U.S. economy in the 1990s because of (1) the flexibility provided by desktop computers, (2) networks of small firms that have the ability to communicate with each other, (3) vast computerized information databases, and (4) computer-controlled machine tools that help small companies provide quality equal to that of large manufacturers.[94]

Although small firms do not have large safety nets and benefits for employees, there is a certain excitement in working for such firms. Employees feel a clear sense of purpose. Lines of communication are short and direct; often the boss walks around the facility several times a day. Employees who are dedicated and care are given serious responsibility. They are trained in numerous jobs and typically are rewarded in ways that encourage their allegiance to their employer.[95]

Interestingly, new entrepreneurial firms have tended to perform better and have a higher survival rate than franchised startup firms. Franchised firms often receive considerable support from the larger businesses from which they are franchised but also must adhere to many of the larger firms' corporate policies and procedures. As such, franchises have less flexibility and are less innovative. Research has shown that over a three-year period, the average net loss for retailing franchising was $4,000 plus, whereas cohort independent entrepreneurial retailing firms had an average net income for the same three-year period of more than $14,000. Similarly, franchise firms had a 45 percent failure rate, whereas young entrepreneurial independent retail firms had a slightly less than 24 percent failure rate for the same time period.[96]

Additionally, entrepreneurs who founded firms are significantly more innovative in their decisions than owners who did not initially establish the firm. These findings suggest that entrepreneurs who operate independent companies are likely to be more innovative and more successful than nonentrepreneurs, particularly those connected to larger firms and operating under their policies and procedures, like franchises.[97]

One of the reasons that entrepreneurs are more innovative than managers in large companies is that they tend to use more heuristics in making decisions. The use of heuristics has been found to be associated with more innovative decisions and outcomes, but the heavy reliance on it is probably why entrepreneurs rarely make effective managers as their firm grows.[98]

As entrepreneurial firms grow, entrepreneurs need to learn the following new skills to manage them well: (1) how to use cash flow to make decisions, (2) how to finance growth, (3) how to increase the value of the business, (4) how to compensate self and associates, (5) how to effectively hire, train, and motivate employees to achieve growth, (6) how to deal with a rapidly changing environment, (7) how to develop management succession, and (8) how to understand the problems of growth.[99] While many entrepreneurs do not seem to have the right skills or mindset to manage their firm after it has grown, Catherine Candland seems to be an exception. Ms. Candland is the founder, owner, and manager of Advantage Staffing Services, a temporary staffing firm. She started the firm in 1983 and now has 17 offices, 200 employees, and almost $70 million in annual revenue. Not only has she developed a successful business, but she also has had three children since founding Advantage.[100]

Successfully innovating and commercializing a new product idea outside large corporations is not an easy task. Putting together the funding, marketing plan, and production facilities, along with completing the regulatory paperwork, is a challenge for entrepreneurs seeking to start their own private company. Nonetheless, small new technology-based firms have fostered the growth of many industries, including semiconductors, CAD, and biotechnology. These examples illustrate the importance of entrepreneurs and small firms in the development of new products and the diffusion of innovation.

What can large firms do to act small and be innovative? First, many firms, through restructuring as described in Chapter 7, are being organized into more manageable units.[101] Accompanying these restructurings, firms are reengineering to reduce organizational processes to the essential functions, share risks with partners, and listen more fully and effectively to customers. Second, large companies are trying to offer attractive places to work and seek to bind employee interests to those of the company. This is accomplished through arrangements such as self-managed teams and customer-satisfaction bonuses. For example, Herbert Kelleher, CEO of Southwest Airlines, has sought to keep a small-firm culture by using traditional profit-sharing plans and a buddy system linking longtime and new employees.

Many large firms have handled decreasing competitiveness by laying off tens of thousands of employees. But downsizing has not realized the gains anticipated. Although head-count cuts happen fast and the stock market sometimes reacts favorably, research indicates that 50 percent or more of the firms end up worse after their downsizing.[102] Much to large firms' chagrin, massive layoffs can sometimes merely erode morale. Divestitures and spin-offs have produced much more favorable results.[103] In the long run, large firms must practice a delicate balancing act that allows autonomy at the lowest levels, while maintaining the advantages of size.

One of the ways large firms contribute to innovation is with the significant resources they can invest in R&D. Table 13.1 lists the top 10 firms throughout the world that have invested the most in R&D. While possibly not the most innovative, these firms should produce a substantial number of new ideas.[104] One way for large firms to make major strategic moves quickly is to link up with smaller, more agile firms. To do this, some large firms provide the venture capital for smaller

TABLE 13.1 *The Largest Investors in R&D in the World*

Company	Dollars Invested (in Billions)	R&D/Sales
1. General Motors (U.S.)	8.8	5.6%
2. Ford (U.S.)	6.8	5.8
3. Siemens (Germany)	4.6	7.7
4. Hitachi (Japan)	4.2	6.1
5. IBM (U.S.)	4.0	5.2
6. Daimler-Benz (Germany)	3.6	5.2
7. Matsushita (Japan)	3.4	5.9
8. Fujitsu (Japan)	3.0	9.2
9. NTT (Japan)	2.8	4.0
10. Novartis (Switzerland)	2.8	10.1

Source: C. Cookson, 1998, Financial community develops a taste for industrial research, *Financial Times,* January 20, 17.

firms to develop a good idea as noted earlier. Larger firms often have more efficient manufacturing and distribution systems as compared to smaller firms. A linkage with smaller firms can also be useful in implementing other strategic moves. This is being done by a number of large firms seeking to establish a presence in the Russian market. Because of their proximity, Finnish firms have operated in Russia for many years and have built a storehouse of knowledge about the Russian culture and markets. Importantly, they also have built numerous contacts. Thus, many large firms from other European and North American countries have established strategic alliances with Finnish firms to enter Russian markets ranging from oil and gas to computer hardware and software.[105]

Still, it seems that many new concepts for business come from small firms. For example, Wawa Inc. started as a family dairy but grew into a five-state chain of new concept convenience stores. In its 515 stores, customers have such upscale choices as kiwi, fresh tomatoes, mineral water, pasta salad, cappuccino, and yogurt. Wawa also serves Taco Bell burritos and Pizza Hut pizzas. The editor-in-chief of *Convenience Store News* states that, "They're on the cutting edge." These new concept convenience stores attract a new type of customer compared to the typical convenience store that sells more beer, gasoline, and tobacco than other products. Wawa founded its first store in 1985. Its current annual sales approximate $850 million.[106] There likely will be other new concepts in service industries in future years. For example, one author predicts that there will be a business and leisure hotel on the moon and other hotels in parts of the solar system. In the shorter term, new hotels are being built in South America, China, Eastern Europe, and lesser known parts of southeast Asia to fill a need for business and tourist travelers.[107]

Thus, large and small firms alike can be innovative. Oftentimes, cooperative efforts between large and small firms may produce the best opportunity to commercialize innovations. The small firms can develop the innovation and the large firms can best get it to the market. This type of cooperative endeavor may be a key link to the ability of both large and small firms to achieve strategic competitiveness and earn above-average returns.[108]

SUMMARY

- Three basic strategic approaches are used to produce and manage innovation. The first approach is called internal corporate venturing. This approach emphasizes the development of autonomous strategic behavior wherein product champions pursue new product ideas and executives help them manage the strategic context to commercialize the new products within a larger firm. Induced strategic behavior is a top-down process wherein incremental product changes and adjustments are made to the original product. This is a process driven by the organization's current corporate strategy, structure, and reward and control systems.
- The innovation process has three stages. Invention is the act of creating and developing a new product idea. The next stage, innovation, is the process of commercializing products from invention. Ultimately, other firms in the industry imitate the new product and diffuse the innovation. Imitation results in product standardization and market acceptance.
- In the past, internal innovation was done serially. Now, more parallel innovation is created through cross-functional teams. Facilitated by cross-functional teams, cross-functional integration can reduce the time a firm needs to introduce innovative products into the marketplace, improve product quality, and ultimately help a firm create value for its targeted customer. When innovations decrease the time to market (speed is a critical competitive factor) and create product quality and customer value, it is likely that a firm will be able to appropriate (or extract) value from the innovation process.

- A second approach used to produce and manage innovation is to obtain innovation through strategic alliances. Because knowledge is exploding and is often located in specialized firms, the only way a firm may be able to obtain the knowledge necessary to create new products is through strategic alliances and/or joint ventures.
- The third basic approach for large firms to produce and manage innovation is to acquire it. Innovation can be acquired either through direct acquisition or through indirect investment. An example of indirect investment is the formation of a wholly owned venture capital division and/or the use of private placement of venture capital. Buying innovation, however, may be risky and detrimental to a firm's internal innovation process.
- The best way to succeed with a wholly owned venture capital operation is to consider the venture capital as an investment and only secondarily as a strategy to acquire innovation. Alternatively, a firm may seek to invest venture capital directly in small firms or to spin off firms into a network of affiliate companies.
- Small firms are particularly well suited for fostering innovation that does not require large amounts of capital (as semiconductors and chemicals do). Small firms have therefore become a vibrant part of industrialized nations, accounting for more job creation than large firms during the last decade. Where there are low-cost ways to invent, for example, through mechanical inventions, small firms are likely to have a higher innovation rate than large firms.
- Large firms are needed to foster innovation due to capital requirements. Small firms are often found to be better at creating specialty products and diffusing the innovation through spin-offs from large corporations. Large firms are seeking ways to think and act smaller in order to become more entrepreneurial. Often, however, the best way for both small and large firms to solve technological problems is to cooperate and collaborate.

REVIEW QUESTIONS

1. What are three strategic approaches firms use to produce and manage innovation?
2. What are the two processes used to engage in internal corporate venturing known as autonomous strategic behavior and induced strategic behavior?
3. What are three types of innovation that are developed in organizations?
4. Some believe that when managed successfully, cross-functional teams facilitate the implementation of internal corporate ventures and a firm's innovation efforts. How should cross-functional teams be managed to achieve these desirable outcomes?
5. Some firms use strategic alliances to contract for innovation. What are the actions taken to use strategic alliances for this purpose?
6. How can a firm create value when it acquires another company to gain access to its innovations and/or its ability to produce innovations?
7. How do large firms use venture capital to create innovations and to identify new product opportunities?
8. What are the differences in the resources, capabilities, and core competencies of large and small firms to produce and manage innovation?

APPLICATION DISCUSSION QUESTIONS

1. In the 1980s and 1990s, the number of acquisitions has accelerated. The number of dollars being spent as venture capital also increased. Discuss whether or not you think there is a relationship between the wave of acquisitions and the increase in venture capital funding.
2. In your opinion, is the term *corporate entrepreneurship* an oxymoron? In other words, is it a contradiction of terms? If so, why?
3. Discuss the reasons for using cross-functional teams as a popular approach to develop new product designs.
4. How would you suggest that developing countries with a tradition of centralized bureaucracy, such as China and Russia, begin to compete in a global economy that emphasizes product innovation? What should be emphasized in these countries to make firms and their countries more competitive on a global basis? Should they encourage entrepreneurial firms (as is the case in Taiwan)? Should they encourage large firms (as is the case in South Korea)? Should both types of firms be emphasized? Be prepared to justify your views.

5. The restructuring movement (e.g., acquisitions, divestitures, and downsizing) of the 1980s and 1990s has apparently made U.S. firms more *productive* (as measured by traditional output-per-employee ratios). But, in your opinion, are U.S. firms more innovative because of the restructuring and downsizing activity? Why or why not?
6. Are strategic alliances a way to increase existing technological capacity, or are strategic alliances used more by firms that are behind technologically and trying to catch up? In other words, are strategic alliances a tool of firms that have a technological advantage, or are they a tool of technologically disadvantaged companies? Please explain.

ETHICS QUESTIONS

1. Is it ethical for a company to purchase another firm in order to gain ownership of its innovative products? Why or why not?
2. Entrepreneurs are sometimes more effective when they work against existing product standards. How do entrepreneurs know when their new products might harm consumers? Should government agencies or trade associations establish guidelines to assist entrepreneurs on this issue? If so, what might some of those guidelines be?
3. Are there any ethical concerns surrounding the use of an internal venturing process to produce and manage innovation? Why or why not?
4. When participating in a strategic alliance, partner firms may legitimately seek to gain knowledge from each other. At what point does it become unethical for a firm to gain additional and competitively relevant knowledge from a strategic alliance partner? Is this point different when partnering with a domestic firm as opposed to a foreign firm? If so, why?
5. Small firms often have innovative products. When is it appropriate for a large firm to buy a small firm for its new products and new product ideas?

INTERNET EXERCISE

Go to Texas Instrument's History of Innovation at:

http://www.ti.com/corp/docs/history/tihistory.html

Texas Instruments (TI) has a rich history of innovation. For example, in 1954 the company produced the first transistor radio, in 1967 the first hand-held calculator, and in 1989, the first quantum-effect transistor. What is particularly striking about TI's legacy of innovation is the diverse set of management techniques that it has used to facilitate the innovation process. These techniques include acquisitions, joint ventures, strategic alliances, and other management initiatives designed to promote and expedite the innovation process.

Visit the Texas Instrument's History of Innovation Web site and make a list of the management techniques that TI has used over the years to facilitate the innovation process. Make special note of the techniques discussed in this chapter.

Strategic Surfing

A number of organizations maintain Web sites that focus on entrepreneurship and innovation. Several of the premier sites include:

EntreWorld, maintained by the Kauffman Foundation:

http://www.entreworld.org

Center for Entrepreneurial Studies at Babson College:

http://www.babson.edu/entrep

EGOPHER, maintained by St. Louis University:

http://www.slu.edu/eweb/egopher.html

Lets Talk Business Network:

http://www.ltbn.com

NOTES

1. H. Lancaster, 1997, A company crisis could be a chance to make your mark, *Wall Street Journal Interactive*, August 29, http://www.wsj.com/edition/current/articles.
2. The expert's corner, 1998, January 19, http://www.benlore.com/files/emexpert2.
3. C. A. Lengnick-Hall, 1992, Innovation and competitive ad-

vantage: What we know and what we need to learn, *Journal of Management* 18: 399–429.

4. M. A. Hitt, B. W. Keats, and S. M. DeMarie, 1998, Navigating in the new competitive landscape: Building strategic flexibility and competitive advantage in the 21st century, *Academy of Management Executive*, in press; R. A. Bettis and M. A. Hitt, 1995, The new competitive landscape, *Strategic Management Journal* 16 (Special Summer Issue): 7–19.
5. R. Price, 1996, Technology and strategic advantage, *California Management Review* 38, no. 3: 38–56; L. G. Franko, 1989, Global corporate competition: Who's winning, who's losing and the R&D factor as one reason why, *Strategic Management Journal* 10: 449–474.
6. G. T. Lumpkin and G. G. Dess, 1996, Clarifying the entrepreneurial orientation construct and linking it to performance, *Academy of Management Review* 21: 135–172; K. M. Kelm, V. K. Narayanan, and G. E. Pinches, 1995, Shareholder value creation during R&D innovation and commercialization stages, *Academy of Management Journal* 38: 770–786.
7. B. C. Reimann, 1995, Leading strategic change: Innovation, value, growth, *Planning Review* 23 (September/October): 6–9.
8. Lumpkin and Dess, Clarifying the entrepreneurial orientation construct.
9. R. C. Solomon, 1995, Marketing heidegger: Entrepreneurship and corporate practices, *Inquiry* 38: 75–81.
10. D. L. Sexton and R. W. Smilor, 1997, Growth strategies in D. L. Sexton and R. W. Smilor (eds.), *Entrepreneurship 2000* (Chicago: Upstart Publishing Company); M. B. Low and E. Abrahamson, 1997, Movements, bandwagons, and clones: Industry evolution and the entrepreneurial process, *Journal of Business Venturing* 12: 435–457.
11. J. M. Stopford and C. W. F. Baden-Fuller, 1994, Creating corporate entrepreneurship, *Strategic Management Journal* 15: 521–536.
12. C. Farrell, 1993, A wellspring of innovation: Factories have changed relentlessly from 18th century mills to today's worker-empowered auto plants, *Fortune* (Special Bonus Issue): 62.
13. J. P. Womack, D. T. Jones, and D. Roos, 1990, *The Machine That Changed the World* (New York: Rawson Associates), 14.
14. R. J. Schonberger, 1996, *World Class Manufacturing: The Next Decade* (New York: The Free Press).
15. J. Schumpeter, 1934, *The Theory of Economic Development* (Cambridge, MA: Harvard University Press).
16. B. Czarniawska-Joerges and R. Wolff, 1991, Leaders, managers, entrepreneurs on and off the organizational stage, *Organization Studies* 12: 529–546.
17. J. Bowles, 1997, Best practices: Driving growth through innovation, alliances, and stakeholder symbiosis, *Fortune*, November 14, S3–S24.
18. Stopford and Baden-Fuller, Creating corporate entrepreneurship.
19. J. P. Kotter, 1990, *A Force for Change* (New York: The Free Press); H. Mintzberg, 1971, Managerial work: Analysis from observation, *Management Science* 18, no. 2: 97–110.
20. R. W. Smilor, 1997, Entrepreneurship: Reflections on a subversive activity, *Journal of Business Venturing* 12: 341–346.
21. F. N. Pieke, 1995, Bureaucracy, friends and money: The growth of capital socialism in China, *Comparative Studies in Society and History* 37: 494–518.
22. M. H. Morris, D. L. Davis, and J. W. Allen, 1994, Fostering corporate entrepreneurship: Cross-cultural comparisons of the importance of individualism versus collectivism, *Journal of International Business Studies* 25: 65–89.
23. P. S. Li, 1993, Chinese investment and business in Canada: Ethnic entrepreneurship reconsidered, *Pacific Affairs* 66: 219–243.
24. D. H. Holt, 1997, A comparative study of values among Chinese and U.S. entrepreneurs: Pragmatic convergence between contrasting cultures, *Journal of Business Venturing* 12: 483–505.
25. T. Bates, 1997, Financing small business creation: The case of Chinese and Korean immigrant entrepreneurs, *Journal of Business Venturing* 12: 109–124.
26. M. Lerner, C. Brush, and R. Hisrich, 1997, Israeli women entrepreneurs: An examination of factors affecting performance, *Journal of Business Venturing* 12: 315–339.
27. P. P. McDougall and B. M. Oviatt, 1997, International entrepreneurship literature in the 1990s and directions for future research in D. L. Sexton and R. W. Smilor (eds.), *Entrepreneurship 2000* (Chicago: Upstart Publishing Co.), 291–321.
28. M. A. Hitt and B. B. Bartkus, 1997, International entrepreneurship in J. A. Katz and R. H. Brockhaus, Sr. (eds.), *Advances in Entrepreneurship, Firm Emergence and Growth* (Greenwich, CT: JAI Press), 7–30.
29. M. A. Hitt, R. E. Hoskisson, and H. Kim, 1997, International diversification: Effects on innovation and firm performance in product-diversified firms, *Academy of Management Journal* 40: 767–798.
30. B. Mascarenhas, 1997, The order and size of entry into international markets, *Journal of Business Venturing* 12: 287–299.
31. R. A. Burgelman, 1983, A model of the interaction of strategic behavior, corporate context, and the concept of strategy, *Academy of Management Review* 8: 61–70.
32. D. Leonard-Barton, 1995, *Wellsprings of Knowledge: Building and Sustaining the Sources of Innovation* (Cambridge, MA: Harvard Business School Press).
33. G. Hamel, 1997, Killer strategies that make shareholders rich, *Fortune*, June 23: 70–88.
34. S. V. Brull, 1997, Sony: A little sensor with a big future, *Business Week Interactive*, June 16, http://www.businessweek.com.
35. P. Coy and R. Grover, 1995, It's Nobuyuki Idei's Sony now, *Business Week*, December 18, 39.
36. G. G. Dess, G. T. Lumpkin, and J. G. Covin, 1997, Entrepreneurial strategy and firm performance: Tests of contingency and configurational models, *Strategic Management Journal* 18: 677–695.
37. L. C. Wright and R. W. Wright, 1997, Developing and deploying corporate resources in the technological race to market in H. Thomas, D. O'Neal, and M. Ghertman (eds.), *Strategy, Structure and Style* (Chichester, GB: John Wiley & Sons), 114–135.
38. R. G. McGrath, 1997, A real options logic for initiating technology positioning investments, *Academy of Management Review* 22: 974–996.
39. D. M. A. Rogers, 1996, The challenge of fifth generation R&D, *Research-Technology Management* July-August: 33–41.
40. B. L. David, 1994, How internal venture groups innovate, *Research-Technology Management* March–April: 38–43.

41. R. C. Shrader and M. Simon, 1997, Corporate versus independent new ventures: Resource, strategy, and performance differences, *Journal of Business Venturing* 12: 47–66.
42. B. O'Reilly, 1997, The secrets of America's most admired corporations: New ideas, new products, *Fortune*, March 3, 60–64.
43. J. A. Byrne, 1993, The horizontal corporation: It's about managing across, not up and down, *Business Week*, December 20, 76–81.
44. J. E. Ettlie, 1988, *Taking Charge of Manufacturing* (San Francisco: Jossey-Bass).
45. A. C. Amason, 1996, Distinguishing the effects of functional and dysfunctional conflict on strategic decision making: Resolving a paradox for top management teams, *Academy of Management Journal* 39: 123–148; P. R. Lawrence and J. W. Lorsch, 1969, *Organization and Environment* (Homewood, IL: Richard D. Irwin).
46. D. Dougherty, 1992, Interpretive barriers to successful product innovation in large firms, *Organization Science* 3: 179–202; D. Dougherty, 1990, Understanding new markets for new products, *Strategic Management Journal* 11 (Special Summer Issue): 59–78.
47. M. A. Hitt, R. D. Nixon, R. E. Hoskisson, and R. Kochhar, 1998, Corporate entrepreneurship and cross-functional fertilization: Activation, process and disintegration of a new product design team, *Entrepreneurship: Theory and Practice*, in press.
48. J. D. Orton and K. E. Weick, 1990, Loosely coupled systems: A reconsideration, *Academy of Management Review* 15: 203–223.
49. S. L. Brown and K. M. Eisenhardt, 1995, Product development: Past research, present findings and future directions, *Academy of Management Review* 20: 343–378.
50. A. Barua, C. H. S. Lee, and A. B. Whinston, 1995, Incentives and computing systems for team-based organizations, *Organization Science* 6: 487–504.
51. I. Sager, 1995, The view from IBM, *Business Week*, October 30, 142–150; IBM says it's ready for networking era, 1995, *Dallas Morning News*, November 14, D4.
52. K. M. Eisenhardt and S. L. Brown, 1998, Time pacing: Competing in markets that won't stand still, *Harvard Business Review* 76, no. 2: 59–69.
53. W. Q. Judge and A. Miller, 1991, Antecedents and outcomes of decision speed in different environmental contexts, *Academy of Management Journal* 34: 449–463.
54. M. B. Lieberman and D. B. Montgomery, 1988, First-mover advantages, *Strategic Management Journal* 9 (Special Summer Issue): 41–58.
55. W. Davidson, 1988, Technology, environments and organizational choice, paper presented at the conference on Managing the High-Tech Firm, Graduate School of Business, University of Colorado.
56. M. J. Chen and D. C. Hambrick, 1995, Speed, stealth and selective attack: How small firms differ from large firms in competitive behavior, *Academy of Management Journal* 38: 453–482.
57. W. M. Bulkeley, 1994, The latest big thing at many companies is speed, speed, speed, *Wall Street Journal*, December 23, A1, A5.
58. M. W. Lawless and P. C. Anderson, 1996, Generational technological change: The effects of innovation and local rivalry on performance, *Academy of Management Journal* 39: 1185–1217; U. Zander and B. Kogut, 1995, Knowledge and the speed of the transfer and imitation of organizational capabilities: An empirical test, *Organization Science* 6: 76–92.
59. K. M. Eisenhardt and B. N. Tabrizi, 1995, Accelerating adaptive processes: Product innovation in the global computer industry, *Administrative Science Quarterly* 40: 84–110.
60. Judge and Miller, Antecedents and outcomes.
61. Hitt, Nixon, Hoskisson, and Kochhar, Corporate entrepreneurship.
62. M. A. Hitt, R. E. Hoskisson, and R. D. Nixon, 1993, A mid-range theory of interfunctional integration, its antecedents and outcomes, *Journal of Engineering Technology Management* 10: 161–185.
63. J. E. Forrest, 1992, Management aspects of strategic partnering, *Journal of General Management* 17, no. 4: 25–40; B. Borys and D. B. Jemison, 1989, Hybrid arrangements as strategic alliances: Theoretical issues in organizational combinations, *Academy of Management Review* 14: 234–249.
64. J. L. Badaracco, Jr., 1991, *The Knowledge Link: How Firms Compete Through Strategic Alliances* (Cambridge, MA: Harvard University School Press).
65. R. Langreth, 1995, Biotech companies abandon go-it-alone approach, *Wall Street Journal*, November 21, B4.
66. R. T. King, Jr., 1995, Pharmaceutical giants are eagerly shopping biotech bargain bin, *Wall Street Journal*, April 19, A1, A10.
67. G. Hamel, 1991, Competition for competence and inter-partner learning within international strategic alliances, *Strategic Management Journal* 12: 83–103.
68. M. T. Dacin, M. A. Hitt, and E. Levitas, 1997, Selecting partners for successful international alliances: Examination of U.S. and Korean firms, *Journal of World Business*, 32, 1: 3–16; M. A. Hitt, M. T. Dacin, B. B. Tyler, and D. Park, 1997, Understanding the differences in Korean and U.S. Executive's strategic orientations, *Strategic Management Journal* 18: 159–167.
69. C. K. Prahalad and G. Hamel, 1990, The core competence of the corporation, *Harvard Business Review* 68, no. 3: 79–93.
70. D. Lei and M. A. Hitt, 1995, Strategic restructuring and outsourcing: The effect of mergers and acquisitions and LBOs on building firm skills and capabilities, *Journal of Management* 21: 835–860.
71. Hamel, Competition for competence.
72. King, Pharmaceutical giants are eagerly shopping.
73. D. C. Mowery and D. J. Teece, 1993, Japan's growing capabilities in industrial technology: Implications for U.S. managers and policy makers, *California Management Review* 35, no. 2: 9–34.
74. M. A. Hitt, R. E. Hoskisson, R. A. Johnson, and D. D. Moesel, 1996, The market for corporate control and firm innovation, *Academy of Management Journal* 39: 1084–1119.
75. M. A. Hitt, R. E. Hoskisson, R. D. Ireland, and J. S. Harrison, 1991, Effects of acquisitions on R&D inputs and outputs, *Academy of Management Journal* 34: 693–706.
76. Hitt et al., The market for corporate control and firm innovation.
77. M. A. Hitt, J. S. Harrison, R. D. Ireland, and A. Best, 1998, Attributes of successful and unsuccessful acquisitions of U.S. firms, *British Journal of Management*, in press; M. A. Hitt,

R. E. Hoskisson, and R. D. Ireland, 1990, Mergers and acquisitions and managerial commitment to innovation in M-form firms, *Strategic Management Journal* 11 (Special Summer Issue): 29–47.

78. B. L. Pandit and N. S. Siddharthan, 1998, Technological acquisition and investment: Lessons from recent Indian experience, *Journal of Business Venturing* 13: 43–55.
79. D. S. Cable and S. Shane, 1997, A prisoner's dilemma approach to entrepreneur-venture capitalist relationships, *Academy of Management Review* 22: 142–176.
80. T. E. Winters and D. L. Murfin, 1988, Venture capital investing for corporate development objectives, *Journal of Business Venturing* 3: 207–222.
81. G. F. Hardymon, M. J. DeNino, and M. S. Salter, 1983, When corporate venture capital doesn't work, *Harvard Business Review* 61, no. 3: 114–120.
82. U. Gupta, 1993, Venture capital investment soars, reversing four-year slide, *Wall Street Journal*, June 1, B2.
83. M. Wright, K. Robbie, and C. Ennew, 1997, Venture capitalists and serial entrepreneurs, *Journal of Business Venturing* 12: 227–249.
84. B. J. Feder, 1998, Good product, sound plans, no sure thing, *New York Times on the Web*, January 19, http://www.search.nytimes.com.
85. P. Patel and K. Pavitt, 1992, Large firms in the production of the world's technology: An important case of non-globalization in O. Granstrand, L. Hakanson, and S. Sjolander (eds.), *Technology Management and International Business: Internationalization of R&D and Technology* (New York: John Wiley & Sons), 53–74.
86. B. O'Reilly, 1994, The new face of small business, *Fortune*, May 2, 82–88.
87. Farrell et al., The boom in IPOs.
88. S. Chartrand, 1998, Women and minorities now account for biggest jump in startup companies, *New York Times* on the Web, January 19: http://www.search.nytimes.com.
89. T. Petzinger, Jr., 1997, Nurse agency thrives taking hard cases in the inner city, *Wall Street Journal* Interactive, October 19: http://www.interactive.wsj.com.
90. C. Boisseau, 1996, Young entrepreneurs finding themselves in good company, *Houston Chronicle*, March 26, C1, C6.
91. R. Rothwell, 1984, The role of small firms in the emergence of new technologies, *International Journal of Management Science* 12, no. 1: 19–29.
92. J. A. Byrne, 1993, Enterprise: Introduction, *Business Week* (Special Bonus Issue): 12; Hitt and Bartkus, International entrepreneurship.
93. G. McWilliams, 1995, Small fry goes on-line, *Business Week*, November 20, 158–164.
94. P. Coy, 1993, Start with some high-tech magic, *Business Week* (Special Bonus Issue): 24–28.
95. C. Burck, 1993, The real world of the entrepreneur, *Fortune*, April 5, 62–81.
96. T. Bates, 1995, Analysis of survival rates among franchise and independent small business startups, *Journal of Small Business Management* 33: 26–36.
97. J. S. Walsh and P. H. Anderson, 1995, Owner-manager adaptations/innovation preference and employment performance: A comparison of founders and non-founders in the Irish small firm sector, *Journal of Small Business Management* 33: 1–8.
98. L. W. Busenitz, 1997, Differences between entrepreneurs and managers in large organizations: Biases and heuristics in strategic decision making, *Journal of Business Venturing* 12: 9–30.
99. D. L. Sexton, N. B. Upton, L. E. Wacholtz, and P. P. Mcdougall, 1997, Learning needs of growth-oriented entrepreneurs, *Journal of Business Venturing* 12: 1–8.
100. Advantage staffing chief has found the right fit, 1997, *Wall Street Journal* Interactive, October 19: http://www.interactive.wsj.com.
101. R. A. Melcher, 1993, How Goliaths can act like Davids, *Business Week* (Special Bonus Issue): 192–201.
102. M. A. Hitt, B. W. Keats, H. F. Harback, and R. D. Nixon, 1994, Rightsizing: Building and maintaining strategic leadership and long-term competitiveness, *Organizational Dynamics* 23, no. 2: 18–32.
103. R. E. Hoskisson and M. A. Hitt, 1994, *Downscoping: Taming the Diversified Firm* (New York: Oxford University Press).
104. C. Cookson, 1998, Financial community develops a taste for industrial research, *Financial Times*, January 20, 17.
105. R. Routamo, 1998, Dragon as a playmate: Small businesses in Finland make big money in Russia, *The EM Global Perspective*, January 19: http://www.benlore.com.
106. A. Westfeldt, 1997, Convenience stores in the 90s: Wawa redefines an American institution, *Waco Tribune-Herald*, December 25, C5.
107. M. Thompson-Noel, 1997, Boldly venturing into virgin territories, *Financial Times*, November 20, 5.
108. Hitt, Keats, and DeMarie, Navigating in the new competitive landscape.

CASES

Contents

INTRODUCTION Preparing an Effective Case Analysis C-1

CASE 1 Amazon.com C-16

CASE 2 Americast: A New Era in Home Entertainment C-32

CASE 3 Anheuser-Busch and Redhook Create Froth in Craft Beers C-38

CASE 4 The Australian Pineapple Industry: An Exporting Case Study C-50

CASE 5 Bank of America and the Carlsbad Highlands Foreclosure C-61

CASE 6 Birra Moretti C-69

CASE 7 Cap Gemini Sogeti: Genesis C-87

CASE 8 Carnival Corporation: 1997 C-120

CASE 9 China Eastern Airlines: Building an International Airline C-134

CASE 10 Ciba-Geigy and Chiron: Partnerships Between Firms in the Pharmaceutical and Biotechnology Industries C-145

CASE 11 Circus Circus Enterprises, Inc., 1997 C-159

CASE 12 Columbia/HCA: One-Stop Shopping in the Health Care Industry C-171

CASE 13 Compaq: Conflicts Between Alliances C-183

CASE 14 Cummins Engine Company, Inc.: Relationship with KamAZ C-197

CASE 15 Dayton Hudson Corporation C-215

CASE 16 Enron Development Corporation C-225

CASE 17 Granada Group: A Successful Story of Mergers and Acquisitions C-239

CASE 18 Harold's Stores, Inc. C-249

CASE 19 Internationalization of Telefónica España, S.A. C-261

CASE 20 Jefferson-Pilot Corporation C-282

CASE 21 Královopolská: The Search for Strategy C-300

CASE 22 The Lincoln Electric Company, 1996 C-315

CASE 23 Lockheed and Martin Marietta: The Defense Megamerger C-338

CASE 24 Motorola in China C-355

CASE 25 Pasta Perfect, Inc. C-367

CASE 26 Prvni Brněnská Strojirna (PBS): The Joint Venture Decision C-378

CASE 27 Rover Group—The Indonesian National Car Programme C-388

CASE 28 Sanyo Manufacturing Corporation: 1977–1990 C-000

CASE 29 Sonic: A Success Story C-400

CASE 30 Southwest Airlines, 1996 C-427

CASE 31 Starbucks Corporation C-443

CASE 32 Steinway & Sons C-461

CASE 33 Textron Inc. and the Cessna 172 C-482

CASE 34 Tootsie Roll, Inc. C-496

CASE 35 Tyson Foods, Inc. C-507

CASE 36 United Colors of Benetton C-527

CASE 37 VOS Industries: Entrepreneurship in the New Russia C-567

CASE 38 Walt Disney Co. C-577

CASE 39 Warner-Lambert Company C-593

CASE 40 Whirlpool's Quest for Global Leadership C-609

Preparing an Effective Case Analysis

In most strategic management courses, cases are used extensively as a teaching tool. A key reason is that cases allow opportunities to identify and solve organizational problems through use of the strategic management process. Thus, by analyzing cases and presenting the results, students learn how to effectively use the tools, techniques, and concepts that combine to form the strategic management process.

The cases that follow involve actual companies. Presented within them are problems and situations that managers must analyze and resolve. As you will see, a strategic management case can focus on an entire industry, a single organization, or a business unit of a large, diversified firm. The strategic management issues facing not-for-profit organizations also can be examined with the case analysis method.

Basically, the case analysis method calls for a careful diagnosis of an organization's current conditions (internal and external) so that appropriate strategic actions can be recommended. Appropriate actions not only allow a firm to survive in the long run, but also describe how it can develop and use core competencies to create sustainable competitive advantages and earn above-average returns. The case method has a rich heritage as a pedagogical approach to the study and understanding of managerial effectiveness.[1]

Critical to successful use of the case method is your *preparation*—that is, the preparation of the student or case analyst. Without careful study and analysis, you will lack the insights required to participate fully in the discussion of a firm's situation and the strategic actions that are appropriate.

Instructors adopt different approaches in their use of the case method. Some require their students to use a specific analytical procedure to examine an organization; others provide less structure, expecting students to learn by developing their own unique analytical method. Still other instructors believe that a moderately structured framework should be used to analyze a firm's situation and make appropriate recommendations. The specific approach you take will be determined by your professor. The approach we present to you here is a moderately structured framework.

Discussion of the case method is divided into four sections. First, it is important for you to understand why cases are used and what skills you can expect to learn through successful use of the case method. Second, a process-oriented framework is provided that can help you analyze cases and effectively discuss the results of your work. Using this framework in a classroom setting yields valuable experiences that can, in turn, help you successfully complete assignments received from your employer. Third, we describe briefly what you can expect to occur during in-class discussions of cases. As this description shows, the relationship and interactions between instructors and students during case discussions are different than they are during lectures. Finally, a moderately structured framework is offered for effective completion of in-depth oral and written presentations. Written and oral communication skills also are attributes valued highly in many organizational settings; hence, their development today can serve you well in the future.

USING THE CASE METHOD

The case method is based on a philosophy that combines knowledge acquisition with significant student involvement. In the words of Alfred North Whitehead, this philosophy "rejects the doctrine that students had first learned passively, and then, having learned should apply knowledge."[2] The case method, instead, is based on principles elaborated by John Dewey:

> Only by wrestling with the conditions of this problem at hand, seeking and finding his own way out, does [the student] think. . . . If he cannot devise his own solution (not, of course, in isolation, but in correspondence with the teacher and other pupils) and find his own way out he will not learn, not even if he can recite some correct answer with a hundred percent accuracy.[3]

The case method brings reality into the classroom. When developed and presented effectively, with rich and interesting detail, cases keep conceptual discussions grounded in reality. Experience shows that simple fictional accounts of situations and collections of actual organizational data and articles from public sources are not as effective for learning as are fully developed cases. A comprehensive case presents you with a partial clinical study of a real-life situation that faced practicing managers. A case presented in narrative form provides motivation for involvement with and analysis of a specific situation. By framing alternative strategic actions and by confronting the complexity and ambiguity of the practical world, case analysis provides extraordinary power for your involvement with a personal learning experience. Some of the potential consequences of using the case method are summarized in Table 1.

As Table 1 suggests, the case method can help you develop your analytical and judgment skills. Case analysis also helps you learn how to ask the right questions—that is, the questions that focus on the core strategic issues included within a case. Students aspiring to be managers can improve their ability to identify underlying problems, rather than focusing on superficial symptoms, through development of the skills required to ask probing, yet appropriate, questions.

The particular set of cases your instructor chooses to assign the class can expose you to a wide variety of organizations and managerial situations. This approach vicariously broadens your experience base and provides insights into many types of managerial situations, tasks, and responsibilities. Such indirect experience can help you make a more informed career

TABLE 1 ***Consequences of Student Involvement with the Case Method***

1. Case analysis requires students to practice important managerial skills—diagnosing, making decisions, observing, listening, and persuading—while preparing for a case discussion.
2. Cases require students to relate analysis and action, to develop realistic and concrete actions despite the complexity and partial knowledge characterizing the situation being studied.
3. Students must confront the *intractability of reality*—complete with absence of needed information, an imbalance between needs and available resources, and conflicts among competing objectives.
4. Students develop a general managerial point of view—where responsibility is sensitive to action in a diverse environmental context.

Source: C. C. Lundberg and C. Enz, 1993, A framework for student case preparation, *Case Research Journal* 13 (Summer): 134.

decision about the industry and managerial situation you believe will prove to be challenging and satisfying. Finally, experience in analyzing cases definitely enhances your problem-solving skills.

Furthermore, when your instructor requires oral and written presentations, your communication skills will be honed through use of the case method. Of course, these added skills depend on your preparation as well as your instructor's facilitation of learning. However, the primary responsibility for learning is yours. The quality of case discussion is generally acknowledged to require, at a minimum, a thorough mastery of case facts and some independent analysis of them. The case method therefore first requires that you read and think carefully about each case. Additional comments about the preparation you should complete to successfully discuss a case appear in the next section.

STUDENT PREPARATION FOR CASE DISCUSSION

If you are inexperienced with the case method, you may need to alter your study habits. A lecture-oriented course may not require you to do intensive preparation for *each* class period. In such a course, you have the latitude to work through assigned readings and review lecture notes according to your own schedule. However, an assigned case requires significant and conscientious *preparation before class.* Without it, you will be unable to contribute meaningfully to in-class discussion. Therefore, careful reading and thinking about case facts, as well as reasoned analyses and the development of alternative solutions to case problems, are essential. Recommended alternatives should flow logically from core problems identified through study of the case. Table 2 shows a set of steps that can help you develop familiarity with a case, identify problems, and propose strategic actions that increase the probability that a firm will achieve strategic competitiveness and earn above-average returns.

Gaining Familiarity

The first step of an effective case analysis process calls for you to become familiar with the facts featured in the case and the focal firm's situation. Initially, you should become familiar with the focal firm's general situation (e.g., who, what, how, where, and when). Thorough familiarization demands appreciation of the nuances as well as the major issues in the case.

Gaining familiarity with a situation requires you to study several situational levels, including interactions between and among individuals within groups, business units, the corporate office, the local community, and the society at large. Recognizing relationships within and among levels facilitates a more thorough understanding of the specific case situation.

It is also important that you evaluate information on a continuum of certainty. Information that is verifiable by several sources and judged along similar dimensions can be classified as a *fact.* Information representing someone's perceptual judgment of a particular situation is referred to as an *inference.* Information gleaned from a situation that is not verifiable is classified as *speculation.* Finally, information that is independent of verifiable sources and arises through individual or group discussion is an *assumption.* Obviously, case analysts and organizational decision makers prefer having access to facts over inferences, speculations, and assumptions.

Personal feelings, judgments, and opinions evolve when you are analyzing a case. It is important to be aware of your own feelings about the case and to evaluate the accuracy of perceived "facts" to ensure that the objectivity of your work is maximized.

Recognizing Symptoms

Recognition of symptoms is the second step of an effective case analysis process. A symptom is an indication that something is not as you or someone else thinks it should be. You may be tempted to correct the symptoms instead of searching for true problems. True problems are the conditions or situations requiring solution before an organization's, unit's, or individual's performance can improve. Identifying and listing symptoms early in the case analysis process tends to reduce the temptation to label symptoms as problems. The focus of your analysis should be on the *actual causes* of a problem, rather than on its symptoms. It is important therefore to remember that symptoms are indicators of problems; subsequent work facilitates discovery of critical causes of problems that your case recommendations must address.

TABLE 2 *An Effective Case Analysis Process*

Step 1: *Gaining Familiarity*	a. In general—determine who, what, how, where, and when (the critical facts of the case). b. In detail—identify the places, persons, activities, and contexts of the situation. c. Recognize the degree of certainty/uncertainty of acquired information.
Step 2: *Recognizing Symptoms*	a. List all indicators (including stated "problems") that something is not as expected or as desired. b. Ensure that symptoms are not assumed to be the problem (symptoms should lead to identification of the problem).
Step 3: *Identifying Goals*	a. Identify critical statements by major parties (e.g., people, groups, the work unit, etc.). b. List all goals of the major parties that exist or can be reasonably inferred.
Step 4: *Conducting the Analysis*	a. Decide which ideas, models, and theories seem useful. b. Apply these conceptual tools to the situation. c. As new information is revealed, cycle back to substeps a and b.
Step 5: *Making the Diagnosis*	a. Identify predicaments (goal inconsistencies). b. Identify problems (discrepancies between goals and performance). c. Prioritize predicaments/problems regarding timing, importance, etc.
Step 6: *Doing the Action Planning*	a. Specify and prioritize the criteria used to choose action alternatives. b. Discover or invent feasible action alternatives. c. Examine the probable consequences of action alternatives. d. Select a course of action. e. Design an implementation plan/schedule. f. Create a plan for assessing the action to be implemented.

Source: C. C. Lundberg and C. Enz, 1993, A framework for student case preparation, *Case Research Journal* 13 (Summer): 144.

Identifying Goals

The third step of effective case analysis calls for you to identify the goals of the major organizations, units, and/or individuals in a case. As appropriate, you should also identify each firm's strategic intent and strategic mission. Typically, these direction-setting statements (goals, strategic intents, and strategic missions) are derived from comments of the central characters in the organization, business unit, or top management team described in the case and/or from public documents (e.g., an annual report).

Completing this step successfully sometimes can be difficult. Nonetheless, the outcomes you attain from this step are essential to an effective case analysis because identifying goals, intent, and mission helps you to clarify the major problems featured in a case and to evaluate alternative solutions to those problems. Direction-setting statements are not always stated publicly or prepared in written format. When this occurs, you must infer goals from other available factual data and information.

Conducting the Analysis

The fourth step of effective case analysis is concerned with acquiring a systematic understanding of a situation. Occasionally cases are analyzed in a less-than-thorough manner. Such analyses may be a product of a busy schedule or the difficulty and complexity of the issues described in a particular case. Sometimes you will face pressures on your limited amounts of time and may believe that you can understand the situation described in a case without systematic *analysis* of all the facts. However, experience shows that familiarity with a case's facts is a necessary, but insufficient, step to the development of effective solutions—solutions that can enhance a firm's strategic competitiveness. In fact, a less-than-thorough analysis typically results in an emphasis on symptoms, rather than problems and their causes. To analyze a case effectively, you should be skeptical of quick or easy approaches and answers.

A systematic analysis helps you understand a situation and determine what can work and probably what will not work. Key linkages and underlying causal networks based on the history of the firm become apparent. In this way, you can separate causal networks from symptoms.

Also, because the quality of a case analysis depends on applying appropriate tools, it is important that you use the ideas, models, and theories that seem to be useful for evaluating and solving individual and unique situations. As you consider facts and symptoms, a useful theory may become apparent. Of course, having familiarity with conceptual models may be important in the effective analysis of a situation. Successful students and successful organizational strategists add to their intellectual tool kits on a continual basis.

Making the Diagnosis

The fifth step of effective case analysis—diagnosis—is the process of identifying and clarifying the roots of the problems by comparing goals to facts. In this step, it is useful to search for predicaments. Predicaments are situations in which goals do not fit with known facts. When you evaluate the actual performance of an organization, business unit, or individual, you may identify over- or under achievement (relative to established goals). Of course, single-problem situations are rare. Accordingly, you should recognize that the case situations you study probably will be complex in nature.

Effective diagnosis requires you to determine the problems affecting longer-term performance and those requiring immediate handling. Understanding these issues will aid your efforts to prioritize problems and predicaments, given available resources and existing constraints.

Doing the Action Planning

The final step of an effective case analysis process is called action planning. Action planning is the process of identifying appropriate alternative actions. Important in the action planning step is selection of the criteria you will use to evaluate the identified alternatives. You may derive these criteria from the analyses; typically, they are related to key strategic situations facing the focal organization. Furthermore, it is important that you prioritize these criteria to ensure a rational and effective evaluation of alternative courses of action.

Typically, managers "satisfice" when selecting courses of actions; that is, they find *acceptable* courses of action that meet most of the chosen evaluation criteria. A rule of thumb that has proved valuable to strategic decision makers is to select an alternative that leaves other plausible alternatives available if the one selected fails.

Once you have selected the best alternative, you must specify an implementation plan. Developing an implementation plan serves as a reality check on the feasibility of your alternatives. Thus, it is important that you give thoughtful consideration to all issues associated with the implementation of the selected alternatives.

WHAT TO EXPECT FROM IN-CLASS CASE DISCUSSIONS

Classroom discussions of cases differ significantly from lectures. The case method calls for instructors to guide the discussion, encourage student participation, and solicit alternative views. When alternative views are not forthcoming, instructors typically adopt one view so students can be challenged to respond thoughtfully to it. Often students' work is evaluated in terms of both the quantity and the quality of their contributions to in-class case discussions. Students benefit by having their views judged against those of their peers and by responding to challenges by other class members and/or the instructor.

During case discussions, instructors listen, question, and probe to extend the analysis of case issues. In the course of these actions, peers or the instructor may challenge an individual's views and the validity of alternative perspectives that have been expressed. These challenges are offered in a constructive manner; their intent is to help students develop their analytical and communication skills. Commonly instructors encourage students to be innovative and original in the development and presentation of their ideas. Over the course of an individual discussion, students can develop a more complex view of the case, benefiting from the diverse inputs of their peers and instructor. Among other benefits, experience with multiple case discussions should help students increase their knowledge of the advantages and disadvantages of group decision-making processes.

Comments that contribute to the discussion are valued by student peers as well as the instructor. To offer *relevant* contributions, you are encouraged to use independent thought and, through discussions with your peers outside of class, to refine your thinking. We also encourage you to avoid using "I think," "I believe," and "I feel" to discuss your inputs to a case analysis process. Instead, consider using a less emotion laden phrase, such as "My analysis shows. . . ." This highlights the logical nature of the approach you have taken to complete the six steps of an effective case analysis process.

When preparing for an in-class case discussion, you should plan to use the case data to explain your assessment of the situation. Assume that the case facts are known to your peers and instructor. In addition, it is good practice to prepare notes before class discussions and use them as you explain your view. Effective notes signal to classmates and the instructor that you are prepared to engage in a thorough discussion of a case. Moreover, thorough notes eliminate the need for you to memorize the facts and figures needed to discuss a case successfully.

The case analysis process described above can help you prepare to effectively discuss a case during class meetings. Adherence to this process results in consideration of the issues required to identify a focal firm's problems and to propose strategic actions through which the firm can increase the probability it will achieve strategic competitiveness.

In some instances, your instructor may ask you to prepare either an oral or a written analysis of a particular case. Typically, such an assignment demands even more thorough study and analysis of the case contents. At your instructor's discretion, oral and written analyses may be completed by individuals or by groups of two or more people. The information and insights gained through completing the six steps shown in Table 2 often are of value in the development of an oral or a written analysis. However, when preparing an oral or written presentation, you must consider the overall framework in which your information and inputs will be presented. Such a framework is the focus of the next section.

PREPARING AN ORAL/WRITTEN CASE PRESENTATION

Experience shows that two types of thinking are necessary to develop an effective oral or written presentation (see Figure 1). The upper part of the model in Figure 1 outlines the *analysis* of case preparation.

In the analysis stage, you should first analyze the general external environmental issues affecting the firm. Next your environmental analysis should focus on the particular industry (or industries, in the case of a diversified company) in which a firm operates. Finally, you should examine the competitive environment of the focal firm. Through study of the three levels of the external environment, you will be able to identify a firm's opportunities and threats. Following the external environmental analysis is the analysis of the firm's internal environment. This analysis results in the identification of the firm's strengths and weaknesses.

As noted in Figure 1, you must then change the focus from analysis to *synthesis*. Specifically, you must *synthesize* information gained from your analysis of the firm's internal and external environments. Synthesizing information allows you to generate alternatives that can resolve the significant problems or challenges facing the focal firm. Once you identify a best alternative, from an evaluation based on predetermined criteria and goals, you must explore implementation actions.

Table 3 outlines the sections that should be included in either an oral or a written presentation: introduction (strategic profile and purpose), situation analysis, statements of strengths/weaknesses and opportunities/threats, strategy formulation, and imple-

FIGURE 1 *Types of Thinking in Case Preparation: Analysis and Synthesis*

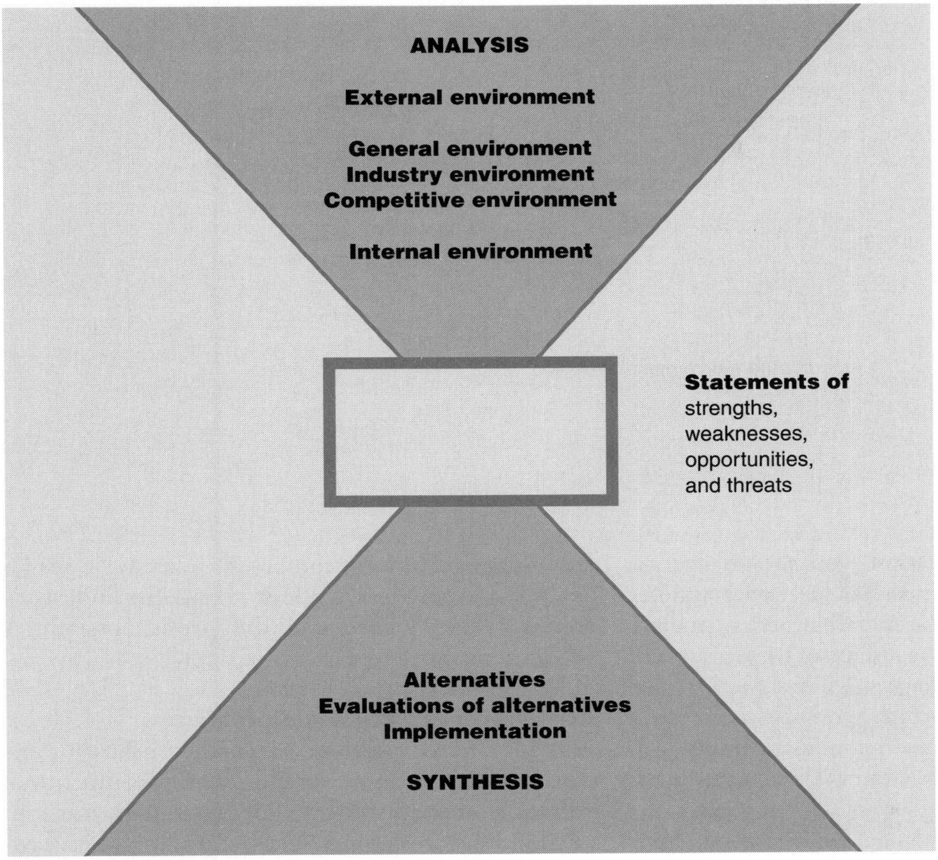

ANALYSIS

External environment

General environment
Industry environment
Competitive environment

Internal environment

Statements of strengths, weaknesses, opportunities, and threats

Alternatives
Evaluations of alternatives
Implementation

SYNTHESIS

mentation. These sections, which can be completed only through use of the two types of thinking featured in Figure 1, are described in the following discussion. Familiarity with the contents of your book's 13 chapters is helpful because the general outline for an oral or a written presentation shown in Table 3 is based on an understanding of the strategic management process detailed in those chapters.

Strategic Profile and Case Analysis Purpose

The strategic profile should state briefly the critical facts from the case that have affected the historical strategic direction and performance of the focal firm. The case facts should not be restated in the profile; rather, these comments should show how the critical facts lead to a particular focus for your analysis. This primary focus should be emphasized in this section's conclusion. In addition, this section should state important assumptions about case facts on which the analyses may be based.

Situation Analysis

As shown in Table 3, a general starting place for completing a situation analysis is the general environment.

General Environmental Analysis First, your analysis of the general environment should consider the *effects of globalization* on the focal firm and its indus-

TABLE 3 ***General Outline for an Oral or a Written Presentation***

I. Strategic Profile and Case Analysis Purpose
II. Situation Analysis
 A. General environmental analysis
 B. Industry analysis
 C. Competitive environmental analysis
 D. Internal analysis
III. Identification of Environmental Opportunities and Threats and Firm Strengths and Weaknesses (SWOT Analysis)
IV. Strategy Formulation
 A. Strategic alternatives
 B. Alternative evaluation
 C. Alternative choice
V. Strategic Alternative Implementation
 A. Action items
 B. Action plan

try. Following that evaluation, you should analyze general environmental trends. Table 4 lists a number of general environmental trends that, when studied, should yield valuable insights. Many of these issues are explained more fully in Chapter 2. These trends need to be evaluated for their impact on the focal firm's strategy and on the industry (or industries) in which it competes in the pursuit of strategic competitiveness.

Industry Analysis Once you analyze the general environmental trends, you should study their effect on the focal industry. Often the same environmental trend may have a significantly different impact on separate industries. Furthermore, the same trend may affect firms within the same industry differently. For instance, with deregulation of the airline industry, older, established airlines had a significant decrease in profitability, while many smaller airlines, with lower cost structures and greater flexibility, were able to aggressively enter new markets.

Porter's five force model is a useful tool for analyzing the specific industry (see Chapter 2). Careful study of how the five competitive forces (i.e., supplier power, buyer power, potential entrants, substitute products, and rivalry among competitors) affect firm strategy is important. These forces may create threats or opportunities relative to the specific business-level strategies (i.e., differentiation, low cost, focus) being implemented. Often a strategic group's analysis reveals how different environmental trends are affecting industry competitors. Strategic group analysis is useful for understanding the industry's competitive structure and the profit possibilities within those structures.

Competitive Environmental Analysis
Firms also need to analyze each of their primary competitors. This analysis should identify competitors' current strategies, strategic intent, strategic mission, capabilities, core competencies, and a competitive response profile. This information is useful to the focal firm in formulating an appropriate strategy and in predicting competitors' probable responses. Sources that can be used to gather information about an industry and companies with whom the focal firm competes are listed in Appendix I. Included in this list is a wide range of publications, such as periodicals, newspapers, bibliographies, directories of companies, industry ratios, forecasts, rankings/ratings, and other valuable statistics.

Internal Analysis Assessing a firm's strengths and weaknesses through a value chain analysis facilitates moving from the external environment to the internal environment. Analysis of the primary and support activities of the value chain provides opportunities to understand how external environmental trends affect the specific activities of a firm. Such analysis helps highlight strengths and weaknesses (see Chapter 3 for an explanation of the value chain).

TABLE 4 ***Sample General Environmental Categories***

Category	Sample
Technology	■ Information technology continues to become cheaper and have more practical applications. ■ Database technology allows organization of complex data and distribution of information. ■ Telecommunications technology and networks increasingly provide fast transmission of all sources of data, including voice, written communications, and video information. ■ Computerized design and manufacturing technologies continue to facilitate quality and flexibility.
Demographic Trends	■ Regional changes in population due to migration ■ Changing ethnic composition of the population ■ Aging of the population ■ Aging of the "baby boom" generation
Economic Trends	■ Interest rates ■ Inflation rates ■ Savings rates ■ Trade deficits ■ Budget deficits ■ Exchange rates
Political/Legal Environment	■ Anti-trust enforcement ■ Tax policy changes ■ Environmental protection laws ■ Extent of regulation/deregulation ■ Developing countries privatizing state monopolies ■ State-owned industries
Sociocultural Environment	■ Increasing number of women in the work force ■ Awareness of health and fitness issues ■ Concern for the environment ■ Concern for customers
Global Environment	■ Currency exchange rates ■ Free trade agreements ■ Trade deficits ■ New or developing markets

For purposes of preparing an oral or a written presentation, it is important to note that strengths are internal resources and capabilities that have the potential to be core competencies. Weaknesses, on the other hand, are internal resources and capabilities that have the potential to place a firm at a competitive disadvantage relative to its rivals. Thus, some of a firm's resources and capabilities are strengths; others are weaknesses.

When evaluating the internal characteristics of the firm, your analysis of the functional activities emphasized is critical. For instance, if the strategy of the firm is primarily technology driven, it is important to evaluate the firm's R&D activities. If the strategy is market driven, marketing functional activities are of paramount importance. If a firm has financial difficulties, critical financial ratios would require careful evaluation. In fact, because of the importance of financial health, most cases require financial analyses. Appendix II lists and operationally defines several common financial ratios. Included are tables describing profitability, liquidity, leverage, activity, and shareholders' return ratios. Other firm characteristics that should be examined to study the internal environment effectively include leadership, organizational culture, structure, and control systems.

Identification of Environmental Opportunities and Threats and Firm Strengths and Weaknesses (SWOT Analysis)

The outcome of the situation analysis is the identification of a firm's strengths and weaknesses and its environmental threats and opportunities. The next step requires that you analyze the strengths and weaknesses and the opportunities and threats for configurations that benefit or do not benefit a firm's efforts to achieve strategic competitiveness. Case analysts, and organizational strategists as well, seek to match a firm's strengths with its external environmental opportunities. In addition, strengths are chosen to prevent any serious environmental threat from affecting negatively the firm's performance. The key objective of conducting a SWOT analysis is to determine how to position the firm so it can take advantage of opportunities, while simultaneously avoiding or minimizing environmental threats. Results from a SWOT analysis yield valuable insights into the selection of strategies a firm should implement to achieve strategic competitiveness.

The *analysis* of a case should not be overemphasized relative to the *synthesis* of results gained from your analytical efforts. There may be a temptation to spend most of your oral or written case analysis on results from the analysis. It is important, however, that you make an equal effort to develop and evaluate alternatives and to design implementation of the chosen strategy.

Strategy Formulation–Strategic Alternatives, Alternative Evaluation, and Alternative Choice

Developing alternatives is often one of the most difficult steps in preparing an oral or a written presentation. Development of three to four alternative strategies is common (see Chapter 4 for business-level strategy alternatives and Chapter 6 for corporate-level strategy alternatives). Each alternative should be feasible (i.e., it should match the firm's strengths, capabilities, and especially core competencies), and feasibility should be demonstrated. In addition, you should show how each alternative takes advantage of the environmental opportunity or avoids/buffers against environmental threats. Developing carefully thought out alternatives requires synthesis of your analyses' results and creates greater credibility in oral and written case presentations.

Once you develop strong alternatives, you must evaluate the set to choose the best one. Your choice should be defensible and provide benefits over the other alternatives. Thus, it is important that both alternative development and evaluation of alternatives be thorough. The choice of the best alternative should be explained and defended.

Strategic Alternative Implementation–Action Items and Action Plan

After selecting the most appropriate strategy (that is, the strategy with the highest probability of enhancing a firm's strategic competitiveness), you must consider effective implementation. Effective synthesis is important to ensure that you have considered and evaluated all critical implementation issues. Issues you might consider include the structural changes necessary to implement the new strategy. In addition, leadership changes and new controls or incentives may be necessary to implement strategic actions. The implementation actions you recommend should be explicit and thoroughly explained. Occasionally, careful evaluation of implementation actions may show the strategy to be less favorable than you thought originally. A strategy is only as good as the firm's ability to implement it effectively. Therefore, effort to determine effective implementation is important.

Process Issues

You should ensure that your presentation (either oral or written) has logical consistency throughout. For example, if your presentation identifies one purpose, but your analysis focuses on issues that differ from the stated purpose, the logical inconsistency will be apparent. Likewise, your alternatives should flow from the configuration of strengths, weaknesses, opportunities, and threats you identified by the internal and external analyses.

Thoroughness and clarity also are critical to an effective presentation. Thoroughness is represented by the comprehensiveness of the analysis and alternative generation. Furthermore, clarity in the results of the analyses, selection of the best alternative strategy, and design of implementation actions are important. For example, your statement of the strengths and weaknesses should flow clearly and logically from the internal analyses presented.

Presentations (oral or written) that show logical consistency, thoroughness, and clarity of purpose, effective analyses, and feasible recommendations (strategy and implementation) are more effective and will receive more positive evaluations. Furthermore, developing the skills necessary to make such presentations will enhance your future job performance and career success.

APPENDIX I: SOURCES FOR INDUSTRY AND COMPETITOR ANALYSES

Abstracts and Indexes

Periodicals	*ABI/Inform*
	Business Periodicals Index
	InfoTrac (CD-ROM computer multidiscipline index)
	Investext (CD-ROM)
	Predicasts F&S Index United States
	Predicasts Overview of Markets and Technology (PROMT)
	Predicasts R&S Index Europe
	Predicasts R&S Index International
	Public Affairs Information Service Bulletin (PAIS)
	Reader's Guide to Periodical Literature
Newspapers	*NewsBank*
	Business NewsBank
	New York Times Index
	Wall Street Journal Index
	Wall Street Journal/Barron's Index
	Washington Post Index

Bibliographies

	Encyclopedia of Business Information Sources
	Handbook of Business Information

Directories

Companies—General	*America's Corporate Families and International Affiliates*
	Hoover's Handbook of American Business
	Hoover's Handbook of World Business
	Million Dollar Directory
	Standard & Poor's Corporation Records
	Standard & Poor's Register of Corporations, Directors, and Executives
	Ward's Business Directory
Companies—International	*America's Corporate Families and International Affiliates*
	Business Asia
	Business China
	Business Eastern Europe
	Business Europe
	Business International

	Business International Money Report
	Business Latin America
	Directory of American Firms Operating in Foreign Countries
	Directory of Foreign Firms Operating in the United States
	Hoover's Handbook of World Business
	International Directory of Company Histories
	Moody's Manuals, International (2 volumes)
	Who Owns Whom
Companies—Manufacturers	*Manufacturing USA: Industry Analyses, Statistics, and Leading Companies*
	Thomas Register of American Manufacturers
	U.S. Office of Management and Budget, Executive Office of the President, *Standard Industrial Classification Manual*
	U.S. Manufacturer's Directory
Companies—Private	*Million Dollar Directory*
	Ward's Directory
Companies—Public	Annual Reports and 10-K Reports
	Disclosure (corporate reports)
	Q-File
	Moody's Manuals:
	Moody's Bank and Finance Manual
	Moody's Industrial Manual
	Moody's International Manual
	Moody's Municipal and Government Manual
	Moody's OTC Industrial Manual
	Moody's OTC Unlisted Manual
	Moody's Public Utility Manual
	Moody's Transportation Manual
	Standard & Poor Corporation, *Standard Corporation Descriptions:*
	Standard & Poor's Handbook
	Standard & Poor's Industry Surveys
	Standard & Poor's Investment Advisory Service
	Standard & Poor's Outlook
	Standard & Poor's Statistical Service
Companies—Subsidiaries and Affiliates	*America's Corporate Families and International Affiliates*
	Ward's Directory
	Who Owns Whom
	Moody's Industry Review
	Standard & Poor's Analyst's Handbook
	Standard & Poor's Industry Report Service
	Standard & Poor's Industry Surveys (2 volumes)
	U.S. Department of Commerce, *U.S. Industrial Outlook*

Industry Ratios

Dun & Bradstreet, *Industry Norms and Key Business Ratios*
Robert Morris Associates Annual Statement Studies
Troy Almanac of Business and Industrial Financial Ratios

Industry Forecasts

International Trade Administration, *U.S. Industrial Outlook Predicasts Forecasts*

Rankings & Ratings

Annual Report on American Industry in *Forbes*
Business Rankings and Salaries
Business One Irwin Business and Investment Almanac
Corporate and Industry Research Reports (CIRR)
Dun's Business Rankings
Moody's Industrial Review
Rating Guide to Franchises
Standard & Poor's Industry Report Service
Value Line Investment Survey
Ward's Business Directory

Statistics

American Statistics Index (ASI) Bureau of the Census, U.S. Department of Commerce, *Economic Census Publications*
Bureau of the Census, U.S. Department of Commerce, *Statistical Abstract of the United States*
Bureau of Economic Analysis, U.S. Department of Commerce, *Survey of Current Business*
Internal Revenue Service, U.S. Treasury Department, *Statistics of Income: Corporation Income Tax Returns*
Statistical Reference Index (SRI)

APPENDIX II: FINANCIAL ANALYSIS IN CASE STUDIES

TABLE A.1 ***Profitability Ratios***

Ratio	Formula	What it Shows
1. Return on total assets	Profits after taxes / Total assets	The net return on total investment of the firm
	or	or
	(Profits after taxes + interest) / Total assets	The return on both creditors' and shareholders' investments
2. Return on stockholders' equity (or return on net worth)	Profits after taxes / Total stockholders' equity	How effectively the company is utilizing shareholders' funds
3. Return on common equity	(Profit after taxes − preferred stock dividends) / (Total stockholders' equity–par value of preferred stock)	The net return to common stockholders
4. Operating profit margin (or return on sales)	Profits before taxes and before interest / Sales	The firm's profitability from regular operations
5. Net profit margin (or net return on sales)	Profits after taxes / Sales	The firm's net profit as a percentage of total sales

TABLE A.2 *Liquidity Ratios*

Ratio	Formula	What it Shows
1. Current ratio	$\frac{\text{Current assets}}{\text{Current liabilities}}$	The firm's ability to meet its current financial liabilities
2. Quick ratio (or acid-test ratio)	$\frac{\text{Current assets} - \text{inventory}}{\text{Current liabilities}}$	The firm's ability to pay off short-term obligations without relying on sales of inventory
3. Inventory to net working capital	$\frac{\text{Inventory}}{\text{Current assets} - \text{current liabilities}}$	The extent to which the firm's working capital is tied up in inventory

TABLE A.3 *Leverage Ratios*

Ratio	Formula	What it Shows
1. Debt-to-assets	$\frac{\text{Total debt}}{\text{Total assets}}$	Total borrowed funds as a percentage of total assets
2. Debt-to-equity	$\frac{\text{Total debt}}{\text{Total shareholders' equity}}$	Borrowed funds versus the funds provided by shareholders
3. Long-term debt-to-equity	$\frac{\text{Long-term debt}}{\text{Total shareholders' equity}}$	Leverage used by the firm
4. Times-interest-earned (or coverage ratio)	$\frac{\text{Profits before interest and taxes}}{\text{Total interest charges}}$	The firm's ability to meet all interest payments
5. Fixed charge coverage	$\frac{\text{Profits before taxes and interest} + \text{lease obligations}}{\text{Total interest charges} + \text{lease obligations}}$	The firm's ability to meet all fixed-charge obligations including lease payments

TABLE A.4 *Activity Ratios*

Ratio	Formula	What it Shows
1. Inventory turnover	$\frac{\text{Sales}}{\text{Inventory of finished goods}}$	The effectiveness of the firm in employing inventory
2. Fixed assets turnover	$\frac{\text{Sales}}{\text{Fixed assets}}$	The effectiveness of the firm in utilizing plant and equipment
3. Total assets turnover	$\frac{\text{Sales}}{\text{Total assets}}$	The effectiveness of the firm in utilizing total assets
4. Accounts receivable turnover	$\frac{\text{Annual credit sales}}{\text{Accounts receivable}}$	How many times the total receivables have been collected during the accounting period
5. Average collection period	$\frac{\text{Accounts receivable}}{\text{Average daily sales}}$	The average length of time the firm waits to collect payments after sales

TABLE A.5 ***Shareholders' Return Ratios***

Ratio	Formula	What it Shows
1. Dividend yield on common stock	$\frac{\text{Annual dividends per share}}{\text{Current market price per share}}$	A measure of return to common stockholders in the form of dividends.
2. Price-earnings ratio	$\frac{\text{Current market price per share}}{\text{After-tax earnings per share}}$	An indication of market perception of the firm. Usually, the faster-growing or less risky firms tend to have higher PE ratios than the slower-growing or more risky firms.
3. Dividend payout ratio	$\frac{\text{Annual dividends per share}}{\text{After-tax earnings per share}}$	An indication of dividends paid out as a percentage of profits.
4. Cash flow per share	$\frac{\text{After-tax profits + depreciation}}{\text{Number of common shares outstanding}}$	A measure of total cash per share available for use by the firm.

NOTES

1. C. Christensen, 1989, *Teaching and the Case Method* (Boston: Harvard Business School Publishing Division); C. C. Lundberg, 1993, Introduction to the case method, in C. M. Vance (ed.), *Mastering Management Education* (Newbury Park, Calif.: Sage).
2. C. C. Lundberg and E. Enz, 1993, A framework for student case preparation, *Case Research Journal* 13 (Summer): 133.
3. J. Soltis, 1971, John Dewey, in L. E. Deighton (ed.), *Encyclopedia of Education* (New York: Macmillan and Free Press).

Name Index

Aaker, D. A., 120
Aaron, H. J., 39
Aaron, H., 267
Abarbanell, J. S., 302, 362
Abdullah, K., 9
Abell, D. F., 158
Abrahamson, E., 468, 500
Adams, C., 198, 242, 346
Aeppel, T., 40, 79, 81, 212
Agee, William, 436
Agle, B. R., 40, 386
Aguilera-Hellweg, M., 453
Ahlstrom, Krister, 464
Albanese, R., 469
Alexander, M., 119, 157–158, 233, 235, 306
Aley, J., 200
Allen, George, 477
Allen, J. W., 501
Allen, L., 307
Allen, Robert E., 147, 351–352, 372, 436–437,454
Allen, Ronald W., 437
Almeida, P., 121
Alsop, Stewart, 492, 493
Alston, L. P., 80
Amason, A. C., 468, 501
Ames, C., 120
Amihud, Y., 235, 387
Amit, R., 40, 90, 119, 121, 234
Anand, J., 266
Anders, G., 266
Anderson, J. C., 158
Anderson, P. C., 120, 468, 502
Anderson, P. H., 503
Angwin, D., 266
Annunziata, Robert, 326
Arbitman, J., 158
Argyres, N., 234
Armacost, R. L., 81
Armstrong, C. Michael, 147, 351–352, 372
Armstrong, L., 104, 307
Arnolod, C., 386
Arnst, C., 4
Arora, A., 40
Artz, K., 432
Asanuma, B., 345
Ashford, S.J., 470
Ashkenas, R.M., 38, 469
Askenas, R. N., 469
Auerback, J. G., 389, 393
Avolio, B. J., 469
Awasthi, V., 387
Axelrod, R., 345, 347

Badaracco, J. L., Jr., 502
Baden-Fuller, C. W. F., 347, 432, 500
Baer, G. R., 200
Bahrami, H., 347
Bailey, E. E., 345
Bailey, J., 389
Bailey, J., 437
Baily, M. N., 267
Baiman, S., 431
Baldwin, T. T., 157
Baliga, B. R., 469
Ball, D., 322
Balu, R., 421
Bank, D., 80, 345
Banks, H., 322
Bannon, L., 266
Bantel, K. A., 200, 469
Barker, V. L., III, 39
Barnathan, J., 61
Barney, J. B., 38–41, 81, 92, 119–121, 233–234, 267–268, 345–346, 348, 431, 470
Barrett, A., 4, 432
Bartkus, B. B., 501–502
Bartlett, C. A., 39–41, 119, 121, 307, 431–432, 470
Barua, A., 501
Batchelor, C., 204
Bates, T., 501, 503
Batholomew, S., 306
Batik, D., 80
Baum, J. A. C., 346
Baum, J. R., 200
Baxter, A., 159
Baysinger, B. D., 267, 388
Beamish, P. W., 198, 307–308
Beatty, R. P., 388
Beatty, S. G., 431
Beaudoin, Laurent, 455
Beck, E., 242
Behling, O. C., 159
Bek, Ole, 125
Belis, G., 41
Bennet, A., 268
Bennett, D. S., 268, 345, 347
Bennett, N., 470
Berger, D. J., 370
Bergh, D. D., 233–234, 266, 269
Bergman, Michael, 154
Berkley, J. D., 468
Berle, A., 387
Bern, Dorrit, J., 56
Berner, R., 158
Bernhardt, K. L., 158
Bernstein, A., 268–269, 305–306
Berton, L., 159
Best, A., 267, 269, 502
Bethel, J. E., 268
Bethune, Gordon, 365
Bettis, R.A., 38–40, 80, 119–121, 157, 198, 233, 345, 468–469, 500
Beyer, J. M., 345, 347
Beyster, Robert, 84
Bezos, Jeff, 17
Bezos, Jeff, 17
Bianco, K., 267, 388
Bickford, D. J., 80
Biddle, F. M., 306, 346
Biggadike, R., 266
Bilimoria, D., 388
Birkinshaw, J., 80, 199, 306
Birnbaum, J. H., 346
Black, B. S., 388
Blackburn, R., 200
Blackmon, D. A., 238, 432
Blake, S., 79
Blalock, D., 470
Bleakley, F. R., 119, 430, 470
Bleeke, J., 346–347

Blumenstein, R., 432
Boeker, W., 119, 233, 468–469
Bogert, J. D., 387
Boisseau, C., 252, 322, 502
Boland, V., 431
Boone, R., Jr., 457
Borgatti, S. P., 347, 432
Borys, B., 502
Bossidy, Lawrence, 11
Boulton, L., 484
Boulton, W. R., 348
Bourassa-Shaw, C., 39
Bowditch, J. L., 267
Bowen, D. E., 200
Bowen, H. K., 120
Bower, J.L., 2 00
Bower, Marvin, 100
Bowles, J., 500
Bowley, G., 158
Bowman, E. H., 235, 268, 345, 469
Bownman, Charles, 142
Box, T., 121, 198
Boyd, B. K., 388, 469
Boyd, Edward F., 30
Boyd, N. G., 39–40, 119, 199, 345
Boynton, A. C., 80
Bradley, S. R., 345
Brahm, R., 346–347
Branch, S., 432
Brandenburger, A. N., 344
Brannigan, M., 346
Branson, Richard, 282
Brass, D. J., 470
Breen, K., 386
Bremner, B., 104, 307, 346
Brett, J. F., 470
Brief, A. P., 470
Brinkley, J., 327, 346
Brockhaus, R. H., Sr., 501
Brocknaus, M., 41
Broder, J. M., 346
Bromiley, P., 41, 233
Brookfield, J., 347
Brooks, G. R., 80
Brophy, T., 215
Browder, S., 27, 81
Brown, Harry, 312–313
Brown, J. M., 305
Brown, L., 38
Brown, P. R., 470
Brown, Ron, 30
Brown, S. L., 200, 501
Brown, S., 234
Browning, L. D., 345, 347
Brownlee, L. L., 212
Bruce, R.K., 470
Bruderer, E., 345, 347
Brull, S. V., 501
Brush, C., 501
Brush, T. H., 233, 234
Bruxelles, M., 80
Bryan, John, 416
Bryant, A., 353, 388
Bryne, H. S., 81, 346
Buchholtz, A. K., 430, 469
Buck, T., 268, 347
Bucker, W., 39
Buckley, M. R., 470
Buckley, P. J., 346
Buckman, Robert, 442
Buerkle, T., 336
Buffett, Warren, 75
Buhner, R., 307
Bulkeley, W. M., 234, 502
Buono, A. F., 267
Burck, C., 503
Burgelman, R.A., 480, 501
Burke, L. M., 431, 468
Burns, G., 235, 267
Burns, T., 286, 306
Burrows, P., 119, 158, 199, 468
Burt, T., 268
Burton, B. K., 470
Busenitz, L. W., 503
Butterfield, Y. D., 470
Buttner, E. H., 80
Byrne, J. A., 121, 269, 305–306, 353, 370, 386–388, 468–469, 501–502

Cable, D. S., 502
Calem, R. E., 80
Callan, S., 266
Calloway, Wayne, 440
Calori, R., 267, 468
Camerer, C., 41
Cameron, K. S., 268
Caminiti, S., 121
Campbell, A., 119, 157–158, 233, 235, 306
Candland, Catherine, 496
Cane, A., 200
Cannella, A. A., 437, 235
Cappelli, P., 85
Capron, L., 266
Carley, W. M., 189, 389, 432
Carper, W. B., 266
Carroll, Ed, 90
Carroll, G. P., 199
Carroll, P. B., 307
Carter, J. C., 470
Carter, M., 430
Caruso, D., 346
Case, Steve, 16
Casson, M., 346
Cauley, L., 327, 346
Caves, E., 307
Cempella, Domenico, 375
Chakrabarti, A. K., 200
Chalmers, Brian, 302
Chambers, John, 451, 453, 490
Champy, J., 470
Chandler, Alfred, 200, 240, 395, 399, 430, 432
Chandler, S., 158, 268
Chang, Y., 235
Chapon, J. P., 345
Charkham, J., 387, 389
Chartrand, S., 502
Chatterjee, S., 200, 233–234
Chen, M. J., 168, 199, 468, 501
Cheng, J. L. C., 39, 199
Chesbrough, H. W., 121, 347
Chi, T., 120
Chilton, K. W., 41, 469
Cho, M., 464
Cho, T. S., 468
Choi, C. J., 345
Choi, J. J., 306
Choi, T. Y., 159
Christensen, C. M., 119, 157, 468
Chung, K. S., 266
Clark, D., 159, 267
Clark, K. B., 120, 200
Clark, L. H., Jr., 266
Clarkson, M. B. E., 40
Clemons, E., K, 198
Clinton, President, 325
Coffee, J. C., 2 3 5
Cohen, D. R., 158
Cohen, W., 81
Cole, J., 80
Coleman, B., 242, 345
Coleman, J. J., Jr., 43 2
Coleman, R., 38, 119,157–158
Collins, G., 432
Collins, J. C., 469
Collis, D. J., 157, 233, 431
Colvin, G., 79, 198
Comes, F. J., 15 7
Comment, R., 387
Conger, J. A., 388
Connor, K. R., 201
Constable, J., 266
Conti, Armando, 493
Contractor, F. J., 345
Coogan, Mark, 172
Cookson, C., 273, 497, 503
Cool, K., 39,201
Cooper, A. C., 235
Cooper, Narri, 84
Cornish, E., 79
Cortese, A., 313, 346, 469
Coss, Lawrence, 373–374
Courtney, H., 79, 157
Covault, C., 346
Covin, J.G., 157, 501
Cowan, David, 492
Cox, T., 79
Coy, P., 502
Crandall, Robert, 69, 437
Cravens, D. W., 345
Crawford, L., 159
Crock, S., 27, 235
Crocker-Hefter, A., 85
Crossen, C., 158
Crutchfield, Edward, 248
Cullen, J. B., 347
Cummings, L. L., 468
Curry, S. R., 266
Cusumano, M. A., 85, 120, 198
Czamiawska-Joerges, B., 500
Czepiec, H., 81

D'Cruz, J., 313, 344, 347
Daberko, David, 248
Dacin, M. T., 40, 80, 306, 308, 347, 469, 502
daCosta, R. C., 307–308

Dailey, C. M., 387, 469
Dallenbach, U. S., 235
Dalton, D. R., 489
Danielson, C., 157
Darlin, D., 67, 113, 121
Datta, D. K., 266–267, 468–469
Daus, C. S., 79
D'Aveni, Richard A., 10, 38, 81, 198, 201, 235, 430
David, B. L., 501
Davidson, N. W., 347–348, 501
Davidson, W. M., 268, 501
Davies, E. M., 120
Davila, A., 233
Davis, A., 231
Davis, D. L., 501
Davis, G. E., 387
Davis, G. F., 266
Davis, J. H., 41, 348, 386–387, 468–469
Davis, W. J., 159
Dawley, H., 9, 38
Day, G. S., 157–158, 198, 200
Day, K., 353, 363
D'Cruz, J., 344, 347
De Backer, P., 468
de Geer, Gerard, 334
Dean, J. W., Jr., 183, 200
Dechant, K., 79
DeFillippi, R. J., 120
deJong, H. W., 234
Delios, A., 306
Dell, Michael, 76, 179, 184, 199, 442, 458–459,470
DeMarie, S.M., 38, 79, 159, 233, 307, 432, 500, 503
Deming, W. Edward, 183, 185
DeMonaco, L. J., 469
DeNino, M. J., 502
Denzier, D. R., 159
Deogan, N., 39, 234
Desmond, E. W., 80
Dess, G. G., 121, 157, 159, 430, 470, 500–501
Deutschman, A., 41
Di Benedetto, C. A., 198
Dial, J., 235, 268
Diamantopoulos, A, 235
Dickie, B. N., 200
Dierick, I., 39, 201
Dobbins, G. H., 388
Dobrzvnski, J. H, 200
Dodge, R., 79
Dodson, Bill, 41
Dollinger, M. J., 348
Dolphin, John, 373
Dominguez, Bernardo, 291
Donaldson, G., 40
Donaldson, L., 348, 386–387, 430, 469
Donaldson, T., 40
Dorfman, J. R., 212
Dos Santos, B. L., 80
Dougherty, D., 501
Douma, S., 382, 389
Dowling, M. J., 346
Drucker, P. F., 157
Druckerman, P., 242
DuBois, M., 346
DuBrin, A. D., 40
Duff, C., 388
Duhaime, I. M., 39, 233
Dukerich, J. M., 470
Duma, S., 382, 389
Dunlap, Albert, 369, 437
Dunne, N., 120, 200
Dutton, J. E., 38–40, 469–470
Dworkin, A., 159, 204, 233, 235, 339, 393
Dyer, J. H., 119, 344–345, 348

Easterwood, J., 268
Eaton, J., 388, 454
Eaton, Robert, 454
Ebbers, Bernard, J.
Echikson, W., 27
Edgerton, D. J., 493
Edmondson, G., 453
Edmundson, G., 348
Edwards, C., 432
Eickhoff, Kathryn, 352
Einhom, B., 234, 307
Eisenberg, M. A., 387
Eisenhardt, K. M., 200, 430, 501–502
Eisner, Michael, 83, 352, 374
Elam, J. J., 121
Elenkov, D. S., 79
Elliott, D., 61
Elliott, M., 61
El-Namaki, M. S. S., 121
Elson, Charles, 369–370
Elstrom, P., 4, 238
Elstrom, T., 353
Emshwiller, J. R., 158
Engardio, N., 61
Ennew, C., 502
Enright, M. J., 306
Eriksson, K., 347
Ernst, D., 346
Ernst, W., 347
Esry, B. C., 430
Ettlie, J. E., 469, 501
Evans, W. N., 199

Fahey, L., 79–80
Faircloth, A., 158
Fairclough, G., 212
Faison, S., 13
Falbe, C. M., 469
Falkenberg, J. S., 79
Fama, E. F., 235, 386–387
Farioun, M., 79, 119
Farkas, C. M., 431, 468
Farnham, A., 75
Farnham, A., 75
Farrell, C., 500, 502
Fatsis, S., 120
Feder, B. J., 502
Fedor, D., 200
Feher, M., 345
Feigenbaum, Armand, 183
Felton, R. F., 389
Fenn, D., 313, 344–345
Ferdows, K, 306
Ferguson, T. W., 109
Fernandez, J. P., 79
Ferris, S. P., 387
Fibbens, B. A., 469
Fidler, S., 198
Filatochev, I., 268, 347
Files, J., 80
Files, J., 80, 238
Finegoid, D., 388
Finkelstein, S., 79, 120, 235, 266, 307, 387–388, 441, 468–469
Fiol, C. M., 470
Firstenberg, P. B., 387
Fisher, A., 79, 85
Fisher, George M. C., 352, 372
Fisher, L. M., 468
Fites, Donald, 191–192
Flanders, S. W., 159
Flynn, J., 4
Fombrun, C. J., 79, 120
Forest, S. A., 199, 235
Forrest, J. E., 502
Forward, Gordon, 101
Foust, D., 198
Francis, S. C., 469
Frank, R., 242, 431, 470
Frank, S. E., 267
Frankenberg, Robert, 247–248
Franko, L. G., 200, 500
Fredrickson, J. W., 468
Freeh, Louis, 74
Freeman, E., 389
Freeman, J., 121, 198
Freeman, S. J., 268
Friedland, J., 81, 158, 306
Frist, Thomas, Jr., 383, 470
Fritsch, P., 266
Frost, P. J., 431
Fruin, W. M., 432
Furchgott, R., 120

Galbraith, J. R., 430–431
Gallagher, Terence J., 364
Galunic, D. C., 430
Galuska, P., 258
Gambardelia, A., 40
Ganitsky, J., 307
Gannon, M. J., 199
Gardner, H., 468
Gardner, W. L., 469
Garland, S. B., 313, 346
Garten, J. E., 157
Garud, R., 159
Gates, Bill, 17, 58, 194, 248, 331, 335
Geber, B., 80
Geczik, Paul, 493
Geer, C. T., 85
Geletkanycz, M. A., 40
Geneen, Harold, 219, 234
Geringer, J.M., 307–308, 347
Gerlach, M. L., 347
Gerstein, M. H., 158
Gerstner, Louis Jr., 45, 48, 443–444, 477
Geyelin, M., 81
Ghemawat, P., 464
Ghertman, M., 501

Ghoshal, S., 39–41, 81, 119, 121, 200, 307, 348, 387, 431–432, 470
Gibson, R., 81, 177, 235, 258, 267, 432
Gilmore, J. H., 80
Gilson, R., 235
Gimeno, J., 199
Ginsberg, A., 199
Glain, S., 80, 307, 346
Glass, David, 449
Glick, W. H., 431, 468
Goalart, F. J., 158
Godfrey, P. C., 119–120, 387
Goizueta, Roberto P., 172, 206, 209, 351, 436
Goldblatt, H., 238
Golden, P. A., 348
Goldhar, J. D., 159, 306
Goldsmith, C., 306, 322
Goldstein, A., 39, 159, 199, 470
Goll, I., 79
Gomes-Casseres, B., 345, 432
Gomez-Mejia, L. R., 235, 387–388
Goodhope, Daniel, 331
Gooding, R. Z., 79
Goold, M., 233, 235
Gorman, Joe, 395
Gotschall, M. G., 75
Govindarajan, V., 266, 273, 307, 431
Graham, G., 430
Granstrand, O., 502
Grant, A. W. H., 157
Grant, L., 189, 199, 267, 290, 432, 453, 470
Grant, R. M., 38–39, 81, 92–93, 119–121, 235
Gray, S. R., 235
Greco, S., 345
Green, J., R., 307
Greenwald, B., 200
Greer, C., R., 470
Greising, D., 267
Griffith, V., 158, 199–200, 393, 430
Griffiths, J., 484
Grimm, C. M., 79, 81, 193, 198–199
Gronhaug, K., 79
Grove, Andrew S., 9, 16, 38–39, 437
Grover, R., 198, 258, 353, 386–388, 501
Gruca, T., 81
Grund, N. E., 120
Gruner, S., 344
Gudridge, K, 235
Gulati, R., 159, 200, 348
Gunz, H. P., 468
Gupta, A., 121, 157, 159, 273, 307, 345, 430
Gupta, U., 346, 502
Gurley, W. J., 81
Gustafson, L. T., 159
Guthrie, J. P., 468–469
Gyllenhammar, P., 38

Hackman, J. R., 159, 200
Hagedoorn, J., 347
Hagel, J., III, 157
Hakanson, L, 502
Hales, C., 430
Haley, J., 121
Halkias, M., 121, 133, 158–159, 199–200, 306, 431
Hall, B. H., 267
Hall, R. H., 93, 120, 430–431
Hall, W. K., 159
Hallaq, J. H., 81
Hambrick, D. C., 79, 235, 307, 387–388, 441, 468–469, 501
Hamel, G., 40–41, 119, 121, 158, 200, 345, 347, 430, 468, 481, 501–502
Hamilton, D. P., 308, 346, 389
Hamilton, M. M., 13
Hamm, S., 313, 346
Hamm, S., 313, 346
Hammer, M., 468, 470
Hanaoka, M., 233
Handy, Charles, 199
Hanlon, S. C., 40, 119, 199, 345
Hannan, M., 121
Hansen, M. H., 41, 346, 348
Hapaaniemi, P., 345
Harback, H. F., 268, 468, 503
Hardee, C., 40, 201, 308
Hardymon, G. F., 502
Harper, Charles, 446
Harris, I. C., 469
Harris, J. S., 41
Harris, K., 80
Harris, M., 38–39
Harris, N., 157, 159, 267, 306
Harrison, D. A., 468
Harrison, D. J., 119
Harrison, J. S., 41, 266–269, 470, 502
Harvey, M. G., 39, 470
Haspeslagh, P. C., 266
Hatmann, Ulrich, 378
Hatsopoulous, George N., 455
Hatsopoulous, John, 455
Haverman, H. A., 233
Hayes, E., 470
Haynes, L., 41
Heene, A., 199
Hegarty, H., 267
Heifetz, R. A., 430, 437
Heilemann, J., 121
Heinzl, M., 234, 345
Heizer, J., 200
Helfat, C. E., 119–120, 157
Helyar, J., 437
Hemmerick, S. S., 364
Henderson, R., 39, 119, 198
Henkoff, R., 79, 121, 159, 234
Hennart, J. F., 121, 157, 159, 267, 307, 346, 430
Hesterly, W. S., 347, 432
Hickman, A., 45
Hilfiger, 158
Hill, C. W. L., 119–121, 157, 159, 234–235, 267–268, 305, 307, 345, 348, 387–388, 430–432, 470
Himelstein, L., 113, 199
Hindery, Leo, 400
Hisrich, R., 501
Hitt, M. A., 38–41, 79–80, 119–121, 157, 159, 198, 200–201, 228, 233–235, 266–269, 306–308, 346–347, 387–389, 431–432, 467–471, 487, 487, 491, 500–503
Hochwarter, W. A., 467
Hodgetts, R. M., 430
Hodgkinson, G. P., 198
Hof, R. D., 113
Hogler, R. L, 388–389
Holbein, G. F., 269
Holl, P., 269
Holloway, C. A., 120
Holm, D. B., 347
Holt, D. H., 501
Holusha, J., 346
Hopkins, S. A., 39
Hopkins, W., 3
Horovitz, B., 199
Hoskisson, R. E., 39, 41, 81, 200, 228, 233–235, 266–269, 306–308, 346–348, 387–389, 431–432, 469–471, 487, 491, 501–503
Hosseini, J. C., 81
Houghton, J. R., 432
Houlder, V., 432
Hout, T. M., 200, 470
Houthoofd, N., 199
Howell, William R., 476
Hrebiniak, G., 120
Huber, G. P., 468
Huber, R. L., 121
Hudnut, A., 389
Huertas, J. C., 345
Huey, J., 120, 233
Huff, A. S., 38–40, 81, 469
Huges, K, 234
Hulland, J., 80
Human, S. E., 313, 344, 430
Human, S. E., 313, 344, 430
Hunt, Michael, S. 71–72, 81
Huselid, M. A., 85, 119
Hutton, B., 242
Hwang, P., 307
Hwang, S. L., 469

Iacocca, Lee, 436
Iams, Paul F., 126, 128
Iansiti, M., 80
Iaquito, A. L., 468
Idei, Noboyuki, 245, 482, 501
Ihlwan, M., 346
Illinitch, A. Y., 198, 430
Ingram, P., 346
Inkpen, A. C., 198, 307
Inman, U. S. Navy Admiral B. R., 84
Ireland, R. D., 38, 40–41, 120–121, 234, 266–269, 306, 308, 389, 430–432, 467–471, 491, 502
Ireland, T. C., 470
Ivester, M. Douglas, 351, 436

Jack, A., 306, 382
Jackson, S. E., 85, 119, 269, 305–306, 469
Jackson, S., 238
Jacob, R., 158, 200, 470
Jaffe, G., 389, 470

Jalland, R. M., 468
Jammine, A. P., 235
Janssen-Bauer, J., 430
Jarrell, G., 387
Jaspin, E., 39
Jeffrey, Kim, 169
Jemison, D. B., 266–267, 502
Jenk, J., 157
Jenkins, H. W., Jr., 119, 469
Jensen, E., 80, 268
Jensen, M. C., 221, 235, 266–268, 386–387
Jick, T., 38
Jobs, Steven, 179, 194, 395
Johaansson, J. K., 307
Johannes, L., 198, 393
Johanson, J., 347
Johns, Doublas, 337
Johns, T. Y., 322, 346
Johnson, A. E., 306
Johnson, David W., 352
Johnson, G., 198, 468
Johnson, J. L., 347
Johnson, R. A., 233, 235, 266–268, 387, 389, 431, 469, 471, 502
Johnson, William R., 420–421
Johnston, R., 345
Johnston, S., 389
Jones, C., 347, 432
Jones, D. T., 500
Jones, G. R., 432
Jones, T. M., 40
Jones, T. O., 157
Jones, T. Y., 346
Joon, Kim Suk, 463
Joplin, J. R. W., 79
Jordan, Michael H., 80, 211
Judge, P, C., 468
Judge, W. Q., Jr., 388, 469, 501–502
Juran, Joseph, 183
Justis, R., 346

Kaback, H., 388
Kahn, J., 80, 345
Kahn, P. H., 61
Kalish, D. E., 4
Kamm, T., 242
Kanter, R. M., 39
Kapferer, J. N., 305
Kapoor, V., 345
Karam, Judith A., 461
Karnani, A., 199, 234
Karrer-Rueedi, E., 234
Kates, W., 9
Katsikeas, C. S., 345
Katz, I., 13
Katz, J. A., 387, 501
Kaufman, S., 120
Kay, N. M, 235
Kayworth, T. R., 430
Keats, B. W., 79, 233, 268, 307, 389, 431–432, 468, 500, 503
Kehoe, L., 199, 430
Kelleher, Herbert, 180, 496
Keller, J. J., 234, 353, 388, 468
Kelm, K. M., 500
Kerr, Steve, 38, 430–431
Kerwin, K., 38, 104, 198, 273, 307, 432
Kerwin, K., 9
Kesner, I. F., 39, 199, 388
Kessides, I. N., 199
Kessler, E. H, 200
Kester, W. C., 267–268
Kets de Vries, M. F. R., 468
Ketwin, K., 38
Khanna, T., 234, 464
Kibazo, J., 430
Kiechel, W., 119
Kierlin, Bob, 456–457, 493
Kilts, James M., 446
Kim, H., 3, 233–235, 307–308, 347, 389, 431, 501
Kim, L., 159
Kim, W. C., 307
King, R. T., Jr., 501
Kinnear, T. C., 158
Kirkland, J., 79, 157
Kirkman, B. L., 305
Kirkpatrick, D., 40, 67, 121, 346, 474
Kirkpatrick, J., 268
Kirsch, L. J., 470
Kitching, J., 267
Klavans, R., A., 198
Klein, K. J., 200
Kline, J. P., 235
Kobrin, S. J., 307
Kochhar, R., 234, 501–502
Kogut, B., 79, 345–346, 502
Koppes, Richard, 363
Koretz, G., 38
Kose, J., 268
Kosnik, R., 387, 389
Kotabe, M., 307, 345
Kotha, S., 38–39, 79–80, 159, 347
Kotter, J. P., 500
Kotulic, A. G., 79
Kramer, Jannifer, 495
Kraar, L., 158
Krebs, M. 104
Krentler, K. A., 158
Kriger, M. P., 469
Krishnan, H. A., 468
Krishnan, R., 200
Kristol, I., 388
Kroll, M., 386, 430
Krug, J. A., 267
Krugman, P., 38
Kuemmerle, W., 306
Kunde, D., 79, 119–120, 453
Kupfer, A., 4
Kurschner, K., 199
Kurtzman, J., 198–199, 233, 430
Kwong, P., 61
Kyriazis, D., 269

Labich, K., 158, 199
Lado, A. A., 39–40, 119, 199, 345
Lagnado, L., 389, 470
Lai, Aling, 182
Lai, L., 79, 119
Lancaster, H., 500
Landers, J., 79, 120
Landro, L., 234
Lane, P. J., 268
Lang, H. P., 268
Langreth, R., 268, 502
Larcker, D. F., 431
Laskawy, Philip, 240
Laurie, D. L., 430, 437
Laverty, K J., 471
Lawler, E. E., III, 200, 388
Lawless, M. W., 502
Lawrence, P. R., 345, 430, 501
Lay, Kenneth, 54, 479
Leavell, H., 386, 430
Leavitt, T., 41
Lee, C. H. S., 501
Lee, Dr., 74
Lee, K. C., 81
Lee, L., 13
Lee, P. M., 268
Lee, S. M., 80
Lee, S., 40
Lei, D., 40, 119–121, 157, 159, 201, 233, 266, 306, 468–469, 502
Lei, L., 79
Leibovitz, M., 75
LeMay, Ronald, T., 437
Lengnick-Hall, C. A., 500
Lenny, Richard H., 447
Leonard-Barton, D., 119–121, 157, 501
Lerner, M., 501
Lev, B., 235, 387
Levering, R., 453
Levine, J., 347
Levitas, E., 347, 502
Lewin, A. Y., 430
Lewis, W. W., 38–39
Li, J., 308, 347
Li, P. S., 501
Li, S., 382
Lieber, R. B., 306
Lieberman, M. B., 199, 501
Liebeskind, J.P., 268
Liedtka, J., 389
Liesman, S., 382
Lim, Y., 159
Lindorff, D., 13
Lipin, S., 258, 266–268, 353, 432
Lippman, J., 80
Liv, R., 113
Livnat, J., 234
Loeb, M., 40–41, 468
Long, W. F., 269
Loomis, C. J., 38
Lopez de Arriortua, Jose Ignacio, 75
Lorange, P., 345
Lorenzoni, G., 347, 432
Lorsch, J. W., 40, 430, 501
Loucks, V. R., Jr., 388
Low, M. B., 500
Lowe, J., 234
Lowenstein, L., 235
Lowenstein, R., 120, 416
Lozano, J. M., 470
Lubatkin, M., 234–235, 266–268
Lublin, J. S., 80, 266, 268, 364, 388, 437, 469

Lubove, S., 158
Luchs, K., 233
Luehrman, T. A., 268
Luldin, J. S., 268
Lumpkin, G. T., 470, 500–501
Lyles, M. A., 307
Lyons, K., 199

MacCormack, A., 80
MacDonald, E., 266
Machalaba, D., 38, 252
Machan, D., 389
MacMillan, I. C., 119–120, 187, 190
Madhavan, R., 347
Madhok, A., 40, 306–307
Madonna, J. C., 38
Magretta, J., 464
Mahindra, J., 198
Mahoney, J. M., 387–389
Mahoney, J. T., 121, 345, 387–389
Makino, S., 306
Malabre, A. L., Jr., 266
Malkiel, B., G., 387
Malkin, E., 199
Mallette, P., 388–389
Malone, M., 347
Mansfield, E., 15 9, 2 66
March, J. G., 43
Marcial, G. G., 234
Maremont, M., 79, 469
Margotin-Roze, V., 157
Marino, K. E., 119
Markides, C. C., 231, 233, 264, 267, 269, 431
Markoczy, L., 41
Marsh, P., 215, 306
Marsh, S. J., 192, 215, 198
Marshall, C., 121
Martin, C. L., 470
Martin, J., 159
Martin, P., 305
Martin, R., 346
Martin, X., 345
Martinez, J. I., 307
Maruca, R. F., 469
Mascarenhas, B., 501
Mathews, A. W., 252
Mathewson, G., F., 346
Mathys, N. J., 467
Matlack, C., 478
Matthews, J. A., 432, 453
Matzer, ,M., 268
Maucher, Helmut, 442
Maxon, T., 158, 199, 431 ,
May D. L., 235
Mayer, R. C., 41, 348, 468
McCardle, F. F., 266
McCarthy D., J., 347
McCarthy, M. J., 158
McCartney, S., 80
McCracken, Edward R., 112
McDougall, P. P., 306, 500–501, 503
McDowell, E., 345
McGahan, A. M., 39, 80
McGee, J. E., 81, 346
McGrath, R. G., 119–120, 346, 501
McGrath, Ted, 167
McHenry David F., 352
McIvor, G., 234, 307
McKay, B., 199
McKenna, R., 157–158
McKinley, W., 268
McLaughlin, M., 79
McMahan, G.C., 158
McNamara, G., 41
McWilliams, G., 4, 468, 474, 502
Means, G., 387
Meckling, W., 387
Megginson, W.L., 347, 389
Mehra, A., 119, 234
Mehta, S. N., 327, 346, 502
Melcher, R. A., 80, 199, 235, 267, 348, 353, 386–387, 416, 503
Melloan, G., 305, 346
Melnyk, S. A., 159
Mentink, H. W., 121
Merchant, H., 234–235, 266
Merchant, K. A., 388
Meyendorff, A., 382
Meyer, A. D., 38–39
Meznar, M. B., 79
Michel, C. H., 157
Michel, J. G., 468
Miesing, P., 469
Milbank, D., 80
Miles, G., 201, 432, 470
Miles, R. E., 347, 432
Miller, A., 159, 501–502
Miller, C. C., 431, 468
Miller, D., 469
Miller, J. P., 410, 416
Miller, K D., 347
Miller, K. L., 157, 305
Miller, L., 267
Miller, Steve, 436–437
Millman, J., 13
Millstein, I. M., 388
Milton-Smith, J., 470
Minow, N., 387, 389
Mintzberg, H., 500
Mishra, A. K, 268
Mitarai, Fujio, 293
Mitchell, J., 470
Mitchell, R. K, 40, 386
Mitchell, W., 39, 119, 198, 266, 345, 347
Mitchener, B., 234–235
Moesel, D. D., 233, 266–268, 387, 389, 431, 502
Moffett, M., 184, 308, 432
Molitoris, Jolene, 8
Moller, J. O., 41
Mondy, R., W., 470
Monks, R. A. G., 387, 389
Monroe, M. J., 235, 437
Monson, R. C., 120
Montgomery, C. A., 38, 119, 157, 233
Montgomery, D. B., 199, 501
Moon, H. J., 81
Moore, A. H., 345
Moore, D. P., 80
Moore, J., 158
Morais, R. C., 120
Moran, P., 348, 387
Morck, R., 347
Morris, B., 39, 80, 119, 470
Morris, M. H., 501
Morris, S. A., 81
Morrison, A., 80
Mosakowski, E., 39, 306
Moskowitz, M., 453
Mowery, D. C., 345, 502
Moxon, R. W., 39
Moyer, R. C., 469
Mroczkowski. T., 233
Mueller, T., 127, 327
Mulhern, C., 39
Mullane, J. V., 159
Murfin, D. L., 502
Murphy, K. J., 235, 268
Murphy, P. E., 470
Murray, A., 382
Murray, M., 235, 267, 431
Murray, S., 470
Mytelka, L. K, 347

Nadler, D. A., 430–432
Naidu, G. M., 307
Naik, G., 327
Nair, A. P., 79, 347
Nakache, P., 453
Nakamoto, M., 198–199, 273
Nakarmi, L., 80
Nalebuff, B. J., 344
Nanda, A., 346
Narayanan, V. K., 79–80, 266, 500
Narisetti, R., 39, 81, 469
Narus, J. A., 158
Nash, R. C., 389
Nash, S., 80
Nath, D., 81
Natuzzi, Pasquale, 98
Naughton, K., 9, 38, 104, 158, 198, 307, 273, 432, 484
Naumov, A., I., 347
Navarro, P., 45
Nayyar, P. R., 80, 199–200, 469
Near, J. P., 470
Neff, R., 80
Nelson, R. R., 157, 430
Newcomb, P., 267
Newmith, J., 39
Nickerson, J. A., 198
Niemond, G. A., 158
Nigh, D., 79
Nirmalya, K., 345
Nishiguchi, T., 347, 432
Nitter, J., 268
Nixon, R. D., 268, 346, 468, 487, 487, 501–503
Nobeoka, K., 198
Nocera, J., 470
Nohria, N., 45, 468
Nokkentved, C., 231, 233–235
Noorda, Raymond, 247–248
Norton, E., 346
Norton, R., 79
Norton, S. W., 346
Novak, David, 258

Nussbaum, B., 469
Nystrom, P. C., 79

O'Reilly, Anthony, 449
O'Reilly, B., 40, 80, 501–502
O'Bannon, D, P., 468
Oberton, Will, 457
Ocasio, W., 198
O'Donnell, S., 388
Ogletree, J., 41
Ohmae, K., 38, 199
Okuda, Hiroshi, 103, 483
O'Leary, Michael, 283
Olian, J. D., 468
Oliver, C., 39, 119, 157
Olk, P., 347
O'Neal, D., 501
O'Neill, H. M, 430
O'Neill, R. M., 470
Ono, Y., 258
O'Reilly, Anthony J. F., 362–363, 420–421, 449
O'Reilly, B., 501–502
Ortega, B., 80, 269
Orton, J. D., 501
Orwell, B., 120
Osnos, E., 158
Oster, S. M., 80
Osterland, A., 382, 389
Ouchi, W. S., 345
Oughton, C., 234
Oum, T. H., 346
Overholt, M. H., 430
Oviatt, B. M., 306, 501
Ovitz, Michael, 365–366
Owen, D., 431
Oxley, J. E., 345
Ozanne, M. R., 121

Paez, B. L., 235
Paine, L. S., 81
Palepu, K., 234, 464
Palia, K. A., 120
Palmer, A. T., 158
Pan, Y., 307, 345
Pandit, B. L., 502
Pantzalis, C., 307
Pappas, B., 457
Parcel, D., 41
Park, D., 40, 80, 201, 306, 308, 347, 42, 502
Park, Seung-Ho., 80, 307, 344–346
Parke, A., 348
Parsons, C. K., 470
Patel, P., 501
Pavitt, K., 502
Pearce, J. A., II, 469
Pearson, A. E., 41
Pearson, Andrall, 215, 258
Peffers, K., 80
Pereira, I., 199
Perry, N. J., 159
Perser, J. H., 200
Person, J., 307
Peteraf, M. A., 81, 119, 199, 233
Petzinger, T., Jr., 40, 502
Pfeffer, J., 119, 266, 469
Pfeifer, Eckhard, 179–180, 439
Phan, P. H., 268
Pieke, F. N., 501
Piercy, N. F., 345
Pinches, G. E., 266, 500
Pine, B. J., II, 80
Pinsker, B., 199
Pisano, G., 40, 79, 119–120, 234, 268, 306, 430
Planck, Max, 284
Platt, Louis E., 368, 370
Poitier, Sidney, 352
Pollack, A., 104
Polonsky, M. J., 4
Pope, K., 327
Porac, J. F., 199
Porras, J. I., 469
Porter, James, 110
Porter, M. E., 38–39, 61, 81, 87, 106, 119–121, 136, 139, 145, 157–159, 198, 233–234, 267, 280, 298, 306–308, 319, 380, 389, 431
Pouder, R., 336, 347, 430
Prahalad, C. K., 38, 40–41, 119, 121, 198, 233, 468, 502
Prasad, S. B., 235, 389
Prasad, V. K, 307
Prasso, S., 234
Preble, J. F., 79
Premeaux, S. R., 470
Prescott, J. E., 347
Pressley, J., 345
Preston, L. F., 40
Price, Michael, 389, 376
Price, R., 500
Price, Sol, 109
Priem, R. L., 79, 119, 468
Provan, K. G., 313, 344, 430
Prudom, J. J., 198
Puffer, S. M., 347
Pulliam, S., 238
Punnett, B. J., 305–307
Puri, S., 388

Quelch, J. A., 307
Quick, R., 238
Quinlan, J. P., 306
Quinn, J. B., 120, 468
Quint, M., 235
Quintanilla, C., 189, 266

Raghavan, A., 266
Rahweddeer, C., 432
Rajagopalan, N., 39–40, 157, 46"69
Rajan, M. V., 306, 431
Ramaswamy, K., 233, 2 66
Ramo, J, C., 39
Ramstad, E., 199, 327, 347, 389, 468
Rangan, U. S., 307, 346
Rasheed, A. M. A., 79, 468
Ravenscraft, D. J., 235, 267, 269
Rawsthorn, A., 231, 235
Rayport, J. F., 157
Reddy, S., 267, 307, 346
Redenbacher, Orville, 158
Rediker, K. J., 387–388
Reed, R., 120
Reger R. K., 81, 159
Rehbeing, K. A., 81
Rehfeld, B., 388
Reibstein, D. J., 157–158, 198, 200
Reichheld, F. F., 120
Reichhng, Gary, 492
Reilly, P. M., 2 34
Reimann, B. C., 500
Reingold, J., 388–389, 468
Reinhardt, A., 38, 119
Reitman, V., 306, 431, 484
Render, B., 200
Reuer, J. J., 347
Reuter, Edzard, 223
Rheem, H., 119
Ricart, J., 346
Rice, F., 158
Richman, L. S., 79
Ricks, D. A., 305–307
Riley, B., 389
Robbie, K., 502
Roberts, H. V., 183, 200
Robey, D., 121
Robins, J., 431
Robinson, G., 79
Roche, Gerard, 436
Rock, L., 268
Rock, R. H., 268
Rodriguez, E. M., 470
Roe, M. J., 388
Roesner, J. B., 80
Rogers, D. M. A., 501
Rohwedder, C., 432
Roll, R., 267
Romer, Paul M., 200
Roos, D., 500
Rose, F., 158
Rose-Ackerman, S., 235
Rosen, B., 200, 388
Roseno, A., 231, 233, 235
Rosenstein, S., 388
Ross, D., 234
Ross, Steven J., 33, 41
Rossan, J. , 4, 234, 242
Roth, K., 388
Rothwell, R., 502
Routamo, R., 503
Rowe, W. G., 233, 430–431
Rowley, T. J., 347
Rudnitsky, H., 470
Rugman, A., 306–307, 313, 344, 347
Rumelt, R. P., 38–41, 157–158, 205, 233–235, 389, 430–431
Rusakova, Ludmila, 495
Russell, R. S., 159, 200
Russo, M., 345

Sager, I., 113, 119, 158, 468–469, 501
Sakakibara, M., 198, 347
Sakano, T., 347
Salk, J. E., 307
Saloner, G., 347
Salter, M. S., 502
Sanchez, C., M., 268

Sanchez, R., 39, 121, 159, 201
Sanders, L., 235
Sankar, C. S., 348
Saporito, B., 157
Sarin, A., 387
Sarnin, P., 468
Sasser, W. E., Jr., 157
Savill, B., 266
Saxenian, A., 307
Saxton, T., 345, 348
Schacht, Henry, 437
Scheilhardt, T., 40
Schendel, D. E., 38–41, 157–158, 234, 389, 430–431
Schendler, B., 345
Schenker, J. L., 345
Scherer, R. M., 234–235, 267
Schick, A. G., 268
Schiller, Z., 40
Schine, E., 387–388
Schlender, B., 307, 345, 474
Schlesinger, L. A., 157
Schmalensee, R., 201
Schmidt, Eric, 442
Schmidt, Rich, 457
Schmidt, Rich, 457
Schoemaker, P. J. H., 40, 90, 119, 121
Scholes, M., 235
Schonberger, R. J., 500
Schonfeld, E., 80
Schoorman, F. D., 41, 348, 386–387, 468–469
Schotchmer, S., 307
Schrempp, Jurgen, 223
Schroeder, D., M., 201
Schroeder, R., G., 200
Schuler, R. S., 85, 119
Schultz, Howard, 153
Schultz, William, 260–261
Schuman, M., 306, 308, 347
Schumpeter, J. A. (Joseph), 170, 179, 199, 476, 500
Schwartz, F. N., 80
Schwartz, M., 266
Schwartz, N. D., 238, 306
Schwartzman, T. A., 393
Schwenk, C. R., 119
Scott, Richard L., 383
Scott, S. G., 470
Scripps, E. W., 410
Scully, J. A., 468
Seligman, P. M., 158, 215, 234
Sellers, P., 119–120, 258, 469
Sergesketter, B. F., 183, 200
Serwer, A. E., 199–200, 389, 470
Sesit, M. R., 267
Seth A., 39, 157, 268, 387–388
Seward, J. K., 235, 386, 388
Sexton, D. L., 500–501, 503
Shan, W., 306, 345
Shane, S. A., 201, 344, 346, 502
Shani, A. B., 200
Shank, J. K., 2 66
Shanley, M., 81
Shapiro, D. L., 305
Shapiro, E., 313
Shaples, S. S., 81
Sharav, B., 159
Sharfman, M. P., 201
Sharma, A., 387
Sharma, V. M., 268
Sharpe, A., 389
Shepard, L., 13
Shepard, S., 79
Shepard, W. G., 234
Shepard, W. G., 234
Sheridan, Kim, 486
Sherman, S., 38, 40, 120–121, 468–470
Sherman, W. S., 38, 120, 200
Shetler, J. C., 345, 347
Shih, Stan, 430
Shirouzu, N., 308, 346, 389
Shleifer, A., 234, 266, 387
Shortell, S. M., 159, 200
Shrader, R. C., 501
Shrivastava, P., 38–40, 469
Shuen, A., 40, 79, 119–120, 234, 306, 430
Siddharthan, N. S., 502
Siekman, P., 474
Sikora, M., 266
Silverman, B. S., 198, 345
Silverman, D., 266
Simmons, J., 158
Simon, M., 501
Simonian, H., 158, 198, 273, 286, 306, 484
Simonin, B. L., 346
Simons, R., 233, 471
Simpson, P., 157
Sims, H. P., Jr., 468
Sinatra, A., 267, 431
Sinegal, James D., 109
Singh, H., 266–269, 431
Singh, K., 80, 346
Singhal, S., 430
Sirois, C., 158
Sitkin, S. B., 200, 267
Sjokander, S., 502
Skaggs, B. C., 470
Skapinker, M., 199, 283, 306
Slevin, D. P., 157
Sloan, Alfred, Jr., 399
Slywotzky, A. J., 157
Smale, John, 382
Smart, D. L., 158, 234, 267, 269
Smart, T., 200, 469
Smilor, R. W., 500–501
Smith, C. G., 235
Smith, D. A., 468
smith, f. i., 199, 234
Smith, G., 307, 470
Smith, H., 45
Smith, Jack, 417, 446, 449
Smith, K. G., 79–81, 198–199, 468
Smith, L., 79–80, 235
Smith, M. P., 387
Smith, M., 234
Smith, Raymond, 325
Snell, S. A., 387, 469
Snider, Susan, 325
Snow, C. C., 120, 201, 347, 430, 432
Snyder, C. A-, 348
Solomon, R. C., 500
Song, J., 306
Sorkin, A. R., 120
Sorra, J. S., 200
Sovern, Michael I., 352
Spender, J.-C., 121
Spreitzer, G. M., 39, 157
Sprout, A. L., 39
Srinivasan, M., 234–235, 266
St. John, C. H., 41, 336, 347
Stadter, G., 120
Stanton, S. A., 468
Starkman, D., 75
Staw, B., 468
Steers, R. M., 80, 346
Steindel, C., 235
Steinhorst, K., 81
Steirunetz, G., 267, 389
Stem, G., 267
Stephens, C., 432
Stevens, K., 199
Stewart, T. A., 38–40, 81, 119–121, 157, 364, 468–469
Stiles, J., 198
Stimpert, J. L., 39, 233
Stodghill, R, 79
Stonham, P., 268
Stopford, J. M., 500
Stout, H., 199
Stout, S. K, 266
Stross, R. E., 40, 119–120, 468
Sturdivant, F. D., 158
Suarez, E. F., 430
Summers, B., 470
Sundaramurthy, C., 387–389
Sutcliffe, K. M., 200
Suzuki, Osamu, 448
Swaminathan, A., 199, 345
Swan, K. S., 345
Swoboda, F., 27
Symonds, W. C., 478
Szulanski, G., 121

Tabrizi, B. N., 200, 502
Tagliabue, J., 345
Tait, N., 307
Takahashi, D., 474
Tallman, S., 308
Talton, J., 2 3 4
Tamangani, Z., 430
Tamburri, R., 267
Tanouye, E., 266, 268
Tanzer, A., 308, 346
Taylor, A., III, 40, 104, 120, 235, 346, 389, 484
Taylor, B. W., III, 159, 200
Taylor, P., 199, 234
Teece, D. J., 39–41, 79, 119–121, 157–158, 234, 306, 347, 389, 430–431, 502
Teitelbaum, R., 7, 38, 487, 457, 493
Templeman, J., 235, 300
Templin, N., 268, 344, 345, 347
Tenti, P., 306
Tetzeli, R., 80

Tezuka, H., 346
Thomas, Charles, 31
Thomas, H., 3 9, 81, 15 7, 199, 235, 501
Thomas, P., 80–81
Thomas, R. E., 345, 347
Thompson, K. R., 467
Thompson, S., 346
Thompson, T. A., 387
Thompson-Noel, M., 503
Thornhill, J., 347
Thorton, E., 9, 38, 453, 484
Thurow, L. C., 38
Timmins, N., 200
Tomkins, R., 273, 306–307, 431
Toombs, L., 386, 430
Topfer, Mort, 459
Topfer, Mort, 459
Torres, C., 80, 346
Tosi, H. L., 235, 387–388
Totty, M., 121
Trotman, Alex, 437
Tse, D. K., 307
Tucker, E., 198
Tully, S., 40–41
Turk, T. A., 235, 387, 389, 431
Turney, R., 234
Tushman, M. L., 430–432
Tyler, B. B., 40, 80, 201, 306, 308, 347, 432, 502
Tyson, L., 200

Uchitelle, L., 388–389
Ulrich, D., 38, 453, 469
Ungson, G. R., 80, 307, 344–346
Upton, D. M., 159
Upton, N. B., 503
Useem, M., 387, 389, 493
Ussery, R. W., 348
Utterback, J. M., 430

van Biema, M., 200
van der Linde, C., 39
van Randenborgh, M., 389
Veiga, J. F., 267
Venables, A. J., 306
Venkataraman, S., 119–120
Venkatraman, N., 199
Verity, J. W., 121, 345
Vernon, Raymond, 274–275, 305
Very, P., 267
Victor, B., 80, 432
Viguerie, P., 157
Vishny, R. W., 234, 266, 387
Visuerie, P., 79
Viswanathan, S., 266
Vitzthum, C., 327
Vlasic, B., 27, 198
Vogel, T., 80
Volberda, H. W., 430
von Krogh, G., 267, 431
Vroman, H. W., 119

Wacholtz, L. E., 503
Wagemen, R., 159, 200
Wagner, J. A., 79
Wagner, S., 266
Wagstyl, S., 192, 215, 306
Wallace, Henry D. G., 400
Waller, M. J., 468
Wally, S., 81, 198, 200
Walsh, J. P., 235, 268, 386–389
Walsh, J. S., 503
Walsh, S., 437
Walter, John, 351–352, 366, 436
Walton, Sam, 283, 449
Wan, W. P., 346
Ward, R. D., 386
Warner, Douglas A., III, 319
Warren, M. E., 41
Waters, R., 268, 430–432
Watson, Thomas, J., Jr., 7
Wayner, P., 345
Webb, S., 364
Webber, J., 470
Weber, T. E., 238, 266
Weick, K. E., 79, 501
Weidenbaum M. L., 41, 464
Weigelt, K, 41
Weimer, D., 192, 306
Weimer, S., 388
Weiner, M., 45
Weisgall, D., 159
Welbourne, T. M., 387
Welch, John F., Jr. (Jack), 30, 83, 90, 96, 181, 189, 200, 257, 262, 469, 373, 375, 395, 437, 440, 449, 453,
Welsh, J., 268
Wernerfelt, B., 119, 199, 234
Westfeldt, A., 503
Westney, D. E., 81
Weston, J. F., 266
Westphal, J. D., 159, 200, 386, 388, 469–470
Wetlaufer, S., 43 1
Wexner, Les, 8
Wheelwright, S. C., 120, 200, 268
Whinston, A. B., 501
Whitman, David, 189, 469
Wierba, E. E., 470
Wiersema, M. F., 268, 431, 469
Wiggenhorn, W., 157
Wiggins, S. F., 157
Wilke, J. R., 80, 327, 346
Willard, G. E., 235
Willcocks, L., 345
William, Kelly, 137
Williams, J. C., 41, 201
Williams, J. R., 39, 200, 235, 345
Williams, M., 9, 38, 308
Williamson, O. E., 234, 375, 386–387, 389, 430
Williamson, P. J., 233–234, 346, 431
Wilson, R. L., 199, 234
Wind, J., 200
Wines, L., 388
Winslow, R., 234,266
Winston, C., 267
Winter, R. H., 346
Winters, T. E., 502
Wiseman, R., 388
Wishart, N. A., 121
Witt., V., 389
Wolff, R., 500
Wolfson, M., 235
Womack, J. P., 500
Woo, C. Y., 199, 235
Wood, D. J., 40, 386
Woodruff, D., 305–307, 469, 484
Woolley, S., 80, 120
Worrell, D. L., 268
Wozniak, Steve, 179
Wright, L. C., 501
Wright, M., 268, 347, 502
Wright, P. M., 158, 233, 430–431
Wright, P., 39–40, 386–387
Wright, Russell W., 501
Wrigley, L., 234
Wyatt, J. G., 266, 388
Wyatt, J., 266
Wyman, Thomas H., 352
Wyser-Pratte, G. Guy, 381
Wysocki, B., Jr., 469

Xie, J. L., 306

Yago, G., 267
Yang, C., , 4, 238
Yang, P. Y., 74
Yasai-Ardekani, M., 79
Yates, R. E., 388
Yeung, B., 347
Yilmaz, M., 200
Yip, G. S., 307
Yoo, S., 80
Yoshino, M. J., 346
Youndt, M. A., 469
Young, C., 347
Young, S., 238
Yuspeh, Alan, 461

Zachary, G. P., 430
Zaheer, S., 39, 306
Zahra, S. A., 80–81, 388, 469
Zajac, E. J., 386, 388, 469–470
Zander, U., 79, 502
Zarrella, Ronald, 446
Zeglis, John, D., 352
Zeithaml, C. P., 469
Zellner, W., 13, 198, 410, 470
Zemen, Jiang, 13
Zesiger, S., 484
Zey, M., 470
Zhang, H., 234
Zhu, T., 382
Zimmerman, M. 157, 348
Zipser, A., 67, 80–81
Zorn, T., 158
Zuckerman, L., 67, 80
Zweig, P. L., 235

Company Index

ABC, 10, 55, 58, 65
Acer, 67, 141, 393
ADAC Laboratories, 197
Adidas, 272
ADM, 324
Advanced Micro Devices (AMD), 144
Advantage Staffing Services, 496
AEROJET, 97
Aerospatiale, 317
Ahlstrom Corporation, 464
Ahold, 12
Air Canada, 321
Air France, 322, 403
Airbus Industrie, 179, 278, 317, 329
AirOne, 321
Alamo, 253
Alcatel, 316–317
Aldi, 12
Alitalia SpA, 321–322, 375, 403
Allen Bradley, 151
Allianz, 242
AlliedSignal, 11–12, 24, 130
Amadeus Fund Management Group, 335
Amazon.com, 17, 68
America Online (AOL), 16–17
American Airlines, 69, 169, 175, 187, 275, 321–322, 409, 437
American Campus Lifestyles, 110
American Eagle, 409, 455
American Express, 52
American Radio Systems, 211
American Society for Industrial Security (ASIS), 75
Ameritech, 319
Ames Rubber Corporation, 197
Amtrak, 409, 455
Amway Corp., 30, 68, 301–302
Andersen Consulting, 32, 116, 319
Andersen Windows, 150–151
Anheuser-Busch, Inc., 55–64, 128, 173, 175, 212, 225–226, 250
Aoki Corp., 291
Apple Computer, 33, 87, 115, 173, 179, 194, 318, 336–337, 454, 458
Aramark, 110
Armstrong & Associates Inc., 206
Arthur Andersen Enterprise Group, 95
Asea Brown Boveri (ABB), 298, 336, 427
Asian Airlines Systems, 321
Asiana Airlines, 329
Assicurazioni General, 242
Assurances Generales De France (AGF), 242
AST Research, Inc., 148
AT&T Corporation, 3–4, 10, 30, 147, 208–209, 237–239, 258, 325–327, 341, 351–353, 362, 366, 372–373, 415, 436–437, 443, 454
AT&T Solutions, 319
Audi, 484
Austrian Airlines, 321
Auto-By-Tel, 108
Avalon Software, Inc., 486
Aveda Corporation, 229
Avery-Dennison Corporation, 74
Avianca, 317
Avis, 253, 261
Avon, 56, 454

B. A. T. Industries, PLC, 242
Bali, 416
Ballard Power Systems, 294
Banana Republic, 104
Banc One Corp., 222
Banco Omego Group, 242
Bang & Olufsen, 125–126, 128–129, 148
BankAmerica, 57
Barclays, 285, 394
Barnes & Noble, 22, 68, 110
BASF, 281
Bath & Body Works, 8
Bausch & Lomb, 446
Baxter International, 371
Bayerische Motoren Werke AG (BMW), 72, 169, 295, 394, 484
BBA Group PLC, 242
BBC, 65
Beatrice Companies, 253
Bell Atlantic Network, 319, 325
Bell Labs, 330, 351
Bellcore, 84
Benetton, 319, 336–337, 424
Bessemer Ventures, 492–493
Bestfoods, 288
Bethlehem Steel, 162–163
Bic, 173
Bidim Ltda, 242
Big Dog Motorcycles, 171
Big Lots, 214
Black & Decker, 401
Blimpies, 110
Blockbuster, 177–178
Bloomingdale's, 146–147
Boeing, 78, 111, 113, 173, 179, 227, 278, 329, 424
Bombardier, 409, 455
Borders, 230
Borland International, 248
Bowmar, 173
Bradesco Seguros, 314
Braun, 478
Bridgestone Corporation, 13, 245
Brion Vega, 126
Bristol-Myers Squibb, 7
British Aerospace, 317
British Airways, 284, 321–322
British Interactive Broadcasting, 181
British Petroleum PLC (BP), 53, 459
British Steel PLC, 162–163
British Telecommunications (BT), 3–4, 181, 237, 316, 327
Broadway Department Stores, 248–249
Brookings Institution, 15
BskyB, 181
Buckman Laboratories, 442
Bucyrus-Erie, 294
Budget, 253
Buick, 417
Burger King, 69, 110, 148, 176–177
Business Week, 78

Cable Europa, 327
Cable News Network (CNN), 65
Cadbury Schweppes, PLC, 261
Caliber Systems Inc., 128, 175

California Public Employees' Retirement System (CalPERS), 352, 362–363, 366, 369
Callahan Associates, 327
Callaway Golf Company, 127
Calyx and Corolla, 108
Camden Property Trust, 110
Campbell Soup Company, 210, 260, 352–353, 362, 417
Campbell Taggart, 225–226, 251
Canada Air, 455
Canada Dry, 173
Canadair, 409
Canon, 24, 135, 173, 230–232, 293
Capital Bank of America, 327
Capital Cities/ABC, 55, 65
Carrefour, 12, 140
Carrus, 164
Cartier International Inc., 126
Catalyst, 370
Caterpillar, 142, 192–192, 241, 244, 286–287, 294, 352
Cathay Pacific Airways, 321
CBS Corporation, 10, 65, 211–212, 260, 352
CBS Records, 245
CCE, 18
Cementos de Mexico (CEMEX), 242, 291
Center for Advanced Fiber Optics Applications, 313
Century Development, 110
Century 21 Real Estate, 94
Cervejaria, 301
Chaparral Steel, 97, 101, 112, 114
Charles Schwab, 331
Charming Shoppes, Inc., 56
Charoen Pokphand, 210
Chase Manhattan, 285, 295, 376
Chemical Bank, 376
Chevrolet, 72, 417
Chevron, 352
Children's General Store, 178
Chiron Corp., 489
Chock Full O'Nuts, 154
Christian Dior, 144
Chrysler Corporation, 13, 24, 26, 102–103, 162, 164, 253, 313–314, 319, 322, 436, 454, 486
Cia, 301
Ciba-Geigy, 253, 489
Cifra, SA, 12
Cisco Systems, 370, 451–452, 493
Cisneros, 165
Citgo, 13
Citibank, 285
Citicorp, 87, 454
CityWeb, 65
CKS Group, 400
Clark Material Handling Company, 211
Clayton, Dubilier & Rice, Inc., 260
CMS Engery, 288
Cobb Theaters, 164
Coca-Cola Corporation, 7, 17–18, 30, 63, 95, 102, 118, 169–170, 173, 187–188, 206, 209, 230, 277–278, 405, 416–418, 436, 457, 493
Coffee Station, Inc., 154
Coldwell Banker Corporation, 58
Colgate-Palmolive (C-P), 188–189
Colliers International Property Consultant, 332
Color Tile, 8–9
Columbia/HCA Health Care Corporation, 35, 321, 383, 461–462
Comcast, 58, 326, 330
Commerce One, 331
Commerzbank, 378
Compagnie Generale des Eaux, 181
Compaq Computer Corporation, 66–67, 113, 115, 147, 169, 173–174, 176, 179–180, 243, 330, 337, 377, 394, 439, 474
CompUSA, 179, 337
Compuserve, 16–17
Computer City, 179
Computer Sciences Corporation, 319
Computer Services, 241
ConAgra, Inc., 446
Conseco, 374
Consolidated Stores, Inc., 212
Construcciones Aeronauticas, 317
Continental Airlines, 322, 365
Continental Bank, 111
Continental Cablevision, 326
Continuum, 241
Contrax, 173
Coopers and Lybrand, 313
Coors, 173
Cordiant Communications Group, 257–259
Cordis, 243
Core States Financial, 248
Corner Bakery, 183
Corning, Inc., 97, 314, 340, 426
Corning Glass, 314
Costco Companies, Inc., 108–109
Cott Corporation, 208–209
Council of Institutional Investors, 364
Cox Communications, 326
Crate & Barrel, 97
Cray Computer, 113
Crystal Geyser, 169
Cummins Engine, 294
Cyrix Corp., 144

Daewoo Motor Co., 129
Daimler-Benz Aerospace (DASA), 329
Daimler-Benz AG, 164, 207, 212, 223–224, 294, 317, 497
Dallas, Garland & Northeastern (DGNO), 147
Dana Corp., 137–138
Dart Group, 210
Dayton Hudson Corporation, 156–157
Debonair, 282, 284
Deere & Co., 88
Delhi Groups, 224
Dell Computer Corporation, 66–67, 76, 113, 115, 118, 169, 173, 176, 179, 184, 204, 337, 442, 458–459
Deloitte & Touche, 75
Delta Airlines, 169, 187, 319, 321–322, 325, 437
Deutsche Telecom AG, 4, 316, 327, 378
Diageo PLC, 286, 447
Dial, 376
Digital Equipment Corporation (DEC), 96, 174, 180, 197, 330, 377, 394, 439, 444
Digital Video Broadcast (DVB), 327
DirecTV, 325
Disco SA, 140
Disney Company, 55, 83, 85, 94, 329, 374
Diversified Pharmaceutical Services, Inc., 218
Dodge, 72
Dofasco, 162
Dollar Rental Car, 253
Douglas, 173
Doumar Products, Inc., 492
Dow Jones, 376
Draw the Line, 494
DreamWorks SKG, 329–330
Dresdner, 378
Dr. Pepper, 261
Dun and Bradstreet, 110
Dunkin' Donuts, 21
DuPont, 169, 395, 399, 427
Duracell, 478

E. W. Scripps, 409
Eagle Hardware, 85–86
Eagle Snacks, 128, 225–226, 250
Eastman Chemical, 197
Eastman Kodak Company, 58, 87, 97, 167, 256–257, 319, 323, 352, 362, 372, 436, 454, 489
EasyJet, 282, 284
EBC Industries, 312
EchoStar Communications, 325
Electrolux, 301, 427
Electronic Data Systems Corp., 204, 241, 245, 259, 319
Eli Lilly and Company, 24, 62, 218, 240
Emerson Electric Co., 137, 140–141
Emhart Glass, 401
Empresa Nationalde Electricidad, 327
Encyclopedia Britannica Inc., 57
Engineering Inc., 97
Enron Corporation, 13, 15, 54, 316
Epson, 330
Ericsson, 215, 427
Erie Bolt, 312
Ernst & Young, 240
ESPN, 10, 94
Estee Lauder, 228
E-Systems, 58
Europipe GmbH, 162–163
Eversharp, 173
Exacta, 173
Excite, 78
Expresso Armando, 493
Exxon, 7, 37

FAG Kugelfischer, 403
Falcon Drilling, 239

Fastenal, 456–457, 493
FBI, 74
FCB, 339
Federal Express (FedEx), 105, 107–108, 128, 175, 197, 337, 420
Federal-Mogul Corporation, 436–437
Federated Department Stores, 248–249
Fender Muscial Instruments, 260–261
Ferguson, 126
Fiat, 219–220
Firestone Tire and Rubber, 13, 245–246
First Bank System, 243
First of America Bank, 248–249
First Union, 248
First USA Inc, 222
Follett College Stores, 110
Foote, Cone & Belding (FCB), 339
Ford Motor Co., 24, 26, 113, 151, 162, 164–165, 179, 253, 279, 194, 314, 317, 400, 437, 497
Forsmann Little, 261
Four Pillars Enterprise Co., 74
Fox Broadcasting Company, 10, 65
France Telecom SA, 4, 181, 316, 327
Franklin Mutual, 376
Fred Myers, 109
Friday's Hospitality Worldwide Inc., 277
Frito-Lay, 128, 251, 277, 340–341
Fruehauf Trailer Corp., 211
Fuji Photo Film Co., 167, 257
Fujitsu, 497

Gadzooks, 132–134
Galaxy Latin America, 165
Gap, The, 97, 104
GapKids, 104
Gateway 2000, 66–67, 76, 173, 176, 337
General Dynamics, 224–225, 257
General Electric (GE), 7, 24, 30, 57, 65, 83, 85, 90, 95, 173, 181, 188, 210, 262, 275, 289, 290, 327, 373, 375, 395, 411–412, 424, 437, 439, 449–450, 457, 486, 489
General Foods, 53, 195, 217
General Instruments, 327
General Mills, 195
General Motors Corp. (GM), 26–28, 37, 75, 94–95, 103, 132, 162, 164, 190, 239, 245, 252, 256, 279, 295, 303, 362, 371, 391, 399, 417, 444, 446, 449, 497
German Opal A.G., 75
Gerber Products, 240
Geric Home Health Care, 494–495
German Chemical Union, 26
Gillette Company, 49, 97, 478–479
Goodyear Tire & Rubber, 444
Great Brands of Europe, 169
Great Canadian Bagel Ltd, The, 21
Green Tree Financial, 373–374
Grundig, 126
Grupo Abril, 165
Grupo Alpha, 325
Grupo Financiero Banamex, 325
Grupo Modelo, 175
Grupo Televisa, 165
GT Bicycles, 92
GTE, 3, 180, 208, 237, 326
Guess, 134
Guicci Group, 126

H. J. Heinz, Inc., 362, 365, 420–421, 449
Haier Group, 189
Hanes, 340, 416
Hanson PLC, 211, 239, 259–260
Harley-Davidson, 65, 92, 94, 170–171
Hay Group, The, 84
HBO, 10
Heidrick & Struggles, Inc., 436
Helene Curtis, 242
Hershey Foods Corp., 210
Hertz, 253
Hewlett-Packard (HP), 66–67, 96–97, 101, 113, 135, 147, 179, 197, 317, 330, 368–369, 448, 450, 455, 458, 473, 487
Hillshire Farm, 340, 416
Hilton Hotels, 321
Hitachi, 151, 328, 334, 497
Hoechst AG, 169, 272–273, 281
Home Depot, 9, 85–86, 109, 149
Honda Motor Company, 8–9, 13, 24, 65, 102–103, 135, 169, 279, 297, 483
Honeywell, 214–215
Hoover's Online, 157
HSBC Midland, 181
Hudson's, 156–157
Hughes Aerospace, 245
Hughes Electronics, 165, 325, 351, 391, 393
Hyundai Group, 59, 463

Iams Company, The, 118, 126, 128, 148
Iams Animal Care Facility, 128
Paul F. Iams Technical Center, 128
IBM Corporation, 7–9, 16, 45, 66–67, 134–135, 141, 147, 169, 173, 176, 179, 186, 190, 197, 241, 256, 312, 318, 330, 336–337, 357, 436, 443–444, 454, 474, 486, 497
Ifil, 219–220
IKEA, 337
Imperial Tobacco, 260
Inc., 78
Industrie Natuzzi SpA, 98
Ingram book group, 22
Integrated Health Services, 213
Intel Corp., 7, 9, 16, 24, 58, 86, 113, 143–144, 174, 317, 330, 437, 450, 473–474, 479, 483
International Co. for Finance & Investment (ICFI), 170
International Harvester, 294
International Paper, 256–257, 259, 295
Ipsco Inc., 163
Issaquah Washington, 109
ITT, 219, 239, 253, 415
Iveco, 164

J. C. Penney Co., 132, 168, 476
Janet's Thingamajigs, 178
Jiangling Motors, 279
Jimmy Dean, 340, 416
Johnson & Johnson, 7, 173, 210, 243–244, 255, 352, 453

Kaiser Wilhelm Institutes, 284
Karossa, 164
Kay-Bee Toys, 177, 214
Kellogg, 187, 195, 210
Kentucky Fried Chicken (KFC), 59, 257–259, 360
KFKI, 316
Khanty-Mansiyskneftegazgeologia (KMNNG), 334
Kimberly-Clark, 71, 87, 257, 454
Kinko's, 109
KLM Royal Dutch Airlines, 284, 322
Kmart, 108, 131–132
KMOC, 334
Kolberg, Kravis and Robert (KKR), 260, 261
Komatsu, 97, 191–192, 286–287, 294, 296
Koninklijke PTT, 314, 327
Korean Air, 329
Korn/Ferry International, 370–371
KPMG Peat Marwick, 240
Kraft Foods, 147, 217, 446
Kubota, 191

L'Eggs, 340, 416
La Madeline, 183
Land Rover, 484
Lands' End, 284, 417
Laurent Kabila, 299
Leica, 173
Levi-Strauss & Co., 84, 87, 96, 134, 150, 167–168, 454
Lexis, 484
Lexis/Nexis, 16
LG Group, 463
Limited, The, 8–9
Liquid Paper, 478
Lockheed Martin Corporation, 27–28, 58, 317, 393
Lockheed, 317
LOT, 403
Louis Vuitton (LVMH), 125–126, 142
Lowe's, 9, 85–86
Luby's Cafeteria, 128
Lucas Varity, 241
Lucent Technologies, 4, 243–244, 258, 319, 437
Lufthansa, 284, 321
Lukens, 162–163

Mabe, 275
Mabuchi Motor, 150, 209
Macy's, 98
Magna International, 319
Mahindra & Mahindra, 165
Maintenance Warehouse America Corp., 149
Mando Machinery, 295
Mannesmann AG, 162
Manpower Inc., 451

Marathon Oil, 224, 245
Marks & Spencer, 284, 319, 321
Marriott, 110
Marshall Field's, 156–157
Martin Marietta, 317
MasterWord Services, 495
Matsushita Electric, 246, 311, 338, 454, 497
MAV rt., 316
Maytag Corporation, 142
Mazda Motor Corporation, 97, 314, 317, 400
MCA, 246
McCaw Cellular Communications, 209
McDonald's, 37, 69, 148, 176–177, 258, 276, 331, 425–426
McDonnell Douglas, 225
MCI WorldCom, 238
MCI, 3–4, 208, 237–238, 316, 325–327, 352
McIlhenny, 187
McKesson, 169, 218
McKinsey & Co., 97, 100, 142, 144, 368
Medco Containment Services Inc., 62, 118, 240
MedPartners, 246–247
Melville, 239
Mercedes-Benz, 72, 102, 164, 223, 276, 484
Merck & Company, 7, 24, 62, 210, 218, 240, 452, 488
Mercury Asset Management group, 244
Merrill Lynch & Company, 244, 326, 410
Mervyn's, 156–157
MicroAge, Inc., 67
Microelectronics Computer Corporation (MCC), 338–339
Microsoft Corporation, 7, 10, 16–17, 24, 58, 65, 85–86, 96, 113, 173, 186, 194, 248, 312, 329–331, 442, 474
Millenium Chemicals, 260
Miller Brewing Co., 173, 216–217, 301, 450
Ministry of International Trade and Investment (MITI), 282
Mitsubishi Consumer Electronics America Inc., 170
Mitsubishi Motors Corp., 58, 314
MKM-Tel, 316
Mobil, 13
MOL rt., 316
Monorail, 337–338
Monsanto, 76
Montgomery Securities, 222
Morgan Stanley & Co., 409–410
Morrison Knudsen Corporation, 436
Motion Control, 97
Motorola, 4, 9, 13, 15, 54, 96, 151, 197, 215, 318, 336, 458–459, 473–474
MSNBC, 65, 330
Mulvision, 165

Nabisco, 446–447
National Car Rental System, 253
National City, 248–249
National Semiconductor, 474
National Small Business United, 95
National Textiles, 416
NationsBank, 222
NBC, 10, 65, 330
NCR, 258, 351
NEC, 311
Nesa Textiles, 286
Nestlé, 289, 442
Netscape Communications, 442
NetSys Technologies, 493
Network Computer, Inc., 58
New Balance Inc., 172
New York Teachers Retirement Fund, 366
Newell Company, 413–414
News Corporation, 10
Nike, 69, 73, 172, 272, 336–337, 416, 481–482
Nikon, 173
Nintendo, 337
Nippon Steel, 162, 224, 245
Nippon Telephone & Telegraph (NTT), 4, 9, 497
Nissan Motor Company, 26, 72, 103, 297, 311, 329, 338, 404–405, 483
Nordstrom, 97, 403
Norrell Corporation, 97
Northern States Power Company, 52
Northern Telecom, 4, 44
Northrop Grumman, 225
Northwest, 322
Norwest, 97
Nova Corporation, 137
Novartis AG, 253, 497
Novell, Inc., 247–248, 330, 442
Nucor Corporation, 163, 313
Nucor Steel, 322
Nutrasweet, 68
Nynex Corp., 325

Octel Communications, 243–244
Odd Lots, 137, 214
Office Depot, 74
Office Max, 179
Old Navy, 104
Olympia & York Developments Ltd., 436
Oracle Corporation, 58, 174, 370, 442
Oral-B, 478
Organizacoes Globo, 165
Orville Redenbacher, 142

Pacific Telesis Group, 325
Packard Bell, 66, 141
Parker Pen, 173, 478
Pasqua Inc., 154
Patek Philippe, 148
Pennzoil, 292
Pep Boys, 24, 75
PepsiCo, 30, 63, 97, 102, 128–129, 169–170, 173, 257–259, 277–278, 340, 405, 440, 453
Perkins Engine, 241, 244
Perrier Group, 169–170
Petroleos de Venezuela, 13, 15
Peugeot-Citroen, 404–405
Pfizer, 173, 352, 364, 483
Philip Morris, 7, 22, 94. 207, 216–217, 364, 446–447, 450
Philips Electronics, 293–294, 451
Phillips Petroleum Company, 24
PhyCor, 246–247
Piemme Atlas Concorde, 284
Pillsbury Corporation, 447
Pinnacle Alliance, 319
Pizza Hut, 257–259, 360, 497
Playtex, 340, 445
Pointcast, 57
Pontiac, 72
Popcorn Institute, The, 142
Power Computing, 337
Pratt and Whitney, 424
Price Club, 108–109
Price/Costco, 324
Primestar Partners, 325
Procter & Gamble (P&G), 7, 11, 24, 59, 71, 94, 109, 115, 188–189, 210, 214, 256, 464
PTT Nederland NV, 4
Publicis of Paris, 339

Quaker Oats, 195
Qualcomm, 4
Quikava, 154

R. H. Macy's, 248–249
R. R. Donnelley & Sons, 351
Radio Shack, 173
Rally's Hamburgers, Inc., 147–148
Ralph Lauren Clothing, 97, 142, 146, 168
Ralston Purina, 126
Raytheon Company, 391–393, 411
Raytheon Systems, 225, 391, 393
RCA, 489
Reading & Bates, 239
Reebok International, 24–25, 69, 73, 172, 272
Reed Elsevier PLC, 242
Regal Cinemas Inc., 164
Renault, 164, 167
Resiassance Capital Group, 170
ResidentSea, 143
Retevision SA, 327
Rheon Automatic Machinery, 293
Ritz-Carlton(Hotel Company, 130
Riverside Cement, 464
Rizal, 242
RJR Nabisco Holdings Corporation, 207, 217, 446
Robert Bosch GmbH, 295
Rolex, 142
Rolls-Royce, 97, 424
Rolodex, 74–75
RoTech Medical Corp., 213
Rover Cars, 295
Royal Crown, 173
Rubbermaid, 29–30, 50, 68, 321, 442
Rupert Murdoch's News Corporation, 165

Rust Belt, 312
Ryanair, 282–284

Saab, 484
Saatchi & Saatchi, 258
Sabena World, 321
Sachs AG, 295
Safeway, 108, 208
Sally Beauty Supply, 148–149
Sam's Club, 108, 324
Samsung Aerospace, 329
Samsung Electronics Co., Ltd., 14, 59, 148, 328
Samsung Group, 329, 463, 474
Sandoz AG, 240, 253
SAP, 331
Sapporo, 173
Sara Lee Corporation, 340–341, 415–416
Sarnoff Research Center, 327
SBC, 3, 325
Scandanavian Airlines, 321
Scania, 164
Schlumberger, 210
Science Applications International Corp. (SAIC), 84–85, 96
Scott Paper Company, 71, 369
Scotts Co., 410–411
Seagate, 370
Seagram's, 246
Sears, Roebuck & Co., 56, 168, 239, 319
Second Cup, 154
Security Passions, 148
Sega, 179
Sematech, 317, 338
Sensormatic, 75
Service Corporation International (SCI), 291, 331
Service Performance Corporation (SPC), 406
7 Up, 218
Shapiro Marketing, 143
Sharp Corporation, 284, 336
Shell, 13
Sherwin-Williams, 147
Shiseido, 242, 289
Siemens, 96, 497
Sigma Circuits, 75
Silicone Graphics, Inc. (SGI), 112–114, 118, 197, 330
Singapore Airlines, 321
SJS-Thomson Electronics, 474
Sky Latin America, 165
SmithKline Beecham PLC, 62, 218, 240
Snap-on Tools, 126, 128, 148
Snappy Rental Car, 253
Solectron Corporation, 97
Solid State Measurements Inc., 31
Solvay Group, 212–213
Sony Corp., 10, 97, 99–100, 141, 179, 245, 246, 272–273, 293–294, 311, 328–329, 477, 482
Southern Pacific Rail Corporation, 251–252
Southwest Airlines, 37, 180, 282, 402–403, 452, 496
Space Imaging, Inc., 58
Spacehab, 58
Spring Corporation, 437
Sprint, 4, 134, 239, 316, 325–327
Ssangyong, 463–464
St. Louis Cardinals, 225–226
Staples, 74, 134
Starbucks, 21, 143, 153–154, 493
Sterilite, 50
Stern Stewart, 249
STET, 4
Sullivan's Toy Store, 178
Sun Microsystems, 113, 174, 197, 330, 337, 370, 442
Sun River, 436
Sunbeam, 369, 376, 437
Suntory International, 169, 173
Svenska Aeroplan Aktiebolaget (Saab), 207, 212, 484
Swiss Bank Group, 242
Swiss Telecom PTT, 4, 314, 327
SwissAir, 321–322

T & N PLC, 437
Taco Bell, 257–259, 360, 497
Tandem Computers, 243, 439
Tandy Corp., 173, 180
TAP Air Portugal, 403
Target, 132, 156–157
Tato, 4
TDA, 329
Teachers Insurance and Annuity Association-College Retirement Equities Fund (TIAA-CREF), 362
Telecom Italia, 327
Tele-Communications Inc. (TCI) 10, 58, 258, 312, 326, 331
Telefónica de España, 327
Telefunken, 126
Teleport Communications, 326, 352
Telia AB, 4, 314, 327
Tengelmann, 12
Tenneco, 210, 239
Terex, 211
Texaco, 13
Texas Industries, 464
Texas Instruments, 173, 225, 334, 391, 393, 474
Texas Oil and Gas, 224, 245
Texmex, 325
Textron, 210
Thai Airways International, 321
Thermo Electron, 180, 455
Thermo King, 211
Thomson Consumer Electronics, 97, 327–328
Thomson Corporation, The, 289–290
Thomson CSF, 329
3M, 180, 239, 393, 477, 483
Thrifty Rental Car, 253
Thunder Tiger, 182
Tibco, 57
Timeless Toys Inc., 178
Time-Warner, 33, 65, 217, 273, 325
Timothy's World Coffee, 154
Timothy's World-News Cafe, 154
Title 9 Sports, 132
Tomkins, 230
Tommy Hilfiger, 142, 144, 168
Toshiba, 311, 474
Toyota Motor Corporation, 13–14, 72, 102–104, 112, 138, 142, 165, 167, 179, 272–273, 279, 303, 311, 338, 424, 483–484
Toys "R" Us, 178, 324–325
Trammel Crow Co., 213
Trans World Airlines, 175
Tricon, 258–259
Trident Precision, 197
True North Communications, 339
True Temper Sports, 401
TRW, 214–215, 256, 395
Tupperware, 277

U.S. Industries, 211
U.S. Postal Service, 128
U.S. Robotics, 57
U.S. Steel, 224, 245
U.S. West, 53, 257–259, 326
Unifi Inc., 137, 140
Unilever Group, 242, 421–422
Union Pacific Corporation, 8, 251–252
Unisource, 316, 327
Unisys, 256
United Airlines, 169, 261, 321
United Biscuits Holdings PLC, 277
United HealthCare, 218
United Parcel Service Inc. (UPS), 128, 175, 203–206, 212
United Technologies, 424
United Utilities, 44
Unix, 113
Unocal Corporation, 24
UPC, 334
UPM-Kummene, 295
USAA, 452
USAir, 166, 321
USI, 260
Usiminas, 162
Usinor, 162
USX Corporation, 224, 313, 322
Utility Empresa Nationalde Electridad, 327

V&S Vin & Spirit AB, 286
Veba AG, 378
Viag, 181
ViaSat, 58
Victoria's Secret, 8
Virgin Express, 282
Visa, 134
Volkswagen, 75, 136
Volvo, 164, 210, 279, 285, 484

Wal-Mart, 9, 12–13, 15, 30, 37, 50, 68, 97, 108–109, 131–132, 140, 187, 208–209, 282–284, 295–297, 321, 413, 440, 449
Washington Construction Group, 436
Waste Management Corporation, 436–437

Wawa Inc., 497
WebTV Networks Inc., 58
Weight Watchers, 421
Wendy's, 69
Werner Enterprises, Inc., 451
Wertkauf hypermarket, 283
Wesray Capital, 253
Westin Hotels Group, 291
Westinghouse Electric Corp., 210, 211
Westinghouse Power Generation, 211
Westinghouse, 489
Whirlpool Corporation, 11–12, 87, 161–162, 188–189, 301, 450, 454
White Rain, 478
Wm. Wrigley Jr. Company, 209, 222
Wolters Kluwer, 242
Woolco, 9
Woolworth, 8–9
WordPerfect, 247–248
World Bank, 276, 381
WorldCom, Inc., 3–4, 7, 9, 17, 37, 208, 237–238, 327, 352
Worldwide Logistics, 203–204, 206
W.R. Grace, 239

Xerox, 24, 180, 210, 231, 256, 319, 492

Yahoo!, 78
Yanmar, 191
Yo!, 398

Zenith, 328, 489
Zurich Insurance Co., 242

Subject Index

above-average return(s), 2, 4–9, 18–23, 25–26, 28, 33–37, 45, 47, 50, 61, 64, 68, 77, 85–86, 88, 90, 104, 111, 114, 118, 127–128, 137, 140–142, 144, 149–150, 153, 155, 164, 167, 170, 180, 182–183, 205–207, 212, 216, 220, 228, 230–231, 239, 242–245, 257, 261, 274, 296, 298, 328, 354, 356, 362, 406, 422, 438, 440, 442–443, 462, 475, 486, 498
acquisition strategies. *See* acquisitions
acquisitions, 116–117, 123, 141, 162, 164, 175, 211–213, 216, 222–223, 225, 227, 229, 238–239, 241–242, 245, 247–250, 252–255, 263, 329, 339, 351–352, 377, 413, 460, 489–490, 492
    cross-border, 238, 241–242, 295
    effective, 254–255
    problems achieving success, 246–254
    reasons for, 240–242, 247
    successful, 256
activity sharing, 212, 214–216, 225–226, 321
Administrative Council of Economic Defense, 301
advertising, 94
agency costs, 360–361, 371
agency relationships, 357–358
agents, 357–358
aggregate output, 14
Aluminum Association, The, 323
American Management Association, 257
antitrust laws (regulations), 212, 221–222, 240, 245
assessing, 48–50, 77
Aufsichtsrat, 378
autonomous strategic behavior, 456, 481
average American, 131
average returns, 5, 29, 36, 88, 140–141, 153, 195, 227, 246, 328
average teenager, 132
awareness (competitor), 167, 170, 195–196

baby boomers' needs, 172
bank-oriented financial system, 379, 381
bargaining power:
    of buyers, 67–68, 140, 146
    of suppliers, 66, 140–141, 146
barriers to entry, 19, 21, 63–65, 78, 141, 146, 179, 240–241, 303
below-average returns, 29, 36, 194, 376
benchmarking, 88, 184–185, 196, 442
best-cost producer strategy, 140
board of directors, 355, 366–371
    insiders, 366–368
    outsiders, 366–368
    related outsiders, 366–368
bondholders, 249
brand equity, 94
brand identification, 253
brand image, 144, 146, 156
brand loyalty, 144, 146–147, 241
brand names, 93–94, 118, 146, 171, 174, 189, 260–261, 286, 420, 482
breakneck expansion plans, 165
broad-based competitor, 147
build to order (BTO) business, 179
bundling, 92
bureaucratic controls, 254
business-level strategy(ies), 34, 104, 116–117, 123–124, 128–129, 135–156, 166–167, 182, 195, 206, 280, 287, 318–319, 393, 395, 401, 406, 424, 458
    generic, 129
    integrated, 290
    international, 287
buyer-centric environment, 68

Cambridge phenomenon, 335
capabilities, 22–25, 31, 33–34, 36, 46, 52, 82, 85–92, 94–102, 104–105, 108, 110–111, 114–117, 124, 127, 134–135, 140, 143–144, 149, 166–167, 182, 187, 191, 194, 207, 209, 213, 216, 222, 230–231, 239–240–241, 243–244, 246, 249, 255, 273–274, 297, 312, 328, 340, 409, 484
    costly-to-imitate, 22, 33, 36, 98–102, 116–117, 225, 442
    difficult-to-imitate, 187
capital allocation, 212, 219, 230, 273
capital gains tax, 221
capital good industries, 12
capital investment, 22, 187
capital markets, 218–219
    external, 219
    internal, 218–219
capital market stakeholders, 26–30, 35
Capital Public Utility Regulatory Policy Act of 1978, 43
capital requirements, 64
cartels, 323
cash flow, 218, 222, 224–225, 243–244, 255, 258
cast-off, 258
casually ambiguous, 101–102, 169–170
Celler-Kefauver Act, 221
Census Bureau, 57
Center for Advanced Fiber Optics Applications, 313
centralization, 288, 401–402, 408, 414
CEO duality, 444–445
chaebols, 329, 463–464
changes in competition, 164–166
Chief Learning Officer (CLO), 95
Chinese economy, 59–61
Chinese entrepreneurial operations, 59
code division multiple access (CDMA), 4
cogeneration technology, 43
combination structure, 421–422
Combined Heat & Power Association, 484
commercial opportunities, 128
commodity-like product, 142
communications technology, 52
competencies, 34, 100, 104, 114, 127, 141, 155, 213, 231, 409
competition, 62
competitive actions, 42, 45, 47, 66, 69–70, 154, 160–172, 174–178, 185, 188, 191–192, 195–197, 217, 224, 301, 325
    speed of, 178, 180–181
competitive advantage, 2, 5, 10, 12, 14, 16, 18, 21–23, 25, 31–37, 46, 52, 75, 83, 85, 85–102, 104–105, 107,

110–112, 114, 116–118, 124, 127–130, 134–137, 146–153, 155–156, 163, 167, 170, 172, 177–178, 184–185, 191–192, 194–197, 204–206, 213, 216, 219, 239–240, 249, 252, 257, 277, 280, 282, 285, 297, 301, 315, 317, 328, 332, 337, 354, 391, 393, 396–397, 401, 409, 423–424, 438, 441–442, 450, 454, 475, 485, 489
sustained/sustainable, 5, 85–87, 89, 92–93, 98–99, 102, 108, 117–118, 135, 149, 166, 171, 181, 185–187, 190, 272, 298, 393, 442, 475
temporary, 166, 190, 196
competitive aggressiveness, 456
competitive analysis, 61, 88
competitive asymmetry, 167
competitive attack, 166–168, 195
competitive challenge, 5, 144, 148, 162, 180
competitive disadvantage, 63, 114
competitive disruption, 166, 191, 196
competitive dynamics, 123, 154, 160, 163, 165–170, 177–179, 182–183, 185, 192, 206
model of, 166–170
competitive environment, 18, 20, 24, 35–36, 45, 48, 61, 87, 93, 115, 118
competitive forces, 42, 144
competitive intelligence, 42, 77, 197
competitive interaction, 70, 170, 178–185, 191, 193
competitive landscape, 2, 5, 9–12, 14–15, 17–18, 21, 31, 34–37, 75, 87–88, 90, 94, 111, 114, 116–117, 124, 127, 132, 137, 149, 163–166, 179, 380, 394, 435, 446, 458
competitive parity, 99, 101–102, 185, 196, 278, 317, 328, 489
competitive position, 13, 19, 45–46, 87, 197, 218, 271, 311
competitive potential, 17
competitive premium, 16
competitive responses, 69, 154, 160, 162–170, 172, 174–177, 191–192, 195–197, 216–217, 288
speed of, 178, 180–181
competitive risk, 340
competitive rivalry, 72, 140, 144, 146, 162, 164, 166–170, 191–192, 197
model of, 166–170, 194–195, 197
competitive scope, 135–136, 149–150, 153, 225
competitive segment, 147–149, 155
competitive strategy, 18, 61, 82, 151, 192, 194, 206, 288
competitive success, 17, 52, 181
competitiveness, 19, 26, 33, 85, 203, 210
competitor analysis, 42, 47–48, 73–77, 167–168, 196
competitor environment, 46–47, 128
competitor intelligence, 74–78
competitors, 63
complementary assets, 254, 339, 341
complementary strategic alliance, 319, 328
horizontal, 319–322
vertical, 319–320, 322
complexity, 89–90
comprehensiveness, 312
computer industry, 3
computer-aided design (CAD), 151, 485
computer-aided manufacturing (CAM), 485
computer-assisted design and development (CADD), 151–152
computer-integrated manufacturing (CIM), 151
Confucian Social Philosophy, 479–480
conglomerates, 210–211, 221, 230, 259, 324, 380, 464
consumer nondurable goods, 64
consumption patterns, 131
contingency workers, 52
continuous improvement, 184
cooperative alliance, 311
cooperative relationship, 312
cooperative strategy(ies), 34, 110, 116–117, 123, 311, 313, 331, 335–336, 339–342, 395, 422
business level. *See* business-level strategies
corporate level. *See* corporate-level strategies
international. *See* international strategies
coopetition, 313
core business, 203, 205, 208, 210–211, 216–217, 223, 230, 253–254, 256–259, 262, 408
core competence(ies), 22–25, 33–34, 36, 43, 50, 77, 82, 85–91, 93–94, 96–99, 104, 107, 110–114, 116–118, 125, 127–130, 134–135, 137, 140, 143–144, 147, 149, 155–156, 167, 171, 182, 204–209, 211–214, 216, 230, 238–240, 249, 259, 261, 271, 273–274, 279, 283, 294, 297, 320, 333, 394, 423, 444, 447, 450, 453–454, 463, 489
core rigidities, 82, 112, 114, 117
core values, 32, 35
corporate control, 356, 367, 376–377
corporate culture, 246, 295, 412, 458
corporate entrepreneurship, 455, 475–476, 479
corporate excellence, 83–84
corporate governance, 36, 261–262, 341, 352–354, 356, 358, 363, 367–370, 383, 396, 463
Germany, 377–379
international, 377
Japan, 379–380
corporate governance mechanisms, 227–228, 354, 355–356, 358, 360–361, 371–376, 393
external, 355
internal, 311, 355, 376
corporate headfake, 76
corporate memory, 130
corporate office, 219, 375
corporate raider, 376
corporate scope, 35
corporate strategy, 282, 288
dominant business, 202, 205–210
single business, 202, 205–209
corporate universities, 118
corporate-level strategy, 34, 116–117, 123, 166, 195, 202, 204, 206–207, 212–213, 229, 231, 238, 273, 318, 328–332, 358, 375, 392–394, 406, 409–410, 424, 426, 481
international, 287, 297, 332–335
cost advantages, 64, 179
cost disadvantages, 64
cost leadership strategy, 19, 124, 129, 135–143, 147, 149, 152, 155–156, 211, 401–402, 458
risks of, 141–142, 155–156
creative destruction, 179
cross-border flow, 271
cross-border focus, 165
cross-functional integration, 484–487
cross-functional organizations, 392
cross-functional work teams, 101, 196, 486
cultural differences, 29
cultural diversity, 55
cultural environment, 59
cultural revolution, 224
cultural superstores, 230
currency fluctuations, 276, 299–300
customer evaluation, 124
customer groups, 126–127, 130–132, 134, 149, 154–155, 215
customer loyalty, 130–131, 146, 170, 172, 195
customer needs, 130, 132, 134–136, 142, 146, 150, 155, 184, 215
customer segment, 126, 131, 135, 178
customer service, 142–143, 178, 437
customer-oriented processes, 130
customers, 67–68, 124, 126–129, 131–132, 134, 136–137, 140–142, 146, 149, 151, 153–155, 161, 178, 183–184, 192–194, 204–205, 208, 226, 230, 243, 252, 279, 282, 285, 335, 460
customers: who, what, how, 129–135, 155–156
customization, 63, 134, 290

debt, 219, 221–222, 246, 248–249, 255, 258, 260–261, 393, 494
decentralization, 18, 272, 287, 289, 401–402
declining competitive advantage, 114
deescalation strategy, 174
deflation, 53
deflationary environment, 276
degree of concentration, 19
Deming's 14 points for management, 184–185
demographic changes, 50–53
age structure, 50, 52
ethnic mix, 50, 52–53
geographic distribution, 50, 52
income distribution, 50, 53
population size, 50–51
demographic variables, 131

denial, 90–91
Department of Defense, 27–28, 35
Department of Transportation, 317
deregulation, 3, 43–45, 54–55, 238, 315–316, 325–327, 455
developing markets, 278
deverticalization, 416
differentiated features, 142–147, 150–151, 155, 272
differentiation, 140, 142–144, 146–147
differentiation strategy, 19, 124, 129, 135–137, 141–147, 149, 153, 155–156, 282, 284, 401, 403–404
  international, 282–284
  risks of, 146–147, 155–156
diffuse ownership, 361, 366
digital transmission technology, 4
distinctive competencies, 96
distribution, 66–67
distribution chain, 204
distribution channels, 64, 126, 144, 226, 229, 439
diversification, 19, 55, 202, 205, 207–209, 211–213, 216, 220–221, 223, 227–230, 246, 331, 359, 367, 398, 400–401
  global, 302
  international, 166, 202, 204, 207–208
  managerial motives, 226–228
  market, 208, 328, 398
  product, 166, 208, 238, 251, 252, 278, 287, 328, 336, 358–360, 398, 406
diversification strategies, 202, 206–208, 211–214, 220, 231, 238, 462
diversified business groups, 463–465
diversified firm, 31, 34, 96, 137, 195, 202, 206–207, 209, 213, 216, 219, 227, 252, 298, 360, 375, 391
diversifying acquisitions, 245
diversifying strategic alliances, 328–329
diversity, 56
divestiture, 207, 211, 221, 223, 239, 255, 257–258, 262, 290, 497
dividends, 221
domestic operation, 13, 170
dominant business, 209–210
downscoping, 256–257, 259–260, 262
downsizing, 255–257, 261, 332, 373, 454, 458, 492, 492

early adopters, 56–57
early advantage, 101–102
E-business, 16
economic environment, 53, 60
Economic Espionage Act of 1996 (EEA), 74
economic output, 14
economic segment, 53–54
economies of scale, 10, 18–19, 63, 70, 139, 196, 218, 241, 254, 276–277, 279, 282, 288, 297, 317, 324, 359
economies of scope, 212–213, 216, 225, 277, 324, 329, 359, 408
electronic mail (E-mail) systems, 16–17
electronic data exchange (EDI), 68
electronic data integration (EDI), 151
emerging economies, 334, 381
emerging entrepreneurial stage. *See* industry life cycle, emerging stage
emerging industries, 192, 196
emerging markets, 58, 129, 186, 191–192, 291, 315, 325, 333
emerging opportunities, 128
employee stock ownership program (ESOP), 84, 451
employment risk, 226–227, 364
employee buyouts (EBO), 260–261
entrepreneurial actions, 193–194, 196
entrepreneurial culture, 456–457, 480
entrepreneurial firm, 65, 496
entrepreneurial orientation (EO), 455–456
entrepreneurial ventures, 179–180, 492
entrepreneurs, 56, 477, 496
entrepreneurship, 35, 180, 223, 475, 492, 494
environment, 21
environmental changes, 18, 49–50, 86, 112, 149, 162–163, 408, 443
  opportunities, 33, 97, 128, 211
  threats, 50, 59, 99, 135, 211
environmental process analyses, 77
environmental trends, 50
equity, 218–219, 222, 249, 258, 260, 370, 383
  corporate, 361
ethical behavior, 76–78, 118, 156, 197, 356, 382–383, 453, 461
ethics, 37, 74, 78
ethnic diversity, 55
ethnic minorities, 55–56
European Community (EC), 291
European Union, 14, 53, 242, 333, 338
executive compensation, 355, 359, 371–375
exit barriers, 70
exporting, 293, 296, 332
exports, 12, 275
export strategy, 161
external environment, 1, 6, 19–20, 22, 34, 36–37, 42, 45–46, 48, 50, 57, 73, 77–78, 85, 112, 114, 116, 127–128, 206, 217, 221, 444
  analysis, 42, 48, 77, 86–87, 114, 117, 127
external opportunities, 34, 97, 114, 117, 127, 135, 209

fast-cycle markets, 166, 186–187, 190–193, 196–197, 315–318, 339
favorable industry position, 135
Federal Communications Commission, 3, 55, 325, 352
Federal Railroad Administration (FRA), 8
federal regulatory agency, 8
financial capital, 96
financial control, 252, 400–401, 458, 462, 465, 490
financial economies, 218, 220
financial resources, 92, 209, 225, 228
financial returns, 228–229
financial slack, 255
firm ability (to take action and respond), 178–185, 195–196
firm infrastructure, 105–107, 139, 145
firm performance, 19, 21, 26, 48, 68, 129, 134, 181–182, 184, 223, 251, 252, 254, 260, 372, 443, 445
firm size, 160, 178, 179, 191, 196, 213, 227, 240, 376, 391
firm strategy, 21, 36, 196
firm-specific loyalty, 130
first mover, 160, 170–172, 190 195, 197, 486
  advantages, 10, 22, 134, 166, 171–172, 196, 279, 455
  disadvantages, 166, 171, 196
five forces model of competition, 19, 61–62, 77–78, 129, 135, 153, 187, 319
flexibility, 18, 151, 225–226, 240, 249, 254–255, 288, 329, 333, 339
flexible manufacturing system (FMS), 150–151
focus strategy, 125, 135, 147, 149, 152–153, 403
focused differentiation, 124, 128, 135–136, 147–149, 154–157, 280, 282, 285, 457
focused diversification, 360
focused low-cost, 124, 135–136, 147–149, 155–157, 280, 282, 284
  international, 284–286
  risks of, 149, 156
followership, 166, 172
forecasting, 48–50, 77
Foreign Corrupt Practices Act, 383
foreign direct investments (FDI), 273, 333
foreign operation, 13
formalization, 401–402
Fortune's Most Admired Corporation list, 8
fragmentation, 132
fragmented firms, 284
fragmented markets, 194
franchising, 207, 331–332
free cash flows, 221, 226–227, 359
free trade, 14, 54, 291–292
free-market economy, 273
free-market reform, 54
function group, 224
functional structure, 397–398, 403–405

GATT agreement, 54
general environment, 42, 43–50, 61, 73, 77–78, 86, 128
  analysis, 61, 88
  demographic segment, 47, 50–53, 77
  economic segment 44, 53–54, 77
  global segment, 47, 58–60, 77
  political/legal segment, 43, 47, 54–55, 77
  sociocultural segment, 47, 55–56, 77
  technological segment, 44, 56–58, 77
geographic diversification, 230, 391
geographic segmentation, 131
geographic(al) markets, 44, 62
glass ceiling, 56
Glass Stegall Act, 381
global changes, 2

global communication, 57
global companies, 13
global competition, 5, 14, 88, 149, 211, 290
global competitive dynamics, 161
global competitive landscape, 14
global distribution system, 18
global economy, 5, 10–12, 31, 34, 37, 45–46, 90, 95–96, 114–115, 128–129, 181–183, 273, 323, 372, 377, 380, 394, 399, 453
global efficiency, 288–290
global environment, 260
global growth, 14
global integration, 276, 299
global markets, 3, 15, 44–45, 58–59, 71, 78, 151, 162, 164–165, 183, 203–204, 238, 273, 279, 286, 295, 297, 300, 302, 314, 475
 choice of entry mode, 292–297
global MTV generation, 276
global proliferation, 17
global rivalry, 71
global scale, 17
global scanning, 298
global segment, 58
global standards, 5, 14
global strategy, 280, 288, 290, 395, 420, 422
global technology, 12
globalization, 11–15, 36, 71, 127, 162–163, 271, 395, 435
 county, 271
 industry, 271–272
 worldwide, 271
globalized industries, 12
globalized market, 12
golden goodbye, 365–366
golden parachute, 227, 365, 376
government policy, 64–65
greenfield venture, 296–297
 international, 333
gross domestic product, 11–12, 16, 53, 381
growth-oriented actions, 193–194, 196
growth-oriented firm, 194, 197
growth-oriented stage. *See* industry life cycle, growth stage
Guanxi, 59

health maintenance organizations (HMOs), 146
horizontal acquisition, 216, 240, 245
horizontal chain alliance, 321
horizontal integration, 221, 224–225
horizontal organization, 484–486
host community, 297
host country, 277, 293, 295
host governments, 277, 297, 303
human capital, 117, 257, 439, 450–451, 454
human resource management, 105, 107, 117, 139, 145
human resources, 84–85, 92, 150, 489
hypercompetition, 9–10, 258, 322
hypercompetitive environment, 10

I/O model. *See* industrial organization model
imitability, 186
imitation, 142, 195, 197, 476
implementation actions, 6–7
imported goods, 15
imports, 12, 279
inbound logistics, 105, 107–108, 139, 145, 214
induced strategic behavior, 482
industrial organization (I/O) model, 2, 6, 19–22, 36
industry analyses, 71–72, 77
industry competition, 42
industry environment, 42, 46–48, 61, 73, 77–78, 86, 128, 207
 analysis, 61, 88, 128
industry evolution, 160, 192, 197
industry life cycle, 193
 emerging stage, 192–194, 196
 growth stage, 192–193, 223
 mature stage, 192–194, 196, 223
 model of, 193
industry segment, 147
industry shakeout, 154
industry structural characteristics, 131
industry, 61
industry-wide competition, 147–149, 155
inertia, 112
inflation rates, 53
inflexibility, 112
information networks, 151–152, 286
information overload, 17
information processing, 220, 226, 252, 408
Information Technology Association of America, 451
information technology, 15–17, 44–45, 64, 96, 110–111, 151, 165, 427
inhwa, 59
initial public offering, 261
innovation, 35, 92–93, 101, 108, 141, 143, 146, 160, 165, 178–179, 181–183, 187, 191, 196–197, 224, 252, 254–255, 258, 261, 271, 288–289, 293–294, 299, 443, 446, 456, 475–476, 483, 489, 498
 process, 194, 196–197, 224, 481
 product, 142, 194, 196–197, 208, 224, 403, 405, 481, 482, 485
institutional environment, 59
institutional investor, 366, 374
institutional owners, 361
intangible resources, 18, 21, 74, 82, 89, 92–94, 116–118, 212, 216, 225–228, 339, 426
integrated low-cost/differentiation strategy, 124, 135, 149–152, 155–156, 272, 282, 290, 401, 404–405
 risks of, 152–153, 155–156
integrated strategy, 129
integration, 239, 246, 248, 254, 288
intellectual capital, 76, 439
interest rates, 53
interfirm rivalry, 167–168, 178, 185, 196–197

internal corporate venture, 480–482, 484
internal environment, 1, 6, 22, 34, 36–37, 46, 82, 116–118, 128, 221
internal environmental analysis, 86–89, 114, 117
internal firm innovation, 486–487
international acquisitions, 242
International Corporate Governance Network, 363
international corporate governance, 356
international diversification, 274–275, 277, 297–298, 300–302
international entrepreneurship, 479
international environment risks, 300
international integration, 12
international markets, 12, 15, 71, 104, 164, 241–242, 245, 251, 274, 277, 279, 282, 293–294, 299, 302, 313, 332
International Monetary Fund (IMB), 333
international strategy, 87, 116–117, 123, 271, 273–274, 277, 279, 291–292, 371, 393, 424, 425, 426
 business, 273, 280
 corporate, 273, 280
international trade, 15
internationalization, 420
Internet trade, 16
Internet, the, 17, 30, 37, 44, 57–58, 64–65, 67–68, 78, 108, 118, 143, 198, 209, 243, 403, 442, 495
intraorganizational conflict, 90–91
introductions, 132–133
invention, 476

Japanese Machine Tool Building Association, 338
Japanese Ministry of Finance, 379
job burnout, 302
joint venture, 12–14, 172, 181, 188, 274–275, 279, 283, 295, 297, 313–314, 316, 325, 329, 333–335, 339, 341, 380, 426, 474
junk bonds, 248
Jurassic Park, 113

keiretsu, 319, 322, 336, 379–380, 480
 horizontal, 337, 379
 vertical 311
knowledge networks, 76
knowledge, 18, 46, 88, 95–96, 105, 111–112, 135, 191, 230–231, 252, 263, 294, 488–489
Korea Soap and Detergent Association, 302

large-block shareholders, 361–363, 366
late mover, 160, 170–172, 174, 195, 197
 advantages, 166, 196
 disadvantages, 166, 196
learning organization, 112
leveraged buyouts (LBO), 256, 460
liability of foreignness, 15
Library of Congress, 57
licensing, 274, 293, 296, 332, 381

lifestyle choices, 131
local responsiveness, 276, 288–289, 299
low-cost leader, 140–142, 146, 155–156
low-cost strategy, 137, 280, 282–283, 401

Malcolm Baldrige National Quality Award, 197
management buyouts (MBO), 260–261
managerial compensation, 213, 226, 332
managerial control, 357, 375, 378
managerial discretion, 441–442
managerial employment risk, 359, 364
managerial frame of reference, 439–440
managerial hubris, 248
managerial incentives, 375
managerial labor market, 445, 447
external 445–446
internal, 445–446
managerial mind-set, 29, 36, 164–165, 440
managerial opportunism, 357, 375, 460
managerial resistance, 263
Manpack, 58
market-based financial system, 379
market activities, 21
market capitalization, 9
market commonality, 168–170, 195
market entry (speed of), 240–241, 315
market for corporate control, 376
market leader, 14, 176
market leadership, 166
market niche, 9, 30, 65, 142, 148, 191, 194, 196, 284
market power, 178–180, 182, 194, 196, 212–213, 217–218, 220, 224–225, 238–242, 246, 315, 320–321, 331
actions, 178–180, 182, 193–194, 196
market segment (segmentation), 65, 125, 126, 132, 149, 285
market share, 14, 50, 63, 69, 113, 115, 143, 148, 151, 164–165, 172, 175, 188, 194, 207, 245, 250, 256, 261, 277, 291, 443, 486
market size, 277
market value added, 7
marketing and sales, 139, 145
marketing, 22, 105–107
marketplace opportunities, 34, 99
matrix organization, 336, 408
matrix structure, 408
mature firm stage. *See* industry life cycle, mature stage
mature industries, 196
Medicare, 35
Merced (Intel), 144, 473–474
merger mania, 238
merger, 221, 239, 243–245, 252, 258, 317, 329, 339, 381
horizontal, 241
related, 241
vertical, 241
minority women, 56
mode of entry, 274, 301
monitoring 48–50, 77, 340, 361, 366–367, 371, 375, 378–379
monopoly, 186–187, 196
motivation, 167–168, 170, 195–196
multidivisional (M-form) structure, 355, 375–376, 391–392, 398–400, 406–413
competitive, 406–407, 412–415
cooperative, 406–410, 414
SBU. *See* strategic business unit
multidomestic strategy, 272, 280, 287–288, 290–291, 395, 412, 420, 422
multinational firms, 208, 275– 276, 290, 298–299, 301, 303, 332, 336, 371, 453
multipoint competition, 169, 207, 212, 217
mutual forbearance, 217, 315, 323
mutual interdependence, 167

national advantage, 280, 282
National Association of Corporate Directors (NACD), 365
National Association of Manufacturers, 95
National Center for Manufacturing Sciences, 183
National Institute of Standards and Technology, 197–198
National Science Foundation, 489
National Tooling and Machining Association, 451
needs, 130, 147
network strategies, 313, 315, 332, 335–337
dynamic, 336
internal, 336–337
stable, 336
network-centered computing, 486
new competitive landscape. *See* competitive landscape
new entrant(s), 63, 78, 141, 144
new generation technologies:
cogeneration, 44
combined-cycle, 44
new process technologies, 143
new product development, 243, 253, 277, 285, 339
speed of, 315
new venture, 241, 243–244, 455, 491
new wholly owned subsidiary, 296
niche, 229, 281
customers, 285
1986 Tax Reform Act, 222
1996 Telecommunications Act, 325
nonfragmented industries, 194
nonstrategic team of resources, 111
nonsubstitutable resources (capabilities), 22, 33, 36, 98, 101–102, 118, 225, 442
North American Free Trade Agreement (NAFTA), 14, 53–54, 165, 291–292

offensive action, 174
oligopolistic markets, 186
online purchasing, 108
online services, 17
OPEC, 323
operational efficiency, 46
operations, 105–107, 139, 145, 214, 262, 273, 275–276, 375
opportunistic managerial behavior, 359
opportunities, 42, 45, 48, 77–78, 85–86, 99, 129, 134, 155, 166, 167, 192–194, 218, 223, 249, 273–274, 277, 279, 298, 333
environmental, 50, 59
Organization of American States (OAS, South America), 291
organizational capability, 85
organizational capital, 21
organizational control, 460–462, 465
organizational culture, 32, 35, 453, 455, 458–459, 461
organizational ethics, 35, 37
organizational resources, 92, 440
organizational size, 131
organizational stakeholders, 27, 28, 30–31, 35
organizational strategists, 7, 31, 36–37
organizational structure, 35, 180–181, 311, 375, 391, 393–396, 397, 403, 406, 409–412, 416, 420–422, 427, 457
outbound logistics, 105, 107–108, 139, 145, 214
outsourcing, 82, 110–111, 117–118, 319–320, 332
overcapacity, 70, 87, 163, 167–168, 257, 315
overdiversification, 227, 239, 252, 256, 400
overdiversify, 15
ownership concentration, 355–356, 361–363

partner (partnership), 311–312, 314, 319–321, 323, 331–333, 339–340, 489
patents, 16, 21, 57, 91, 243
Pentium Pro Intel microprocessors, 113, 473–474
perceived acceptable alternative, 146
perpetual innovation, 15
personality traits, 131
physical resources, 92, 150
poison pill, 227, 368
political/legal environment, 54
political/legal segment, 54
portfolio matrix, 207
portfolio of businesses, 207, 211, 213, 218, 229, 239, 244, 256, 259, 273, 359, 377
Porsche, 72
potential entrants, 141, 146
premium price, 196, 248, 377, 457
price predator, 176
price sensitivity, 144
price-quality positioning, 10
primary activities, 104–106, 108, 110–111, 117, 129, 138, 144, 149, 214, 217, 423
principals, 357–358, 360
private synergy, 249
privatization, 316, 322, 380–382
proactiveness, 456
procurement, 105–107, 139, 145
product champion, 481
product development teams, 484–485
product differentiation, 19, 63–64, 66, 68–70, 148

product life cycle, 10, 16, 274–275
product markets, 43, 128, 155, 206, 213
product market stakeholder, 26–28, 30, 35, 381
product obsolescence, 278
product quality, 183, 185
product segment, 135
product standardization, 194, 287–288
product substitutes, 141, 146
productivity, 28
profit margin, 113, 115
profit maximizing behavior, 19
profitability, 21, 26, 45, 48, 54, 63–64, 66, 69–70, 111, 132, 179, 205, 218, 225, 227, 243–244, 256, 263
protected markets, 87, 187

quality, 140, 160, 178, 183–185, 191–192, 196, 230

rapid technology diffusion, 16
rare resources (capabilities), 22, 33, 36, 98–99, 102, 104, 117, 225, 442
rate of return, 19, 151
red directors, 381
reengineering, 88, 442, 458
refocus, 258, 260
regionalization, 290–292
regulated markets, 43, 87
regulation, 55
regulatory barriers, 44
related acquisition, 240
related diversification, 202, 209–210, 212–213, 217, 222, 225–226, 228–229, 240–241, 245, 252
  related constrained, 205, 207, 209–211, 214, 406–408
  related linked, 205, 207, 210–211, 215, 391–392, 406, 411
relatedness, 225, 410
reputation, 92–93, 118, 171, 195–196, 227, 340, 358, 482
research and development (R&D), 165, 182, 190, 196, 241, 243, 254–255, 261, 276–278, 288, 298, 317–318, 321, 325, 336, 338–339, 367, 372, 398, 402–403, 425, 452, 482–483, 490, 494, 497
reseller, 66–67
resource dissimilarity, 170
resource mobility, 19
resources, 21–25, 31, 33–34, 36, 63–66, 82, 85–94, 96–97, 105, 108, 110–111, 114–118, 127, 135, 140, 146, 167, 178, 187, 194–195, 202, 207, 209–210, 213, 216, 219, 227–228, 231, 239–241, 244, 249, 278, 294, 297
  costly-to-imitate, 22, 33, 36, 98–102, 116–117
  difficult-to-imitate, 187
  sharing, 216, 226, 287, 290
resource similarity, 168–170
resource-based model, 6, 21–23, 36,
restructuring, 116–117, 123, 208, 212, 220,–221, 227, 239, 254–256, 261–262, 329, 372–373, 442, 463–464, 492
  outcomes, 262–263
retaliation, 63, 67, 78
retrenchment, 261
return on investment (ROI), 27–28, 252, 278, 401
reverse engineering, 278
Right Guard, 478
rightsizing, 257
risk, 5, 29, 31, 35, 124, 129, 141, 146, 171, 195, 207, 209, 216, 218, 220–221, 223, 225, 243–245, 252, 295, 298, 325, 339, 342, 359, 475, 486
  economic, 274, 276, 299–301
  financial, 276
  political, 274, 276, 299–300
risk aversion, 225, 253, 261, 462
risk bearing, 357
risk taking, 456
rivalry, 68–71, 86, 113, 144, 178, 185, 188, 197, 217, 246
Russian consumer revolution, 128

sales, 105–107
satellite imaging, 58
scanning, 48–50, 77
scope, 135
second mover, 160, 170–172, 195, 197
  advantages, 166, 196
  disadvantages, 166, 196
Secretary of Commerce, 30
Security and Exchange Commission (SEC), 57, 363–364
seller-centric environment, 68
service, 105–107, 127, 139–140, 142, 144–146, 153, 331
service differentiation, 68–69
service quality dimensions, 183
shareholder activism, 362–363, 368, 380
shareholder empowerment, 364
shareholder value, 18, 259, 353–354, 368, 378–379, 381
shareholder wealth, 225, 227, 355, 358, 361, 373, 375
shareholders, 26–29, 35, 108, 112, 221, 223, 227, 239, 245, 248, 249–250, 254, 262–263, 340, 352, 356, 358, 361, 364, 374, 377, 444, 457
sheltered markets, 186
shielded advantage, 186–187
simple structure, 396–398, 405–406
Six Sigma, 375
slack resources, 18
slow-cycle market, 166, 186–187, 190, 196, 315–316
smart bomb strategy, 289–290
social complexity, 101–103, 169
social culture, 295
sociocultural segment, 55
sociological changes, 45
solutions-oriented approach, 180
special administrative region (SAR), 60
specialization, 312, 401
speed to market, 234
speed, 181, 474
spending patterns of teenagers, 133
spinoff, 258–260, 311, 351, 360, 455, 492, 497
spying, 74
stakeholders, 2, 7, 18, 25–30, 32–33, 35–37, 46, 76, 84, 90, 93, 183, 220, 243, 353–354, 357, 372–373, 443–444
standard-cycle markets, 166, 186–190, 196, 315–317
standardized product, 288
statistical process control (SPC), 183
stewardship theory, 444
stock swap, 249
strategic acquisitions, 277
strategic actions, 5–6, 19, 22, 25, 34, 47, 59, 82, 97, 114, 117, 123, 128, 162, 174–177, 195–197, 217, 227, 241, 262, 323, 326, 342, 421, 438, 454
strategic advantage, 74, 302
strategic alliance, 10, 110, 165, 175, 181, 207, 241, 254, 294, 296–297, 303, 314–318, 325, 329, 331, 339–340, 425–426, 488–489
  approaches to managing, 341–342
  complementary. See complementary strategic alliance
  international, 333
  nonequity, 314
  reasons for, 316
strategic analyses, 52
strategic asset, 96, 340, 408
strategic business unit (SBU), 273, 287, 289, 392, 406–407, 410–412
strategic center, 337
strategic center firm, 422–426
strategic change, 219, 393, 438, 443
strategic competitiveness, 1–2, 4–9, 10–11, 14–15, 18, 21–23, 25, 30, 33–35, 37, 48, 50, 61, 68, 77, 85–90, 96, 111–112, 114, 125, 127–128, 134, 149, 151, 154–155, 163–165, 167, 180, 183, 186, 192, 205–209, 211–216, 218, 227–229, 231, 239, 245, 249, 252, 254, 257, 273–274, 277–278, 282–283, 289–290, 294, 298–299, 315, 320, 328, 332, 342, 354, 372, 382, 393–394, 409, 438, 440, 462, 489, 498
strategic control, 252, 400, 458, 462, 465, 490
strategic decision, 28, 35, 90, 126, 160, 181, 197, 277, 354, 391
strategic dimensions, 72
strategic direction, 45, 364, 370, 443–444, 448, 453
strategic equivalents, 101–102, 104
strategic flexibility, 18–19, 150–151, 192, 412
strategic group, 42, 71–73, 77, 78, 194
strategic implications, 17
strategic inputs, 5–6, 19, 34, 82, 114, 117, 128
strategic intent, 2, 6, 7, 24–26, 31, 33–37, 47, 70, 86–87, 114–117, 127, 141, 206, 302, 334, 339, 357

strategic leadership, 32, 35, 259, 394, 435, 437–443, 446, 448–450, 453–454, 458–459, 461–463, 477
strategic management challenge, 9
strategic management inputs, 1
strategic management, 1, 2, 38, 50
strategic management process, 2, 5–7, 31, 33–37, 86, 88, 166, 271, 353, 357, 377, 394–395, 428, 438
strategic mission, 2, 6–7, 24–26, 34–37, 47, 86–87, 114, 116–117, 127, 153, 206, 357
strategic myopia, 112
strategic network, 422–424
strategic opportunities, 17
strategic options, 15
strategic orientation, 25–26, 32
strategic outcomes, 5, 26, 31, 34–36, 128
strategic outsourcing, 422–423
strategic reorientation, 18
strategic response, 251
strategic responsiveness, 151
strategic value, 113
strategic vision, 23, 153
strategically competitive, 15, 26, 36, 130
strategically relevant, 113
strategy, 22, 31–32, 124, 127
strategy formulation, 5–7, 20, 23, 34, 86–88, 116–117, 123, 127, 443
strategy implementation, 5, 20, 23, 34, 87, 116–117, 127, 183, 443, 450, 460, 462, 465
strategists, 2, 31–34, 36, 73, 86, 89–91. *See also* organizational strategists
stretch goals, 115–116
structural flexibility, 412
structural integration mechanisms, 406
  direct contact, 406–408
  integrated department, 406–408
  liaison role, 406–408
  task forces, 406–408
stuck-in-the-middle, 153–155
subsidiary business, 239
substitute products (threat of), 68
superior value, 130
suppliers, 66, 93, 141, 146, 151, 161, 184, 244, 272, 276, 314, 320, 413
supply chain management process, 116
support activities, 104–106, 108–110–111, 117, 129, 138, 144, 149, 214, 217, 423
switching costs, 64, 66, 68, 70
symmetric multi-processing, 113
synergistic strategic alliances, 329–331
synergy, 225–226, 231, 241, 246, 249, 251–252, 254–255, 257–258, 279, 297

tacit collusion, 315, 323
tactical action, 174–177, 179, 195–197
takeover, 227, 240, 245, 263, 365, 368, 376
  hostile, 263, 339
tangible resources, 21, 82, 89, 92–94, 97, 116–118, 212–213, 225–226, 228
target customers, 131–132, 134, 137, 148, 251
target firm, 244, 248–249, 253–254, 263
tariffs, 277, 293
tax laws, 221–222
Teamsters Union, 26
Technical Workstation Alliance, 338
technological change, 2, 5, 10, 11, 15, 36, 45, 56–57, 127, 192, 225, 243
  technology and, 10–11, 15
technological development, 105–107, 145, 151, 335
technological diffusion, 16
technological innovation, 141
technological leadership, 142
technological obsolescence, 298
technological resources, 92–93
technological segment, 56
technological trends, 15
technology, 15
technology development, 139, 214
technology, diffusion, 482
telecommunications industry, 3, 4, 44
threat(s), 42, 45, 48, 77–78, 135, 167, 225
tier-one supplier, 312
time-based competition, 88
top management team (TMT), 219, 259, 299, 356, 376, 439, 442–445, 447, 458
  heterogeneous, 443
  homogeneous, 447
top-level managers, 31–33, 36, 134, 156, 163, 181, 204, 206
total quality management (TQM), 84, 88, 151–152, 156, 184–185, 196–197, 442
trade agreements, 291
trade associations, 14
trade barriers, 301–302
trade deficits, 53
trade laws, 324
trading blocks, 14
transaction costs, 252
transnational strategy, 280, 288–290, 299, 395, 421–422
triad competition, 168
trust, 32, 315, 340, 342
trustmark, 174
trustworthiness, 340

U.S. Commerce Department, 57, 198
U.S. Department of Justice, 55, 238, 313
U.S. Government, 27
U.S. National Cooperative Research Act of 1984, 338
unattractive industry, 71
uncertainty reduction strategies, 325–326, 328
uncertainty, 89–90, 220, 224–225, 318, 325–326, 328, 338, 487
unique historical conditions, 99
unique materials, 146
unique(ness), 142, 146
Unisource consortium, 4, 316, 327
United Auto Workers (UAW) Union, 26
unrelated businesses, 259
unrelated diversification, 202, 205, 209–213, 218–221, 225–226, 239–240, 245, 252, 406, 412–413
urbanization, 59
utilities, 44

valuable capabilities. *See* valuable resources
valuable resources (capabilities), 22, 33, 36, 98–99, 102, 104, 117, 225, 442
value chain, 104–105, 108, 129, 138, 144, 214, 320, 423
  analysis, 82, 89, 98, 108, 117
value investor, 376
value, 82, 88, 117–118, 130–131, 134–138, 140, 142, 147, 155, 178, 191, 194, 202, 206, 213, 217–219, 225, 228–230, 248, 262–263
value-creating strategy (activity), 4–5, 35, 85–86, 88, 90, 98–99, 101–102, 105, 110, 117, 128, 134, 139, 142–143, 217, 486
value-creation opportunities, 340
Velo Glide, 92 (product)
venture capital, 491–492, 494
vertical acquisition, 240
vertical integration, 43, 55, 153, 161–162, 173, 207, 212, 217–218, 221, 319, 331, 408
  backward integration, 62, 217
  forward integration, 62, 66, 217–218
videoconferencing, 57
videotape VHS Alliance, 338
virtual company, 338
Vorstand, 378

Wa, 59
Windows NT, 113
Wintel standard, 113
World Trade Organization (WTO), 3, 333
World Wide Web, 17
worldwide geographic area structure, 420, 422
worldwide product divisional structure, 420, 422

Photo Credits

pp. 1, 3: © Bob Krist/Tony Stone Images; **p. 14:** Courtesy of Toyota; **p. 17:** Courtesy of Amazon.com; **p. 32:** © Michael Newman/PhotoEdit; **pp. 1, 43:** © Jake Rajs/Tony Stone Images; **p. 51:** © Alan Levinson/Tony Stone Images; **p. 57:** © Michael Rosenfeld/Tony Stone Images; **p. 65:** Courtesy of American Honda Motor Company, Inc.; **pp. 1, 83:** © Alan Brown/Photonics; **p. 91:** © SWCP; **p. 100:** © Sony Electronics, Inc.; **p. 115:** © David Butow/SABA; **pp. 123, 125:** Courtesy Bang & Olufsen America, Inc.; **p. 133:** © Kirstin Finnegan/Tony Stone Images; **p. 152:** © Bruno De Hogues/Tony Stone Images; **pp. 123, 161:** © Jeff Greenberg/PhotoEdit; **p. 171:** © Spencer Grant/PhotoEdit; **p. 180:** Courtesy of Southwest Airlines; **pp. 123, 203:** Photography by Cary Benbow; **p. 222:** Photography by Nicholas Communications; **p. 229:** © Jeff Greenberg; **pp. 123, 237:** © James Leynse/SABA; **p. 250:** © Tom Tracy/Tony Stone Images; **p. 259:** Courtesy of Kentucky Fried Chicken; **p. 261:** © Tony Freeman/PhotoEdit; **pp. 123, 271:** © Jeff Greenberg; **p. 275:** © Keith Dannemiller/SABA; **p. 292:** © Jeff Greenberg; **pp. 123, 311:** © A. Ramey/PhotoEdit; **p. 324:** Photography by Nicholas Communications; **p. 337:** Courtesy of Monorail; **pp. 349, 351:** © Mark Peterson/SABA; **p. 355:** © 1997 PhotoDisc, Inc.; **p. 365:** © 1997 PhotoDisc, Inc.; **p. 374:** © Christopher Brown/Stock, Boston; **pp. 349, 393:** © George Hall/Check Six; **p. 405:** © Rob Nelson/Black Star Publishing; **p. 412:** © Rob Crandall/Stock, Boston/P.N.I.; **p.425:** © 1997 PhotoDisc, Inc.; **pp. 349, 435:** © 1997 PhotoDisc, Inc.; **p. 444:** © Frank Fournier/Contact Press Images; **p. 458:** © Reuters/Toshiyuki Aizawa/Archive Photos; **pp. 349, 473:** © Tom Tracy/Photo Network/P.N.I.; **p. 477:** © Bob Daemmrich/Stock, Boston; **p. 503:** © 1997 PhotoDisc, Inc.